2020 EDITION | PRIDE & FERRELL

MARKETING

WILLIAM M. PRIDE

Texas A & M University

O.C. FERRELL

Auburn University

CENGAGE

Australia • Brazil • Mexico • Singapore • United Kingdom • United States

CENGAGE

Marketing 2020, **Twentieth Edition**
William M. Pride and O.C. Ferrell

Senior Vice President, Higher Ed Product,
Content, and Market Development: Erin Joyner

Product Director: Bryan Gambrel

Product Manager: Heather Mooney

Content Manager: Allie Janneck

Manager, Content Delivery: John Rich

Product Assistant: Lucia Hermo del Teso

Marketing Manager: Andrew Miller

Production Service/Composition: SPi Global

Senior Designer: Bethany Bourgeois

Text/Cover Designer: Joe Devine/Red Hangar Design

Cover Image: Leigh Prather/Shutterstock.com

Tree Image: marilyn barbone/Shutterstock.com

Target: stuar/Shutterstock.com

Camera: licccka/Shutterstock.com

Arrows: your/Shutterstock.com

Light bulb: Sergey Nivens/Shutterstock.com

Rocket launching: adike/Shutterstock.com

Intellectual Property Analyst: Diane Garrity

Intellectual Property Project Manager: Nick Barrows

For product information and technology assistance, contact us at
Cengage Customer & Sales Support, 1-800-354-9706
or **support.cengage.com.**
For permission to use material from this text or product,
submit all requests online at **www.cengage.com/permissions.**

Library of Congress Control Number: 2018961055

Soft-cover Edition ISBN: 978-0-357-03379-1

Loose-Leaf Edition ISBN: 978-1-337-91065-1

Cengage
20 Channel Center Street
Boston, MA 02210
USA

Cengage is a leading provider of customized learning solutions with employees residing in nearly 40 different countries and sales in more than 125 countries around the world. Find your local representative at **www.cengage.com.**

Cengage products are represented in Canada by
Nelson Education, Ltd.

To learn more about Cengage platforms and services, register or access your online learning solution, or purchase materials for your course, visit **www.cengage.com.**

Printed at CLDPC, USA, 08-19

To Nancy, Allen, Carmen, Gracie, Mike, Ashley,
Charlie, J.R., and Anderson Pride

To James Collins Ferrell and
George Collins Ferrell

Brief Contents

Contents

PART 4   Buying Behavior, Global Marketing, and Digital Marketing 183

Contents

Contents

PART 6 — Distribution Decisions 393

PART 7 Promotion Decisions 465

Preface

MARKETING: A KEY TO SUCCESS

This edition of *Marketing* has been revised to capture changes that will determine the future of marketing. Marketing knowledge is important to every student's success, regardless of their career path. There is significant evidence that marketing is becoming a more important function in organizations, and students will need to be prepared to understand opportunities and challenges from a marketing perspective. This new edition provides the concepts, frameworks, and engagement in decision-making experiences that will prepare students for their careers. It is not enough to learn terminology and memorize concepts. What we teach students today could be obsolete in five or ten years. We need to prepare them to engage in critical thinking and engage in continuous self-development.

Active learning requires a holistic understanding with examples, exercises, and cases facilitated by MindTap, our online teaching experience. MindTap provides relevant assignments that guide students to analyze, apply, and improve thinking, allowing them to measure skills and outcomes with ease. This means that students using this book should develop respect for the importance of marketing and understand that the learning of marketing requires in-depth knowledge and the mastering of essential concepts. We have made the learning experience as fresh as possible with available research, new examples and boxes, as well as illustrations.

We address how technology is changing the marketing environment. As students prepare for the new digital world, they will also need to practice developing communication skills, especially teamwork, that go beyond their personal interaction with digital devices. As internet retailing and online business-to-business marketing advances, the importance of supply chain management becomes important in connecting and integrating members of the distribution system. Marketing analytics and artificial intelligence (AI) are defining how decisions are made and implemented. For example, UPS is delivering packages with drones, and driverless cars may be widespread by 2021. All of these advances related to technology are changing marketing activities, strategies, and business models. We address all of these developments to prepare students for the future.

We also provide numerous ancillary materials to aid in student comprehension of marketing concepts as well as to increase instructor resources for teaching this important material. The MindTap materials include building a marketing plan, concept check quizzes on the reading, self-assessments, homework assignments, PowerPoint presentations practice exam preparation tests, videos of real companies, branching activities, flashcards, and more! Additionally, on the instructor companion site, YouTube videos are available for each chapter with worksheets to engage students in applying concepts. Our marketing video case series enables students to learn about how real-world companies address marketing challenges. Our Marketing Plan activities and video program provide students with practical knowledge of the challenges and the planning process of launching a new product. Together these revisions and additional materials will assist students in gaining a full understanding of pertinent marketing practices.

Online social networking has become an increasingly powerful tool for marketers. Most discussions about marketing today bring up issues such as how digital media can lower costs, improve communications, provide better customer support, and achieve improved marketing research. All elements of the marketing mix should be considered when using digital media and social networking. We discuss how digital media and social networking tools can create effective digital marketing strategies that can enhance marketing efforts. In addition, the entire book integrates important digital marketing concepts and examples where appropriate.

We have paid careful attention to enhancing all key concepts in marketing and have built this revision to be current and to reflect important changes in marketing. Our book is a market leader because students find it readable and relevant. Our text reflects the real world of marketing and provides the most comprehensive coverage possible of important marketing topics.

Specific details of this extensive revision are available in the transition guide in the *Instructor's Manual*. We have also made efforts to improve all teaching ancillaries and student learning tools. PowerPoint presentations continue to be a very popular teaching device, and a special effort has been made to upgrade the PowerPoint program to enhance classroom teaching. The *Instructor's Manual* continues to be a valuable tool, updated with engaging in-class activities and projects. The authors and publisher have worked together to provide a comprehensive teaching package and ancillaries that are unsurpassed in the marketplace.

The authors have maintained a hands-on approach to teaching this material and revising the text and its ancillaries. This results in an integrated teaching package and approach that is accurate, sound, and successful in reaching students. The outcome of this involvement fosters trust and confidence in the teaching package and in student learning outcomes. Student feedback regarding this textbook is highly favorable.

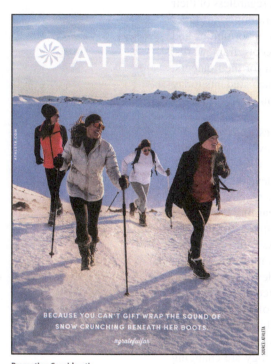

Promotion Considerations
Athleta uses Instagram to spread its #gratefulfor campaign which encourages Athleta fans to share stories of positivity and gratitude.

WHAT'S NEW TO THIS EDITION?

Our goal is to provide the most up-to-date content—concepts, examples, cases, exercises, and data—possible. Therefore, in this revision there are significant changes that make learning more engaging and interesting to the students. The following highlight the types of changes that were made in this revision.

- **Foundational content.** Each chapter has been updated with the latest knowledge available related to frameworks, concepts, and academic research. These additions have been seamlessly integrated into the text. Many examples are new and a review of footnotes at the ends of chapters will reveal where new content has been added.
- **Opening vignettes:** *Marketing Insights*. All of the chapter-opening vignettes are new or updated. They are written to introduce the theme of each chapter by focusing on actual entrepreneurial companies and how they deal with real-world situations.

- **Boxed features.** Each chapter includes two new boxed features that highlight disruptive marketing, creative marketing, integrity in marketing, or entrepreneurship in marketing. Three of these themes are new to this edition.
- **New Snapshot features.** The Snapshot features are new and engage students by highlighting interesting, up-to-date statistics that link marketing theory to the real world.
- **New research.** Throughout the text we have updated content with the most recent research that supports the frameworks and best practices for marketing.
- **New illustrations and examples.** New advertisements from well-known firms are employed to

How Do Employees Spend Time on Their Personal Mobile Devices at Work?

	According to Employees	According to Managers
Personal Email	30%	28%
Social Networks	28%	62%
Sports Sites	9%	1%
Mobile Games	6%	2%
Online Shopping Sites	5%	4%
Entertainment Sites	3%	1%

SNAPSHOT

Source: "Working Hard or Hardly Working? Employees Waste More Than One Day a Week on Non-Work Activities," Robert Half, July 19, 2017, http://rh-us.mediaroom.com/2017-07-19-WORKING-HARD-OR-HARDLY-WORKING-Employees-Waste-More-Than-One-Day-a-Week-on-Non-Work-Activities (accessed January 27, 2018).

illustrate chapter topics. Experiences of real-world companies are used to exemplify marketing concepts and strategies throughout the text. Most examples are new or updated to include digital marketing concepts as well as several new sustainable marketing illustrations.

- **End-of-chapter cases.** Each chapter contains two cases, including a video case, profiling firms to illustrate concrete application of marketing strategies and concepts. Many of our video cases are new to this edition and are supported by current and engaging videos.

- **YouTube videos.** Each chapter has a YouTube video related to a concept. Student worksheets are available for application. These are all available on the instructor companion site.

FEATURES OF THE BOOK

As with previous editions, this edition of the text provides a comprehensive and practical introduction to marketing that is both easy to teach and to learn. *Marketing* continues to be one of the most widely adopted introductory textbooks in the world. We appreciate the confidence that adopters have placed in our textbook and continue to work hard to make sure that, as in previous editions, this edition keeps pace with changes. The entire text is structured to excite students about the subject and to help them learn completely and efficiently.

- An *organizational model* at the beginning of each part provides a "road map" of the text and a visual tool for understanding the connections among various components.

- *Objectives* at the start of each chapter present concrete expectations about what students are to learn as they read the chapter.
- Every chapter begins with an *opening vignette*. This feature provides an example of the real world of marketing that relates to the topics covered in the chapter. After reading the vignette, the student should be motivated to want to learn more about concepts and strategies that relate to the varying topics. Students will have an opportunity to learn more about organizations such as Chipotle, L'Oréal, Dunkin' Donuts, Alibaba, and Spotify.

CREATIVE MARKETING

Tiffany Rings Up More through Mobile Marketing

Building on a distinctive brand image forged over more than 180 years, Tiffany & Co. is polishing its marketing strategy for the next generation of fine-jewelry buyers. The firm, known worldwide for diamond rings and other luxury jewelry items, began with a single store in New York City. Today, Tiffany operates more than 300 full-service stores in dozens of countries and rings up $4 billion in annual sales.

Although the technology and the product designs have changed over the decades, Tiffany's timeless brand has retained its strong upscale

firm's website or checking its popular accounts on Pinterest, Facebook, Google+, YouTube, Twitter, or Instagram. All are awash in Tiffany Blue, which is also the color of its official Snapchat icon.

When the firm first developed its mobile marketing strategy, Lacaze says company marketers were "scared of showing expensive products on a tiny screen," fearing the impact would be lost. However, Tiffany quickly discovered that smartphone users don't just look, they actually click to see more. As a result, the firm now posts extra-

- Boxed features—*Creative Marketing* and *Disruptive Marketing*—capture dynamic changes in marketing. These changes are influencing marketing strategies and customer behavior. Strong feedback from adopters indicated the need for coverage in these areas.

- The *Creative Marketing* feature explores unique marketing approaches at Tiffany's, Airbnb, ipsy, and Volition.

- The *Disruptive Marketing* boxes cover such marketing phenomena as Blockchain, apparel rental, and flash sales. Featured companies include IKEA, Amazon, Google, and Zappos.

DISRUPTIVE MARKETING

Making Meaning Out of Big Data: Marketing Analytics

The field of marketing research is changing. Where it was once dominated by focus groups and surveys, today's marketers are increasingly turning to marketing analytics to glean customer insights. Big data and marketing analytics are being used to disrupt industries across the board. A report found that large business-to-consumer firms are planning to increase their spending on marketing analytics by almost 100 percent in a three-year period. Eighty-three percent of business leaders pursue big data proj-

is important in identifying marketing channels that increase ROI.

It is not enough simply to record big data. The hard part is determining which small bits of information among massive data files will reveal significant customer insights. However, interpreting big data correctly can help marketers recognize trends they never would have realized existed otherwise. For instance, one analytics firm helped a mobile phone manufacturer determine that the major reason consumers bought its phone

INTEGRITY IN MARKETING

Patagonia Unzips Its Advertising Strategy: Don't Buy This Jacket

One of apparel store Patagonia's most popular advertisements features its popular R2 coat with the headline: "Don't Buy This Jacket." In the copy, the advertisement explains that although the R2 uses recycled materials, it is still harmful to the environment. Patagonia advocates for decreased consumption where consumers purchase less (also termed green demarketing).

Patagonia was founded upon environmental principles with a three-part mission: sell quality products, cause no unnecessary harm, and find business solutions to environmental issues. Because excessive consumption generates waste, encouraging consumers to purchase less demonstrates Patagonia's environmental commitment. Patagonia wants consumers

developed a film showing fans wearing old Patagonia clothing held together by duct tape, demonstrating the value of less consumption. Patagonia also announced it would donate 100 percent of proceeds from sales generated on the day after Thanksgiving to environmental causes.

Because Patagonia clothing lasts a long time, its marketing indirectly promotes its own products as a solution to the constant need to replace worn-out apparel. The company even urges consumers to return worn-out merchandise so Patagonia can recycle it into something else. This approach resonates with consumers as sustainable consumption becomes an important sociocultural value.

- In the *Integrity in Marketing* boxed features, topics such as ethics, sustainability, privacy, and social responsibility are considered. Featured companies include Chick-fil-A, Flowers for Dreams, Unilever, Starbucks, REI, and Patagonia.

- The *Entrepreneurship in Marketing* feature focuses on the role of entrepreneurship and the need for creativity in developing successful marketing strategies by featuring successful entrepreneurial companies such as Blue Bottle Coffee, Harmless Harvest, Halo Top Ice Cream, Haney's Appledale Farm, Louisville Slugger, and Tastefully Simple.

ENTREPRENEURSHIP IN MARKETING

Halo Top Ice Cream Tops Pint Sales Charts

How does an entrepreneur with no food or marketing experience create an ice cream brand that holds its own with industry giants like Häagen-Dazs and Ben & Jerry's? Smart target marketing. Justin Woolverton was a sweets-loving lawyer when he started testing recipes for a lower-calorie, higher-protein ice cream. After months of experimentation, he settled on a recipe sweetened with stevia to slash the calorie count without sacrificing flavor—a key benefit desired by health-conscious Millennials. In fact, a pint of Halo Top has fewer calories and more protein than a pint of traditional ice cream.

Packaging reflects another of Woolverton's insights. Consumers in his target market want to spoon their way through the whole pint in one sitting, without guilt. As a result, Halo Top is sold only in pints

prominently labeled with the calorie count for product differentiation. Under the lid, the foil seal encourages buyers to go ahead and indulge: "Stop when you hit the bottom." And, to tempt variety-seeking Millennial palates, Halo Top comes in buzz-worthy flavors like cinnamon roll, rainbow swirl, and pancakes and waffles, as well as perennial favorites like vanilla bean.

As Halo Top appeared on store shelves, Woolverton revved up outreach to his target market via Facebook and Instagram. Fans quickly added their comments and images, building word-of-mouth authenticity for the young brand, and sending its total follower count over the one-million mark. Before Halo Top reached its fifth birthday, its pint sales had outstripped the pint sales of the best-established brand names in the ice-cream industry for the first time.[a]

- *Key term definitions* appear in the margins to help students build their marketing vocabulary.

- Figures, tables, photographs, advertisements, and Snapshot features increase comprehension and stimulate interest.

- A complete *chapter summary* reviews the major topics discussed, and the list of important terms provides another end-of-chapter study aid to expand students' marketing vocabulary.

- *Discussion and review questions* at the end of each chapter encourage further study and exploration of chapter content.

- The *Developing Your Marketing Plan* feature allows students to explore each chapter topic in relation to developing and implementing a marketing plan.

- Two *cases* at the end of each chapter help students understand the application of chapter concepts. One of the end-of-chapter cases is related to a video segment. Some examples of companies highlighted in the cases are Crayola, Salesforce.com, Netflix, Instagram, Rebecca Minkoff, and Louis Vuitton.

- A *strategic case* at the end of each part helps students integrate the diverse concepts that have been discussed within the related chapters. Examples include Whole Foods, Uber, Nike, and Gelson's Market.

- *Online appendices* discuss marketing career opportunities, explore financial analysis in marketing, and present a sample marketing plan. All of these appendices appear online on the instructor and student companion sites and in MindTap.

- A comprehensive *glossary* defines more than 600 important marketing terms.

TEXT ORGANIZATION

We have organized the eight parts of *Marketing* to give students a theoretical and practical understanding of marketing decision making.

Part 1   **Marketing Strategy and Customer Relationships**

In *Chapter 1*, we define marketing and explore several key concepts: customers and target markets, the marketing mix, relationship marketing, the marketing concept, and value-driven marketing. In *Chapter 2*, we look at an overview of strategic marketing topics, such as the strategic planning process; corporate, business-unit, and marketing strategies; the implementation of marketing strategies; performance evaluation of marketing strategies; and the components of the marketing plan.

Part 2   **Environmental Forces and Social and Ethical Responsibilities**

We examine competitive, economic, political, legal and regulatory, technological, and sociocultural forces that can have profound effects on marketing strategies in *Chapter 3*. In *Chapter 4*, we explore social responsibility and ethical issues in marketing decisions.

Part 3   **Marketing Research and Target Market Analysis**

In *Chapter 5*, we provide a foundation for analyzing buyers with a look at marketing information systems and the basic steps in the marketing research process. We look at elements that affect buying decisions to better analyze customers' needs and evaluate how specific marketing strategies can satisfy those needs. In *Chapter 6*, we deal with how to select and analyze target markets—one of the major steps in marketing strategy development.

Part 4   **Buying Behavior, Global Marketing, and Digital Marketing**

We examine consumer buying decision processes and factors that influence buying decisions in *Chapter 7*. In *Chapter 8*, we explore business markets, business customers, the buying center, and the business buying decision process. *Chapter 9* focuses on the actions, involvement, and strategies of marketers that serve international customers. In *Chapter 10*, we discuss digital marketing, social media, and social networking.

Part 5   **Product Decisions**

In *Chapter 11*, we introduce basic concepts and relationships that must be understood to make effective product decisions. Also, we discuss a number of dimensions associated with branding and packaging. We analyze a variety of topics regarding product management in *Chapter 12*, including line extensions and product modification, new-product development, and product deletions. *Chapter 13* discusses services marketing.

Part 6   **Distribution Decisions**

In *Chapter 14*, we look at supply chain management, marketing channels, and the decisions and activities associated with the physical distribution of products, such as order processing, materials handling, warehousing, inventory management, and transportation. *Chapter 15* explores retailing and wholesaling, including types of retailers and wholesalers, direct marketing and selling, and strategic retailing issues.

Part 7   **Promotion Decisions**

We discuss integrated marketing communications in *Chapter 16*. The communication process and major promotional methods that can be included in promotion mixes are described. In *Chapter 17*, we analyze the major steps in developing an advertising campaign. We also define public relations and how it can be used. *Chapter 18* deals with personal selling and the role it can play in a firm's promotional efforts. We also explore the general characteristics of sales promotion and describe sales promotion techniques.

Part 8   **Pricing Decisions**

In *Chapter 19*, we discuss the importance of price and look at some characteristics of price and nonprice competition. We explore fundamental concepts such as demand, elasticity, marginal analysis, and breakeven analysis. We then examine the major factors that affect marketers' pricing decisions. In *Chapter 20*, we look at the six major stages of the process marketers use to establish prices.

A COMPREHENSIVE INSTRUCTIONAL RESOURCE PACKAGE

For instructors, this edition of *Marketing* includes an exceptionally comprehensive package of teaching materials.

Instructor's Manual

The *Instructor's Manual* has been revamped to meet the needs of an engaging classroom environment. It has been updated with diverse and dynamic discussion starters, classroom activities, and group exercises. It includes such tools as:

- Quick Reference Guide to see the available key terms, overview of the learning objectives, and major topic in each chapter
- What's New in Each Chapter?
- Purpose Statements
- Integrated Lecture Outlines
- Discussion Starter recommendations that encourage active exploration of the in-text examples
- Class Exercises and Semester Project Activities
- Suggested Answers to end-of-chapter exercises, cases, and strategic cases

Test Bank

The test bank provides more than 4,000 test items, including true/false, multiple-choice, and essay questions. In this edition, you will find several new questions for each learning objective. Each objective test item is accompanied by the correct answer, appropriate Learning Objective, level of difficulty, Bloom's level of thinking, Program Interdisciplinary Learning Outcomes, and Marketing Disciplinary Learning Outcomes. Cengage Learning Testing powered by Cognero is a flexible, online system that allows you to:

- Author, edit, and manage test bank content from multiple Cengage Learning solutions
- Create multiple test versions in an instant
- Deliver tests from your LMS, your classroom, or wherever you want

American Marketing Association Professional Certified Marketer®

The American Marketing Association has recently started offering marketing graduates the opportunity of adding the AMA PCM® credentials to their undergraduate or MBA degree, which can serve as a symbol of professional excellence that affirms mastery of marketing knowledge and commitment to quality in the practice of marketing. Certification, which is voluntary, requires passing a rigorous and comprehensive exam and then maintaining the certification through continuing education. Earning an AMA PCM certification demonstrates to employers, peers, and clients that the holder:

- Has mastered essential marketing knowledge and practices
- Goes the extra mile to stay current in the marketing field
- Follows the highest professional standards

The AMA recommends Pride and Ferrell's *Marketing* as a suggested resource for AMA PCM students to utilize as they prepare for taking the AMA PCM certification exam, and the text was used as a source to design the course and as a source for suitable examination questions. Now, more than ever, you need to stand out in the marketplace. AMA's Professional Certified Marketer (PCM®) program is the perfect way to showcase your expertise and set yourself apart.

To learn more about the American Marketing Association and the AMA PCM exam, visit https://www.ama.org/events-training/Certification/Pages/digital-marketing-certification.aspx.

PowerPoint Slides

PowerPoint continues to be a very popular teaching device, and a special effort has been made to upgrade the PowerPoint program to enhance classroom teaching. Premium lecture slides, containing such content as advertisements, and unique graphs and data, have been created to provide instructors with up-to-date, unique content to increase student application and interest.

Marketing Video Case Series

This series contains videos specifically tied to the video cases found at the end of each chapter. The videos include information about exciting companies such as Apple, Tesla, Ford, Instagram, and Warby Parker. MindTap video exercises provide students with opportunities to use the videos to test and expand their knowledge. Also included are YouTube videos that have been selected by the authors specifically to be used in the classroom to engage students and illustrate marketing concepts.

MindTap for Marketing

MindTap is a personalized teaching experience with relevant assignments that guide students to analyze, apply, and improve thinking, allowing them to measure skills and outcomes with ease.

- Personalized Teaching: Becomes yours with a learning path that is built with key student objectives. Control what students see and when they see it. Use it as-is or match to your syllabus exactly—hide, rearrange, add, and create your own content.

MINDTAP *From Cengage*

MINDTAP MARKETING, 20TH EDITION   SHOW HIDDEN ✕   EDIT ✕

Expand all ↓   **+ Add / Create**   Filters ▼

Watch Before You Begin...
Ready to start your digital course experience? Watch this quick video to learn just how easy it is to dive right in!

📁 Part 1: Marketing Strategy and Customer Relationships (Chs. 1-2)   33 activities ⌄

📁 Part 2: Environmental Forces and Social and Ethical Responsibilities (Chs. 3-4)   31 activities ⌄

📁 Part 3: Marketing Research and Target Market Analysis (Chs. 5-6)   32 activities ⌄

📁 Part 4: Buying Behavior, Global Marketing, and Digital Marketing (Chs. 7-10)   58 activities ⌄

📁 Part 5: Product Decisions (Chs. 11-13)   46 activities ⌄

📁 Part 6: Distribution Decisions (Chs. 14-15)   31 activities ⌄

📁 Part 7: Promotion Decisions (Chs. 16-18)   49 activities ⌄

📁 Part 8: Pricing Decisions (Chs. 19-20)   31 activities ⌄

📁 Appendices   3 activities ⌄

- Guide Students: A unique learning path of relevant readings, multimedia, and activities that move students up the learning taxonomy from basic knowledge and comprehension to analysis and application.
- Promote Better Outcomes: Empower instructors and motivate students with analytics and reports that provide a snapshot of class progress, time in course, and engagement and completion rates.

Author's Website

The authors also maintain a website at *http://prideferrell.net* to provide additional video resources that can be used as supplements and class exercises. The videos have been developed as marketing labs with worksheets for students to use after observing the videos. Some of the videos are accessible through links, and there is also information on where some of the videos can be obtained. These videos are in addition to the new set of YouTube videos described earlier.

Building a Marketing Plan

The marketing plan has been expanded into eight parts that walk students through the steps of building a marketing plan as they finish relevant content in the book. These flexible, modular assignments allow you to assign a complete marketing plan in stages—or pick only specific sections to assign. Featuring fill-in-the-blank response fields for quick review of student-provided information and corresponding templates for students to complete and upload, these assignments present a flexible, course-integrated way to give students experience thinking through and building out a marketing plan.

In addition, there is a section entitled Developing Your Marketing Plan at the end of each chapter. These application-focused sections contain exercises that help students to relate chapter content to the development of marketing plans.

SUPPLEMENTS TO MEET STUDENT NEEDS

The MindTap has been updated with key features to help address your students' needs and engage them in the material. It is the digital learning solution that powers students from memorization to mastery by challenging students to apply what they have learned, instead of just recalling the information, with activities such as You Make the Decision and Video Quizzes. It gives you complete control of your course—to provide engaging content, to challenge every individual, and to build their confidence.

Other MindTap activities include:

- Self-Assessments
- Chapter Assignments
- Concept Checks
- Adaptive Test Prep (Test Your Knowledge)
- Flashcards
- PowerPoint slides
- And more!

YOUR COMMENTS AND SUGGESTIONS ARE VALUED

As authors, our major focus has been on teaching and preparing learning materials for introductory marketing students. We have traveled extensively to work with students and to understand the needs of professors of introductory marketing courses. We both teach this marketing course on a regular basis and test the materials included in the book, test bank, and other ancillary materials to make sure they are effective in the classroom.

Through the years, professors and students have sent us many helpful suggestions for improving the text and ancillary components. We invite your comments, questions, and criticisms. We want to do our best to provide materials that enhance the teaching and learning of marketing concepts and strategies. Your suggestions will be sincerely appreciated. Please write us, or e-mail us at **w-pride@tamu.edu** or **ocferrell@gmail.com**, or call 979-845-5857 (Bill Pride).

Acknowledgments

Like most textbooks, this one reflects the ideas of many academicians and practitioners who have contributed to the development of the marketing discipline. We appreciate the opportunity to present their ideas in this book. A number of individuals have made helpful comments and recommendations in their reviews of this or earlier editions.

Zafar U. Ahmed, *Lebanese American University*
Thomas Ainscough, *University of South Florida*
Sana Akili, *U.S. Department of Commerce*
Katrece Albert, *Southern University*
Joe F. Alexander, *Belmont University*
Mark I. Alpert, *University of Texas at Austin*
David M. Ambrose, *University of Nebraska*
David Andrus, *Kansas State University*
Linda K. Anglin, *Minnesota State University*
George Avellano, *Central State University*
Emin Babakus, *University of Memphis*
Siva Balasubramanian, *Illinois Institute of Technology*
Joseph Ballenger, *Stephen F. Austin State University*
Frank Barber, *Cuyahoga Community College*
Joseph Barr, *Framingham State College*
Thomas E. Barry, *Southern Methodist University*
Richard C. Becherer, *University of Tennessee–Chattanooga*
Walter H. Beck, Sr., *Reinhardt College*
Russell Belk, *York University*
John Bennett, *University of Missouri–Columbia*
W. R. Berdine, *California State Polytechnic Institute*
Karen Berger, *Pace University*
Stewart W. Bither, *Pennsylvania State University*
Roger Blackwell, *Blackwell Business Advisors*
Nancy Bloom, *Nassau Community College*
Paul N. Bloom, *Duke University*
James P. Boespflug, *Arapahoe Community College*
Joseph G. Bonnici, *Central Connecticut State University*
John Boos, *Ohio Wesleyan University*
Peter Bortolotti, *Johnson & Wales University*
Chris D. Bottomley, *Ocean County College*
Jenell Bramlage, *University of Northwestern Ohio*
James Brock, *Pacific Lutheran University*
John R. Brooks, Jr., *Houston Baptist University*
John Buckley, *Orange County Community College*
Pat J. Calabros, *University of Texas–Arlington*
Linda Calderone, *State University of New York College of Technology at Farmingdale*
Joseph Cangelosi, *University of Central Arkansas*
William J. Carner, *University of Texas–Austin*
Nancy M. Carr, *Community College of Philadelphia*
James C. Carroll, *University of Central Arkansas*
Terry M. Chambers, *Westminster College*

Lawrence Chase, *Tompkins Cortland Community College*
Larry Chonko, *Baylor University*
Ernest F. Cooke, *Loyola College–Baltimore*
Robert Copley, *University of Louisville*
Robert Corey, *West Virginia University*
Deborah L. Cowles, *Virginia Commonwealth University*
William L. Cron, *Texas Christian University*
Gary Cutler, *Dyersburg State Community College*
Bernice N. Dandridge, *Diablo Valley College*
Sally Dibb, *Open University*
Katherine Dillon, *Ocean County College*
Ralph DiPietro, *Montclair State University*
Paul Dishman, *Utah Valley University*
Casey L. Donoho, *Northern Arizona University*
Todd Donovan, *Colorado State University*
Kent Drummond, *University of Wyoming*
Tinus Van Drunen, *University Twente (Netherlands)*
Robert F. Dwyer, *University of Cincinnati*
Roland Eyears, *Central Ohio Technical College*
Cheryl A. Fabrizi, *Broome Community College, State University of New York*
Kathleen Ferris-Costa, *Bridgewater State University*
James Finch, *University of Wisconsin–La Crosse*
Renée Florsheim, *Loyola Marymount University*
Charles W. Ford, *Arkansas State University*
John Fraedrich, *Southern Illinois University, Carbondale*
Terry Gabel, *Monmouth College*
Robert Garrity, *University of Hawaii*
Geoffrey L. Gordon, *Northern Illinois University*
Sharon F. Gregg, *Middle Tennessee University*
Charles Gross, *University of New Hampshire*
John Hafer, *University of Nebraska at Omaha*
David Hansen, *Texas Southern University*
Richard C. Hansen, *Ferris State University*
Nancy Hanson-Rasmussen, *University of Wisconsin–Eau Claire*
Robert R. Harmon, *Portland State University*
Michael Hartline, *Florida State University*
Salah S. Hassan, *George Washington University*
Manoj Hastak, *American University*
Dean Headley, *Wichita State University*
Esther Headley, *Wichita State University*

Debbora Heflin-Bullock, *California State Polytechnic University–Pomona*

Tony Henthorne, *University of Nevada, Las Vegas*

Charles L. Hilton, *Eastern Kentucky University*

Elizabeth C. Hirschman, *Rutgers, State University of New Jersey*

Charlie Hofacker, *Florida State University*

Deloris James, *Howard University*

Ron Johnson, *Colorado Mountain College*

Theodore F. Jula, *Stonehill College*

Peter F. Kaminski, *Northern Illinois University*

Jerome Katrichis, *University of Hartford*

Garland Keesling, *Towson University*

James Kellaris, *University of Cincinnati*

Alvin Kelly, *Florida A&M University*

Sylvia Keyes, *Bridgewater State College*

William M. Kincaid, Jr., *Oklahoma State University*

Hal Koenig, *Oregon State University*

Kathleen Krentler, *San Diego State University*

John Krupa, Jr., *Johnson & Wales University*

Barbara Lafferty, *University of South Florida*

Patricia Laidler, *Massasoit Community College*

Bernard LaLonde, *Ohio State University*

Richard A. Lancioni, *Temple University*

Geoffrey P. Lantos, *Stonehill College*

Charles L. Lapp, *University of Texas at Dallas*

Virginia Larson, *San Jose State University*

John Lavin, *Waukesha County Technical Institute*

Marilyn Lavin, *University of Wisconsin Whitewater*

Hugh E. Law, *East Tennessee State University*

Monle Lee, *Indiana University–South Bend*

Ron Lennon, *University of South Florida–Sarasota-Manatee*

Richard C. Leventhal, *Ashford University*

Marilyn L. Liebrenz-Himes, *George Washington University*

Terry Loe, *Kennesaw State University*

Mary Logan, *Global University*

Paul Londrigan, *Mott Community College*

Anthony Lucas, *Community College of Allegheny County*

George Lucas, *U.S. Learning, Inc.*

William Lundstrom, *Cleveland State University*

Rhonda Mack, *College of Charleston*

Stan Madden, *Baylor University*

Patricia M. Manninen, *North Shore Community College*

Gerald L. Manning, *Des Moines Area Community College*

Lalita A. Manrai, *University of Delaware*

Franklyn Manu, *Morgan State University*

Allen S. Marber, *University of Bridgeport*

Gayle J. Marco, *Robert Morris College*

Marilyn Martin Melchiorre, *College of Idaho*

Carolyn A. Massiah, *University of Central Florida*

James McAlexander, *Oregon State University*

Donald McCartney, *University of Wisconsin–Green Bay*

Jack McNiff, *State University of New York College of Technology at Farmington*

Lee Meadow, *Eastern Illinois University*

Jeffrey A. Meier, *Fox Valley Technical College*

James Meszaros, *County College of Morris*

Brian Meyer, *Minnesota State University*

Martin Meyers, *University of Wisconsin–Stevens Point*

Stephen J. Miller, *Oklahoma State University*

Carol Morris-Calder, *Loyola Marymount University*

David Murphy, *Madisonville Community College*

Keith Murray, *Bryant University*

Sue Ellen Neeley, *University of Houston–Clear Lake*

Carolyn Y. Nicholson, *Stetson University*

Francis L. Notturno, Sr., *Owens Community College*

Terrence V. O'Brien, *Northern Illinois University*

James R. Ogden, *Kutztown University of Pennsylvania*

Shannon Ogden, *Black River Technical College*

Lois Bitner Olson, *San Diego State University*

Robert S. Owen, *Texas A&M University—Texarkana*

David P. Paul, III, *Monmouth University*

Terry Paul, *Ohio State University*

Teresa Pavia, *University of Utah*

John Perrachione, *Truman State University*

Lana Podolak, *Community College of Beaver County*

William Presutti, *Duquesne University*

Daniel Rajaratnam, *University of Texas at Dallas*

Mohammed Rawwas, *University of Northern Iowa*

James D. Reed, *Louisiana State University–Shreveport*

John Reed, *University of New Mexico*

William Rhey, *Florida Southern College*

Glen Riecken, *College of Charleston*

Ed Riordan, *Wayne State University*

Bruce Robertson, *San Francisco State University*

Robert A. Robicheaux, *University of Alabama–Birmingham*

Linda Rose, *Westwood College Online*

Bert Rosenbloom, *Drexel University*

Robert H. Ross, *Wichita State University*

Tom Rossi, *Broome Community College*

Vicki Rostedt, *The University of Akron*

Catherine Roster, *University of New Mexico*

Don Roy, *Middle Tennessee State University*

Catherine Ruggieri, *St. John's University*

Rob Salamida, *SUNY Broome Community College*

Ronald Schill, *Middlebury Institute of International Studies at Monterey*

Bodo Schlegelmilch, *Vienna University of Economics and Business Administration*

Edward Schmitt, *Villanova University*

Donald Sciglimpaglia, *San Diego State University*

Stanley Scott, *University of Alaska—Anchorage*

Beheruz N. Sethna, *University of West Georgia*

Abhay Shah, *Colorado State University—Pueblo*

Morris A. Shapero, *Eckerd College*

Mark Siders, *Southern Oregon University*

Carolyn F. Siegel, *Eastern Kentucky University*
Lyndon Simkin, *University of Reading*
Roberta Slater, *Cedar Crest College*
Paul J. Solomon, *University of South Florida*
Sheldon Somerstein, *City University of New York*
Eric R. Spangenberg, *University of Mississippi*
Rosann L. Spiro, *Indiana University*
William Staples, *University of Houston–Clear Lake*
Carmen Sunda, *University of New Orleans*
Crina Tarasi, *Central Michigan University*
Ruth Taylor, *Texas State University*
Steven A. Taylor, *Illinois State University*
Ira Teich, *Lander College for Men*
Debbie Thorne, *Texas State University*
Sharynn Tomlin, *Angelo State University*

James Underwood, *University of Louisiana–Lafayette*
Barbara Unger, *Western Washington University*
Dale Varble, *Indiana State University*
Bronis Verhage, *Georgia State University*
R. "Vish" Viswanathan Iyer, *University of Northern Colorado*
Kirk Wakefield, *Baylor University*
Harlan Wallingford, *Pace University*
Jacquelyn Warwick, *Andrews University*
James F. Wenthe, *Georgia College*
Sumner M. White, *Massachusetts Bay Community College*
Janice Williams, *University of Central Oklahoma*
Alan R. Wiman, *Rider College*
John Withey, *St. Edwards University*

We would like to thank Charlie Hofacker and Michael Hartline, both of Florida State University, for many helpful suggestions and insights in developing the chapter on digital marketing and social networking. Michael Hartline also assisted in the development of the marketing plan outline and provided suggestions throughout the text.

We thank Gwyn Walters and Kelsey Reddick for their research and editorial assistance in the revision of the chapters. We appreciate the efforts of Marian Wood and Jennifer Sawayda for developing and revising a number of boxed features and cases. We also thank Dianne Kroncke, Shelby Wyatt, Lauren Grantham, and Mark Zekoff for their research and assistance. We deeply appreciate the assistance of Alexa Garcia, Siarra Waddy, Brenda Aram, Jaime Mitash, Clarissa Means, Amy Handlin, and Susan Leshnower for providing editorial technical assistance and support.

We express appreciation for the support and encouragement given to us by our colleagues at Texas A&M University and Auburn University. We are also grateful for the comments and suggestions we received from our own students, student focus groups, and student correspondents who provided feedback through the website.

A number of talented professionals at Cengage Learning and SPi Global have contributed to the development of this book. We are especially grateful to Heather Mooney, Allie Janneck, Stephanie Hall, Bethany Bourgeois, Megan Guiliani, and Lucia Hermo del Teso. Their inspiration, patience, support, and friendship are invaluable.

William M. Pride
O. C. Ferrell

About the Authors

William M. Pride
Texas A&M University

William M. Pride is Professor of Marketing, Mays Business School, at Texas A&M University. He received his PhD from Louisiana State University. In addition to this text, he is the coauthor of Cengage Learning's *Business* text, a market leader. Dr. Pride teaches Principles of Marketing at both undergraduate and graduate levels and constantly solicits student feedback important to revising a Principles of Marketing text.

Dr. Pride's research interests are in advertising, promotion, and distribution channels. His research articles have appeared in major journals in the fields of marketing, such as the *Journal of Marketing*, the *Journal of Marketing Research*, the *Journal of the Academy of Marketing Science*, and the *Journal of Advertising*.

Dr. Pride is a member of the American Marketing Association, Academy of Marketing Science, Society for Marketing Advances, and the Marketing Management Association. He has received the Marketing Fellow Award from the Society for Marketing Advances and the Marketing Innovation Award from the Marketing Management Association. Both of these are lifetime achievement awards.

O.C. Ferrell
Auburn University

O. C. Ferrell is The James T. Pursell Sr. Eminent Scholar in Ethics and Director of the Center for Ethical Organizational Cultures, Auburn University. He served as the Distinguished Professor of Leadership and Ethics at Belmont University and University Distinguished Professor of Marketing at the Anderson School of Management at University of New Mexico. He has also been on the faculties of the University of Wyoming, Colorado State University, University of Memphis, Texas A&M University, Illinois State University, and Southern Illinois University. He received his PhD in marketing from Louisiana State University.

He is past president of the Academic Council of the American Marketing Association, and he chaired the American Marketing Association Ethics Committee. Under his leadership, the committee developed the AMA Code of Ethics and the AMA Code of Ethics for Marketing on the Internet. In addition, he is a former member of the Academy of Marketing Science Board of Governors and is a Society of Marketing Advances and Southwestern Marketing Association Fellow and an Academy of Marketing Science Distinguished Fellow. He was the vice president of publications and is president for the Academy of Marketing Science. He was the first recipient of the Marketing Education Innovation Award from the Marketing Management Association. He received a Lifetime Achievement Award from the Macromarketing Society and a special award for service to doctoral students from the Southeast Doctoral Consortium. He received the Harold Berkman Lifetime Service Award from the Academy of Marketing Science and, more recently, the Cutco/Vector Distinguished Marketing Educator Award.

Dr. Ferrell is the co-author of 20 books and more than 100 published articles and papers. His articles have been published in the *Journal of Marketing Research*, the *Journal of Marketing*, the *Journal of Business Ethics*, the *Journal of Business Research*, the *Journal of the Academy of Marketing Science*, *AMS Review*, and the *Journal of Public Policy & Marketing*, as well as other journals.

Marketing Strategy and Customer Relationships

1 An Overview of Strategic Marketing

2 Planning, Implementing, and Evaluating Marketing Strategies

PART 1 introduces the field of marketing and offers a broad perspective from which to explore and analyze various components of the marketing discipline.

CHAPTER 1 defines *marketing* and explores some key concepts, including customers and target markets, the marketing mix, relationship marketing, the marketing concept, and value.

CHAPTER 2 provides an overview of strategic marketing issues, such as the effect of organizational resources and opportunities on the planning process; the role of the mission statement; corporate, business-unit, and marketing strategies; and the creation of the marketing plan.

ECONOMIC FORCES

COMPETITIVE FORCES

POLITICAL FORCES

PRODUCT

PRICE   CUSTOMER   DISTRIBUTION

PROMOTION

SOCIOCULTURAL FORCES

LEGAL AND REGULATORY FORCES

TECHNOLOGICAL FORCES

CHAPTER

1

An Overview of Strategic Marketing

LEARNING OBJECTIVES

1-1 Define marketing.

1-2 Explain the different variables of the marketing mix.

1-3 Describe how marketing creates value.

1-4 Briefly explore the marketing environment.

1-5 Summarize the marketing concept.

1-6 Identify the importance of building customer relationships.

1-7 Explain why marketing is important to our global economy.

JERAMEY LENDE/SHUTTERSTOCK.COM

Amazon Sells Everything from A to Z

Jeff Bezos came up with the idea for an online bookstore after hearing about the rapid growth of web usage. Before Google or eBay came on the scene, Bezos quit his job in finance and founded Amazon in 1994. When books proved to be a successful product, he asked some of his customers what else he should sell on the site. The response was overwhelming. Bezos realized Amazon met a customer need that was greater than books: convenience.

Today, Amazon sells everything from toys and clothing to ebooks and groceries. Amazon's market orientation has led to its growth beyond retail to content as consumer behavior on the web continues to evolve. The site is now the source of original, award-winning shows such as *Transparent* as part of its Amazon Prime offering. Bezos attributes Amazon's success to its focus on the customer instead of the competition. For example, in order to maintain and build an exchange relationship with its customers, Amazon offers an A-to-z Guarantee that protects against damaged goods and late deliveries.

Amazon provides products that satisfy customer needs; and, despite its immense success, the company believes it can create even more value for more customers. For instance, Amazon offers a reduced Prime membership to consumers with an Electronic Benefit Transfer (EBT) card to attract low-income customers. With its vast network of partnerships and cost efficiencies, Amazon often uses price as a competitive tool. The company has also set its sights on Generation Z with a feature that allows users to create supervised accounts for their teenagers so they can make parent-approved purchases.

In another move to become an indispensable part of every household, Amazon has continued to evolve the Amazon Echo, a voice-controlled digital assistant. Through the Echo, users can check the weather, get news alerts, play games, control connected smart home devices, and more. Prime users, roughly two-thirds of U.S. households, can also order prime-eligible items. Additionally, Amazon is transforming grocery shopping with its recent purchase of Whole Foods. The company plans to integrate various aspects of Whole Foods, Prime Now two-hour delivery, and AmazonFresh grocery delivery to explore new ways to meet customer needs.[1]

Like all organizations, Amazon strives to provide products that customers want, communicate useful information about them to excite interest, make them available when and where customers want to buy them, and price them appropriately. Even if an organization does all these things well, however, competition from marketers of similar products, economic conditions, and other factors can affect the company's success. Such factors influence the decisions that all organizations must make in strategic marketing.

This chapter introduces the strategic marketing concepts and decisions covered throughout the text. First, we develop a definition of *marketing* and explore each element of the definition in detail. Next, we explore the importance of value-driven marketing. We also introduce the marketing concept and consider several issues associated with its implementation. Additionally, we take a look at the management of customer relationships and relationship marketing. Finally, we examine the importance of marketing in a global society.

1-1 DEFINING MARKETING

If you ask several people what *marketing* is, you are likely to hear a variety of descriptions. Although many people think marketing is advertising or selling, marketing is much more complex than most people realize. In this book, we define **marketing** as the process of creating, distributing, promoting, and pricing goods, services, and ideas to facilitate satisfying exchange relationships with customers and to develop and maintain favorable relationships with stakeholders in a dynamic environment. Our definition is consistent with that of the American Marketing Association (AMA), which defines *marketing* as "the activity, set of institutions, and processes for creating, communicating, delivering, and exchanging offerings that have value for customers, clients, partners, and society at large."[2]

The essence of marketing is to develop satisfying exchanges from which both customers and marketers benefit. The customer expects to gain a reward or benefit greater than the costs incurred in a marketing transaction. The marketer expects to gain something of value in return, generally the price charged for the product. Through buyer–seller interaction, a customer develops expectations about the seller's future behavior. To fulfill these expectations, the marketer must deliver on promises made. Over time, this interaction results in relationships between the two parties. Fast-food restaurants such as Wendy's and Chick-fil-A depend on repeat purchases from satisfied customers—many often live or work a few miles from these restaurants—whereas customer expectations revolve around tasty food, value, and dependable service.

The marketing-mix variables—which include product, distribution, promotion, and price—are often viewed as controllable because they can be modified. However, there are limits to how much marketing managers can alter them. Competitive forces, economic conditions, political forces, laws and regulations, technology, and sociocultural forces shape the decision-making environment for controllable variables. While some products are tangible goods, services are also products and represent a significant part of the economy. Entire industries such as health care, entertainment, sports, hospitality, and tourism provide services.

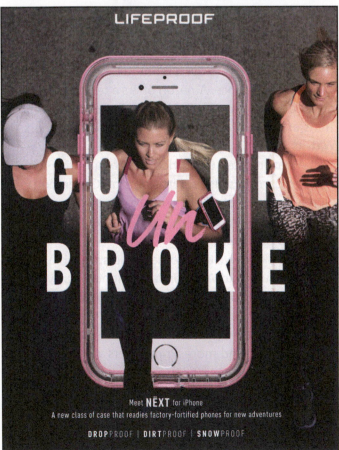

SOURCE: LIFEPROOF.COM

Appealing to Target Markets
LifeProof appeals to consumers with an active lifestyle.

1-1a **Marketing Focuses on Customers**

As the purchasers of the products that organizations develop, distribute, promote, and price, **customers** are the focal point of all marketing activities (see Figure 1.1). Organizations have to define their products not as what the companies make or produce but as what they do to satisfy customers. As the advertisement indicates, LifeProof phone cases are designed for consumers that want a durable case for an active lifestyle. The case provides an advantage to consumers that want a dropproof, dirtproof, and snowproof phone case.

Organizations generally focus their marketing efforts on a specific group of customers, called a **target market**. Marketing managers may define a target market as a vast number of people or a relatively small group. For instance, marketers are increasingly interested in Hispanic consumers as they constitute a population of more than 59 million and buying power of more than $1.5 trillion.[3] Within the last decade, Hispanics made up more than half of the population gains in the United States. As a result, marketers are developing new ways to reach this demographic. For instance, online retail giant Amazon includes Spanish language options to its site.[4] Some companies target multiple markets with different products, distribution systems, promotions, and prices for each one while others focus on a smaller niche market. Comcast, for example, offers solutions for consumers as well as small businesses and larger enterprises. While consumer-oriented products and services make up the majority of its business, business services is their fastest growing segment.[5] Home Depot, on the other hand, targets a number of markets with thousands of items. It provides home improvement products for both household consumers and contractors.

customers The purchasers of organizations' products; the focal point of all marketing activities

target market A specific group of customers on whom an organization focuses its marketing efforts

Figure 1.1	**Components of Strategic Marketing**

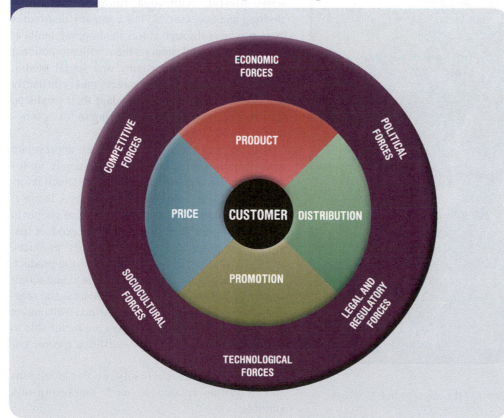

1-2 MARKETING DEALS WITH PRODUCTS, DISTRIBUTION, PROMOTION, AND PRICE

Marketing is more than simply advertising or selling a product; it involves developing and managing a product that will satisfy customer needs. It focuses on communicating availability in the right place and at the right price. It also requires promotion, communicating information that helps customers learn about the product and determine if the product will satisfy their needs. These activities are planned, organized, implemented, and controlled to meet the needs of customers within the target market. Marketers refer to these activities—product, distribution, promotion, and pricing—as the **marketing mix** because they decide what type of each variable to use and how to coordinate the variables. Marketing creates value through the marketing mix. A primary goal of a marketing manager is to create and maintain the right mix of these variables to satisfy customers' needs for a general product type. Amazon is well-known for its implementation of the marketing mix. It routinely engages in research and development to create new products such as its digital assistant, Echo. It promotes its products through advertising, social media, and media events. Best Buy and other retailers provide these products at a premium price to convey their quality and effectiveness. Note in Figure 1.1 that the marketing mix is built around the customer.

marketing mix Four marketing activities—product, distribution, promotion, and pricing—that a firm can control to meet the needs of customers within its target market

Marketing managers strive to develop a marketing mix that matches the needs of customers in the target market. Clothing retailer lululemon athletica, for example, targets shoppers with an active lifestyle with yoga, running, and fitness clothing and accessories. The company distributes these products through stores in shopping malls at premium prices and supports them with promotional activities such as advertising and social media. Additionally, marketing managers must constantly monitor the competition and adapt their products, distribution, promotion, and pricing to foster long-term success.

Before marketers can develop an appropriate marketing mix, they must collect in-depth, up-to-date information about customer needs. Such information might include data about the age, income, ethnicity, gender, and educational level of people in the target market, their preferences for product features, their attitudes toward competitors' products, and the frequency with which they use the product. SAP operates in the digital marketplace and monitors every consumer's needs, preferences, and reactions to adjust its marketing mix. Armed with market information, marketing managers are better able to develop a marketing mix that satisfies a specific target market.

Let's look more closely at the decisions and activities related to each marketing-mix variable.

IT'S TODAY'S BEST SELLER. AND ALREADY YESTERDAY'S NEWS.

PRODUCTS ARE LIVE.
In a digital marketplace, a great product is only a start. With SAP, you can monitor every consumer's needs, preferences and reactions live. So you can change your product experience, not just with the times, but with the moment. And take each consumer on the exact journey they're looking for.
sap.com/livebusiness

SAP   Run Simple

SOURCE: SAP

Promotional Activities
This SAP advertisement informs the audience of the ways in which its service can help businesses learn about consumers.

1-2a **The Product Variable**

Successful marketing efforts result in products that become part of everyday life. Consider the satisfaction customers have had over the years from Pepsi, Mastercard credit cards, Folgers coffee, and professional sports such as baseball, basketball, hockey, and football. The product variable of the marketing mix deals with researching customers' needs and wants and designing a product that satisfies them. A product could be considered a bundle of satisfaction that provides value to the consumer. A **product** can be a good, a service, or an idea. A good is a physical entity you can touch. Marc Jacobs sunglasses, Subaru hatchbacks, and Beats by Dre headphones are all examples of products. In the advertisement on the left, Breyers highlights its creamy Gelato Indulgences as an alternative to ice cream. Breyers Gelato Indulgences is an example of a tangible good that consumers can enjoy. Consumers can select from multiple flavors with sauces and gourmet toppings. In contrast, the advertisement on the right promotes the BigCommerce e-commerce software and shopping cart platform to business owners as a way to sell products online. The platform includes beautiful, responsive themes to help e-commerce retailers grow their businesses. This software is an example of an intangible product. A service is the application of human and mechanical efforts to people or objects to provide intangible benefits to customers. Air travel, education, insurance, banking, health care, and day care are examples of services. Ideas include concepts, philosophies, images, and issues. For instance, a marriage counselor, for a fee, gives spouses ideas to help improve their relationship. Other marketers of ideas include political parties, churches, and animal protection groups.

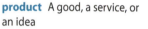

product A good, a service, or an idea

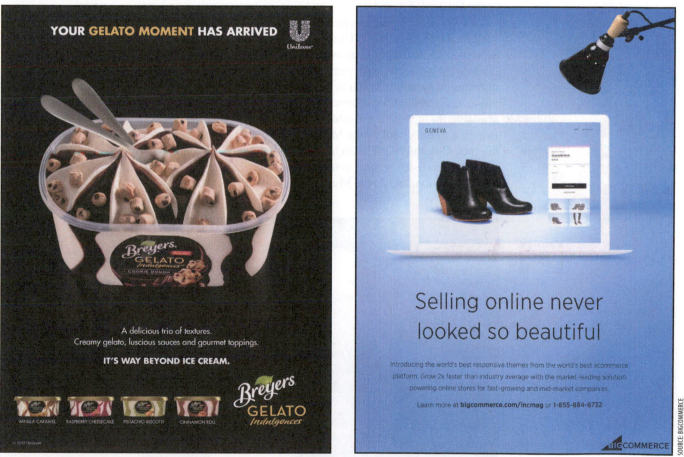

Types of Products
Breyers Gelato Indulgences are tangible goods that consumers enjoy for pleasure. Online software, such as the BigCommerce e-commerce software and shopping cart platform, represents intangible products that provide business owners a way to retail products online.

The product variable also involves creating or modifying brand names and packaging and may include decisions regarding warranty and repair services. For example, Icelandic Provisions introduced paper-wrapped cups for its skyr, a yogurt-like dairy product, because they can be recycled easier than printed shrink-sleeved cups.[6] The company adapted its product's packaging to provide a healthier and "greener" offering.

Product variable decisions and related activities are important because they directly relate to customers' needs and wants. Apple continues to upgrade its iPhone using different model identifiers such as 7, 8, and X to signal new modifications. To maintain an assortment of products that helps an organization achieve its goals, marketers must develop new products, modify existing ones, and eliminate those that no longer satisfy enough buyers or that yield unacceptable profits.

1-2b The Distribution Variable

To satisfy customers, products must be available at the right time and in appropriate locations. Subway, for example, locates its restaurants not only in strip malls but also inside Walmarts, Home Depots, laundromats, churches, and hospitals, as well as inside Goodwill stores, car dealerships, and appliance stores. There are more than 44,800 Subways in 112 different countries, surpassing McDonald's as the world's largest chain.[7]

In dealing with the distribution variable, a marketing manager makes products available in the quantities desired to as many target-market customers as possible, keeping total inventory, transportation, and storage costs as efficient as possible. A marketing manager also may select and motivate intermediaries (wholesalers and retailers), establish and maintain inventory control procedures, and develop and manage transportation and storage systems.

Supply chain management (SCM) involves maintaining a flow of products through physical distribution activities. This includes acquiring resources, inventory, and the interlinked networks that make products available to customers through purchasing, logistics, and operations. SCM has become very important to the success of online marketers. Consider Amazon's distribution system that is now integrating its own warehousing and transportation to deliver products—sometimes the same day they are ordered. Companies now can make their products available throughout the world without maintaining facilities in each country. For instance, Pandora, Spotify, and Apple Music have benefited from the ability to stream music over the internet. Customers can listen to music for free with commercial interruptions, or they can pay to upgrade to listen without commercials. Pandora has 73.3 million active users, while Spotify has 140 million, and Apple Music has 1 million.[8]

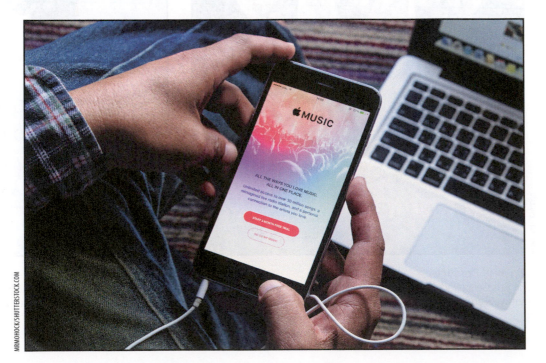

Distribution
Apple Music uses digital distribution to allow consumers to stream ad-free music online or off.

MRMOHOCK/SHUTTERSTOCK.COM

1-2c The Promotion Variable

The promotion variable relates to activities used to inform and persuade to create a desired response. Promotion can increase public awareness of the organization and of new or existing products. It can help create a direct response by including a link to access a website or order a product. Consider Geico's television and radio advertising that encourages people to spend 15 minutes "to save 15% or more on car insurance." Geico's tagline is meant to elicit a direct response from consumers, encouraging them to take 15 minutes to make a sales call to a Geico representative.

Promotional activities can inform customers about product features. It is a mistake to think promotion just involves advertising. Personal selling is needed for almost every type of product and provides the revenue that the firm must have to be successful. Sales promotions such as coupons and other incentives such as online discount codes keep sales dynamic. Publicity that provides information, often in the mass media, is another form of promotion that firms try to manage. The promotion mix focuses integrated marketing communication to inform and persuade consumers to purchase a product.[9]

Promotion can also help to sustain interest in established products that have been available for decades, such as M&M'S or Tide detergent. Many companies are using the internet to communicate information about themselves and their products. L'Oréal operates Makeup. com, a beauty website that discusses beauty trends and shares makeup tutorials using products from L'Oréal brands like Urban Decay, Maybelline, and NYX.[10]

1-2d The Price Variable

The price variable relates to decisions and actions associated with pricing objectives and policies and actual product prices. Price is a critical component of the marketing mix because customers are concerned about the value obtained in an exchange. Price is often used as a competitive tool, and intense price competition sometimes leads to price wars. Higher prices can be used competitively to establish a product's premium image. Rolex, for example, has an image of high quality and high price that has given it significant status. Other companies are skilled at providing products at prices lower than others, for example, global discount supermarket chain Aldi. Amazon and Walmart use a vast network of partnerships and cost efficiencies to provide products at low prices. Many retailers, such as Macy's and Nordstrom, have had to close stores because of the inability to provide lower prices.

The marketing-mix variables are often viewed as controllable because they can be modified. However, there are limits to how much marketing managers can alter them. Economic conditions, competitive structure, and government regulations may prevent a manager from adjusting prices frequently or significantly. Making changes in the size, shape, and design of most tangible goods is expensive; therefore, such product features cannot be altered very often. In addition, promotional campaigns and methods used to distribute products ordinarily cannot be rewritten or revamped overnight. But dramatic changes in price can be made any time. This makes price the most flexible variable in the marketing mix.

1-3 MARKETING CREATES VALUE

Learning Objective 1-3
Describe how marketing creates value.

Value is an important element of managing long-term customer relationships and implementing the marketing concept. We view **value** as a customer's subjective assessment of benefits relative to costs in determining the worth of a product (customer value = customer benefits − customer costs). Consumers develop a concept of value through the integration of their perceptions of product quality and financial sacrifice.[11] From a company's perspective, there is a trade-off between increasing the value offered to a customer and maximizing the profits from a transaction.[12]

Customer benefits include anything a buyer receives in an exchange. Hotels and motels, for example, basically provide a room with a bed and bathroom, but each firm provides a different level of service, amenities, and atmosphere to satisfy its guests. Motel 6 offers the minimum

value A customer's subjective assessment of benefits relative to costs in determining the worth of a product

NORTHFOTO/SHUTTERSTOCK.COM

Value-Driven Marketing
Nordstrom creates value for customers with its liberal return policies and strong customer service.

services necessary to maintain a quality, efficient, low-price overnight accommodation. In contrast, The Ritz-Carlton provides every imaginable service a guest might desire. The hotel even allows its staff members to spend up to $2,000 to settle customer complaints.[13] Customers judge which type of accommodation offers the best value according to the benefits they desire and their willingness and ability to pay for the costs associated with the benefits.

Customer costs include anything a buyer must give up to obtain the benefits the product provides. The most obvious cost is the monetary price of the product, but nonmonetary costs can be equally important in a customer's determination of value. Two nonmonetary costs are the time and effort customers expend to find and purchase desired products. To reduce time and effort, a company can increase product availability, thereby making it more convenient for buyers to purchase the firm's products. Another nonmonetary cost is risk, which can be reduced by offering good basic warranties or extended warranties for an additional charge.[14] Another risk-reduction strategy is the offer of a 100 percent satisfaction guarantee. This strategy is increasingly popular in today's internet shopping environment. Bath & Body Works, for example, uses such a guarantee to reduce the risk involved in ordering merchandise from its stores and website.

The processes which people use to determine the value of a product may differ widely. All of us tend to get a feel for the worth of products based on our own expectations and previous experience. We can, for example, compare the value of tires, batteries, and computers directly with the value of competing products. We evaluate movies, sporting events, and performances by entertainers on the more subjective basis of personal preferences and emotions. For most purchases, we do not consciously try to calculate the associated benefits and costs. It becomes an instinctive feeling that General Mills' Cheerios is a good value or that McDonald's is a good place to take children for a quick lunch. The purchase of an automobile or a mountain bike may have emotional components, but more conscious decision making also may figure in the process of determining value.

In developing marketing activities, it is important to recognize that customers receive benefits based on their experiences. For example, many computer buyers consider services such as fast delivery, ease of installation, technical advice, and training assistance to be important elements of the product. Each marketing activity has its own benefits and costs and must be adapted for its contribution to value.[15] For example, hotels and restaurants are based on experience and atmosphere. Hilton hotels maintain a high standard of service from the minute a consumer walks in the lobby. Customers also derive benefits from the act of shopping and selecting products. These benefits can be affected by the atmosphere or environment of a store, such as Red Lobster's nautical/seafood theme. Even the ease of navigating a website can have a tremendous impact on perceived value.

The marketing mix can be used to enhance perceptions of value. A product that demonstrates value usually has a feature or an enhancement that provides benefits. Promotional activities can also help to create image and prestige characteristics that customers consider in their assessment of a product's value. In some cases, value may be perceived simply as the lowest price. Many customers may not care about the quality of the paper towels they buy; they simply want the cheapest ones for use in cleaning up spills because they plan to throw them in the trash anyway. On the other hand, more people are looking for the fastest, most convenient way to achieve a goal and therefore become insensitive to pricing. For example, many busy customers are buying more prepared meals in supermarkets to take home and serve quickly, even though these meals cost considerably more than meals prepared from scratch. In such cases the products with the greatest convenience may be perceived as having the greatest value. The availability or distribution of products also can enhance their value. Taco Bell wants to have its Mexican-inspired fast-food products available at any time and any place people are thinking about consuming food. It therefore has introduced Taco Bell products into supermarkets, vending machines, college campuses, and other convenient locations. Thus, the development of an effective marketing strategy requires understanding the needs and desires of customers and designing a marketing mix to satisfy them and provide the value they want.

1-3a Marketing Builds Relationships with Customers and Other Stakeholders

Marketing also creates value through the building of stakeholder relationships. Individuals and organizations engage in marketing to facilitate **exchanges**, the provision or transfer of goods, services, or ideas in return for something of value. Any product (good, service, or even idea) may be involved in a marketing exchange. We assume only that individuals and organizations expect to gain a reward in excess of the costs incurred.

For an exchange to take place, four conditions must exist. First, two or more individuals, groups, or organizations must participate, and each must possess something of value that the other party desires. Second, the exchange should provide a benefit or satisfaction to both

exchanges The provision or transfer of goods, services, or ideas in return for something of value

MARKUS MAINKA/SHUTTERSTOCK.COM

Satisfying Stakeholder Needs
Southwest Airlines continues to excel at offering services that satisfy customers, generate jobs, and create shareholder wealth.

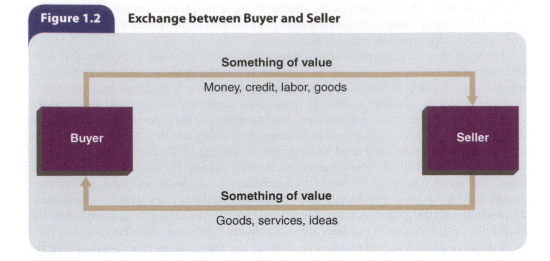

Figure 1.2 Exchange between Buyer and Seller

parties involved in the transaction. Third, each party must have confidence in the promise of the "something of value" held by the other. If you go to a Taylor Swift concert, for example, you go with the expectation of a great performance. Finally, to build trust, the parties to the exchange must meet expectations.

Figure 1.2 depicts the exchange process. The arrows indicate that the parties communicate that each has something of value available to exchange. An exchange will not necessarily take place just because these conditions exist; marketing activities can occur even without an actual transaction or sale. You may see an ad for a Samsung refrigerator, for instance, but you might never buy the luxury appliance. When an exchange occurs, products are traded for other products or for financial resources.

Marketing activities should attempt to create and maintain satisfying exchange relationships. To maintain an exchange relationship, buyers must be satisfied with the good, service, or idea obtained, and sellers must be satisfied with the financial reward or something else of value received. The customer relationship often endures over an extended time period, and repeat purchases are critical for the firm. A dissatisfied customer who lacks trust in the relationship often searches for alternative organizations or products.

Marketers are concerned with building and maintaining relationships not only with customers but also with relevant stakeholders. **Stakeholders** include those constituents who have a "stake," or claim, in some aspect of a company's products, operations, markets, industry, and outcomes; these include customers, employees, investors and shareholders, suppliers, governments, communities, competitors, and many others. While engaging in marketing activities, the firm should be proactive and responsive to stakeholder concerns. This engagement has been found to increase financial performance.[16] Therefore, developing and maintaining favorable relations with stakeholders is crucial to the long-term growth of an organization and its products. For example, well-satisfied employees directly improve customer satisfaction, and dependable suppliers are necessary to make quality products. Communities can be positive contributors to a firm's reputation, and in turn these communities provide opportunities for a firm to make social and economic contributions. Customers and competitors are often considered to be core stakeholders in developing a marketing strategy.[17]

stakeholders Constituents who have a "stake," or claim, in some aspect of a company's products, operations, markets, industry, and outcomes

marketing environment The competitive, economic, political, legal and regulatory, technological, and sociocultural forces that surround the customer and affect the marketing mix

Learning Objective 1-4

Briefly explore the marketing environment.

1-4 MARKETING OCCURS IN A DYNAMIC ENVIRONMENT

Marketing activities do not take place in a vacuum. The **marketing environment**, which includes competitive, economic, political, legal and regulatory, technological, and sociocultural forces, surrounds the customer and affects the marketing mix (see Figure 1.1). The effects of these forces on buyers and sellers can be dramatic and difficult to predict. Their impact on value can be extensive as market changes can easily influence how stakeholders perceive certain products. They can create threats to marketers but also can generate opportunities for new products and new methods of reaching customers.

The forces of the marketing environment affect a marketer's ability to facilitate value-driven marketing exchanges in three general ways. First, they influence customers by affecting their lifestyles, standards of living, and preferences and needs for products. Because a marketing manager tries to develop and adjust the marketing mix to satisfy customers, effects of environmental forces on customers also have an indirect impact on marketing-mix components. Second, marketing environment forces can determine whether and how a marketing manager can perform certain marketing activities. Third, environmental forces may shape a marketing manager's decisions and actions by influencing buyers' reactions to the firm's marketing mix.

Marketing environment forces can fluctuate quickly and dramatically, which is one reason why marketing is so interesting and challenging. Because these forces are closely interrelated, changes in one may cause changes in others. For example, evidence linking children's consumption of soft drinks and fast foods to health issues has exposed marketers of such products to negative publicity and generated calls for legislation regulating the sale of soft drinks in public schools. Some companies have responded to these concerns by voluntarily reformulating products to make them healthier or even introducing new products. For example, Pepsi reformulated its Diet Pepsi product by replacing the sweetener aspartame with sucralose and acesulfame potassium. Although the Food and Drug Administration (FDA) has ruled aspartame as safe, many consumers view aspartame as having health risks. Despite Pepsi's attempt to appeal to changing consumer preferences, the initial reactions of Diet Pepsi loyalists after the company reformulated the product were often negative. Pepsi reintroduced an aspartame-sweetened version, now called Diet Pepsi Classic, after the backlash.[18] Changes in the marketing environment produce uncertainty for marketers and at times hurt marketing efforts, but they also create opportunities. For example, when oil and gasoline prices increase, consumers shift to potential alternative sources of transportation including bikes, buses, light rail, trains, carpooling, more energy-efficient vehicle purchases, or telecommuting when possible. When those prices decrease, consumers purchase more SUVs, drive more, and may have more money for other purchases.

Marketers who are alert to changes in environmental forces not only can adjust to and influence these changes but can also capitalize on the opportunities such changes provide. Marketing-mix variables—product, distribution, promotion, and price—are factors over which an organization has control; the forces of the environment, however, are subject to far less control. Even though marketers know that they cannot predict changes in the marketing environment with certainty, they must nevertheless plan for them. Because these environmental forces have such a profound effect on marketing activities, we explore each of them in considerable depth in Chapter 3.

1-5 UNDERSTANDING THE MARKETING CONCEPT

Learning Objective 1-5

Summarize the marketing concept.

Firms frequently fail to attract customers with what they have to offer because they define their business as "making a product" rather than as "helping potential customers satisfy their needs and wants." Drones provide an example of a product that is satisfying many needs and wants from being a toy or recreational product to commercial applications. The marketing concept is based on the philosophy that consumers purchase the satisfaction and value they derive from a product not the product itself. Companies that do not pursue such opportunities struggle to compete.

According to the **marketing concept**, an organization should try to provide products that satisfy customers' needs through a coordinated set of activities that also allows the organization to achieve its goals. Customer satisfaction is the major focus of the marketing concept.

marketing concept A managerial philosophy that an organization should try to satisfy customers' needs through a coordinated set of activities that also allows the organization to achieve its goals

To implement the marketing concept, an organization strives to determine what buyers want and uses this information to develop satisfying products. It focuses on customer analysis, competitor analysis, and integration of the firm's resources to provide customer value and satisfaction, as well as to generate long-term profits.[19] For example, Kellogg's knows its customers want a fast breakfast. As the advertisement suggests, Kellogg's Nutri-Grain Soft Baked Breakfast Bars are ideal for a wholesome breakfast that won't slow customers down. The breakfast bars, made with whole grains and real fruit, satisfy consumers' desires for a quick and healthy breakfast option.

Howard Schultz, founder and former CEO of Starbucks, demonstrated the company's grasp on the marketing concept by explaining that Starbucks is not a coffee business that serves people, but rather a "people business serving coffee." Starbucks' leadership sees the company as being "in the business of humanity," emphasizing the fact that Starbucks is not only concerned about customers but society as well.[20] Thus, the marketing concept emphasizes that marketing begins and ends with customers. Research has found a positive association between customer satisfaction and shareholder value, and high levels of customer satisfaction also tend to attract and retain high-quality employees and managers.[21]

The marketing concept is not a second definition of marketing. It is a management philosophy guiding an organization's overall activities. This philosophy affects all organizational activities, not just marketing. Production, finance, accounting, human resources, and marketing departments must work together. For example, at Procter & Gamble the marketing function coordinates research and development, distribution, and resource deployment to focus on providing consumer products for households.

The marketing concept is a strategic concept to achieve objectives. A firm that adopts the marketing concept must satisfy not only its customers' objectives but also its own, or it will not stay in business long. The overall objectives of a business usually relate to profits, market share, sales, or probably a combination of all three. The marketing concept stresses that an organization can best achieve these objectives by being customer-oriented. Thus, implementing the marketing concept should benefit the organization as well as its customers.

It is important for marketers to consider not only their current buyers' needs but also the long-term needs of society. Striving to satisfy customers' desires by sacrificing society's long-term welfare is unacceptable. For instance, there is significant demand for large SUVs and trucks. However, environmentalists and federal regulators are challenging automakers to produce more fuel-efficient vehicles with increased miles-per-gallon standards. The question that remains is whether Americans are willing to give up their spacious SUVs for the good of the environment. Automakers are addressing environmental concerns with smaller, more fuel-efficient SUVs. Demand for these SUVs shows that these vehicles are not going away anytime soon. So, implementing the marketing concept and meeting the needs of society is a balancing act.

BREAKFASTER.

Made with invigorating whole grains and real fruit to help you move at the speed of morning.

THE BREAKFAST BAR

SOURCE: KELLOGG'S

The Marketing Concept
Kellogg's introduced the Nutri-Grain Soft Baked Breakfast Bars to satisfy consumers' desires for a quick and easy breakfast.

DISRUPTIVE MARKETING

Zappos' Customer Service Strategy Is a Perfect Fit

In 2000, Tony Hsieh became the CEO of Zappos, the online shoe retailer, at age 26. Hsieh saw an opportunity to create value for customers by using the company's resources to provide a stellar customer service experience to shoppers. Although the company initially struggled to make a profit, things took a positive turn in 2007 after the company reached annual sales of $840 million, and in 2009 Amazon acquired the company for $1.2 billion.

Zappos strives to make the shopping experience easy and enjoyable. It provides a 100 percent satisfaction guaranteed return policy to build and maintain strong customer relationships. Recognizing the hesitancy of many shoppers to purchase shoes online, Zappos encourages customers to order several styles and return items if needed. This strategy may seem expensive but tends to work in Zappos' favor and satisfies a customer's needs that

many retailers do not. It also allows customers to feel confident when shopping with the company as they are able to return unwanted products easily. The company has disrupted the way consumers purchase shoes from department stores and specialty shoe stores.

Zappos' customer relationship management strategy focuses on building customer relationships through human interaction. For example, if a customer experiences a problem with an order or has a question about a product, Zappos responds honestly, authentically, and in a timely manner. The company recently used several of its customer success stories in a series of ads that highlight Zappos' ability to satisfy its customers. With this type of customer service, the company builds satisfying, long-term customer relationships and increases customer lifetime value as happy customers make repeat purchases.[a]

1-5a Evolution of the Marketing Concept

The marketing concept may seem like an obvious approach to running a business. Yet, while satisfied consumers are necessary for business success, historically not all firms were successful in implementing this concept. The evolution of marketing has gone through three time periods, including production, sales, and market orientation. While this is an oversimplification, these frameworks help to understand marketing over time. There have always been companies that embraced the marketing concept and focused on the interests of consumers.

The Production Orientation

During the second half of the 19th century, the Industrial Revolution was in full swing in the United States. Electricity, rail transportation, division of labor, assembly lines, and mass production made it possible to produce goods more efficiently. With new technology and new ways of using labor, products poured into the marketplace, where demand for manufactured goods was strong. Although mass markets were evolving, firms were developing the ability to produce more products, and competition was becoming more intense.

The Sales Orientation

While sales have always been needed to make a profit, during the first half of the 20th century competition increased and businesses realized that they would have to focus more on selling products to many buyers. Businesses viewed sales as the major means of increasing profits, and this period came to have a sales orientation. Businesspeople believed that the most important marketing activities were personal selling, advertising, and distribution. Today, some people incorrectly equate marketing with a sales orientation and are still guided by this approach.

The Market Orientation

Although marketing history reveals that some firms have always produced products that consumers desired, by the 1950s, both businesses and academics developed new philosophies and terminology to explain why this approach is necessary for organizational success.[22] This perspective emphasized that marketers first need to determine what customers want and then produce those products rather than making the products first and then trying to persuade customers that they need them. As more organizations realized the importance of satisfying customers' needs, U.S. businesses entered the marketing era called market orientation.

A **market orientation** requires the "organizationwide generation of market intelligence pertaining to current and future customer needs, dissemination of the intelligence across departments, and organizationwide responsiveness to it."[23] Market orientation is linked to new product innovation by developing a strategic focus to explore and develop new products to serve target markets.[24] For example, the popular outdoor store REI allows consumers to return most products within one year for a full refund. Electronics have a shorter window for returns. A "user friendly" return policy helps REI better serve its customers' desires to return merchandise without time pressures.[25] Top managers, marketing managers, nonmarketing managers (those in production, finance, human resources, and so on), and customers are all important in developing and carrying out a market orientation. Trust, openness, honoring promises, respect, collaboration, and listening are six values required by organizations striving to become more market oriented.[26]

A market orientation should recognize the need to create specific types of value-creating capabilities that enhance organizational performance.[27] For example, a bank needs to use its resources to provide the desired level of customer service to a market that is increasingly made up of online users. Unless marketing managers provide continuous customer-focused leadership with minimal interdepartmental conflict, achieving a market orientation will be difficult. Nonmarketing managers must communicate with marketing managers to share information important to understanding the customer.

Finally, a market orientation involves being responsive to ever-changing customer needs and wants. For example, Weight Watchers made its program easier for consumers to use by adapting its points system. The "Freestyle" program builds upon understanding a "healthy lifestyle" with more than 200 ingredients deemed healthy as opposed to penalizing members with higher points for less healthy options. The sustainability and results exceed those of its other programs.[28] Today, businesses want to satisfy customers and build meaningful long-term relationships. Doing so helps a firm boost its own financial value. For example, Oprah Winfrey bought a 10 percent stake in Weight Watchers because she believes in the company.

1-5b Implementing the Marketing Concept

A philosophy may sound reasonable and look good on paper, but this does not mean that it can be put into practice easily. To implement the marketing concept, a market-oriented organization must accept some general conditions and recognize and deal with several problems. Consequently, the marketing concept has yet to be fully accepted by all businesses.

Management must first establish an information system to discover customers' real needs and then use the information to create satisfying products. SAP offers enterprise software to help clients manage their business operations and customer relationships. One of its clients, the German Football Association, used SAP software to improve communication with fans and personalize marketing activities.[29] Listening and responding to consumers' frustrations and appreciation is the key in implementing the marketing concept. An information system is usually expensive; management must commit money and time for its development and

market orientation An organizationwide commitment to researching and responding to customer needs maintenance. Without an adequate information system, however, an organization cannot be market oriented.

To satisfy customers' objectives as well as its own, a company also must coordinate all of its activities. This may require restructuring its internal operations, including production, marketing, and other business functions. This requires the firm to adapt to a changing external environment, including changing customer expectations. Companies that monitor the external environment can often predict major changes and adapt successfully. Elon Musk has been a leader in supporting the research and development for driverless cars. Consumers increasingly do not wish to drive and use ride-sharing services. The development of Artificial Intelligence at Tesla, they believe, will result in a global businesses advantage at a lower cost than the competition.[30]

If marketing is not included in the organization's top-level management, a company could fail to address actual, and evolving, customer needs and desires. Implementing the marketing concept demands the support not only of top management but also of managers and staff at all levels of the organization.

1-6 CUSTOMER RELATIONSHIP MANAGEMENT

Customer relationship management (CRM) focuses on using information about customers to create marketing strategies that develop and sustain desirable customer relationships. Achieving the full profit potential of each customer relationship should be the fundamental goal of every marketing strategy. Marketing relationships with customers are the lifeblood of all businesses. At the most basic level, profits can be obtained through relationships in the following ways: (1) by acquiring new customers, (2) by enhancing the profitability of existing customers, and (3) by extending the duration of customer relationships. In addition to retaining customers, companies also should focus on regaining and managing relationships with customers who have abandoned the firm.[31] Implementing the marketing concept means optimizing the exchange relationship, otherwise known as the relationship between a company's financial investment in customer relationships and the return generated by customers' loyalty and retention.

1-6a Relationship Marketing

Maintaining positive relationships with customers is a crucial goal for marketers. The term **relationship marketing** refers to "long-term, mutually beneficial arrangements in which both the buyer and seller focus on value enhancement through the creation of more satisfying exchanges."[32] Relationship marketing continually deepens the buyer's trust in the company, and as the customer's confidence grows, this, in turn, increases the firm's understanding of the customer's needs. Buyers and marketers can thus enter into a close relationship in which both participate in the creation of value.[33] Successful marketers respond to customer needs and strive to increase value to buyers over time. Eventually, this interaction becomes a solid relationship that allows for cooperation and mutual dependency. Relationship marketing begins with creating a product image and impression. HBO won awards for *Game of Thrones* brand building that created awareness and built excitement for the upcoming season and for allowing greater use of user-generated content and connectedness to the show and other fans.[34]

Relationship marketing strives to build satisfying exchange relationships between buyers and sellers by gathering useful data at all customer contact points and analyzing that data to better understand customers' needs, desires, and habits. It focuses on building and using databases and leveraging technologies to identify strategies and methods that will maximize the lifetime value of each desirable customer to the company. It is imperative that marketers educate themselves about their customers' expectations if they are to satisfy their needs; customer dissatisfaction will only lead to defection.[35]

customer relationship management (CRM) Using information about customers to create marketing strategies that develop and sustain desirable customer relationships

relationship marketing Establishing long-term, mutually satisfying buyer-seller relationships

To build these long-term customer relationships, marketers are increasingly turning to marketing research and data analytics. By increasing customer value over time, organizations try to retain and increase long-term profitability through customer loyalty. The airline industry is a key player in CRM efforts with its frequent-flyer programs. Frequent-flyer programs enable airlines to track individual information about customers, using databases that can help airlines understand what different customers want, and treat customers differently depending on their flying habits and overall value to the company. Airlines, hotels, and other service providers are also increasingly gathering a greater "share of customer," as discussed below, by tying a company-branded credit card to enhance overall value for the user and the customer. Many airlines require that the customer fly certain levels of mileage and charge a minimum dollar value to his or her credit card to retain premium benefits. Relationship-building efforts such as frequent-flyer and credit card programs have been shown to increase customer value.[36]

Through the use of e-marketing strategies, companies can personalize customer relationships on a nearly one-on-one basis. A wide range of products, such as electronics, jeans, golf clubs, cosmetics, and entertainment, can be tailored for specific customers. CRM provides a strategic bridge between data analytics and marketing strategies aimed at long-term relationships. This involves finding and retaining customers by using information to improve customer value and satisfaction. At the same time, ensuring customer satisfaction is not just a one-way street. Customers themselves contribute to the relationship by their purchase behaviors and their use of resources to maximize customer satisfaction. For example, customers can do pre-purchase research and spend time experiencing or examining the product before purchasing it.[37]

1-6b Customer Lifetime Value

customer lifetime value (CLV)
A key measurement that forecasts a customer's lifetime economic contribution based on continued relationship marketing efforts

Managing customer relationships requires identifying patterns of buying behavior and using that information to focus on the most promising and profitable customers.[38] Companies must be sensitive to customers' requirements and desires and must establish communication to build their trust and loyalty. **Customer lifetime value (CLV)** predicts the net value (profit or loss) for the future relationship with the customer. Starbucks, for example, is estimated to have a lifetime customer value of more than $14,000.[39] A customer's value over a lifetime represents an intangible asset to a marketer that can be augmented by addressing the customer's varying needs and preferences at different stages in his or her relationship with the firm.[40] In general, when marketers focus on customers chosen for their lifetime value, they earn higher profits in future periods than when they focus on customers selected for other reasons.[41]

The ability to identify individual customers allows marketers to shift their focus from targeting groups of similar customers to increasing their share of an individual customer's purchases. The emphasis changes from *share of market* to *share of customer*. Focusing on share of customer requires recognizing that all customers have different needs and that not all customers weigh the value of a company equally. The most basic application of this idea is the 80/20 rule: 80 percent

What Are Your Company's Top Marketing Challenges?

Generating traffic and leads	63%
Proving the ROI of our marketing activities	40%
Securing enough budget	28%
Identifying the right technologies for our needs	26%
Managing our website	26%
Targeting content for an international audience	21%
Training our team	19%
Hiring top talent	16%
Finding an executive sponsor	7%

SNAPSHOT

Source: Lindsay Kolowich, "8 of the Top Marketing Challenges Marketers Will Face This Year [New Data]," HubSpot, May 26, 2017, https://blog.hubspot.com/blog/tabid/6307/bid/33820/5-major-challenges-marketers-face-and-how-to-solve-them.aspx (accessed January 6, 2018).

of business profits come from 20 percent of customers. The goal is to assess the worth of individual customers and thus estimate their lifetime value to the company. The concept of customer lifetime value (CLV) may include not only an individual's tendency to engage in purchases but also his or her strong word-of-mouth communication about the company's products. Some customers—those who require considerable hand-holding or who return products frequently—may simply be too expensive to retain due to the low level of profits they generate. Companies can discourage these unprofitable customers by requiring them to pay higher fees for additional services.

CLV is a key measurement that forecasts a customer's lifetime economic contribution based on continued relationship marketing efforts. It can be calculated by taking the sum of the customer's present value contributions to profit margins over a specific time frame. For example, the lifetime value of a Buick customer could be predicted by how many new automobiles Buick could sell the customer over a period of years and a summation of the contribution to margins across the time period. Although this is not an exact science, knowing a customer's potential lifetime value can help marketers determine how best to allocate resources to marketing strategies to sustain that customer over a lifetime.

1-7 THE IMPORTANCE OF MARKETING IN OUR GLOBAL ECONOMY

Learning Objective 1-7

Explain why marketing is important to our global economy.

Our definition of marketing and discussion of marketing activities reveal some of the obvious reasons the study of marketing is relevant in today's world. In this section, we look at how marketing affects us as individuals and its role in our increasingly global society.

1-7a Marketing Costs Consume a Sizable Portion of Buyers' Dollars

Studying marketing will make you aware that many marketing activities are necessary to provide satisfying goods and services. Obviously, these activities cost money. About one-half of a buyer's dollar goes toward marketing costs. If you spend $300 on a new smartphone, more than half goes toward marketing expenses, such as promotion and distribution, as well as profit margins. A family with a monthly income of $3,000 that allocates $600 to taxes and savings spends about $2,400 for goods and services. On average, $1,200 goes toward marketing activities. If marketing expenses consume that much of your dollar, you should know how this money is being used. Marketing costs have an impact on the economy and the standard of living for consumers.

1-7b Marketing Is Used in Nonprofit Organizations

Although the term *marketing* may bring to mind advertising for AT&T, Microsoft, and UPS, marketing is also important in organizations working to achieve goals other than ordinary business objectives (such as profit). Government agencies at the federal, state, and local levels engage in marketing activities to fulfill their mission and goals. Universities and colleges engage in marketing activities to recruit new students, as well as to obtain donations from alumni and businesses.

In the private sector, nonprofit organizations also employ marketing activities to create, distribute, promote, and price programs that benefit particular segments of society. The Red Cross provides disaster relief throughout the world and offers promotional messages to encourage donations to support its efforts. Nonprofits operate just like businesses in that they serve a client base and have to create revenue to meet their needs. Marketing activities are necessary to create effective exchange relationships with donors and those served by the nonprofit.

1-7c **Marketing Is Important to Businesses and the Economy**

Businesses must engage in marketing to survive and grow, and marketing activities are needed to reach customers and provide products. Marketing is the business function responsible for creating revenue to sustain the operations of the organization and to provide financial returns to investors. Innovation in operations and products drive business success and customer loyalty. Nonprofit businesses need to understand and use marketing to survive and provide services to their target market.

Marketing activities help to produce the profits that are essential to the survival of individual businesses. Without profits, businesses would find it difficult, if not impossible, to buy more raw materials, hire more employees, attract more capital, and create additional products that, in turn, make more profits. Without profits, marketers cannot continue to provide jobs and contribute to social causes. Companies promote their support of social causes through promotional activities such as the FEED Projects advertisement. In the advertisement, FEED Projects explains that the company provides one child with school meals for one year with the purchase of each Anniversary FEED 1 Bag. Therefore, marketing helps create a successful economy and contributes to the well-being of society.

BAGS WITH A MISSION FOR WOMEN ON A MISSION

The **Anniversary FEED 1 Bag** gives
1 child school meals for **1 year**.

FEED
FEEDPROJECTS.COM

Social Marketing
Marketing is used by companies such as FEED Projects to create awareness of the social causes they support to improve society.

1-7d **Marketing Fuels Our Global Economy**

Marketing is necessary to advance a global economy. Advances in technology, along with falling political and economic barriers and the universal desire for a higher standard of living, have made marketing across national borders commonplace while stimulating global economic growth. As a result of worldwide communications and increased international travel, many global brands have achieved widespread acceptance around the world. At the same time, customers in the United States have greater choices among the products they buy because foreign brands such as Audi (Germany), Honda (Japan), and Swatch (Switzerland) sell alongside U.S. brands such as Ford, Converse, and Hewlett-Packard. People around the world watch CNN and HGTV on Samsung and Panasonic televisions they purchased at Walmart. Social media and the internet now enable businesses of all sizes to reach buyers worldwide. We explore the international markets and opportunities for global marketing in Chapter 9.

1-7e **Marketing Knowledge Enhances Consumer Awareness**

Besides contributing to the well-being of our global economy, marketing activities help to improve the quality of our lives. Studying marketing allows us to understand the importance of marketing to customers, organizations, and our economy. Thus, we can analyze marketing efforts that need improvement and how to attain that goal. Today the consumer has more power from information available through websites, social media, and required disclosure. As you become more knowledgeable, it is possible to improve career options as well as purchasing decisions. In general, you have more accurate information about a product before you purchase it than at any other time in history. Understanding marketing enables us to evaluate corrective measures (such as laws, regulations, and industry guidelines) that could stop unfair, damaging, or unethical marketing practices. Also, knowledge of marketing helps you to evaluate public policy toward marketing that could potentially affect economic well-being. Thus, understanding how marketing activities work can help you to be a better consumer, increase your ability to maximize value from purchases, and understand how marketing is a necessary function in all organizations.

1-7f Marketing Connects People through Technology

Technology, especially information technology, helps marketers to understand and satisfy more customers than ever before. Access to the internet has changed the daily lives of consumers. Mobile devices, emails, and office management systems are almost universally used. Facebook, Instagram, and Google have changed the way consumers communicate, learn about products, make purchases, and share their opinions with others. The global spread of mobile devices has enabled marketers and consumers to forge new relationships that challenge how the traditional marketing-mix variables are implemented. Evolving software tools make it easy to create, store, share, and collaborate.[42]

Technology has also enabled firms like Lyft and TaskRabbit to create successful new-product concepts by harnessing peer-to-peer power and sharing underutilized resources such as automobiles, boats, and houses to earn income. This economic model is called the sharing economy. It is also referred to as the "gig economy" because firms specializing in peer-to-peer services are using independent contractors to provide services. These contractors essentially run their own businesses and take on service jobs, or "gigs," whenever they desire to earn income using their own resources. While some gig workers do this to earn extra income, more and more are pursuing this as a full-time job.[43] This has led to a rise in independent contracting; it is estimated that independent contractors grew by almost 40 percent in the last decade.[44] This disruptive technology challenges traditional industries such as taxis and hotels.

Additionally, marketers have new methods to store, communicate, and share information through advanced platforms that access what has been termed as "big data." We define big data as massive data files that can be obtained from both structured and unstructured databases. Companies such as Salesforce.com have used big data to provide CRM services. A new generation of consumers are using social networks and mobile messaging applications rather than email.[45]

The internet allows companies to provide tremendous amounts of information about their products to consumers and to interact with them through email and websites as well as Instagram and Twitter. A consumer shopping for a new car, for example, can access automakers' webpages, configure an ideal vehicle, and get instant feedback on its cost. Consumers can visit TrueCar, Edmunds, and other websites to find professional reviews and obtain comparative pricing information on both new and used cars to help them find the best value. They can also visit a consumer review site, such as Yelp, to read other consumers' reviews of the products. They can then purchase a vehicle online or at a dealership. A number of companies employ social media to connect with their customers, utilizing blogs and social networking sites such as Facebook and Twitter. We consider social networking and other digital media in Chapter 10.

1-7g Socially Responsible Marketing: Promoting the Welfare of Customers and Stakeholders

The success of our economic system depends on marketers whose values promote trust and cooperative relationships in which customers and other stakeholders are proactively engaged and their concerns are addressed through marketing activities. Social responsibility and ethical conduct are a part of strategic planning and the implementation of marketing activities. Although some marketers' irresponsible or unethical activities end up on the front pages of *The New York Times* or *The Wall Street Journal*, more firms are working to develop a responsible approach to developing long-term relationships with customers and other stakeholders. Firms recognize that trust is built on ethical conduct.

In the area of the natural environment, companies are increasingly embracing the notion of **green marketing**, which is a strategic process involving stakeholder assessment to create meaningful long-term relationships with customers while maintaining, supporting, and enhancing the natural environment. For example, Greenpeace recognized Fairphone and Apple for the sustainability of their smartphones. Apple leads the smartphone industry in renewable energy for the manufacturing of its devices and was the first to make a commitment to closed-loop production.[46] Such initiatives not only reduce the negative impact that businesses have on the environment but also serve to enhance their reputations as sustainability concerns continue to grow.

By addressing concerns about the impact of marketing on society, a firm can contribute to society through socially responsible activities as well as increase its financial performance. For example, studies have revealed that market orientation combined with social responsibility improves overall business performance.[47] We examine these issues and many others as we develop a framework for understanding more about marketing in the remainder of this book.

1-7h Marketing Offers Many Exciting Career Prospects

From 25 to 33 percent of all civilian workers in the United States perform marketing activities. The marketing field offers a variety of interesting and challenging career opportunities throughout the world, such as personal selling, advertising, packaging, transportation, storage, marketing research, product development, social media management, wholesaling, and retailing. All industries have marketing positions, including health care, sports, consumer products, nonprofits, government, as well as agriculture and commodities such as the oil and gas industry. When unemployment is high, sales positions remain among the most attractive job opportunities. Marketing positions are among the most secure positions because of the need to manage customer relationships. In addition, many individuals working for nonbusiness organizations

green marketing A strategic process involving stakeholder assessment to create meaningful long-term relationships with customers while maintaining, supporting, and enhancing the natural environment

ENTREPRENEURSHIP IN MARKETING

Blue Bottle Coffee: Not Your Typical Daily Grind

At Blue Bottle Coffee Company in Oakland, California, coffee is more than a commodity. Blue Bottle, founded by James Freeman, embraces the third-wave movement, a movement that makes premium coffee into an exquisite experience of purity, flavor, and artisanship, similar to wine and cigars. To show that this experience is worth paying for, Blue Bottle has adopted a different marketing style than that of traditional coffee shops or even Starbucks.

Blue Bottle cafés emphasize the coffee experience above all else. For example, beverages only come in one size. With the exception of its Palo Alto location, stores do not have Wi-Fi so as to prevent distraction and encourage real-life interaction. Beans for each order are freshly ground and brewed from scratch right in front of the customer. Likewise, online orders are shipped within 48 hours of their beans' roasting to ensure freshness. The price: between $4 and $7 per cup.

While this may seem expensive for the average coffee lover, Blue Bottle shows that its niche target market is those who appreciate the quality and experience of coffee. Nestlé, who recently acquired a majority stake in the coffee company, sees growth opportunities in this market. Blue Bottle has more than 45 locations from Washington D.C. to Tokyo with ongoing expansion plans in the works.[b]

engage in marketing activities to promote political, educational, cultural, church, civic, and charitable activities. It is a mistake to believe that the only way to contribute to society is to work for a nonprofit. Without businesses, the economic system that supports jobs and contributes to a standard of living would not exist. Consider that 5 percent of charitable contributions are corporate donations from companies such as Wells Fargo. Many large companies also form foundations to serve their communities. Foundations donate 10 percent of all charitable contributions in the United States.[48] Two major foundations formed by business founders include the Arthur M. Blank Family Foundation (founder of Home Depot) and the Bill and Melinda Gates Foundation (founder of Microsoft). Successful businesses provide the resources necessary to sustain nonprofits and governments. While most charitable contributions are from individuals, most of these people earned their wealth as entrepreneurs or corporate managers. Therefore, marketing plays a key role in supporting philanthropy. Whether a person earns a living through marketing activities or performs them voluntarily for a nonprofit group, marketing knowledge and skills are valuable personal and professional assets.

Summary

1-1 Define marketing.

Marketing is the process of creating, pricing, distributing, and promoting goods, services, and ideas to facilitate satisfying exchange relationships with customers and to develop and maintain favorable relationships with stakeholders in a dynamic environment. The essence of marketing is to develop satisfying exchanges from which both customers and marketers benefit. Organizations generally focus their marketing efforts on a specific group of customers called a target market. A target market is the group of customers toward which a company directs a set of marketing efforts.

1-2 Explain the different variables of the marketing mix.

Marketing involves developing and managing a product that will satisfy customer needs, making the product available at the right place and at a price acceptable to customers, and communicating information that helps customers determine if the product will satisfy their needs. These variables—product, distribution, promotion, and price—are known as the marketing mix because marketing managers decide what type of each element to use and in what amounts. Marketing managers strive to develop a marketing mix that matches the needs of customers in the target market. Before marketers can develop a marketing mix, they must collect in-depth, up-to-date information about customer needs. The product variable of the marketing mix deals with researching customers' needs and wants and designing a product that satisfies them. A product can be a good, a service, or an idea. In dealing with the distribution variable, a marketing manager tries to make products available in the quantities desired to as many customers as possible. The promotion variable relates to activities used to inform individuals or groups about the organization and its products. The price variable involves decisions and actions associated with establishing pricing policies and determining product prices. These marketing-mix variables are often viewed as controllable because they can be changed, but there are limits to how much they can be altered.

1-3 Describe how marketing creates value.

Individuals and organizations engage in marketing to facilitate exchanges—the provision or transfer of goods, services, and ideas in return for something of value. Four conditions must exist for an exchange to occur. First, two or more individuals, groups, or organizations must participate, and each must possess something of value that the other party desires. Second, the exchange should provide a benefit or satisfaction to both parties involved in the transaction. Third, each party must have confidence in the promise of the "something of value" held by the other. Finally, to build trust, the parties to the exchange must meet expectations. Marketing activities should attempt to create and maintain satisfying exchange relationships.

1-4 Briefly explore the marketing environment.

The marketing environment, which includes competitive, economic, political, legal and regulatory, technological, and sociocultural forces, surrounds the customer and the marketing mix. These forces can create threats to marketers, but they also generate opportunities for new products and new methods of reaching customers. These forces can fluctuate quickly and dramatically.

1-5 Summarize the marketing concept.

According to the marketing concept, an organization should try to provide products that satisfy customers' needs through a coordinated set of activities that also allows the organization to achieve its goals. Customer satisfaction is the marketing concept's major objective. The philosophy of the marketing concept emerged in the United States during the 1950s after the production and sales eras. Organizations that develop activities consistent with the marketing concept become market-oriented organizations. To implement the marketing concept, a market-oriented organization must establish an information system to discover customers' needs and use the information to create satisfying products. It must also coordinate all its activities and develop marketing mixes that create value for customers in order to satisfy their needs.

1-6 Identify the importance of building customer relationships.

Relationship marketing involves establishing long-term, mutually satisfying buyer–seller relationships. Customer relationship management (CRM) focuses on using information about customers to create marketing strategies that develop and sustain desirable customer relationships. Managing customer relationships requires identifying patterns of buying behavior and using that information to focus on the most promising and profitable customers. A customer's value over a lifetime represents an intangible asset to a marketer that can be augmented by addressing the customer's varying needs and preferences at different stages in his or her relationship with the firm. Customer lifetime value is a key measurement that forecasts a customer's lifetime economic contribution based on continued-relationship marketing efforts. Knowing a customer's potential lifetime value can help marketers determine how to best allocate resources to marketing strategies to sustain that customer over a lifetime.

1-7 Explain why marketing is important to our global economy.

Marketing is important to our economy in many ways. Marketing costs absorb about half of each buyer's dollar. Marketing activities are performed in both business and nonprofit organizations. Marketing activities help business organizations to generate profits, and they help fuel the increasingly global economy. Knowledge of marketing enhances consumer awareness. New technology improves marketers' ability to connect with customers. Socially responsible marketing can promote the welfare of customers and society. Green marketing is a strategic process involving stakeholder assessment to create meaningful, long-term relationships with customers while maintaining, supporting, and enhancing the natural environment. Finally, marketing offers many exciting career opportunities.

Important Terms

marketing 4	value 9	marketing concept 13	relationship marketing 17
customers 5	exchanges 11	market orientation 16	customer lifetime
target market 5	stakeholders 12	customer relationship	value (CLV) 18
marketing mix 6	marketing environment 12	management (CRM) 17	green marketing 22
product 7			

Discussion and Review Questions

1. What is *marketing*? How did you define the term before you read this chapter?
2. What is the focus of all marketing activities? Why?
3. What are the four variables of the marketing mix? Why are these elements known as variables?
4. What is value? How can marketers use the marketing mix to enhance the perception of value?
5. What conditions must exist before a marketing exchange can occur? Describe a recent exchange in which you participated.
6. What are the forces in the marketing environment? How much control does a marketing manager have over these forces?

7. Discuss the basic elements of the marketing concept. Which businesses in your area use this philosophy? Explain why.
8. How can an organization implement the marketing concept?
9. What is customer relationship management? Why is it so important to "manage" this relationship?
10. Why is marketing important in our society? Why should you study marketing?

Developing Your Marketing Plan

Successful companies develop strategies for marketing their products. The strategic plan guides the marketer in making many of the detailed decisions about the attributes of the product, its pricing, distribution, and promotional activities. A clear understanding of the foundations of marketing is essential in formulating a strategy and in the development of a specific marketing plan. To guide you in relating the information in this chapter to the development of your marketing plan, consider the following:

1. Discuss how the marketing concept contributes to a company's long-term success.
2. Describe the level of market orientation that currently exists in your company. How will a market orientation contribute to the success of your new product?
3. What benefits will your product provide to the customer? How will these benefits play a role in determining the customer value of your product?

Video Case 1.1

Apple Inc.: The Future of Retailing, Education, and Entertainment

Headquartered in Cupertino, California, Apple Inc. has experienced many challenges throughout its business history. In 1997, the company's share price was $3.30. By checking the price today, you can see the unbelievable gains in price. Apple regularly places very highly on lists of "most admired companies," and to millions of consumers, the Apple brand embodies quality, prestige, and innovation. Its ability to anticipate and fulfill customer needs has made the company the world's most valuable publicly traded company, with a market value of about $776 billion. This ability has also established the company as a leader in retail stores for electronic products. Apple creates significant value for its customers with its finely tuned in-store experience.

Apple's success can be attributed in part to its strong marketing mix consisting of product, distribution, promotion, and price. Although Apple started out as a computer company, former CEO Steve Jobs had the foresight to redirect the company's goal to consumer electronics by developing and protecting intellectual property and creating a decentralized culture. The result was Apple's expansion into new product lines within the electronics industry. In 2001, Apple satisfied customers' desires for portable music with the launch of the iPod—a portable music player that forever changed the music industry. The company also introduced iTunes, a type of "jukebox" software that allowed users to upload songs from CDs onto their computers and then organize and manage their personalized song libraries. Two years later Apple introduced the online iTunes Store, in which users could download millions of their favorite songs for $0.99 each.

In 2007, Jobs announced that Apple Computer, Inc. would be renamed Apple Inc., demonstrating the company's grasp on the marketing concept. However, in order for a company to remain competitive, it must continually focus its efforts on planning and goal setting. Apple continued to expand its product lines as part of the strategic plan. That same year it introduced the iPhone, which revolutionized the cellular phone industry. Apple did the same to the computer industry in 2010 with the introduction of the iPad. While the iPod was not the first MP3 player and the iPad wasn't the first tablet, these products are viewed as the industry standard, highlighting that you don't have to be the first to succeed.

Under CEO Tim Cook, who has retained Jobs' executive team, Apple released the Apple Watch in 2015, a smartwatch at the forefront of wearable technology. The company announced its first smart home speaker, HomePod, in 2017. Looking forward, Apple is working on a self-driving car and incorporating augmented reality into its iOS to not only stay ahead of technology trends but also to support the growth of those industries. The company is also opening its first next-generation retail stores.

As Apple continued to introduce products, the company developed and incorporated a creative tactical goal of evangelizing. The concept of evangelism has been an important component of Apple's culture, and this was particularly true under Steve Jobs. Corporate evangelists are people who extensively promote a corporation's products. Apple even had a chief evangelist whose job was to spread the message about Apple and gain support for its products. However, as the name evangelism implies, the role of an evangelist takes on greater meaning. Evangelists believe strongly in the company and will spread that belief to others, who in turn will convince other people. Therefore, evangelists are not only employees but loyal customers as well. In this way, Apple was able to form what it refers to as a "Mac cult"—customers who were very loyal to Apple's Mac computers and who spread a positive message about Macs to their friends and families.

After 15 years with retail stores, Apple has defined the future of retailing. The new flagship retail store in San Francisco has massive doors that bring the outdoors indoors. A courtyard with trees provides a relaxed environment. Creative pros in the Genius Grove assist with music and service. Twenty percent of the space is just for education and entertainment. The store is designed to be a place to hang out and have fun. Apple has also announced plans to redesign many of its current retail stores as "town squares" where people can attend free in-store classes such as photography workshops, music production classes, and iPhone editing tutorials. This experience-based strategy elevates the Apple brand and its products, turning its stores into centers of learning, gathering, and creating. Apple's innovation as an experience-based electronics retailer makes the company stand out as other retailers struggle.

Apple recognizes that in adopting the marketing concept it must satisfy not only its customers' objectives but also its own, or it will not continue to be successful. In order to support the efforts of the tactical goals, Apple ensures its operational goals are set in place. One example is the design of the retail locations and the hiring of employees for these locations. Apple looks for retail employees who work well in its culture, and ensures that its retail employees make each consumer feel welcome. Inside Apple retail locations are stations where customers can test and experiment with the latest Apple products. Employees, who can directly influence customer satisfaction, have been trained to speak with customers within two minutes of them entering the store. To ensure that its retail employees feel motivated, Apple provides extensive training, greater compensation than employees might receive at similar stores, and opportunities to move up to manager, genius (an employee trained to answer the more difficult customer questions), or creative (an employee who trains customers one-on-one or through workshops). All of this planning, which includes strategic, tactical, and operational goals, has contributed to Apple's distinctive competence and success.[49]

Questions for Discussion

1. How has a market orientation contributed to Apple's success?
2. Describe how Apple embraces the marketing concept.
3. How would you describe Apple's strategy in the highly competitive consumer electronics industry?

Case 1.2

TOMS: Purchase One and Give One

Most firms do not want other companies to copy their successful business model. However, the shoe retailer TOMS is not your typical retailer. While many organizations try to incorporate social entrepreneurship into their business operations, TOMS takes the concept of philanthropy one step further by blending a for-profit business with a philanthropic component in what it terms the One for One® model. For every product purchased, TOMS donates products or resources to help those in need. Under founder Blake Mycoskie's inspirational leadership, the company's One for One concept has inspired other firms—such as eyeglass retailer Warby Parker—to adopt similar models as a way to give back to society. Rather than feel threatened, Mycoskie is funding social entrepreneurship firms with similar missions.

For every product purchased, including TOMS Shoes, TOMS Eyewear, and coffee bags from TOMS Roasting Co., TOMS will help a person in need. For every pair of shoes sold, a child in need receives a pair of shoes. For every pair of glasses sold, TOMS provides a person in need with a full eye exam and treatment including prescription glasses, sight-saving surgery, or medical treatment to restore his or her sight. For each bag of TOMS Roasting Co. Coffee, TOMS provides an entire week's supply of safe drinking water to a person in need. When consumers buy a TOMS product, they get the value of an extra philanthropic component.

Unlike many nonprofits, TOMS' for-profit business enables the company to support its philanthropic component, which keeps the company from having to solicit donations. The idea for TOMS occurred after founder Blake Mycoskie witnessed the immense poverty in Argentinean villages, poverty so bad that many families could not afford to purchase shoes for their children. Recognizing the importance of shoes to health and education, Mycoskie decided to create a new for-profit business with a socially focused mission. For each pair of shoes TOMS sold, it would deliver a free pair of shoes to children in need across the world.

For his original product, Mycoskie decided to adopt the alpargata shoe worn in Argentina. The alpargata is a slip-on shoe made from canvas or fabric with rubber soles. After a *Los Angeles Times* article featured Mycoskie's new business, demand for the shoes exploded. Unfortunately for Mycoskie, he did not have enough shoes to fill the orders. He was able to work out the product shortage, and today TOMS is a thriving business.

Mycoskie wanted customers to become active participants in the One for One movement by using their purchases to change the world. This inspirational business model provided TOMS with a competitive advantage, and the company was able to distribute its one-millionth pair of shoes in 2010. After distributing its one-millionth pair of shoes, TOMS began to consider other products that could be used in the One for One model. "When I thought about launching another product with the TOMS model, vision seemed the most obvious choice," Mycoskie explained. Because 80 percent of vision impairment in developing countries is preventable or curable, TOMS decided that for every pair of eyewear it sold, the company would provide treatment or prescription glasses for those in need. TOMS chose Nepal as the first country in which to apply its One for One model.

In 2012, Mycoskie took a sabbatical from TOMS, moving to Austin, Texas with his wife to reflect on his "why" for leading the company. After recommitting to his original mission to improve the lives of others with his business, he returned with a renewed sense of passion and energy. The desire to help others resonates with both TOMS employees and customers, so Mycoskie recognized how important it was to return to a purpose-focused mindset. Customers who do business with TOMS feel committed to the company because they know that their purchases are going toward a good cause, even if they might pay a bit more in the process. TOMS also goes to great lengths to educate the public about the importance of its mission. Every year, the company promotes the One Day Without Shoes campaign, in which participants spend one day without shoes to understand what children in developing countries must undergo daily. These events have been supported by celebrities such as Charlize Theron, Kris Ryan, and the Dallas Cowboys Cheerleaders.

In 2014, TOMS made the decision to expand the One to One model into the coffee business and started TOMS Roasting Co. Each purchase of a bag of TOMS Roasting Co. Coffee provides an entire week's supply of safe drinking water to a person in need. However, as TOMS expanded, it began to experience problems that plague more traditional firms, such as slower decision making and more internal conflict. Because Mycoskie's long-term goal is for TOMS to be recognized as "the most influential, inspirational company in the world," he knew the company needed someone to tackle management so he could focus on leadership. He sold half of the business to Bain Capital in 2014 and hired Jim Alling as CEO to improve stability and strategic thinking. Mycoskie then used $100 million from the sale of his share to start TOMS Social Entrepreneurship Fund. This fund provides financial support to like-minded companies who want to focus on social entrepreneurship. Mycoskie continues to demonstrate authentic leadership with his passion for TOMS's objectives and his willingness to model corporate values and form relationships with customers, employees, and other social entrepreneurs in using business as a force for good.

Led by Mycoskie's vision, TOMS has provided more than 35 million pairs of shoes to children in need in over 60 countries, restored sight to more than 250,000 people across 13 countries, and provided 175,000 weeks of clean drinking water to people in five countries. Despite its success, TOMS's mission is far from complete. As its expansion into coffee demonstrates, the company is looking for new opportunities to apply its One for One model. It has even adopted a new logo, "For One, Another," to demonstrate the importance of caring for one another. TOMS demonstrates how a unique marketing strategy and a vision supported by employees and customers can create a successful company that makes a difference.[50]

Questions for Discussion

1. How has TOMS implemented the marketing concept?
2. Describe the benefits and value that TOMS provides to consumers and other stakeholders.
3. Explain how for-profit and nonprofit organizations can have an integrated marketing strategy.

TUMSASEDGARS/ISTOCK/GETTY IMAGES

2

Planning, Implementing, and Evaluating Marketing Strategies

LEARNING OBJECTIVES

2-1 Explain the strategic planning process.

2-2 Understand the importance of a firm's mission statement and corporate and business-unit strategy.

2-3 Discuss how analyzing organizational resources and the marketing environment can help identify opportunities and create competitive advantage.

2-4 Explore how a firm develops marketing objectives and strategies that contribute to overall objectives.

2-5 Identify what is necessary to manage the effective implementation of marketing strategies.

2-6 Describe the four major elements of strategic performance evaluation.

2-7 Outline the development of a marketing plan.

JIA LI/SHUTTERSTOCK.COM

Tesla's Electric-Driven Strategy

Is Tesla Motors a luxury car company, an electric car company, or an electric battery company? Headed by CEO Elon Musk, the entrepreneur behind the rocket firm Space-X, Tesla has spent billions of dollars developing, building, and marketing all-electric cars that offer style and status, as well as sustainability. Tesla has also spent billions to create its own state-of-the-art factory for lithium-ion car batteries, supporting the company's mission of accelerating the transition to renewable-energy vehicles.

Tesla wasn't the first automaker to market an all-electric vehicle, but its made-in-America cars definitely stand out in a growing field of competitors that includes Ford and General Motors. The distinctively designed Model S and Model X cars have been snapped up by affluent drivers willing to pay nearly $100,000 to put a Tesla in their driveway. Building on its brand strength and technical expertise, the company has now expanded the target market with the Model 3, a more affordable electric car with a starting price of $35,000. Months before the 2017 introduction of the Model 3, Tesla had received more than 400,000 reservations, each with a $1,000 deposit, from eager buyers.

As the Model 3 launched, the company struggled to meet demand for all three of its vehicle models, in part because it couldn't produce batteries quickly enough. Still, with its factories increasing output month after month, Tesla continues to aim high, expecting to sell hundreds of thousands of all-electric cars yearly to eco-minded consumers around the world.[1]

Whether it's Tesla or your local print shop, an organization must be able to create customer value and achieve its goals. This occurs through successful strategic marketing management. **Strategic marketing management** is the process of planning, implementing, and evaluating the performance of marketing activities and strategies, both effectively and efficiently. Effectiveness and efficiency are key concepts to understanding strategic marketing management. *Effectiveness* is the degree to which long-term customer relationships help achieve an organization's objectives. *Efficiency* refers to minimizing the resources an organization uses to achieve a specific level of desired customer relationships. Thus, the overall goal of strategic marketing management is to facilitate highly desirable customer relationships and to minimize the costs of doing so.

We begin this chapter with an overview of the strategic planning process and a discussion of the nature of marketing strategy. These elements provide a framework for an analysis of the development, implementation, and evaluation of marketing strategies. We conclude with an examination of how to create a marketing plan.

Learning Objective 2-1

Explain the strategic planning process.

2-1 THE STRATEGIC PLANNING PROCESS

Through the process of **strategic planning**, a company establishes an organizational mission and formulates goals, a corporate strategy, marketing objectives, and a marketing strategy.[2] A market orientation should guide the process of strategic planning to ensure that a concern for customer satisfaction is an integral part of the entire company, leading to the development of successful marketing strategies and planning processes.[3]

Figure 2.1 shows the various components of the strategic planning process, which begins with the establishment or revision of an organization's mission and goals. The corporation and individual business units then develop strategies to achieve these goals. The company performs a detailed analysis of its strengths and weaknesses and identifies opportunities and threats

strategic marketing management The process of planning, implementing, and evaluating the performance of marketing activities and strategies, both effectively and efficiently

strategic planning The process of establishing an organizational mission and formulating goals, a corporate strategy, marketing objectives, and a marketing strategy

Figure 2.1	Components of the Strategic Planning Process

within the external marketing environment. Next, each functional area of the organization (marketing, production, finance, human resources, and so forth) establishes its own objectives and develops strategies to achieve them, which must support the organization's overall goals and mission and should be focused on market orientation. Because this is a marketing book, we are most interested in marketing objectives and strategies. We will examine the strategic planning process by taking a closer look at each component, beginning with organizational mission statements and goals.

2-2 ESTABLISHING MISSION, GOALS, AND STRATEGIES

Learning Objective 2-2

Understand the importance of a firm's mission statement and corporate and business-unit strategy.

The strategic planning process begins with deciding on the firm's organizational mission—its *raison d'etre*—and goals. These give meaning and direction to the organization.

2-2a Developing Organizational Mission and Goals

The goals of any organization should derive from its **mission statement**, a long-term view, or vision, of what the organization wants to become. For instance, Facebook's mission, "to give people the power to build community and bring the world closer together," speaks to the company's desire to transform the way the world communicates.[4] When an organization decides on its mission, it is answering two questions: *Who are our customers?* and *What is our core competency?* Although these questions appear very simple, they are two of the most important questions for any company to address. Defining customers' needs and wants gives direction to what the company must do to satisfy them.

Mission statements, goals, and objectives must be properly implemented to achieve the desired result. It is advantageous to broadcast them to the public, customers, employees, and other stakeholders so that they know what they may expect from the firm. Companies try to develop and manage a consistent *corporate identity*—their unique symbols, personalities, and philosophies—to support all corporate activities, including strategic planning and marketing. For example, Slack, a cloud-based team collaboration service, has established this mission: "To make people's working lives simpler, more pleasant, and more productive." This statement drives Slack's strategies and activities, and it is reiterated in every interview given by the firm's CEO. Hiring managers underscore the mission to prospective employees at the beginning of the hiring process, and they strive to find new employees who share that mission and the firm's expressed values. This mission also fosters a culture of inclusion, transparency, direct feedback, learning from mistakes, and continuous improvement, which have helped make Slack the fastest growing workplace software.[5]

Consider the advertisement for De Beers jewellery, which conveys the corporate identity the company desires to project. De Beers, which is

mission statement A long-term view, or vision, of what the organization wants to become

SOURCE: FORBES MEDIA LLC

Corporate Identity
De Beers has established a corporate identity associated with the mining and cutting of diamonds. The De Beers name is almost synonymous with diamonds. This company has been in business for more than 125 years.

nearly synonymous with diamonds, wants its target market of affluent shoppers to see the company as the go-to retailer of upscale diamond jewelry. The company's advertisement, which spotlights three exquisite diamond rings, reminds potential buyers that De Beers is "the home of diamonds since 1888." The corporate identity is further reinforced by the ad's simplicity, the exclusivity of De Beers' products (the ad lists the only five locations in North America), and its use of the company's long-time name-mark in a distinctive font.

An organization's goals and objectives, derived from its mission statement, guide its planning efforts. Goals focus on the end results the organization seeks. Each level of management and department within the firm should have goals that stem from the mission statement and provide direction for the firm's activities.

2-2b Developing Corporate and Business-Unit Strategies

In most organizations, strategic planning begins at the corporate level and proceeds downward to the business-unit and marketing levels. However, organizations are increasingly developing strategies and conducting strategic planning that moves in both directions. When conducting strategic planning, a firm is likely to seek out experts from many levels of the organization to take advantage of in-house expertise and a variety of opinions.

Figure 2.2 shows the relationships among three planning levels: corporate, business unit, and marketing. Corporate strategy is the broadest of the three levels and should be developed with the organization's overall mission in mind. Business-unit strategy should be consistent with the corporate strategy while also serving the unit's needs. Marketing strategy utilizes the marketing mix to develop a message that is consistent with the business-unit and corporate strategies.

CREATIVE MARKETING

Tiffany Rings Up More through Mobile Marketing

Building on a distinctive brand image forged over more than 180 years, Tiffany & Co. is polishing its marketing strategy for the next generation of fine-jewelry buyers. The firm, known worldwide for diamond rings and other luxury jewelry items, began with a single store in New York City. Today, Tiffany operates more than 300 full-service stores in dozens of countries and rings up $4 billion in annual sales.

Although the technology and the product designs have changed over the decades, Tiffany's timeless brand has retained its strong upscale appeal. Now the company is extending its signature Tiffany Blue color beyond packaging to its entire digital presence, including mobile marketing. The goal, according to marketing executive Catherine Lacaze, is to "remind you that you're in the Tiffany world," whether browsing the firm's website or checking its popular accounts on Pinterest, Facebook, Google+, YouTube, Twitter, or Instagram. All are awash in Tiffany Blue, which is also the color of its official Snapchat icon.

When the firm first developed its mobile marketing strategy, Lacaze says company marketers were "scared of showing expensive products on a tiny screen," fearing the impact would be lost. However, Tiffany quickly discovered that smartphone users don't just look, they actually click to see more. As a result, the firm now posts extra-large photos and videos on its mobile-optimized website to showcase detail. It also offers an engagement-ring finder app, featuring a virtual "try on" function to help mobile users envision themselves wearing a special piece of Tiffany jewelry.[a]

Figure 2.2	**Levels of Strategic Planning**

Corporate Strategies

Corporate strategy determines the means for utilizing resources in the functional areas of marketing, production, finance, research and development, and human resources to achieve the organization's goals. A corporate strategy outlines the scope of the business and such considerations as resource deployment, competitive advantages, and overall coordination of functional areas. When John Flannery took over as CEO of General Electric (GE) in 2017, for example, he refocused the century-old corporation on three core divisions—aviation, power, and health care. Implementing this strategy required directing the huge firm's resources toward those areas and potentially divesting some weaker divisions, such as lighting and locomotives, in order to maximize growth in the core businesses.[6] Top management's level of marketing expertise and ability to deploy resources to address the company's markets can affect sales growth and profitability. Corporate strategy addresses the two questions posed in the organization's mission statement: *Who are our customers?* and *What is our core competency?* The term *corporate* in this case does not apply solely to corporations. In this context, it refers to the top-level (i.e., highest) strategy and is used by organizations of all sizes and types.

Corporate strategy planners are concerned with broad issues such as organizational culture, competition, differentiation, diversification, interrelationships among business units, and environmental and social issues. They attempt to match the resources of the organization with the opportunities and threats in the environment. Consider that Ford Motor's new CEO, Jim Hackett, shifted the automaker's priorities to capitalize on marketing opportunities as well as the firm's strengths in certain product categories. For example, the company planned to divert some resources from automobile development and put them instead into trucks and SUVs, categories in which Ford is already a leader in U.S. sales. Additionally, the firm planned to invest greater resources into developing more electric and hybrid vehicles, which have been gaining sales at the expense of conventional gas-combustion vehicles. Finally, Ford planned to make 100 percent of all new Fords sold in the United States with internet connectivity, such as in-vehicle Wi-Fi.[7] These decisions and priorities will guide Ford's strategies and activities for the years to come.

corporate strategy A strategy that determines the means for utilizing resources in the various functional areas to reach the organization's goals

Business-Unit Strategies
Pantene products represent a business unit within Procter & Gamble. Marketers at Procter & Gamble develop a specific business-unit strategy for Pantene hair care products.

strategic business unit (SBU) A division, product line, or other profit center within the parent company

market A group of individuals and/or organizations that have needs for products in a product class and have the ability, willingness, and authority to purchase those products

market share The percentage of a market that actually buys a specific product from a particular company

market growth/market share matrix A helpful business tool, based on the philosophy that a product's market growth rate and its market share are important considerations in determining its marketing strategy

Business-Unit Strategies

After analyzing corporate operations and performance, the next step in strategic planning is to determine future business directions and develop strategies for individual business units. A **strategic business unit (SBU)** is a division, product line, or other profit center within the parent company. PepsiCo, for example, has SBUs for Frito-Lay, Quaker, and North American Beverages as well as global divisions for its products.[8] Each SBU sells a distinct set of products to an identifiable group of customers and each competes with a well-defined set of competitors. The revenues, costs, investments, and strategic plans of each SBU can be separated from those of the parent company and evaluated. SBUs face different market growth rates, opportunities, competition, and profit-making potential. Business strategy should seek to create value for the company's target markets and attain greater performance, which marketing research suggests requires implementing appropriate strategic actions and targeting appropriate market segments.[9]

Take a look at the ad for Pantene's 3 Minute Miracle conditioner. Pantene—part of Procter & Gamble's Hair Care group—identified an opportunity in the marketing environment to target young women who want stronger hair. This ad depicts actress/singer Selena Gomez holding a bottle of 3 Minute Miracle conditioner along with the tag line, "makes hair stronger in just 3 minutes." The ad emphasizes Gomez's sleek hairstyle to convey the product's benefits. Pantene's promotion highlights Procter & Gamble's Hair Care unit's efforts to innovate in order to continue to satisfy the changing needs of its business customers.

Strategic planners should recognize the performance capabilities of each SBU and carefully allocate resources among them. Several tools allow a company's planners to classify and visually display its portfolio of SBUs, or even individual products, according to the attractiveness of markets and the business's relative market share. A **market** is a group of individuals and/or organizations that have needs for products in a product class and have the ability, willingness, and authority to purchase those products. The percentage of a market that actually buys a specific product from a particular company is referred to as that product's (or business unit's) **market share**. Google, for example, has a dominant share of the search engine market in the United States, at nearly 89 percent.[10] Product quality, order of entry into the market, and market share have been associated with SBU success.[11]

One of the most helpful tools for a marketer is the **market growth/market share matrix**, developed by the Boston Consulting Group (BCG). This approach is based on the philosophy that a product's market growth rate and its market share are important considerations in determining marketing strategy. To develop such a tool, all of the company's SBUs and products are integrated into a single matrix and compared and evaluated to determine appropriate strategies for individual products and overall portfolio strategies. Managers use this model to determine and classify each product's expected future cash contributions and future cash requirements. However, the BCG analytical approach is more of a diagnostic tool than a guide for making strategy prescriptions.

Figure 2.3, which is based on work by the BCG, enables a strategic planner to classify a company's products into four basic types: stars, cash cows, dogs, and question marks. *Stars* are products with a dominant share of the market and good prospects for growth. However, they

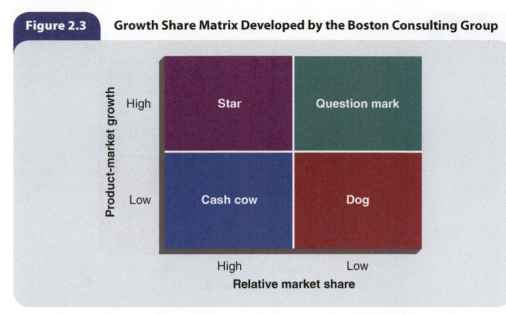

Figure 2.3   **Growth Share Matrix Developed by the Boston Consulting Group**

Source: *Perspectives*, No. 66, "The Product Portfolio." Reprinted by permission from The Boston Consulting Group, Inc., Boston, MA, Copyright © 1970.

use more cash than they generate to finance growth, add capacity, and increase market share. Amazon's Fire tablet computers might be considered stars because they are gaining market share quickly but remain well behind Apple, the leader. *Cash cows* have a dominant share of the market, but low prospects for growth. They typically generate more cash than is required to maintain market share. Bounty paper towels represent a cash cow for Procter & Gamble because it is a product that consistently sells well. *Dogs* have a subordinate share of the market and low prospects for growth. Dogs are often found in established markets. The MP3 player would probably be considered a dog by a company like Apple, as most customers prefer to listen to music on their smartphones. *Question marks,* sometimes called "problem children," have a small share of a growing market and generally require a large amount of cash to build market share. The Google Home voice-activated speaker, for example, is a question mark relative to Amazon's Echo with Alexa.

The long-term health of an organization depends on having a range of products, some that generate cash (and generate acceptable profits) and others that use cash to support growth. The major indicators of a firm's overall health are the size and vulnerability of the cash cows, the prospects for the stars, and the number of question marks and dogs. Particular attention should be paid to products that require large cash flows, as most firms cannot afford to sponsor many such products. If resources are spread too thin, the company will be unable to finance promising new product entries or acquisitions. Polaris Industries, for example, shut down its Victory line of motorcycles after the 18-year-old brand never achieved market share goals. The company had introduced the motorcycle line in an effort to diversify its portfolio of sporting vehicles, but the brand was outshined by the company's newer Indian brand of motorcycles.[12]

Competitive Growth Strategies

Based on analyses of each product or business unit, a firm may choose one or more competitive strategies. Figure 2.4 shows these competitive strategies on a product-market matrix. The matrix can help in determining growth that can be implemented through marketing strategies.

Market penetration is a strategy of increasing sales in current markets with current products. Coca-Cola, for example, boosted sales due to a promotion that offered soft-drink bottles and cans labeled with hundreds of different personal names, song lyrics, and phrases such as "Friends," "Family," and "BFF." The personalized labels were especially popular with younger consumers, who shared photos of personalized bottles on Instagram along with the

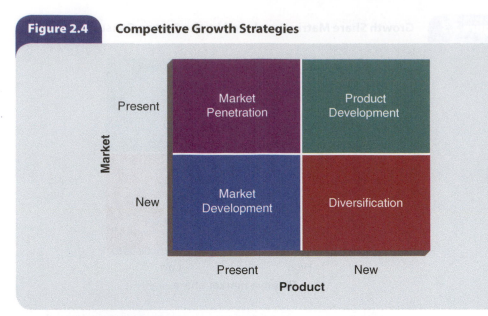

| Figure 2.4 | Competitive Growth Strategies |

Source: Adapted from Ansoff's Matrix (New Corporate Strategy), (New York: Wiley, 1988), p. 109.

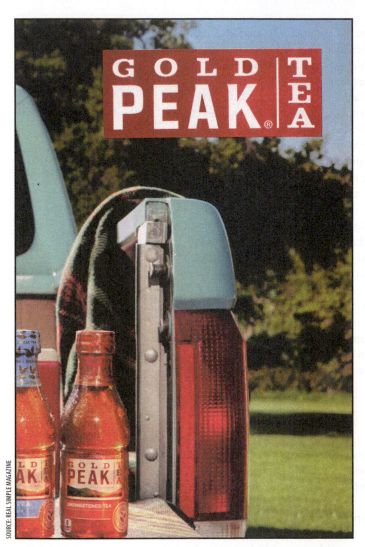

Diversification
The Coca-Cola Company created Gold Peak Tea to diversify its product portfolio.

hashtag #shareacoke.[13] *Market development* is a strategy of increasing sales of current products in new markets. Arm & Hammer, for example, successfully introduced its baking soda, the firm's basic product, into new markets for use as a carpet deodorizer, as a freshener for litter boxes, as a laundry detergent, as deodorant, and as a toothpaste. Market development also occurs when a company introduces its products into international markets for the first time. When Baskin Robbins opened its first ice cream shop in South Africa, it paid special attention to local tastes for its flavors and planned to swap out flavors regularly.[14]

Product development is a strategy of increasing sales by improving present products or developing new products for current markets. Electric guitar maker Fender, for example, introduced an online guitar lesson service to help ensure that new buyers of Fender guitars learn to play well enough to want to buy more Fender guitars.[15] Perhaps the most common example of product development occurs in the automotive industry, in which car manufacturers regularly introduce redesigned or completely new models to their current markets. Finally, *diversification* is a strategy of developing new products to be sold in new markets. Diversification allows firms to make better and wider use of their managerial, technological, and financial resources. Consider Nokia, best known as a cell phone maker until it sold that business to Microsoft, which has introduced a number of internet-connected health devices, including blood-pressure monitors, scales, and thermometers under the Nokia brand name and logo.[16] As shown in the ad, Coca-Cola employed a diversification strategy when it introduced Gold Peak, a line of iced tea products that capitalized on the growing demand for beverages other than sweetened sodas. The ad presents two flavors of Gold Peak iced tea in front of a cooler in the back of a pickup truck, suggesting that the beverage is a good choice to accompany leisure activities. That idea is reinforced by the ad's tagline, "You make memories. We'll make the home-brewed taste." Diversification also offers some advantages over single-business firms because it allows firms to spread their risk across a number of markets.

2-3 ASSESSING ORGANIZATIONAL RESOURCES AND OPPORTUNITIES

Learning Objective 2-3
Discuss how analyzing organizational resources and the marketing environment can help identify opportunities and create competitive advantage.

core competencies Things a company does extremely well, which sometimes give it an advantage over its competition

The next phase of the strategic planning process is an analysis of the marketing environment, including the industry in which the company operates or intends to sell its products. As we will see in Chapter 3, the marketing environment (which includes economic, competitive, political, legal and regulatory, sociocultural, and technological forces) can threaten an organization and influence its overall goals, affecting the amount and type of resources the company can acquire. However, these forces can also create favorable opportunities that can help an organization achieve its goals and marketing objectives.

Any strategic planning effort must take into account the organization's available financial and human resources and capabilities and how these resources are likely to change over time, as changes may affect the organization's ability to achieve its mission and goals. Adequate resources can help a firm generate customer satisfaction and loyalty, goodwill, and a positive reputation, all of which impact marketing through creating well-known brands and strong financial performance. Coca-Cola, Apple, and Google all benefit from high levels of brand recognition and goodwill. Such strengths also include **core competencies**, things a company does extremely well—sometimes so well that they give the company an advantage over its competition.

Analysis of the marketing environment also includes identifying opportunities in the marketplace, which requires a solid understanding of the company's industry. When the right combination of circumstances and timing permits an organization to take action to reach a particular target market, a **market opportunity** exists. To illustrate, Tommy Hilfiger saw an opportunity in the underserved market for clothing for children and adults with disabilities. The company, which is owned by PVH Corp. (formerly known as Phillips-Van Heusen Corporation), introduced multiple clothing collections for children and, later, adults. The clothing includes modifications such as Velcro closures and adjustable leg openings to facilitate dressing no matter what abilities a person might have.[17] Such opportunities are often called **strategic windows**, temporary periods of optimal fit between the key requirements of a market and the particular capabilities of a company competing in that market.[18]

When a company matches a core competency to opportunities in the marketplace, it is said to have a **competitive advantage**. Some companies possess manufacturing, technical, or marketing skills that they can tie to market opportunities to create a competitive advantage. As shown in the ad, Larabar gained a significant advantage over

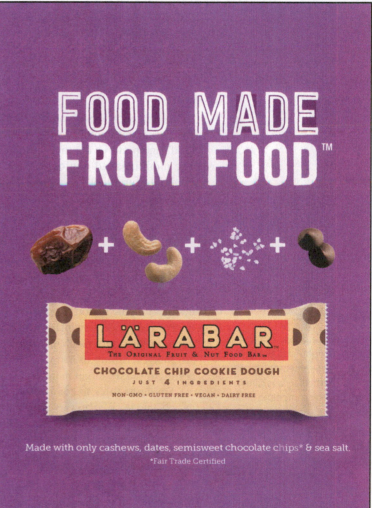

SOURCE: WOMEN'S HEALTH

Competitive Advantage
The competitive advantage of the Larabar, the original fruit and nut bar, is that it is made from just a few ingredients, such as dates, semisweet chocolate chips, and sea salt, and all of them are real foods.

DISRUPTIVE MARKETING

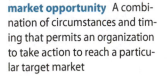

Amazon's Alexa Brings More Retailing Disruptions

Will Alexa, the voice-activated artificial intelligence (AI) agent, give Amazon.com a special edge in disrupting both traditional *and* online retailing? As Amazon approaches its 25th anniversary, technological innovations such as Alexa are helping the pioneering e-tailer to attract new customers, reinforce loyalty among existing customers, and challenge competitors day after day.

Amazon first introduced Alexa in 2014 as a hands-free digital assistant accessed through its Echo smart speaker for the home. Always listening for a voice command, Alexa is programmed to answer questions, play music, check weather reports, turn on lights, and—of course—order merchandise from Amazon. Unlike Siri, the AI assistant built into Apple's iPhones, Alexa remained tethered to Amazon's speakers until 2017, when it debuted in the very popular Amazon shopping app for iPhone users. Alexa can also "chat"

with Microsoft's AI assistant, Cortana, enabling Amazon to reach the millions of people who have downloaded the Cortana app. Already, more than 25 million U.S. consumers call on Alexa for assistance every month.

Now that Amazon owns Whole Foods Market, its retail empire extends beyond e-commerce into the hyper-competitive world of brick-and-mortar grocery retailing. Alongside fruits and vegetables, Whole Foods stores prominently display Amazon's Echo speakers with built-in Alexa functionality, beckoning traditional shoppers to enjoy the convenience of voice-command shopping. Looking ahead, Alexa's ever-increasing market penetration will only strengthen Amazon's ability to disrupt traditional retailing practices by smoothing the way for millions of consumers to order from Amazon businesses with just a few words.[b]

---

competing energy bar brands by appealing to the growing market for foods that are minimally processed and contain few ingredients. In the ad, Larabar touts that it is "food made from food" and pictures the four ingredients in the chocolate chip cookie dough flavor of Larabar. The minimalist ad reinforces the idea that Larabars are a healthy option for those desiring minimal ingredient lists; non-GMO ingredients; Fair Trade ingredients; and vegan, dairy-free, and/or gluten-free products.

2-3a SWOT Analysis

market opportunity A combination of circumstances and timing that permits an organization to take action to reach a particular target market

strategic windows Temporary periods of optimal fit between the key requirements of a market and the particular capabilities of a company competing in that market

competitive advantage The result of a company matching a core competency to opportunities it has discovered in the marketplace

SWOT analysis Assessment of an organization's strengths, weaknesses, opportunities, and threats

A SWOT analysis can be helpful for gauging a firm's capabilities and resources relative to the industry. The **SWOT analysis** assesses an organization's strengths, weaknesses, opportunities, and threats. It can provide a firm with insights into such factors as timing market entry into a new geographic region or product category. Figure 2.5 depicts the SWOT analysis as a four-cell matrix and shows how marketers must seek to convert weaknesses into strengths, threats into opportunities, and match internal strengths with external opportunities to develop competitive advantages. Strengths and weaknesses are internal factors that can influence an organization's ability to satisfy target markets.

Strengths refer to competitive advantages, or core competencies, that give the company an advantage. *Weaknesses* are limitations a company faces in developing or implementing a marketing strategy. Consider Walmart, a company that was so dominant for decades that it almost did not need to worry about competitors. However, Amazon has grown into such a threat recently, with its low costs and high customer satisfaction, that Walmart has been forced to acknowledge it has a serious weakness in online sales and technological innovation. To respond to this threat, Walmart has made numerous acquisitions, such as Jet.com, to help the company improve its online shopping experience and delivery.[19] Both strengths and weaknesses should be examined from a customer perspective. Only those strengths that relate to satisfying customers should be considered true competitive advantages. Likewise, weaknesses that directly affect customer satisfaction should be considered disadvantages.

Figure 2.5 **The Four-Cell SWOT Matrix**

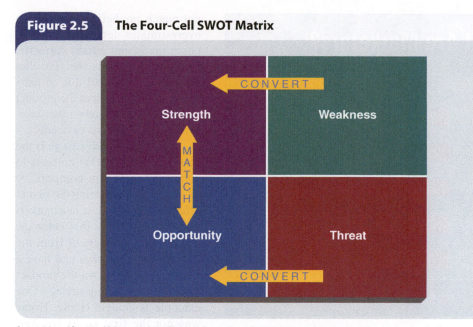

Source: Adapted from Nigel F. Piercy, *Market-Led Strategic Change.* Copyright 1992, Butterworth-Heinemann Ltd., p. 371. Reprinted with permission.

Opportunities and threats affect all organizations within an industry, market, or geographic region because they exist outside of and independently of the company. *Opportunities* refer to favorable conditions in the environment that could produce rewards for the organization if acted upon. Opportunities are situations that exist but must be exploited for the company to benefit from them. *Threats,* on the other hand, refer to barriers that could prevent the company from reaching its objectives. Threats must be acted upon to prevent them from limiting the organization's capabilities. Opportunities and threats can stem from many sources within the environment. When a competitor's introduction of a new product threatens a company, a firm may require a defensive strategy. If the company can develop and launch a new product that meets or exceeds the competition's offering, it can transform the threat into an opportunity. It is important to use SWOT analysis to explore the internal organization and the marketing environment without judgment, focusing on issues that could lead to the greatest possibilities of success. This means using some resources for open-minded examination rather than looking for information to confirm current beliefs.[20]

2-3b First-Mover and Late-Mover Advantage

An important factor that marketers must consider when identifying organizational resources and opportunities is whether the firm has the resources to cultivate a first-mover advantage, or is in a position to choose between developing a first-mover or late-mover advantage. A **first-mover advantage** is the ability of an innovative company to achieve long-term competitive advantages by being the first to offer a certain product in the marketplace. Being the first to enter a market helps a company build a reputation as a pioneer and market leader. Amazon and eBay were both first-mover start-ups that remain leaders as they grow and innovate ahead of the competition. For a first mover, the market is, for at least a short period, free of competition as potential competitors work to develop a rival product. Because consumers have no choice initially, being a first mover also helps establish customer brand loyalty in cases when switching to another brand later may be costly or difficult. The first to develop a new product can also protect secrets and technology through patents.

There are risks, however, of being the first to enter a market. There are usually high cost outlays associated with creating a new product, including market research, product development, production, and marketing—or buyer education—costs. Also, early sales growth may

first-mover advantage The ability of an innovative company to achieve long-term competitive advantages by being the first to offer a certain product in the marketplace

How Confident Are Marketers?

How confident are you that your organization's marketing team...

	Not Confident	Confident
...has a clear and well-understood brand positioning in place to be competitive?	28%	48%
...has the right capabilities to be competitive?	25%	43%
...is doing the right things to drive growth?	29%	40%
...is Investing in the customers who matter?	30%	39%
...has a clear and well-understood strategy in place to be competitive?	32%	37%

SNAPSHOT

■ Not Confident ■ Confident

Source: The Marketers' Confidence Index, 2016.

not match predictions if the firm overestimates demand or fails to target marketing efforts correctly. The company runs the risk that the product will fail due to market uncertainty, or that the product might not completely meet consumers' expectations or needs.

A **late-mover advantage** is the ability of later market entrants to achieve long-term competitive advantages by not being the first to offer a certain product in a marketplace. Competitors that enter the market later can benefit from the first mover's mistakes and have a chance to improve on the product design and marketing strategy. One example is Google Home. Home was not the first smart speaker/ home automation device, but Google's technology and experience with voice search along with richer features may give Home a late-mover advantage over first mover Amazon Echo.[21] A late mover is also likely to have lower initial investment costs than the first mover because the first mover has already developed a distribution infrastructure and educated buyers about the product. By the time a late mover enters the market, there is also more data, and therefore more certainty, about product success.

There are disadvantages of being a late mover too, though. The company that entered the market first may have patents and other protections on its technology and trade secrets that prevent the late mover from producing a similar product. If customers who have already purchased the first mover's product believe that switching to the late mover's product will be expensive or time-consuming, it may be difficult for the late mover to gain market share.

It is important to note that the timing of entry into the market is crucial. Companies that are relatively quick to enter the market after the first mover have a greater chance of building market share and brand loyalty. Companies that enter the market later on, after many other companies have done so, face stronger competition and have more disadvantages.

Learning Objective 2-4

Explore how a firm develops marketing objectives and strategies that contribute to overall objectives.

late-mover advantage The ability of later market entrants to achieve long-term competitive advantages by not being the first to offer a certain product in a marketplace

marketing objective A statement of what is to be accomplished through marketing activities

2-4 DEVELOPING MARKETING OBJECTIVES AND MARKETING STRATEGIES

The next phase in strategic planning is the development of marketing objectives and marketing strategies, which are used to achieve overall objectives. A **marketing objective** states what is to be accomplished through marketing activities. These objectives can be given in terms of product introduction, product improvement or innovation, sales volume, profitability, market share, pricing, distribution, advertising, or employee training activities. A marketing objective of Ritz-Carlton hotels, for example, is to have more than 90 percent of its customers indicate that they had a memorable experience at the hotel. Marketing objectives should be based on a careful study of the SWOT analysis, matching strengths to opportunities, eliminating weaknesses, and minimizing threats.

Marketing objectives should possess certain characteristics. First, a marketing objective should be expressed in clear, simple terms so all marketing and non-marketing personnel in the company understand exactly what they are trying to achieve. Second, an objective should be measurable, which allows the organization to track progress and compare outcomes against beginning benchmarks. For instance, if an objective is to increase market share by 10 percent in the United States, the company should be able to measure market share changes accurately to ensure that it is making gains toward that objective. Third, a marketing objective should specify a time frame for its accomplishment, such as six months or one year. Finally, a marketing objective should be consistent with both business-unit and corporate strategies. This ensures that the company's mission is carried out consistently at all levels of the organization by all personnel. Marketing objectives should be achievable and use company resources effectively, and successful accomplishment should contribute to the overall corporate strategy. A marketing strategy ensures that the firm has a plan in place to achieve its marketing objectives.

A **marketing strategy** is the selection of a target market and the creation of a marketing mix that will satisfy the needs of target-market members. A marketing strategy articulates the best use of the company's resources to achieve its marketing objectives. It also directs resource deployment so as to boost competitive advantage. Marketing strategy is the key variable in strengthening organizational competitiveness.[22]

Marketing strategies may need to be adapted as the environment changes. Some organizations fail to adapt their strategy in response to competition, consumer behavior, or other factors that may create the need for a new modified strategy.[23] For instance, as Android smartphones became popular, Samsung had to adapt its strategy to compete in the market with new features and variations. Samsung developed its Galaxy S9 in response to competition and consumer demand.

2-4a **Selecting the Target Market**

Selecting an appropriate target market may be the most important decision a company makes in the strategic planning process and is crucial for strategic success. The target market must be chosen before the organization can adapt its marketing mix to meet the customers' needs and preferences. If a company selects the wrong target market, all other marketing decisions are likely to be in vain. The local U.K. TV channel London Live, for example, was launched with much fanfare and targeted at the youth market. Within five months of its launch, the station was struggling severely. The programs aired on London Live did not appear to resonate with younger audiences, prompting the network to try to reposition itself by changing its target market to focus on an older demographic.[24]

Careful and accurate target-market selection is crucial to productive marketing efforts. Products, and even whole companies, sometimes fail because marketers misidentify the best target market for their products. Organizations that try to be all things to all people rarely satisfy the needs of any customer group very well. Identification and analysis of a target market provide a foundation on which the company can develop its marketing mix.

When exploring possible target markets, marketing managers try to evaluate how entry could affect the company's sales, costs, and profits. Marketing information should be organized to facilitate a focus on the chosen target customers. Accounting and information systems, for example, can be used to track revenues and costs by customer (or customer group). The firm should offer rewards to managers and employees who focus efforts on profitable customers. Firms should develop teamwork skills that promote a flexible customer orientation that allows the firm to adapt to changes in the marketing environment.

Compare the target markets for the Special K and KTM products featured in the accompanying advertisements. This *Women's Health* magazine ad directly targets women who want to eat heathy products with fewer ingredients. The ad pictures a woman enjoying a bowl of Special K cereal, describes the cereal's ingredients, and presents Special K's motto, "Own it." The KTM ad, on the other hand, appeared in *Dirt Bike* magazine and features a motorcycle racer riding a KTM 350 EXC-F at the front of the pack in an off-road race. The target market for this ad, which depicts the 350 EXC-F in the thrill of an off-road race, is clearly off-rode motorcycle enthusiasts.

marketing strategy A plan of action for identifying and analyzing a target market and developing a marketing mix to meet the needs of that market

Target Market Selection
Who are the target markets for Special K and for KTM products? Are they targeting the same customers?

Marketers should determine whether a selected target market aligns with the company's overall mission and objectives. If it does, they should assess whether the company has the appropriate resources to develop a marketing mix (product, price, promotion, and distribution) that meets the needs of that target market. The size and number of competitors already marketing products in potential target markets are concerns as well. For example, the market for mobile gaming has become so competitive that new entrants must carefully evaluate whether their smartphone and tablet games represent a new product that would be in demand by the target market or a genuine improvement over what already exists. This market is estimated to reach $65 billion by 2020.[25]

2-4b Creating the Marketing Mixes

Using all relevant information available to conduct in-depth research allows a firm to select the most appropriate target market, which is the basis for creating a marketing mix that satisfies the needs of that market. Tesla Motors selected a unique segment of the battery electric vehicle market and created a marketing mix of new technology that included not only a sleek electric automobile but also distribution direct from the manufacturer. It selected promotional methods and price points that suitably reflected the upper end of the electric car market.[26]

An organization should analyze demographic information, customer needs, preferences, and behaviors with respect to product design, pricing, distribution, and promotion. For example, to grow beyond its core Baby Boomer market, Thor Industries developed a new Airstream recreational vehicle to target Millennials. To meet the needs and desires of Millennials, the

Airstream Basecamp is smaller, solar powered, and can be towed with a variety of mid-size SUVs. The $36,000 Basecamp includes Bluetooth speakers, Italian cabinetry, and a panoramic window for taking in Instagram-ready views.[27]

Marketing-mix decisions should have two additional characteristics: consistency and flexibility. All marketing-mix decisions should be consistent with the business-unit and corporate strategies. Such consistency allows the organization to achieve its objectives on all three levels of planning. Flexibility, on the other hand, permits the organization to alter the marketing mix in response to changes in market conditions, competition, and customer needs. Marketing strategy flexibility has a positive influence on organizational performance.

Utilizing the marketing mix as a tool set, a company can detail how it will achieve a sustainable competitive advantage. A **sustainable competitive advantage** is one that the competition cannot copy in the foreseeable future. Amazon maintains a sustainable competitive advantage in shipping because of its high-tech logistics system and extensive network of distribution centers, which allows the online giant to offer low prices and fast delivery. Many retailers struggle to compete with Amazon in terms of low-cost products and fast, low-cost shipping. Maintaining a sustainable competitive advantage requires flexibility in the marketing mix when facing uncertain competitive environments.

2-5 MANAGING MARKETING IMPLEMENTATION

Marketing implementation is the process of putting marketing strategies into action. Through planning, marketing managers provide purpose and direction for an organization's marketing efforts and are positioned to implement specific marketing strategies. The effective implementation of any and all marketing activities depends on a well-organized marketing department that is capable of motivating personnel, communicating effectively, employing good coordination efforts, and setting reasonable and attainable timetables for activity completion. Managers play a key role in creating desired outcomes through supervisory actions that provide rewards, reduce risks, and recognize behaviors that implement the marketing strategy.[28]

2-5a Organizing the Marketing Unit

The structure and relationships of a marketing unit—including lines of authority and communication that connect and coordinate individuals—strongly affect marketing activities. Companies that truly adopt the marketing concept develop an organizational culture that is based on a shared set of beliefs that places the customer's needs at the center of decisions about strategy and operations. Technology can help companies adopt the marketing concept. For example, firms increasingly use online tracking and related technology to gather and analyze information from every interaction with customers to improve their understanding of customers' needs and wants. Though some worry that such tracking may violate individual privacy, the "big data" generated and analyzed help marketers build detailed profiles for their target markets, which helps them identify and better satisfy the needs and wants of the target market.

Firms must decide whether to centralize or decentralize operations, a choice that directly affects marketing decision making and strategy. In a **centralized organization**, top-level managers delegate little authority to lower levels. In a **decentralized organization**, decision-making authority is delegated as far down the chain of command as possible. In centralized organizations, marketing decisions are made at the top levels. However, centralized decision making may prove ineffective in firms that must respond quickly to fluctuations in customer demand. In these organizations, decentralized authority allows the company to adapt more rapidly to customer needs.

sustainable competitive advantage An advantage that the competition cannot copy

marketing implementation The process of putting marketing strategies into action

centralized organization A structure in which top-level managers delegate little authority to lower levels

decentralized organization A structure in which decision-making authority is delegated as far down the chain of command as possible

Recognition
Recognizing outstanding performance is one approach to motivating marketing personnel.

How effectively a company's marketing management can implement marketing strategies also depends on how the marketing unit is organized. Organizing marketing activities to align with the overall strategic marketing approach enhances organizational efficiency and performance. A marketing department should clearly outline the hierarchical relationships between personnel and who is responsible for performing certain activities and making decisions.

2-5b Coordinating and Communicating

Marketing managers must coordinate diverse employee actions to achieve marketing objectives and work closely with management in many areas, including research and development, production, finance, accounting, and human resources to ensure that marketing activities align with other functions of the firm. They must also coordinate the activities of internal marketing staff with the marketing efforts of external organizations, including advertising agencies, resellers (wholesalers and retailers), researchers, and shippers. Marketing managers can improve coordination by making each employee aware of how his or her job relates to others and how his or her actions contribute to the achievement of marketing objectives. This requires effective communication and motivation of everyone involved in the marketing process.

Marketing managers must be in clear communication with the firm's upper-level management to ensure that they are aware of the firm's goals and achievements and that marketing activities are consistent with the company's overall goals and strategies. The marketing unit should also take steps to ensure that its activities are in sync with those of other departments, such as finance or human resources. For instance, marketing personnel should work with the production staff to design products that have the features that marketing research indicates are what customers desire.

It is important that communication flow upward, from the front lines of the organization to upper management. Customer-contact employees are in a unique position to understand customers' wants and needs, and pathways should be open for them to communicate this knowledge to marketing managers. In this way, marketing managers can gain access to a rich source of information about what customers require, how products are selling, the effectiveness of marketing activities, and any issues with marketing implementation. Upward communication also allows marketing managers to understand the problems and requirements of lower-level employees, a critical group to keep satisfied, as they are the ones who interact with customers.

Training is an essential element of communicating with marketing employees. An effective training program provides employees with a forum to learn and ask questions, and results in employees who are empowered and can be held accountable for their performance. Many firms utilize a formalized, high-tech information system that tracks data and facilitates communication between marketing managers, sales managers, and sales personnel. Information systems expedite communications within and between departments and support other activities, such as allocating scarce organizational resources; planning; budgeting; and preparing sales analyses, performance evaluations, and reports.

To motivate marketing personnel, managers must address their employees' needs to maintain a high level of workplace satisfaction. Employee motivation and reward programs should be fair, ethical, and well understood to maintain a high level of workplace satisfaction. Employee rewards should also be tied to organizational goals. A firm can motivate its workers through a variety of methods, including by informing workers how their performance affects department and corporate results and their own compensation, providing appropriate and competitive compensation, linking pay with performance, implementing a flexible benefits program, and adopting a participative management approach.

Diversity in the workplace can complicate employee motivational strategies, as different generations and cultures may be motivated by different things. A specific employee might value autonomy or recognition more than a pay increase. Managers can compensate employees, not just with money and fringe benefits, but also with nonfinancial rewards, such as prestige or recognition, job autonomy, skill variety, task significance, increased feedback, or a more relaxed dress code. It is crucial for management to show that it takes pride in its workforce and to motivate employees to take pride in their company.

2-5c Establishing a Timetable for Implementation

Successful marketing implementation requires that employees know the specific activities for which they are responsible and the timetable for completing them. Establishing an implementation timetable involves several steps: (1) identifying the activities to be performed, (2) determining the time required to complete each activity, (3) separating the activities to be performed in sequence from those to be performed simultaneously, (4) organizing the activities in the proper order, and (5) assigning responsibility for completing each activity to one or more employees, teams, or managers. Completing all implementation activities on schedule requires tight coordination within the marketing unit and among other departments that contribute to marketing activities, such as production. Pinpointing which activities can be performed simultaneously will reduce the total amount of time needed to put a given marketing strategy into practice. Because scheduling can be a complicated task, some organizations use sophisticated computer programs to plan the timing of marketing activities.

2-6 EVALUATING MARKETING STRATEGIES

Learning Objective 2-6
Describe the four major elements of strategic performance evaluation.

To achieve marketing objectives, marketing managers must evaluate marketing strategies effectively. **Strategic performance evaluation** consists of establishing performance standards, measuring actual performance, comparing actual performance with established standards, and modifying the marketing strategy, if needed.

2-6a Establishing Performance Standards

A **performance standard** is an expected level of performance against which actual performance can be compared. A performance standard might be a 20 percent reduction in customer complaints, a monthly sales quota of $150,000, or a 10 percent increase per month in new-customer accounts. Performance standards are derived from marketing objectives that are set while developing the marketing strategy. By establishing marketing objectives, a firm indicates what a marketing strategy is supposed to accomplish. Marketing objectives directly or indirectly set forth performance standards, usually in terms of sales, costs, or communication dimensions, such as brand awareness or product feature recall. Actual performance should be measured in similar terms to facilitate comparisons.

2-6b Analyzing Actual Performance

The principal means by which a marketer can gauge whether a marketing strategy has been effective in achieving objectives is by analyzing the actual performance of the marketing strategy. Analyzing actual performance associated with communication dimensions is usually achieved by conducting customer research. Generally speaking, technological advancements have made it easier for firms to analyze actual performance. Firms such as IRI, featured in the advertisement, can help companies analyze actual performance using high-tech tools. This ad states that IRI's Personalization Suite can help marketers harness their data to target customers

strategic performance evaluation Establishing performance standards, measuring actual performance, comparing actual performance with established standards, and modifying the marketing strategy, if needed

performance standard An expected level of performance against which actual performance can be compared

Analyzing Actual Performance
Products, such as services sold by IRI, can help firms better analyze actual performance to improve their marketing plans.

more precisely and efficiently. The ad humorously depicts a fake advertisement offering hair products to a bald motorcycle rider to illustrate how poor targeting efforts are wasteful to marketers and annoying to consumers. The ad describes how IRI's product solutions help marketers improve the quality of decision making and marketing implementation. In this section, we focus on two bases—sales and cost—for evaluating the actual performance of marketing strategies.

Sales Analysis

Sales analysis uses sales figures to evaluate a firm's current performance. It is a common method of evaluation because sales data are readily available, at least in aggregate form, and can reflect the target market's reactions to a marketing mix. If sales spike after a particular marketing mix is implemented, marketers can be reasonably certain that the marketing mix was effective at reaching the target audience. Consider the sales spike that McDonald's experienced in the same quarter after it began selling larger and smaller versions of its famous Big Mac burger.[29] Information gleaned from sales data alone is not sufficient, however. To be useful, marketers must compare current sales data with forecasted sales, industry sales, specific competitors' sales, and the costs incurred from marketing efforts to achieve the sales volume. For example, knowing that a specialty store attained a $600,000 sales volume this year does not tell management whether its marketing strategy has succeeded. However, if managers know expected sales were $550,000, they are in a better position to determine the effectiveness of the firm's marketing efforts. In addition, if they know the marketing costs needed to achieve the $600,000 volume were 12 percent less than budgeted, they are in an even better position to analyze their marketing strategy precisely.

Although sales may be measured in several ways, the basic unit of measurement is the sales transaction. A sales transaction results in an order for a specified quantity of the organization's product sold under specified terms by a particular salesperson or sales team on a certain date. Organizations should record all information related to a transaction so that they can analyze sales in terms of dollar volume or market share. Firms frequently use dollar volume in their sales analyses because the dollar is a common denominator of sales, costs, and profits. A marketing manager who uses dollar-volume analysis should factor out the effects of price changes, which can skew the numbers by making it seem that more or fewer sales have been made than is the actual case.

As mentioned earlier, a firm's market share is its sales of a product stated as a percentage of industry sales of competing products. Market share analysis lets a company compare its marketing strategy with competitors' strategies. The primary reason for using market share analysis is to estimate whether sales changes have resulted from the firm's marketing strategy or from uncontrollable environmental forces. When a company's sales volume declines but its share of the market stays the same, the marketer can assume that industry sales declined because of outside factors. However, if a company experiences a decline in both sales and market share, it should consider making changes to its marketing strategy to make it more effective.

sales analysis Analysis of sales figures to evaluate a firm's performance

Even though market share analysis can be helpful in evaluating the performance of a marketing strategy, the user must exercise caution when interpreting results. When attributing a sales decline to uncontrollable factors, a marketer must keep in mind that factors in the external marketing environment do not impact all firms equally because firms have varying strategies and objectives. Changes in the strategies of one company can affect the market shares of one or all companies in that industry. Within an industry, the entrance of new firms, the launch of new products by competing firms, or the demise of established products also affects a firm's market share. Market share analysts should attempt to account for these effects. In one case, Apple caused its competitors to reevaluate their marketing strategies when it introduced the iPad and iPhone, spurring competitor innovation and revised marketing strategies.

Marketing Cost Analysis

Although sales analysis is critical for evaluating the performance of a marketing strategy, it provides only a partial picture. A marketing strategy that successfully generates sales may nevertheless be deemed ineffective if it is extremely costly. A firm must take into account the marketing costs associated with a strategy to gain a complete understanding of its effectiveness at achieving a desired sales level. **Marketing cost analysis** breaks down and classifies costs to determine which are associated with specific marketing efforts. Comparing costs of previous marketing activities with results allows a marketer to allocate the firm's marketing resources better in the future. Marketing cost analysis lets a company evaluate the performance of marketing strategy by comparing sales achieved and costs sustained. By pinpointing exactly where a company incurs costs, this form of analysis can help isolate profitable or unprofitable customers, products, and geographic areas. A company that understands and manages its costs appropriately has a competitive advantage. Evidence shows that a low-cost provider is in a position to engage in aggressive price competition.

One way to analyze costs is to compare a company's costs with industry averages. Many companies check the amount of money they spend on marketing efforts and other operations against average levels for the industry to identify areas in need of improvement. For example, a business could compare its advertising costs as a percentage of its sales with the industry average. A company might determine it spends 6 percent of its sales on advertising, while the industry average is 2 percent. When looking at industry averages, however, a company should take into account its own unique situation. The company's costs can differ from the industry average for several reasons, including its own marketing objectives, cost structure, geographic location, types of customers, and scale of operations. When comparing its advertising costs with the industry average, for instance, the company just mentioned might be spending a larger proportion on advertising because it is a smaller company competing against industry giants. Or perhaps this firm's advertising objectives are much more aggressive than those of other firms in the industry.

Costs can be categorized in different ways when performing marketing cost analysis. One way is to identify which ones are affected by sales or production volume. Some costs are fixed, meaning they do not change between different units of time, regardless of a company's production or sales volume. Fixed costs are expenses such as rent and employees' salaries, which are not affected by fluctuations in production or sales. Fixed costs are generally not very illuminating when determining how to use marketing funds more effectively. For example, it does little good to know that $80,000 is spent for rent annually. The marketing analyst must conduct additional research to determine that, of the $80,000 spent on rent, $32,000 is spent on facilities associated with marketing efforts.

Some costs are directly attributable to production and sales volume. These costs are known as variable costs and are stated as a per quantity (or unit) cost. Variable costs include the cost to produce or sell each unit of a specific product, such as the materials and labor, or the amount of commissions that are paid to salespeople when they sell products.

Another way to categorize costs is based on whether or not they can be linked to a specific business function. Costs that can be linked are allocated, using one or several criteria, to the functions that they support. If the firm spends $80,000 to rent space for production, storage, and sales facilities, the total rental cost can be allocated to each of the three functions using a

marketing cost analysis
Analysis of costs to determine which are associated with specific marketing efforts

measurement, such as square footage. Some costs cannot be assigned according to any logical criteria. These are costs such as interest paid on loans, taxes paid to the government, and the salaries of top management.

2-6c Comparing Actual Performance with Performance Standards and Making Changes If Needed

When comparing actual performance with established performance standards, a firm may find that it exceeded or failed to meet performance standard benchmarks. When actual performance exceeds performance standards, marketers will likely be satisfied and a marketing strategy will be deemed effective. It is important that a firm seek to gain an understanding of why the strategy was effective, because this information may allow marketers to adjust the strategy tactically to be even more effective.

When actual performance does not meet performance standards, marketers should seek to understand why a marketing strategy was less effective than expected. Perhaps a marketing mix variable, such as price, was not ideally suited to the target market, which could result in lower performance. Environmental changes and aggressive competitive behavior can both cause a marketing strategy to underperform.

When a marketer finds that a strategy is underperforming expectations, a question sometimes arises as to whether the marketing objective, against which performance is measured, is realistic. After studying the problem, the firm may find that the marketing objective is indeed unrealistic. In this case, marketers must alter the marketing objective to bring it in line with more sensible expectations. It is also possible that the marketing strategy is underfunded, which can result in lower performance.

Learning Objective 2-7

Outline the development of a marketing plan.

2-7 CREATING THE MARKETING PLAN

The strategic planning process ultimately yields a marketing strategy that is the framework for a **marketing plan**, a written document that specifies the marketing activities to be performed to implement and evaluate the organization's marketing strategies. Developing a clear and well-written marketing plan, though time-consuming, is important. It provides a uniform marketing vision for the firm and is the basis for internal communications. It delineates marketing responsibilities and tasks and outlines schedules for implementation. The plan presents objectives and specifies how resources are to be allocated to achieve them. Finally, the marketing plan helps marketing managers monitor and evaluate the performance of a marketing strategy.

A single marketing plan can be developed and applied to the business as a whole, but it is more likely that a company will choose to develop multiple marketing plans, with each relating to a specific brand or a product. Multiple marketing plans are part of a larger strategic business plan and are used to implement specific parts of the overall strategy.

Organizations use many different formats when producing a marketing plan. They may be written for strategic business units, product lines, individual products or brands, or specific markets. The key is to make sure that the marketing plan aligns with corporate and business-unit strategies and is accessible by, and shared with, all key employees. A marketing plan represents a critical element of a company's overall strategy development, and it should reflect the company's culture and be representative of all functional specialists in the firm.

Marketing planning and implementation are closely linked in successful companies. The marketing plan provides a framework to stimulate thinking and provide strategic direction. Implementation is an adaptive response to day-to-day issues, opportunities, and unanticipated situations—such as an economic slowdown that dampens sales—that cannot be incorporated into marketing plans.

marketing plan A written document that specifies the activities to be performed to implement and evaluate the organization's marketing strategies

Table 2.1 describes the major parts of a typical marketing plan. Each component builds on the previous one. The first component is the executive summary, which provides an overview of the entire marketing plan so that readers can quickly identify the key issues and their roles in the planning and implementation process. The executive summary includes an introduction, an explanation of the major aspects of the plan, and a statement about the costs.

The next component of the marketing plan is the environmental analysis, which supplies information about the company's current situation with respect to the marketing environment, the target market, and the firm's current objectives and performance. The environmental analysis includes an assessment of all the environmental factors—competitive, economic, political, legal, regulatory, technological, and sociocultural—that can affect marketing activities. It then examines the current needs of the organization's target markets. In the final section of the environmental analysis, the company evaluates its marketing objectives and performance to ensure that objectives are consistent with the changing marketing environment.

The next component of the marketing plan is the SWOT analysis (strengths, weaknesses, opportunities, and threats), which uses the information gathered in the environmental analysis. The marketing objectives section of the marketing plan states what the company wants to accomplish through marketing activities, using the SWOT analysis as a guide to where the firm stands in the market. The marketing strategies component outlines how the firm plans to achieve its marketing objectives and discusses the company's target market selection(s) and marketing mix. The marketing implementation component of the plan outlines how marketing strategies will be implemented. The success of the marketing strategy depends on the feasibility of marketing implementation. Finally, the performance evaluation section establishes the standards for how results will be measured and evaluated, and what actions the company should take to reduce the differences between planned and actual performance.

It is important to note that most organizations use their own unique formats and terminology to describe the marketing plan. Every marketing plan is, and should be, unique to the

Table 2.1 Components of the Marketing Plan

Plan Component	Component Summary	Highlights
Executive Summary	One- to two-page synopsis of the entire marketing plan	1. Stress key points 2. Include one to three key points that make the company unique
Environmental Analysis	Information about the company's current situation with respect to the marketing environment	1. Assessment of marketing environment factors 2. Assessment of target market(s) 3. Assessment of current marketing objectives and performance
SWOT Analysis	Assessment of the organization's strengths, weaknesses, opportunities, and threats	1. Strengths of the company 2. Weaknesses of the company 3. Opportunities in the environment and industry 4. Threats in the environment and industry
Marketing Objectives	Specification of the company's marketing objectives	1. Qualitative measures of what is to be accomplished 2. Quantitative measures of what is to be accomplished
Marketing Strategies	Outline of how the company will achieve its objectives	1. Target market(s) 2. Marketing mix
Marketing Implementation	Outline of how the company will implement its marketing strategies	1. Marketing organization 2. Activities and responsibilities 3. Implementation timetable
Performance Evaluation	Explanation of how the company will evaluate the performance of the implemented plan	1. Performance standards 2. Financial controls 3. Monitoring procedures (audits)

organization for which it was created. Creating and implementing a marketing plan allows the organization to achieve its marketing objectives and its business-unit and corporate goals. However, a marketing plan is only as good as the information it contains and the effort and creativity that went into its development. Therefore, the importance of having a good marketing information system that generates robust and reliable data cannot be overstated. Equally important is the role of managerial judgment throughout the strategic planning process. Although the creation of a marketing plan is an important milestone in strategic planning, it is by no means the final step. To succeed, a company must have a plan that is closely followed, yet flexible enough to allow for adjustments to reflect the changing marketing environment.

Summary

2-1 Explain the strategic planning process.

Through the process of strategic planning, a company identifies or establishes an organizational mission and goals, corporate strategy, marketing objectives, marketing strategy, and a marketing plan. To achieve its marketing objectives, an organization must develop a marketing strategy, which includes identifying a target market and creating a plan of action for developing, distributing, promoting, and pricing products that meet the needs of customers in that target market. The strategic planning process ultimately yields the framework for a marketing plan, a written document that specifies the activities to be performed for implementing and controlling an organization's marketing activities.

2-2 Understand the importance of a firm's mission statement and corporate and business-unit strategy.

An organization's goals should align with its mission statement—a long-term view, or vision, of what the organization wants to become. A well-formulated mission statement gives an organization a clear purpose and direction, distinguishes it from competitors, provides direction for strategic planning, and fosters a focus on customers. An organization's goals, which focus on the end results sought, guide the remainder of its planning efforts.

Corporate strategy determines the means for using resources in the areas of production, finance, research and development, human resources, and marketing to reach the organization's goals. Business-unit strategy focuses on strategic business units (SBUs)—divisions, product lines, or other profit centers within the parent company used to define areas for consideration in a specific strategic marketing plan. The Boston Consulting Group's market growth/market share matrix integrates a company's products or SBUs into a single, overall matrix for evaluation to determine appropriate strategies for individual products and business units. Based on its analysis, a firm may choose one or more competitive

strategies: market penetration, market development, product development, and/or diversification.

2-3 Discuss how analyzing organizational resources and the marketing environment can help identify opportunities and create competitive advantage.

The marketing environment, including economic, competitive, political, legal and regulatory, sociocultural, and technological forces, can affect the resources available to a company to create favorable opportunities. Resources may help a firm develop core competencies, which are things that a company does extremely well, sometimes so well that it gives the company an advantage over its competition. When the right combination of circumstances and timing permits an organization to take action toward reaching a particular target market, a market opportunity exists. Strategic windows are temporary periods of optimal fit between the key requirements of a market and the particular capabilities of a company competing in that market. When a company matches a core competency to opportunities it has discovered in the marketplace, it is said to have a competitive advantage. A marketer can use SWOT analysis to assess a firm's ability to achieve a competitive advantage.

If marketers want to understand how the timing of entry into a marketplace can create competitive advantage, they can examine and compare first-mover and late-mover advantages.

2-4 Explore how a firm develops marketing objectives and strategies that contribute to overall objectives.

The next phase of strategic planning involves the development of marketing objectives and strategies. Marketing objectives state what is to be accomplished through marketing activities and should be consistent with both business-unit and corporate strategies. Marketing strategies, the most detailed and specific of the three levels of strategy, are composed of two elements: the selection of a target market and the creation of a marketing mix that will satisfy the needs of the target-market members. The selection of a target market serves as the basis for the creation of the marketing mix to satisfy the needs of that market. Marketing-mix decisions should also be consistent with business-unit and corporate strategies and be flexible enough to respond to changes in market conditions, competition, and customer needs. Different elements of the marketing mix can be changed to accommodate different marketing strategies.

2-5 Identify what is necessary to manage the effective implementation of marketing strategies.

Marketing implementation is the process of putting marketing strategies into action. Through planning, marketing managers provide purpose and direction for an organization's marketing efforts. Marketing managers must understand the problems and elements of marketing implementation before they can effectively implement specific marketing activities.

The marketing unit must have a coherent internal structure in order to organize marketing efforts. In a centralized organization, top-level managers delegate very little authority to lower levels, whereas in decentralized organizations, decision-making authority is delegated as far down the chain of command as possible. Marketing managers must also be able to effectively coordinate marketing activities. This entails both coordinating the activities of the marketing staff within the firms and integrating those activities with the marketing actions of external organizations that are also involved in implementing the marketing strategies. Proper communication should move both down (from top management to the lower-level employees) and up (from lower-level employees to top management). Marketing managers learn marketing employees' needs and develop different methods to motivate those employees to help the organization meet its goals.

Finally, successful marketing implementation requires that a timetable be established. Establishment of an implementation timetable involves several steps and ensures that employees know the specific activities for which they are responsible and the timeline for completing each activity. Completing all activities on schedule requires tight coordination among departments. Many organizations use sophisticated computer programs to plan the timing of marketing activities.

2-6 Describe the four major elements of strategic performance evaluation.

Strategic performance evaluation consists of establishing performance standards, analyzing actual performance, comparing actual performance with established standards, and modifying the marketing strategy when needed. When actual performance is compared with performance standards, marketers must determine whether a discrepancy exists and, if so, whether it requires corrective action, such as changing the performance standard or improving actual performance.

Two possible ways to evaluate the actual performance of marketing strategies are sales analysis and marketing cost analysis. Sales analysis uses sales figures to evaluate a firm's current performance. It is the most common method of evaluation because sales data are a good indication of the target market's reaction to a marketing mix. Marketing cost analysis breaks down and classifies costs to determine which are associated with specific marketing efforts. Marketing cost analysis helps marketers decide how to best allocate the firm's marketing resources.

2-7 Outline the development of a marketing plan.

A key component of marketing planning is the development of a marketing plan, which outlines all the activities necessary to implement marketing strategies. The plan fosters communication among employees, assigns responsibilities and schedules, specifies how resources are to be allocated to achieve objectives, and helps marketing managers monitor and evaluate the performance of a marketing strategy.

Important Terms

strategic marketing
 management 30
strategic planning 30
mission statement 31
corporate strategy 33
strategic business unit
 (SBU) 34
market 34
market share 34

market growth/market
 share matrix 34
core competencies 37
market opportunity 37
strategic windows 37
competitive advantage 37
SWOT analysis 38
first-mover advantage 39
late-mover advantage 40

marketing objective 40
marketing strategy 41
sustainable competitive
 advantage 43
marketing
 implementation 43
centralized organization 43
decentralized
 organization 43

strategic performance
 evaluation 45
performance
 standard 45
sales analysis 46
marketing cost
 analysis 47
marketing
 plan 48

Discussion and Review Questions

1. Identify the major components of strategic planning, and explain how they are interrelated.
2. Explain how an organization can create a competitive advantage at the corporate strategy level and at the business-unit strategy level.
3. How might a planner decide on competitive growth strategies using tools such as the market growth/market share matrix (Figure 2.3) and product-market matrix (Figure 2.4)?
4. What are some issues to consider in analyzing a company's resources and opportunities? How do these issues affect marketing objectives and marketing strategy?
5. What is SWOT analysis and why is it important?
6. How can an organization make its competitive advantages sustainable over time? How difficult is it to create sustainable competitive advantages?

7. How should organizations set marketing objectives?
8. What are the two major parts of a marketing strategy?
9. When considering the strategic planning process, what factors influence the development of a marketing strategy?
10. Identify and explain the major managerial actions that are a part of managing the implementation of marketing strategies.
11. Which element of the strategic planning process plays a major role in the establishment of performance standards? Explain.
12. When assessing actual performance of a marketing strategy, should a marketer perform marketing cost analysis? Why or why not?
13. Identify and explain the major components of a marketing plan.

Developing Your Marketing Plan

One of the foundations of a successful marketing strategy is a thorough analysis of your company. To make the best decisions about what products to offer, which markets to target, and how to reach those target market members, you must recognize your company's strengths and weaknesses. The information collected in this analysis should be referenced when making many of the decisions in your marketing plan. While writing the beginning of your plan, the information in this chapter can help you with the following:

1. Can you identify the core competencies of your company? Do they currently contribute to a competitive advantage? If not, what changes could your company make to establish a competitive advantage?
2. Conduct a SWOT analysis of your company to identify its strengths and weaknesses. Continue your analysis to include the business environment, discovering any opportunities that exist or threats that may affect your company.
3. Using the information from your SWOT analysis, have you identified any opportunities that are a good match with your company's core competencies? Likewise, have you discovered any weaknesses that could be converted to strengths through careful marketing planning?

Video Case 2.1

Inside Tesla's Strategy for Growth

Tesla has been pursuing a strategy of aggressive growth since its founding in 2003. The company's mission is to accelerate the move to vehicles that will save energy while saving the planet. The key word here is *accelerate*. Tesla's strategy combines a long-term vision of a world fueled by renewable energy with a sense of urgency about creating Earth-friendly vehicles that customers will want to drive now.

Because it relies heavily on technology, it's not surprising that Tesla is based in Palo Alto, California, home to tech giants like Hewlett Packard and Facebook. The firm operates a single, highly automated manufacturing plant in Fremont, California. It also built its own massive production facility to supply lithium-ion batteries for its vehicles and developed a network of charging stations from coast to coast. Instead of selling through dealers, Tesla's strategy is to sell directly to consumers. This unusual arrangement allows more control over the sales process and yields a higher profit margin per vehicle, because dealers aren't part of the distribution channel.

In planning its products, Tesla has gone beyond the "green" appeal to showcase the style, speed, and status of its vehicles, marketing to people who want a special driving experience. Consider the Roadster, a snappy, low-slung sports car introduced in 2008. The attractive and sporty Roadster broke the mold for traditional electric cars and rocketed Tesla into the public eye.

The company stopped selling the Roadster in 2011 as it focused on launching the Model S, a stylish, high-end, high-performance sedan with self-driving capabilities. The head designer knew he had to create an all-electric sedan that would stand out in a crowded field of competing vehicles made by international giants such as Audi, BMW, and Mercedes. His design blends the best of today and tomorrow, creating a classically elegant yet forward-looking exterior. Just as important, the Model S has an extended driving range, thanks to the company's advanced battery technology.

Next, Tesla introduced the head-turning Model X, a luxury SUV with unique "falcon wing" passenger doors that open upward for access to rear seating. Thousands of consumers rushed to put down a deposit for this new product, eager to be among the first owners. Despite strong demand, the company struggled to increase production output because of the complexities of manufacturing the unique vehicle and because of parts shortages. Tesla delayed deliveries for months while it ironed out these problems.

Expanding the product line and targeting a new customer segment, Tesla then introduced the Model 3. This sedan is more affordably priced than the firm's previous vehicles, part of the strategy to enter the mainstream of high-volume, all-electric car marketing. The Model 3 has a modern, uncluttered look with curb appeal. The dashboard is similarly uncluttered, replacing the usual gaggle of gadgets and buttons with one touch-screen control panel. Enhancing Tesla's reputation for technology, the Model 3's "autopilot" feature allows for some driverless operations. More than 450,000 people have already submitted a deposit of $1,000 each to reserve a Model 3. Still, Tesla has had difficulty bringing production to full throttle and, as a result, has been forced to delay some deliveries.

Looking ahead to the long-term goal of producing 500,000 vehicles per year and profiting from economies of scale, Tesla is hiring thousands of employees and revamping facilities for higher output. It is preparing for several product introductions, including a new Roadster sports car, a Model Y crossover vehicle, and a Semi truck. Can Tesla achieve sustained profitability as it races to meet its ambitious goals, tries to outpace competitors, and seeks to accelerate the transition to renewable energy?[30]

Questions for Discussion

1. How would you describe Tesla's strengths, weaknesses, opportunities, and threats?
2. What are Tesla's core competencies, and how do they help the company compete with long-established car companies?
3. What performance standards has Tesla set, and what other standards would you recommend that Tesla use for strategic performance evaluation? Explain your answer.

Case 2.2

Crayola's Colorful Marketing Strategy for the Digital Age

New products, new technologies, and new partnerships—these are some of the elements in Crayola's marketing strategy for continued success in the digital age. The original founders of Crayola marketed their first boxed set of eight crayons in 1903, seeking to compete with more expensive imported coloring sticks. Crayola's products caught on quickly because they were affordable and child-friendly. Over time, the company introduced additional colors, and it scored a big hit with the now-iconic box of 64 crayons, launched in 1958.

KARENFOLEYPHOTOGRAPHY/SHUTTERSTOCK.COM

More than a century after being founded, Crayola—now owned by Hallmark Cards—dominates its market, selling three billion crayons every year. Its marketing plan focuses on a diverse range of products that facilitate creativity and personal expression, including crayons, markers, paints, coloring books, craft activity sets, toys, and modeling compounds like clay and Silly Putty. Crayola targets multiple audiences, including children and adults, retailers, schools, educational distributors, and international distributors. Communicating through traditional and social media allows the company to engage customers of all ages in all markets, and keeps brand awareness high.

Crayola constantly scans the marketing environment to identify new trends and opportunities. When the adult coloring craze swept the nation, Crayola developed and promoted a line of Color Escapes coloring books for people who like to relax with a crayon or marker in hand. As apps became increasingly popular, Crayola introduced its Color Alive product line, which works with a proprietary app. With Color Alive, children color and scan a picture of a character or superhero, and then use the app to see the drawing spring to life.

The company's marketing plan also calls for refreshing existing products from time to time, such as by "retiring" a few older colors and inviting consumers to help name new colors. In one marketing communications campaign, Crayola planned to announce it was retiring a classic yellow crayon on National Crayon Day, during a special live event streamed on Facebook. One day before, however, a consumer who noticed that a certain yellow was missing from a Crayola box in a New Jersey store tweeted about his discovery. That tweet, including the consumer's #SpoilerAlert hashtag, went viral, revealing that the color Dandelion was being dropped.

Far from spoiling the surprise, the consumer's spontaneous tweet riveted public interest and prompted comments all over social media, as well as news coverage in print and broadcast media. Crayola was ready to join the conversation with an immediate video upload about Dandelion's "retirement tour" of schools. It also paved the way for the follow-up marketing communications campaign requesting that consumers submit names for a new blue crayon color. When the company measured final results against performance standards, it found these marketing activities had reached five times the number of people projected in the original plan.

To attract, entertain, and inspire digital-savvy children and parents, Crayola has a robust online presence, including a website and posts on Instagram, Facebook, Twitter, Pinterest, and YouTube. It also offers free downloadable coloring pages for every season and every interest. Outside the digital realm, it has opened four Crayola Experience attractions featuring creative hands-on activities. To expand the brand's horizons, Crayola has partnered with Clinique on a line of lip-balm crayons. Watch for more partnerships and more creativity in marketing as Crayola aims to grow revenues and profits in the digital age.[31]

Questions for Discussion

1. Which competitive growth strategy was Crayola pursuing when it retired old crayon colors and launched new colors? Which strategy was it pursuing when it introduced coloring books for adults?

2. From the perspective of a SWOT analysis, how is Crayola using its strengths to make the most of potential opportunities and to convert potential threats into opportunities?

3. Can Crayola transfer its first-mover advantage from the crayon market to creative and artistic products for digital-savvy consumers? Why or why not?

Strategic Case 1

Amazonization of Whole Foods

In 1978, two entrepreneurs, John Mackey and Renee Lawson Hardy, began a challenging venture to create a company that incorporated the values of healthy living and conscious capitalism, all with a $45,000 loan. Their efforts led them to open a small natural foods store named Safer Way Natural Foods, founded in Austin, Texas in 1980. The two founders had a difficult time beginning the company and later merged with Clarksville Natural Grocery, which culminated in the two companies becoming the world's largest retailer of organic and natural food and personal care products. The company was called Whole Foods. Whole Foods has grown, not only domestically but also internationally, since its initial expansion in 1984.

Starting the business was no easy feat; the company has faced many challenges along the way. Less than a year after opening, a devastating flood hit central Austin, which wiped out the store's entire inventory. The company faced more than $400,000 worth of damages. After weighing options, the employees banded together to work as a team. With the help of the community, they were able to reopen their store in four weeks. From the beginning, Mackey instilled company core values in all aspects of the organization.

A Commitment to Quality

Whole Foods' mission and goals resulted in core values to turn its mission into a reality. The company's values involve meeting customer needs and describe the company's commitment toward selling the highest quality natural and organic products. Whole Foods also aims to create positive and ethical ongoing partnerships with suppliers, while simultaneously creating wealth through profits and growth as well as caring about the community and environment. The company also aims to delight customers by promoting the health of all stakeholders through healthy eating education. Along with management striving to implement these core values, employees help to create this environment through daily interactions with

customers. Employees are highly valued at Whole Foods and are labeled team members to empower them through their everyday contributions.

Whole Foods' marketing strategy is focused on being a specialty grocery store. The core competencies address a market opportunity to develop high-quality products and experiences of both suppliers and consumers. A competitive advantage comes from providing local brands from smaller suppliers. Often, these smaller suppliers do not have the resources to reach national markets. Whole Foods has provided an opportunity for some of these local brands to reach national markets.

Competing on Premium

Whole Foods' target market is people who purchase organic brands and health-conscious consumers. This market includes those that care about sustainability and prefer all-natural products. Therefore, most of their customers have a college degree and are in the middle class. Because organic foods and a focus on sustainability come at a higher price, Whole Foods is a premium-price grocer and this has resulted in being called "whole paycheck" by some consumers. Therefore, a competitive advantage comes from providing unique, expensive gourmet foods that are considered beneficial to their target market. This includes a fast-growing health and wellness market that is willing to pay for high-quality organic and natural foods.

Focusing on Team Members

Team members of Whole Foods are highly regarded and are given personal stakes in the company through stock options. Company leaders realize that the success of the company depends on Whole Foods Market team members and believe in motivating and rewarding them for quality performance. At each Whole Foods store, individuals are divided into eight to ten teams and are the backbone of the store. Initially, when an individual is hired, he or she is hired on a provisional basis. Before candidates are hired on a provisional basis, they undergo a 60-day process of interviews on the phone, with team members, and with leaders. If two-thirds of the team members vote in favor of the candidate at the end of the provisional period, the candidate becomes part of the team. Those who do not receive two-thirds of the votes can redo the provisional period with another team or choose to leave the company.

This element is an important part of the Whole Foods culture because the company believes that working together is the most important thing that occurs during business hours. This team approach has been adopted throughout the entire chain of command. Regional leaders are arranged into teams, and even founder John Mackey shared his CEO title with former co-CEO Walter Robb for a number of years. Hard work and positive attitudes are essential among team members because additional pay and profit sharing is based on team performance. Each individual relies on the productivity of the members in their team to receive these benefits. They cannot reach them alone.

Whole Foods also uses the talents of employees to improve company operations. It implements an open-door policy that allows employees to provide feedback to managers and other team members, which ensures that clear and concise communication is constantly occurring in the store. In addition to this, Whole Foods strives to enrich the lives of Whole Foods employees and incentivizes employees to participate in a team member healthy discount incentive program. The company rewards employees for living healthy lifestyles when employees and team members reach certain benchmarks. To reach the goals of the program, team members are prompted to work together while simultaneously encouraging one another through positive reinforcement.

Self-directed work teams consisting of employees make many of the decisions in the day-to-day operations of the different stores. For instance, teams have control over their scheduling and aim to work with each other to provide an optimal schedule for everyone. The company provides its team members with extensive training and resources of educational information, including information on the company's gain sharing program and the company's quality standards. By empowering its employees through teams, perks, and education, Whole Foods has been able to turn its workers into significant contributors of value for the company.

The Age of Amazon

Despite Whole Foods' success, the company has struggled to get rid of its "whole paycheck" reputation in recent years. Many consumers viewed Whole Foods products as

unaffordable. Even its 365 Everyday Value brand failed to shake off this image. Due in part to financial struggles, Whole Foods agreed to be acquired by Amazon.com in 2017 for $13.7 billion. How Amazon's management of Whole Foods will influence team decision making is unclear, but there are signs that Whole Foods is becoming a more centralized company. For instance, rather than allowing local stores to decide whether to carry regional items, these decisions will now be made by Whole Foods executives at headquarters. These changes might take away some of the team autonomy that has been practiced at individual stores. Amazon and Whole Foods will need to find a balance between a more centralized approach—which might lead to decreased costs, greater control, as well as faster and more consistent decision making—and the team approach practiced at individual stores that has provided Whole Foods with its own distinctive flair and made it a great place for employees to work.

Changes since Amazon acquired Whole Foods include Prime Now Whole Foods delivery in select markets and the addition of Amazon Locker. Prime Now is a grocery delivery service similar to Instacart that uses contractors to shop and deliver groceries. Amazon has installed its lockers in all Whole Foods stores giving its customers a secure place to pick up and return items ordered on Amazon.

Another major change is more emphasis on efficiency with consistent and high-quality experiences for both suppliers and customers. This includes more centralized purchasing operations to save on costs. In an attempt to reduce inefficiency, Amazon is requiring Whole Foods to provide more national brands and cut back on local suppliers. This results in more shelf space for national brands that are focused on maximizing revenue and lowering operating costs. One reason for this is some consumer-voiced frustration in finding no national brands for products like paper towels and shaving cream. The goal for Amazon is to leverage their low prices on national brands with the core competency of fresh organic products such as produce and meat. Amazon also introduced some everyday low prices on bananas and yogurt to help change the high-price images. The important question for the future is whether changes in merchandising will change the identity of Whole Foods.[32]

Questions for Discussion

1. How has Amazon changed the Whole Foods marketing strategy?
2. What is the role of teamwork in implementing the Whole Foods marketing strategy?
3. Will national brands and a centralized approach to product decisions help or harm the future success of Whole Foods?

Environmental Forces and Social and Ethical Responsibilities

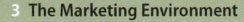

3 The Marketing Environment

4 Social Responsibility and Ethics in Marketing

PART 2 deals with the marketing environment, social responsibility, and marketing ethics.

CHAPTER 3 examines competitive, economic, political, legal and regulatory, technological, and sociocultural forces in the marketing environment, which can have profound effects on marketing strategies.

CHAPTER 4 explores the role of social responsibility and ethical issues in marketing decisions.

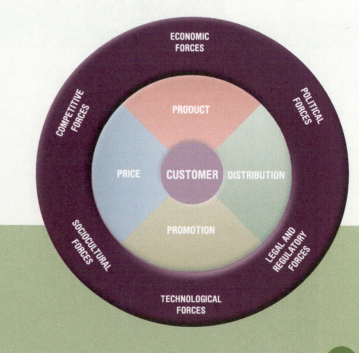

CHAPTER

3

The Marketing Environment

LEARNING OBJECTIVES

3-1 Summarize why it is important to examine and respond to the marketing environment.

3-2 Explain how competitive factors affect an organization's ability to compete.

3-3 Articulate how economic factors influence a customer's ability and willingness to buy products.

3-4 Identify the types of political forces in the marketing environment.

3-5 Explain how laws, government regulations, and self-regulatory agencies affect marketing activities.

3-6 Describe how new technology impacts marketing and society.

3-7 Outline the sociocultural issues marketers must deal with as they make decisions.

STUDIO BARCELONA/SHUTTERSTOCK.COM

Chipotle Defends "Food with Integrity" Promise

Chipotle Mexican Grill has always done things a bit differently from other restaurant chains. Steve Ells, founder and former CEO, established the first Chipotle restaurant in 1993 as a high-end fast-casual restaurant chain offering higher-quality items than fast-food restaurants. Ells set Chipotle apart in the competitive environment by creating a customer-service-oriented atmosphere where customers could see their food being prepared with fresh ingredients.

Chipotle's "food with integrity" offering appeals to the growing cultural values related to eating food that is healthy and sustainable. Despite the company's focus on its ingredients, Chipotle found itself in the midst of an *E. Coli* outbreak that was traced to a small number of stores. With a heightened consumer focus on food safety, Chipotle has focused on changing employee training and winning back consumer confidence.

Competition has also been increasing, requiring Chipotle to constantly analyze the marketing environment. Chipotle must monitor the activities of brand competitors operating in the fast-casual Mexican food market like Qdoba as well as product competitors like low-cost fast-food chains McDonald's, Wendy's, and Burger King. These chains are also recognizing that consumers desire to eat healthier and are beginning to offer healthier menu options. In response to competitor offerings, Chipotle introduced queso free of artificial flavors, colors, and preservatives. The queso was so disliked, the company began reformulating it just a few months after it was introduced.

Chipotle continues to struggle in its recovery. Ells stepped down and was replaced by former Taco Bell CEO Brian Niccol. Niccol needs a strong understanding of the environment to maintain customers as well as grow sales beyond its original state.[1]

Companies like Chipotle are modifying marketing strategies in response to changes in the marketing environment. Because recognizing and addressing such changes in the marketing environment are crucial to marketing success, we will focus in detail on the forces that contribute to these changes.

This chapter explores the competitive, economic, political, legal and regulatory, technological, and sociocultural forces that constitute the marketing environment. First, we define the marketing environment and consider why it is critical to scan and analyze it. Next, we discuss the effects of competitive forces and explore the influence of general economic conditions: prosperity, recession, depression, and recovery. We also examine buying power and look at the forces that influence consumers' willingness to spend. We then discuss the political forces that generate government actions that affect marketing activities and examine the effects of laws and regulatory agencies on these activities. After analyzing the major dimensions of the technological forces in the environment, we consider the impact of sociocultural forces on marketing efforts.

Learning Objective 3-1

Summarize why it is important to examine and respond to the marketing environment.

3-1 EXAMINING AND RESPONDING TO THE MARKETING ENVIRONMENT

The marketing environment consists of external forces that directly or indirectly influence an organization's acquisition of inputs (human, financial, natural resources and raw materials, and information) and creation of outputs (goods, services, or ideas). As we saw in Chapter 1, the marketing environment includes six such forces: competitive, economic, political, legal and regulatory, technological, and sociocultural.

Whether fluctuating rapidly or slowly, environmental forces are always dynamic. Changes in the marketing environment create uncertainty, threats, and opportunities for marketers. Firms providing digital products such as software, music, and movies face many environmental threats as well as opportunities. Advancing technology provides digital delivery of these products, which is an efficient and effective way to reach global markets. On the other hand, technology has made it easier for file-sharing websites to infringe on others' intellectual property. The Walt Disney Co. and Redbox recently came head-to-head when the home video kiosk company began selling digital copies of Disney movies. Redbox purchased DVD and Blu-ray packages that included digital download codes and resold them to its customers. The primary issue is that Redbox is undercutting Disney's retail prices.[2] The marketing environment constantly fluctuates, requiring marketers to monitor it regularly.

Although the future is sometimes hard to predict, marketers try to forecast what may happen. We can say with certainty that marketers continue to modify their marketing strategies and plans in response to dynamic environmental forces. Consider how technological changes have affected the products offered by the mobile phone industry and how the public's growing concern with health and fitness has influenced clothing, food, exercise equipment, and healthcare companies. Wearable technology such as the Garmin Vivosport linked to a smartphone can monitor many vital signs of health and exercise. Marketing managers who fail to recognize changes in environmental forces leave their firms unprepared to capitalize on marketing opportunities or to cope with threats created by those changes. For instance, BlackBerry, one of the original leaders of the smartphone industry, failed to keep up with technology trends like the transition to full touchscreens. The company's sales went from more than 50 million devices in 2011 to just 4 million five years later.[3] Monitoring the environment is crucial to an organization's survival and to the long-term achievement of its goals.

3-1a Environmental Scanning and Analysis

environmental scanning The process of collecting information about forces in the marketing environment

To monitor changes in the marketing environment effectively, marketers engage in environmental scanning and analysis. **Environmental scanning** is the process of collecting information about forces in the marketing environment. Scanning involves observation; secondary

INTEGRITY IN MARKETING

Chick-fil-A Rules the Roost

From the day it was founded, Chick-fil-A has served communities differently than other fast-food chains. The founder, S. Truett Cathy, created a culture founded on integrity. Having previously worked in the restaurant industry, Cathy decided that he did not want his restaurants open 7 days a week or 24 hours a day. He saw the importance of being closed on Sundays so that employees could set aside one day to rest or engage in religious activities if they chose. This practice continues today.

Chick-fil-A also takes a different approach to the preparation of the food: "Cook less, more often." Quality is emphasized over quantity. In an industry with monopolistic competition, Chick-fil-A is able to make its chicken sandwiches stand out from competitors such as McDonald's, Wendy's, and Burger King.

Although it still holds true to its founding principles, Chick-fil-A has responded to technological forces by releasing the Chick-fil-A One app to enhance its services. The app allows customers to preorder their meals to bypass lines and pay at the counter by scanning their phones for a fast and easy experience. Chick-fil-A's foray into mobile technology is just one of many initiatives it has adopted to extend its top-notch customer service.[a]

sources such as business, trade, government, and general-interest publications; and marketing research. The internet has become a popular scanning tool because it makes data more accessible and allows companies to gather needed information quickly. Environmental scanning gives companies an edge over competitors in allowing them to take advantage of current trends. However, simply gathering information about competitors and customers is not enough; companies must know how to *use* that information in the strategic planning process. Managers must be careful not to gather so much information that sheer volume makes analysis impossible.

Environmental analysis is the process of assessing and interpreting the information gathered through environmental scanning. A manager evaluates the information for accuracy, tries to resolve inconsistencies in the data, and, if warranted, assigns significance to the findings. Evaluating this information should enable the manager to identify potential threats and opportunities linked to environmental changes. Understanding the current state of the marketing environment and recognizing threats and opportunities that might arise from changes within it help companies in their strategic planning. A threat could be rising interest rates or commodity prices. An opportunity could be increases in consumer income, decreases in the unemployment rate, or a sudden drop in commodity prices. For example, in recent years, unemployment rates have dropped to record lows.

3-1b Responding to Environmental Forces

Marketing managers take two general approaches to environmental forces: accepting them as uncontrollable or attempting to influence and shape them.[4] An organization that views environmental forces as uncontrollable remains passive and reactive toward the environment. Instead of trying to influence forces in the environment, its marketing managers adjust current marketing strategies to environmental changes. They approach market opportunities discovered through environmental scanning and analysis with caution. On the other hand, marketing managers who believe environmental forces can be shaped adopt a more proactive approach. If a market opportunity is blocked by environmental constraints, proactive marketing managers may use their political skills to overcome obstacles. For example, if a company decides to align itself with social interests, it should be proactive

environmental analysis
The process of assessing and interpreting the information gathered through environmental scanning

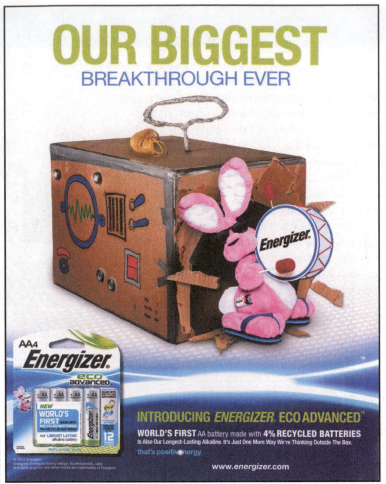

Responding to the Marketing Environment
Energizer proactively pursues sustainable innovation to enhance its positive reputation with consumers.

and disclose its social responsibility activities to maintain transparent communication with stakeholders.[5] Kraft Heinz released its first corporate social responsibility plan outlining its initiatives such as using only eggs from cage-free hens by 2025. These efforts have the potential to improve sales, attract and retain employees, and satisfy stakeholders.[6]

A proactive approach can be constructive and bring desired results. To influence environmental forces, marketing managers seek to identify market opportunities or to extract greater benefits relative to costs from existing market opportunities. For instance, Energizer identified an opportunity to increase its reputation for sustainability. The company's advertisement draws attention to its latest breakthrough: Energizer EcoAdvanced batteries, the world's first AA battery made with 4 percent recycled batteries. The battery is also its longest-lasting alkaline. Energizer promotes sustainable innovation which generates goodwill toward the brand.

Political action is another way to affect environmental forces. The pharmaceutical industry, for example, has lobbied very effectively for fewer restrictions on prescription drug marketing. However, managers must recognize that there are limits to the degree that environmental forces can be shaped. Although an organization may be able to influence legislation through lobbying—as the movie and music industries are doing to try and stop the piracy of their products—it is unlikely that a single organization can significantly change major economic factors such as recessions, interest rates, or commodity prices.

Whether to take a reactive or a proactive approach to environmental forces is a decision for a firm to make based on its strengths or weaknesses. For some organizations, the passive, reactive approach is more appropriate, but for others the aggressive approach leads to better performance. Selection of a particular approach depends on an organization's managerial philosophies, objectives, financial resources, customers, and human resources skills, as well as on the environment within which the organization operates. Both organizational factors and managers' personal characteristics affect the variety of responses to changing environmental conditions. Facebook, for instance, has the means to take a proactive approach because of its financial resources and the highly visible image of its founder, Mark Zuckerberg. However, the social media giant came under fire regarding privacy violations when it was discovered that the data analytics firm Cambridge Analytica used personal information from Facebook profiles without permission for politically fueled ads. This demonstrates that even Facebook is limited in how far it can influence the business environment.

In the remainder of this chapter, we explore in greater detail the six environmental forces—competitive, economic, political, legal and regulatory, technological, and sociocultural—that interact to create opportunities and threats that must be considered in strategic planning.

3-2 COMPETITIVE FORCES

Learning Objective 3-2
Explain how competitive factors affect an organization's ability to compete.

Few firms, if any, operate free of competition. In fact, for most goods and services, customers have many alternatives from which to choose. For instance, a customer in the market for an oil change could choose from Jiffy Lube, Tires Plus, Grease Monkey, and more. The customer could also choose an alternative such as a dealership. Thus, when marketing managers define the target market(s) their firms will serve, they simultaneously establish a set of competitors.[7] In addition, marketing managers must consider the type of competitive structure in which the firm operates. In this section, we examine types of competition and competitive structures, as well as the importance of monitoring competitors' actions.

3-2a Types of Competitors

Broadly speaking, all firms compete with one another for customers' dollars. More practically, however, a marketer generally defines **competition** as other firms that market products that are similar to or can be substituted for its products in the same geographic area. These competitors can be classified into one of four types. **Brand competitors** market products with similar features and benefits to the same customers at similar prices. Pantene, for example,

competition Other organizations that market products that are similar to or can be substituted for a marketer's products in the same geographic area

brand competitors Firms that market products with similar features and benefits to the same customers at similar prices

FUEL YOUR HAIR

PANTENE
PRO-V

DAILY
moisture
RENEWAL

DREAM*care*
SHAMPOO

ESSENTIAL HYDRATION
FROM ROOT TO TIP

STRONG IS BEAUTIFUL

SOURCE: PANTENE

KEEP MOROCCAN AND ROLLIN'

LET LIFE IN
to your hair and your head

Herbal Essences
bio:renew

0%

REPAIR
argan oil
of morocco
SHAMPOO

SOURCE: HERBAL ESSENCES

Brand Competition
Pantene and Herbal Essences compete head-to-head in the hair-care market.

competes with Herbal Essences in the hair-care market. In its advertisement, Pantene emphasizes the Pro-V vitamin formula for strong, beautiful hair. In contrast, the Herbal Essences advertisement touts the use of argan oil of Morocco in its shampoo for repairing damaged hair. Both products are available at retailers like Walgreens and Ulta Beauty. Another example is rental cars. Travelers may choose a car rental company like Hertz or Alamo. However, these companies face competition from other transportation services like Lyft or Uber. **Product competitors** compete in the same product class but market products with different features, benefits, and prices. The thirsty dieter might purchase iced tea, juice, a sports beverage, or bottled water instead of a soda.

Generic competitors provide very different products that solve the same problem or satisfy the same basic customer need. Our travelers might simply use public transportation to get to where they need to go. **Total budget competitors** compete for the limited financial resources of the same customers.[8] Total budget competitors for Hertz, for example, might include firms which provide meals, lodging, and air travel. Although all four types of competition can affect a firm's marketing performance, brand competitors are the most significant because buyers typically see the different products of these firms as direct substitutes for one another. Consequently, marketers tend to concentrate environmental analyses on brand competitors.

3-2b **Types of Competitive Structures**

The number of firms that supply a product may affect the strength of competitors. When just one or a few firms control supply, competitive factors exert a different form of influence on marketing activities than when many competitors exist. Table 3.1 presents four general types of competitive structures: monopoly, oligopoly, monopolistic competition, and pure competition.

A **monopoly** exists when an organization offers a product that has no close substitutes, making that organization the sole source of supply. Because the organization has no competitors, it controls the supply of the product completely and, as a single seller, can erect barriers to potential competitors. Sirius XM Radio, for example, has a monopoly on the satellite radio market, but still faces competition from AM/FM radio and online streaming services like Pandora. In reality, most monopolies surviving today are local utilities, which are heavily regulated by local, state, or federal agencies.

An **oligopoly** exists when a few sellers control the supply of a large proportion of a product. In this case, each seller considers the reactions of other sellers to changes in marketing activities. Products facing oligopolistic competition may be homogeneous, such as aluminum, or differentiated, such as packaged delivery services. The airline industry is an example of an oligopoly. However, even an industry dominated by a few companies must still compete and release promotional materials. Usually barriers of some sort make it difficult to enter the market and compete with oligopolies. For example, because of the enormous financial outlay required, few companies or individuals could afford to enter the oil-refining or steel-producing industry.

product competitors Firms that compete in the same product class but market products with different features, benefits, and prices

generic competitors Firms that provide very different products that solve the same problem or satisfy the same basic customer need

total budget competitors Firms that compete for the limited financial resources of the same customers

monopoly A competitive structure in which an organization offers a product that has no close substitutes, making that organization the sole source of supply

oligopoly A competitive structure in which a few sellers control the supply of a large proportion of a product

Table 3.1   Selected Characteristics of Competitive Structures

Type of Structure	Number of Competitors	Ease of Entry into Market	Product	Examples
Monopoly	One	Many barriers	Almost no substitutes	Water utilities
Oligopoly	Few	Some barriers	Homogeneous or differentiated (with real or perceived differences)	UPS, FedEx, U.S. Postal Service (package delivery)
Monopolistic competition	Many	Few barriers	Product differentiation, with many substitutes	Wrangler, Levi Strauss, Diesel, Lee Jeans (jeans)
Pure competition	Unlimited	No barriers	Homogeneous products	Vegetable farm (sweet corn)

Moreover, some industries demand special technical or marketing skills, a qualification that deters the entry of many potential competitors.

Monopolistic competition exists when a firm with many potential competitors attempts to develop a marketing strategy to differentiate its product. For example, Wrangler and True Religion have established an advantage for their blue jeans through well-known trademarks, design, advertising, and a reputation for quality. Wrangler is associated with a cowboy image, while True Religion tries to maintain a premium designer image. Although many competing brands of blue jeans are available, these firms have carved out market niches by emphasizing differences in their products, especially style and image. Lee releases advertising to demonstrate its blue jeans from its budget line, Riders by Lee. The Riders by Lee ad uses models of various sizes and body types jumping and dancing to emphasize its range of styles and fits. Lee recognizes the importance consumers place on good fitting clothing and has found these benefits help differentiate it from rival jean competitors.

Pure competition, if it existed at all, would entail an extremely large number of sellers, none of which could significantly influence price or supply. Products would be homogeneous, and entry into the market would be easy. The closest thing to an example of pure competition is an unregulated farmers' market, where local growers gather to sell their produce. Commodities such as soybeans, corn, and wheat have their markets subsidized or regulated by the government. Pure competition is an ideal at one end of the continuum, and a monopoly is at the other end. Most marketers function in a competitive environment somewhere between these two extremes.

monopolistic competition
A competitive structure in which a firm has many potential competitors and tries to develop a marketing strategy to differentiate its product

pure competition A market structure characterized by an extremely large number of sellers, none strong enough to significantly influence price or supply

3-2c **Monitoring Competition**

Marketers need to monitor the actions of major competitors to determine what specific strategies competitors are using and how those strategies affect their own. Competitive intensity influences a firm's strategic approach to markets. Delta developed a pricing strategy to compete more effectively with discount airlines such as Southwest. Delta offers "basic economy" to compete with discount carriers and attract more price-sensitive customers. Other airlines are adopting this pricing strategy as well. Monitoring guides marketers in developing competitive advantages and in adjusting current marketing strategies and planning new ones. When two large companies such as Walgreens and Rite Aid merge, there is the potential for less competition.

In monitoring competition, it is not enough to analyze available information; the firm must develop a system for gathering ongoing information about competitors and potential competitors. Understanding the market and what customers want, as well as what the competition is providing, will assist in maintaining a market orientation.[9] Information about competitors allows marketing managers to assess the performance of their own marketing efforts and to recognize the strengths and weaknesses in their own marketing strategies. Data about market shares, product movement, sales volume, and expenditure levels can be useful. However, accurate information on these matters is often difficult to obtain.

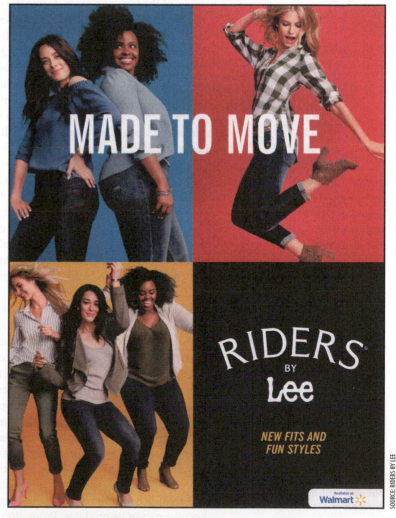

SOURCE: RIDERS BY LEE

Monopolistic Competition
The blue jeans market is an example of monopolistic competition. Lee competes against many competitors and uses its advertisement to emphasize its wide variety of fits and styles for different body types.

Articulate how economic factors influence a customer's ability and willingness to buy products.

3-3 ECONOMIC FORCES

Economic forces in the marketing environment influence both marketers' and customers' decisions and activities. In this section, we examine the effects of general economic conditions as well as buying power and the factors that affect people's willingness to spend.

3-3a Economic Conditions

The overall state of the economy fluctuates in all countries. Even downturns in large countries, such as China, can affect the global economy. Changes in general economic conditions affect (and are affected by) supply and demand, buying power, willingness to spend, consumer expenditure levels, and intensity of competitive behavior. Therefore, current economic conditions and changes in the economy have a broad impact on the success of organizations' marketing strategies.

Fluctuations in the economy follow a general pattern, often referred to as the **business cycle**. In the traditional view, the business cycle consists of four stages: prosperity, recession, depression, and recovery. From a global perspective, different regions of the world may be in different stages of the business cycle during the same period. Throughout much of the 1990s, for example, the United States experienced growth (prosperity). The U.S. economy began to slow in 2000, with a brief recession, especially in high-technology industries, in 2001, when many dot-com or internet companies failed. Japan, however, endured a recession during most of the 1990s and into the early 2000s. Economic variation in the global marketplace creates a planning challenge for firms that sell products in multiple markets around the world. In 2007, the United States experienced an economic downturn due to higher energy prices, falling home values, increasing unemployment, the financial crisis in the banking industry, and fluctuating currency values. That recession was the longest since the Great Depression of the 1930s and has been called the Great Recession. As the United States was recovering from the Great Recession, Europe's and Japan's economies continued to struggle. By 2018, unemployment levels in the United States were back down to early 2007 levels. The world economy is so integrated that if one region has an economic problem, it affects all the other countries.[10]

During **prosperity**, unemployment is low and total income is relatively high. Assuming a low inflation rate, this combination ensures high buying power. If the economic outlook remains prosperous, consumers generally are willing to buy. In the prosperity stage, marketers often expand their product offerings to take advantage of increased buying power. They can sometimes capture a larger market share by intensifying distribution and promotion efforts.

Because unemployment rises during a **recession**, total buying power declines. These factors, usually accompanied by consumer pessimism, often stifle both consumer and business spending. As buying power decreases, many customers may become more price and value conscious, and look for basic, functional products. When buying power decreased during the most recent recession, department store sales dropped. Consumers began shopping at off-price retailers such as TJ Maxx and Ross. In the years following the recession, Nordstrom opened more off-price Nordstrom Rack stores while Macy's introduced its own off-price concept, Backstage. Appealing to bargain shoppers, however, could negatively impact luxury brands.[11] Online retailers such as Amazon also attract consumers desiring low prices.

During a recession, some firms make the mistake of drastically reducing their marketing efforts, thus damaging their ability to survive. Obviously, however, marketers should consider some revision of their marketing activities during a recessionary period. Because consumers are more concerned about the functional value of products, a company should focus its marketing research on determining precisely what functions buyers want and make sure those functions become part of its products. Promotional efforts should emphasize value and utility. Marketers must also carefully monitor the needs and expectations of their companies' target markets.

A prolonged recession may become a **depression**, a period in which unemployment is extremely high, wages are very low, total disposable income is at a minimum, and consumers

business cycle A pattern of economic fluctuations that has four stages: prosperity, recession, depression, and recovery

prosperity A stage of the business cycle characterized by low unemployment and relatively high total income, which together ensure high buying power (provided the inflation rate stays low)

recession A stage of the business cycle during which unemployment rises and total buying power declines, stifling both consumer and business spending

depression A stage of the business cycle during which unemployment is extremely high, wages are very low, total disposable income is at a minimum, and consumers lack confidence in the economy

lack confidence in the economy. A depression usually lasts for an extended period, often years, and has been experienced by Russia, Mexico, and Brazil in the 2000s. Although evidence supports maintaining or even increasing spending during economic slowdowns, marketing budgets are more likely to be cut in the face of an economic downturn.

During **recovery**, the economy moves from recession or depression toward prosperity. During this period, high unemployment begins to decline, total disposable income increases, and the economic gloom that reduced consumers' willingness to buy subsides. The U.S. economy went through a long recovery from a deep recession during 2011–2016. Both the ability and the willingness to buy rose slowly. Marketers face some problems during recovery, as it is difficult to ascertain how quickly and to what level prosperity will return. Large firms such as Procter & Gamble must try to assess how quickly consumers will increase their purchase of higher-priced brands versus economy brands. In this stage, marketers should maintain as much flexibility in their marketing strategies as possible so they can make the needed adjustments.

3-3b Buying Power

The strength of a person's **buying power** depends on economic conditions and the size of the resources—money, goods, and services that can be traded in an exchange—that enable the individual to make purchases. The major financial sources of buying power are income, credit, and wealth. For an individual, **income** is the amount of money received through wages, rents, investments, pensions, and subsidy payments for a given period, such as a month or a year. Normally this money is allocated among taxes, spending for goods and services, and savings. The median annual household income in the United States is approximately $59,039.[12] However, because of differences in people's educational levels, abilities, occupations, and wealth, income is not equally distributed in this country.

Marketers are most interested in the amount of money left after payment of taxes because this **disposable income** is used for spending or saving. Because disposable income is a ready source of buying power, the total amount available in a nation is important to marketers. Several factors determine the size of total disposable income. One is the total amount of income, which is affected by wage levels, the rate of unemployment, interest rates, and dividend rates. Because disposable income is income left after taxes are paid, the number and amount of taxes directly affect the size of total disposable income. When taxes rise, disposable income declines; when taxes fall, disposable income increases.

Disposable income that is available for spending and saving after an individual has purchased the basic necessities of food, clothing, and shelter is called **discretionary income**. People use discretionary income to purchase entertainment, vacations, automobiles, education, pets, furniture, appliances, and so on. Changes in total discretionary income affect sales of these products, especially automobiles, furniture, large appliances, and other costly durable goods. Versace—known as a luxury fashion brand—sells products that are often purchased with discretionary income. Inspired by Greek mythology, the advertisement depicts a model wearing a Grecian robe holding a larger-than-life bottle of Versace Eros Eau de Toilette spray to create an image of strength, desirability, and luxury.

Credit enables people to spend future income now or in the near future. However, credit increases current buying power at the expense of future buying power. Several factors determine whether people use, acquire, or forgo credit. First, credit must be available. Interest rates also affect buyers' decisions to use credit, especially for expensive purchases such as homes, appliances, and automobiles. When interest rates are low, the total cost of automobiles and houses becomes more affordable. In the United States, low interest rates in the 2000s induced many buyers to take on the high level of debt necessary to own a home, fueling a tremendous boom in the construction of new homes and the sale of older homes. In contrast, when interest rates are high, consumers are more likely to delay buying such expensive items. Use of credit is also affected by credit terms, such as size of the down payment and amount and number of monthly payments.

recovery A stage of the business cycle during which the economy moves from recession or depression toward prosperity

buying power The size of the resources, such as money, goods, and services that can be traded in an exchange, that enable the individual to make purchases

income For an individual, the amount of money received through wages, rents, investments, pensions, and subsidy payments for a given period

disposable income After-tax income

discretionary income Disposable income available for spending and saving after an individual has purchased the basic necessities of food, clothing, and shelter

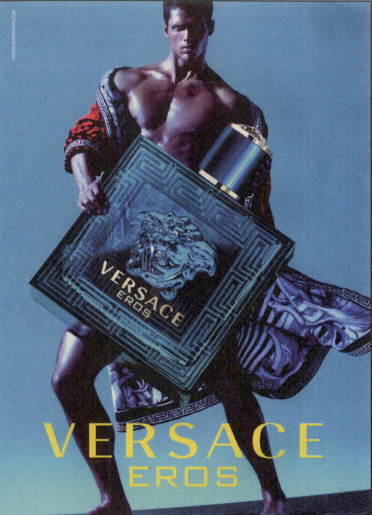

Discretionary Income
Versace, an Italian luxury fashion company, sells everything from men's and women's clothing to home goods and fragrance. Versace fragrances would be purchased using discretionary income.

wealth The accumulation of past income, natural resources, and financial resources

willingness to spend An inclination to buy because of expected satisfaction from a product, influenced by the ability to buy and numerous psychological and social forces

Wealth is the accumulation of past income, natural resources, and financial resources. It exists in many forms, including cash, securities, savings accounts, gold, jewelry, and real estate. Global wealth is increasing, with 16.5 million millionaires worldwide.[13] Like income, wealth is unevenly distributed. A person can have a high income and very little wealth. It is also possible, but not likely, for a person to have great wealth but little income. The significance of wealth to marketers is that as people become wealthier, they gain buying power in three ways: They can use their wealth to make current purchases, to generate income, and to acquire large amounts of credit. Knowing that Maryland ranks as the richest state and Mississippi the poorest state according to the U.S. Census Bureau would be helpful if selling Tesla high-end electric sports cars.

Income, credit, and wealth equip consumers with buying power to purchase goods and services. Marketing managers must be aware of current levels and expected changes in buying power in their own markets because buying power directly affects the types and quantities of goods and services customers purchase. Information about buying power is available from government sources, trade associations, and research agencies. One of the most current and comprehensive sources of buying-power data is the *Consumer Expenditure Survey*, published by the U.S. Bureau of Labor Statistics. Having buying power, however, does not mean consumers will buy. They must also be willing to use their buying power.

3-3c **Willingness to Spend**

People's **willingness to spend**—their inclination to buy because of expected satisfaction from a product—is, to some degree, related to their ability to buy. That is, people are sometimes more willing to buy if they have the buying power. However, a number of other elements also influence willingness to spend. Some elements affect specific products; others influence spending in general. A product's price and value influence almost all of us. A. Lange & Söhne, for instance, appeals to customers who are willing to spend more for watches even when lower-priced ones are readily available. The amount of satisfaction received from a product already owned may also influence customers' desires to buy other products. Satisfaction depends not only on the quality of the currently owned product but also on numerous psychological and social forces. The American Customer Satisfaction Index, computed by the National Quality Research Center at the University of Michigan (see Figure 3.1), offers an indicator of customer satisfaction with a wide variety of businesses. The American Customer Satisfaction Index (ACSI) helps marketers to understand how consumers perceive their industries and businesses and to adapt their marketing strategies accordingly.

Factors that affect consumers' general willingness to spend are expectations about future employment, income levels, prices, family size, and general economic conditions. Willingness to spend ordinarily declines if people are unsure whether or how long they will be employed, and it usually increases if people are reasonably certain of higher incomes in the future.

Figure 3.1 National Customer Satisfaction Index

National ACSI Score
Baseline 1994 to Q3 2017
(0–100 Scale)

Source: American Customer Satisfaction Index, "U.S. Overall Customer Satisfaction," www.theacsi.org/national-economic-indicator/us-overall-customer-satisfaction (accessed December 28, 2017).

Expectations of rising prices in the near future may also increase willingness to spend in the present. For a given level of buying power, the larger the family, the greater the willingness to spend. One reason for this relationship is that as the size of a family increases, more dollars must be spent to provide the basic necessities to sustain family members.

3-4 POLITICAL FORCES

Learning Objective 3-4

Identify the types of political forces in the marketing environment.

Political, legal, and regulatory forces of the marketing environment are closely interrelated. Legislation is enacted, legal decisions are interpreted by courts, and regulatory agencies are created and operated, for the most part, by elected or appointed officials. Legislation and regulations (or the lack thereof) reflect the current political outlook. After the financial crisis caused a worldwide recession, the government passed the Dodd-Frank Wall Street Reform and Consumer Protection Act of 2010. This act was created to increase accountability and transparency in the financial industry.[14] The legislation established a new Bureau of Consumer Financial Protection to protect consumers from deceptive financial practices.[15] But many political leaders blamed this legislation for slowing down the economic recovery and adding extra costs and uncertainty to business decision making. This example shows that the political forces of the marketing environment have the potential to influence marketing decisions and strategies.

Marketing organizations strive to maintain good relations with elected and appointed political officials for several reasons. Political officials well disposed toward particular firms or industries are less likely to create or enforce laws and regulations unfavorable to those companies. Consequently, political officials who believe oil companies are making honest efforts to control pollution are unlikely to create and enforce highly restrictive pollution-control laws.

Government contracts can be very profitable, so understanding the competitive bidding process for obtaining contracts is important. Finally, political officials can play key roles in helping organizations secure foreign markets. Government officials will sometimes organize trade missions in which business executives go to foreign countries to meet with potential clients or buyers.[16]

Many marketers view political forces as beyond their control and simply adjust to conditions that arise from those forces. Some firms, however, seek to influence the political process. In some cases, organizations publicly protest the actions of legislative bodies. More often, organizations help elect individuals, who regard them positively, to political offices. Much of this help is in the form of campaign contributions. AT&T is an example of a company that has attempted to influence legislation and regulation over a long period of time. Since 1990, AT&T has made more than $74 million in corporate donations for use in supporting the campaign funds of political candidates.[17] Until recently, laws have limited corporate contributions to political campaign funds for specific candidates, and company-sponsored political advertisements could primarily focus only on topics (e.g., health care) and not on candidates. In the 2010 ruling for *Citizens United vs. Federal Election Commission*, the U.S. Supreme Court ruled that the government is not authorized to ban corporate spending in candidate elections.[18] This means that elections can be affected by large corporate donations to candidates. Marketers also can influence the political process through political action committees (PACs) that solicit donations from individuals and then contribute those funds to candidates running for political office.

Companies can also participate in the political process through lobbying to persuade public and/or government officials to favor a particular position in decision making. Many organizations concerned about the threat of legislation or regulation that may negatively affect their operations employ lobbyists to communicate their concerns to elected officials. Case in point: as the U.S. government debates whether to pass stricter laws regulating marketing activities over the internet, social media firms such as Facebook are sending lobbyists to give their respective viewpoints regarding the proposed legislation.

Learning Objective 3-5

Explain how laws, government regulations, and self-regulatory agencies affect marketing activities.

3-5 LEGAL AND REGULATORY FORCES

A number of federal laws influence marketing decisions and activities. Table 3.2 lists some of the most important laws. In addition to discussing these laws, which deal with competition and consumer protection, this section examines the effects of regulatory agencies and self-regulatory forces on marketing efforts.

3-5a Procompetitive Legislation

Procompetitive laws are designed to preserve competition. Most of these laws were enacted to end various antitrade practices deemed unacceptable by society. The Sherman Antitrust Act, for example, was passed in 1890 to prevent businesses from restraining trade and monopolizing

Table 3.2   Major Federal Laws That Affect Marketing Decisions

Name and Date Enacted	Purpose
Sherman Antitrust Act (1890)	Prohibits contracts, combinations, or conspiracies to restrain trade; establishes as a misdemeanor monopolizing or attempting to monopolize
Clayton Act (1914)	Prohibits specific practices such as price discrimination, exclusive-dealer arrangements, and stock acquisitions whose effect may noticeably lessen competition or tend to create a monopoly
Federal Trade Commission Act (1914)	Created the Federal Trade Commission; also gives the FTC investigatory powers to be used in preventing unfair methods of competition

Name and Date Enacted	Purpose
Robinson-Patman Act (1936)	Prohibits price discrimination that lessens competition among wholesalers or retailers; prohibits producers from giving disproportionate services or facilities to large buyers
Wheeler-Lea Act (1938)	Prohibits unfair and deceptive acts and practices regardless of whether competition is injured; places advertising of foods and drugs under the jurisdiction of the FTC
Lanham Act (1946)	Provides protections for and regulation of brand names, brand marks, trade names, and trademarks
Celler-Kefauver Act (1950)	Prohibits any corporation engaged in commerce from acquiring the whole or any part of the stock or other share of the capital assets of another corporation when the effect would substantially lessen competition or tend to create a monopoly
Fair Packaging and Labeling Act (1966)	Prohibits unfair or deceptive packaging or labeling of consumer products
Magnuson-Moss Warranty (FTC) Act (1975)	Provides for minimum disclosure standards for written consumer product warranties; defines minimum consent standards for written warranties; allows the FTC to prescribe interpretive rules in policy statements regarding unfair or deceptive practices
Consumer Goods Pricing Act (1975)	Prohibits the use of price maintenance agreements among manufacturers and resellers in interstate commerce
Foreign Corrupt Practices Act (1977)	Prohibits American companies from making illicit payments to foreign officials in order to obtain or keep business
Trademark Counterfeiting Act (1980)	Imposes civil and criminal penalties against those who deal in counterfeit consumer goods or any counterfeit goods that can threaten health or safety
Trademark Law Revision Act (1988)	Amends the Lanham Act to allow brands not yet introduced to be protected through registration with the Patent and Trademark Office
Nutrition Labeling and Education Act (1990)	Prohibits exaggerated health claims; requires all processed foods to contain labels with nutritional information
Telephone Consumer Protection Act (1991)	Establishes procedures to avoid unwanted telephone solicitations; prohibits marketers from using an automated telephone dialing system or an artificial or prerecorded voice to certain telephone lines
Federal Trademark Dilution Act (1995)	Grants trademark owners the right to protect trademarks and requires relinquishment of names that match or parallel existing trademarks
Digital Millennium Copyright Act (1996)	Refined copyright laws to protect digital versions of copyrighted materials, including music and movies
Children's Online Privacy Protection Act (2000)	Regulates the collection of personally identifiable information (name, address, email address, hobbies, interests, or information collected through cookies) online from children under age 13
Do Not Call Implementation Act (2003)	Directs the FCC and FTC to coordinate so their rules are consistent regarding telemarketing call practices including the Do Not Call Registry and other lists, as well as call abandonment; in 2008, the FTC amended its rules and banned prerecorded sales pitches for all but a few cases
Credit Card Act (2009)	Implements strict rules on credit card companies regarding topics such as issuing credit to youths, terms disclosure, interest rates, and fees
Dodd-Frank Wall Street Reform and Consumer Protection Act (2010)	Promotes financial reform to increase accountability and transparency in the financial industry, protects consumers from deceptive financial practices, and establishes the Bureau of Consumer Financial Protection

markets. Examples of illegal anticompetitive practices include stealing trade secrets or obtaining other confidential information from a competitor's employees, trademark and copyright infringement, price fixing, false advertising, and deceptive selling methods such as "bait and switch" and false representation of products. The Lanham Act (1946) and the Federal Trademark Dilution Act (1995) help companies protect their trademarks (brand names, logos, and other registered symbols) against infringement. The latter also requires users of names that match or parallel existing trademarks to relinquish them to prevent confusion among consumers. Antitrust laws also authorize the government to punish companies that engage in such anticompetitive practices. For instance, Mallinckrodt ARD Inc., formerly known as Questcor Pharmaceuticals, Inc., and its parent company, Mallinckrodt plc, reached a $100 million settlement with the Federal Trade Commission due to accusations that Questcor illegally acquired the rights to a drug that stifled competition in the market for adrenocorticotropic hormone (ACTH) drugs.[19]

Laws have also been created to prevent businesses from gaining an unfair advantage through bribery. The U.S. Foreign Corrupt Practices Act (FCPA) prohibits American companies from making illicit payments to foreign officials in order to obtain or keep business. To illustrate, Telia Company, a Sweden-based telecommunications provider, was fined $965 million to settle allegations that it paid more than $331 million in bribes to an Uzbek government official in an effort to build its telecommunications business in Uzbekistan.[20] The FCPA does allow for small facilitation ("grease") payments to expedite routine government transactions. However, the passage of the U.K. Bribery Act does not allow for facilitation payments.[21] The U.K. Bribery Act is more encompassing than the FCPA and has significant implications for global business. Under this law companies can be found guilty of bribery even if the bribery did not take place within the U.K., and company officials without explicit knowledge about the misconduct can still be held accountable. The law applies to any business with operations in the U.K. However, the U.K. Bribery Act does allow for leniency if the company has an effective compliance program and undergoes periodic ethical assessments.[22] In 2017, Canada repealed its facilitation payments exception under the Corruption of Foreign Public Officials Act.[23] In response, companies have begun to strengthen their compliance programs related to bribery. For instance, Lockheed Martin publicly changed its internal compliance procedures to ban facilitation payments in adherence to the new law.[24]

Political Forces
The Federal Trade Commission regulates a variety of business practices and curbs false advertising, misleading pricing, and deceptive packaging and labeling.

3-5b **Consumer Protection Legislation**

Consumer protection legislation is not a recent development. During the mid-1800s, lawmakers in many states passed laws to prohibit adulteration of food and drugs. However, consumer protection laws at the federal level mushroomed in the mid-1960s and early 1970s. A number of them deal with consumer safety, such as the food and drug acts, and are designed to protect people from actual and potential physical harm caused by adulteration or mislabeling. Other laws prohibit the sale of various hazardous products, such as flammable fabrics and toys that may injure children. Others concern automobile safety.

Congress has also passed several laws concerning information disclosure. Some require that information about specific products, such as textiles, furs, cigarettes, and automobiles, be provided on labels. Other laws focus on particular marketing activities: product development and testing, packaging, labeling, advertising, and consumer financing. Concerns about companies' online collection and use of personal information, especially about children, resulted in the passage of the Children's Online Privacy Protection Act (COPPA), which prohibits websites and internet providers from seeking personal information from children under age 13 without parental consent. Fines for violating COPPA can be severe. TRUSTe, now known as TrustArc, was fined $100,000 by the Federal Trade Commission after it was discovered that many of the company's customers who made use of TrustArc certification program, permitted third-party tracking technology that was not in compliance with COPPA.[25]

3-5c **Encouraging Compliance with Laws and Regulations**

Marketing activities are sometimes at the forefront of organizational misconduct, with fraud and antitrust violations the most frequently sentenced organizational crimes. Legal violations usually begin when marketers develop programs that unwittingly overstep legal bounds. Many marketers lack experience in dealing with complex legal actions and decisions. Some test the limits of certain laws by operating in a legally questionable way to see how far they can get

Credit Card Security
Credit card theft has created the need for consumer vigilance and regulatory agencies' assistance in preventing fraud.

away with certain practices before being prosecuted. Other marketers interpret regulations and statutes very strictly to avoid violating a vague law. When marketers interpret laws in relation to specific marketing practices, they often analyze recent court decisions both to better understand what the law is intended to do and to predict future court interpretations.

Many companies are choosing to provide incentives that foster a culture of ethics and responsibility that encourages compliance with laws and regulations. Developing best practices and voluntary compliance creates rules and principles that guide decision making. Many companies are encouraging their employees to take responsibility for avoiding legal misconduct themselves. The New York Stock Exchange, for example, requires all member companies to have a code of ethics, and some firms try to go beyond what is required by the law. Many firms are trying to develop ethical cultures based on values and proactive assessments of risks to prevent misconduct.

3-5d Regulatory Agencies

Federal regulatory agencies influence many marketing activities, including product development, pricing, packaging, advertising, personal selling, and distribution. Usually these bodies have the power to enforce specific laws, as well as some discretion in establishing operating rules and regulations to guide certain types of industry practices. Because of this discretion and overlapping areas of responsibility, confusion or conflict regarding which agencies have jurisdiction over which marketing activities is common.

Of all the federal regulatory units, the **Federal Trade Commission (FTC)** most heavily influences marketing activities. Although the FTC regulates a variety of business practices, it allocates a large portion of resources to curbing false advertising, misleading pricing, and deceptive packaging and labeling. For instance, the FTC opened a preliminary probe into whether Google was using its Android operating system to require handsets to prominently display its maps, search, and other features. The agency believed this requirement incentivized handsets to favor Google services on smartphones' home screens, placing Google's rivals at a disadvantage.[26] When it has reason to believe a firm is violating a law, the commission typically issues a complaint stating that the business is in violation. If, after it is issued a complaint, a company continues the questionable practice, the FTC can issue a cease-and-desist order demanding that the business stop doing whatever caused the complaint. The firm can appeal to the federal courts to have the order rescinded. However, the FTC can seek civil penalties in court, up to a maximum penalty of $10,000 a day for each infraction if a cease-and-desist order is violated. The commission can require companies to run corrective advertising in response to previous ads deemed misleading (see Figure 3.2).

The FTC also assists businesses in complying with laws and evaluates new marketing methods every year. The agency has held hearings to help firms establish guidelines for avoiding charges of price fixing, deceptive advertising, and questionable telemarketing practices.

Federal Trade Commission (FTC) An agency that regulates a variety of business practices and curbs false advertising, misleading pricing, and deceptive packaging and labeling

Figure 3.2	**Federal Trade Commission Enforcement Tools**

Cease-and-desist order	Consent decree	Redress	Corrective advertising	Civil penalties
A court order to a business to stop engaging in an illegal practice	An order for a business to stop engaging in questionable activities to avoid prosecution	Money paid to customer to settle or resolve a complaint	A requirement that a business make new advertisement to correct misinformation	Court-ordered civil fines for up to $10,000 per day for violating a cease-and-desist order

It has also held conferences and hearings on electronic (internet) commerce, identity theft, and childhood obesity. When general sets of guidelines are needed to improve business practices in a particular industry, the FTC sometimes encourages firms within that industry to establish a set of trade practices voluntarily. The FTC may even sponsor a conference that brings together industry leaders and consumers for this purpose.

Unlike the FTC, other regulatory units are limited to dealing with specific goods, services, or business activities. Consider the Food and Drug Administration (FDA), which enforces regulations that prohibit the sale and distribution of adulterated, misbranded, or hazardous food and drug products. After the Blue Bell ice cream recall—in which bacteria-contaminated ice cream led to three deaths—the FDA finalized rules to make it mandatory for food manufacturers to adopt detailed plans for how to prevent foodborne illnesses.[27] Table 3.3 outlines the areas of responsibility of seven federal regulatory agencies.

In addition, all states, as well as many cities and towns, have regulatory agencies that enforce laws and regulations regarding marketing practices within their states or municipalities. State and local regulatory agencies try not to establish regulations that conflict with those of federal regulatory agencies. They generally enforce laws dealing with the production and sale of particular goods and services. The utility, insurance, financial, and liquor industries are commonly regulated by state agencies. Among these agencies' targets are misleading advertising and pricing. Recent legal actions suggest that states are taking a firmer stance against perceived deceptive pricing practices and are using basic consumer research to define deceptive pricing.

State consumer protection laws offer an opportunity for state attorneys general to deal with marketing issues related to fraud and deception. Most states have consumer protection laws that are very general in nature and provide enforcement when new schemes evolve that injure consumers. The New York Consumer Protection Board, for instance, is proactive in monitoring consumer protection and providing consumer education. New York became the first state to implement an airline passenger rights law. In addition, New York City has banned trans fats and tried to ban large soft drinks.

Table 3.3 Major Federal Regulatory Agencies

Agency	Major Areas of Responsibility
Federal Trade Commission (FTC)	Enforces laws and guidelines regarding business practices; takes action to stop false and deceptive advertising, pricing, packaging, and labeling
Food and Drug Administration (FDA)	Enforces laws and regulations to prevent distribution of adulterated or misbranded foods, drugs, medical devices, cosmetics, veterinary products, and potentially hazardous consumer products
Consumer Product Safety Commission (CPSC)	Ensures compliance with the Consumer Product Safety Act; protects the public from unreasonable risk of injury from any consumer product not covered by other regulatory agencies
Federal Communications Commission (FCC)	Regulates communication by wire, radio, and television in interstate and foreign commerce
Environmental Protection Agency (EPA)	Develops and enforces environmental protection standards and conducts research on the adverse effects of pollution
Federal Power Commission (FPC)	Regulates rates and sales of natural gas producers, thereby affecting the supply and price of gas available to consumers; also regulates wholesale rates for electricity and gas, pipeline construction, and U.S. imports and exports of natural gas and electricity
Bureau of Consumer Financial Protection	Regulates the offering and provision of consumer financial products and serves to protect consumers from deceptive financial practices

Source: "Subtitle A—Bureau of Consumer Financial Protection," *One Hundred Eleventh Congress of the United States of America*, 589.

3-5e Self-Regulatory Forces

Various forms of self-regulation that promote cooperation, along with voluntary ethics and social responsibility standards, create accountability and transparency that go beyond government regulation.[28] In an attempt to be good corporate citizens and prevent government intervention, some businesses try to regulate themselves. Similarly, a number of trade associations have developed self-regulatory programs. Though these programs are not a direct outgrowth of laws, many were established to stop or stall the development of laws and governmental regulatory groups that would regulate the associations' marketing practices. Sometimes trade associations establish ethics codes by which their members must abide or risk censure or exclusion from the association. For instance, the National Association of Home Builders has adopted a code of ethics and guiding principles by which its members must abide.[29] The Direct Selling Association and the Direct Marketing Association also require compliance with detailed codes of ethics in order for member organizations to retain their membership.

Perhaps the best-known self-regulatory group is the **Better Business Bureau (BBB)**, which is a system of nongovernmental, independent, local regulatory agencies that are supported by local businesses. More than 128 bureaus help settle problems between consumers and specific business firms. Each bureau also acts to preserve good business practices in a locality, although it usually lacks strong enforcement tools for dealing with firms that employ questionable practices. When a firm continues to violate what the Better Business Bureau believes to be good business practices, the bureau warns consumers through local newspapers or broadcast media. If the offending organization is a BBB member, it may be expelled from the local bureau. Table 3.4 describes some of the major self-regulatory issues that often occur in the marketing industry.

The Council of Better Business Bureaus is a national organization composed of all local Better Business Bureaus. The National Advertising Division (NAD) of the council operates a self-regulatory program that investigates claims regarding alleged deceptive advertising. For instance, NAD prompted Comcast to discontinue a set of ads that claimed its internet services were faster than Verizon's FiOS service. While certain tiers are in fact faster, the statements did not specify this, and were therefore deemed misleading.[30]

Another self-regulatory entity, the **National Advertising Review Board (NARB)**, considers cases in which an advertiser challenges issues raised by the NAD about an advertisement. Cases are reviewed by panels drawn from NARB members that represent advertisers, agencies, and the public. In one case, the NARB recommended that personal-care company Philosophy, Inc. modify its claims regarding "Time in a Bottle Age-Defying Serum." The claims had already been reviewed by the NAD, but Philosophy, Inc. took the case to the NARB. The NARB determined that the study Philosophy, Inc. had relied upon to make its claims was reliable, but still recommended it modify or discontinue certain claims that could potentially be misleading.[31] The NARB, sponsored by the Council of Better Business Bureaus and three advertising trade organizations, has no official enforcement powers. However, if a firm refuses to comply with its decision, the NARB may publicize the questionable practice and file a complaint with the FTC. For example, NARB referred Rust-Oleum to the FTC for further investigation after the company failed to comply with the NARB's recommendation that Rust-Oleum stop using the "2X" classification from its Painter's Touch Ultra Cover product branding. Sherwin-Williams originally brought its concerns to NARB challenging its competitors claim that you get twice the coverage in a single application.[32]

Self-regulatory programs have several advantages over governmental laws and regulatory agencies. Establishment and implementation are usually less expensive, and

Better Business Bureau (BBB) A system of nongovernmental, independent, local regulatory agencies supported by local businesses that helps settle problems between customers and specific business firms

National Advertising Review Board (NARB) A self-regulatory unit that considers challenges to issues raised by the National Advertising Division (an arm of the Council of Better Business Bureaus) about an advertisement

Table 3.4   Self-Regulatory Issues in Marketing

1	Truthful Advertising Messages
2	Health and Childhood Obesity
3	Internet Tracking/User Privacy
4	Concern for Vulnerable Populations
5	Failure to Deliver on Expectations and Promises
6	Sustainable Marketing Practices and Greenwashing
7	Transparent Pricing
8	Understandable Labeling and Packaging
9	Supply Chain Relationships/Ethical Sourcing
10	Marketing of Dangerous Products
11	Product Quality Failures
12	Nonresponse to Customer Complaints

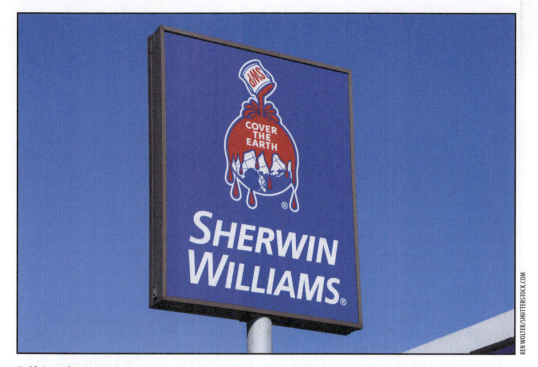

KEN WOLTER/SHUTTERSTOCK.COM

Self-Regulatory Forces
Sherwin-Williams voiced concerns to the National Advertising Review Board about Rust-Oleum's claim that its "2X" spray paints have twice the coverage of competing brands.

guidelines are generally more realistic and operational. In addition, effective self-regulatory programs reduce the need to expand government bureaucracy. However, these programs have several limitations. When a trade association creates a set of industry guidelines for its members, nonmember firms do not have to abide by them. Furthermore, many self-regulatory programs lack the tools or authority to enforce guidelines. Finally, guidelines in self-regulatory programs are often less strict than those established by government agencies.

3-6 **TECHNOLOGICAL FORCES**

Learning Objective 3-6
Describe how new technology impacts marketing and society.

The word *technology* brings to mind scientific advances such as electric vehicles, smartphones, drones, lifestyle drugs, radio frequency identification tags, and more. Technology has revolutionized the products created and offered by marketers and the channels by which they communicate about those products. However, even though these innovations are outgrowths of technology, none of them *are* technology. **Technology** is the application of knowledge and tools to solve problems and perform tasks more efficiently. Technology grows out of research performed by businesses, universities, government agencies, and nonprofit organizations. More than half of this research is paid for by the federal government, which supports research in such diverse areas as health, defense, agriculture, energy, and pollution.

The rapid technological growth of the last several decades is expected to accelerate. It has transformed the U.S. economy into the most productive in the world and provided Americans with an ever-higher standard of living and tremendous opportunities for sustained business expansion. Disruptive technologies and innovations often create a new market or greater value for consumers. This new market often replaces older industry leaders. Instacart and Airbnb are examples of firms using peer-to-peer internet platforms to challenge existing markets. Technology and technological advancements clearly influence buyers' and marketers' decisions, so let's take a closer look at the impact of technology and its use in the marketplace.

technology The application of knowledge and tools to solve problems and perform tasks more efficiently

3-6a Impact of Technology

Technology determines how we, as members of society, satisfy our physiological needs. In various ways and to varying degrees, eating and drinking habits, sleeping patterns, sexual activities, health care, and work performance are all influenced by both existing technology and changes in technology. Because of the technological revolution in communications, for example, marketers can now reach vast numbers of people more efficiently through a variety of media. Social networks, smartphones, and tablet computers help marketers stay in touch with clients, make appointments, and handle last-minute orders or cancellations. A growing number of U.S. households, as well as many businesses, have given up their land-lines in favor of using cell phones as their primary phones. Currently, more than 50 percent of Americans have exchanged their land-lines for cell phones.[33]

The growth of information technology (IT) is staggering. IT is changing the lives of consumers across the globe. Not only does it offer lucrative career opportunities, it also provides business opportunities for the entrepreneur. For instance, entrepreneur Marc Benioff built an entire organization around the cloud computing industry. Today Salesforce.com continues to be listed among the world's most innovative companies.[34] The internet also improves supply chain management (SCM) as it allows manufacturers, distributors, retailers, and other members of the supply chain to collaborate more closely and serve their customers more efficiently.[35] The importance of the internet will only increase in the future. It is estimated that more than 50 billion things, including cars, refrigerators, medical devices, and more, will be hooked up to the internet infrastructure within the next few years. South Korea is making significant progress in this pursuit. This phenomenon—known as the Internet of Things—will greatly impact how we do business and live our daily lives.[36] However, it also requires significant investment in security systems to protect these devices from cybercriminals.

Computers have become a staple in American homes, but the type of computer has been changing drastically in this past decade. Traditional desktop computers appear to be on the decline. Laptops became immensely popular due to their mobility, but analysts estimate that laptops might be entering the maturity stage of the product life cycle. Tablet computers are in the growth stage of the product life cycle, but it seems that this growth is already slowing down. In response many companies are creating apps specifically made for the iPad and similar devices. The rapidly evolving state of technology requires marketers to familiarize themselves with the latest technological changes.

In most households, the internet has become a major tool for communicating, researching, shopping, and entertaining. It is estimated that U.S. adults spend an average of five hours per day on digital devices.[37] Time spent on social networks makes up a significant portion of a consumer's online activities. One study estimates that users worldwide spend 22 percent of their time online on social networking sites.[38] The growth of online retailing is resulting in many brick-and-mortar retailers closing shop. It's estimated that over the next 10 years, about 25 percent of shopping malls in the United States will close.[39]

Although technology has had many positive impacts on our lives, there are also many negative

Do You Get News from Social Media?

HARDLY EVER 20%
NEVER 33%
OFTEN 20%
SOMETIMES 27%

SNAPSHOT

Note: Percent of U.S. adults who get news from social media sites.
Source: Pew Research Center. Survey conduction Aug. 8–21, 2017. "News Use across Social Media Platforms."

impacts to consider. We enjoy the benefits of communicating through the internet; however, we are increasingly concerned about protecting our privacy and intellectual property. Hackers and those who steal digital property are also using advanced technology to harm others. Likewise, technological advances in the areas of health and medicine have led to the creation of new drugs that save lives; however, such advances have also led to cloning and genetically modified foods that have become controversial issues in many segments of society. Consider the impact of cell phones. The ability to call from almost any location has many benefits, but it also has negative side effects, including increases in traffic accidents, increased noise pollution, and fears about potential health risks.[40]

The effects of technology relate to such characteristics as dynamics, reach, and the self-sustaining nature of technological progress. The *dynamics* of technology involve the constant change that often challenges the structures of social institutions, including social relationships, the legal system, religion, education, business, and leisure. *Reach* refers to the broad nature of technology as it moves through society.

The *self-sustaining* nature of technology relates to the fact that technology acts as a catalyst to spur even faster development. As new innovations are introduced, they stimulate the need for more advancement to facilitate further development. CenturyLink's advertisement promotes the speed and capacity of its services by highlighting that the company delivers 2,000 eCards per minute on behalf of the world's largest eCard brand, including 5 million deliveries on Valentine's Day. The advertisement suggests CenturyLink's data is secure, reliable, and fast. Our increasing reliance on computer technology for business purposes has led to an increased risk of hacking or data theft. This, in turn, has caused more demand for internet security services that combat hacking attempts. Technology initiates a change process that creates new opportunities for new technologies in every industry segment or personal life experience that it touches. At some point, there is a multiplier effect that causes still greater demand for more change to improve performance.[41]

Impact of Technology
CenturyLink provides communication and data services like data, voice, cloud, and managed services for businesses. As new innovations are introduced, they stimulate the need for more advancement to facilitate further development.

The expanding opportunities for online retailing and e-commerce, the sharing of business information, the ability to maintain business relationships, and the ability to conduct business transactions via digital networks are changing the relationship between businesses and consumers.[42] Many people use the internet to purchase consumer electronics, clothing, software, books, furniture, and music. Amazon is the third-largest retailer in the world behind Walmart and CVS.[43] More people now opt to purchase music online or simply listen for free on social networking sites. As a result, CD sales have decreased over the years. In addition, consumers go online to acquire travel-related services, financial services, and information. The forces unleashed by the internet are particularly important in business-to-business relationships, where uncertainties are being reduced by improving the quantity, reliability, and timeliness of information.

3-6b **Adoption and Use of Technology**

Many companies lose their status as market leaders because they fail to keep up with technological changes. It is important for firms to determine when a technology is changing the industry and to define the strategic influence of the new technology. For example, driverless cars, which are projected to be road ready by 2021, will disrupt the transportation and automobile markets. The result will be fewer accidents, reduced carbon emissions, fewer cars on the road, and companies like Uber will be positioned to eliminate drivers. To remain competitive, companies today must keep up with and adapt to technological advances.

The extent to which a firm can protect inventions that stem from research also influences its use of technology. How secure a product is from imitation depends on how easily others can copy it without violating its patent. If groundbreaking products and processes cannot be protected through patents, a company is less likely to market them and make the benefits of its research available to competitors.

Through a procedure known as *technology assessment*, managers try to foresee the effects of new products and processes on their firm's operations, on other business organizations, and on society in general. With information obtained through a technology assessment, management tries to estimate whether benefits of adopting a specific technology outweigh costs to the firm and to society at large. The degree to which a business is technologically based also influences its managers' response to technology.

Learning Objective 3-7

Outline the sociocultural issues marketers must deal with as they make decisions.

3-7 **SOCIOCULTURAL FORCES**

Sociocultural forces are the influences in a society and its culture(s) that bring about changes in people's attitudes, beliefs, norms, customs, and lifestyles. Profoundly affecting how people live, these forces help determine what, where, how, and when people buy products. Like the other environmental forces, sociocultural forces present marketers with both challenges and opportunities. For a closer look at sociocultural forces, we examine three major issues: demographic and diversity characteristics, cultural values, and consumerism.

3-7a **Demographic and Diversity Characteristics**

Changes in a population's demographic characteristics—age, gender, race, ethnicity, marital and parental status, income, and education—have a significant bearing on relationships and individual behavior. These shifts lead to changes in how people live and ultimately in their consumption of such products as food, clothing, housing, transportation, communication, recreation, education, and health services. We'll look at a few of the changes in demographics and diversity that are affecting marketing activities.

One demographic change that is affecting the marketplace is the increasing proportion of older consumers. According to the U.S. Bureau of the Census, the number of people age 65 and older is expected to more than double by the year 2060, reaching 98.2 million.[44] Consequently, marketers can expect significant increases in the demand for health-care services, recreation, tourism, retirement housing, and selected skin-care products. Even online companies are trying to take advantage of the opportunities baby boomers present. Several online dating sites directed toward boomers have been launched, such as BabyBoomerPeopleMeet .com and SeniorPeopleMeet.com.[45] To reach older customers effectively, of course, marketers must understand the diversity within the mature market with respect to geographic location, income, marital status, and limitations in mobility and self-care.

The number of singles is also on the rise. Singles currently comprise more than half of American households.[46] Single people have quite different spending patterns than couples and families with children. They are less likely to own homes, and thus they buy less furniture and fewer appliances. They spend more heavily on convenience foods, restaurants, travel, entertainment, and recreation. In addition, they tend to prefer smaller packages, whereas families often buy bulk goods and products packaged in multiple servings.

sociocultural forces The influences in a society and its culture(s) that change people's attitudes, beliefs, norms, customs, and lifestyles

DISRUPTIVE MARKETING

De Vegetarische Slager Disrupts the Global Meat Market

De Vegetarische Slager (The Vegetarian Butcher), a Dutch vegetarian food producer, started with Jaap Korteweg's initiative toward an organic and animal-friendly diet. At the end of the 20th century, swine fever and mad cow disease had killed many people in the Netherlands. Korteweg's environmental analysis highlighted a lack of tasty vegetarian alternatives, so he responded by searching and developing meat-like vegetarian products.

Since its launch in 2010, De Vegetarische Slager has become a sizable business with 3,500 stores in 15 countries. Its commitment to producing plant-based products resembling meats is disrupting Europe's meat industry. According to Korteweg, the company receives letters from meat lovers who have stated they prefer De Vegetarische Slager's vegetarian chicken alternative over the taste of real chicken. Additionally, cultural values have shifted, and people today are more concerned about the foods they eat. Combined with a focus on sustainability, more and more consumers are seeking plant-based products. Worldwide, livestock farms

emit about 18 percent of human-caused greenhouse gases. Hence, switching from a meat-based diet to a plant-based one reduces the pressure of livestock production on the environment.

Despite its success, De Vegetarische Slager faces legal and regulatory issues. The Dutch Food and Consumer Product Safety Authority (NVWA) has accused the company of misleading consumers with meat names. After one consumer complained that De Vegetarische Slager is using meaty terms for its plant-based products, the NVWA decided to force the company to change all of their product names. It is necessary for De Vegetarische Slager to maintain its competitive advantage for meat-like products—especially since the Dutch authorities have placed limitations on how these "meat-tasting" vegetarian products can be marketed. Yet the company is up to the challenge. If De Vegetarische Slager can overcome the current regulatory challenges, global consumers can expect to have tastier vegetarian "meats" in the future.[b]

Despite these trends, the United States is facing a baby bust with its lowest fertility rate ever. This means that without immigration, the United States will fail to grow.[47] In the last decade, the U.S. population experienced the slowest rate of growth since the Great Depression at 9.7 percent growth. Today, the U.S. population is about 327 million. While the birth rate is declining, new immigrants help with population gains.[48] It is estimated that those in the U.S. population that were born in other countries has more than doubled since the 1960s, with more than 43 million foreign-born individuals.[49]

The number of immigrants in the United States has steadily risen during the last 50 years. In the 1960s, 3.3 million people immigrated to the United States; in the 1970s, 4.4 million immigrated; in the 1980s, 7.3 million arrived; in the 1990s, the United States received 9.1 million immigrants; and in the 2000s, more than 8.3 million people have immigrated to the United States.[50] In contrast to earlier immigrants, very few recent ones are of European origin. One reason for the increasing cultural diversification of the United States is that most recent immigrants are relatively young, whereas U.S. citizens of European origin are growing older. These younger immigrants tend to have more children than their older counterparts, further shifting the population balance. By the turn of the 20th century, the U.S. population had shifted from one dominated by whites to one consisting largely of three racial and ethnic groups: whites, blacks, and Hispanics. The U.S. government projects that by the year 2065, approximately 107 million Hispanics, 57 million blacks or African Americans, and 61 million Asians will call the United States home.[51] Table 3.5 provides a glimpse into the multicultural nature of the U.S. population. Although the majority of the population still identify themselves as white, Hispanic and Asian ethnicities are expected to grow in the next 50 years, while white non-Hispanic ethnicities are estimated to decrease.

Table 3.5 **The Multicultural Nature of the U.S. Population**

Race	% Population 2015	Estimated % 2065
White	62	46
Hispanic	18	24
Black or African American	12	13
Asian	6	14

Source: Pew Research Center, "Projected U.S. Population by Race and Hispanic Origin, 2015–2065, with and without Immigrants Entering 2015–2065," September 24, 2015, www.pewhispanic.org/2015/09/28/modern-immigration-wave-brings-59-million-to -u-s-driving-population-growth-and-change-through-2065/ph_2015-09-28_immigration-through-2065-a2-06/ (accessed December 28, 2017).

Marketers recognize that these profound changes in the U.S. population bring unique problems and opportunities. But a diverse population means a more diverse customer base, and marketing practices must be modified—and diversified—to meet its changing needs. For instance, Mattel has started releasing Barbie dolls with more average waistlines and individual style trends. This is in response to parents' desires to have dolls for their children that do not depict unrealistic standards (such as the impossible proportions of Barbie) and that stress individuality so children are encouraged to be themselves.[52]

3-7b **Cultural Values**

Changes in cultural values have dramatically influenced people's needs and desires for products. Although cultural values do not shift overnight, they do change at varying speeds. Marketers try to monitor these changes. Knowing this information can equip them to predict changes in consumers' needs for products, at least in the near future. For instance, automakers are adapting their strategies to appeal to the younger demographic because fewer young adults are choosing to purchase vehicles or get their driver's licenses. An alternative some teens are pursuing is opening up an Uber account at age 16 so they can get where they want to go without their parents and without having to go through the hassle of obtaining a license.[53]

Starting in the late 1980s, issues of health, nutrition, and exercise grew in importance. People today are more concerned about the foods they eat and thus are choosing healthier

Sociocultural Forces
Consumers' busy schedules often require them to grab ready-to-cook meals, but there is also a growing shift toward eating more natural, organic foods. Progresso introduced a range of organic soups, turning both of these trends into opportunities.

products. Compared to those in the previous two decades, Americans today are more likely to favor smoke-free environments and to consume less alcohol. They have also altered their sexual behavior to reduce the risk of contracting sexually transmitted diseases. Marketers have responded with a proliferation of foods, beverages, and exercise products that fit this new lifestyle; with programs to help people quit smoking; and with contraceptives that are safer and more effective. Americans are also becoming increasingly open to alternative medicines and nutritionally improved foods. As a result, sales of organic foods, herbs and herbal remedies, vitamins, and dietary supplements have escalated. In addition to the proliferation of new organic brands, such as Earthbound Farm, Horizon Organic Dairy, and Whole Foods 365 Everyday Value, many conventional marketers have introduced organic versions of their products, including Orville Redenbacher, Heinz, and Walmart.

The major source of cultural values is the family. For years, when asked about the most important aspects of their lives, adults specified family issues and a happy marriage. Today, however, only one out of two marriages is predicted to last. Values regarding the permanence of marriage are changing. Because a happy marriage is prized so highly, more people are willing to give up an unhappy one and seek a different marriage partner or opt to stay single.

Children continue to be very important. Marketers have responded with safer, upscale baby gear and supplies, children's electronics, and family entertainment products. Marketers are also aiming more marketing efforts directly at children because children often play pivotal roles in purchasing decisions. A study in Austria reported that children influence twice as many purchase decisions in the supermarket than parents are aware of, and the majority of items children requested are products positioned at their eye level.[54]

Children and family values are also factors in the trend toward more eat-out and take-out meals. Busy families in which both parents work generally want to spend less time in the kitchen and more time together enjoying themselves. Beneficiaries of this trend have primarily been fast-food and casual restaurants like McDonald's, Taco Bell, and Ruby Tuesday, but most supermarkets have added more ready-to-cook and ready-to-serve meal components to meet the needs of busy customers. Some also offer dine-in cafés.

Green marketing helps establish long-term consumer relationships by maintaining, supporting, and enhancing the natural environment. One of society's environmental hurdles is proper disposal of waste, especially of nondegradable materials such as disposable diapers and polystyrene packaging. Companies have responded by developing more environmentally sensitive products and packaging. Procter & Gamble, for example, uses recycled materials in some of its packaging and sells environmentally friendly refills. Companies like Seventh Generation, which sells products like paper towels and bathroom tissue made from recycled paper as well as eco-friendly cleaning products, have entered the mainstream. Everything the company produces is as environmentally friendly as it can be, in hopes of having as little impact on the next seven generations as possible.[55] A number of marketers sponsor recycling programs and encourage their customers to take part in them.

3-7c Consumerism

Consumerism involves organized efforts by individuals, groups, and organizations to protect consumers' rights. The movement's major forces are individual consumer advocates, consumer organizations and other interest groups, consumer education, and consumer laws.

To achieve their objectives, consumers and their advocates write letters or send emails to companies, post on social media sites, lobby government agencies, broadcast public service announcements, and boycott companies whose activities they deem irresponsible. Consider that a number of consumers would like to eliminate telemarketing and email spam, and some of them have joined organizations and groups attempting to stop these activities. Businesses that engage in questionable practices invite additional regulation. Several organizations, for instance, evaluate children's products for safety, often announcing dangerous products before Christmas so parents can avoid them. Other actions by the consumer movement have resulted in seat belts and air bags in automobiles, dolphin-friendly tuna, the banning of unsafe three-wheel motorized vehicles, and numerous laws regulating product safety and information. We take a closer look at consumerism in the next chapter.

consumerism Organized efforts by individuals, groups, and organizations to protect consumers' rights

Summary

3-1 Summarize why it is important to examine and respond to the marketing environment.

The marketing environment consists of external forces that directly or indirectly influence an organization's acquisition of inputs (personnel, financial resources, raw materials, and information) and generation of outputs (goods, services, and ideas). The marketing environment includes competitive, economic, political, legal and regulatory, technological, and sociocultural forces.

Environmental scanning is the process of collecting information about forces in the marketing environment; environmental analysis is the process of assessing and interpreting information obtained in scanning. This information helps marketing managers predict opportunities and threats associated with environmental fluctuation. Marketing managers may assume either a passive, reactive approach or a proactive, aggressive approach in responding to these environmental fluctuations. The choice depends on the organization's structures and needs and on the composition of environmental forces that affect it.

3-2 Explain how competitive factors affect an organization's ability to compete.

All businesses compete for customers' dollars. A marketer, however, generally defines *competition* as other firms in the same geographic area that market products that are similar to or can be substituted for its products. These competitors can be classified into one of four types: brand competitors, product competitors, generic competitors, and total budget competitors. The number of firms controlling the supply of a product may affect the strength of competitors. The four general types of competitive structures are monopoly, oligopoly, monopolistic competition, and pure competition. Marketers monitor what competitors are currently doing and assess changes occurring in the competitive environment.

3-3 Articulate how economic factors influence a customer's ability and willingness to buy products.

General economic conditions, buying power, and willingness to spend can strongly influence marketing decisions and activities. The overall state of the economy fluctuates in a general pattern known as the business cycle, which consists of four stages: prosperity, recession, depression, and recovery. Consumers' goods, services, and financial holdings make up their buying power, or ability to purchase. Financial sources of buying power are income, credit, and wealth. After-tax income used for spending or saving is disposable income. Disposable income left after an individual has purchased the basic necessities of food, clothes, and shelter is discretionary income. Factors affecting buyers' willingness to spend include product price; level of satisfaction obtained from currently used products; family size; and expectations about future employment, income, prices, and general economic conditions.

3-4 Identify the types of political forces in the marketing environment.

The political, legal, and regulatory forces of the marketing environment are closely interrelated. Political forces may determine what laws and regulations affecting specific marketers are enacted, how much the government purchases, and from which suppliers. They can also be important in helping organizations secure foreign markets. Companies influence political forces in several ways, including maintaining good relationships with political officials; protesting the actions of legislative bodies; helping to elect to public office, through campaign contributions, those individuals who regard them positively; and employing lobbyists to communicate their concerns to elected officials.

3-5 Explain how laws, government regulations, and self-regulatory agencies affect marketing activities.

Federal legislation affecting marketing activities can be divided into procompetitive legislation—laws designed to preserve and encourage competition—and consumer protection laws, which generally relate to product safety and information disclosure. Actual effects of legislation are determined by how marketers and courts interpret the laws. Federal guidelines for sentencing concerning violations of these laws represent an attempt to force marketers to comply with the laws.

Federal, state, and local regulatory agencies usually have power to enforce specific laws. They also have some discretion in establishing operating rules and drawing up regulations to guide certain types of industry practices. Industry self-regulation represents another regulatory force; marketers view this type of regulation more favorably than government action because they have more opportunity to take part in creating guidelines. Self-regulation may be less expensive than government regulation, and its guidelines are generally more realistic. However, the groups providing such regulation generally cannot ensure compliance as effectively as government agencies.

3-6 Describe how new technology impacts marketing and society.

Technology is the application of knowledge and tools to solve problems and perform tasks more efficiently. Consumer demand, buyer behavior, product development, packaging, promotion, prices, and distribution systems are all influenced directly by technology. The rapid technological growth of the last few decades is expected to accelerate. Revolutionary changes in communication technology have allowed marketers to reach vast numbers of people; however, with this expansion of communication has come concern about privacy and intellectual property. And while science and medical research have brought many great advances, cloning and genetically modified foods are controversial issues in many segments of society. Home, health, leisure, and work are all influenced to varying degrees by technology and technological advances. The *dynamics* of technology involves the constant change that challenges every aspect of our society. *Reach* refers to the broad nature of technology as it moves through and affects society.

Many companies lose their status as market leaders because they fail to keep up with technological changes. The ability to protect inventions from competitor imitation is also an important consideration when making marketing decisions.

3-7 Outline the sociocultural issues marketers must deal with as they make decisions.

Sociocultural forces are the influences in a society and its culture that result in changes in attitudes, beliefs, norms, customs, and lifestyles. Major sociocultural issues directly affecting marketers include demographic and diversity characteristics, cultural values, and consumerism.

Changes in a population's demographic characteristics, such as age, income, race, and ethnicity, can lead to changes in that population's consumption of products. Changes in cultural values, such as those relating to health, nutrition, family, and the natural environment, have had striking effects on people's needs for products and therefore are closely monitored by marketers. Consumerism involves the efforts of individuals, groups, and organizations to protect consumers' rights. Consumer rights organizations inform and organize other consumers, raise issues, help businesses develop consumer-oriented programs, and pressure lawmakers to enact consumer protection laws.

Important Terms

environmental scanning 60
environmental analysis 61
competition 63
brand competitors 63
product competitors 64
generic competitors 64
total budget competitors 64

monopoly 64
oligopoly 64
monopolistic competition 65
pure competition 65
business cycle 66
prosperity 66
recession 66
depression 66

recovery 67
buying power 67
income 67
disposable income 67
discretionary income 67
wealth 68
willingness to spend 68
Federal Trade Commission (FTC) 74

Better Business Bureau (BBB) 76
National Advertising Review Board (NARB) 76
technology 77
sociocultural forces 80
consumerism 83

Discussion and Review Questions

1. Why are environmental scanning and analysis important to marketers?
2. What are the four types of competition? Which is most important to marketers?
3. In what ways can each of the business cycle stages affect consumers' reactions to marketing strategies?
4. What business cycle stage are we experiencing currently? How is this stage affecting business firms in your area?
5. Define *income, disposable income,* and *discretionary income.* How does each type of income affect consumer buying power?

6. How do wealth and consumer credit affect consumer buying power?
7. What factors influence a buyer's willingness to spend?
8. Describe marketers' attempts to influence political forces.
9. What types of problems do marketers experience as they interpret legislation?
10. What are the goals of the Federal Trade Commission? List the ways in which the FTC affects marketing activities. Do you think a single regulatory agency should have such broad jurisdiction over so many marketing practices? Why or why not?
11. Name several nongovernmental regulatory forces. Do you believe self-regulation is more or less

effective than governmental regulatory agencies? Why?
12. What does the term *technology* mean to you? Do the benefits of technology outweigh its costs and potential dangers? Defend your answer.
13. Discuss the impact of technology on marketing activities.
14. What factors determine whether a business organization adopts and uses technology?
15. What evidence exists that cultural diversity is increasing in the United States?
16. In what ways are cultural values changing? How are marketers responding to these changes?
17. Describe consumerism. Analyze some active consumer forces in your area.

Developing Your Marketing Plan

A marketing strategy is dynamic. Companies must continually monitor the marketing environment, not only to create their marketing strategy, but also to revise it if necessary. Information about various forces in the marketplace is collected, analyzed, and used as a foundation for several marketing plan decisions. The following questions will help you to understand how the information in this chapter contributes to the development of your marketing plan:

1. Describe the current competitive market for your product. Can you identify the number of brands or the market share that they hold? Expand your analysis to include other products that are similar or could be substituted for yours.

2. Using the business-cycle pattern, in which of the four stages is the current state of the economy? Can you identify changes in consumer buying power that would affect the sale and use of your product?
3. Referring to Tables 3.2 and 3.3, do you recognize any laws or regulatory agencies that would have jurisdiction over your type of product?
4. Conduct a brief technology assessment, determining the impact that technology has on your product and its sale or use.
5. Discuss how your product could be affected by changes in social attitudes, demographic characteristics, or lifestyles.

Video Case 3.1

Apple vs. Samsung: Gloves Are Off

Both Apple and Samsung have been at the forefront of technology innovation. Technological forces are pushing for newer and better products, and tech companies must constantly pursue product development to compete effectively against each other. As a result, the tech environment has become highly aggressive with firms going to great lengths to protect their patents. A patent rewards an innovator for a new invention or technology by providing the innovator the sole rights to develop and sell that product for 20 years. Patents offer the owner legal protection. If during that time

competitors try to sell the product, they can be sued for damages.

In the United States, whoever files a patent first gets legal protection. This can get complicated, however, when it is hard to determine which company obtained a patent first, or when a firm accuses another firm of violating their patent by copying certain product features protected under the patent. This was the case between Apple and Samsung, leading to a legal battle that would take multiple years to resolve. It started in 2011, when Apple accused Samsung of violating its iPhone patent by copying certain iPhone features for its Galaxy S. In its allegations, Apple accused Samsung of copying the iPhone shape; color; tap-to-zoom, flip-to-rotate, and slide-to-scroll features; and more. It also claimed that Samsung violated the patent for its iPad.

Samsung claimed the opposite. It claimed that it had patented these components before Apple and that therefore Apple's iPhone violated Samsung's intellectual property rights. Samsung countersued. Soon the lawsuit had taken on global proportions as lawsuits were filed in the United States, South Korea, Germany, Japan, the United Kingdom, and other countries. Since the legal and regulatory environments differ in each country, the courts often came up with different verdicts. For instance, South Korea courts found that Apple had violated two of Samsung's patents, while Samsung violated one of Apple's. The United Kingdom ruled in favor of Samsung.

In the United States, Apple wanted more than $2 billion in damages from Samsung. In the original verdict, U.S. courts ruled that Samsung had violated Apple's patents and ordered Samsung to pay $1 billion in damages. Later appeals reduced this amount. In 2012 Apple filed a new lawsuit against Samsung claiming it had copied five features protected under Apple's patent. Samsung sued Apple, claiming it had violated two of the patents it owned.

This time the jury issued a mixed verdict. "Among the popular features, it found Samsung copied the slide-to-unlock button on some of its phones and autocorrect," said Betty Yu, a reporter from KPIX 5 CBS who covered the outcome. "Samsung accused Apple of infringing two of its patents and in the end was found guilty of just one. It involves photo and video organization in folders."

As a result of the verdict, Samsung was ordered to pay $120 million in damages to Apple, whereas Apple was told to pay Samsung $158,000. Analysts see the legal battle as being a fight over dominance rather than a concern over money. Both companies hold a large share of the smartphone market, and neither is willing to give up market share.

For consumers the verdict is likely to have little impact. Sometimes legal battles over intellectual property can result in the losing company being ordered to stop selling the product within the country. However, this did not happen with the Apple vs. Samsung case.

"What does all this mean for you and me? Well, experts say that this really doesn't mean anything for us," Betty Yu says. "You can still use your phones involved in this case, and the newest devices aren't an issue."

As this case demonstrates, intellectual property is not always an easy path to navigate, especially for global companies who operate in countries with different laws. In China, for instance, intellectual property rights laws are more lax, and copying is more common. Although some might view Apple as being overly aggressive, maintaining control over intellectual property in the tech industry could mean the difference between company failure and success. Currently, Samsung overshadows Apple in the global smartphone market. However, newer competitors including Chinese firms Huawei, Lenovo, and Xiaomi are quickly gaining in market share.[56]

Questions for Discussion

1. In what type of competitive environment do you think Apple and Samsung operate?
2. How do technological forces impact how Apple and Samsung operate when it comes to protecting their intellectual property?
3. Why is it important for international tech firms to be familiar with the laws and regulations of the countries in which they operate?

Case 3.2

Dollar General Uses Buying Power to Target Markets

Dollar General has a strong understanding of the economic forces that impact its customers. The company has overtaken the competition by recognizing that the large income gap in the United States leaves a significant number of locations untouched by rival stores. As such, Dollar General's business model focuses on selling small-ticket items to a target market of low-income consumers on tight budgets. Many stores are not able to justify entering into a low-income market with a customer base that has low buying power and largely relies on government assistance to buy necessities. However, understanding this market is where Dollar General found its niche.

Larger chain stores—such as Walmart or Whole Foods—along with smaller local stores find it difficult to sustain

JONATHAN WEISS/SHUTTERSTOCK.COM

operations in these markets. Even low-cost retailer Walmart faces a start-up cost of $15 million when creating a new Supercenter, in contrast with the $250,000 that Dollar General spends on a new store. Dollar General makes good use of its shelving space, fitting a variety of different products within a space one-tenth the size of a Walmart store. This large assortment of products helps offset the setbacks in customer service some Dollar General stores experience as it keeps costs low by hiring fewer workers.

Although sales per square foot of Dollar General are about half of Walmart's and far below the industry average, its gross profit margins are often higher. In addition to the low start-up costs and higher margins, Dollar General does not carry large-ticket purchases like bikes and appliances; instead, it focuses on the basics such as toilet paper and laundry detergent. Understanding that its leading target market shops paycheck-to-paycheck, the store avoids selling items in bulk like many competitors in the industry.

Thorough environmental analysis led CEO Todd Vasos to target opportunities in the United States and add to its more than 14,000 stores. The idea was to seek out small and very small towns consisting of low-income households and individuals that rely on government assistance. These are areas that are not looking to thrive economically, but primarily to survive in a prosperous economy. Dollar General announced the intention to add around 1,000 new stores as part of its $22 billion expansion plan.

Dollar General is not the only company with intentions to expand, however. It faces intense competition from many facets of the industry, ranging from current competitors to new entrants. Historically, its most direct competitor has been Dollar Tree Inc., which also owns Family Dollar and has a similar business model to Dollar General. According to Dollar Tree Inc., it expects that the U.S. economy can sustain an additional 10,000 Dollar Trees and 15,000 Family Dollars on top of their current 14,500 stores.

Despite its higher costs of operations, Walmart could also become a formidable competitor to Dollar General. For example, as Walmart reduced prices, Dollar General, which closely monitors its competition, cut prices on hundreds of items. Dollar General must keep prices low, so it has to be aware of products that could be substitutes for the products it sells. Dollar General also knows that as its footprint expands, its costs will likely increase and it will have to find different ways to compete. After Walmart announced a $2.7 million investment into better employee training and benefits, Dollar General began to boost compensation for managers at some of its stores. This has begun to reduce turnover costs.

Dollar General could face even more change in legal and regulatory forces as the U.S. Food and Drug Administration is piloting a program allowing those with food assistance cards to order their groceries online. This program could potentially allow larger chains to penetrate low-income areas by bypassing many of the previous barriers. Ten companies have signed on, including Walmart and Amazon.com Inc.

Recently, Amazon.com Inc. has made inroads in the grocery market with its acquisition of Whole Foods Market Inc. Despite the fact that these big players may not find immediate success in the rural market, Dollar General has many current and future environmental factors to consider.

Although it may not be providing numerous high-salary jobs or offering top-notch health products, Dollar General offers an option for those that would not otherwise have one. It is committed to continuing its strategy of recognizing and catering to "Anytown, USA."[57]

Questions for Discussion

1. Describe how Dollar General monitors and responds to its competition.

2. What overall impact do you think the U.S. Food and Drug Administration's pilot program will have on Dollar General?

3. How should Dollar General change its marketing strategies to cope with increasing competition from larger retailers like Walmart?

4

Social Responsibility and Ethics in Marketing

LEARNING OBJECTIVES

4-1 Define the four dimensions of social responsibility.

4-2 State the importance of marketing ethics.

4-3 Describe the three factors of ethical decision making.

4-4 Comment on the requirements for improving ethical decision making.

4-5 Critique the role of social responsibility and ethics in improving marketing performance.

JONATHAN WEISS/SHUTTERSTOCK.COM

Volkswagen Defeated by its Own Device

Volkswagen, the world's largest automaker, saw its green reputation crumble after it was discovered the company had used a "defeat device" to alter emissions testing results. During this testing, the software made the vehicles run below performance, which released fewer emissions and met requirements. However, on the road the cars ran at maximum performance and gave off up to 40 times the allowable limit for emissions in the United States.

Until the scandal broke, VW had promoted itself as an eco-friendly company. Its commercials featured VW rally driver and *Top Gear* USA host Tanner Foust driving elderly women around in a TDI VW to dispel the myth that diesel is slow. As a result of its marketing, VW made large inroads in gaining acceptance for its clean diesel vehicles. This green image was highly beneficial for VW as consumer values are changing to favor greener products.

Because of the scandal, VW agreed to pay up to $17.5 billion to compensate consumers affected by its defeat devices, which included retrofitting and buying back impacted vehicles. Perhaps the worst impact the scandal has caused has been to VW's reputation. Many VW customers felt betrayed by the company. Its reputation for sustainability has been shattered, and two awards it had been given for "Green Car of the Year" were pulled.

Because it operates in an oligopoly, other global car companies may benefit from the scandal and gain market share from VW. At the same time, VW's conduct has caused problems for the industry as a whole. Consumers are now questioning the environmental claims of other car brands, and automakers will have to work harder to prove that their claims are accurate. Consumer trust is easily lost and is not restored overnight.[1]

Most businesses operate responsibly and within the limits of the law, but organizations often walk a fine line between acting ethically and engaging in questionable behavior. Research shows that ethical companies often have better stock performance, but too often companies are distracted by the short-term costs of implementing ethics programs and the fleeting benefits of cutting ethical corners. Another common mistake companies make is a tendency to believe that because an activity is legal, it is also ethical. In fact, ethics often goes above and beyond the law and should, therefore, be a critical concern of marketers.

Some of the most common types of unethical practices among companies include deceptive sales practices, bribery, price discrimination, deceptive advertising, misleading packaging, and marketing defective products. Deceptive advertising in particular causes consumers to become defensive toward all promotional messages and distrustful of all advertising, so it hurts not only consumers but marketers as well.[2] Practices of this kind raise questions about marketers' obligations to society. Inherent in these questions are the issues of social responsibility and marketing ethics.

Because social responsibility and ethics often have profound impacts on the success of marketing strategies, we devote this chapter to their role in marketing decision making. We begin by defining social responsibility and exploring its dimensions. We then discuss social responsibility issues, such as sustainability and the marketer's role as a member of the community. Next, we define and examine the role of ethics in marketing decisions. We consider ethical issues in marketing, the ethical decision-making process, and ways to improve ethical conduct in marketing. Finally, we incorporate social responsibility and ethics into strategic market planning.

social responsibility
An organization's obligation to maximize its positive impact and minimize its negative impact on society

Learning Objective 4-1
Define the four dimensions of social responsibility.

4-1 THE NATURE OF SOCIAL RESPONSIBILITY

Social Responsibility
American Airlines partnered with Stand Up to Cancer to support cancer research and raise awareness.

In marketing, **social responsibility** refers to an organization's obligation to maximize its positive impact and minimize its negative impact on society. Social responsibility thus deals with the total effect of all marketing decisions on society. In marketing, social responsibility includes the managerial processes needed to monitor, satisfy, and even exceed stakeholder expectations and needs.[3] Remember from Chapter 1 that stakeholders are groups that have a "stake," or claim, in some aspect of a company's products, operations, markets, industry, and outcomes. CEOs such as Dan Amos, CEO of Aflac, are increasingly recognizing the importance of business ethics and social responsibility.[4]

Ample evidence demonstrates that ignoring stakeholders' demands for responsible marketing can destroy customers' trust and even prompt government regulation. Irresponsible actions that anger customers, employees, or competitors may not only jeopardize a marketer's financial standing but have legal repercussions as well. Corporate social responsibility can have a direct, observable effect on both employees and customers. If employees perceive that management and customers support social responsibility activities, they positively identify with the firm. This means social responsibility activities can improve employee performance and customer loyalty to the organization.[5]

Socially responsible activities can generate positive publicity and boost sales. For example, 3M, the maker of Post-it, developed the 3Mgives program to contribute to education, community, and the environment in areas with 3M operations. The company has invested more than $1.45 billion and 350,000 hours in service through the program.

Initiatives include improving access to quality education and improving standards of living. Although the program is costly in both time and money for the company, 3M's efforts have likely improved its relationships with stakeholders and generated significant goodwill worldwide.[6]

Socially responsible efforts such as 3M's have a positive impact on local communities; at the same time, they indirectly help the sponsoring organization by attracting goodwill, publicity, and potential customers and employees. Thus, although social responsibility is certainly a positive concept in itself, most organizations embrace it in the expectation of indirect long-term benefits. For example, American Airlines partnered with the organization Stand Up to Cancer to support cancer research. Its advertisement features popular celebrity Bradley Cooper alongside American Airlines team members affected by cancer as endorsers for the organization. Because Bradley Cooper is a figure that many people admire, having him as an endorser encourages others to support the movement. Our own research suggests that an organizational culture that supports social responsibility generates greater employee commitment and improved business performance.[7] Table 4.1 provides a sampling of companies that have chosen to make social responsibility a strategic long-term objective.

Table 4.1	Best Corporate Citizens
1	Hasbro, Inc.
2	Intel Corp.
3	Microsoft Corp.
4	Altria Group Inc.
5	Campbell Soup Co.
6	Cisco Systems, Inc.
7	Accenture plc
8	Hormel Foods Corp.
9	Lockheed Martin Corp.
10	Ecolab, Inc.

Source: "CR's 100 Best Corporate Citizens 2017," *CR*, www.thecro.com/wp-content/uploads/2017/05/CR_100Bestpages_digitalR.pdf (accessed January 21, 2018).

4-1a The Dimensions of Social Responsibility

Socially responsible organizations strive for **marketing citizenship** by adopting a strategic focus for fulfilling the economic, legal, ethical, and philanthropic social responsibilities that their stakeholders expect of them. Marketing citizenship is also defined as corporate social responsibility (CSR). Companies that consider the diverse perspectives of stakeholders in their daily operations and strategic planning are said to have a *stakeholder orientation*, an important element of social responsibility.[8] A stakeholder orientation in marketing goes beyond

marketing citizenship The adoption of a strategic focus for fulfilling the economic, legal, ethical, and philanthropic social responsibilities expected by stakeholders

| Figure 4.1 | The Pyramid of Corporate Social Responsibility |

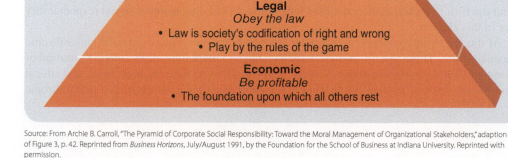

Source: From Archie B. Carroll, "The Pyramid of Corporate Social Responsibility: Toward the Moral Management of Organizational Stakeholders," adaption of Figure 3, p. 42. Reprinted from *Business Horizons*, July/August 1991, by the Foundation for the School of Business at Indiana University. Reprinted with permission.

customers, competitors, and regulators to include understanding and addressing the needs of all stakeholders, including communities and special-interest groups. As a result, organizations are now under pressure to undertake initiatives that demonstrate a balanced perspective on stakeholder interests.[9] Panera has many CSR programs exhibiting its marketing citizenship. One such program is Day-End Dough-Nation. At the end of each day, leftover items are shared with food banks, homeless shelters, and other charitable organizations to help those in need.[10] As Figure 4.1 shows, the economic, legal, ethical, and philanthropic dimensions of social responsibility can be viewed as a pyramid.[11]

At the most basic level, all companies have an economic responsibility to be profitable so that they can provide a return on investment to their owners and investors, create jobs for the community, and contribute goods and services to the economy. How organizations relate to stakeholders affects the economy. When economic downturns or poor decisions lead companies to lay off employees, communities often suffer as they attempt to absorb the displaced employees. Customers may experience diminished levels of service as a result of fewer experienced employees. Stock prices often decline when layoffs are announced, reducing the value of shareholders' investment portfolios. An organization's sense of economic responsibility is especially significant for employees, raising such issues as equal job opportunities, workplace diversity, job safety, health, and employee privacy. Economic responsibilities require finding a balance in stakeholder interests while recognizing that a firm must make a profit to be sustainable in the long run.

Marketers also have an economic responsibility to engage in fair competition and build ethical customer relationships. Government regulatory agencies often define the activities that constitute fair competition along with unethical issues such as price fixing, deceptive sales practices, false advertising, bribery, and questionable distribution practices. This misconduct can be considered unfair competition that is also damaging to consumers. Companies that engage in questionable conduct damage their reputation and can destroy customer trust. On the other hand, the "World's Most Ethical Companies"—a designation given by the Ethisphere Institute—have a track record of avoiding these types of issues. Starbucks, Aflac, Mastercard, Adobe, and Waste Management are profitable and have excellent reputations with their customers. Marketers are also expected, of course, to obey laws and regulations. Laws and regulations are designed to keep U.S. companies' actions within the range of acceptable conduct and fair competition. When customers, interest groups, or businesses become outraged over what they perceive as misconduct on the part of a marketing organization, they may urge their legislators to draft new legislation to regulate the behavior or engage in litigation to force the organization to "play by the rules."

Economic and legal responsibilities are the most basic aspects of social responsibility for a good reason: Failure to consider them may mean that a marketer does not operate long enough to engage in ethical or philanthropic activities. Beyond these dimensions lies **marketing ethics**, principles and standards that define acceptable conduct in marketing as determined by various stakeholders, including the public, government regulators, private-interest groups, consumers, industry, and the organization itself. The most basic of these principles have been codified as laws and regulations to encourage marketers to conform to society's expectations for conduct. However, marketing ethics goes beyond legal issues. Ethical marketing decisions foster trust, which helps build long-term marketing relationships. Trust is a key part of developing customer relationships. It has been found that transparency about how products are produced, as well as how a firm's philanthropic activities give back to the community, creates trust and intentions to purchase. This also creates positive word-of-mouth communication about the firm.[12] We take a more detailed look at the ethical dimension of social responsibility later in this chapter.

At the top of the pyramid of corporate responsibility (see Figure 4.1) are philanthropic responsibilities. These responsibilities, which go beyond marketing ethics, are not required of a company, but they promote human welfare or goodwill, as do the economic, legal, and ethical dimensions of social responsibility. That many companies have demonstrated philanthropic

marketing ethics Principles and standards that define acceptable marketing conduct as determined by various stakeholders

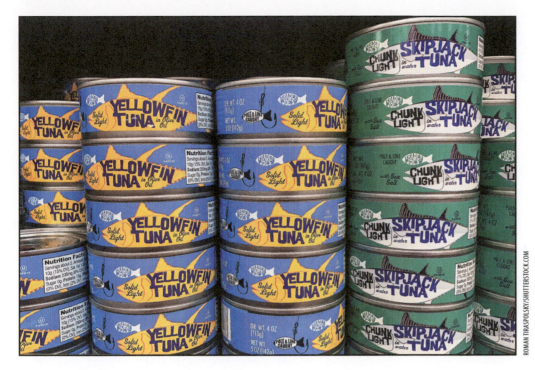

ROMAN TIRASPOLSKY/SHUTTERSTOCK.COM

The Nature of Social Responsibility
Trader Joe's maintains high quality and sustainability standards for its seafood. They have committed to offering a seafood selection that is exclusively from sustainable sources.

responsibility is evidenced by $18.5 billion in annual corporate donations and contributions to environmental and social causes.[13] For example, New Belgium Brewing partners with local nonprofits through its Grant Program with donations totaling more than $9 million to date. Grant Program initiatives include sustainable agriculture, youth environmental education, and water conservation and restoration. New Belgium Brewing has developed an ethical culture with respect for all stakeholders including the communities it serves.[14] Even small companies participate in philanthropy through donations and volunteer support of local causes and national charities, such as the Red Cross and the United Way.

More companies than ever are adopting a strategic approach to corporate philanthropy. Many firms link their products to a particular social cause on an ongoing or short-term basis, a practice known as **cause-related marketing**. Marketers like the programs because well-designed ones increase sales and create feelings of respect and admiration for the companies involved. The BMW Ultimate Drive program involves specially marked BMWs that drive across the United States to increase breast cancer awareness and raise funds for breast cancer research. BMW donates $1 to the Susan G. Komen Breast Cancer Foundation for every mile these cars are test-driven by participants.[15] Indeed, research suggests that 91 percent of Millennials (those born between the early 1980s and 2000) are willing to switch to a brand associated with a cause.[16]

On the other hand, some companies are beginning to extend the concept of corporate philanthropy beyond financial contributions by adopting a **strategic philanthropy** approach, the synergistic use of organizational core competencies and resources to address key stakeholders' interests and achieve both organizational and social benefits. Strategic philanthropy involves employees, organizational resources and expertise, and the ability to link those assets to the concerns of key stakeholders, including employees, customers, suppliers, and social needs. Strategic philanthropy involves both financial and nonfinancial contributions to stakeholders (employee time, goods and services, company technology and equipment, etc.), while also benefiting the company.[17] Warby Parker, an American brand of prescription eyewear, donates one pair of eyeglasses to the nonprofit VisionSpring for each pair that is sold. This socially responsible initiative is a core part of Warby Parker's mission and business model.[18]

cause-related marketing The practice of linking products to a particular social cause on an ongoing or short-term basis

strategic philanthropy The synergistic use of organizational core competencies and resources to address key stakeholders' interests and achieve both organizational and social benefits

ROMAN TIRASPOLSKY/SHUTTERSTOCK.COM

Cause-Related Marketing
JetBlue partnered with FirstBook to provide books to children in low-income households through its Soar with Reading program.

4-1b Social Responsibility Issues

Although social responsibility may seem to be an abstract ideal, managers make decisions related to social responsibility every day. To be successful, a business must determine what customers, government regulators, competitors, and society want or expect in terms of social responsibility. Table 4.2 summarizes three major categories of social responsibility issues: sustainability, consumerism, and community relations.

Sustainability

One of the more common ways marketers demonstrate social responsibility is through programs designed to protect and preserve the natural environment. **Sustainability** is the potential for the long-term well-being of the natural environment, including all biological entities, as

sustainability The potential for the long-term well-being of the natural environment, including all biological entities, as well as the interaction among nature and individuals, organizations, and business strategies

Table 4.2   Social Responsibility Issues

Issue	Description	Major Social Concerns
Sustainability	Consumers insisting not only on a good quality of life but also on a healthful environment so they can maintain a high standard of living during their lifetimes	Conservation Water pollution Air pollution Land pollution
Consumerism	Activities undertaken by independent individuals, groups, and organizations to protect their rights as consumers	The right to safety The right to be informed The right to choose The right to be heard
Community relations	Society eager to have marketers contribute to its well-being, wishing to know what marketers do to help solve social problems	Equality issues Disadvantaged members of society Safety and health Education and general welfare

well as the interaction among nature and individuals, organizations, and business strategies. Sustainability includes the assessment and improvement of business strategies, economic sectors, work practices, technologies, and lifestyles—all while maintaining the natural environment. Vegetarian food producer MorningStar Farms uses advertising to promote its veggie patties and a vegetarian lifestyle using the tagline, "Just What the World Ordered." The advertisement states that eating less meat and more vegetable-based protein is good for consumer health and the environment. Many companies are making contributions to sustainability by adopting more eco-friendly business practices and/or supporting environmental initiatives. Method has been largely successful in selling green cleaning supplies. Its success prompted other firms in the industry, such as SC Johnson, to begin their own green product lines. SC Johnson also has a Greenlist™ process by which it ranks the sustainability of ingredients it uses in its product formulas.[19] Such efforts generate positive publicity and often increase sales for the companies involved. The consumption of green products can be promoted by emphasizing the shared responsibility between the firm and consumers in protecting the environment.[20] For example, some retailers will assist consumers in recycling used electrical equipment.

Many products have been certified as "green" by environmental organizations such as Green Seal and carry a special logo identifying their organization as green marketers. Kimberly-Clark became the first consumer-products company to become certified by the Forest Stewardship Council (FSC). Its tissues carry the FSC label to indicate that they were harvested from sustainable forests using environmentally friendly methods.[21] In Europe, companies can voluntarily apply for the EU Ecolabel to indicate that their products are less harmful to the environment than competing products, based on scientifically determined criteria (see Figure 4.2). On the other hand, consumers are becoming very skeptical of greenwashing, which occurs when firms claim to protect the environment but fail to demonstrate their commitment.[22]

Although demand for economic, legal, and ethical solutions to environmental problems is widespread, the environmental movement in marketing includes many different groups whose values and goals often conflict. Some environmentalists and marketers believe companies should work to protect and preserve the natural environment by implementing the following goals:

1. *Eliminate the concept of waste.* Recognizing that pollution and waste usually stem from inefficiency, the question is not what to do with waste but how to make things without waste.

2. *Reinvent the concept of a product.* Products should be reduced to only three types and eventually just two. The first type is

SOURCE: MORNING STAR FARM

Green Marketing
MorningStar Farms promotes its 100 percent vegetarian Spicy Indian Veggie Patties while informing consumers that eating less meat is good for the environment.

| **Figure 4.2** | **The EU Ecolabel** |

© EU Ecolabel

consumables, which are eaten or, when placed in the ground, turn into soil with few harm-ful side effects. The second type is durable goods—such as cars, televisions, computers, and refrigerators—that should be made, used, and returned to the manufacturer within a closed-loop system. Such products should be designed for disassembly and recycling. The third category is unsalables and includes such products as radioactive materials, heavy metals, and toxins. These products should always belong to the original makers, who should be responsible for the products and their full life-cycle effects. Reclassify-ing products in this way encourages manufacturers to design products more efficiently.

3. *Make prices reflect the cost.* Every product should reflect or at least approximate its actual cost—not only the direct cost of production but also the cost of air, water, and soil. To illustrate, the cost of a gallon of gasoline is higher when pollution, waste disposal, health effects, and defense expenditures are factored in. There have been tax credits for electric cars to reflect their positive impact on the environment.

4. *Make environmentalism profitable.* Consumers are beginning to recognize that competition in the marketplace should not occur between companies that are harming the environment and those that are trying to save it.[23]

Consumerism

Another significant issue in socially responsible marketing is consumerism, which we defined in Chapter 3 as the efforts of independent individuals, groups, and organizations to protect the rights of consumers. A number of interest groups and individuals have taken action against companies they consider irresponsible by lobbying government officials and agencies, engag-ing in letter-writing campaigns and boycotts, and making public-service announcements. Some consumers choose to boycott firms and products out of a desire to support a cause and make a difference.[24] How a firm handles customer complaints affects consumer evaluations and, in turn, customer satisfaction and loyalty.[25]

The consumer movement has been helped by news-format television programs, such as *Dateline, 60 Minutes*, and *ABC World News Tonight*, as well as by 24-hour news coverage from CNN, MSNBC, and Fox News. The internet too has changed the way consumers obtain infor-mation about companies' goods, services, and activities. Consumers can share their opinions about goods and services and about companies they see as irresponsible at consumer-oriented websites, such as epinions.com and Angie's List, and through blogs and social networking sites.

Ralph Nader, one of the best-known consumer activists, continues to crusade for consumer rights. Consumer activism by Nader and others has resulted in legislation requiring many fea-tures that make cars safer: seat belts, air bags, padded dashboards, stronger door latches, head restraints, shatterproof windshields, and collapsible steering columns. Activists' efforts have also facilitated the passage of several consumer protection laws, including the Wholesome Meat Act of 1967, the Radiation Control for Health and Safety Act of 1968, the Clean Water Act of 1972, and the Toxic Substance Act of 1976.

Also of great importance to the consumer movement are four basic rights spelled out in a consumer "bill of rights" that was drafted by President John F. Kennedy. These rights include the right to safety, the right to be informed, the right to choose, and the right to be heard.

Ensuring consumers' *right to safety* means marketers are obligated not to market a product that they know could harm consumers. This right can be extended to imply that all products must be safe for their intended use, include thorough and explicit instructions for proper and safe use, and have been tested to ensure reliability and quality. Johnson & John-son suspended sales of a surgical tool known as a power morcellator used to remove uterine fibroids in women. Although a minimally invasive surgical procedure, studies indicate that in patients with undetected uterine cancer, the morcellators can spread the cancer. There was an investigation into how much Johnson & Johnson knew about potential hazards beforehand.[26]

ENTREPRENEURSHIP IN MARKETING

No Harm, No Foul: Harmless Harvest Connects with Stakeholders

In recent years, sociocultural preferences have changed to embrace healthier foods, leading to high demand for products such as coconut water. Today, the coconut water industry is a $2.2 billion market. However, with great demand comes high competition. Because they operate in a monopolistic competitive environment, players in the coconut water industry must differentiate their products. Coconut water company Harmless Harvest uses two characteristics to differentiate its products from competitors: taste and a socially responsible focus.

When Harmless Harvest founders Justin Guilbert and Douglas Riboud decided to start a company, they wanted the organization to create value not only for owners and customers, but also for every stakeholder in the supply chain—including the environment. After settling on a coconut variety from Thailand, the men used a proprietary multi filter process to maintain the fresh, nutty richness of the coconut in its product.

The company also became Fair for Life certified. This certification has higher criteria than fair trade products. Harmless Harvest must adhere to higher standards to protect workers on coconut farms, pay fair wages, and use best farming practices to preserve the environment. Harmless Harvest's great taste and socially responsible practices have resonated with consumers. Not only did its product become one of Whole Foods' top sellers, it was also nominated by CircleUp25 as one of the most innovative brands of the year.[a]

Continuing to use a tool or product that could cause unnecessary harm is a violation of the consumer's right to safety.

Consumers' *right to be informed* means consumers should have access to, and the opportunity to review, all relevant information about a product before buying it. Many laws require specific labeling on product packaging to satisfy this right. In addition, labels on alcoholic and tobacco products must inform consumers that these products may cause illness and other problems.

The *right to choose* means consumers should have access to a variety of products at competitive prices. They should also be assured of satisfactory quality and service at a fair price. Activities that reduce competition among businesses in an industry might jeopardize this right.

The *right to be heard* ensures that consumers' interests will receive full and sympathetic consideration in the formulation of government policy. The right to be heard also promises consumers fair treatment when they complain to marketers about products. For example, the Consumer Financial Protection Bureau provides the opportunity to submit a complaint and get answers to questions. This right benefits marketers, too, because when consumers complain about a product, the manufacturer can use this information to modify the product and make it more satisfying.

The Federal Trade Commission provides a wealth of consumer information at its website (www.consumer.ftc.gov/) on a variety of topics ranging from automobiles and the internet to diet, health, fitness, and identity theft.

Community Relations

Being a good community citizen also means avoiding harmful actions that could damage the community. Examples include pollution, urban sprawl, and exploitation of the workforce. A firm that participates in the economic viability of the community improves community relations. This supports local businesses and helps build good relationships with the community. Burlington Coat Factory has a program called Burlington Gives Back that donates

DIGITALREFLECTIONS/SHUTTERSTOCK.COM

Corporate Contributions

Tyson Foods makes a positive contribution to society through its Project A+ program. The Tyson Project A+ logo can often be found on the back of product bags such as Tyson Any'tizers Snacks and Tyson Fun Nuggets. Customers can clip the label and send them to Tyson to support a school of their choice. The schools are provided 24 cents for every label.

sample merchandise to local nonprofits and organizations in Burlington store communities nationwide.[27]

Although most charitable donations come from individuals, corporate philanthropy is on the rise. CenturyLink, for example, hosts a food drive every summer to help local food banks that see a spike in traffic as a result of kids no longer receiving school lunches. The company invites both employees and customers to participate in the annual Backpack Buddies Food Drive. CenturyLink provides a $1 million match to food banks and to date has contributed more than 50 million pounds of food and equivalent financial donations to community food banks.[28]

Smaller firms can also make positive contributions to their communities. Indie beauty brand Thrive Causemetics donates one item for every product purchased to women in need and hosts giving events with makeup artists at local hospitals and shelters through its Beauty with a Purpose program.[29] From a positive perspective, a marketer can significantly improve its community's quality of life through employment opportunities, economic development, and financial contributions to educational, health, cultural, and recreational causes.

Learning Objective 4-2

State the importance of marketing ethics.

4-2 MARKETING ETHICS

As noted earlier, marketing ethics is a dimension of social responsibility that involves principles and standards that define acceptable conduct in marketing. Acceptable standards of conduct in making individual and group decisions in marketing are determined by various stakeholders and by an organization's ethical climate. Marketers must also use their own values and knowledge of ethics to act responsibly and provide ethical leadership for others.

Marketers should be aware of stakeholders, including customers, employees, regulators, suppliers, and the community. When marketing activities deviate from accepted standards, the exchange process can break down, resulting in customer dissatisfaction, lack of trust, and lawsuits. In recent years, a number of ethical scandals have resulted in a massive loss of confidence in the integrity of U.S. businesses. About 48 percent of U.S. consumers trust businesses today.[30] Trust is an important concern for marketers because it is the foundation for long-term relationships. Consumer lack of trust has increased in recent years due to the financial crisis and deep recession. The questionable conduct of high-profile financial institutions and banks has caused many consumers to critically examine the conduct of all companies. Trust must be built or restored to gain the confidence of customers. Figure 4.3 describes the trust global consumers have for different institutions. Once trust is lost, it can take a lifetime to rebuild. The way to deal with ethical issues is proactively during the strategic planning process, not after major problems materialize.

Our focus here is on the ethical conduct of marketers. It is not our purpose to examine the conduct of consumers, although some do behave unethically (engaging, for instance, in coupon fraud, shoplifting, intellectual property piracy, and other abuses). We discuss consumer

Figure 4.3   **Global Trust in Different Industries**

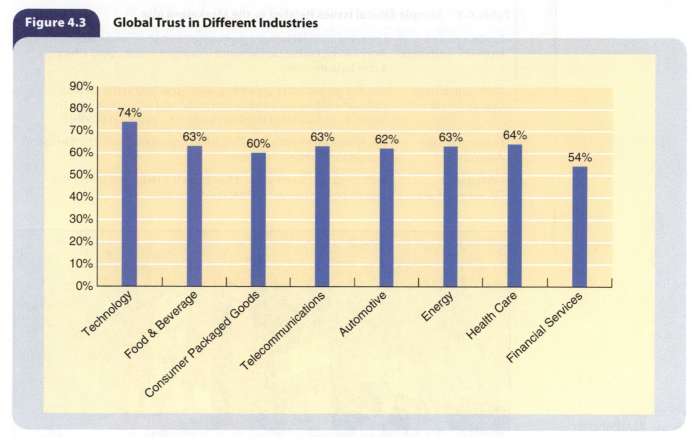

Source: Edelman, *2018 Edelman Trust Barometer Global Report,* http://cms.edelman.com/sites/default/files/2018-01/2018_Edelman_Trust_Barometer_Global_Report_Jan.PDF (accessed January 27, 2018).

misbehavior and ethical issues associated with this misconduct in Chapter 7. Our goal in this chapter is to underscore the importance of resolving ethical issues in marketing and to help you learn about marketing ethics.

4-2a **Ethical Issues in Marketing**

An **ethical issue** is an identifiable problem, situation, or opportunity that requires an individual or organization to choose from among several actions that must be evaluated as right or wrong, ethical or unethical. Any time an activity causes marketing managers or customers in their target market to feel manipulated or cheated, a marketing ethical issue exists, regardless of the legality of that activity. For instance, GT's Kombucha, a naturally fermented beverage, faced criticism for using misleading labels that claimed its fermented tea was nonalcoholic. Kombucha can contain trace amounts of alcohol, and alcohol levels have the potential to increase during its shelf life. The company was required to update its labels to include an alcohol warning.[31]

Regardless of the reasons behind specific ethical issues, marketers must be able to identify those issues and decide how to resolve them. Doing so requires familiarity with the many kinds of ethical issues that may arise in marketing. Research suggests that the greater the consequences associated with an issue, the more likely it will be recognized as an ethics issue and the more important it will be in making an ethical decision.[32] Some examples of ethical issues related to product, distribution, promotion, and price (the marketing mix) appear in Table 4.3.

Product-related ethical issues generally arise when marketers fail to disclose risks associated with a product or information regarding the function, value, or use of a product. Pressures can build to substitute inferior materials or product components to reduce costs. Ethical issues also arise when marketers fail to inform customers about existing conditions or changes in product quality; such failure is a form of dishonesty about the nature of the product. *Product recalls* occur when companies ask customers to return products found to be defective. Companies that issue product recalls are often criticized for not having adequate quality controls

ethical issue An identifiable problem, situation, or opportunity requiring a choice among several actions that must be evaluated as right or wrong, ethical or unethical

Table 4.3   Sample Ethical Issues Related to the Marketing Mix

Product Issue *Product information*	Covering up defects that could cause harm to a consumer; withholding critical performance information that could affect a purchase decision
Distribution Issue *Counterfeiting*	Counterfeit products are widespread, especially in the areas of computer software, clothing, and audio and video products. The internet has facilitated the distribution of counterfeit products.
Promotion Issue *Advertising*	Deceptive advertising or withholding important product information in a personal-selling situation
Pricing Issue *Deceptive Pricing*	Indicating that an advertised sale price is a reduction below the regular price when in fact that is not the case

LESTER BALAJADIA/SHUTTERSTOCK.COM

Ethical Issue

The use of antibiotics on animals used for food has become controversial because of the increase in drug-resistant bacteria. KFC, Burger King, Popeyes, Tim Hortons, and Tyson have all made announcements that they will no longer use meat treated with antibiotics in light of this growing concern.

to catch the defective product before it was released. For instance, Chipotle suffered a major reputational blow after an *E.coli* outbreak forced it to temporarily close 43 of its restaurants in the Seattle and Portland areas. The failure to maintain product quality and integrity in production is a significant ethical issue, and Chipotle continues to work hard to improve food safety and handling procedures to reassure consumers.[33]

Promotion can create ethical issues in a variety of ways, among them false or misleading advertising and manipulative or deceptive sales promotions, tactics, and publicity. One controversial issue in the area of promotion is *greenwashing*, which occurs when products are promoted as being more environmentally friendly than they really are. As green products gain in popularity, companies are increasingly selling products that they claim to be "green." However, there are no formal criteria for what constitutes a green product, so it is hard to determine whether a company's product is truly green. Another major ethical issue is promoting products that might be construed as harmful, such as violent video games or fatty foods, to children.

Many other ethical issues are linked to promotion, including the use of bribery in personal selling situations. *Bribery* occurs when an incentive (usually money or expensive gifts) is offered in exchange for an illicit advantage. Even a bribe that is offered to benefit the organization is usually considered unethical. Because it jeopardizes trust and fairness, it hurts the organization in the long run. For this reason, sales promotion activities such as games, contests, and other sales attempts must be communicated accurately and transparently.

In pricing, common ethical issues are price fixing, predatory pricing, and failure to disclose the full price of a purchase. The emotional and subjective nature of price creates many situations in which misunderstandings between the seller and buyer cause ethical problems. Marketers have the right to price their products to earn a reasonable profit, but ethical issues may crop up when a company seeks to earn high profits at the expense of its customers. Some pharmaceutical companies, for example, have been accused of *price gouging*, or pricing products at exorbitant levels, and taking advantage of customers who must purchase the medicine to survive or to maintain their quality of life. Various forms of *bait-and-switch* pricing schemes attempt to gain consumer interest with a low-priced product, but then switch the buyer to a more expensive product or add-on service. One way companies do this is by telling customers that the lower-priced product they wanted is unavailable. Another issue relates to quantity surcharges that occur when consumers are effectively overcharged for buying a larger package size of the same grocery product.[34]

Ethical issues in distribution involve relationships among producers and marketing intermediaries. Marketing intermediaries, or middlemen (wholesalers and retailers), facilitate the flow of products from the producer to the ultimate customer. Each intermediary performs a different role and agrees to certain rights, responsibilities, and rewards associated with that role. For example, producers expect wholesalers and retailers to honor agreements and keep them informed of inventory needs. Serious ethical issues with regard to distribution include manipulating a product's availability for purposes of exploitation and using coercion to force intermediaries to behave in a specific manner. Several companies have been accused of *channel stuffing*, which involves shipping surplus inventory to wholesalers and retailers at an excessive rate, typically before the end of a quarter. The practice may conceal declining demand for a product or inflate financial statement earnings, which misleads investors.[35] Another ethical issue that has become a worldwide problem is *counterfeiting*. Counterfeit products not only cost the firm, but they can also be dangerous to the consumer. For instance, while legitimate sellers of pharmaceuticals are using call centers to sell to consumers, a number of call centers have arisen that sell counterfeit drugs—particularly in the Philippines, which employs the greatest number of call center employees. These counterfeits could seriously jeopardize public safety.[36]

As this section has shown, the nature of marketing ethics involves the ethics of all marketing channel members. However, the member managing the product is often held accountable for ethical conduct throughout the total supply chain. Party City was placed near the bottom of the list that ranks compliance with conflict minerals laws. Party City reported that some of its balloons might have utilized tin from areas that are involved in serious conflicts and/or civil wars. Although this violates conflict minerals laws, Apple, General Electric, Microsoft, and Ford claim they also might have used tainted materials, demonstrating how difficult it is to trace all the materials used in a product throughout the supply chain.[37]

4-2b Ethical Dimensions of Managing Supply Chain Relationships

Managing supply chains responsibly is one of the greatest difficulties of marketing ethics and, therefore, needs some additional explanation. Supply chains require constant vigilance on the part of marketers as well as the need to anticipate unforeseen circumstances. Consider Costco, a well-known firm with a strong reputation. Lawsuits were filed against the firm alleging it had sold farmed prawns from Thailand that made use of slave labor. According to reports, there is concern that the food used to feed the prawns is caught at sea using unpaid labor. Costco claims that it does not tolerate human suffering, and, though the case was dismissed, the company said it will work with the Thai government to get to the bottom of the issue. The Thai government has since extended labor rights to workers on fishing vessels.[38]

The issues that Costco has faced highlight the numerous risks that occur in global supply chains. Although companies often create a Supplier Code of Conduct, this requires regular audits to ensure that factories are following compliance standards—which in turn can incur significant costs to companies in both time and finances. Countries with lax labor laws, such as China and Russia, require even more diligent monitoring. Often suppliers hire subcontractors to do some of the work, which increases a company's network of suppliers and the costs of trying to monitor all of them. Finally, company compliance requirements may conflict with the mission of the procurement office. Because it is the procurement division's job to procure resources at the lowest price possible, the division may very well opt to source from less expensive suppliers with questionable ethical practices rather than from more expensive ethical suppliers. British fashion brands ASOS and Marks & Spencer recently faced this problem when they were implicated in a child labor scandal.[39]

Managing supply chain ethical decision making is important because many stakeholders hold the firm responsible for all ethical conduct related to product availability. This requires the company to exercise oversight over all of the supplies used in producing a product. Developing good supply chain ethics is important because it ensures the integrity of the product and the firm's operations in serving customers. For instance, leading health-care supply company Novation has been recognized for its strong corporate governance and reporting mechanisms in its supply chain. To encourage its suppliers to report misconduct, the company has instituted a vendor grievance and feedback system. This allows vendors to report potential problems before they reach the next level of the supply chain, which reduces the damage such problems will cause if the products continue down the supply chain unchecked.[40]

Fortunately, organizations have been coming up with solutions to promote ethical sourcing practices. First, it is essential for all companies that work with global suppliers to adopt a Global Supplier Code of Conduct and ensure that it is effectively communicated to suppliers. Additionally, companies should encourage compliance and procurement employees to work together to find ethical suppliers at reasonable costs. Marketers must also work to make certain that their company's supply chains are diverse. This can be difficult because sometimes the best product manufacturers are located in a single country. Yet, although it is expensive to diversify a company's supply chain, disasters can incapacitate a country.[41] Finally, and perhaps most importantly, companies must perform regular audits on its suppliers and, if necessary, discipline those found to be in violation of company standards.[42] More on supply chain management will be discussed in Chapter 14.

Learning Objective 4-3

Describe the three factors of ethical decision making.

4-3 THE NATURE OF MARKETING ETHICS

To grasp the significance of ethics in marketing decision making, it is helpful to examine the factors that influence the ethical decision-making process. As Figure 4.4 shows, individual factors, organizational relationships, and opportunity interact to determine ethical decisions in marketing.

Figure 4.4   **Factors That Influence the Ethical Decision-Making Process**

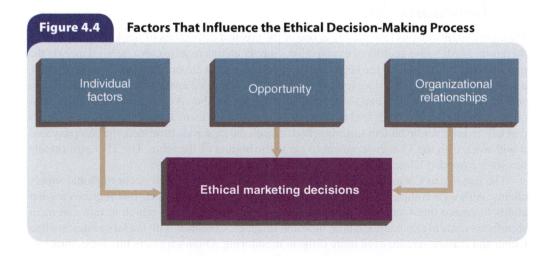

4-3a Individual Factors

When people need to resolve ethical conflicts in their daily lives, they often base their decisions on their own values and principles of right or wrong. People learn values and principles through socialization by family members, social groups, religion, and formal education. Because of different levels of personal ethics in any organization, there will be significant ethical diversity among employees. Most firms do not attempt to change an individual's personal ethics but try to hire employees with good character. Therefore, shared ethical values and compliance standards are required to prevent deviation from desired ethical conduct. In the workplace, however, research has established that an organization's culture often has more influence on marketing decisions than an individual's own values.[43]

4-3b Organizational Relationships

Although people can and do make ethical choices pertaining to marketing decisions, no one operates in a vacuum.[44] Ethical choices in marketing are most often made jointly, in work groups and committees, or in conversations and discussions with coworkers. Marketing employees resolve ethical issues based not only on what they learned from their own backgrounds but also on what they learn from others in the organization. The outcome of this learning process depends on the strength of each individual's personal values, opportunity for unethical behavior, and exposure to others who behave ethically or unethically. Superiors, peers, and subordinates in the organization influence the ethical decision-making process. While individuals may have good ethics, they often face new and complex decisions in the business environment. Although people outside the organization, such as family members and friends, also influence decision makers, organizational culture and structure operate through organizational relationships to influence ethical decisions.

Organizational (corporate) culture, is a set of values, beliefs, goals, norms, and rituals that members of an organization share. These values also help shape employees' satisfaction with their employer, which may affect the quality of the service they provide to customers. A firm's culture may be expressed formally through codes of conduct, memos, manuals, dress codes, and ceremonies, but it is also conveyed informally through work habits, extracurricular activities, and stories. An organization's culture gives its members meaning and suggests rules for how to behave and deal with problems within the organization.

organizational (corporate) culture A set of values, beliefs, goals, norms, and rituals that members of an organization share

With regard to organizational structure, most experts agree that the chief executive officer or vice president of marketing sets the ethical tone for the entire marketing organization. Lower-level managers obtain their cues from top managers, but they too impose some of their personal values on the company. Top-performing sales representatives may influence the conduct of other salespersons as they serve as role models for success. This interaction between corporate culture and executive leadership helps determine the firm's ethical value system.

Coworkers' influence on an individual's ethical choices depends on the person's exposure to unethical behavior. Especially in gray areas, the more a person is exposed to unethical activity by

How Do Employees Spend Time on Their Personal Mobile Devices at Work?

	According to Employees	According to Managers
Personal Email	30%	28%
Social Networks	28%	62%
Sports Sites	9%	1%
Mobile Games	6%	2%
Online Shopping Sites	5%	4%
Entertainment Sites	3%	1%

SNAPSHOT

Source: "Working Hard or Hardly Working? Employees Waste More Than One Day a Week on Non-Work Activities," Robert Half, July 19, 2017, http://rh-us.mediaroom.com/2017-07-19-WORKING-HARD-OR-HARDLY-WORKING-Employees-Waste-More-Than-One-Day-a-Week-on-Non-Work-Activities (accessed January 27, 2018).

others in the organizational environ-ment, the more likely he or she is to behave unethically. Most marketing employees take their cues from coworkers in learning how to solve problems, including ethical problems.[45] The most recent Global Business Ethics Survey (GBES) found that 30 percent of employees in the United States observe some form of misconduct. About 24 percent choose not to report the misconduct.[46] Table 4.4 describes observed ethical conduct in the United States. Moreover, research suggests that marketing employees who perceive their work environment as ethical experience less role conflict and ambiguity, are more satisfied with their jobs, and are more committed to their employer.[47]

Table 4.4   Observed Misconduct in the U.S. Workforce

Misconduct Facts	Percentages
Observed misconduct	30%
Abusive behavior	22%
Lying to stakeholders	22%
Conflict of interest	19%
Pressure to compromise standards	22%
Report observed misconduct	76%
Experience retaliation for reporting	53%

Source: Ethics and Compliance Initiative, *2016 Global Business Ethics Survey™: Measuring Risk and Promoting Workplace Integrity* (Arlington, VA: Ethics and Compliance Initiative, 2016), p. 43.

Organizational pressure plays a key role in creating ethical issues. For example, because of pressure to meet a schedule, a superior may ask a salesperson to lie to a customer over the phone about a late product shipment. Similarly, pressure to meet a sales quota may result in overly aggressive sales tactics. Research in this area indicates that superiors and coworkers can generate organizational pressure, which plays a key role in creating ethical issues. Additionally, bullying, when a person or group is targeted and threatened, harassed, belittled, verbally abused, or overly criticized, may create a hostile environment. As Table 4.5 indicates, bullying can use a mix of verbal, nonverbal, and manipulative threatening expressions to damage workplace productivity. Nearly all marketers face difficult issues whose solutions are not obvious or that present conflicts between organizational objectives and personal ethics.

4-3c Opportunity

Another factor that may shape ethical decisions in marketing is opportunity—that is, conditions that limit barriers or provide rewards. A marketing employee who takes advantage of an opportunity to act unethically and is rewarded or suffers no penalty may repeat such acts as other opportunities arise. For instance, a salesperson who receives a raise after using a

Table 4.5   Actions Associated with Bullies

1.	Spreading rumors to damage others
2.	Blocking others' communication in the workplace
3.	Flaunting status or authority to take advantage of others
4.	Discrediting others' ideas and opinions
5.	Using email to demean others
6.	Failing to communicate or return communication
7.	Insults, yelling, and shouting
8.	Using terminology to discriminate by gender, race, or age
9.	Using eye or body language to hurt others or their reputation
10.	Taking credit for others' work or ideas

Source: O. C. Ferrell, 2017

INTEGRITY IN MARKETING

A Real Pain: McKesson Corporation

Opioids and other addicting drugs are often over-prescribed by health professionals and abused by patients. Social responsibility requires oversight to address the opioid crisis. McKesson Corporation, a legitimate drug wholesaler to hospitals and pharmacies, is the nation's largest distributor of opioids and has a long history of ignoring the Drug Enforcement Agency (DEA) regulations regarding opioid distribution practices. In 2008, the government sued the company for these violations. After settling the charges and paying a fine of $13.3 million they continued opioid shipments with little monitoring.

McKesson attempted to divert DEA scrutiny by overstating the size of the markets to which they were selling. As a result, many small towns received an exorbitant number of pain killers. In 2017, McKesson was fined $150 million for failing to comply with its prior narcotic distribution agreements. McKesson hired many former DEA investigators and attorneys from the government to work for them, which compromised the litigation. In addition, McKesson has spent more than a billion dollars annually with lobbying groups to influence government policy that supports the pharmaceutical industry.

As part of a new Department of Justice settlement, McKesson agreed to suspend sales of controlled substances for several years to its distribution centers in Colorado, Florida, Michigan, and Ohio. It also agreed to have periodic audits by an independent monitor that would track and report on its compliance. As opioid deaths climb, McKesson's opioid sales continue to increase. In the past decade, McKesson's CEO, John Hammergren, received compensation exceeding $692 million, making him one of the highest paid executives in the country.

McKesson is not the only corporate villain contributing to the opioid epidemic. Recently, in a united law enforcement effort, 41 state attorneys general, as a group, filed subpoenas on Endo International plc, Janssen Pharmaceuticals, Teva Pharmaceuticals, Allergan, and Purdue Pharma.

McKesson's contribution to the opioid crisis demonstrates the importance of incorporating social responsibility and ethics into strategic marketing planning and highlights the potential negative impact marketing decisions can have on society.[b]

deceptive sales presentation to increase sales is being rewarded and thus will probably continue the behavior. Indeed, opportunity to engage in unethical conduct is often a better predictor of unethical activities than are personal values.[48] Beyond rewards and the absence of punishment, other elements in the business environment may create opportunities. Professional codes of conduct and ethics-related corporate policy also influence opportunity by prescribing what behaviors are acceptable. The larger the rewards and the milder the punishment for unethical conduct, the greater is the likelihood that unethical behavior will occur.

However, just as the majority of people who go into retail stores do not try to shoplift at each opportunity, most marketing managers do not try to take advantage of every opportunity for unethical behavior in their organizations. Although marketing managers often perceive many opportunities to engage in unethical conduct in their companies and industries, research suggests that most refrain from taking advantage of such opportunities. Moreover, most marketing managers do not believe that unethical conduct in general results in success.[49] Individual factors as well as organizational culture may influence whether an individual becomes opportunistic and tries to take advantage of situations unethically.

4-4 IMPROVING MARKETING ETHICS

Learning Objective 4-4

Comment on the requirements for improving ethical decision making.

It is possible to improve ethical conduct in an organization by hiring ethical employees and eliminating unethical ones, and by improving the organization's ethical standards. One way to approach improvement of an organization's ethical standards is to use a "bad apple–bad barrel" analogy. Some people always do things in their own self-interest, regardless of organizational goals or accepted moral standards; they are sometimes called "bad apples." To eliminate unethical conduct, an organization must rid itself of bad apples through screening techniques and enforcement of the firm's ethical standards. However, organizations sometimes become "bad barrels" themselves, not because the individuals within them are unethical but because the pressures to survive and succeed create conditions (opportunities) that reward unethical behavior. One way to resolve the problem of the bad barrel is to redesign the organization's image and culture so that it conforms to industry and societal norms of ethical conduct.[50]

Without ethics and compliance programs and uniform standards and policies regarding conduct, it is hard for employees to determine what conduct is acceptable within the company. In the absence of such programs and standards, employees will generally make decisions based on their observations of how coworkers and superiors behave. To improve ethics, many organizations have developed **codes of conduct** (also called *codes of ethics*) that consist of formalized rules and standards that describe what the company expects of its employees. Most large corporations have formal codes of conduct, but codes are not effective if they are implemented improperly. Codes must be periodically revised to identify and eliminate weaknesses in the company's ethical standards and policies. Most codes address specific ethical risk areas in marketing. For instance, Pfizer's code of conduct has a bribery policy that prohibits both the bribing of foreign officials as well as commercial bribery. In its more detailed policy, Pfizer also prohibits facilitation payments, or small payments paid out to expedite an activity, and any type of gift or service of nominal value.[51] Codes of conduct promote ethical behavior by reducing opportunities for unethical behavior; employees know both what is expected of them and what kind of punishment they face if they violate the rules. Codes help marketers deal with ethical issues or dilemmas that develop in daily operations by prescribing or limiting specific activities.

Codes of conduct do not have to be so detailed that they take every situation into account, but they should provide guidelines that enable employees to achieve organizational objectives in an ethical manner. The American Marketing Association Code of Ethics, reprinted in Table 4.6, does not cover every possible ethical issue, but it provides a useful overview of what marketers believe are sound principles for guiding marketing activities. This code serves as a helpful model for structuring an organization's code of conduct.

codes of conduct Formalized rules and standards that describe what the company expects of its employees

Table 4.6   **Code of Ethics of the American Marketing Association**

Ethical Norms and Values for Marketers
PREAMBLE
The American Marketing Association commits itself to promoting the highest standard of professional ethical norms and values for its members (practitioners, academics, and students). Norms are established standards of conduct that are expected and maintained by society and/or professional organizations. Values represent the collective conception of what communities find desirable, important and morally proper. Values also serve as the criteria for evaluating our own personal actions and the actions of others. As marketers, we recognize that we not only serve our organizations but also act as stewards of society in creating, facilitating and executing the transactions that are part of the greater economy. In this role, marketers are expected to embrace the highest professional ethical norms and the ethical values implied by our responsibility toward multiple stakeholders (e.g., customers, employees, investors, peers, channel members, regulators, and the host community).
ETHICAL NORMS
As Marketers, we must:
1. **Do no harm.** This means consciously avoiding harmful actions or omissions by embodying high ethical standards and adhering to all applicable laws and regulations in the choices we make.
2. **Foster trust in the marketing system.** This means striving for good faith and fair dealing so as to contribute toward the efficacy of the exchange process as well as avoiding deception in product design, pricing, communication, and delivery of distribution.
3. **Embrace ethical values.** This means building relationships and enhancing consumer confidence in the integrity of marketing by affirming these core values: honesty, responsibility, fairness, respect, transparency, and citizenship.

Ethical Values

Honesty—to be forthright in dealings with customers and stakeholders. To this end, we will:

- Strive to be truthful in all situations and at all times.

- Offer products of value that do what we claim in our communications.

- Stand behind our products if they fail to deliver their claimed benefits.

- Honor our explicit and implicit commitments and promises.

Responsibility—to accept the consequences of our marketing decisions and strategies. To this end, we will:

- Strive to serve the needs of customers.

- Avoid using coercion with all stakeholders.

- Acknowledge the social obligations to stakeholders that come with increased marketing and economic power.

- Recognize our special commitments to vulnerable market segments such as children, seniors, the economically impoverished, market illiterates and others who may be substantially disadvantaged.

- Consider environmental stewardship in our decision making.

Fairness—to balance justly the needs of the buyer with the interests of the seller. To this end, we will:

- Represent products in a clear way in selling, advertising, and other forms of communication; this includes the avoidance of false, misleading, and deceptive promotion.

- Reject manipulations and sales tactics that harm customer trust.
  Refuse to engage in price fixing, predatory pricing, price gouging, or "bait-and-switch" tactics.

- Avoid knowing participation in conflicts of interest.
  Seek to protect the private information of customers, employees, and partners.

Respect—to acknowledge the basic human dignity of all stakeholders. To this end, we will:

- Value individual differences and avoid stereotyping customers or depicting demographic groups (e.g., gender, race, sexual orientation) in a negative or dehumanizing way.

- Listen to the needs of customers and make all reasonable efforts to monitor and improve their satisfaction on an ongoing basis.

- Make every effort to understand and respectfully treat buyers, suppliers, intermediaries, and distributors from all cultures.

- Acknowledge the contributions of others, such as consultants, employees, and coworkers, to marketing endeavors.

- Treat everyone, including our competitors, as we would wish to be treated.

Transparency—to create a spirit of openness in marketing operations. To this end, we will:

- Strive to communicate clearly with all constituencies.

- Accept constructive criticism from customers and other stakeholders.

- Explain and take appropriate action regarding significant product or service risks, component substitutions or other foreseeable eventualities that could affect customers or their perception of the purchase decision.

- Disclose list prices and terms of financing as well as available price deals and adjustments.

Citizenship—to fulfill the economic, legal, philanthropic, and societal responsibilities that serve stakeholders. To this end, we will:

- Strive to protect the ecological environment in the execution of marketing campaigns.

- Give back to the community through volunteerism and charitable donations.
  Contribute to the overall betterment of marketing and its reputation.

- Urge supply chain members to ensure that trade is fair for all participants, including producers in developing countries.

(continued)

Table 4.6   (continued)

Implementation
We expect AMA members to be courageous and proactive in leading and/or aiding their organizations in the fulfillment of the explicit and implicit promises made to those stakeholders. We recognize that every industry sector and marketing sub-discipline (e.g., marketing research, e-commerce, internet selling, direct marketing, and advertising) has its own specific ethical issues that require policies and commentary. An array of such codes can be accessed through links on the AMA Web site. Consistent with the principle of subsidiarity (solving issues at the level where the expertise resides), we encourage all such groups to develop and/or refine their industry and discipline-specific codes of ethics to supplement these guiding ethical norms and values.

Source: Copyright © 2016 by the American Marketing Association, https://archive.ama.org/archive/AboutAMA/Pages/Statement%20of%20Ethics.aspx (accessed January 27, 2018).

If top management develops and enforces ethical and legal compliance programs to encourage ethical decision making, this becomes a force to help individuals make better decisions. A company's ethical culture is the greatest determinant of future misconduct. Thus, a well-implemented ethics program and a strong corporate culture result in the greatest decrease in ethical risks for an organization. Companies that wish to improve their ethics, then, should implement a strong ethics and compliance program and encourage organizationwide commitment to an ethical culture.[52] Ethics programs that include written standards of conduct, ethics training, and hotlines increase the likelihood that employees will report misconduct observed in the workplace. When top managers talk about the importance of ethics and model ethical behavior themselves, employees observe significantly fewer instances of unethical conduct. When marketers understand the policies and requirements for ethical conduct, they can more easily resolve ethical conflicts. However, marketers can never fully abdicate their personal ethical responsibility in making decisions. Claiming to be an agent of the business ("the company told me to do it") is unacceptable as a legal excuse and is even less defensible from an ethical perspective.[53] It is also unacceptable for managers to punish those who do report ethical misconduct, although retaliation is still fairly prevalent. From a global perspective, the GBES study shows that approximately one-third of whistle-blowers experience some type of retaliation.[54] Figure 4.5 shows the rate of retaliation whistle-blowers face in different countries.

Figure 4.5   Retaliation against Whistle-Blowers

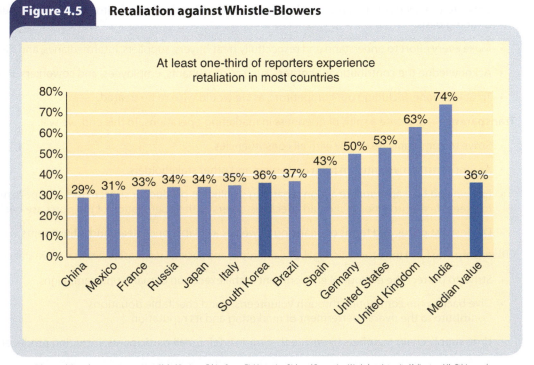

Source: Ethics and Compliance Initiative, *2016 Global Business Ethics Survey™: Measuring Risk and Promoting Workplace Integrity* (Arlington, VA: Ethics and Compliance Initiative, 2016), p. 18.

4-5 INCORPORATING SOCIAL RESPONSIBILITY AND ETHICS INTO STRATEGIC PLANNING

Although the concepts of marketing ethics and social responsibility are often used interchangeably, it is important to distinguish between them. *Ethics* relates to individual and group decisions—judgments about what is right or wrong in a particular decision-making situation—whereas *social responsibility* deals with the total effect of marketing decisions on society. The two concepts are interrelated because a company that supports socially responsible decisions and adheres to a code of conduct is likely to have a positive effect on society. Because ethics and social responsibility programs can be profitable as well, an increasing number of companies are incorporating them into their overall strategic market planning. When company strategies are implemented, they must align with the organization's core beliefs and values.

As we have emphasized throughout this chapter, ethics is one dimension of social responsibility. Being socially responsible relates to doing what is economically sound, legal, ethical, and socially conscious. One way to evaluate whether a specific activity is ethical and socially responsible is to ask other members of the organization if they approve of it. Contact with concerned consumer groups and industry or government regulatory groups may be helpful. A check to see whether there is a specific company policy about an activity may help resolve ethical questions. If other organizational members approve of the activity and it is legal and customary within the industry, chances are that the activity is acceptable from both an ethical and a social responsibility perspective.

A rule of thumb for resolving ethical and social responsibility issues is that if an issue can withstand open discussion that results in agreement or limited debate, an acceptable solution

Social Responsibility and Strategic Planning
IKEA employs a Chief Sustainability Officer and incorporates social responsibility into its strategies. IKEA built socially responsible principles into its original business model.

Ethical Treatment of Stakeholders
Natural American Spirit advertises its cigarettes as "natural" and "additive-free." The company must also inform consumers that these products are not safer than other cigarettes and may cause illness and other problems.

may exist. Nevertheless, even after a final decision is reached, different viewpoints on the issue may remain. Openness is not the end-all solution to the ethics problem. However, it creates trust and facilitates learning relationships.[55]

Many of society's demands impose costs. For example, society wants a cleaner environment and the preservation of wildlife and their habitats, but it also wants low-priced products. Consider the plight of the gas station owner who asked his custom-ers if they would be willing to spend an additional 1 cent per gallon if he instituted an air filtration system to eliminate harmful fumes. The majority indicated they supported his plan. However, when the system was installed and the price increased, many customers switched to a lower-cost competitor across the street. Thus, companies must carefully balance the costs of providing low-priced products against the costs of manufacturing, packaging, and distributing their products in an environmentally responsible manner.

In trying to satisfy the desires of one group, marketers may dissatisfy others. Regarding the smoking debate, for instance, marketers must balance nonsmokers' desire for a smoke-free environment against smokers' desires, or needs, to continue to smoke. In the advertisement, Natural American Spirit emphasizes that its cigarettes are 100 percent additive-free, made from U.S.-grown, natural tobacco. The company, however, must still disclose that organic tobacco and additive-free tobacco does not mean a safer cigarette. Some anti-tobacco crusaders call for the complete elimination of tobacco products to ensure a smoke-free world. However, this attitude fails to consider the difficulty smokers have in quitting (now that tobacco marketers have admitted their product is addictive)

and the impact on U.S. communities and states that depend on tobacco crops for their economic survival. Thus, this issue, like most ethical and social responsibility issues, cannot be viewed in black and white. Although some people believe that electronic cigarettes are a responsible alternative to smoking, e-cigarettes remain controversial due to continued health concerns.

Balancing society's demands to satisfy all members of society is difficult, if not impossible. Marketers must evaluate the extent to which members of society are willing to pay for what they want. For instance, customers may want more information about a product but be unwilling to pay the costs the firm incurs in providing the data. Marketers who want to make socially responsible decisions may find the task a challenge because, ultimately, they must ensure their economic survival.

4-5a Social Responsibility and Ethics Improve Marketing Performance

The challenges of ethical conduct are an important part of marketing success. Increasing evidence indicates that being socially responsible and ethical results in increased profits. Research suggests that a relationship exists between a stakeholder orientation and an organizational climate that supports marketing ethics and social responsibility. Marketing is often the most visible interaction that consumers have with a firm. Also, stakeholders observe marketing activities such as promotion and learn about their activities through the mass media. Anytime there is a product recall or potential unethical act, reputational damage can occur. On the other hand, firms that are highly ethical and build trust with customers are usually not headline stories in the mass media.

The evidence is strong that a broad stakeholder view of the firm can help improve marketing practices that contribute to improved financial, social, and ethical performance.[56] This relationship implies that being ethically and socially concerned is consistent with meeting the demands of customers and other stakeholders. By encouraging employees to understand their markets, companies can help them respond to stakeholders' demands.[57] A stakeholder orientation helps to broaden and redefine marketing beyond a market orientation that focuses on customers and competitors by considering primary stakeholders such as employees, suppliers, regulators, shareholders, customers, and the community. Marketers need to analyze stakeholder relationships to maximize value for specific target markets.

This creates a need to prioritize stakeholders, deal with conflicting demands, and respond with a marketing strategy to provide balance. For instance, global engineering company CH2M incorporates values and stakeholder needs into all facets of its operations. In fact, the company has been named one of the "World's Most Ethical Companies" by Ethisphere Institute for nine years running. CH2M's business practices benefit both clients and employees as well as the environment and the economy. The company implemented sustainable management practices at hundreds of municipal water facilities; improved environmental, health, and safety performance at project sites; and contributed more than $1 million to support STEM education.[58] By incorporating ethics into its marketing strategy, CH2M has balanced the needs of its

ROMAN TIRASPOLSKY/SHUTTERSTOCK.COM

Social Responsibility Improves Marketing
Seventh Generation has developed its entire reputation around its socially responsible and environmentally friendly products made from plant-based ingredients.

stakeholders and developed a solid reputation of trust. All of these actions should be grounded in social responsibility and marketing ethics. The results should be positive relationships with customers and increased financial performance.[59]

A direct association exists between corporate social responsibility and customer satisfaction, profits, and market value.[60] In a survey of consumers, 89 percent indicated that when quality and price are similar among competitors, they would be more likely to buy from the company associated with a good cause. In addition, 79 percent of consumers look for products that are socially or environmentally responsible. Consumers want to align themselves with companies that share their values, and 73 percent of consumers say they would boycott a company if it had a different stance on social justice issues.[61]

Thus, recognition is growing that the long-term value of conducting business in an ethical and socially responsible manner far outweighs short-term costs.[62] Companies that fail to develop strategies and programs to incorporate ethics and social responsibility into their organizational culture may pay the price with poor marketing performance and the potential costs of legal violations, civil litigation, and damaging publicity when questionable activities are made public. Because marketing ethics and social responsibility are not always viewed as organizational performance issues, many managers do not believe they need to consider them in the strategic planning process. Individuals also have different ideas as to what is ethical or unethical, leading them to confuse the need for workplace ethics and the right to maintain their own personal values and ethics. Although the concepts are undoubtedly controversial, it is possible—and desirable—to incorporate ethics and social responsibility into the planning process.

Summary

4-1 Define the four dimensions of social responsibility.

Social responsibility refers to an organization's obligation to maximize its positive impact and minimize its negative impact on society. It deals with the total effect of all marketing decisions on society. Although social responsibility is a positive concept, most organizations embrace it in the expectation of indirect long-term benefits. Marketing citizenship involves adopting a strategic focus for fulfilling the economic, legal, ethical, and philanthropic social responsibilities expected of organizations by their stakeholders, those constituents who have a stake, or claim, in some aspect of the company's products, operations, markets, industry, and outcomes.

At the most basic level, companies have an economic responsibility to be profitable so that they can provide a return on investment to their stockholders, create jobs for the community, and contribute goods and services to the economy. Marketers are also expected to obey laws and regulations. Marketing ethics refers to principles and standards that define acceptable conduct in marketing as determined by various stakeholders, including the public, government regulators, private-interest groups, industry, and the organization itself. Philanthropic responsibilities go beyond marketing ethics; they are not required of a company, but they promote human welfare or goodwill. Many firms use cause-related marketing, the practice of linking products to a social cause on an ongoing or short-term basis. Strategic philanthropy is the synergistic use of organizational core competencies and resources to address key stakeholders' interests and achieve both organizational and social benefits.

Three major categories of issues that fit into the four dimensions of social responsibility are sustainability, consumerism, and community relations. One of the more common ways marketers demonstrate social responsibility is through programs designed to protect and preserve the natural environment. Sustainability is the potential for the long-term well-being of the natural environment, including all biological entities, as well as the interaction among nature and individuals, organizations, and business strategies. Consumerism consists of the efforts of independent individuals, groups, and organizations to protect the rights of consumers. Consumers expect to have the right to safety, the right to be informed, the right to choose, and the right to be heard. Many marketers view social responsibility as including contributions of resources (money, products, and time) to community causes such as the natural environment, arts and recreation, disadvantaged members of the community, and education.

4-2 State the importance of marketing ethics.

Whereas social responsibility is achieved by balancing the interests of all stakeholders in the organization, ethics relates to acceptable standards of conduct in making individual and group decisions. Marketing ethics goes beyond legal issues. Ethical marketing decisions foster mutual trust in marketing relationships.

An ethical issue is an identifiable problem, situation, or opportunity requiring an individual or organization to choose from among several actions that must be evaluated as right or wrong, ethical or unethical. A number of ethical issues relate to the marketing mix (product, distribution, promotion, and price).

4-3 Describe the three factors of ethical decision making.

Individual factors, organizational relationships, and opportunity interact to determine ethical decisions in marketing. Individuals often base their decisions on their own values and principles of right or wrong. However, ethical choices in marketing are most often made jointly, in work groups and committees, or in conversations and discussions with coworkers. Organizational culture and structure operate through organizational relationships (with superiors, peers, and subordinates) to influence ethical decisions. Organizational, or corporate, culture is a set of values, beliefs, goals, norms, and rituals that members of an organization share. The more a person is exposed to unethical activity by others in the organizational environment, the more likely he or she is to behave unethically. Organizational pressure plays a key role in creating ethical issues, as do opportunity and conditions that limit barriers or provide rewards.

4-4 Comment on the requirements for improving ethical decision making.

It is possible to improve ethical behavior in an organization by hiring ethical employees and eliminating unethical ones, and by improving the organization's ethical standards. If top management develops and enforces ethics and legal compliance programs to encourage ethical decision making, it becomes a force to help individuals make better decisions. To improve company ethics, many organizations have developed codes of conduct—formalized rules and standards that describe what the company expects of its employees. To nurture ethical conduct in marketing, open communication is essential. Firms should also periodically monitor and audit their operations, including their supply chains, to ensure the integrity of the product and the firm's activities. Companies must consistently enforce standards and impose penalties or punishment on those who violate codes of conduct.

4-5 Critique the role of social responsibility and ethics in improving marketing performance.

An increasing number of companies are incorporating ethics and social responsibility programs into their overall strategic marketing planning. To promote socially responsible and ethical behavior while achieving organizational goals, marketers must monitor changes and trends in society's values. They must determine what society wants and attempt to predict the long-term effects of their decisions. Costs are associated with many of society's demands, and balancing those demands to satisfy all of society is difficult. However, increasing evidence indicates that being socially responsible and ethical results in valuable benefits: an enhanced public reputation (which can increase market share), cost savings, and greater profits.

Important Terms

social responsibility 92
marketing citizenship 93
marketing ethics 94

cause-related marketing 95
strategic philanthropy 95
sustainability 96

ethical issue 101
organizational (corporate)
culture 105

codes of conduct 108

Discussion and Review Questions

1. What is social responsibility? Why is it important?
2. What are stakeholders? What role do they play in strategic marketing decisions?
3. What are four dimensions of social responsibility? What impact do they have on marketing decisions?
4. What is strategic philanthropy? How does it differ from more traditional philanthropic efforts?
5. What are some major social responsibility issues? Give an example of each.
6. What is the difference between ethics and social responsibility?

7. Why is ethics an important consideration in marketing decisions?
8. How do the factors that influence ethical or unethical decisions interact?
9. What ethical conflicts may exist if business employees fly on certain airlines just to receive benefits for their personal frequent-flyer programs?
10. Give an example of how ethical issues can affect each component of the marketing mix.

11. How can the ethical decisions involved in marketing be improved?
12. How can people with different personal values work together to make ethical decisions in organizations?
13. What trade-offs might a company have to make to be socially responsible and responsive to society's demands?
14. What evidence exists that being socially responsible and ethical is worthwhile?

Developing Your Marketing Plan

Because social responsibility and ethics often have significant impacts on the success of marketing strategies, companies must consider the impact of their marketing plan. A marketing strategy is dynamic. Companies must continually monitor the marketing environment not only to create their marketing strategy, but also to revise it if necessary. The following questions will help you to understand how the information in this chapter contributes to the development of your marketing plan:

1. What values, beliefs, goals, norms, and rituals are central to your marketing plan?

2. Referring to Table 4.2, do you recognize any sustainability issues that would have an impact on your type of product?
3. How do you plan to incorporate socially responsible activities to generate positive publicity and boost product sales?
4. Discuss how you would promote socially responsible and ethical behavior while achieving organizational goals related to your product.

Video Case 4.1

Cruising to Success: The Tale of New Belgium Brewing

In 1991 electrical engineer Jeff Lebesch and Kim Jordan began making Belgian-style ales in their basement. The impetus for the brewery occurred after Lebesch had spent time in Belgium riding throughout the country on his mountain bike. He believed he could manufacture high-quality Belgian beers in America. After spending time in the Colorado Rockies deciding the values and direction of their new company, the two launched New Belgium Brewing (NBB), with Kim Jordan as marketing director. The company's first beer was named Fat Tire in honor of Lebesch's Belgian mountain biking trek. Fat Tire remains one of NBB's most popular ales.

NBB has come far from its humble basement origins. Today, the Fort Collins–based brewery is the fourth-largest craft brewer in the country with products available in all 50 states, as well as Canada, Sweden, Norway, South Korea, Japan, and Australia. Kim Jordan was one of the few female CEOs of a large beer firm before she stepped down from the role in 2015. "This entrepreneurial thing sneaks up on you," Jordan states. "And even after 20 years, I still have those pinch me moments where I think, wow, this is what we've created here together." While total beer sales remain flat, craft beer sales are growing. Today craft

beers constitute 12.3 percent of the total beer market in the United States.

Creating such success required a corporate culture that stressed creativity and an authentic approach to treating all stakeholders with respect. While the New Belgium product is a quality craft beer, just as important to the company is how it treats employees, the community, and the environment. Each variable of the marketing mix was carefully considered. The company spends a significant amount of time researching and creating its beers, even collaborating with other craft brewers to co-create new products. This collaboration has led to products such as the New England IPA and Bière de Garde. NBB's culture is focused on making a quality product and satisfying customers. It has even ventured into organic beer with its creation of Mothership Wit Organic Wheat Beer. The company has several product line varieties, including its more popular beers Fat Tire, 1554, Dayblazer, Voodoo Ranger IPA, Pilsener, and Citradelic; seasonal beers such as Voodoo Ranger Atomic Pumpkin and Accumulation; and its Lips of Faith line, a series of experimental beers including La Folie, Transatlantique Kriek, and Le Terroir.

The distribution element of the product mix was complex at the outset. In her initial role as marketing director, Jordan needed to convince distributors to carry their products. Often, new companies must work hard to convince distributors to carry their brands because distributors are fearful of alienating more established rivals. However, Jordan tirelessly got NBB beer onto store shelves, even delivering beer in her Toyota station wagon. As a craft brewer, NBB uses a premium pricing strategy. Its products are priced higher than domestic brands such as Coors or Budweiser and have higher profit margins. The popularity of NBB beers has prompted rivals to develop competitive products such as MillerCoors' Blue Moon Belgian White.

Perhaps the most notable dimension of NBB's marketing mix is promotion. From the beginning, the company based its brand on its core values, including practicing environmental stewardship and forming a participative environment in which all employees can exert their creativity. "For me, brand is absolutely everything we are. It's the people here. It's how we interact with one another. And then there's the other piece of that creativity, obviously, which is designing beers," Kim Jordan said. NBB promotion has attempted to portray the company's creativity and its harmony with the natural environment. For instance, one NBB video features a tinkerer repairing a bicycle and riding down the road, while another features NBB "rangers" singing a hip-hop number to promote the company's Ranger IPA (now known as the Voodoo Ranger IPA). The company has also heavily promoted its brand through Facebook and Twitter. This "indie" charm has served to position NBB as a company committed to having fun and being socially responsible.

NBB also markets itself as a company committed to sustainability. Sustainability has been a core value at NBB from day one. The company was the first fully wind-powered brewery in the United States. NBB recycles cardboard boxes, keg caps, office materials, and amber glass. The brewery stores spent barley and hop grains in an on-premise silo and invites local farmers to pick up the grains, free of charge, to feed their pigs. The company also provides employees with a cruiser bicycle after one year of employment so they can bike to work instead of drive.

NBB's popularity allowed it to open up a second brewery in Asheville, North Carolina. This new brewery helps NBB expand throughout the Eastern United States. Amidst the changes, it was announced that the CEO position would be turned over to Steve Fechheimer, former chief strategy officer at Beam Suntory, a liquor company. Kim Jordan assumed the role of Executive Chair of the company's Board of Directors so she can continue to impact NBB on a strategic level and work with the New Belgium Family Foundation. The combination of a unique brand image, strong marketing mix, and an orientation that considers all stakeholders has turned NBB into a multimillion-dollar success, and Kim Jordan wants this success to inspire other firms to adopt progressive and socially responsible business practices.[63]

Questions for Discussion

1. How has New Belgium's focus on employees, community, and the environment impacted the company?
2. What has Kim Jordan done to create success at New Belgium?
3. How does New Belgium's focus on sustainability as a core value contribute to its corporate culture and success?

Case 4.2

Sseko Helps Women Get a Step Ahead

Liz Forkin Bohannon, Founder and CEO of Sseko Designs, a socially minded fashion and design company from Portland, Oregon, uses the company as a platform to empower women in Uganda and East Africa. In 2008, after traveling to Kampala, the capital city of Uganda, she was appalled to see the extreme poverty of the people, especially that of its women. She discovered that the top 2 percent of high school girls who were eligible to go to a university were required to return to their villages and work for nine months while saving money for tuition. Most of these girls did not continue their education because the families needed the money for their subsistence. She also learned that these women preferred to work rather than receive a handout.

Her first attempt at a socially conscious for-profit business was a short-lived chicken farm. It was then that Liz recalled an incident from her college days. She wanted to avoid the noise made by flip-flops, so she redesigned them by purchasing rubber flip-flop bottoms and tying them with ribbon, making a quieter sandal. Liz believed she could improve upon her original design using materials obtained locally. For two weeks she traveled through Kampala looking for suppliers while gaining skills in sandal making through tutorial videos on YouTube. She developed a business idea for a work-study model for Ugandan women who showed college potential. Liz would offer women employment during the nine-month period they had to earn enough revenues for college; the women would make sandals and other products that could be sold to consumers in the United States, thus learning new skills while they earned their tuition.

When she returned to the United States, she married Ben Bohannon, who left his job to help her run Sseko and become a co-founder. Of course, making the sandals was only half the battle. The Bohannons also had to find buyers. Together the couple traveled the nation for six months in their Honda Odyssey minivan—often sleeping in the van and showering at truck stops to save money—to try and convince stores to purchase sandals from Sseko Designs. In 2009, the sandals, the first product offered by Sseko Designs, became an immediate success when Martha Stewart recommended them in her gift ideas, and their inventory was soon depleted.

To continue the company's growth, Liz and Ben sought funding via the popular ABC reality show *Shark Tank*. Entrepreneurs Mark Cuban, Barbara Corcoran, Kevin O'Leary, Lori Grainer, and Robert Herjavec were offered a 10 percent stake in Sseko for a $300,000 investment. Sseko had suffered a $90,000 loss in 2014 and anticipated it would lose money in 2015 as well. The Bohannons explained that the reason for the loss is that they were putting more money into development and hiring more salespeople. They expressed their belief that as more Americans learned about Sseko, its unique products, and its social mission, sales would increase, and the firm would recoup its losses. The sharks maintained that was too high a value, especially for a company that, in their judgment, was too focused on its social mission and philanthropy and not enough on profitability. The Bohannons countered that many of today's retailers and their customers value companies with a social mission. This, they maintained, is especially the case with Millennials, their target customers. They noted that younger consumers are less concerned about brand names and more interested in the story behind the brand. They believe that many customers prefer buying from firms that share their values and that if a company supports a cause the consumer

cares about, then the company's brand will be viewed more favorably.

While the sharks declined the opportunity to invest in Sseko, its exposure on the show resulted in a 500-fold increase in traffic on its website and a 1,000 percent increase in sales in one month. In addition, other investors came forward, and they received the entire investment that they initially wanted from *Shark Tank* without having to decrease their estimation of the value of their company. Sseko Designs has already had a major impact on Uganda. Not only is it the largest footwear manufacturer—resulting in more jobs for Uganda as well as for the Ethiopian and Kenyan artisans who create crafted products for Sseko to sell—it also serves to empower women. Currently, Sseko employs 65 women in Uganda and is the country's largest footwear manufacturer. Its product offerings have expanded to include apparel, footwear, jewelry, accessories, and leather bags.

Today, the company supports the education of women by providing scholarships for their employees. Each employee is encouraged to save 50 percent of their salary which goes into their personal Sseko savings accounts for nine months, after which the account receives a 200 percent match from the company. Additional funding for these scholarships comes from the Sseko Fellows program. This program began a few years ago and has 300 Fellows. Sseko Fellows are U.S. social entrepreneurs who sell the company's products direct. Every Sseko Fellow is matched with a Sole Sister in Uganda; every dollar of Sseko product sold in the United States by one of these fellows provides income for the fellow and generates funding that helps contribute to sending a Sole Sister to the university. To date, 87 female employees have been able to get a university education, thanks to Sseko Designs.[64]

Questions for Discussion

1. Discuss Sseko's social entrepreneurship model and how it differs from traditional charitable initiatives that other companies might take.
2. Do you believe the Bohannons are too focused on their social mission? Should they compromise on their values in favor of profit?
3. Are there ethical risks associated with the implementation of Sseko's strategy?

Strategic Case 2

Not So Well: The Case of Wells Fargo

Wells Fargo, one of the largest banks in the United States, is in hot water. The Consumer Financial Protection Bureau fined the bank $185 million after it opened 2.1 million unauthorized client accounts and services that lowered

customer's credit scores. About 5,300 employees were fired for falsely opening accounts and forging client signatures. Wells Fargo reached a $110 million settlement to resolve a civil class action complaint. The bank issued a statement that "this agreement is another step in our journey to make things right with consumers and rebuild trust."

A Culture for Fraud

Organizational pressure plays a key role in creating ethical issues. After the discovery, it soon became clear that misconduct at Wells Fargo went way beyond fraudulent bank accounts. Subsequent investigations paint a picture of a toxic corporate culture where fraudulent activities were encouraged to meet sales goals. A letter addressed to former CEO John Stumpf from 2007 was discovered describing how employees were opening fake bank accounts and forging signatures to meet the bank's aggressive sales quotas. Those who did not meet quotas were fired.

Evidence also suggests managers approved of these activities. When misconduct was identified, the bank's solution was often to terminate employees without investigating into the root cause. An investigation by a special board committee, which included 100 interviews from current and former employees, attributed the scandal to a "sales-oriented culture or a decentralized corporate structure." The review also placed blame on the former head of the community bank unit, Carrie Tolstedt. It became evident that sales goals were too high, and retail scorecards, instituted by Tolstedt, and sales promotions added significant pressure. Employees felt the goals could only be reached by cheating.

Without ethics and compliance programs and uniform standards and policies regarding conduct, it is hard for employees to determine what conduct is acceptable within the company. An investigation by the Securities and Exchange Commission (SEC) revealed that Wells Fargo failed to report on suspicious activities related to money laundering. The Surveillance and Investigations group, which had previously been applauded for its diligence in reporting such incidences, received different directives under new management. They were instructed to only record facts and final decisions in the bank's internal case management system. Wells Fargo paid a penalty of $3.5 million.

With regard to organizational structure, chief executive officers often set the ethical tone for the entire marketing organization. Although the former CEO claims he never saw early emails describing the fraud, numerous employees claim they became whistle-blowers, sending letters to the board's audit committee and calling the ethics hotline about the fraud. The result? They were fired.

Whistle-Blower Retaliation

Many employees are concerned about retribution when making a decision to report potential misconduct externally. Wells Fargo conducted an investigation of terminated employees who had made calls to the ethics hotlines with concerns over sales practices at the company. Its initial internal investigation showed that there was "cause for concern" and admitted there was evidence of retaliation. Corporate retaliation against whistle-blowers is illegal, but only 2 percent of whistle-blower cases favor the employee. Yet, one whistle-blower has already won a lawsuit against Wells Fargo, suggesting more may follow. The former employee won $5.4 million to cover back pay, compensatory damages, and legal feels. This is the largest individual award ordered to date under the Occupational Safety and Health Administration's (OSHA) whistle-blower protection program. OSHA also ordered the bank to rehire the employee. More employees began to tell of horrific stories of bullying, being disciplined, or retaliated against, for complaining about being, or refusing to be, forced to make quotas by signing up customers for new accounts without their consent which led to more public attention. As a result, Stumpf publically stated his shock at the management practices and immediately fired more than 5,300 employees.

Stumpf resigned as CEO and was replaced by Timothy Sloan. Under Sloan, Wells Fargo reviewed calls made to its ethics line over the past five years in which callers identified themselves more than 40 percent of the time. A third party also investigated cases where employees were terminated within 12 months of making a call to the ethics line. Sloan confirmed a few cases "raised questions."

Consumer Trust

Many consumers and companies lost trust in Wells Fargo. Once trust is lost, it can take a long time to rebuild. The scandal was so widespread that nearly a year after the initial fallout, more than 1 million additional possible fraudulent accounts were discovered bringing the number of potentially unauthorized accounts to 3.5 million. In addition to these

SUNDRY PHOTOGRAPHY/SHUTTERSTOCK.COM

accounts, it was uncovered that more than 500,000 accounts were also enrolled in the bank's online bill pay. The service previously charged fees to certain accounts, and the bank has stated it will refund $910,000 to customers who were charged. It will take many years for consumers to regain confidence in Wells Fargo.

The Road to Recovery

In an effort to recover financially, Wells Fargo has replaced many members of its board, refocused on internal controls and risk management policies, and reoriented its branch employees to focus on customer service. When Stumpf resigned, he took with him $133.1 million as part of his payment package, the majority of which came from about 2.4 million shares in the company he earned over his tenure. To regain some of what Wells Fargo had lost, the company's independent directors initiated "clawbacks" to recover money that had already been disbursed totaling more than $69 million. The bank also closed about 1,000 branches to cut costs while it continues to incur legal expenses which total more than $3.1 billion.

The company eliminated lofty sales goals so employees no longer feel intense pressure to sell products. The company introduced a new compensation structure that centers around customer service and customer satisfaction to realign employee incentives. Oversight and accountability are core components of the new plan. The result: new customer checking account openings dropped by 41 percent over the next year, and credit card applications dropped by 45 percent.

The depth of company involvement in the scandal is so great that regulators may hold the bank's board of directors accountable. It will be important for the bank to establish an ethics program that includes written standards of conduct, ethics training, and truly confidential hotlines. This will help establish an ethical culture, improve the likelihood that employees will report observed misconduct, and decrease chances for retaliation. Wells Fargo has a long road ahead in trying to reestablish trust with consumers, regulators, and—perhaps most of all—employees.[65]

Questions for Discussion

1. Evaluate how Wells Fargo treated its primary stakeholders.
2. How can a division, like sales, operate with such a different "ethical subculture"?
3. How can Wells Fargo, going forward, prevent unethical subcultures from damaging its brand and reputation?

5 Marketing Research and Information Systems

6 Target Markets: Segmentation and Evaluation

PART 3 examines how marketers use information and technology to better understand and reach customers.

CHAPTER 5 provides a foundation for analyzing buyers through a discussion of marketing information systems and the basic steps in the marketing research process. Understanding elements that affect buying decisions enables marketers to better analyze customers' needs and to evaluate how specific marketing strategies can satisfy those needs.

CHAPTER 6 deals with selecting and analyzing target markets, which is one of the major steps in marketing strategy development.

CHAPTER

5

Marketing Research and Information Systems

LEARNING OBJECTIVES

5-1 Define marketing research and its importance to decision makers.

5-2 Distinguish between exploratory and conclusive research.

5-3 Name the five basic steps in conducting marketing research, including the two types of data and four survey methods.

5-4 Describe the tools, such as databases, big data, marketing analytics, and decision support systems, useful to marketing decision making.

5-5 Identify ethical and international issues in marketing research.

SHEILA FITZGERALD/SHUTTERSTOCK.COM

Food for Thought: General Mills Embraces Marketing Research

General Mills has adopted a "consumer first" brand strategy that requires the consumer foods manufacturer to make costly investments to keep up with consumers' rapidly changing values. The company has turned to marketing research in order to learn more about its customers and how its products satisfy their needs.

Marketing research often focuses on identifying and defining market opportunities or changes in the environment. For example, marketing research indicates an increase in consumer snacking due to increasingly busy lifestyles, highlighting a big opportunity for General Mills. The company is using this trend as well as the growing demand for wholesome snacks to guide its product development strategy. General Mills understands the importance of marketing research to meet the needs of its customers. General Mills' Betty Crocker team members attempted to feed their families for under $100 per week to gain insight on budgeting and decision making for its low-income customers.

General Mills wants its customer-centric focus to differentiate it from rival firms. According to recent studies, 20 percent of U.S. consumers say they are "very" or "extremely" concerned about genetically modified food. In keeping with this customer emphasis, General Mills has agreed to adopt GMO labeling for some of its products. While General Mills believes GMO products are safe, it wants customers to know that it is listening to their concerns. In fact, General Mills became a first mover in this endeavor by reformulating its Cheerios to be GMO-free. As competitors also turn toward organic and natural ingredients, General Mills continues to monitor marketing research and adapt is products accordingly to maintain its competitive position.[1]

Marketing research enables marketers to implement the marketing concept by helping them acquire information about whether and how their goods and services satisfy the desires of target market customers. When used effectively, such information facilitates relationship marketing by helping marketers focus their efforts on meeting and even anticipating the needs of their customers. Marketing research and information systems that can provide practical and objective information to help firms develop and implement marketing strategies are, therefore, essential to effective marketing.

In this chapter, we focus on how marketers gather information needed to make marketing decisions. First, we define marketing research and examine the individual steps of the marketing research process, including various methods of collecting data. Next, we look at how technology aids in collecting, organizing, and interpreting marketing research data. In addition, we explore how big data and marketing analytics are used in marketing research today. Finally, ethical and international issues in marketing research are considered.

Learning Objective 5-1

Define marketing research and its importance to decision makers.

5-1 THE IMPORTANCE OF MARKETING RESEARCH

Marketing research is the systematic design, collection, interpretation, and reporting of information to help marketers solve specific marketing problems or take advantage of marketing opportunities. As the word *research* implies, it is a process for gathering information that is not currently available to decision makers. The purpose of marketing research is to inform an organization about customers' needs and desires, marketing opportunities for products, and changing attitudes and purchase patterns of customers. Market information increases the marketer's ability to respond to customer needs, which leads to improved organizational performance. Detecting shifts in buyers' behaviors and attitudes helps companies stay in touch with the ever-changing marketplace. Some retail stores, for instance, are redesigning their selling floors to keep customers in the store longer. Studies have shown that slower shoppers tend to buy more, and offering amenities such as lounges are one way retailers can differentiate the shopping experience from purchasing items online.[2] Strategic planning requires marketing research to facilitate the process of assessing such opportunities or threats from competitors.

Marketing research can help a firm better understand market opportunities, ascertain the potential for success for new products, and determine the feasibility of a particular marketing strategy. It can also reveal some surprising trends. For example, the average television viewership for NASCAR has declined more than 45 percent since 2006 when it attracted close to 20 million viewers. In addition, the audience is becoming older. This finding could indicate the need for additional research to determine approaches to increase viewership.[3] Failing to conduct research can prevent companies from maintaining a competitive advantage.

Many types of organizations use marketing research to help them develop marketing mixes to match the needs of customers. Supermarkets have learned from marketing research that roughly half of all Americans prefer to have their dinners ready in 15 to 30 minutes. Such information highlights a tremendous opportunity for supermarkets to offer high-quality "heat-and-eat" meals to satisfy this growing segment of the food market. Political candidates also depend on marketing research to understand the scope of issues their constituents view as important. National political candidates may spend millions surveying voters to better understand their views and then craft their images accordingly.

Changes in the economy have dramatically changed marketers' decision-making strategies. Increasingly, businesses need speed and agility to survive and to react quickly to changing consumer behaviors. Understanding the market is crucial for effective marketing strategies. Evidence shows that automakers use information about consumer vehicle preferences to determine what features are important in the development of new vehicles. Marketing research has shifted its focus toward smaller studies like test marketing, small-scale surveys,

marketing research The systematic design, collection, interpretation, and reporting of information to help marketers solve specific marketing problems or take advantage of marketing opportunities and short-range forecasting in order to learn about changing dynamics in the marketplace. However, large, high-value research projects remain necessary for long-term success. Though it is acceptable to conduct studies that take six months or more, many companies need real-time information to help them make good decisions. Firms may benefit from historical or secondary data, but due to changes in the economy and buyer behavior, such data are not as useful in today's decision-making environment. As we discuss in this chapter, the use of big data and marketing analytics are helping to integrate findings in order to help companies make tactical and strategic decisions. In the future, the marketing researcher will need to be able to identify the most efficient and effective ways of gathering information.[4]

The real value of marketing research is measured by improvements in a marketer's ability to make decisions. IKEA, for instance, is testing products for their suitability for small, cramped homes. In order to test the products, the company refurbished a small apartment and invited several families to stay there. The families were provided with iPads so they could write down their impressions of what it was like to live there. IKEA hopes to use this information to expand into a wider market for furniture.[5] Marketers should treat information the same way they treat other resources; they must weigh the costs and benefits of obtaining information. Information should be considered worthwhile if it results in marketing activities that better satisfy the firm's target customers, leads to increased sales and profits, or helps the firm achieve some other goal. Take a look at the advertisement for MorningStar Farms' Spicy Black Bean burger. MorningStar Farms used insights gleaned from marketing research to determine that this product is the top-selling veggie burger in the United States. The advertisement uses this information to encourage product trial among new users, using the phrase, "grill it to believe it." MorningStar Farms relies on market research and insights from Nielsen, a global information and data company. This type of marketing research can be crucial in developing and adapting marketing strategies to connect with customers.

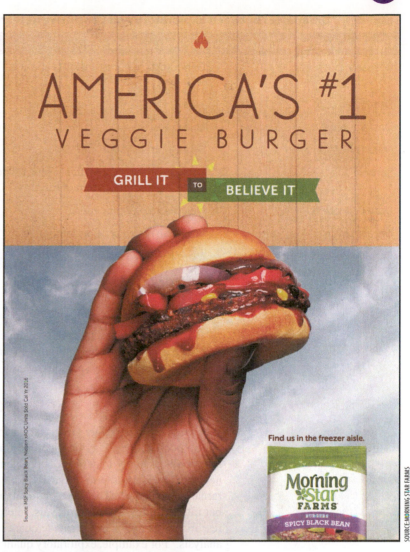

Importance of Marketing Research
MorningStar Farms used data from marketing research to determine that its Spicy Black Bean burgers are America's top-selling veggie burger.

SOURCE: MORNING STAR FARMS

5-2 TYPES OF RESEARCH

Learning Objective 5-2

Distinguish between exploratory and conclusive research.

The nature and type of research vary based on the research design and the hypotheses under investigation. Marketing research can involve two forms of data. *Qualitative data* yields descriptive non-numerical information. *Quantitative data* yields empirical information that can be communicated through numbers. Marketers may choose to collect either, depending upon the research required.

Table 5.1   **Differences between Exploratory and Conclusive Research**

Research Project Components	Exploratory Research	Conclusive Research
Research purpose	General: to generate insights about a situation	Specific: to verify insights and aid in selecting a course of action
Data needs	Vague	Clear
Data sources	Ill-defined	Well-defined
Data collection form	Open-ended, rough	Usually structured
Sample	Relatively small; subjectively selected to maximize generalization of insights	Relatively large; objectively selected to permit generalization of findings
Data collection	Flexible; no set procedure	Rigid; well-laid-out procedure
Data analysis	Informal; typically nonquantitative	Formal; typically quantitative
Inferences/ recommendations	More tentative than final	More final than tentative

To collect this data, marketers conduct either exploratory research or conclusive research. Although each has a distinct purpose, the major differences between them are formalization and flexibility rather than the specific research methods used. Table 5.1 summarizes the differences.

5-2a   Exploratory Research

When marketers need more information about a problem or want to make a tentative hypothesis more specific, they may conduct **exploratory research**. The main purpose of exploratory research is to better understand a problem or situation and/or to help identify additional data needs or decision alternatives.[6] Exploratory research is usually associated with qualitative research techniques. The focus of qualitative research is not metrics and complex data analysis but rather stories, visual portrayals, interpretations, and expressive descriptions. Exploratory research does not usually provide quantitative data that assigns numeric values for statistical analysis.[7] For example, exploratory qualitative research could include online participant observation or even netnography, which is involvement in social networks to understand brand perceptions. For instance, a researcher may get involved in an online PlayStation community to better understand the brand and consumer interests. This type of exploratory research helps marketers better understand consumers and opens up the opportunity for additional research hypotheses about options for retail pricing.

Some organizations utilize **customer advisory boards**, which are small groups of actual customers who serve as sounding boards for new product ideas and offer insights into their feelings and attitudes toward a firm's products, promotion, pricing, and other elements of marketing strategy. These advisory boards provide qualitative exploratory information. Though these advisory boards help companies maintain strong relationships with valuable customers, they can also provide great insight into marketing research questions. Oracle maintains customer advisory boards that allow customers to use the products, engage in collaborative sessions with Oracle executives and product experts, and offer feedback.[8]

One common method for conducting exploratory research is through a focus group. A **focus group** brings together multiple people to discuss a certain topic in a group setting led by a moderator. For example, CVS maintains a mock-up store where it not only tests new products but also conducts focus groups with consumers.[9] Focus groups are often conducted informally, without a structured questionnaire. Using focus groups is a common technique associated with qualitative research. They allow customer attitudes, behaviors, lifestyles, needs, and desires to be explored in a flexible and creative manner. Questions are open-ended and stimulate respondents to answer in their own words. A traditional focus group session consists

exploratory research Research conducted to gather more information about a problem or to make a tentative hypothesis more specific

customer advisory boards Small groups of actual customers who serve as sounding boards for new product ideas and offer insights into their feelings and attitudes toward a firm's products and other elements of its marketing strategy

focus group A small group of 8 to 12 people who are brought together to participate in an interview that is often conducted informally, without a structured questionnaire, to observe interaction when members are exposed to an idea or a concept

of approximately eight to 12 individuals and is led by a moderator, an independent individual hired by the research firm or the company. The moderator encourages group discussion among all of the participants and can direct the discussion by occasionally asking questions.

Focus groups can provide companies with ideas for new products or be used for initial testing of different marketing strategies for existing products. Illustrative of this, Ford may use focus groups to determine whether to change its advertising to emphasize a vehicle's safety features rather than its style and performance. The less-structured format of focus groups, where participants can interact with one another and build on each other's comments, is beneficial to marketers because it can yield more detailed information to researchers, including information that they might not have necessarily thought to ask participants about beforehand.

Focus Groups
Focus groups consist of multiple people discussing a certain topic in a group setting. Usually, focus groups are led by a moderator who encourages group discussion.

A current trend for researchers is online focus groups. In this method, participants sign in to a website and type their comments and responses there. Online focus groups can gather data from large and geographically diverse groups in a less intensive manner than focus-group interviews. Online focus groups are also more convenient for the participants than traditional focus groups. However, this method makes it more difficult to ask participants about a product's smell or taste, if that is relevant to the product being tested. Researchers also cannot observe the participants' nonverbal cues and body language in this setting, which can often reveal "gut" reactions to questions asked or topics discussed.

Focus groups do have a few disadvantages for marketers. Sometimes, the focus group's discussion can be hindered by overly talkative, confrontational, or shy individuals. Some participants may be less than honest in an effort to be sociable or to receive money and/or food in exchange for their participation.[10] For these reasons, focus groups provide only qualitative, not quantitative, data and are thus best used to uncover issues that can then be explored using quantifiable marketing research techniques.

Other forms of exploratory qualitative research include observation, conversation, and depth interviews that can last over an hour. Depth interviews provide more insight into an individual's perceptions than focus groups.[11] While these exploratory research techniques provide qualitative information, conclusive research provides quantitative in-depth analysis of problems and opportunities.

5-2b **Conclusive Research**

Conclusive research is designed to verify insights through an objective procedure to help marketers make decisions. It is helpful in reaching conclusions and provides quantitative information. It is used when the marketer has one or more alternatives in mind and needs assistance in the final stages of decision making. Consider exploratory research that has revealed that the terms *clearance* and *sale* send different signals to consumers. To make a decision about how to use this information, marketers would benefit from a well-defined and structured research project that will help them decide which approach is best for a specific set of products and target consumers. Conclusive research studies are typically formal, specific, and have verifiable methods. Two such types of conclusive research are descriptive research and experimental research.

If marketers need to understand the characteristics of certain phenomena to solve a particular problem, **descriptive research** can aid them. Descriptive studies may range from general surveys of customers' education, occupations, or ages to specifics on how often teenagers

conclusive research Research designed to verify insights through objective procedures and to help marketers in making decisions

descriptive research Research conducted to clarify the characteristics of certain phenomena to solve a particular problem

consume sports drinks or how often customers buy new pairs of athletic shoes. For example, if Nike and Reebok want to target more young women, they might ask 15- to 35-year-old females how often they work out, how frequently they wear athletic shoes for casual use, and how many pairs of athletic shoes they buy in a year. Such descriptive research can be used to develop specific marketing strategies for the athletic-shoe market. Descriptive studies generally demand much prior knowledge and assume that the problem or issue is clearly defined. Some descriptive studies require statistical analysis and predictive tools. The marketer's major task is to choose adequate methods for collecting and measuring data.

Descriptive research is limited in providing evidence necessary to make causal inferences (i.e., that variable X causes a variable Y). **Experimental research** allows marketers to make these causal deductions about relationships between variables. The experiment controls one variable and randomizes one or more other variables. Such experimentation requires that an independent variable (one not influenced by or dependent on other variables) be manipulated and the resulting changes in a dependent variable (one contingent on, or restricted to, one value or set of values assumed by the independent variable) be measured. For instance, McDonald's has been testing a number of new menu items in its restaurants as part of a turnaround strategy, including sales of energy drinks, breakfast at all hours, and chef-crafted sandwiches.[12] To truly determine whether these products are successful, McDonald's will have to hold other variables such as promotion constant. Manipulation of the causal variable and control of other variables are what make experimental research unique. As a result, they can provide much stronger evidence of cause and effect than data collected through descriptive research.

5-3 THE MARKETING RESEARCH PROCESS

We will examine a generalized approach to the research process that should be adapted to a specific project. Marketing research should be customized to use methods that provide the best information for the marketing decision. Analytical approaches provide flexible and insightful information.[13]

To maintain the control needed to obtain accurate information, marketers approach marketing research as a process with logical steps: (1) locating and defining problems or issues, (2) designing the research project, (3) collecting data, (4) interpreting research findings, and (5) reporting research findings (see Figure 5.1). These steps should be viewed as an overall approach to conducting research rather than as a rigid set of rules to be followed in each project. In planning research projects, marketers must consider each step carefully and determine how they can best adapt the steps to resolve the particular issues at hand.

5-3a Locating and Defining Problems or Research Issues

The first step in launching a research study is problem or issue definition, which focuses on uncovering the nature and boundaries of a situation or question related to marketing strategy or implementation. The first sign of a problem is typically a departure from some normal function, such as the failure to attain objectives. If a corporation's objective is a 12 percent sales increase and the current marketing strategy resulted in a 6 percent increase, this discrepancy should

experimental research
Research that allows marketers to make causal inferences about relationships between variables

Figure 5.1   **The Five Steps of the Marketing Research Process**

be analyzed to help guide future marketing strategies. A decrease in sales is a symptom of the problem, not the problem itself. Declining sales, increasing expenses, and decreasing profits all signal problems that could merit research. Customer relationship management (CRM) is frequently based on analysis of existing customers. Armed with the results of this analysis, a firm could define a problem as (1) finding a way to adjust for the biases uncovered when gathering data from existing customers or (2) developing methods for gathering information to help find new customers. Conversely, when an organization experiences a dramatic rise in sales or some other positive event, it may conduct marketing research to discover the reasons and maximize the opportunities stemming from them. Often, the discrepancy relates to marketing-related issues.

Marketing research often focuses on identifying and defining market opportunities or changes in the environment. When a firm discovers a market opportunity, it may need to conduct research to understand the situation more precisely so it can craft an appropriate marketing strategy. For example, UPS may want to know if it can deliver packages using a drone. This may require a survey of existing customers.

To pin down the specific boundaries of a problem or an issue through research, marketers must define the nature and scope of the situation in a way that requires probing beneath the superficial symptoms. The interaction between the marketing manager and the marketing researcher should yield a clear definition of the research needed. Researchers and decision makers should remain in the problem or issue definition stage until they have determined precisely what information they want from marketing research and how they will use it. Deciding how to refine a broad, indefinite problem or issue into a precise, researchable statement is a prerequisite for the next step in the research process.

5-3b Designing the Research Project

Once the problem or issue has been defined, the next step is to create a **research design**, an overall plan for obtaining the information needed to address it. This step requires formulating a hypothesis and determining what type of research is most appropriate for testing the hypothesis to ensure the results are reliable and valid. The project should not be limited to a small set of research approaches or methods. Marketers should recognize that a large diversity of approaches is available and should be customized to address the most important research questions.[14]

Developing a Hypothesis

The objective statement of a marketing research project should include a hypothesis based on both previous research and expected research findings. A **hypothesis** is an informed guess or assumption about a certain problem or set of circumstances. It is based on all the insight and knowledge available about the problem or circumstances from previous research studies and other sources. So, because data suggest that salsa sales have surpassed ketchup sales in the United States, a food marketer at H. J. Heinz Company might develop a hypothesis that consumers perceive salsa to be a healthier alternative. As information is gathered, the researcher can test the hypothesis. For example, a marketer at a cosmetics company might propose the hypothesis that the fragrance of its scented beauty products will influence in-store purchase patterns. A marketing researcher would then gather data, perhaps through testing scents in the store and seeing whether sales change. The researcher would then analyze the data and draw conclusions as to whether the hypothesis is correct. Sometimes, several hypotheses are developed over the course of a research project. The hypotheses that are accepted or rejected become the study's conclusions.

Research Reliability and Validity

In designing research, marketing researchers must ensure that research techniques are both reliable and valid. A research technique has **reliability** if it produces almost identical results in repeated trials. However, a reliable technique is not necessarily valid. To have **validity**, the research method must measure what it is supposed to measure, not something else. For example, although a group of customers may express the same level of satisfaction based on

research design An overall plan for obtaining the information needed to address a research problem or issue

hypothesis An informed guess or assumption about a certain problem or set of circumstances

reliability A condition that exists when a research technique produces almost identical results in repeated trials

validity A condition that exists when a research method measures what it is supposed to measure

a rating scale, as individuals they may not exhibit the same repurchase behavior because of different personal characteristics. If the purpose of rating satisfaction was to estimate potential repurchase behavior, this result may cause the researcher to question the validity of the satisfaction scale.[15] A study to measure the effect of advertising on sales would be valid if advertising could be isolated from other factors or from variables that affect sales. The study would be reliable if replications of it produced the same results.

5-3c **Collecting Data**

primary data Data observed and recorded or collected directly from respondents

secondary data Data compiled both inside and outside the organization for some purpose other than the current investigation

The next step in the marketing research process is collecting data to help prove (or disprove) the research hypothesis. The research design must specify what types of data to collect and how they will be collected.

Types of Data

Marketing researchers have two types of data at their disposal. **Primary data** are observed and recorded or collected directly from respondents. This type of data must be gathered by observing phenomena or surveying people of interest. **Secondary data** are compiled both inside and outside the organization for some purpose other than the current investigation. Secondary data include general reports supplied to an enterprise by various data services and internal and online databases. Such reports might concern market share, retail inventory levels, and customers' buying behavior. Commonly, secondary data are already available in private or public reports or have been collected and stored by the organization itself. Due to the opportunity to obtain data via the internet, more than half of all marketing research now comes from secondary sources.

SOURCE: PARDOT.COM

Sales and Marketing –
together at last.

Lifecycle Report

12,033   115   112

Pipeline   Velocity

salesforce pardot

B2B Marketing Automation
by Salesforce

www.pardot.com

Sources of Secondary Data
Internal sources of secondary data like CRM systems can contribute to research. Businesses can use platforms like Salesforce's B2B marketing automation tool Pardot to gather analytics and run sales reports.

Sources of Secondary Data

Marketers often begin the data-collection phase of the marketing research process by gathering secondary data. They may use available reports and other information from both internal and external sources to study a marketing problem.

Internal sources of secondary data can contribute tremendously to research. An organization's own database may contain information about past marketing activities, such as sales records and research reports, which can be used to test hypotheses and pinpoint problems. From sales reports, a firm may be able to determine not only which product sold best at certain times of the year but also which colors and sizes customers preferred. Such information may have been gathered using customer relationship management tools for marketing, management, or financial purposes. Consider the advertisement for Pardot by Salesforce. The platform equips businesses with powerful analytics that can be used as secondary data for marketing research. The advertisement highlights one of many reports that can be found in the platform to help marketers use sales data to make business decisions.

Accounting records are also an excellent source of data but, surprisingly, are often overlooked. The large volume of data an accounting department collects does not automatically flow to other departments. As a result, detailed information about costs, sales, customer accounts, or profits by product category may not be easily accessible to the marketing area. This condition develops particularly in organizations that do not store marketing information on a systematic basis. A third source of internal secondary data is competitive information gathered by the sales force.

External sources of secondary data include trade associations, periodicals, government publications, unpublished sources, and online databases. Trade associations, such as the American Marketing Association, offer guides and directories that are full of information. Periodicals such as *Bloomberg Businessweek, The Wall Street Journal, Sales & Marketing Management, Advertising Age, Marketing Research*, and *Direct Selling News* publish general information that can help marketers define problems and develop hypotheses. *Survey of Buying Power*, an annual supplement to *Sales & Marketing Management*, contains sales data for major industries on a county-by-county basis. Many marketers also consult federal government publications such as the *Statistical Abstract of the United States*, the *Census of Business*, the *Census of Agriculture*, and the *Census of Population*; most of these government publications are available online. Although the government still conducts its primary census every 10 years, it also conducts the American Community Survey, an ongoing survey sent to population samples on a regular basis.[16] This provides marketers with a more up-to-date demographic picture of the nation's population every year. A company might use survey census data to determine whether to construct a shopping mall in a specific area.[17]

In addition, companies may subscribe to services such as Nielsen or Information Resources Inc. (IRI) that track retail sales and other information. For example, IRI tracks consumer purchases using in-store, scanner-based technology. Marketing firms can purchase information from IRI about a product category, such as frozen orange juice, as secondary data.[18] Small businesses may be unable to afford such services, but they can still find a wealth of information through industry publications and trade associations.

Companies such as TiVo are challenging services like Nielsen by offering year-round second-by-second information about the show and advertising viewing habits of consumers who own the company's DVRs. The data are anonymous and are recorded by the TV viewers' boxes. Nielsen only measures local program viewing for four months a year. However, TiVo's data gathering is limited. Its privacy-protection policies prevent the company from collecting information that Nielson can provide, such as demographic breakdowns and the number of people watching each TV set. On the other hand, TiVo information can aid local TV news programs in their programming decisions by helping them choose when to air sports and weather and how much time to devote to each segment.[19]

The internet can be especially useful to marketing researchers. Search engines such as Google can help marketers locate many types of secondary data or research topics of interest. Amazon.com, for instance, has built a relationship with its customers by tracking the types of books, music, and other products they purchase. Each time a customer logs on to the website, the company can offer recommendations based on the customer's previous purchases. Such a marketing system helps the company track the changing desires and buying habits of its most valued customers. Furthermore, marketing researchers are increasingly monitoring blogs to discover what consumers are saying about their products—both positive and negative. Some, including yogurt maker Stonyfield Farms, have even established its own blogs as a way to monitor consumer dialogue on issues of their choice. There are many reasons people go online, which can make the job of using the internet complicated for marketers. Table 5.2 summarizes the external sources of secondary data, excluding syndicated services.

Table 5.2   Examples of Secondary Sources

Government Sources	
Economic census	https://www.census.gov/EconomicCensus
Export.gov—country and industry market research	https://www.export.gov/welcome
National Technical Information Services	www.ntis.gov
Industry Canada	http://www.ic.gc.ca/eic/site/icgc.nsf/eng/home
Trade Associations and Shows	
American Society of Association Executives	www.asaecenter.org
Directory of Associations	http://www.marketingsource.com/directories/associations/us
Trade Show News Network	www.tsnn.com
Magazines, Newspapers, Video, and Audio News Programming	
Resource Library	http://findarticles.com
Google Video Search	https://www.google.com/videohp
Google News Directory	www.news.google.com
Yahoo! Video Search	www.video.search.yahoo.com
Corporate Information	
Annual Report Service	www.annualreportservice.com
Bitpipe	www.bitpipe.com
Business Wire—press releases	www.businesswire.com
Hoover's Online	www.hoovers.com
PR Newswire—press releases	www.prnewswire.com

Source: Adapted from "Data Collection: Low-Cost Secondary Research," *KnowThis.com*, www.knowthis.com/principles-of-marketing-tutorials/data-collection-low-cost-secondary
-research (accessed February 6, 2018).

population All the elements, units, or individuals of interest to researchers for a specific study

sample A limited number of units chosen to represent the characteristics of a total population

sampling The process of selecting representative units from a total population

probability sampling A type of sampling in which every element in the population being studied has a known chance of being selected for study

random sampling A form of probability sampling in which all units in a population have an equal chance of appearing in the sample, and the various events that can occur have an equal or known chance of taking place

Methods of Collecting Primary Data

Collecting primary data is a lengthier, more expensive, and more complex process than collecting secondary data. To gather primary data, researchers use sampling procedures, survey methods, and observation. These efforts can be handled in-house by the firm's own research department or contracted to a private research firm such as Nielsen, Information Resources Inc., or IMS International. Consider the advertisement for marketing research firm FocusVision. FocusVision uses an image of a multitool to describe its suite of products that can be used to collect both quantitative and qualitative data. For instance, FocusVision clients can use its Decipher platform to collect primary data through mobile and web surveys.

Sampling Because the time and resources available for research are limited, it is almost impossible to investigate all the members of a target market or other population. A **population**, or "universe," includes all the elements, units, or individuals of interest to researchers for a specific study. Consider a Gallup poll designed to predict the results of a presidential election. All registered voters in the United States would constitute the population. By systematically choosing a limited number of units—a **sample**—to represent the characteristics of a total population, researchers can project the reactions of a total market or market segment. (In the case of the presidential poll, a representative national sample of several thousand registered voters would be selected and surveyed to project the probable voting outcome.) **Sampling** in marketing research, therefore, is the process of selecting representative units from a total population. Sampling techniques allow marketers to predict buying behavior fairly accurately on the basis of the responses from a representative portion of the population of interest. Most types of marketing research employ sampling techniques.

There are two basic types of sampling: probability sampling and nonprobability sampling. With **probability sampling**, every element in the population being studied has a known chance of being selected for study. Random sampling is a form of probability sampling. When marketers employ **random sampling**, all the units in a population have an equal chance of appearing in the sample. The various events that can occur have an equal or known chance of taking place. For instance, a specific card in a regulation deck has a one in 52 probability of being drawn at any one time. Sample units are ordinarily chosen by selecting from a table of random numbers statistically generated so that each digit, zero through nine, will have an equal probability of occurring in each position in the sequence. The sequentially numbered elements of a population are sampled randomly by selecting the units whose numbers appear in the table of random numbers.

Another type of probability sampling is **stratified sampling**, in which the population of interest is divided into groups according to a common attribute, and a random sample is then chosen within each group. The stratified sample may reduce some of the error that could occur in a simple random sample. By ensuring that each major group or segment of the population receives its proportionate share of sample units, investigators avoid including too many or too few sample units from each group. Samples are usually stratified when researchers believe there may be variations among different types of respondents. As an example, many political opinion surveys are stratified by gender, race, age, and/or geographic location.

The second type of sampling, **nonprobability sampling**, is more subjective than probability sampling because there is no way to calculate the likelihood that a specific element of the population being studied will be chosen. Quota sampling, for example, is highly judgmental because the final choice of participants is left to the researchers. In **quota sampling**, researchers divide the population into groups and then arbitrarily choose participants from each group. In quota sampling, there are some controls—usually limited to two or three variables, such as age, gender, or race—over the selection of participants. The controls attempt to ensure that representative categories of respondents are interviewed. A study of people who wear eyeglasses, for instance, may be conducted by interviewing equal numbers of men and women who wear eyeglasses. Because quota samples are not probability samples, not everyone has an equal chance of being selected, and sampling error, therefore, cannot be measured statistically. Quota samples are used most often in exploratory studies, when hypotheses are being developed. Often a small quota sample will not be projected to the total population, although the findings may provide valuable insights into a problem. Quota samples are useful when

Collecting Primary Data
FocusVision offers a number of tools companies can use to collect both primary qualitative and quantitative market research.

stratified sampling A type of probability sampling in which the population is divided into groups with a common attribute, and a random sample is chosen within each group

nonprobability sampling A sampling technique in which there is no way to calculate the likelihood that a specific element of the population being studied will be chosen

quota sampling A nonprobability sampling technique in which researchers divide the population into groups and then arbitrarily choose participants from each group

people with some common characteristic are found and questioned about the topic of interest. A probability sample used to study people who are allergic to cats would be highly inefficient while quota sampling would produce much more useful information.

Survey Methods   Marketing researchers often employ sampling to collect primary data through mail, telephone, personal interview, online, or with social networking surveys. The results of such surveys are used to describe and analyze buying behavior. The survey method chosen depends on the nature of the problem or issue; the data needed to test the hypothesis; and the resources, such as funding and personnel, available to the researcher. Marketers may employ more than one survey method depending on the goals of the research. Surveys can be quite expensive, although online survey services have made the method much more affordable even for small firms. There are many companies that offer free or low-cost survey services, such as SurveyMonkey or Qualtrics.[20] Table 5.3 summarizes and compares the advantages of the various survey methods.

Gathering information through surveys is becoming increasingly difficult because fewer people are willing to participate. Many people believe responding to surveys requires too much scarce personal time, especially as surveys become longer and more detailed. Others have concerns about how much information marketers are gathering and whether their privacy is being invaded. The unethical use of selling techniques disguised as marketing surveys has also led to decreased cooperation. These factors cause an increase in the nonresponse rates for any type of survey.

In a **mail survey**, questionnaires are sent to respondents, who are encouraged to complete and return them. Mail surveys are used most often when the individuals in the sample are spread over a wide area and funds for the survey are limited. A mail survey is less expensive than a telephone or personal interview survey as long as the response rate is high enough to produce reliable results. The main disadvantages of this method are the possibility of a low response rate and of misleading results if respondents differ significantly from the population being sampled. One

mail survey A research method in which respondents answer a questionnaire sent through the mail

Table 5.3   Comparison of the Four Basic Survey Methods

	Mail Surveys	Telephone Surveys	Online Surveys	Personal Interview Surveys
Economy	Potentially lower in cost per interview than telephone or personal surveys. Low response rate is a limitation.	Avoids interviewers' travel expenses. Limited by large part of population with cell phones.	The least expensive method. Nonresponse and privacy limit access to respondents.	The most expensive survey method; shopping mall and focus-group interviews have lower costs than in-home interviews.
Flexibility	Inflexible; questionnaire must be short and easy for respondents to complete.	Flexible because interviewers can ask probing questions, but observations are impossible.	Less flexible. Must be easy for online users to receive and return; short, concise questions work best.	Most flexible method; respondents can react to visual materials; demographic data are more accurate; in-depth probes are possible.
Interviewer bias	Interviewer bias is eliminated; questionnaires can be returned anonymously.	Some anonymity; may be hard to develop trust in respondents.	Interviewer bias is often eliminated, but privacy issues exist.	Interviewers' personal characteristics or inability to maintain objectivity may result in bias.
Sampling and respondents' cooperation	Obtaining a complete mailing list is difficult; nonresponse is a major disadvantage.	Sample limited to respondents with accessible telephones. Refusals are a problem.	The available email address list may not be a representative sample for some purposes. Nonresponse is an issue.	Not-at-homes are a problem, which may be overcome by focus-group and shopping mall interviewing.

method of improving response rates involves attaching a brief personal message on a Post-it® Note to the survey packet. Response rates to these surveys are higher, and the quality and timeliness of the responses are also improved.[21] As a result of these issues, companies are increasingly moving to internet surveys and automated telephone surveys.

Premiums or incentives that encourage respondents to return questionnaires have been effective in developing panels of respondents who are interviewed regularly by mail. Such mail panels, selected to represent a target market or market segment, are especially useful in evaluating new products and providing general information about customers, as well as records of their purchases (in the form of purchase diaries). Mail panels and purchase diaries are much more widely used than custom mail surveys, but both panels and purchase diaries have shortcomings. People who take the time to fill out a diary may differ from the general population based on income, education, or behavior, such as the time available for shopping activities. Internet and social networking surveys have also greatly gained in popularity, although they are similarly limited as well—given that not all demographics utilize these media equally.

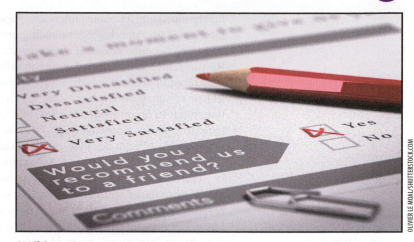

Mail Survey
Mailing surveys to consumers to fill out and send back can be highly useful for reaching a widespread sample over a large geographic area. However, this survey method often has a low response rate, prompting some marketers to offer some sort of incentive for taking the survey.

In a **telephone survey**, an interviewer records respondents' answers to a questionnaire over a phone line. A telephone survey has some advantages over a mail survey. The rate of response is higher because it takes less effort to answer the telephone and talk than to fill out and return a questionnaire. If enough interviewers are available, a telephone survey can be conducted very quickly. Thus, political candidates or organizations that want an immediate reaction to an event may choose this method. In addition, a telephone survey permits interviewers to gain rapport with respondents and ask probing questions. Automated telephone surveys, also known as interactive voice response or "robosurveys," rely on a recorded voice to ask the questions while a computer program records respondents' answers. The primary benefit of automated surveys is the elimination of any bias that might be introduced by a live researcher.

Another option is the **telephone depth interview**, which combines the traditional focus group's ability to probe with the confidentiality provided by a telephone survey. This type of interview is most appropriate for qualitative research projects among a small targeted group that is difficult to bring together for a traditional focus group because of members' professions, locations, or lifestyles. Respondents can choose the time and day for the interview. Many companies are using Skype so that interviewers can have personal interaction with respondents and show products. Although this method is difficult to implement, it can yield revealing information from respondents who otherwise would be unwilling to participate in marketing research.

A major shortcoming is that only a small proportion of the population likes to participate in telephone surveys or interviews. This can significantly limit participation and distort representation. Many households are excluded from telephone directories by choice (unlisted numbers) or because the residents moved after the directory was published. Potential respondents often use telephone answering machines, voice mail, or caller ID to screen or block calls; additionally, millions have signed up for "Do Not Call Lists." Moreover, an increasing number of Americans are giving up their fixed telephone lines in favor of cellular or wireless phones. In fact, 52 percent of households have a cell phone but no landline telephones.[22] These issues have serious implications for the use of telephone samples in conducting surveys or interviews. Additionally, surveys and interviews conducted over the telephone are limited to oral communication; visual aids or observation cannot be included. Interpreters of results must make adjustments for individuals who are not at home or do not have telephones.

In a **personal interview survey**, participants respond to questions face-to-face. Various audiovisual aids—pictures, products, diagrams, or prerecorded advertising copy—can be

telephone survey A research method in which respondents' answers to a questionnaire are recorded by an interviewer on the phone

telephone depth interview An interview that combines the traditional focus group's ability to probe with the confidentiality provided by telephone surveys

personal interview survey A research method in which participants respond to survey questions face-to-face

incorporated into a personal interview. Rapport gained through direct interaction usually permits more in-depth interviewing, including probes, follow-up questions, or psychological tests. In addition, because personal interviews can be longer, they may yield more information. Respondents can be selected more carefully, and reasons for nonresponse can be explored. One such research technique is the **in-home (door-to-door) interview**. The in-home interview offers a clear advantage when thoroughness of self-disclosure and elimination of group influence are important. In an in-depth interview of 45 to 90 minutes, respondents can be probed to reveal their true motivations, feelings, behaviors, and aspirations. Door-to-door interviewing is increasingly difficult due to respondent and interviewer security and safety issues. This method is particularly limited in gated communities such as condos or apartments.

The nature of personal interviews has changed. In the past, most personal interviews, which were based on random sampling or prearranged appointments, were conducted in the respondent's home. Today, many personal interviews are conducted in shopping malls. **Shopping mall intercept interviews** involve interviewing a percentage of individuals who pass by an "intercept" point in a mall. Like any face-to-face interviewing method, mall intercept interviewing has many advantages. The interviewer is in a position to recognize and react to respondents' nonverbal indications of confusion. Respondents can view product prototypes, videos of commercials, and the like, and provide their opinions. The mall environment lets the researcher deal with complex situations. In taste tests, for instance, researchers know that all the respondents are reacting to the same product, which can be prepared and monitored from the mall test kitchen. In addition to the ability to conduct tests requiring bulky equipment, lower cost and greater control make shopping mall intercept interviews popular.

An **on-site computer interview** is a variation of the shopping mall intercept interview in which respondents complete a self-administered questionnaire displayed on a computer monitor. A computer software package can be used to conduct such interviews in shopping malls. After a brief lesson on how to operate the software, respondents proceed through the survey at their own pace. Questionnaires can be adapted so that respondents see only those items (usually a subset of an entire scale) that may provide useful information about their attitudes.

Online and Social Media Surveys We give online surveys and internet research its own section because as more and more consumers gain internet access, internet surveys are likely to become the predominant tool for general population sampling. In an **online survey**, questionnaires can be transmitted to respondents either through email or through a website. Marketing researchers often send these surveys to online panel samples purchased from professional brokers or put together by the company. Marketing research firms that specialize in internet research can also be used to conduct digital research for their client organizations. Many offer tools that complement or enhance online surveys. One of the largest online survey providers is Qualtrics. Qualtrics provides software to firms who want to develop their own surveys that they can circulate online. The company also offers services such as concept testing, data collection, and employee feedback. It has clients in 12 countries and runs approximately 2.1 million surveys each day.[23] Qualtrics' flexibility and research capabilities have caught the attention of many companies who want to learn more about their customers, including JetBlue. JetBlue used Qualtrics software to understand customer opinions on individual flights.[24]

in-home (door-to-door) interview A personal interview that takes place in the respondent's home

shopping mall intercept interview A research method that involves interviewing a percentage of individuals passing by "intercept" points in a mall

on-site computer interview A variation of the shopping mall intercept interview in which respondents complete a self-administered questionnaire displayed on a computer monitor

online survey A research method in which respondents answer a questionnaire via email or on a website

Online Surveys
Online surveys are becoming increasingly common as they offer a low-cost and convenient way to survey a large number of customers over vast geographic areas.

Because email is semi-interactive, recipients can ask for clarification of specific questions or pose questions of their own. The potential advantages of online surveys are quick response and lower cost than traditional mail, telephone, and personal interview surveys if the response rate is adequate. More firms are using their websites to conduct surveys. They may include a premium, such as a chance to win a prize, to encourage participation. In addition, online surveys can be completed via mobile devices. For example, apps on smartphones can collect online information without active moment-to-moment participation by respondents.[25]

Social networking sites can also be used to conduct surveys. Marketers can use digital media forums such as chat rooms, blogs, newsgroups, social networks, and research communities to identify trends in interests and consumption patterns. However, using these forums for conducting surveys has some limitations. Often consumers choose to go to a particular social media site or blog and then take the survey; this eliminates randomness and makes it more difficult to obtain a representative sample size. On the other hand, they can provide a general idea of consumer trends and preferences. Movies, consumer electronics, food, and computers are popular topics in many online communities. Indeed, by "listening in" on these ongoing conversations, marketers may be able to identify new product opportunities and consumer needs. Moreover, this type of online data can be gathered at little incremental cost compared to alternative data sources.

Crowdsourcing combines the words *crowd* and *outsourcing* and calls for taking tasks usually performed by a marketer or researcher and outsourcing them to a crowd, or potential market, through an open call. In the case of digital marketing, crowdsourcing is often used to obtain the opinions or needs of the crowd (or potential markets). Consider Lego's crowdsourcing platform Lego Ideas. Lego Ideas is a site that invites consumers to submit ideas for Lego sets. Those ideas that get 10,000 votes are reviewed by the firm for possible development. If the Lego set is chosen for development, the creator gets 1 percent of the product's total net sales.[26] Crowdsourcing is a way for marketers to gather input straight from willing consumers and to actively listen to people's ideas and evaluations on products. It is also important for organizations to harness all of their internal information, and internal social networks can be helpful for that. On the other hand, results appear to show that internal social networks are not very popular with employees. A major reason is thought to be that top executives do not use internal collaboration platforms, which convinces employees that they are not necessary. It is, therefore, important to have top management's support and participation for companies that want to adopt strong digital internal social networks.[27]

One internet system that uses crowdsourcing to connect people from across the world is Amazon's Mechanical Turk (MTurk). MTurk is an online marketplace that connects requesters for someone to perform tasks with workers willing to complete them. MTurk operates on the premise that there are still various tasks that only humans, and not computers, can complete. Based on this idea, MTurk allows companies and entrepreneurs to crowdsource human intelligence tasks (HITs) to workers worldwide. Workers who are equipped to complete these tasks have the flexibility to work their own hours from their homes. Money for the tasks is deposited into MTurk accounts.[28] Some have found the data generated from these crowdsourcing processes to be just as reliable as data gathered through more traditional methods.[29] However, others have criticized MTurk because it is sometimes impossible to determine if respondents are representing themselves accurately. There has been a tendency for more respondents to be from countries outside of the United States. Freelancers who use MTurk have also complained that they are seen as little more than algorithms rather than skilled workers.[30]

Marketing research will likely rely heavily on online panels and surveys in the future. Furthermore, as negative attitudes toward telephone surveys render that technique less representative and more expensive, the integration of email and voice mail functions into one computer-based system provides a promising alternative for survey research. However, there are some ethical issues to consider when using the internet for marketing research, such as unsolicited email, which could be viewed as "spam," and privacy, as some potential survey respondents fear their personal information will be given or sold to third parties

crowdsourcing Combines the words *crowd* and *outsourcing* and calls for taking tasks usually performed by a marketer or researcher and outsourcing them to a crowd, or potential market, through an open call

without their knowledge or permission. Additionally, as with direct mail, internet surveys have a good chance of being discarded, particularly with users who receive dozens of emails every day.

Another challenge for researchers is obtaining a sample that is representative of the desired population. Although internet surveys allow respondents to retain their anonymity and flexibility, they can also enable survey takers to abuse the system. For instance, some survey takers take multiple surveys or pose as other people to make more money. To get around this problem, companies are developing screening mechanisms and instituting limits on how many surveys one person can take.[31] Survey programs such as Qualtrics can also delete surveys that appear suspicious.

Questionnaire Construction A carefully constructed questionnaire is essential to the success of any survey. Questions must be clear, easy to understand, and directed toward a specific objective; that is, they must be designed to elicit information that meets the study's data requirements. Researchers need to define the objective before trying to develop a questionnaire because the objective determines the substance of the questions and the amount of detail. A common mistake in constructing questionnaires is to ask questions that interest the researchers but do not yield information useful in deciding whether to accept or reject a hypothesis. Finally, the most important rule in composing questions is to maintain impartiality. The questions are usually of three kinds: open-ended, dichotomous, and multiple-choice. Problems may develop in the analysis of dichotomous or multiple-choice questions when responses for one outcome outnumber others. For example, a dichotomous question that asks respondents to choose between "buy" or "not buy" might require additional sampling from the disproportionately smaller group if there were not enough responses to analyze.[32] Researchers must also be very careful about questions that a respondent might consider too personal or that might require an admission of activities that other people are likely to condemn. Questions of this type should be worded to make them less offensive.

Observation Methods In using observation methods, researchers record individuals' overt behavior, taking note of physical conditions and events. Direct contact with them is avoided; instead, their actions are examined and noted systematically. For instance, researchers might use observation methods to answer the question, "How long does the average McDonald's restaurant customer have to wait in line before being served?" Observation may include the use of ethnographic techniques, such as watching customers interact with a product in a real-world environment. Interestingly, many online retailers are starting to open physical stores, not simply to extend their reach but also as a way of observing customers in ways that cannot be done online. Being able to observe how customers interact with products in-store helps marketers of online firms like Bonobos understand consumer likes and dislikes—information that is integral to improving its product offerings, both in-store and online. Even online maverick Amazon.com opened a physical store in Seattle.[33] Observation may also be combined with interviews. For instance, during a personal interview, the condition of a respondent's home or other possessions may be observed and recorded. The interviewer can also directly observe and confirm such demographic information as race, approximate age, and gender.

Data gathered through observation can sometimes be biased if the subject is aware of the observation process. However, an observer can be placed in a natural market environment, such as a grocery store, without influencing shoppers' actions. If the presence of a human observer is likely to bias the outcome or if human sensory abilities are inadequate, mechanical means may be used to record behavior. Mechanical observation devices include cameras, recorders, counting machines, scanners, and equipment that records physiological changes. A special camera can be used to record the eye movements of people as they look at an advertisement. Tracking the eye movements of online shoppers has revealed that functional and nonfunctional product characteristics result in greater eye movement and intensity, suggesting that using these attributes in product descriptions could engage viewers more thoroughly.[34] The camera detects the sequence of reading and the parts of the advertisement that receive the greatest attention. The electronic scanners used in supermarkets are very useful in marketing research: They provide accurate data on sales and customers' purchase patterns, and marketing researchers may buy such data from the supermarkets.

Observation is straightforward and avoids a central problem of survey methods: motivating respondents to state their true feelings or opinions. However, observation tends to be descriptive. When it is the only method of data collection, it may not provide insights into causal relationships. Another drawback is that analyses based on observation are subject to the observer's biases or the limitations of the mechanical device.

5-3d Interpreting Research Findings

After collecting data to test their hypotheses, marketers need to interpret the research findings. Interpretation of the data is easier if marketers carefully plan their data analysis methods early in the research process. They should also allow for continual evaluation of the data during the entire collection period. Marketers can then gain valuable insights into areas that should be probed during the formal analysis. Table 5.4 shows that interpreting analytics and implementing insights—as well as research and data collection—are among the top 10 marketing challenges.

The first step in drawing conclusions from most research is to display the data in table format. If marketers intend to apply the results to individual categories of the things or people being studied, cross-tabulation may be useful, especially in tabulating joint occurrences. Using the two variables of gender and purchase rates of automobile tires, for instance, a cross-tabulation could show how men and women differ in purchasing automobile tires. The advertisement promoting marketing research firm NPD Group's Checkout Tracking service emphasizes the need to understand the customer. Checkout Tracking tracks consumer purchases online and in-store. By linking these purchases to consumer patterns and demographics, Checkout Tracking aids businesses in both collecting and interpreting purchase data.

After the data are tabulated, they must be analyzed. **Statistical interpretation** focuses on what is typical and what deviates from the average. It indicates how widely responses vary and how they are distributed in relation to the variable being measured. When marketers interpret statistics, they must take into account estimates of expected error or deviation from the true values of the population. The analysis of data may lead researchers to accept or reject the hypothesis being studied. Data require careful interpretation by the marketer. If the results of a study are valid, the decision maker should take action; if a question has been incorrectly or poorly worded, however, the

SOURCE: NPD GROUP, INC.

Interpreting Research Findings
NPD Group uses the image of a man with a black bar covering his eyes to symbolize how its Checkout Tracking service can help businesses interpret customer purchase data to truly know their customers.

Table 5.4   Biggest Marketing Challenges

	Marketing Challenge
1.	Traffic and leads
2.	Metrics/performance measurement
3.	Budget
4.	Technology
5.	Website
6.	International content marketing
7.	Training
8.	Hiring top talent
9.	Finding an executive sponsor

Source: Lindsay Kolowich, "8 of the Top Marketing Challenges Marketers will Face This Year," *HubSpot*, July 28, 2017, https://blog.hubspot.com/blog/tabid/6307/bid/33820/5-major-challenges-marketers-face-and-how-to-solve-them.aspx (accessed February 6, 2018).

results may produce poor decisions. Consider the research conducted for a food marketer that asked respondents to rate a product on criteria such as "hearty flavor," as well as how important each criterion was to the respondent. Although such results may have had utility for advertising purposes, they are less helpful in product development because it is not possible to discern each respondent's meaning of the phrase "hearty flavor." Managers must understand the research results and relate them to a context that permits effective decision making.

5-3e   Reporting Research Findings

The final step in the marketing research process is to report the research findings. Before preparing the report, the marketer must take a clear, objective look at the findings to see how well the gathered facts answer the research question or support or negate the initial hypotheses. In most cases, it is extremely doubtful that the study can provide everything needed to answer the research question. Thus, the researcher must point out the deficiencies in the research and their causes in the report. Research should be meaningful to all participants, especially top managers who develop strategy. Therefore, researchers must try to make certain that their findings are relevant and not just interesting. Research is not useful unless it supports the organization's overall strategy objectives. The more knowledge researchers have about the opportunities and challenges facing an organization, the more meaningful their research report will be. If an outside research agency conducts research, it is even more important to understand the client's business. After conducting research, a research report is the next step. Those responsible for preparing the report must facilitate adjusting the findings to the environment, as elements change over time. Most importantly, the report should be helpful to marketers and managers on an ongoing basis.[35]

The report of research results is usually a formal, written document. Researchers must allow time for the writing task when they plan and schedule the project. Because the report is a means of communicating with the decision makers who will use the research findings, researchers need to determine beforehand how much detail and supporting data to include. They should keep in mind that corporate executives prefer reports that are short, clear, and simply expressed. Researchers often give their summary and recommendations first, especially if decision makers do not have time to study how the results were obtained. A technical report allows its users to analyze data and interpret recommendations because it describes the research methods and procedures and the most important data gathered. Thus, researchers must recognize the needs and expectations of the report user and adapt to them.

Marketing researchers want to know about behavior and opinions, and they want accurate data to help them in making decisions. Careful wording of questions is very important because a biased or emotional word can dramatically change the results. Marketing research and marketing information systems can provide an organization with accurate and

statistical interpretation
Analysis of what is typical and what deviates from the average

How Fortune 1000 Executives Report Using Big Data

	Started and seen value	Started and not seen value	Not started
Decrease expenses	49.2%	23.4%	27.4%
Find new innovation avenues	44.3%	20.2%	35.5%
Launch new products/services	36.1%	26.8%	37.1%
Add revenue	32.8%	22.0%	45.2%
Increase the speed of current efforts	31.1%	33.4%	35.5%
Transform business for the future	27.9%	23.7%	48.4%
Establish a data-driven culture	27.9%	41.5%	30.6%

SNAPSHOT

Source: Newvantage Partners Big Data Executive Survey (2017), *Harvard Business Review*, April 28, 2017, https://hbr.org/2017/04/how-companies-say-theyre-using-big-data (accessed February 8, 2018).

reliable customer feedback, which a marketer must have to understand the dynamics of the marketplace. As managers recognize the benefits of marketing research, they assign it a much larger role in decision making.

5-4 USING TECHNOLOGY TO IMPROVE MARKETING INFORMATION GATHERING AND ANALYSIS

Describe the tools, such as databases, big data, marketing analytics, and decision support systems useful to marketing decision making.

Technology makes information for marketing decisions increasingly accessible. The ability of marketers to track customer buying behavior and to better discern what buyers want is changing the nature of marketing. Information technology permits internal research and quick information gathering to help marketers better understand and satisfy customers. The use of data is helping marketers discover customer insights that would have been hard to discover through traditional methods. Company responses to email complaints—as well as to communications through mail, telephone, and personal contact—can be used to improve customer satisfaction, retention, and value. Armed with such information, marketers can fine-tune marketing mixes to satisfy their customers' needs.

Consumer feedback is an important aspect of marketing research, and new technology such as digital media is enhancing this process. Online retailers such as Amazon, Netflix, and Priceline are capitalizing on these ratings and reviews by allowing consumers to post comments on its sites concerning books, movies, hotels, and more. Marketers can use these social media forums to closely monitor what their customers are saying. In the case of negative feedback, marketers can communicate with consumers to address problems or complaints more easily than with traditional marketing channels. In one survey, it was noted that a business has the opportunity to turn 18 percent of negative reviewers into loyal customers by responding to their negative feedback. In addition, more than 60 percent of those who receive a reply will replace their negative comments with positive ones.[36] By researching what consumers are saying about their products, companies can understand what features of their product mixes should be promoted or modified.

Finally, the integration of telecommunications and computer technologies allows marketers to access a growing array of valuable information sources related to industry forecasts, business trends, and customer buying behavior. Electronic communication tools can be effectively used to gain accurate information with minimal customer interaction. Most marketing researchers have electronic networking at their disposal. In fact, many firms use marketing information systems and CRM technologies to network all these technologies and organize all the marketing data available to them. In this section, we look at marketing information systems and specific technologies that are helping marketing researchers obtain and manage marketing research data.

5-4a Marketing Information Systems

A **marketing information system (MIS)** is a framework for the day-to-day management and structuring of information gathered regularly from sources both inside and outside the organization. As such, an MIS provides a continuous flow of information about prices, advertising expenditures, sales, competition, and distribution expenses. Marketing information systems can be an important asset for developing effective marketing strategies. Procter & Gamble (P&G) managers, for instance, search through P&G's proprietary MIS for data to help the company predict which products will work best in different countries.[37] The main purposes of the MIS are data storage and retrieval, computer capabilities, and management's information requirements. Regular reports of sales by product or market categories, data on

marketing information system (MIS) A framework for managing and structuring information gathered regularly from sources inside and outside the organization

inventory levels, and records of salespeople's activities are examples of information that is useful in making decisions. In the MIS, the means of gathering data receive less attention than do the procedures for expediting the flow of information. Most firms develop a dashboard display where data can be integrated into useful management reports for strategic and tactical decisions.

An effective MIS starts by determining the objective of the information—that is, by identifying decision needs that require certain information. The firm can then specify an information system for continuous monitoring to provide regular, pertinent information on both the external and internal environments. FedEx, for instance, has interactive marketing systems that provide instantaneous communication between the company and customers. Customers can track their packages and receive immediate feedback concerning delivery via the internet. The company's website provides information about customer usage and allows customers to convey what they think about company services. The evolving telecommunications and computer technologies allow marketers to use information systems to cultivate one-to-one relationships with customers.

5-4b Databases

Most marketing information systems include internal databases. A **database** is a collection of information arranged for easy access and retrieval. It is a structured set of data that can be used in many ways. Databases allow marketers to tap into an abundance of information useful in making marketing decisions: internal sales reports, newspaper articles, company news releases, government economic reports, bibliographies, and more, often accessed through a computer system.

Information technology has made it possible for firms to develop databases that are vastly enhanced in their speed and storage capacity to guide strategic planning and improve customer service.

Customer relationship management (CRM) employs database marketing techniques to identify different types of customers and develop specific strategies for interacting with each customer. CRM incorporates these three elements:

1. Identifying and building a database of current and potential consumers, including a wide range of demographic, lifestyle, and purchase information.

2. Delivering differential messages according to each consumer's preferences and characteristics through established and new media channels.

3. Tracking customer relationships to monitor the costs of retaining individual customers and the lifetime value of their purchases.[38]

Many commercial websites require consumers to register and provide personal information to access the site or to make a purchase. Frequent-flyer programs permit airlines to ask loyal customers to participate in surveys about their needs and desires and to track their best customers' flight patterns by time of day, week, month, and year. Also, supermarkets gain a significant amount of data through checkout scanners tied to store discount cards.

Marketing researchers can also use databases, such as LexisNexis, to obtain useful information for marketing decisions. Many commercial databases are accessible online for a fee. Sometimes, they can be obtained in printed form or digitally. With most commercial databases, the user typically conducts a computer search by keyword, topic, or company, and the database service generates abstracts, articles, or reports that can then be printed out.

Information provided by a single firm on household demographics, purchases, television viewing behavior, and responses to promotions such as coupons and free samples is called **single-source data**. For example, BehaviorScan Rx ad testing, offered by IRI, allows different TV advertisements to be played in the same market. It is also able to discover important links between TV viewing behaviors and consumer activities.[39] It is important to gather longitudinal (long-term) information on customers to maximize the usefulness of single-source data.

database A collection of information arranged for easy access and retrieval

single-source data Information provided by a single marketing research firm

5-4c **Big Data**

Big data has the potential to revolutionize the way businesses gather marketing research and develop tailored campaigns. **Big data** involves massive data files that can be obtained from both structured and unstructured databases. Big data often consists of high-volume data that marketers can use to discover unique insights and make more knowledgeable marketing decisions.[40] Big data can include mountains of data collected from social networks, RFID, retailer scanning, purchases, logistics, and production.[41] The amount of data that can be gleaned from consumer activities and purchase patterns yields significant insights for marketers. The complexity of big data requires sophisticated software to store and analyze it.[42] It also requires marketers to identify and understand how to use this data to develop stronger customer relationships. Many firms like Walmart, Whole Foods, and General Electric are adopting centralized systems to integrate disparate data and glean the most insights about consumers.[43]

Big data presents a new opportunity to use IT-enabled information to assist in marketing decision making. The amount of data is rapidly increasing through an array of generating sources, including mobile devices, internet searches, behavioral observations, and tracking of purchase behavior. Marketers want to use this data to create competitive advantages that will help them discover new insights into customer

big data Massive data files that can be obtained from both structured and unstructured databases

behavior. Many companies are optimistic that increasingly advanced methodologies for analyzing and interpreting big data will lead to the development of new innovations with major impacts for society.[44]

The positive impact that big data has had upon marketing is undeniable. A McKinsey study showed that companies which incorporated big data into their marketing decisions saw their return on investment (ROI) improve between 15 and 20 percent. Big data is also important in giving firms a competitive advantage. According to research studies, 80 percent of companies that utilize big data effectively in marketing have seen positive results.[45] Unlike other forms of marketing research, using big data can reveal specific details about consumers that would be hard to discover in other ways. The marketing vice president at DataSift—an organization that analyzes social data—has determined that his company's software can mine 400 pieces of data from a 280-character tweet.[46] For these reasons, Johnson & Johnson is partnering with IBM to use IBM's big data service, Watson, to assess the probability of success for drugs before their release to the market. Johnson & Johnson hopes this partnership will help speed up its development of new drugs.[47] In the advertisement, IBM promotes its partnership with *Sesame Street* to create a personalized learning experience for children by using the machine-learning platform to adapt to each child's learning style, ability, and needs. *Sesame Street* is using big data to transform education.

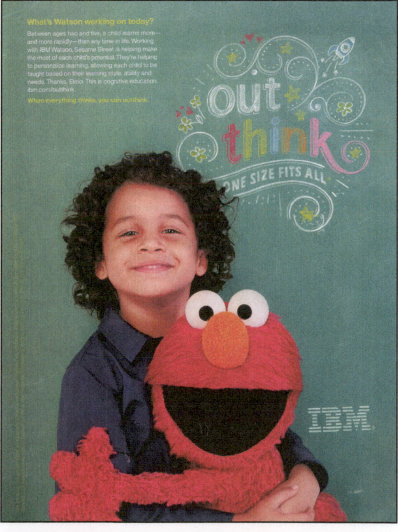

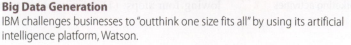

Big Data Generation
IBM challenges businesses to "outthink one size fits all" by using its artificial intelligence platform, Watson.

Big data is important because marketers can look at patterns of consumption behavior and discover trends that predict future buying behaviors. Not all of these patterns would be as visible through traditional marketing research methods. It is obvious, for instance, that a woman buying baby supplies is likely pregnant or has a new baby. However, other consumption patterns are less obvious. Target has found that purchases of larger quantities of unscented lotions, cotton balls, scent-free soap, and supplements are also predictors of pregnancy. Target discovered these trends by analyzing its collection of data on consumer purchases. These discoveries have allowed the firm to accurately predict pregnancy. As a result, it has been able to send out marketing materials, such as coupons for diapers, to this demographic in the hopes that they will become future loyal customers.[48] Big data can, therefore, improve the relationship between company and consumer.

Despite the benefits of big data to marketing research, the challenge for marketers is to figure out how to use pieces of data to develop more targeted marketing strategies. Marketers must know what data to examine, which analytical tools to use, and how to translate this data into customer insights.[49] Big data is useless if an organization's marketers do not know how to use it. Mining big data for customer insights takes much time and energy. In one research study surveying marketers, a little more than half indicated that their organizations had a good understanding of big data. A major reason is that many marketers do not understand the definition of big data or its benefits.[50] Additionally, as with marketing research, big data can still be subject to bias, projection error, and sampling issues.[51]

Although big data yields tremendous insights into consumer preferences, lifestyles, and behaviors, it also creates serious privacy issues. Many consumers do not like to have their purchasing behavior tracked, and sometimes using big data for marketing purposes creates conflict. On the other hand, social media networks such as Facebook and Twitter provide listening centers to monitor conversation about product and companies. Listening to different social media can indicate what consumers say about a specific brand, about competitors, or about an industry.[52] Pinpointing the desires and needs of the target market creates big data files that require marketing analytics to aid in strategy development and to learn how to adjust implementation of existing strategies. Although the benefits of big data for marketing are numerous, and many consumers appreciate the added benefits of receiving marketing materials specifically targeted toward their needs, others feel uncomfortable with companies knowing so much about them. At the same time, companies that ignore big data miss out on the opportunity to develop stronger marketing strategies and customer relationships. Avoiding big data could cause a business to sacrifice a competitive advantage. Although there is no easy solution to this issue, consumers can do one thing if they do not want their store purchases tracked: pay in cash. However, some stores still track purchases by recording customer account numbers for frequent purchase awards.

5-4d Marketing Analytics

Big data is of little use without tools to measure and interpret the data to glean insights and develop better-targeted campaigns. As digital marketing has become more popular, adding more complexity to the field of marketing, organizations have found the need to focus more extensively on how to measure the effectiveness of their marketing strategies. **Marketing analytics** uses tools and methods to measure and interpret the effectiveness of a firm's marketing activities. The purpose of marketing analytics is to evaluate the company's ROI on its marketing strategies and make adjustments when necessary. This usually involves investing in software that can track, store, and analyze data. Big data linked to analytics software unlocks insights with decision-ready intelligence. For example, SAP provides advanced marketing analytics software with predictive features. Investing in marketing analytics involves the following four steps: (1) defining what to measure and which tools to use, (2) collecting data,

marketing analytics The use of tools and methods to measure and interpret the effectiveness of a firm's marketing activities

(3) developing reporting capabilities, and (4) implementing the campaign and analyzing the results.[53] Having the right data and the right methods is necessary in our data-rich business environment.[54]

Marketing analytics is considered one of the most important marketing research tools to aid strategic decisions and implementation. Developments in software can automate analysis of massive amounts of data available to marketers. Databases provide the opportunity to engage in data mining to better understand the attitudes and behaviors of consumers. Retailers create data from checkout scanners that can be used to determine purchasing patterns. For example, in a supermarket, if consumers are regularly buying Kashi cereal and Silk soy milk at the same time, maybe there could be a joint promotion.

Dashboards are a data management tool to visually communicate important information for decision making. Dashboards can convert data analytics to easy-to-use key performance indicators (KPIs). The dashboard is a way to provide a report of findings and make it available so a variety of marketers in different positions can use the data to make decisions. For example, Wave Analytics is an IT company that provides self-service analytics that the marketer can see instantly on any device. Therefore, decision makers can gain knowledge and take action. The ability to harness trillions of gigabytes of data and convert to useable information provides marketing research findings on demand.

Using marketing analytics is becoming an increasingly important part of companies' marketing activities, even among mid-sized and smaller organizations. More than 30 percent of companies have integrated marketing analytics into the daily activities of the marketing function, and marketing professionals believe that an increasing percentage of the marketing budget should go toward analytics. Web analytics has become highly important for measuring marketing effectiveness. More than 82 percent of marketers that use analytics tools measure their website traffic and performance.[55] Google Analytics is the most popular web analytics software and can be helpful for small businesses without a large marketing budget because its basic functions are free to use. Marketers use Google Analytics to measure website visitors, page views, the percentage of new visits, the average amount of time spent during a visit, and more.[56] Even more sophisticated marketing analytics software is available for marketers who want a more in-depth look at the effectiveness of their marketing activities that can be tied to ROI.

The highest goal marketers appear to have with marketing analytics is identifying how to develop better-targeted campaigns.[57] British Airways, for example, has successfully used marketing analytics to increase activities geared toward forming relationships with customers. It adopted a marketing analytics program that combined information on customer loyalty with information on the online behavior and buying patterns of the company's 20 million customers. The software has enabled the company to target thank-you messages to their most loyal customers and offer incentives.[58] The successful deployment of marketing analytics positively relates to favorable and sustainable marketing performance. Research shows that a one-unit increase in marketing analytics deployment results in an 8 percent increase in a company's return on assets.[59] It is, therefore, imperative that marketers investigate which marketing analytics metrics would best work for their companies to improve marketing performance and maintain competitive advantages.

Marketing Analytics
Google Analytics is the most popular web analytics software.

DISRUPTIVE MARKETING

Making Meaning Out of Big Data: Marketing Analytics

The field of marketing research is changing. Where it was once dominated by focus groups and surveys, today's marketers are increasingly turning to marketing analytics to glean customer insights. Big data and marketing analytics are being used to disrupt industries across the board. A report found that large business-to-consumer firms are planning to increase their spending on marketing analytics by almost 100 percent in a three-year period. Eighty-three percent of business leaders pursue big data projects in the belief that it will provide their firms with a competitive advantage. The advantages of marketing analytics are not limited to business-to-consumer firms; approximately 79 percent of businesses that sell to other businesses believe analytics is important in identifying marketing channels that increase ROI.

It is not enough simply to record big data. The hard part is determining which small bits of information among massive data files will reveal significant customer insights. However, interpreting big data correctly can help marketers recognize trends they never would have realized existed otherwise. For instance, one analytics firm helped a mobile phone manufacturer determine that the major reason consumers bought its phone was not because of the camera, which is what the firm thought, but because of a certain app built into the phone. There is no doubt that marketing analytics has begun to revolutionize marketers' understanding of customer trends and preferences.[a]

5-4e Marketing Decision Support Systems

A **marketing decision support system (MDSS)** is customized computer software that aids marketing managers in decision making by helping them anticipate the effects of certain decisions. MDSS is linked to the availability of big data and marketing analytics. An MDSS offers great computational and modeling capabilities and has a broad range and advanced marketing analytics, allowing managers to explore a wide range of alternatives. For instance, an MDSS can determine how sales and profits might be affected by higher or lower interest rates or how sales forecasts, advertising expenditures, production levels, and the like might affect overall profits. For this reason, MDSS software is often a major component of a company's marketing information system. Some decision support systems incorporate artificial intelligence and other advanced computer technologies.

Learning Objective 5-5

Identify ethical and international issues in marketing research.

5-5 ISSUES IN MARKETING RESEARCH

Marketers should identify concerns that influence the integrity of research. Ethical issues are a constant risk in gathering and maintaining the quality of information. International issues relate to environmental differences, such as culture, legal requirements, level of technology, and economic development.

5-5a The Importance of Ethical Marketing Research

marketing decision support system (MDSS) Customized computer software that aids marketing managers in decision making

Marketing managers and other professionals are relying more and more on marketing research, marketing information systems, and new technologies to make better decisions. Therefore, it is essential that professional standards be established by which to judge the reliability of marketing research. Such standards are necessary because of the ethical and legal issues that develop in gathering marketing research data. In the area of online interaction, for example, consumers remain wary of how the personal information collected by marketers will be used, especially whether it will be sold to third parties. In addition, the relationships between research suppliers, such as marketing research agencies, and the marketing managers who make strategy decisions require ethical behavior. Organizations such as the Marketing Research Association have developed codes of conduct and guidelines to promote ethical marketing research. To be effective, such guidelines must instruct marketing researchers on how to avoid misconduct. Table 5.5 provides sample steps researchers should follow when introducing a questionnaire to a customer in order to ensure respondent cooperation and satisfaction.

Consumer privacy has also become a significant issue. Firms now have the ability to purchase data on customer demographics, interests, and more personal matters such as bankruptcy filings and past marriages. This information has allowed companies to predict customer behavior or current life changes more accurately but may also infringe upon consumer privacy.[60] Videotaping customers in retail stores or tracking shoppers' mobile phones helps retailers understand store traffic, repeat customers, and eye movement. It also raises serious concerns about whether the stores are violating the rights of "honest shoppers."[61] The popularity of the internet has enabled marketers to collect data on internet users who visit their websites. Many companies have been able to use this to their advantage. For instance, Amazon, Netflix, and eBay use data to make customized recommendations based on their customers' interests, ratings, or past purchases. Although such data enable companies to offer more personalized services, policy makers fear that it could also allow them to discriminate among consumers who do not appear to be "valuable" customers.[62]

5-5b International Issues in Marketing Research

As we shall see in Chapter 9, sociocultural, economic, political, legal, and technological forces vary in different regions of the world. These variations create challenges for the organizations that are attempting to understand foreign customers through marketing research. The marketing research process we describe in this chapter is used globally, but to ensure the research is valid and reliable, data-gathering methods may have to be modified to allow for regional differences. To make certain that global and regional differences are satisfactorily addressed, many companies retain a research firm with experience in the country of interest.

Table 5.5 Guidelines for Questionnaire Introduction

- Allow interviewers to introduce themselves by name.
- State the name of the research company.
- Indicate that this questionnaire is a marketing research project.
- Explain that no sales will be involved.
- Note the general topic of discussion (if this is a problem in a "blind" study, a statement such as "consumer opinion" is acceptable).
- State the likely duration of the interview.
- Assure the anonymity of the respondent and the confidentiality of all answers.
- State the honorarium, if applicable (for many business-to-business and medical studies, this is done up-front for both qualitative and quantitative studies).
- Reassure the respondent with a statement such as, "There are no right or wrong answers, so please give thoughtful and honest answers to each question" (recommended by many clients).

Source: The Marketing Research Association

CREATIVE MARKETING

Marketing Research Reveals Marketing Opportunities in the Baby Boomer Generation

For many years, marketers have focused on consumers between the ages of 18 and 34 to promote products in the hopes of creating lifetime loyal customers. However, statistics show that spending among these Millennials is actually shrinking, and Baby Boomer spending has been increasing. Baby Boomers are estimated to have $3.2 trillion in annual buying power. With approximately 20 percent of the U.S. population estimated to be 65 years or older by 2030, marketers are seeking creative marketing ideas to reach these Baby Boomers.

In one study, researchers attempted to understand how older consumers shop and interact in stores by using neck braces, blurry goggles, and other equipment to simulate what a person in his or her 70s with arthritis would experience. This research has been shared with many businesses, which have interpreted the findings to create a retail environment better suited to this demographic. CVS, for instance, has lowered its shelves, made its store lighting softer, and installed magnifying glasses for hard-to-read

labels. Other businesses are using this information to redesign their products.

Additionally, Baby Boomers have created an opportunity for businesses to market entirely new products. Technology firms are seeing an opportunity to develop products to be installed in the homes of older consumers to monitor the movements of the inhabitants and alert family or experts if there are any changes in the inhabitants' movements. Many Baby Boomers are also concerned with preserving their more youthful appearance. Lingerie maker Maidenform has created shapewear, or clothes that help to tone the body, targeted toward those of ages 35 to 54.

Although marketers have long focused on Millennials, the demand for products by Baby Boomers is causing companies to get more creative with their marketing. Marketing research is key to understanding the Baby Boomer demographic and creating the goods and services that best meet their needs.[b]

Most of the largest marketing research firms derive a significant share of their revenues from research conducted outside the United States. Table 5.6 includes Kantar, one of the largest marketing research firms in the world, a U.S. company with a market presence in 100 different countries. About 74.2 percent of its revenue is generated from outside of the United States.[63]

Experts recommend a two-pronged approach to international marketing research. The first phase involves a detailed search for, and analysis of, secondary data to gain a greater understanding of a particular marketing environment and to pinpoint issues that must be taken into account in gathering primary research data. Secondary data can be particularly helpful in building a general understanding of the market, including economic, legal, cultural, and demographic issues; in assessing the risks of doing business in that market; and in forecasting

Table 5.6 Top U.S. Marketing Research Firms

Company Rank	Global Revenues (in Millions of U.S. Dollars)	Percent of Revenues from Outside the United States
1 The Nielsen Co.	$6,300	42.5%
2 QuintilesIMD	3,300	58.9
3 Kantar	3,894	74.2
4 IRI	1,026	38.5
5 Ipsos	1,968	71

Source: Diane Bowers and Michael Brereton, "The 2017 AMA Gold Top 50 Report," *Marketing News*, https://www.ama.org/publications/MarketingNews/Pages/the-ama-gold-report-2017-top-50-market-research-firms.aspx (accessed February 5, 2018).

demand. Marketing researchers often begin by studying country trade reports from the U.S. Department of Commerce as well as country-specific information from local sources, such as a country's website, and trade and general business publications, such as *The Wall Street Journal*. These sources can offer insights into the marketing environment in a particular country and can even indicate untapped market opportunities abroad.

The second phase involves field research using many of the methods described earlier, including focus groups and telephone surveys, to refine a firm's understanding of specific customer needs and preferences. Specific differences among countries can have a profound influence on data gathering. In-home (door-to-door) interviews are illegal in some countries. In developing countries, few people have landline telephones as many opt for cell phones, making telephone surveys less practical and less representative of the total population. Primary data gathering may have a greater chance of success if the firm employs local researchers who better understand how to approach potential respondents and can do so in their own languages.[64] Regardless of the specific methods used to gather primary data, whether in the United States or abroad, the goal is to recognize the needs of specific target markets in order to craft the best marketing strategy to satisfy the needs of customers in each market, as we will see in Chapter 6.

Summary

5-1 Define marketing research and its importance to decision makers.

Marketing research is the systematic design, collection, interpretation, and reporting of information to help marketers solve specific marketing problems or take advantage of marketing opportunities. It is a process for gathering information not currently available to decision makers. Marketing research can help a firm better understand market opportunities, ascertain the potential for success for new products, and determine the feasibility of a particular marketing strategy. The value of marketing research is measured by improvements in a marketer's ability to make decisions.

5-2 Distinguish between exploratory and conclusive research.

There are two types of marketing research: exploratory research and conclusive research. When marketers need more information about a problem or want to make a tentative hypothesis more specific, they may conduct exploratory research. The main purpose of exploratory research is to better understand a problem or situation and/or to help identify additional data needs or decision alternatives. More organizations are starting customer advisory boards, small groups of actual customers who serve as sounding boards for new product ideas and offer insights into their feelings and attitudes toward a firm's products, promotion, pricing, and other elements of marketing strategy. Another common method for conducting exploratory research is through a focus group. A focus group brings together multiple people to discuss a certain topic in a group setting led by a moderator.

Conclusive research is designed to verify insights through an objective procedure to help marketers make decisions. It is used when the marketer has one or more alternatives in mind and needs assistance in the final stages of decision making. Conclusive research can be descriptive or experimental. If marketers need to understand the characteristics of certain phenomena to solve a particular problem, descriptive research can aid them. Experimental research allows marketers to make causal deductions about relationships. Such experimentation requires that an independent variable (one not influenced by, or dependent on, other variables) be manipulated and the resulting changes in a dependent variable (one contingent on, or restricted to, one value or set of values assumed by the independent variable) be measured.

5-3 Name the five basic steps in conducting marketing research, including the two types of data and four survey methods.

To maintain the control needed to obtain accurate information, marketers approach marketing research as a process with logical steps: (1) locating and defining problems or issues, (2) designing the research project, (3) collecting data, (4) interpreting research findings, and (5) reporting research findings.

The first step in launching a research study, the problem or issue definition, focuses on uncovering the nature and boundaries of a situation or question related to marketing strategy or implementation. When a firm discovers a market opportunity, it may need to conduct research to understand the situation more precisely so it can craft an appropriate marketing strategy.

In the second step, marketing researchers design a research project to obtain the information needed to address it. This step requires formulating a hypothesis and determining what type of research to employ to test the hypothesis so the results are reliable and valid. A hypothesis is an informed guess or assumption about a problem or set of circumstances. Marketers conduct exploratory research when they need more information about a problem or want to make a tentative hypothesis more specific; they use conclusive research to verify insights through an objective procedure. Research is considered reliable if it produces almost identical results in repeated trials; it is valid if it measures what it is supposed to measure.

For the third step of the research process, collecting data, two types of data are available. Primary data are observed and recorded or collected directly from respondents; secondary data are compiled inside or outside the organization for some purpose other than the current investigation. Sources of secondary data include an organization's own database and other internal sources, periodicals, government publications, unpublished sources, and online databases. Methods of collecting primary data include sampling, surveys, observation, and experimentation. Sampling involves selecting representative units from a total population. In probability sampling, every element in the population being studied has a known chance of being selected for study. Nonprobability sampling is more subjective than probability sampling because there is no way to calculate the likelihood that a specific element of the population being studied will be chosen. Marketing researchers employ sampling to collect primary data through mail, telephone, online, or personal interview surveys. A carefully constructed questionnaire is essential to the success of any survey. In using observation methods, researchers record respondents' overt behavior and take note of physical conditions and events. In an experiment, marketing researchers attempt to maintain certain variables while measuring the effects of experimental variables.

To apply research data to decision making, marketers must interpret and report their findings properly—the final two steps in the marketing research process. Statistical interpretation focuses on what is typical or what deviates from the average. After interpreting the research findings, the researchers must prepare a report on the findings that the decision makers can understand and use. Researchers must also take care to avoid bias and distortion.

5-4 Describe the tools, such as databases, big data, marketing analytics, and decision support systems useful to marketing decision making.

Many firms use computer technology to create a marketing information system (MIS), a framework for managing and structuring information gathered regularly from sources both inside and outside the organization. A database is a collection of information arranged for easy access and retrieval. Big data involves massive data files that can be obtained from both structured and unstructured databases. Marketing analytics is the use of tools and methods to measure and interpret the effectiveness of a firm's marketing activities. A marketing decision support system (MDSS) is customized computer software that aids marketing managers in decision making by helping them anticipate the effects of certain decisions. Online information services and the internet also enable marketers to communicate with customers and obtain information.

5-5 Identify ethical and international issues in marketing research.

Eliminating unethical marketing research practices and establishing generally acceptable procedures for conducting research are important goals of marketing research. Both domestic and international marketing use the same marketing research process, but international marketing may require modifying data-gathering methods to address regional differences.

Important Terms

marketing research 124
exploratory research 126
customer advisory
   boards 126
focus group 126
conclusive research 127
descriptive research 127
experimental
   research 128
research design 129
hypothesis 129
reliability 129
validity 129

primary data 130
secondary data 130
population 132
sample 132
sampling 132
probability
   sampling 133
random sampling 133
stratified
   sampling 133
nonprobability
   sampling 133
quota sampling 133

mail survey 134
telephone survey 135
telephone depth
   interview 135
personal interview
   survey 135
in-home (door-to-door)
   interview 136
shopping mall intercept
   interviews 136
on-site computer
   interview 136
online survey 136

crowdsourcing 137
statistical
   interpretation 139
marketing information
   system (MIS) 141
database 142
single-source
   data 142
big data 143
marketing analytics 144
marketing decision
   support system
   (MDSS) 146

Discussion and Review Questions

1. What is marketing research? Why is it important?
2. Describe the five steps in the marketing research process.
3. What is the difference between defining a research problem and developing a hypothesis?
4. Describe the different types of approaches to marketing research, and indicate when each should be used.
5. Where are data for marketing research obtained? Give examples of internal and external data.
6. What is the difference between probability sampling and nonprobability sampling? In what situation would random sampling be best? Stratified sampling? Quota sampling?
7. Suggest some ways to encourage respondents to cooperate in mail surveys.
8. If a survey of all homes with listed telephone numbers is to be conducted, what sampling design should be used?
9. Describe some marketing problems that could be solved through information gained from observation.
10. What is a marketing information system, and what should it provide?
11. Define database. What is its purpose, and what does it include?
12. What is *big data?* Why is it important to marketing research?
13. How can marketers use online services and the internet to obtain information for decision making?
14. What role do ethics play in marketing research? Why is it important that marketing researchers be ethical?
15. How does marketing research in other countries differ from marketing research in the United States?

Developing Your Marketing Plan

Decisions about which market opportunities to pursue, what customer needs to satisfy, and how to reach potential customers are not made in a vacuum. The information provided by marketing research activities is essential in developing both the strategic plan and the specific marketing mix. Focus on the following issues as you relate the concepts in this chapter to the development of your marketing plan.

1. Define the nature and scope of the questions you must answer with regard to your market. Identify the types of information you will need about the market to answer those questions. For example, do you need to know about the buying habits, household income levels, or attitudes of potential customers?
2. Determine whether or not this information can be obtained from secondary sources.
3. Using Table 5.3, choose the appropriate survey method(s) you would use to collect primary data for one of your information needs. What sampling method would you use?

Video Case 5.1

Picture Perfect: How Instagram Uses Big Data

Instagram is a photo-sharing app that has surpassed 800 million daily active users. In contrast, rival Snapchat has 173 million. Instagram allows its users to manipulate their photos with different filters and share them with friends and the greater Instagram community with hashtags and location tags. One thing that makes the platform so engaging for its active users is the personalized experience Instagram creates using artificial intelligence and big data.

With more than 70 million new photos posted to the app each day, Instagram has endless data logged from the ways users engage with posts. Instagram uses machine learning to populate its Discover tab, an area in the app where users can explore content on the platform. According to Dan Toffey, Head of Community Lab, Instagram dives into vast amounts of data to understand how people use the platform and to create a curated experience for users. For example, Instagram is able to adjust a user's feed based on likes, comments, follows, search preferences, and more. The app continuously learns from user behavior and adapts over time.

"We have this rich diversity of data that we're able to use to look for constellations of accounts. Then we can go in with humans and look at it and understand what they're doing," Toffey said.

Instagram's Community Lab team works to unearth insights from data trends. Big data is valuable but it is useless when a company doesn't know how to use it. Mining big data for customer insights can take a lot of time and resources. Instagram prioritizes this and is able to drive product development and extract community insights as a result. Instagram strikes a balance between artificial intelligence and human curation to deliver personalized content as well as subject matter that may be outside of a user's interests to create new opportunities for engagement.

Instagram also uses this data to sell advertising to companies who want to reach various user groups. Facebook purchased Instagram for $1 billion in 2012 with the intention of breaking into the mobile industry. With more people using mobile apps or accessing the internet through their smartphones, the use of photo sharing through mobile devices is increasing. This also adds to the data pool Instagram has to work with to offer highly targeted advertising.

Instagram also uses artificial intelligence to filter out spam posts and comments. The system, called DeepText, was created by Facebook to remove fake messages across nine different languages: English, Chinese, Russian, Arabic,

and more. It has the ability to understand not just bad words but the context in which they are used. DeepText was trained by humans who sorted through messages and classified them as spam or not spam. It has expanded to also remove messages that fall into the categories of bullying, racism, or sexual harassment. While it's not a perfect system, the filter outperforms static algorithms because it is always learning.

"The whole idea of machine learning is that it's far better about understanding those nuances than any algorithm has in the past, or than any single human being could," said Kevin Systrom, Instagram's CEO and co-founder. "And I think what we have to do is figure out how to get into those gray areas and judge the performance of this algorithm over time to see if it actually improves things. Because, by the way, if it causes trouble and it doesn't work, we'll scrap it and start over with something new."

Above all, Instagram's use of big data is aimed at enhancing the user experience to ensure users keep coming back for more. The influx of content and users on a daily basis requires the platform to be nimble when it comes to learning from its findings and adapting the app.[65]

Questions for Discussion

1. Describe Instagram's process for populating content on the Discover page.
2. Why is it important for Instagram to create a tailored app experience for each user?
3. In what other ways could Instagram use big data to improve its platform?

Case 5.2

No Mystery Here: Why Market Force Is a Leading Market Research Firm

What if someone could consolidate the fragmented customer experience measurement industry? This is the question Market Force Information co-founders Karl Maier, Paul Berberian, and Rushton McGarr asked themselves when they set out to create a customer experience management company in 2005. Market Force combines services like mystery shopping, social media monitoring, employee surveys, market research, and in-store audits to help stores with multiple locations measure and improve the customer experience.

This data and insights firm, based in Louisville, Colorado, has been hired by companies to provide a look into their shoppers. Rent-A-Center; a rent-to-own retailer of furniture, electronics, appliances, and more; plans to employ Market Force's mystery shopping services. Mystery

shopping is when shoppers pose as regular customers while evaluating and reporting on their experience. Market Force's KnowledgeForce platform is capable of gathering and analyzing the data gathered from mystery shoppers to reveal areas for improvement at the location level. The company has amassed a mystery shopper database of more than 200,000 that report on in-store, online, and phone shopping experiences. Using data from mystery shops helps businesses improve customer loyalty. Retaining existing customers is often less expensive than acquiring new customers.

With the desire to increase beverage sales, Church's Chicken partnered with Market Force to create an employee incentive program that used mystery shoppers to reward team members instantly when an employee successfully executed trained upselling behavior. The program was successful with a 5.6 percent increase in beverage sales, benefiting both Church's Chicken as well as its beverage supplier. It allowed the restaurant to emphasize the right behaviors for its employees while gathering insights into customer service, speed of service, cleanliness, food quality, order accuracy, and upselling combo meals and beverages.

Market Force also relies heavily on consumer surveys. For example, a recent Customer Loyalty Index survey of 12,774 consumers revealed Publix and Wegmans are America's favorite grocery stores. Supermarkets were rated based on value, cashier courtesy, checkout speed, product availability, ease of finding products, specialty services, and cleanliness. In order to collect the data, Market Force uses a sample that represents the characteristics of a total population to project the reactions of the market and predict buying behavior. Grocery stores can use this data to determine whether their goods and services satisfy the desires of target market customers.

It is important for businesses to monitor customer buying behavior, industry forecasts, and business trends in order to anticipate consumer demand. By analyzing click-and-collect grocery services, where consumers order groceries online and pick up at the store, Market Force found that consumer use of these services has doubled in recent years and more than a quarter of those surveyed used the service at least once per month. Similarly, Market Force is able to use its data to forecast that food delivery services like GrubHub, UberEats, and Postmates will grow to $76 billion by 2022. This data, which suggests there will be fewer in-store shoppers in the near future, is important for stores like Walmart, Kroger, Whole Foods, and Harris Teeter so they can adjust their marketing strategy accordingly. Such information highlights an opportunity for supermarkets to offer online ordering, curbside grocery

KEN WOLTER/SHUTTERSTOCK.COM

pickup, and meal delivery to satisfy this growing segment of the market.

Market Force now has offices in the United States, Canada, U.K., France, and Spain as it continues to grow globally. It serves more than 350 clients, completes more than 100,000 mystery shops per month, and was recently named in the American Marketing Association's Gold Report of top 50 market research firms. Market research is central to Market Force's operations. It has the potential to help its clients develop and implement marketing strategies to increase sales and customer satisfaction. Market Force's use of marketing research to glean insights on behalf of multi-location businesses is critical to determining new ways to improve the customer experience.[66]

Questions for Discussion

1. Discuss how retailers can use the insights from mystery shoppers to alter their marketing strategy.
2. How does Market Force leverage marketing research to help its clients?
3. Why is it important for businesses to continually gather market research from their target markets?

6

Target Markets: Segmentation and Evaluation

LEARNING OBJECTIVES

6-1 Define what markets are and explain how they are generally classified.

6-2 List the five steps of the target market selection process.

6-3 Compare three targeting strategies.

6-4 Identify the major segmentation variables.

6-5 Explain what market segment profiles are and how they are used.

6-6 Describe how to evaluate market segments.

6-7 Identify the factors that influence the selection of specific market segments for use as target markets.

6-8 Discuss sales forecasting methods.

JPSTOCK/SHUTTERSTOCK.COM

L'Oréal Targets More Than Just Pretty Faces

So many brands, so many target markets. L'Oréal, based in France, is the global leader in beauty brands, offering L'Oréal Paris, Lancôme, Maybelline New York, Essie, and Garnier, among other famous names. It has grown annual revenues beyond $27 billion by aiming to reach a wider range of consumers interested in personal-care products that pamper the skin and express individual style. In the "selfie" era, L'Oréal's marketing reflects the many faces of cosmetics users today, targeting men as well as women, from preteens to seniors, around the world.

For example, to reach men who are using or want to try cosmetics, L'Oréal has featured makeup artist Gary Thompson in its advertising, bringing its brands to the attention of his large social-media following as "ThePlasticBoy." The company offers beard shampoo, face moisturizers, skin cleansers, and other products developed especially for men. L'Oréal's Giorgio Armani beauty brand offers unisex cosmetics products, suitable for both men and women. Looking ahead, L'Oréal envisions men's cosmetics counters in department stores and drug stores, as a place to try and buy different products that meet their needs.

L'Oréal also has expanded the number of makeup shades it offers in its True Match face foundation line, a part of its strategy to target women from diverse backgrounds. Some of its cosmetics products are geared toward younger women interested in personal expression, while others appeal to older women seeking anti-aging benefits. As a result, L'Oréal's ads focus on ageless beauty, from 20-something actress Elle Fanning to 70-something actress Helen Mirren.[1]

Like most organizations that are trying to compete effectively, L'Oréal must identify specific customer groups, such as women and men of all ages, toward which they will direct marketing efforts. This process includes developing and maintaining marketing mixes that satisfy the needs of those customers. In this chapter, we define and explore the concepts of markets and market segmentation. First, we discuss the major requirements of a market. Then, we examine the steps in the target market selection process, including identifying the appropriate targeting strategy, determining which variables to use for segmenting consumer and business markets, developing market segment profiles, evaluating relevant market segments, and selecting target markets. We conclude with a discussion of the various methods for developing sales forecasts.

Learning Objective 6-1

Define what markets are and explain how they are generally classified.

6-1 WHAT ARE MARKETS?

In Chapter 2, we defined a *market* as a group of individuals and/or organizations that have a desire or need for products in a product class and have the ability, willingness, and authority to purchase those products. You, as a student, are part of the market for textbooks. You are part of other markets as well, such as for computers, clothes, food, and music. To truly be a market, consumers must possess all four characteristics. For instance, teenagers are not part of the market for alcohol. They may have the desire, willingness, and ability to buy liquor, but they do not have the authority to do so because teenagers are prohibited by law from buying alcoholic beverages.

Markets fall into one of two categories: consumer markets and business markets. These categories are based on the characteristics of the individuals and groups that make up a specific market and the purposes for which they buy products. A **consumer market** consists of purchasers and household members who intend to consume or benefit from the purchased products and do not buy products to make a profit. Consumer markets are sometimes referred to as *business-to-consumer (B2C) markets.* Each of us belongs to numerous consumer markets for all the purchases we make in categories such as housing, food, clothing, vehicles, personal services, appliances, furniture, recreational equipment, and other products.

A **business market** consists of individuals, organizations, or groups that purchase a specific kind of product for one of three purposes: resale, direct use in producing other products, or use in general daily operations. For instance, a producer that buys electrical wire to use in the production of lamps is part of a business market for electrical wire. Some products can be part of either the business or consumer market, depending on their end use. For instance, if you purchase a chair for your home, that chair is part of the consumer market. However, if an office manager purchases the same chair for use in a business office, it is part of the business market. Business markets may be called *business-to-business (B2B), industrial,* or *organizational markets* and can be sub-classified into producer, reseller, government, and institutional markets, as we shall see in Chapter 8.

The advertisements show a product targeted at the consumer market and one targeted at the business market. The photo in the Oui French Style Yogurt advertisement shows a pair of hands dishing yogurt out of the product's distinctive glass package. The ad emphasizes the newness of the product, its simplicity, and the fact that it comes from a traditional French recipe. The Supermicro ad, on the other hand, pictures a room full of MicroBlade servers in a data center. The ad promotes the features of MicroBlade servers and highlights the fact that they enabled a Fortune 100 company to achieve one of the world's highest efficiency data centers. You can see from these two advertisements that the one for Supermicro focuses on the practical application of the product in the business world, while the advertisement for Oui yogurt highlights the product's French simplicity, illustrating how marketers will have different objectives depending on which market they target.

consumer market Purchasers and household members who intend to consume or benefit from the purchased products and do not buy products to make a profit

business market Individuals, organizations, or groups that purchase a specific kind of product for resale, direct use in producing other products, or use in general daily operations

Types of Markets

Oui yogurt targets a consumer market by emphasizing that its new yogurt is inspired by its traditional French recipe, while Supermicro focuses on a business market by showing how its products can be used in data centers.

6-2 TARGET MARKET SELECTION PROCESS

As indicated earlier, the first of two major components of developing a marketing strategy is to select a target market. Although marketers may employ several methods for target market selection, generally they follow a five-step process. This process is shown in Figure 6.1, and we explore these steps in the following sections.

Figure 6.1	Target Market Selection Process

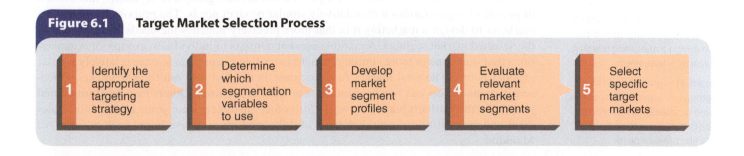

1. Identify the appropriate targeting strategy
2. Determine which segmentation variables to use
3. Develop market segment profiles
4. Evaluate relevant market segments
5. Select specific target markets

6-3 STEP 1: IDENTIFY THE APPROPRIATE TARGETING STRATEGY

A target market is a group of people or organizations for which a business creates and maintains a marketing mix specifically designed to satisfy the needs of group members. The strategy used to select a target market is affected by target market characteristics, product attributes, and the organization's objectives and resources. Figure 6.2 illustrates the three basic targeting strategies: undifferentiated, concentrated, and differentiated.

6-3a Undifferentiated Targeting Strategy

An organization sometimes defines an entire market for a product as its target market. When a company designs a single marketing mix and directs it at the entire market for a particular product, it is using an **undifferentiated targeting strategy**. As Figure 6.2 shows, the strategy assumes that all customers in the target market have similar needs, and thus the organization can satisfy most customers with a single marketing mix with little or no variation. Products marketed successfully through the undifferentiated strategy include commodities and staple food items, such as sugar, salt, and conventionally raised produce.

The undifferentiated targeting strategy is effective under two conditions. First, a large proportion of customers in a total market must have similar needs for the product, a situation termed a **homogeneous market**. A marketer using a single marketing mix for a total market of customers with a variety of needs would find that the marketing mix satisfies very few people. For example, marketers would have little success using an undifferentiated strategy to sell a "universal car" because different customers have varying needs. Second, the organization must have the resources to develop a single marketing mix that satisfies customers' needs in a large portion of a total market and the managerial skills to maintain it.

The reality is that although customers may have similar needs for a few products, for most products their needs are different enough to warrant separate marketing mixes. In such instances, a company should use a concentrated or a differentiated strategy.

6-3b Concentrated Targeting Strategy through Market Segmentation

Although most people will be satisfied with the same white sugar, not everyone wants or needs the same car, furniture, or clothes. A market comprised of individuals or organizations with diverse product needs is called a **heterogeneous market**. Some individuals, for instance, want a Ford truck because they have to haul heavy loads for their work, while others live in the city and enjoy the ease of parking and the good gas mileage of a Smart car. The automobile market thus is heterogeneous.

For heterogeneous markets, market segmentation is the best approach. **Market segmentation** is the process of dividing a total market into groups, or segments, that consist of people or organizations with relatively similar product needs. The purpose is to enable a marketer to design a marketing mix that more precisely matches the needs of customers in the selected market segment. A **market segment** consists of individuals, groups, or organizations that share one or more similar characteristics that cause them to have relatively similar product needs. The total market for blue jeans is divided into multiple segments. Price-sensitive customers can buy bargain jeans at Walmart or Ross. Others may need functional jeans, like the Carhartt brand, for work. Still other customers wear jeans as a fashion statement and are willing to spend hundreds of dollars on an exclusive brand such as 7 for All Mankind.

undifferentiated targeting strategy A strategy in which an organization designs a single marketing mix and directs it at the entire market for a particular product

homogeneous market A market in which a large proportion of customers have similar needs for a product

heterogeneous market A market made up of individuals or organizations with diverse needs for products in a specific product class

market segmentation The process of dividing a total market into groups consisting of people or organizations with relatively similar product needs in order to design a marketing mix that matches those needs

market segment Individuals, groups, or organizations sharing one or more similar characteristics that cause them to have similar product needs

Figure 6.2   **Targeting Strategies**

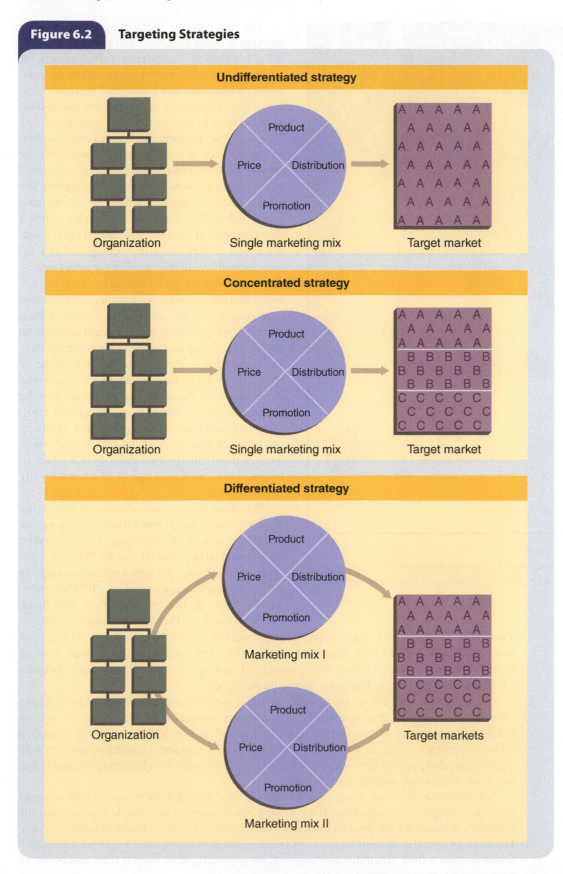

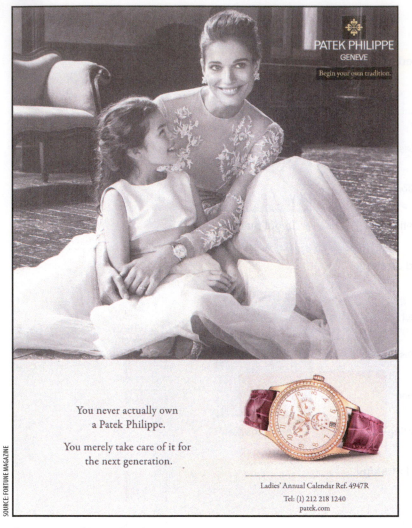

PATEK PHILIPPE
GENEVE

Begin your own tradition.

You never actually own
a Patek Philippe.

You merely take care of it for
the next generation.

Ladies' Annual Calendar Ref. 4947R

Tel: (1) 212 218 1240
patek.com

Concentrated Targeting Strategy
Patek Philippe uses a concentrated targeting strategy, aiming at individuals who purchase high-end watches that are intended to be passed from one generation to the next.

The rationale for segmenting heterogeneous markets is that a company will be most successful in developing a satisfying marketing mix for a portion of a total market whose needs are relatively similar, because customers' needs tend to vary. The majority of organizations use market segmentation to best satisfy their customers.

For market segmentation to succeed, five conditions must exist. First, customers' needs for the product must be heterogeneous. Otherwise, there is no reason to waste resources segmenting the market. Second, segments must be identifiable and divisible. The company must be able to find a characteristic, or variable, for effectively separating a total market into groups comprised of individuals with relatively uniform product needs. Third, marketers must be able to compare the different market segments with respect to estimated sales potential, costs, and profits. Fourth, at least one segment must have enough profit potential to justify developing and maintaining a special marketing mix for it. Finally, the company must be able to reach the chosen segment with a particular marketing mix. Some market segments may be difficult or impossible to reach because of legal, social, or distribution constraints. For instance, producers of tobacco products cannot legally promote or distribute their products to U.S. children because those under the age of 18 cannot legally purchase them.

When an organization directs its marketing efforts toward a single market segment using one marketing mix, it is employing a **concentrated targeting strategy**. Recall that in Figure 6.2 the organization using the concentrated strategy is aiming its marketing mix only at "B" customers. Take a look at the advertisement for Patek Philippe watches. This brand is using a concentrated marketing strategy to reach a specific target market: those who can afford very high-end watches that sell for tens of thousands of dollars. The ad pictures a smiling woman wearing the high-end luxury watch sitting with a young girl to illustrate that this is meant to become a family heirloom, hinting that price should be no object.

As you can see with this ad, the chief advantage of the concentrated strategy is that it allows a firm to specialize. The firm analyzes the characteristics and needs of a distinct customer group and then focuses all its energies on satisfying that group's needs. If the group is big enough, a firm may generate a large sales volume by reaching a single segment. Concentrating on a single segment can also permit a firm with limited resources to compete with larger organizations that may have overlooked smaller segments.

Specialization, however, means that a company allocates all of its resources for one target segment, which can be hazardous. If a company's sales depend on a single segment and the segment's demand for the product declines, the company's financial health also deteriorates. The strategy can also prevent a firm from targeting other segments that might be successful, because when a firm penetrates one segment, its popularity may keep it from extending its marketing efforts into other segments.

concentrated targeting strategy A market segmentation strategy in which an organization targets a single market segment using one marketing mix

6-3c Differentiated Targeting Strategy through Market Segmentation

With a **differentiated targeting strategy**, an organization directs its marketing efforts at two or more segments by developing a marketing mix for each segment (see Figure 6.2). After a firm uses a concentrated targeting strategy successfully in one market segment, it may expand its efforts to include additional segments. For instance, Adidas is primarily considered to be a man's brand of athletic shoes and apparel. Recognizing additional growth opportunities among female consumers, Adidas recently introduced a number of athleisure products that can outfit women from work to the gym. The company, which hired a former Lululemon executive as an advisor, is also airing prime-time commercials featuring more women.[2]

A benefit of a differentiated approach is that a firm may increase sales within the total market because its marketing mixes are aimed at more customers. For this reason, a company with excess production capacity may find a differentiated strategy advantageous because the sale of products to additional segments can help to absorb excess capacity. On the other hand, a differentiated strategy often demands more production processes, materials, and people because the different ingredients in each marketing mix will vary. Thus, production costs for a differentiated strategy may be higher than with a concentrated strategy.

6-4 STEP 2: DETERMINE WHICH SEGMENTATION VARIABLES TO USE

Learning Objective 6-4

Identify the major segmentation variables.

Segmentation variables are the characteristics of individuals, groups, or organizations used to divide a market into segments. Location, age, gender, and rate of product usage can all be bases for segmenting markets. Marketers may use several variables in combination when segmenting a market. As an example, Cheerwine is a soda brand manufactured in North Carolina. It is targeted at soda drinkers in its primary distribution area of southern and mid-Atlantic states and at young people through heavy use of online and social media for advertising and promotional efforts. Because of its relatively limited availability, the soda has maintained a desirability among fans of cool, regional products.[3] Segmentation variables should be used to select the most attractive segments. The criteria for selection include areas where there is a sustainable competitive advantage that creates profitability. Therefore, a competitive analysis can be a strong predictor in finding the best segmentation variables.[4]

To select a segmentation variable, markets consider several factors. The segmentation variable should relate to customers' needs for, uses of, or behavior toward the product. Consider that an automobile marketer is likely to segment the market for cars by income, age, and gender but not by religion, because people's car preferences do not vary much because of religion. Marketers must select measurable segmentation variables, such as age, location, or gender, if individuals or organizations in a total market are to be classified accurately.

There is no best way to segment markets, and the approach will vary depending on a number of factors. A company's resources and capabilities affect the number and size of segment variables used. The type of product and degree of variation in customers' needs also dictate the number and size of segments targeted. No matter what approach is used, choosing one or more segmentation variables is a critical step in effectively targeting a market. Selecting an inappropriate variable limits the chances of developing a successful marketing strategy. To help you better understand potential segmentation variables, we next examine the differences between the major variables used to segment consumer and business markets.

differentiated targeting strategy A strategy in which an organization targets two or more segments by developing a marketing mix for each segment

segmentation variables Characteristics of individuals, groups, or organizations used to divide a market into segments

6-4a Variables for Segmenting Consumer Markets

A marketer that is using segmentation to reach a consumer market can choose one or several variables. As Figure 6.3 shows, segmentation variables can be grouped into four major categories: demographic, geographic, psychographic, and behavioristic.

Demographic Variables

Demographers study aggregate population characteristics such as the distribution of age and gender, fertility rates, migration patterns, and mortality rates. Demographic characteristics that marketers commonly use include age, gender, race, ethnicity, income, education, occupation, family size, family life cycle, religion, and social class. Marketers segment markets by demographic characteristics because they are often closely linked to customers' needs and purchasing behaviors and can be readily measured.

Age is a common variable for segmentation purposes. A trip to the shopping mall highlights the fact that many retailers, including Zara, Forever 21, and American Eagle Outfitters, target teens and very young adults. If considering segmenting by age, marketers need to be aware of age distribution, how that distribution is changing, and how it will affect the demand for different types of products. The proportion of consumers under age 55 is expected to continue to decrease over time as Baby Boomers (born between 1946 and 1964) age. Meanwhile, Millennials (born between 1981 and 1997) now total 79.8 million, surpassing Baby Boomers.[5] In 1970, the median age of a U.S. citizen was 28.1. It is currently 37.9.[6] Because of the increasing average age of Americans, many marketers are searching for ways to market their products to older adults. As Figure 6.4 shows, Americans in different age groups have different product needs because of their different lifestyles, family status, and health situations. Citizens age 65 and older, for instance, spend the most on health care, while those under age 35 spend the most on entertainment and transportation. Hilton Hotels is trying to reach those under 35 with a new hotel concept—as yet unnamed—that will have flexible, small rooms and smaller prices as well as access to trendy restaurants and bars. The hotel company, which has a hotel product for nearly every demographic, hopes the new concept will lure Millennials away from Airbnb and other vacation rental websites.[7]

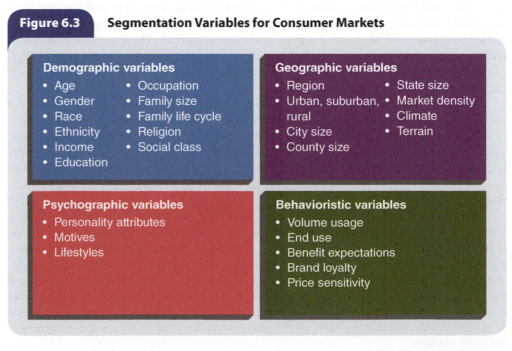

Figure 6.3   Segmentation Variables for Consumer Markets

Demographic variables
- Age
- Gender
- Race
- Ethnicity
- Income
- Education
- Occupation
- Family size
- Family life cycle
- Religion
- Social class

Geographic variables
- Region
- Urban, suburban, rural
- City size
- County size
- State size
- Market density
- Climate
- Terrain

Psychographic variables
- Personality attributes
- Motives
- Lifestyles

Behavioristic variables
- Volume usage
- End use
- Benefit expectations
- Brand loyalty
- Price sensitivity

| Figure 6.4 | Spending Levels by Age Groups for Selected Product Categories |

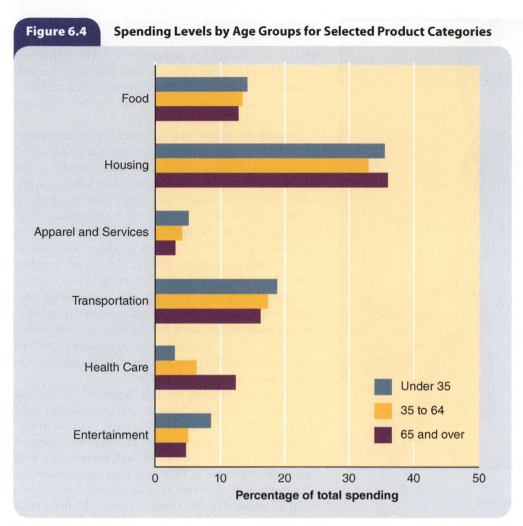

Source: Derived from Ann C. Foster, "Consumer Expenditures by Age," Beyond the Numbers (U.S. Department of Labor, Bureau of Labor Statistics), December 2015, Table 2, http://www.bls.gov/opub/btn/volume-4/consumer-expenditures-vary-by-age.htm (accessed February 7, 2018).

Gender is another demographic variable that is commonly used to segment markets, including clothing, soft drinks, nonprescription medications, magazines, some food items, and personal care products. The U.S. Census Bureau reports that females account for 50.8 percent, and males for 49.2 percent, of the total U.S. population.[8] Although they represent only slightly more than half of the population, women disproportionately influence buying decisions. It is estimated that women account for 85 percent of all consumer purchases, causing many marketers to consider female customers when making marketing decisions.[9] Consider the advertisement for St. Ives. The ad touts that St. Ives Face Scrub is made only from natural exfoliants like walnut shell powder, not plastic microbeads. The images—a young woman making a face and a pile of apricots—are predominantly feminine colors.

Marketers also use race and ethnicity as variables for segmenting markets for such products as food, music, clothing, cosmetics, banking, and insurance. Cosmetics, for example, is an industry in which it is important to match the shade of the products with the skin colors of the target market to maintain customer satisfaction and loyalty. IMAN Cosmetics is a line created by the Ethiopian supermodel Iman, with deeper colors designed to flatter the skin tones of women of color, be they Black, Hispanic, or Asian. These products are not made for, nor marketed to, light-skinned women.[10]

Because income strongly influences people's product purchases, it often provides a way to divide markets. Income affects customers' lifestyles and what they can afford to buy. Product

SOURCE: ST. IVES

Gender Segmentation
St. Ives targets its marketing efforts at women.

markets segmented by income include sporting goods, housing, furniture, cosmetics, clothing, jewelry, home appliances, automobiles, and electronics. Although it may seem obvious to target higher-income consumers because of their larger purchasing power, many marketers choose to target lower-income segments because they represent a much larger population globally.

Among the factors that influence household income and product needs are marital status and the presence and age of children. These characteristics, often combined and called the *family life cycle,* affect needs for housing, appliances, food and beverages, automobiles, and recreational equipment. Transitions between life cycle stages, such as weddings, can also be lucrative for marketers. Consider that there are more than 2 million weddings performed in the U.S. each year, and the average cost of each wedding is $35,329. Marketers know that engaged couples will be highly receptive to wedding-related marketing messages, much like parents-to-be will be receptive to baby-themed marketing, making them a very desirable market segment.[11] Family life cycles can be divided in various ways, as Figure 6.5 shows. This figure depicts the process broken down into nine categories.

The composition of the U.S. household in relation to the family life cycle has changed considerably over the last several decades. Single-parent families are on the rise, with one quarter of all children under age 18 living with a single parent. In fact, households with two married parents in their first marriage account for 46 percent of all households in the United States, down from 73 percent in the 1960s.[12] Nearly 15 percent of

Figure 6.5   **Family Life Cycle Stages as a Percentage of All Households**

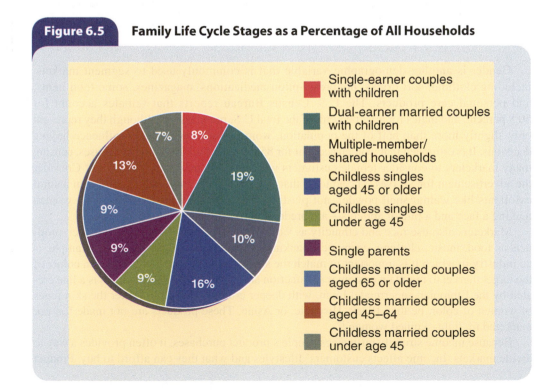

Americans live alone, though that figure is skewed toward the elderly.[13] Previously small groups have risen in prominence, prompting an interest from marketers. For example, more than 8 million households are comprised of unmarried couples living together; three times as many as in 1996.[14] Nearly 800,000 households include same-sex partners.[15] Thus, people live in many different situations, all of which have different requirements for goods and services. Tracking demographic shifts such as these helps marketers be informed and prepared to satisfy the needs of target markets through new marketing mixes that address consumers' changing lifestyles.

Geographic Variables

Geographic variables—climate, terrain, city size, population density, and urban/rural areas— also influence consumer product needs. Markets may be divided using geographic variables because differences in location, climate, and terrain will influence consumers' needs. Consumers in the South, for instance, rarely have a need for snow tires. A company that sells products to a national market might divide the United States into Pacific, Southwest, Central, Midwest, Southeast, Middle Atlantic, and New England regions. A firm that is operating in one or several states might regionalize its market by counties, cities, zip code areas, or other units.

City size can be an important segmentation variable. Many firms choose to limit marketing efforts to cities above a certain size because small populations have been calculated to generate inadequate profits. Other firms actively seek opportunities in smaller towns. A classic example is Walmart, which initially was located only in small towns and even today can be found in towns where other large retailers stay away. If a marketer chooses to divide by a geographic variable, such as city size, the U.S. Census Bureau provides reports on population and demographics that can be of considerable assistance.

Because cities often cut across political boundaries, the U.S. Census Bureau developed a system to classify metropolitan areas (any area with a city or urbanized area with a population of at least 50,000 and a total metropolitan population of at least 100,000). Metropolitan areas are categorized as one of the following: a metropolitan statistical area (MSA), a primary metropolitan statistical area (PMSA), or a consolidated metropolitan statistical area (CMSA). An MSA is an urbanized area encircled by nonmetropolitan counties and is neither socially nor economically dependent on any other metropolitan area. A metropolitan area within a complex of at least 1 million inhabitants can elect to be named a PMSA. A CMSA is a metropolitan area of at least 1 million that has two or more PMSAs. Of the 20 CMSAs, the five largest—New York, Los Angeles, Chicago, San Francisco, and Philadelphia—account for 20 percent of the U.S. population. The federal government provides a considerable amount of socioeconomic information about MSAs, PMSAs, and CMSAs that can aid in market analysis and segmentation.

Market density refers to the number of potential customers within a unit of land area, such as a square mile. Although market density relates generally to population density, the correlation is not exact. For instance, in two different geographic markets of approximately equal size and population, market density for office supplies would be much higher in an area containing a large number of business customers, such as a city downtown, than in another area that is largely residential. Market density may be a useful segmentation variable for firms because low-density markets often require different sales, advertising, and distribution activities than do high-density markets.

Marketers may also use geodemographic segmentation. **Geodemographic segmentation** clusters people by zip codes or neighborhood units based on lifestyle and demographic information. Targeting this way can be effective because people often choose to live in an area that shares their basic lifestyle and political beliefs. Information companies such as Nielsen provide geodemographic data services and products. PRIZM, for example, classifies zip code areas into 66 different cluster types, based on demographic information of residents.[16]

Geodemographic segmentation allows marketers to engage in micromarketing. **Micromarketing** involves focusing precise marketing efforts on very small geographic

market density The number of potential customers within a unit of land area

geodemographic segmentation A way of segmenting the market that clusters people by zip codes or neighborhood units based on lifestyle and demographic information

micromarketing A way of segmenting a market that focuses precise marketing efforts on very small geographic markets, such as communities or neighborhoods

Segmentation Based on Climate
Eddie Bauer targets its EverTherm Down Jackets at individuals who live in cold weather climates.

markets, such as communities and even individual neighborhoods. Providers of financial and health-care services, retailers, and consumer product companies use micromarketing. Many retailers use micromarketing to determine the merchandise mix for individual stores. Increasingly, firms can engage in micromarketing in online retailing, given the internet's ability to target precise interest groups. Unlike traditional micromarketing, online micromarketing is not limited by geography. The wealth of consumer information available online allows marketers to appeal efficiently and effectively to very specific consumer niches.

Climate is commonly used as a geographic segmentation variable because of its broad impact on people's behavior and product needs. Product markets affected by climate include air-conditioning and heating equipment, fireplace accessories, clothing, gardening equipment, recreational products, and building materials. Look at the advertisement for the Eddie Bauer EverTherm Down jacket, which targets consumers who need a coat for extremely cold climates. The ad emphasizes that the EverTherm can keep wearers warm down to −15 degrees (F), better than most down jackets by comparing thermal images of a body in an EverTherm jacket and one in a conventional quilted jacket. The picture of EverTherm-clad hikers walking comfortably in snowy mountains further illustrates the product's benefits for those seeking a performance coat for cold-weather activities.

Psychographic Variables

Marketers sometimes use psychographic variables, such as personality characteristics, motives, and lifestyles, to segment markets. A psychographic variable can be used by itself or in combination with other types of segmentation variables. For example, parents' attitudes and motives shape their purchases of software and technology for their children in ways that go beyond demographics. Using psychographic variables, marketing researchers can divide the family tech market into three segments. Enablers, who have confidence in their children's ability to make their own technology decisions, tend to seek out products based on their entertainment value. Limiters, who strive to minimize their children's screen time, generally focus on products that can further their children's academic skills. Finally, parents who prefer to actively spur and guide their children's technology use typically look for products that promote a balance of fun and educational value. Such segmentation suggests different strategies for reaching the different segments than those used based on basic demographics.[17]

Personality characteristics can be a useful means of segmentation when a product resembles many competing products and consumers' needs are not significantly related to other segmentation variables. However, segmenting a market according to personality traits can be risky. Although marketing practitioners have long believed consumer choice and product use vary with personality, marketing research has generally indicated only a weak relationship. It is difficult to measure personality traits accurately, especially because most personality tests were developed for clinical use, not for segmentation purposes.

When appealing to a personality characteristic, a marketer almost always selects one that many people view positively. Individuals with this characteristic, as well as those who aspire to have it, may be influenced to buy that marketer's brand. Marketers taking this approach do not worry about measuring how many people have the positively valued characteristic. They assume a sizable proportion of people in the target market either have it or aspire to have it.

When motives are used to segment a market, the market is divided according to consumers' reasons for making a purchase. Personal appearance, affiliation, status, safety, and health are examples of motives affecting the types of products purchased and the choice of stores in which they are bought. Marketing efforts based on particular motives can be a point of competitive advantage for a firm. Lifestyle segmentation groups individuals according to how they spend their time, the importance of things in their surroundings (homes or jobs, for example), beliefs about themselves and broad issues, and some demographic characteristics, such as income and education.[18] Lifestyle analysis provides a broad view of buyers because it encompasses numerous characteristics related to people's activities (e.g., work, hobbies, entertainment, sports),

Release yourself back into the wild.

The newly redesigned 2018 Subaru Outback. With Symmetrical All-Wheel Drive + 32 mpg, it's a trustworthy traveling companion. And Subaru has the 2017 lowest 5-Year Cost to Own of all brands, according to Kelley Blue Book. Love. It's what makes a Subaru, a Subaru.

Outback. Well-equipped at $25,895.

SUBARU
Confidence in Motion

Lifestyle Segmentation
Subaru aims its Subaru Outback with all-wheel drive at customers that embrace an outdoor lifestyle.

interests (e.g., family, home, fashion, food, technology), and opinions (e.g., politics, social issues, education, the future). The advertisement for the Subaru Outback, for example, targets consumers who enjoy outdoor activities, telling potential buyers to "Release yourself back into the wild." The ad's depiction of an Outback on a rutted road in the woods along with a description of how its features make it a "trusted traveling companion" are likely to appeal to those adopting an outdoor lifestyle.

PRIZM, by Nielsen, is commonly used by marketers to segment by demographic variables. It can also be used to segment by lifestyles. PRIZM combines demographics, consumer behavior, and geographic data to help marketers identify, understand, and reach their customers and prospects, resulting in a highly robust tool for marketers.[19] PRIZM divides U.S. households into demographically and behaviorally distinct segments that take into account such factors as likes, dislikes, lifestyles, and purchase behaviors. Used by thousands of marketers, including many within Fortune 500 companies, PRIZM provides marketers with a common tool for understanding and reaching customers in a highly diverse and complex marketplace.

Behavioristic Variables

Firms can divide a market according to consumer behavior toward a product, which commonly involves an aspect of product use. Therefore, a market may be separated into users—classified as heavy, moderate, or light—and nonusers. To satisfy a specific group, such as heavy users, marketers may create a distinctive product and price or initiate special promotion and distribution activities. Per capita consumption data help determine different levels of usage by product category. To satisfy customers who use a product in a certain way, some feature—packaging, size, texture, or color—may be designed precisely to make the product easier to use, safer, or more convenient.

Benefit segmentation is the division of a market according to benefits that consumers want from the product. Although most types of market segmentation assume a relationship between the variable and customers' needs, benefit segmentation differs in that the benefits customers seek *are* their product needs. Consider that a customer who purchases over-the-counter cold relief medication may be specifically interested in two benefits: stopping a runny nose and relieving chest congestion. Thus, individuals are segmented directly according to their needs. By determining the desired benefits, marketers can divide people into groups by the benefits they seek. The effectiveness of such segmentation depends on three conditions: (1) the benefits sought must be identifiable, (2) using these benefits, marketers must be able to divide people into recognizable segments, and (3) one or more of the resulting segments must be accessible to the firm's marketing efforts.

Marketers can segment consumer markets using many characteristics. They do not, however, use the same variables to segment business characteristics. We will learn about business market segmentation in the next section.

6-4b   Variables for Segmenting Business Markets

benefit segmentation The division of a market according to benefits that consumers want from the product

Like consumer markets, business markets are frequently segmented for marketing purposes. Marketers segment business markets according to geographic location, type of organization, customer size, and product use.

ENTREPRENEURSHIP IN MARKETING

Halo Top Ice Cream Tops Pint Sales Charts

How does an entrepreneur with no food or marketing experience create an ice cream brand that holds its own with industry giants like Häagen-Dazs and Ben & Jerry's? Smart target marketing. Justin Woolverton was a sweets-loving lawyer when he started testing recipes for a lower-calorie, higher-protein ice cream. After months of experimentation, he settled on a recipe sweetened with stevia to slash the calorie count without sacrificing flavor—a key benefit desired by health-conscious Millennials. In fact, a pint of Halo Top has fewer calories and more protein than a pint of traditional ice cream.

Packaging reflects another of Woolverton's insights. Consumers in his target market want to spoon their way through the whole pint in one sitting, without guilt. As a result, Halo Top is sold only in pints,

prominently labeled with the calorie count for product differentiation. Under the lid, the foil seal encourages buyers to go ahead and indulge: "Stop when you hit the bottom." And, to tempt variety-seeking Millennial palates, Halo Top comes in buzz-worthy flavors like cinnamon roll, rainbow swirl, and pancakes and waffles, as well as perennial favorites like vanilla bean.

As Halo Top appeared on store shelves, Woolverton revved up outreach to his target market via Facebook and Instagram. Fans quickly added their comments and images, building word-of-mouth authenticity for the young brand, and sending its total follower count over the one-million mark. Before Halo Top reached its fifth birthday, its pint sales had outstripped the pint sales of the best-established brand names in the ice-cream industry for the first time.[a]

Geographic Location

Earlier we noted that the demand for some consumer products can vary considerably among geographic areas because of differences in climate, terrain, or regional customer preferences. Demand for business products also varies according to geographic location. For instance, producers of lumber may divide their markets geographically because customers' needs vary by region. Geographic segmentation may be especially appropriate for producers seeking to reach industries concentrated in certain locations, such as furniture and textile producers concentrated in the Southeast.

Type of Organization

A company sometimes segments a market by types of organizations within that market because they often require different product features, distribution systems, price structures, and selling strategies. Given these variations, a firm may either concentrate on a single segment with one marketing mix (a concentrated targeting strategy) or focus on several groups with multiple mixes (a differentiated targeting strategy). A carpet producer could segment potential customers into several groups, such as automobile makers, commercial carpet contractors (firms that carpet large office buildings), apartment complex developers, carpet wholesalers, and large retail carpet outlets.

Customer Size

An organization's size may affect its purchasing procedures and the types and quantities of products it wants. Size can thus be an effective variable for segmenting a business market. To reach a segment of a particular size, marketers may have to adjust one or more marketing mix ingredients. For instance, marketers may want to offer customers who buy in large quantities a discount as a purchase incentive. Personal selling is common and expected in business markets, where a higher level of customer service may be required—larger customers may require a higher level of customer service because of the size and complexity of their orders. Because the needs of large and small buyers tend to be distinct, marketers frequently use different marketing practices to reach target customer groups. Examine the advertisement for FedEx Express. The ad features Varun Ramesh, managing director of Pothys, a leading Indian silk textiles retailer. Amid an image of bolts of colorful silk ready to be made into sarees and sent around the world to satisfy growing demand, the ad informs business owners seeking to expand into international markets that FedEx Express can help them reach customers in 220 countries and territories so that they can become as successful as Pothys. The ad also refers business owners to a web page for additional information relevant to their international distribution needs.

TAKING LOCAL TRADITIONS TO GLOBAL DESTINATIONS.

Representing the roots of Indian culture, the saree's popularity saw an international demand and a need to export.

FedEx Express provides access to over 220 countries and territories, giving Pothys the global distribution network they need to reach customers the world over.

FedEx connects you to a world of opportunity.

Learn more at fedex.com/in/global

Varun Ramesh
Managing Director, Pothys

FedEx. Express

SOURCE: FORTUNE MAGAZINE

Segmenting Business Markets
FedEx focuses on several business segments. In this advertisement, FedEx is communicating with a segment consisting of small businesses that want to reach customers in other countries.

Product Use

Certain products, particularly raw materials like steel, petroleum, plastics, and lumber, can be used in numerous ways in the production of goods. These variations will affect the types and amounts of products purchased, as well as the purchasing method. An industrial paint manufacturer, for example, might target different paint products at construction companies for painting bridges and at automakers for painting vehicles.

Learning Objective 6-5

Explain what market segment profiles are and how they are used.

6-5 STEP 3: DEVELOP MARKET SEGMENT PROFILES

A market segment profile describes the similarities among potential customers within a segment and explains the differences among people and organizations in different segments. A profile may cover aspects such as demographic characteristics, geographic factors, product benefits sought, lifestyles, brand preferences, and usage rates. Individuals and organizations within segments should be relatively similar with respect to several characteristics and product needs and differ considerably from those within other market segments. Marketers use market segment profiles to assess the degree to which their products fit potential customers' product needs. Market segment profiles support marketers in understanding how they can use their firms' capabilities to serve potential customer groups.

Market segment profiles help a marketer determine which segment or segments are most attractive relative to the firm's strengths, weaknesses, objectives, and resources. Although marketers may initially believe certain segments are attractive, a market segment profile may unveil new information that makes a segment less attractive than expected. Market segment profiles can be useful in helping a firm make marketing decisions relating to a specific market segment or segments.

INTEGRITY IN MARKETING

Flowers for Dreams Blossoms by Giving Back

Steven Dyme and Joseph Dickstein feel so strongly about giving back to the community that they signaled their intention by naming their Chicago-based business Flowers for Dreams. The two friends became entrepreneurs during a summer break from college, when they teamed up to sell flowers at high school graduations. The goal was to make a bit of extra cash for themselves and earn money to buy and donate backpacks to low-income students.

After graduation, Dyme and Dickstein built on their experience to found Flowers for Dreams as an online floral delivery service with a social conscience. Targeting consumers in Chicago and its suburbs, Flowers for Dreams offers competitive-priced bouquets wrapped in burlap and delivered to the buyer's door. The firm seeks

out local sources of fresh flowers, including dahlias and other blooms grown by inmates in the Cook County Jail's urban flower farm program. Flowers for Dreams also donates 25 percent of its profits to a different local charity every month. "We fundamentally integrated giving and social conscience into our DNA," says Dyme.

As the business prospers and expands to new markets, it can send larger checks to charities chosen by the co-founders and their 25 employees. With more than $3 million in annual sales, Flowers for Dreams has already donated nearly $250,000 to charities like Alive Rescue, Mercy Home, and the Chicago Parks Foundation. The firm's social media accounts publicize its charitable connections, giving customers a good feeling about buying fresh flowers from a local business that never stops giving back to the community.[b]

6-6 STEP 4: EVALUATE RELEVANT MARKET SEGMENTS

Learning Objective 6-6
Describe how to evaluate market segments.

After analyzing the market segment profiles, a marketer should be able to narrow his or her focus to several promising segments that warrant further analysis. Marketers should examine sales estimates, competition, and estimated costs associated with each of these segments.

6-6a Sales Estimates

Potential sales for a market segment can be measured along several dimensions, including product level, geographic area, time, and level of competition.[20] With respect to product level, potential sales can be estimated for a specific product item (e.g., Diet Coke) or an entire product line (e.g., Coca-Cola Classic, Diet Coke, and Coca-Cola Zero Sugar comprise goods in a product line). A manager must also determine the geographic area to include in the estimate. In relation to time, sales estimates can be short range (one year or less), medium range (one to five years), or long range (longer than five years). The competitive level specifies whether sales are being estimated for a single firm or for an entire industry.

Market potential is the total amount of a product that customers will purchase within a specified period at a specific level of industry-wide marketing activity. Market potential can be stated in terms of dollars or units. A segment's market potential is affected by economic, sociocultural, and other environmental forces. The specific level of marketing effort will vary from one firm to another, and all firms' marketing activities together add up to the industry-wide marketing effort total. A marketing manager must also estimate whether, and to what extent, industry marketing efforts will change over time.

Company sales potential is the maximum percentage of a market that an individual firm within an industry can expect to capture for a specific product. Several factors influence company sales potential for a market segment. First, the market potential places absolute limits on the size of the company's sales potential—a firm cannot exceed the market potential. Second, the magnitude of industry-wide marketing activities has an indirect but definite impact on the company's sales potential. When Domino's Pizza advertises home-delivered pizza, for instance, it indirectly promotes pizza in general. Maybe you see the ad and it sparks a craving for pizza, but you call the Pizza Hut down the street because it is more familiar to you. Third, the intensity and effectiveness of a company's marketing activities relative to competitors' activities affect the size of the company's sales potential. If a company spends twice as much as any of its competitors on marketing efforts, and if each dollar spent is more effective in generating sales, the firm's sales potential will be high relative to competitors' sales potential.

Two general approaches that measure company sales potential are breakdown and buildup. In the **breakdown approach**, the marketing manager first develops a general economic forecast for a specific time period. Next, the manager estimates market potential based on this forecast. The manager derives the company's sales potential from the forecast and an estimate of market potential. In the **buildup approach**, the marketing manager begins by estimating how much of a product a potential buyer in a specific geographic area, such as a sales territory, will purchase in a given period. The manager then multiplies that amount by the total number of potential buyers in that area. The manager performs the same calculation for each geographic area in which the firm sells products and then adds the totals for each area to calculate market potential. To determine company sales potential, the manager must estimate, based on planned levels of company marketing activities, the proportion of the total market potential the company can reasonably attain.

6-6b Competitive Assessment

Besides obtaining sales estimates, it is crucial to assess competitors that are already operating in the segments being considered. A market segment that initially seems attractive based on sales estimates may turn out to be much less so after a competitive assessment. Such an assessment

market potential The total amount of a product that customers will purchase within a specified period at a specific level of industry-wide marketing activity

company sales potential The maximum percentage of a market that an individual firm within an industry can expect to obtain for a specific product

breakdown approach Measuring company sales potential based on a general economic forecast for a specific period and the market potential derived from it

buildup approach Measuring company sales potential by estimating how much of a product a potential buyer in a specific geographic area will purchase in a given period, multiplying the estimate by the number of potential buyers, and adding the totals of all the geographic areas considered

"My boy has food sensitivities
so I started feeding him BLUE Basics.
Now he's happy and I'm even happier."

BLUE Basics® is a limited-ingredient diet designed to minimize the food
sensitivities some dogs experience, while providing them with a delicious
and nutritious meal.

We always feature salmon, turkey or duck– proteins not common in dog
foods, and BLUE Basics does not include many of the ingredients that
can trigger allergic reactions in some dogs.

• NO chicken or beef • NO corn, wheat or soy • NO dairy or eggs

If your dog or cat has food sensitivities, ask your veterinarian about BLUE
Basics. With both traditional and grain-free recipes, you're sure to find one
that's perfect for your pet.

BlueBasicsPets.com
Love them like family. Feed them like family.®

Available for dogs and cats.

Competitive Assessment
Marketers conducted an assessment and determined that Blue Basics dog food can maintain an advantage in a market filled with competing brands by offering a dog food made specifically for dogs with food sensitivities.

should ask several questions about competitors: How many exist? What are their strengths and weaknesses? Do several competitors already have major market shares and together dominate the segment? Can our company create a marketing mix to compete effectively against competitors' marketing mixes? Is it likely that new competitors will enter this segment? If so, how will they affect our firm's ability to compete successfully? Answers to such questions are important for proper assessment of the competition in potential market segments.

The market for dog food, for instance, has many competitors with a variety of products at many price points. Blue Basic, featured in the advertisement, competes against these other brands by highlighting how its product has limited ingredients and is designed to reduce food sensitivities in some dogs. The ad explains that the product does not contain ingredients known to trigger allergic reactions such as chicken, corn, wheat, and dairy and instead contains proteins like salmon and turkey that are less commonly found in commercial dog foods. The image of a happy dog running with a ball along with one user's positive review of the food reinforces the idea that Blue Basic is good for sensitive dogs and helps the product stand out in a crowded field of dog food products.

6-6c Cost Estimates

To fulfill the needs of a target segment, an organization must develop and maintain a marketing mix that precisely meets the wants and needs of that segment, which can be expensive. Distinctive product features, attractive package design, generous product warranties, extensive advertising, attractive promotional offers, competitive prices, and high-quality personal service use considerable organizational resources. In some cases, marketers may conclude that the costs to reach some segments are so high that they are essentially inaccessible. Marketers also must consider whether the organization can reach a segment at costs equal to or below competitors' costs. If the firm's costs are likely to be higher, it will be unable to compete in that segment in the long run.

Identify the factors that influence the selection of specific market segments for use as target markets.

6-7 STEP 5: SELECT SPECIFIC TARGET MARKETS

An important initial consideration in selecting a target market is whether customers' needs differ enough to warrant the use of market segmentation. If segmentation analysis shows customer needs to be homogeneous, the firm's management may decide to use the undifferentiated approach, discussed earlier. However, if customer needs are heterogeneous, which is more likely, marketers must select one or more target markets.

Assuming one or more segments offer significant opportunities to achieve organizational objectives, a marketer must decide which offer the most potential at reasonable costs. Ordinarily, information gathered in the previous step—concerning sales estimates, competitors, and cost estimates—requires careful review in this final step to determining long-term marketing opportunities. At this time, the firm's management must investigate whether the organization has sufficient financial resources, managerial skills, employee expertise, and facilities to compete effectively in selected segments. The firm must also consider the possibility that the requirements of some market segments are at odds with the firm's overall objectives, and that possible legal problems, conflicts with interest groups, and technological advancements will render certain segments unattractive. Finally, marketers must consider long-term versus short-term growth. If long-term prospects look poor, a marketer may ultimately choose not to target a segment because it would be difficult to recoup expenses.

Selecting appropriate target markets is important to an organization's effective adoption and use of the marketing concept philosophy. Identifying the right target market is the key to implementing a successful marketing strategy. Failure to do so can lead to low sales, high costs, and severe financial losses. A careful target market analysis places an organization in a strong position to serve customers' needs and achieve its objectives.

6-8 DEVELOPING SALES FORECASTS

Learning Objective 6-8
Discuss sales forecasting methods.

After a company selects a target market or markets, it must develop a **sales forecast**—the amount of a product the company expects to sell during a specific period at a specified level of marketing activity. The sales forecast differs from the company sales potential in that it concentrates on what actual sales will be at a certain level of company marketing effort. The company sales potential assesses what sales are possible at various levels of marketing activities, assuming certain environmental conditions exist. Businesses use the sales forecast for planning, organizing, implementing, and controlling activities. The success of numerous activities depends on this forecast's accuracy. Common problems in failing companies are improper planning and lack of realistic sales forecasts. Overly ambitious sales forecasts can lead to overbuying, overinvestment, and higher costs that weaken a firm's strength and position.

To forecast sales, a marketer can choose from a number of forecasting methods, some arbitrary and quick and others more scientific, complex, and time-consuming. A firm's choice of method or methods depends on the costs involved, type of product, market characteristics, time span and purpose of the forecast, stability of the historical sales data, availability of required information, managerial preferences, and forecasters' expertise and experience.[21] Common forecasting techniques fall into five categories: executive judgment, surveys, time series analysis, regression analysis, and market tests.

6-8a Executive Judgment

Executive judgment is the intuition of one or more executives. This is an unscientific but expedient and inexpensive approach to sales forecasting. It is not a very accurate method, but executive judgment may work reasonably well when product demand is relatively stable and the forecaster has years of market-related experience. However, because intuition is heavily influenced by recent experience, the forecast may weight recent sales booms or slumps excessively. Another drawback to executive judgment is that the forecaster has only past experience as a guide for deciding where to go in the future.

6-8b Surveys

Another way to forecast sales is to question customers, sales personnel, or experts regarding their expectations about future purchases. In a **customer forecasting survey**, marketers ask customers what types and quantities of products they intend to buy during a specific period.

sales forecast The amount of a product a company expects to sell during a specific period at a specified level of marketing activity

executive judgment A sales forecasting method based on the intuition of one or more executives

customer forecasting survey A survey of customers regarding the types and quantities of products they intend to buy during a specific period

When You Purchase Products, How Important Is Environmental Impact?

Environmental Impact at Least Moderately Important

Packaged Foods/Beverages	86%
Health and Beauty	80%
Home Appliances	76%
Electronics	72%
Clothing	53%

SNAPSHOT

Source: Chris Medenwald, "Keen on Green? Shopper Attitudes toward EcoFriendly Products [Survey]," Field Agent, April 19, 2016, https://blog .fieldagent.net/keen-on-green-shopper-attitudes-toward-eco-friendly-products-survey (accessed February 7, 2018).

This approach may be useful to a business with relatively few customers. Consider Lockheed Martin, the U.S. government's largest contractor. Because most of its contracts come from the same customer, the government, Lockheed Martin could conduct customer forecasting surveys effectively. PepsiCo, by contrast, has millions of customers and could not feasibly use a customer survey to forecast future sales.

In a **sales force forecasting survey**, the firm's salespeople estimate anticipated sales in their territories for a specified period. The forecaster combines these territorial estimates to arrive at a tentative forecast. A marketer may survey the sales staff for several reasons, the most important being that the sales staff are the company personnel closest to customers on a daily basis. They, therefore, have first-hand knowledge about customers' product needs. Moreover, when sales representatives assist in developing the forecast, they are invested in the process and are more likely to work toward its achievement. Forecasts can be prepared for single territories, divisions consisting of several territories, regions made up of multiple divisions, and the total geographic market.

When a company wants an **expert forecasting survey**, it hires professionals to help prepare the sales forecast. These experts are usually economists, management consultants, advertising executives, college professors, or other individuals outside the firm with experience in a specific market. Drawing on this experience and their analyses of available information about the company and the market, experts prepare and present forecasts or answer questions. Using experts is a quick way to get information and is relatively inexpensive. However, because they work outside the firm, these forecasters may be less motivated than company personnel to do an effective job.

A more complex form of the expert forecasting survey incorporates the Delphi technique. In the **Delphi technique**, experts create initial forecasts, submit them to the company for averaging, and have the results returned to them so they can make individual refined forecasts. When making calculations using the Delphi technique, experts use the averaged results to eradicate outliers and to refine predictions. The procedure can be repeated several times until the experts, each working separately, reach a consensus. Because this technique gets rid of extreme data, the ultimate goal in using the Delphi technique is to develop a highly reliable sales forecast.

6-8c Time Series Analysis

With **time series analysis**, the forecaster uses the firm's historical sales data to discover a pattern or patterns in sales over time. If a pattern is found, it can be used to forecast sales. This forecasting method assumes that past sales patterns will continue into the future. The accuracy, and thus usefulness, of time series analysis hinges on the validity of this assumption.

In a time series analysis, a forecaster usually performs four types of analyses: trend, cycle, seasonal, and random factor. **Trend analysis** focuses on aggregate sales data, such as the

sales force forecasting survey A survey of a firm's sales force regarding anticipated sales in their territories for a specified period

expert forecasting survey Sales forecasts prepared by experts outside the firm, such as economists, management consultants, advertising executives, or college professors

Delphi technique A procedure in which experts create initial forecasts, submit them to the company for averaging, and then refine the forecasts

time series analysis A forecasting method that uses historical sales data to discover patterns in the firm's sales over time and generally involves trend, cycle, seasonal, and random factor analyses

trend analysis An analysis that focuses on aggregate sales data over a period of many years to determine general trends in annual sales

company's annual sales figures, covering a period of many years to determine whether annual sales are generally rising, falling, or staying about the same. Through **cycle analysis**, a forecaster analyzes sales figures (often monthly sales data) for a three- to five-year period to ascertain whether sales fluctuate in a consistent, periodic manner. When performing a **seasonal analysis**, the analyst studies daily, weekly, or monthly sales figures to evaluate the degree to which seasonal factors, such as climate and holiday activities, influence sales. In a **random factor analysis**, the forecaster attempts to attribute erratic sales variations to random, nonrecurring events, such as a regional power failure, a natural disaster, or political unrest in a foreign market. After performing each of these analyses, the forecaster combines the results to develop the sales forecast. Time series analysis is an effective forecasting method for products with reasonably stable demand, but not for products with erratic demand.

6-8d Regression Analysis

Like time series analysis, regression analysis requires the use of historical sales data. In **regression analysis**, the forecaster seeks to find a relationship between past sales (the dependent variable) and one or more independent variables, such as population, per capita income, or gross domestic product. Simple regression analysis uses one independent variable, whereas multiple regression analysis includes two or more independent variables. The objective of regression analysis is to develop a mathematical formula that accurately describes a relationship between the firm's sales and one or more variables. However, the formula indicates only an association, not a causal relationship. Once an accurate formula is established, the analyst plugs the necessary information into the formula to derive the sales forecast.

Regression analysis is useful when a precise association can be established. However, a forecaster seldom finds a perfect correlation. Furthermore, this method can be used only when available historical sales data are extensive. Thus, regression analysis is futile for forecasting sales of new products.

6-8e Market Tests

A **market test** involves making a product available to buyers in one or more test areas and measuring purchases and consumer responses to the product, distribution, promotion, and price. Test areas are often midsized cities with populations of 200,000 to 500,000, but they can be towns or small cities with populations of 50,000 to 200,000. Test areas are chosen for their representativeness of a firm's target markets.

A market test provides information about consumers' actual, rather than intended, purchases. In addition, purchase volume can be evaluated in relation to the intensity of other marketing activities such as advertising, in-store promotions, pricing, packaging, and distribution. Forecasters base their sales estimates for larger geographic units on customer response in test areas. Chick-fil-A, for example, test-marketed two new spicy entrees—Spicy Chick-n-Strips and a Grilled Spicy Chicken Deluxe Sandwich—at select Chick-fil-A restaurants in Central and South Texas as well as Philadelphia. Less piquant versions of the two items were already on Chick-fil-A menus, but the company decided to test spicier versions based on customer requests.[22] The company will use data from the market tests in Texas and Pennsylvania to determine whether the new items will generate enough sales to warrant offering them at all Chick-fil-As.

Because it does not require historical sales data, a market test is effective for forecasting sales of new products or of existing products in new geographic areas. A market test also gives a marketer an opportunity to test the success of various elements of the marketing mix, including product ingredients and pricing. However, these tests are often time-consuming and expensive. In addition, a marketer cannot be certain that consumer response during a market test represents the total market response or that such a response will continue in the future.

cycle analysis An analysis of sales figures for a three- to five-year period to ascertain whether sales fluctuate in a consistent, periodic manner

seasonal analysis An analysis of daily, weekly, or monthly sales figures to evaluate the degree to which seasonal factors influence sales

random factor analysis An analysis attempting to attribute erratic sales variations to random, nonrecurring events

regression analysis A method of predicting sales based on finding a relationship between past sales and one or more independent variables, such as population or per capita income

market test Making a product available to buyers in one or more test areas and measuring purchases and consumer responses to marketing efforts

6-8f **Using Multiple Forecasting Methods**

Although some businesses depend on a single sales forecasting method, most firms use several techniques. Sometimes a company is forced to use multiple methods when marketing diverse product lines, but even a single product line may require several forecasts, especially when the product is sold to different market segments. Thus, a producer of automobile tires may rely on one technique to forecast tire sales for new cars and on another to forecast sales of replacement tires. Variation in the length of forecasts may call for several forecasting methods as well. A firm that employs one method for a short-range forecast may find it inappropriate for long-range forecasting. Sometimes a marketer verifies results of one method by using one or more other methods and comparing outcomes.

Summary

6-1 Define what markets are and explain how they are generally classified.

A market is a group of people who, as individuals or as organizations, have needs for products in a product class and have the ability, willingness, and authority to purchase such products. Markets can be categorized as consumer markets or business markets, based on the characteristics of the individuals and groups that make up a specific market and the purposes for which they buy products. A consumer market, also known as a *business-to-consumer (B2C) market,* consists of purchasers and household members who intend to consume or benefit from the purchased products and do not buy products for the main purpose of making a profit. A business market, also known as *business-to-business (B2B), industrial,* or *organizational market,* consists of individuals or groups that purchase a specific kind of product for one of three purposes: resale, direct use in producing other products, or use in general daily operations.

6-2 List the five steps of the target market selection process.

In general, marketers employ a five-step process when selecting a target market. Step one is to identify the appropriate targeting strategy. Step two is determining which segmentation variables to use. Step three is to develop a market segment profile. Step four is evaluating relevant market segments. Finally, step five is selecting specific target markets. Not all marketers will follow all of these five steps in this order, but this process provides a good general guide.

6-3 Compare three targeting strategies.

Step one of the target market selection process is to identify the appropriate targeting strategy. When a company designs a single marketing mix and directs it at the entire market for a particular product, it is using an undifferentiated targeting strategy. The undifferentiated strategy is effective in a homogeneous market, whereas a heterogeneous market needs to be segmented through a concentrated targeting strategy or a differentiated targeting strategy. Both of these strategies divide markets into segments consisting of individuals, groups, or organizations that have one or more similar characteristics and can be linked to similar product needs. When using a concentrated strategy, an organization directs marketing efforts toward a single market segment through one marketing mix. With a differentiated targeting strategy, an organization directs customized marketing efforts at two or more segments.

Certain conditions must exist for market segmentation to be effective. First, customers' needs for the product should be heterogeneous. Second, the segments of the market should be identifiable and divisible. Third, the total market should be divided so segments can be compared with respect to estimated sales, costs, and profits. Fourth, at least one segment must have enough profit potential to justify developing and maintaining a special marketing mix for that segment. Fifth, the firm must be able to reach the chosen segment with a particular marketing mix.

6-4 Identify the major segmentation variables.

The second step is determining which segmentation variables to use, which are the characteristics of individuals, groups, or organizations used to divide a total market into segments. The segmentation variable should relate to customers' needs for, uses of, or behavior toward the product. Segmentation variables for consumer markets can be grouped into four categories: demographic (e.g., age, gender, income, ethnicity, family life cycle), geographic (e.g., population, market density, climate), psychographic (e.g., personality traits, motives, lifestyles), and behavioristic (e.g., volume usage, end use, expected benefits, brand loyalty, price sensitivity). Variables for segmenting business markets include geographic location, type of organization, customer size, and product use.

6-5 Explain what market segment profiles are and how they are used.

Step three in the target market selection process is to develop market segment profiles. Such profiles describe the similarities among potential customers within a segment and explain the differences among people and organizations in different market segments. They are used to assess the degree to which the firm's products can match potential customers' product needs. Segments, which may seem attractive at first, may be shown to be quite the opposite after a market segment profile is completed.

6-6 Describe how to evaluate market segments.

Step four is evaluating relevant market segments. Marketers analyze several important factors, such as sales estimates, competition, and estimated costs, associated with each segment. Potential sales for a market segment can be measured along several dimensions, including product level, geographic area, time, and level of competition. Besides obtaining sales estimates, it is crucial to assess competitors that are already operating in the segments being considered. Without competitive information, sales estimates may be misleading. The cost of developing a marketing mix that meets the wants and needs of individuals in that segment must also be considered. If the firm's costs to compete in that market are very high, it may be unable to compete in that segment in the long run.

6-7 Identify the factors that influence the selection of specific market segments for use as target markets.

The final step involves the actual selection of specific target markets. In this step, the company considers whether customers' needs differ enough to warrant segmentation and which segments to target. If customers' needs are heterogeneous, the decision must be made whether to enter the market at all and if so which segment to target. The firm's available resources, managerial skills, employee expertise, facilities, the firm's overall objectives, possible legal problems, conflicts with interest groups, and technological advancements must be considered when deciding which segments to target.

6-8 Discuss sales forecasting methods.

A sales forecast is the amount of a product the company actually expects to sell during a specific period at a specified level of marketing activity. To forecast sales, marketers can choose from a number of methods. The choice depends on various factors, including the costs involved, type of product, market characteristics, and time span and purposes of the forecast. There are five categories of forecasting techniques: executive judgment, surveys, time series analysis, regression analysis, and market tests. Executive judgment is based on the intuition of one or more executives. Surveys include customer, sales force, and expert forecasting. Time series analysis uses the firm's historical sales data to discover patterns in the firm's sales over time and employs four major types of analysis: trend, cycle, seasonal, and random factor. With regression analysis, forecasters attempt to find a relationship between past sales and one or more independent variables. Market testing involves making a product available to buyers in one or more test areas and measuring purchases and consumer responses to distribution, promotion, and price. Many companies employ multiple forecasting methods.

Important Terms

consumer market 156
business market 156
undifferentiated targeting
   strategy 158
homogeneous market 158
heterogeneous market 158
market segmentation 158
market segment 158
concentrated targeting
   strategy 160

differentiated targeting
   strategy 161
segmentation variables
   161
market density 165
geodemographic
   segmentation 165
micromarketing 165
benefit segmentation 168
market potential 171

company sales potential
   171
breakdown approach 171
buildup approach 171
sales forecast 173
executive judgment 173
customer forecasting
   survey 173
sales force forecasting
   survey 174

expert forecasting survey
   174
Delphi technique 174
time series analysis 174
trend analysis 174
cycle analysis 175
seasonal analysis 175
random factor analysis 175
regression analysis 175
market test 175

Discussion and Review Questions

1. What is a market? What are the requirements for a market?
2. In your local area, identify a group of people with unsatisfied product needs who represent a market. Could this market be reached by a business organization? Why or why not?
3. Outline the five major steps in the target market selection process.
4. What is an undifferentiated strategy? Under what conditions is it most useful? Describe a present market situation in which a company is using an undifferentiated strategy. Is the business successful? Why or why not?
5. What is market segmentation? Describe the basic conditions required for effective segmentation. Identify several firms that use market segmentation.
6. List the differences between concentrated and differentiated strategies, and describe the advantages and disadvantages of each.
7. Identify and describe four major categories of variables that can be used to segment consumer markets. Give examples of product markets that are segmented by variables in each category.
8. What dimensions are used to segment business markets?
9. Define *geodemographic segmentation*. Identify several types of firms that might employ this type of market segmentation, and explain why.
10. What is a market segment profile? Why is it an important step in the target market selection process?
11. Describe the important factors that marketers should analyze to evaluate market segments.
12. Why is a marketer concerned about sales potential when trying to select a target market?
13. Why is selecting appropriate target markets important for an organization that wants to adopt the marketing concept philosophy?
14. What is a sales forecast? Why is it important?
15. What are the two primary types of surveys a company might use to forecast sales? Why would a company use an outside expert forecasting survey?
16. Under what conditions are market tests useful for sales forecasting? What are the advantages and disadvantages of market tests?
17. Under what conditions might a firm use multiple forecasting methods?

Developing Your Marketing Plan

Identifying and analyzing a target market is a major component of formulating a marketing strategy. A clear understanding and explanation of a product's target market is crucial to developing a useful marketing plan. References to various dimensions of a target market are likely to appear in several locations in a marketing plan. To assist you in understanding how information in this chapter relates to the creation of your marketing plan, focus on the following considerations:

1. What type of targeting strategy is being used for your product? Should a different targeting strategy be employed?
2. Select and justify the segmentation variables that are most appropriate for segmenting the market for your product. If your product is a consumer product, use Figure 6.3 for ideas regarding the most appropriate segmentation variables. If your marketing plan focuses on a business product, review the information in the section entitled "Variables for Segmenting Business Markets."
3. Discuss how your product should be positioned in the minds of customers in the target market relative to the product positions of competitors.

Video Case 6.1

How Nike Uses Targeting in the High-Stakes Race for Sales

Nike, the company behind the famous swoosh logo and the classic "Just do it" ad campaign, has long been a major force in marketing athletic footwear, clothing, and equipment. It targets professionals and other consumers with innovative shoes and apparel for running, basketball, soccer, tennis, skateboarding, football, and

lacrosse, among other sports. In recent years, the Oregon-based company's annual sales have increased beyond $30 billion as it progresses toward its 2022 goal of achieving annual sales of $50 billion. In this high-stakes race, Nike must also stay ahead of Adidas, Puma, and other competitors seeking to capture a higher share of the market for athletic footwear.

for improving its sneakers to give athletes at all levels a real performance edge.

Nike dominates the U.S. market for basketball shoes, with branded product lines by NBA legends Michael Jordan and LeBron James. Nike Air Jordan sneakers have been selling well for more than 30 years, regularly updated with new features that enhance performance and stylish touches that bring today's looks to these classic shoes. And every time LeBron James wears his newest Nike shoes on the basketball court, sports-minded fans focus on the functional improvements while fashion-conscious consumers check for the latest colors, patterns, and materials.

Careful targeting is a key element in Nike's strategy for marketing shoes. Consider the company's Zoom Vaporfly 4%, a high-performance sneaker designed to help marathon runners speed ahead through 26.2 miles. This special shoe incorporates lightweight foam for effective cushioning and a shaped carbon-fiber insert for putting spring in every step, mile after mile. Nike invested heavily in developing and testing the advanced components of this product, which it promotes as being capable of boosting a racer's efficiency by as much as four percent.

The target market is both elite runners and weekend athletes who know that saving even a fraction of a second can make all the difference as they approach the finish line. Nike markets one version of the shoe, the Zoom Vaporfly Elite, for top athletes who run in the world's most competitive marathons. The less-expensive, but still pricey, Zoom Vaporfly 4% is for serious runners seeking to boost personal performance.

Prior to the product launch, the company staged an unofficial marathon event, "Breaking2," featuring leading marathoners Eliud Kipchoge, Lelisa Desisa, and Zersenay Tadese wearing Zoom Vaporfly Elite shoes. Their goal: to complete the course in two hours or less, a feat unprecedented in marathon history. The winner was Olympic marathon champ Kipchoge, with the impressively fast time of 2 hours and 25 seconds. A number of world-class runners have since won official marathons wearing Zoom Vaporfly Elite shoes, adding to the product's reputation and desirability within the target market. The company continues to solicit feedback from elite runners as input

In addition, Nike targets "sneakerheads"—consumers who are sneaker enthusiasts and want to be among the first to have the newest, "must-have" products. With this market in mind, the company is expanding its range of unisex sizing to make hot new styles accessible to anyone, male or female, who wants to buy. In some key stores, stylists are on hand to help buyers select shoes that fit their lifestyle and express their personality. Nike also offers an app called Snkrs that informs sneakerheads when and where highly coveted limited-edition sneakers can be purchased. This keeps sneakerheads happy and, in turn, reinforces loyalty to the Nike brand.[23]

Questions for Discussion

1. When Nike segments the market for athletic shoes, what types of variables is it using? Why are these variables appropriate?
2. Is Nike using a differentiated, an undifferentiated, or a concentrated strategy for targeting buyers of athletic shoes? Explain your answer.
3. How should Nike assess competitors that market to the segment of consumers who buy high-performance running shoes such as the Zoom Vaporfly?

Case 6.2

Looking for a BFF? Umpqua Bank Can Help!

Since 1953, Oregon-based Umpqua Bank has worked hard to earn a regional reputation as a friendly, responsive, and responsible community bank. Headquartered in Portland, the bank serves consumers, small businesses, and corporations in its home state as well as in Washington, Idaho, California, and Nevada. Umpqua prides itself on understanding its customers and its communities. It offers personalized service in more than 300 stores (bank branches), positioning these locations as neighborhood hubs for community events, not just places to make a deposit or apply for a loan. Every store has a hotline available for any customer who wants to personally chat with the CEO, whether to complain, give a compliment, or ask a question.

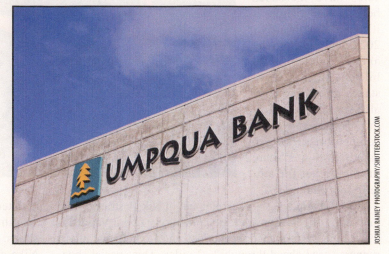

Umpqua has formulated a separate marketing mix to meet the needs of each customer segment it targets. For small businesses, it provides a variety of checking and savings accounts, credit-card processing, loans, and other products and services to help owners manage their financial resources for ongoing growth. Larger companies can choose from a broad range of banking and financial services, including some especially tailored to five particular industries: retailing, manufacturing, health care, agriculture, and professional services. The bank offers financial products such as checking, savings, and credit and debit cards for consumers, along with a menu of specialized services for more affluent consumers.

Although Umpqua operates more than 300 stores across five states, it has closed 30 stores in recent years and begun redesigning dozens of other stores. This is part of the bank's shift to a "human-digital" strategy aligned with the needs and preferences of targeted customer segments. Leading up to the change, Umpqua researched its customers' banking behavior and reviewed industry studies indicating that 46 percent of consumers do most of their banking without going to a branch.

Umpqua had been offering online banking and mobile banking for some time, including an app that allowed customers to check balances and handle other bank transactions in automated fashion. The "human-digital" strategy takes this to a more human level, with an app powered by Engage software. Because customers using the app select a particular employee to be their personal banker, Umpqua insiders call this the BFF app, which stands for Best Financial Friend. Participants can either text or video chat with their chosen bank employee via the app, completing all kinds of transactions—except, of course, for making a cash withdrawal.

Testing the BFF app in Portland, Umpqua was ready for 1,000 downloads. Instead, demand was so high it had to cap the first part of the pilot at 1,700 customers. Through testing, the bank learned that 99 percent of the participants preferred to text their chosen banker. It also found that the bankers were able to build rapport with customers without in-person conversations.

Behind the scenes, the app allows bankers to access customer account analyses and summaries of previous interactions. This provides the background to deliver "circumstances-based banking" connected to events that occur in a consumer's life or in the course of running a business. Whether a customer is thinking about the financial consequences of a new baby or steering a company through a rocky economy, the Umpqua banker has the data and the knowledge to offer timely and relevant tools, advice, and services.

As a result of implementing its "human-digital" strategy, Umpqua is restructuring its stores to enable employees to serve customers via app and in person. But don't expect Umpqua to become a branchless bank. "We are always going to have stores," the CEO states. "There are always going to be people who want to know there's a human being behind the bank."[24]

Questions for Discussion

1. Is Umpqua Bank using a concentrated, a differentiated, or an undifferentiated targeting strategy? How do you know?

2. Identify the categories of variables used by Umpqua Bank to segment the business and consumer markets. What additional variables might help the bank define suitable segments for marketing attention?

3. Do you agree with Umpqua Bank's decision to use a market test before launching its BFF app in the wider marketplace? Explain your answer.

Strategic Case 3

Uber Attempts to Make a Right Turn

Uber Technologies Inc. is a tech startup that provides ride sharing services by connecting independent contractors (drivers) and riders with the use of an app. Uber has expanded its operations to 674 cities in 83 countries around the world. It has become a key player in the sharing economy, a new economic model in which independent contractors rent out their underutilized resources such as vehicles or lodging to other consumers. The company has experienced resounding success and is looking toward expansion both internationally and within the United States.

Understanding Its Target Market

Like all companies, Uber must understand its target market and maintain a strong marketing mix to be successful. Due to its technology, Uber does not have as many constraints as taxi cabs, although it has encountered regulatory obstacles and some public resistance. A major reason Uber is so popular is because its app allows users to contact any drivers in the near vicinity. The Uber business model takes advantage of the smartphone technology of consumers and links them with independent drivers as their cabs. These drivers act as their own entrepreneurs. They pay Uber a commission but are free to run their businesses as they see fit. This provides a potentially more efficient and less expensive way for consumers to purchase transportation.

Uber's target market is focused on Generation Z and Millennials because of their lifestyle, interests, and low interest in auto ownership. While the market is similar to the taxi cab market, anyone who does not have a car or does not want to engage in driving is in the market. Research indicates the core U.S. market is 65 percent age 16–34, 17 percent age 35–44, and only 18 percent over 45. The market is split evenly between males and females with 48 percent suburban and 46 percent urban and only 6 percent rural. Because all are using the Uber app there is big data available for analytics.

Available Locally, Expanding Globally

Uber has adopted the motto "Available locally, expanding globally" to describe the opportunities it sees in global expansion. As it expands into different countries, Uber is engaging in strategic partnerships with local companies. These alliances with local firms are especially important as Uber expands internationally because it allows the company to utilize the resources and knowledge of domestic firms familiar with the country's culture. Uber has partnered with Times Internet in India, Baidu in China, and America Movil in Latin America. International expansion is a major part of Uber's marketing strategy, and it believes that consumers from other countries will appreciate its low cost, convenience, and freedom.

Despite its international success, many countries have regulatory hurdles that have caused trouble for Uber. Perhaps the biggest is the failure to obtain licenses even though Uber drivers offer many of the same services as a taxi. Governments have responded by banning Uber or Uber services due to the lack of professional licenses for drivers. For instance, in Spain, Uber shut down its ride-sharing service after a judge ruled that Uber drivers are not legally authorized to transport passengers and that it unfairly competes against licensed taxi drivers. Because the taxi industry is an important industry in many cities, governments like France, Spain, and Germany are not looking favorably at what they view as an unfair competitive advantage that could potentially bankrupt the industry. Uber has since returned to some countries with UberX, which uses licensed drivers and places it more on par with licensed taxi drivers.

Driving Trust and Safety

Uber operates in an industry where trust between strangers is vital. This trust ensures a safe and comfortable ride for both passenger and driver. Uber has developed a rating system to help assure this trust and reliability between passengers and drivers, called a rideshare ratings system. Rideshare ratings systems pose a unique challenge for Uber because of the way they are set up and the level of rider objectivity. Uber's insistent policy of maintaining a five-star fleet can put drivers at a disadvantage. Uber rivals have similar policies; for instance, Lyft tells customers that anything less than 5 stars indicates unhappiness with the ride.

Low driver scores can mean drivers are forced to take remedial classes where they learn about safe driving techniques and driver etiquette. Those who fail to increase their scores risk suspension or permanent deactivation. Because consumers have different views of what constitutes quality, it can be argued that Uber drivers are placed at the mercy of the consumer's mood.

Operating on Cost Leadership

Uber uses its app to determine pricing. Once the passenger completes his or her ride with an Uber partner–driver, the person's credit card is charged automatically. Fees charged for speeds more than 11 miles per hour are charged by the distance traveled. Uber operates on a cost leadership basis, claiming that it offers lower rates than taxis. However, the app OpenStreetCab suggests that Uber might be more cost-efficient only when the fare is more than $35.

Uber uses an algorithm to estimate fees charged when demand is high. Called surge pricing, Uber has even applied for a patent for this type of system. This "peak pricing" strategy is not too different than when utilities or flights charge higher prices when demand is high. Passengers are alerted during times when the price is higher. However, the extent of the pricing increase has been questioned as some consumers believe Uber uses this high demand to "price gouge" passengers.

Spreading Awareness and Creating Buzz

Uber has engaged in a number of promotional activities to make its brand known. Often it adopts buzz marketing strategies to draw attention to its services. For instance, to celebrate National Ice Cream Month one year, Uber launched on-demand ice cream trucks in seven major cities. In one promotion Uber partnered with General Electric to offer free DeLorean rides to San Francisco users reminiscent of the movie *Back to the Future*. Uber also uses promotion to portray its benefits compared to its rivals. For instance, Uber assumed a combative advertising approach to its major rival Lyft through a Facebook ad campaign. Uber advertising often stresses the convenience and low cost of its ridesharing services.

More recently, Uber has come under criticism for an aggressive—and some say toxic—corporate culture. Some prominent executives at Uber have left the firm, claiming that the corporate culture conflicted with their values. Former CEO Travis Kalanick was well-known for his aggressive strategies, and according to critics, this behavior trickled down to employees. Uber is now trying to build a new culture with its CEO Dara Khosrowshahi while attempting to clean up its public image.

What's Around the Next Turn

Uber's business model can be found in similar rides-for-hire services, such as Lyft and the Indian ride-sharing service Ola. More rides-for-hires could emerge, in addition to the everyday competition from taxi cabs, limos, rental car businesses, air travel, trains, and city and chartered buses. Switching costs for customers are low, and because ride-sharing companies do not own their own fleets, costs of operating are much less than in other industries. This means that Uber must remain competitive if it wants to keep its customers loyal. Lyft is probably Uber's biggest competitor in the United States with 20 percent market share. Its smaller size makes it easier for Lyft to subsidize drivers and to lower fares. Expanding into the autonomous car industry has also placed Uber in competition with Google, Tesla, and major automobile manufacturers that are also trying to enter the industry. The company temporarily halted road-testing of its autonomous vehicles in Phoenix, Pittsburgh, San Francisco, and Toronto after a pedestrian was struck and killed in Tempe.

Despite Uber's challenges, the company has become widely popular among consumers and independent contractors. Supporters claim that Uber is revolutionizing the transportation service industry. Investors clearly believe Uber is going to be strong in the market in the long run. One lesson that Uber will hopefully take to heart is the need to ensure that independent contractors using its app obey relevant country laws. Uber has to address these issues to uphold the trust of its customers and achieve long-term market success in different countries.[25]

Questions for Discussion

1. What are the ethical challenges that Uber faces in using app-based peer-to-peer sharing technology?
2. Describe Uber's core market. Why is Uber targeting these groups in particular?
3. Why would consumers question Uber's pricing strategy?

Buying Behavior, Global Marketing, and Digital Marketing

PART 4 continues our focus on the customer. Understanding elements that affect buying decisions enables marketers to analyze customers' needs and evaluate how specific marketing strategies can satisfy those needs.

CHAPTER 7 examines consumer buying behavior, the decision processes, and factors that influence buying decisions.

CHAPTER 8 stresses business markets, organizational buyers, the buying center, and the organizational buying decision process.

CHAPTER 9 looks at how marketers can reach global markets and the actions, involvement, and strategies that marketers employ internationally.

CHAPTER 10 examines how online social networking and digital media have affected marketing strategies with the creation of new communication channels and the consumer behavior related to these emerging technologies and trends.

ECONOMIC FORCES

COMPETITIVE FORCES

POLITICAL FORCES

PRODUCT

PRICE CUSTOMER DISTRIBUTION

PROMOTION

SOCIOCULTURAL FORCES

LEGAL AND REGULATORY FORCES

TECHNOLOGICAL FORCES

LORDN/GETTY IMAGES

EVA-KATALIN/GETTY IMAGES

CHAPTER 7

Consumer Buying Behavior

LEARNING OBJECTIVES

7-1 Recognize the stages of the consumer buying decision process.

7-2 Classify the types of consumer decision making and the level of involvement.

7-3 Explore how situational influences may affect the consumer buying decision process.

7-4 Identify the psychological influences that may affect the consumer buying decision process.

7-5 Describe the social influences that may affect the consumer buying decision process.

7-6 Discuss consumer misbehavior.

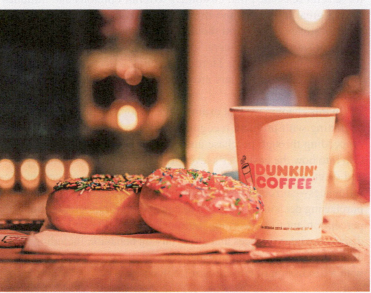

PERE RUBI/SHUTTERSTOCK.COM

Dunkin' Donuts Brews Up New Strategy to Reflect Changes in Consumer Lifestyles and Preferences

Founded in 1950, Massachusetts-based Dunkin' Donuts has built a large and loyal following for its fresh-baked doughnuts and fresh-brewed coffees. Over the years, it has had to adapt to changing consumer lifestyles and food preferences as well as more intense competition. One major influence was the rise of Starbucks, which riveted consumer attention on nuances of beans, brewing, and flavor. Another factor bringing competition to the boiling point was McDonald's introduction of specialty coffees and new breakfast items, followed by its decision to serve breakfast all day. Then regional doughnut companies like Krispy Kreme began expanding across the country, even as Dunkin' Donuts moved beyond its New England roots into southern and western states.

Now that consumers have more coffee and breakfast choices than ever, Dunkin' Donuts has been rethinking its offerings. After a few years of adding fancy coffees and trendier breakfast and lunch sandwiches, the company is slowly rolling out a slimmed-down menu. Rather than offering several dozen doughnut varieties, Dunkin' Donuts is experimenting with a core line of 18 top-selling doughnut varieties. It also eliminated artificial dyes from its donut recipes. Former CEO Nigel Travis says the company still aims to be the "number one retailer of doughnuts," but it also wants a simpler menu to speed in-store customer service, accuracy, and consistency. In addition, Dunkin' Donuts has partnered with Coca-Cola to market bottled, ready-to-drink iced coffees through other retail outlets. Finally, building on its decade-long "America Runs on Dunkin'" advertising campaign, the company is testing new stores branded only as "Dunkin.'"[1]

Dunkin' Donuts and many other traditional and online marketers go to great lengths to understand their customers' needs and wants so that they can develop and modify products to satisfy them. This information provides insights into **buying behavior**, which is the decision processes and actions of people involved in buying and using products. **Consumer buying behavior** refers to the buying behavior of ultimate consumers—those who purchase products for personal or household use and not for business purposes. Marketers attempt to understand buying behavior for several reasons. First, customers' overall opinions and attitudes toward a firm's products have a great impact on the firm's success. Second, as we saw in Chapter 1, the marketing concept stresses that a firm should create a marketing mix that meets customers' needs. To find out what satisfies consumers, marketers must examine the main influences on what, where, when, and how they buy. Third, by gaining a deeper understanding of the factors that affect buying behavior, marketers are better positioned to predict how consumers will respond to marketing strategies.

In this chapter, we first examine the major stages of the consumer buying decision process, beginning with problem recognition, information search, and evaluation of alternatives, and proceeding through purchase and postpurchase evaluation. We follow this with an investigation into how the customer's level of involvement affects the type of decision making they use and discuss the types of consumer decision-making processes. Next, we explore situational influences—surroundings, time, purchase reason, and buyer's mood and condition—that affect purchasing decisions. We go on to consider psychological influences on purchasing decisions: perception, motives, learning, attitudes, personality and self-concept, and lifestyles. Next, we discuss social influences that affect buying behavior, including roles, family, reference groups, digital influences, opinion leaders, social classes, and culture and subcultures. We conclude with a discussion of consumer misbehavior.

buying behavior The decision processes and actions of people involved in buying and using products

consumer buying behavior The decision processes and purchasing activities of people who purchase products for personal or household use and not for business purposes

consumer buying decision process A five-stage purchase decision process that includes problem recognition, information search, evaluation of alternatives, purchase, and postpurchase evaluation

Learning Objective 7-1

Recognize the stages of the consumer buying decision process.

7-1 CONSUMER BUYING DECISION PROCESS

The **consumer buying decision process**, shown in the bottom of Figure 7.1, includes five stages: problem recognition, information search, evaluation of alternatives, purchase, and postpurchase evaluation. Before we examine each stage, consider these important points. First, as shown in

| Figure 7.1 | Consumer Buying Decision Process and Possible Influences on the Process |

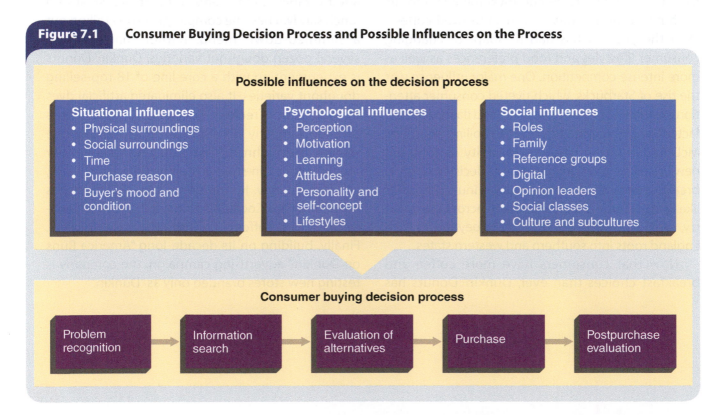

Figure 7.1, this process can be affected by numerous influences, which are categorized as situational, psychological, and social. Second, the actual act of purchasing is usually not the first stage of the process. Third, not all decision processes result in a purchase—individuals can end the process at any stage. Finally, not all consumer decisions include all five stages. The increasing use of mobile technology, especially smartphones, is speeding up the buying decision process for those who use them, in part by providing more opportunities to engage in the process whenever and wherever consumers happen to be.

7-1a Problem Recognition

Problem recognition occurs when a buyer becomes aware of a difference between a desired state and an actual condition. For example, a person may recognize a desire for clean floors, but lack a working vacuum cleaner to fulfill that need. The speed of consumer problem recognition can be quite rapid or rather slow. A person may not recognize a problem or need until marketers point it out. Marketers use sales personnel, advertising, and packaging to help trigger recognition of such needs or problems. Consider the Tidy Cats advertisement, which uses humor to highlight the fact that its product can solve the not-so-funny problem of smelly litter boxes. The ad presents before and after pictures of a woman's face—before using the product and after—to show cat owners that the product is a solution to their stinky litter box problem.

Problem Recognition
This advertisement is attempting to stimulate problem recognition.

7-1b Information Search

After recognizing the problem or need, a buyer will decide whether to pursue satisfying that need. If the consumer chooses to move forward, he or she will next search for product information to help resolve the problem or satisfy the need. If, for example, a consumer realizes that he wants clean floors, he will conduct a search on different products that could fulfill this need.

An information search has two aspects. In an **internal search**, buyers search their memories for information about products that might solve their problem. If they cannot retrieve enough information from memory to make a decision, they seek additional information from outside sources in an **external search**. The external search may focus on communication with friends or relatives, comparison of available brands and prices, marketer-dominated sources, and/or public sources. An individual's personal contacts—friends, relatives, and coworkers—often are influential sources of information because the person trusts and respects them. However, consumers should take care not to overestimate the product knowledge of family and friends. Consumers may also use marketer-dominated sources of information, such as salespeople, advertising, websites, package labeling, and in-store demonstrations and displays because they typically require little effort.

The internet has become a major resource during the consumer buying decision process, and buyers often begin their search online to research buying guides, product descriptions, reviews, prices, and more. Buyers can also obtain information from independent sources: government reports, news presentations, publications such as *Consumer Reports,* and reports from product-testing organizations, for instance. Consumers frequently view information from

internal search An information search in which buyers search their memories for information about products that might solve their problem

external search An information search in which buyers seek information from sources other than their memories

these sources as credible because of their factual and unbiased nature. For services that are hard to evaluate even after consumption (e.g., legal advice), consumers rely more on salespeople, friends and family, and independent consumer reports.[2] Buyers today routinely turn to user review sites and apps such as Yelp, Zagat, TripAdvisor, and Angie's List for insights into both goods and services. Increasingly, consumers begin their information search on a mobile device.

Repetition, a technique often used by advertisers, increases consumers' information retention and recall. When they see or hear an advertising message for the first time, recipients may not grasp all its important details, but they recall more particulars as the message is repeated. However, marketers should take care not to repeat a message too many times, as consumers can tire of it and begin to respond unfavorably. Information can be presented verbally, numerically, or visually. Marketers pay great attention to the visual components of their advertising materials.

consideration set A group of brands within a product category that a buyer views as alternatives for possible purchase

evaluative criteria Objective and subjective product characteristics that are important to a buyer

7-1c **Evaluation of Alternatives**

A successful information search within a product category yields a group of brands that a buyer views as possible alternatives. This group of brands is sometimes called a **consideration set** (or an *evoked set*). Consumers assign a greater value to a brand they have heard of than to one they have not—even when they do not know anything else about the brand other than the name. For example, a consideration set of laptop computers might include devices from Apple, Microsoft, Dell, and Lenovo. A consumer will probably lean initially toward the one with which he or she is most familiar, or that his or her friends prefer, before conducting any additional searches.

To assess the products in a consideration set, the buyer uses **evaluative criteria**: objective characteristics (such as the size, speed, and capacity) and subjective characteristics (such as style and color) that are important to him or her. Consider that one laptop buyer may prefer a large display, whereas another may want one with a lot of memory. The buyer assigns a certain level of importance to each criterion. However, some features and characteristics carry more weight than others, depending on consumer preferences. The buyer rates, and eventually ranks, brands in the consideration set using the selected evaluative criteria. It is possible that the evaluation stage may yield no brand the buyer is willing to purchase. In that case, a further information search may be necessary.

Marketers may influence consumers' evaluations by *framing* the alternatives—that is, describing the alternatives and their attributes in a certain manner. Framing can make a characteristic seem more important to a consumer and facilitate its recall from memory. For instance, by stressing a car's superior comfort and safety features over those of a competitor's, a carmaker can direct consumers' attention toward these points. The advertisement for Kraft's P3 Portable Protein Packs engages in framing by highlighting the fact that the products contain 60 percent more food and 17 grams of protein as well as four unique tastes in each pack. The

Framing
Kraft attempts to influence a customer's evaluation of alternatives by framing the important characteristics of P3 Portable Protein Packs.

ad also displays a Portable Protein Pack surrounded by loose pieces of turkey, almonds, cheese, and yogurt-covered fruit to illustrate the quality of foods contained in each pack. After seeing the ad, a consumer interested in a high-protein snack will likely judge competing products in relation to the information given in the ad. You have experienced the framing effect if you have ever walked into a gourmet grocery or high-end clothing store where the displays make the products seem so appealing that you feel you just have to buy them, only to return home and be less satisfied than you were in the store. Framing has a stronger influence on the decision processes of inexperienced buyers. If the evaluation of alternatives yields one or more brands that the consumer is willing to buy, he or she is ready to move on to the next stage of the decision process: the purchase.

7-1d **Purchase**

In the purchase stage, the consumer chooses to buy the product or brand yielded by the evaluation of alternatives. However, product availability may influence which brand is ultimately purchased. If the brand that ranked highest in evaluation is unavailable and the buyer is unwilling to wait until it is available again, the buyer may choose to purchase the brand that ranked second. So, if a consumer is at the mall shopping for jeans and the preferred Levis in her size are out of stock but the Lucky brand jeans are not, the consumer may opt to purchase the Lucky brand to save another trip to the mall later.

During this stage, buyers also pick the seller from which they will buy the product—it could be a specific retail shop, chain, or online retailer. The choice of seller may affect final product selection and, therefore, the terms of sale, which, if negotiable, are determined at this stage. Consumers also settle other issues, such as price, delivery, warranties, maintenance agreements, installation, and credit arrangements, at this time. Finally, the actual purchase takes place (although the consumer can still decide to terminate the buying decision process even at this late stage).

7-1e **Postpurchase Evaluation**

After the purchase, the buyer evaluates the product to ascertain if its actual performance meets expected levels. Many criteria used in evaluating alternatives are applied again during postpurchase evaluation in order to make a comparison. The outcome of this stage is either satisfaction or dissatisfaction, which influences whether the consumer will repurchase the brand or product, complain to the seller, or communicate positively or negatively with other possible buyers. Postpurchase intent may differ between consumers. For example, the perceived value of the purchase has a weaker effect on the repurchase intent for women than for men. On the other hand, the costs and efforts of switching to a new store affect men's repurchase decisions much more than women's.[3]

cognitive dissonance A buyer's doubts shortly after a purchase about whether the decision was the right one

The postpurchase evaluation stage is especially important for high-priced items. Shortly after the purchase of an expensive product, evaluation may result in **cognitive dissonance**, which involves doubts in the buyer's mind about whether purchasing the product was the right decision. Cognitive dissonance is most likely to arise when a person recently bought an expensive, high-involvement product that is found to be lacking some of the desirable features of competing brands. A buyer who is experiencing cognitive

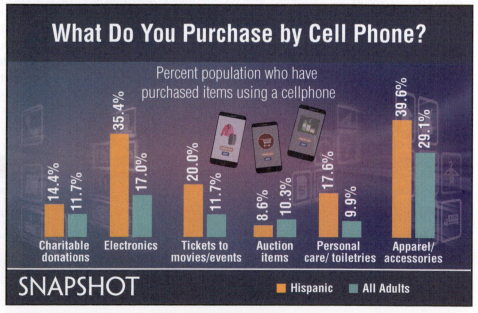

What Do You Purchase by Cell Phone?

Percent population who have purchased items using a cellphone

	Hispanic	All Adults
Charitable donations	14.4%	11.7%
Electronics	35.4%	17.0%
Tickets to movies/events	20.0%	11.7%
Auction items	8.6%	10.3%
Personal care/ toiletries	17.6%	9.9%
Apparel/ accessories	39.6%	29.1%

SNAPSHOT

Source: Simmons Media Behavior Trends (formerly Simmons New Media Study), Fall 2016.

dissonance may attempt to return the product or may seek out positive information, such as reviews, to justify choosing it. For instance, a person would likely experience cognitive dissonance if he or she bought a pair of Nike shoes for full price and then found them on sale a week later. Marketers sometimes attempt to reduce cognitive dissonance by having salespeople telephone or e-mail recent purchasers to make sure they are satisfied with their new purchases. Salespeople may send recent buyers results of studies showing that other consumers are very satisfied with the brand.

As Figure 7.1 shows, three major categories of influences are believed to affect the consumer buying decision process: situational, psychological, and social. Although we discuss each major influence separately later in the chapter, their effects on the consumer decision process are interrelated.

7-2 TYPES OF CONSUMER DECISION MAKING AND LEVEL OF INVOLVEMENT

To acquire products that satisfy their current and future needs, consumers engage in different types of decision-making processes that vary depending on the nature of the product. The amount of effort, both mental and physical, that buyers expend in solving problems also varies considerably with the cost and type of product.

7-2a Types of Consumer Decision Making

There are three types of consumer decision making, which vary in involvement level and other factors: routinized response behavior, limited decision making, or extended decision making (Table 7.1).

A consumer uses **routinized response behavior** when buying frequently purchased, low-cost items that require very little search-and-decision effort. A consumer may have a brand preference, but will be satisfied with several brands in the product class. Typically, low-involvement products are bought through routinized response behavior—that is, almost automatically. For example, buyers spend little time or effort selecting most supermarket items such as soft drinks or batteries. If the preferred brand is out of stock, they will select a competing product with little thought.

Buyers engage in **limited decision making** when they buy products occasionally, or from unfamiliar brands in a familiar product category. This type of decision making requires slightly more time for information gathering and deliberation. For instance, if Procter & Gamble introduces a new Pantene brand shampoo, interested buyers will seek additional information about the product, perhaps by asking a friend who has used it, watching a commercial about it, or visiting the company's website, before making a trial purchase.

The most complex type of decision making, **extended decision making**, occurs with high-involvement, unfamiliar, expensive, or infrequently purchased items—for instance, a computer, a car, or the services of a doctor or a lawyer. The buyer uses many criteria to evaluate alternative

routinized response behavior
A consumer decision-making process used when buying frequently purchased, low-cost items that require very little search-and-decision effort

limited decision making
A consumer decision-making process used when purchasing products occasionally or needing information about an unfamiliar brand in a familiar product category

extended decision making
A consumer decision-making process employed when purchasing unfamiliar, expensive, or infrequently bought products

Table 7.1 Consumer Decision Making

	Routinized Response	Limited	Extended
Product cost	Low	Low to moderate	High
Search effort	Little	Little to moderate	Extensive
Time spent	Short	Short to medium	Lengthy
Brand preference	More than one is acceptable, although one may be preferred	Several	Varies, usually many

brands or choices and spends much time seeking information and deciding before making the purchase.

Purchase of a particular product does not elicit the same type of decision-making process every time. We may engage in extended decision making the first time we buy a product, but find that limited decision making suffices when we buy it again. If a routinely purchased brand is discontinued or no longer satisfies us, we may use limited or extended decision making to switch to a new brand. Thus, if we notice that the brand of pain reliever we normally buy is no longer working well, we may seek out a different brand through limited decision making.

It is important to note that consumer decision making is not always rational. Most consumers occasionally make purchases solely on impulse and not on the basis of any of these three decision-making processes. **Impulse buying** involves no conscious planning and stems from a powerful urge to buy something immediately. Research indicates that 83 percent of U.S. shoppers admit to having purchased something impulsively, and about 68 percent of those impulse buys were made in brick-and-mortar stores.[4] Retailers set up gum, beef jerky, peanuts, and magazines close to the cash registers to encourage impulse buying.

Low-Involvement Products
Candy products, such as Skittles, are low-involvement products because they are inexpensive and purchased frequently by candy buyers. When buying candy, consumers usually employ routinized response behavior.

ANTONIO GRAVANTE/ISTOCK EDITORIAL/GETTY IMAGES

7-2b Consumer Level of Involvement

A major factor in the type of decision-making process employed depends on the customer's **level of involvement**, which is the degree of interest in a product and the importance the individual places on that product. As an example, involvement with wine can be used to segment consumers who will visit a winery. Those consumers with high involvement with wine differ significantly in visitation motives and patterns than those identified as low involvement.[5] High-involvement products tend to be those that are visible to others (e.g., real estate, high-end electronics, or automobiles) and are more expensive. High-importance issues, such as health care, are also associated with high levels of involvement. Low-involvement products are much less expensive and have less associated social risk (e.g., grocery or drugstore items).

A person's interest in a product or product category that is ongoing and long term is referred to as *enduring involvement*. Most consumers have an enduring involvement with very few activities or items—the product categories in which they have the most interest. Many consumers, for instance, have an enduring involvement with Apple products, a brand that inspires loyalty and trust. These consumers will expend a great deal of effort to purchase and learn about Apple products, such as waiting in line for the latest iPhone release and reading articles about the various features of the latest MacBook. In contrast, *situational involvement* is temporary and dynamic, and results from a particular set of circumstances, such as the sudden need to buy a new laptop after the current one starts malfunctioning right before a research project is due. For a short period of time the consumer will research computer types, brands, models, retailers, and prices, but will settle on a choice relatively quickly because the consumer needs a functional computer as soon as possible. Once the purchase is made, the consumer's interest and involvement wane quickly. Consumer involvement may be attached to product categories (e.g., sports), loyalty to a specific brand, interest in a specific advertisement (e.g., a funny commercial) or a medium (e.g., a television show), or to certain decisions and behaviors (e.g., a love of shopping). Interest, such as finding an advertisement entertaining, does not necessarily mean the consumer will become involved with the brand. It may not satisfy a need the customer currently has, or he or she may be loyal to another brand.

impulse buying An unplanned buying behavior, involving no conscious planning, resulting from a powerful urge to buy something immediately

level of involvement An individual's degree of interest in a product and the importance of the product for that person

There are several factors that influence a buyer's level of involvement. The most significant is the perceived risk of a purchase. In particular, high-priced items have greater risk of financial loss of future purchasing power. Buying a new car, for example, generally requires a monthly payment that will significantly reduce your purchasing power for other items in your monthly budget. Thus, high-priced products tend to be associated with a higher level of involvement. On the other hand, previous experience with a product is usually associated with lower levels of involvement because buyers do not need to engage in extensive decision making for a product they have purchased several times before. Finally, a buyer who is highly interested in something is likely to have a higher level of involvement than someone who is not. Consider an avid runner who likes to compete in marathons; he is more likely than most to be interested in running shoes and sports drinks, as well as magazines and blogs devoted to running and marathons. His level of involvement in a pair of running shoes is likely to be higher than that of a college student who is just buying shoes to wear around campus.

Learning Objective 7-3

Explore how situational influences may affect the consumer buying decision process.

7-3 SITUATIONAL INFLUENCES ON THE BUYING DECISION PROCESS

Situational influences result from circumstances, time, and location that affect the consumer buying decision process. Imagine buying an automobile tire after noticing, while washing your car, that the current tire is badly worn. This is a different experience from buying a tire right after a blowout on the highway spoils your road trip because in the prior scenario you can take the time to conduct research and select the best product and supplier for your needs. Situational factors can influence the buyer during any stage of the consumer buying decision process and may cause the individual to shorten, lengthen, or terminate the process. Situational factors can be classified into five categories: physical surroundings, social surroundings, time perspective, reason for purchase, and the buyer's momentary mood and condition.[6]

Physical surroundings include location, store atmosphere, scents, sounds, lighting, weather, and other factors in the physical environment in which the decision process occurs. A sports stadium, for example, includes not only the playing field and seats but also concession stands, souvenir shops, entertainment, music, and the energy of the audience. Retail chains try to design their store environment and layout in a way that makes shopping as enjoyable and easy as possible, so consumers are more inclined to linger and make purchases. Marketers at banks, department stores, and specialty stores go to considerable effort and expense to create physical settings that are conducive to making purchase decisions. Abercrombie & Fitch, for example, is introducing new fitting room "suites" in some stores that allow shoppers to try on clothes together while still changing in private. They can also adjust the fitting room's lighting and sound and charge their phones while they try on clothing. The clothing chain hopes these and other changes will bring customers back to the Abercrombie & Fitch brand.[7] Restaurant chains, such as Olive Garden and Chili's, invest heavily in facilities, often building from the ground up, to provide surroundings that are distinctive to the chain and that enhance customers' experiences. Even remodeling the physical surroundings of a store can directly affect sales. Remodeling tends to increase the sales to new customers, who will spend more per visit and return to the store more frequently than existing customers.[8]

However, dimensions such as weather, traffic sounds, and odors are clearly beyond the marketers' control in some settings. General climatic conditions, for example, may influence a customer's decision to buy a specific type of vehicle (e.g., an SUV) with certain features (e.g., four-wheel drive). Current weather conditions, or other external factors, may be either encouraging or discouraging to consumers when they seek out specific products. Such factors may be favorable to retailers, as when forecasted bad weather causes customers to stock up and even hoard staples. Although traffic is generally beyond marketers' control, McDonald's found a way to exploit traffic congestion in the U.K. with a digital billboard that changes based on traffic conditions. When traffic slows down, the billboards ask, "Stuck in a jam? There's light

situational influences Influences that result from circumstances, time, and location that affect the consumer buying decision process

at the end of the tunnel." along with an image of the fast-food company's golden arches to stimulate desire for McDonald's products.[9]

Social surroundings include characteristics and interactions of others who are present during a purchase decision, such as friends, relatives, salespeople, and other customers. Buyers may feel pressured to behave in a certain way because they are in a public place such as a restaurant, store, or sports arena. Thoughts about who will be around when the product is used or consumed are another dimension of the social setting. Negative elements of physical surroundings, such as an overcrowded store or an argument between a customer and a salesperson, may cause consumers to leave the store before purchasing anything.

The time dimension influences the buying decision process in several ways. It takes varying amounts of time to progress through the steps of the buying decision process, including learning about, searching for, purchasing, and using a product. Time also plays a major role when consumers consider the frequency of product use, the length of time required to use it, and the overall product life. Other time dimensions that can influence purchases include time of day, day of the week or month, seasons, and holidays. Thus, a customer under time constraints is likely to either make a quick purchase decision or delay a decision. On the other hand, consumers may be willing to wait longer to purchase certain products depending upon their desire for them. An Apple enthusiast might spend a considerable time waiting for the newest iPhone to be released.

The reason for purchase involves what, exactly, the product purchase should accomplish and for whom. Generally, consumers purchase an item for their own use, for household use, or as a gift. Purchase choices are likely to vary depending on the reason. For example, you will likely choose a nicer product brand for a gift than you would for yourself. If you own a Mont Blanc pen, which is a very expensive brand, it is likely that you received it as a gift from someone very close to you. On the other hand, a wedding dress is usually worn just once and often costs hundreds or even thousands of dollars, so brides tend to spend considerable time looking through magazines, considering style and prices, long before trying on a single dress. **Thus**, the advertisement for Rebecca Ingram bridal gowns presents a model wearing a beautiful wedding dress in a garden setting with the tagline "Timeless Elegance. Modern Value." Retail outlets where Rebecca Ingram gowns are sold are likely to encourage purchases through situational influences, such as appealing displays, highly attentive salespeople, dressing areas large enough to accommodate friends and family of the bride, lighting calculated to enhance the look of the dresses, and strategic positioning of products to catch consumers' eyes.

The buyer's mood (e.g., anger, anxiety, or contentment) or condition (e.g., fatigue, illness, or having cash on hand) may also affect the consumer buying decision process. Such mood or condition is momentary and occurs immediately before the situation in which a buying decision will be made. They can affect a person's ability and desire to search for or receive information, or seek

Situational Influences
Due to the fact that a wedding is a very important event in a person's life, the purchase of a wedding gown will require considerable time and deliberation compared to many other purchase decisions.

and evaluate alternatives. Moods can also significantly influence a consumer's postpurchase evaluation. If you are happy immediately after purchase, you may be more likely to attribute the mood to the product and will judge it favorably.

7-4 PSYCHOLOGICAL INFLUENCES ON THE BUYING DECISION PROCESS

Psychological influences partly determine people's general behavior and thus influence their behavior as consumers. Primary psychological influences on consumer behavior are perception, motivation, learning, attitudes, personality and self-concept, and lifestyles. Even though these psychological factors operate internally, they are affected strongly by external social forces.

7-4a **Perception**

People perceive the same event or thing at the same time in different ways. When you first look at the illustration with the caption "Perception?" for instance, do you see people or columns? Similarly, the same individual may perceive an item in different ways at different times. **Perception** is the process of selecting, organizing, and interpreting information inputs to produce meaning. **Information inputs** are sensations received through sight, taste, hearing, smell, and touch. When we hear an advertisement on the radio, see a friend, smell food cooking at a restaurant, or touch a product, we receive information inputs. Some inputs are more effective in attracting attention than others. For instance, research has shown that advertisements for food items that appeal to multiple senses at once are more effective than ones that focus on taste alone.[10]

Selection is the first step in the perceptual process. Perception can be interpreted in different ways because, although we constantly receive pieces of information, only some reach our awareness. We would be completely overwhelmed if we paid equal attention to all sensory inputs, so we select some and ignore others. This process is called **selective exposure** because an individual selects (mostly unconsciously) which inputs will reach awareness. If you are concentrating on this paragraph, you probably are not aware that cars outside are making noise, that the room light is on, that a song is playing in the background, or even that you are touching the page. Even though you receive these inputs, they do not reach your awareness until they are brought to your attention. An individual's current set of needs affects selective exposure.

psychological influences Factors that in part determine people's general behavior, thus influencing their behavior as consumers

perception The process of selecting, organizing, and interpreting information inputs to produce meaning

information inputs Sensations received through sight, taste, hearing, smell, and touch

selective exposure The process by which some inputs are selected to reach awareness and others are not

selective distortion An individual's changing or twisting of information that is inconsistent with personal feelings or beliefs

Information inputs that relate to one's strongest needs are more likely to reach conscious awareness. It is not by chance that many fast-food commercials are aired near mealtimes. Customers are more likely to pay attention to these advertisements at times when they are hungry.

The selective nature of perception may also result in two other conditions: selective distortion and selective retention. **Selective distortion** is changing or twisting received information. It occurs when a person receives information inconsistent with personal feelings or beliefs and he or she selectively interprets the information, changing its meaning to align more closely with expectations. Selective distortion explains why people will reject logical information, even when presented with supporting evidence. Selective distortion can both help and hurt marketers. For instance, a consumer may become loyal to a brand and remain loyal, even when confronted with evidence that another brand

Perception?
Do you see two women or three columns?

JURIAH MOSIN/SHUTTERSTOCK.COM

is superior. However, selective distortion can also lessen the impact of the message on the individual substantially. For instance, consumers are less likely to purchase a green product if they learn that the product was intentionally redesigned to benefit the environment. They prefer any environmental benefits to be unintentional side effects. Consumers tend to believe that products intentionally designed to be more sustainable require product developers to take resources away from other areas, such as product quality.[11] In **selective retention**, a person remembers information inputs that support personal feelings and beliefs and forgets inputs that do not. After hearing a sales presentation and leaving a store, for example, a customer may quickly forget many selling points if they contradict personal beliefs or preconceived notions about a product.

The second step in the process of perception is perceptual organization. Information inputs that reach awareness are not received in an organized form. To produce meaning, an individual must organize and integrate new information with what is already stored in memory. People use several methods to achieve this. One method is called *figure-ground*. When an individual uses figure-ground, a portion of the information inputs that reach awareness stands out as the figure and others become the background. For example, when looking back at the image of the women and columns, when you mentally allow the columns to stand out as the figure, the women become the background. If you allow the women to stand out as the figure, the columns become the background. Another method, called *closure,* occurs when a person fills in missing information in a way that conforms to a pattern or statement. In an attempt to draw attention to its brand, a marketer may capitalize on closure by using incomplete images, sounds, or statements in advertisements.

Interpretation, the third step in the perceptual process, is the assignment of meaning to what has been organized. A person interprets information according to what he or she expects or what is familiar. For this reason, a manufacturer who changes a product or its package may face consumer backlash from customers looking for the old, familiar product or package and who do not recognize, or do not like, the new one. PepsiCo, for example, faced a significant backlash after it redesigned the look of the packaging for its popular Tropicana Pure Premium orange juice. The new juice cartons featured cleaner text and simple graphics, but consumers

selective retention Remembering information inputs that support personal feelings and beliefs and forgetting inputs that do not

INTEGRITY IN MARKETING

Unilever Grows "Sustainable Living" Brands

From Lifebuoy to Lipton, a growing number of Unilever's best-selling brands are serving a larger purpose beyond revenues and profits. Based in London, Unilever rings up $58 billion in annual revenues, selling its food and household products to 2.5 billion customers worldwide. During the past decade, the Anglo-Dutch company has been working toward aggressive targets for reducing its environmental footprint and increasing its social impact. Year after year, it has added top-selling brands like Lifebuoy, Hellmann's, Ben & Jerry's, and Dove to its "Sustainable Living" initiative, investing in earth-friendly production and marketing programs as well as socially-responsible activities that benefit local communities worldwide.

But do brands with purpose have a competitive edge in the marketplace? Unilever's research indicates that many consumers consider the well-being of the planet and its people when making buying decisions. More specifically, its research shows that one in three consumers places a high priority on sustainability when choosing among competing products. And this translates into better revenues and profits for Unilever, because its "Sustainable Living" brands are now growing 50 percent more quickly than the rest of its brands.

Given the high number of competing products in categories like food and personal care, building brands with purpose helps Unilever differentiate itself and forge a closer connection with customers. Just as important, Unilever is innovating with sustainability in mind, to improve its products and its profits as it seeks to make the world a little better every day.[a]

quickly rejected—or simply failed to recognize—them. After sales fell 20 percent, the company hastily returned to its more familiar packaging.[12] Unless a product or package change is accompanied by a promotional program that makes people aware of the change, an organization may suffer a sales decline.

Although marketers cannot control buyers' perceptions, they often try to influence them. Several problems may arise from such attempts, however. First, a consumer's perceptual process may operate such that a seller's information never reaches the target. For example, a buyer may block out and not notice an advertisement in a magazine. Second, a buyer may receive information but perceive it differently from what was intended, as occurs in selective distortion. For instance, when a toothpaste producer advertises that "35 percent of the people who use this toothpaste have fewer cavities," a customer could potentially infer that 65 percent of users have more cavities. Third, a buyer who perceives information inputs to be inconsistent with prior beliefs is likely to forget the information quickly, as is the case with selective retention.

7-4b Motivation

Motivation refers to the inner driving forces or reasons behind an individual's actions and behaviors. Generally, people are motivated to maintain a current acceptable state of being, to improve their state of being to a more ideal level, or to avoid negative consequences. For example, a person might be motivated to seek a raise to maintain his current state of living if his rent goes up or to purchase a new smartphone that has more desirable features to improve his state of being to a more ideal level. Motivation can derive from physical feelings, states of mind, or emotions. Indeed, motivation is strongly interrelated with emotion. It is also influenced by perceived risk as well as self-concept, values, needs, goals, and self-control. When consumers are motivated to achieve a particular goal, they will expend significant effort to research products and solutions, think about and process information on those potential solutions, and feel some level of involvement, as we discussed earlier.[13]

Some motives may help an individual achieve his or her goals, whereas others create barriers to achievement. Motivation also affects the direction and intensity of behavior. At any point in time, certain motives will have a stronger influence on the person than others will. For example, the sensation of being cold is a strong motivator on the decision to purchase a new coat, making the motivation more urgent in the winter than it is in the summer.

With online shopping increasing annually, marketers have increasingly found a need to understand the motivation of online shoppers and how the new shopping medium affects their buying behavior. One research project divided online shoppers by two basic motivations: utilitarian (or functional) shoppers and hedonic (or nonfunctional) shoppers. Utilitarian consumers shop online because it is a useful and fast way to purchase certain items, whereas hedonic consumers shop online because it is a fun and enjoyable way to find bargains. The research found that hedonic consumers spent more time on the internet for each purchase and shopped online more often than utilitarian consumers. Hedonic consumers were also more likely to make impulse buys online and engage in bidding wars on sites like eBay.[14]

Motivation may drive a person to satisfy a recognized want or need. Abraham Maslow, an American psychologist, conceived a theory of motivation based on a hierarchy of needs. According to Maslow, humans seek to satisfy five levels of needs, from most basic for survival to lofty, as shown in Figure 7.2. This pyramid is known as **Maslow's hierarchy of needs**. Maslow proposed that people are constantly striving to move up the hierarchy, fulfilling one level of needs, then aspiring to fulfill the next.

At the most basic level are *physiological needs,* requirements for survival such as food, water, sex,

motivation The inner driving forces or reasons behind an individual's actions and behaviors.

Maslow's hierarchy of needs The five levels of needs that humans seek to satisfy, from most to least important

Figure 7.2   Maslow's Hierarchy of Needs

- Self-actualization needs
- Esteem needs
- Social needs
- Safety needs
- Physiological needs

clothing, and shelter, which people try to satisfy first. Food and beverage marketers often appeal to physiological needs, such as sex appeal or hunger. At the next level are *safety needs,* which include security and freedom from physical and emotional pain and suffering. Life insurance, automobile air bags, carbon monoxide detectors, vitamins, and decay-fighting toothpastes are products that consumers purchase to ensure their safety needs are met. Next are *social needs*—the human requirements for love and affection and a sense of belonging. Advertisements for beauty products, jewelry, and even cars often suggest that purchasing these products will bring love and social acceptance. At the level of *esteem needs,* people require respect and recognition from others as well as self-esteem, a sense of one's own worth. Owning a Lexus automobile, purchasing a Michael Kors handbag, or flying first class can satisfy esteem needs. At the top of the hierarchy are *self-actualization needs.* These refer to people's needs to grow and develop and to become all they are capable of becoming. Some products that may send messages that they satisfy these needs include fitness center memberships, education, and self-improvement workshops.

Physiological Needs
Crest brand toothpaste appeals to safety needs because it fights tooth decay, resulting in better health for the user.

7-4c **Learning**

Learning refers to changes in a person's thought processes and behavior caused by information and experience. Consequences of behavior strongly influence the learning process. Behaviors that result in positive consequences tend to be repeated. For instance, a consumer who buys a Kind snack bar, enjoys the taste, and feels satisfied after eating it is more likely to buy a Kind bar again. The individual will probably continue to purchase that product until it no longer provides satisfaction. When outcomes of the behavior are no longer satisfying or stand in the way of achieving a desired goal, such as weight loss, the person may switch to a less fattening brand or stop eating candy bars altogether.

Purchasing decisions require customers to process information, an ability that varies by individual. The type of information inexperienced buyers use may differ from the type used by experienced shoppers who are familiar with the product and purchase situation. Thus, two potential buyers of an antique desk may use different types of information in making their purchase decisions. The inexperienced buyer may judge the desk's value by price and appearance, whereas the more experienced buyer may look at the construction and condition of the desk and seek information about the manufacturer, period, and place of origin to assess the desk's quality and value. Consumers who lack experience may seek information from others when making a purchase and even take along an informed friend with experience. Experienced buyers have greater self-confidence and more knowledge about the product and can recognize which product features are reliable cues to quality.

Marketers help customers learn about their products by facilitating opportunities to gain experience with them, which makes customers feel more comfortable. They engage in *shaping* potential buyers' early experience through free samples, sometimes coupled with coupons, to encourage product trial and reduce purchase risk. For instance, because some consumers may be wary of trying new products outside of their routine, Costco, H-E-B's Central Market, and Whole Foods permit companies to offer samples of their products in the stores' aisles. Personal-care products sometimes include a sample of another product in the package. In-store demonstrations foster knowledge of product uses. A software producer may use point-of-sale product demonstrations to introduce a new product. Test drives give potential new-car purchasers some experience with the automobile's features.

Consumers also learn by experiencing products indirectly through information from salespeople, advertisements, websites, internet videos, social media, friends, and relatives. Through

learning Changes in an individual's thought processes and behavior caused by information and experience

sales personnel and advertisements, marketers offer information before (and sometimes after) purchases that can create favorable consumer attitudes toward the product. However, marketers may encounter problems in attracting and holding consumers' attention, providing them with information for making purchase decisions, and convincing them to try the product.

7-4d Attitudes

An **attitude** is an individual's enduring evaluation of feelings about, and behavioral tendencies toward, an object or idea. The objects toward which we have attitudes may be tangible or intangible, living or nonliving. For example, we have attitudes toward sex, religion, politics, and music, just as we do toward cars, football, and hamburgers. Although attitudes can change over time, they tend to remain stable and do not vary, particularly in the short term. A person's attitudes toward different things do not have equal impact at any one time, and some are stronger than others. Individuals acquire attitudes through experience and interaction with other people.

An attitude consists of three major components: cognitive, affective, and behavioral. The cognitive component is the person's knowledge and information about the object or idea. For example, as consumers have become more knowledgeable about health, obesity, and quality ingredients, their attitudes toward soft drinks and fast food have declined along with the sales of companies like McDonald's and Coca-Cola. The affective component comprises the individual's feelings and emotions toward the object or idea. Emotions involve both psychological and biological elements. They relate to feelings and can create visceral responses related to behavior. Love, hate, anger, and fear are emotions that can influence behavior. For some people, certain brands, such as Apple, Starbucks, or REI, elicit an emotional response. Firms that successfully create an emotional experience or connection with customers establish a positive brand image that can result in customer loyalty. Southwest Airlines, for example, has forged an emotional connection with many of its customers through creative use of humor both during flights and on its website. The airline extends this playful focus and personal touches in every interaction to demonstrate its commitment to people—both customers and employees.[15] This means it is important for marketers to generate authentic messages that consumers can relate to on an emotional level. The behavioral component manifests itself in the person's actions regarding the object or idea. Changes in cognitive, affective, or behavioral components may possibly affect other components.

Consumer attitudes toward a company and its products greatly influence success or failure of the firm's marketing strategy. When consumers have strong, negative attitudes toward one or more aspects of a firm's marketing practices, they may not only stop using its products but also urge relatives and friends to do likewise. Because attitudes play an important part in determining consumer behavior, marketers should regularly measure consumer attitudes toward prices, package designs, brand names, advertisements, salespeople, repair services, store locations, features of existing or proposed products, and social responsibility efforts.

Efforts to understand attitudes have resulted in two major academic models: the attitude toward the object model (known as the Fishbein model) and the behavioral intentions model (also known as the Theory of Reasoned Action). These models provide an understanding of the role of attitudes in decision making. The attitude toward the object model can be used to understand, and possibly predict, a consumer's attitude. It consists of three elements: beliefs about product attributes, the strength of beliefs, and the evaluation of beliefs. These elements combine to form what is called the overall attitude toward the object.[16]

The behavioral intentions model, rather than focusing on attributes, focuses on intentions to act or purchase. This model considers consumer perceptions of what other people, particularly peers, believe is the best choice among a set of alternatives. As its name indicates, this model focuses on attitudes toward the buying behavior, not toward the object. The subjective norm component is important in recognizing that individuals live in an inherently social environment and are influenced by what others think and believe. Consider attitudes toward personal appearance (e.g., what clothes people wear, hairstyles, or body modifications such as piercings or tattoos). Consumers will take into account what others may think of their decisions before committing to products that alter appearance. Many people are motivated to comply with what

attitude An individual's enduring evaluation of feelings about, and behavioral tendencies toward, an object or idea

others hold to be an acceptable norm and stay in close communication through word of mouth and traditional and digital media.

Several methods help marketers gauge consumer attitudes. One of the simplest ways is to question people directly. The internet and social networking sites are useful tools for marketers seeking to garner information on attitudes directly from consumers. Using sites such as Facebook, companies can ask consumers for feedback and product reviews.

Marketers also evaluate attitudes through attitude scales. An **attitude scale** usually consists of a series of adjectives, phrases, or sentences about an object. Respondents indicate the intensity of their feelings toward the object by reacting to the adjectives, phrases, or sentences. For example, a marketer who is measuring people's attitudes toward shopping might ask respondents to indicate the extent to which they agree or disagree with a number of statements, such as "shopping is more fun than watching television."

When marketers determine that a significant number of consumers have negative attitudes toward an aspect of a marketing mix, they may try to change those attitudes. This task is generally lengthy, expensive, and difficult and can require extensive promotional efforts. To alter responses so that more consumers purchase a certain brand, a firm might launch an information-focused campaign to change the cognitive component of a consumer's attitude, or a persuasive (emotional) campaign to influence the affective component. Distributing free samples might help change the behavioral component.

Both business and nonbusiness organizations try to change people's attitudes about many things, from health and safety to prices and product features. Look at the advertisement for Toyota, for instance. In recent years, Toyota experienced negative publicity after it recalled millions of cars for mechanical and safety issues, damaging its long-time reputation for quality. To rebuild its brand, the company invested heavily in safety redesigns. Now, it is using promotion to restore favorable attitudes toward the brand, promising that "Safety just comes naturally." The ad, which pictures a new Toyota Camry, lets potential buyers know that Toyota Safety Sense features like Lane Departure Alert and Pre-Collision System, now are standard on many Toyota vehicles. The ad targets buyers who are looking for the best safety features available in a new vehicle.

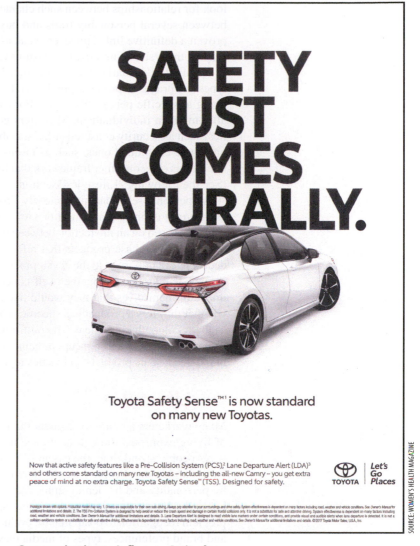

Communication to Influence Attitudes
Toyota experienced negative news coverage regarding the safety of its cars. This advertisement, along with other Toyota marketing communications, is attempting to make consumers' attitudes more favorable regarding the safety of Toyota vehicles.

7-4e **Personality and Self-Concept**

Personality is a set of internal traits and distinct behavioral tendencies that result in consistent patterns of behavior in certain situations. An individual's personality is a unique combination of hereditary characteristics and personal experiences. Personalities typically are described as having one or more characteristics, such as compulsiveness, ambition, gregariousness, dogmatism, authoritarianism, introversion, extroversion, and competitiveness. Marketing researchers

attitude scale A means of measuring consumer attitudes by gauging the intensity of individuals' reactions to adjectives, phrases, or sentences about an object

personality A set of internal traits and distinct behavioral tendencies that result in consistent patterns of behavior in certain situations

look for relationships between such characteristics and buying behavior. Although a few links between several personality traits and buyer behavior have been identified, studies have not proven a definitive link. However, weak association between personality and buying behavior may be the result of unreliable measures rather than a true lack of a relationship.

A number of marketers are convinced that consumers' personalities do indeed influence types and brands of products purchased. Because of this believed relation, marketers aim advertising at specific personality types. For example, truck commercials often highlight rugged, all-American individualism. Marketers generally focus on positive personality characteristics, such as security consciousness, sociability, independence, or competitiveness, rather than on negatively valued ones, such as insensitivity or timidity. The PRIZM program, owned by Nielsen, is one consumer framework that takes into account individual personality differences. (See the following "Lifestyles" section.)

A person's self-concept is closely linked to personality. **Self-concept** (sometimes called *self-image*) is one's perception or view of oneself. Individuals develop and alter their self-concepts based on an interaction between psychological and social dimensions. Research shows that buyers purchase products that reflect and enhance their self-concepts and that purchase decisions are important to the development and maintenance of a stable self-concept.[17] Consumers who feel insecure about their self-concept may purchase products that help them bolster the image of themselves that they would like to project. Consumers' self-concepts may influence whether they buy a product in a specific product category and may affect brand selection as well as the retailers they frequent. The outfitting company Patagonia, for example, appeals to consumers who have a self-concept of being outdoor enthusiasts. Many consumers are loyal to the brand because its products and values represent their lifestyle.

7-4f Lifestyles

Many marketers attempt to segment markets by lifestyle. A **lifestyle** is an individual's pattern of living expressed through activities, interests, and opinions. Lifestyle patterns include the ways people spend time, the extent of their interaction with others, and their general outlook on life and living. People partially determine their own lifestyles, but lifestyle is also affected by personality and by demographic factors such as age, education, income, and social class. Lifestyles have a strong impact on many aspects of the consumer buying decision process, from problem recognition to postpurchase evaluation. Lifestyles influence consumers' product needs and brand preferences, types of media they use, and how and where they shop.

One of the most popular frameworks for understanding consumer lifestyles and their influences on purchasing behavior is a product called PRIZM (see also Chapter 6). Originally developed by Claritas, PRIZM was acquired by Nielsen, one of the leading research companies in the world. It divides consumers in the United States into 66 distinct groups based on numerous variables such as education, income, technology use, employment, and social groups.[18] These groups can help marketers understand consumers and how things like lifestyle and education will influence their purchasing habits. Because technology is increasingly important to marketers and plays a huge role in many consumers' lives, Nielsen also released another product, ConneXions, which uses the same lifestyle groups as PRIZM to analyze consumer communications behavior. This information can be valuable to marketers, as it reveals how consumers choose to access information.[19]

self-concept A perception or view of oneself

lifestyle An individual's pattern of living expressed through activities, interests, and opinions

social influences The forces other people exert on one's buying behavior

---

Learning Objective 7-5

Describe the social influences that may affect the consumer buying decision process.

7-5 SOCIAL INFLUENCES ON THE BUYING DECISION PROCESS

Forces that other people exert on buying behavior are called **social influences**. As Figure 7.1 (located near the beginning of this chapter) shows, they are divided into seven major groups: roles, family, reference groups, digital, opinion leaders, social classes, and culture and subcultures.

7-5a Roles

All of us occupy positions within groups, organizations, and institutions. In these positions, we play one or more **roles**, which are sets of actions and activities a person in a particular position is supposed to perform based on the expectations of both the individual and surrounding people. Because every person occupies numerous positions, they have many roles. A man may perform the roles of son, husband, father, employee, employer, church member, civic organization member, and student in an evening college class. Thus, multiple sets of expectations are placed on each person's behavior.

An individual's roles influence both general behavior and buying behavior. The demands of a person's many roles may be diverse, and even at times inconsistent or at odds. Consider the various types of clothes that you buy and wear depending on whether you are going to class, to work, to a party, or to the gym. You and others in these settings have expectations about what is acceptable attire for these activities. Thus, the expectations of those around us affect our purchases of many different types of products.

7-5b Family Influences

Parents teach children how to cope with a variety of problems, including those that help with purchase decisions. Thus, family influences have a direct impact on the consumer buying decision process. **Consumer socialization** is the process through which a person acquires the knowledge and skills to function as a consumer. Often, children gain this knowledge and set of skills by observing parents and older siblings in purchase situations. Children observe brand preferences and buying practices in their families and, as adults, will retain some of these brand preferences and buying practices as they establish and raise their own families. Buying decisions made by a family are a combination of group and individual decision making.

The extent to which family members take part in family decision making varies among families and product categories. Traditionally, family decision-making processes have been grouped into four categories: autonomic, husband dominant, wife dominant, and syncratic, as shown in Table 7.2.[20] Although female roles have changed over time, women still make the majority of purchase decisions in households. Indeed, research indicates that women remain the primary decision makers for 85 percent of all consumer buying decisions.[21]

The family life-cycle stage affects individual and joint needs of family members. Family life-cycle stage influences purchases ranging from housing, clothing, and personal-care items to entertainment and investment products. For example, consider how the car needs of recently married "twenty-somethings" compare to those of the same couple when they are "thirty-somethings" with a baby or "forty-somethings" with teenagers. Chrysler is developing an electric minivan, the Portal, which buyers can reconfigure as needed to

Table 7.2 Types of Family Decision Making

Decision-Making Type	Decision Maker	Types of Products
Husband dominant	Male head of household	Lawnmowers, hardware and tools, stereos, automobile parts
Wife dominant	Female head of household	Children's clothing, women's clothing, groceries, household furnishings
Autonomic	Equally likely to be made by the husband or wife, but not by both	Men's clothing, luggage, toys and games, sporting equipment, cameras
Syncratic	Made jointly by husband and wife	Vacations, TVs, living room furniture, carpets, financial planning services, family cars

roles Actions and activities that a person in a particular position is supposed to perform based on expectations of the individual and surrounding people

consumer socialization The process through which a person acquires the knowledge and skills to function as a consumer

ZORANM/GETTY IMAGES

Family Influences

The consumer decision processes related to the purchase of numerous products are influenced by both parents and children. Children learn about buying many products from their families, and they apply this learning when making similar decisions when they are adults.

match their changing life-cycle stages.[22] Family life-cycle changes can affect which family members are involved in purchase decisions and the types of products purchased. Children also have a strong influence on household purchase decisions.

When two or more family members participate in a purchase, their roles may dictate that each is responsible for performing certain purchase-related tasks, such as initiating the idea, gathering information, determining if the product is affordable, deciding whether to buy the product, or selecting the specific brand. The specific purchase tasks performed depend on the types of products being considered, the kind of family purchase decision process typically employed, and the presence and amount of influence children have in the decision process. Thus, different family members may play different roles in the family buying process.

Within a household, an individual may perform one or more roles related to making buying decisions. The gatekeeper is the household member who collects and controls information, including price and quality comparisons, locations of sellers, and assessment of which brand best suits the family's needs. For example, if a family is planning a summer vacation, the gatekeeper might compare prices for hotels and airfare to determine the best deal. The influencer is a family member who expresses his or her opinions. In the vacation example, an influencer might be a child who wants to go to Disney World or a teenager who wants to go snowboarding. The decider is a member who makes the buying choice. This role switches based on the type and expense of the product being purchased. In the case of a vacation, the decider will more likely be the adults, who possess information, influence, and their own preferences. The buyer is a member who actually makes the purchase. The user is a household member who consumes or uses the product. In this Disney World example, all members of the family are users.

7-5c Reference Groups

A **reference group** is a group, either large or small, with which a person identifies so strongly that he or she adopts the values, attitudes, and behavior of group members. Most people have several reference groups, such as families, work-related groups, fraternities or sororities, civic clubs, professional organizations, or church-related groups.

In general, there are three major types of reference groups: membership, aspirational, and disassociative. A membership reference group is one to which an individual actually belongs. The individual identifies intensely enough with this group to take on the values, attitudes, and behaviors of people in that group. An aspirational reference group is one to which a person aspires to belong. The aspiring member desires to be like group members. This is why companies may partner with celebrities to market their brands or products. Sprint, for example, partnered with Jay-Z, Lele Pons, Gerard Adams, and other young social influencers with its #LiveUnlimited campaign, which let the social influencers deliver their own take on the brand's message.[23] A group that a person does not wish to be associated with is a disassociative, or negative, reference group. The individual does not want to take on the values, attitudes, and behavior of group members.

reference group A group that a person identifies with so strongly that he or she adopts the values, attitudes, and behavior of group members

A reference group may serve as an individual's point of comparison and source of information. A customer's behavior may change to be more in line with actions and beliefs of group members. For instance, a person may switch to a different brand of shirt based on reference group members' advice and preferences. An individual may also seek information from the reference group about other factors regarding a prospective purchase, such as where to buy a certain product.

Reference groups can affect whether a person does or does not buy a product at all, buys a type of product within a product category, or buys a specific brand. The extent to which a reference group affects a purchase decision depends on the product's conspicuousness and on the individual's susceptibility to reference group influence. Generally, the more conspicuous a product, the more likely that reference groups will influence a consumer's purchase decision. A product's conspicuousness is determined by whether others can see it and whether it attracts attention. A marketer sometimes tries to use reference group influence in advertisements by suggesting that people in a specific group buy a product and are satisfied with it. Whether this kind of advertising succeeds depends on three factors: how effectively the advertisement communicates the message, the type of product, and the individual's susceptibility to reference group influence. In this type of appeal, the advertiser hopes that many people will accept the suggested group as a reference group and buy (or react more favorably to) the product.

7-5d Digital Influences

A generation ago, buyers were influenced by word-of-mouth referrals from a few neighbors, coworkers, or friends for each purchase. Today, however, buyers are strongly influenced by the opinions of hundreds or even thousands through digital sources such as social media networks, reviews on e-commerce sites, and review apps such as Yelp. A PricewaterhouseCoopers survey found that nearly half of online shoppers reported that reading reviews, comments, and feedback on social media influenced their shopping decisions.[24] Among women, 81 percent say they often purchase products they've seen shared on Facebook, Instagram, Pinterest, and other social networks. Nearly three-quarters of women surveyed say the ability to find recommendations on social media reduces the risk of buying a new product.[25]

Buyers are emotional, whether they realize it or not, and tapping into the experiences and opinions of others plays into that aspect of the buying decision process. By exploring the experiences of others as relayed on Amazon.com comments or Yelp reviews, shoppers can reduce their risk in trying an unknown product by gaining information from others. Online, consumers can not only find opinions but also obtain feedback as well as photos, videos, experiences, and how-to ideas that can lead them to particular brands or retailers.

Computers, smartphones, and wearables, as well as in-store kiosks and mobile payment devices affect both online and in-store shopping behaviors all around the world. These tools are profoundly altering in-store customer behavior but at different rates of impact, depending on the country.[26] Consumers today are increasingly online all the time no matter where they are. In the time it takes to stand in line at a coffee shop, a buyer in the information-search stage can read reviews on a product, find a store that sells it, and see a map showing the nearest store. When they log into Instagram, Facebook, or Twitter, they can see what their friends or favorite celebrities are wearing; they can also see whether their favorite brands might be introducing new products or having a sale. Thus, digital influences on the buying decision process have become increasingly important to marketers.

7-5e Opinion Leaders

An **opinion leader** is a member of an informal group who provides information about a specific topic, such as smartphones, to other group members seeking information. The opinion leader is in a position, or has knowledge or expertise, that makes him or her a credible source of information about a few topics. Opinion leaders are easily accessible—often through social media—and are viewed by other group members as being well informed about one or multiple topics. Opinion leaders are not the foremost authority on all topics, but because such

opinion leader A member of an informal group who provides information about a specific topic to other group members

CREATIVE MARKETING

Picture This: Target and Pinterest Team Up for Visual Search

Point, tap, match, shop. That's the idea behind putting Pinterest Lens visual search technology into Target's apps and website. Pinterest is a popular social media site where users seek out and save images related to interests like home decorating, cooking, holiday gifts, fashion, and more. When consumers tap the Pinterest Lens icon to photograph a product they spot somewhere, such as a lamp or a T-shirt, the software searches for images of items that match or look very similar. Through the deal with Pinterest, Target customers can point the store app's camera icon at anything they like, and then browse the matching images at Target.com, along with complementary items related to the matching products.

The partnership between Target and Pinterest builds on a trend toward more consumers using images, as well as voice commands, to search via mobile devices for products and information online. "When it comes to shopping, what we hear time and again is the importance of ease and convenience," says the chief marketing officer.

The retailer also understands that consumers can identify and comprehend images more quickly than words. By incorporating Pinterest's technology into its shopping apps, the retailer helps consumers speed up the search process by narrowing the focus to just those items that match what they have in mind. And, of course, the pictured matches are drawn from Target.com, encouraging browsers to take the next step and make a purchase from the retailer's website.[b]

individuals know they are opinion leaders, they feel a responsibility to remain informed about specific topics, and thus seek out advertisements, manufacturers' brochures, salespeople, and other sources of information. Opinion leaders have a strong influence on the behavior of others in their group, particularly relating to product adoption and purchases.

An opinion leader is likely to be most influential when consumers have high product involvement but low product knowledge, when they share the opinion leader's values and attitudes, and when the product details are numerous or complicated. Possible opinion leaders and topics are shown in Table 7.3.

7-5f **Social Classes**

In all societies, people rank others into higher or lower positions of respect. This ranking process, called social stratification, results in social classes. A **social class** is an open aggregate of people with similar social rank. A class is referred to as *open* because people can move into and out of it. Criteria for grouping people into classes vary from one society to another. In the United States, we take into account many factors, including occupation, education, income, wealth, race, ethnic group, and possessions. A person who is ranking someone into a class does not necessarily apply all of a society's criteria. Sometimes, too, the role of income tends to be

social class An open group of individuals with similar social rank

Table 7.3   Examples of Opinion Leaders and Topics

Opinion Leader	Possible Topics
Spiritual acquaintance	Charities to support, political ideas, lifestyle choices
"Movie buff" friend	Movies to see in theaters, rent, stream or buy
Medical friend	Prescription drugs, vitamins, health products
"Techie" acquaintance	Computer and other electronics purchases, software purchases, internet service choices, video game purchases

overemphasized in social class determination. Although income does help determine social class, the other factors also play a role. Within social classes, both incomes and spending habits differ significantly among members.

To some degree, individuals within social classes develop and assume common behavioral patterns. They may have similar attitudes, values, language patterns, and possessions. Social class influences many aspects of people's lives. Because people most frequently interact with others within their own social class, people are more likely to be influenced by others within their own class than by those in other classes. Social class can influence choice of religion, financial planning decisions, and access to education, occupation, and leisure time activities.

Social class also influences people's spending, saving, and credit practices. It can determine the type, quality, and quantity of products a person buys and uses. For instance, it affects purchases of clothing, foods, financial and health-care services, travel, recreation, entertainment, and home furnishings. Behaviors within a social class can influence others as well. Most common is the "trickle-down" effect, in which members of lower classes attempt to emulate members of higher social classes, such as by purchasing desirable automobiles, large homes, and even selecting certain names for their children. Couture fashions designed for the upper class influence the clothing sold in department stores frequented by the middle class, which eventually is sold to the working class who shop at discount clothing stores. Less often, status float will occur, when a product that is traditionally associated with a lower class gains status and popularity among upper classes. Blue jeans, for example, were originally worn exclusively by the working class. Youth of the 1950s began wearing them as a symbol of rebellion against their parents. By the 1970s and 1980s, jeans had also been adopted by upper-class youth when they began to acquire designer labels. Today, blue jeans are acceptable attire for all social classes and cost anywhere from a few dollars to thousands of dollars, depending on the brand.

Social class also affects an individual's shopping patterns and types of stores patronized. In some instances, marketers attempt to focus on certain social classes through store location and interior design, product design and features, pricing strategies, personal sales efforts, and advertising. Many companies focus on the middle and working classes because they account for such a large portion of the population. Outside the United States, the middle class is growing rapidly in places such as India, China, and Brazil, making these consumers desirable targets for marketing messages. For example, Hilton Hotels and Resort is acquiring hotels in major cities in Africa and converting them into Hilton branded hotels, including Hilton Hotels, DoubleTree by Hilton, Garden Inn, and Curio Collection by Hilton. The acquisition and conversion strategy gives Hilton access to Africa's growing middle class at the expense of U.S. competitors who have yet to recognize the opportunities there.[27]

Some firms target different classes with a range of products at different price points. Even designers who previously only made clothing for the wealthy have learned about the benefits of offering items at different price points. For instance, luxury fashion designers Victoria Beckham, Phillip Lim, and Missoni have created limited edition collections for sale exclusively at Target.[28]

7-5g Culture and Subcultures

Culture is the accumulation of values, knowledge, beliefs, customs, objects, and concepts that a society uses to cope with its environment and passes on to future generations. Culture permeates most things you do and objects you interact with, from the style of buildings in your town, to the type of education you receive, to the laws governing your country. Culture also includes society-specific core values and the degree of acceptability of a wide range of behaviors. For example, in U.S. culture, customers as well as businesspeople are expected to behave ethically.

Culture influences buying behavior because it permeates our daily lives. Our culture determines what we wear and eat and where we reside and travel. Society's interest in the healthfulness of food affects food companies' approaches to developing and promoting their products. Culture also influences how we buy and use products and the satisfaction we get from them.

When U.S. marketers sell products in other countries, they must be aware of the tremendous impact specific cultures have on product purchases and use. Global marketers will find that people in other regions of the world have different attitudes, values, and needs, which call for

culture The accumulation of values, knowledge, beliefs, customs, objects, and concepts that a society uses to cope with its environment and passes on to future generations

SOURCE: ESSENCE MAGAZINE

Subcultures

Design Essentials is appealing to the subculture of African American women who like to style their hair with minimal effort.

different methods of doing business and different marketing mixes. Some international marketers fail because they do not, or cannot, adjust to cultural differences.

A culture consists of various subcultures. A **subculture** is a group of individuals whose characteristics, values, and behavioral patterns are similar within the group and different from those of people in the surrounding culture. U.S. culture is marked by many different subcultures, such as punk, rocker, gamer, biker, endurance sports enthusiast, cowboy, and business professional. Within subcultures, greater similarities exist in people's attitudes, values, and actions than within the broader culture. Relative to other subcultures, individuals in one subculture may have stronger preferences for specific types of clothing, furniture, food, or consumer electronics. Take a look at the advertisement for the Design Essentials Sweet Almond and Avocado line of hair products, for example. The ad, which pictures an African American woman along with all the products in the Sweet Almond and Avocado line of Design Essentials Natural products, stresses that using the products saves styling time for all hair textures. Busy women of color who like to style their hair with less effort are the subculture targeted by this advertisement.

Subcultures can play a significant role in how people respond to advertisements, particularly when pressured to make a snap judgment. It is important for marketers to understand that a person can be a member of more than one subculture and that the behavioral patterns and values attributed to specific subcultures do not necessarily apply to all group members.

Subcultural boundaries are often based on geographic designations and demographic characteristics, such as age, religion, race, and ethnicity. The percentage of the U.S. population consisting of ethnic and racial subcultures has grown and is expected to continue to grow. By 2050, about one-half of the U.S. population will be members of racial and ethnic minorities. The three largest and fastest-growing ethnic U.S. subcultures are African Americans, Hispanics, and Asians.[29] The population growth of these racial and ethnic subcultures represents a tremendous opportunity for marketers because of cultural-specific tastes and desires. Businesses recognize that, to succeed, their marketing strategies have to take into account the values, needs, interests, shopping patterns, and buying habits of these various subcultures. Consider Procter & Gamble's Tide, which is popular among many subcultures in the United States, with an overall market share of 43 percent. One way Procter & Gamble holds onto Tide's market share is by deliberately fostering diversity and inclusion with positive representations of race and gender in all its promotion and striving to avoid stereotypes long common in advertising. While Tide ads all have a common look, the actors and models reflect Tide customers' diversity.[30]

subculture A group of individuals whose characteristics, values, and behavioral patterns are similar within the group and different from those of people in the surrounding culture

African American Subculture

In the United States, the African American subculture represents 13.3 percent of the population.[31] That figure is expected to grow to 14.3 percent by 2060.[32] African American consumers are more likely to shop online and interact with brands via social media, making this an effective route for marketers targeting this lucrative subculture. Younger African Americans have become trendsetters for all young American consumers regardless of race or ethnicity. The combined buying power of African American consumers is estimated to be approximately $1.5 trillion by 2021, up 98 percent since 2000.[33]

With young African Americans having so much buying power and growing influence, it's no surprise that companies are increasing their focus on the African American community. Allstate, for example, launched a national campaign on its YouTube, Instagram, and Facebook pages to highlight the contributions of African Americans who are making a positive impact on society. The "Worth Telling" campaign employs images and videos to celebrate the positive impact these individuals have had and strives to connect with black consumers with regard to insurance products.[34]

Hispanic Subculture

Hispanics represent 17.6 percent of the U.S. population, but that figure is projected to grow to 28.6 percent by 2060. Hispanic buying power is estimated to be approximately $1.8 trillion by 2021.[35] When considering the buying behavior of Hispanics, marketers must keep in mind that this subculture is really composed of many diverse cultures coming from a huge geographic region that encompasses nearly two dozen nationalities, including Cuban, Mexican, Puerto Rican, Caribbean, Spanish, and Dominican. Each has its own history and unique culture that affect consumer preferences and buying behavior. Four clusters of the Hispanic market have been identified based upon language preferences, classified as retainers (those who speak Spanish as their main language), biculturals (alternate between Spanish and English), assimilators (speak English but acknowledge Hispanic background), and non-identifiers.[36] Marketers should also recognize that the terms *Hispanic* and *Latino* refer to an ethnic category rather than a racial distinction.

Hispanics represent a large and powerful subculture, and are an attractive consumer group for marketers. Target, for example, created its "Sin Traducción" ("Without Translation") campaign solely for its Hispanic customers to forge deeper connections. The Spanish-language campaign, which plays off Spanish words that do not have an easy English translation, strives to foster a dialog with Latino customers on social media. The retailer spends about 3 percent of its total advertising campaign funds on Hispanic media.[37] Macy's is reaching out to Latino customers in a variety of ways, but particularly through mobile media. The retailer has also introduced a collection of clothing, shoes, and jewelry from popular singer and telenovela star Ariadna Thalía Sodi Miranda (Thalía). The line features trendy items and includes colors and patterns designed to appeal to Latinas of different cultures.[38] Marketers should recognize that simply translating an English-speaking ad into Spanish may not resonate with Hispanic consumers—and may even backfire. Consider that when the California Milk Processing Board sought to translate its popular and long-running "Got Milk?" campaign into Spanish, it did not consult with actual Spanish speakers, and the resulting campaign, "Are You Lactating?" failed.[39]

Asian American Subculture

The term *Asian American* includes Filipinos, Chinese, Japanese, South Asian Indians, Koreans, and Vietnamese, encompassing people from more than 40 countries of origin. This group represents 5.7 percent of the U.S. population, and their combined buying power is expected to reach $1.1 trillion by 2020.[40] Asian Americans tend to identify strongly with their culture of origin; most prefer to refer to themselves by their country of origin (e.g., Japanese or Japanese American) rather than being referred to as Asian American.[41] The individual language, religion, and value system of each group influences its members' purchasing decisions.

Although Asian Americans are a smaller subculture than African Americans and Hispanics in the United States, they are growing faster. However, Asian Americans appear to be underserved relative to other subcultures.[42] For instance, advertisers spend less to reach this important segment.[43] However, ignoring such an important segment represents missed opportunities for marketers. Some companies are beginning to remedy this. Insurance company AIG, for example, opened a branch in California that targets Chinese Americans specifically but strives to appeal to all Asian American consumers. The opening ceremony for the branch featured an auspicious lion dance. The office has signs in both Chinese and English, and all employees speak English and at least one Asian language. To make its customers feel comfortable, it hosts meeting spaces that feel like tea rooms.[44]

Learning Objective 7-6

Discuss consumer misbehavior.

7-6 CONSUMER MISBEHAVIOR

Approaching the topic of inappropriate consumer behavior requires some caution because of varying attitudes and cultural definitions of what comprises misbehavior. However, it is generally agreed that some conduct, such as shoplifting or purchasing illegal drugs, falls under the category of activities that are not accepted by established norms. Therefore, we will define consumer misbehavior as behavior that violates generally accepted norms of a particular society. Shoplifting is one of the most obvious misconduct areas. U.S. retailers lose nearly $49 billion annually due to individuals shoplifting grocery items, electronics, and more, as well as employee thefts, and the cost of these losses is passed on to consumers as higher prices.[45] Organized retail crime—where criminal groups engage in large-scale theft from retail and online stores—has become a major threat, not only to retailers, but to all organizations including governments. Experts estimate that organized retail crime alone costs businesses about $30 billion annually.[46] Aside from selling goods on the black market, consumer motivation for shoplifting includes the low risk of being caught, a desire to be accepted by a group of peers (particularly among young people), and the excitement associated with the activity.

Consumer fraud includes purposeful actions to take advantage of and/or damage others during a transaction. Using fraudulently obtained credit cards, debit cards, checks, or bank accounts falls into this category, as does making false insurance claims. Although few realize it, purchasing a dress for a special event, wearing it once with the tags hidden, and then returning it is also fraud. Returning items for cash when those items were actually received as gifts or even stolen is another example of fraud. Retailers lose an estimated $15 billion annually to return fraud.[47] Some consumers engage in identity theft, which is a serious and growing legal problem—particularly as more shopping is conducted online, where regulations and security are more difficult to enforce.

Piracy is copying computer software, video games, movies, or music without paying the producer for them. It is estimated that global businesses spend approximately $500 billion to fix security issues arising from malware associated with pirated software. Global consumers spend approximately $25 billion and waste 1.2 billion hours to fix problems resulting from downloaded pirated software.[48] The recording industry broadcasts messages explaining why sharing music is not acceptable, but it remains a serious problem. Understanding motivations for piracy can be helpful in developing a plan to combat the issue (see Table 7.4).

Yet another area of concern with consumer misbehavior is abusive consumers. Rude customers engage in verbal or physical abuse, can be uncooperative, and may even break policies. Airlines remove abusive customers if they represent a threat to employees and other passengers. Belligerently drunk customers, especially in environments such as bars and airplanes, have to be removed in order to protect others. Understanding the psychological and social reasons for consumer misconduct can be helpful in preventing or responding to the problem.

Table 7.4 Motivations for Unethical or Illegal Misbehavior

Justification/rationalization	The thrill of getting away with it
Economic reasons	There is little risk of getting caught
It is accepted by peers	People think they are smarter than others

Source: Kevin J. Shanahan and Michael J. Hyman, "Motivators and Enablers of SCOURing: A Study of Online Piracy in the US and UK," *Journal of Business Research* 63 (September–October 2010): 1095–1102.

consumer misbehavior
Behavior that violates generally accepted norms of a particular society

Summary

7-1 Recognize the stages of the consumer buying decision process.

The consumer buying decision process includes five stages: problem recognition, information search, evaluation of alternatives, purchase, and postpurchase evaluation. Not all decision processes culminate in a purchase, nor do all consumer decisions include all five stages. Problem recognition occurs when buyers become aware of a difference between a desired state and an actual condition. After recognizing the problem or need, buyers search for information about products to help resolve the problem or satisfy the need. In the internal search, buyers search their memories for information about products that might solve the problem. If they cannot retrieve from memory sufficient information to make a decision, they seek additional information through an external search. A successful search yields a group of brands, called a consideration set, which a buyer views as possible alternatives. To evaluate the products in the consideration set, the buyer establishes certain criteria by which to compare, rate, and rank different products. Marketers can influence consumers' evaluations by framing alternatives. In the purchase stage, consumers select products or brands on the basis of results from the evaluation stage and on other dimensions. Buyers also choose the seller from whom they will buy the product. After the purchase, buyers evaluate the product to determine if its actual performance meets expected levels.

7-2 Classify the types of consumer decision making and the level of involvement.

Buying behavior consists of the decision processes and acts of people involved in buying and using products. Consumer buying behavior is the buying behavior of ultimate consumers. An individual's level of involvement—the importance of, and intensity of interest in, a product in a particular situation—affects the type of decision-making process used. Enduring involvement is an ongoing interest in a product class because of personal relevance, whereas situational involvement is a temporary interest that stems from the particular circumstance or environment in which buyers find themselves. There are three kinds of consumer decision making: routinized response behavior, limited decision making, and extended decision making. Consumers rely on routinized response behavior when buying frequently purchased, low-cost items requiring little search-and-decision effort. Limited decision making is used for products purchased occasionally or when buyers need to acquire information about an unfamiliar brand in a familiar product category. Consumers

engage in extended decision making when purchasing an unfamiliar, expensive, or infrequently bought product. Purchase of a certain product does not always elicit the same type of decision making. Impulse buying is not a consciously planned buying behavior but involves a powerful urge to buy something immediately.

7-3 Explore how situational influences may affect the consumer buying decision process.

Three major categories of influences affect the consumer buying decision process: situational, psychological, and social. Situational influences are external circumstances or conditions existing when a consumer makes a purchase decision. Situational influences include surroundings, time, reason for purchase, and the buyer's mood and condition.

7-4 Identify the psychological influences that may affect the consumer buying decision process.

Psychological influences partly determine people's general behavior, thus influencing their behavior as consumers. The primary psychological influences on consumer behavior are perception, motivation, learning, attitudes, personality and self-concept, and lifestyles. Perception is the process of selecting, organizing, and interpreting information inputs (sensations received through sight, taste, hearing, smell, and touch) to produce meaning. The three steps in the perceptual process are selection, organization, and interpretation. Individuals have numerous perceptions of packages, products, brands, and organizations that affect their buying decision processes. Motivation refers to the inner driving forces or reasons behind an individual's actions and behaviors. Learning refers to changes in a person's thought processes and behavior caused by information and experience. Marketers try to shape what consumers learn to influence what they buy. An attitude is an individual's enduring evaluation, feelings, and behavioral tendencies toward an object or idea and consists of three major components: cognitive, affective, and behavioral. Personality is the set of traits and behaviors that make a person unique. Self-concept, closely linked to personality, is one's perception or view of oneself. Researchers have found that buyers purchase products that reflect and enhance their self-concepts. Lifestyle is an individual's pattern of living expressed through activities, interests, and opinions. Lifestyles influence consumers' needs, brand preferences, and how and where they shop.

7-5 Describe the social influences that may affect the consumer buying decision process.

Social influences are forces that other people exert on buying behavior. They include roles, family, reference groups, social media, opinion leaders, social class, and culture and subcultures. Everyone occupies positions within groups, organizations, and institutions, and each position involves playing a role—a set of actions and activities that a person in a particular position is supposed to perform based on expectations of both the individual and surrounding persons. Consumer socialization is the process through which a person acquires the knowledge and skills to function as a consumer. The consumer socialization process is partially accomplished through family influences.

A reference group is a group that a person identifies with so strongly that he or she adopts the values, attitudes, and behavior of group members. The three major types of reference groups are membership, aspirational, and disassociative. Buyers are increasingly influenced by the opinions of hundreds or even thousands through digital sources such as social media networks, reviews on e-commerce sites, and review apps. An opinion leader is a member of an informal group who provides information about a specific topic to other group members.

A social class is an open group of individuals with similar social rank. Social class influences people's spending, saving, and credit practices. Culture is the accumulation of values, knowledge, beliefs, customs, objects, and concepts that a society uses to cope with its environment and passes on to future generations. A culture is made up of subcultures, groups of individuals whose characteristic values and behavior patterns are similar to one another but different from those of the surrounding culture. U.S. marketers focus on three major ethnic subcultures: African American, Hispanic, and Asian American.

7-6 Discuss consumer misbehavior.

Consumer misbehavior is defined as behavior that violates generally accepted norms of a particular society. One form of consumer misbehavior involves shoplifting, or stealing goods from retail stores. Another form of consumer misbehavior is consumer fraud, which involves purposeful actions to take advantage of, and/or damage, others. Piracy, the copying or sharing of music, movies, video games, and computer software, is another form of misbehavior. One final area of concern with regard to consumer misbehavior is abusive consumers, which include customers who are rude, verbally or physically abusive, and/or uncooperative, which may violate some companies' policies. To respond to, or even prevent, these growing problems, organizations need to understand the psychological and social reasons for consumer misbehavior.

Important Terms

buying behavior 186	limited decision making 190	selective exposure 194	lifestyle 200
consumer buying behavior 186	extended decision making 190	selective distortion 194	social influences 200
consumer buying decision process 186	impulse buying 191	selective retention 195	roles 201
internal search 187	level of involvement 191	motivation 196	consumer socialization 201
external search 187	situational influences 192	Maslow's hierarchy of needs 196	reference group 202
consideration set 188	psychological influences 194	learning 197	opinion leader 203
evaluative criteria 188	perception 194	attitude 198	social class 204
cognitive dissonance 189	information inputs 194	attitude scale 199	culture 205
routinized response behavior 190		personality 199	subculture 206
		self-concept 200	consumer misbehavior 208

Discussion and Review Questions

1. What are the major stages in the consumer buying decision process? Are all these stages used in all consumer purchase decisions? Why or why not?
2. How does a consumer's level of involvement affect his or her choice of decision-making process?
3. Name the types of consumer decision-making processes. List some products you have bought using

each type. Have you ever bought a product on impulse? If so, describe the circumstances.
4. What are the categories of situational factors that influence consumer buying behavior? Explain how each of these factors influences buyers' decisions.
5. What is selective exposure? Why do people engage in it?

6. How do marketers attempt to shape consumers' learning?
7. Why are marketers concerned about consumer attitudes?
8. In what ways do lifestyles affect the consumer buying decision process?
9. How do roles affect a person's buying behavior? Provide examples.
10. What are family influences, and how do they affect buying behavior?
11. What are reference groups? How do they influence buying behavior? Name some of your own reference groups.
12. How does an opinion leader influence the buying decision process of reference group members?
13. In what ways does social class affect a person's purchase decisions?
14. What is culture? How does it affect a person's buying behavior?
15. Describe the subcultures to which you belong. Identify buying behavior that is unique to one of your subcultures.
16. What is consumer misbehavior? Describe the various forms of consumer misbehavior.

Developing Your Marketing Plan

Understanding the process that an individual consumer goes through when purchasing a product is essential for developing marketing strategy. Knowledge about the potential customer's buying behavior will become the basis for many of the decisions in the specific marketing plan. Using the information from this chapter, you should be able to determine the following:

1. See Table 7.1. What types of decision making are your customers likely to use when purchasing your product?

2. Determine the evaluative criteria that your target market(s) would use when choosing between alternative brands.

3. Using Table 7.2, what types of family decision making, if any, would your target market(s) use?

4. Identify the reference groups or subcultures that may influence your target market's product selection.

Video Case 7.1

How Ford Drives Future Innovation

What do consumers care about today, what will they think about tomorrow, and what does it all mean for automotive manufacturers? Sheryl Connelly, Ford's manager of global consumer trends—the company's chief trend-watcher—has been studying consumer behavior worldwide, with an eye toward determining what consumers will want and need long before they know. By surveying consumers, and analyzing emerging social trends, technological developments, political issues, environmental concerns, and economic changes, Connelly provides Ford's marketers with insights that shape and refine the company's future innovations.

For example, when Connelly looked at technological trends, she found that medical advances are allowing seniors to lead active lifestyles far longer than ever before. Yet as they age, drivers will need vehicles with features that help them adapt to changes in their physical and mental capabilities. Based on Connelly's conclusions, Ford has been adding features such as automated parking assistance systems

and ergonomic seats that enable drivers—old and young—to stay safe and comfortable behind the wheel.

Another trend Connelly recently identified is growing demand for products that are "more anticipatory and self-sufficient" in fulfilling consumers' needs. Self-driving cars will do this by steering themselves and maintaining a safe distance between other vehicles, freeing drivers from having to concentrate on the road as they travel. The company plans to have a self-driving car on the market within a few years, with a popular price tag. According to Connelly's research, buyers in the United States and the U.K. have less-positive attitudes about self-driving cars than buyers in China and India. Why? Because commuters in India and China battle more traffic congestion and face more challenging road conditions than drivers in the Western nations. Ford is also working on a voice-command system that will allow drivers to handle specific tasks such as opening a garage door simply by speaking instead of using their hands.

STEVE LAGRECA/SHUTTERSTOCK.COM

Increasingly, consumers want the benefits of mobility without the expense and responsibility of owning and maintaining vehicles individually. Especially in urban areas, consumers are flocking to alternatives such as hailing a ride to be driven somewhere or hiring a car to drive themselves for a few hours or a few days. In response, Ford has created a suite of mobility services branded "Ford Pass" to give customers and non-customers alike more alternatives when they're deciding how to get where they want to go. For example, consumers who install the Ford Pass app can use it to locate a parking lot or spot, pay for parking, and arrange to share a ride with other people.

In addition, Connelly has noticed how many consumers are interested in environmental issues, such as conserving natural resources. Showcasing its sustainability initiatives, Ford looks carefully at its impact from raw materials to finished products and beyond. For example, the manufacturer is experimenting with ways to incorporate recycled materials as car parts.

Finally, Connelly's research has revealed a strong emphasis on self-reliance, which in turn means that buyers place a high value on product quality, versatility, and durability. Research shows that 76 percent of U.S. adults expect to keep and drive the same car for a decade or longer. As a result, Ford must be sure its cars, sport-utility vehicles, vans, and pickup trucks will deliver dependable transportation for years and years to first-time buyers, adults with families, seniors, and other consumer segments.[49]

Questions for Discussion

1. How does Ford take into account the diversity of consumer roles as it plans its future marketing? Explain Ford's approach in understanding two or more roles that can affect the buying decision process for vehicles.
2. In terms of psychological influences on buying, why would Ford make its "Ford Pass" app available to both customers and non-customers?
3. Ford widely publicizes Sheryl Connelly's research findings about the broad trends affecting consumer behavior. During which stages of the consumer buying decision process is this publicity likely to prove influential, and why?

Case 7.2

Campbell's Soup Company Cooks Up New Marketing

Eyeing the way today's consumers buy, prepare, and consume food products, Campbell's Soup has been busy cooking up new marketing for new lifestyles and demographics. The 150-year-old company still offers its traditional condensed soups in cans with the familiar red-and-white label, as well as Chunky heat-and-eat canned soups. It also markets other foods under well-known brands such as Pepperidge Farms, Prego, Swanson, and V8. However, with revenues plateauing, Campbell's has had to develop a new recipe for long-term growth, which includes refreshing its pantry and responding to the buying patterns of Millennials and young families.

Over the past decade, the company has acquired several successful brands and products associated with healthy eating. For example, it purchased Bolthouse Farms, which markets carrots, salad dressings, smoothies, and fruit juices. This enhanced Campbell's strength in food categories that consumers perceive as fresh and nutritious. It also acquired Plum Organics, which makes all-natural baby foods and snacks, allowing it to expand into a fast-growing niche favored by health-conscious parents. Then it bought Garden Fresh Gourmet, which makes refrigerated salsas, hummus, and dips, appealing to consumers who prefer authentic, flavorful, and fresh ingredients. And it purchased Pacific Foods, known for all-natural soups, broths, and non-dairy beverages made from locally sourced ingredients.

Another trend Campbell's Soup's marketers spotted is the rise of anytime, all-the-time snacking by on-the-go consumers. In response, the company has been introducing new snack products under its existing Pepperidge Farm brand. It also bought Snyder's-Lance, the parent company of Cape Cod chips, Pop Secret popcorn, Snyder's pretzels, and other popular snacks. With these acquired products, Campbell's revenues now exceed $10 billion. Just as important, the acquisition tilts the company's product portfolio toward foods that fit contemporary tastes and lifestyles.

Campbell's Soup is working hard to identify new flavors that will tempt the taste buds of increasingly adventurous consumers. Its chefs travel the world visiting restaurants, food trucks, and farms, sampling local produce and unique spices. Then they spend time learning to make local dishes as inspiration for new products in the Campbell portfolio. This research helps uncover new ingredients or sources of ingredients, such as a special potato grown only in one region, for use in a new product or to add extra zest to an existing product's recipe.

Internal archives are another source of product inspiration. John Dorrance, who headed Campbell's Soup a century ago, was the inventor of condensed soup. Based on Dorrance's recipe for tomato soup, company chefs recently used New Jersey tomatoes to create a limited-edition Beefsteak Tomato Soup. Lately, the head of Campbell's Culinary & Baking Institute has been studying the original recipes of Margaret Rudkin, founder of Pepperidge Farm, as he thinks about how to combine old-fashioned goodness with innovative flavors for today's palates.

DJCLASSEN/ISTOCK UNRELEASED/GETTY IMAGES

Consumers often buy food products online as well as shopping in supermarkets and specialty grocery stores. With this in mind, Campbell's Soup has begun testing the online sale of premium, ready-to-heat soups, packaged in glass jars and delivered to the consumer's door. The soups are made from ingredients freshly grown near the company's production plants, and the packaging is designed to reflect an upscale positioning in contrast with that of more traditional canned soups. The test will not only provide feedback on the new product's appeal, it will help Campbell's Soup gain more experience in e-commerce that it can apply to selling a wider range of the foods, beverages, and snacks in its product pantry.[50]

Questions for Discussion

1. How high a level of involvement is the typical consumer likely to have with Campbell's Soup's adult food products, compared with its baby food products? What are the implications for the company's marketing efforts?

2. Which social influences on the buying decision process are reflected in Campbell's Soup's marketing activities, and why?

3. Which psychological influences on the buying decision process are being addressed by Campbell's Soup's marketing efforts?

8 Business Markets and Buying Behavior

LEARNING OBJECTIVES

8-1 Distinguish among the four types of business markets.

8-2 Define the North American Industry Classification System and describe how it can be used to identify and analyze business markets.

8-3 Identify the major characteristics of business customers and transactions.

8-4 Describe the buying center, stages of the business buying decision process, and the factors that affect this process.

8-5 Explore how the internet facilitates business buying and marketing.

SPVVK/ISTOCK EDITORIAL/GETTY IMAGES

Google Targets AI at Business Customers

Artificial intelligence (AI) has been part of Google's technological toolkit for more than 20 years. Back when Google was known only for its search engine, the company began applying AI to make its search capabilities even more powerful. Now Google is developing and marketing cutting-edge services, including AI technology, for businesses in a variety of industries.

One business customer is the global engineering and manufacturing firm Rolls-Royce. In addition to making aircraft engines and power systems, the firm manufactures specialized ships for cargo transport, coastal patrol, commercial fishing, and other functions. With safety in mind, Rolls-Royce is training its proprietary software, with Google's AI technology, to prevent collisions by detecting and monitoring a wider array of objects in the water around its vessels. As Rolls-Royce's software learns to identify new objects, all of its vessels will have access to the upgrades via Google's cloud-computing service.

Google is also partnering with Cisco to provide customized cloud-computing services to Cisco's business customers, large and small. The selling point is that each business can pick and choose which of Google's cloud services it wants and make a smooth transition to that configuration on a "pay as you go" basis. For businesses that have already invested heavily in information technology, this approach serves as a bridge to the future by combining the customer's existing technology with Google's advanced cloud capabilities. Thanks to partnerships like this and to Google's AI-fueled breakthroughs, the company aims to add more *Fortune 500* corporations to its roster of business customers in the coming years.[1]

Marketers are just as concerned with meeting the needs of business customers as they are of meeting those of consumers. Marketers at Google, for instance, go to considerable lengths to understand their business customers so they can provide better, more satisfying products and develop and maintain long-term customer relationships.

In this chapter, we look at business markets and business buying decision processes. We first discuss various kinds of business markets and the types of buyers that comprise those markets. Next, we explore several dimensions of business buying, such as the characteristics of transactions, attributes and concerns of buyers, methods of buying, and distinctive features of demand for business products. We then examine how business buying decisions are made and who makes the purchases. Finally, we consider how businesses rely on technology and the internet when marketing and building relationships with business customers.

8-1 BUSINESS MARKETS

As defined in Chapter 6, a business market (also called a *business-to-business market* or *B2B market*) consists of individuals, organizations, or groups that purchase a specific kind of product for one of three purposes: resale, direct use in producing other products, or use in general daily operations. Marketing to businesses employs the same concepts—defining target markets, understanding buying behavior, and developing effective marketing mixes—as marketing to ultimate consumers. However, there are important structural and behavioral differences in business markets. A company that markets to another company must be aware of how its product will affect other firms in the marketing channel, such as resellers and other manufacturers. Business products can also be technically complex, and the market often consists of sophisticated buyers.

Because the business market consists of relatively smaller customer populations, a segment of a market could be as small as a few customers—or even just one. The market for railway equipment in the United States, for example, is limited to a few major carriers, such as CSX. Some products can be both business and consumer products, especially commodities like corn, bolts, or screws, or supplies like light bulbs or furniture. An Apple iPad might customarily be thought of as a consumer product, but some restaurants are using them to list menu items or take orders. Salespeople at many car dealerships are also using iPads for personal selling purposes. However, the quantity purchased and the buying methods differ significantly between the consumer and business markets, even for the same products. Business marketing is often based on long-term mutually profitable relationships across members of the marketing channel based on cooperation, trust, and collaboration. Manufacturers may even co-develop new products, with business customers sharing marketing research, production, scheduling, inventory management, and information systems. Business marketing can take a variety of forms, ranging from long-term buyer–seller relationships to quick exchanges of basic products at competitive market prices. For most business marketers, the goal is to understand customer needs and provide a value-added exchange that shifts from attracting customers to keeping customers and developing relationships.

The four categories of business markets are producer, reseller, government, and institutional. In the remainder of this section, we discuss each of these types of markets.

8-1a Producer Markets

Individuals and business organizations that purchase products for the purpose of making a profit by using them to produce other products or using them in their operations are classified as **producer markets**. Producer markets include buyers of raw materials, as well as purchasers of semi-finished and finished items, used to make other products. Producer markets include a broad array of industries, including agriculture, forestry, fisheries, mining, construction, transportation, communications, and utilities. As Table 8.1 indicates, the number of business establishments in national producer markets is enormous. For instance, manufacturers buy raw materials and component parts for direct use in product creation. Grocery stores and supermarkets are part of producer markets for numerous support products, such as paper and plastic

producer markets Individuals and business organizations that purchase products to make profits by using them to produce other products or using them in their operations

Table 8.1   Number of Establishments in Industry Groups

Industry	Number of Establishments
Agriculture, forestry, fishing, and hunting	22,368
Mining, quarrying, and oil/gas extraction	29,225
Construction	682,390
Manufacturing	292,825
Transportation and warehousing	228,382
Utilities	17,990
Finance and insurance	470,062
Real estate	321,871

Source: "SUSB Annual Data Tables by Establishment Industry," U.S. Census Bureau, https://www.census.gov/data/tables/2015/econ/susb/2015-susb-annual.html (accessed January 18, 2018).

BOYKPC/ISTOCK/GETTY IMAGES

Producer Markets
Chemical plants are part of a producer market because they produce goods that organizations purchase to use as ingredients in the production of other goods.

bags, shelves, counters, and scanners. Farmers are part of producer markets for farm machinery, fertilizer, seed, and livestock. Chemical manufacturing plants are also part of producer markets, as they produce materials and ingredients that other firms use in the production of other goods. Service providers such as delivery services, banks, and airlines are also an important part of producer markets.

8-1b Reseller Markets

Reseller markets consist of intermediaries, such as wholesalers and retailers, that buy finished goods and resell them for a profit. Aside from making minor alterations, resellers do not change the physical characteristics of the products they handle. Resellers also exist for services and intangible products. For instance, there are reseller markets for financial products such as stocks and bonds. Priceline, Orbitz, and Kayak act as resellers for hotel services. Except for items producers sell directly to consumers, all products sold to consumer markets are first sold to reseller markets.

reseller markets Intermediaries that buy finished goods and resell them for a profit

Wholesalers purchase products for resale to retailers, other wholesalers, producers, governments, and institutions. Like manufacturers, wholesalers can also be geographically concentrated. Of the 413,437 wholesale establishments in the United States, a large number are located in New York, California, Illinois, Texas, Ohio, Pennsylvania, New Jersey, and Florida.[2] Although some products are sold directly to end users, many manufacturers sell their products to wholesalers, which then sell the products to other firms in the distribution system. Seafood, for example, goes through a number of intermediaries, including producer, processor, and wholesaler or distributor all the way down to the retailer and final customer. Thus, wholesalers play a very important role in helping producers get their products to customers.

Retailers purchase products and resell them to final consumers. There are more than 1 million retailers in the United States, employing more than 15 million people and generating approximately $5 trillion in annual sales.[3] The United States continues to be a powerful force in retailing. Seven of the top 10 largest retail companies in the world are based in the United States: Walmart, Costco, The Kroger Co., Walgreens Boots Alliance, Amazon, The Home Depot Inc., and CVS Health.[4] Some retailers—Home Depot, PetSmart, and Staples, for example—carry a large number of items. Supermarkets may handle as many as 50,000 different products. In small, individually owned retail stores, owners or managers make purchasing decisions. In chain stores, a central office buyer or buying committee frequently decides whether store managers will stock a product on their shelves. For many products, however, local managers make the actual buying decisions for a particular store.

When making purchase decisions, resellers consider several factors. They evaluate the level of demand for a product to determine the quantity and the price at which the product can be resold. Retailers assess the amount of space required to handle a product relative to its potential profit, sometimes on the basis of sales per square foot of selling area. Because customers often depend on resellers to have products available when needed, resellers typically appraise a supplier's ability to provide adequate quantities when and where they are needed. Colgate Palmolive, for example, has an oral care division that helps retail customers such as Target assess their space and merchandise involving toothpaste, mouthwash, and other oral care products. Resellers also take into account the ease of placing orders and whether producers offer technical assistance or training programs. Before resellers buy a product for the first time, they will try to determine whether the product competes with or complements products they currently handle. These types of concerns distinguish reseller markets from other markets. Producers may even help resellers market the product to their end customers. Colgate-Palmolive has an office in Minnesota to assist Target in marketing oral care products.

8-1c Government Markets

Federal, state, county, and local governments make up **government markets**. These markets spend billions of dollars annually for a wide range of goods and services—from office supplies and health-care services to vehicles, heavy equipment, and weapons—to support their internal operations and provide citizens with products such as highways, education, water service, energy, and national defense. Government spending accounts for about 36 percent of the U.S. total gross domestic product (GDP).[5] The government also purchases services such as hotel rooms, food services, vehicle rentals, and legal and consulting services. The amount spent by federal, state, and local governments over the decades has gone up on average because the total number of government units and the services they provide have both increased. Costs of providing these services have also risen.

Because government agencies spend public funds to buy the products needed to provide services, they are accountable to the public. This accountability explains their relatively complex buying procedures. Some firms choose not to sell to government buyers because of the additional time and expense the red tape costs them. However, many marketers benefit enough from government contracts that they do not find these procedures to be a stumbling block. For certain products, such as defense-related items, the government may be the only customer.

government markets Federal, state, county, or local governments that buy goods and services to support their internal operations and provide products to their constituencies

Governments advertise their product needs through releasing bids or negotiated contracts. Although companies may be reluctant to approach government markets because of the complicated bidding process, once they understand the rules of this process, firms can routinely penetrate government markets. To make a sale under the bid system, firms must apply and be approved for placement on a list of qualified bidders. When a government unit wants to buy, it sends out a detailed description of the products to qualified bidders. Businesses whose products fit with the needs described will submit bids. The government unit is usually required to accept the lowest bid. When buying nonstandard or highly complex products, a government unit often uses a negotiated contract. Under this procedure, the government unit selects only a few firms and then negotiates specifications and terms. It eventually awards the contract to one of the negotiating firms.

8-1d Institutional Markets

Organizations with charitable, educational, community, or other nonbusiness goals comprise **institutional markets**. Members of institutional markets include churches, some hospitals, fraternities and sororities, charitable organizations, and private colleges. Institutions purchase millions of dollars' worth of products annually to support their activities and provide goods, services, and ideas to various audiences. Because institutions often have different goals and fewer resources than other types of organizations, firms may use special marketing efforts to serve them. For example, Aramark provides a variety of services and products to institutional markets, including schools, hospitals, sporting arenas, and senior living centers. It frequently ranks as one of the most admired companies in its industry. For areas like university food service, Aramark aims its marketing efforts directly at students.[6] Another example is the pictured pipe organ manufacturer. Because most businesses or individuals have no need for pipe organs, the producer mainly targets its marketing efforts at churches.

STEPHAN ZABEL/ISTOCK/GETTY IMAGES

Institutional Markets
The producer of this pipe organ supplies products mainly to churches, which are a part of institutional markets.

8-2 USING THE NORTH AMERICAN INDUSTRY CLASSIFICATION SYSTEM TO IDENTIFY AND ASSESS BUSINESS CUSTOMERS

Marketers have access to a considerable amount of information about potential business customers through government and industry publications and websites. Marketers use this information to identify potential business customers and to estimate their purchase potential. The **North American Industry Classification System (NAICS)** is a single industry classification system used by the United States, Canada, and Mexico to generate comparable statistics among the three North American Free Trade Agreement partners. The NAICS classification is based on production activities. NAICS is also similar to the International Standard Industrial Classification (ISIC) system used in Europe and many other parts of the world.

Learning Objective 8-2

Define the North American Industry Classification System and describe how it can be used to identify and analyze business markets.

institutional markets
Organizations with charitable, educational, community, or other nonbusiness goals

North American Industry Classification System (NAICS)
An industry classification system that generates comparable statistics among the United States, Canada, and Mexico

Table 8.2   **Examples of NAICS Classification**

NAICS Hierarchy for AT&T Inc.		NAICS Hierarchy for Apple Inc.	
Sector 51	Information	Sector 31–33	Manufacturing
Subsector 517	Telecommunications	Subsector 334	Computer and Electronic Manufacturing
Industry Group 5173	Wired & Wireless Telecommunication Carriers	Industry Group 3341	Computer and Peripheral Equipment Manufacturing
Industry 51731	Wired & Wireless Telecommunication Carriers	Industry 33411	Computer and Peripheral Equipment Manufacturing
Industry 517311	Wired Telecommunication Carriers	U.S. Industry 334111	Electronic Computer Manufacturing
Industry 517312	Wireless Telecommunications Carriers		

Source: "North American Industry Classification System," U.S. Census Bureau, http://www.census.gov/eos/www/naics/ (accessed January 19, 2018).

NAICS divides industrial activity into 20 sectors with 1,170 industry classifications. NAICS is comprehensive and up-to-date, and it provides considerable information about service industries and high-tech products.[7] Table 8.2 shows some NAICS codes for Apple Inc. and AT&T Inc. Industry classification systems provide a consistent means of categorizing organizations into groups based on such factors as the types of goods and services provided. Although an industry classification system is a vehicle for segmentation, it is best used in conjunction with other types of data to determine exactly how many and which customers a marketer can reach.

A business marketer can identify and locate potential customers in specific groups by using state directories or commercial industrial directories, such as *Standard & Poor's Register* and Dun & Bradstreet's *Million Dollar Database*. These sources contain information about a firm, including its name, NAICS classification, address, phone number, and annual sales. By referring to one or more of these sources, marketers locate potential business customers by industry classification numbers, determine their locations, and develop lists of prospective customers by desired geographic area.

A more expedient, although more expensive, approach is to use a commercial data service. Dun & Bradstreet, for example, can provide a list of organizations that fall into a particular industry classification group. For each company on the list, Dun & Bradstreet provides the name, location, sales volume, number of employees, types of products handled, names of chief executives, and other pertinent information. Either method can identify and locate effectively a group of potential customers by industry and location. Because some companies on the list will have greater potential than others, marketers must conduct further research to determine which customer or customer group to pursue.

To estimate the purchase potential of business customers or groups of customers, a marketer must find a relationship between the size of potential customers' purchases and a variable available in industrial classification data, such as the number of employees. Thus, a paint manufacturer might attempt to determine the average number of gallons purchased by a type of potential customer relative to the number of employees. Once this relationship is established, it can be applied to customer groups to estimate the size and frequency of potential purchases. After deriving these estimates, the marketer is in a position to select the customer groups with the most sales and profit potential.

Learning Objective 8-3

Identify the major characteristics of business customers and transactions.

8-3 DIMENSIONS OF MARKETING TO BUSINESS CUSTOMERS

Now that we have considered different types of business customers and how to identify them, we look at several dimensions of marketing related to them, including transaction characteristics, attributes of business customers and some of their primary concerns, buying methods, major types of purchases, and the characteristics of demand for business products (see Figure 8.1).

| Figure 8.1 | Dimensions of Marketing to Business Customers |

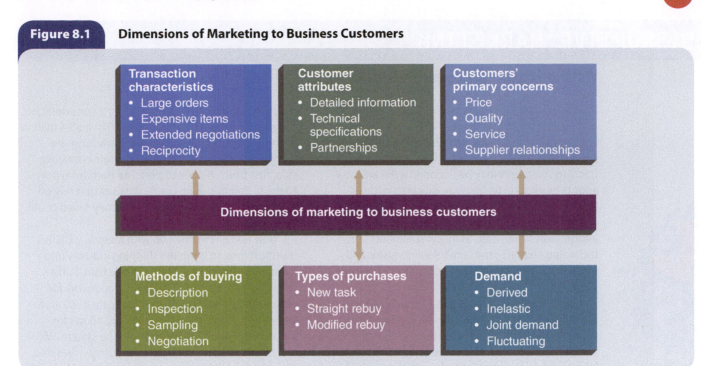

Transaction characteristics
- Large orders
- Expensive items
- Extended negotiations
- Reciprocity

Customer attributes
- Detailed information
- Technical specifications
- Partnerships

Customers' primary concerns
- Price
- Quality
- Service
- Supplier relationships

Dimensions of marketing to business customers

Methods of buying
- Description
- Inspection
- Sampling
- Negotiation

Types of purchases
- New task
- Straight rebuy
- Modified rebuy

Demand
- Derived
- Inelastic
- Joint demand
- Fluctuating

8-3a Characteristics of Transactions with Business Customers

Transactions between businesses differ from consumer sales in several ways. Orders by business customers tend to be much larger than individual consumer sales. Major government contractor Booz Allen Hamilton is sometimes awarded contracts worth up to half a billion dollars to supply medical and IT support assessments and services to various government agencies.[8] Suppliers of large, expensive, or complex goods often must sell products in large quantities to make profits. Consequently, they may prefer not to sell to customers who place small orders.

Some business purchases involve expensive items, such as complex aircraft. For instance, Seattle-based Boeing signed a contract with flydubai, a United Arab Emirates airline, to supply one hundred seventy-five 737 Max aircraft as well as the rights to an additional fifty aircraft, with a combined list price of $27 billion. However, the UAE airline secured discounts by contracting for them during the Dubai Air Show.[9] Other products, such as raw materials and component items, are used continuously in production, and their supply may need frequent replenishing. The contract regarding terms of sale of these items is likely to be a long-term agreement.

Discussions and negotiations associated with business purchases can require considerable marketing time and selling effort. Purchasing decisions are often made by committee, orders are frequently large and expensive, and products may be custom built. Several people or departments in the purchasing organization are often involved. For instance, one department expresses a need for a product, a second department develops the specifications, a third stipulates maximum expenditures, and a fourth places the order.

Business customers look for solutions to reach their objectives. Therefore, suppliers need to identify and promote their competencies to position their products so as to indicate how they provide customer value. Staples recognized this need when it ran a television advertising campaign illustrating how the office-supply retailer can help small businesses succeed.[10] To be successful, suppliers also have to differentiate their products from competitors. Building a brand reputation is an effective way to develop long-term relationships.[11] For instance, Federal Express develops long-term relationships with business customers by integrating customer solutions as a provider of many tracking, transportation, and delivery services.

DISRUPTIVE MARKETING

Will Blockchain Disrupt the Shipping Industry?

Day in and day out, thousands of U.S. businesses send and receive shipments of merchandise, materials, and supplies across the country and around the world. Now, traditional ways of documenting and tracking shipments may be upended if the industry adopts blockchain technology. Blockchain, the technology behind digital currencies like Bitcoin, utilizes encrypted data to better secure and speed information. When used to follow shipments, this technology replaces the cumbersome, costly, and error-prone paper trail that stretches from the point of shipment to the point of receipt.

Manufacturers, retailers, and other businesses that ship and receive, as well as all the entities that facilitate shipping throughout the supply chain, stand to benefit from fewer delays, fewer errors, and stronger data security as blockchain is adopted by the shipping industry. Money is also a consideration: by one estimate, blockchain could shave $5.4 million from the cost of documenting and tracking the many products transported by a single container ship, first from shipper to port and then from port to the recipient's door. For businesses that rely on multiple sourcing, the time and money saved could be substantial.

Now IBM has teamed up with Maersk, a Danish transport firm, to bring the shipping industry into the digital age in a big way via blockchain. Rather than deal with dozens of pieces of paperwork for each container-shipping transaction, their solution streamlines electronic processing and allows for instant tracking of any shipment in the system. Will blockchain disrupt the shipping industry—and if so, how quickly will business customers see the benefits?[a]

One practice unique to business markets is **reciprocity**, an arrangement in which two organizations agree to buy from each other. Reciprocal agreements that threaten competition are illegal. The Federal Trade Commission and the Justice Department monitor and take actions to stop anticompetitive reciprocal practices, particularly among large firms. Nonetheless, a certain amount of reciprocal activity occurs among small businesses and, to a lesser extent, among larger companies. Because reciprocity influences purchasing agents to deal only with certain suppliers, it can lead to less-than-optimal purchases.

8-3b Attributes of Business Customers

Business customers also differ from consumers in their purchasing behavior because they are generally better informed about the products they purchase. They typically demand detailed information about a product's functional features and technical specifications to ensure that it meets their needs. Personal goals, however, may also influence business buying behavior. Most purchasing agents seek the psychological satisfaction that comes with organizational advancement and financial rewards. Agents who consistently exhibit rational business buying behavior are likely to attain their personal goals because they help their firms achieve organizational objectives. Suppliers need to take into account organizational behavior in the form of individual-level decisions. Often the reaction of an individual buyer triggers the purchase of products and affects the broader organizational acceptance of them.[12]

Today, many suppliers and their customers build and maintain mutually beneficial relationships, sometimes called *partnerships*. Researchers find that even in a partnership between a small vendor and a large corporate buyer, a strong partnership can exist because high levels of interpersonal trust can lead to higher levels of commitment to the partnership by both organizations.[13] Consider JetBlue Airways' program to mentor small food businesses and prepare them for success, hopefully as future JetBlue suppliers

reciprocity An arrangement unique to business marketing in which two organizations agree to buy from each other

of sustainable food items. The BlueBud program connects promising small firms with resources and opportunities to work with its leaders to develop business strategies aligned with JetBlue's.[14]

8-3c Primary Concerns of Business Customers

When making purchasing decisions, business customers take into account a variety of factors. Among their chief considerations are price, product quality, service, and supplier relationships. Price is an essential consideration for business customers because it influences operating costs and costs of goods sold, which affects selling price, profit margin, and ultimately the ability to compete. A business customer is likely to compare the price of a product with the benefits the product will yield to the organization, often over a period of years. When purchasing major equipment, a business customer views price as the amount of investment necessary to obtain a certain level of return or savings on business operations. On the other hand, excellent service and product quality also enter into the decision. A product with a higher price could yield lower operating costs for the buyer in terms of service and quality. For instance, Caterpillar construction equipment may be sold at a higher price with superior service and parts availability.

Most business customers try to maintain a specific level of quality in the products they buy. To achieve this goal, most firms establish standards (usually stated as a percentage of defects allowed) for these products and buy them on the basis of a set of expressed characteristics. These standards, commonly called **product specifications**, are written statements describing a product's necessary characteristics, standards of quality, and other information essential to identifying the best supplier for the needed product. The auto industry, for instance, is turning toward aluminum to build vehicles because it is a lighter metal, which can help boost fuel efficiency. Metal companies, such as Alcoa, wanting to sell aluminum to automakers must meet certain specifications in strength and lightness. A customer evaluates the quality of the products being considered to determine whether they meet specifications. In Alcoa's case, its success will depend on how automakers view the price and quality of its metal sheets. If a product fails to meet specifications or malfunctions for the ultimate consumer, the customer may drop that product's supplier and switch to a different one. On the other hand, customers are ordinarily cautious about buying products that exceed specifications because such products often cost more, which increases the organization's overall costs. Business customers, therefore, must strike a balance between quality and price when making purchasing decisions. Specifications are designed to meet a customer's wants, and anything that does not contribute to meeting those wants may be considered wasteful.

Because their purchases tend to be large and sometimes complicated, business buyers value service. Services offered by suppliers directly and indirectly influence customers' costs, sales, and profits. Typical services business customers desire from suppliers are market information, inventory maintenance, on-time delivery, and repair services. Business buyers may need technical product information, data regarding demand, information about general economic conditions, or supply and delivery information. Purchasers of machinery are especially concerned about obtaining repair services and replacement parts quickly because inoperable equipment is costly, in terms of both repairs and lost productivity. Offering quality customer service can be a means of gaining a competitive advantage over other firms, which leads some businesses to seek out ways to improve their customer service. Long known for its quality customer service and strong customer devotion, Bain & Company targets these businesses with programs to improve its clients' service operations in retail establishments, call centers, and a variety of other service situations. For example, it has developed multiple frameworks of different steps their clients can take to become customer-centered service providers.[15]

Maintaining adequate inventory is critical to quality, customer service, customer satisfaction, and managing inventory costs and distribution efficiency. Furthermore, on-time delivery is crucial to ensuring that products are available as needed. Reliable on-time delivery saves

product specifications Written statements describing a product's necessary characteristics, standards of quality, and other information essential to identifying the best supplier for the needed product

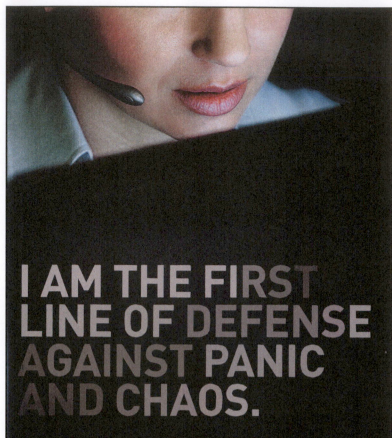

I AM THE FIRST LINE OF DEFENSE AGAINST PANIC AND CHAOS.

When the customer service line rings at 3AM, chances are the person on the other end doesn't want to talk to a machine. Or listen to excuses. That's why I'm here 24/7. I am a curator of solutions. I know your business and what you need. I specialize in answers. And results. I'm not here just to listen to your problems, I own them. I am *Piloting Business*

pilotdelivers.com / 1-800-HI-PILOT

PILOT *FREIGHT SERVICES*

Concerns of Business Customers
No matter what the shipping need, Pilot Freight Services promises to deliver a high level of service through 24/7 personal attention.

business customers money because it enables them to carry only the inventory needed at any given time. Consider the advertisement for Pilot Freight Services, which illustrates the company's commitment to customer service. The ad includes the partial image of a woman wearing a headset along with the text, "I am the first line of defense against panic and chaos." The ad goes on to describe how Pilot is available 24/7 to answer customer questions and solve problems so that its business customers can achieve their goals and have confidence that their shipments will be delivered properly and on time.

Customer expectations about quality of service have increased and broadened over time. Using traditional service quality standards based only on traditional manufacturing and accounting systems is not sufficient. Customers also expect to have access to communication channels that allow them to ask questions, voice complaints, submit orders, and track shipments. Increasingly, they expect to be able to do that on the fly through their cell phones or other mobile devices. Marketers should develop customer service objectives and monitor customer service programs, striving for uniformity of service, simplicity, truthfulness, and accuracy. Firms can observe service by formally surveying customers or informally calling on customers and asking questions about the service they receive. Spending the time and effort to ensure that customers are satisfied can greatly benefit marketers by increasing customer retention.

Businesses are also increasingly concerned about ethics and social responsibility. Sustainability in particular is rising as a consideration among customers making purchases. Managers are playing a key role in green marketing strategies through the integration of environmental values into the organizational culture.[16]

This results in purchase decisions that favor sustainable and environmentally friendly products. In fact, improvement of environmental performance can indirectly improve financial performance. For instance, the government places a high priority on sustainable purchasing. The Environmental Protection Agency created an Environmentally Preferable Purchasing program to help the federal government comply with green purchasing guidelines and support suppliers selling eco-friendly products.[17]

Finally, business customers are concerned about the costs of developing and maintaining relationships with their suppliers. By building trust with a particular supplier, buyers can reduce their search efforts and uncertainty about prices. Business customers have to keep in mind the overall fit of a supplier and its products with marketing objectives, including distribution and inventory-maintenance costs and efficiency.

8-3d Methods of Business Buying

Although no two business buyers do their jobs the same way, most use one or more of the following purchase methods: *description, inspection, sampling,* and *negotiation.* The most straightforward is description. When products are standardized and graded according to certain characteristics such as size, shape, weight, and color, a business buyer may be able to purchase simply by describing or specifying quantity, grade, and other attributes. Commodities and raw materials may be purchased this way. Sometimes buyers specify a particular brand or its equivalent when describing the desired product. Purchases based on description are especially common between a buyer and a seller with an ongoing relationship built on trust.

Certain products, such as industrial equipment, used vehicles, and buildings, have unique characteristics and may vary with regard to condition. Depending on how they were used and for how long, two products may be in very different conditions, even if they look identical on paper. Consequently, business buyers of such products should base purchase decisions on inspection.

Sampling entails evaluating a portion of the product on the assumption that its characteristics represent the entire lot. This method is appropriate when the product is homogeneous—for instance, grain—and examining the entire lot is not physically or economically feasible.

Some purchases by businesses are based on negotiated contracts. In certain instances, buyers describe exactly what they need and ask sellers to submit bids. They then negotiate with the suppliers that submit the most attractive bids. This approach is generally used for very large or expensive purchases, such as commercial vehicles. This is frequently how government departments conduct business. In other cases, the buyer may be unable to identify specifically what is to be purchased and can provide only a general description, as might be the case for a piece of custom-made equipment. A buyer and seller might negotiate a contract that specifies a base price and provides for the payment of additional costs and fees. These contracts are most commonly used for one-time projects such as buildings, capital equipment, and special projects.

new-task purchase An organization's initial purchase of an item to be used to perform a new job or solve a new problem

8-3e Types of Business Purchases

Most business purchases are one of three types: new-task, straight rebuy, or modified rebuy. Each type is subject to different influences and requires business marketers to modify their selling approaches appropriately. For a **new-task purchase**, an organization makes an initial purchase of an item to be used to perform a new job or solve a new problem. A new-task purchase may require development of product specifications, vendor specifications, and procedures for future product purchases. To make the initial purchase, the business buyer usually needs to acquire a lot of information. New-task purchases are important to suppliers because they can result in a long-term buying relationship if customers are satisfied. Examine the ad for Altergy backup power solutions. The ad, which pictures a storm over a cityscape with lightning striking multiple buildings, promotes how Altergy's fuel-cell technology can help businesses maintain power even during hurricanes and earthquakes. With the tagline, "Clean | Safe | Proven," Altergy is targeting businesses that might be exploring alternative power backup systems.

Fear no storm. You've already modernized your communications network and embraced sustainability. Continuous connectivity requires reliability and runtime not available with batteries and generators. It's time to upgrade – with a modern solution – and save hundreds of thousands of dollars in the process.

Altergy's advanced fuel cell systems provide more reliable, compact, longer-lasting backup power. Our solutions can also exceed the 24-hour-plus runtime FirstNet demands. For more information visit **www.altergy.com/upgrade**

altergy®
Leading the Fuel Cell Revolution

Types of Business Purchases
When purchasing a backup power system, it is likely that business customers would treat this purchase as a new-task purchase.

A **straight rebuy purchase** occurs when buyers purchase the same products routinely under approximately the same terms of sale. Buyers require little information for routine purchase decisions and tend to use familiar suppliers that have provided satisfactory service and products in the past. These marketers may set up automatic systems to make reordering easy and convenient for business buyers. A supplier may even monitor the business buyer's inventories and communicate to the buyer what should be ordered and when.

For a **modified rebuy purchase**, a new-task purchase is altered after two or three orders, or requirements associated with a straight rebuy purchase are modified. A business buyer might seek faster delivery, lower prices, or a different quality level of product specifications. Retaining existing customers should receive more attention than attracting new customers. If a long-term purchase contract does not exist, a firm should use all information available to develop retention strategies.[18] This means knowing what customers are likely to purchase and how their purchases might change over time. Orders are likely to be similar over time, but demand for specific business products and supplies may fluctuate in cycles that mirror periods of higher and lower customer demand. A modified rebuy situation may cause regular suppliers to compete to keep the account. When a firm changes the terms of a service contract, such as modifying the speed or comprehensiveness of a telecommunication services package, it has made a modified rebuy purchase.

8-3f Demand for Business Products

Demand for business products (also called *industrial demand*) can be characterized as (1) derived, (2) inelastic, (3) joint, or (4) fluctuating.

Derived Demand

Because business customers, especially producers, buy products for direct or indirect use in the production of goods and services to satisfy consumers' needs, the demand for business products derives from the demand for consumer products—it is, therefore, called **derived demand**. In the long run, no demand for business products is totally unrelated to the demand for consumer products. The derived nature of demand is usually multilevel in that business marketers at different levels are affected by a change in consumer demand for a product. For example, demand for Velositol protein booster derives from the demand for protein powders used by athletes and others. As shown in the ad, the "Now Made with Velositol" sticker on protein powder brands is meant to stimulate derived demand by encouraging customers to choose a brand of protein powder with Velositol as an ingredient to improve protein synthesis. The ad describes how Velositol can improve the performance of protein powder in the hopes that consumers will seek out brands that have Velositol as an ingredient, boosting demand. Change in consumer demand for a product affects demand for all firms involved in the production of that product.

Derived Demand

In this advertisement, the maker of Velositol encourages the buyers of protein powder to make sure the product contains Velositol. The demand for Velositol derives from the purchase of protein powders containing it.

Inelastic Demand

With **inelastic demand**, a price increase or decrease does not significantly alter demand for a business product. A product has inelastic demand when the buyer is not sensitive to price or when there are no ready substitutes. Because many business products are more specialized than consumer products, buyers will continue to make purchases even as the price goes up. Some business products contain a large number of parts that each comprises a small portion of the overall cost, so price increases that affect only one or two parts may yield only a slightly higher per-unit production cost. However, when a sizable price increase for a component represents a large proportion of the product's cost, demand may become more elastic because the price increase in the component causes the price at the consumer level to rise sharply. If manufacturers of a key part of solar panels, for instance, substantially increase their prices, forcing the cost of solar photovoltaic panel units to skyrocket, the demand for that source of renewable energy will decrease (or become more elastic) as businesses and consumers reconsider whether there will be a return on investment in installing a solar energy system.

Inelasticity of demand in the business market applies at the industry level, while demand for an individual firm's products may fluctuate. Suppose a spark plug producer increases the price of spark plugs sold to small-engine manufacturers, but its competitors continue to maintain lower prices. The spark plug company that raised its prices will experience reduced unit sales because most small-engine producers will switch to lower-priced brands. A specific firm, therefore, remains vulnerable to elastic demand, while demand across the industry as a whole will not fluctuate drastically.

Joint Demand

Certain business products, especially raw materials and components, are subject to joint demand. **Joint demand** occurs when two or more items are used in combination to produce a product. For example, when you buy a new printer, you also have to purchase printer ink in order for it to operate. Understanding the effects of joint demand is particularly important for a marketer that sells multiple jointly demanded items. Such a marketer realizes that when a customer begins purchasing one of the jointly demanded items, a good opportunity exists to sell related products.

Fluctuating Demand

Because the demand for business products is derived from consumer demand, it is subject to dramatic fluctuations. In general, when consumer products are in high demand, producers buy large quantities of raw materials and components to ensure that they meet long-run production requirements. These producers may expand production capacity to meet demands as well, which entails acquiring new equipment and machinery, more workers, and more raw materials and component parts. Conversely, a decline in demand for certain consumer goods reduces demand for business products used to produce those goods. Declining consumer preference for sodas and processed foods with sugar has resulted in a significant decline in the demand for raw sugar.[19]

Sometimes, price changes lead to surprising temporary changes in demand. A price increase for a business product initially may cause business customers to buy more of the item in an attempt to stock up because they expect the price to continue to rise. Similarly, demand for a business product may decrease significantly following a price cut because buyers are waiting for further price reductions. Fluctuations in demand can be substantial in industries in which prices change frequently.

inelastic demand Demand that is not significantly altered by a price increase or decrease

joint demand Demand involving the use of two or more items in combination to produce a product

business (organizational) buying behavior The purchase behavior of producers, government units, institutions, and resellers

Learning Objective 8-4

Describe the buying center, stages of the business buying decision process, and the factors that affect this process.

8-4 BUSINESS BUYING DECISIONS

Business (organizational) buying behavior refers to the purchase behavior of producers, government units, institutions, and resellers. Although several factors that affect consumer buying behavior (discussed in Chapter 7) also influence business buying behavior, a number of

Business Concerns About Cyber Risks

Worried Somewhat or a Great Deal (%)

Security breach: someone hacking into computer system	49%
Someone gaining access to banking accounts or financial control systems	46%
Having the resources and know-how to recover from data-related breaches	42%
Remote access or hacking into supervisory control systems or other business operational software systems	40%
Using online cloud storage data or information	34%
Company being a victim of cyber extortion	31%

SNAPSHOT

Source: *Inbound Logistics*, January 2017, p. 244.

factors are unique to businesses. In this section, we analyze the buying center to learn who participates in business buying decisions. Then we focus on the stages of the buying decision process and the factors that affect it.

8-4a The Buying Center

Relatively few business purchase decisions are made by just one person. Often purchases are made through a buying center. The **buying center** is the group of people within the organization who make business buying decisions. They include users, influencers, buyers, deciders, and gatekeepers.[20] One person may perform several roles within the buying center, and participants share goals and risks associated with their decisions.

Users are the organizational members who will actually use the product. They frequently initiate the purchase process and/or generate purchase specifications. After the purchase, they evaluate product performance relative to the specifications.

Influencers are often technical personnel, such as engineers, who help develop product specifications and evaluate alternatives. Technical personnel are especially important influencers when the products being considered involve new, advanced technology.

Buyers select suppliers and negotiate terms of purchase. They may also be involved in developing specifications. Buyers are sometimes called purchasing agents or purchasing managers. Their choices of vendors and products, especially for new-task purchases, are heavily influenced by others in the buying center. For straight rebuy purchases, the buyer plays a major role in vendor selection and negotiations.

Deciders actually choose the products. Although buyers may be deciders, it is not unusual for different people to occupy these roles. For routinely purchased items, buyers are commonly deciders. However, a buyer may not be authorized to make purchases that exceed a certain dollar limit, in which case higher-level management personnel are deciders.

Finally, *gatekeepers*, such as administrative assistants and technical personnel, control the flow of information to and among the different roles in the buying center. Buyers who deal directly with vendors also may be gatekeepers because they can control information flows. The flow of information from a supplier's sales representatives to users and influencers is often controlled by personnel in the purchasing department.

The number and structure of an organization's buying centers are affected by the organization's size and market position, the volume and types of products being purchased, and the firm's overall managerial philosophy on who should make purchase decisions. The size of a buying center is influenced by the stage of the buying decision process and by the type of purchase (new task, straight rebuy, or modified rebuy). The size of the buying center is generally larger for a new-task purchase than for a straight rebuy. A marketer attempting to sell to a business customer should first determine who the people in the buying center are, the roles they play, and which individuals are most influential in the decision process. Although it may not be feasible to contact all those involved in the buying center, marketers should contact a few of the most influential people.

buying center The people within an organization who make business purchase decisions

8-4b Stages of the Business Buying Decision Process

Like consumers, businesses follow a buying decision process. This process is summarized in the lower portion of Figure 8.2.

In the first stage, one or more individuals recognize that a problem or need exists. *Problem recognition* may arise under a variety of circumstances—for instance, when machines malfunction or a firm modifies an existing product or introduces a new one. It may be individuals in the buying center or other individuals in the firm who initially recognize that a problem exists.

The second stage of the process, *development of product specifications,* requires that buying center participants assess the problem or need and determine what is necessary to resolve or satisfy it. During this stage, users and influencers, such as engineers, provide information and advice for developing product specifications. By assessing and describing needs, the organization should be able to establish product specifications.

Searching for and evaluating potential products and suppliers is the third stage in the decision process. Search activities may involve looking in company files and trade directories, websites, contacting suppliers for information, soliciting proposals from known vendors, and examining various online and print publications. It is common for organizations, particularly those with a reputation for having open hiring policies, to specify a desire to work with diverse vendors, such as those owned by women or by minorities.

During this third stage, some organizations engage in value analysis, an evaluation of each component of a potential purchase. **Value analysis** examines quality, design, materials, and possibly item reduction or deletion to acquire the product in the most cost-effective way. Some vendors may be deemed unacceptable because they are not large enough to supply needed quantities. Others may be excluded because of poor delivery and service records. Sometimes the product is not available from any vendor and the buyer will work with an innovative supplier to design and produce it. Buyers evaluate products to make sure they meet or exceed

value analysis An evaluation of each component of a potential purchase

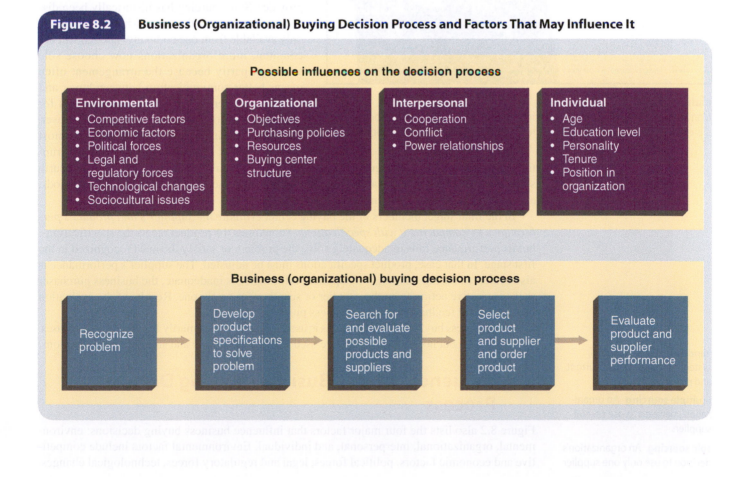

| Figure 8.2 | Business (Organizational) Buying Decision Process and Factors That May Influence It |

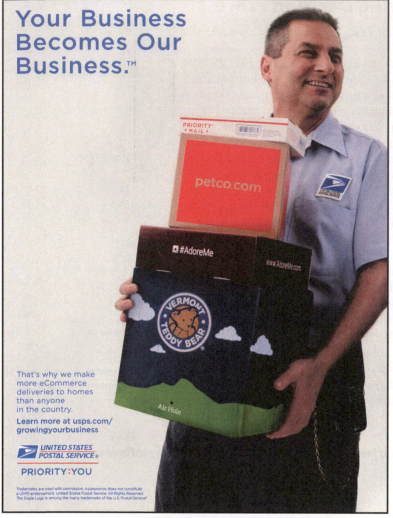

Multiple Sourcing
Many organizations use multiple sourcing for both goods and services. For example, it is common for organizations to use multiple sourcing for shipping services.

product specifications developed in the second stage of the business buying decision process. Usually suppliers are judged according to multiple criteria. A number of firms employ **vendor analysis**, a formal, systematic evaluation of current and potential vendors, focusing on such characteristics as price, product quality, delivery service, product availability, and overall reliability.

The results of deliberations and assessments in the third stage are used during the fourth stage of the process to *select the product to be purchased and the supplier*. In some cases, the buyer selects and uses several suppliers, a process known as **multiple sourcing**. Firms with federal government contracts are generally required to have several sources for an item to ensure a steady supply. The U.S. Postal Service advertisement, which pictures a postal employee carrying boxed online orders, focuses on the shipping solutions that USPS can provide small businesses. The company knows that most companies use more than one shipping company, so the ad reminds businesses that the organization delivers more e-commerce shipments than any other shipper. At times, only one supplier is selected, a situation called **sole sourcing**. For organizations that outsource their insurance services, many of these companies will use just one provider. Sole sourcing has historically been discouraged except in the cases where a product is only available from one company. Though still not common, more organizations now choose sole sourcing, partly because the arrangement often means better communication between buyer and supplier, greater stability and higher profits for suppliers, and lower prices for buyers. However, multiple sourcing remains preferable for most firms because it lessens the possibility of disruption caused by strikes, shortages, or bankruptcies. The actual product is ordered in this fourth stage, and specific details regarding terms, credit arrangements, delivery dates and methods, and technical assistance are finalized.

In the final stage, members of the buying center *evaluate the supplier's and product's performance by comparing it with specifications*. Sometimes the product meets the specifications, but its performance fails to adequately solve the problem or satisfy the need recognized in the first stage. In that case, product specifications must be adjusted. The supplier's performance is also evaluated during this stage. If supplier performance is inadequate, the business purchaser seeks corrective action from the supplier or searches for a new one. Results of the evaluation become useful feedback in future business purchase decisions.

This business buying decision process is used in its entirety primarily for new-task purchases. Several stages, but not necessarily all, are used for modified rebuy and straight rebuy situations.

vendor analysis A formal, systematic evaluation of current and potential vendors

multiple sourcing An organization's decision to use several suppliers

sole sourcing An organization's decision to use only one supplier

8-4c Influences on the Business Buying Decision Process

Figure 8.2 also lists the four major factors that influence business buying decisions: environmental, organizational, interpersonal, and individual. Environmental factors include competitive and economic factors, political forces, legal and regulatory forces, technological changes, and sociocultural issues. These factors can generate considerable uncertainty for an organization, including in buying decisions. Changes in one or more environmental forces, such as new government regulations or increased competition, can create opportunities and threats that affect purchasing decisions.

Organizational factors that influence the buying decision process include the company's objectives, purchasing policies, resources, and the size and composition of its buying center. An organization may also have certain buying policies to which buying center participants must conform that limit buying decisions. For instance, a firm's policies may mandate contract lengths that are undesirable to many sellers. An organization's financial resources may require special credit arrangements. Any of these conditions could affect purchase decisions.

Interpersonal factors are the relationships among people in the buying center. Trust is crucial in collaborative partnerships. This is especially true when customized products are involved—the buyer may not see the product until it is finished and must trust that the producer is creating it to specifications. Trust and clear communication will ensure that all parties are satisfied with the outcome. Interpersonal dynamics and varying communication abilities within the buying center may complicate processes.

Individual factors are the personal characteristics of participants in the buying center, such as age, education level, personality, and tenure and position in the organization. Consider a 55-year-old manager who has been in the organization for 25 years. This manager is likely to have a greater influence and power over buying center decisions than a 30-year-old employed at the firm only two years. The influence of various factors, such as age and tenure, on the buying decision process depends on the buying situation, the type of product, and the type of purchase (new task, modified rebuy, or straight rebuy). Employees' negotiating styles will vary, as well. To be effective, marketers must know customers well enough to be aware of these individual factors and their potential effects on purchase decisions.

Promotion targeted to individuals in the buying center can influence individual decision making as well. Most trade publications carry advertising to influence buyers. Cintas, for example, launched its first-ever national advertising campaign using television, radio, print, and online ads to show how the commercial laundry and uniform provider can help a variety of businesses be "ready."[21] Trade shows are very popular when products can be

ENTREPRENEURSHIP IN MARKETING

Meet Brittni Brown of the Bee Agency

Public relations expert Brittni Brown started down the path to marketing entrepreneurship during her undergraduate years at Eastern Michigan University. As co-founder of the university's Fashion Week, she needed to devise a plan for attracting an audience of 1,500 students. Brown took the story to local radio and television outlets and successfully obtained advance coverage of the event. Not only did the media attention draw students, the experience convinced her to pursue a public relations career, with a special focus on her peers, Millennial consumers.

Brown founded the Bee Agency after graduation and began her business-to-business marketing to acquire beauty, fashion, and lifestyle public-relations clients in the Detroit area and beyond. When she met Tommy Walker Jr., the entrepreneur behind the Detroit vs. Everybody brand, she arranged to handle his firm's public relations in exchange for having him mentor her business. The high-profile work Brown did for Detroit vs. Everybody demonstrated her agency's capabilities to other businesses and enabled her to sign new clients year after year.

Now Brown wants to help up-and-coming Millennial entrepreneurs sharpen their branding skills and their professionalism through a program she calls Bee-Coming Your Brand University. She tells new entrepreneurs to set daily and weekly goals for achievement and reevaluate every "win" with an eye toward even bigger accomplishments. And, looking back on how she successfully established the Bee Agency, she urges young entrepreneurs to network, attend industry events, and look for opportunities to build relationships with potential clients.[b]

demonstrated and samples provided. Personal selling is by far the most important influence of trust in maintaining strong relationships. Interestingly, business-to-business marketers seem to hesitate in embracing social media as a relationship marketing tool. When they use social media, they tend to focus on relationships rather than on functional or rational appeals for purchases.[22] When using Twitter or other social media sites, business-to-business marketers should try to craft messages to convey useful information and develop trust rather than close the sale.

Learning Objective 8-5

Explore how the internet facilitates business buying and marketing.

8-5 RELIANCE ON THE INTERNET AND OTHER TECHNOLOGY

Whereas in the past, an organization seeking a type of product might contact product suppliers, speak with someone on the sales force, and request a catalog or brochure, business customers today first turn to the internet to search for information and find sources. The internet has become a major channel in organizational buying, accounting for nearly $900 billion in sales.[23] Indeed, 68 percent of business buyers now purchase products online, and 94 percent of B2B buyers engaged in online research prior to purchasing a product.[24] In many cases, business buyers' needs and wants have been shaped by their experiences as consumers shopping at sites such as Amazon.com, LandsEnd.com, and Walmart.com. Paper Enterprises USA, which has supplied paper products for more than 100 years, created an e-commerce site that functions more like a retail website for its primarily small business customers. The company's software integrates online catalogs and sales with its own warehouse. Customers do not have to do anything special other than log in using their computer web browsers. The system now accounts for more than $2 million in sales.[25]

Organizational buyers often begin searching for a product after recognizing a need or problem. The internet allows buyers to research potential solutions, communicate with peers about their experiences with those products, read blogs, consult webinars and watch YouTube videos, examine specifications, and even find reviews of potential products long before beginning a formal buying process. Interactions with a sales representative now may occur much later in the process than in the past. B2B marketers should, therefore, take care that the content they post on their blogs, webinars, videos, eBooks, whitepapers, and even responses to forum queries include useful information about how their products might solve customers' problems or address their needs. John Deere, for example, uses its comprehensive website to showcase its products so that business buyers can research product details and find the right one to match their needs.

For most firms, online marketing efforts make the buying process far more efficient because it saves time and reduces costs. For example, after Intelligentsia Coffee upgraded its e-commerce system to coordinate functions and improve its mobile features, it experienced greater mobile traffic and fewer service calls from its coffee shop customers. The new system streamlines the ordering process and gives customers more information about their orders so that sales representatives can spend more time selling coffee. Now, about 90 percent of the wholesaler's business is done online.[26] As we shall see in Chapter 14, internet technology has streamlined physical distribution and other supply chain activities, resulting in significant cost savings.

Organizations can make purchases directly from a firm's website, such as computers from dell.com or hp.com. Like many larger companies, Dell and Hewlett Packard offer special access through a password-protected portal to B2B customers where they can track orders, see past orders, and access relevant information. Organizations can also purchase supplies from a retailer's website. Amazon Business, for example, offers business buyers 5 million products using the successful and secure e-commerce platform of its parent, Amazon.com. Business buyers even have their own version of Amazon Prime, giving them free two-day shipping on most Amazon Business products.[27]

Increasingly, businesses are turning to **B2B e-commerce sites**, which serve as online marketplaces where business buyers and sellers from around the world can exchange information, goods, services, ideas, and payments. Variously known as trading exchanges, B2B exchanges, and ehubs, B2B e-commerce sites may be independent or private. Independent sites act as a neutral third party and charge a fee for providing a trading forum. Some sites may be focused on a specific industry, while others may offer products and attract businesses from many industries. AutoWurld.com, for example, is an independent e-commerce site for wholesale and retail buying and selling of motor vehicles.[28] Alibaba, on the other hand, connects buyers from all over the world with Chinese manufacturing firms offering millions of products in forty categories for many industries and purposes.[29] Such exchanges are especially beneficial for small businesses because they allow them to expand their customer base while reducing the costs of marketing to and buying from other companies. Private B2B exchanges connect member firms, who typically share supply chains or complex customers, through a secure system that permits all the organizations to share significant information as well as facilitate exchanges. Exostar, for example, serves as a private exchange for companies in the aerospace, defense, health-care, pharmaceutical, and financial markets.

Businesses may also turn to online auctions, such as B-Stock Solutions and TradeOut.com, to find products. As with a traditional auction, a seller posts an item to an online auction, and potential buyers bid on the item against each other; the highest bidder wins the right to buy the item. Such auctions are especially popular for liquidating unsold, returned, and used merchandise. In a reverse auction, a buyer invites businesses to bid to supply the specified good or service in competition with each other; the lowest bidder wins the right to sell the product. FedBid, for example, offers reverse online auctions for government agencies. As shown in the screenshot of FedBid.com, the site connects tens of thousands of suppliers—many of them small businesses—with 75 federal government agencies. The site offers a number of tools and resources to facilitate exchanges with no subscription fees.

B2B e-commerce sites Online marketplaces where business buyers and sellers from around the world can exchange information, goods, services, ideas, and payments

Reverse Online Auctions FedBid provides reverse online auction services to government agencies. Through FedBid, government agencies are able to bid prices lower.

SOURCE: FEDBID.COM

Summary

8-1 Distinguish among the four types of business markets.

Business (B2B) markets consist of individuals, organizations, and groups that purchase a specific kind of product for resale, direct use in producing other products, or use in day-to-day operations. Producer markets include those individuals and business organizations that purchase products for the purpose of making a profit by using them to produce other products or as part of their operations. Intermediaries that buy finished products and resell them to make a profit are classified as reseller markets. Government markets consist of federal, state, county, and local governments, which spend billions of dollars annually for goods and services to support internal operations and to provide citizens with needed services. Organizations with charitable, educational, community, or other nonprofit goals constitute institutional markets.

8-2 Define the North American Industry Classification System and describe how it can be used to identify and analyze business markets.

Business marketers have a considerable amount of information available for use in planning marketing strategies. The North American Industry Classification System (NAICS) is a single industry classification system used by the United States, Canada, and Mexico to generate comparable statistics. It provides marketers with information needed to identify business customer groups. It can best be used for this purpose in conjunction with other information. After identifying target industries, a marketer can obtain the names and locations of potential customers by using government and commercial data sources. Marketers then must estimate potential purchases of business customers by finding a relationship between a potential customer's purchases and a variable available in industrial classification data.

8-3 Identify the major characteristics of business customers and transactions.

Transactions that involve business customers differ from consumer transactions in several ways. Business transactions tend to be larger and require greater negotiation. They may involve more than one person or department in the purchasing organization. They may also involve reciprocity, an arrangement in which two organizations agree to buy from each other.

Business customers are usually better informed than ultimate consumers and are more likely to seek information about a product's features and technical specifications.

Business customers are particularly concerned about quality, service, price, and supplier relationships. Quality is important because it directly affects the quality of products the buyer's firm produces. To achieve an exact level of quality, organizations often buy products on the basis of a set of expressed characteristics, called specifications. Because services have such a direct influence on a firm's costs, sales, and profits, factors such as market information, on-time delivery, and availability of parts are crucial to a business buyer. Although business customers do not depend solely on price to decide which products to buy, price is of primary concern because it directly influences profitability.

Business buyers use several purchasing methods, including description, inspection, sampling, and negotiation. Most organizational purchases are new-task, straight rebuy, or modified rebuy. In a new-task purchase, an organization makes an initial purchase of items to be used to perform new jobs or solve new problems. A straight rebuy purchase occurs when a buyer purchases the same products routinely under approximately the same terms of sale. In a modified rebuy purchase, a new-task purchase is changed the second or third time it is ordered or requirements associated with a straight rebuy purchase are modified.

Industrial demand differs from consumer demand along several dimensions. Industrial demand derives from demand for consumer products. At the industry level, industrial demand is inelastic. If an industrial item's price changes, product demand will not change as much proportionally. Some industrial products are subject to joint demand, which occurs when two or more items are used in combination to make a product. Finally, because organizational demand derives from consumer demand, the demand for business products can fluctuate significantly.

8-4 Describe the buying center, stages of the business buying decision process, and the factors that affect this process.

Business (or organizational) buying behavior refers to the purchase behavior of producers, resellers, government units, and institutions. Business purchase decisions are made through a buying center, the group of people involved in making such purchase decisions. Users are those in the organization who actually use the product. Influencers help develop specifications and evaluate alternative products for possible use. Buyers select suppliers and negotiate purchase terms. Deciders choose the products. Gatekeepers control the flow of information to and among individuals occupying other roles in the buying center.

The stages of the business buying decision process are problem recognition, development of product specifications to solve problems, search for and evaluation of products and suppliers, selection and ordering of the most appropriate product, and evaluation of the product's and supplier's performance.

Four categories of factors influence business buying decisions: environmental, organizational, interpersonal, and individual. Environmental factors include competitive forces, economic conditions, political forces, laws and regulations, technological changes, and sociocultural factors. Business factors include the company's objectives, purchasing policies, and resources, as well as the size and composition of its buying center. Interpersonal factors are the relationships among people in the buying center. Individual factors are personal characteristics of members of the buying center, such as age, education level, personality, and tenure and position in the organization.

8-5 Explore how the internet facilitates business buying and marketing.

The internet has become a major facilitator of business transactions with business buyers often beginning the buying process informally by searching online for information to solve a problem or address a need. They may find useful information in online catalogs, blogs, videos, webinars, white papers, and peer reviews to help them find the best products and suppliers. Online marketing efforts make the buying process more efficient by saving time and reducing costs. Organizational buyers can purchase directly from a company's website, from an online retailer, from a B2B e-commerce site, or through an online auction. A B2B e-commerce site is an online marketplace where buyers and sellers from around the world can exchange information, goods, services, ideas, and payments.

Important Terms

producer markets 216
reseller markets 217
government markets 218
institutional markets 219
North American Industry
    Classification System
    (NAICS) 219

reciprocity 222
product specifications 223
new-task purchase 225
straight rebuy
    purchase 226
modified rebuy purchase
    226

derived demand 226
inelastic demand 227
joint demand 227
business (organizational)
    buying behavior
    227
buying center 228

value analysis 229
vendor analysis 230
multiple sourcing
    230
sole sourcing 230
B2B e-commerce
    sites 233

Discussion and Review Questions

1. Identify, describe, and give examples of the four major types of business markets.
2. What function does an industrial classification system help marketers perform?
3. Why might business customers generally be considered more rational in their purchasing behavior than ultimate consumers?
4. What are the primary concerns of business customers?
5. List several characteristics that differentiate transactions involving business customers from consumer transactions.
6. What are the commonly used methods of business buying?

7. Why do buyers involved in straight rebuy purchases require less information than those making new-task purchases?
8. How does demand for business products differ from consumer demand?
9. What are the major components of a firm's buying center?
10. Identify the stages of the business buying decision process. How is this decision process used when making straight rebuys?
11. How do environmental, business, interpersonal, and individual factors affect business purchases?
12. How has the internet facilitated the organizational buying process?

Developing your Marketing Plan

When developing a marketing strategy for business customers, it is essential to understand the process the business goes through when making a buying decision. Knowledge of business buying behavior is important when developing several aspects of the marketing plan. To assist you in relating the information in this chapter to the creation of a marketing plan for business customers, consider the following issues:

1. What are the primary concerns of business customers? Could any of these concerns be addressed with the strengths of your company?

2. Determine the type of business purchase your customer will likely be using when purchasing your product. How would this impact the level of information required by the business when moving through the buying decision process?

3. Discuss the different types of demand that the business customer will experience when purchasing your product.

Video Case 8.1

Will Apple Pay Pay Off for Retailers?

When Apple introduced its mobile payment system in 2014, the company was looking to leverage the popularity of its iPhone by adding more functionality and convenience for millions of customers. With Apple Pay, iPhone owners and Apple Watch wearers first enter their credit- or debit-card information, which Apple confirms with the banks. Once this information is on file, Apple creates a digital "token" that will be electronically transmitted to the retailer when an iPhone owner pays for something. To complete a purchase, the customer simply waves the phone or taps it at the checkout, uses the iPhone's Touch or Face ID security to activate Apple Pay, and the phone instantly transfers the token as payment.

Even though Apple Pay offers consumers the benefits of convenience and security, Apple knew it wouldn't succeed without a large network of retailers, restaurants, and other businesses agreeing to accept its mobile payments. Among the earliest businesses to sign up with Apple was McDonald's, which agreed to honor Apple Pay in its 14,000 U.S. restaurants and drive-through locations. "We serve 27 million customers every day. This is a clear and compelling business opportunity for us," explained McDonald's chief information officer. Compared with cash transactions, Apple Pay transactions cost McDonald's a few pennies more to process because of bank fees. Yet the fast-food giant was willing to sign on because it saw competitive advantage and profit potential in wooing iPhone users interested in speedy checkout.

Another early business supporter was Walgreens, the nationwide drug-store chain with 85 million customers enrolled in its frequent-buyer rewards program. Walgreens sells snacks, household products, and health and beauty items in addition to health-care products. Not only did Walgreens agree to accept Apple Pay at its checkout counters, but it was also the first U.S. retailer to add its rewards program to Apple Pay's easy sign-on system. As a result, Walgreens' customers tap twice at the checkout, once to activate the rewards account and display their savings, the second time to process the actual payment. By deciding to honor Apple Pay, Walgreens said it was "enabling a simple and convenient customer experience."

Several hundred thousand businesses had signed on to participate by the time Apple Pay launched in October 2014.

PRIMAKOV/SHUTTERSTOCK.COM

Apple's ongoing efforts to increase business participation paid off: Eighteen months later, the network of participating businesses topped 2 million, and major companies like Starbucks, Domino's, and Crate & Barrel were preparing to participate. Eyeing international expansion, Apple also initiated talks with banks in China to bring Apple Pay to millions of iPhone users there. Today, Apple Pay is accepted at more than 50 percent of all U.S. retail locations and in many retail stores in twenty countries.

Even though more consumers are making more mobile payments year after year, not every U.S. retailer is willing or able to work with Apple Pay. Some aren't satisfied with the amount of consumer information that Apple Pay shares with participating merchants. Others would have to upgrade to new checkout technology for Apple Pay. Still others are locked into exclusive mobile payment deals with competing services.

Today, mobile payments represent a small fraction of all purchase transactions, dwarfed by cash as well as by credit and debit payments. And Apple Pay faces strong competition from Google, Samsung, and others operating in the mobile-payment market. To remain a leader, Apple will have to keep signing more participating businesses and showing consumers the benefits of paying by iPhone or Apple Watch whenever they make a purchase.[30]

Questions for Discussion

1. When a retailer is considering whether to participate in Apple Pay, is the decision process like a new-task purchase, a straight rebuy purchase, or a modified rebuy purchase? Explain your answer.

2. Which of the four categories of business markets is Apple Pay best suited for, and why?

3. Which environmental influences on the decision process seem to have been most important to McDonald's when it decided to honor Apple Pay?

Case 8.2

Salesforce.com Uses Dreamforce to Reach Business Customers

Founded in 1999, Salesforce.com has become a forceful player in the world of business technology, specializing in software that helps organizations manage customer relationships, handle marketing contacts, coordinate and analyze sales, and manage customer service. Salesforce.com was an early believer in cloud-based software, offering its sophisticated applications via remote access rather than having business customers pay hefty upfront fees to acquire and install the software on individual computers. As a result, businesses don't have to worry about outdated or mismatched versions of the software their employees use to track contacts with prospects and customers, process orders, analyze service inquiries, and manage other functions. They rely on Salesforce.com for the technology to meet the needs of *their* customers. In fact, on any given day, 150,000 business customers use Salesforce.com's software to generate 1.4 billion email messages, track 2.4 million sales leads, manage 3 million customer orders, and enable 600 million e-commerce pageviews.

Salesforce.com targets startups, small businesses, medium-sized businesses, and corporate giants, as well as nonprofit organizations. It has also introduced software tailored to the specific needs of particular industries, including financial services and health care. Through a strategic partnership with IBM, Salesforce.com offers its own Salesforce Einstein artificial intelligence along with IBM's Watson artificial intelligence to give businesses more analytic and predictive capabilities for better decision making. Through a strategic partnership with Google, Salesforce.com offers businesses the option of integrating G Suite office software tools and Google Cloud storage for added productivity.

JONATHAN WEISS/SHUTTERSTOCK.COM

Behind the scenes, Salesforce.com invests heavily in marketing to businesses and nonprofit organizations through in-person sales, workshops, webinars, product trials, and other activities. One of its biggest budget items is an annual four-day conference called Dreamforce, which attracts 170,000 attendees to the company's headquarters city of San Francisco. Dreamforce includes more than 2,500 "how to" training sessions for business and nonprofit customers, plus prominent keynote speakers to motivate and inspire the audience. Attendees can earn certification credits and gain practical knowledge from technical experts and customers that use Salesforce.com's software products. Dreamforce even offers a CEO track, with special sessions geared to the needs and interests of senior business leaders.

Dreamforce also includes an exhibit hall where businesses can browse the latest product innovations and meet with partners who can customize Salesforce.com's software to individual specifications. Throughout the conference, attendees are exposed to volunteer opportunities benefiting good causes such as Room to Read and RED. After hours, Salesforce.com puts on concerts and parties to encourage networking and make Dreamforce a fun event to remember. Although Dreamforce costs an estimated $30 million to plan and implement every year, it generates worldwide publicity and serves as a highly visible symbol of Salesforce.com's commitment to the success of its business customers. Just as important, the company sees Dreamforce as a vital opportunity to answer customers' questions, ask about new customer problems and needs, obtain product feedback, and cement relations with partners.

Today, Salesforce.com rings up $10 billion in annual revenues. It gives out millions of dollars in grants to support educational initiatives in elementary schools, for science and technology programs aimed at teenagers, and for internships and other workforce-readiness training. It also encourages involvement in local communities by giving every employee seven days of paid leave yearly to pursue volunteer pursuits. Looking ahead, the company has announced its intention to reach $20 billion in annual revenues by 2022, $40 billion by 2028, and $60 billion by 2034. To achieve these ambitious milestones of future growth, Salesforce.com must continue to understand and meet the needs of its business customers worldwide, creating software that allows them to serve *their* customers.[31]

Questions for Discussion

1. How does Dreamforce help Salesforce.com market to business buyers in multiple stages of the business buying decision process?
2. Why would Dreamforce include a special series of sessions for the CEOs of customer companies? Explain your answer in terms of the organizational influences on the buying decision process.
3. Is Salesforce.com's involvement with philanthropy and volunteerism a good way to show that the company understands the primary concerns of business customers? Explain your answer.

CHAPTER

9

Reaching Global Markets

LEARNING OBJECTIVES

9-1 Define international marketing.

9-2 Differentiate between the environmental forces that affect international marketing efforts.

9-3 List important international trade agreements.

9-4 Identify methods of international market entry.

9-5 Examine various forms of global organizational structures.

9-6 Describe the use of the marketing mix internationally.

DMITRY BIRIN/SHUTTERSTOCK.COM

Emirates Airline Soars Beyond the Turbulence

Emirates is the largest airline in the Middle East, with 265 aircraft that travel to more than 155 destinations across 80 countries. Recently, Emirates was recognized as the "Best Airline in the World" by TripAdvisor's Travelers' Choice Awards, and on social media the company became the first airline to reach 1 million Instagram followers. In the United States, airlines operate as private companies. Emirates, however, is owned by the government of Dubai, although it operates as a commercial enterprise that does not receive government financial support.

Despite its high standing as an industry favorite, Emirates president Tim Clark says the airline has experienced a flat line in demand due to the ever-changing sociocultural, economic, political, legal, and regulatory forces including an economic embargo on Qatar and a diplomatic dispute between the United Arab Emirates (UAE) and Qatar. In response to a decline in demand, Emirates often decreases capacity and eliminates routes.

Despite these diplomatic disputes and the slowing of growth, the company has had 29 consecutive years of profitability and is still one of the fastest-growing carriers globally. Emirates has a reputation for its world-class flying experience, from superior in-flight entertainment to premium first-class amenities. The company recently invested $15.1 billion for a fleet of 40 Boeing 787 Dreamliners, which Clark says will be "gainfully employed" across both new and existing destinations, hinting at further expansion. He believes investing in these aircraft helps the airline address different segments in demand. Emirates has responded quickly and efficiently to fluctuation in demand and has proven that it can withstand uncertainty in the political landscapes of the countries in which it operates.[1]

Technological advances and rapidly changing political and economic conditions are making it easier than ever for companies to market their products overseas as well as at home. With most of the world's population and two-thirds of total purchasing power outside the United States, international markets represent lucrative opportunities for growth. For example, Procter & Gamble obtains only 45 percent of its net sales from North America.[2] Accessing international markets can promote innovation, while intensifying competition can spur companies to develop global strategies.

Due to the increasingly global nature of marketing, we devote this chapter to the unique aspects of global markets and international marketing. We begin by considering the nature of global marketing strategy and the environmental forces that create opportunities and threats for international marketers. Next, we explore several regional trade alliances, markets, and agreements. Then we examine the modes of entry into international marketing and companies' degree of involvement in it, as well as some of the structures that can be used to organize multinational enterprises. Finally, we examine how firms may alter their marketing mixes when engaging in international marketing efforts. All of these factors must be considered in any marketing plan that includes an international component.

Learning Objective 9-1

Define international marketing.

international marketing
Developing and performing marketing activities across national boundaries

9-1 THE NATURE OF GLOBAL MARKETING STRATEGY

International marketing involves developing and performing marketing activities across national boundaries. Global marketing strategies require knowledge about the marketing environment and customers. For instance, Walmart operates 11,695 stores in 28 countries; Starbucks serves tens of millions of customers a week at more than 24,000 shops in more than 75 markets.[3] The advertisement for Le Petit Marseillais body wash is trying to attract users in the United States by appealing to consumers with a fondness for France with its "true-to-nature fragrances" that are inspired by the South of France. The *OK!* Magazine Award icon adds reputability to the product by leveraging the power of a well-known U.S. publication.

Firms are finding that international markets provide strong prospects for growth. To encourage international growth, many countries offer practical assistance and valuable research to help their domestic firms become more competitive globally. One example is Export.gov, a website managed by the U.S. Department of Commerce's International Trade Administration, which collects a variety of resources to help businesses that want to export to other countries.[4] A major element of the assistance that government organizations can provide for firms (especially small and medium-sized firms) is knowledge of the internationalization process.

Traditionally, most companies have entered the global marketplace gradually and incrementally as they gained knowledge and experience about various markets and opportunities. However, some firms—such as eBay, Google, and Twitter—were founded with the knowledge and resources to accelerate their participation and investment in the global marketplace. These "born globals"—typically small technology-based firms earning as much as 70 percent of their sales outside the domestic home market—export their products almost immediately after being established in market niches in which they compete with larger, more established firms.[5] Whether a firm chooses to adopt the traditional approach, the born global approach, or an approach that merges attributes of both, international

SOURCE: LE PETIT MARSEILLAIS

POP OPEN A BOTTLE AND VOILÀ!

DELIGHTFUL SCENTS INSPIRED BY THE SOUTH OF FRANCE

DISCOVER OUR NEW BODY WASH RANGE WITH TRUE-TO-NATURE FRAGRANCES.

Sunny. It's our nature.

International Marketing
Le Petit Marseillais, the top body wash brand in France, uses advertisements such as this one to attract the interest of consumers in the United States.

marketing strategy is a critical element of a firm's global operations. Today, global competition in most industries is intense and becoming increasingly fierce with the addition of newly emerging markets and firms.

9-2 ENVIRONMENTAL FORCES IN GLOBAL MARKETS

Learning Objective 9-2

Differentiate between the environmental forces that affect international marketing efforts.

Firms that enter international markets must often make significant adjustments to their marketing strategies. The environmental forces that affect foreign markets may differ dramatically from those that affect domestic markets, and failure to understand them can result in significant costs. Alphabet Inc.'s Google faces unique competition, regulatory issues, and consumer use patterns in the foreign markets it serves. Thus, a successful international marketing strategy requires a careful environmental analysis. Conducting research to understand the needs and desires of international customers is crucial to global marketing success. Many firms have demonstrated that such efforts can generate tremendous financial rewards, increase market share, and heighten customer awareness of their products around the world. In this section, we explore how differences in the sociocultural; economic; political, legal, and regulatory; social and ethical; competitive; and technological forces in other countries can profoundly affect marketing activities.

9-2a Sociocultural Forces

Cultural and social differences among nations can have profound effects on marketing activities. Because marketing activities are primarily social in purpose, they are influenced by beliefs and values regarding family, religion, education, health, and recreation. By identifying, understanding, and respecting sociocultural differences among countries, marketers lay the groundwork for effective adjustments of marketing strategy. When Taco Bell originally expanded into South Korea, the menu was largely the same as in the United States, but more recently it has grown to include items like kimchi quesadillas, designed to appeal to local tastes. The kimchi quesadilla launch was a success, and the menu item now makes up 10 percent of sales in the country.[6] McDonald's was one of the first U.S. brands to be successful in China, but in 2017 sold an 80 percent interest in its 2,400 Chinese stores to a state-owned enterprise. Chinese consumers became more concerned about their health and have less confidence in fast food.[7]

Local preferences, tastes, and idioms can prove complicated for international marketers. For example, although football is a popular sport in the United States and a major opportunity for many television advertisers, soccer is the most popular televised sport in Europe and Latin America. Indeed, outside of the United States, the term "football" actually refers to soccer. Additionally, while middle-class consumers in some countries prefer to create their own unique fashion styles to demonstrate their individuality, in Turkey middle-class consumers accept fashion themes and demonstrate their creativity by "rotating" items in their wardrobes.[8] And, of course, marketing communications often must be translated into other languages. Sometimes, the true meaning of translated messages can be misinterpreted or lost. Consider some translations that went awry in foreign markets: KFC's long-running slogan "Finger lickin' good" was translated in China as "Eat your fingers off," while Coors' "Turn it loose" campaign was translated into Spanish as "Drink Coors and get diarrhea."[9]

It can be difficult to transfer marketing symbols, trademarks, logos, and even products to international markets, especially if these are associated with objects that have profound religious or cultural significance in a particular culture. Consider the problem Kellogg had with its Corn Flakes brand in South Africa. Because South Africans are used to hot porridge for breakfast, many of them were boiling Kellogg's corn flakes and ruining the meal. To adapt to this cultural expectation, Kellogg's reformulated the product and released Corn Flakes Instant Porridge to the South African market.[10]

Cultural differences may also affect marketing negotiations and decision-making behavior. Differences in the emphasis placed on personal relationships, status, and decision-making styles have been known to complicate dealings between Americans and businesspeople from other countries. In many parts of Asia, a gift may be considered a necessary introduction before negotiation, whereas in the United States or Canada, a gift may be misconstrued as an illegal bribe.

Buyers' perceptions of other countries can influence product adoption and use. Consumers who have a global orientation tend to have a positive attitude toward purchasing global brands. On the other hand, when consumers think local and are ethnocentric, they are more negative toward global brands.[11] Multiple research studies have shown that consumer preferences for products depend on both the country of origin and the product category of competing products.[12] When people are unfamiliar with products from another country, their perceptions of the country as a whole may affect their attitude toward the product and influence whether they will buy it. If a country has a reputation for producing quality products and therefore has a positive image in consumers' minds, marketers of products from that country will want to make the country of origin well known. BMW is a respected German brand that manufactures many of its vehicles in the United States, Mexico, and South Africa. In the case of BMW, the brand is more important than the country of origin to most consumers. BMW produces more than 400,000 X models in South Carolina each year with 70 percent exported outside the U.S. This makes BMW the largest exporter of cars in the U.S.[13] On the other hand, marketers may want to distance themselves from a particular country in order to build a brand's reputation as truly global or because that country does not have a good reputation for quality. Traditionally, Chinese brands have been viewed as being of low quality. However, the global success of companies such as Lenovo, Xiaomi, and Alibaba are not only increasing China's brand reputation but are also challenging top competitors such as Hewlett-Packard, Apple, and Amazon. The extent to which a product's brand image and country of origin influence purchases is subject to considerable variation based on national culture characteristics.

When products are introduced from one nation into another, acceptance is far more likely if similarities exist between the two cultures. In fact, many similar cultural characteristics exist across countries. For international marketers, cultural differences have implications for product development, advertising, packaging, and pricing. When Walmart expanded into China, for instance, it quickly found that it had to adapt its stores' seafood section because Chinese shoppers like to select their own seafood. This required the stores to build large tanks containing live fish so customers could choose which ones they wanted to purchase.

INTEGRITY IN MARKETING

Going Green: China Addresses Greenhouse Gas Emissions

China may have been slow on the environmental uptake, but it has made up for lost time. As the world's largest producer of greenhouse gases, the country had a tough job ahead of it. It responded by creating a Ministry of Environmental Protection with goals to clean up China's air and water and establish the country as an alternative energy powerhouse.

In a short amount of time, China launched a number of green initiatives. China has adopted stringent fuel economy standards and is encouraging manufacturers to develop electric vehicles. It also launched an extensive program investing in renewables. China has installed more wind and solar power farms than any other country in the world. It is also increasing fines for dumping waste. Six companies were fined $26 million for polluting rivers, the largest fine at the time.

Though China plans to scale back investments in wind and solar power because of slow economic growth and a slump in electricity demands, the country continues to set new goals. Recently, China's National Energy Administration set a goal for clean energy to meet 20 percent of China's energy demand by 2030. China has no plans to abandon its sustainability initiatives, pledging to invest more than $367 billion in renewable energy in the next few years.[a]

9-2b Economic Forces

Global marketers also need to understand the international trade system, particularly the economic stability of individual nations, as well as trade barriers that may stifle marketing efforts. Economic differences among nations—differences in standards of living, credit, buying power, income distribution, national resources, exchange rates, and the like—dictate many of the adjustments firms must make in marketing internationally. Country-specific factors such as economic wealth and national culture have a direct influence on the success of a new product in specific countries.[14]

Instability is a constant in the global business environment. The United States and the European Union are more stable economically than many other regions of the world. However, even these economies have downturns in regular cycles. A number of other countries, including Greece, Russia, Spain, and Thailand, have all experienced economic problems, such as recessions, high unemployment, corporate bankruptcies, instabilities in banking systems, and trade imbalances. The rising price of raw materials could increase inflation in developing countries where demand is growing.[15] Fluctuating economic conditions in different countries require that marketers carefully monitor the global environment and adjust their marketing strategies accordingly. Economic instability can disrupt the markets for U.S. products in places that otherwise might provide excellent marketing opportunities. On the other hand, competition from the sustained economic growth of countries like China and India can disrupt markets for U.S. products.

An important economic factor in the global business environment is currency valuation. The value of the dollar, euro, and yen has a major impact on the prices of products in many countries. Many countries have a floating exchange rate, which means the currencies of those countries fluctuate, or float, according to the foreign exchange market. Table 9.1 compares the value of the dollar, euro, yen, and yuan. China has been criticized for devaluing its currency, or setting its currency's value below market value. This gives it an advantage in selling exports, as the Chinese yuan has a lower value than other nations' currencies. It also decreases demand for manufacturers and exporters from other countries. Devaluing currency worries investors because it suggests that China's economy is slowing down.[16] The value of the U.S. dollar is also important. In the last few years, the value of the dollar has been strong relative to other currencies. This means that U.S. exports cost more if purchased using euros or yen. Because many countries float their exchange rates around the dollar, too much or too little U.S. currency in the economy could create inflationary effects or harm exports.[17] On the other hand, because imports are cheaper, a 10 percent increase in the value of the U.S. dollar increases the trade deficit by 1 percent of the gross domestic product. The strong dollar damages companies like Boeing, 3M, and Caterpillar that have significant global sales.[18]

In terms of the value of all products produced by a nation, the United States has the largest gross domestic product in the world at more than $19 trillion.[19] **Gross domestic product (GDP)** is an overall measure of a nation's economic standing; it is the market value of a nation's total output of goods and services for a given period. However, it does not take into account the

gross domestic product (GDP) The market value of a nation's total output of goods and services for a given period; an overall measure of economic standing

Table 9.1 **Exchange Rates of Global Currencies**

	1 USD (U.S. dollar)	1 EUR (euro)	1 JPY (Japanese yen)	1 CNY (China yuan renminbi)
1 USD	1.00	1.23	0.0092	0.16
1 EUR	0.81	1.00	0.0075	0.13
1 JPY	108.69	133.52	1.00	17.26
1 CNY	6.30	7.74	0.058	1.00

Floating Currency
Morocco recently started the gradual floating of its currency with plans to move toward a free-floating currency.

concept of GDP in relation to population (GDP per capita). The United States has a GDP per capita of $59,500.[20] Switzerland is roughly 230 times smaller than the United States—a little larger than the state of Maryland—but its population density is six times greater than that of the United States. Although Switzerland's GDP is much smaller than the United States' GDP, its GDP per capita is slightly higher. On the other hand, Canada, which is comparable in size to the United States, has a lower GDP and GDP per capita.[21] Table 9.2 provides a comparative economic analysis of 15 countries, including the United States. Knowledge about per capita income, credit, and the distribution of income provides general insights into market potential.

Opportunities for international trade are not limited to countries with the highest incomes. The countries of Brazil, Russia, India, China, and South Africa (BRICS) have attracted attention as their economies are rapidly advancing. Relationship marketing has proven to be a highly effective tool in reaching these emerging markets. This is because businesses in these countries value long-term and close interactions with marketers that they can trust. Relationship marketing has been shown to be 55 percent more effective in the growing economies of Brazil, Russia, India, and China than in the United States.[22] Other nations are progressing at a much faster rate than they were a few years ago, and these countries—especially in Latin America, Africa, eastern Europe, and the Middle East—have great market potential. Myanmar offers significant expansion opportunities for global

BRICS
CVS Health operates retail locations in 49 states as well as Brazil. BRICS countries consisting of Brazil, Russia, India, China, and South Africa offer lucrative opportunities for businesses like CVS to expand globally.

Table 9.2 **Comparative Analysis of Selected Countries**

Country	Population (in Millions)	GDP (U.S. $ in Billions)	Exports (U.S. $ in Billions)	Imports (U.S. $ in Billions)	Internet Users (in Millions)	Cell Phones (in Millions)
Brazil	207.4	$ 2,080.9	$ 215.4	$ 151.9	149.1	280.7
Canada	35.6	$ 1,640.4	$ 433.0	$ 443.7	33.0	29.5
China	1,379.3	$11,937.6	$ 2,157.0	$ 1,731.0	772.0	1,300.0
Honduras	9.0	$ 22.7	$ 8.2	$ 10.9	2.7	7.7
India	1,281.9	$ 2,439.0	$ 299.3	$ 426.8	462.1	944.0
Japan	126.5	$ 4,884.5	$ 683.3	$ 625.7	118.6	152.7
Jordan	10.2	$ 40.5	$ 7.7	$ 17.6	6.3	11.1
Kenya	47.6	$ 78.4	$ 6.4	$ 14.5	43.3	33.6
Mexico	124.6	$ 1,142.5	$ 406.5	$ 417.3	85.0	102.2
Russia	142.3	$ 1,469.3	$ 336.8	$ 212.7	109.6	221.0
South Africa	54.8	$ 344.1	$ 78.3	$ 80.2	29.9	79.5
Switzerland	8.2	$ 680.6	$ 336.8	$ 286.7	7.6	11.5
Turkey	80.8	$ 841.2	$ 157.3	$ 196.8	56.0	71.9
Thailand	68.4	$ 437.8	$ 228.2	$ 190.0	57.0	97.1
U.S.	326.6	$19,362.1	$ 1,576.0	$ 2,352.0	312.3	317.4

Note: Cell phone user data is current as of 2016 according to statistics used from the World Factbook.

Source: Central Intelligence Agency, "Guide to Country Comparisons," *World Factbook*, https://www.cia.gov/library/publications/the-world-factbook/rankorder/rankorderguide.html (accessed February 11, 2018); "World GDP Ranking 2017," *Knoema*, https://knoema.com/nwnfkne/world-gdp-ranking-2017-gdp-by-country-data-and-charts (accessed February 11, 2018); Internet World Stats, https://www.internetworldstats.com/top20.htm (accessed February 22, 2018).

firms, including Gap, Coca-Cola, and General Electric (GE). Until recently, U.S. sanctions against Myanmar prohibited the United States from shipping goods into or out of the country. A temporary removal of sanctions increases opportunities for other U.S. companies to engage in trade with the country.[23] Marketers must also understand the political and legal environments before they can convert buying power of customers in these countries into actual demand for specific products.

9-2c Political, Legal, and Regulatory Forces

The political, legal, and regulatory forces of the environment are closely intertwined in the United States. To a large degree, the same is true in many countries internationally. Typically, legislation is enacted, legal decisions are interpreted, and regulatory agencies are operated by elected or appointed officials. A country's legal and regulatory infrastructure is a direct reflection of its political climate. In some countries, this political climate is decided by the people via elections, whereas in other countries leaders are appointed or have assumed leadership based on

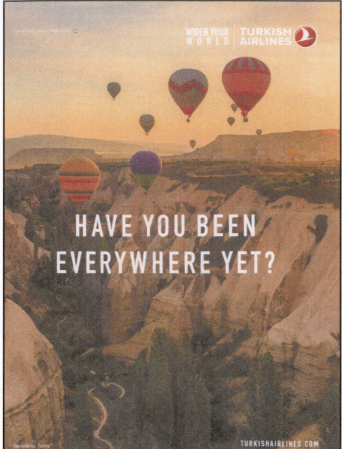

SOURCE: TURKISH AIRLINES

Turkish Airlines
Turkish Airlines has laid out aggressive growth plans. The advertisement features hot air balloons in Cappadocia, Turkey, to highlight one of the many destinations the airline services.

Table 9.3   The Best Countries for Starting a Business

Rank	Country
1	United Kingdom
2	New Zealand
3	Netherlands
4	Sweden
5	Canada
6	Hong Kong
7	Denmark
8	Ireland
9	Singapore
10	Switzerland

Source: "The Best Countries for Business 2017 Ranking," *Forbes*, www.forbes.com/best-countries-for-business/list/#tab:overall (accessed February 11, 2018).

certain powers. Although laws and regulations have direct effects on a firm's operations in a country, political forces are indirect and often not clearly known in all countries. China is an example of state-directed or national capitalism. The government owns a majority of, or has a partial stake in, many businesses. State-backed firms accounted for one-third of the emerging world's foreign direct investment in the last decade. An issue with state-owned enterprises versus private ones is the nature of competition. State-backed companies do not have as many competitors because the government is supporting them. Unless state-owned firms work hard to remain competitive, costs for these companies will most likely increase.[24]

Additionally, businesses from different countries might be similar in nature but operate differently based on legal, political, or regulatory conditions in their home countries. For instance, in the United States airlines operate as private companies while Emirates airlines is owned by the government of Dubai, although it operates as a commercial enterprise that does not receive government financial support.[25] This advertisement for Turkish Airlines speaks to the desire for adventure and exploration, challenging consumers to "widen your world." Instead of speaking to airplane features or loyalty program benefits, Turkish Airlines highlights the destination of Cappadocia, Turkey. Aside from Turkey, the airline services Russia, Greece, the United States, and more. On the other hand, some countries have political climates that make it easier for international entrepreneurs to start their own businesses. Table 9.3 lists some of the best countries in which to start a business, according to *Forbes*. The United States is not in the top 10, possibly due to regulations, taxes, and fewer incentives.

The political climate in a country or region, political officials in a country, and political officials in charge of trade agreements directly affect the legislation and regulations (or lack thereof). Within industries, elected or appointed officials of influential industry associations also set the tone for the regulatory environment that guides operations in a particular industry. Consider the American Marketing Association, which has one of the largest professional associations for marketers with more than 30,000 members worldwide in every area of marketing. It has established a statement of ethics, called "Ethical Norms and Values for Marketers," that guides the marketing profession in the United States.[26]

A nation's political system, laws, regulatory bodies, special-interest groups, and courts all have a great impact on international marketing. Laws regarding competition may serve as trade barriers. For example, the European Union has stronger antitrust laws than does the United States. Being found guilty of anticompetitive behavior has cost companies like Intel billions of dollars. Because some companies do not have the resources to comply with more stringent laws, this can act as a barrier to trade.

Some countries have established import barriers, such as tariffs. An **import tariff** is any duty levied by a nation on goods bought outside its borders and brought into the country. Because they raise the prices of foreign goods, tariffs impede free trade between nations. Tariffs are usually designed either to raise revenue for a country or to protect domestic products. In the

United States, tariff revenues account for a small percentage of total federal revenues, down from about 50 percent of total federal revenues in the early 1900s.

Nontariff trade barriers include quotas and embargoes. A **quota** is a limit on the amount of goods an importing country will accept for certain product categories in a specific period of time. The United States maintains tariff-rate quotas on imported raw cane sugar, refined and specialty sugar, and sugar-containing products. An **embargo** is a government's suspension of trade in a particular product or with a given country. Embargoes are generally directed at specific goods or countries and are established for political, health, or religious reasons. An embargo may be used to suspend the purchase of a commodity like oil from a country that is involved in questionable conduct, such as human rights violations or terrorism. Products that were created in the United States or by U.S. companies or those containing more than 20 percent of U.S.-manufactured parts cannot be sold to Cuba. Until recently, most Americans were banned from visiting Cuba because of the embargo. However, diplomatic relations between the United States and Cuba have resumed, and the Obama administration supported an end to the embargo.[27] As the advertisement shows, access to Cuba is increasing, and cruise companies like Pearl Seas Cruises are offering trips to the island.

Exchange controls, government restrictions on the amount of a particular currency that can be bought or sold, may also limit international trade. They can force businesspeople to buy and sell foreign products through a central agency, such as a central bank. Developing economies use exchange control to limit speculation against their currencies and to limit foreign investment. For example, Greece placed restrictions on how much cash could be withdrawn from banks and restrictions on transfer of capital abroad during a financial crisis. On the other hand, to promote international trade, some countries have joined to form free trade zones, multinational economic communities that eliminate tariffs and other trade barriers. Such regional trade alliances are discussed later in the chapter. As mentioned earlier, foreign currency exchange rates also affect the prices marketers can charge in foreign markets. Fluctuations in the international monetary market can change the prices charged across national boundaries on a daily basis. Thus, these fluctuations must be considered in any international marketing strategy.

Countries may establish barriers to limit imports in order to maintain a favorable balance of trade. The **balance of trade** is the difference in value between a nation's exports and its imports. When a nation exports more products than it imports, a favorable balance of trade exists because money is flowing into the country. The United States has a negative balance of trade for goods and services of more than $502 billion.[28] A negative balance of trade is considered harmful because it means U.S. dollars are supporting foreign economies at the expense of U.S. companies and workers. At the same time, U.S. citizens benefit from the assortment of imported products and their typically lower prices.

import tariff A duty levied by a nation on goods bought outside its borders and brought into the country

quota A limit on the amount of goods an importing country will accept for certain product categories in a specific period of time

embargo A government's suspension of trade in a particular product or with a given country

exchange controls Government restrictions on the amount of a particular currency that can be bought or sold

balance of trade The difference in value between a nation's exports and its imports

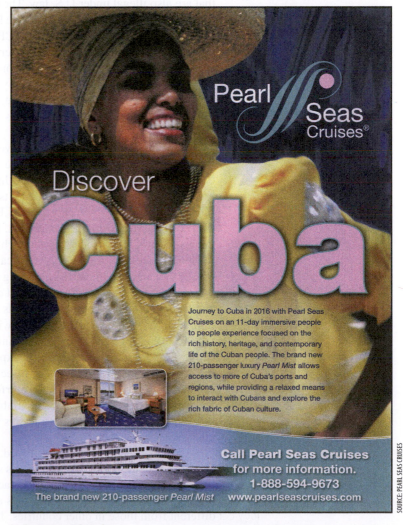

Journey to Cuba in 2016 with Pearl Seas Cruises on an 11-day immersive people to people experience focused on the rich history, heritage, and contemporary life of the Cuban people. The brand new 210-passenger luxury *Pearl Mist* allows access to more of Cuba's ports and regions, while providing a relaxed means to interact with Cubans and explore the rich fabric of Cuban culture.

Call Pearl Seas Cruises for more information.
1-888-594-9673
www.pearlseascruises.com

The brand new 210-passenger *Pearl Mist*

SOURCE: PEARL SEAS CRUISES

Relations with Cuba
With the reestablishment of diplomatic relations with Cuba, more U.S. consumers are having the opportunity to visit the country. Pearl Seas Cruises has seized upon this opportunity to promote an 11-day cruise to Cuba.

Many nontariff barriers, such as quotas, minimum price levels set on imports, port-of-entry taxes, and stringent health and safety requirements, still make it difficult for U.S. companies to export their products. For instance, the collectivist nature of Japanese culture and the high-context nature of Japanese communication make some types of direct marketing messages through the internet and mass media less effective and may predispose many Japanese to support greater regulation of direct marketing practices.[29] Because of their collectivist culture, direct selling involving face-to-face communication may be more acceptable. A government's attitude toward importers has a direct impact on the economic feasibility of exporting to that country.

9-2d Ethical and Social Responsibility Forces

Differences in national standards are illustrated by what the Mexicans call *la mordida*: "the bite." The use of payoffs and bribes is deeply entrenched in many parts of the world. Because U.S. trade and corporate policy, as well as U.S. law, prohibits direct involvement in payoffs and bribes, it may be difficult for U.S. companies to compete with foreign firms that engage in these practices. Some U.S. businesses that refuse to make payoffs are forced to hire local consultants, public relations firms, or advertising agencies, which results in indirect payoffs that are also illegal under U.S. law. The ultimate decision about whether to give small tips or gifts where they are customary must be based on a company's code of ethics. However, under the Foreign Corrupt Practices Act (FCPA) of 1977, it is illegal for U.S. firms to attempt to make large payments or bribes to influence policy decisions of foreign governments. Walmart spent $791 million on legal fees and on internal investigation and to revamp its compliance systems.[30] Nevertheless, facilitating payments, or small payments to support the performance of standard tasks, are often acceptable. The FCPA also subjects all publicly held U.S. corporations to rigorous internal controls and record-keeping requirements for their overseas operations.

Many other countries have outlawed bribery. As we discussed in Chapter 3, the U.K. Bribery Act redefined what many companies consider to be bribery versus gift-giving. Companies with operations in the United Kingdom could still face penalties for bribery, even if the bribery occurred outside the country and managers were not aware of the misconduct. In this case, the U.K. Bribery Act might be considered stricter than the U.S. Foreign Corrupt Practices Act. It is thus essential for global marketers to understand the major laws in the countries in which their companies operate.

Differences in ethical standards can also affect marketing efforts. In China and Vietnam, for example, standards regarding intellectual property differ dramatically from those in the United States, creating potential conflicts for marketers of computer software, music, and books. Trade in counterfeit goods has been estimated to be anywhere from $200 billion to more than $1.7 trillion worldwide, but the full scope is unknown according to the U.S. Chamber of Commerce.[31] This influx of counterfeit goods is presenting a hurdle for Chinese internet firm Alibaba as it expands globally. Although Alibaba claims it is building systems that allow it to more effectively detect counterfeit goods, it has been heavily criticized for the number of counterfeit goods found through its site.[32] The enormous amount of counterfeit products available worldwide, the time it takes to track them down, and legal barriers in certain countries make the pursuit of counterfeiters challenging for many companies.

When marketers do business abroad, they sometimes perceive that other business cultures have different modes of operation. This sensitivity is especially pronounced in marketers who have not traveled extensively or interacted much with foreigners in business or social settings. For example, a perception exists among many in the United States that U.S. firms are different from those in other countries. This implied perspective of "us" versus "them" is also common in other countries. In business, the idea that "we" differ from "them" is called the self-reference criterion (SRC). The SRC is the unconscious reference to one's own cultural values, experiences, and knowledge. When confronted with a situation, we react on the basis of knowledge we have accumulated over a lifetime, which is usually grounded in our culture of origin. Our reactions are based on meanings, values, and symbols that relate to our culture but may not have the same relevance to people of other cultures.

Many companies try to conduct global business based on the local culture. These businesspeople adapt to the cultural practices of the country they are in and use the host country's cultural practices as the rationalization for sometimes straying from their own ethical values when doing business internationally. For instance, by defending the payment of bribes or "greasing the wheels of business" and other questionable practices in this fashion, some businesspeople are resorting to **cultural relativism**—the concept that morality varies from one culture to another and that business practices are, therefore, differentially defined as right or wrong by particular cultures. Table 9.4 indicates the countries that business people, risk analysts, and the general public perceive as having the most and least corrupt public sectors. Most global companies are recognizing that they must establish values and standards that are consistent throughout the world.

Because of differences in cultural and ethical standards, many companies work both individually and collectively to establish ethics programs and standards for international business conduct. Levi Strauss' code of ethics, for example, bars the firm from manufacturing in countries where workers are known to be abused. Many firms, including Texas Instruments, Coca-Cola, DuPont, Hewlett-Packard, and Walmart, endorse following international business practices responsibly. These companies support a globally based resource system called Business for Social Responsibility (BSR). BSR tracks emerging issues and trends, provides information on corporate leadership and best practices, conducts educational workshops and training, and assists organizations in developing practical business ethics tools.[33]

cultural relativism The concept that morality varies from one culture to another and that business practices are, therefore, differentially defined as right or wrong by particular cultures

Table 9.4 Ranking of Countries Based Upon Corruption of Public Sector

Country Rank	CPI Score[*]	Least Corrupt	Country Rank	CPI Score[*]	Most Corrupt
1	89	New Zealand	180	10	Somalia
2	88	Denmark	179	12	South Sudan
3	85	Finland	178	14	Syria
3	85	Norway	177	15	Afghanistan
3	85	Switzerland	175	16	Yemen
6	84	Singapore	175	16	Sudan
6	84	Sweden	171	17	Libya
8	82	Canada	171	17	North Korea
8	82	Luxembourg	171	17	Equatorial Guinea
8	82	Netherlands	169	18	Venezuela
8	82	United Kingdom	169	18	Iraq
12	81	Germany	167	19	Turkmenistan
13	77	Australia	167	19	Angola

[*]CPI score relates to perceptions of the degree of public sector corruption as seen by business people and country analysts and ranges between 100 (highly clear) and 0 (highly corrupt). The United States is perceived as the 16th least-corrupt nation.
Source: Data from Transparency International, Corruption Perceptions Index 2017 (Berlin, Germany, 2018).

9-2e Competitive Forces

Competition is often viewed as a staple of the global marketplace. Customers thrive on the choices offered by competition, and firms constantly seek opportunities to outmaneuver their competition to gain customers' loyalty. Firms typically identify their competition when they establish target markets worldwide. Customers who are seeking alternative solutions to their product needs find the firms that can solve those needs. However, the increasingly interconnected international marketplace and advances in technology have resulted in competitive forces that are unique to the international marketplace.

Each country has unique competitive aspects—often founded in the other environmental forces (i.e., sociocultural, technological, political, legal, regulatory, and economic forces)—that are often independent of the competitors in that market. The most globally competitive countries are listed in Table 9.5. Although competitors drive competition, nations establish the infrastructure and the rules for the types of competition that can take place. For example, the privacy laws in the European Union are stricter than those in the United States. Over the last seven years, Alphabet Inc.'s Google has experienced the European Union's antitrust regulators' claims that Google is restricting competition. The claim is that the search feature restricts advertisements sold by other companies. Also, there is a claim that Google pre-installs its search engine as a default on mobile devices.[34] However, like the United States, other countries allow some monopoly structures to exist. In Sweden, for example, all alcoholic beverage sales are made through the government store Systembolaget, which is legally supported by the Swedish Alcohol Retail Monopoly. According to Systembolaget, the Swedish Alcohol Retail Monopoly exists for one reason: "to minimize alcohol-related problems by selling alcohol in a responsible way."[35]

A new breed of customer—the global customer—has changed the landscape of international competition drastically. In the past, firms simply produced goods or services and provided local markets with information about the features and uses of their goods and services. Customers seldom had opportunities to compare products from competitors, know details about the competing products' features, and compare other options beyond the local (country or regional) markets. Now, however, not only do customers who travel the globe expect to be able to buy the same product in most of the world's 200 countries, but they also expect that the product they buy in their local store in Miami will have the same features as similar products sold in London or even in Beijing. If either the quality of the product or the product's features are more advanced in an international market, customers will soon demand that their local markets offer the same product at the same or lower prices.

Table 9.5 Ranking of the Most Competitive Countries in the World

Rank	Country
1	Switzerland
2	United States
3	Singapore
4	Netherlands
5	Germany
6	Hong Kong SAR
7	Sweden
8	United Kingdom
9	Japan
10	Finland

Source: World Economic Forum, "The Global Competitiveness Report 2017–2018," https://www.weforum.org/reports/the-global-competitiveness-report-2017-2018 (accessed February 11, 2018).

9-2f Technological Forces

Advances in technology have made international marketing much easier. Interactive websites, instant messaging, and podcast downloads (along with the traditional vehicles of voice mail, email, and smart phones) make international marketing activities more affordable and convenient. Internet use and social networking activities have accelerated dramatically within the United States and abroad. In Japan, more than 118 million have internet access, and more than 109 million Russians, 462 million Indians, and 772 million Chinese are logging on to the internet (refer back to Table 9.2).[36]

In many developing countries that lack the level of technological infrastructure found in the United States and Japan, marketers are beginning to capitalize on opportunities to leap-frog existing technology. For example, cellular and wireless phone technology is reaching many countries at a more affordable rate than traditional hard-wired telephone systems. Consequently, opportunities for growth in the cell phone market remain strong in Southeast Asia, Africa, and the Middle East. One opportunity created by the rapid growth in mobile devices in Kenya is mobile payment services. London-based Vodafone partnered with Kenyan telecom firm Safaricom to take advantage of this market opportunity with its M-PESA money transfer service, the most popular money transfer service in Kenya. It is estimated that twice as many Kenyans use their mobile phones for financial activities than have bank accounts.[37]

Despite the enormous benefits of digital technology, however, the digital economy may actually be increasing the divide between skilled wealthy workers and the rest of the labor force. Instead of increasing wages overall, wages have remained relatively flat. There is also the fear that technology will take over people's jobs. At a Foxconn factory in China, auto-

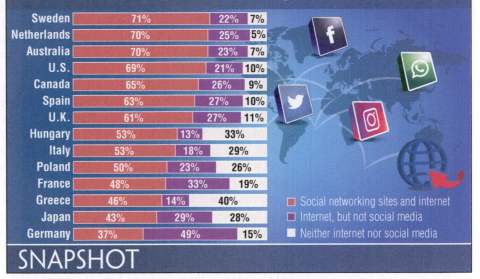

Social Media and Internet Usage Around the World

Country	Social networking sites and internet	Internet, but not social media	Neither internet nor social media
Sweden	71%	22%	7%
Netherlands	70%	25%	5%
Australia	70%	23%	7%
U.S.	69%	21%	10%
Canada	65%	26%	9%
Spain	63%	27%	10%
U.K.	61%	27%	11%
Hungary	53%	13%	33%
Italy	53%	18%	29%
Poland	50%	23%	26%
France	48%	33%	19%
Greece	46%	14%	40%
Japan	43%	29%	28%
Germany	37%	49%	15%

SNAPSHOT

Source: Pew Research Center. Spring 2016 Global Attitudes Survey. Q79, Q81, Q82. U.S. data from a Pew Research Center Survey conducted Sept. 29–Nov. 6, 2016.

mation replaced many workers to reduce the risk of injury. However, technology also leads to the hire of skilled individuals to work on the automation. Despite the labor imbalance that some technologies are causing, they offer a great opportunity for entrepreneurs in developing countries to reach the rest of the world.[38]

9-3 REGIONAL TRADE ALLIANCES, MARKETS, AND AGREEMENTS

Learning Objective 9-3

List important international trade agreements.

Although many more firms are beginning to view the world as one huge marketplace, various regional trade alliances and specific markets affect companies engaging in international marketing; some create opportunities, and others impose constraints. In fact, while trade agreements in various forms have been around for centuries, the last century can be classified as the trade agreement period in the world's international development. Today, there are nearly 200 trade agreements around the world compared with only a select handful in the early 1960s. In this section, we examine several of the more critical regional trade alliances, markets, and changing conditions affecting markets. These include the North American Free Trade Agreement (NAFTA), European Union (EU), Southern Common Market (MERCOSUR), Asia-Pacific Economic Cooperation (APEC), Association of Southeast Asian Nations (ASEAN), and World Trade Organization (WTO).

9-3a The North American Free Trade Agreement (NAFTA)

The **North American Free Trade Agreement (NAFTA)**, implemented in 1994, effectively merged Canada, Mexico, and the United States into one market of nearly 454 million consumers. NAFTA eliminated virtually all tariffs on goods produced and traded among Canada, Mexico, and the United States to create a free trade area. The estimated annual output for this trade alliance is more than $17 trillion.[39]

NAFTA makes it easier for U.S. businesses to invest in Mexico and Canada; provides protection for intellectual property (of special interest to high-technology and entertainment industries); expands trade by requiring equal treatment of U.S. firms in both countries; and

North American Free Trade Agreement (NAFTA) An alliance that merges Canada, Mexico, and the United States into a single market simplifies country-of-origin rules, hindering Japan's use of Mexico as a staging ground for further penetration into U.S. markets. Although most tariffs on products coming to the United States were lifted, duties on more sensitive products, such as household glassware, footwear, and some fruits and vegetables, were phased out over a 15-year period.

Canada's more than 36 million consumers are relatively affluent, with a per capita GDP of $48,100.[40] Canada is the single largest trading partner of the United States, which in turn supports 1.7 million U.S. jobs.[41] NAFTA has also facilitated additional trade between Canada and Mexico. Mexico is Canada's fifth-largest export market and third-largest import market.[42]

With a per capita GDP of $18,900, Mexico's more than 123 million consumers are less affluent than Canadian consumers.[43] The United States receives imports totaling $295 billion from Mexico.[44] Many U.S. companies, including GE, Hewlett-Packard, IBM, and General Motors, have taken advantage of Mexico's low labor costs and close proximity to the United States to set up production facilities, sometimes called *maquiladoras*. Production at the *maquiladoras*, especially in the automotive, electronics, and apparel industries, has grown rapidly as companies as diverse as Ford, John Deere, Motorola, Kimberly-Clark, and VF Corporation set up facilities in north-central Mexican states. Although Mexico suffered financial instability throughout the 1990s—as well as the more recent drug cartel violence—privatization of some government-owned firms and other measures instituted by the Mexican government and businesses have helped Mexico's economy. Moreover, increasing trade between the United States and Canada constitutes a strong base of support for the ultimate success of NAFTA.

Mexico's membership in NAFTA links the United States and Canada with other Latin American countries, providing additional opportunities to integrate trade among all the nations in the Western Hemisphere. Indeed, efforts to create a free trade agreement among the 34 nations of North and South America are under way. A related trade agreement—the Dominican Republic–Central American Free Trade Agreement (CAFTA-DR)—among Costa Rica, the Dominican Republic, El Salvador, Guatemala, Honduras, Nicaragua, and the United States has also been ratified in all those countries except Costa Rica. The United States exports $29 billion to the CAFTA-DR countries annually.[45]

9-3b **The European Union (EU)**

The **European Union (EU)**, sometimes also referred to as the *European Community* or *Common Market*, was established in 1958 to promote trade among its members, which initially included Belgium, France, Italy, West Germany, Luxembourg, and the Netherlands. Today the Euro Zone (countries that have adopted the euro as their currency) consists of 19 separate countries with varying political landscapes.[46] In 1991, East and West Germany united, and by 2015, the EU included the United Kingdom, Spain, Denmark, Greece, Portugal, Ireland, Austria, Finland, Sweden, Cyprus, Poland, Hungary, the Czech Republic, Slovenia, Estonia, Latvia, Lithuania, Slovakia, Malta, Romania, Bulgaria, Belgium, France, Germany, Italy, Luxembourg, The Netherlands, and Croatia. The Former Yugoslav Republic of Macedonia, Montenegro, Serbia, and Turkey are candidate countries that hope to join the European Union in the near future.[47]

In 2016, the United Kingdom voted to exit the European Union. This decision to exit, called "Brexit," resulted in the value of the pound falling sharply. There remains many questions about the impact of the proposed exit on trade relationships with other countries. The European Union consists of more than half a billion consumers and has a combined GDP of nearly $17.1 trillion.[48] In recent years, a worldwide recession has slowed Europe's economic growth and created a debt crisis. Several members have budget deficits and are struggling to recover. Exiting the EU could have an even greater impact on the economy. For instance, economists are predicting that Brexit will slow growth in the U.K., create barriers to trade, and lead to conflict among the U.K. and other countries in the EU.

The EU is a relatively diverse set of democratic European countries. It is not a state that is intended to replace existing country states, nor is it an organization for international cooperation. Instead, its member states have common institutions to which they delegate some of their

European Union (EU) An alliance that promotes trade among its member countries in Europe

TOBIAS ARHELGER/SHUTTERSTOCK.COM

European Union
While the economies of Spain, Italy, and Greece have struggled in recent years, other countries such as Poland have prospered. Germany has the largest economy in the European Union.

sovereignty to allow specific matters of joint interest to be decided at the European level. The primary goals of the EU are to establish European citizenship; ensure freedom, security, and justice; promote economic and social progress; and assert Europe's role in world trade.[49] To facilitate free trade among members, the EU is working toward standardizing business regulations and requirements, import duties, and value-added taxes; eliminating customs checks; and creating a standardized currency for use by all members. Many European nations (Austria, Belgium, Finland, France, Germany, Ireland, Italy, Luxembourg, the Netherlands, Portugal, Greece, and Spain) are linked to a common currency, the *euro*, but several EU members have rejected the euro in their countries (e.g., Denmark, Sweden, and the United Kingdom). Although the common currency may necessitate that marketers modify their pricing strategies and subjects them to increased competition, it also frees companies that sell products among European countries from the complexities of exchange rates. The European Central Bank is committed to supporting the value of the euro, even in countries in the Euro Zone like Greece that required financial support. The long-term goals are to eliminate all trade barriers within the EU, improve the economic efficiency of the EU nations, and stimulate economic growth, thus making the union's economy more competitive in global markets, particularly against Japan and other Pacific Rim nations and North America.

As the EU nations attempt to function as one large market, consumers in the EU may become more homogeneous in their needs and wants. Marketers should be aware, however, that cultural differences among the nations may require modifications in the marketing mix for customers in each nation. Differences in tastes and preferences in these diverse markets are significant for international marketers. But there is evidence that such differences may be diminishing, especially within the younger population that includes teenagers and young professionals. Gathering information about these distinct tastes and preferences is likely to remain a very important factor in developing marketing mixes that satisfy the needs of European customers.

Although the United States and the EU do not always agree, partnerships between the two have been profitable and the two entities generally have a positive relationship. Much of this success can be attributed to the shared values of the United States and EU. The EU is mostly democratic and has a strong commitment to human rights, fairness, and the rule of law. As a result, the United States and EU have been able to collaborate on mutually beneficial projects with fewer problems than partnerships with other trade alliances that do not share similar values.[50] There have been discussions about the possibility of a trade agreement between the two entities. In many respects, the United States, the EU, and Asia have become largely interdependent in trade and investment. For instance, the United States and the EU have adopted the "Open Skies" agreement to remove some of the restrictions on transatlantic flights, and the two often collaborate on ways to prevent terrorist attacks, cyber hacking, and other types of crime. The United States and the EU hope that by working together, they can create mutually beneficial relationships that will provide benefits to millions of their citizens.[51]

9-3c The Southern Common Market (MERCOSUR)

The **Southern Common Market (MERCOSUR)** was established in 1991 under the Treaty of Asunción to unite Argentina, Brazil, Paraguay, and Uruguay as a free trade alliance. Venezuela and Bolivia joined in 2006 and 2015, respectively.[52] Currently, Chile, Colombia, Ecuador, and Peru are associate members. The alliance represents two-thirds of South America's population and has a combined GDP of more than $3.3 trillion, making it the fourth-largest trading bloc behind NAFTA, the EU, and ASEAN. Like NAFTA, MERCOSUR promotes "the free circulation of goods, services, and production factors among the countries" and establishes a common external tariff and commercial policy.[53]

South America and Latin America are drawing the attention of many international businesses. The region is advancing economically with an estimated growth rate of 4 to 5 percent. Another trend is that several of the countries, including some of the MERCOSUR alliance, are starting to experience more stable democracies. Even Cuba, one of the traditionally harshest critics of capitalism in Latin America, is accepting more privatization. For example, while there is a growing flow of funds (remittances from the United States) and tourists from the United States, there is much uncertainty about the future economic relations. About a third of Cubans are in the private sector, but the money for starting most of these businesses came from Cuban Americans' remittances that are greater than all of Cuba's exports.[54] Despite governmental restrictions, entrepreneurship is growing in Cuba.[55]

9-3d The Asia-Pacific Economic Cooperation (APEC)

The **Asia-Pacific Economic Cooperation (APEC)**, established in 1989, promotes open trade and economic and technical cooperation among member nations, which initially included Australia, Brunei Darussalam, Canada, Indonesia, Japan, South Korea, Malaysia, New Zealand, the Philippines, Singapore, Thailand, and the United States. Since its introduction, the alliance has grown to include China, Hong Kong, Taiwan, Mexico, Papua New Guinea, Chile, Peru, Russia, and Vietnam. The 21-member alliance represents approximately 40 percent of the world's population, 54 percent of the world's GDP, and nearly 44 percent of global trade.[56] APEC differs from other international trade alliances in its commitment to facilitating business and its practice of allowing the business/private sector to participate in a wide range of APEC activities.[57] Companies of the APEC have become increasingly competitive and sophisticated in global business in the last few decades. Moreover, the markets of the APEC offer tremendous opportunities to marketers who understand them. In fact, the APEC region has consistently been one of the most economically dynamic parts of the world.

Japanese firms in particular have made tremendous inroads on world markets for automobiles, motorcycles, watches, cameras, and audio and video equipment. Products from Sony, Sanyo, Toyota, Mitsubishi, Canon, Suzuki, and Toshiba are sold all over the world and have set standards of quality by which other products are often judged. Despite the high volume of trade between the United States and Japan, the two economies are less integrated than the U.S. economy is with Canada and the European Union. If Japan imported goods at the same rate as other major nations, the United States would sell billions of dollars more each year to Japan.

The most important emerging economic power in APEC is China, which has become one of the most productive manufacturing nations. China, which is now the United States'

Southern Common Market (MERCOSUR) An alliance that promotes the free circulation of goods, services, and production factors, and has a common external tariff and commercial policy among member nations in South America

Asia-Pacific Economic Cooperation (APEC) An alliance that promotes open trade and economic and technical cooperation among member nations throughout the world

second-largest trading partner, has initiated economic reforms to stimulate its economy by privatizing many industries, restructuring its banking system, and increasing public spending on infrastructure. Many foreign companies, including Apple and Samsung, have opened factories in China to take advantage of its low labor costs, and China has become a major global supplier in virtually every product category. For international businesses, the potential of China's consumer market is so vast that it is almost impossible to measure. However, doing business in China entails many risks. Political and economic instability—especially inflation, corruption, and erratic policy shifts—have undercut marketers' efforts to stake a claim in what could become the world's largest market. Piracy, in particular, is a major issue, and protecting a brand name in China is difficult. Because copying is a tradition in China, and laws that protect copyrights and intellectual property are weak and minimally enforced, the country is flooded with counterfeit media, computer software, furniture, and clothing. However, there are signs that piracy laws are beginning to be better enforced in China. China's National Copyright Administration is taking an active role in combating music piracy, removing 2.2 million songs from online music platforms deemed to be unlicensed.[58]

Pacific Rim regions like South Korea, Thailand, Singapore, Taiwan, and Hong Kong are also major manufacturing and financial centers. Even before Korean brand names, such as Samsung, Daewoo, and Hyundai, became household words, these products prospered under U.S. company labels, including GE, GTE, RCA, and JCPenney. Singapore boasts huge global markets for rubber goods and pharmaceuticals. Hong Kong is still a strong commercial center after being transferred to Chinese control. Vietnam is one of Asia's fastest-growing markets for U.S. businesses, and more businesses are choosing to open factories in Vietnam as China's labor costs continue to grow.[59] Taiwan, given its stability and high educational attainment, has the most promising future of all the Pacific Rim nations as a strong local economy, and low import barriers draw increasing imports. The markets of APEC offer tremendous opportunities to marketers who understand them.

Another important trade agreement involving countries bordering the Pacific was the Trans-Pacific Partnership (TPP), a trade agreement that was proposed between Singapore, Brunei, Chile, New Zealand, Vietnam, Malaysia, Japan, Peru, the United States, Canada, Mexico, and Australia.[60] The agreement would have created standards for state-owned enterprises, labor, international property, and the environment.[61] While the Obama administration supported the agreement, the Trump administration officially removed the U.S. from the partnership. Without the U.S., the remaining 11 countries signed a deal to eliminate trade barriers under a new name: the Comprehensive and Progressive Agreement for Trans-Pacific Partnership (also known as CPTPP or TPP-11).[62]

9-3e Association of Southeast Asian Nations (ASEAN)

The **Association of Southeast Asian Nations (ASEAN)**, established in 1967, promotes trade and economic integration among member nations in Southeast Asia. The trade pact includes Malaysia, the Philippines, Indonesia, Singapore, Thailand, Brunei Darussalam, Vietnam, Laos, Myanmar, and Cambodia.[63] The advertisement for Microsoft Cloud details how putting Temenos banking software in the cloud has expanded its international reach to "underbanked" people all over the globe. An image of a woman in the Philippines is used to highlight one of the many places that benefit from

Association of Southeast Asian Nations (ASEAN) An alliance that promotes trade and economic integration among member nations in Southeast Asia

This cloud opens doors **of opportunity.**

The Microsoft Cloud has helped Temenos lower the cost of borrowing by 90%. By putting their core banking software in the cloud, microfinance institutions are able to reduce the need for infrastructure and management. In turn, this opens the doors of opportunity for millions of underbanked people all over the globe.

This is the Microsoft Cloud.

learn more at microsoftcloud.com

■■ Microsoft Cloud

SOURCE: MICROSOFT CLOUD

International Growth Opportunities
Switzerland-based Temenos partnered with Microsoft Cloud to put its core banking software in the cloud to lower the cost of borrowing by 90 percent and expand the international reach of the banking industry.

258

cloud-based banking. The ASEAN region is home to more than 660 million people with a combined GDP of $2.5 trillion.[64] With its motto "One Vision, One Identity, One Community," member nations have expressed the goal of encouraging free trade, peace, and collaboration between member countries.[65] ASEAN's three pillars are political-security, economic, and sociocultural. The ASEAN Economic Community (AEC) attempts to unite the regional economy.[66]

Despite the positive growth potential, ASEAN faces many obstacles in becoming a unified trade bloc. There have been conflicts among members themselves and concerns over issues such as human rights and disputed territories.[67] Therefore, there are great opportunities but also substantial risk. The state-owned oil and gas company in Thailand, PTT Chemical Company, is one organization that looks to prosper from growth in the ASEAN trade bloc. With the population of Southeast Asia estimated to hit 690 million by 2020, the growing need for energy bodes well for PTT Chemical.[68]

While many choose to compare ASEAN with the European Union, ASEAN members are careful to point out their differences. Although members hope to increase economic integration, they expressed that there will be no common currency or fully free labor flows between members. In this way, ASEAN plans to avoid some of the pitfalls that occurred among nations in the EU during the latest worldwide recession.[69]

9-3f The World Trade Organization (WTO)

The **World Trade Organization (WTO)** is a global trade association that promotes free trade among 164 member nations. The WTO is the successor to the **General Agreement on Tariffs and Trade (GATT)**, which was originally signed by 23 nations in 1947 to provide a forum for tariff negotiations and a place where international trade problems could be discussed and resolved. Rounds of GATT negotiations reduced trade barriers for most products and established rules to guide international commerce, such as rules to prevent **dumping**, the selling of products at unfairly low prices. The WTO came into being in 1995 as a result of the Uruguay Round (1988–1994) of GATT negotiations. Broadly, WTO is the main worldwide organization that deals with the rules of trade between nations; its main function is to ensure that trade flows as smoothly, predictably, and freely as possible between nations.[70]

Fulfilling the purpose of the WTO requires eliminating trade barriers; educating individuals, companies, and governments about trade rules around the world; and assuring global markets that no sudden changes of policy will occur. At the heart of the WTO are agreements that provide legal ground rules for international commerce and trade policy. Based in Geneva, Switzerland, the WTO also serves as a forum for dispute resolution.[71] For example, the WTO ruled against the United States regarding country-of-origin labeling rules for meat products that required information on where the animals were born, raised, and slaughtered. Canada and Mexico argued that these laws discriminated against their livestock. The WTO agreed, which authorized Mexico and Canada to seek retaliatory measures against the United States if the law continues.[72]

World Trade Organization (WTO) An entity that promotes free trade among member nations by eliminating trade barriers and educating individuals, companies, and governments about trade rules around the world

General Agreement on Tariffs and Trade (GATT) An agreement among nations to reduce worldwide tariffs and increase international trade

dumping Selling products at unfairly low prices

Learning Objective 9-4

Identify methods of international market entry.

9-4 MODES OF ENTRY INTO INTERNATIONAL MARKETS

Marketers enter international markets and continue to engage in marketing activities at several levels of international involvement. Traditionally, firms have adopted one of four different modes of entering an international market; each successive "stage" represents different degrees of international involvement.

- Stage 1: No regular export activities
- Stage 2: Export via independent representatives (agents)
- Stage 3: Establishment of one or more sales subsidiaries internationally
- Stage 4: Establishment of international production/manufacturing facilities[73]

As Figure 9.1 shows, companies' international involvement today covers a wide spectrum, from purely domestic marketing to global marketing. Domestic marketing involves marketing strategies aimed at markets within the home country; at the other extreme, global marketing entails developing marketing strategies for the entire world (or at least more than one major region of the world). Many firms with an international presence start out as small companies serving local and regional domestic markets and expand to national markets before considering opportunities in foreign markets (the born global firm, described earlier, is one exception to this internationalization process). Companies like HSBC use experience in international markets as a selling point. In the advertisement, HSBC touts 150 years of experience in the banking and financial services industry in more than 60 countries. The advertisement suggests that HSBC offers a seamless experience from country to country to make international growth easier. Limited exporting may occur even if a firm makes little or no effort to obtain foreign sales. Foreign buyers may seek out the company and/or its products, or a distributor may discover the firm's products and export them. The level of commitment to international marketing is a major variable in global marketing strategies. In this section, we examine importing and exporting, trading companies, licensing and franchising, contract manufacturing, joint ventures, direct ownership, and some of the other approaches to international involvement.

Entry into International Markets
HSBC encourages businesses to become a part of its global network because it has a presence in more than 60 countries.

9-4a Importing and Exporting

Importing and exporting require the least amount of effort and commitment of resources. **Importing** is the purchase of products from a foreign source. **Exporting**, the sale of products to foreign markets, enables firms of all sizes to participate in global business. A firm may also find an exporting intermediary to take over most marketing functions associated with marketing to other countries. This approach entails minimal effort and cost. Modifications in packaging, labeling, style, or color may be the major expenses in adapting a product for the foreign market.

Export agents bring together buyers and sellers from different countries and collect a commission for arranging sales. Export houses and export merchants purchase products from different companies and then sell them abroad. They are specialists at understanding customers' needs in global markets. Using exporting intermediaries involves limited risk because no foreign direct investment is required. For example, China has an insatiable appetite for pork and pork imports, while Poland exports more apples than any other country.

Buyers from foreign companies and governments provide a direct method of exporting and eliminate the need for an intermediary. These buyers encourage international exchange by contacting overseas firms about their needs and the opportunities available in exporting to them. Indeed, research suggests that many small firms tend to rely heavily on such native contacts, especially in developed markets, and remain production-oriented rather than market-oriented

importing The purchase of products from a foreign source

exporting The sale of products to foreign markets

Figure 9.1   **Levels of Involvement in Global Marketing**

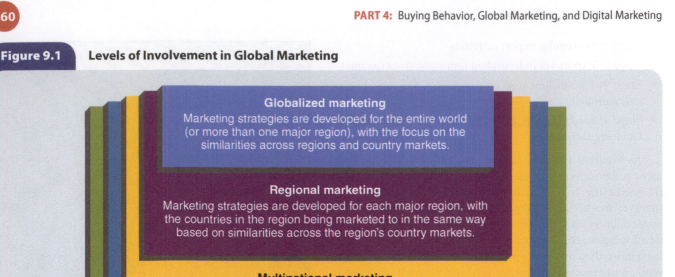

in their approach to international marketing.[74] Domestic firms that want to export with minimal effort and investment should seek out export intermediaries. Once a company becomes involved in exporting, it usually develops more knowledge of the country and becomes more confident in its competitiveness.[75]

9-4b   Trading Companies

Marketers sometimes employ a **trading company**, which links buyers and sellers in different countries but is not involved in manufacturing and does not own assets related to manufacturing. Trading companies buy products in one country at the lowest price consistent with quality and sell them to buyers in another country. For instance, the World Trade System (WTSC) offers a 24-hour-per-day online world trade system that connects 20 million companies in 245 countries, offering more than 60 million products.[76] A trading company acts like a wholesaler, taking on much of the responsibility of finding markets while facilitating all marketing aspects of a transaction. An important function of trading companies is taking title to products and performing all the activities necessary to move the products to the targeted foreign country.

    Trading companies reduce risk for firms that want to get involved in international marketing. A trading company provides producers with information about products that meet quality and price expectations in domestic and international markets. Additional services a trading company may provide include consulting, marketing research, advertising, insurance, product research and design, legal assistance, warehousing, and foreign exchange.

trading company A company that links buyers and sellers in different countries

9-4c Licensing and Franchising

When potential markets are identified across national boundaries, and when production, technical assistance, or marketing know-how is required, **licensing** is an alternative to direct investment. The licensee (the owner of the foreign operation) pays commissions or royalties on sales or supplies used in manufacturing. The licensee may also pay an initial down payment or fee when the licensing agreement is signed. Exchanges of management techniques or technical assistance are primary reasons for licensing agreements. Yoplait, for example, is a French yogurt that is licensed for production in the United States; the Yoplait brand tries to maintain a French image. Similarly, sports organizations like the International Olympic Committee (IOC), which is responsible for the Olympic Games, typically concentrate on organizing their sporting events while licensing the merchandise and other products that are sold.

Licensing is an attractive alternative when resources are unavailable for direct investment or when the core competencies of the firm or organization are not related to the product being sold (such as in the case of Olympics merchandise). Licensing can also be a viable alternative when the political stability of a foreign country is in doubt. In addition, licensing is especially advantageous for small manufacturers wanting to launch a well-known brand internationally.

Franchising is a form of licensing in which a company (the franchisor) grants a franchisee the right to market its product, using its name, logo, methods of operation, advertising, products, and other elements associated with the franchisor's business, in return for a financial commitment and an agreement to conduct business in accordance with the franchisor's standard of operations. This arrangement allows franchisors to minimize the risks of international marketing in four ways: (1) the franchisor does not have to put up a large capital investment, (2) the franchisor's revenue stream is fairly consistent because franchisees pay a fixed fee and royalties, (3) the franchisor retains control of its name and increases global penetration of its product, and (4) franchise agreements ensure a certain standard of behavior from franchisees, which protects the franchise name.[77]

9-4d Contract Manufacturing

Contract manufacturing occurs when a company hires a foreign firm to produce a designated volume of the firm's product (or a component of a product) to specification and the final product carries the domestic firm's name. The Gap, for example, relies on contract manufacturing for

licensing An alternative to direct investment that requires a licensee to pay commissions or royalties on sales or supplies used in manufacturing

contract manufacturing The practice of hiring a foreign firm to produce a designated volume of the domestic firm's product, or a component of it, to specification; the final product carries the domestic firm's name

Franchising
With more than 1,400 locations, Canada-based Yogen Früz frozen yogurt is one of the top global franchises.

some of its apparel; Nike uses contract manufacturers in Vietnam to produce many of its athletic shoes. Marketing may be handled by the contract manufacturer or by the contracting company.

Three specific forms of contract manufacturing have become popular in the last decade: outsourcing, offshoring, and offshore outsourcing. **Outsourcing** is defined as the contracting of noncore operations or jobs from internal production within a business to an external entity that specializes in that operation. For example, outsourcing certain elements of a firm's operations to China and Mexico has become popular. The majority of all footwear is now produced in China, regardless of the brand name on the shoe you wear. Services can also be outsourced. Recent years, however, have seen an increase in domestic manufacturing within the United States. On the other hand, higher costs make domestic manufacturing difficult for smaller organizations, and many are forced to outsource overseas to keep costs down. Conflicts between globalism and protectionism associated with nationalism have emerged, but most economists believe all trade is beneficial.[78]

Offshoring is defined as moving a business process that was done domestically at the local factory to a foreign country, regardless of whether the production accomplished in the foreign country is performed by the local company (e.g., in a wholly owned subsidiary) or a third party (e.g., subcontractor). Typically, the production is moved to reap the advantages of lower cost of operations in the foreign location. **Offshore outsourcing** is the practice of contracting with an organization to perform some or all business functions in a country other than the country in which the product will be sold. Today, some manufacturers that previously engaged in offshore outsourcing are moving production back to the United States to maintain quality and tighter inventory control, a process known as reshoring. However, offshoring still outpaces reshoring for U.S. manufacturers.[79]

9-4e Joint Ventures

In international marketing, a **joint venture** is a partnership between a domestic firm and a foreign firm or government. Joint ventures are especially popular in industries that require large investments, such as natural resources extraction or automobile manufacturing. Control of the joint venture may be split equally, or one party may control decision making. Joint ventures are often a political necessity because of nationalism and government restrictions on foreign ownership. Qualcomm formed a joint venture with Chinese chip maker Semiconductor Manufacturing International Corporation to produce semiconductors. It is believed that this joint venture will allow Qualcomm to gain a foothold in selling chips in the Chinese market.[80] Joint ventures may also occur when acquisition or internal development is not feasible or when the risks and constraints leave no other alternative.

Joint ventures also provide legitimacy in the eyes of the host country's citizens. Local partners have firsthand knowledge of the economic and sociopolitical environment and the workings of available distribution networks, and they may have privileged access to local resources (raw materials, labor management, and so on). However, joint venture relationships require trust throughout the relationship to provide a foreign partner with a ready means of implementing its own marketing strategy. Joint ventures are assuming greater global importance because of cost advantages and the number of inexperienced firms that are entering foreign markets. They may be the result of a trade-off between a firm's desire for completely unambiguous control of an enterprise and its quest for additional resources.

Strategic alliances are partnerships formed to create a competitive advantage on a worldwide basis. They are very similar to joint ventures, but while joint ventures are defined in scope, strategic alliances are typically represented by an agreement to work together (which can ultimately mean greater involvement than a joint venture). In an international strategic alliance, the firms in the alliance may have been traditional rivals competing for the same market. They may also be competing in certain markets while working together in other markets where it is beneficial for both parties. One such strategic alliance was formed between accounting firm Ernst & Young and career networking site LinkedIn. The purpose of the relationship is to help companies with their ability to use technology, social networking, and sales.[81] Whereas joint ventures are formed to create a new identity, partners in strategic alliances often retain their distinct identities, with each partner bringing a core competency to the union.

outsourcing The practice of contracting noncore operations with an organization that specializes in that operation

offshoring The practice of moving a business process that was done domestically at the local factory to a foreign country, regardless of whether the production accomplished in the foreign country is performed by the local company (e.g., in a wholly owned subsidiary) or a third party (e.g., subcontractor)

offshore outsourcing The practice of contracting with an organization to perform some or all business functions in a country other than the country in which the product will be sold

joint venture A partnership between a domestic firm and a foreign firm or government

strategic alliances Partnerships that are formed to create a competitive advantage on a worldwide basis

The success rate of international alliances could be higher if a better fit between the companies existed. A strategic alliance should focus on a joint market opportunity from which all partners can benefit. In the automobile, computer, and airline industries, strategic alliances are becoming the predominant means of competing internationally. Competition in these industries is so fierce and the costs of competing on a global basis are so high that few firms have all the resources needed to do it alone. Firms that lack the internal resources essential for international success may seek to collaborate with other companies. A shared mode of leadership among partner corporations combines joint abilities and allows collaboration from a distance. Focusing on customer value and implementing innovative ways to compete create a winning strategy.

9-4f Direct Ownership

Once a company makes a long-term commitment to marketing in a foreign country that has a promising market as well as a suitable political and economic environment, **direct ownership** of a foreign subsidiary or division is a possibility. Most foreign investment covers only manufacturing equipment or personnel because the expenses of developing a separate foreign distribution system can be tremendous. The opening of retail stores in Europe, Canada, or Mexico can require a staggering financial investment in facilities, research, and management.

The term **multinational enterprise**, sometimes called *multinational corporation (MNC)*, refers to a firm that has operations or subsidiaries in many countries. Often, the parent company is based in one country and carries on production, management, and marketing activities in other countries. The firm's subsidiaries may be autonomous so they can respond to the needs of individual international markets, or they may be part of a global network led by the headquarters' operations.

At the same time, a wholly owned foreign subsidiary may be allowed to operate independently of the parent company to give its management more freedom to adjust to the local environment. Cooperative arrangements are developed to assist in marketing efforts, production, and management. A wholly owned foreign subsidiary may export products to the home country, its market may serve as a test market for the firm's global products, or it may be a component of the firm's globalization efforts. Some U.S. automobile manufacturers, for example, import cars built by their foreign subsidiaries. A foreign subsidiary offers important tax, tariff, and other operating advantages. Table 9.6 lists some major multinational companies around the world.

direct ownership A situation in which a company owns subsidiaries or other facilities overseas

multinational enterprise A firm that has operations or subsidiaries in many countries

Table 9.6 Multinational Corporations from Around the World

Company	Country	Description
Royal Dutch Shell	Netherlands	Oil and gas
Toyota	Japan	Automobiles
Walmart	United States	Retail
Siemens	Germany	Electronics and engineering
Nestlé	Switzerland	Nutritional, snack-food, and health-related consumer goods
Samsung	South Korea	Subsidiaries specializing in electronic components, telecommunications equipment, medical equipment, and more
Unilever	United Kingdom	Consumer goods including cleaning and personal care, foods, beverages, and more
Boeing	United States	Aerospace and defense
Lenovo	China	Computer technology
Subway	United States	Largest fast-food chain

One of the greatest advantages of a multinational enterprise is the ability to adopt a cross-cultural approach. A subsidiary usually operates under foreign management so it can develop a local identity. In particular, the firm (i.e., seller) is often expected to adapt, if needed, to the buyer's culture. This may become less of an advantage over time as the cultural values of younger consumers (under 30 years of age) are becoming increasingly similar around the world. Today, a 20-year-old in Russia is increasingly similar in mindset to a 20-year-old in China and a 20-year-old in the United States, especially with regard to their tastes in music, clothes, cosmetics, and technology. This makes marketing goods and services to the younger population easier today than it was only a generation ago. Nevertheless, there is still great danger involved in having a wholly owned subsidiary in some parts of the world due to political uncertainty, terrorism threats, and economic instability. After the terrorist attacks in Paris, France, for instance, many large firms, including Coca-Cola Enterprises and Priceline Group, became more concerned about geopolitical risk because they receive 30 percent or more of their revenue from Europe.[82]

Whereas the most well-known multinational corporations come from developed countries, the world is seeing a rise in MNCs from emerging economies as well. Brazil's Embraer (an aircraft company) and South Africa's MTN (a mobile phone company) are two examples. India's Tata Group is even beginning to rival more established MNCs. Tata owns several firms that qualify as MNCs, specializing in such diverse products as cars, hotels, steel, and chemicals.

Learning Objective 9-5

Examine various forms of global organizational structures.

9-5 GLOBAL ORGANIZATIONAL STRUCTURES

Firms develop their international marketing strategies and manage their marketing mixes (i.e., product, distribution, promotion, and price) by developing and maintaining an organizational structure that best leverages their resources and core competencies. This organizational structure is defined as the way a firm divides its operations into separate functions and/or value-adding units and coordinates its activities. Most firms undergo a step-by-step development in their internationalization efforts of the firm's people, processes, functions, culture, and structure. The pyramid in Figure 9.2 symbolizes how deeply rooted the international operations and values are in the firm, with the base of the pyramid—structure—being the most difficult to change (especially in the short term). Three basic structures of international organizations exist: export departments, international divisions, and internationally integrated structures (e.g., product division structures, geographic area structures, and matrix structures). The existing structure of the firm, or the structure that the firm chooses to adopt, has implications for international marketing strategy.

9-5a Export Departments

As we described earlier, the early stages of international development for most firms are often informal and not fully planned. During this early stage, sales opportunities in the global marketplace motivate a company to engage internationally. For instance, born global firms make exporting a primary objective from their inceptions. A unique case of developing a successful export operation early after its inception is the born global firm of Logitech International. Founded in 1981, Logitech is a Swiss company that designs personal computer peripherals that enable people to effectively work, play, and communicate in the digital world. For most firms, however, very minimal, if any, organizational adjustments take place to accommodate international sales. Foreign sales are typically so small that many firms cannot justify allocating structural or other resources to the internationalization effort in the infancy of internationalization. Exporting, licensing, and using trading companies are preferred modes of international market entry for firms with an export department structure.

Figure 9.2	Organizational Architecture

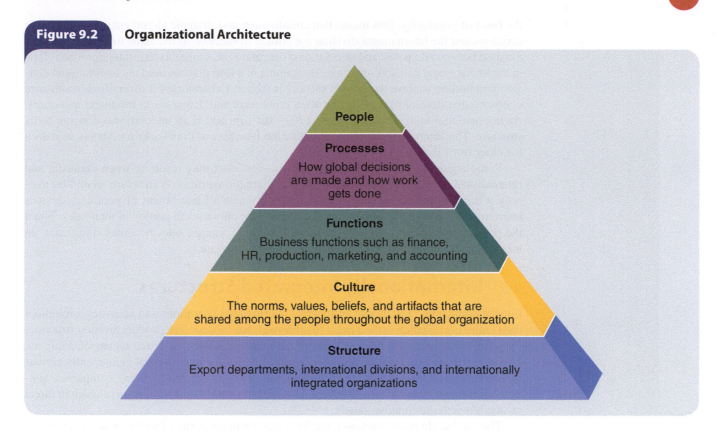

People

Processes
How global decisions
are made and how work
gets done

Functions
Business functions such as finance,
HR, production, marketing, and accounting

Culture
The norms, values, beliefs, and artifacts that are
shared among the people throughout the global organization

Structure
Export departments, international divisions, and internationally
integrated organizations

Some firms develop an export department as a subunit of the marketing department, whereas others organize it as a separate department at an equal level with the other functional units. Some companies choose to hire outside export departments to handle their international operations. Lone Star Distribution, a distributor for sports and nutritional supplements, has an export department that helps its clients transport their goods internationally.[83]

As demand for a firm's goods and services grows or its commitments increase due to its internationalization efforts, it develops an international structure. Many firms evolve from using their export department structure to forming an international division.

9-5b International Divisions

As a company gains greater international exposure and sales, it may centralize all of the responsibility for international operations and all international activities into an international division. The typical international division concentrates human resources (with international expertise) into one unit and serves as the central point for all information flow related to international operations, such as international market opportunities or international research and development. At the same time, firms with an international division structure take advantage of economies of scale by keeping manufacturing and related functions within the domestic divisions. Firms may develop international divisions at any stage of their international development. However, an increasing number of firms are recognizing the importance of going global early on. As such, these firms use exporting, licensing and franchising, trading companies, contract manufacturing, and joint ventures as possible modes of international market entry.

The implementation of an international division highlights the importance of coordination and cooperation among domestic and international operations within a firm. Frequent interaction and strategic planning meetings are required to make this structure work effectively. In particular, firms that use an international division structure are often organized domestically on the basis of functions or product divisions, while the international division is organized on the basis of geography. This means that coordination and strategic alignment across domestic divisions and the international division are critical to success. At the same time, lack of coordination between domestic and international operations is commonly the most significant flaw in the international division structure. An example of a firm that has used the international division structure to achieve worldwide success is Abbott Laboratories, a diversified health-care company that develops products that span prevention and diagnosis to treatment and cures. As international sales grew in the late 1960s, the firm added an international division to its structure. This international division structure has benefits and drawbacks for Abbott, as it does for other firms that use it.[84]

Some argue that to offset the natural "isolation" that may result between domestic and international operations in this structure, the international division structure should be used only when a company (1) intends to market only a small assortment of goods or services internationally and (2) when foreign sales account for only a small portion of total sales. When the product assortment increases or the percentage of foreign sales becomes significant, an internationally integrated structure may be more appropriate.

9-5c Internationally Integrated Structures

Finally, companies may choose to integrate international operations and activities throughout their entire organization in their quest to achieve global success. The product division structure, the geographic area structure, and the global matrix structure are three means of doing so. Firms with these varied structures have multiple choices for international market entry similar to international divisions (e.g., exporting, licensing and franchising, trading companies, contract manufacturing, and joint ventures). However, they are the most likely to engage in direct ownership activities internationally.

The product division structure is the form used by the majority of multinational enterprises. This structure lends itself to firms that are diversified, often driven by their current domestic operations. Each division is a self-contained entity with responsibility for its own operations, whether it is based on a country or regional structure. The worldwide headquarters maintains the overall responsibility for the strategic direction of the firm, while each product division is in charge of its implementation. Procter & Gamble has a long-standing tradition of operating in a product division structure, with leading brands like Pampers, Tide, Pantene, Bounty, Charmin, Downy, Crest, and Olay.

The geographic area structure is well suited to firms with a low degree of diversification. Under this domestically influenced functional structure, the world is divided into logical geographical areas based on the firms' operations and the customers' characteristics. Accenture, a global management consulting firm, operates worldwide largely based on a geographic area structure. Each area tends to be relatively self-contained, and integration across areas is typically via the worldwide or the regional headquarters. This structure facilitates local responsiveness, but it is not ideal for reducing global costs and transferring core knowledge across the firm's geographic units. A key issue in geographic area structures, as in almost all multinational corporations, is the need to become more regionally and globally integrated.

The global matrix structure was designed to achieve both global integration and local responsiveness. Asea Brown Boveri (ABB), a Swedish-Swiss engineering multinational, is the best-known firm to implement a global matrix structure. ABB is an international leader in power and automation technologies that enable customers to improve their performance while lowering environmental impact. Global matrix structures theoretically facilitate a simultaneous focus on realizing local responsiveness, cost efficiencies, and knowledge transfers. However, few firms can operate a global matrix well, because the structure is based on, for example, product and geographic divisions simultaneously (or a combination of any two traditional structures). This means that employees belong to two divisions and often report to two managers throughout the hierarchies of the firm. An effectively implemented global matrix structure has the benefit of being global in scope while also being nimble and responsive locally. However, a poorly implemented global matrix structure results in added bureaucracy and indecisiveness in leadership and implementation.

9-6 CUSTOMIZATION VERSUS GLOBALIZATION OF INTERNATIONAL MARKETING MIXES

Learning Objective 9-6
Describe the use of the marketing mix internationally.

Like domestic marketers, international marketers develop marketing strategies to serve specific target markets. Traditionally, international marketing strategies have customized marketing mixes according to cultural, regional, and national differences. Table 9.7 provides a sample of international issues related to product, distribution, promotion, and price. For example, many developing countries lack the infrastructure needed for expansive

Table 9.7 **Marketing-Mix Issues Internationally**

Sample International Issues	
PRODUCT ELEMENT	
Core Product	Is there a commonality of the customer's needs across countries? What will the product be used for and in what context?
Product Adoption	How is awareness created for the product in the various country markets? How and where is the product typically bought?
Managing Products	How are truly new products managed in the country markets vis-á-vis existing products or products that have been modified slightly?
Branding	Is the brand accepted widely around the world? Does the home country help or hurt the brand perception of the consumer?
DISTRIBUTION ELEMENT	
Marketing Channels	What is the role of the channel intermediaries internationally? Where is value created beyond the domestic borders of the firm?
Physical Distribution	Is the movement of products the most efficient from the home country to the foreign market or to a regional warehouse?
Retail Stores	What is the availability of different types of retail stores in the various country markets?
Retailing Strategy	Where do customers typically shop in the targeted countries—in department stores, specialty stores, online, or through direct selling?
PROMOTION ELEMENT	
Advertising	Some countries' customers prefer firm-specific advertising instead of product-specific advertising. How does this affect advertising?
Public Relations	How is public relations used to manage the stakeholders' interests internationally? Are the stakeholders' interests different worldwide?
Personal Selling	What product types require personal selling internationally? Does it differ from how those products are sold domestically?
Sales Promotion	Is coupon usage a widespread activity in the targeted international markets? What other forms of sales promotion should be used?
PRICING ELEMENT	
Core Price	Is price a critical component of the value equation of the product in the targeted country markets?
Analysis of Demand	Is the demand curve similar internationally and domestically? Will a change in price drastically change demand?
Demand, Cost, and Profit Relationships	What are the fixed and variable costs when marketing the product internationally? Are they similar to the domestic setting?
Determination of Price	How do the pricing strategy, environmental forces, business practices, and cultural values affect price?

distribution networks, which can make it harder to get the product to consumers. Realizing that both similarities and differences exist across countries is a critical first step to developing the appropriate marketing strategy effort targeted to particular international markets. Today, many firms strive to build their marketing strategies around similarities that exist instead of customizing around differences.

For many firms, **globalization** of marketing is the goal; it involves developing marketing strategies as though the entire world (or its major regions) were a single entity: a globalized firm markets standardized products in the same way everywhere. Global brands are emerging that are rapidly losing their associations with individual countries.[85] Nike and Adidas shoes, for example, are standardized worldwide. Other examples of globalized products include electronic communications equipment, Western-style clothing, movies, soft drinks, music, cosmetics, and toothpaste. In this advertisement, UPS demonstrates globalization through its depiction of flags from various countries. UPS is using this advertisement to inform consumers that it is a global logistics firm that reaches across the world.

For many years, organizations have attempted to globalize their marketing mixes as much as possible by employing standardized products, distribution channels, promotion campaigns, and prices for all markets. The economic and competitive payoffs for globalized marketing strategies are certainly great. Brand name, product characteristics, packaging, and labeling are among the easiest marketing-mix variables to standardize; media allocation, retail outlets, and price may be more difficult. In the end, the degree of similarity among the various environmental and market conditions determines the feasibility and degree of globalization. A successful globalization strategy often depends on the extent to which a firm is able to implement the idea of "think globally, act locally."[86] Even take-out food lends itself to globalization: McDonald's, KFC, and Taco Bell restaurants satisfy hungry customers in both hemispheres, although menus may be altered slightly to satisfy local tastes. When 7-Eleven opened stores in the United Arab Emirates, it sold its signature Slurpee drinks but also offered more local fare such as hummus, curries, and samosas.[87]

International marketing demands some strategic planning if a firm is to incorporate foreign sales into its overall marketing strategy. International marketing activities often require customized marketing mixes to achieve the firm's goals. Globalization requires a total commitment to the world, regions, or multinational areas as an integral part of the firm's markets; world or regional markets become as important as domestic ones. Global brands exist in an increasingly local world where consumer behavior, economic conditions, and distribution systems differ. Therefore, global brands may shift to local responsibility for marketing strategy implementation.[88] Regardless of the extent to which a firm chooses to globalize its marketing strategy, extensive environmental analysis and marketing research are necessary to understand the needs and desires of the target market(s) and successfully implement the chosen marketing strategy.

A global presence does not automatically result in a global competitive advantage. However, a global presence generates five opportunities for creating value: (1) to adapt to local market differences, (2) to exploit economies of global scale, (3) to exploit economies of global scope, (4) to mine optimal locations for activities and resources, and (5) to maximize the transfer of knowledge across locations.[89] To exploit these opportunities, marketers need to conduct marketing research and work within the constraints of the international environment and regional trade alliances, markets, and agreements.

globalization The development of marketing strategies that treat the entire world (or its major regions) as a single entity

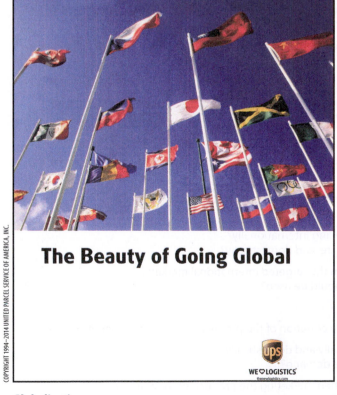

The Beauty of Going Global

UPS
WE ♥ LOGISTICS
thenewlogistics.com

Globalization
UPS demonstrates that it is a global firm by depicting flags from various countries waving in the wind.

CREATIVE MARKETING

Airbnb: Flying High Globally

Airbnb has come a long way since it was founded by Brian Chesky and Joe Gebbia when they turned their apartment into a bed and breakfast so they could afford to pay rent. They recognized that a customer need existed that was not being met: the desire to stay in less expensive but homier lodgings. Like Uber, Airbnb embraces the sharing economy concept that promotes the sharing of human and physical resources. The target market was initially conference attendees but soon expanded to all types of travelers. Today Airbnb connects travelers to lodgings in 65,000 cities across 191 countries.

Those who wish to rent their extra room or house can set their own prices, and Airbnb takes 3 percent of the booking price. Airbnb believes it can create more value for more customers. For example, the company launched Experiences where hosts can offer events and classes to create local activities for travelers. Since its launch, Airbnb global weekly bookings increased more than 2,000 percent.

Some regulators believe Airbnb encourages owners of multiple properties to rent them in the short-term rather than turning them into long-term residences—thus disrupting urban housing. For example, Detroit, with more than 430 Airbnb hosts, banned the rental of many residential properties. While Airbnb has been successful in many countries, the company has struggled in China due to turnover in management and competition from similar, locally based services. However, with international expansions and acquisitions, Airbnb doesn't plan to slow down anytime soon.[b]

Summary

9-1 Define international marketing.

International marketing involves developing and performing marketing activities across national boundaries. International markets can provide tremendous opportunities for growth and renewed opportunity for the firm.

9-2 Differentiate between the environmental forces that affect international marketing efforts.

A detailed analysis of the environment is essential before a company enters an international market. Environmental aspects of special importance include sociocultural; economic; political, legal, and regulatory; social and ethical; competitive; and technological forces. Because marketing activities are primarily social in purpose, they are influenced by beliefs and values regarding family, religion, education, health, and recreation. Cultural differences may affect marketing negotiations, decision-making behavior, and product adoption and use. A nation's economic stability and trade barriers can affect marketing efforts. Significant trade barriers include import tariffs, quotas, embargoes, and exchange controls. Gross domestic product (GDP) and GDP per capita are common measures of a nation's economic standing. Political and legal forces include a nation's political system, laws, regulatory bodies, special-interest groups, and courts. In the area of ethics, cultural relativism is the concept that morality varies from one culture to another and that business practices are, therefore, differentially defined as right or wrong by particular cultures. In addition to considering the types of competition and the types of competitive structures that exist in other countries, marketers also need to consider the competitive forces at work and recognize the importance of the global customer who is well informed about product choices from around the world. Advances in technology have greatly facilitated international marketing.

9-3 List important international trade agreements.

Various regional trade alliances and specific markets create both opportunities and constraints for companies engaged in international marketing. Important trade agreements include the North

American Free Trade Agreement, European Union, Southern Common Market, Asia-Pacific Economic Cooperation, Association of Southeast Asian Nations, and World Trade Organization.

9-4 Identify methods of international market entry.

There are several ways to enter international marketing. Importing (the purchase of products from a foreign source) and exporting (the sale of products to foreign markets) are the easiest and most flexible methods. Marketers may employ a trading company, which links buyers and sellers in different countries but is not involved in manufacturing and does not own assets related to manufacturing. Licensing and franchising are arrangements whereby one firm pays fees to another for the use of its name, expertise, and supplies. Contract manufacturing occurs when a company hires a foreign firm to produce a designated volume of the domestic firm's product to specification, and the final product carries the domestic firm's name. Joint ventures are partnerships between a domestic firm and a foreign firm or government. Strategic alliances are partnerships formed to create competitive advantage on a worldwide basis. Finally, a firm can build its own marketing or production facilities overseas. When companies have direct ownership of facilities in many countries, they may be considered multinational enterprises.

9-5 Examine various forms of global organizational structures.

Firms develop their international marketing strategies and manage their marketing mixes by developing and maintaining an organizational structure that best leverages their resources and core competencies. Three basic structures of international organizations include export departments, international divisions, and internationally integrated structures (e.g., product division structures, geographic area structures, and matrix structures).

9-6 Describe the use of the marketing mix internationally

Although most firms adjust their marketing mixes for differences in target markets, some firms standardize their marketing efforts worldwide. Traditional full-scale international marketing involvement is based on products customized according to cultural, regional, and national differences. Globalization, however, involves developing marketing strategies as if the entire world (or its major regions) were a single entity; a globalized firm markets standardized products in the same way everywhere. International marketing demands some strategic planning if a firm is to incorporate foreign sales into its overall marketing strategy.

Important Terms

international marketing 242
gross domestic product (GDP) 245
import tariff 248
quota 249
embargo 249
exchange controls 249
balance of trade 249
cultural relativism 251
North American Free Trade Agreement (NAFTA) 253

European Union (EU) 254
Southern Common Market (MERCOSUR) 256
Asia-Pacific Economic Cooperation (APEC) 256
Association of Southeast Asian Nations (ASEAN) 257
World Trade Organization (WTO) 258

General Agreement on Tariffs and Trade (GATT) 258
dumping 258
importing 259
exporting 259
trading company 260
licensing 261
contract manufacturing 261
outsourcing 262

offshoring 262
offshore outsourcing 262
joint venture 262
strategic alliances 262
direct ownership 263
multinational enterprise 263
globalization 268

Discussion and Review Questions

1. How does international marketing differ from domestic marketing?
2. What factors must marketers consider as they decide whether to engage in international marketing?
3. Why are the largest industrial corporations in the United States so committed to international marketing?

4. Why do you think this chapter focuses on an analysis of the international marketing environment?
5. If you were asked to provide a small tip (or bribe) to have a document approved in a foreign nation where this practice is customary, what would you do?

6. How will NAFTA affect marketing opportunities for U.S. products in North America (the United States, Mexico, and Canada)?
7. What should marketers consider as they decide whether to license or enter into a joint venture in a foreign nation?
8. Discuss the impact of strategic alliances on international marketing strategies.

9. Contrast globalization with customization of marketing strategies. Is one practice better than the other?
10. What are some of the product issues that need to be considered when marketing luxury automobiles in Australia, Brazil, Singapore, South Africa, and Sweden?

Developing Your Marketing Plan

When formulating marketing strategy, one of the issues a company must consider is whether or not to pursue international markets. Although international markets present increased marketing opportunities, they also require more complex decisions when formulating marketing plans. To assist you in relating the information in this chapter to the development of your marketing plan, focus on the following:

1. Review the environmental analysis that was completed in Chapter 3. Extend the analysis for each of the seven factors to include global markets.

2. Using Figure 9.1 as a guide, determine the degree of international involvement that is appropriate for your product and your company.
3. Discuss the concepts of customization and globalization for your product when moving to international markets. Refer to Table 9.7 for guidance in your discussion.

Video Case 9.1

Alibaba and Global E-Commerce: Should Amazon Be Afraid?

From rural farmers to multimillionaires, millions of people in China are reaping economic opportunities from the growing e-commerce market. One entrepreneur earns $5 million in sales annually from his ladies' handbag e-commerce business—a far cry from his humble origins. Although his success might be the exception to the norm, many Chinese consumers with similar backgrounds have found jobs working in e-commerce.

"We grew up in a rural area which left us few choices. I never thought about my future or had any belief in it," the entrepreneur says.

At the center of this is Alibaba, an online marketplace founded by entrepreneur Jack Ma in 1999. Jack Ma conceived of an online portal that could connect Chinese manufacturers with buyers from other countries. He chose the name Alibaba because it was globally recognized based upon the famous character in the collection *Arabian Nights*. Today, this multibillion-dollar company serves more than 600 million customers in 240 nations. Alibaba has held tightly to its top spot in China where non-Chinese e-commerce

sites like eBay and Amazon have struggled. Alibaba, with a 47 percent market share in China's online retail market, has made it more difficult for businesses to compete on price. Ma's vision for expanding international business includes plans to increase Alibaba's revenue outside China from 10 percent of total revenues to 50 percent.

Alibaba has a number of trading platforms that sell to both business-to-business (B2B) and business-to-consumer (B2C) markets. Its B2C market portal, Taobao, has been termed the Chinese version of Amazon.com or eBay. Taobao has enabled rural farmers to start their own businesses and created employment opportunities for locals. Because of its influence, entire Taobao Villages have sprung up across China. These villages consist of residents who operate in e-commerce. Today, there are estimated to be 780 Taobao Villages in China.

This is just the beginning for Alibaba. In 2014 it was listed on the U.S. stock exchange with an initial public offering (IPO) of $25 billion, the largest IPO to date. To emphasize its global intentions, Alibaba opened offices in

France, Germany, and Italy. It is also focused on selling more international brands such as Macy's, Apple, and L'Oréal. In its quest to expand into media, Alibaba entered into a licensing agreement with Disney to sell a streaming device that will broadcast movies, television shows, e-books, games, and more.

TESTING/SHUTTERSTOCK.COM

Although it is listed on the U.S. stock exchange, investing in Alibaba differs from the traditional model due to regulatory and legal barriers. The Chinese government restricts foreign investment in certain areas, meaning that global investors outside of China cannot own shares of Alibaba outright. In reality, investors purchase shares of a shell corporation in the Cayman Islands. Alibaba itself owns all of its non-Chinese assets. Jack Ma has the most power in the company, and some investors are concerned about his tendency to make large decisions or transfer ownership without consulting many other people.

Another issue that Alibaba is coming across as it expands involves counterfeit products. In China, counterfeit goods have traditionally been more accepted than in other countries. Its international e-commerce site AliExpress has gained widespread popularity in Russia, the United States, and Brazil, but its rise in popularity has been accompanied by a rise in counterfeit goods sold through the site. Regulators are worried that the site is allowing counterfeits to

go straight from Chinese manufacturers to consumers on a global scale. In fact, Kering SA—a French luxury group—filed a lawsuit against Alibaba accusing the firm of knowingly allowing the sale of counterfeit products. Alibaba denies the charges and is working with government bodies to improve counterfeiting controls.

Despite the risks of investing in a firm that they cannot actually own, investors were eager to purchase shares during Alibaba's initial public offering. China, with approximately 890 million online shoppers, is overtaking the United States as the largest e-commerce market, and the opportunities are too good for many investors to pass up. They believe Alibaba has the potential for massive global growth as it is less capital intensive and, therefore, more flexible than global rivals such as Amazon.com.[90]

Questions for Discussion

1. What are some of the barriers Alibaba is facing as it expands globally?
2. How has Taobao created economic opportunities for Chinese entrepreneurs that were inaccessible to them before?
3. Why would the sale of counterfeit products through its sites be damaging to Alibaba?

Case 9.2

Netflix Stream Becomes a Global River

When Netflix was launched in 1997, few people could envision it would one day topple the former market leader for video rental, Blockbuster. Customers were attracted to Netflix's low subscription prices and lack of late fees. Netflix used the U.S. Postal Service to mail DVDs straight to the home, saving consumers a trip to the video store. Its superiority in price and distribution were only the beginning of Netflix's marketing prowess. Netflix is taking on the world as it becomes available in more countries. It became one of the first U.S. companies to expand into Cuba, and with a presence in about 190 countries, Netflix

has announced its intention to enter into every country in the world.

The key to Netflix's rapid international expansion is its globalized approach. Because Netflix is an internet streaming service, it is easily obtained by any household with a strong enough internet connection. Its products and distribution channels are, therefore, highly standardized. As more consumers become connected to the internet worldwide, Netflix is taking advantage of the opportunity to reach them. Currently, it has more than 117 million subscribers who watch more than 140 million hours of content daily.

Netflix is also moving its marketing strategy to focus less on pricing and more on its original content programming, including international content. For example, the company announced its first Polish original series directed by Agnieszka Holland and Kasia Adamik. Additionally, a collaboration with the Australian Broadcasting Corporation resulted in a six-hour international political thriller by screenwriter Greg Haddrick and Felicity Packard. Netflix's original content is rivaling traditional television shows and movies. Today, Netflix has not only conquered the rental movie industry, it is convincing more people around the globe to give up cable and direct television in favor of streaming.

DANIEL KRASON/SHUTTERSTOCK.COM

Despite Netflix's advantage, competitors like Amazon Prime are making inroads in the streaming industry. This requires Netflix to continually improve its marketing strategy and adapt to cultural differences. For instance, consumers in some countries favor using mobile devices over computers. Netflix has adapted its streaming services to display effectively on mobile devices. It has also adopted mobile payment options such as Google Play and iTunes so subscribers can complete transactions straight from their phones. Netflix's constantly evolving marketing strategy is key to the firm maintaining its strong competitive edge.

However, even companies with a globalization approach face certain challenges that vary by country. U.S. sanctions on Syria and North Korea currently prevent Netflix from entering those countries. It was also forced to abandon its original plans to launch in China due to the country's government restrictions. Instead, Netflix has decided to license content to local firms rather than launching its own service. In Cuba, the price for its services is about half the monthly salary of the average Cuban worker. Payments must be made with credit or debit cards that are not accessible to the majority of Cubans. Netflix may, therefore, have to customize its payment options. Finally, Netflix's success depends upon how much of the population has sufficient internet connections. Only about 34 percent of Cubans have internet access. Despite these struggles, there is still plenty of room for international growth and expansion.[91]

Questions for Discussion

1. Why do you think Netflix has an easier time expanding into some countries than others?
2. Describe some of the forces acting as barriers to Netflix in various countries.
3. Do you think Netflix's international original content will contribute to international growth? Why or why not?

CHAPTER

10

Digital Marketing and Social Networking

LEARNING OBJECTIVES

10-1 Define digital media, digital marketing, and electronic marketing.

10-2 Summarize the growth and importance of digital marketing.

10-3 Describe different types of digital media and how they can be used for marketing.

10-4 Describe how marketers can measure the success of a digital strategy.

10-5 Describe how digital media affect the four variables of the marketing mix.

10-6 Identify legal and ethical considerations in digital marketing.

VDOVICHENKO DENIS/SHUTTERSTOCK.COM

Best Buy Uses Digital Marketing to Live Up to Its Name

Retail is a fast-paced environment that can be difficult to handle, and Best Buy is no exception. With the rise of e-commerce, the company saw revenue fall while operating costs increased. To combat online giant Amazon, Best Buy's CEO introduced a turnaround strategy that placed an emphasis on online sales and the shopping experience.

Best Buy has used single text messages (SMS), mobile banner ads, and apps to better connect to relevant consumers. Keeping its customers' needs and desires in mind, Best Buy designed its mobile app to easily allow users to research products and connect with a sales associate, creating a seamless shopping experience via mobile, desktop, and its traditional retail spaces. Best Buy has been recognized as a leader in mobile marketing strategy with aggressive mobile marketing initiatives that support its omni-channel retailing efforts. The company recognizes that many shoppers research products both online and in-store before making a final purchase.

Best Buy is turning its attention to enhanced SMS communication. The company has partnered with 3C Interactive to expand on its text message communication systems and go beyond basic text-based messages. The new technology will allow the tech retailer to send product images, maps for store pick-up, and more purchase details. This initiative will provide customers with more information as well as a more personalized shopping experience.

By matching prices with Amazon and providing a stellar in-store as well as online experience, Best Buy has increased sales significantly. CEO Hubert Joly announced a new initiative that looks to not just sell products but solve its customers' needs by improving the customer experience across channels.[1]

Since the 1990s, the internet and information technology have dramatically changed the marketing environment and the strategies that are necessary for marketing success. Digital media have created exciting opportunities for companies to target specific markets more effectively, develop new marketing strategies, and gather more information about customers. Using digital media channels, marketers are better able to analyze and address consumer needs. Fueled by changing technology, consumer behavior has changed with internet-enabled consumer empowerment. This has resulted in a shift in the balance of power between consumer and marketer.[2]

One of the defining characteristics of information technology in the 21st century is accelerating change. New systems and applications advance so rapidly that unexpected new innovations appear that can change existing assumptions about digital marketing opportunities. For example, digital assistants that function as a personal information manager were not in wide use a few years ago. Now, Amazon and Google are connecting consumers to the internet based on voice commands. Now you can order products, create a shopping list, and of course obtain music, news, and weather. How this will affect digital marketing will evolve. Email, smartphones, social networking, drones, and even driverless vehicles are shaping the marketing environment. All of these advances in technology relate to how consumers make decisions about products. In this chapter we focus more on social media marketing but digital marketing is a broad field that provides opportunity to develop relationships with consumers.

While digital marketing has many benefits and opportunities, there are also challenges. Today, consumers often have to sacrifice their privacy to use and engage digital technology. As firms gather information on consumers to employ in marketing research, there are dangers of data breaches and online crime. Data analytics associated with big data to understand consumers opens the door to identity theft, online fraud, and other cybercrimes. There are regulatory issues relating to what types of consumer data can be stored and what firms should do to protect consumer data. We address these issues later in the chapter. With more than 3.8 billion people accessing the internet worldwide, marketers are seeing their digital marketing strategies reach consumers from different parts of the world like never before.[3]

In this chapter, we focus on digital marketing strategies—particularly communication channels such as social networks—and discuss how consumers are changing their information searches and consumption behaviors to fit with the emerging technologies and trends. Most importantly, we analyze how marketers can use new media to their advantage to connect with consumers, gather more information about their target markets, and convert this information into successful marketing strategies.

Learning Objective 10-1

Define digital media, digital marketing, and electronic marketing.

digital media Electronic media that function using digital codes—media available via computers, cellular phones, smartphones, and other digital devices that have been released in recent years

digital marketing The use of all digital media, including the internet and mobile and interactive channels, to develop communication and exchanges with customers

electronic marketing or **e-marketing** The strategic process of distributing, promoting, and pricing products, and discovering the desires of customers using digital media and digital marketing

10-1 DEFINING DIGITAL MARKETING

Before we move on, we must first provide a definition of digital media. **Digital media** are electronic media that function using digital codes—when we refer to digital media, we are referring to media available via computers, smartphones, and other smart devices, including wearable technology and televisions that have been released in recent years. A number of terms have been coined to describe marketing activities on the internet. **Digital marketing** uses all digital media, including the internet and mobile and interactive channels, to develop communication and exchanges with customers. In this chapter, we focus on how the internet relates to all aspects of marketing, including strategic planning. Thus, we use the term **electronic marketing**, or **e-marketing**, to refer to the strategic process of distributing, promoting, and pricing products, and discovering the desires of customers using digital media and digital marketing. Although there are differences between the terms, many people use *digital marketing* and *electronic marketing* interchangeably. In addition, we sometimes use the term *e-tailing* to describe online retailing. Our definition of e-marketing goes beyond the internet and also includes mobile phones, banner ads, digital outdoor marketing, and social networks.

10-2 GROWTH AND BENEFITS OF DIGITAL MARKETING

The phenomenal growth of the internet has provided unprecedented opportunities for marketers to forge interactive relationships with consumers. As the internet and digital communication technologies have advanced, they have made it possible to target markets more precisely and reach markets that were previously inaccessible. As the world of digital media continues to develop, e-marketing has developed strategies that include all digital media, including television advertising and other mobile and interactive media that do not use the internet (advertising media are discussed in detail in Chapter 17). In fact, marketers are using the term *digital marketing* as a catch-all for capturing all digital channels for reaching customers. This area is progressing rapidly, and the digital world is evolving into effective marketing strategy integration.[4]

One of the most important benefits of e-marketing is the ability of marketers and customers to share information. Through websites, social networks, and other digital media, consumers can learn about everything they consume and use in life. As a result, the internet is changing the way marketers communicate and develop relationships. Today's marketers can use the internet to form relationships with a variety of stakeholders, including customers, employees, and suppliers. For example, IBM's digital assistant allows IBM customers to identify and digitally interact with key experts through a variety of platforms. IBM's Watson is an assistant in cognitive computing impacting fields as diverse as finance, medicine, and education. This results in the need to adjust marketing strategies to the digital world. Digital marketing and social media permit innovative forms of communication and co-created content in relationship-based interactions.[5]

For many businesses, engaging in digital and online marketing activities is essential to maintaining competitive advantages. Increasingly, small businesses can use digital media to develop strategies to reach new markets and access inexpensive communication channels. In addition, large companies like Target use online catalogs and company websites to supplement their brick-and-mortar stores. At the other end of the spectrum, companies like Amazon.com and Alibaba, which have traditionally lacked physical stores and sell products solely online, are challenging traditional brick-and-mortar businesses. Amazon is taking on department stores and big-box stores such as Walmart and Home Depot. Department stores such as Macy's and Sears have had to close hundreds of stores and some shopping centers have gone out of business.[6] Social networking sites are advancing e-marketing by providing features to aid in commerce, such as the ability to view daily deals or purchase items using Facebook. Finally, some corporate websites and social media sites provide feedback mechanisms through which customers can ask questions, voice complaints, indicate preferences, and otherwise communicate about their needs and desires.

Blue Bottle Coffee uses Slack, an easy-to-use messaging app that integrates with your existing tools and gathers all your communication in one place. It's teamwork made simpler, more pleasant, and more productive.

brewbetter .slack.com

✳ slack
work on purpose

SOURCE: SLACK

New Business Opportunities
Businesses are using the messaging app Slack to integrate their communication tools and bring all of their communication to one place.

Table 10.1   Characteristics of Online Media

Characteristic	Definition	Example
Addressability	The ability of the marketer to identify customers before they make a purchase	Amazon installs cookies on a user's computer that allow the company to identify the user when he or she returns to the website.
Interactivity	The ability of customers to express their needs and wants directly to the firm in response to its marketing communications	Texas Instruments interacts with its customers on its Facebook page by answering concerns and posting updates.
Accessibility	The ability for marketers to obtain digital information	Google can use web searches done through its search engine to learn about customer interests.
Connectivity	The ability for consumers to be connected with marketers along with other consumers	Mary Kay offers users the opportunity to sign up for MyMK, a system that connects customers with beauty consultants and allows them to develop their own personalized space.
Control	The customer's ability to regulate the information they view as well as the rate and exposure to that information	Consumers use Kayak.com to discover the best travel deals.

This increase in digital promotions is providing new business opportunities for internet services. Slack is a messaging app that brings all communication together into one place. This is particularly helpful for businesses because it enables them to engage in real-time messaging. As the advertisement demonstrates, Blue Bottle—a U.S. coffee roaster and retailer in Oakland, California—uses Slack to enhance communication and teamwork.

One of the biggest mistakes a marketer can make when engaging in digital marketing is to treat it like a traditional marketing channel. Digital media offer a whole new dimension to marketing that marketers must consider when concocting their companies' marketing strategies. The quality of a website will have a major impact on whether the customer exhibits loyalty to the site. Website aesthetics, navigational quality, information content, and information quality positively impact the level of a customer's relative loyalty to the e-tailer website.[7] Some of the characteristics that distinguish online media from traditional marketing include addressability, interactivity, accessibility, connectivity, and control, as defined in Table 10.1.

Learning Objective 10-3

Describe different types of digital media and how they can be used for marketing.

10-3   TYPES OF CONSUMER-GENERATED MARKETING AND DIGITAL MEDIA

Although digital and e-marketing have generated exciting opportunities for producers of products to interact with consumers, it is essential to recognize that social media are more consumer-driven than traditional media. Consumer-generated material is having a profound effect on marketing. As the internet becomes more accessible worldwide, consumers are creating and reading consumer-generated content like never before. Social networks and advances in software technology provide an environment for marketers to utilize consumer-generated content.

Two major trends have caused consumer-generated information to gain importance:

1. The increased tendency of consumers to publish their own thoughts, opinions, reviews, and product discussions through blogs or digital media.

2. Consumers' tendencies to trust other consumers over corporations. Consumers often rely on the recommendations of friends, family, and fellow consumers when making purchasing decisions.

By understanding where online users are likely to express their thoughts and opinions, marketers can use these forums to interact with consumers, address problems, and promote their companies. It is also helpful for targeting certain demographics. For example, young adults aged 16 to 24 favor Instagram, Twitter, Snapchat, Pinterest, and Tumblr, though many use other sites including blogs, wikis, media-sharing sites, virtual reality gaming, mobile devices, applications and widgets, and more.

10-3a Social Media Marketing

Social media marketing involves establishing communications with consumers through social media sites. Social media marketing enables firms to promote a message and create online conversations through multiple platforms. Large markets can be targeted and reached through paid media, owned media, and earned media.[8] Traditional paid media includes traditional print and broadcast but is now joined by paid advertising on social networks such as Facebook and Twitter. Marketers can place ads on Google just like they place an ad on television. On Facebook, which has more than 5 million advertisers, brands can pay to boost posts, create compelling photo carousel ads, promote their page, and more.[9] In addition to placing ads, marketers can own their own media outlets and create messages on social networks. Most firms have owned websites but can also develop websites through such social networking services as Facebook and LinkedIn. Finally, markets can have earned media when consumers are communicating on social media sites. These digital word-of-mouth posts or interactions can promote a product or firm. Although it is not controllable like advertising, if the communication is positive, it increases sales.[10]

User-generated content relates to consumers that create, converse, rate, collect, join, or simply read online materials. For example, when a consumer posts a selfie on Instagram with a Mountain Dew in hand, this is user-generated content. Marketers can access the creative efforts of consumers that post or publish on publicly accessible websites, such as blogs, like *A Beautiful Mess* and *Modern Martha*, or on social networking sites such as LinkedIn. These user-generated sites often involve self-disclosure where consumers share their knowledge, interests, and desire to join or associate with others. Participating in discussions to connect and network with others is a major motivating factor to influence others or to promote an interest or cause. There are many critics involved in user-generated content. These consumers comment on different subjects, post evaluations on blogs, and post ratings and reviews. If you have ever posted a product review or rated a movie, you have engaged in this activity. Evaluating what critics post should be an important part in a company's digital marketing strategy. Of course consumers read ratings to aid their shopping purchases. Yelp is one of the most comprehensive review sites on products and businesses. Yelp, with more than 140 million reviews, continues to expand its platform, adding "Questions and Answers" for users to ask venue-specific questions for other users to answer.[11] Therefore, these rating sites can be helpful to collect information to be used in marketing research and to monitor firm reputation.

Marketers need to analyze their target markets and determine the best social media approach to support marketing objectives. Social media should be included in both the corporate and marketing strategy. It should be a part of the firm's marketing plan and implementation efforts. Social media can be used to monitor target market competitors and understand the social and economic environment as a whole. Social media has the potential to build campaigns that produce advocates and enthusiasts of a firm's products. For example, Dodge uses social media to release product teasers and news to its engaged fans. The brand rewarded its most engaged social media fans by inviting a limited number to the unveiling of the 2018 Dodge Challenger SRT Demon.[12] Marketing should be focused on relationship building, and social media can influence consumer behavior and deliver value to the firm.

Social networks have been integrated into marketing strategies. A **social network** is a website where users can create a profile and interact with other users, post information, and engage in other forms of web-based communication. Marketing is evolving from digital into strategic interactive marketing that facilitates two-way communication. Allowing consumers to opt-in or opt-out of programs facilitates communication without intruding on privacy.[13]

social network A website where users can create a profile and interact with other users, post information, and engage in other forms of web-based communication

Another benefit of social networking is marketers' ability to reach out to new target markets. Snapchat is a mobile photo messaging application that allows users to send photos, messages, or videos to their friends for a certain amount of time. After that time the post is deleted from both the recipient's phone and Snapchat servers. Snapchat has grown immensely popular with Millennials, a popular but difficult demographic for marketers to reach. When Snap Inc., Snapchat's parent company, debuted on the stock market, the stock value was up 44 percent by the end of its first day of trading, giving the company a $33 billion valuation.[14] Many countries also have their own, much smaller, social networking sites that marketers should consider when trying to reach global populations. For instance, VK, based in Russia, is a popular social networking site in Europe; while QZone, which has 632 million users, is popular in China.[15] More information on how marketers use social networks is provided in later sections of this chapter.

Social networks are building business models for economic success. As Figure 10.1 demonstrates, the majority of social network users are between the ages of 18 and 29, but other age groups are not that far behind. Seventy-nine percent of online adults use Facebook, which continues to be the most popular social media platform by far. The second most popular platform, Instagram, attracts 32 percent of online adults.[16] As social networks evolve, both marketers and the owners of social networking sites are realizing the incredible opportunities such networks offer—an influx of advertising dollars for social networking owners and a large reach for the advertiser. The challenge to improve the brand is to expand the range of social media used and to target various stakeholders that should be a part of the dialogue. Therefore, social media is a part of corporate communication and brand-building strategy.[17] The following social networks we examine are among the most important to marketers worldwide.

Facebook

Facebook is the most popular social networking site in the world. When it was launched in 2004 by Harvard student Mark Zuckerberg and four of his classmates, it was initially limited to Harvard students. In 2006, the site was opened to anyone aged 13 or older. Internet users create Facebook profiles and then search the network for people with whom to connect. The social networking giant has surpassed 2 billion users and is still growing. It has also acquired

Figure 10.1 **Social Networking Use by Age and Year**

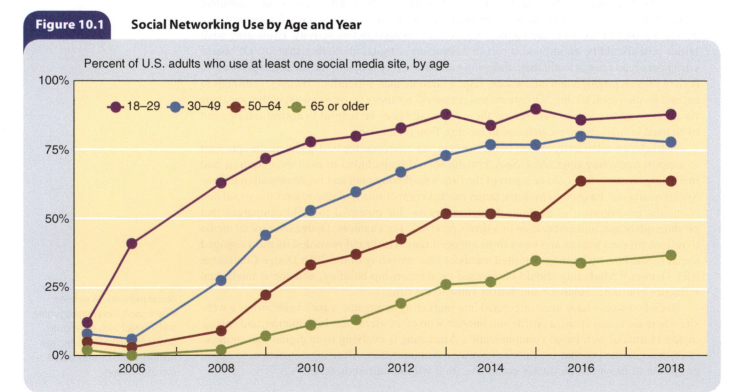

Source: Pew Research Center surveys, 2005–2018. No data are available for 2007 and 2017.

a number of companies as it expands into other services, including Instagram, WhatsApp, and Oculus.[18]

Organizations also use Facebook and other digital media sites to give special incentives to customers. Doritos released 11,500 limited-edition rainbow chip bags in support of the LGBTQ community, only the chips were never available for sale. To receive a bag, customers had to donate a sum of $10 or more to the It Gets Better Project and post a supportive quote on social media using #boldandbetter. This not only engaged customers, resulting in 30 times more Facebook shares than the brand's average, but also made the Doritos brand

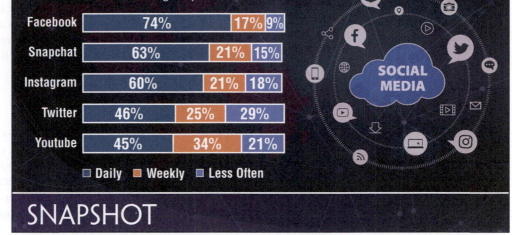

How Often Do You Use Social Media?

Among the users of each social media site, the percent who use that site with the following frequencies.

	Daily	Weekly	Less Often
Facebook	74%	17%	9%
Snapchat	63%	21%	15%
Instagram	60%	21%	18%
Twitter	46%	25%	29%
Youtube	45%	34%	21%

SNAPSHOT

Source: Pew Research Center study conducted January 3–10, 2018.

Note: Numbers may not add up to 100 due to rounding.

appear more authentic to the public.[19] Advertising on Facebook has also been increasing. The firm generates more than $12 billion in annual advertising revenues and allows advertisers to target ads to users based upon their web-browsing habits.[20]

Additionally, social networking sites are useful for relationship marketing, or the creation of relationships that mutually benefit the marketing business and the customer. A poll revealed that 30 percent of consumers claim social media has some influence on their purchasing decisions. This is leading firms to focus more on the quality of their Facebook interactions rather than simply their quantity. Ritz-Carlton, for instance, now spends more time analyzing its social media conversations and reaching out to noncustomers. The emphasis is shifting from simply selling a product or promoting a brand to developing a mutually beneficial relationship in which the brand provides the user with a positive outcome.[21] Thanks to Facebook, companies that are focused upon building and enhancing customer relationships are better able to understand who their customers are and how they can meet their needs.

Twitter

Twitter is a hybrid mix of a social networking site and a microblogging site that asks viewers one simple question: "What's happening?" Users can post answers of up to 280 characters, which are then available for their "followers" to read. A limitation of 280 characters may not seem like enough for companies to send an effective message, but some have become experts at using Twitter in their marketing strategies. For instance, American Airlines was ranked as the top airline on Twitter due to its customer engagement and responsiveness.[22] For sports enthusiasts, the National Football League developed a deal with Twitter to feature football video highlights, pictures, and clips on the site. Twitter also sells all of the advertising for the NFL that is tied to tweets.[23]

Snapchat

While Snap Inc. admits it may never achieve profitability, posting a net loss of approximately $514 million in recent years, investors see value in Snapchat, which has more than 187 million daily active users.[24] The mobile app, launched in 2011, allows users to send messages and disappearing photos and videos to friends. The parent company prefers to think of itself as a camera company rather than a social media company, and plans to release more lifestyle products like Spectacles, camera glasses sold at Snapchat pop-up shops, outside of its social media platform.[25] Marketers are looking at Snapchat as an opportunity to reach their young, highly engaged audience. Brands like Taco Bell, Sour Patch Kids, and Birchbox have taken to Snapchat to engage with their audiences.

Snapchat, which features skippable, vertical video ads and custom photo filters, is used mostly by users under the age of 34. In fact, 85 percent of daily users are between 18 and 34.[26] Universal Pictures created a custom lens in the app, a special filter that alters a user's picture, to promote the movie *Fifty Shades Darker*, enabling users to add a masquerade mask to their photo. Other films promoted on Snapchat include *Office Christmas Party*, *Ghostbusters*, and *Sing*.[27] One of Snapchat's biggest challenges will be scaling its advertising dollars to achieve its revenue goals.

YouTube

Purchased by Google for $1.65 billion, YouTube allows users to upload and share videos worldwide. Users watch a billion hours of YouTube videos every day, making this popular video platform an important part of marketing strategy.[28] Though brands use the platform to release original video content, consumers far outnumber them on the platform. For example, beauty brands on YouTube are outnumbered by beauty vloggers in beauty searches by 14 to 1.[29] This makes it challenging for brands to control messaging about their products on the platform.

YouTube continues to diversify its video offering with YouTube Red and YouTube TV. YouTube Red expands upon the original platform allowing users to pay for uninterrupted music, ad-free and offline video, and original programming from top creators. As more homes cancel their cable packages, YouTube TV is an affordable alternative. For $35 per month users can watch ABC, CBS, and NBC among other top networks, positioning the service as a competitor to Sling TV and DirecTV Now.[30]

LinkedIn

LinkedIn is the top networking site for businesses and business professionals. This networking tool allows users to post a public profile, similar to a resume, connect with colleagues, find job listings, and join private groups. Eighty percent of B2B marketers say LinkedIn is an effective business lead generator.[31] This platform can also be used to spread brand awareness and for corporate recruiting. HubSpot, an inbound marketing and sales platform with more than 200,000 followers, uses LinkedIn to spread its content, promote free webinars, and increase awareness around inbound marketing.[32]

10-3b Blogs and Wikis

Today's marketers must recognize the impact of consumer-generated material like blogs and wikis, as their significance to online consumers has increased a great deal. **Blogs** (short for "weblogs") are web-based journals in which writers can editorialize and interact with other internet users. It is estimated that 33 percent of Millennials read blogs before they make a purchase.[33] Many bloggers use Twitter and Facebook to announce a new blog post with a link and a photo to encourage users to click on it. The blogging site Tumblr, which allows anyone to post text, hyperlinks, pictures, and other media for free, is particularly popular with younger consumers. The site has approximately 396 million blogs. In 2013, Yahoo! purchased Tumblr for $1.1 billion. Although marketers are eager to reach the younger demographic that uses Tumblr, many are unsure how to market effectively through the site. To make it easier, Tumblr set up a network that pairs advertisers with Tumblr artists and bloggers.[34]

Blogs give consumers control, sometimes more control than companies would like. Whether or not the blog's content is factually accurate, bloggers can post whatever opinions they like about a company or its products. Although companies have filed lawsuits against bloggers for defamation, they usually cannot prevent the blog from going viral. Responding

blogs Short for "weblogs," these are web-based journals in which writers editorialize and interact with other internet users

INTEGRITY IN MARKETING

Social Media Advertisers Fight Fake News

Social networks have changed the marketing discipline, in many ways benefiting companies that use their services. However, there are always those who take advantage of social media to earn money through fraudulent means. A more recent concern is the propagation of fake news. During major events such as elections, fake news stories abound. The more popular the story shared on social media sites—whether factual or false—the higher up it is in users' news feeds. This has allowed fake news stories to spread virally across social media.

Although some of these perpetrators have their own personal agendas, many spread fake news on social media sites because it directs interested users to their own websites. Once users are on the fraudsters' websites, they are presented with a number of ads that earn the fraudsters money from advertisers if clicked on. Hence, fraudsters disseminating fake news want to convince users to visit their phony news websites because they hope users will click on ads posted there.

CEO Mark Zuckerberg originally denied fake news claims, alleging that 99 percent of Facebook posts were authentic; however, due to the criticism Facebook and Google have faced, they started to take steps to identify fake news stories. Google announced that it would ban fake news from its advertising platform, while Facebook is relying on its users to vet news sources to improve news feed integrity through ongoing quality surveys. Facebook is also reducing the amount of news appearing in the news feed to 4 percent.[a]

to a negative blog posting is a delicate matter. For instance, although companies sometimes force bloggers to remove blogs, readers often create copies of the blog and spread it across the internet after the original's removal. In other cases, a positive review of a product posted on a popular blog can result in large increases in sales. Thus, blogs can represent a potent threat to corporations as well as an opportunity.

Many businesses use blogs to their advantage. Rather than trying to eliminate blogs that cast their companies in a negative light, some marketers are using such blogs to answer consumer concerns or defend their corporate reputations. Many major corporations have created their

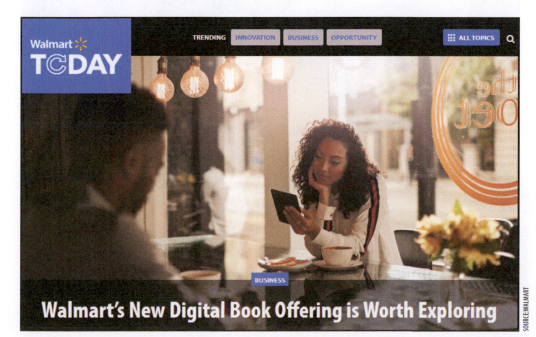

Walmart's New Digital Book Offering is Worth Exploring

Blogging
Many businesses, such as Walmart, create their own blogs to drive web traffic, provide product education, and encourage loyalty.

own blogs or encourage employees to blog about the company. Bill Marriott, current Executive Chairman of Marriott International, maintains a blog called "Marriott on the Move" where he not only discusses the hotel business but posts on a number of insightful business and inspirational topics to engage his readers.[35] As blogging changes the face of media, companies like Marriott are using blogs to build enthusiasm for their products and develop customer relationships.

A **wiki** is a type of software that creates an interface that enables users to add to or edit the content of some types of websites. One of the best known is Wikipedia, an online encyclopedia with more than 40 million articles in 293 languages on nearly every subject imaginable.[36] Wikipedia is consistently one of the top 10 most popular sites on the web. Like all social media, wikis have advantages and disadvantages for companies. Wikis on controversial companies like Walmart and Nike often contain negative publicity about the companies. However, some companies have begun to use wikis as internal tools for teams working on a project requiring lots of documentation.[37] Additionally, monitoring wikis provides companies with a better idea of how consumers feel about the company brand.

There is too much at stake financially for marketers to ignore blogs and wikis. Despite this fact, statistics show that only about a third of *Fortune* 500 companies have a corporate blog.[38] Marketers who want to form better customer relationships and promote their company's products must not underestimate the power of these two tools as new media outlets.

10-3c **Media-Sharing Sites**

Marketers share their corporate messages in more visual ways through media-sharing sites. Media-sharing sites allow marketers to share photos, videos, and podcasts but are more limited in scope in how companies interact with consumers. They tend to be more promotional-oriented. This means that while firms can promote their products through videos or photos, they usually do not interact with consumers through personal messages or responses. At the same time, the popularity of these sites has the potential to reach a global audience of consumers.

Photo-sharing sites allow users to upload and share their photos with the world. Well-known photo-sharing sites include Flickr, Shutterfly, Snapfish, and Instagram. Flickr is a popular photo-sharing site on the internet. A Flickr user can upload images, edit them, classify the

wiki Type of software that creates an interface that enables users to add to or edit the content of some types of websites

SAITALAT PHUKKUM/SHUTTERSTOCK.COM

Social Photo Sharing
Flickr, Shutterfly, Snapfish, and Instagram allow users to share photos with a variety of other people on the internet.

images, create photo albums, and share photos or videos with friends without having to email bulky image files or send photos through the mail. Instagram is a mobile photo-sharing site that has surpassed Flickr in popularity. Instagram allows its 800 million users to manipulate their photos with different tints and share them with their friends.[39] To compete against Snapchat, Instagram introduced Instagram Stories, a way for its users to send their friends messages that disappear in 24 hours.[40] Facebook purchased Instagram for $1 billion with the intention of breaking into the mobile industry.[41] With more people using mobile apps or accessing the internet through their smartphones, the use of photo sharing through mobile devices is increasing.

Other sites are emerging that take photo sharing to a new level. Pinterest is a photo-sharing bulletin board that combines photo sharing with elements of bookmarking and social networking. Users can share photos and images with other internet users, communicating mostly through images that they "pin" to their boards. Other users can "repin" these images to their boards, follow each other, "like" images, and make comments. Marketers have found that an effective way of marketing through Pinterest is to post images conveying a certain emotion that represents their brand.[42] It has become so popular that it has surpassed Google+ in number of users. Because Pinterest users create boards that deal with their interests, marketers also have a chance to develop marketing messages encouraging users to purchase the product or brand that interests them. Pinterest hopes to learn how to influence a customer to proceed from showing interest in a product to having an intent to purchase. This knowledge will be helpful to advertisers marketing through Pinterest's website.[43] Pinterest added a feature called Lens that allows users to take a picture of an object and find a list of pins with similar looking objects, further establishing the platform as a discovery tool for shopping.[44]

Photo sharing represents an opportunity for companies to market themselves visually by displaying snapshots of company events, company staff, and/or company products. For example, pasta brand Buitoni has purchased advertising through Pinterest and features recipes on its board. Pinterest offers tools for support and consultations to advertisers in the retailing and consumer-packaging industries.[45] Digital marketing companies are also scanning photos and images on photo-sharing sites to gather insights about how brands are being displayed or used. These companies hope to offer these insights to big-name companies such as Kraft.[46] The opportunities for marketers to use photo-sharing sites to gather information and promote brands appear limitless.

Another popular form of media sharing is video-sharing sites. These sites allow virtually anybody to upload videos, from professional marketers at *Fortune* 500 corporations to the average internet user. Some of the most popular video-sharing sites include YouTube and Vimeo along with live streaming video platform Twitch. Video-sharing sites give companies the opportunity to upload ads and informational videos about their products. A few videos become viral at any given time, and although many of these gain popularity because they embarrass the subject in some way, others reach viral status because people find them entertaining (viral marketing will be discussed in more detail in Chapter 16). Marketers are seizing upon opportunities to use this viral nature to promote awareness and use of their products.

A new trend in video marketing is the use of amateur filmmakers. Entrepreneurs have begun to realize that they can use consumer-generated content to their advantage. Video-sharing websites give businesses the chance to capitalize on consumer-generated content. They also provide would-be video bloggers with the chance to create a name for themselves, which in turn could catch the attention of major companies. Consider the case of Bethany Mota, who started uploading videos to YouTube when she was 13. Since then she has started weekly videos featuring the makeup and clothing that she wears. As a charismatic presenter with 10.5 million subscribers, she has promoted different fashion brands, written a book, and even developed her own fashion, accessory, and fragrance collection at Aéropostale.[47] These types of videos are more authentic and create enthusiasm for products among consumer participants. They become an electronic word-of-mouth form of communication that supports brand image.

With the rise of bloggers and social media stars like Michelle Phan and Eva Gutowski, brands are turning to influencers to promote their products. Brands identify influencers who align with their brand image and often pay them for an endorsement or send complimentary product in exchange for a review. Roughly 22 percent of businesses are seeing higher customer acquisition rates through influencer marketing than traditional channels like email and search marketing.[48] Brands can contact influencers directly or use paid platforms like TapInfluence and BrandBacker to identify ideal partners and manage campaigns. Influenster is a product sampling program that puts products in the hands of influencers and micro-influencers in exchange for authentic, user-generated content on social media. With a community of more than 4 million, brands are able to identify users who fall into their target demographic through data collected on the platform along with pre-qualification surveys. Once a user receives a set of products, Influenster drives social posts, in-store actions, and product reviews by incentivizing the influencers with a "Brand Badge." To receive the digital badge and retain membership privileges, users must participate in activities dictated by the brand, such as writing a review on a blog, posting a photo on Instagram, or uploading video using the products on YouTube.[49]

podcasts Audio or video files that can be downloaded from the internet with a subscription that automatically delivers new content to listening devices or personal computers

Podcasting, traditionally used for music and radio broadcasts, is also an important digital marketing tool. **Podcasts** are audio or video files that can be downloaded from the internet with a subscription that automatically delivers new content to listening devices or personal computers. Podcasts offer the benefit of convenience, giving users the ability to listen to or view content when and where they choose. American Public Media's Marketplace is a business news show on the radio that has downloadable podcasts. The advertisement describes three podcasts involving different topics in business news that users can download. If they choose to subscribe, they will automatically get new content when it is uploaded. Companies can use podcasts to demonstrate how to use their products or understand certain features. As podcasting continues to catch on, radio and television networks like CBC Radio, NPR, MSNBC, and PBS are creating podcasts of their shows to profit from this growing trend. Through podcasting, many companies hope to create brand awareness, promote their products, and encourage customer loyalty.

Podcasts
Consumers interested in business news can subscribe to Marketplace's three new podcasts and get updated content automatically.

10-3d Mobile Marketing

Mobile devices, such as smartphones, mobile computing devices, and tablet computers, allow customers to leave their desktops and access digital networks from anywhere. About 95 percent of American adults have a mobile device.[50] Many of these mobile devices are smartphones, which have the ability to access the internet, download apps, listen to music, take photographs, and more. It is estimated that 90 percent of those who use Facebook access the site through their phones.[51] Figure 10.2 breaks down smartphone ownership by age and activity. Mobile marketing is exploding—marketers worldwide spend about $206 billion on mobile advertising.[52]

Mobile marketing has proven effective in grabbing consumers' attention. In one study, 45 percent of consumers recalled a full-page ad shown through a smartphone device, compared to 38 percent who saw it on a desktop.[53] Capital One

Figure 10.2   **Smartphone Activities by Age**

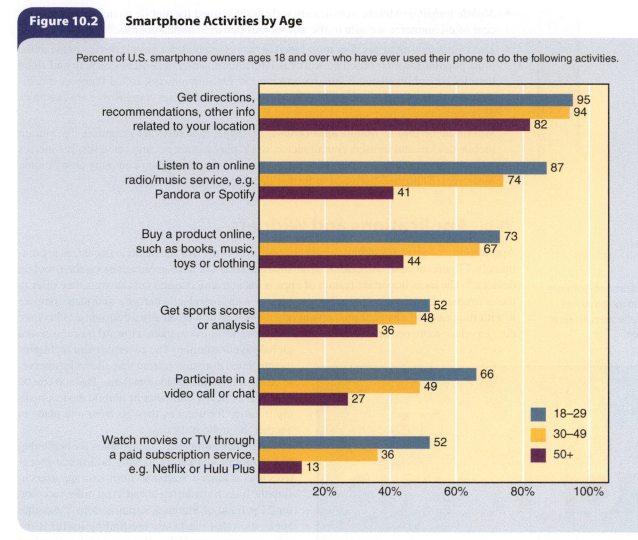

Percent of U.S. smartphone owners ages 18 and over who have ever used their phone to do the following activities.

Get directions, recommendations, other info related to your location
- 18–29: 95
- 30–49: 94
- 50+: 82

Listen to an online radio/music service, e.g. Pandora or Spotify
- 18–29: 87
- 30–49: 74
- 50+: 41

Buy a product online, such as books, music, toys or clothing
- 18–29: 73
- 30–49: 67
- 50+: 44

Get sports scores or analysis
- 18–29: 52
- 30–49: 48
- 50+: 36

Participate in a video call or chat
- 18–29: 66
- 30–49: 49
- 50+: 27

Watch movies or TV through a paid subscription service, e.g. Netflix or Hulu Plus
- 18–29: 52
- 30–49: 36
- 50+: 13

Legend: ■ 18–29   ■ 30–49   ■ 50+

Source: Pew Research Center survey conducted June 10–July 12, 2015.

saw its brand recall increase by 16 percent after it began advertising through the mobile social service Instagram.[54] Despite these promising trends, many brands have yet to take advantage of mobile marketing opportunities. Although most major businesses have websites, not all of these websites are easily viewable on mobile devices. It is also important for marketers to understand what types of promotions users prefer and when to show them. For instance, studies show that app users tend to dislike advertisements that show up while the app is in use but do like when brands provide them with information during the processing time of the app.[55]

To avoid being left behind, brands must recognize the importance of mobile marketing. Some of the more common mobile marketing tools include the following:

- *SMS messages:* SMS messages are single text messages of 160 characters or less. SMS messages can be used to send coupons to prospective customers.

- *Multimedia messages:* Multimedia messaging (MMS) takes SMS messaging a step further by allowing companies to send video, audio, photos, and other types of media over mobile devices. The MMS market is estimated to be a $20 billion market. Approximately 98 percent of all U.S. cell phones can receive MMS.[56]

- *Mobile advertisements:* Mobile advertisements are visual advertisements that appear on mobile devices. Companies might choose to advertise through search engines, websites, or games accessed on mobile devices. Mobile accounts for over half of digital advertising spending.[57]

- *Mobile websites:* Mobile websites are websites designed for mobile devices. Over 50 percent of e-commerce website traffic now comes through mobile devices.[58]

- *Location-based networks:* Location-based networks are built for mobile devices. One of the most popular location-based networks is Foursquare, which lets users check in and share their location with others. It introduced a new advertising network called Pinpoint specifically for marketers. Samsung Galaxy, Olive Garden, and Jaguar Land Rover are examples of companies that have used its new service.[59]

- *Mobile applications:* **Mobile applications,** or "apps," are software programs that run on mobile devices and let users communicate, work, play games, or carry out tasks. Businesses release apps to help consumers access more information about their company or to provide incentives. These are discussed in further detail in the next section.

10-3e **Applications and Widgets**

Applications, or apps, are adding an entirely new layer to the marketing environment, as approximately 77 percent of all American, adult smartphone users have applications on their mobile devices.[60] The most important feature of apps is the convenience and cost savings they offer to the consumer. Certain apps permit consumers to scan a product's barcode and then compare it with the prices of identical products in other stores or download store discounts. Others are developed for more personal purposes. The Hyperwallet app is marketed toward businesses as a global payout solution. The advertisement highlights its integrated donation feature that allows businesses to easily make charitable donations. The app can be accessed from any computer or mobile device, making it easier for users as they go from one place to another throughout the day.

mobile applications Software programs that run on mobile devices and give users access to certain content

To remain competitive, companies are beginning to use mobile marketing to offer additional incentives to consumers. Starbucks allows its app users to skip the lines by ordering ahead. App orders account for 21 percent of Starbuck's transactions.[61] Another application that marketers are finding useful is the QR scanning app. QR codes are black-and-white squares that sometimes appear in magazines, posters, and storefront displays. Smartphone users that have downloaded the QR scanning application can open their smartphones and scan the code, which contains a hidden message accessible with the app. The QR scanning app recognizes the code and opens the link, video, or image on the phone's screen. Marketers are using QR codes to promote their companies and offer consumer discounts.[62]

Increasingly, companies are taking advantage of beacon technology to target and communicate with app users based on their location. For example, retailers can place beacons throughout their stores, so when a shopper approaches one, it activates the retailer's app on the shopper's smartphone with custom messages and promotions. Macy's uses this technology in all of its U.S. stores to detect shopper's locations and present personalized offers.[63] Similarly, Marriott's LocalPerks initiative locates the mobile devices of Marriott guests to determine their location and send them daily deals and other marketing messages.[64] One large barrier is that consumers need the company's app installed on their

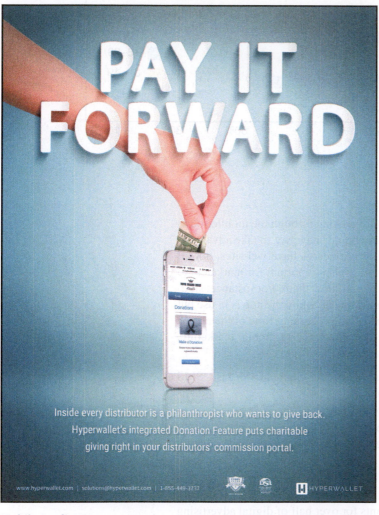

SOURCE: HYPERWALLET

Mobile Applications
The Hyperwallet app allows businesses to manage payments, transfer money, and make donations.

phone in order to receive beacon signals. Google aims to lower this barrier by sending Chrome browser-based notifications.[65] The applications for location-based technology will continue to expand as companies determine the new ways to deliver value to their customers.

Mobile technology is also making inroads in transforming the shopping experience. Not only can shoppers use mobile applications to compare prices or download electronic discounts, but they can also use mobile applications to tally up purchases and pay through their smartphones. Mobile payments are gaining traction, and companies like Google and Apple are working to capitalize on this opportunity.[66] Google Wallet and Apple Pay are mobile apps that allow users to pay with their phones. When the shopper is ready to check out, he or she can tap the phone at the point of sale for the transaction to be registered.[67] Square is a company that provides organizations with smartphone swiping devices for credit cards and tablets that can be used to tally purchases. Bitcoin is a virtual peer-to-peer currency used to make a payment via a smartphone. Smaller organizations have begun to accept Bitcoin at some of their stores. The success of digital payment systems in revolutionizing the shopping experience will largely depend upon retailers adopting this payment system, and companies like Starbucks are already rising to the opportunity.

Widgets are small bits of software on a website, desktop, or mobile device that perform a simple task, such as providing stock quotes or weather updates. Marketers might use widgets to display news headlines, clocks, or games on their webpages.[68] CNBC uses widgets to send alerts and financial news to subscribers. Widgets downloaded to a user's desktop can update the user on the latest company or product information, enhancing relationship marketing between companies and their fans. For instance, Toyota used a widget to place a social-media-driven photo gallery on one of its sites. Approximately 34 percent of users that visited the site clicked on the gallery.[69] Widgets are an innovative digital marketing tool to personalize webpages, alert users to the latest company information, and spread awareness of the company's products.

10-4 MONITORING DIGITAL MEDIA BEHAVIORS OF CONSUMERS

Learning Objective 10-4
Describe how marketers can measure the success of a digital strategy.

Consumers now have a greater ability to regulate the information that they view as well as the rate and sequence of their exposure to that information. The internet is sometimes referred to as a *pull* medium because users determine which websites they are going to view; the marketer has only limited ability to control the content to which users are exposed, and in what sequence. Today, blogs, wikis, podcasts, and ratings sites such as Yelp and Angie's List are used to publicize, praise, or challenge companies. Digital media require marketers to approach their jobs differently compared to traditional marketing. However, most companies in the United States do not routinely monitor consumers' postings to online social networking sites. In many cases, this represents a missed opportunity to gather information.

On the other hand, some companies are using the power of the consumer to their advantage. While negative ratings and reviews are damaging to a company, positive customer feedback is free publicity that often helps the company more than corporate messages do. Because consumer-generated content appears more authentic than corporate messages, it can go far in increasing a company's credibility. Additionally, while consumers can use digital media to access more information, marketers can also use the same sites to get information on the consumer—often more information than could be garnered through traditional marketing venues. They can examine how consumers are using the internet to target marketing messages to their audience. Finally, marketers are also using the internet to track the success of their online campaigns, creating an entirely new way of gathering marketing research.

10-4a Online Monitoring and Analytics

Without digital media monitoring and evaluation, it is not possible to maximize resources and minimize costs in social media marketing. The strength of measurement relates to the ability to have online analytics and metrics. Social media monitoring involves activities to track, measure, and evaluate a firm's digital marketing initiatives.[70] An advantage of digital marketing evaluations

widgets Small bits of software on a website, desktop, or mobile device that perform a simple task, such as providing stock quotes or blog updates

is that there are methods of capturing the metrics that indicate the outcomes of strategies. Therefore, establishing an expected level of performance creates a benchmark against which performance can be compared. Metrics develop from listening and tracking. For example, a firm could set up a hashtag and promote it. Metrics can be quantitative or qualitative. For example, click-through rate (CTR) determines the percentage of consumers who clicked on a link on a site as a quantitative measure. In addition, a qualitative metric could relate how consumers feel about a product.

Key Performance Indicators (KPIs) should be embedded at the onset of a social media strategy that can allow almost real-time measurement and evaluation. This provides a foundation for making iterative changes to implementation and tactical execution. Marketing analytics uses tools and methods to measure and interpret the effectiveness of marketing activities. Applying analytics to social media performance can help develop better-targeted social media campaigns. Selecting valid metrics requires specific objectives that the social media strategy is to obtain. Objectives that are quantitative could include the number of likes on an Instagram post or the CTR of a Facebook post. Table 10.2 provides a list of metrics based on exposure, engagement, influence, impact, and advocacy.

Table 10.2   Social Media Metrics

Exposure	Engagement	Influence	Impact	Advocacy
Quantitative	**Quantitative**	**Quantitative**	**Quantitative**	**Quantitative**
Page Visits	Repeat Visits	Links	New Subscribers	Online Ratings
Visitors, Unique Visitors	Time Spent on Site	Association with Brand Attributes	Number of Referrals to Website	Ratio Mentions to Recommendations
Visits per Channel (Source)	Total Interactions on Post/Page	Purchase Consideration	Number of Content Downloads	Number of Brand Fans/Advocates
Reach Total Follower (Audience Count)	Likes, Shares Comments, + 1s	Likelihood to Recommend	Number of App Downloads	
	Click-Throughs		Abandoned Shopping Carts (−)	
Opportunity-to-See	Number of Followers, Friends		Number of Sales Leads	
			Conversion Rate	
CPM (cost per thousand exposures)	Total Audience of All Shares		Sales	
			Repeat Sales	
	Interaction with Profile		Purchase Frequency	
	Use of Hashtags		Cost Savings	
	Qualitative	**Qualitative**	**Qualitative**	**Qualitative**
	Mentions	Sentiment (Positive, Neutral, Negative)	Satisfaction	Content of Ratings/Reviews
	People Talking About Brand		Loyalty	
		Net Promoter Score		Organic Posts by Advocates
		Klout Score		Employee Ambassadors

Table 10.3   Google Analytics

Real-Time	Data updates live so you can see pageviews, top social traffic, top referrals, top keywords, top active pages, and top locations in real-time.
Audience	Audience reports provide insight into demographics, interested, geography, behavior, mobile use, and more.
Acquisition	In-bound traffic is monitored through acquisition reports, allowing you to compare traffic from search, referrals, email, and social media.
Behavior	Evaluates your site's content by seeing how visitors interact with your content. Monitors landing pages, exit pages, site speed, bounce rate, and more.
Conversions	Google Analytics allows users to set goals and objectives to monitor web conversions, like signing up for an email newsletter or completing a purchase.

A comprehensive performance evaluation requires gathering all valid metrics and understanding the way the strategy meets performance standards or underperforms based on expectations. One way to approach this is to use Google Analytics, the largest analytics platform monitoring more than 30 million websites.[71] The Google Analytics dashboard is broken down into five sections: Real-Time, Audience, Acquisition, Behavior, and Conversions. Table 10.3 explains the function of each section. Using this tool allows you to identify your website's strengths and weaknesses and uncover opportunities for growth. For example, you may find that organic search traffic is very high, but that your social media traffic is quite low, or you may see a spike in weekday traffic while weekends are slow. KPIs for your social media strategy can include likes, shares, reach, engagement rate, click-through rate (CTR), and conversions. In the conversions dashboard, marketers can set up custom conversion goals to see the impact social media has on their business.

By analyzing rich site traffic data, marketers can better understand their customers and measure the effectiveness of their marketing efforts. For example, PBS uses Google Analytics to monitor the web performance for multiple properties and track key events such as user registrations and video views. After analyzing search engine trends, PBS experienced 30 percent more site traffic in the first year after implementation.[72] Google Analytics is arguably the most robust web analytics tool available, and it's free to anyone with a Google account. A premium version, Google Analytics 360 Suite, designed to help companies target potential customers, is available for even more in-depth analytics. The tool identifies someone's habits from web and television to mobile, competing with companies like Salesforce and Oracle.

10-5   E-MARKETING STRATEGY

Learning Objective 10-5
Describe how digital media affect the four variables of the marketing mix.

More than one-fourth of the world's population uses the internet, and this number is growing at a high rate. This trend displays a growing need for businesses to use the internet to reach an increasingly technology-savvy population. As more shoppers go online for purchases, the power of traditional brick-and-mortar businesses is lessening.

This makes it essential for businesses, small and large alike, to learn how to effectively use new social media. Most businesses are finding it necessary to use digital marketing to gain or maintain market share. When Amazon.com first became popular as an online bookstore in the 1990s, the brick-and-mortar bookseller chain Barnes & Noble quickly made online shopping possible through its website, but did not abandon its physical stores. This "brick-and-clicks" model is now standard for businesses from neighborhood family-owned restaurants to national chain retailers. The following sections will examine how businesses are effectively using these social media forums to create effective marketing strategies on the web.

10-5a Product Considerations

In traditional marketing, marketers must anticipate consumer needs and preferences and then tailor their products to meet these needs. The same is true with marketing products using digital media. Digital media provide an opportunity to add a service dimension to traditional products and create new products that could only be accessible on the internet. For example, the digital platform Steam provides gamers access to thousands of video games for PC and Mac. These represent products that can only be found in the digital realm.

The ability to access information for any product can have a major impact on buyer decision making. However, with larger companies now launching their own extensive campaigns, and with the constant increase of sophistication of digital technology, many businesses are finding it necessary to continually upgrade their product offerings to meet consumer needs. In managing a product, it is important to pay attention to consumer-generated brand stories that address quality and performance and impact image.[73] As has been discussed throughout this chapter, the internet represents a large resource to marketers for learning more about consumer wants and needs.

Some companies now use online advertising campaigns and contests to help develop better products. For example, Volition, a skin care and cosmetics company, crowdsources its new product ideas from its customers. If an idea makes it past the Volition team, tens of thousands of people in the Volition community will vote online whether the product should be produced and then receive a discount if the product is voted in. Using their fan base for new ideas has led to unique and innovative products, and as consumers share their product ideas with their social networks for support from friends and family, awareness increases for this beauty community.[74]

Distribution Considerations

1-800-Flowers.com must consider distribution challenges including shipping times and costs to ensure fresh bouquets are delivered to its customers.

10-5b Distribution Considerations

The role of distribution is to make products available at the right time, at the right place, and in the right quantities. Digital marketing can be viewed as a new distribution channel that helps businesses increase efficiency. The ability to process orders electronically and increase the speed of communications via the internet reduces inefficiencies, costs, and redundancies while increasing speed throughout the marketing channel. Shipping times and costs have become an important consideration in attracting consumers, prompting many companies to offer consumers low shipping costs or next-day delivery. In the advertisement, 1-800-Flowers.com promises the season's freshest bouquets, plants, and gifts. 1-800-Flowers.com uses local florists to offer same-day delivery options for its floral arrangements and fruit bouquets.[75]

Many online retailers, such as Birchbox, Blue Nile, and Warby Parker, have established a presence in the traditional brick-and-mortar world to create a physical presence and increase awareness. Unlike most, Blue Nile's shops, called a "Webroom," are showrooms only, meaning customers can touch and feel the products, but all orders are placed online, saving the company money in distribution costs and real estate costs associated with large storefronts. This trend is a result of increased online competition as well as a trend toward **omni-channel** retailing where retailers offer a seamless experience on mobile, desktop, or traditional retail spaces. For example, many retailers aim to offer consistent product assortments and pricing on all channels as well as streamline the return process. A customer may research a purchase online, shop in-store, browse an in-store digital catalog, and then use a coupon from the retailer's app at checkout. Seventy-three percent of shoppers use multiple channels while shopping, making a seamless shopping experience a way to differentiate a retailer from its competitors. The survey revealed that research online before in-store shopping led to 13 percent more in sales among omni-channel shoppers.[76]

10-5c **Promotion Considerations**

The majority of this chapter has discussed ways that marketers use digital media to promote products, from creating profiles on social networks for connecting with consumers to inserting brands into virtual social games. Social networking sites also allow marketers to approach promotion in entirely new, creative ways. ColourPop is an example of a digital marketing

omni-channel Various marketing channels, including mobile, desktop, or traditional retail spaces, providing seamless customer experiences

success story. The company is online only and does no traditional advertising. Instead, it relies on social buzz developed through digital marketing. The company, known for its low price point, became popular through Instagram and YouTube and has a number of Millennial fans, including 5.6 million followers on its Instagram account, 762,000 followers on Twitter, and 1.6 million likes on Facebook. As a result, ColourPop is thriving at a time when the beauty market is more crowded than ever.[77] In the advertisement for Athleta, the women's athletic clothing company features #gratefulfor, tying in with its holiday Instagram challenge which encourages women to share stories of gratitude. The ad says, "you can't gift wrap the sound of snow crunching beneath her boots," suggesting that gifting her Athleta is about the experience. By promoting its campaign hashtag, the company encourages user-generated content that promotes the brand and reinforces the company's mission to empower women.[78] Marketers who choose to engage in these opportunities have the chance to boost their firms' brand exposure. Califia Farms, a natural beverage company, uses Instagram as a platform to showcase its iconic, award-winning packaging, teach consumers new ways to enjoy Califia Farms beverages, and educate consumers on the benefits of their ingredients.[79]

Online advertising includes many types of display advertising, including the use of text, logos, animation, video, photographs, or any other type of graphic display. Currently, internet advertising revenues surpass $72 billion and continue to grow. A major advantage of internet advertising is being able to track advertising statistics. High-impact digital advertisements featuring large and interactive formats drive higher response ratios. Marketers are tracking and maximizing internet advertising to

ATHLETA.COM

BECAUSE YOU CAN'T GIFT WRAP THE SOUND OF SNOW CRUNCHING BENEATH HER BOOTS.

#gratefulfor

SOURCE: ATHLETA

Promotion Considerations
Athleta uses Instagram to spread its #gratefulfor campaign which encourages Athleta fans to share stories of positivity and gratitude.

CREATIVE MARKETING

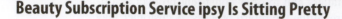

Beauty Subscription Service ipsy Is Sitting Pretty

After Michelle Phan was rejected for a job at a Lancôme Cosmetics, she used YouTube to display her passion for makeup. Within three years of posting videos, she had 690,000 subscribers. She became such a sensation that Lancôme, which had previously rejected her for employment, signed Phan up as its first video makeup artist. In 2012, Phan founded online subscription service ipsy.

The idea for ipsy came when Phan noticed how women prefer to purchase smaller samples of unfamiliar beauty products. Because beauty products are expensive, purchasing an unfamiliar cosmetic can be risky. Ipsy allows subscribers to try these products for a low monthly fee. The company acquires small samples from well-known beauty brands and makes them available to subscribers. For $10 a month, subscribers get a monthly "glam" bag of five beauty product samples.

To differentiate itself from its rivals, ipsy uses online beauty influencers on social media sites to market its services. Women who look up to these online celebrities are more likely to use ipsy's services. Due to its creative marketing strategy, Ipsy has surpassed 3 million subscribers.[b]

improve the value of their products.[80] Google's AdWords is the dominant player in the online advertising market, and the company wants to take its success into the mobile realm as well. To achieve its goals, Google launched an initiative called Enhanced Campaigns and required users of its AdWords service to participate. Enhanced Campaigns requires advertisers to bid on advertisements across a number of devices, including mobile and tablets.[81] Despite the extensive use of online promotion from all types of industries, small businesses do not engage in paid internet advertising as much due to smaller budgets. Facebook and other digital companies are studying ways to communicate to smaller businesses how paid advertising can create value for their companies.[82]

Digital media has also opened opportunities for business-to-business promotions. As more companies adopt digital marketing strategies, the need for better platforms and digital solutions have grown. Digital promotions all attempt to increase brand awareness and market to consumers. As a result of online promotion, consumers are more informed, reading user-generated content before making purchasing decisions and increasingly shopping at internet stores. Consumer consumption patterns are changing radically, and marketers must adapt their promotional efforts to meet these new patterns.

10-5d **Pricing Considerations**

Pricing relates to perceptions of value and is the most flexible element of the marketing mix. Digital media marketing facilitates both price and nonprice competition, because internet marketing gives consumers access to more information about products and prices. As consumers become more informed about their options, the demand for low-priced products has grown, leading to the creation of daily deal sites. ShopStyle is an online destination that informs users about fashion trends and connects them with fashion brands and websites. Users can filter their searches by price as well as other criteria. ShopStyle competes on its wide product offering as well as price with its promise of exclusive offers provided to shoppers daily. Several marketers also use buying incentives like online coupons or free samples to generate consumer demand for their product offerings.

Digital connections can help the customer find the price of the product available from various competitors in an instant. Websites provide price information, and mobile applications can help the customer find the lowest price. Consumers can even bargain with retailers in the store by using a smartphone to show the lowest price available during a transaction. Although this new access to price information benefits the consumer, it also places new pressures on the seller to be competitive and to differentiate products so that customers focus on attributes and benefits rather than price.

Retailers and other organizations are beginning to develop e-commerce stores on Facebook and social media sites so that customers can purchase the product they want directly. Facebook partnered with BigCommerce to create a "Shop" section on Facebook pages to allow merchants to share merchandise on the social platform and direct consumers to their websites.[83] Brands like Smartwool, YETI, and Polkadot Alley have taken advantage of the integration. For the business that wants to compete on price, digital marketing provides unlimited opportunities.

Learning Objective 10-6
Identify legal and ethical considerations in digital marketing.

10-6 ETHICAL AND LEGAL ISSUES

How marketers use technology to gather information—both online and offline—raises numerous legal and ethical issues. The popularity and widespread use of the internet grew so quickly in the 1990s that global regulatory systems were unable to keep pace. The global regulatory environment is not uniform, with areas such as Europe more concerned about privacy than the United States. Even today, courts are debating over laws that would affect consumer internet activities. For instance, are threats posted on Facebook protected speech according to the First Amendment? The U.S. Supreme Court ruled that a person could not be convicted based on threats unless there is evidence that a reasonable person would regard the communications as a threat, but protected speech is evaluated on a case-by-case basis. The Federal Trade Commission (FTC) regulates and makes rules for privacy, fraud, and misappropriation of copyrighted intellectual property, as well as other illicit internet activities.

The FTC's rules for online marketing are the same as for any other form of communication or advertising. These rules help maintain the credibility of the internet as an advertising medium. To avoid deception, all online communication must tell the truth and cannot mislead consumers. In addition, all claims must be substantiated. If online communication is unfair and causes injury that is substantial and not reasonably avoidable and is not outweighed by other benefits, it is considered deceptive. The FTC identifies risk areas for online communication and issues warnings to consumers as misconduct is reported. Some of the areas include testimonials and endorsements, warranties and guarantees, free products, and mail and telephone orders. The FTC periodically joins with other law enforcement agencies to monitor the internet for potentially false or deceptive online claims, including fraud, privacy, and intellectual property issues.

Influencer marketing is relatively new compared with other forms of digital marketing, so it should be no surprise there have been road bumps for early adopters. Due to concerns about dishonest advertising, the FTC requires influencers to clearly disclose any connection they have with brands they promote. Neglecting to make a disclosure is viewed as deceptive advertising. Cases have been filed against Warner Bros. Home Entertainment, who paid PewDiePie, YouTube's number one most subscribed channel, for an endorsement of its video game *Middle-Earth: Shadow of Mordor*, and Lord & Taylor, who paid various influencers to promote their dresses, all without disclosures. According to the FTC, any level of compensation must be disclosed, whether a partner is paid or an influencer strictly receives free product.[84]

10-6a Privacy

Unfortunately, consumers or firms that try to protect their privacy cannot control the internet environment where cybercrime exists. The FTC attempts to regulate and prevent identity theft and online fraud and to provide information on privacy to consumers and marketers. The use of consumer data associated with marketing analytics sets the stage for hackers to steal or demand ransom for files. A data breach at Yahoo! compromised at least 500 million users' data. Yahoo! is still under investigation over the incident because it took the company two years to disclose the incident. There is a regulatory guideline that firms need to disclose material information about cybersecurity incidents once they determine it could affect investors.[85]

Determining what data is needed and how to protect it is the first step for protecting consumers. In our current environment, data breaches and piracy will continue to occur. All organizations involved in social media marketing have a responsibility to protect the consumer by understanding risks and the development of effective cybersecurity. All organizations need a contingency or crisis management plan to respond if a data breach occurs.[86]

One of the most significant privacy issues involves the use of personal information companies collect from website visitors in their efforts to foster long-term customer relationships. Some people fear that the collection of personal information from website users violates users' privacy, especially when it is done without their knowledge. Additionally, governments have issued subpoenas to companies like Google and Microsoft for user information when pursuing legal action. Smartphone companies like Apple Inc. resist sharing code that provides access to a person's phone records. On the other hand, the U.S. Justice Department gets some of its most effective evidence from emails in processing cases.

Due to consumer concerns over privacy, the FTC is considering developing regulations that would protect consumer privacy by limiting the amount of consumer information that businesses can gather online. Other countries are pursuing similar actions. The European Union passed a law requiring companies to get users' consent before using cookies to track their information. In the United States, some government officials have called for a "do not track" bill, similar to the "do not call" bill for telephones, to allow users to opt out of having their information tracked. Legislators reintroduced a Do Not Track Kids bill that would make it illegal for companies to track children between the ages 13 and 15 over the internet or mobile devices without parental permission (currently, marketers are prohibited from gathering information about consumers aged 13 or younger without parental permission). They also desire a system that would erase information that these teenagers found to be embarrassing.[87] Certain laws pertaining to privacy have also taken on new meanings with the increase in digital marketing. For instance, the Federal Video Privacy Protection Act requires that any marketers who wish to disclose or share information about a consumer's video content consumption must obtain separate, independent consent from the consumer. This means that a company cannot share information about videos that users watched on their sites with other parties without permission.[88] Marketers are also seeing opportunities to capitalize on users' discontent with having their data collected. Social networking site Ello markets the fact that they do not collect customer data. Ello, created for artists, designers, musicians, illustrators, and architects, never sells ads or personal data to third parties. Wickr, a mobile messaging app, refuses to store information on its central server, preventing the organization from keeping a digital record of user activity, claiming no conversation can be tracked.[89]

While consumers may welcome such added protections, web advertisers, who use consumer information to target advertisements to online consumers, see it as a threat. In response to impending legislation, many web advertisers are attempting self-regulation in order to stay ahead of the game. For instance, the Digital Advertising Alliance (DAA) has adopted privacy guidelines for online advertisers. The DAA has created a "trusted mark" icon that websites adhering to their guidelines can display. However, because it is self-regulatory, not all digital advertisers may choose to participate in its programs.[90] Table 10.4 describes industry best practices for digital marketers to consider before launching digital campaigns. It is important for digital marketers to craft campaigns that comply with FTC rules.

10-6b **Online Fraud**

Online fraud includes any attempt to conduct dishonest activities online. Online fraud includes, among other things, attempts to deceive consumers into releasing personal information. It is becoming a major source of frustration with social networking sites. Cybercriminals are discovering ways to use sites like Facebook and Twitter to carry out fraudulent activities. Hacking attacks—in which criminals break into company computers to steal information—have almost become the norm. Companies including Target, Home Depot, and Sony have experienced

online fraud Any attempt to conduct dishonest activities online, including deceiving consumers into releasing personal information

Table 10.4   Best Practices for Digital Campaigns

1. Implement privacy during the conceptualization phase of the campaign.

2. Disclose all passive tracking systems used to collect information.

3. Data collection involving third parties should involve clear guidelines regarding how the data will be used and who owns it. Provide ways for users to opt out of tracking or email marketing through visible notices.

4. Screen age of users if appropriate for the campaign. Collecting personal information of children under 13 requires parental consent. If marketing to children is allowed, ensure that the content and language is appropriate for the age range targeted.

5. Ensure that all tracking or data collection activities that occur do not conflict with the company's online privacy policy.

6. Adopt security measures for any data collected from users. User information must be protected, particularly if it is identifiable.

7. Be aware of all legal requirements and industry codes of ethics on digital marketing.

Source: Adapted from Jesse Brody, "Terms and Conditions," *Marketing News*, November 2014, pp. 34–41; Direct Marketing Association, *Direct Marketing Association's Guidelines for Ethical Business Practice*, January 2014, http://thedma.org/wp-content/uploads/DMA_Guidelines_January_2014.pdf (accessed February 17, 2018).

wide-scale hacking attacks. Hackers may break into websites and steal users' personal information, enabling them to commit identity theft. In one of the worst cybercrimes to date, three individuals were able to steal data on more than 100 million people from the computers of 11 companies, including J.P. Morgan, Dow Jones & Co., and E*Trade Financial Corp. The men used the stolen information to make more than $100 million.[91] The FTC considers ransomware as the most challenging cybersecurity issue at this time. Cybercriminals gain access to consumer and business computers, encrypt files, and then demand a ransom payment for providing a key to unlock the files.[92]

Organizations and social networking sites alike are developing ways to combat fraudulent activity on digital media sites. For instance, organizations known as brand-protection firms monitor social networks for fraudulent accounts.[93] ForgeRock is an identity and access management software firm. In its advertising, it assures companies that it secures their identities to protect against identity theft. However, the best protection for consumers is to be careful when divulging information online. Privacy advocates advise that the best way to stay out of trouble is to avoid giving out personal information, such as social security numbers or credit card information, unless the site is definitely legitimate.

10-6c Intellectual Property

The internet has also created issues associated with intellectual property, the copyrighted or trademarked ideas and creative materials developed to solve problems, carry out applications,

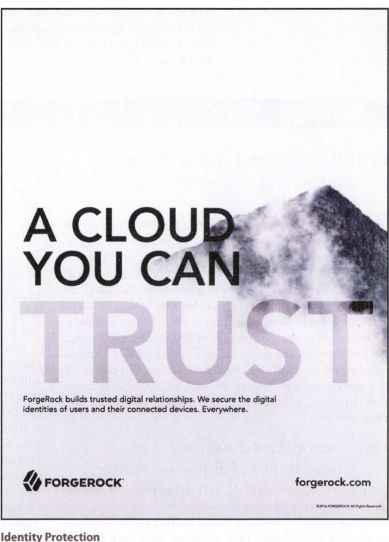

Identity Protection
ForgeRock offers protection services that can be used to secure the identities of users and their connected devices.

and educate and entertain others. Each year, intellectual property losses in the United States total billions of dollars stemming from the illegal copying of computer programs, movies, compact discs, and books. YouTube has often faced lawsuits on intellectual property infringement. With millions of users uploading content to YouTube, it can be hard for Google to monitor and remove all the videos that may contain copyrighted materials.

The software industry is particularly hard-hit when it comes to the pirating of materials and illegal file sharing. The Business Software Alliance estimates that the global computer software industry loses more than $400 billion a year to illegal theft.[94] Consumers view illegal downloading in different ways, depending on the motivation for the behavior. If the motivation is primarily utilitarian, or for personal gain, then the act is viewed as less ethically acceptable than if it is for a hedonistic reason, or just for fun.[95]

Consumers rationalize pirating software, video games, and music for a number of reasons. First, many consumers feel they just do not have the money to pay for what they want. Second, because their friends engage in piracy and swap digital content, they feel influenced to engage in this activity. Third, for some, the attraction is the thrill of getting away with it and the slim risk of consequences. Fourth, to some extent, there are people who think they are smarter than others; engaging in piracy allows them to show how technology-savvy they are.[96]

As digital media continues to evolve, more legal and ethical issues will certainly arise. As a result, marketers and all other users of digital media should make an effort to learn and abide by ethical practices to ensure that they get the most out of the resources available in this growing medium. Doing so will allow marketers to maximize the tremendous opportunities digital media has to offer.

Summary

10-1 Define digital media, digital marketing, and electronic marketing.

Digital media are electronic media that function using digital codes—when we refer to digital media, we are referring to media available via computers, cellular phones, smartphones, and other digital devices that have been released in recent years. Digital marketing uses all digital media, including the internet and mobile and interactive channels, to develop communication and exchanges with customers. Electronic marketing refers to the strategic process of distributing, promoting, and pricing products, and discovering the desires of customers using digital media and digital marketing. Our definition of e-marketing goes beyond the internet and also includes mobile phones, banner ads, digital outdoor marketing, and social networks.

10-2 Summarize the growth and importance of digital marketing.

The phenomenal growth of the internet has provided unprecedented opportunities for marketers to forge interactive relationships with consumers. As the internet and digital communication technologies have advanced, they have made it possible to target markets more precisely and reach markets that were previously inaccessible. One of the most important benefits of e-marketing is the ability of marketers and customers to share information. Through websites, social networks, and other digital media, consumers can learn about everything they consume and use in life. As a result, the internet is changing the way marketers communicate and develop relationships. For many businesses, engaging in digital marketing activities is essential to maintaining competitive advantages.

10-3 Describe different types of digital media and how they can be used for marketing.

Many types of digital media can be used as marketing tools. A social network is a website where users can create a profile and interact with other users, post information, and engage in other forms of web-based communication. Blogs (short for "weblogs") are web-based journals in which writers can editorialize and interact with other internet users. A wiki is a type of software that creates an interface that enables users to add to or edit the content of some types of websites. Media-sharing sites allow marketers to share photos, videos, and podcasts but are more limited in scope in how companies interact with consumers. One type of media sharing is podcasts, which are audio or video files that can be downloaded from the internet with a subscription that automatically delivers new content to listening devices or personal computers. Virtual-gaming sites are three-dimensional game sites that are social in nature and often involve role-playing. Advertising over mobile devices is becoming increasingly common. Mobile applications are software programs that run on mobile devices and give users access to certain content. Widgets are small bits of software on a website, desktop, or mobile device that performs a simple task such as displaying stock updates.

As a result of these new marketing channels, digital marketing is moving from a niche strategy to becoming a core consideration in the marketing mix. At the same time, digital technologies are largely changing the dynamic between marketer and consumer. Consumers use social networking sites and mobile applications to do everything from playing games to engaging in commerce. The menu of digital media alternatives continues to grow, requiring marketers to make informed decisions about strategic approaches.

10-4 Describe how marketers can measure the success of a digital strategy.

It is essential that marketers focus on the changing social behaviors of consumers and how they interact with digital media. Consumers now have a greater ability to regulate the information that they view as well as the rate and sequence of their exposure to that information. This is why the internet is sometimes referred to as a *pull* medium because users determine which websites they are going to view; the marketer has only limited ability to control the content to which users are exposed, and in what sequence. Marketers must modify their marketing strategies to adapt to the changing behaviors of online consumers.

Monitoring and evaluating digital media helps marketers maximize resources and minimize costs. Key Performance Indicators (KPIs) related to specific objectives are defined at the onset of a social media strategy for real-time measurement and evaluation. Tools like Google Analytics help marketers to measure and interpret the effectiveness of marketing activities. Applying analytics to social media performance, from likes to clicks, can help develop better targeted social media campaigns.

10-5 Describe how digital media affect the four variables of the marketing mix.

The reasons for a digital marketing strategy are many. The low costs of many digital media channels can provide major savings in promotional budgets. Digital marketing is allowing companies to connect with market segments that are harder to reach with traditional media. Despite the challenges involved in such a strategy, digital marketing is opening up new avenues in the relationship between businesses and consumers.

The marketing mix of product, distribution, promotion, and price continues to apply in digital marketing. From a product perspective, digital media provide an opportunity to add a service dimension to traditional products and create new products that could only be accessible on the internet. Many businesses find it necessary to continually upgrade their product offerings to meet consumer needs. For distribution, the ability to process orders electronically and increase the speed of communications via the internet reduces inefficiencies, costs, and redundancies while increasing speed throughout the marketing channel. Marketers can promote their products to consumers in new and creative ways using digital media. Finally, from a pricing dimension, digital media facilitate both price and nonprice competition, because internet marketing gives consumers access to more information about products and prices.

10-6 Identify legal and ethical considerations in digital marketing.

How marketers use technology to gather information—both online and offline—has raised numerous legal and ethical issues. Privacy is one of the most significant issues, involving the use of personal information that companies collect from website visitors in their efforts to foster long-term relationships with customers. Some people fear that the collection of personal information from website users may violate users' privacy, especially when it is done without their knowledge. Another concern is that hackers may break into websites and steal users' personal information, enabling them to commit identity theft.

Online fraud includes any attempt to conduct dishonest activities online. Online fraud includes, among other things, attempts to deceive consumers into releasing personal information. It is becoming a major source of frustration with social networking sites. Cybercriminals are discovering entirely new ways to use sites like Facebook and Twitter to carry out fraudulent activities. The best way for users to combat fraudulent activity is not to give out personal information except on trustworthy sites.

The internet has also created issues associated with intellectual property, the copyrighted or trademarked ideas and creative materials developed to solve problems, carry out applications, and educate and entertain others. Each year, intellectual property losses in the United States total billions of dollars stemming from the illegal copying of computer programs, movies, compact discs, and books. The software industry is particularly hard-hit when it comes to pirating material and illegal file sharing.

Important Terms

digital media 276	social network 279	podcasts 286	omni-channel 293
digital marketing 276	blogs 282	mobile applications 288	online fraud 296
electronic marketing, or e-marketing 276	wiki 284	widgets 289	

Discussion and Review Questions

1. How does digital marketing differ from traditional marketing?
2. Define *interactivity* and explain its significance. How can marketers exploit this characteristic to improve relations with customers?
3. Explain the distinction between push and pull media. What is the significance of control in terms of using websites to market products?
4. Why are social networks becoming an increasingly important marketing tool? Find an example online in which a company has improved the effectiveness of its marketing strategy by using social networks.
5. How has digital media changed consumer behavior? What are the opportunities and challenges that face marketers with this in mind?

6. Describe the ways marketers can measure digital strategy success.
7. How can marketers exploit the characteristics of the internet to improve the product element of their marketing mixes?
8. How do the characteristics of digital marketing affect the promotion element of the marketing mix?
9. How have digital media affected the pricing of products? Give examples of the opportunities and challenges presented to marketers in light of these changes.
10. Name and describe the major ethical and legal issues that have developed in response to the internet. How should policy makers address these issues?

Developing Your Marketing Plan

When developing a marketing strategy using new digital media, a marketer must be aware of the strengths and weaknesses of these new media. Digital media are relatively new to the field of marketing and have different pros and cons relative to traditional media sources. Different products and target markets may be more or less suited for different digital media outlets.

1. Review the key concepts of addressability, interactivity, accessibility, connectivity, and control in Table 10.1, and explain how they relate to social media. Think

about how a marketing strategy focused on social media differs from a campaign reliant on traditional media sources.
2. No matter what marketing media are used, determining the correct marketing mix for your company is always important. Think about how social media might affect the marketing mix.
3. Discuss different digital media and the pros and cons of using each as part of your marketing plan.

Video Case 10.1

Zappos Runs with Social Media

Zappos the world's largest online shoe retailer, was one of the first companies to incorporate social media into its business, and it has established itself as a leader in its use. Zappos sells women's, men's, and kid's shoes as well as clothing, bags, and more. The Amazon-owned company focuses on building customer relationships through human interaction and emphasizes comments related to service and fun. For example, if a customer experiences a problem with an order or has a question about a product, the Zappos team ensures that these comments are responded to honestly, authentically, and in a timely manner. Sometimes customers will leave fun comments about their experience with the company. Zappos takes these comments just as seriously. Both instances are at the heart of its operations, which is to "deliver happiness."

Zappos does not maintain a specific strategy for marketing on social media, nor does it have a policy for responding to customers. As with any Zappos activity, marketing is guided by the company's core values, including creating "WOW" customer experiences and a culture characterized by fun and a little weirdness. If customers are congregating on Facebook, Zappos makes sure to have a presence there so it can engage them in conversation. In fact, Kenshoo, a digital marketing specialist, has recognized Zappos' Facebook activity for its effectiveness. Over a 2-month period, the company initiated 85,000 visits to its webpage through status updates. Forty-two percent of these updates led to purchases, while the other 58 percent left comments or likes on the webpage.

Rob Siefker, Senior Director of Customer Loyalty, emphasizes the importance of using Twitter. He states, "Most people went on Twitter as a way to interact with friends. Some companies went on there and solely focused on the business or service aspect. For us, part of service is being playful . . . it makes it much more human to the customer . . . it makes it much more personal." Most companies that use social media use it for promotion rather than for truly interacting with customers. This creates a distance between the company and the customer. Siefker points out that customers "feel when they are being marketed to, and they know there is a reason for it." However, Zappos strives to go beyond using digital media simply for promotion purposes. The company wants to forge a real connection with customers, create the best customer experience possible, and describe itself as a human company, requiring strong interactions between customers and the organization.

The company has been able to achieve rapid growth through its use of values in its marketing activities. Zappos offers free shipping as well as free, full refund returns within a year of purchase eliminate any hesitancy consumers may feel about shopping for shoes online. Zappos even created a set of ads reenacting real customer stories highlighting the lengths the company will go to satisfy its customers. It is a large company with a small business feel when it comes to how it treats its customers and how its customers feel about Zappos. This is due in large part to its presence on social media and the way it cross-promotes its activities across platforms. For example, if it receives or posts a comment on Facebook, Zappos will also share it on other networks like Twitter, Snapchat, and Instagram in order to reach other current or potential customers. While the company focuses mainly on current customers, this activity generates wide-spread effects such as word-of-mouth marketing that brings in new customers. The current customers in this sense serve as brand advocates or brand enthusiasts.

Zappos also generates interest by encouraging customers to share promotions and purchases with friends. One campaign it used on Facebook was to ask people to like its page. It read, "Let's be in a Like-Like relationship." Then it asked users to sign up for its email list. The order in which it made these requests gave people the impression that Zappos was indeed concerned about building relationships. The company also has exclusive content for people who opt to become fans. Once deemed a fan, people are able to see special offers, videos, and promotions and share comments about Zappos. Finally, another major campaign Zappos launched was its engagement strategy called "Fan of the Week Contest," where people were encouraged to take and post photos of themselves with Zappos products. Then users voted on the best photo, and the one with the most votes won. Zappos posted the photo on its website for all to see. Overall, Zappos ensures that it is using social media to build relationships by bringing customers closer to the company. Marketing for Zappos is an authentic and human activity that is not about selling products but building relationships.[97]

Questions for Discussion

1. Describe some ways in which Zappos uses digital media tools.
2. How does Zappos encourage word-of-mouth marketing through digital media?
3. How does Zappos use digital media to create an authentic relationship with consumers?

Case 10.2

Dollar Shave Club Faces Sharp Competition

The idea for Dollar Shave Club (DSC) emerged from a conversation entrepreneur Michael Dubin was having with his co-founder about the annoyances of shaving. They found it inconvenient and costly to have to purchase brand-name blades each month. They decided to create DSC, a subscription-based service headquartered in Venice, California. Consumers that become members of DSC are mailed razors for $1, $6, or $9 per month. Since the company launched, it has expanded its offerings to include personal-care products like hand cream, shave butter, and hair gel.

The entrepreneurs had to find a low-cost way of communicating with customers. For $4,500 Michael Dubin developed and starred in a humorous video marketing the benefits of Dollar Shave razors, while poking fun at the extra bells-and-whistles that come with brand-name razors. The video was posted on YouTube, where it went viral. Sales for DSC's subscription service soared to 12,000 orders in a single day and caused the company's website to crash. To date the video has more than 25 million views. Video-sharing sites like YouTube are free for companies to use, giving them an easy, affordable way to upload advertisements and informational videos about their products. DSC's video undoubtedly went viral because it was funny and it struck a chord with viewers.

Beyond its digital marketing strategies, in the beginning DSC relied heavily on focus groups. The company discussed grooming with small consumer panels which resulted in new products. For example, after one panel complained about rough toilet paper, DSC launched One Wipe Charlies, flushable towelettes. To promote the launch, DSC turned back to YouTube with a video titled "Let's Talk about #2." Today, the firm is estimated to have $200 million in revenues. DSC communicates with customers frequently to measure customer satisfaction, and it continues to utilize promotional strategies through press releases and low-cost videos on YouTube. DSC's success eventually caught the attention of Unilever, which purchased DSC for $1 billion.

DSC believes educational content is a big part of the value they create for consumers. On its blog, "DSC Original Content," the company covers everything from grooming and style tips to fitness guides. "There's a very big trend around 'manscaping' at the moment," said Bart Kuppens, DSC Europe General Manager. The company publishes articles that address topics men may not readily talk about with their friends. DSC also releases a weekly podcast to address similar topics to engage with its customers. Podcasts offer a convenient way for companies to discuss how to use their products or understand certain features. It also creates brand awareness, promotes their products, and encourages customer loyalty.

To encourage new member signups and create brand awareness, DSC turned to Facebook advertising. Facebook advertising allows business owners to target Facebook and Instagram users based on geography, age, preferences, and shopping behavior. Using the platform's Canvas ad format, DSC used existing creative content to target men ages 18 to 65. The company reached 1.6 million Facebook users and decreased the cost per subscription acquired by 30 percent. Despite DSC's success with the platform, Unilever, who has spent more than $9 billion on advertising in recent years, has threatened to stop using Facebook advertising if the social media giant doesn't address the fake news epidemic.

Beyond the United States, DSC ships to Australia and Canada. The global market for men's razors is $15 billion, and DSC wants a bigger slice of the pie. The company selected the U.K. as its next international venture because online shopping behavior and online subscription services are similar to those in the United States. Competition for the razor subscription model is building, with New York–based Harry's recently launching in the U.K. as well. To support their U.K. launch, DSC implemented TV, outdoor, cinema, Facebook, and Google AdWords advertising campaigns.

Brazil's and India's shaving markets are forecast to grow by $620 million over the next several years, making these two countries excellent candidates for expansion. For DSC, next steps include further expansion across Europe and diversification of its product lines.[98]

Questions for Discussion

1. How is Dollar Shave Club using digital marketing to reach its customers?
2. How does Dollar Shave Club foster loyalty with its blog and podcast?
3. Discuss the challenges Dollar Shave Club may face with international expansion and how they should address these issues.

Strategic Case 4

Need a Place to Stay? InterContinental Hotels Group Has One Just for You

With nearly 800,000 guest rooms in 100 cities worldwide marketed under 13 different hotel and resort brands, the InterContinental Hotels Group (IHG) is appealing to multiple target markets of customers, families, and business travelers. The multinational company's brands include InterContinental, Kimpton Hotels, Hotel Indigo, Even Hotels, Crowne Plaza, Holiday Inn, Holiday Inn Resorts, Holiday Inn Club Vacations, Holiday Inn Express, Avid, Candlewood Suites, Staybridge Suites, and Hualuxe Hotels. Each brand has its own image, decor, and services geared to the needs of a specific market segment.

Brands Target Specific Markets

The upscale InterContinental hotels are luxurious and located in internationally known metropolitan areas. They feature a full range of services to fit the needs of affluent consumers and business executives. Kimpton Hotels and Hotel Indigo are two of IHG's boutique brands, marketed to consumers and businesspeople who want distinctive accommodations and amenities. The buildings are unique, the rooms have stylish flair, and the on-site restaurants reflect the heritage and flavors of their city locations. The Even Hotel brand caters

TREASUREGALORE/SHUTTERSTOCK.COM

to health-conscious guests, with fitness and food options that enhance wellness and promote healthy lifestyles.

Crowne Plaza hotels, located in major gateway cities, have the latest digital conveniences and meeting accommodations needed by business travelers, both domestic and international. The lobbies and other public spaces have the space and flexibility to accommodate either work or social activities. Holiday Inn, Holiday Inn Resorts, and Holiday Inn Vacations are marketed to consumers, particularly families, seeking an affordable and fun getaway experience, while Holiday Inn Express targets consumers and business travelers who want a simple but comfortable room at an affordable price. Customers in this market segment are not interested in the full range of services usually offered at upscale hotels and prefer not to pay the higher room rates.

Avid, a recent addition to the IHG portfolio, is marketed to price-conscious, technology-savvy consumers who appreciate the convenience of mobile check-in and check-out and want to be able to stream entertainment from their own digital devices through the hotel's smart TV. Guests at Avid Hotels enjoy a quality mattress and soundproofing for a good night's sleep, and they have the option of sipping premium-brand coffee along with the complimentary breakfast. Rooms at Avid are priced up to $15 less than Holiday Inn Express, with "grab-and-go" food items for travelers who are headed home or to a meeting.

Both Candlewood Suites and Staybridge Suites are designed for travelers—in many cases, businesspeople—who will be spending more than a few days away from home. Each guest suite has a kitchen and a comfortable sitting area for after-hours relaxation during a long-term stay. Hualuxe hotels, new and exclusive to China, offer luxury rooms and services tailored to the needs of business managers and individuals at various status levels. The entire experience of staying in a Hualuxe property has been planned with local customs and perceptions in mind, as well as meeting the expectations of what a well-known, multinational hotel corporation should offer to its guests.

Global Expansion and Marketing

Although more than half of IHG's $1.7 billion in annual revenue comes from its properties in North and South America, China is the company's second-largest market, and its fastest-growing. Hualuxe is one of six hotel brands that IHG markets in China, where the company sees significant opportunity based on trends such as rising middle-class income and higher demand for business and tourist travel. As a result, IHG has been steadily expanding its presence in China. In 2013, the company had 200 hotels across the country; today, it has more than 400 hotels, with dozens more being built every year. New IHG hotels will be opening in time to host the influx of sports fans who will attend the 2022 Winter Olympics in Beijing, for example. The company also operates an intensive hospitality training program to educate new employees and managers so they can deliver customer service as required by IHG's quality and performance standards.

In China, as in other markets, IHG invites customers to download a proprietary app for reserving hotel rooms via smartphones and tablet computers, getting driving directions to the hotels, and receiving discount offers. The company's analysis reveals that customers in China book a higher percentage of hotel reservations through the app than customers in any other market, reflecting especially high penetration and usage of mobile devices within China. In addition, IHG's cloud-based reservations system can be customized to each customer's personal preferences and usage patterns, adding convenience and speeding transactions for customers in all markets.

When communicating with customers in both consumer and business markets worldwide, IHG relies on a combination of digital marketing and social media, as well as traditional advertising and personal selling. For example, the global campaign "Stories of the InterContinental Life" consisted of online videos and podcasts showcasing exciting and unusual travel possibilities in destinations like Beijing, Panama City, and Montreal—cities where InterContinental hotels are located. Another campaign, "Neighborhood 15," highlighted fascinating things to see and do within 15 minutes of Hotel Indigo properties in Bali, Singapore, and other areas. This digital campaign was supported by social media promotions and tied into the hotel's tag line, "The Color of Discovery."

Holiday Inn targets families that travel with young children with a special website, "Little Big Travellers" (https://littlebigtravellers.holidayinn.com/en), focusing on Asian, Australian, and Middle Eastern markets. The site is positioned as a resource for Millennial parents seeking inspiration, ideas, and practical advice for traveling as a family. Parents can view videos, learn more about particular destinations, and download activity starters like Chatterbox Conversation Cards, cards with specific words or phrases to stimulate family discussions about travel. For the Chinese market, Crowne Plaza has implemented several digital marketing communications campaigns focusing on the brand's sophisticated image and promoting specific benefits desired by domestic travelers in that market.

All IHG brands are active on social networks. Holiday Inn, for instance, posts on Facebook, Instagram, Twitter, and YouTube. Crowne Plaza, Kimpton Hotels, and Avid Hotels, among other IHG brands, also use LinkedIn to connect with business travelers and recruit job candidates. Hotel Indigo has generated social media conversations by partnering with the ASOS fashion brand to promote specially designed clothing for men and women inspired by the culture and neighborhoods surrounding its hotel locations. The ASOS clothing collection for Hotel Indigo Denver Downtown, for example, is designed with a nod to Denver's Gold Rush heritage. Consumers who see or buy the clothing can join the conversation by tagging their social media comments with #HotelIndigo, #ASOSxHotelIndigo, or #ASOS.

Rewarding Loyalty, Meeting Needs

Through the IHG Rewards Club, visitors at any of the company's hotels and resorts can earn points for each night they stay. Club members also enjoy extras like bonus points and discounts. They can also earn points through travel partners like Hertz and through thousands of restaurants, then redeem points to pay for hotel stays or airline tickets. All of the hotel's brands participate in the rewards program, which encourages loyalty and gives customers yet another incentive to choose IHG every time they travel.

Recently, the rewards program was expanded to include restaurant meals booked via OpenTable and food deliveries ordered via Grubhub. Knowing that some customers are at Candlewood Suites and Staybridge Suites for weeks at a time, this arrangement offers "the chance to explore the neighborhood and try new restaurants when they don't want to cook in their suite," says IHG's head of loyalty, partnerships, and portfolio marketing. She adds that IHG is always looking for new ways to meet customers' needs "throughout the entire travel process, not just when they're staying at our hotels."[99]

Questions for Discussion

1. How do IHG's multiple brands enable the company to address the needs of specific consumer and business markets?
2. In which stage(s) of the consumer buying decision process would IHG's digital marketing and social media activities likely have a significant influence? Explain your answer.
3. Why would IHG create a separate hotel brand specifically for China?
4. What are the advantages and disadvantages of each IHG brand having its own social network accounts?

11 Product Concepts, Branding, and Packaging
12 Developing and Managing Products
13 Services Marketing

We are now prepared to analyze the decisions and activities associated with developing and maintaining effective marketing mixes.

PART 5 explores the product and price ingredients of the marketing mix.

CHAPTER 11 focuses on basic product concepts and on branding and packaging decisions.

CHAPTER 12 analyzes various dimensions regarding product management, including line extensions and product modification, new-product development, product deletions, and the management of services as products.

In **CHAPTER 13**, we discuss services marketing, including its importance, key characteristics, marketing strategies for services, and the nature of nonprofit marketing.

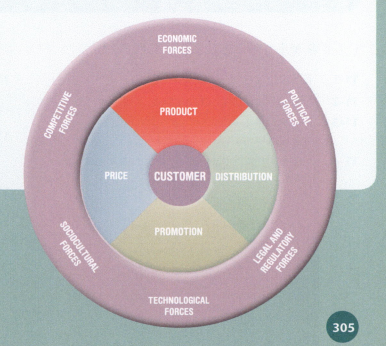

Product Concepts, Branding, and Packaging

LEARNING OBJECTIVES

11-1 Define the concept of a product.

11-2 Discuss how products are classified.

11-3 Explain the concepts of product line and product mix and how they are related.

11-4 Explore the product life cycle and its impact on marketing strategies.

11-5 Discuss the product adoption process.

11-6 Explain the major components of branding, including brand types, branding strategies, and brand protection.

11-7 Describe the major packaging functions, design considerations, and how packaging is used in marketing strategies.

11-8 Identify the functions of labeling and legal issues related to labeling.

DENNIZN/SHUTTERSTOCK.COM

Basics, Essentials, and Elements Are All Parts of Amazon's Private Brands

From Mama Bear diapers and Goodsport clothing to Happy Belly foods and Rivet sofas, Amazon.com is launching a raft of new brands exclusive to its retail website. It is also marketing various product lines branded with a variation of the Amazon name, such as Amazon Essentials and Amazon Elements. AmazonBasics, another brand available only through the pioneering online retailer, already rings up more than $250 million in annual sales of computer accessories, batteries, and other goods.

These fast-growing Amazon-only brands offer value to consumers and return a significant profit margin to the retailer every time customers click to buy. Consider Rivet, an Amazon brand covering sofas and other home furnishings. Consumers can return any Rivet product for free within 30 days, taking the risk out of buying without seeing the product in person. Rivet furniture also carries a one-year warranty, another way to reassure consumers they risk nothing by buying. And because Amazon sells these brands directly to consumers, the prices can be lower than nationally advertised brands, even as the margin is higher.

One of Amazon's strengths is its ability to analyze mountains of customer data. By putting private brands on its own versions of frequently purchased items like batteries and diapers, Amazon can offer the right products to the right buyers at the right time and the right price, reinforcing customer loyalty while it increases revenues. Since Amazon acquired Whole Foods, customers have also been able to buy products featuring the 365 Everyday Value brand exclusive to Whole Foods Market.[1]

307

AmazonBasics and Happy Belly are brands that consumers use to identify specific products. In this chapter, we first define a product and discuss how products are classified. Next, we examine the concepts of product line and product mix. We then explore the stages of the product life cycle and the effect of each life-cycle stage on marketing strategies. Next, we outline the product adoption process. Then, we discuss branding, its value to customers and marketers, brand loyalty, and brand equity. We examine the various types of brands and consider how companies choose and protect brands, the various branding strategies employed, brand extensions, co-branding, and brand licensing. We also look at the role of packaging, the functions of packaging, issues to consider in packaging design, and how the package can be a major element in marketing strategy. We conclude with a discussion of labeling and some related legal issues.

Learning Objective 11-1

Define the concept of a product.

good A tangible physical entity

service An intangible result of the application of human and mechanical efforts to people or objects

idea A concept, philosophy, image, or issue

11-1 WHAT IS A PRODUCT?

As defined in Chapter 1, a *product* is a good, a service, or an idea received in an exchange. It can be either tangible or intangible and includes functional, social, and psychological utilities or benefits. A **good** is a tangible physical entity, such as an Apple iPhone or a Subway sandwich. A **service**, in contrast, is intangible. It is the result of the application of human and mechanical efforts to people or objects. Examples of services include a concert performance by Beyoncé, online car insurance, a medical examination, an airline flight, and child day care. Many marketers of intangible products try to make them seem more tangible to consumers through advertisements that employ tangible images that provoke ideas. Skin treatments and cosmetic dermatology are another example of services. In the advertisement for Westlake Dermatology, the business primarily displays a large image of a young woman in a swimsuit. The ad implies that users of its SmartLipo service will be able to dress similarly because they will have great skin to show off.

An **idea** is a concept, philosophy, image, or issue. Ideas provide the psychological stimulation that aids in solving problems or adjusting to the environment. Charity: water, for example, uses traditional marketing and social media activities to raise money to dig wells that bring safe drinking water to 663 million people around the world who lack access to clean water.[2]

It is useful to think of a total product offering as having three interdependent elements: the core product, its supplemental features, and its symbolic or experiential benefits. The core product consists of a product's fundamental utility or main benefit and usually addresses a fundamental need of the consumer. Most consumers, however, appreciate additional features and services. For instance, a basic cell phone allows consumers to make calls and exchange texts, but consumers today expect smart phones with supplemental features, such as widely available high-speed internet access, high-resolution cameras, and apps. Consumers also may seek out symbolic benefits, such as a trendy brand name, when purchasing a phone.

Supplemental features provide added value or attributes that are in addition to the product's core utility or

WESTLAKE DERMATOLOGY®
SmartLipo

Services
Westlake Dermatology offers a variety of dermatological services including SmartLipo.

benefit. These features often include perks such as free installation, guarantees, product information, promises of repair or maintenance, delivery, training, or financing. These supplemental attributes are not required to make the core product function effectively, but they help to differentiate one product brand from another and may increase customer loyalty. For instance, Drury Hotels creates customer loyalty through strong customer service and supplemental benefits. In addition to its core product, the hotel's value package offers supplemental product features including free breakfast, free Wi-Fi, free popcorn and soda in the hotel lobby, and a snack and beverage social in the evenings, which reinforce its tagline, "the extras aren't extra."[3] These supplemental benefits differentiate the hotel chain in customers' minds, making them feel as if they are getting a better deal than they would receive at rival hotels.

Finally, customers also receive benefits based on their experiences with the product, which give symbolic meaning to many products (and brands) for buyers. For some consumers, the simple act of shopping gives them pleasure, which lends to its symbolic value and improves their attitudes about the products they consider buying. Some retailers capitalize on this by striving to create a special, personalized experience for customers. Even well-established retail chains are recognizing the importance of an individualized customer experience for gaining a competitive advantage. McDonald's, known for its quick service, introduced Signature Crafted Recipe sandwiches that allow customers to customize their burgers by choosing bun, protein (beef, grilled or crispy chicken), and various topping bundles, such as Pico Guacamole, Maple Bacon Dijon, and Sweet BBQ Bacon. Although customization takes more time and may conflict with McDonald's reputation for quick service, Millennials—McDonald's key target market for this venture—appear to value customization over time.[4]

The atmosphere and décor of a retail store, the variety and depth of product choices, the customer support, and even the sounds and smells all contribute to the experiential element. Thus, when buyers purchase a product, they are really buying the benefits and satisfaction they think the product will provide. A Rolex or Patek Philippe watch is purchased to make a statement that the wearer has high status or has achieved financial success—not just for telling time. Services, in particular, are purchased on the basis of expectations. Expectations, suggested by images, promises, and symbols, as well as processes and delivery, help consumers to make judgments about tangible and intangible products. Often symbols and cues are used to make intangible products more tangible, or real, to the consumer. Prudential Insurance, for example, features the Rock of Gibraltar on its logo to symbolize strength and permanency.

11-2 CLASSIFYING PRODUCTS

Learning Objective 11-2

Discuss how products are classified.

Products fall into one of two general categories. Products purchased to satisfy personal and family needs are **consumer products**. Those bought to use in a firm's operations, to resell, or to make other products are **business products**. Consumers buy products to satisfy their personal wants, whereas business buyers seek to satisfy the goals of their organizations. Product classifications are important because they may influence pricing, distribution, and promotion decisions. In this section, we examine the characteristics of consumer and business products and explore the marketing activities associated with some of these products.

11-2a Consumer Products

The most widely accepted approach to classifying consumer products is based on characteristics of consumer buying behavior. It divides products into four categories: convenience, shopping, specialty, and unsought products. However, not all buyers behave in the same way when

consumer products Products purchased to satisfy personal and family needs

business products Products bought to use in a firm's operations, to resell, or to make other products

purchasing a specific type of product. Thus, a single product might fit into several categories. To minimize complexity, marketers think in terms of how buyers *generally* behave when purchasing a specific item. Examining the four traditional categories of consumer products can provide further insight.

Convenience Products

Convenience products are relatively inexpensive, frequently purchased items for which buyers exert only minimal purchasing effort. They range from bread, soft drinks, and chewing gum to gasoline and newspapers. The buyer spends little time planning the purchase or comparing available brands or sellers. Even a buyer who prefers a specific brand will generally choose a substitute if the preferred brand is not conveniently available. A convenience product is normally marketed through many retail outlets, such as gas stations, drugstores, and supermarkets. Coca-Cola products, for instance, are available in grocery stores, convenience stores, gas stations, restaurants, and airports—among many other outlets. Because sellers experience high inventory turnover, per-unit gross margins can be relatively low. Producers of convenience products, such as Wrigley's chewing gum, expect little promotional effort at the retail level and thus must provide it themselves with advertising and sales promotion. Packaging and displays are also important because many convenience items are available only on a self-service basis at the retail level, and thus the package plays a major role in selling the product.

convenience products
Relatively inexpensive, frequently purchased items for which buyers exert minimal purchasing effort

SOURCE: MAXIM MAGAZINE

SOURCE: MEN'S FITNESS

Convenience versus Shopping Products
Convenience products such as Propel electrolyte water do not require much shopping effort. However, a consumer might expend considerable effort when deciding on, locating, and purchasing a pair of Samuel Hubbard Uptown Maverick street boots.

Shopping Products

Shopping products are items for which buyers are willing to expend considerable effort in planning and making the purchase. Buyers spend significant time comparing stores and brands with respect to prices, product features, qualities, services, and perhaps warranties. Shoppers may compare products at a number of outlets such as Best Buy, Amazon.com, Lowe's, or Home Depot; they may begin their buying process at the websites of these stores. Appliances, bicycles, furniture, stereos, cameras, and shoes exemplify shopping products. These products are expected to last a fairly long time and are more expensive than convenience products. These products, however, are still within the budgets of most consumers and are purchased less frequently than convenience items. Shopping products are distributed via fewer retail outlets than convenience products.

Because shopping products are purchased less frequently, inventory turnover is lower, and marketing channel members expect to receive higher gross margins to compensate for the lower turnover. In certain situations, both shopping products and convenience products may be marketed in the same location. For instance, retailers such as Target or Walmart carry shopping products like televisions, furniture, and cameras as well as groceries and other convenience products. Take a look at the two advertisements for convenience versus shopping products. Propel electrolyte water is a convenience product that is inexpensive and widely available. The advertisement—which highlights that Propel differs from conventional bottled water—does not even mention where Propel is sold because it is so widely available. Samuel Hubbard Uptown Maverick boots, on the other hand, are a shopping product. This ad depicts a pair of street boots and emphasizes their comfort and craftsmanship. Consumers who purchase this product are likely to have conducted research and will seek out these specific Samuel Hubbard boots because of their features and comfort.

A marketer must consider several key issues to market a shopping product effectively, including how to allocate resources, whether personal selling is needed, and cooperation within the supply chain. Although advertising for shopping products often requires a large budget, an even larger percentage of the overall budget is needed if marketers determine that personal selling is required. The producer and the marketing channel members usually expect some cooperation from one another with respect to providing parts and repair services and performing promotional activities. Marketers should consider these issues carefully so that they can choose the best course for promoting these products.

Specialty Products

Specialty products possess one or more unique characteristics, and generally buyers are willing to expend considerable effort to obtain them. On average, this is the most expensive category of products. Buyers conduct research, plan the purchase of a specialty product, know exactly what they want, and will not accept a substitute. Examples of specialty products include fine jewelry or limited-edition collector's items. When searching for specialty products, buyers do not compare alternatives and are unlikely to base their decision on price. They are concerned primarily with finding an outlet that sells the preselected product. This

shopping products Items for which buyers are willing to expend considerable effort in planning and making purchases

specialty products Items, with unique characteristics, that buyers are willing to expend considerable effort to obtain

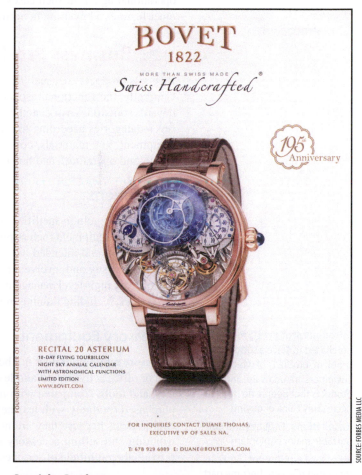

Specialty Product
A Swiss-made watch, such as this Bovet brand, is a specialty product. It is expensive ($30,000 and above), exclusive, and is meant to be treasured for a long time.

advertisement for the Bovet Récital 20 Astérium watch underscores the fact that it is a specialty product. The advertisement has only an image of a Bovet Récital 20 Astérium watch along with brief text highlighting its features, including 10-day flying tourbillon, night sky annual calendar, and astronomical functions. The ad refers interested buyers to the U.S. vice president of sales rather than a retailer, hinting that price should be no object. The watch is very expensive and available only at exclusive outlets.

Marketers will approach their efforts for specialty products differently from convenience or shopping products in several ways. Specialty products are often distributed through a very limited number of retail outlets. Similar to shopping products, they are purchased infrequently, causing lower inventory turnover and thus requiring high gross margins to be profitable.

Unsought Products

Unsought products are those purchased when a sudden problem must be solved, products of which customers are unaware until they see them in a store or online, and products that people do not plan on purchasing. Emergency medical services and automobile repairs are examples of products needed quickly and suddenly to solve a problem. A consumer who is sick or injured has little time to plan to go to an emergency medical center or hospital and will find the closest location to receive service. Likewise, in the event of a broken fan belt in a car, a consumer likely will seek the nearest auto repair facility or call AAA to minimize the length of time before the car is operational again. In such cases, speed of problem resolution is more important than price or other features a buyer might normally consider if there were more time for making a decision.

11-2b Business Products

Business products are usually purchased on the basis of an organization's goals and objectives. Generally, the functional aspects of the product are more important than the psychological rewards sometimes associated with consumer products. Business products can be classified into seven categories according to their characteristics and intended uses: installations, accessory equipment, raw materials, component parts, process materials, MRO supplies (maintenance, repair, and operating), and business services.

Installations

Installations include facilities, such as office buildings, factories, warehouses, and major nonportable equipment such as production lines and very large machines. Normally, installations are expensive and intended to be used for a considerable length of time. Because installations tend to be costly and involve a long-term investment of capital, these purchase decisions often are made by high-level management. Marketers of installations must frequently provide a variety of services, including training, repairs, maintenance assistance, and even aid in financing.

Accessory Equipment

Accessory equipment does not become part of the final physical product but is used in production or office activities. Examples include file cabinets, fractional-horsepower motors, calculators, and tools. Compared with major equipment, accessory items usually are less expensive, purchased routinely with less negotiation, and are often treated as expense items rather than capital items because they are not expected to last as long. More outlets are required for distributing and selling accessory equipment than for installations, but sellers do not have to provide the multitude of services expected of installations marketers.

Raw Materials

Raw materials are the basic natural materials that actually become part of a physical product. They include minerals, chemicals, agricultural products, and materials from forests and oceans. Corn, for instance, is a raw material that is found in many different products, including food (in many forms), beverages (as corn syrup), and even fuel (as ethanol).

unsought products Products purchased to solve a sudden problem, products of which customers are unaware, and products that people do not necessarily think of buying

installations Facilities and nonportable major equipment

accessory equipment Equipment that does not become part of the final physical product but is used in production or office activities

raw materials Basic natural materials that become part of a physical product

Component Parts

Component parts become part of the physical product and are either finished items ready for assembly or products that need little processing before assembly. Although they become part of a larger product, component parts often can be identified and distinguished easily, even after the product is assembled. Spark plugs, tires, clocks, brakes, and headlights are all component parts of an automobile. Buyers purchase such items according to their own specifications or industry standards, and they expect the parts to be of a specified quality and delivered on time so that production is not slowed or stopped. Producers that are primarily assemblers, such as auto or computer manufacturers, depend heavily on suppliers of component parts. Apple, for example, procures component parts from companies in eight different Asian countries—including Foxconn, Pegatron, Sharp, Japan Display, Largan Precision, Alps Electric, and Cowell Electronics—in order to manufacture its iPhone.[5]

Process Materials

Process materials are used directly in the production of other products. Unlike component parts, however, process materials are not readily identifiable. Case in point, a salad dressing manufacturer includes vinegar as an ingredient in dressing. The vinegar is a process material because it is not identifiable or extractable from the other ingredients in the dressing. As with component parts, process materials are purchased according to industry standards or the purchaser's specifications.

MRO Supplies

MRO supplies are maintenance, repair, and operating items that facilitate production and operations, but do not become part of the finished product. Many products that were purchased as consumer products could also be considered MRO supplies to businesses. These might include paper, pencils, cleaning supplies, and paints. MRO supplies are sold through numerous outlets and are purchased routinely, much like convenience products in the consumer market. To ensure supplies are available when needed, buyers often deal with more than one seller.

Business Services

Business services are the intangible products that many organizations use in their operations. They include financial, legal, marketing research, information technology, and janitorial services. Firms must decide whether to provide these services internally or obtain them from outside the organization. This decision depends on the costs associated with each alternative and how frequently the services are needed. In this advertisement, EY promotes its consulting services by asking "Is your strategy planning for the future or creating it?" It pictures a woman writing on a glass board while describing EY's analytics solutions. It targets businesses looking to get ahead through planning and big data analytics.

component parts Items that become part of the physical product and are either finished items ready for assembly or items that need little processing before assembly

process materials Materials that are used directly in the production of other products but are not readily identifiable

MRO supplies Maintenance, repair, and operating items that facilitate production and operations but do not become part of the finished product

business services Intangible products that many organizations use in their operations

ey.com/consulting

EY
Building a better working world

Is your strategy planning for the future or creating it?

Navigate the Transformative Age with analytics solutions from the better-connected consultants.

The better the question. The better the answer. The better the world works.

SOURCE: FORBES MEDIA LLC

Business Services
EY provides consulting services to businesses.

Learning Objective 11-3

Explain the concepts of product line and product mix and how they are related.

11-3 PRODUCT LINE AND PRODUCT MIX

Marketers must understand the relationships among all the products of their organization to coordinate the marketing of the total group of products. The following concepts help to describe the relationships among an organization's products.

A **product item** is a specific version of a product that can be designated as a distinct offering among an organization's products. An American Eagle Outfitters T-shirt represents a product item. A **product line** is a group of closely related product items that are considered to be a unit because of marketing, technical, or end-use considerations. Starbucks, for example, has product lines for beverages, food, mugs and tumblers, and coffee making equipment. Within its beverage product line, the Mocha Frappuccino is a product item.

Specific product items in a product line, such as different lipstick shades or shampoos for oily and dry hair, usually reflect the desires of different target markets or the varying needs of consumers. Thus, to develop the optimal product line, marketers must understand buyers' goals. Firms with high market share are more likely to expand their product lines aggressively, as are marketers with relatively high prices or limited product lines.[6] This pattern can be seen in many industries—including the computer industry, where companies are likely to expand their product lines when industry barriers are low or perceived market opportunities exist.

A **product mix** is the composite, or total, group of products that an organization makes available to customers. The **width of product mix** is measured by the number of product lines a company offers. Deere & Co. offers multiple product lines for the agricultural industry, including tractors and loaders, farm equipment and technology, tools and used equipment, and utility vehicles.[7] The **depth of product mix** is the average number of different product items offered in each product line. Procter & Gamble offers a broad product mix, comprised of all the health-care, beauty-care, laundry and cleaning, food and beverage, and paper products the firm manufactures, some of which are quite deep. Figure 11.1 shows the width and depth of part of Procter & Gamble's product mix. Procter & Gamble is known for using distinctive branding, packaging, segmentation, and consumer advertising to promote individual items in its product lines. Tide, Bold, Gain, Cheer, and Era, for example, are all Procter & Gamble detergents that share the same distribution channels and similar manufacturing facilities, but each is promoted as a distinctive product, adding depth to the product line.

product item A specific version of a product that can be designated as a distinct offering among a firm's products

product line A group of closely related product items viewed as a unit because of marketing, technical, or end-use considerations

product mix The composite, or total, group of products that an organization makes available to customers

width of product mix The number of product lines a company offers

depth of product mix The average number of different products offered in each product line

Figure 11.1 **The Concepts of Product Mix Width and Depth Applied to U.S. Procter & Gamble Products**

Laundry	Oral Care	Bar Soaps	Deodorants	Shampoos	Tissue/Towel	Health
Dreft 1933	Crest 1955	Ivory 1879	Old Spice 1948	Pantene 1947	Charmin 1928	Pepto-Bismol 1901
Tide 1946	Scope 1966	Safeguard 1963	Secret 1956	Head & Shoulders 1961	Puffs 1960	Vicks 1905
Cheer 1950	Oral-B 2006	Olay 1993			Bounty 1965	Prilosec OTC 2003
Downy 1960				Herbal Essences 2001		
Bold 1965				Aussie 2003		
Gain 1966						
Era 1972						
Febreze 2000						

Depth

Width

11-4 PRODUCT LIFE CYCLES AND MARKETING STRATEGIES

Product life cycles follow a similar trajectory to biological life cycles, progressing from birth to death. As Figure 11.2 shows, a **product life cycle** has four major stages: introduction, growth, maturity, and decline. As a product moves through each cycle, the strategies relating to competition, pricing, distribution, promotion, and market information must be evaluated and possibly adjusted. Astute marketing managers use the life-cycle concept to make sure that strategies relating to the introduction, alteration, and deletion of products are timed and executed properly. By understanding the typical life-cycle pattern, marketers can maintain profitable product mixes.

11-4a Introduction

The **introduction stage** of the product life cycle begins at a product's first appearance in the marketplace. Sales start at zero and profits are negative because companies must invest in product development and launch prior to selling. Profits may remain low or below zero because initial revenues will be low while the company covers large expenses for promotion and distribution. Notice in Figure 11.2 how, as sales move upward from zero over time, profits also increase.

Sales may be slow at first because potential buyers must be made aware of a new product's features, uses, and advantages through marketing. Efforts to highlight a new product's value can create a foundation for building brand loyalty and customer relationships.[8] Two difficulties may arise during the introduction stage. First, sellers may lack the resources, technological knowledge, and marketing expertise to launch the product successfully. Large companies often launch new products with advertising and social media campaigns to inform potential buyers about the value of their new offerings. When PepsiCo introduced its Bubly line of flavored, unsweetened sparkling water, it ran commercials during the much-watched Academy Awards to showcase its lighthearted take on the product category. In contrast, National Beverage

product life cycle The progression of a product through four stages: introduction, growth, maturity, and decline

introduction stage The initial stage of a product's life cycle; its first appearance in the marketplace, when sales start at zero and profits are negative

Figure 11.2 **The Four Stages of the Product Life Cycle**

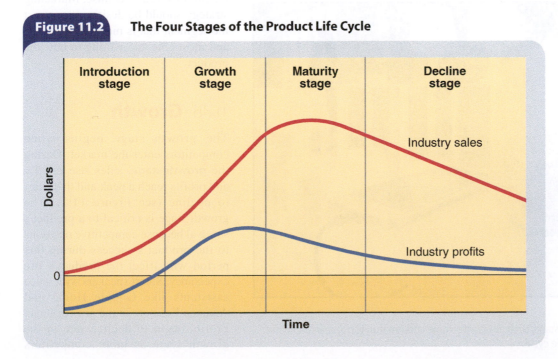

Market Shares for the Largest Consumer Packaged Goods Companies

PepsiCo	5.6%
Kraft Heinz	5.1%
Nestlé	3.4%
General Mills	2.9%
Kellogg's	2.6%
Mars	2.5%
ConAgra Foods	2.2%
Hershey	2.2%
Mondelez Intl.	2.2%
Campbell's	1.6%

SNAPSHOT

Source: Euromonitor.

Corporation achieved rapid sales and loyal following for its LaCroix sparkling water product using an aggressive social media campaign.[9] However, a large marketing budget is not required to launch a successful product. Marketers can attract attention through such techniques as giving away free samples or through media appearances. Websites, such as Retailmenot.com, help firms with low-cost promotion by listing coupons and samples for thousands of companies—exposing customers to great deals and new brands. Some firms also choose to host online brand communities to promote the new product and predict its success. Apple and eBay have become experts in hosting online brand communities to promote products.[10] Second, the initial product price may have to be high to recoup expensive marketing research or development costs, which can depress sales. Given these difficulties, it is not surprising that many products never last beyond the introduction stage.

Most new products start off slowly and seldom generate enough sales to bring immediate profits. Although new-product success rates vary a great deal between companies and in different industries, it is estimated that only 15 to 25 percent of new products succeed in the marketplace.[11] Even among established and successful companies, new-product success rates are rarely above 50 percent. As buyers learn about the new product and express interest, the firm should constantly monitor the product and marketing strategy for weaknesses and make corrections quickly to prevent the product's early demise. Marketing strategy should be designed to attract the segment that is most interested in, and most able and willing to buy, the product.

growth stage The product life-cycle stage during which sales rise rapidly, profits reach a peak, and then profits start to decline

Growth Stage
Smart speaker AI personal assistants such as Google Home and Amazon Echo are in the market growth stage of the product life cycle.

ZAPP2PHOTO/SHUTTERSTOCK.COM

11-4b Growth

The growth stage begins when competitors enter the market. During the **growth stage**, sales rise rapidly and profits reach a peak and then start to decline (see Figure 11.2). The growth stage is critical to a product's survival because competitive reactions to the product's success during this period will affect the product's life expectancy. Smart speakers with voice assistants like Google Home and Amazon Echo are in the growth stage. Profits begin to decline late in the growth stage as more competitors enter the market, driving prices down and creating the need for heavy promotional expenses. At this point, a typical marketing strategy seeks to strengthen market share and position the product favorably against aggressive competitors by emphasizing product benefits. Marketers should analyze competing brands' product positions relative to their own and adjust the marketing mix in response to their findings. Aggressive pricing, including price cuts, is also typical during this stage as a means of gaining market share—even if it means short-term loss of profits. The goal of the marketing strategy in the growth stage is to establish and fortify the product's market position by encouraging adoption and brand loyalty. To achieve greater market penetration, marketers may choose to use segmentation strategies more intensively, which requires developing product variations to satisfy the needs of consumers in several different market segments. For example, a packaged goods company might introduce new flavors of a successful cookie to appeal to different tastes or allergy-free versions to target those with food sensitivities.

Firms should seek to fill gaps in geographic market coverage during the growth period. As a product gains market acceptance, new distribution outlets usually become easier to secure. Marketers sometimes move from an exclusive or a selective exposure to a more intensive network of dealers to achieve greater market penetration. Marketers must also make sure the physical distribution system is running efficiently so that customers' orders are processed accurately and delivered on time.

Promotion expenditures in the growth stage may be slightly lower than during the introductory stage, but are still large. As sales continue to increase, promotion costs should drop as a percentage of total sales, which contributes significantly to increased profits. Advertising messages should stress brand benefits.

maturity stage The stage of a product's life cycle during which the sales curve peaks and starts to level off or decline, and profits continue to fall

11-4c **Maturity**

During the **maturity stage**, sales peak and start to level off or decline, and profits continue to fall (see Figure 11.2). DVDs and DVD players are examples of products in the maturity phase. This stage is characterized by intense competition because many brands are now in the market. Competitors emphasize improvements and differences in their versions of the product. Another example of a product that has many competitors and many variations available on the market is toothpaste and related dental hygiene products. The advertisement for Colgate Total toothpaste and mouthwash, both products in the maturity stage, touts that Colgate Total removes 24 times more bacteria than ordinary, nonantibacterial mouthwash. The advertisement, which pictures a bottle of Colgate Total mouthwash, a tube of Colgate Total whitening toothpaste, and a brand new toothbrush, further distinguishes Colgate Total as supporting "whole mouth health." Weaker competitors are squeezed out of the market during the maturity stage.

During the maturity phase, the producers who remain in the market are likely to change their promotional and distribution efforts. Advertising and dealer-oriented promotions are typical during this stage of the product life cycle. Marketers also must take into account that as maturity is reached, buyers' knowledge of the product is likely to be high. Consumers are no longer inexperienced generalists. They have become experienced specialists. Marketers of

Product Maturity

Dental hygiene products such as Colgate are in the maturity stage of the product life cycle. There are a large number of brands. Many of these brands attempt to distinguish themselves on a specific product feature such as whitener, decay fighter, breath freshener, or tarter control.

mature products sometimes expand distribution into global markets, in which case products may have to be adapted to fit differing needs of global customers more precisely. For instance, as Barbie doll sales decline in the United States, Mattel has been trying to increase interest for Barbie in China. Because parents in China have a different view of toys than parents in the United States have, Mattel has had to adapt Barbie to focus more on learning and intellectual pursuits.[12] If the iconic doll fails to take off there, Mattel may have to shift to a decline strategy for Barbie.

Because many products are in the maturity stage of their life cycles, marketers must know how to deal with them and be prepared to adjust their marketing strategies. There are many approaches to altering marketing strategies during the maturity stage. To increase the sales of mature products, marketers may suggest new uses for them. As customers become more experienced and knowledgeable about products during the maturity stage (particularly about business products), the benefits they seek may change as well, necessitating product modifications. Stonyfield, for example, reformulated its yogurt products so that they would contain less sugar. Because many consumers are concerned about the amount of sugar in consumer packaged goods, Stonyfield recognized this as an opportunity to differentiate its mature products from rivals.[13]

During the maturity stage, marketers actively encourage resellers to support the product. Resellers may be offered promotional assistance to lower their inventory costs. In general, marketers go to great lengths to serve resellers and provide incentives for displaying and selling their brand. Maintaining market share during the maturity stage requires promotion expenditures, which can be large if a firm seeks to increase a product's market share through new uses. Advertising messages in this stage may focus on differentiating a brand from the field of competitors, and sales promotion efforts may be aimed at both consumers and resellers.

11-4d Decline

During the **decline stage**, sales fall rapidly (see Figure 11.2). When this happens, the marketer must consider eliminating items from the product line that no longer earn a profit. The marketer may cut promotion efforts, eliminate marginal distributors, and finally, plan to phase out the product. This can be seen in the decline in demand for most sweetened carbonated beverages such as soda, which has been continuing for decades as consumers turn instead to bottled teas and flavored waters. Companies have responded to this shift in consumer preference by expanding their offerings of juices, waters, and healthier drink options.

In the decline stage, marketers must decide whether to reposition the product to extend its life, or whether it is better to eliminate it. Usually a declining product has lost its distinctiveness because similar competing or superior products have been introduced. Competition engenders increased substitution and brand switching among consumers as they become increasingly insensitive to minor product differences. For these reasons, marketers do little to change a product's style, design, or other attributes during its decline. New technology or social trends, product substitutes, or environmental considerations may also indicate that the time has come to delete the product.

During a product's decline, spending on promotion efforts is usually reduced considerably. Advertising of special offers and sales promotions, such as coupons and premiums, may slow the rate of decline temporarily. Firms will maintain outlets with strong sales volumes and eliminate unprofitable outlets. An entire marketing channel may be eliminated if it does not contribute adequately to profits. A channel not used previously, such as a factory outlet or internet retailer, can help liquidate remaining inventory of a product that is being eliminated. As sales decline, the product becomes harder for consumers to find, but loyal buyers will seek out resellers who still carry it. As the product continues to decline, the sales staff at outlets where it is still sold will shift emphasis to more profitable products.

decline stage The stage of a product's life cycle during which sales fall rapidly

11-5 PRODUCT ADOPTION PROCESS

Learning Objective 11-5
Discuss the product adoption process.

Acceptance of new products—especially new-to-the-world products—usually does not happen quickly. It can take a very long time for consumers to become aware of and overcome skepticism about a new product, particularly if it represents a dramatic innovation. Many consumers prefer to wait to adopt a new product until the "second generation," when kinks are more likely to have been worked out. Customers come to accept new products through an adoption process, detailed in Figure 11.3. The stages of the **product adoption process** are as follows:

Awareness: The buyer becomes aware of the product.

Interest: The buyer seeks information and is receptive to learning about the product.

Evaluation: The buyer considers the product's benefits and decides whether to try it, considering its value versus the competition.

Trial: The buyer examines, tests, or tries the product to determine if it meets his or her needs.

Adoption: The buyer purchases the product and can be expected to use it again whenever the need for this product arises.[14]

In the first stage, when consumers initially become aware that the product exists, they possess little information and are not yet concerned about obtaining more. Consumers enter the interest stage when they become motivated to learn about the product's features, uses, advantages, disadvantages, price, or location. During the evaluation stage, individuals consider whether the product will address the criteria that are crucial to meeting their specific needs. In the trial stage, consumers use or experience the product for the first time, possibly by purchasing a small quantity, taking advantage of free samples, or borrowing the product from someone else. Individuals move into the adoption stage when they need a product of that general type and choose to purchase the new product on a trial basis. However, entering the adoption stage does not mean that the person will eventually adopt the new product. Rejection may occur at any stage. Both product adoption and product rejection can be temporary or permanent.

When an organization introduces a new product, consumers in the target market enter into and move through the adoption process at different rates. For most products, there is also a group of non-adopters who never begin the process. For business marketers, success in managing production innovation, diffusion, and adoption requires great adaptability and significant effort in understanding customers.[15]

Depending on the length of time it takes them to adopt a new product, consumers tend to fall into one of five major adopter categories: innovators, early adopters, early majority, late majority, and laggards.[16] **Innovators** are the first to adopt a new product because they enjoy trying new products and do not mind taking a risk. **Early adopters** choose new products carefully and are viewed as people who are in-the-know by those in the remaining adopter categories. People in the **early majority** adopt just prior to the average person. They are deliberate and cautious in trying new products. Individuals in the **late majority** are skeptical of new products, but eventually adopt them because of economic necessity or social pressure. **Laggards**, the last to adopt a new product, are oriented toward the past. They are suspicious of new products, and when they finally adopt them, the products may already have been replaced by even newer products.

product adoption process The five-stage process of buyer acceptance of a product: awareness, interest, evaluation, trial, and adoption

innovators First adopters of new products

early adopters People who adopt new products early, choose new products carefully, and are viewed as "the people to check with" by later adopters

early majority Individuals who adopt a new product just prior to the average person

late majority Skeptics who adopt new products when they feel it is necessary

laggards The last product adopters, who distrust new products

---

Figure 11.3	**Production Adoption Process**

Awareness → Interest → Evaluation → Trial → Adoption

Learning Objective 11-6

Explain the major components of branding, including brand types, branding strategies, and brand protection.

11-6 **BRANDING**

Marketers must make many decisions about products, including choices about brands, brand names, brand marks, trademarks, and trade names. A **brand** is a name, term, design, symbol, or any other feature that identifies one marketer's product as distinct from those of other marketers.[17] A brand may identify a single item, a family of items, or all items of that seller. Some have defined a brand as not just the physical good, name, color, logo, or ad campaign, but everything associated with the product, including its symbolism and experiences.[18] Firms that try to shift the image of a brand risk losing market share. Coca-Cola learned this the hard way with its failed New Coke brand. The casual dining restaurant chain Applebee's also stumbled when it tried to rebrand itself as a modern bar and grill to appeal more to affluent Millennial consumers. New dishes and remodeled stores didn't bring in younger consumers, but they did drive away Applebee's older regular customers. The chain was forced to close 130 restaurants when sales fell. The remaining stores are bringing back old favorites like all-you-can-eat specials in hopes of bringing back Applebee's core regular customers.[19] However, simple brand changes have also led to major marketing successes.

A **brand name** is the part of a brand that can be spoken—including letters, words, and numbers—such as 7UP or V8. A brand name is essential, as it is often a product's only distinguishing characteristic without which a firm could not differentiate its products. To consumers, a brand name is as fundamental as the product itself. Indeed, many brand names have become synonymous with the product, such as Scotch Tape, Xerox copiers, and Kleenex tissues. Marketers must make efforts, through promotional activities, to ensure that such brand names do not become generic terms, which are not protected under the law.

The element of a brand that is not comprised of words—often a symbol or design—is a **brand mark**. Examples of brand marks include the McDonald's Golden Arches, Nike's "swoosh," and Apple's silhouette of an apple with a bite missing. A **trademark** is a legal designation indicating that the owner has exclusive use of a brand or a part of a brand and that others are prohibited by law from its use. To protect a brand name or a brand mark in the United States, an organization must register it as a trademark with the U.S. Patent and Trademark Office. Finally, a **trade name** is the full and legal name of an organization, such as Ford Motor Company, rather than the name of a specific product.

11-6a **Value of Branding**

Both buyers and sellers benefit from branding. Brands help buyers, during the buying decision process, to recognize specific products that meet their criteria for quality, which reduces the time needed to identify and purchase products by facilitating identification of products that satisfy consumer needs. Without brands, product selection would be more difficult because buyers would have fewer guideposts indicating quality and product features. For many consumers, purchasing certain brands is a form of self-expression. For instance, clothing brand names, such as The North Face or Ralph Lauren, are important to many consumers because they convey signals about their lifestyle or self-image. Especially when a customer is unable to judge a product's quality, a brand indicates a quality level and image to the customer and reduces a buyer's perceived risk of purchase. Customers want to purchase brands whose quality they trust, such as Coca-Cola, Nike, and Panera. In addition, customers might receive a psychological reward from purchasing and owning a brand that symbolizes high status, such as Aston Martin or Chanel. On the other hand, conspicuous brand usage that is considered to be attention-getting can cause dilution in some cases. Some brand users with a low self-brand connection may have a harder time connecting with the brand. For example, showing-off behaviors such as wearing Gucci sunglasses indoors may be perceived negatively by brand users.[20]

Sellers also benefit from branding because brands are identifiers that make repeat purchasing easier for customers, thereby fostering brand loyalty. Furthermore, branding helps a firm

brand A name, term, design, symbol, or other feature that identifies one seller's product as distinct from those of other sellers

brand name The part of a brand that can be spoken, including letters, words, and numbers

brand mark The part of a brand that is not made up of words, such as a symbol or design

trademark A legal designation of exclusive use of a brand

trade name The full legal name of an organization

introduce a new product by carrying the name and image of one or more existing products. Buyers are more likely to experiment with the new product because of familiarity with products carrying the firm's existing brand names. It also facilitates promotional efforts because the promotion of each branded product indirectly promotes all other products bearing the same brand. As consumers become loyal to a specific brand, the company's market share will achieve a level of stability, allowing the firm to use its resources more efficiently.

Branding also involves a cultural dimension in that consumers confer their own social meanings onto them. A brand appeals to customers on an emotional level based on its symbolic image and key associations.[21] For some brands, such as Harley-Davidson and Apple, this can result in an almost cult-like following. These brands may develop communities of loyal customers that communicate through get-togethers, online forums, blogs, podcasts, and other means. They may even help consumers to develop their identity and self-concept and serve as a form of self-expression. In fact, the term *cultural branding* has been used to explain how a brand conveys a powerful myth that consumers find useful in cementing their identities.[22] It is also important for marketers to recognize that brands are not completely within their control because a brand exists independently in the consumer's mind. Every aspect of a brand is subject to a consumer's emotional involvement, interpretation, and memory. By understanding how branding influences purchases, marketers can foster customer loyalty.[23]

11-6b Brand Equity

A well-managed brand is an asset to an organization. The value of this asset is often referred to as brand equity. **Brand equity** is the marketing and financial value associated with a brand's strength in a market. In addition to actual proprietary brand assets, such as patents and trademarks, four major elements underlie brand equity: brand-name awareness, brand loyalty, perceived brand quality, and brand associations (see Figure 11.4).[24]

Being aware of a brand leads to brand familiarity, which results in a level of comfort with the brand. A consumer is more likely to select a familiar brand than an unfamiliar one because the familiar brand is more likely to be viewed as reliable and of an acceptable level of quality. The familiar brand is also likely to be in a customer's consideration set, whereas the unfamiliar brand is not.

Brand loyalty is a customer's favorable attitude toward a specific brand. If brand loyalty is sufficiently strong, customers will purchase the brand consistently when they need a product in that specific product category. Customer satisfaction with a brand is the most common reason for loyalty to that brand.[25] Companies with the most brand loyalty include Delta (airlines), Amazon (online retailer), Lyft (app-based ride share), Red Bull (energy drinks), Advil (pain relievers), ExxonMobil (gasoline), AT&T (wireless phone service), and Discover

brand equity The marketing and financial value associated with a brand's strength in a market

brand loyalty A customer's favorable attitude toward a specific brand

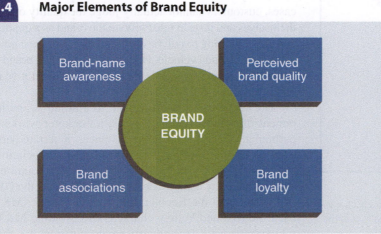

Figure 11.4   Major Elements of Brand Equity

(credit cards).[26] Brand loyalty has advantages for the customer as well as the manufacturer and the seller. It reduces a buyer's risks and shortens the time spent deciding which product to purchase. The degree of brand loyalty is highly variable among product categories. For instance, it is challenging for a firm to foster brand loyalty for products such as fruits or vegetables, because customers can readily judge their quality by looking at them in the grocery store without referring to a brand. However, when consumers perceive products as being green or sustainable, their attitude toward the brand tends to improve.[27]

The rapid pace of technological transformation also presents challenges for marketers. With new computers, apps, and other digital devices entering the market at an ever more rapid pace, it can be difficult for marketers to sustain a high level of emotional engagement with consumers, and therefore retain their loyalty from year to year. Brand loyalty also varies by country, as different cultures may identify with a certain brand to a greater or lesser degree. Globally, international tech brands Apple and Google have a higher degree of brand loyalty than brands in other product categories.[28]

brand recognition The degree of brand loyalty in which a customer is aware that a brand exists and views the brand as an alternative purchase if their preferred brand is unavailable

brand preference The degree of brand loyalty in which a customer prefers one brand over competitive offerings

brand insistence The degree of brand loyalty in which a customer strongly prefers a specific brand and will accept no substitute

There are three degrees of brand loyalty: recognition, preference, and insistence. **Brand recognition** occurs when a customer is aware that the brand exists and views it as an alternative purchase if the preferred brand is unavailable or if the other available brands are unfamiliar. This is the weakest form of brand loyalty. **Brand preference** is a stronger degree of brand loyalty. A customer has a definite preference for one brand over competitive offerings, and will purchase this brand if it is available. However, if the brand is not available, the customer will accept a substitute rather than expending the additional effort required to find and purchase the preferred brand. **Brand insistence** is the strongest and least common level of brand loyalty. A customer will accept no substitute and is willing to spend a great deal of time and effort to acquire that brand. If a brand-insistent customer goes to a store and finds the brand unavailable, he or she will seek the brand elsewhere rather than purchase a substitute. Brand insistence also can apply to service products, such as Hilton Hotels, or sports teams, such as the Dallas Cowboys. Although rare, marketers aspire to achieve brand insistence.

Brand loyalty is an important component of brand equity because it reduces a brand's vulnerability to competitors' actions. It allows an organization to retain existing customers and avoid expending significant resources to gain new ones. Loyal customers help to promote a brand by providing visibility and reassuring potential new customers of the brand's quality. Retailers strive to carry the brands known for their strong customer following to satisfy customers because they expect these brands to be available when and where they shop.

Customers associate a particular brand with a certain level of overall quality. As mentioned, customers frequently use a brand name as a proxy for an actual assessment of a product's quality. In many cases, customers cannot actually judge the quality of the product for themselves and instead must rely on the brand as a quality indicator. A consumer looking to purchase a new car might have never purchased a Toyota or Honda vehicle. However, because the brands rank among the highest in quality, a potential car buyer might give preference to them over other brands.[29]

The set of associations linked to a brand is another key component of brand equity. At times, a marketer works to connect a particular lifestyle or, in some instances, a certain personality type with a specific brand. These types of brand associations contribute significantly to the brand's equity. Brand associations sometimes are facilitated by using trade characters, such as the GEICO Gecko, Mr. Clean, and the Keebler Elves. For instance, M&Ms has long used the Red and Yellow characters to promote M&M candies in a humorous way. This advertisement portrays the characters with

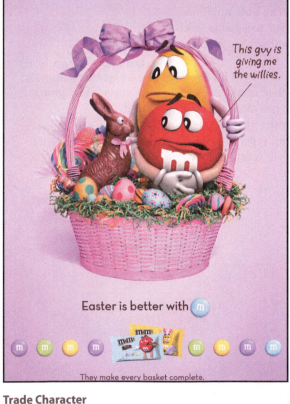

SOURCE: GOOD HOUSEKEEPING

Trade Character
The M&M Red and Yellow characters are used as trade characters. They are used to create positive brand associations in the minds of customers.

a chocolate bunny in an Easter basket with the tag line, "Easter is better with M&Ms." The Red and Yellow trade characters help establish positive brand associations in the minds of consumers. Placing these trade characters in advertisements and on packaging helps consumers to link the ads and packages with the brands. This practice is particularly effective with younger consumers, which is why many cereals and candies feature licensed characters such as Dora the Explorer.[30]

Although difficult to measure, brand equity represents the value of a brand to an organization—it includes both tangible assets and intangibles such as public perception and consumer loyalty. Table 11.1 lists the top 10 brands with the highest economic value. Any company that owns a brand listed in Table 11.1 would agree that equity is likely to be the greatest single asset in the organization's possession.

11-6c Types of Brands

There are three categories of brands: manufacturer, private distributor, and generic. **Manufacturer brands** are initiated by producers and ensure that producers are identified with their products at the point of purchase—for example, Green Giant, Dell Computer, and Levi's jeans. A manufacturer brand usually requires a producer to become involved in distribution, promotion, and to some extent, pricing decisions.

Private distributor brands (also called *private brands, store brands*, or *dealer brands*) are initiated and owned by resellers—wholesalers or retailers. The major characteristic of private brands is that the manufacturers are not identified on the products. Retailers and wholesalers use private distributor brands to develop more efficient promotion, generate higher gross margins, and change store image. Private distributor brands give retailers or wholesalers freedom to purchase products of a specified quality at the lowest cost without disclosing the identities of the manufacturers. Wholesaler brands include IGA (Independent Grocers' Alliance) and Price Chopper. Successful private brands are distributed nationally, and many rival the quality of manufacturer brands. Familiar retailer brand names include Target's Archer Farms and Up & Up, Walmart's Great Value, and Whole Foods' 365 Everyday Value. Sometimes retailers with successful private distributor brands start manufacturing their own products to gain more control over product costs, quality, and design in the hope of increasing profits. Sales of private labels have reached $115 billion, now accounting for one out of every four products sold in supermarkets. In recent years, store brand sales have grown by 1.8 percent while the leading

manufacturer brands A brand initiated by producers to ensure that producers are identified with their products at the point of purchase

private distributor brands Brands initiated and owned by a reseller

Table 11.1 **The 10 Most Valuable Brands in the World**

Rank	Brand	Brand Value ($ Billions)
1	Google	245.6
2	Apple	234.7
3	Microsoft	143.2
4	Amazon	139.3
5	Facebook	129.8
6	AT&T	115.1
7	Visa	111.0
8	Tencent	108.3
9	IBM	102.1
10	McDonald's	97.7

Source: Millward Brown, "2017 BrandZ Top 100 Global Brands," http://www.millwardbrown.com/brandz/top-global-brands/2017 (accessed February 12, 2018).

national manufacturer brands have seen sales growth of just 1.1 percent.[31] Quality and benefits relative to price are a significant reason many shoppers choose store brands over manufacturer ones. These factors simplify the consumers buying decision process when confronted with multiple brands—many now opt for the private brand knowing that quality is on par with leading manufacturer brands.[32]

Some products, on the other hand, are not branded at all, which is often called *generic branding*. **Generic brands** indicate only the product category and do not include the company name or other identifying terms. These items are typically staples that would be marketed using an undifferentiated strategy because they lack special features, such as sugar, salt, or aluminum foil. Generic brands usually are sold at lower prices than comparable branded items and compete on the basis of price and value. The prevalence of generic brands has decreased over time, particularly as the quality and value of private brands has increased.

11-6d Selecting a Brand Name

Marketers consider several factors in selecting a brand name. First, the name should be easy for customers (including foreign buyers if the firm intends to market its products in other countries) to say, spell, and recall. Short, one-syllable names, such as Cheer, often satisfy this requirement. Second, the brand name should indicate in some way the product's major benefits and, if possible, should suggest the product's uses and special characteristics. Marketers should always avoid negative or offensive references. Thus, the brand names of household cleaning products such as Ajax dishwashing liquid, Vanish toilet bowl cleaner, Formula 409 multipurpose cleaner, Cascade dishwasher detergent, and Wisk laundry detergent connote strength and effectiveness. There is evidence that consumers are more likely to recall and to evaluate favorably names that convey positive attributes or benefits.[33] Third, to set it apart from competing brands, the brand should be distinctive. Further research findings have shown that creating a brand personality that aligns with the products sold and the target market's self-image is important to brand success—if the target market feels aligned with the brand, they are more likely to develop brand loyalty.[34] If a marketer intends to use a brand for a product line, that brand must be compatible with all products in the line. Finally, a brand should be designed to be used and recognized in all types of media. Finding the right brand has become an increasingly challenging task because many obvious names have already been used.

Marketers can devise brand names from single or multiple words—for example, Dodge Nitro. Letters and numbers, alone or in combination, are used to create such brands as the Honda CR-V or iPhone X. Words, numbers, and letters are combined to yield brand names, such as Samsung Galaxy S8+ or Audi S3 sedan. To avoid terms that have negative connotations, marketers sometimes use fabricated words that have absolutely no meaning when created—for example, Häagen-Dazs. For marketing in China, U.S. brands strive to use names that translate well and have significant meaning in Chinese, but stay true to their U.S. identities. Thus, Starbucks goes by Starry Hope, which is consistent with its U.S. logo. Nike calls itself "Nai ke," which translates to "endurance and perseverance" but sounds like its U.S. name; rival Reebok is called "Rui bu," which means "fast steps."[35]

Who actually creates brand names? Brand names are generally created by individuals or a team within the organization. Sometimes a name is suggested by individuals who are close to the development of the product. Some organizations have committees that participate in brand-name creation and approval. Large companies that introduce numerous new products annually are likely to have a department that develops brand names. At times, outside consultants and companies that specialize in brand-name development are used.

11-6e Protecting a Brand

generic brands Brands indicating only the product category

A marketer should also design a brand that can be protected easily through registration. A series of court decisions has created a broad hierarchy of protection based on brand type. From most protectable to least protectable, these brand types are fanciful (Exxon), arbitrary (Dr Pepper),

CREATIVE MARKETING

What Does Coach, Kate Spade, and Stuart Weitzman Have in Common? Tapestry!

Since Coach was founded in 1941, the company has built an international reputation for high-quality wallets, handbags, briefcases, and other leather goods. Over time, Coach has steadily expanded into other product categories, including fashion apparel for men and women. It also operates 950 Coach stores around the world. The brand's strength has been a real plus for the company, its products, and its stores. So why would the company rebrand itself after more than three-quarters of a century?

The answer has to do with the company's changing product mix and brand portfolio. A few years ago, it branched out beyond wallets and handbags by acquiring Stuart Weitzman, a luxury shoe manufacturer. Not long afterward, it bought Kate Spade, an upscale marketer of stylish handbags, shoes,

clothing, and accessories. At that point, "Coach Inc. was now also the parent of two other brands, but only represented one of the three brands," said CEO Victor Luis.

Coach wanted its corporate name to reflect the widening product mix and growing number of brands under its ownership. With the help of a branding agency, Coach executives considered a number of new names, checking which were eligible for multinational trademark protection and how each would sound as a website name or social-media account. After weeks of deliberation, they chose Tapestry as the new corporate name. The CEO explained this rebranding by noting that "Tapestry can grow with our portfolio and with our current brands as they extend into new categories and markets."[a]

suggestive (Spray 'n Wash), and descriptive (Minute Rice). Generic terms, such as aluminum foil, are not protectable. Surnames and descriptive, geographic, or functional names are difficult to protect.[36] However, research findings show that consumers prefer these descriptive and suggestive brand names and find them easier to recall compared with fanciful and arbitrary brand names.[37] A firm should take steps so that its brands are protected and trademarks are renewed as needed.

To guard its exclusive rights to a brand, a company must ensure that the brand is not likely to be considered an infringement on any brand already registered with the U.S. Patent and Trademark Office. Actually proving that patent infringement has occurred may be complex because infringement is determined by the courts, which base their decisions on whether a brand causes consumers to be confused, mistaken, or deceived about the source of the product. McDonald's is the company probably most famous for aggressively protecting its trademarks against infringement by launching legal charges against a number of companies with *Mc* names. It fears that use of the prefix will give consumers the impression that these companies are associated with or owned by McDonald's.

A marketer should guard against allowing a brand name to become a generic term because these cannot be protected as exclusive brand names. For example, *aspirin, escalator,* and *shredded wheat*—all brand names at one time—eventually were declared generic terms that refer to product classes. Thus, they could no longer be protected. To keep a brand name from becoming a generic term, the firm should spell the name with a capital letter and use it as an adjective to modify the name of the general product class, as in Kool-Aid Brand Soft Drink Mix or Kleenex Brand Tissues.[38] An organization can deal with this problem directly by advertising that its brand is a trademark and should not be used generically. The firm also can indicate that the brand is a registered trademark by using the symbol ®.

A U.S. firm that tries to protect a brand in a foreign country is likely to encounter additional problems. In many countries, brand registration is not possible. In such places, the first firm to use a brand in such a country automatically has the rights to it. In some instances, U.S. companies actually have had to buy their own brand rights from a firm in a foreign country because the foreign firm was the first user in that country. Consider that in China, "trademark squatters" look for valuable foreign brands and rush to register them as trademarks there. When the actual brand owners attempt to launch their products in China, they are forced to buy back their trademark for huge sums, rebrand their product, or spend considerable time and money fighting the infringement in Chinese courts.[39]

Marketers trying to protect their brands also must contend with brand counterfeiting. In the United States, for instance, one can purchase fake General Motors parts, Cartier and Rolex watches, Louis Vuitton handbags, Walt Disney character dolls, Microsoft software, Warner Brothers clothing, Mont Blanc pens, and a host of other products illegally marketed by manufacturers that do not own the brands. The global trade in counterfeit and pirated goods is estimated at $1.7 trillion while the criminal enforcement, social, and investment costs of dealing with these goods are estimated at $2.5 trillion. Counterfeit products not only harm manufacturers, but can also harm consumers when their manufacture is subpar or they are made of harmful ingredients.[40]

11-6f Branding Strategies

Before establishing branding strategies, a firm must decide whether to brand its products at all. If a company's product is homogeneous and similar to competitors' products, it may be difficult to brand in a way that will result in consumer loyalty. Raw materials and commodities such as coal, carrots, or gravel are hard to brand because of their homogeneity and their physical characteristics.

If a firm chooses to brand its products, it may use individual or family branding, or a combination. **Individual branding** is a policy of naming each product differently. Nestlé S.A., the world's largest food and nutrition company, uses individual branding for many of its more than 2,000 different brands, such as Nescafé coffee, PowerBar nutritional food, Maggi soups, and Häagen-Dazs ice cream. A major advantage of individual branding is that, if an organization introduces a product that fails in the marketplace, the negative images associated with it do not influence consumers' decisions to purchase the company's other products. An individual branding strategy may also facilitate market segmentation when a firm wishes to enter many segments of the same market. Separate, unrelated names can be used, and each brand can be aimed at a specific segment. With individual branding, however, a firm cannot capitalize on the positive image associated with successful products.

When using **family branding**, all of a firm's products are branded with the same name, or part of the name, such as the cereals Kellogg's Frosted Flakes, Kellogg's Rice Krispies, and Kellogg's Corn Flakes. In some cases, a company's name is combined with other words, such as with Arm & Hammer Heavy Duty Detergent, Arm & Hammer Pure Baking Soda, and Arm & Hammer Carpet Deodorizer, which uses the "Arm & Hammer" name followed by a description. Unlike individual branding, family branding means that the promotion of one item with the family brand promotes the firm's other products. Family branding can be a benefit when consumers have positive associations with brands, or a drawback if something happens to make consumers think negatively of the brand.

An organization is not limited to a single branding strategy. A company that uses primarily individual branding for many of its products also may use family branding for a specific product line. Branding strategy is influenced by the number of products and product lines the company produces, the number and types of competing products available, and the size of the firm.

11-6g Brand Extensions

A **brand extension** occurs when an organization uses one of its existing brands to brand a new product in a different product category. For example, Baileys extended its well-known Baileys Irish Cream liqueur brand when it introduced Baileys Iced Coffee, single serving

individual branding A branding strategy in which each product is given a different name

family branding Branding all of a firm's products with the same name or part of the name

brand extension An organization uses one of its existing brands to brand a new product in a different product category

canned iced coffees flavored with Baileys Irish Cream, to capitalize on the growing category of iced coffee.[41] Mont Blanc has long been known for its luxury writing instruments that can cost hundreds or thousands of dollars. The advertisement shows that Mont Blanc has extended the brand and its trademark logo to a number of other product categories including fragrances. The tagline of the ad, "Mont Blanc Legend," over an image of two bottles of Mont Blanc Legend fragrances, reminds consumers of the renowned Mont Blanc reputation for quality and strives to attach it to entirely new types of products in the minds of consumers. A brand extension should not be confused with a line extension, which will be discussed in greater detail in Chapter 12. A line extension refers to using an existing brand on a new product in the same product category, such as new flavors or sizes.

If a brand is extended too many times or extended too far outside its original product category, it can be weakened through dilution of its image and symbolic impact. Table 11.2 describes brand extensions that failed because they were too dissimilar to their core product. For example, Harley Davidson's cake decorating kit has been voted one of the worst brand extensions because cake decorating does not appear to relate to its iconic motorcycle product.[42] Research has found that a line extension into premium categories can be an effective strategy to revitalize a brand, but the extension needs to be closely linked to the core brand.[43] Successful branding strategies for new product categories depend largely on how they fit with the product categories of the parent brand, as well as how the positioning of the new product is similar to how the parent brand is positioned.[44]

Brand Extensions

Writing instruments were the first products to carry the Mont Blanc name. Today the brand has been extended to watches, leather products, smart devices, jewelry, and fragrances.

Table 11.2 Worst Brand Extensions

Brand Name	Core Product	Failed Brand Extension
Smith & Wesson	Firearms	Mountain Bikes
BIC	Pens	BIC Underwear
Cosmopolitan	Magazine	Yogurt
Wrigley	Candy	Life Savers Soda
Coors	Beer	Rocky Mountain Spring Water
Colgate	Consumer products	Colgate Kitchen Entrees
Frito-Lay	Snack foods	Lemonade
Harley-Davidson	Motorcycles	Perfume

Source: "Top 25 Biggest Product Flops of All Time," *AOL*, https://www.aol.com/article/finance/2016/05/25/top-25-biggest-product-flops-of-all-time/21383586/ (accessed February 12, 2018).

11-6h Co-Branding

Co-branding is the use of two or more brands on one product. Marketers employ co-branding to capitalize on the brand equity of multiple brands. For instance, Benjamin Moore partnered with the retailer, Target, to release a co-branded line of paint colors that coordinate with Target's kids' furniture and accessories collection.[45] Co-branding is popular in several processed-food categories and in the credit card industry. The brands used for co-branding can be owned by the same company. Many food items are co-branded initially. Cinnabon has released co-branded items with Kellogg's (cereal) and Pillsbury (Toaster Strudel).

Effective co-branding capitalizes on the trust and confidence customers have in the brands involved. For instance, Harley Davidson successfully teamed up with Best Western to develop a rewards program for motorcycle enthusiasts. At more than 1,200 hotels throughout the United States, motorcycle enthusiasts can receive a free wipe-down motorcycle towel and other benefits. The partnership was so successful that it was extended for three years and expanded to areas outside of the United States.[46] The brands should not lose their identities, and it should be clear to customers which brand is the main brand. It is important for marketers to understand before entering a co-branding relationship that when a co-branded product is unsuccessful, both brands are implicated in the failure. To gain customer acceptance, the brands involved must represent a complementary fit in the minds of buyers. Trying to link a brand such as Harley-Davidson with a brand such as Healthy Choice would not achieve co-branding objectives because customers are not likely to perceive these brands as compatible.

co-branding Using two or more brands on one product

brand licensing An agreement whereby a company permits another organization to use its brand on other products for a licensing fee

11-6i Brand Licensing

A popular branding strategy involves **brand licensing**, an agreement in which a company permits another organization to use its brand on other products for a licensing fee. Royalties may be as low as 2 percent of wholesale revenues or higher than 10 percent. The licensee is responsible for all manufacturing, selling, and advertising functions and bears the costs if the

INTEGRITY IN MARKETING

John Deere Brand Drives Eco Rigs Toys

When BeginAgain of Fort Collins, Colorado, began planning a line of eco-friendly toys, co-founders Chris Clemmer and David Bowen approached Deere & Company with the idea of licensing its famous brand. The Deere brand has a long association with American agriculture, stretching back to the firm's original plows introduced in the 1830s. By licensing the brand, BeginAgain aims to "tell the story of farmers and factories coming together to create a great product," says Clemmer.

Once BeginAgain secured the brand license, the co-founders designed a dump truck and a front-loader as the first two toys in the product line because so many U.S. farmers use those types of trucks. They arranged to manufacture the toy trucks in Illinois, Maine, and Nebraska, using bioplastic materials created from corncobs and sugar cane harvested in the American heartland. To emphasize the use of plant-based materials rather than traditional oil-based plastics, they named the product line "Eco Rigs." The trucks even smell a little like toasted corn, reinforcing their "farm-to-factory" back story.

Today, BeginAgain's John Deere-branded toys are sold in stores from coast to coast as well as through online retailers. Even JohnDeere.com sells the Eco Rigs. What's more, BeginAgain is winning recognition and industry awards for its use of regionally produced, sustainable agricultural materials instead of non-biodegradable plastics to make this line of toys. Watch for more Eco Rigs as BeginAgain expands the product line to meet demand in the coming years.[b]

licensed product fails. The top U.S. licensing company is Disney Consumer Products, the products arm of the Walt Disney Company, with $56.6 billion in licensing revenue.[47] Sports is an industry that engages in much licensing, with the NFL, the NCAA, NASCAR, and MLB all leaders in the retail sales of licensed sports-related products. The advantages of licensing range from extra revenues and the low cost of brand expansion to generating free publicity, developing a new image, or protecting a trademark. The major disadvantages are a lack of manufacturing control and the risks of making consumers feel bombarded with too many unrelated products bearing the same name.

11-7 PACKAGING

Learning Objective 11-7

Describe the major packaging functions, design considerations, and how packaging is used in marketing strategies.

Packaging involves the development of a container to hold a product. A package can be a vital part of a product, making it more versatile, safer, and easier to use. It also conveys vital information about the product and is an opportunity to display interesting graphic design elements. Like a brand name, a package can influence customers' attitudes toward a product and their decisions to purchase. Consequently, packaging convenience can be a major factor in purchase. Producers of jellies, sauces, and ketchups package their products in squeezable plastic containers that can be stored upside down, which make dispensing and storing the product more convenient. Package characteristics help to shape buyers' impressions of a product at the time of purchase and during use. In this section, we examine the main functions of packaging and consider several major packaging decisions. We also analyze the role of the package in a marketing strategy.

11-7a Packaging Functions

At the most basic level, packaging materials serve the basic purpose of protecting the product and maintaining its functional form. Fluids, like milk or orange juice, require packages that are waterproof and durable to preserve and protect their contents. Packaging should prevent damage that could affect the product's usefulness, which leads to higher costs. Packaging techniques have also been developed to prevent product tampering, as this has been a major problem for many firms. Some packages are also designed to deter shoplifting through the inclusion of antitheft devices.

Another function of packaging is to offer convenience to consumers. For instance, single-serving containers for food and drinks that do not require refrigeration appeal to children, parents, and those with active lifestyles because they are easily portable. Packaging can prevent product waste, make storage easier for retailers and for consumers, and even promote greater consumption. Additionally, packaging can promote a product by communicating its features, uses, benefits, and image. Sometimes a reusable package can make the product more desirable. SC Johnson encourages consumers to reuse their Windex bottles by selling smaller recyclable refill packages. These refills help reduce the waste that comes with purchasing an entirely new bottle of Windex each time the old one runs out.[48] Finally, packaging can be used to communicate symbolically the quality or premium nature of a product. When Colorado-based MM Local rebranded itself as Farmhand Organics, it modified the packaging of its pickled and fermented products to reflect their simple ingredients and highlight the farms that produced them. The products are packaged in clear glass jars with clear labels so consumers can see exactly what's in them, and each product has a traceability sticker that indicates what farm grew the products inside.[49] Packaging can also evoke an emotional response.

11-7b Major Packaging Considerations

Marketers must take many factors into account when designing and producing packages. Obviously, a major consideration is cost. Although a number of different packaging materials, processes, and designs are available, costs can vary greatly. In recent years, buyers have shown a willingness to pay more for improved packaging, but there are limits. Marketers should conduct research to determine exactly how much customers are willing to pay for effective and efficient package designs.

Increasingly, firms are finding that they can cut down on the cost of packaging and be more environmentally friendly through developing minimalist packaging. Redesigned packaging requires fewer materials, is easier and cheaper to ship because it is lighter, and consumers appreciate the lower carbon footprint. As part of its long-term plan, McCormick & Co. was able to save costs, reduce its carbon footprint, and achieve longer spice freshness by changing the packaging for its black pepper and Old Bay seasonings from tin to Polyethylene Terephthalate (PET) containers.[50]

As mentioned previously, developing tamper-resistant packaging is very important for certain products. Although no package is completely tamperproof, marketers can develop packages that are difficult to contaminate. At a minimum, all packaging must comply with the Food and Drug Administration's (FDA) packaging regulations. However, packaging should also make any product tampering evident to resellers and consumers. Although effective tamper-resistant packaging may be expensive to develop, when compared to the potential costs of lost sales, loss of consumer confidence and company reputation, and potentially expensive product liability lawsuits, the costs of ensuring consumer safety through safer packaging are relatively small.

Marketers should consider how much consistency is desirable between the package designs of different products produced by an organization. If a firm's products are unrelated or aimed at very different target markets, no consistency may be the best policy. In many cases, however, packaging uniformity may be best. To promote an overall company image, a firm may decide that all packages should be similar or should all feature a major design element. This approach is called **family packaging**. It is generally used for lines of products, as with Campbell's soups, Weight Watchers' foods, or Planters Nuts.

A package's promotional role is an important consideration. Through verbal and nonverbal symbols, the package can inform potential buyers about the product's content, features, uses, advantages, and hazards. A firm can create desirable images and associations by its choice of color, design, shape, and texture. Many cosmetics manufacturers, for example, design their packages to create impressions of luxury and exclusivity. A package performs a promotional function when it is designed to be safer or more convenient to use if such characteristics help stimulate demand.

A package designer must consider size, shape, texture, color, and graphics—as well as functionality—to develop a package that has a definite promotional value. Clever design can make a package appear taller or shorter or larger or smaller, depending on the desire of the marketer and expectations of consumers. Marketers often carefully consider what colors to use on packages to attract attention and positively influence customers' emotions. People associate specific colors with certain feelings and experiences. Here are some examples:

- White represents sincerity, simplicity, and purity.
- Yellow is associated with cheerfulness, optimism, and friendliness.
- Red connotes excitement and stimulation.
- Pink is considered soft, nurturing, and feminine.
- Blue is soothing; it is also associated with intelligence, trust, and security.
- Black represents power, status, and sophistication.
- Purple is associated with dignity, quality, and luxury.
- Brown is linked to seriousness, ruggedness, and earthiness.
- Green is associated with nature and sustainability.[51]

family packaging Using similar packaging for all of a firm's products or packaging that has one common design element

When opting for color on packaging, marketers must judge whether a particular color will evoke positive or negative feelings when linked to a specific product. Thus, marketers are not likely to package meat or bread in green materials because customers may associate green with mold. Marketers must also determine whether a specific target market will respond favorably or unfavorably to a color.

Packaging also must meet the needs of resellers. Wholesalers and retailers consider whether a package facilitates transportation, storage, and handling. Resellers may refuse to carry certain products if their packages are cumbersome or require too much shelf space. For instance, concentrated versions of laundry detergents and fabric softeners aid retailers and shoppers alike by offering products in smaller containers that are easier to transport, store, and display.

A final consideration is whether to develop packages that are viewed as environmentally responsible. Nearly one-half of all garbage consists of discarded plastic packaging, such as polystyrene containers, plastic soft-drink bottles, and carryout bags. Plastic packaging material does not biodegrade, and paper requires the destruction of valuable forests. Consequently, many companies have changed to environmentally sensitive packaging that is recycled, lighter weight, and uses fewer materials.

11-7c **Packaging and Marketing Strategy**

Packaging can be a major component of a marketing strategy. A new cap or closure, a better box or wrapper, or a more convenient container may give a product a competitive advantage. The right type of package for a new product can help it gain market recognition very quickly. This advertisement for Meow Mix Simple Servings single-use cups emphasizes the product's ease of use. The advertisement pictures a cat playing in a paper bag looking at an open serving of the Meow Mix Simple Servings single-use cup, while promoting, "No mess. No leftovers. So simple." The individually packaged servings of cat food represent an innovation in an industry and target cat owners looking for convenience options for feeding their furry friends.

In the case of existing brands, marketers should reevaluate packages periodically. Marketers should view packaging as a strategic tool, especially for consumer convenience products. When considering the strategic uses of packaging, marketers must also analyze the cost of packaging and package changes. In this section, we will examine several ways to use packaging strategically in marketing efforts.

Altering the Package

At times, a marketer changes a package or labeling because the existing design is no longer in style, especially when compared with the packaging of competitive products. As an example, after years of falling sales, Lean Cuisine redesigned the packaging for its reduced-calorie frozen dinners as part of a campaign to reposition the brand from a diet product to a health-and-wellness one. Nestlé, the brand's owner, made significant changes to the color, images, and descriptions, such as photographing the food on a black restaurant style plate, unlike other frozen food products, and dropping

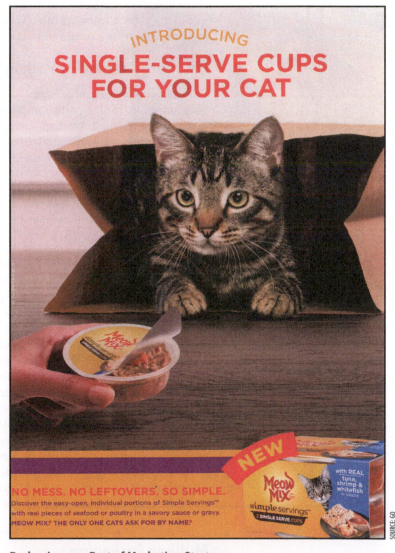

SOURCE: GQ

Packaging as a Part of Marketing Strategy
The marketer of Meow Mix cat food uses single-serve packaging as a part of its marketing strategy.

the word "diet." Within a year, sales jumped by $58 million and the redesign won the first Nielsen Design Impact Award.[52] A package may be redesigned because new product features need to be highlighted or because new packaging materials have become available. Cleaning supply company Seventh Generation sells its 4x concentrated laundry detergent in a paper bottle, which encloses a plastic pouch that contains the detergent. The design is innovative, completely recyclable, and requires fewer materials to make.[53]

An organization may also decide to change a product's packaging to make the product safer or more convenient to use. When Procter & Gamble released its popular Tide Pods product, it did not anticipate that children would mistake the colorful packaging and pods as candy or deliberately ingest them. After a number of children were poisoned by the pods, Procter & Gamble developed a double safety latch for the packaging and redesigned the transparent container to make it opaque. These moves were meant to make the pods look less like candy and harder for children to access. However, continued ingestions led Procter & Gamble and other laundry pod manufacturers to make additional modifications to make the packaging safer.[54]

Secondary-Use Packaging

A secondary-use package can be reused for purposes other than its initial function. For example, a margarine container can be reused to store leftovers, and a jelly container can serve as a drinking glass. Customers often view secondary-use packaging as adding value to products, in which case its use should stimulate unit sales.

Category-Consistent Packaging

With category-consistent packaging, the product is packaged in line with the packaging practices associated with a particular product category. Some product categories—for example, mayonnaise, mustard, ketchup, and peanut butter—have traditional package shapes. Other product categories are characterized by recognizable color combinations, such as red and white for soup and red, white, and blue for Ritz-like crackers. When an organization introduces a brand in one of these product categories, marketers will often use traditional package shapes and color combinations to ensure that customers will recognize the new product as being in that specific product category.

Innovative Packaging

Sometimes a marketer employs a unique cap, design, applicator, or other feature to make a product distinctive. Such packaging can be effective when the innovation makes the product safer, easier to use, or provides better protection. Valvoline, for instance, modified its motor oil 5-quart jug, closure, spout, and labels to make it easier for those who change their own oil.[55] Marketers also use innovative or unique packages that are inconsistent with traditional packaging practices to make the brand stand out from its competitors. Basing their packaging on research findings that wine drinkers tend to decide which product to purchase in the store, not in advance, Stack Wine offers its products in unique single-serve cups. The cups are filled with wine, sealed, and come stacked together in four packs. The unique packaging is eye-catching and practical, designed for parties, camping, or other situations where wine glasses are not readily available. It is also a convenient product for the occasional wine drinker, who may not want to open an entire bottle just to have one glass.[56] Unusual packaging sometimes requires expending considerable resources, not only on designing the package but also on making customers aware of the unique package and why it is an improvement. Researchers suggest that uniquely shaped packages that attract attention are likely to be perceived as containing a higher volume of product than comparable products that generate less attention.[57]

Multiple Packaging

Rather than packaging a single unit of a product, marketers sometimes use twin packs, tri-packs, six-packs, or other forms of multiple packaging. For certain types of products, multiple packaging may increase demand because it increases the amount of the product available at the point of consumption (e.g., in one's house). It may also increase consumer acceptance of the product by encouraging the buyer to try the product several times. Multiple packaging can make products easier to handle and store, as in the case of six-packs for soft drinks, and it can facilitate special price offers, such as two-for-one sales. However, multiple packaging does not work well for all types of products. One would not use additional table salt, for example, simply because an extra box is in the pantry.

Handling-Improved Packaging

A product's packaging may be changed to make it easier to handle in the distribution channel—for example, by altering the outer carton or using special bundling, shrink-wrapping, or pallets. In some cases, the shape of the package itself is changed. An ice cream producer, for instance, may adopt a rectangular-shaped package over a cylindrical one to facilitate handling. In addition, at the retail level, the ice cream producer may be able to get more shelf facings with a rectangular package than with a round one. Outer containers for products are sometimes altered so they will proceed more easily through automated warehousing systems.

11-8 **LABELING**

Labeling is very closely related with packaging and is used for identification, promotional, informational, and legal purposes. Labels can be small or large relative to the size of the product and carry varying amounts of information. The stickers on a banana or an apple, for example, are small and display only the brand name of the fruit, the type, and perhaps a stock-keeping unit number. A label can be part of the package itself or a separate feature attached to the package. The label on a can of Coke is actually part of the can, whereas the label on a two-liter bottle of Coke is separate and can be removed.

Information presented on a label may include the brand name and mark, the registered trademark symbol, package size and content, product features, nutritional information, presence of potential allergens, type and style of the product, number of servings, care instructions, directions for use and safety precautions, the name and address of the manufacturer, expiration dates, seals of approval, and other facts.

Labels can facilitate the identification of a product by displaying the brand name in combination with a unique graphic design. For instance, Heinz ketchup and Coca-Cola are both easy to identify on a supermarket shelf because of their iconic labels, which feature the name and recognizable brand marks. By drawing attention to products and their benefits, labels can strengthen an organization's promotional efforts. Labels may contain promotional messages, such as "Thirty percent more at no additional cost." Also, a label might be about a new or improved product feature, such as "New, improved scent."

Several federal laws and regulations specify information that must be included on the labels of certain products. Garments must be labeled with the name of the manufacturer, country of manufacture, fabric content, and cleaning instructions. Labels on nonedible items, such

Learning Objective 11-8

Identify the functions of labeling and legal issues related to labeling.

labeling Providing identifying, promotional, or other information on package labels

Strategic Labeling
Labeling can be an important part of a marketing strategy. The label can be attached to the packaging to communicate that the product is natural. Labeling can include claims about sustainability as well as other information that is potentially valuable to the buyer.

as shampoos and detergents, must include both safety precautions and directions for use. The Nutrition Labeling Act of 1990 requires the FDA to review food labeling and packaging for nutrition content, label format, ingredient labeling, food descriptions, and health messages. Any food product making a nutritional claim must follow standardized nutrition labeling. Food product labels must state the number of servings per container, serving size, number of calories per serving, number of calories derived from fat, number of carbohydrates, and amounts of specific nutrients such as vitamins. Many firms that used to feature the word "Natural" on their product labels are retracting that claim in an effort to protect themselves from lawsuits. Though natural food products are popular and profitable, the claim is problematic because there are no regulations for what is natural. Until the FDA issues clearer guidelines for what constitutes natural, it is likely that more companies will change their labels to downplay their "natural" ingredients.[58]

Another concern for many manufacturers is the Federal Trade Commission's (FTC) guidelines regarding "Made in USA" labels, a problem owing to the increasingly global nature of manufacturing. Additionally, consumers in many countries attach high brand value to American-made brands, including Russia, India, Brazil, and China, giving U.S. firms an even greater incentive to adopt the "Made in USA" label.[59] The FTC requires that "all or virtually all" of a product's components be made in the United States if the label says "Made in USA."[60] The "Made in USA" labeling issue remains complicated, as so many products involve parts sourced, produced, or assembled in places around the globe. Because business shows little sign of becoming less international, the FTC criteria for "Made in USA" are likely to be challenged and may be changed or adapted over time.

Summary

11-1 Define the concept of a product.

A product is a good, a service, an idea, or any combination of the three received in an exchange. It can be either tangible or intangible and includes functional, social, and psychological utilities or benefits. When consumers purchase a product, they are buying the benefits and satisfaction they think the product will provide.

11-2 Discuss how products are classified.

Products can be classified on the basis of the buyer's intentions. Consumer products are those purchased to satisfy personal and family needs. Business products are purchased for use in a firm's operations, to resell, or to make other products. Consumer products can be subdivided into convenience, shopping, specialty, and unsought products. Business products can be classified as installations, accessory equipment, raw materials, component parts, process materials, MRO supplies, and business services.

11-3 Explain the concepts of product line and product mix and how they are related.

A product item is a specific version of a product that can be designated as a distinct offering among an organization's

products. A product line is a group of closely related product items that are considered a unit because of marketing, technical, or end-use considerations. The composite, or total, group of products that an organization makes available to customers is called the product mix. The width of the product mix is measured by the number of product lines the company offers. The depth of the product mix is the average number of different products offered in each product line.

11-4 Explore the product life cycle and its impact on marketing strategies.

The product life cycle describes how product items in an industry move through four stages: introduction, growth, maturity, and decline. The sales curve is at zero at introduction, rises at an increasing rate during growth, peaks during the maturity stage, and then declines. Profits peak toward the end of the growth stage of the product life cycle.

11-5 Discuss the product adoption process.

When customers accept a new product, they usually do so through a five-stage adoption process. The first stage is awareness, when buyers become aware that a product exists. Interest, the second stage, occurs when buyers seek information and are receptive to learning about the product. The third stage is evaluation—buyers consider the product's benefits and decide whether to try it. The fourth stage is trial, during which buyers examine, test, or try the product to determine if it meets their needs. The last stage is adoption, when buyers purchase the product and use it whenever a need for this general type of product arises.

11-6 Explain the major components of branding, including brand types, branding strategies, and brand protection.

A brand is a name, term, design, symbol, or any other feature that identifies one seller's good or service and distinguishes it from those of other sellers. Branding helps buyers to identify and evaluate products, helps sellers to facilitate product introduction and repeat purchasing, and fosters brand loyalty. Brand equity is the marketing and financial value associated with a brand's strength. It represents the value of a brand to an organization. The four major elements underlying brand equity include brand-name awareness, brand loyalty, perceived brand quality, and brand associations.

There are three degrees of brand loyalty. Brand recognition occurs when a customer is aware that the brand exists and views it as an alternative purchase if the preferred brand is unavailable or if the other available brands are unfamiliar. Brand preference is a stronger degree of brand loyalty. Brand insistence is the strongest and least common level of brand loyalty.

A manufacturer brand is initiated by a producer. A private distributor brand is initiated and owned by a reseller, sometimes taking on the name of the store or distributor. A generic brand indicates only the product category and does not include the company name or other identifying terms. When selecting a brand name, a marketer should choose one that is easy to say, spell, and recall and that alludes to the product's uses, benefits, or special characteristics. Brand names can be devised from words, letters, numbers, nonsense words, or a combination of these. Companies protect ownership of their brands through registration with the U.S. Patent and Trademark Office.

Individual branding designates a unique name for each of a company's products. Family branding identifies all of a firm's products with a single name. A brand extension is the use of an existing name on a new or improved product in a different product category. Co-branding is the use of two or more brands on one product. Through a licensing agreement and for a licensing fee, a firm may permit another organization to use its brand on other products. Brand licensing enables producers to earn extra revenue, receive low-cost or free publicity, and protect their trademarks.

11-7 Describe the major packaging functions, design considerations, and how packaging is used in marketing strategies.

Packaging involves the development of a container and a graphic design for a product. Effective packaging offers protection, economy, safety, and convenience. It can influence a customer's purchase decision by promoting features, uses, benefits, and image. When developing a package, marketers must consider the value to the customer of efficient and effective packaging, offset by the price the customer is willing to pay. Other considerations include how to make the package tamper resistant, whether to use multiple packaging and family packaging, how to design the package as an effective promotional tool, and how best to accommodate resellers. Packaging can be an important part of an overall marketing strategy and can be used to target certain market segments. Modifications in packaging can revive a mature product and extend its product life cycle. Producers alter packages to convey new features or to make them safer or more convenient. If a package has a secondary use, the product's value to the consumer may increase. Innovative packaging enhances a product's distinctiveness.

11-8 Identify the functions of labeling and legal issues related to labeling.

Labeling is closely interrelated with packaging and is used for identification, promotional, informational, and legal purposes. Various federal laws and regulations require that certain products be labeled or marked with warnings, instructions, nutritional information, manufacturer's identification, and perhaps other information.

Important Terms

good 308
service 308
idea 308
consumer products 309

business products 309
convenience products 310
shopping products 311
specialty products 311

unsought products 312
installations 312
accessory equipment 312
raw materials 312

component parts 313
process materials 313
MRO supplies 313
business services 313

Discussion and Review Questions

1. Is a personal computer sold at a retail store a consumer product or a business product? Defend your answer.
2. How do convenience products and shopping products differ? What are the distinguishing characteristics of each type of product?
3. How does an organization's product mix relate to its development of a product line? When should an enterprise add depth to its product line rather than width to its product mix?
4. How do industry profits change as a product moves through the four stages of its life cycle?
5. What are the stages in the product adoption process, and how do they affect the commercialization phase?
6. How does branding benefit consumers and marketers?
7. What is brand equity? Identify and explain the major elements of brand equity.
8. What are the three major degrees of brand loyalty?
9. Compare and contrast manufacturer brands, private distributor brands, and generic brands.
10. Identify the factors a marketer should consider in selecting a brand name.
11. What is co-branding? What major issues should be considered when using co-branding?
12. Describe the functions a package can perform. Which function is most important? Why?
13. What are the main factors a marketer should consider when developing a package?
14. In what ways can packaging be used as a strategic tool?
15. What are the major functions of labeling?

Developing Your Marketing Plan

Identifying the needs of consumer groups and developing products that satisfy those needs are essential when creating a marketing strategy. Successful product development begins with a clear understanding of fundamental product concepts. The product concept is the basis on which many of the marketing plan decisions are made. When relating the information in this chapter to the development of your marketing plan, consider the following:

1. Using Figure 11.1 as a guide, create a matrix of the current product mix for your company.

2. Discuss how the profitability of your product will change as it moves through each of the phases of the product life cycle.

3. Create a brief profile of the type of consumer who is likely to represent each of the product adopter categories for your product.

4. Discuss the factors that could contribute to the failure of your product. How will you define product failure?

Video Case 11.1

Impossible Foods Cooks Up Meatless Burgers in Silicon Valley

Silicon Valley in California is home to countless high-tech startups. So why is it the headquarters of Impossible Foods? Because the company is using sophisticated technology to invent a meatless burger that looks, smells, cooks, and tastes like a flavorful, beefy, ground-meat hamburger.

Dr. Patrick O. Brown founded Impossible Foods in 2011 with the mission of creating nutritious, healthy foods that are based on plants rather than made from animals. However, the company is not creating products specifically for vegetarians. Its long-term business goal is much more ambitious: By 2035, it envisions a world in which affordable and tasty plant-derived foods have replaced more expensive animal-derived foods. A transition away from meat would free up land and other resources for sustainable farming of grains and other foods for the growing world population. If Impossible Foods can entice billions of consumers to switch to plant-based foods, it expects to dramatically reduce global hunger, save a lot of water compared with traditional meat-production methods, and profit from increased demand.

NATASHAPHOTO/ISTOCK/GETTY IMAGES

Because the hamburger is the most popular meat product in the United States, the company decided to focus its initial efforts on developing a good-tasting meatless burger. Its scientists carefully studied the physical properties of ground meat and analyzed how consumers experience the sensory aspects of a juicy, delicious hamburger, both on the grill and in the mouth. They discovered that heme is what gives a hamburger its characteristic meaty aroma, flavor, and color.

As company scientists searched for particular protein elements in plants that could deliver that same aroma, flavor, and color, they zeroed in on the heme which is present in soybean roots. Given the millions of pounds of meatless meat Impossible Foods plans to market every year, extracting a sufficient quantity of heme from plants would be impractical. That's why the scientists used genetic engineering to create a yeast that can produce a great deal of heme. Add some coconut oil to mimic the fat in a burger and mix in textured wheat protein, plus other ingredients and nutrients, and the result is the beef-like yet meatless Impossible Burger.

The next step was to make thousands of mouths water for this meatless burger. Rather than package its new product for supermarkets to sell to consumers, Impossible Foods introduced the burger by selling first to trendy restaurants like Momofuku Nishi in New York City. Foodies started to notice the new burger and food critics spread the word with their reviews. To reach a wider audience, the company then began selling through upscale burger restaurant chains like Umami Burger and Fatburger. Soon after, Impossible Foods took the product mainstream by selling through White Castle, which cooked up a $1.99 version of the burger it called the Impossible Slider, complete with cheese, pickles, and onions.

Impossible Foods recently introduced the meatless burger in Hong Kong by partnering with high-profile chefs to showcase the appealing taste. Watch for further international distribution as the company increases production. Looking ahead, its scientists have already analyzed the technical characteristics of chicken, fish, and pork, and patented proprietary methods of creating similar-tasting foods from plant-derived ingredients. This will allow Impossible Foods to cook up an expanded menu of meat alternatives and gain more fans, year after year.[61]

Questions for Discussion

1. Is the Impossible Burger a convenience product, a shopping product, or a specialty product? What are the implications for marketing this meatless burger?

2. What are the advantages and disadvantages of marketing a meatless burger under the Impossible brand?

3. How do you think Impossible Foods' decision to introduce its meatless burger through restaurants first influenced the product adoption process?

Case 11.2

Hilton Worldwide Expands to New Brands and New Markets

Hilton Worldwide was founded in 1919, and the lodging giant is expanding by adding new brands and opening in new markets to continue its aggressive growth. Based in McLean, Virginia, Hilton has a wide product mix covering multiple brands. Its line of luxury hotels includes two brands, Waldorf Astoria and Conrad. It markets lifestyle hotels under the Canopy by Hilton brand and full-service hotels under four brands: Hilton, Curio Collection by Hilton, Doubletree by Hilton, and Embassy Suites by Hilton. Hilton's hotel brands with limited services include Hilton Garden Inn, Hampton Inn by Hilton, Homewood Suites by Hilton, Home2 Suites by Hilton, and Tru by Hilton.

Hilton is currently opening the doors to the first of more than two dozen Canopy boutique hotels. These are hotels in locations like Reykjavik, Iceland, and Bethesda, Maryland, where customers can use mobile devices for convenient check-in, then check out the neighborhood using the hotel's on-site bikes. Canopy hotels have open lobbies to invite lingering, a free gift waiting in every room, and free wine tastings in the evening to encourage mingling.

Another of Hilton's newer brands is Tru, a group of more than 100 mid-priced hotels designed with Millennials in mind. Introducing the brand, Hilton's CEO stated: "We have a very large swath of demand that indexes very young, and we're not serving it." The company's analysis indicates that 40 percent of demand for hotel rooms comes from customers seeking affordable accommodations. Tru is geared to travelers in their twenties and thirties who want accommodations with a modern design and a reasonable price, plus opportunities to personalize the experience for individual needs.

Each Tru hotel has flexible public-space areas for customers to enjoy as they choose: some may want to play foosball, others may do a bit of work, while still others will relax in easy chairs or get a snack from the "grab and go" eatery. Tru's guest rooms are smaller than typical U.S. hotel rooms but carefully set up with amenities preferred by the target market, such as free Wi-Fi, 55-inch televisions, and showers rather than bathtubs. Tru will compete in the mid-priced market with rival brands such as Comfort Inn by Choice Hotels and Marriott's Fairfield Inn & Suites.

Meanwhile, the marketing environment continues to evolve, leading to challenges and opportunities for Hilton and its competitors. To achieve economies of scale and build their product portfolios, competitors are buying up hotel brands at a rapid pace. InterContinental Hotels acquired Kimpton Hotels, for instance, to take advantage of growing interest in boutique hotels and to plant its brands in more cities. Marriott International acquired Starwood Hotels, and AccorHotels acquired Fairmont, among other hotel brands. The industry is also feeling competitive pressure from rental services such as Airbnb, which link owners of apartments, condos, and homes with customers who want to rent for a day or longer.

Rather than buy an existing brand, Hilton is developing its own hotel brands from scratch so it can build in the features and services desired by particular target markets, with appropriate pricing. It is also entering new markets, such as Bolivia and Chad, bringing its total to more than 100 countries. With a portfolio of 13 brands covering hundreds of thousands of rooms worldwide, Hilton is well positioned to meet the needs of a wide range of customers in a wide range of locations, now and in the future.[62]

Questions for Discussion

1. Which branding strategy is Hilton using? Why is this appropriate for Hilton?

2. How does the state of competition among hotels indicate where this category is in the product life cycle?

3. Is Hilton's product mix deep as well as wide? Explain your answer.

Developing and Managing Products

LEARNING OBJECTIVES

12-1 Explain how companies manage existing products through line extensions and product modifications.

12-2 Explore how businesses develop a product idea into a commercial product.

12-3 Discuss the importance of product differentiation and the elements that differentiate one product from another.

12-4 Explain how businesses position their products.

12-5 Discuss how product deletion is used to improve product mixes.

12-6 Describe organizational structures used for managing products.

Coca-Cola: A "Total Beverage Company"

KEITH HOMAN/SHUTTERSTOCK.COM

Coca-Cola has been transforming itself from a marketer of carbonated soft drinks like Coke to a company offering everything from bottled waters and fruit juices to premium mixers for specialty drinks. Despite the traditional strength of the company's Coca-Cola flagship brand, consumers are increasingly seeking out a variety of beverages, often with little or no sugar. So by pouring on the new products and updating existing products, the company—founded in the nineteenth century—aims to appeal to twenty-first century preferences.

For example, Coca-Cola has designated its Venturing and Emerging Brands unit to invest in new products and emerging brands, serving as an entrepreneurial incubator for products with solid profit potential. This unit worked on the global expansion of Honest Tea after Coca-Cola acquired it. Now the unit is guiding the country-by-country introduction of another product which Coca-Cola recently purchased—Topo Chico sparkling water bottled in Mexico. To accelerate new-product development, the company is also partnering with local Coca-Cola bottlers to identify promising ideas, speed products to market, and drop underperforming products quickly.

In a U.K. market test, the company tested a revamped Coke Zero with a new taste formulation and new packaging, as well as a new name, Coke Zero Sugar. That test was so successful that Coca-Cola is rolling out Coke Zero Sugar worldwide, with positive results. In all, Coca-Cola plans to launch or relaunch 500 new products per year in the quest to become what its CEO describes as a "total beverage company" for today's global marketplace.[1]

To provide products that satisfy target markets and achieve the firm's objectives, marketers like those at Coca-Cola must develop, alter, and maintain an effective product mix. An organization's product mix may require adjustment for a variety of reasons. Because customers' attitudes and product preferences change over time, their desire for certain products may wane. For instance, Americans' breakfast preferences are shifting from cold cereals, such as Frosted Flakes and Cheerios, toward healthier and more varied fare like yogurt and snack bars as well as fast-food breakfast items. Cereal makers have responded to the decline in sales of traditional cereals by introducing new products such as cereal-based snack bars as well as reformulating cereals to make them more appealing to more consumers. Kellogg, for example, introduced Special K Crustless Quiche.[2] In other cases, a company may need to alter its product mix for competitive reasons. A marketer may have to delete a product from the mix because a competitor dominates the market for that product. IBM, for example, sold its personal computer product line to Lenovo because of intense competition in that area. Similarly, a firm may have to introduce a new product or modify an existing one to compete more effectively. A marketer may expand the firm's product mix to take advantage of excess marketing and production capacity.

In this chapter, we examine several ways to improve an organization's product mix. First, we discuss managing existing products through effective line extension and product modification. Next, we examine the stages of new-product development, including idea generation, screening, concept testing, business analysis, product development, test marketing, and commercialization. Then, we go on to discuss the ways companies differentiate their products in the marketplace and follow with a discussion of product positioning and repositioning. Next, we examine the importance of deleting weak products and the methods companies use to eliminate them. Finally, we look at the organizational structures used to manage products.

line extension Development of a product that is closely related to existing products in the line but is designed specifically to meet different customer needs

12-1   MANAGING EXISTING PRODUCTS

An organization can benefit by capitalizing on its existing products. By assessing the composition of the current product mix, a marketer can identify weaknesses and gaps. This analysis can then lead to improvement of the product mix through line extensions and product modifications.

Line Extension
The maker of Oreos has created more than 50 line extensions based on the original Oreo cookie.

12-1a   Line Extensions

A **line extension** is the development of a product that is closely related to one or more products in the existing product line but designed specifically to meet somewhat different customer needs. For example, in addition to classic Coca-Cola, the Coca-Cola Company markets Diet Coke, Coke Zero Sugar, and caffeine-free Coca-Cola to appeal to customers who have differing needs and wants with regard to cola drinks. Occasionally, the firm will extend the line when it introduces a new flavor of Diet Coke, such as Twisted Mango, or a Coca-Cola product with slightly different ingredients, such as stevia in Coca-Cola Life, to better appeal to a market segment.

Many of the so-called new products introduced each year are in fact line extensions. Line extensions are more common than new products because they are a less-expensive, lower-risk alternative for increasing sales. A line extension may focus on a different market segment or attempt to increase sales within the same market segment by more precisely satisfying the needs of people in that segment. For example, B&G Foods introduced Wild Tings, baked crunchy corn sticks, as well as new flavors of its popular Pirate's Booty rice and corn puffs to extend the Pirate's Booty line of "better for you" snacks.[3] Firms should be careful which lines they choose to extend and how. The success of a line extension is enhanced if the parent brand has a high-quality brand image and if there is a good fit between the line extension and its parent.[4] Line extensions, when successfully applied, can take market share from competitors.

12-1b **Product Modifications**

Product modification means changing one or more characteristics of a product. A product modification differs from a line extension in that the original product does not remain in the line. Automakers, for instance, use product modifications annually when they create new models of the same brand. The advertisement for the Volkswagen Tiguan introduces the newly redesigned vehicle with new features like premium leather seating and a Digital Cockpit navigation system. The ad playfully shows off the new features by having a group of tourists on "safari" view the new Tiguan in its "natural habitat," the city. Makers of running shoes also follow this practice, releasing new shoe models nearly every year and retiring old ones. Once the new models are introduced, the manufacturers stop producing the previous model. Like line extensions, product modifications entail less risk than developing new products.

Product Modification
Automobile manufacturers employ product modification. They engage in quality improvements, feature improvements, and aesthetic improvements.

Product modification can indeed improve a firm's product mix, but only under certain conditions. First, the product must be modifiable. Second, customers must be able to perceive that a modification has been made. Third, the modification should make the product more consistent with customers' desires so it provides greater satisfaction. One drawback to modifying a successful product is that a consumer who had experience with the original version of the product may view a modified version as a riskier purchase. There are three major types of modifications that can be made to products: quality, functional, and aesthetic.

Quality Modifications

Quality modifications are changes relating to a product's dependability and durability. Usually, the changes are executed by altering the materials or the production process. Reducing a product's quality may allow an organization to lower its price and direct the item at a different target market. In contrast, increasing the quality of a product may give a firm an advantage over competing brands. Higher quality may enable a company to charge a higher price by creating customer loyalty and lowering customer sensitivity to price. Case in point, many firms, including Campbell Soup Company and General Mills, are modifying their products to eliminate artificial colors and flavors in response to growing consumer preference for natural and simple ingredients. General Mills modified its Trix, Golden Grahams, and Reese's Puffs to replace the artificial colors with ones made from annatto and turmeric.[5] However, higher quality may require the use of more expensive ingredients, components, and processes, which

product modification Changes in one or more characteristics of a product

quality modifications Changes relating to a product's dependability and durability

may force the organization to cut costs in other areas. Some firms, such as Caterpillar, are finding ways to increase quality while reducing costs.

Functional Modifications

Changes that affect a product's versatility, effectiveness, convenience, or safety are called **functional modifications**, and they usually require that the product be redesigned. Product categories that have undergone considerable functional modification include agricultural equipment, appliances, cleaning products, and telecommunications services. Functional modifications can increase the number of users of a product and thus enlarge its market. For instance, the iPhone is always adding new features. The iPhone X has OLED display, wireless charging, better cameras, facial and fingerprint recognition and unlocking, and animated emojis.[6] This technology, along with other modifications, makes the iPhone X significantly different from previous models. Companies can place a product in a favorable competitive position by providing benefits that competing brands do not offer.

Additionally, functional modifications can help an organization achieve and maintain a progressive image. Finally, functional modifications are sometimes made to reduce the possibility of product liability lawsuits, such as adding a kill switch on a machine in case it malfunctions.

Aesthetic Modifications

Aesthetic modifications change the sensory appeal of a product by altering its taste, texture, sound, smell, or appearance. A buyer making a purchase decision is swayed by sensory inputs, and an aesthetic modification may thus strongly affect purchases. The fashion industry relies heavily on aesthetic modifications from season to season. For example, Louis Vuitton clothing, handbags, and leather goods are leaders in the haute couture industry. In order to maintain its reputation for the utmost level of quality and style, the company performs aesthetic modifications on its products regularly. This ensures that Louis Vuitton maintains its reputation for cutting-edge design and high quality. In addition, aesthetic modifications attempt to minimize the amount of illegal product counterfeiting that occurs through constant change in design.

Aesthetic modifications can help a firm differentiate its product from competing brands and thus gain a sizable market share. The major drawback in using aesthetic modifications is that their value is determined subjectively. Although a firm may strive to improve the product's sensory appeal, some customers actually may find the modified product less attractive.

Learning Objective 12-2

Explore how businesses develop a product idea into a commercial product.

12-2 DEVELOPING NEW PRODUCTS

A firm develops new products as a means of enhancing its product mix and adding depth to a product line. Developing and introducing new products is frequently expensive and risky. However, failure to introduce new products is also risky. Consider the case of Kodak, once one of the world's best-known brands, which marketed film and other products for cameras and imaging products. Although Kodak invested significant resources into developing a line of digital cameras, it persisted in trying to make them function like the conventional cameras it knew so well. Even after it became clear that consumers were shifting rapidly to digital cameras and later to smartphones, Kodak continued to define itself as a film company and failed to adapt to the disruption of digital technology and consumers' changing preferences. Although Kodak survives as an imaging company, consumers seldom describe the digital images they share on social media as "Kodak moments."[7]

The term *new product* can have more than one meaning. A genuinely new product offers innovative benefits. For example, BUDDY is a robot for the home that can serve as a personal

functional modifications
Changes affecting a product's versatility, effectiveness, convenience, or safety

aesthetic modifications
Changes relating to the sensory appeal of a product

assistant and multimedia station, provide social interaction and home patrol, play games with children, and more.[8] However, products that are different and distinctly better are often viewed as new, even if they do not represent a truly new product. For instance, Barry Callebaut AG's new ruby chocolate is slightly pink with a natural berry flavor and is made from a special type of cocoa bean. Other companies market red cocoa powder, but Barry Callebaut's is the first naturally reddish chocolate.[9] This advertisement for One Two Cosmetics' magnetic false eyelashes illustrates a product that represents an innovation over existing false eyelashes. The ad shows a woman applying false eyelashes while describing the innovations of the product, such as no glue or mess, relative to conventional false eyelashes. Some popular product innovations of recent decades include cell phones, tablet computers, electric cars, digital video recorders, satellite radio, and drones.

A new product can also be one that a given firm has not marketed previously, although similar products are available from other companies. Android Pay, for example, is not the first digital wallet available, but it is a new product offering from Google. This advertisement for the Spanx Arm Tights represents a product that is new to Spanx but not totally new to the market. Other companies, such as Leonisa and Lymphedema, market similar products that let the wearer layer and slim the arms. This is the first such product released by Spanx, however, which is underscored by the phrase "a Wardrobe Game-Changer" written out in the ad. The ad also showcases a diverse group of women wearing Arm Tights with a variety of outfits. Finally, a product can be viewed as new when it is brought to one or more markets from another market.

In recent years, a growing number of companies have found success by identifying ways to change how things are done in an industry and then developing products to lead the way. **Disruptive innovation**, first described by Professor Clayton Christensen of Harvard Business School, identifies old technologies that can be exploited in new ways or that develop new business models to give customers more than they've come to expect from current products in a specific market. Companies like Google, Netflix, iTunes, Uber, Lyft, and Warby Parker have become successful by recognizing unmet or poorly satisfied needs and developing products to satisfy them. Michael Dubin, for example, founded Dollar Shave Club after recognizing that buying refill cartridges for men's razors was boring, expensive, and often frustrating when retailers kept them locked up. He also realized that most men don't change their cartridges often enough. Dollar Shave Club is a subscription service that sends four or five cartridges every month for as little as $1/month for the first month. Its more than 3 million subscribers can also get other skin care products shipped as well. The company's great success has spawned imitators and spurred shaving giant Gillette to launch its own subscription service.[10]

Before a product is introduced, it goes through the seven phases of the **new-product development process** shown in Figure 12.1: (1) idea generation, (2) screening, (3) concept testing, (4) business analysis, (5) product development, (6) test marketing, and (7) commercialization. A product may be dropped at any stage of development. In this section, we look at the process through which products are developed, from idea inception to fully commercialized product.

disruptive innovation A new way of exploiting old technologies - or a new business model developed - to give customers more than they've come to expect from current products in a specific market

new-product development process A seven-phase process for introducing products: idea generation, screening, concept testing, business analysis, product development, test marketing, and commercialization

SOURCE: COSMOPOLITAN MAGAZINE

Product Innovation
Although false eyelashes is a well-established product category, One Two Cosmetics has created a product innovation by developing magnetic eyelashes.

SOURCE: COSMOPOLITAN MAGAZINE

New Product for a Firm

Spanx has developed a new product called Arm Tights. Arm Tights is viewed as a new product for Spanx, even though it may not be viewed as a new-to-the-world product generally.

idea generation Seeking product ideas to achieve organizational objectives

12-2a **Idea Generation**

Businesses and other organizations seek product ideas that will help them achieve their objectives. This activity is **idea generation**. The fact that only a few ideas are good enough to be commercially successful underscores the challenge of the task.

Although some organizations get their ideas by chance, firms that are most successful at managing their product mixes usually develop systematic approaches for generating new product ideas. At the heart of innovation is a purposeful, focused effort to identify new ways to serve a market.[11] New product ideas can come from several sources. They may stem from internal sources—marketing managers, researchers, sales personnel, engineers, franchisees, or other organizational personnel. Brainstorming and incentives for good ideas are typical intra-firm devices for stimulating the development of ideas. For instance, the idea for 3M Post-it adhesive-backed notes came from an employee. As a church choir member, he used slips of paper to mark songs in his hymnal. Because the pieces of paper kept falling out, he suggested developing an adhesive-backed note. Over time, employees have become more empowered to express their own product ideas to their supervisors. This collaborative process can be particularly useful to help marketers iron out the details of a new product concept.[12]

New product ideas may also arise from sources outside the firm, such as customers, competitors, advertising agencies, management consultants, and private research organizations. Increasingly, firms are bringing consumers into the product idea development process through online campaigns. The internet gives marketers the chance to tap into consumer ideas by building online communities and listening to their product needs and wants. These communities provide consumers with a sense of empowerment and allow them to provide insight for new product ideas that can prove invaluable to the firm.[13] The internet and social media have become very important tools for gathering information from stakeholders, particularly when a firm is targeting younger consumers. Frito-Lay, for example, holds an annual contest inviting consumers to submit their ideas for a new potato chip flavor idea via website or social media. The winner receives a substantial cash prize, and Frito-Lay gets a fresh new flavor.[14] The interactivity of the internet allows other stakeholders not only to suggest and analyze new product ideas but also to interact with one another on evaluating and filtering these ideas.

Many firms offer product development consulting and can be good sources for stimulating new product ideas. As an example, Kaleidoscope offers product design, engineering, and development services to companies in the health-care, medical, consumer goods, electronics, and high-tech industries.[15] When outsourcing new-product development activities to outside organizations, firms should spell out the specific details of the arrangement and include detailed contractual specifications. Asking customers what they want from products has helped many firms become successful and remain competitive. As more global consumers become interconnected through the internet, marketers have the chance to tap into consumer ideas by building online communities with them.

12-2b Screening

In the process of **screening**, the ideas with the greatest potential are selected for further review. During screening, product ideas are analyzed to determine if they match the organization's mission, objectives, and resources. A firm's overall ability to produce and market the product are also analyzed. Other aspects of an idea to be weighed are the nature and wants of buyers and possible environmental changes. At times, a checklist of new-product requirements is used when making screening decisions. This practice encourages evaluators to be systematic and thus reduces the chances of overlooking some pertinent fact. Most new product ideas are rejected during the screening phase.

12-2c Concept Testing

To evaluate ideas properly, it may be necessary to test product concepts. In **concept testing**, a small sample of potential buyers is presented with a product idea through a written or oral description (and perhaps a few drawings) to determine their attitudes and initial buying intentions regarding the product. Chipotle, for example, operates the NEXT Kitchen in Manhattan to try out new recipes, ingredients, and technology on paying customers. The NEXT Kitchen made it possible for Chipotle to develop a long-demanded queso product while remaining true to its commitment not to use additives and artificial colors and flavors in its products.[16] For a single product idea, an organization can test one or several concepts of the same product. Concept testing is a low-cost procedure that allows a company to determine customers' initial reactions to a product idea before it invests considerable resources in research and development.

Figure 12.2 shows a concept test for a proposed tick and flea control product. During concept testing, the concept is described briefly, and then a series of questions is presented to a test panel. For a potential food product, a sample may be offered. The questions vary considerably depending on the type of product being tested. Typical questions can include the following: In general, do you find this proposed product attractive? Which benefits are especially attractive to you? Which features are of little or no interest to you? Do you feel that this proposed product would work better for you than the product you currently use? Compared with your current product, what are the primary advantages of the proposed product? If this product were available at an appropriate price, would you buy it? How often would you buy this product? How could the proposed product be improved?

12-2d Business Analysis

During the **business analysis** stage, the product idea is evaluated to determine its potential contribution to the firm's sales, costs, and profits. In the course of a business analysis, evaluators ask a variety of questions: Does the product fit in with the organization's existing product mix? Is demand strong enough to justify entering the market, and will this demand endure? What types of environmental and competitive changes can be expected, and how will these changes affect the product's future sales, costs, and profits?

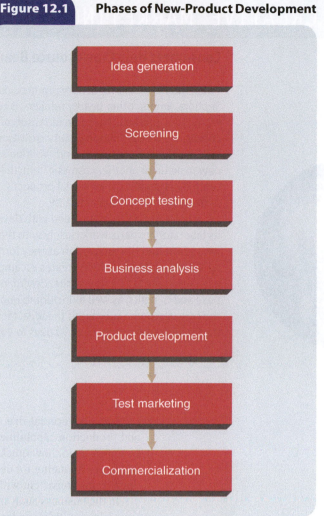

Figure 12.1 Phases of New-Product Development

- Idea generation
- Screening
- Concept testing
- Business analysis
- Product development
- Test marketing
- Commercialization

screening Selecting the ideas with the greatest potential for further review

concept testing Seeking a sample of potential buyers' responses to a product idea

business analysis Evaluating the potential impact of a product idea on the firm's sales, costs, and profits

CREATIVE MARKETING

Consumers Help Crowdsource Beauty at Volition

Where do new ideas for beauty products come from? Sephora, among other beauty retailers, is currently selling new products based on ideas submitted by consumers via the Volition Beauty crowdsourcing website. When a consumer sends Volition an idea for new makeup or another cosmetic item, the company carefully evaluates the potential product's quality, originality, safety, and practicality.

If Volition decides to proceed with development, its laboratory experts work closely with the consumer who submitted the suggestion as they formulate the new product. Next, Volition creates a "campaign" for each new product on its website, describing the purpose and benefits, as well as including quotes from the consumer who submitted the idea. Members of the Volition community have 90 days to vote for their favorite campaigns. Then Volition tallies the totals and commercializes the winners, with the creators sharing in the sales revenue. And, as an incentive to vote, consumers who supported a winning campaign can buy that new product at a discount.

In addition to selling via its own website, Volition has successfully marketed some of its new products through Sephora stores and QVC. Now sales are growing rapidly as more members join the Volition community to vote and to buy. Cofounder Brandy Hoffman says Volition is intended "to give the customer a true voice in driving the direction of a brand" by proposing ideas for innovative beauty products they really want to buy. At the same time, she says Volition solves a critical problem for beauty marketers: How to develop a "truly differentiated product in a sea of sameness."[a]

It is also crucial that a firm determine whether its research, development, engineering, and production capabilities are adequate to develop the product; whether new facilities must be constructed, how quickly they can be built, and how much they will cost; and whether the necessary financing for development and commercialization is on hand or is obtainable based upon terms consistent with a favorable return on investment.

In the business analysis stage, firms seek market information. The results of customer surveys, along with secondary data, supply the specifics needed to estimate potential sales, costs, and profits. For many product ideas in this stage, forecasting sales accurately is difficult. This is especially true for innovative and completely new products. Organizations sometimes employ breakeven analysis to determine how many units they would have to sell to begin making a profit. At times, an organization also uses payback analysis, in which marketers compute the time period required to recover the funds that would be invested in developing the new product. Because breakeven and payback analyses are based on estimates, they are usually viewed as useful but not particularly precise tools.

12-2e Product Development

Product development is the phase in which the organization determines if it is technically feasible to produce the product and if it can be produced at costs low enough to make the final price reasonable. To test its acceptability, the idea or concept is converted into a prototype, or working model. When Dyson was working to develop its Supersonic hair dryer, it went through 600 prototypes before it found the right one.[17] The prototype should reveal tangible and intangible attributes associated with the product in consumers' minds. The product's design, mechanical features, and intangible aspects must be linked to wants in the marketplace. Through marketing research and concept testing, product attributes that are important to buyers are identified. These characteristics must be communicated to customers through the design of the product.

product development
Determining if producing a product is technically feasible and cost effective

| **Figure 12.2** | **Concept Test for a Tick and Flea Control Product** |

Product description

An insecticide company is considering the development and introduction of a new tick and flea control product for pets. This product would consist of insecticide and a liquid-dispensing brush for applying the insecticide to dogs and cats. The insecticide is in a cartridge that is installed in the handle of the brush. The insecticide is dispensed through the tips of the bristles when they touch the pet's skin (which is where most ticks and fleas are found). The actual dispensing works very much like a felt-tip pen. Only a small amount of insecticide actually is dispensed on the pet because of this unique dispensing feature. Thus, the amount of insecticide that is placed on your pet is minimal compared to conventional methods of applying a tick and flea control product. One application of insecticide will keep your pet free from ticks and fleas for 14 days.

Please answer the following questions:

1. In general, how do you feel about using this type of product on your pet?

2. What are the major advantages of this product compared with the existing product that you are currently using to control ticks and fleas on your pet?

3. What characteristics of this product do you especially like?

4. What suggestions do you have for improving this product?

5. If it is available at an appropriate price, how likely are you to buy this product?

        Very likely   Semi-likely   Not likely

6. Assuming that a single purchase would provide 30 applications for an average-size dog or 48 applications for an average-size cat, approximately how much would you pay for this product?

After a prototype is developed, its overall functioning must be assessed. Its performance, safety, convenience, and other functional qualities are tested both in a laboratory and in the field. Functional testing should be rigorous and lengthy enough to test the product thoroughly. Studies have revealed that the form or design of a product can actually influence how consumers view the product's functional performance.[18] Manufacturing issues that come to light at the prototype stage may require adjustments.

A crucial question that arises during product development is how much quality to build into the product. Thus, a major dimension of quality is durability. Higher quality often calls for better materials and more expensive processing, which increase production costs and, ultimately, the product's price. In determining the specific level of quality that is best for a product, a marketer must ascertain approximately what price the target market views as acceptable. In addition, a marketer usually tries to set a quality level consistent with that of the firm's other products. The quality of competing brands is also a consideration.

The development phase of a new product is often a lengthy and expensive process. As a result, only a relatively small number of product ideas are put into development. If the product appears sufficiently successful during this stage to merit test marketing, then, during the latter part of the development stage, marketers begin to make decisions regarding branding, packaging, labeling, pricing, and promotion for use in the test marketing stage.

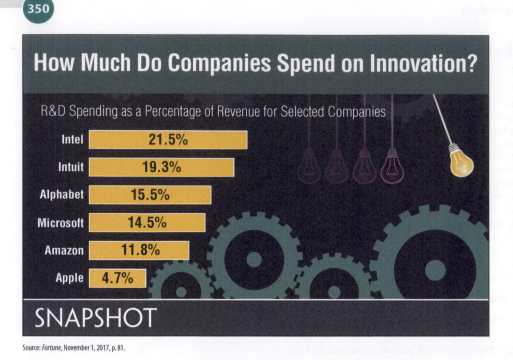

How Much Do Companies Spend on Innovation?

R&D Spending as a Percentage of Revenue for Selected Companies

Company	R&D Spending
Intel	21.5%
Intuit	19.3%
Alphabet	15.5%
Microsoft	14.5%
Amazon	11.8%
Apple	4.7%

SNAPSHOT

Source: *Fortune*, November 1, 2017, p. 81.

12-2f Test Marketing

Test marketing is a limited introduction of a product in geographic areas chosen to represent the intended market. Fast-food chain KFC, for example, test marketed Hot Honey Chicken—crispy chicken tenders doused with honey pepper sauce—at its Bronx, New York, locations.[19] The aim of test marketing is to determine the extent to which potential customers will buy the product. Test marketing is not an extension of the development stage, but rather a sample launching of the entire marketing mix. It should be conducted only after the product has gone through development and initial plans have been made regarding the other marketing mix variables. Companies use test marketing to lessen the risk of product failure. The dangers of introducing an untested product include undercutting already profitable products and, should the new product fail, loss of credibility with distributors and customers.

Test marketing provides several benefits. It lets marketers expose a product in a natural marketing environment to measure its sales performance. The company can strive to identify weaknesses in the product or in other parts of the marketing mix. Planet Smoothie, for example, recognized in test marketing that its new Lemon Cayenne Kick smoothie was spicier than its customers preferred, so the firm dialed back the amount of cayenne. On the other hand, Wing Zone found that its new Mango Fire flavor wasn't spicy enough for its patrons, so it ramped up the heat in the final product.[20] A product weakness discovered after a nationwide introduction can be expensive to correct. Moreover, if consumers' early reactions are negative, marketers may be unable to persuade consumers to try the product again. Thus, making adjustments after test marketing can be crucial to the success of a new product. On the other hand, test marketing results may be positive enough to warrant accelerating the product's introduction. Test marketing also allows marketers to experiment with variations in advertising, pricing, and packaging in different test areas and to measure the extent of brand awareness, brand switching, and repeat purchases resulting from these alterations in the marketing mix.

Selection of appropriate test areas is very important because the validity of test marketing results depends heavily on selecting test sites that provide accurate representations of the intended target market. U.S. cities commonly used for test marketing appear in Table 12.1. The criteria used for choosing test cities depend upon the product's attributes, the target market's characteristics, and the firm's objectives and resources.

Test marketing is not without risks. It is expensive, and competitors may try to interfere. A competitor may attempt to "jam" the test program by increasing its own advertising or promotions, lowering prices, and offering special incentives, all to combat consumer recognition and purchase of the new brand. Such tactics can invalidate test results. Sometimes, competitors copy the product in the testing stage and rush to introduce a similar product. It is, therefore, desirable to move to the commercialization phase as soon as possible after successful testing.

Because of these risks, many companies use alternative methods to measure customer preferences. One such method is simulated test marketing. Typically, consumers at shopping centers are asked to view an advertisement for a new product and are given a free sample to take home. These consumers are subsequently interviewed over the phone or through online

test marketing A limited introduction of a product in geographic areas chosen to represent the intended market

Table 12.1   Popular Test Markets in the United States

Rank	City
1	Columbus, Ohio
2	Peoria, Illinois
3	Albany, New York
4	Jacksonville, Florida
5	Lexington, Kentucky
6	Des Moines, Iowa
7	Battle Creek, Michigan
8	Greensboro, North Carolina
9	Cleveland, Ohio
10	Phoenix, Arizona

panels and asked to rate the product. The major advantages of simulated test marketing are greater speed, lower costs, and tighter security, which reduce the flow of information to competitors and reduce jamming. Several marketing research firms, such as the Nielsen Company, offer test marketing services to provide independent assessment of proposed products. Not all products that are test-marketed are launched. At times, problems discovered during test marketing cannot be resolved.

12-2g Commercialization

During the **commercialization** phase, plans for full-scale manufacturing and marketing must be refined and settled and budgets for the project prepared. Early in the commercialization phase, marketing management analyzes the results of test marketing to find out what changes in the marketing mix are needed before introducing the product. The results of test marketing may suggest the need to change one or more of the product's physical attributes, modify the distribution plans to include more retail outlets, alter promotional efforts, or change the product's price. However, as more and more changes are made based on test marketing findings, the test marketing projections may become less valid.

During the early part of this stage, marketers must not only gear up for larger-scale production, but also make decisions about warranties, repairs, and replacement parts. The type of warranty a firm provides can be a critical issue for buyers, especially for expensive, technically complex goods, such as appliances, or frequently used items, such as mattresses. Establishing an effective system for providing repair services and replacement parts is necessary to maintain favorable customer relationships. Although the producer may furnish these services directly to buyers, it is more common for the producer to provide such services through regional service centers. Regardless of how services are provided, it is important to customers that they be performed quickly and correctly.

The product enters the market during the commercialization phase. When introducing a product, a firm may spend enormous sums on advertising, personal selling, and other types of promotion, as well as on manufacturing and equipment costs. Such expenditures may not be recovered for several years. Smaller firms may find this process difficult, but even so they may use press releases, blogs, podcasts, and other tools to capture quick feedback as well as to promote the new product. Another low-cost promotional tool is product reviews in newspapers, magazines, or blogs, which can be especially helpful when these reviews are positive and target the same customers.

Products are not usually launched nationwide overnight, but are introduced in stages through a process called a *rollout*. With a rollout, a product is introduced starting in one geographic area or set of areas and gradually expanding into adjacent ones. It may take several

commercialization Refining and finalizing plans and budgets for full-scale manufacturing and marketing of a product

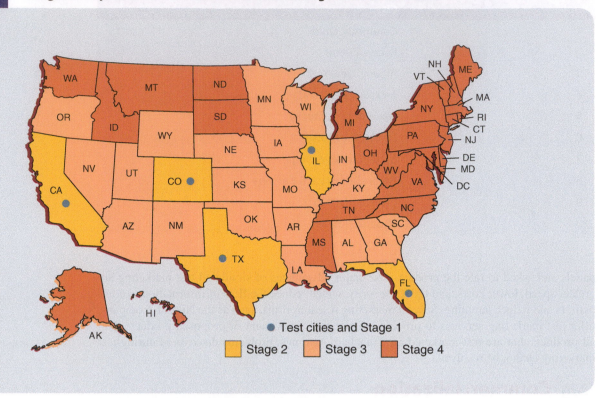

Figure 12.3　　**Stages of Expansion into a National Market during Commercialization**

Test cities and Stage 1

Stage 2　　　Stage 3　　　Stage 4

years to reach national marketing coverage. Sometimes, the test cities are used as initial market-ing areas, and the introduction of the product becomes a natural extension of test marketing. A product test-marketed in Sacramento, California, and Fort Collins, Colorado, could be intro-duced first in those cities. After the stage 1 introduction is complete, stage 2 usually includes market coverage of the states where the test cities are located. In stage 3, marketing efforts might be extended to adjacent states. All remaining states would then be covered in stage 4. Figure 12.3 shows these four stages of commercialization.

Product rollouts do not always occur state by state. Other geographic combinations, such as groups of counties that overlap across state borders, are sometimes used. Products destined for multinational markets may also be rolled out one country or region at a time. Gradual product introduction is desirable for several reasons. First, it reduces the risks of introducing a new product. If the product fails, the firm will experience smaller losses if it introduced the item in only a few geographic areas than if it marketed the product nationally. Second, a company cannot introduce a product nationwide overnight, because a system of wholesalers and retailers to distribute the product cannot be established so quickly. Developing a distribution network can take considerable time. Third, if the product is successful from launch, the number of units needed to satisfy nationwide demand for it may be too large for the firm to produce in a short time. Finally, gradual introduction allows for fine-tuning of the marketing mix to satisfy target customers.

Despite the good reasons for introducing a product gradually, marketers realize this approach creates problems. A gradual introduction allows competitors to observe what the firm is doing and monitor results just as the firm's own marketers are doing. If competitors see that the newly introduced product is successful, they may quickly enter the same target market with similar products. In addition, as a product is introduced region by region, competitors may expand their marketing efforts to offset promotion of the new product. Marketers should realize that too much delay in launching a product can cause the firm to miss out on seizing market opportunities, creating competitive offerings, and forming cooperative relationships with channel members.[21]

Learning Objective 12-3

12-3 PRODUCT DIFFERENTIATION THROUGH QUALITY, DESIGN, AND SUPPORT SERVICES

Discuss the importance of product differentiation and the elements that differentiate one product from another.

Some of the most important characteristics of products are the elements that distinguish them from one another. **Product differentiation** is the process of creating and designing products so customers perceive them as different from competing products. Customer perception is critical in differentiating products. Perceived differences might include quality, features, styling, price, or image. In this section, we examine three aspects of product differentiation that companies must consider when creating and offering products for sale: product quality, product design and features, and product support services. These aspects involve the company's attempt to create real differences among products.

product differentiation Creating and designing products so customers perceive them as different from competing products

quality The overall characteristics of a product that allow it to perform as expected in satisfying customer needs

level of quality The amount of quality a product possesses

consistency of quality The degree to which a product has the same level of quality over time

12-3a Product Quality

Quality refers to the overall characteristics of a product that allow it to perform as expected in satisfying customer needs. The words *as expected* are very important to this definition because quality usually means different things to different customers. For some, durability signifies quality. The Stanley Black & Decker line of tools at Lowe's is an example of a product with a reputation for durability. Indeed, Stanley provides a lifetime guarantee on its tools.

The concept of quality also varies between consumer and business markets. Consumers consider high-quality products to be reliable, durable, and easy to maintain. For business markets, technical suitability, ease of repair, and company reputation are important characteristics. Unlike consumers, most organizations place far less emphasis on price than on product quality.

One important dimension of quality is **level of quality**, the amount of quality a product possesses. The concept is a relative one because the quality level of one product is difficult to describe unless it is compared to that of other products. As an example, the advertisement for Sargento sliced cheese stresses the product's level of quality, comparing it to American singles. The advertisement insists that "real cheese people believe the only cheese is 100% real, natural cheese" like that made by Sargento and includes a photo of a generous sandwich. To reinforce the idea of quality as measured by precision, the ad informs consumers that American singles sliced cheese are required to have just 51 percent real cheese compared to Sargento's 100 percent.

The American Customer Satisfaction Index (ACSI) ranks customer satisfaction among a wide variety of businesses in the United States. For instance, Amazon is the highest-ranked online retailer according to the ACSI.[22]

A second important dimension is consistency. **Consistency of quality** refers to the degree to which a product has the same level of quality over time. Consistency means giving consumers the quality they expect every time they purchase the product. As with level of quality, consistency is a relative concept. It implies a quality comparison within the same brand over time.

Level of Quality

This advertisement for Sargento cheese focuses on the level of product quality by indicating that Sargento cheese is 100 percent real natural cheese.

The consistency of product quality can also be compared across competing products. It is at this stage that consistency becomes critical to a company's success. Companies that can provide quality on a consistent basis have a major competitive advantage over rivals. FedEx, for example, offers reliable delivery schedules and a variety of options, ranking it at the top of consumer shipping companies.[23] No company has ever succeeded by creating and marketing low-quality products that do not satisfy consumers. Many companies have taken major steps, such as implementing total quality management (TQM), to improve the quality of their products and become more competitive.

Higher product quality means firms will have to charge a higher price for the product. Marketers must, therefore, consider the balance of quality and price carefully in their planning efforts.

12-3b Product Design and Features

Product design refers to how a product is conceived, planned, and produced. Design is a very complex topic because it involves the total sum of all the product's physical characteristics. Many companies are known for the outstanding designs of their products: Apple for electronics and computers, Cuisinart for kitchen appliances, and Merrell for hiking shoes. Good design is one of the best competitive advantages any brand can possess.

One component of design is **styling**, or the physical appearance of the product. The style of a product is one design feature that can allow certain products to sell very rapidly. Good design, however, means more than just appearance—design also encompasses a product's functionality and usefulness. For instance, a pair of jeans may look great, but if they fall apart after three washes, the design was poor. Most consumers seek out products that both look good and function well.

Product features are specific design characteristics that allow a product to perform certain tasks. By adding or subtracting features, a company can differentiate its products from those of the competition. Product features can also be used to differentiate products within the same company. For instance, Nike offers a range of shoes designed for purposes from walking, to running, to weightlifting, to cross-training in a gym. In general, the more features a product has, the higher its price and often the higher its perceived quality.

For a brand to have a sustainable competitive advantage, marketers must determine the product designs and features that customers desire. Information from marketing research efforts and databases can help in assessing customers' product design and feature preferences. Being able to meet customers' desires for product design and features at prices they can afford is crucial to a product's long-term success. Marketers must be careful not to misrepresent or overpromise regarding product features or product performance.

12-3c Product Support Services

Many companies differentiate their product offerings by providing support services. Usually referred to as **customer services**, these services include any human or mechanical efforts or activities a company provides that add value to a product. Examples of customer services include delivery and installation, financing arrangements, customer training, warranties and guarantees, repairs, layaway plans, convenient hours of operation, adequate parking, and information through toll-free numbers and websites. Trader Joe's stands out among supermarkets for its stellar customer service. Marketers at Trader Joe's strive to ensure that nothing interrupts the positive experience and to create opportunities for employees to connect with customers. This approach ensures that shoppers find and purchase exactly what they want. To create a more personal environment, the store does not even have loudspeakers. As a result, Trader Joe's customers are highly loyal and sales per square foot frequently are triple that of competitors.[24]

Whether as a major or minor part of the total product offering, all marketers of goods sell customer services. In the case of markets where all products have essentially the same quality,

product design How a product is conceived, planned, and produced

styling The physical appearance of a product

product features Specific design characteristics that allow a product to perform certain tasks

customer services Human or mechanical efforts or activities that add value to a product

design, and features, providing good customer service may be the only way a company can differentiate its products. This is especially true in the computer industry. When buying a laptop computer, for example, consumers are likely to shop more for fast delivery, technical support, warranties, and price than for product quality and design, as witnessed by the high volume of "off-the-shelf," non-customized lower-priced laptops sold at retailers such as Best Buy, Costco, Walmart, and Target. Through research, a company can discover the types of services customers want and need. The level of customer service a company provides can profoundly affect customer satisfaction. Additionally, the mere availability of add-on features can enhance the value and quality of a product in the eyes of the consumer.[25]

> **product positioning** The decisions and activities intended to create and maintain a certain concept of the firm's product, relative to competitive brands, in customers' minds

12-4 PRODUCT POSITIONING AND REPOSITIONING

Learning Objective 12-4

Explain how businesses position their products.

Once a target market is selected, a firm must consider how to position its product. **Product positioning** refers to the decisions and activities intended to create and maintain a certain concept of the firm's product, relative to competitive brands, in customers' minds. When marketers introduce a product, they try to position it so that it appears to have the characteristics that the target market most desires. This projected image is crucial. For instance, this advertisement for Six Star Whey Protein positions the brand as the choice for athletes who want fast absorbing protein and a low cost per serving. By picturing athletes from a variety of sports in the background, Six Star conveys that the product is appropriate for all types of athletes, while the ad's text describes the benefits of the product and distinguishes it from competing protein products.

12-4a **Perceptual Mapping**

A product's position is the result of customers' perceptions of the product's attributes relative to those of competitive brands. Buyers make numerous purchase decisions on a regular basis. To simplify buying decisions and avoid a continuous reevaluation of numerous products, buyers tend to group, or "position," products in their minds. Rather than allowing customers to position products independently, marketers often try to influence and shape consumers' concepts or perceptions of products through advertising. Marketers sometimes analyze product positions by developing perceptual maps, as shown in Figure 12.4. Perceptual maps are created by questioning a sample of consumers about their perceptions of products, brands, and organizations with respect to two or more dimensions. To develop a perceptual map like the one in Figure 12.4, respondents would be asked how they perceive selected pain relievers in regard to price and type of pain for which the products are used.

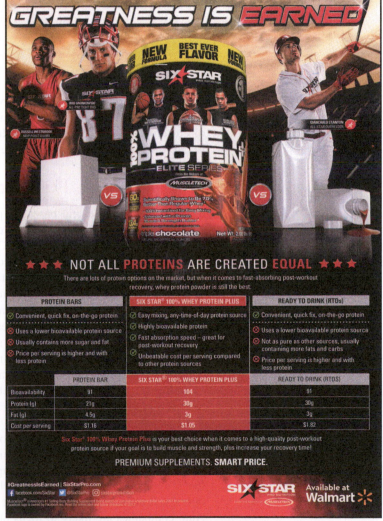

SOURCE: MEN'S FITNESS

Product Positioning

Six Star Whey Protein is positioned against protein bars and ready-to-drink products by pointing out that it is higher in bioavailability, higher in grams of protein, lower in fat, and lower in cost.

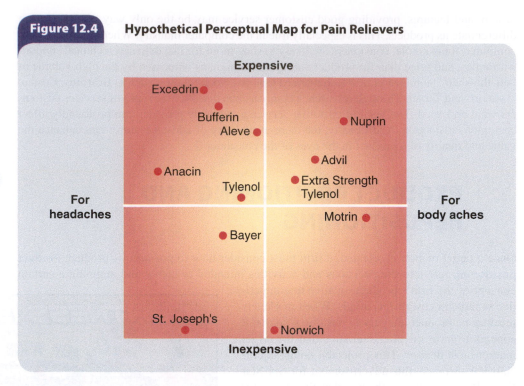

Figure 12.4   Hypothetical Perceptual Map for Pain Relievers

Also, respondents would be asked about their preferences for product features to establish "ideal points" or "ideal clusters," which represent a consensus about what a specific group of customers desire in terms of product features. Then, marketers can compare how their brand is perceived compared with the ideal points.

12-4b Bases for Positioning

Marketers can use several bases for product positioning. A common basis for positioning products is to use competitors. A firm can position a product to compete head-on with another brand, as PepsiCo has done against Coca-Cola, or to avoid competition, as 7 Up has done relative to Coca-Cola. Head-to-head competition may be a marketer's positioning objective if the product's performance characteristics are at least equal to those of competitive brands and if the product is priced lower. Head-to-head positioning may be appropriate even when the price is higher if the product's performance characteristics are superior. Interestingly, smaller or less well-known brands in industries that have dominant competitors can actually increase visibility and sales by emphasizing the size and proximity of their competitor's brand compared to their own.[26] SodaStream, which manufactures a consumer home-carbonation product, uses a head-to-head positioning strategy against the dominant players in the soda market, Pepsi and Coca-Cola. SodaStream positions itself as a healthier, more eco-friendly brand, and portrays its top competitors as environmentally harmful due to the large amounts of plastic bottle waste that ends up in landfills.

Conversely, positioning to avoid competition may be best when the product's performance characteristics do not differ significantly from competing brands. Moreover, positioning a brand to avoid competition may be appropriate when that brand has unique characteristics that are important to some buyers. Prius, for example, does not compete directly with other hybrids. Rather, marketers position it as an eco-friendly hybrid that is also family-friendly. Auto companies are likely to focus on style, fuel efficiency, performance, terms of sale, or safety in their advertisements. Avoiding competition is critical when a firm introduces a brand into a market in which the company already has one or more brands. Marketers usually want to avoid cannibalizing sales of their existing brands, unless the new brand generates substantially larger profits.

A product's position can be based on specific product attributes or features. Apple's iPhone, for instance, is positioned based on product attributes such as its sleek design and compatibility with other Apple products and accessories, such as apps and music through the iTunes store. Style, shape, construction, and color help create the image and generate appeal. If buyers can easily identify the benefits, they are more likely to purchase the product. When the new product does not offer certain preferred attributes, there is room for another new product.

Other bases for product positioning include price, quality level, and benefits provided by the product. The target market can also be a positioning basis for marketers. This type of positioning relies heavily on promoting to the types of people who use the product.

12-4c Repositioning

Positioning decisions are not only for new products. Evaluating the positions of existing products is important because a brand's market share and profitability may be strengthened by product repositioning. Repositioning requires changes in perception and usually changes in product features. When introducing a new product into a product line, one or more existing brands may have to be repositioned to minimize cannibalization of established brands and ensure a favorable position for the new brand.

Repositioning can be accomplished by physically changing the product, its price, or its distribution. Rather than making any of these changes, marketers sometimes reposition a product by changing its image through promotional efforts. Wyndham Hotel Group repositioned each of its 16 lodging brands to broaden their appeal and distinguish them in an increasingly crowded hospitality market. In addition to updating and refreshing individual hotels, the company also gave the brands new slogans backed by promotional efforts. Travelodge, for example, now has the slogan, "Your Basecamp for Adventure," and has partnered with the National Parks Conservation Association to highlight nearby national parks.[27] Finally, a marketer may reposition a product by aiming it at a different target market.

INTEGRITY IN MARKETING

Inside the Positioning of Starbucks Coffee

On National Coffee Day in late September, U.S. coffee shops and doughnut stores typically give away free cups of coffee or advertise deep discounts. But that's not what Starbucks did recently. Rather than offer free or discounted coffee, the company took the unusual step of changing every one of its in-store menu boards to feature photos and text explaining the importance of sustainability. "We want our customers to know that they can feel good about their Starbucks purchase, which is positively impacting coffee growing communities around the world," said a company executive.

With $22 billion in annual sales, Starbucks can zig when competitors zag because it positions its products on the basis of sustainability and social responsibility, not just quality and taste. It knows many customers care about the deeper meaning of the products they buy, seeking out Starbucks because of its support of the environment and social justice. In fact, 99 percent of the coffee it sells is ethically sourced, meaning the growers are paid fairly and apply eco-friendly agricultural techniques. Starbucks is also a cofounder of the Sustainable Coffee Challenge, which brings businesses, conservation groups, and government experts together to help coffee growers worldwide improve sustainability.

Since 2015, Starbucks has been planting one coffee tree for every bag of coffee it sells. On National Coffee Day, it launched a new product, Single-Origin Guatemala Huehuetenango, made from the beans of trees it planted as part of this initiative. This product introduction emphasized both taste and sustainability and tapped into Starbucks' competitive differentiation as a company that cares.[b]

Learning Objective 12-5

Discuss how product deletion is used to improve product mixes.

12-5 PRODUCT DELETION

Generally, a product cannot satisfy target market customers and contribute to the achievement of the organization's overall goals indefinitely. **Product deletion** is the process of eliminating a product from the product mix, usually because it no longer satisfies a sufficient number of customers. Best Buy, for instance, announced that it would discontinue sales of CDs due to flagging sales. Sales have been declining since the early 2000s as more people prefer to stream their music or buy it on vinyl records.[28] A declining product reduces an organization's profitability and drains resources that could be used to modify other products or develop new ones. A marginal product may require shorter production runs, which can increase per-unit production costs. Finally, when a dying product completely loses favor with customers, the negative feelings may transfer to some of the company's other products.

Most organizations find it difficult to delete a product. A decision to drop a product may be opposed by managers and other employees who believe that the product is necessary to the product mix. Salespeople who still retain loyal customers may be especially upset when a product is dropped. Companies may spend considerable resources and effort to revive a slipping product with a changed marketing mix and thus avoid having to eliminate it.

Some organizations wait to delete products until after they have become heavy financial burdens. A better approach is some form of systematic review in which each product is evaluated periodically to determine its impact on the overall effectiveness of the firm's product mix. This review should analyze the product's contribution to the firm's sales for a given period, as well as estimate future sales, costs, and profits associated with the product. It should also gauge the value of making changes in the marketing strategy to improve the product's performance. A systematic review allows an organization to improve product performance and ascertain when to delete products. General Motors decided to delete the Hummer, Saturn, Saab, and Pontiac brands in order to lower costs, improve reputation, and become more profitable.

There are three basic ways to delete a product: phase it out, run it out, or drop it immediately (see Figure 12.5). A *phase-out* allows the product to decline without a change in the marketing strategy. With this strategy, no attempt is made to give the product new life. A *run-out* exploits any strengths left in the product. Intensifying marketing efforts in core markets or eliminating some marketing expenditures, such as advertising, may cause a sudden temporary jump in profits. This approach is commonly taken for technologically obsolete products, such

product deletion Eliminating a product from the product mix when it no longer satisfies a sufficient number of customers

---

©JIM R. BOUNDS/ BLOOMBERG VIA GETTY IMAGES

Figure 12.5 Product Deletion Process

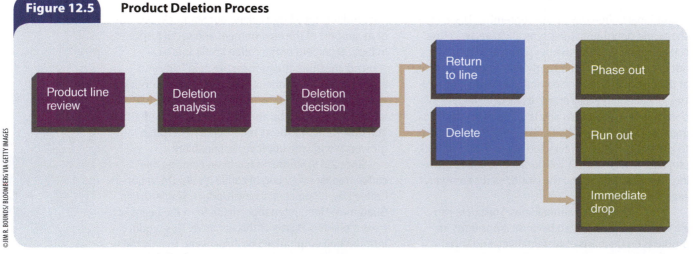

Source: Martin L. Bell, *Marketing: Concepts and Strategy*, 3rd ed., p. 267; Copyright © 1979, Houghton Mifflin Company. Reprinted by permission of Mrs. Martin L. Bell.

as older models of computers. Often, the price is reduced to generate a sales spurt. The third alternative, an *immediate drop* of an unprofitable product, is the best strategy when losses are too great to prolong the product's life.

12-6 ORGANIZING TO DEVELOP AND MANAGE PRODUCTS

Learning Objective 12-6

Describe organizational structures used for managing products.

It should be obvious by now that managing products is a complex task. Often, the traditional functional form of an organization does not fit a company's needs. In this case, management must find an organizational approach that accomplishes the tasks necessary to develop and manage products. Alternatives to functional organization include the product or brand manager approach, the market manager approach, and the venture team approach.

A **product manager** is responsible for a product, a product line, or several distinct products that make up an interrelated group within a multiproduct organization. A **brand manager** is responsible for a single brand. Kraft, for example, has one brand manager for Nabisco Oreos, its number-one-selling cookie, and another for Oscar Mayer Lunchables. Both product and brand managers operate cross-functionally to coordinate the activities, information, and strategies involved in marketing an assigned product. Product managers and brand managers plan marketing activities to achieve objectives by coordinating a mix of distribution, promotion (especially sales promotion and advertising), and price. They must consider packaging and branding decisions and work closely with personnel in research and development, engineering, and production. Marketing researchers help product managers understand consumers and find target markets. Because the brand names of luxury brands like Aston Martin and Porsche can be negatively impacted by association with producers' other mass-market brands, brand managers must balance their brands' independent image with associated brands of the firm. The product or brand manager approach to organization is used by many large, multiproduct companies.

A **market manager** is responsible for managing the marketing activities that serve a particular group of customers. This organizational approach is effective when a firm engages in different types of marketing activities to provide products to diverse customer groups. A company might have one market manager for business markets and another for consumer markets. Markets can also be divided by geographic region. Thus, the Jack-in-the-Box fast-food chain offers different menu items in New Mexico than it does in Oregon. Worldwide, McDonald's offers lamb and vegetarian options in lieu of beef and pork products at its restaurants in some countries to accommodate cultural and religious preferences. The chains recognize that different markets have different preferences. These broad market categories might be broken down into more limited market responsibilities.

A **venture team** creates entirely new products that may be aimed at new markets. Unlike a product or market manager, a venture team is responsible for all aspects of developing a product: research and development, production and engineering, finance and accounting, and marketing. Venture team members are brought together from different functional areas of the organization. In working outside established divisions, venture teams have greater flexibility to apply inventive approaches to develop new products that can take advantage of opportunities in highly segmented markets. Companies are increasingly using such cross-functional teams for product development in an effort to boost product quality. Quality may be positively related to information integration within the team, customers' influence on the product development process, and a quality orientation within the firm. When a new product has demonstrated commercial potential, team members may return to their functional areas, or they may join a new or existing division to manage the product.

product manager The person within an organization who is responsible for a product, a product line, or several distinct products that make up a group

brand manager The person responsible for a single brand

market manager The person responsible for managing the marketing activities that serve a particular group of customers

venture team A cross-functional group that creates entirely new products that may be aimed at new markets

Summary

12-1 Explain how companies manage existing products through line extensions and product modifications.

Organizations must be able to adjust their product mixes to compete effectively and achieve their goals. Using existing products, a product mix can be improved through line extension and through product modification. A line extension is the development of a product closely related to one or more products in the existing line but designed specifically to meet different customer needs. Product modification is the changing of one or more characteristics of a product. This approach can be achieved through quality modifications, functional modifications, and aesthetic modifications.

12-2 Explore how businesses develop a product idea into a commercial product.

Before a product is introduced, it goes through a 7-phase new-product development process. In the idea generation phase, new product ideas may come from internal or external sources. In the process of screening, ideas are evaluated to determine whether they are consistent with the firm's overall objectives and resources. Concept testing, the third phase, involves having a small sample of potential customers review a brief description of the product idea to determine their initial perceptions of the proposed product and their early buying intentions. During the business analysis stage, the product idea is evaluated to determine its potential contribution to the firm's sales, costs, and profits. In the product development stage, the organization determines if it is technically feasible to produce the product and if it can be produced at a cost low enough to make the final price reasonable. Test marketing is a limited introduction of a product in areas chosen to represent the intended market. Finally, in the commercialization phase, full-scale production of the product begins and a complete marketing strategy is developed.

12-3 Discuss the importance of product differentiation and the elements that differentiate one product from another.

Product differentiation is the process of creating and designing products so that customers perceive them as different from competing products. Product quality, product design and features, and product support services are three aspects of product differentiation that companies consider when creating and marketing products. Product quality includes the overall characteristics of a product that allow it to perform as expected in satisfying customer needs. The level of quality is the amount of quality a product possesses. Consistency of quality is the degree to which a product has the same level of quality over time. Product design refers to how a product is conceived, planned, and produced. Components of product design include styling (the physical appearance of the product) and product features (the specific design characteristics that allow a product to perform certain tasks). Companies often differentiate their products by providing support services, usually called customer services. Customer services are human or mechanical efforts or activities that add value to a product.

12-4 Explain how businesses position their products.

Product positioning relates to the decisions and activities that create and maintain a certain concept of the firm's product in customers' minds. Buyers tend to group, or "position," products in their minds to simplify buying decisions. Marketers try to position a new product so that it appears to have all the characteristics that the target market most desires. Positioning plays a role in market segmentation. Organizations can position a product to compete head-to-head with another brand or to avoid competition. Positioning a product away from competitors by focusing on a specific attribute not emphasized by competitors is one strategy. Other bases for positioning include price, quality level, and benefits provided by the product. Repositioning by making physical changes in the product, changing its price or distribution, or changing its image can boost a brand's market share and profitability.

12-5 Discuss how product deletion is used to improve product mixes.

Product deletion is the process of eliminating a product that no longer satisfies a sufficient number of customers. Although a firm's personnel may oppose product deletion, weak products are unprofitable, consume too much time and effort, may require shorter production runs, and can create an unfavorable impression of the firm's other products. A product mix should be systematically reviewed to determine when to delete products. Products to be deleted can be phased out, run out, or dropped immediately.

12-6 Describe organizational structures used for managing products.

Often, the traditional functional form of organization does not lend itself to the complex task of developing and managing products. Alternative organizational forms include the product or brand manager approach, the market manager approach, and the venture team approach. A product manager is responsible for a product, a product line, or several distinct products that make up an interrelated group within a multiproduct organization. A brand manager is responsible for a single brand.

A market manager is responsible for managing the marketing activities that serve a particular group or class of customers. A venture team is sometimes used to create entirely new products that may be aimed at new markets.

Important Terms

line extension 342
product modification 343
quality modifications 343
functional modifications 344
aesthetic modifications 344
disruptive innovation 345

new-product development process 345
idea generation 346
screening 347
concept testing 347
business analysis 347
product development 348
test marketing 350

commercialization 351
product differentiation 353
quality 353
level of quality 353
consistency of quality 353
product design 354
styling 354

product features 354
customer services 354
product positioning 355
product deletion 358
product manager 359
brand manager 359
market manager 359
venture team 359

Discussion and Review Questions

1. What is a line extension, and how does it differ from a product modification?
2. Compare and contrast the three major approaches to modifying a product.
3. Identify and briefly explain the seven major phases of the new-product development process.
4. Do small companies that manufacture just a few products need to be concerned about developing and managing products? Why or why not?
5. Why is product development a cross-functional activity—involving finance, engineering, manufacturing, and other functional areas—within an organization?
6. What is the major purpose of concept testing, and how is it accomplished?
7. What are the benefits and disadvantages of test marketing?
8. Why can the process of commercialization take a considerable amount of time?

9. What is product differentiation, and how can it be achieved?
10. Explain how the term *quality* has been used to differentiate products in the automobile industry in recent years. What are some makes and models of automobiles that come to mind when you hear the terms *high quality* and *poor quality?*
11. What is product positioning? Under what conditions would head-to-head product positioning be appropriate? When should head-to-head positioning be avoided?
12. What types of problems does a weak product cause in a product mix? Describe the most effective approach for avoiding such problems.
13. What type of organization might use a venture team to develop new products? What are the advantages and disadvantages of such a team?

Developing Your Marketing Plan

A company's marketing strategy may be revised to include new products as it considers its SWOT analysis and the impact of environmental factors on its product mix. When developing a marketing plan, the company must decide whether new products are to be added to the product mix or if existing ones should be modified. The information in this chapter will assist you in the creation of your marketing plan as you consider the following:

1. Identify whether your product will be a modification of an existing one in your product mix or a completely new product.

2. If the product is an extension of one in your current product mix, determine the type(s) of modifications that will be performed.
3. Using Figure 12.1 as a guide, discuss how your product idea would move through the stages of new-product development. Examine the idea, using the tests and analyses included in the new-product development process.
4. Discuss how the management of this product will fit into your current organizational structure.

Video Case 12.1

Cutting Edge Quality: Cutco "Knives for Life"

What if you could have a high-quality kitchen knife that would last forever? Look no further than Cutco. Cutco began manufacturing knives in Olean, New York, in 1949 when two companies, Alcoa Corp. and Case Cutlery, formed a joint venture to begin creating high-quality cutlery. Since then, Cutco has grown to become a nationally recognized brand known for its high-quality, American-made products. All Cutco knives come with a "Forever Guarantee" where customers can get their knives serviced for free, no matter how long ago the knives were purchased. Cutco knives pass from generation to generation.

Since 1949, Cutco has used a direct sales channel. In 1981, Vector was founded in Philadelphia as the sales division. It has grown to more than 250 district sales offices. The management team at Vector started as sales representatives. Sales representatives and managers gain skills needed for their future careers. Cutco's direct sales force is largely college students looking to make extra money during the summer. These students learn how to manage their time, how to interface with others, and how to express unique product attributes which set Cutco apart from the competition.

There are two models of direct selling compensation: multilevel and single-level marketing. Multilevel compensation means direct sellers earn commission from their own sales as well as commissions from those they have recruited and trained. In the case of Cutco, it uses a single-level method of compensation. This means that the sales representatives only earn a commission on the sales they make themselves and they do not recruit other sales representatives.

While the driver of the Cutco distribution model is direct selling, it has begun to experiment with different sales methods. Cutco has opened 16 retail locations since 2005 in order to give existing customers a place to service their knives while allowing potential customers a place to view and handle its products. These stores are focused on giving a "Cutco experience" where customers can try out knives, take classes on cooking, floral arrangement, gardening, and more. These Cutco stores also offer more than 100 kinds of kitchen cutlery products in addition to its knives. On the shelves in one of Cutco's retail stores, you might find utensils, kitchen shears, flatware, cookware, and a full line of sporting knives.

Cutco's retail stores were designed to help Cutco maintain long-term relationships with customers. Because the sales force for Cutco is mainly college students who stop selling after a year or two, it is easy for customers to lose contact with Cutco. Through its retail stores, Cutco maintains better customer relationships and a very visible presence on the retail front.

In addition to opening retail stores, Cutco now sells its products online, directly to customers. Cutco has also entered into a relationship with Costco Warehouse where the Cutco product is being sold in its roadshow program. These alternative distribution initiatives that Cutco has implemented allow consumers to have more exposure to Cutco products and are governed in a way to work synergistically with Cutco's direct sales model.

Cutco is proud of its history and heritage as an American knife manufacturer. Quality and fair treatment of employees and the community are, first and foremost, the priorities for the company. Cutco's knives are made from high-quality materials. Its blades are made from a high-carbon stainless steel, which goes through a three-stage heat treatment process to ensure that blades can take a sharp edge, maximize their resistance to corrosion, and won't snap under pressure. All knives have "full-tang construction," which means that the blade's metal extends all the way through the handle of the knife to create stability. The handles are made from an acetal copolymer thermo-resin, which gives the handles high strength, toughness, and resistance to abrasion. Rivets that hold the

SOURCE: CUTCO CORPORATION

handle together are made of a nickel-silver alloy that doesn't expand or contract from heat. This process creates a high-quality knife that is built to last. However, wear and tear is inevitable, so customers can get their knives serviced at any time.

Cutco is now one of the few American cutlery companies to keep its manufacturing in the United States. Cutco's American-made commitment has not always been easy to abide by. After the company entered the flatware business, its American supplier went bankrupt and closed down its operation. All other flatware manufacturing was outside of the United States. In order to uphold its commitment to American-made knives it purchased the fabricating equipment for its stainless table knives and insourced the product into its own factory in Olean, New York. That is an unparalleled commitment to American jobs and American made.

Cutco believes in social responsibility and making a positive difference, particularly in its hometown community. The Cutco Foundation was founded in 1996 with the mission to contribute to the growth and betterment of the Olean community. The foundation focuses its charitable work in the areas of education, quality of life improvement, and support of key organizations. The foundation supports many organizations, from the local hospital and

university to the small non-profits that make a difference for the less fortunate. For more than 20 years, employees at Cutco have volunteered hundreds of hours annually during the holiday season to support the Red Kettle Campaign for the Salvation Army. Cutco employees also participate in an annual toy drive for underprivileged children, an annual food drive for the local food pantries, and various charity walks.

Thanks to Cutco's high-quality products and unique business model, it is a nationally recognized brand for cutlery that is synonymous with quality. Cutco continues to expand its product offerings and has begun complementing its direct sales distribution with retail and internet sales. Even with its marketing strategy evolving, the high quality of its knives and its commitment to direct sales has remained constant since Cutco began in 1949.[29]

Questions for Discussion

1. How has Cutco used quality to differentiate its products?
2. How does Cutco add value to its products through the "Forever Guarantee"?
3. Does the direct selling channel help position Cutco's high-quality knives in the marketplace?

Case 12.2

Quesalupa! Crunchy and All that Cheese from Taco Bell

Remember Doritos Locos Tacos? Introduced in 2012, this one product increased Taco Bell's revenues by a whopping $1 billion during its first year on the market. No wonder the fast-food restaurant company never stops cooking up ideas to change and expand its menu. Taco Bell's research shows that adding new items, even those available for a limited time only, will bring consumers back to its 6,500 outlets again and again. That kind of brand loyalty is especially important in today's competitive marketplace, which is why Taco Bell aims to launch a new product every five weeks. In recent years, the firm has used co-branding for new breakfast items like the "Chocoladilla," a quesadilla stuffed with melted Kit Kats or Twix candies. It has also experimented with different ingredients and spices by introducing lunch and dinner items such as spicy, tortilla-wrapped DareDevil Loaded Grillers.

The new-product process at Taco Bell begins with brainstorming, experimentation, and discussion. Top executives scan the overall marketing environment, including

social-media sites, seeking inspiration for new flavor sensations or untraditional food combinations that will attract customer interest and fit with Taco Bell's brand personality. Food experts from top suppliers regularly step into the company's test kitchens to whip up innovative creations based on the latest food trends and consumer research. Taco Bell's marketers nibble away, and as the conversation flows, they come away with ideas to shape into specific product concepts. Two Taco Bell restaurants near the company's headquarters also serve as idea generators, by encouraging buyers to creatively customize their food orders. Marketers carefully analyze the frequency of requests for different combinations to gain insights into how consumers' tastes are changing. Although Taco Bell's customers often favor crunchy and cheesy products, the firm is always on the lookout for other ideas that will add a bit of variety to the menu.

Once the company has screened the ideas, tested product concepts, and developed prototypes of new menu items, it puts the best into test marketing. The crunchy, cheese-stuffed

SWEETBABEEJAY/ISTOCK EDITORIAL/GETTY IMAGES

Quesalupa, a cross between a quesadilla and chalupa, was tested in 36 Taco Bell restaurants around Toledo, Ohio, the same city where Dorito Locos Tacos were test-marketed before being launched nationally. Through test marketing, Taco Bell was able to evaluate customer reaction to the Quesalupa and, just as important, be sure the new product could be prepared to look and taste as it should, every time customers placed an order. The firm also assessed whether it could get sufficient supplies for a large-scale launch, if and when the product was chosen for commercialization. Taco Bell supported its test marketing with Toledo-area ads to encourage product trial.

After months of test marketing in Toledo, Taco Bell determined that customer response was enthusiastic enough to move ahead with a national launch of the Quesalupa. Rather than introduce the new product with a traditional marketing campaign, Taco Bell created a buzz in mass media and social media by trumpeting a big introduction to coincide with the Super Bowl—without saying which product was being added to the menu. During the Super Bowl, Taco Bell cleared up the mystery by revealing the Quesalupa in a national ad and five regional ads for targeted markets. This got the launch off to a strong start by bringing consumers into restaurants across the country for a taste and a chance to tell their friends all about the satisfying crunch and the bridges of hot, stringy cheese with taco toppings in the middle.[30]

Questions for Discussion

1. In terms of product differentiation, why does Taco Bell test-market its new products for months before deciding whether to introduce them in a wider area?
2. What are the advantages and disadvantages of Taco Bell introducing a product simultaneously in all outlets nationwide rather than in stages through a rollout?
3. Which product attributes or features does Taco Bell appear to be using to position the Quesalupa, and why?

CHAPTER

13

Services Marketing

LEARNING OBJECTIVES

13-1 Discuss the growth and importance of services.

13-2 Identify the characteristics of services that differentiate them from goods.

13-3 Analyze how the characteristics of services influence the development of marketing mixes for services.

13-4 Explain the importance of service quality and explain how to deliver exceptional service quality.

13-5 Describe the nature of nonprofit marketing.

VECTORHOT/SHUTTERSTOCK.COM

PEJK/SHUTTERSTOCK.COM

Spotify Spots Product Opportunities Beyond Streaming Services

In 2005, serial entrepreneurs Daniel Ek and Martin Lorentzon realized that technology was disrupting the music industry. While some consumers bought CDs in stores or online, paid for digital music on sites like iTunes, or used streaming radio like Pandora, many others obtained digital music illegally, without paying. Ek and Lorentzon set out to create Spotify as a new kind of streaming music service, with two priorities. First, they wanted to ensure proper payment to publishers and artists, encouraging participation in their service and helping to strengthen the industry. Second, they wanted to give consumers free or affordable access to millions of songs for streaming anywhere, at any time.

After years of negotiating with music publishers, Spotify went live in Europe with a free, ad-supported streaming service in 2008. The company later introduced a fee-based, ad-free version. Next, Spotify launched in the United States, offering both a free version with ads and a paid, ad-free version. To attract more subscribers while raising revenue, the company added a lower-priced student option and a family subscription priced for up to six members. Still, more than half of Spotify's 140 million users worldwide use the free, ad-supported version.

The major competitor in streaming services is Apple Music, although giants such as Microsoft and Sony have tried and then discontinued streaming music. To maintain its growth, Spotify plans a steady stream of service innovations to satisfy consumers, music publishers, and artists. For instance, artists can now sell merchandise to fans via the Spotify platform. What's next for Spotify?[1]

Intangible services like Spotify involve a deed, performance, or effort that cannot be physically possessed. This chapter explores concepts that apply specifically to products that are services. The organizations that market services include for-profit firms (e.g., those offering financial, personal, and professional services) and nonprofit organizations (e.g., educational institutions, churches, charities, and governments).

We begin this chapter with a discussion of the huge importance of service industries in economies, particularly in developed countries like the United States. We then address the unique characteristics of services. Next, we deal with the challenges these characteristics pose in developing and managing marketing mixes for services. We then discuss customers' judgment of service quality and the importance of delivering high-quality services. Finally, we define nonprofit marketing and examine the development of nonprofit marketing strategies.

Learning Objective 13-1

Discuss the growth and importance of services.

13-1 THE GROWTH AND IMPORTANCE OF SERVICES

All products—whether goods, services, or ideas—are, to some extent, intangible. We previously defined a service as an intangible product that involves a deed, a performance, or an effort that cannot be physically possessed.[2] Services are usually provided through the application of human and/or mechanical efforts that are directed at people or objects. For example, a service such as education involves the efforts of service providers (teachers) that are directed at people (students), whereas janitorial and interior decorating services direct their efforts at objects. Services can also involve the use of mechanical efforts directed at people (air or public transportation) or objects (freight transportation). A wide variety of services, such as health care and landscaping, involve both human and mechanical efforts. Although many services entail the use of tangibles such as tools and machinery, the primary difference between a service and a good is that a service is dominated by the intangible portion of the total product.

The importance of services in the U.S. economy led the United States to be known as the world's first service economy. In most developed countries, including Germany, Japan, Australia, and Canada, services account for about 70 percent of the gross domestic product (GDP). More than one-half of new businesses in the United States are service businesses, and service employment is expected to continue to grow. A practice that has gained popularity among U.S. businesses as telecommunications technology has improved is **homesourcing**, in which customer-contact jobs, such as at call centers, are outsourced to the homes of workers. Staffing agencies such as Rhema Business Solutions are dedicated to providing homesourcing employees to organizations in a variety of industries, including nursing, marketing and sales, advertising, web development, and writing.[3] Companies as diverse as 1-800-FLOWERS, J.Crew, and Office Depot all utilize homesourcing for some tasks.

A major catalyst in the growth of consumer services has been long-term economic growth (slowed by a few recessions) in the United States, which has led to increased prosperity and interest in financial services, travel, entertainment, and personal care. The need for child care, domestic services, online dating services, and other time-saving services has increased during the late 20th and early 21st centuries. Many busy consumers want to minimize or avoid such tasks as meal preparation, house cleaning, yard maintenance, and tax preparation in order to focus on other activities, such as work or family time. Because Americans tend to be health, fitness, and recreation oriented, the demand for services related to exercise and recreation has escalated. Another driver of services is the aging population in the United States, which has spurred expansion of health-care services. Finally, the increasing number and complexity of high-tech goods have spurred demand for support services. Indeed, dramatic changes in information technology have influenced and expanded the services sector in the 21st century. Consider service companies like Google Pay, Instacart, Tinder, and Uber, which use technology to provide services that are responsive and well-targeted to customer needs and that have challenged traditional ways of conducting business.

Business services have grown as well. Business services include support and maintenance, consulting, installation, equipment leasing, marketing research, advertising, temporary office

homesourcing A practice whereby customer-contact jobs are outsourced into workers' homes

assistance, and janitorial services. The growth in business services can be attributed to the increasingly complex, specialized, and competitive business environment.

A way that might help you view services is using the metaphor of a theater. A play features production elements (such as actors, audience, a setting) and a performance. The actors (service workers) create a performance (service) for the audience (customers) in a setting (service environment) where the performance unfolds. Costumes (uniforms), props (devices, music, machines), and the setting (face-to-face or indirect through telephone or internet) help complete the metaphor.[4] A service provider such as Disney World illustrates the metaphor: Employees wear costumes, there is an entertainment setting, and most service contact with employees involves playing roles and engaging in planned skits.

Services as products should not be confused with the related topic of customer service. Customer service involves any human, mechanical, or electronic activity that adds value to the product. Although customer service is a part of the marketing of goods, service marketers also provide customer services. Many service companies offer service quality guarantees to their customers in an effort to increase value. La Quinta Inns & Suites, a national chain of hotels, gives its guests a free night if they are not 100 percent satisfied with their stay.[5] In some cases, a 100 percent satisfaction guarantee or similar service commitment can motivate employees to provide consistently high-quality service because they are proud to be part of an organization that is so committed to good service.

intangibility The characteristic that a service is not physical and cannot be perceived by the senses

> **Learning Objective 13-2**
>
> Identify the characteristics of services that differentiate them from goods.

13-2 CHARACTERISTICS OF SERVICES

The issues associated with marketing service products are not exactly the same as those associated with marketing goods. To understand these differences, it is first necessary to understand the distinguishing characteristics of services. Services have six basic characteristics: intangibility, inseparability of production and consumption, perishability, heterogeneity, client-based relationships, and customer contact.[6]

13-2a Intangibility

As already noted, one of the major characteristics that distinguish a service from a good is intangibility. **Intangibility** means a service is not physical and, therefore, cannot be touched. It is impossible, for instance, to touch the education that students derive from attending classes—the intangible benefit is becoming more knowledgeable in a chosen field of study. In addition, services cannot be physically possessed. Students cannot physically touch knowledge as they can a smartphone or a car. The level of intangibility of a service increases the overall importance of the brand image when a customer is deciding which to purchase. A customer trying to select an intangible product usually relies more heavily on the brand to act as a cue to the nature and quality of the service. Consider the advertisement for GEICO insurance. Insurance is an intangible service and challenging to describe and market. In this advertisement, GEICO focuses on educating buyers that GEICO insurance products can save them money that they can spend on what they really love, such as exercise. The ad, which pictures an exercise bike and playfully tells potential buyers, "That spin class won't pay for itself," reinforces the GEICO brand.

Intangibility

GEICO provides auto, home, renter, cycle, and boat insurance products. Insurance products possess a very high level of intangibility.

Figure 13.1   **The Tangibility Continuum**

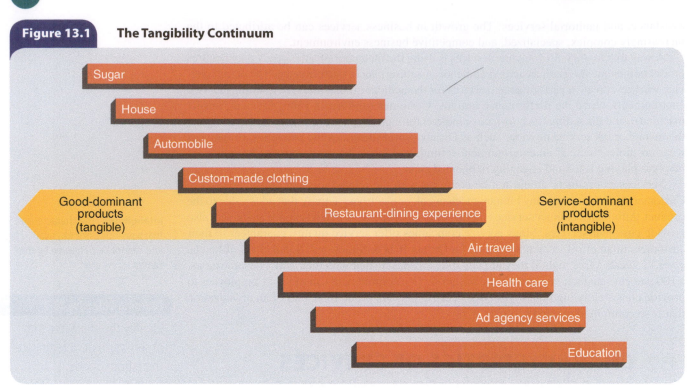

Figure 13.1 depicts a tangibility continuum from pure goods (tangible) to pure services (intangible). Pure goods, if they exist at all, are rare because practically all marketers of goods also provide customer services. Even a tangible product like sugar must be delivered to the store, priced, and placed on a shelf before a customer can purchase it. Intangible, service-dominant products such as education or health care are clearly service products. Most products fall somewhere in the middle of this continuum. Products such as a restaurant meal or a hotel stay have both tangible and intangible dimensions. Knowing where the product lies on the continuum is important in creating marketing strategies for service-dominant products.

inseparability The quality of being produced and consumed at the same time

Inseparability of Production and Consumption

An airline flight is characterized by inseparability. That is, production and consumption occur simultaneously and cannot be separated.

13-2b Inseparability of Production and Consumption

Another important characteristic of services that creates challenges for marketers is **inseparability**, which refers to the fact that the production of a service cannot be separated from its consumption by customers. For instance, an airline flight is produced and consumed simultaneously—that is, services are produced, sold, and consumed at the same time. In goods marketing, a customer can purchase a good, take it home, and store it until ready for use. The manufacturer of the good may never see an actual customer. Customers, however, often must be present at the production of a service (such as investment consulting or surgery) and cannot take the service home. Indeed, both the service provider and the customer must work together to provide and receive the service's full value. Because of inseparability, customers not only want a specific type of service but expect it to be provided in a specific way by a specific individual. For instance, the production and consumption of a medical exam occur simultaneously, and the patient knows in advance who the physician is and generally understands how the exam will be conducted. Inseparability implies a shared responsibility between the customer and the service provider. Training programs for employees in the service sector should stress the importance of the customer in the service experience so that employees understand that the shared responsibility exists.

13-2c **Perishability**

Services are characterized by **perishability** because the unused service capacity of one time period cannot be stored for future use. For instance, empty seats on an airline flight today cannot be stored and sold to passengers at a later date. Other examples of service perishability include unsold basketball tickets, unscheduled dentists' appointment times, and empty hotel rooms. Although some goods (e.g., meat, milk, or produce) are perishable, goods generally are less perishable than services. If a pair of jeans has been sitting on a department store shelf for a month, the quality is not affected. Goods marketers can handle the supply–demand problem through production scheduling and inventory techniques. Service marketers do not have the same advantage and face several hurdles in trying to balance supply and demand. They can, however, plan for demand that fluctuates according to day of the week, time of day, or season.

13-2d **Heterogeneity**

Services delivered by people are susceptible to **heterogeneity**, or variation in quality. The quality of manufactured goods is easier to control with standardized procedures, and mistakes are easier to isolate and correct. Because of the nature of human behavior, however, it is very difficult for service providers to maintain a consistent quality of service delivery. This variation in quality can occur from one organization to another, from one service person to another within the same service facility, and from one service facility to another within the same organization. Consequently, the staff at one bookstore location may be more knowledgeable

perishability The inability of unused service capacity to be stored for future use

heterogeneity Variation in quality

and, therefore, more helpful than those at another bookstore owned by the same chain. The quality of the service a single employee provides can vary from customer to customer, day to day, or even hour to hour. Although many service problems are one-time events that cannot be predicted or controlled ahead of time, employee training and the establishment of standard procedures can help increase consistency and reliability. Training should offer ways that will help employees provide quality service consistently to customers, thus mitigating the issue of heterogeneity. Thus, a business that provides services in a cross-cultural environment may want to train its employees to be more sensitive toward people of different countries and cultures.

Heterogeneity usually increases as the degree of labor intensiveness increases. Many services, such as auto repair, education, and hairstyling, rely heavily on human labor. Other services, such as telecommunications, health clubs, and public transportation, are more

Heterogeneity
Do you like to go to the same hair care professional most of the time? If so, it is probably because you want the same quality of hair care, such as a haircut that you have received from this individual in the past.

equipment intensive. People-based services are often prone to fluctuations in quality from one time period to the next. For instance, the fact that a hairstylist gives a customer a good haircut today does not guarantee that customer a haircut of equal quality from the same hairstylist at a later time. Equipment-based services suffer from this problem to a lesser degree than people-based services. For instance, automated teller machines have high consistency in the quality of services compared to receiving the same service in person at a bank, and bar-code scanning has improved the accuracy of service at checkout counters in grocery stores.

13-2e **Client-Based Relationships**

The success of many services depends on creating and maintaining **client-based relationships**, which are interactions that result in satisfied customers who use a service repeatedly over time.[7] In fact, some service providers such as lawyers, accountants, and financial advisors call their customers *clients* and often develop and maintain close, long-term relationships with them. For such service providers, it is not enough to attract customers. They are successful only to the degree to which they can maintain a group of clients who use their services on an ongoing basis. For example, an accountant may serve a family in his or her area for decades. If the members of this family like the quality of the accountant's services, they are likely to recommend the accountant to other families. If several families repeat this positive word-of-mouth communication, the accountant will likely acquire a long list of satisfied clients.

Service companies are increasingly using social media, especially Facebook and Instagram, to build customer relationships by sharing useful information, responding to communications, and generally demonstrating the company's personality and brand. Wendy's, for example, has become renowned for its witty tweets and taunts of competitors like McDonald's on Twitter, where Wendy's has more than 2 million followers.[8] Social media have made it easier for customers to share information about service companies. Word-of-mouth (or going viral, which is the online equivalent) is a key factor in creating and maintaining client-based relationships. To ensure that it actually occurs, the service provider must take steps to build trust, demonstrate customer commitment, and satisfy customers so well that they become very loyal to the provider and unlikely to switch to competitors.

13-2f **Customer Contact**

Not all services require a high degree of customer contact, but many do. **Customer contact** refers to the level of interaction between the service provider and the customer necessary to deliver the service. High-contact services include health care, real estate, and legal services. Examples of low-contact services are tax preparation, auto repair, travel reservations, and dry cleaning. Technology has enabled many service-oriented businesses to reduce their level of customer contact. Most airlines, for example, have apps through which fliers can book flights, choose seats, check in, and more on their phone or tablet. Note that high-contact services generally involve actions directed toward people, who must be present during production. A hairstylist's customer, for example, must be physically present at the salon during the styling process. When the customer must be present, the process of production may be just as important as its final outcome. Although it is sometimes possible for the service provider to go to the customer, high-contact services typically require that the customer go to the production facility. Thus, the physical appearance of the facility may be a major component of the customer's overall evaluation of the service. Even in low-contact service situations, the appearance of the facility is important because the customer likely will need to be present to initiate and finalize the service transaction. Consider customers of auto-repair services. They bring in the vehicle and describe its symptoms but often do not remain during the repair process.

Employees of high-contact service providers represent a very important ingredient in creating satisfied customers. A fundamental precept of customer contact is that satisfied employees lead to satisfied customers. Employee satisfaction is one of the most important factors in

client-based relationships
Interactions that result in satisfied customers who use a service repeatedly over time

customer contact The level of interaction between provider and customer needed to deliver the service

DISRUPTIVE MARKETING

Can't Get It Together? IKEA's TaskRabbit Can

With 403 stores in 49 countries, IKEA is the biggest furniture marketer on the planet. It's known for marketing affordable, stylish furniture like desks and bed frames packed flat for do-it-yourself customers to assemble at home. However, not every customer has the time or the know-how to complete the assembly process.

Now IKEA has made an acquisition that will put assembly services a click or two away for customers who don't want to do it themselves. The Swedish-based company acquired TaskRabbit, an online marketplace where freelancers offer their services for hire. Even before the acquisition, TaskRabbit received so many inquiries about assembling IKEA furniture that it created a special web page just for those services. IKEA had previously teamed up with TaskRabbit

to pilot a program offering assembly services to customers at its London stores. The pilot was so successful that IKEA followed up by buying TaskRabbit to be able to offer assembly services, on demand, to customers in a much wider market area.

IKEA has conducted research, and it knows its customers want more than just a great product at a great price. The U.K. CEO explains: "People are saying there's value to time—'I don't have the time to assemble it myself. I don't necessarily have the time to install things myself. Actually, I'm looking for services from you.'" In other words, customers trust IKEA and expect it to provide services that complement the products it sells. And that's why TaskRabbit is now part of IKEA, adding to the furniture company's competitive strength.[a]

providing high service quality to customers. Thus, to minimize potential problems, service organizations must take steps to understand and meet the needs of employees by training them adequately, empowering them to make decisions, and rewarding them for customer-oriented behavior.[9] Southwest Airlines encourages customer loyalty and employee retention through training their staff and broadcasting instances of customer satisfaction and standout customer service through social media channels. Social media can be an inexpensive and effective means of training and engaging employees, as well as spreading awareness of stellar service to customers.[10]

13-3 DEVELOPING AND MANAGING MARKETING MIXES FOR SERVICES

Learning Objective 13-3

Analyze how the characteristics of services influence the development of marketing mixes for services.

The characteristics of services discussed in the previous section create a number of challenges for service marketers (see Table 13.1). These challenges are especially evident in the development and management of marketing mixes for services. Although such mixes contain the four major marketing-mix variables—product, distribution, promotion, and price—the characteristics of services require that marketers consider additional issues.

13-3a Development of Services

A service offered by an organization is generally a package, or bundle, of services consisting of a core service and one or more supplementary services. A *core service* is the basic service experience or commodity that a customer expects to receive. A *supplementary service* supports the core service and is used to differentiate the service bundle from those of competitors. For example, when a student attends a tutoring session for a class, the core service is the tutoring. Bundled with the core service might be access to outlines with additional information, handouts or apps with practice questions, or online services like a chat room or wiki to address questions that arise outside the designated tutoring time.

Table 13.1   **Service Characteristics and Marketing Challenges**

Service Characteristics	Resulting Marketing Challenges
Intangibility	Difficult for customer to evaluate. Customer does not take physical possession. Difficult to advertise and display. Difficult to set and justify prices. Service process is usually not protectable by patents.
Inseparability of production and consumption	Service provider cannot mass-produce services. Customer must participate in production. Other consumers affect service outcomes. Services are difficult to distribute.
Perishability	Services cannot be stored. Balancing supply and demand is very difficult. Unused capacity is lost forever. Demand may be very time sensitive.
Heterogeneity	Service quality is difficult to control. Service delivery is difficult to standardize.
Client-based relationships	Success depends on satisfying and keeping customers over the long term. Generating repeat business is challenging. Relationship marketing becomes critical.
Customer contact	Service providers are critical to delivery. Requires high levels of service employee training and motivation. Changing a high-contact service into a low-contact service to achieve lower costs is difficult to achieve without reducing customer satisfaction.

Sources: K. Douglas Hoffman and John E. G. Bateson, *Services Marketing: Concepts, Strategies, and Cases*, 5th ed. (Mason, OH: Cengage Learning, 2017); Valarie A. Zeithaml, A. Parasuraman, and Leonard L. Berry, *Delivering Quality Service: Balancing Customer Perceptions and Expectations* (New York: Free Press, 1990); Leonard L. Berry and A. Parasuraman, *Marketing Services: Competing through Quality* (New York: Free Press, 1991), p. 5.

As discussed earlier, heterogeneity results in variability in service quality and makes it difficult to standardize services. As an example, an Uber ride varies depending on the customer's origination and destination, time of day, the driver's vehicle, and traffic. However, heterogeneity provides one advantage to service marketers: It allows them to customize their services to match the specific needs of individual customers. Customization plays a key role in providing competitive advantage for the service provider. Being able to personalize the service to fit the exact needs of the customer accommodates individual needs, wants, or desires.[11] Chipotle, Subway, and Freebirds, for example, allow each customer to participate in developing his or her own customized taco, sandwich, or burrito.

Such customized services can be expensive for both provider and customer, and some service marketers, therefore, face a dilemma: how to provide service at an acceptable level of quality in an efficient and economic manner and still satisfy individual customer needs. To cope with this problem, some service marketers offer standardized packages. Thus, a lawyer may offer a divorce package at a specified price for an uncontested divorce. When service bundles are standardized, the specific actions and activities of the service provider usually are highly specified. Automobile quick-lube providers frequently offer a service bundle for a single price. The specific work to be done on a customer's car is spelled out in detail. Various other equipment-based services are also often standardized into packages. For instance, cable television providers offer several packages, such as "Basic," "Standard," and "Premier."

The characteristic of intangibility makes it difficult for customers to evaluate a service prior to purchase. Intangibility requires service marketers, such as stylists or attorneys, to market promises to customers. The customer must place some degree of trust in the service provider to perform the service in a manner that meets or exceeds those promises. Service marketers should take steps to avoid sending messages that consumers might construe as promises that raise customer expectations beyond what the firm can provide.

To cope with the problem of intangibility, marketers employ tangible cues (such as well-groomed, professional-appearing contact personnel and clean, attractive physical facilities) to assure customers about the quality and professionalism of the service. Most service providers require that at least some of their high-contact employees wear uniforms, which help make the service experience more tangible and serve as physical evidence to signal quality, create consistency, and send cues that suggest a desired image.[12] Consider the professionalism, experience, and competence conveyed by an airline pilot's uniform. Life insurance companies sometimes try to make the quality of their policies more tangible by printing them on premium paper and enclosing them in sheaths or high-quality folders. Because customers often rely on brand names as an indicator of product quality, service marketers at organizations whose names are the same as their service brand names should strive to build a strong national image for their companies. For example, USAA insurance, Ritz Carlton hotels, and Starbucks coffee maintain strong, positive national company images because these names are the brand names of the services they provide.

The inseparability of production and consumption and the level of customer contact also influence the development and management of services. The fact that customers are present and may take part in the production of a service means that other customers can affect the outcome of the service. For instance, a restaurant might give a small discount if children are well-behaved. Service marketers can reduce problems by encouraging customers to share the responsibility of maintaining an environment that allows all participants to receive the intended benefits of the service environment.

13-3b **Distribution of Services**

Marketers deliver services in various ways. In some instances, customers go to a service provider's facility. For instance, most health-care, dry-cleaning, and spa services are delivered at the provider's facilities. Some services are provided at the customer's home or business. Lawn care, air-conditioning and heating repair, and carpet cleaning are examples. Other services are delivered primarily at "arm's length," meaning no face-to-face contact occurs between the customer and the service provider. A number of equipment-based services can be delivered at arm's length, including electric, online, cable television, and telephone services. It can be costly for a firm to install the systems required to deliver high-quality customer service at arm's length, but this can be essential in keeping customers satisfied and maintaining market share.

Marketing channels for services usually are short and direct, meaning the producer delivers the service directly to the end user. Credit cards are a service that is frequently offered directly, with customers dealing directly with credit card companies. This advertisement, for example, promotes the Capital One Venture credit card, which offers double airline miles in its reward program. The image in the ad—a spinning Ferris wheel over the water—underscores that Capital One's Venture credit card gives consumers rewards and choices,

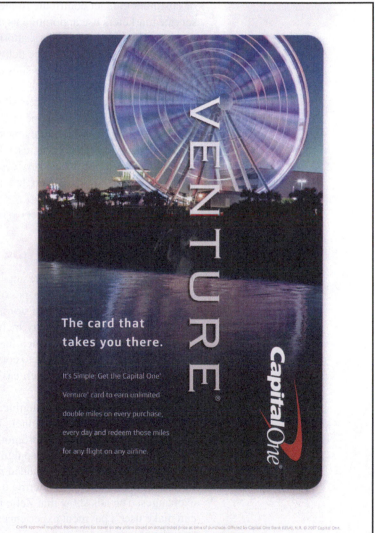

Direct Marketing Channel
Most credit card companies provide credit services through direct marketing channels. Credit card holders deal directly with their credit card companies.

such as using their reward miles on any airline and any flight, which may help Capital One stand out in a crowded field of credit card companies.

Some services, however, use intermediaries. For example, travel agents facilitate the delivery of airline services, independent insurance agents participate in the marketing of a variety of insurance policies, and financial planners market investment services. The internet has allowed some service providers to alter marketing and distribution channels. Restaurants are increasingly using third-party intermediaries to deliver hot meals to customers who prefer not (or are unable) to leave their homes, workplaces, or hotel rooms. A growing number of services, such as GrubHub, DoorDash, and UberEats, connect restaurants and customers with website or smartphone ordering and swift delivery. In some cases, the popularity of such delivery services has led some restaurants to expand or open kitchens without dining rooms to handle growing delivery sales.[13] Similarly, Stitch Fix is an online personal shopping service, which ships clothing items to subscribers based on a detailed questionnaire. Personal shopping used to be a high-touch service, but the internet has allowed Stitch Fix to offer a high-quality service at arm's length.[14]

Service marketers are less concerned with warehousing and transportation than are goods marketers. They are very concerned, however, about inventory management, especially balancing supply and demand for services. The service characteristics of inseparability and level of customer contact contribute to the challenges of demand management. In some instances, service marketers use appointments and reservations as approaches for scheduling delivery of services. Health-care providers, attorneys, accountants, and restaurants often use appointments or reservations to plan and pace delivery of their services. To increase the supply of a service, marketers use multiple service sites and also increase the number of contact service providers at each site.

To make delivery more accessible to customers and increase the supply of a service, as well as reduce labor costs, some service providers have replaced some contact personnel with equipment. In other words, they have changed a high-contact service into a low-contact one. By installing ATMs, banks increased production capacity and reduced customer contact. The transition to more automated services is not always seamless, however. Some customers do not like that automated services are less personal and would prefer to talk to a staff person. When designing service delivery, marketers must pay attention to the degree of personalization that customers in their target market desire.

13-3c **Promotion of Services**

The intangibility of services results in several promotion-related challenges to service marketers. Because it may not be possible to depict the actual performance of a service in an advertisement or display it in a store, explaining a service to customers can be a difficult task. Promotion of services typically includes tangible cues that symbolize the service. Consider Liberty Mutual Insurance, which features the Statue of Liberty on its logo. This image symbolizes strength and reliability to consumers. Although this symbol has nothing to do with the actual service, it makes it much easier for customers to understand the intangible attributes associated with the service.

To make a service more tangible, promotions for services may show pictures of facilities, equipment, and service personnel. Thus, advertisements for fitness centers may depict the equipment available. Service promotions may show people using the service, often in humorous ways. The advertising campaign used to introduce Zelle, a digital payment service, used an amusing campaign that included rapper/actor Daveed Diggs being frustrated by his inability to use cash while encountering a variety of people using Zelle to do convenient financial exchanges. The ads show that Zelle is available through a number of large banking firms and can make user's payment experiences easier and faster, boosting awareness of the service and app downloads.[15]

Marketers may also promote their services as a tangible expression of consumers' lifestyles. The advertisement for Choctaw Casino & Resort highlights the resort services available, which is targeted at consumers who want to gamble and feel like they are being treated like millionaires. The image of a woman laughing while apparently winning highlights that Choctaw Casino customers can "live like a millionaire, and maybe leave as one." The ad emphasizes that the services offered by Choctaw Casino & Resort are an extension of the lifestyle and types of trips taken by target consumers.

Branded marketing can help service firms hone their messages for maximum impact. JPMorgan Chase & Co. kept this in mind when it revamped its banking website in part to create a consistent message across all available channels, including its smartphone app. The redesigned website employs a simple, responsive, and personal design to echo the bank's highly used Chase Mobile App. Many of the website's buttons and menus are identical to those used in the app. The website also includes discussions and advice about financial health and stories about neighborhoods. The changes have already resulted in longer stays on the website, allowing Chase to build stronger relationships with its customers.[16] When preparing advertisements, service marketers should be careful to use concrete, specific language to help make services more tangible in customers' minds. Service companies are also careful not to promise too much regarding their services so that customer expectations do not rise to unattainable levels.

Compared with goods marketers, service providers are more likely to promote price, guarantees, performance documentation, availability, and training and certification of contact personnel. It is common, for example, for gyms and yoga or aerobics studios to promote their trainers' degrees and certifications as a way to ensure customers that their trainers are well-qualified to help them reach their fitness goals.

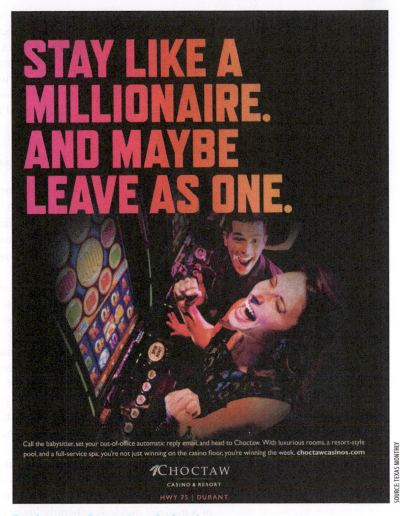

Services as an Expression of Lifestyles
Casinos provide a variety of services, some of which are an expression of lifestyle.

Through their actions, service contact personnel can be directly or indirectly involved in the personal selling of services. Personal selling may be important because personal influence can help the customer visualize the benefits of a given service. Because service contact personnel may engage in personal selling, some companies invest heavily in training. To improve its poor customer complaint rate, Spirit Airlines turned to the Disney Institute, an offshoot of the Walt Disney Company that provides training and development services. Disney helped the airline develop the Spirit Signature Service training program that included new service standards and additional training for all personnel to help improve its reputation.[17]

As noted earlier, intangibility makes experiencing a service prior to purchase difficult, if not impossible, in some cases. A car can be test-driven, a snack food can be sampled in a supermarket, and a new brand of bar soap can be distributed as a free sample. Some services can also be offered on a trial basis at little or no risk to the customer, but a number of services cannot be sampled before purchase. Promotional programs that encourage trial use of insurance, health care, or auto repair are difficult to design because, even after purchase of such services, assessing their quality may require a considerable length of time. For instance, an individual may purchase auto insurance from the same provider for 10 years before filing a claim, but the quality of the coverage is based primarily on how the customer is treated and protected when a claim is made.

Because of the heterogeneity and intangibility of services, word-of-mouth communication is particularly important in service promotion. What other people say about a service provider can have a tremendous impact on whether an individual decides to use that provider. Some service marketers attempt to stimulate positive word-of-mouth communication by asking satisfied customers to tell their friends and associates about the service and give a high rating on Yelp. Groupon and Living Social, which offer discounted deals at local businesses in participating cities, offer a free deal to customers who refer friends who then become new customers.

13-3d **Pricing of Services**

Services should be priced with consumer price sensitivity, the nature of the transaction, and its costs in mind.[18] Prices for services can be established on several different bases. The prices of such services as pest-control, dry cleaning, carpet cleaning, and health consultations are usually based on the performance of specific tasks. Other service prices are based on time spent on the task. For example, attorneys, consultants, counselors, piano teachers, and plumbers usually charge by the hour or day.

Some services use demand-based pricing. When demand for a service is high, the price is also high. Conversely, when demand for a service is low, so is the price. The perishability of services means that, when demand is low, the unused capacity cannot be stored and is lost—resulting in forgone revenues for the firm. Every empty seat on an airline flight or in a movie theater represents lost revenue. Some services are time sensitive, meaning that a significant number of customers desire the service around the same time. This point in time is called *peak demand*. A provider of time-sensitive services brings in most of its revenue during peak demand. For an airline, peak demand is usually early and late in the day. For cruise lines, peak demand occurs in the winter for Caribbean cruises and in the summer for Alaskan or European cruises. Customers can receive better deals on services by purchasing during nonpeak times.

Providers of time-sensitive services can use demand-based pricing to manage the problem of balancing supply and demand. They charge top prices during peak demand and lower prices during off-peak demand to encourage more customers to use the service. This is why the price of a matinee movie is generally lower than the same movie shown at a later time. The city of San Francisco adopted demand-based pricing with regard to city-owned on-street parking. The city raised the rates on parking meters that were routinely above 80 percent occupancy and reduced them on those spaces regularly below 60 percent occupancy. Hopefully, drivers will choose to reduce the time parked in the higher-priced spaces freeing them up sooner. The goal of the pricing structure is to decrease the amount of time people spend searching for parking spaces and thereby reduce congestion and greenhouse emissions.[19] **Off-peak pricing** is the practice of reducing prices of services used during slow periods in order to boost demand. Off-peak pricing has long been used by hotels and airlines, but other industries are looking to the practice to smooth out peak traffic. The upscale London restaurant Bob Ricard introduced off-peak pricing to bring in diners who rarely eat at luxury restaurants because of the high prices. The restaurant now charges 25 percent less for à la carte menu items during off-peak times and 15 percent less during "mid-peak" times. The strategy has doubled the number of customers coming in during normally slow hours.[20]

In cases where customers tend to purchase services in a bundle, marketers must decide whether to offer the services at one price, price them separately, or use a combination of the two methods. Some service providers offer a one-price option for a specific bundle of services and make add-on services available at additional charges. Most cable television providers offer a standard package, and customers can add services according to their needs, for additional fees. However, the trend of à la carte television services is growing as more consumers choose to forgo cable or satellite and pay only for those channels they want to stream. As a result, some networks like HBO and CBS are offering stand-alone streaming services for customers who do not want the full package.[21]

off-peak pricing The practice of reducing prices of services used during slow periods in order to boost demand

Because of the intangible nature of services, customers sometimes rely heavily on price as an indicator of quality. If customers perceive the available services in a service category as being similar in quality, and if the quality of such services is difficult to judge even after these services are purchased, customers may seek out the lowest-priced provider. For example, many customers search for auto insurance providers with the lowest rates because insurance companies tend to offer packages that are easily comparable between firms. If the quality of different service providers is likely to vary, customers may rely heavily on the price–quality association. For instance, if you have to have an appendectomy, will you choose the surgeon who charges $1,500 or the surgeon who only charges $399?

For certain types of services, market conditions may limit how much can be charged for a specific service, especially if the services in this category are perceived as generic in nature. Thus, the prices charged by a self-serve Laundromat are likely to be limited by the competitive rates for laundry services in a given community. Also, state and local government regulations may reduce price flexibility in some industries, such as for auto insurance, utilities, cable television service, and even housing rentals in rent-controlled communities.

13-4 SERVICE QUALITY

Learning Objective 13-4
Explain the importance of service quality and explain how to deliver exceptional service quality.

Delivery of high-quality services is one of the most important and difficult tasks any service organization faces. Because of their characteristics, services are very difficult to evaluate. Hence, customers must look closely at service quality when comparing services. **Service quality** is defined as customers' perceptions of how well a service meets or exceeds their expectations.[22] Research findings by American Express state that 70 percent of surveyed American consumers would spend an average of 17 percent more for a product from a company that provides good customer service. On the other hand, more than half of those consumers reported abandoning a planned purchase because of poor service.[23] Customers, not the organization, evaluate service quality—a critical distinction because it forces service marketers to examine quality from the customer's viewpoint. Thus, it is important for service organizations to determine what customers expect and then develop service products that meet or exceed those expectations.

13-4a Customer Evaluation of Service Quality

The biggest obstacle for customers in evaluating service quality is the intangible nature of the service. How can customers evaluate something they cannot see, feel, taste, smell, or hear? Evaluation of a good is much easier because all goods possess **search qualities**, tangible attributes like color, style, size, feel, or fit that can be evaluated prior to purchase. Trying on a new coat and taking a car for a test drive are examples of how customers evaluate search qualities. Services, on the other hand, have very few search qualities. Instead, they possess experience and credence qualities. **Experience qualities** are attributes, such as taste, satisfaction, or pleasure that can be assessed only during the purchase and consumption of a service.[24] Restaurants and vacations are examples of services high in experience qualities. **Credence qualities** are attributes that customers may be unable to evaluate even after the purchase and consumption of the service. Examples of services high in credence qualities are surgical operations, automobile repairs, and legal representation. Most consumers lack the knowledge or skills to evaluate the quality of these types of services. Consequently, they must place a great deal of faith in the integrity and competence of the service provider.

Despite the difficulties in evaluating quality, service quality may be the only way customers can choose one service over another. For this reason, successful service marketers must understand how consumers judge service quality. Table 13.2 defines five dimensions consumers use when evaluating service quality: tangibles, reliability, responsiveness, assurance, and empathy.

service quality Customers' perceptions of how well a service meets or exceeds their expectations

search qualities Tangible attributes that can be judged before the purchase of a product

experience qualities Attributes that can be assessed only during purchase and consumption of a service

credence qualities Attributes that customers may be unable to evaluate even after purchasing and consuming a service

Table 13.2 Dimensions of Service Quality

Dimension	Evaluation Criteria	Examples
Tangibles: Physical evidence of the service	Appearance of physical facilities Appearance of service personnel Tools or equipment used to provide the service	A clean and professional-looking doctor's office A clean and neatly attired repairperson The freshness of food in a restaurant The equipment used in a medical exam
Reliability: Consistency and dependability in performing the service	Accuracy of billing or recordkeeping Performing services when promised	An accurate bank statement A confirmed hotel reservation An airline flight departing and arriving on time
Responsiveness: Willingness or readiness of employees to provide the service	Returning customer phone calls Providing prompt service Handling urgent requests	A server refilling a customer's cup of coffee without being asked An ambulance arriving within 3 minutes
Assurance: Knowledge/competence of employees and ability to convey trust and confidence	Knowledge and skills of employees Company name and reputation Personal characteristics of employees	A highly trained financial advisor A known and respected service provider A doctor's bedside manner
Empathy: Caring and individual attention provided by employees	Listening to customer needs Caring about customers' interests Providing personalized attention	A store employee listening to and trying to understand a customer's complaint A nurse counseling a heart patient

Sources: Adapted from Leonard L. Berry and A. Parasuraman, *Marketing Services: Competing through Quality* (New York: Free Press, 1991); Valarie A. Zeithaml, A. Parasuraman, and Leonard L. Berry, *Delivering Quality Service: Balancing Customer Perceptions and Expectations* (New York: Free Press, 1990); A. Parasuraman, Leonard L. Berry, and Valarie A. Zeithaml, "An Empirical Examination of Relationships in an Extended Service Quality Model," *Marketing Science Institute Working Paper Series*, Report no. 90–112 (Cambridge, MA: Marketing Science Institute, 1990), p. 29.

Note that all of these dimensions have links to employee performance. Of the five, reliability is the most important in determining customer evaluations of service quality.[25]

Service marketers pay a great deal of attention to the tangibles of service quality. Tangible elements, such as the appearance of facilities and employees, are often the only aspects of a service that can be viewed before purchase and consumption. Therefore, service marketers must ensure that these tangible elements are consistent with the overall image of the service. When it comes to the appearance of service personnel, something that an organization might want to consider is whether service personnel workers have visible tattoos. Research findings indicate that consumers draw conclusions based on visible tattoos that can affect their overall expectations of the service. In general, visible tattoos on white-collar workers, such as those in the medical and financial services sectors, are still viewed as inappropriate and unprofessional. However, attitudes about tattoos are changing as they become more common. More than 12 percent of workers age 30 and younger have a tattoo, meaning the level of acceptance of body modifications in the service industry, even in traditionally buttoned-up industries like accounting, is bound to increase over time.[26]

Except for the tangibles dimension, the criteria customers use to judge service quality are intangible. For instance, how does a customer judge reliability? Because dimensions like reliability cannot be examined with the senses, customers must rely on other ways of judging service. One of the most important factors in customer judgments of service quality is service expectations. Service expectations are influenced by past experiences with the service, word-of-mouth communication from other customers, and the service company's own advertising. For instance, customers are usually eager to try a new restaurant, especially when friends recommend it. These same customers may have also seen advertisements or tweets or Instagram photos from the restaurant. As a result, they have a preconceived idea of what to expect before they visit the restaurant for the first time. When they finally dine there, the quality they experience will change the expectations they have for their next visit. That is why providing consistently high service quality is important. If the quality of a restaurant, or of any service, begins to deteriorate, customers will alter their own expectations and change their word-of-mouth communication to others accordingly. Charles Schwab is a financial institution with independent financial advisors as shown in the advertisement. This advertisement underscores the high level of service quality provided by informing potential customers that "Investors trust independent advisors with $4 trillion of their money." The image of a woman financial advisor and additional text explains why Charles Schwab supports independent financial advisors. The ad helps convey quality by explaining how financial advisors' independence means they serve their customers rather than trying to sell them more products.

Service Quality

Charles Schwab promotes the quality of its services by focusing on the qualification and training of its registered investment advisors.

13-4b Delivering Exceptional Service Quality

Providing high-quality service consistently is very difficult. All consumers have experienced examples of poor service: late flight departures and arrivals, inattentive restaurant servers, rude bank employees, and long waits. Obviously, it is impossible for a service organization to ensure exceptional service quality 100 percent of the time. However, an organization can take many steps to increase the likelihood of providing high-quality service. First, though, the service company must consider the four factors that affect service quality: (1) analysis of customer expectations, (2) service quality specifications, (3) employee performance, and (4) management of service expectations (see Figure 13.2).[27]

13-4c Analysis of Customer Expectations

Providers need to understand customer expectations when designing a service to meet or exceed those expectations. Only then can they deliver good service. Customers usually have two levels of expectations: desired and acceptable. The desired level of expectations is what the customer really wants. If this level of expectations is provided, the customer will be very satisfied. The acceptable level of expectations is what the customer views as adequate. The difference between these two levels of expectations is called the customer's *zone of tolerance*.[28]

Service companies sometimes use marketing research, such as surveys and focus groups, to discover customer needs and expectations. They can also listen to customers on social media. Analyzing complaints, feedback, and questions to Facebook, Twitter, and other social channels can help a firm identify patterns that may indicate corrective action is needed or suggest market opportunities that a firm can capitalize on. Customer reviews posted to Yelp or local review sites can also yield useful insights. Other service marketers, especially restaurants, may use comment cards on which customers can complain or provide suggestions. Still another approach is to ask employees. Because customer-contact employees interact daily with customers, they are in good positions to know what customers want from the company. Service managers should interact with their employees regularly by asking their opinions on the best way to serve customers.

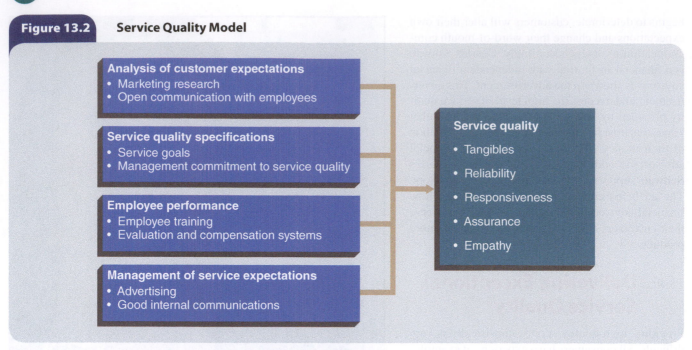

Figure 13.2   Service Quality Model

Source: Adapted from A. Parasuraman, Leonard L. Berry, and Valarie A. Zeithaml, "An Empirical Examination of Relationships in an Extended Service Quality Model," Marketing Science Institute Working Paper Series, Report no. 90–112, 1990.

Service Quality Specifications

After an organization understands its customers' needs, it must establish goals to help ensure good service delivery. These goals, or service specifications, are typically set in terms of employee or machine performance. For example, a bank may require its employees to conform to a dress code. Likewise, the bank may require that all incoming phone calls be answered by the third ring or that emails be answered within two hours. Specifications like these can be very important in providing quality service as long as they are tied to the needs expressed by customers.

Perhaps the most critical aspect of service quality specifications is managers' commitment to service quality. Service managers who are committed to quality become role models for all employees in the organization. Such commitment motivates customer-contact employees to comply with service specifications. It is crucial that all managers within the organization embrace this commitment, especially frontline managers, who are much closer to customers than higher-level managers.

Employee Performance

Once an organization sets service quality standards and managers are committed to them, the firm must find ways to ensure that customer-contact employees perform their jobs well. Contact employees in most service industries (bank tellers, flight attendants, servers, sales clerks, etc.) are often the least-trained and lowest-paid members of the organization. Service organizations that excel realize that contact employees are the most important link to the customer, and thus their performance is critical to customer perceptions of service quality. There is a direct relationship between the satisfaction of a company's contact employees, which is manifested in a positive attitude and a good work ethic, and the satisfaction of its customers. Employee and customer satisfaction levels also have a direct relationship with customer retention and loyalty.[29] The way to ensure that employees perform well is to train them effectively so they understand how to do their jobs. Providing information about customers, service specifications, and the organization itself during the training promotes this understanding.

The evaluation and compensation system the organization uses also plays a part in employee performance. Many service employees are evaluated and rewarded on the basis of output measures, such as sales volume (automobile salespeople) or a low error rate (bank tellers). Systems using output measures may overlook other major aspects of job performance, including friendliness, teamwork, effort, and customer satisfaction. These customer-oriented measures of performance might be a better basis for evaluation and reward. In fact, a number of service marketers use customer satisfaction ratings to determine a portion of service employee compensation.

Management of Service Expectations

Because expectations play such a significant role in customer evaluations of service quality, service companies must set

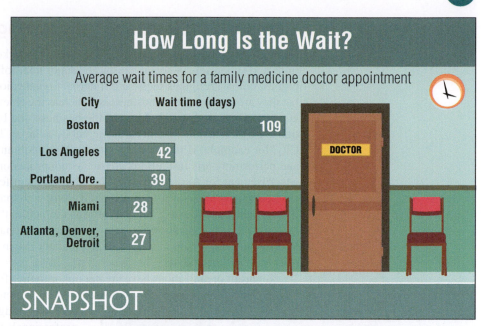

How Long Is the Wait?

Average wait times for a family medicine doctor appointment

City	Wait time (days)
Boston	109
Los Angeles	42
Portland, Ore.	39
Miami	28
Atlanta, Denver, Detroit	27

SNAPSHOT

Source: Merritt Hawkins. "2017 Survey of Physician Appointment Wait Times." 2017, www.merritthawkins.com/uploadedFiles/MerrittHawkins /Content/Pdf/mha2017waittimesurveyPDF.pdf (accessed May 7, 2018).

realistic expectations about the service they provide. They can set these expectations through advertising and good internal communication. In their advertisements, service companies make promises about the kind of service they will deliver. As already noted, a service company is forced to make promises because the intangibility of services prevents the organization from showing the benefits in the advertisement. However, the advertiser should not promise more than it can deliver. Doing so will likely mean disappointed customers.

To deliver on promises made, a company needs to have thorough internal communication among its departments, especially management, advertising, and store operations. Assume, for example, that a restaurant's radio advertisements guarantee service within 15 minutes or the meal is free. If top management or the advertising department fails to inform store operations about the 15-minute guarantee, the restaurant will very likely fail to meet its customers' service expectations. Even though customers might appreciate a free meal, the restaurant will lose some credibility as well as revenue. As mentioned earlier, word-of-mouth communication and online viral communication from other customers also shapes customer expectations. However, service companies cannot manage this "advertising" directly. The best way to ensure positive word-of-mouth communication is to provide exceptional service quality. It has been estimated that customers tell four times as many people about bad service as they do about good service.

13-5 NONPROFIT MARKETING

Nonprofit marketing refers to marketing activities that are conducted by individuals and organizations to achieve some goal other than ordinary business goals such as profit, market share, or return on investment. Nonprofit marketing is divided into two categories: nonprofit-organization marketing and social marketing. Nonprofit-organization marketing is the use of marketing concepts and techniques by organizations whose goals do not include making profits. Social marketing promotes social causes, such as AIDS research or recycling.

Most of the previously discussed concepts and approaches to service products also apply to nonprofit organizations. Indeed, many nonprofit organizations mainly provide service products. In this section, we examine the concept of nonprofit marketing to determine how it differs from marketing activities in for-profit business organizations. We also explore the marketing objectives of nonprofit organizations and the development of their product strategies.

Learning Objective 13-5

Describe the nature of nonprofit marketing.

nonprofit marketing
Marketing activities conducted to achieve some goal other than ordinary business goals such as profit, market share, or return on investment

13-5a How Is Nonprofit Marketing Different?

Many nonprofit organizations strive for effective marketing activities. Charitable organizations and supporters of social causes are major nonprofit marketers in this country. Political parties, unions, religious sects, and fraternal organizations also perform marketing activities, but they are not considered businesses. Whereas the chief beneficiaries of a business enterprise are the owners and stockholders of the business, the beneficiaries of a nonprofit organization are its clients, its members, or the public at large. The Metropolitan Opera in New York City, for example, is run by the nonprofit Metropolitan Opera Association. Many museums and performing arts institutions are run as nonprofits or have a nonprofit arm. Consider this advertisement for Autism Speaks. The advertisement features an artistic image of the world as experienced by an overwhelmed child along with that child's statement, "I am very sensitive to lights and sounds." The ad informs the public that sensory sensitivity may be a sign of autism. The organization hopes to create an emotional reaction among those who view the advertisement and help more people learn about autism, perhaps leading to more diagnoses or at least understanding.

Nonprofit organizations have greater opportunities for creativity than most for-profit business organizations, but trustees or board members of nonprofit organizations are likely to have difficulty judging the performance of the trained professionals they oversee. It is harder for administrators to evaluate the performance of professors or social workers than it is for sales managers to evaluate the performance of salespeople in a for-profit organization.

Another way nonprofit marketing differs from for-profit marketing is that nonprofit marketing is sometimes quite controversial. Large national nonprofit organizations, such as Greenpeace, the National Rifle Association, and the National Association for the Reform of Marijuana Laws, allocate lobbying efforts in their budgets to inform Congress, the White House, and others of their interests and to gain their support. Some nonprofits must devote a large amount to lobbying because their mission is controversial or misunderstood by the general public. However, marketing as a field of study does not attempt to state what an organization's goals should be or to debate the issue of nonprofit versus for-profit business goals. Marketing only tries to provide a body of knowledge and concepts to help further an organization's goals. Individuals must decide whether they approve or disapprove of a particular organization's goal orientation. Most marketers would agree that profit and consumer satisfaction are appropriate goals for business enterprises but may disagree about appropriate goals for a nonprofit organization.

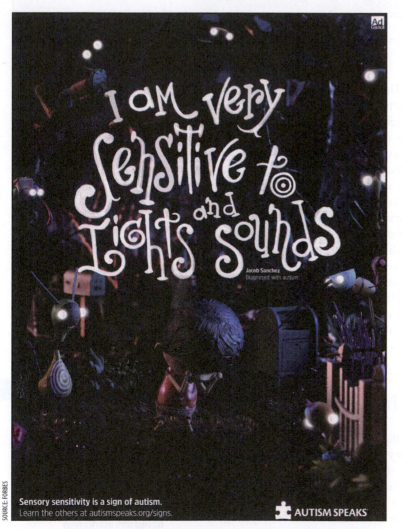

Marketing in Nonprofit Organizations
Autism Speaks is a nonprofit organization that helps individuals with autism and their families by raising awareness and providing information regarding available resources.

13-5b Nonprofit Marketing Objectives

The basic aim of nonprofit organizations is to obtain a desired response from a target market. The response could be a change in values, a financial

INTEGRITY IN MARKETING

Nonprofits Help Nonprofits Plan Marketing

How can nonprofit organizations, with their limited marketing budgets, find the experienced, professional help they need to craft effective marketing programs? Now they can post their requests on the Create For Change website (https://createforchange.org). Create For Change was established by two nonprofits, the Ad Council and the Taproot Foundation, to help other nonprofits connect with volunteers who have the skills and expertise to assist in identifying target markets and developing suitable marketing-mix programs for traditional or digital media. In announcing the initiative, the president of the Ad Council said, "Create For Change will allow our industry to lend their 'day job' skills for good in ways that will make a lasting impact on American life."

The Ad Council is the group behind such memorable marketing campaigns as "Love Has No Labels"

(promoting diversity and inclusion) and "McGruff the Crime Dog" (crime prevention). The mission of the Taproot Foundation is to support social change by encouraging and facilitating professionals to volunteer their skills for the benefit of nonprofits that need a helping hand. Together, the groups are smoothing the way for nonprofit organizations to attract volunteers who can help with web design, media planning, advertising, marketing technology, and other assistance.

Create For Change also hosts free webinars and posts informational content for nonprofit marketers who want to learn new skills or brush up on the basics. A few of the topics covered include: successful fundraising, data-driven target marketing, and e-mail marketing. By volunteering, marketing professionals can feel good about applying what they know and helping the nonprofits of their choice.[b]

contribution, the donation of services, or some other type of exchange. Nonprofit marketing objectives are shaped by the nature of the exchange and the goals of the organization. These objectives should state the rationale for the organization's existence. An organization that defines its marketing objective as providing a product can be left without a purpose if the product becomes obsolete. However, servicing and adapting to the perceived needs and wants of a target public, or market, enhance an organization's chance to survive and achieve its goals.

13-5c **Developing Nonprofit Marketing Strategies**

Nonprofit organizations develop marketing strategies by defining and analyzing a target market and creating and maintaining a total marketing mix that appeals to that market.

Target Markets

We must revise the concept of target markets slightly to apply it to nonprofit organizations. Whereas a business seeks out target groups that are potential purchasers of its product, a non-profit organization may attempt to serve many diverse groups. For our purposes, a **target public** is a collective of individuals who have an interest in or a concern about an organization, a product, or a social cause. The terms *target market* and *target public* are difficult to distinguish for many nonprofit organizations. For instance, the target public for Accion International is anyone interested in supporting international development and relief work. However, the target market for Accion's advertisements consists of people in developing nations who want microloans to start businesses and spur economic development.[30]

In nonprofit marketing, direct consumers of the product are called **client publics** and indirect consumers are called **general publics**.[31] For example, the client public for a university is its student body, and its general public includes parents, alumni, and trustees. The client public usually receives most of the attention when an organization develops a marketing strategy.

target public A collective of individuals who have an interest in or concern about an organization, product, or social cause

client publics Direct consumers of a product of a nonprofit organization

general publics Indirect consumers of a product of a nonprofit organization

Developing Marketing Mixes

A marketing strategy directs marketing activities and resources toward achieving organizational goals. The strategy should include a blueprint for making decisions about product, distribution, promotion, and price. These decision variables should be combined in the best way possible to serve the target market.

In developing the product, nonprofit organizations usually deal with ideas and services. Problems may arise when an organization fails to define what it provides. What product, for example, does the Peace Corps provide? Its services include vocational training, health services, nutritional assistance, and community development. It also markets the ideas of international cooperation and U.S. foreign policy ideals. The product of the Peace Corps is more difficult to define than the average business product. The marketing of ideas and concepts is more abstract than the marketing of tangibles, and much effort is required to present benefits.

Distribution decisions in nonprofit organizations relate to how ideas and services will be made available to clients. If the product is an idea, selecting the right media to communicate the idea will facilitate distribution. By nature, services consist of assistance, convenience, and availability. Availability is thus part of the total service. Making a product such as health services available calls for knowledge of such retailing concepts as site location analysis.

Developing a channel of distribution to coordinate and facilitate the flow of nonprofit products to clients is necessary, but in a nonprofit setting, marketers may need to revise the traditional concept of the marketing channel because the independent wholesalers available to a business enterprise do not exist in most nonprofit situations. Instead, a very short channel—nonprofit organization to client—is the norm because production and consumption of ideas and services are often simultaneous.

Making promotional decisions may be the first sign that a nonprofit organization is performing marketing activities. Nonprofit organizations use advertising and publicity to communicate with clients and the public. PACER's National Center for Bullying Prevention utilizes a variety of resources and media to promote its mission. It hosts National Bullying Prevention Month every October, in which thousands of schools participate. It also distributes coloring books to children, has websites geared toward educating kids and teens, and even hosts a fun run. Facebook, Instagram, and TLC are multimedia partners of the group.[32] Direct mail continues to be used for fundraising by many social service organizations, such as the Red Cross and Special Olympics. Though direct mail remains important, some organizations have reduced their volume of direct mail in favor of emails or other digital communications.

Increasingly, nonprofits are using the internet to reach fundraising and promotional goals through email, websites, social media, and software that permits online donations. For example, the March of Dimes educates the public about its mission to give babies a healthy start in life on multiple social media sites and encourages people to share their inspirational stories of how the nonprofit has helped save their children.[33] More recently, online crowdfunding sites like GoFundMe, Indiegogo, and Kickstarter, have given nonprofits a new channel for targeting many potential donors at once. Crowdfunding enables many people to go online and donate small amounts to a fundraising project. Such efforts allow people to give to a very targeted cause or project and, therefore, to feel more connected to where their donations go.[34] Mobile forms of marketing help nonprofits raise more money quickly, particularly among younger target publics.

Many nonprofit organizations also use personal selling, although they may call it by another name. Churches and charities rely on personal selling when they send volunteers to recruit new members or request donations. The U.S. Army uses personal selling when its recruiting officers attempt to persuade men and women to enlist. Special events to obtain funds, communicate ideas, or provide services are also effective promotional activities. Amnesty International, for example, has held worldwide concert tours featuring well-known musical artists to raise funds and increase public awareness of political prisoners around the world.

Although product and promotional techniques may require only slight modification when applied to nonprofit organizations, pricing is generally different and decision making is more complex. The different pricing concepts the nonprofit organization faces include pricing in user and donor markets. Two types of monetary pricing exist: *fixed* and *variable.* There may be a fixed fee for users, or the price may vary depending on the user's ability to pay. When a donation-seeking organization will accept a contribution of any size, it is using variable pricing.

The broadest definition of price (valuation) must be used to develop nonprofit marketing strategies. Financial price, an exact dollar value, may or may not be charged for a nonprofit product. Economists recognize giving up alternatives as a cost. **Opportunity cost** is the value of the benefit given up by selecting one alternative over another. According to this traditional economic view of price, if a nonprofit organization persuades someone to donate time to a cause or to change his or her behavior, the alternatives given up are a cost to (or a price paid by) the individual. Volunteers who answer phones for a university counseling service or a suicide hotline, for example, give up the time they could spend studying or doing other things as well as the income they might earn from working at a for-profit business organization.

For other nonprofit organizations, financial price is an important part of the marketing mix. Nonprofit organizations today raise money by increasing the prices of their services or charging for previously free services. They are using marketing research to determine what kinds of products people will pay for. Pricing strategies of nonprofit organizations often stress public and client welfare over equalization of costs and revenues. If additional funds are needed to cover costs, the organization may solicit donations, contributions, or grants.

opportunity cost The value of the benefit given up by choosing one alternative over another

Summary

13-1 Discuss the growth and importance of services.

Services are intangible products that involve deeds, performances, or efforts that cannot be physically possessed. They are the result of applying human or mechanical efforts to people or objects. Services are a growing part of the U.S. economy. They have six fundamental characteristics: intangibility, inseparability of production and consumption, perishability, heterogeneity, client-based relationships, and customer contact.

13-2 Identify the characteristics of services that differentiate them from goods.

Intangibility means that a service cannot be seen, touched, tasted, or smelled. Inseparability refers to the fact that the production of a service cannot be separated from its consumption by customers. Perishability means unused service capacity of one time period cannot be stored for future use. Heterogeneity is variation in service quality. Client-based relationships are interactions with customers that lead to the repeated use of a service over time. Customer contact is the interaction between providers and customers needed to deliver a service.

13-3 Analyze how the characteristics of services influence the development of marketing mixes for services.

Core services are the basic service experiences customers expect. Supplementary services are those that relate to, and support, core services. Because of the characteristics of services, service marketers face several challenges in developing and managing marketing mixes. To address the problem of intangibility, marketers use cues that help assure customers about the quality of their services. The development and management of service products are also influenced by the service characteristics of inseparability and level of customer contact. Some services require that customers come to the service provider's facility, and others are delivered with no face-to-face contact. Marketing channels for services are usually short and direct, but some services employ intermediaries. Service marketers are less concerned with warehousing and transportation than are goods marketers, but inventory management and balancing supply and demand for services are important issues. The intangibility of services poses several promotion-related challenges. Advertisements with tangible cues that symbolize the service and depict facilities, equipment, and personnel help address these challenges. Service providers are likely to promote price, guarantees, performance documentation, availability, and training and certification of contact personnel. Through their actions, service personnel can be involved directly or indirectly in the personal selling of services.

Intangibility makes it difficult to experience a service before purchasing it. Heterogeneity and intangibility make word-of-mouth communication an important means of promotion. The prices of services are based on task performance, time required, or demand. Perishability creates difficulties in balancing supply and demand because unused capacity cannot be stored. The point in time when a significant number of customers desire a service is called peak demand. Demand-based pricing results in higher prices charged for services during peak demand. Off-peak pricing is the practice of reducing prices of services used during slow periods in order to boost demand. When services are offered in a bundle, marketers must decide whether to offer them at one price, price them separately, or use a combination of the two methods. Because services are intangible, customers may rely on price as a sign of quality. For some services, market conditions may dictate the price. For others, state and local government regulations may limit price flexibility.

13-4 Explain the importance of service quality and explain how to deliver exceptional service quality.

Service quality is customers' perception of how well a service meets or exceeds their expectations. Although one of the most important aspects of service marketing, service quality is very difficult for customers to evaluate because the nature of services renders benefits impossible to assess before actual purchase and consumption. These benefits include experience qualities, such as taste, satisfaction, or pleasure, and credence qualities, which customers may be unable to evaluate even after consumption. When competing services are very similar, service quality may be the only way for customers to distinguish among them. Service marketers can increase the quality of their services by following the four-step process of understanding customer expectations, setting service specifications, ensuring good employee performance, and managing customers' service expectations.

13-5 Describe the nature of nonprofit marketing.

Nonprofit marketing is marketing aimed at nonbusiness goals, including social causes. It uses most of the same concepts and approaches that apply to business situations. Whereas the chief beneficiary of a business enterprise is whoever owns or holds stock in it, the beneficiary of a nonprofit enterprise should be its clients, its members, or its public at large. The goals of a nonprofit organization reflect its unique philosophy or mission. Some nonprofit organizations have very controversial goals, but many organizations exist to further generally accepted social causes.

The marketing objective of nonprofit organizations is to obtain a desired response from a target market. Developing a nonprofit marketing strategy consists of defining and analyzing a target market and creating and maintaining a marketing mix. In nonprofit marketing, the product is usually an idea or a service. Distribution is aimed at the communication of ideas and the delivery of services. The result is a very short marketing channel. Promotion is very important to nonprofit marketing. Nonprofit organizations use advertising, publicity, and personal selling to communicate with clients and the public. Direct mail remains the primary means of fundraising for social services, but some nonprofits use the internet for fundraising and promotional activities. Price is more difficult to define in nonprofit marketing because of opportunity costs and the difficulty of quantifying the values exchanged.

Important Terms

homesourcing 368	client-based relationships	search qualities 379	target public 385
intangibility 369	372	experience qualities 379	client publics 385
inseparability 370	customer contact 372	credence qualities 379	general publics 385
perishability 371	off-peak pricing 378	nonprofit marketing	opportunity cost
heterogeneity 371	service quality 379	383	387

Discussion and Review Questions

1. How important are services in the U.S. economy?
2. Identify and discuss the major characteristics of services.
3. For each marketing-mix element, which service characteristics are most likely to have an impact? Explain.
4. What is service quality? Why do customers find it difficult to judge service quality?
5. Identify and discuss the five components of service quality. How do customers evaluate these components?

6. What is the significance of tangibles in service marketing?
7. How do search, experience, and credence qualities affect the way customers view and evaluate services?
8. What steps should a service company take to provide exceptional service quality?
9. How does nonprofit marketing differ from marketing in for-profit organizations?
10. What are the differences among clients, publics, and customers? What is the difference between a target public and a target market?
11. Discuss the development of a marketing strategy for a university. What marketing decisions must be made as the strategy is developed?

Developing Your Marketing Plan

Products that are services rather than tangible goods present unique challenges to companies when they formulate marketing strategy. A clear comprehension of the concepts that apply specifically to service products is essential when developing the marketing plan. These concepts will form the basis for decisions in several plan areas. To assist you in relating the information in this chapter to the development of your marketing plan for a service product, focus on the following:

1. Using Figure 13.1, determine your product's degree of tangibility. If your product lies close to the tangible end of the continuum, then you may proceed to the questions in the next chapter. If your product is more intangible, then continue with this chapter's issues.

2. Discuss your product with regard to the six service characteristics. To what degree does it possess the qualities that make up each of these characteristics?

3. Using Table 13.1 as a guide, discuss the marketing challenges you are likely to experience.

4. Determine the search, experience, and credence qualities that customers are likely to use when evaluating your service product.

5. Consider how your service product relates to each of the dimensions of service quality. Using Table 13.2 as a guide, develop the evaluation criteria and examples that are appropriate for your product.

Video Case 13.1

Mike Boyle's Services Are Not for Everyone

Everyone wants to be strong, healthy, and fit. But not everyone is in the target market for Mike Boyle Strength & Conditioning (MBSC). With two Massachusetts locations, MBSC offers a variety of services to help athletes at all levels build strength, improve endurance, and enhance performance. Cofounder Mike Boyle developed his approach to athletic training as a result of working as a trainer for various sports teams and with Boston University. He's also trained Olympic athletes, professional athletes, and celebrities.

Over the years, Boyle noticed how many people join a gym with good intentions but then lose their motivation and rarely use the facilities. So when Boyle opened his first gym, he went down a different marketing path. He wants to provide services to customers who expect to actively train, customers who will set personal goals and then come to the gym for regular one-on-one or group training. Boyle recognizes that his business doesn't just provide equipment and space for workouts—it also offers social support and professional guidance, encouraging customers to make progress toward their fitness and performance goals, week after week.

For school athletes in their teens and twenties, MBSC offers services such as middle-school athletic training, high-school performance training, and college-break workout sessions. For adults, MSBC offers small-group strength and training services and private or semi-private personal training geared to each customer's individual needs and goals, including weight loss, better stamina, and better mobility. In addition, MBSC provides services to help adults improve capabilities and performance in specific sports, such as golf. Prices vary, depending on the duration of the service programs and whether customers receive private or group training.

As they age, professional athletes who want to continue their high-performance careers see MBSC's services as a way to keep up their strength, speed, and endurance. Even adults who aren't athletes see MBSC as a resource for taking fitness to the next level, learning to prevent injuries, and getting in shape to look their best. Customers also have the option of requesting services such as massage therapy and physical therapy to regain strength and improve agility.

FATCAMERA/E+/GETTY IMAGES

members in their 80s. A small percentage of customers are professional athletes, and many of his customers are young men and women who want training to supplement their school sports activities. Because he was known for his work with the Boston Bruins hockey team and with Boston University's hockey team, Boyle attracts many varsity hockey players from the Boston area. These days, Boyle has little extra time for the kind of extended workouts he once enjoyed. Still, he makes the rounds of his gyms every day, training in brief, intensive stints and serving as a role model for the ongoing benefits of maintaining strength and conditioning at all ages and for all lifestyles.[35]

Boyle reaches out to a wider audience with "how to" videos that educate and encourage people who want to know about his training and services. His Facebook page has nearly 45,000 likes, his Twitter account has 35,800 followers, and his YouTube channel has 11,000 subscribers. Boyle maintains a dialogue with customers and prospects by posting notes and videos on his blog and social-media accounts about diverse topics, including effective training techniques and the benefits of school athletics.

Today, MBSC offers services to customers as young as 11 years old, and at the other end of the spectrum, to

Questions for Discussion

1. In terms of services marketing, why is it important for customers to see Mike Boyle working out and supervising trainers at his gym facilities every day?
2. Mike Boyle only wants to attract customers who will be frequent users of his facilities and training services. What does this suggest about how MBSC manages service expectations?
3. How, specifically, can customers evaluate the search qualities, experience qualities, and credence qualities of MBSC?

Case 13.2

FedEx Courts Customers with Convenience, Not Just Speed

During nearly four decades of business operations, Memphis-based FedEx has earned a reputation for reliable, on-time delivery of packages to homes and offices around the country. Founder Fred Smith originally focused on overnight deliveries, choosing Memphis as the company's headquarters because the airport rarely closes due to bad weather. With FedEx's planes departing and arriving on schedule nearly all the time, its express shipments usually remained on schedule, then and now. To reassure customers that delivery will take place when and where promised, the firm offers a money-back guarantee on time-sensitive express shipments, among other services.

FedEx has steadily expanded its portfolio of services since the 1970s. Its original overnight express delivery is currently available to U.S. customers in various forms, including "first-overnight" delivery, next-morning delivery, next-afternoon delivery, and budget-pleasing two- or three-day delivery. The company's services also include cost-effective ground delivery for parcels and extra-speedy same-day delivery for urgent deliveries within 1,800 cities.

Over the years, FedEx has widened its delivery network to more than 220 countries. It has purchased more cargo jets and acquired specialized shipping firms, including Tiger International, Roberts Express, RPS, and TNT Express, to support global growth. For international business customers needing products, parts, or raw materials shipped across countries or continents, the company now offers time-saving services such as commercial freight forwarding and cross-border logistical support.

To add the convenience of local drop-off and pickup points for U.S. consumers and small businesses, FedEx acquired the Kinko's office services company in 2004 and later rebranded it as FedEx Office. This acquisition also added printing and copying to the menu of services offered. Then the company arranged for large U.S. retailers such as Walgreens, Albertsons, Kroger, and Safeway to accept packages for shipment and receive package delivery for customer pickup in thousands of store locations. This means people who want to send a package can head to a nearby retailer and ship where they shop, rather than making a separate trip to the

FedEx location. It's also a safe alternative for packages to be picked up by people who don't want FedEx shipments left by the front door.

Another service FedEx offers to small and mid-sized businesses, including retailers, is FedEx Fulfillment. The purpose is to expedite order fulfillment by having each business store its products in a FedEx warehouse. Then, when the business's customers place orders, FedEx puts the products into boxes bearing the business's own logo and ships directly to those customers. The business doesn't need a separate warehouse or staff for fulfillment, and packages are on their way to customers more quickly because the products were in FedEx's warehouse, ready to be packed and shipped. This service puts FedEx into direct competition with Amazon.com, which offers a similar service to merchants that sell through the online Amazon Marketplace. But it also gives businesses that don't sell via Amazon a fast and professional fulfillment alternative.

FedEx is careful to let customers know, through media and social-media announcements, when it anticipates that extreme weather or other conditions will cause delays or force it to halt pickups and deliveries. For the duration of Hurricane Irma, for example, FedEx said it would suspend deliveries in Florida. Some Florida customers who had ordered generators to be delivered via FedEx were unhappy, because they worried about being without power during and after the storm. But one FedEx employee loaded several generator orders into his car and took them to customers himself. When a customer posted a grateful compliment to FedEx on Facebook, the message generated thousands of likes, shares, and positive comments. The company also received positive comments for its donations of cash and transportation services to areas devastated by Hurricanes Irma, Harvey, and Maria.

PHILIP LANGE/SHUTTERSTOCK.COM

According to the American Customer Satisfaction Index (ACSI), FedEx often tops the list of U.S. shipping companies as ranked by customers surveyed. Every day, the company delivers 13 million packages—and during the busy year-end holiday season, it delivers many more. By meeting customers' expectations for on-time deliveries, FedEx has increased annual revenues beyond $60 billion and positioned itself for continued growth in the future.[36]

Questions for Discussion

1. How does FedEx's money-back guarantee address customers' concerns about heterogeneity?
2. Are FedEx's services more closely associated with experience qualities or credence qualities? What are the implications for the company's marketing activities?
3. What are the customer-contact pros and cons of FedEx offering package pickup and drop-off through local locations of Walgreens, Kroger, and other retailers?

Strategic Case 5

Nike Runs the Innovation Race Every Day

Nike, the long-time market leader in athletic shoes, apparel, and gear, has been racing into innovation for more than 50 years. Co-founders Phil Knight and Bill Bowerman met at the University of Oregon, where Knight was a student athlete and Bowerman was a veteran coach and trainer. For years, Bowerman had been experimenting with developing homemade running shoes, some of which Knight tested on the track. After Knight graduated, he decided the U.S. market needed an alternative to the high-priced German shoes that many athletes preferred at the time. He formed Blue Ribbon Sports with Bowerman as his partner and became the U.S. distributor for a Japanese sneaker firm, selling shoes from the trunk of his car.

While Knight handled business operations, Bowerman applied his knowledge of running to product development, testing and improving one type of running shoe after another. The breakthrough came when he created an entirely new design by grafting a waffle-patterned rubber sole to a lightweight, cushioned sneaker. These shoes were the first of Bowerman's innovations to carry the now-iconic swoosh logo, and they burst into the marketplace just as running became a major fitness trend. By 1978, when the company was renamed Nike, after the Greek goddess of victory, it was marketing its shoes on the basis of performance and fashion.

Athlete Endorsers Add Star Power

Former CEO Phil Knight believed that endorsements and product input from athletes were the key to attracting consumer attention and building credibility for Nike's quality performance. He raised eyebrows in the 1980s by arranging a $250,000 endorsement deal with a two-time All-American North Carolina basketball player who went on to become NBA Rookie of the Year. It didn't take long for this deal with the now-legendary Michael Jordan to begin paying off in the form of publicity and profits. Nike introduced an entire sneaker line named after Jordan and, later, added Jordan-branded clothing. Today, the Nike Jordan brand rings up annual sales of nearly $3 billion.

Following the strategy Knight pioneered, Nike now markets a number of product lines designed in collaboration with star athletes in key sports. For example, basketball endorsers such as Russell Westbrook and Chris Paul have their own shoe and clothing product lines within the Nike Jordan portfolio, with products influenced by their professional prowess and individual styles. Nike has a lifetime deal with the NBA's LeBron James, reflecting not only his basketball achievements but also his potential influence on sports, fashion, and entertainment in the coming years. Tennis champ Serena Williams has her own Nike shoe and clothing product lines, based on her ideas, aesthetic preferences, and performance requirements.

Aiming to Achieve Aggressive Growth

Co-founder Phil Knight relinquished the CEO position in 2006 and remained Nike's chairman until 2016. Current CEO Mark Parker heads a more than $34 billion company that aims to achieve $50 billion in annual sales by 2020 by continuing its track record of innovation in branded goods and services. Nike's brand portfolio includes Converse, Jordan, and Hurley, as well as brands that include the Nike name, such as NIKEiD (personalized versions of Nike products) and Nike+ (apps and online tools for tracking and improving personal athletic performance). The Nike+ product line originally included the FuelBand wristband for performance tracking, but the company dropped the hardware in favor of software as competitors such as FitBit entered the market. Looking ahead, digital services are a priority as Nike seeks to enhance connections with customers by enabling them to

SORBIS/SHUTTERSTOCK.COM

chart their progress, compare fitness statistics with friends, and connect with other performance-minded consumers.

In recent years, dozens of high-profile product introductions have fueled Nike's growth and increased brand awareness throughout the 190 countries where it does business. Nike already offers many types of products for men, women, and children, in many variations of sizes, colors, and materials. That's why Nike's CEO works closely with the product-development teams "to edit down our opportunities to the ones that will make the most impact for the company." He challenges Nike marketers to be sure any new offering will represent an improvement, satisfy an actual need, inspire or motivate customers, and enhance the brand.

One lucrative market opportunity the company sees is increasing sales to women. Although Nike currently generates $6.6 billion in yearly revenue from sales of products for women, this is a small fraction of the revenue generated from its sales of products for men. To appeal to women, Nike is offering new products designed by women athletes, free apps for athletic training, newsletters with advice and tips, and YouTube videos about workouts and motivation. With rivals like Under Armour and Lululemon also targeting women, Nike never stops running the innovation race, always looking for the next hit combination of performance and fashion.[37]

Questions for Discussion

1. How would you describe Nike's product mix? Why would the CEO talk about editing down opportunities when he's aiming for aggressive growth?
2. What is Nike's branding strategy, and what are the implications for its investment in athlete endorsements?
3. How is Nike using differentiation to distinguish its products in a crowded and competitive marketplace?

Distribution Decisions

Developing products that satisfy customers is important, but that is not enough to guarantee successful marketing strategies. Products must also be available in adequate quantities in accessible locations at the times when customers desire them.

PART 6 deals with the distribution of products and the marketing channels and institutions that help to make products available.

CHAPTER 14 discusses supply chain management, marketing channels, and the decisions and activities associated with the logistics of products, such as order processing, materials handling, warehousing, inventory management, and transportation.

CHAPTER 15 explores retailing and wholesaling, including types of retailers and wholesalers, direct marketing and selling, and strategic retailing issues.

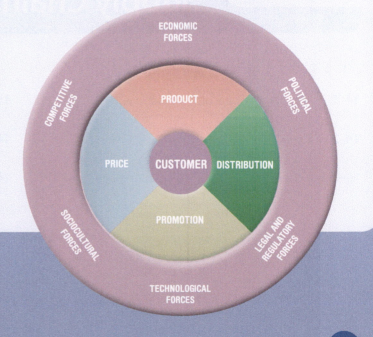

CHAPTER

14

Marketing Channels and Supply Chain Management

LEARNING OBJECTIVES

14-1 Describe the foundations of supply chain management.

14-2 Explain the role and significance of marketing channels and supply chains.

14-3 Identify the intensity of market coverage.

14-4 Explore strategic issues in marketing channels, including leadership, cooperation, and conflict.

14-5 Explain logistics as being a part of supply chain management.

14-6 Examine legal issues in channel management.

PHOTOMIKA-COM/SHUTTERSTOCK.COM

Championship Gear Is a Supply Chain Touchdown

Fifteen minutes. That's all the time Fanatics needs to post official championship-logo caps and clothing for sale after a major league sports or college team wins a big game. The company aims to have clothing available "at internet speed," an executive explains. Once the company had NCAA tournament apparel for sale online four minutes after the buzzer sounded. The company prepares by creating designs in advance when possible. Right after the game, Fanatics sends the design to the winning team or league for approval. Minutes later, with responses in hand, Fanatics finalizes and posts the product online, ready to manufacture on demand when customers order.

For traditional retailers, stocking the right team merchandise can be more challenging. Before the AFC and NFC championship football games, Dick's Sporting Goods orders T-shirts showing all four teams as winners, knowing it will sell only the winning team shirts and donate losing shirts to charity. "Providing excited fans with championship gear immediately following big games outweighs the costs of being prepared for both outcomes," explains a Dick's manager.

When the Chicago Cubs played in the World Series, retailers ordered merchandise in anticipation of the final game and opened their doors immediately after the game ended. Many retailers had trucks on the road overnight, picking up additional Cubs merchandise to sell the next morning, while fans continued to celebrate the victory. Recently, Fanatics partnered with American Express to create the NBA Jersey Assurance Program, which allows Amex users to return NBA jerseys if a player is traded within 90 days of purchase. Next, Fanatics plans to expand its model internationally.[1]

The **distribution** component of the marketing mix focuses on the decisions and activities involved in making products available to customers when and where they want to purchase them. Fanatics has become an expert at making trendy products available when they are wanted—as soon as a team wins big—through a variety of marketing channels. Choosing which channels of distribution to use to reach customers in a timely manner is a major decision in the development of marketing strategies.

In this chapter, we focus on marketing channels and supply chain management. First, we explore the concept of the supply chain and its various activities. Second, we elaborate on marketing channels and the need for intermediaries and the primary functions they perform. Next, we outline the types and characteristics of marketing channels, discuss how they are selected, and explore how marketers determine the appropriate intensity of market coverage for a product. We then examine the strategic channel issues of leadership, cooperation, and conflict. We also look at the role of logistics within the supply chain, including its objectives and basic functions. Finally, we look at several legal issues that affect channel management.

Learning Objective 14-1

Describe the foundations of supply chain management.

14-1 FOUNDATIONS OF THE SUPPLY CHAIN

An important function of distribution is to create an effective **supply chain**, which includes all the organizations and activities involved with the flow and transformation of products from raw materials through to the end customer. It may help to think of the firms involved in a total distribution system as existing along a conceptual line, the combined impact of which results in an effective supply chain. Firms that are "upstream" in the supply chain (e.g., suppliers) and "downstream" (e.g., wholesalers and retailers) work together to serve customers and generate competitive advantage. Historically, marketing focused solely on certain downstream supply chain activities, but today marketing professionals recognize that they can reduce costs, boost profits, and better serve customers by effectively integrating activities along the entire length of the supply chain. Doing so requires marketing managers to work with other managers in operations, logistics, and procurement.

Procurement (sometimes called supply management) actually involves the processes used to obtain resources to create value through sourcing, purchasing, and recycling, including materials and information. Procurement for many is synonymous with "buying" or "purchasing," but this is only a small part of what goes into the procurement activities within a supply chain. Procurement, including the delivery of services, is important for all organizations.

Sourcing is concerned not only with what materials a firm needs, but where those materials come from. Are the materials safe? How are we gathering them, and what effect are we having on the environment? Should the materials be sourced locally or abroad? These questions are about more than price—in reality, they are largely concerned with marketing integrity, which leads to performance and profits. **Purchasing** is the act of negotiating and executing transactions to buy and sell goods, materials, and services. **Recycling** is converting waste into reusable material, reprocessing, reclaiming, or reusing supplies and final products and is very important. Therefore, the supply chain should consider how to deal with the impact of its products after consumption.

It is important to note that supply management doesn't just happen at the beginning—these are activities which can be found at all levels of the supply chain. When these functions align, there is a strong foundation from which to build a value proposition. Creating a digital platform to link everything from production to consumer involves sensors, mobile devices, cameras, and other systems that capture information for supply management.[2]

Logistics management involves planning, implementing, and controlling the efficient and effective flow and storage of products and information, from the point of origin to consumption, to meet customers' needs and wants. There is sometimes a misconception that logistics are just about the physical transport of goods and materials. However, there is also an enormous burden on firms to quickly and accurately share information with their suppliers, customers, and even among themselves. While these intangible assets are often overlooked, digital connections that provide information can be very important to forecast inventory requirements, provide maintenance alerts, and handle client requests, production schedules, and

distribution The decisions and activities that make products available to customers when and where they want to purchase them

supply chain All the organizations and activities involved with the flow and transformation of products from raw materials through to the end customer

procurement Processes to obtain resources to create value through sourcing, purchasing, and recycling, including materials and information

sourcing The process of determining what materials a firm needs, where those materials come from, and how they impact marketing integrity

purchasing The act of negotiating and executing transactions to buy and sell goods, materials, and services

recycling Converting waste into reusable material, reprocessing, reclaiming, or reusing supplies and final products

logistics management Managing the efficient and effective flow of materials, products, and information from the point of origin to consumption

transportation itineraries. The more effectively firms can communicate these things, the more efficiently they can respond.

Logistical concerns involve physical distribution and the selection of transportation modes. In transportation, digital networks that integrate the movement of products provide insights to improve service and reduce cost. Manufacturers, distributors, and retailers need to communicate with their supply chain partners to provide real-time information. This provides the opportunity to advance capabilities and efficiencies in the supply chain. For these same reasons, and with so many variables, logistical disruptions can be massively harmful to the ability to adequately satisfy customer expectations and can even be fatal to the firm.

Logistics management is just as important in managing services and enabling and communicating with partners. For example, health-care providers must rely on manufacturers and distributors to perform many supply chain activities for many different unrelated items. Food, medicine, and supplies all need to meet required standard logistics involving deliveries from vendors with inventories that accommodate the ability to provide health-care services.[3]

Operations management concerns are different from sourcing and transportation but intimately related to the supply chain. We have the materials where they should be, but what do we do with them now? These activities can range anywhere from services to manufacturing, and even to the final delivery of a service or consumption of a product.

Historically, firms have been mainly concerned with workplace efficiency and costs. How can this item be produced? Should we use manual labor or invest in automation? How many varieties of product is it profitable to make? When should we produce, and when does it make sense to replenish inventory? When to fill orders or reduce inventory because of obsolescence are important decisions. Sporting goods producer Acushnet, maker of gold balls, clubs, and bags under the Titleist and Pinnacle brands, faced these questions. For better knowledge of up-to-date inventory levels, a platform was developed to monitor production, transportation, and storage at each stage of the supply chain pipeline.[4]

Operations are often the most public and visible aspect of the supply chain. Consumers are increasingly concerned with an important question: "How are our products being made?" Fair trade, organic food products, working conditions, child labor, concerns with sending jobs overseas, and regulatory mandates create major factors in decision making about operations.

Technology in operations is driving a more digital enterprise system. Robotics, predictive analytics, the Internet of Things (IOT), driverless cars, drones, automation in identification of inventory, and network inventory optimization tools are changing the landscape of operations.[5] By making profitable and responsible use of the materials and products sourced to them, and utilizing the information and capabilities afforded them through logistics, operations personnel can create extensive financial and brand value.

The marketing channel involves directing the flow of product from producer to consumer in the supply chain. There are many strategic options for the structure of the marketing channel. These can involve complex and legal commitments, long-term contracts, sizeable investments, loyalty to channel members, and transparency in communications. Because of the commitments among channel members, there can be inflexible elements of the marketing channel among marketing intermediaries that link procedures to ultimate consumers or users of products. Channel arrangements can assure movement directly from producer to consumer, but most channels are indirect, involving intermediaries. Marketing channels are a strategic part of a supply chain.

Supply chain management (SCM) refers to the coordination of all the activities involved with the flow and transformation of supplies, products, and information throughout the supply chain to the ultimate consumer. It integrates the functions of operations management, logistics management, procurement, and marketing channel management so that products are produced and distributed in the right quantities, to the right locations, and at the right times. It includes activities such as manufacturing, research, sales, advertising, and shipping. SCM involves all entities that facilitate product distribution and benefit from cooperative efforts, including suppliers of raw materials and other components to make goods and services, logistics and transportation firms, communication firms, and other firms that indirectly take part in marketing exchanges. The key tasks involved in supply chain management are outlined in Table 14.1. Supply chain managers must encourage cooperation between organizations in the supply chain and understand the trade-offs required to achieve optimal levels of efficiency and service.

operations management Managing activities from production to final delivery through system-wide coordination

supply chain management (SCM) The coordination of all the activities involved with the flow and transformation of supplies, products, and information throughout the supply chain to the ultimate consumer

Table 14.1   **Key Tasks in Supply Chain Management**

Marketing Activities	Sample Activities
Operations management	Managing activities from production to final delivery through system-wide coordination
Procurement	Processes to obtain resources to create value through sourcing, purchasing, and recycling, including materials and information
Logistics management	Managing the efficient and effective flow of materials, products, and information from the point of origin to consumption
Channel management	Directing the flow of products

In an efficient supply chain, upstream firms provide direct or indirect input to make the product, and downstream firms are responsible for delivery of the product and after-market services to the ultimate customers. To ensure quality and customer satisfaction, firms must be involved in the management of every aspect of their supply chain, in close partnership with all involved upstream and downstream organizations.

Supply chain management should begin with a focus on the customer, who is the ultimate consumer and whose satisfaction should be the goal of all the efforts of channel members. Cooperation between channel members should improve customer satisfaction while also increasing coordination, reducing costs, and increasing profits. When the buyer, the seller, marketing intermediaries, and facilitating agencies work together, the cooperative relationship results in compromise and adjustments that meet customers' needs regarding delivery, scheduling, packaging, or other requirements. Consider that today's technology-savvy consumer expects retailers such as Office Depot to offer multiple options for fulfilling orders—in the store, online via desktop computer or smartphone, or shipped to a nearby store—and to be able to deliver their orders quickly, even the very same day. Retailers must adjust their physical distribution strategies in response or risk losing their customers to other retailers who will provide what they want.[6] Figure 14.1 shows the material and information flows for a cereal manufacturer's supply chain.

Figure 14.1   **A Cereal Manufacturer's Supply Chain**

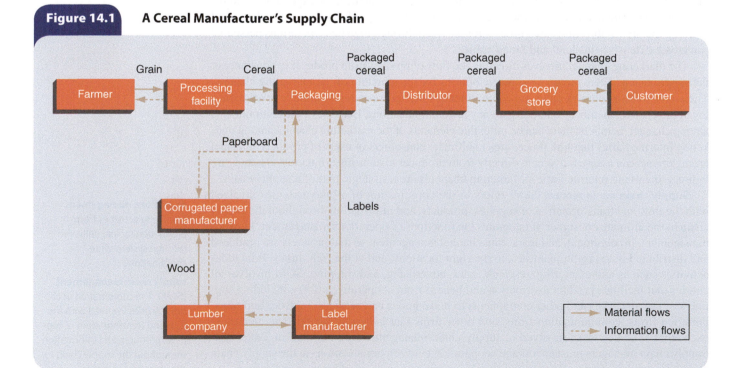

Each supply chain member requires information from other channel members. For instance, suppliers need order and forecast information from the manufacturer. They also may need availability information from their own suppliers. Customer relationship management (CRM) systems exploit the information in supply chain partners' information systems and make it available for easy reference. CRM systems can help all channel members make better marketing strategy decisions that develop and sustain desirable customer relationships. Companies now offer online software that integrates business data into a social networking site format. Tibbr and Yammer are two such programs. By entering all data into a single, easy-to-use online system, businesses can achieve greater efficiencies and improve their CRM.[7]

Demand for innovative goods and services has increased and changed over time. Marketers need to be flexible in order to respond to the fluctuating needs and desires of customers by developing and distributing new products and modifying existing ones. Supply chain managers can exploit data available through improved information technology to learn about a firm's customers, which helps to improve products in the downstream portion of the supply chain. Marketers now understand that managing the entire supply chain is critically important in ensuring that customers get the products when, where, and how they want them. In fact, supply chain management is one of the industries poised for strong future growth because of the increasing importance of getting the right products where they need to go safely and on time.[8] Amazon has set the gold standard for supply chain management—offering customers nearly anything they can imagine at low prices, through a user-friendly website that features product reviews and ratings, perks like offering a variety of shipping options, and an easy return policy. Amazon has even moved into selling and distributing everyday items, like toilet paper or cleaning supplies, teaming up with suppliers all over the country to create a seamless distribution system that can even provide same-day delivery in some areas.[9] Many companies have struggled to compete with, and adapt to, such a large and flexible competitor.

Technology has improved supply chain management capabilities globally. Advances in information technology, in particular, have created an almost seamless distribution process for matching inventory needs to manufacturer requirements in the upstream portion of the supply chain and to customers' requirements in the downstream portion of the chain. With integrated information sharing among chain members, firms can reduce costs, improve services, and provide increased value to the end customer. Information is a crucial component in operating supply chains efficiently and effectively.

14-2 THE ROLE OF MARKETING CHANNELS IN SUPPLY CHAINS

Learning Objective 14-2
Explain the role and significance of marketing channels and supply chains.

A **marketing channel** (also called a *channel of distribution* or *distribution channel*) is a group of individuals and organizations that direct the flow of products from producers to customers within the supply chain. The major role of marketing channels is to make products available at the right time, at the right place, in the right quantities. This is accomplished through achieving synergy among operations management, logistics management, and procurement. Providing customer satisfaction should be the driving force behind marketing channel decisions. Buyers' needs and behavior are, therefore, important concerns of channel members.

Some marketing channels are direct, meaning that the product goes directly from the producer to the customer. For instance, when you order pears online from Harry & David, the product is sent from the manufacturer to the customer. Most channels, however, are indirect and have one or more **marketing intermediaries** that link producers to other intermediaries or to ultimate consumers through contractual arrangements or through the purchase and reselling of products. Marketing intermediaries perform the activities described in Table 14.2. They also play key roles in customer relationship management, not only through their distribution activities but also by maintaining databases and information systems to help all members of the marketing channel maintain effective customer relationships.

marketing channel A group of individuals and organizations that direct the flow of products from producers to customers within the supply chain

marketing intermediaries Middlemen that link producers to other intermediaries or ultimate consumers through contractual arrangements or through the purchase and resale of products

Table 14.2   **Marketing Channel Activities Performed by Intermediaries**

Marketing Activities	Sample Activities
Marketing information	Analyze sales data and other information in databases and information systems. Perform or commission marketing research.
Marketing management	Establish strategic and tactical plans for developing customer relationships and organizational productivity.
Facilitating exchanges	Choose product assortments that match the needs of customers. Cooperate with channel members to develop partnerships.
Promotion	Set promotional objectives. Coordinate advertising, personal selling, sales promotion, publicity, and packaging.
Price	Establish pricing policies and terms of sales.
Logistics	Manage transportation, warehousing, materials handling, inventory control, and communication.

For example, MercuryGate provides transportation management software to firms to streamline logistics. The company also works directly with shippers and third-party logistics companies and brokers to ensure that its customers have effective and efficient supply chains, using analytics and a robust information database pulled from its many clients. Its methods work—as its clients, such as Walmart and Siemens, are known for their exemplary supply chain management.[10]

Wholesalers and retailers are examples of intermediaries. Wholesalers buy and resell products to other wholesalers, retailers, and industrial customers. Retailers purchase products and resell them to end consumers. Consider your local supermarket, which probably purchased the Advil on its shelves from a wholesaler. The wholesaler purchased that pain medicine, along with other over-the-counter and prescription drugs, from manufacturers like McNeil Consumer Healthcare. Chapter 15 discusses the functions of wholesalers and retailers in marketing channels in detail.

14-2a **The Significance of Marketing Channels**

Although it is not necessary to make marketing channel decisions before other marketing decisions, they can have a strong influence on the other elements of the marketing mix (i.e., product, promotion, and pricing). Channel decisions are critical because they determine a product's market presence and accessibility. Without marketing channel operations that reach the right customers at the right time, even the best goods and services will not be successful. For example, in spite of spending massive amounts on marketing efforts, Target abandoned the Canadian market after losing a billion dollars in large part due to a poor distribution system. The retail company opened 133 stores in just two years, but Canadian shoppers routinely found empty shelves due to supply chain issues the company might have identified sooner had it opened just a few stores at a time. Pricing issues and intense competition further hamstrung the U.S. retailer's first foray into a foreign market.[11]

Marketing channel decisions have strategic significance because they generally entail long-term commitments among a variety of firms (e.g., suppliers, logistics providers, and operations firms). Furthermore, distribution channels are the least flexible component of the marketing mix. Once a firm commits to a distribution channel, it is difficult to change. Marketing channels serve many functions, including creating utility and facilitating exchange efficiencies. Although some of these functions may be performed by a single channel member, most functions are accomplished through both independent and joint efforts of channel members.

Marketing Channels Create Utility

Marketing channels create four types of utility: time, place, possession, and form. *Time utility* is having products available when the customer wants them. Services like Netflix allow customers to watch a movie or TV show whenever they want. *Place utility* is making products available in locations where customers wish to purchase them. For example, Zappos allows customers to shop for shoes and accessories anywhere they have access to a mobile device and an internet connection. *Possession utility* means that the customer has access to the product to use or to store for future use. Possession utility can occur through ownership or through arrangements that give the customer the right to use the product, such as a lease or rental agreement. Channel members sometimes create *form utility* by assembling, preparing, or otherwise refining the product to suit individual customer needs.

Marketing Channels Facilitate Exchange Efficiencies

Even if producers and buyers are located in the same city, there are costs associated with exchanges. Marketing intermediaries can reduce the costs of exchanges by performing certain services or functions efficiently. As Figure 14.2 shows, when four buyers seek products from four producers, 16 separate transactions are possible. If one intermediary serves both producers and buyers, the number of possible transactions is cut in half. Intermediaries are specialists in facilitating exchanges. They provide valuable assistance because of their access to, and control over, important resources used in the proper functioning of marketing channels. Many firms exist to assist firms with creating supply chain efficiencies. Take a look at the advertisement for

Figure 14.2 **Efficiency in Exchanges Provided by an Intermediary**

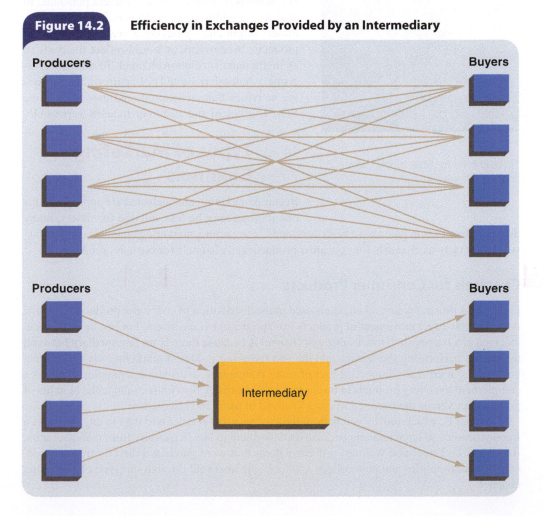

Supply Chain Efficiencies
Logistics firms such as Fidelitone can help businesses to create supply chain efficiencies, distributing their goods quickly and affordably.

Fidelitone. It shows a man and a woman reviewing a document and informs customers that Fidelitone is paying attention to what matters in your business. Firms such as Fidelitone have expert knowledge and have developed distribution networks that can help other firms to create supply chain efficiencies.

Nevertheless, the media, consumers, public officials, and even other marketers freely criticize intermediaries, especially wholesalers. Critics accuse wholesalers of being inefficient and adding to costs. Buyers often think that making the distribution channel as short as possible will decrease the prices for products, but this is not the case.

Critics who suggest that eliminating wholesalers will lower prices for customers fail to recognize that this would not eliminate the need for the services the wholesalers provide. Although wholesalers can be eliminated, their functions cannot. Other channel members would have to perform those functions, perhaps not as efficiently, and customers still would have to pay for them. In addition, all producers would deal directly with retailers or customers, meaning that every producer would have to keep voluminous records and hire sufficient personnel to deal with a multitude of customers. In the end, customers might end up paying a great deal more for products, because prices would reflect the costs of an inefficient distribution channel. To mitigate criticisms, wholesalers should only perform the marketing activities that are desired, and they must strive to be as efficient and customer-focused as possible.

14-2b Types of Marketing Channels

Because marketing channels that are appropriate for one product may be less suitable for others, many different distribution paths have been developed. The various marketing channels can be classified generally as channels for consumer products and channels for business products.

Channels for Consumer Products

Figure 14.3 illustrates several channels used in the distribution of consumer products. Channel A depicts the direct movement of products from producer to consumers. For instance, a haircut received at a barber shop moves through channel A because there is no intermediary between the person performing the service and the one receiving it. Direct marketing via the internet has become a critically important part of some companies' distribution strategies, often as a complement to selling products in traditional retail stores. A firm must evaluate the benefits of going direct versus the transaction costs involved in using intermediaries.

Channel B, which moves goods from the producer to a retailer and then to customers, is a frequent choice of large retailers because it allows them to buy in quantity from manufacturers. Retailers like Target and Walmart sell many items that were purchased directly from producers. New automobiles and new college textbooks are also sold through this type of marketing channel.

| Figure 14.3 | Typical Marketing Channels for Consumer Products |

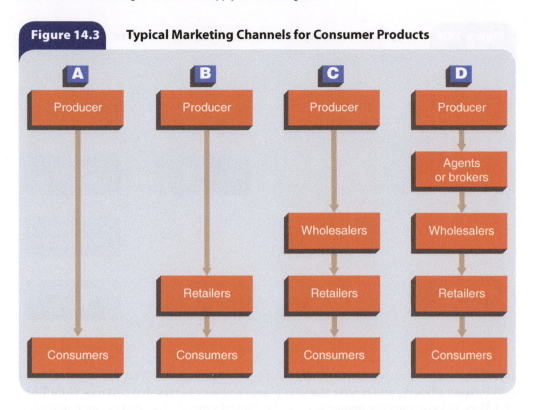

Channel C is a common distribution channel for consumer products. It takes goods from the producer to a wholesaler, then to a retailer, and finally to consumers. It is a practical option for producers that sell to hundreds of thousands of customers through thousands of retailers. Some home appliances, hardware, and many convenience goods are marketed through this type of channel. Consider the number of retailers marketing KitchenAid mixers. It would be rather difficult, if not impossible, for KitchenAid to deal directly with each of the many retailers that sell its brand.

Channel D, wherein goods pass from producer, to agents, to wholesalers, to retailers, and finally to consumers, is used frequently for products intended for mass distribution, such as processed foods. Consequently, to place its Wheat Thins crackers in specific retail outlets, supply chain managers at Nabisco may hire an agent (or a food broker) to sell the crackers to wholesalers. Wholesalers then sell the Wheat Thins to supermarkets, vending-machine operators, and convenience stores.

Contrary to what you might think, a long channel may actually be the most efficient distribution channel for some goods. When several channel intermediaries perform specialized functions, costs are likely to be lower than when one channel member tries to perform them all. Efficiencies arise when firms that specialize in certain elements of producing a product or moving it through the channel are more effective at performing specialized tasks than the manufacturer. This results in added value to customers and reduced costs throughout the distribution channel.

Channels for Business Products

Figure 14.4 shows four of the most common channels for business products. As with consumer products, manufacturers of business products sometimes work with more than one level of wholesaler.

Channel E illustrates the direct channel for business products. In contrast to consumer goods, business products, especially expensive equipment, are most likely to be sold through direct channels. Business customers prefer to communicate directly with producers,

| Figure 14.4 | Typical Marketing Channels for Business Products |

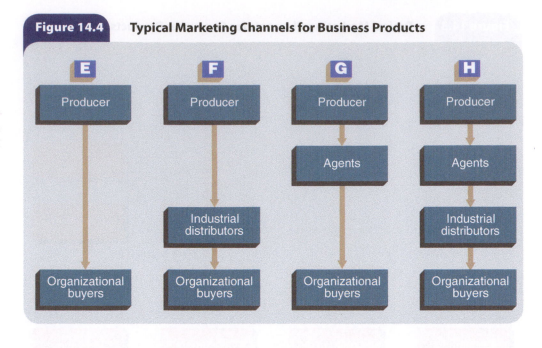

especially when expensive or technically complex products are involved. For instance, business buyers of Boeing jets receive not only planes and accessories that cost tens of millions of dollars, but also ongoing maintenance and technical support. This makes communication and customer support even more significant and would be impossible to obtain through an intermediary.[12]

In channel F, an industrial distributor facilitates exchanges between the producer and the customer. An **industrial distributor** is an independent business that takes title to products and carries inventories. Industrial distributors usually sell standardized items, such as maintenance supplies, production tools, and small operating equipment. Some industrial distributors carry a wide variety of product lines. Applied Industrial Technologies Inc., for instance, carries millions of products from more than 4,000 manufacturers and works with a wide variety of companies from small janitorial services companies to giant manufacturers such as Boeing.[13] Other industrial distributors specialize in one or a small number of lines. Industrial distributors carry an increasing percentage of business products. Overall, these distributors can be most effective when a product has broad market appeal, is easily stocked and serviced, is sold in small quantities, and is needed on demand to avoid high losses.

Industrial distributors offer sellers several advantages. They can perform the needed selling activities in local markets at a relatively low cost to a manufacturer and reduce a producer's financial burden by providing customers with credit services. Also, because industrial distributors usually maintain close relationships with their customers, they are aware of local needs and can pass on market information to producers. By holding adequate inventories in local markets, industrial distributors reduce producers' capital requirements.

Using industrial distributors has several disadvantages. They may be difficult to manage because they are independent firms. They often stock competing brands, so a producer cannot depend on them to sell its brand aggressively. Furthermore, industrial distributors incur expenses from maintaining inventories and are less likely to handle bulky or slow-selling items, or items that need specialized facilities or extraordinary selling efforts. In some cases, industrial distributors lack the specialized knowledge necessary to sell and service technical products.

The third channel for business products, channel G, employs a *manufacturers' agent*, an independent businessperson who sells complementary products of several producers in assigned territories and is compensated through commissions. Unlike an industrial distributor, a manufacturers' agent does not acquire title to the products and usually does not take

industrial distributor An independent business organization that takes title to industrial products and carries inventories

ENTREPRENEURSHIP IN MARKETING

Haney's Appledale Farm Taps into Experiential Logistics

The aroma of fresh baked apple pies with a hint of cinnamon fills the doorway to Haney's Appledale Farm and Market. This small Kentucky family-owned business is a producer to customer channel; folks come from near and far to pick their own apples and peaches. Located in Nancy, Kentucky, this family-farm business has been in operation since 1870. Currently Haney's is run by brothers Don and Mark, the fifth generation of the Haney family to operate the business.

Today, it is a sustainable 450-acre family farm that grows 35 varieties of apples and 15 varieties of peaches. As a product to consumer channel, Haney's Appledale Farm sells produce directly to consumers with no involvement of intermediaries,

so its supply chain is more focused on the supplies it needs to operate the farm efficiently to provide products and experiences for customers who visit the farm. In season, customers can pick their own apples or peaches in the farm's orchards. The trees are cultivated to provide a staggered and longer growing season. Their retail market sells apple-related items such as cookies, cakes, jams, jellies, and more.

Although the Haneys have had offers to go national with this product, they have declined the opportunity so that product integrity can be maintained. They tried selling product online, but it did not work for them. Now in their 60s, the Haney brothers' lives are just like their supply chain: simple. Their mantra is "Be honest and give more than you take."[a]

possession. Acting as a salesperson on behalf of the producers, a manufacturers' agent has little or no latitude in negotiating prices or sales terms.

Using manufacturers' agents can benefit an organizational marketer. They usually possess considerable technical and market information and have an established set of customers. A manufacturers' agent can be an asset for an organization with seasonal demand because the seller does not have to support a year-round sales force. The fact that manufacturers' agents are typically paid on a commission basis may also be an economical alternative for a firm that has highly limited resources and cannot afford a full-time sales force. The use of manufacturers' agents also has drawbacks. The seller has little control over the actions of manufacturers' agents. Because they work on commission, manufacturers' agents prefer to concentrate on larger accounts. They are often reluctant to spend time following up with customers after the sale, putting forth special selling efforts, or providing sellers with market information because they are not compensated for these activities and they reduce the amount of productive selling time. Because they rarely maintain inventories, manufacturers' agents have a limited ability to provide customers with parts or repair services quickly.

Finally, channel H includes both a manufacturers' agent and an industrial distributor. This channel may be appropriate when the producer wishes to cover a large geographic area, but maintains no sales force due to highly seasonal demand or because it cannot afford one. This channel can also be useful for a business marketer that wants to enter a new geographic market without expanding its sales force.

Multiple Marketing Channels

To reach diverse target markets, manufacturers may use more than one marketing channel simultaneously, with each channel involving a different group of intermediaries. A manufacturer often uses multiple channels when the same product is directed to both consumers and business customers. For example, when Heinz markets ketchup for household use, the product is sold to supermarkets through grocery wholesalers or, in some cases, directly to retailers, whereas ketchup being sold to restaurants or institutions follows a different distribution channel.

SOURCE: OGX

Multichannel Distribution
Many companies, including OGX, use multichannel distribution—meaning products are targeted at the same group of consumers via multiple channels. In this case, shampoo is made available to consumers in drugstores and online.

A **strategic channel alliance** exists when the products of one firm are distributed through the marketing channels of another. The products of the two firms are often similar with respect to target markets or uses, but they are not direct competitors. A brand of bottled water might be distributed through a marketing channel for soft drinks, or a cereal producer in the United States might form a strategic channel alliance with a European food processor to facilitate international distribution. Such alliances can provide benefits for both the organization that owns the marketing channel and the company whose brand is being distributed through the channel.

Quite often, companies today use multiple channels to reach the same target market. For example, consumers can purchase a Dell computer directly from the company by calling a toll-free number or going through its website as well as indirectly through select retailers such as Best Buy. Likewise, L.L. Bean markets products through its longstanding catalog, its website, and through its own retail stores. In such cases, the firm is using **multichannel distribution**—the use of a variety of marketing channels to ensure maximum distribution. The primary reason for using a multichannel strategy is to reach target customers wherever and whenever they may choose to interact with a company or its products. Some consumers may prefer to shop in a brick-and-mortar store where they can personally compare and sample products, while others prefer the instant gratification of shopping for an item on their smartphone as soon as they recognize a need for the product. Even marketers for hair care products, such as the OGX shampoo featured in the advertisement, employ multichannel distribution. This product—which the ad informs was developed for people with dry and damaged hair—is available in drugstores,

strategic channel alliance An agreement whereby the products of one organization are distributed through the marketing channels of another

multichannel distribution The use of a variety of marketing channels to ensure maximum distribution

digital distribution Delivering content through the internet to a computer or other device

but customers can also purchase it on the producer's website, which is displayed on the advertisement.

Some products can forgo physical distribution altogether. **Digital distribution** involves delivering content through the internet to a computer or other device. For example, when you watch a TV show on Netflix or Hulu or listen to music on Pandora or Spotify, those networks stream the content to your device so that you can consume them at the same time that they are streamed. In today's high-tech world, it is also possible to rent digital content, such as a textbook, or subscribe to software, such as Office 365, for a specific period of time after downloading them to a computer, tablet, or smartphone. Some services can also be distributed through digital channels such as booking travel services through Expedia.com or Hotels.com.

It is important to recognize that the line between different marketing channels is becoming increasingly blurred. Consider that today's consumer expects to be able to order a product online from, say, Home Depot or Target, and pick up the order at their nearest retail store to avoid paying a shipping charge. Many companies have distribution channels that include physical retail stores as well as Amazon.com or eBay. Younger consumers today have learned to shop online wherever they may be through their smartphones, though they may visit a retail store to assess a product for themselves, and then order it directly from the manufacturer's website or Amazon. Marketers are having to adjust their strategies to respond to the blurred lines between multiple marketing channels by ensuring they are using every channel their target market prefers to use and sending a consistent message across all distribution channels.

14-2c Selecting Marketing Channels

Selecting appropriate marketing channels is important because they are difficult to change once chosen. Although the process varies across organizations, channel selection decisions are usually affected significantly by one or more of the following factors: customer characteristics, product attributes, type of organization, competition, marketing environmental forces, and characteristics of intermediaries (see Figure 14.5).

Customer Characteristics

Marketing managers must consider the characteristics of target market members in channel selection. As we have already seen, the channels that are appropriate for consumers are different from those for business customers. Because of variations in product use, product complexity, consumption levels, and need for services, firms develop different marketing strategies for each group. Business customers often prefer to deal directly with producers (or very knowledgeable channel intermediaries such as industrial distributors), especially for highly technical or expensive products, such as mainframe computers, jet airplanes, or heavy machinery that require strict specifications and technical assistance. Businesses also frequently buy in large quantities.

Consumers, on the other hand, generally buy limited quantities of a product, purchase from retailers, and often do not mind limited customer service. When customers are concentrated in a small geographic area, a direct channel may be best, but when many customers are spread across an entire state or nation, distribution through multiple intermediaries is likely to be more efficient.

Figure 14.5 **Selecting Marketing Channels**

Product Attributes

The attributes of the product can have a strong influence on the choice of marketing channels. Marketers of complex and expensive products (like automobiles) will likely employ short channels, as will marketers of perishable products (such as dairy and produce). Less-expensive standardized products with long shelf lives, such as soft drinks and canned goods, can go through longer channels with many intermediaries. Fragile products that require special handling are likely to be distributed through short channels to minimize the amount of handling and risk of damage. Firms that desire to convey an exclusive image for their products may wish to limit the number of outlets available.

Type of Organization

The characteristics of the organization will have a great impact on the distribution channels chosen. Owing to their size, larger firms are in a better position to deal with vendors or other channel members. They are also likely to have more distribution centers, which reduces delivery times to customers. Large companies can also use an extensive product mix as a competitive tool. A smaller company that uses regional or local channel members, on the other hand, might be in a strong position to cater its marketing mix to serve customers in that particular area, compared with a larger and less-flexible organization. However, smaller firms may not have the resources to develop their own sales force, ship their products long distances, maintain a large inventory, or extend credit. In such cases, they might consider including other channel members that have the resources to provide these services to customers.

Competition

Competition is another important factor for supply chain managers to consider. The success or failure of a competitor's marketing channel may encourage or dissuade an organization from taking a similar approach. In a highly competitive market, it is important for a company to maintain low costs so it can offer lower prices than its competitors if necessary to maintain a competitive advantage.

Environmental Forces

Environmental forces can play a role in channel selection. Adverse economic conditions might force an organization to use a low-cost channel, even though it reduces customer satisfaction. In contrast, a growing economy may allow a company to choose a channel that previously had been too costly. New technology might allow an organization to add to or modify its channel strategy, such as by adding online retailing. Government regulations can also affect channel selection. As labor and environmental regulations change, an organization may be forced to modify its existing distribution channel structure to comply with new laws. Firms might choose to enact such changes before they are mandated in order to appear proactive. International governmental regulations can complicate the supply chain a great deal, as laws vary from country to country.

Characteristics of Intermediaries

When an organization believes that an intermediary is not promoting its products adequately or does not offer the correct mix of services, it may reconsider its channel choices. In these instances, the company may choose another channel member to handle its products, it may select a new intermediary, or it might choose to eliminate intermediaries altogether and perform the functions itself.

INTEGRITY IN MARKETING

REI: A Consumer-Owned Retailer

Recreational Equipment Inc. (REI), known for its quality outdoor gear and equipment, places consumers first—so much so that it is organized as a consumer cooperative. A cooperative consists of small businesses or, as in REI's case, consumers who want to save money and develop a high-integrity organization without the pressure of profits. For $20, consumers can become lifelong members of REI. Although different from corporate shareholders, REI members receive annual dividends in the form of member rebates and REI Visa card rebates. The amount depends on how much consumers purchase during the year, rewarding them for their loyalty. Members also receive product discounts and are able to vote for REI's board members. REI customers seem to enjoy the benefits that membership has to offer; the company has more than 6 million active members.

While REI's supply chain is similar to other retailers, this structure encourages REI to be customer-oriented by offering quality services, an inviting store environment, and superior products. For example, many REI stores have bike trails and rock climbing walls so that consumers can test products. In addition to many well-known outdoor brands, the company offers its own branded items that are high in quality.

For some time, REI found itself behind the curve in its supply chain operations, so it began to ask itself questions regarding capacity requirements, customer service, technology, and sustainability. To improve its automation and distribution, the company opened a 400,000-square-foot facility in Phoenix and effectively increased capacity by 40 percent. REI's commitment to the environment and its customers allows the company to operate with integrity and influence the outdoor industry.[b]

14-3 INTENSITY OF MARKET COVERAGE

Learning Objective 14-3

Identify the intensity of market coverage.

In addition to deciding which marketing channels to use to distribute a product, marketers must determine the appropriate intensity of coverage—that is, the number and kinds of outlets in which a product will be sold. This decision depends on the characteristics of the product and the target market. To achieve the desired intensity of market coverage, distribution must correspond to behavior patterns of buyers. In Chapter 11, we divided consumer products into four categories—convenience, shopping, specialty, and unsought—according to how consumers make purchases. In considering products for purchase, consumers take into account such factors as replacement rate, product adjustment (services), duration of consumption, and time required to find the product.[14] These variables directly affect the intensity of market coverage. As shown in Figure 14.6, the three major levels of market coverage are intensive, selective, and exclusive distribution.

14-3a Intensive Distribution

Intensive distribution uses all available outlets for distributing a product. Intensive distribution is appropriate for products that have a high replacement rate, require almost no service, and are often bought based on price cues. Most convenience products like bread, chewing gum, soft drinks, and newspapers are marketed through intensive distribution. Multiple channels may be used to sell through all possible outlets. For example, goods such as soft drinks, snacks, laundry detergent, and pain relievers are available at convenience stores, service stations, supermarkets, discount stores, and other types of retailers. To satisfy consumers seeking to buy these

intensive distribution Using all available outlets to distribute a product

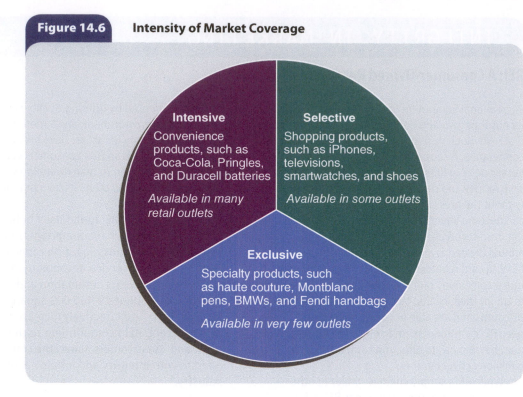

Figure 14.6   **Intensity of Market Coverage**

Intensive
Convenience products, such as Coca-Cola, Pringles, and Duracell batteries

Available in many retail outlets

Selective
Shopping products, such as iPhones, televisions, smartwatches, and shoes

Available in some outlets

Exclusive
Specialty products, such as haute couture, Montblanc pens, BMWs, and Fendi handbags

Available in very few outlets

products, they must be available at a store nearby and be obtained with minimal search time. For these products, consumers want speed in obtaining them while receiving a reliable level of quality and flexibility to buy the product wherever it is most convenient for them at the lowest price possible. Sales of low-cost convenience products may be directly related to product availability.

14-3b   Selective Distribution

Selective distribution uses only some available outlets in an area to distribute a product. Selective distribution is appropriate for shopping products, which include durable goods like televisions or computers. Shopping products are more expensive than convenience goods, and consumers are willing to spend more time and possibly visit several retail outlets and websites to compare prices, designs, styles, and other features.

Selective distribution is desirable when a special effort, such as customer service from a channel member, is important to customers. Shopping products require differentiation at the point of purchase. Selective distribution is often used to motivate retailers to provide adequate service. Dealers can offer higher-quality customer service when products are distributed selectively. Consider the advertisement for Samuel Hubbard. Samuel Hubbard is a moderately high-end brand of men's shoe that is distributed selectively. Samuel Hubbard shoes are available at department stores such as Nordstrom. This advertisement seeks to cultivate a high-end image that also speaks to comfort. Most perfumes and colognes and some cosmetics are marketed using selective distribution in order to maintain a particular image.

14-3c   Exclusive Distribution

Exclusive distribution uses only one outlet in a relatively large geographic area. This method is suitable for products purchased infrequently, consumed over a long period of

selective distribution Using only some available outlets in an area to distribute a product

exclusive distribution Using a single outlet in a fairly large geographic area to distribute a product

time, or that require a high level of customer service or information. It is also used for expensive, high-quality products with high profit margins, such as Porsche, BMW, and other luxury automobiles. It is not appropriate for convenience products and many shopping products because an insufficient number of units would be sold to generate an acceptable level of profits on account of those products' lower profit margins.

Exclusive distribution is often used as an incentive to sellers when only a limited market is available for products. Consider Patek Philippe watches that may sell for $10,000 or more. These watches, like luxury automobiles, are available in only a few select locations. Tourneau, featured in the advertisement, is an exclusive retail outlet that sells new and preowned high-end luxury watches, including Patek Philippe. There are only a few Tourneau outlets, all located in very large cities. Items can retail for tens of thousands of dollars, and the available brands shown in the ad are frequently worn as a status symbol. A producer using exclusive distribution expects dealers to carry a complete inventory, train personnel to ensure a high level of product knowledge and quality customer service, and participate in promotional programs.

Some products are appropriate for exclusive distribution when first introduced, but as competitors enter the market and the product moves through its life cycle, other types of market coverage and distribution channels become necessary. A problem that can arise with exclusive (and selective) distribution is that unauthorized resellers acquire and sell products or counterfeits, violating the agreement between a manufacturer and its exclusive authorized dealers.

MY MOTHER WAS A SNEAKER, MY FATHER WAS A DRESS SHOE

I can't help it. I was born this way. Insanely comfortable and ready for a day in the office. Think of me as the Un-Sneaker.™

SAMUELHUBBARD.COM
SHOEMAKERS SINCE 1930

30 colors, 9 styles, 1 free catalog. 844.482.4800

SOURCE: SAMUELHUBBARD.COM

Selective Distribution
Samuel Hubbard shoes are distributed selectively. Salespeople will be knowledgeable and willing to assist a customer in making a selection.

14-4 STRATEGIC ISSUES IN MARKETING CHANNELS

Learning Objective 14-4
Explore strategic issues in marketing channels, including leadership, cooperation, and conflict.

To maintain customer satisfaction and an effective supply chain, managers must retain a strategic focus on certain competitive priorities, including developing channel leadership, fostering cooperation between channel members, managing channel conflict, and possibly consolidating marketing channels through channel integration.

14-4a Competitive Priorities in Marketing Channels

Increasingly, firms are recognizing that supply chains can be a source of competitive advantage and a strong market orientation because supply chain decisions cut across all functional areas of business. Building the most effective and efficient supply chain can sustain a business and help it to use resources effectively and be more efficient. Many well-known firms, including Amazon, Dell, FedEx, Toyota, and Walmart, owe much of their success to outmaneuvering rivals with unique supply chain capabilities. Many countries offer firms

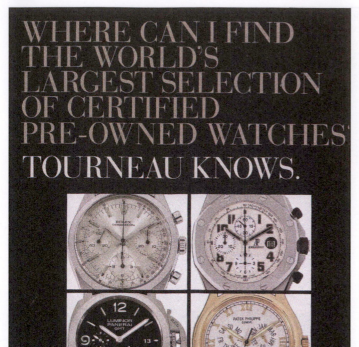

Exclusive Distribution

Tourneau is an exclusive outlet of high-end luxury watches, selling products only in large cities.

opportunities to create an effective and efficient supply chain to support the development of competitive national industries. Although developed nations like Germany, the United States, and Canada remain highly competitive manufacturing countries, China has ranked number one on Deloitte's annual survey of global manufacturing competitiveness for years, indicating the country's superior capabilities to produce goods at a low price and efficiently distribute them.[15] India, Mexico, and Taiwan have risen to prominence as well.

To unlock the potential of a supply chain, firms must integrate activities so that all functions are coordinated into an effective system. Supply chains driven by firm-established goals focus on the "competitive priorities" of speed, quality, cost, and flexibility as the performance objectives. Managers must remember, however, to keep a holistic view of the supply chain so that goals such as "speed" or "cost" do not result in dissatisfied or underpaid workers or other such abuses in factories. This should be a particular concern among firms that use international manufacturers because it can be more difficult to monitor working conditions internationally.

14-4b Channel Leadership, Cooperation, and Conflict

Each channel member performs a specific role in the distribution system and agrees (implicitly or explicitly) to accept rights, responsibilities, rewards, and sanctions for nonconformity. Moreover, each channel member holds certain expectations of other channel members. Retailers, for instance, expect wholesalers to maintain adequate inventories and deliver goods on time. Wholesalers expect retailers to honor payment agreements and keep them informed of inventory needs. Manufacturers, wholesalers, and retailers expect shipping companies to deliver products on schedule and at a reasonable cost. Any one organization's failure to meet expectations can disrupt the entire supply chain. After South Korea's Hanjin Shipping Company declared bankruptcy, ports around the world refused entry to Hanjin ships until the firm could secure funding to pay the port fees. As a result, Hanjin ships loaded with millions of dollars of merchandise from around the world were left anchored offshore unable to be offloaded for months, disrupting supply chains for a large variety of products.[16]

Channel partnerships can facilitate effective supply chain management when partners agree on objectives, policies, and procedures for physical distribution efforts associated with the supplier's products. Such partnerships eliminate redundancies and assign tasks for maximum system-wide efficiency. Channel cooperation reduces wasted resources, such as time, energy, or materials. A coordinated supply chain can also be more environmentally friendly, a consideration that is increasingly important to many organizations and their stakeholders. In fact, research findings show that companies with environmentally responsible supply chains tend to be more profitable, particularly when a firm's marketing efforts point out the fact that it has a sustainable supply chain.[17] In order to reduce the carbon footprint of the U.S. auto industry's production processes, equipment manufacturers and suppliers partnered with the Environmental Protection Agency to form the Suppliers Partnership for the Environment. It is a forum for companies and their supply chain partners to share environmental best practices and optimize supply chain productivity. The result is a more efficient and less polluting supply chain.[18] In this section, we discuss channel member behavior—including leadership, cooperation, and conflict—that marketers must understand to make effective channel decisions.

Channel Leadership

Many marketing channel decisions are determined through channel member compromise with a better marketing channel as an end goal. Some marketing channels, however, are organized and controlled by a single leader, or **channel captain** (also called *channel leader*). The channel captain may be a producer, wholesaler, or retailer. Channel captains may establish channel policies and coordinate development of the marketing mix. To attain desired objectives, the captain must possess **channel power**, the ability to influence another channel member's goal achievement. The member that becomes the channel captain will accept the responsibilities and exercise the power associated with this role.

When a manufacturer is a channel captain and it determines that it must increase sales volume to achieve production efficiency, it may encourage growth through offering channel members financing, business advice, ordering assistance, advertising services, sales and service training, and support materials. These benefits usually come with requirements related to sales volume, service quality, training, and customer satisfaction.

Retailers may also be channel captains. Walmart, for example, dominates the supply chain for its retail stores by virtue of the magnitude of its resources (especially information management) and a strong, nationwide customer base. To be part of Walmart's supply chain, other channel members must agree to Walmart's rules. Small retailers, too, may assume leadership roles when they gain strong customer loyalty in local or regional markets. Retailers that are channel captains control many brands and sometimes replace uncooperative producers. Increasingly, leading retailers are concentrating their buying power among fewer suppliers, which makes it easier to coordinate and maintain a high level of quality and transparency along the entire supply chain. These more selective relationships often involve long-term commitments, which enable retailers to place smaller and more frequent orders as needed, rather than waiting for large-volume discounts, or placing large orders and assuming the risks associated with carrying more inventory than needed.

Wholesalers can assume channel leadership roles as well. Wholesaler leaders may form voluntary chains with several retailers, which they supply with bulk buying or management services, and which may also market their own brands. In return, the retailers shift most of their purchasing to the wholesaler leader. The Independent Grocers Alliance (IGA) is one of the best-known wholesaler leaders in the United States with nearly 5,000 outlets in more than 30 countries.[19] IGA's power is based on its expertise in advertising, pricing, and purchasing knowledge that it makes available to independent business owners. Wholesaler channel leaders may help retailers with store layouts, accounting, and inventory control.

Channel Cooperation

Because the supply chain is an interrelated system, the success of one firm in the channel depends in part on other member firms. Cooperation enables retailers, wholesalers, suppliers, and logistics providers to speed up inventory replenishment, improve customer service, and cut the costs of bringing products to the consumer.[20] Without cooperation, neither overall channel goals nor individual member goals can be realized. Thus, marketing channel members should make a coordinated effort to satisfy market requirements. Channel cooperation leads to greater trust among channel members and improves the overall functioning of the channel. Cooperation also leads to more satisfying relationships among channel members.

There are several ways to improve channel cooperation. If a marketing channel is viewed as a unified supply chain competing with other systems, individual members will be less likely to take actions that create disadvantages for other members. Channel members should agree to

channel captain The dominant leader of a marketing channel or a supply channel

channel power The ability of one channel member to influence another member's goal achievement

#DontCrackUnderPressure

TAGHeuer
SWISS AVANT-GARDE SINCE 1860

TAG HEUER CARRERA CALIBRE HEUER 01
Chris Hemsworth works hard and chooses his roles carefully. He handles pressure by
taming it, and turning it to his advantage. #DontCrackUnderPressure was coined with
him in mind.

Available at Macy's and Macys.com

Channel Conflict

Exclusive brands like Tag Heuer, which previously were only available at authorized retailers, risk channel conflict now that they are also sold online via the company's website.

direct efforts toward common objectives, and their tasks should be defined precisely so that roles can be structured for maximum effectiveness in working toward achieving objectives. Starting from a common basis allows channel members to set benchmarks for reviewing intermediaries' performance and helps to reduce conflicts as each channel member knows what is expected of it.

Channel Conflict

Although all channel members work toward the same general goal—distributing products profitably and efficiently—members sometimes may disagree about the best methods for attaining this goal. The internet has increased the potential for conflict and resentment between manufacturers and intermediaries. When a manufacturer such as Apple or Dell makes its products available through the internet, it is employing a direct channel that competes with the retailers that also sell its products. Take a look at the advertisement for Tag Heuer watches. This is a very exclusive brand, which is underscored by featuring the famous actor Chris Hemsworth as a model. The brand was previously only available via authorized jewelers. Consumers can now purchase the watches directly from the producer via the company's website, creating potential resentment among brick-and-mortar stores if they lose business.

Channel conflicts also arise when intermediaries overemphasize competing products or diversify into product lines traditionally handled by other intermediaries. When a producer that has traditionally used franchised dealers broadens its retailer base to include other types of retail outlets, for example, conflict can arise with the traditional outlets. Sometimes conflict develops because producers strive to increase efficiency by circumventing intermediaries.

If self-interest creates misunderstanding about role expectations, the end result is frustration and conflict for the whole channel. For individual organizations to function together, each channel member must clearly communicate and understand role expectations. For example, using social media to communicate helps supplier-retailer partners achieve common goals, develop relationships, increase customer interaction, and promote the supplier, brand, and competitive environment across the different levels.[21] On the other hand, communication difficulties are a potential form of channel conflict because ineffective communication leads to frustration, misunderstandings, and ill-coordinated strategies, jeopardizing further coordination.

Although there is no single method for resolving conflict, partnerships can be reestablished if two conditions are met. First, the role of each channel member must be clearly defined and followed. Channel members must have a clear understanding of goals and expectations as well as the metrics that different members will use to measure progress and determine incentive rates.[22] To minimize misunderstanding, all members must be able to expect unambiguous performance levels from one another. Second, members of channel partnerships must agree on means of coordinating channels, which requires strong, but not polarizing, leadership. To prevent channel conflict, producers or other channel members may provide competing resellers with different brands, allocate markets among resellers, define policies for direct sales to avoid potential conflict over large accounts, negotiate territorial issues among regional distributors, and provide recognition to certain resellers for their importance in distributing to others.

14-4c Channel Integration

Channel members can either combine and control activities or pass them to another channel member. Channel functions may be transferred between intermediaries and producers, even to customers. As mentioned earlier in the chapter, supply chain functions cannot be eliminated. Unless buyers themselves perform the functions, they must pay for the labor and resources needed to perform them. Various channel stages may be combined, either horizontally or vertically, under the management of a channel captain. Such integration may stabilize supply, reduce costs, and increase channel member coordination.

Vertical Channel Integration

Vertical channel integration combines two or more stages of the channel under one management. This may occur when one member of a marketing channel purchases the operations of another member or simply performs the functions of another member, eliminating the need for that intermediary. Tesla, for example, manufactures electric vehicles which it sells directly to the consumer rather than through dealerships. The company is also building and operating its own Supercharger stations across the nation where Tesla owners can recharge their electric cars in just a few minutes.[23]

Vertical channel integration represents a more progressive approach to distribution, in which channel members become extensions of one another as they are combined under a single management. Vertically integrated channels can be more effective against competition because of increased bargaining power and the ease of sharing information and responsibilities. At one end of a vertically integrated channel, a manufacturer might provide advertising and training assistance. At the other end, the retailer might buy the manufacturer's products in large quantities and actively promote them.

Integration has been successfully institutionalized in a marketing channel called the **vertical marketing system (VMS)**, in which a single channel member coordinates or manages all activities to maximize efficiencies, resulting in an effective and low-cost distribution system that does not duplicate services. Vertical integration brings most or all stages of the marketing channel under common control or ownership. It can help speed the rate at which goods move through a marketing channel. VMSs account for a large share of retail sales in consumer goods. Most vertical marketing systems take one of three forms: corporate, administered, or contractual.

A *corporate VMS* combines all stages of the marketing channel, from producers to consumers, under a single owner. For example, the Inditex Group, which owns popular clothing retailer Zara, utilizes a corporate VMS to achieve channel efficiencies and maintain a maximum amount of control over the supply chain. Zara's clothing is trendy, requiring the shortest time possible from product development to offering the clothing in stores. Inventory is characterized by very high turnover and frequent changes. Because it has control over all stages of the supply chain, Inditex can maintain an advantage through speed and keeping prices low.[24]

In an *administered VMS*, channel members are independent, but informal coordination achieves a high level of interorganizational management. Members of an administered VMS may adopt uniform accounting and ordering procedures and cooperate in promotional activities for the benefit of all partners. Although individual channel members maintain autonomy, as in conventional marketing channels, one channel member (such as a producer or large retailer) dominates the administered VMS so that distribution decisions take the whole system into account.

A *contractual VMS* is the most popular type of vertical marketing system. Channel members are linked by legal agreements spelling out each member's rights and obligations. Franchise organizations, such as McDonald's and KFC, are contractual VMSs. Other contractual

vertical channel integration Combining two or more stages of the marketing channel under one management

vertical marketing system (VMS) A marketing channel managed by a single channel member to achieve efficient, low-cost distribution aimed at satisfying target market customers

VMSs include wholesaler-sponsored groups, such as IGA stores, in which independent retailers band together under the contractual leadership of a wholesaler. Retailer-sponsored cooperatives, which own and operate their own wholesalers, are a third type of contractual VMS. Ace Hardware is a retail cooperative of more than 5,000 stores with revenues of $5.4 billion and strong growth despite competition from so-called big-box stores like Home Depot and Lowe's. Each Ace Hardware store contributes to advertising and marketing for the whole group and can capitalize on the well-known brand to build their neighborhood stores.[25]

Horizontal Channel Integration

Combining organizations at the same level of operation under one management constitutes **horizontal channel integration**. An organization may integrate horizontally by merging with other organizations at the same level in the marketing channel. The owner of a dry cleaning firm, for example, might buy and combine several other existing dry-cleaning establishments. Likewise, Sherwin-Williams acquired rival paint firm Valspar for $11.3 billion in part to fast-track its move into international markets.[26]

Although horizontal integration permits efficiencies and economies of scale in purchasing, marketing research, advertising, and specialized personnel, it is not always the most effective method of improving distribution. Problems that come with increased size often follow, resulting in decreased flexibility, difficulties coordinating among members, and the need for additional marketing research and large-scale planning. Unless distribution functions for the various units can be performed more efficiently under unified management than under the previously separate managements, horizontal integration will neither reduce costs nor improve the competitive position of the integrating firm.

Learning Objective 14-5

Explain logistics as being a part of supply chain management.

14-5 LOGISTICS IN SUPPLY CHAIN MANAGEMENT

Logistics, involving physical distribution, relates to planning, implementing, and controlling the efficient flow and storage of products. Physical distribution is an important part of logistics and includes activities used to move products from producers to customers and other end users. These activities include order processing, inventory management, materials handling, warehousing, and transportation. Logistics systems must meet the needs of both the supply chain and customers. Distribution activities are thus an important part of supply chain planning and can require a high level of cooperation among partners.

Within the marketing channel, physical distribution activities may be performed by a producer, wholesaler, or retailer, or they may be outsourced. In the context of distribution, *outsourcing* is the contracting of physical distribution tasks to third parties. **Third-party logistics (3PL) firms** have special expertise in core physical distribution activities such as warehousing, transportation, inventory management, and information technology and can often perform these activities more efficiently. In recent years, 3PL firms have become increasingly sophisticated in their offerings. Today, outsourcing logistics to third-party organizations, such as trucking companies, warehouses, and data-service providers, can reduce marketing channel costs, improve information flow and analysis, and boost service and customer satisfaction for all supply chain partners.[27]

The internet and technological advancements have revolutionized logistics, allowing many manufacturers to carry out actions and services entirely online, bypassing shipping and warehousing considerations, and transforming logistics by facilitating just-in-time delivery, precise inventory visibility, and instant shipment-tracking capabilities. For example, video game and computer software manufacturers such as Microsoft and Sony have increasingly made their products available for download. Emerging technologies such as autonomous vehicles—forklifts, robots, drones, and even self-driving trucks—will further advance logistics.[28]

horizontal channel integration Combining organizations at the same level of operation under one management

third-party logistics (3PL) firms Firms that have special expertise in core logistics activities such as warehousing, transportation, inventory management, and information technology and can often perform these activities more efficiently

Technological advances create new challenges for manufacturers, such as how to maintain a high level of customer service when customers never enter a store or meet with a salesperson and how to deal with returns of a product that does not exist in a physical form. However, technology enables companies to avoid expensive mistakes, reduce costs, and generate increased revenues. Moreover, information technology enhances the transparency of the supply chain, allowing all marketing channel members to track the movement of goods throughout the supply chain and improve their customer service.

Planning an efficient logistics system is crucial to developing an effective marketing strategy because it can decrease costs and increase customer satisfaction. When making distribution decisions, firms keep in mind that speed of delivery, flexibility, and quality of service are often as important to customers as price. Companies that offer the right goods, in the right place, at the right time, in the right quantity, and with the right support services are able to sell more than competitors that do not. Even when the demand for products is unpredictable, suppliers must be able to respond quickly to inventory needs. In such cases, logistics costs may be a minor consideration when compared with service, dependability, and timeliness.

Although logistics managers try to minimize the costs associated with order processing, inventory management, materials handling, warehousing, and transportation, decreasing the costs in one area often raises them in another. Figure 14.7 shows the percentage of total costs that the individual logistics functions represent. A total-cost approach to logistics that takes into account all these different functions enables managers to view logistics as a system and shifts the emphasis from lowering the costs of individual activities to minimizing overall costs.

Logistics managers must, therefore, be sensitive to the issue of cost trade-offs. Trade-offs are strategic decisions to combine (and recombine) resources for greatest cost-effectiveness. The goal is not always to find the lowest cost, but rather to find the right balance of costs. Higher costs in one functional area of a distribution system may be necessary to achieve lower costs in another. When distribution managers regard the system as a network of integrated functions, trade-offs become useful tools in implementing a unified, cost-effective distribution strategy.

Another important goal of logistics involves **cycle time**, the time needed to complete a process. For instance, reducing cycle time while maintaining or reducing costs and/or maintaining or increasing customer service is a winning combination in supply chains and ultimately results in greater customer satisfaction. Firms should look for ways to reduce cycle time while

cycle time The time needed to complete a process

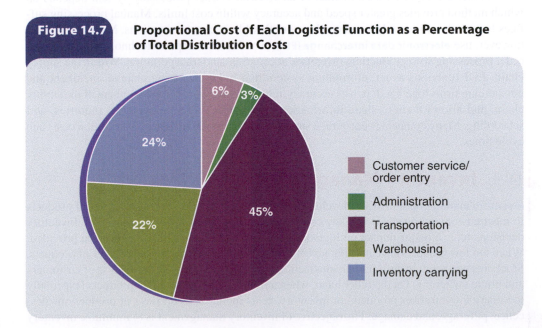

| Figure 14.7 | **Proportional Cost of Each Logistics Function as a Percentage of Total Distribution Costs** |

6% 3%

24%

22%

45%

Customer service/order entry

Administration

Transportation

Warehousing

Inventory carrying

maintaining or reducing costs and maintaining or improving customer service. Consider Dollar Shave Club, which grew from a tiny business with a highly popular viral video to a large business that ships razor blades to subscribers across the country. To reduce cycle time while maintaining high customer satisfaction and quality, the Venice, California, company turned to a third-party logistics specialist, which allowed it to focus on providing excellent customer service while ensuring on-time deliveries to subscribers.[29] In the rest of this section, we take a closer look at a variety of logistics activities, including order processing, inventory management, materials handling, warehousing, and transportation.

14-5a Order Processing

Order processing is the series of steps from receipt of a sales order to the successful delivery of the product or service. Although management sometimes overlooks the importance of these activities, efficient order processing facilitates product flow. Computerized order processing provides a platform for information management, allowing all supply chain members to increase their productivity. When carried out quickly and accurately, order processing contributes to customer satisfaction, decreased costs and cycle time, and increased profits.

Order processing entails three main tasks: order entry, order handling, and order delivery. Order entry begins when customers or salespeople place purchase orders via a customer-service counter, telephone, regular mail, email, or website. Electronic ordering has become the most common. It is less time-consuming than a paper-based ordering system and reduces costs. In some companies, sales representatives receive and enter orders personally and also handle complaints, prepare progress reports, and forward sales order information.

Order handling involves several tasks. Once an order is entered, it is transmitted to a warehouse to verify product availability and, if necessary, to the credit department to set terms and prices and to check the customer's credit rating. If the credit department approves the purchase, warehouse personnel assemble the order. In many warehouses, automated machines carry out this step. If the requested product is not in stock, a production order is sent to the factory, or the customer is offered a substitute.

When the order has been assembled and packed for shipment, the warehouse schedules delivery with an appropriate carrier. If the customer pays for rush service, overnight delivery by an overnight carrier is used. The customer is sent an invoice, inventory records are adjusted, and the order is delivered.

Whether a company uses a manual or an electronic order processing system depends on which method provides greater speed and accuracy within cost limits. Manual processing suffices for small-volume orders and can be more flexible in certain situations. Most companies, however, use **electronic data interchange (EDI)**, which uses computer technology to integrate order processing with production, inventory, accounting, and transportation. Within the supply chain, EDI functions as an information system that links marketing channel members and outsourcing firms together. It boosts accuracy, reduces paperwork for all members of the supply chain, and allows them to share information on invoices, orders, payments, inquiries, and scheduling. Many companies encourage suppliers to adopt EDI to reduce distribution costs and cycle times.

14-5b Inventory Management

Inventory management involves developing and maintaining adequate assortments of products to meet customers' needs. It is a key component of any effective logistics system. Inventory decisions have a major impact on logistics costs and the level of customer service provided. When too few products are carried in inventory, the result is *stockouts*, or shortages of products. Stockouts can result in customer dissatisfaction that leads to lower sales, even loss of customers and brand switching. On the other hand, when a firm maintains too many products (especially too many low-turnover products) in inventory, costs increase, as do risks of product obsolescence, pilferage, and damage. The objective of inventory management is to minimize inventory

order processing The receipt and transmission of sales order information

electronic data interchange (EDI) A computerized means of integrating order processing with production, inventory, accounting, and transportation

inventory management Developing and maintaining adequate assortments of products to meet customers' needs

costs while maintaining an adequate supply of goods to satisfy customers. To achieve this objective, marketers focus on two major issues: when to order and how much to order.

To determine when to order, a marketer calculates the *reorder point:* the inventory level that signals the need to place a new order. To calculate the reorder point, the marketer must know the order lead time, the usage rate, and the amount of safety stock required. The *order lead time* refers to the average time lapse between placing the order and receiving it. The *usage rate* is the rate at which a product's inventory is used or sold during a specific time period. *Safety stock* is the amount of extra inventory a firm keeps to guard against stockouts resulting from above-average usage rates and/or longer-than-expected lead times. The reorder point can be calculated using the following formula:

$$\text{Reorder Point} = (\text{Order Lead Time} \times \text{Usage Rate}) + \text{Safety Stock}$$

Thus, if order lead time is 10 days, usage rate is 3 units per day, and safety stock is 20 units, the reorder point is 50 units.

Efficient inventory management with accurate reorder points is crucial for firms that use a **just-in-time (JIT)** approach, in which supplies arrive just as they are needed for use in production or for resale. Companies that use JIT (sometimes referred to as *lean distribution*) can maintain low inventory levels and purchase products and materials in small quantities only when needed. Usually there is no safety stock in a JIT system. Suppliers are expected to provide consistently high-quality products exactly when they are needed. JIT inventory management requires a high level of coordination between producers and suppliers, but it eliminates waste and reduces inventory costs. This approach is popular among many well-known firms, including Toyota, Dell Computer, and Harley-Davidson. More recently, Trinity Health, which operates 94 U.S. hospitals, began to apply JIT distribution methods to save an estimated $20 million in inventory carrying costs and improvements in supply chain efficiency with the help of 3PL partner XPO Logistics.[30] When a JIT approach is used in a supply chain, suppliers may move operations close to their major customers in order to provide goods as quickly as possible.

14-5c Materials Handling

Materials handling, the physical handling of tangible goods, supplies, and resources, is an important factor in warehouse operations, as well as in transportation from points of production to points of consumption. Efficient procedures and techniques for materials handling minimize inventory management costs, reduce the number of times a good is handled, improve customer service, and increase customer satisfaction. Systems for packaging, labeling, loading, and movement must be coordinated to minimize costs and maximize customer satisfaction.

Increasingly, companies are using **radio frequency identification (RFID)** —a wireless system composed of tags and readers which use radio waves to communicate information (tags communicate to readers)—through every phase of handling. The types of readers can include handheld readers, door portals, and overhead readers. RFID has greatly improved shipment tracking and reduced cycle times. It's also used in inventory control, equipment tracking, personnel tracking, asset tracking, and manufacturing. It can also be used in preventing distribution of counterfeit drugs and medical devices as well as diverted product. Hundreds of RFID tags can be read at a time, which represents an advantage over barcodes. Firms are discovering that RFID technology has very broad applications. Inditex, for example, uses RFID chips inside the larger security tags of its clothes in more than 2,000 Zara stores in 48 countries. When an item is sold, the RFID tag records the time and orders an identical product from the company's stockroom. This has streamlined the inventory process and made inventory management easier.[31] The growth of omni-channel marketing and the need for organizations to be more accurate than ever with inventory has led to rapid adoption. The increase in sharing data among the entire supply chain and the many potential solutions for RFID tags will continue to support the growth of this technology.[32]

Product characteristics often determine handling. For example, the characteristics of bulk liquids and gases dictate how they can be moved and stored. Internal packaging is also an

just-in-time (JIT) An inventory management approach in which supplies arrive just when needed for production or resale

materials handling Physical handling of tangible goods, supplies, and resources

radio frequency identification (RFID) Using tags and readers that use radio waves to identify and track tagged materials

Challenges in Supply Chain Management

	Over the past 3 years	Over the next 5 years
Increasing volatility of customer demand	37%	21%
Increasing consumer expectations about customer service/product quality	32%	28%
Increasing cost pressure in logistics/transportation	30%	25%
Increasing pressure from global competition	27%	35%
Increasing volatility of commodity prices	25%	24%
Increasingly complex patterns of customer demand	24%	27%
Increasing financial volatility (eg. currency fluctuations, higher inflation)	22%	24%
Increasingly global markets for labor and talent, including rising wage rates	17%	23%
Growing exposure to differing regulatory requirements in the areas where we operate	14%	24%
Increasing complexity in supplier landscape	14%	15%
Increasing environmental concerns	12%	21%
Geopolitical instability	2%	7%

SNAPSHOT

Source: McKinsey & Company Survey, n=639, respondents who answered "other" or "don't know" are not shown.

important consideration in materials handling—goods must be packaged correctly to prevent damage or breakage during handling and transportation. Many companies employ packaging consultants during the product design process to help them decide which packaging materials and methods will result in the most efficient handling.

Unit loading and containerization are two common methods used in materials handling. With *unit loading*, one or more boxes are placed on a pallet or skid. These units can then be loaded efficiently by mechanical means, such as forklifts, trucks, or conveyer systems. *Containerization* is the consolidation of many items into a single, large container that is sealed at its point of origin and opened at its destination. Containers are usually 8 feet wide, 8 feet high, and 10 to 40 feet long. Their uniform size means they can be stacked and shipped via train, barge, or ship. Once containers reach their destinations, wheel assemblies can be added to make them suitable for ground transportation by truck. Because individual items are not handled in transit, containerization greatly increases efficiency and security in shipping.

14-5d **Warehousing**

Warehousing, the design and operation of facilities for storing and moving goods, is another important logistics function. Warehousing provides time utility by enabling firms to compensate for dissimilar production and consumption rates. When mass production creates a greater stock of goods than can be sold immediately, companies warehouse the surplus until customers are ready to buy it. Warehousing also helps to stabilize prices and to facilitate the availability of seasonal items. The advertisement for Magaya, a logistics software company that provides software for managing inventory in warehouses, highlights the importance of effective inventory management. The image of a worker carrying boxes clearly marked fragile illustrates the importance of effective inventory management systems that minimize product handling and maximize efficient warehouse operations.

Choosing appropriate warehouse facilities is an important strategic consideration because these facilities allow a company to reduce transportation and inventory costs and improve service to customers. The wrong type of warehouse can lead to inefficient logistics and added costs. Warehouses fall into two general categories: private and public. In many cases, a combination of private and public facilities provides the most flexible warehousing approach.

Companies operate **private warehouses** for shipping and storing their own products. A firm usually leases or purchases a private warehouse when its warehousing needs in a given geographic market are substantial and stable enough to warrant a long-term commitment to a fixed facility. Private warehouses are also appropriate for firms that require special handling and storage and that want control of warehouse design and operation. Retailers such as Sears find it economical to integrate private warehousing with purchasing and distribution for their retail outlets. When sales volumes are fairly stable, ownership and control of a private warehouse may be most convenient and offer cost benefits. Private warehouses, however, face fixed costs, such as insurance, taxes, maintenance, and debt expense. They limit firms' flexibility if they wish to move inventories to different locations. Many private warehouses are being eliminated by direct links between producers and customers, reduced cycle times, and outsourcing to third-party logistics firms with warehousing services.

warehousing The design and operation of facilities for storing and moving goods

private warehouses Company-operated facilities for storing and shipping their own products

Public warehouses lease storage space and related logistics facilities to other companies. They sometimes provide distribution services, such as receiving, unloading, inspecting, filling orders, financing, displaying products, and coordinating shipments. Distribution Unlimited Inc., for example, offers a wide range of such services through its facilities in New York, which contain more than 8 million square feet of warehouse space.[33] Public warehouses are especially useful to firms that have seasonal production or demand, low-volume storage needs, and inventories that must be maintained in many locations. They are also useful for firms that are testing or entering new markets or require additional storage space. Additionally, public warehouses serve as collection points during product recall programs. Whereas private warehouses have fixed costs, public warehouses offer variable (and possibly lower) costs because users rent space and purchase warehousing services only as needed.

Many public warehouses furnish security for products that are used as collateral for loans, a service provided at either the warehouse or the site of the owner's inventory. *Field public warehouses* are established by public warehouses at the owner's inventory location. The warehouser becomes custodian of the products and issues a receipt that can be used as collateral for a loan. Public warehouses also provide *bonded storage*, a warehousing arrangement in which imported or taxable products are not released until the products' owners pay U.S. customs duties, taxes, or other fees. Bonded warehouses enable firms to defer tax payments on such items until they are delivered to customers.

Distribution centers are large facilities used for receiving, warehousing, and redistributing products to stores or customers. They are specially designed for rapid flow of products and are usually one-story buildings with access to transportation networks, such as major highways and/or railway lines. Many distribution centers are automated, with computer-directed robots, forklifts, and hoists that collect and move products to loading docks. Amazon, for example, relies on "fulfillment centers" around the world, each using robots, computer systems, and hundreds of employees to process and fulfill customer orders.[34] Distribution over large geographic areas can be complicated, and having strategically located distribution centers can help a company meet consumer demand. Even Walmart had to build more distribution centers to accommodate a greater number of online sales as it positioned itself to compete directly with Amazon, especially in terms of next-day delivery.[35] Although some public warehouses offer such specialized services, most distribution centers are privately owned. They serve customers in regional markets and, in some cases, function as consolidation points for a company's branch warehouses.

Warehousing and Inventory Management
Magaya helps firms manage their warehouse operations efficiently.

14-5e **Transportation**

Transportation, the movement of products from where they are made to intermediaries and end users, is the most expensive logistics function. Transportation costs in the United States reached $907 billion, 62.6 percent of total logistics activities' costs.[36] Because product availability and timely deliveries depend on transportation functions, transportation decisions directly affect customer service. In some cases, a firm may choose to build its distribution and marketing strategy around a unique transportation system if that system can ensure on-time deliveries and give the firm a competitive edge. Companies may build their own transportation fleets (private carriers) or outsource the transportation function to a common or contract carrier.

public warehouses Storage space and related logistics facilities that can be leased by companies

distribution centers Large, centralized warehouses that focus on moving rather than storing goods

transportation The movement of products from where they are made to intermediaries and end users

Transportation Modes

The basic transportation modes for moving physical goods are railroads, trucks, waterways, airways, and pipelines. Each has distinct advantages. Many companies adopt physical handling procedures that facilitate the use of two or more modes in combination. Table 14.3 gives more detail on the characteristics of each transportation mode.

Railroads such as Union Pacific and Canadian National carry heavy, bulky freight that must be shipped long distances over land. Railroads commonly haul minerals, sand, lumber, chemicals, and farm products, as well as automobiles and low-value manufactured goods. Railroads are especially efficient for transporting full carloads, which can be shipped at lower rates than smaller quantities, because they require less handling. Many companies locate factories or warehouses near rail lines for convenient loading and unloading.

Trucks provide the most flexible schedules and routes of all major transportation modes in the United States, because they can go almost anywhere. Because trucks do not have to conform to a set schedule and can move goods from factory or warehouse to customer, wherever there are roads, they are often used in conjunction with other forms of transport that cannot provide door-to-door deliveries, such as waterways and railroads. Trucks are more expensive and somewhat more vulnerable to bad weather than trains. They are also subject to size and weight restrictions on the loads they carry. Trucks are sometimes criticized for high levels of loss and damage to freight and for delays caused by the rehandling of small shipments.

Waterways are the cheapest method of shipping heavy, low-value, nonperishable goods. Water carriers offer considerable capacity. Powered by tugboats and towboats, barges that travel along intra-coastal canals, inland rivers, and navigation systems can haul at least 10 times the weight of one rail car, and oceangoing vessels can haul thousands of containers. The vast majority of international cargo is transported by water at least part of the way. However, many markets are inaccessible by water transportation, and shipping must be supplemented by rail or truck. Droughts and floods also may create difficulties for users of inland waterway transportation. Nevertheless, the growing need to transport goods long distances across the globe will likely increase its use in the future.

Air transportation is the fastest but most expensive form of shipping. It is used most often for perishable goods, for high-value and/or low-bulk items, and for products that require quick delivery over long distances. Some air carriers transport combinations of passengers, freight, and mail. Despite its expense, air transit can reduce warehousing and packaging costs and losses from theft and damage, thus helping the aggregate cost of the mode. Although air

Table 14.3   Characteristics and Ratings of Transportation Modes by Selection Criteria

Selection Criteria	Railroads	Trucks	Pipelines	Waterways	Airplanes
Cost	Moderate	High	Low	Very low	Very high
Speed	Average	Fast	Slow	Very slow	Very fast
Dependability	Average	High	High	Average	High
Load flexibility	High	Average	Very low	Very high	Low
Accessibility	High	Very high	Very limited	Limited	Average
Frequency	Low	High	Very high	Very low	Average
Products carried	Coal, grain, lumber, paper and pulp products, chemicals	Clothing, computers, books, groceries and produce, livestock	Oil, processed coal, natural gas	Chemicals, bauxite, grain, motor vehicles, agricultural implements	Flowers, food (highly perishable), technical instruments, emergency parts and equipment, overnight mail

transport accounts for a small minority of total cargo carried, it is an important form of transportation in an increasingly time-sensitive business environment.[37] In fact, the success of many businesses is now based on the availability of overnight air delivery service provided by such organizations as UPS, FedEx, DHL, RPS Air, and the U.S. Postal Service. Many firms offer overnight or same-day shipping to customers.

Pipelines, the most automated transportation mode, usually belong to the shipper and carry the shipper's products. Most pipelines carry petroleum products or chemicals. Slurry pipelines carry pulverized coal, grain, or wood chips suspended in water. Pipelines move products slowly but continuously and at relatively low cost. They are dependable and minimize the problems of product damage and theft. However, contents are subject to as much as 1 percent shrinkage, usually from evaporation—which can result in profit losses. Pipelines also have been a concern to environmentalists, who fear that pipelines disrupt animals' migratory routes and that leaks can harm plants and animals and threaten water quality.

Choosing Transportation Modes

Logistics managers select a transportation mode based on the combination of cost, speed, dependability, load flexibility, accessibility, and frequency that is most appropriate for their products and generates the desired level of customer service. Table 14.3 shows relative ratings of each transportation mode by these selection criteria.

intermodal transportation
Two or more transportation modes used in combination

Marketers compare alternative transportation modes to determine whether the benefits from a more expensive mode are worth the higher costs. A firm wishing to establish international distribution may consider a large logistics firm for its vast network of global partners. Expeditors International, for instance, has 16,000 associates in 331 locations throughout the world. The company provides tailored solutions and integrated information systems to perform supply chain management functions at locations around the globe.[38] Look at the MercuryGate International advertisement—it is an international logistics company that helps firms identify the optimal modes of transportation for distributing their products around the world. You can see from the advertisement that MercuryGate International offers a transportation management system for developing seamless global distribution using all available options, including air, rail, and trucks.

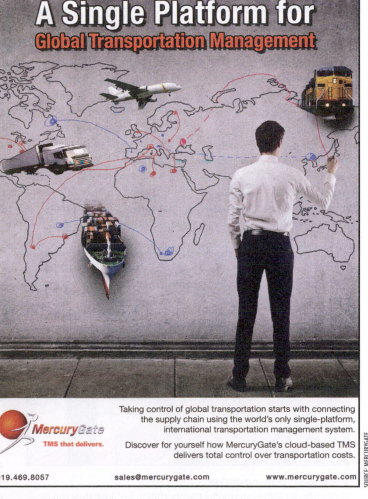

Transportation Modes
A logistics company such as MercuryGate International can help firms to develop efficient distribution that utilizes available modes of transportation.

Coordinating Transportation

To take advantage of the benefits offered by various transportation modes and compensate for shortcomings, marketers often combine and coordinate two or more modes. **Intermodal transportation** is easier than ever because of developments within the transportation industry. It combines the flexibility of trucking with the low cost or speed of other forms of transport. Containerization facilitates intermodal transportation by consolidating shipments into sealed containers for transport by *piggyback* (using truck trailers and railway flatcars), *fishyback* (using water carriers), and *birdyback* (using air carriers). As transportation costs have increased and firms seek to find the most efficient methods possible, intermodal shipping has gained popularity.

Specialized outsourcing agencies provide other forms of transport coordination. Known as **freight forwarders**, these firms combine shipments from several organizations into efficient lot sizes. Small loads (less than 500 pounds) are much more expensive to ship than full carloads or truckloads and may make shipping cost-prohibitive for smaller firms. Freight forwarders help such firms by consolidating small loads from various organizations to allow them to qualify collectively for lower rates. Freight forwarders' profits come from the margin between the higher rates firms would have to pay and the lower carload rates the freight forwarder pays for full loads. Because large shipments also require less handling, freight forwarders can reduce delivery time and the likelihood of shipment damage. Freight forwarders also have the insight to determine the most efficient carriers and routes and are useful for shipping goods to foreign markets. Shipping firms such as UPS and FedEx offer freight-forwarding services, as do dedicated freight forwarders such as Vista Global Logistics or Worldwide Express. Some companies may prefer to outsource their shipping to freight forwarders because the forwarders provide door-to-door service.

Another transportation innovation is the development of **megacarriers**, freight transportation companies that offer several shipment methods, including rail, truck, and air service. Prior to the development of megacarriers, transportation companies generally only specialized in one mode. To compete with megacarriers, air carriers have increased their ground transportation services. As the range of transportation alternatives expands, carriers also put greater emphasis on customer service in order to gain a competitive advantage.

Learning Objective 14-6

Examine legal issues in channel management.

freight forwarders Organizations that consolidate shipments from several firms into efficient lot sizes

megacarriers Freight transportation firms that provide several modes of shipment

14-6 LEGAL ISSUES IN CHANNEL MANAGEMENT

The numerous federal, state, and local laws governing distribution channel management in the United States are based on the principle that the public is best served by protecting competition and free trade. Under the authority of such federal legislation as the Sherman Antitrust Act and the Federal Trade Commission Act, courts and regulatory agencies determine under what circumstances channel management practices violate this underlying principle and must be restricted. Although channel managers are not expected to be legal experts, they should be aware that attempts to control distribution functions might have legal repercussions. When shipping internationally, managers must also be aware of international laws and regulations that might affect their distribution activities. The following practices are among those frequently subject to legal restraint.

Intermodal Transportation
Containers facilitate intermodal transportation because they can be transported by ships, trains, and trucks.

14-6a Restricted Sales Territories

To tighten control over product distribution, a manufacturer may try to prohibit intermediaries from selling outside of designated sales territories. Intermediaries themselves often favor this practice, because it provides them with exclusive territories where they can minimize competition. Over the years, the courts have adopted conflicting positions in regard to restricted sales territories. Although the courts have deemed restricted sales territories a restraint of trade among intermediaries handling the same brands (except for small or newly established companies), they have also held that exclusive territories can actually promote competition among dealers handling different brands. At present, the producer's intent in establishing restricted territories and the overall effect of doing so on the market must be evaluated for each individual case.

14-6b Tying Agreements

When a supplier (usually a manufacturer or franchiser) furnishes a product to a channel member with the stipulation that the channel member must purchase other products as well, it has negotiated a **tying agreement**. Suppliers may institute tying agreements as a means of getting rid of slow-moving inventory, or a franchiser may tie the purchase of equipment and supplies to the sale of franchises, justifying the policy as necessary for quality control and protection of the franchiser's reputation.

A related practice is *full-line forcing*, in which a supplier requires that channel members purchase the supplier's entire line to obtain any of the supplier's products. Manufacturers sometimes use full-line forcing to ensure that intermediaries accept new products and that a suitable range of products is available to customers.

The courts accept tying agreements when the supplier is the only firm able to provide products of a certain quality, when the intermediary is free to carry competing products as well, and when a company has just entered the market. Most other tying agreements are considered illegal.

14-6c Exclusive Dealing

When a manufacturer forbids an intermediary to carry products of competing manufacturers, the arrangement is called **exclusive dealing**. Manufacturers receive considerable market protection in an exclusive-dealing arrangement and may cut off shipments to intermediaries that violate the agreement.

The legality of an exclusive-dealing contract is determined by applying three tests. If the exclusive dealing blocks competitors from as much as 15 percent of the market, the sales volume is large, and the producer is considerably larger than the retailer, then the arrangement is considered anticompetitive. If dealers and customers in a given market have access to similar products or if the exclusive-dealing contract strengthens an otherwise weak competitor, the arrangement is allowed.

14-6d Refusal to Deal

For nearly a century, courts have held that producers have the right to choose or reject the channel members with which they will do business. Within existing distribution channels, however, suppliers may not legally refuse to deal with wholesalers or dealers merely because these wholesalers or dealers resist policies that are anticompetitive or in restraint of trade. Suppliers are further prohibited from organizing some channel members in refusal-to-deal actions against other members that choose not to comply with illegal policies.

tying agreement An agreement in which a supplier furnishes a product to a channel member with the stipulation that the channel member must purchase other products as well

exclusive dealing A situation in which a manufacturer forbids an intermediary from carrying products of competing manufacturers

Summary

14-1 Describe the foundations of supply chain management.

The distribution component of the marketing mix focuses on the decisions and activities involved in making products available to customers when and where they want to purchase them. An important function of distribution is the joint effort of all involved organizations to be part of creating an effective supply chain, which includes all the organizations and activities involved with the flow and transformation of products from raw materials through to the end customer. Operations management is the total set of managerial activities used by an organization to transform resource inputs into goods, services, or both. Logistics management involves planning, implementing, and controlling the efficient and effective flow and storage of goods, services, and information from the point of origin to consumption in order to meet customers' needs and wants. Procurement in its broadest form refers to the processes that enable the progress of value from raw material to final customer and back to redesign and final disposition. Supply chain management (SCM) refers to the coordination of all the activities involved with the flow and transformation of supplies, products, and information throughout the supply chain to the ultimate consumer. It integrates the functions of operations management, logistics management, procurement, and marketing channel management so that goods and services are produced and distributed in the right quantities, to the right locations, and at the right time. The supply chain includes all entities—shippers and other firms that facilitate distribution, as well as producers, wholesalers, and retailers—that distribute products and benefit from cooperative efforts.

14-2 Explain the role and significance of marketing channels and supply chains.

A marketing channel, or channel of distribution, is a group of individuals and organizations that direct the flow of products from producers to customers. The major role of marketing channels is to make products available at the right time, at the right place, and in the right amounts. In most channels of distribution, producers and consumers are linked by marketing intermediaries. The two major types of intermediaries are retailers, which purchase products and resell them to ultimate consumers, and wholesalers, which buy and resell products to other wholesalers, retailers, and business customers.

Marketing channels serve many functions. They create time, place, and possession utilities by making products available when and where customers want them and by providing customers with access to product use through sale or rental. Marketing intermediaries facilitate exchange efficiencies, often reducing the costs of exchanges by performing certain services and functions. Although some critics suggest eliminating wholesalers, the functions of the intermediaries in the marketing channel must be performed. As such, eliminating one or more intermediaries results in other organizations in the channel having to do more. Because intermediaries serve both producers and buyers, they reduce the total number of transactions that otherwise would be needed to move products from producer to the end customer.

Channels of distribution are broadly classified as channels for consumer products and channels for business products. Within these two broad categories, different channels are used for different products. Although consumer goods can move directly from producer to consumers, consumer channels that include wholesalers and retailers are usually more economical and knowledge-efficient. Distribution of business products differs from that of consumer products in the types of channels used. A direct distribution channel is common in business marketing. Also used are channels containing industrial distributors, manufacturers' agents, and a combination of agents and distributors. Most producers have

multichannel distribution systems that can be adjusted for various target markets.

A strategic channel alliance exists when the products of one firm are distributed through the marketing channels of another. Multichannel distribution—the use of a variety of marketing channels to ensure maximum distribution—is increasingly used to reach target customers wherever and whenever they may choose to interact with a company or its products. Some products use digital distribution to deliver content through the internet to a computer or other device. It is important to recognize that the line between different marketing channels is becoming increasingly blurred.

Selecting an appropriate marketing channel is a crucial decision for supply chain managers. To determine which channel is most appropriate, managers must think about customer characteristics, the type of organization, product attributes, competition, environmental forces, and the availability and characteristics of intermediaries. Careful consideration of these factors will assist a supply chain manager in selecting the correct channel.

14-3 Identify the intensity of market coverage.

A marketing channel is managed such that products receive appropriate market coverage. In choosing intensive distribution, producers strive to make a product available to all possible dealers. In selective distribution, only some outlets in an area are chosen to distribute a product. Exclusive distribution usually gives a single dealer rights to sell a product in a large geographic area.

14-4 Explore strategic issues in marketing channels, including leadership, cooperation, and conflict.

Each channel member performs a different role in the system and agrees to accept certain rights, responsibilities, rewards, and sanctions for nonconformance. Although many marketing channels are determined by consensus, some are organized and controlled by a single leader, or channel captain. A channel captain may be a producer, wholesaler, or retailer. A marketing channel functions most effectively when members cooperate. When they deviate from their roles, channel conflict can arise.

Integration of marketing channels brings various activities under one channel member's management. Vertical integration combines two or more stages of the channel under one management. The vertical marketing system (VMS) is managed centrally for the mutual benefit of all channel members. Vertical marketing systems may be corporate, administered, or contractual. Horizontal integration combines institutions at the same level of channel operation under a single management.

14-5 Explain logistics as being a part of supply chain management.

Logistics, involving physical distribution, relates to planning, implementing, and controlling the efficient flow and storage of products. Physical distribution is an important part of logistics and includes activities used to move products from producers to customers and other end users. These activities include order processing, inventory management, materials handling, warehousing, and transportation. An efficient logistics system is an important component of an overall marketing strategy because it can decrease costs and increase customer satisfaction. Within the marketing channel, logistics activities are often performed by a wholesaler, but they may also be performed by a producer or retailer or outsourced to a third party. Third-party logistics (3PL) firms have special expertise in core logistics activities such as warehousing, transportation, inventory management, and information technology and can often perform these activities more efficiently. Efficient logistics systems can decrease costs and transit time while increasing customer service.

Order processing is the series of steps from receipt of a sales order to the successful delivery of the product or service. It consists of three main tasks—order entry, order handling, and order delivery—that may be done manually but are more often handled through electronic data interchange (EDI) systems. Inventory management involves developing and maintaining adequate assortments of products to meet customers' needs. Logistics managers must strive to find the optimal level of inventory to satisfy customer needs while keeping costs down. Materials handling, the physical handling of products, is a crucial element in warehousing and transporting products. Radio frequency identification (RFID) uses radio waves to identify and track materials tagged with special microchips through every phase of handling. Warehousing involves the design and operation of facilities for storing and moving goods. Such facilities may be privately owned or public. Transportation, the movement of products from where they are made to where they are purchased and used, is the most expensive logistics function. The basic modes of transporting goods include railroads, trucks, waterways, airways, and pipelines.

14-6 Examine legal issues in channel management.

Federal, state, and local laws regulate channel management to protect competition and free trade. Courts may prohibit or permit a practice depending on whether it violates this underlying principle. Channel management practices frequently subject to legal restraint include restricted sales territories, tying agreements, exclusive dealing, and refusal to deal. When these practices strengthen weak competitors or increase competition among dealers, they may be permitted. In most other cases, when competition may be weakened considerably, they are deemed illegal.

Important Terms

distribution 396
supply chain 396
procurement 396
sourcing 396
purchasing 396
recycling 396
logistics management 396
operations management 397
supply chain management (SCM) 397
marketing channel 399
marketing intermediaries 399

industrial distributor 404
strategic channel alliance 406
multichannel distribution 406
digital distribution 406
intensive distribution 409
selective distribution 410
exclusive distribution 410
channel captain 413
channel power 413
vertical channel integration 415

vertical marketing system (VMS) 415
horizontal channel integration 416
third-party logistics (3PL) firm 416
cycle time 417
order processing 418
electronic data interchange (EDI) 418
inventory management 418
just-in-time (JIT) 419
materials handling 419

radio frequency identification (RFID) 419
warehousing 420
private warehouses 420
public warehouses 421
distribution centers 421
transportation 421
intermodal transportation 423
freight forwarders 424
megacarriers 424
tying agreement 425
exclusive dealing 425

Discussion and Review Questions

1. Define supply chain management. Why is it important?
2. Describe the major functions of marketing channels. Why are these functions better accomplished through combined efforts of channel members?
3. List several reasons consumers often blame intermediaries for distribution inefficiencies.
4. Compare and contrast the four major types of marketing channels for consumer products. Through which

type of channel is each of the following products most likely to be distributed?

    a. New automobiles
    b. Saltine crackers
    c. Cut-your-own Christmas trees
    d. New textbooks
    e. Sofas
    f. Soft drinks

5. Outline the four most common channels for business products. Describe the products or situations that lead marketers to choose each channel.

6. Describe an industrial distributor. What types of products are marketed through an industrial distributor?

7. Under what conditions is a producer most likely to use more than one marketing channel?

8. Identify and describe the factors that may influence marketing channel selection decisions.

9. Explain the differences among intensive, selective, and exclusive methods of distribution.

10. "Channel cooperation requires that members support the overall channel goals to achieve individual goals." Comment on this statement.

11. Explain the major characteristics of each of the three types of vertical marketing systems (VMSs): corporate, administered, and contractual.

12. Discuss the cost and service trade-offs involved in developing a logistics system.

13. What are the main tasks involved in order processing?

14. Explain the trade-offs that inventory managers face when they reorder products or supplies. How is the reorder point computed?

15. Explain the major differences between private and public warehouses. How do they differ from a distribution center?

16. Compare and contrast the five major transportation modes in terms of cost, speed, and dependability.

17. Under what conditions are tying agreements, exclusive dealing, and refusal-to-deal judged illegal?

Developing Your Marketing Plan

One of the key components in a successful marketing strategy is the plan for getting the products to your customer. To make the best decisions about where, when, and how your products will be made available to the customer, you need to know more about how these distribution decisions relate to other marketing-mix elements in your marketing plan. To assist you in relating the information in this chapter to your marketing plan, consider the following issues:

1. Marketing intermediaries perform many activities. Using Table 14.1 as a guide, discuss the types of activities for which a channel member could provide needed assistance.

2. Using Figure 14.3 (or 14.4 if your product is a business product), determine which of the channel distribution paths is most appropriate for your product. Given the nature of your product, could it be distributed through more than one of these paths?

3. Determine the level of distribution intensity that is appropriate for your product. Consider the characteristics of your target market(s), the product attributes, and environmental factors in your deliberation.

4. Discuss the physical functions that will be required for distributing your product, focusing on materials handling, warehousing, and transportation.

Video Case 14.1

The Cocoa Exchange's Sweet Spot in the Supply Chain

In May 2017, Mars, Incorporated, the world's largest chocolate company, announced the launch of a new stand-alone subsidiary called The Cocoa Exchange. While Mars focuses on mass producing products like Snickers and M&M'S that are available in all distribution channels, The Cocoa Exchange aims to sell exclusive and premium chocolate products directly to consumers through a commission-based sales force under three product lines: Pod & Bean, Dove Signature, and Pure Dark. The Cocoa Exchange's mission is to create incremental, noncannibalizing growth for Mars through niche products targeting individual consumers rather than the mass market. The company accomplishes this by creating supply chain efficiencies, thanks to its parent company, and using the direct selling business model. Direct selling can be a more relational, customized form of selling and allows for even greater market reach and segmentation.

Procurement is one of the most important, mutually beneficial aspects of the Mars and The Cocoa Exchange relationship. Chocolate is made from cocoa, which can only be grown in very few places around the world. The Cocoa Exchange sources most of its cocoa from farmers in developing countries like the Ivory Coast and Ghana in West Africa. Most of these farms are family run with the women of the family doing most of the work. Harvesting cocoa begins by removing ripened pods from the trunk and branches of a cocoa tree. Next, the pods are opened and cocoa beans are removed. Afterward, beans are fermented and dried before they can be processed into chocolate. The Cocoa Exchange has the benefit of using Mars' robust supply chain. The Cocoa Exchange is able to source their cocoa beans directly from farmers, just like Mars. However, once production of the chocolate products is complete, The Cocoa Exchange uses independent contractors and the go-to-market strategy is selling directly to customers. This is different from Mars, which uses marketing intermediaries like wholesalers and retailers. The Cocoa Exchange's goal is to make specialty chocolate products, such as Pod & Bean Cappuccino Caramel S'mores or Dove Signature Sea Salt Caramel Collection that appeal to a much more targeted slice of the market. Having less-intense market coverage adds to the exclusivity of the company's premium products and adds more allure to the luxury brand.

The concept of marketing and selling directly to the consumer, through an independent contractor salesforce, is called direct selling. The Cocoa Exchange embraces the direct selling model and has created a commission-based labor force called "curators" to sell its products through in-house parties. Party attendees can sample a range of products from The Cocoa Exchange and purchase the products they like online. Curators receive a 25 to 40 percent commission on products sold from their individual online store and gain access to exclusive discounts of up to 50 percent depending on performance. Curators also have the opportunity to increase their earning power by building and training a team, receiving 3 to 5 percent commission on team sales. The Cocoa Exchange subsidizes the starter kits and curators host parties and provide free shipping on the items ordered. Additionally, as curators' sales grow, they earn credits they can use to shop. The company also ships products directly to the consumer, so curators aren't burdened with inventory management and protection. Premium chocolates and other Cocoa Exchange products are carefully handled so that they arrive fresh and in "mint" condition. Direct selling encourages an entrepreneurial spirit in their chocolate sellers, allows The Cocoa Exchange to find new customers, and helps the company maintain a robust and efficient supply chain.

Businesses are continually putting more emphasis on environmental issues, and The Cocoa Exchange is no exception. The company believes that sustainability has to be at the heart of everything they do, especially as they are invested in the agricultural industry. Demand continues to grow for chocolate, especially in developing parts of the world like India. However, sourcing cocoa sustainably is limited because the crop can only grow in certain areas near the equator. Because of these challenges, The Cocoa Exchange aims to improve conditions for farmers so that they can create a larger supply of cocoa. By partnering with the humanitarian group, CARE, whose goal is to end global poverty, The Cocoa Exchange aims to establish Savings & Loan Associations in West African villages to give farmers more access to capital and the ability to improve their business skills. Additionally, Mars has made a commitment to only using certified sources of cocoa. By investing in the suppliers from which The Cocoa Exchange sources and purchases its chocolate, the company has greater influence over the sustainability of its supply chain.

The Cocoa Exchange is a unique company designed to sell premium and exclusive chocolate and unique food products directly to consumers. As a subsidiary of Mars, Incorporated, The Cocoa Exchange benefits from an established supply chain where it can align all of the resources necessary to create luxury chocolate products and food items. Distribution through its direct selling channel allows curators to receive commissions on the products they distribute to customers. The Cocoa Exchange also puts a strong emphasis on the sustainability of cocoa sourcing. In addition, by partnering with Care and helping rural farmers set up loans and build capital, The Cocoa Exchange helps to increase the supply of cocoa and improve sustainability.[39]

Questions for Discussion

1. How is The Cocoa Exchange different than its parent company (Mars, Inc.)?
2. What are the benefits of the direct selling model? How does this impact the supply chain?
3. How are The Cocoa Exchange's sustainability efforts impactful?

Case 14.2

ADM: The Link from Farm to Table

Archer Daniels Midland (ADM), one of the world's largest agricultural processors, is a vital link between farm, factory, and table. The Chicago-based multinational rings up almost $62 billion in annual net sales of soybeans, corn, gluten, and other agricultural products provided by farmers worldwide. ADM's focus on agriculture and energy requires the adjustment of organizational behavior while operating in a very dynamic and competitive environment. External forces such as changes in technology related to innovation in the supply chain, online purchasing, and digital marketing are complex and require changes in tactics and strategy to help its supply chain operate efficiently. Its vast network of processing plants and distribution centers as well as its extensive transportation network must all work together.

ADM's clients include several well-known companies. Unilever, for instance, purchases oil from soybeans procured and processed by ADM. Unilever uses this oil to produce its mayonnaise products. As ADM's executives know, Unilever and other clients are concerned with more than just price. To stay ahead of demand for sustainable agricultural processes, ADM has partnered with Unilever to enroll its farmers in the Iowa Sustainable Soy Fieldprint Project to monitor factors such as soil conservation and land use. In the project's first year, 43 farms with land totaling more than 44,000 acres were enrolled. ADM also introduced a cost-share initiative to soybean farmers in Iowa to increase the pool of farms with sustainably grown soybeans and provide financial assistance to farmers. These efforts to deliberately structure operations and behaviors in anticipation of environmental forces are a good example of planned change. The initiative works hand-in-hand with Unilever's Sustainable Living Plan, which includes a commitment to source all agricultural raw materials sustainably in the coming years. These factors make ADM an ideal soybean oil supplier for Unilever's Hellmann's mayonnaise. The emphasis on documentation allows companies like Unilever to measure progress and improvements, making it easier for all parties in the supply chain to communicate with customers and stakeholders.

KATHERINE WELLES/SHUTTERSTOCK.COM

To support its global operations and growth, ADM buys from 220,000 suppliers and processes more than 2.5 million payments yearly. The company also manages a vast land, water, and rail transportation network to ensure that raw materials and processed products arrive when and where scheduled. Such a large organization requires ADM's management to make changes that may impact company stakeholders both positively and negatively. Recently, ADM announced internal organizational changes likely to encounter resistance. The firm planned a series of layoffs to streamline the company's efforts and redistribute resources as it struggled with its grain trading business. The agricultural giant employs about 32,000 employees in more than 170 countries, with more than 4,000 in Decatur, Illinois. ADM Chairman and CEO Juan Luciano spoke to shareholders about cutting costs and selling assets as a way to make a "strong recovery." Additionally, the company closed its energy trading operations and changed staff in its Switzerland office, which handles commodities such as wheat and soybeans. ADM emailed affected employees to tell them about the decision and claims it is handling layoffs respectfully with consideration for employees. One way it is trying to overcome resistance is by offering some eligible employees early retirement. If these changes continue, ADM will have to work hard to overcome resistance from employees as it introduces incremental changes and makes small adjustments to fine-tune the organization.

An excess of corn, soybeans, and wheat has disrupted the supply chain. Many farmers have chosen to store grain to wait for better profits, and some food companies are placing smaller orders because prices are low. In response to these changing external forces, ADM is also making changes to its product lines. As part of its ever-changing nature, the company recently introduced Nutriance, a new range of wheat protein concentrates that are vegetarian and vegan-friendly—a business market in which it sees great potential for future profit. The increase in consumers following a more holistic approach to their health has been an ongoing external force that has prompted ADM to expand its portfolio to meet the needs of health-conscious consumers. Looking ahead, ADM is exploring natural flavors and nutritional ingredients such as protein and vitamins. By recognizing potential new areas of profitability, ADM demonstrates that it is carefully monitoring the external environment and changing accordingly.[40]

Questions for Discussion

1. How has the oversupply of grain impacted the supply chain?
2. Describe how Archer Daniels Midland can diversify its portfolio to protect itself from external forces?
3. How is Archer Daniels Midland staying ahead of demand for sustainable agriculture?

CHAPTER

15

Retailing, Direct Marketing, and Wholesaling

LEARNING OBJECTIVES

15-1 Explain the purpose and function of retailers in the marketing channel.

15-2 Describe online retailing and explain how it is changing the field of retailing.

15-3 Classify the major types of retailers.

15-4 Explore strategic issues in retailing.

15-5 Identify the various forms of direct marketing, direct selling, and vending.

15-6 Explain the nature and functions of wholesalers.

HELEN89/SHUTTERSTOCK.COM

Like Treasure Hunts? TJX Is Looking for You

At a time when many consumers choose to buy with a click or a swipe, crowds still search for bargains in the aisles of T.J. Maxx, Marshalls, HomeGoods, and HomeSense. T.J. Maxx and Marshalls both feature name-brand clothing for men, women, and children, as well as household goods like specialty foods and linens. HomeGoods and HomeSense offer an ever-changing array of decorative accessories, casual furniture, and other home merchandise. All four retailers are owned by TJX, a Massachusetts-based company that buys out-of-season branded fashions and limited-run merchandise, prices items low for quick resale, and sends frequent shipments of fresh merchandise to its branches. In all, TJX rings up $33 billion in annual revenue through 3,800 stores worldwide.

The company's idea is to get price-conscious consumers excited about the "treasure hunt" aspect of the in-person shopping experience. Consumers never know exactly what specially priced merchandise will be in stock when they walk through the door. They do know that prices will be well below what they'd pay in a department or specialty store. They also know that new items come and go so quickly that if they don't buy something when they first see it, it will likely be sold out the next time they stop in.

TJX has aggressive global expansion plans, opening hundreds of new stores year after year even as full-priced retailers like department stores are closing stores. Within a few years, the company expects to be operating 5,600 stores around the world, attracting consumers who like roaming the aisles in their hunt for bargains.[1]

Retailers like T.J. Maxx and HomeGoods are the most visible and accessible marketing channel members to consumers. They represent an important link in the marketing channel because they are both marketers for, and customers of, producers and wholesalers. They perform many supply chain functions, such as buying, selling, grading, risk taking, and developing and maintaining information databases about customers. Retailers are in a strategic position to develop relationships with consumers and partnerships with producers and intermediaries in the marketing channel.

In this chapter, we examine the nature of retailing, direct marketing, and wholesaling and their roles in supplying consumers with goods and services. First, we explore the growing use of online retailing. Then, we identify the major types of retail stores and explore strategic issues in retailing: location, franchising, retail technology, retail positioning, store image, and category management. Next, we discuss direct marketing, including catalog marketing, direct-response marketing, telemarketing, and television home shopping. We also explore direct selling and vending. Finally, we examine the importance of wholesalers in marketing channels, including their functions and classifications.

Learning Objective 15-1

Explain the purpose and function of retailers in the marketing channel.

15-1 RETAILING

Retailing includes all transactions in which the buyer is the ultimate consumer and intends to use the product for personal, family, or household purposes. A **retailer** is an organization that purchases products for the purpose of reselling them to ultimate consumers. Although most retailers' sales are made directly to the consumer, nonretail transactions occur occasionally when retailers sell products to other businesses. Retailing is vital to the U.S. economy. Every time you buy a meal, a smartphone, a movie ticket, or some other product from a retailer, the money you spend flows through the economy to the store's employees, to the government, and to other businesses and consumers. There are more than 1 million retail establishments in the United States, and they employ nearly 16 million people. Retailers contribute $1.1 trillion, or 5.9 percent, directly to the U.S. gross domestic product.[2]

Retailers add value for customers by providing services and assisting in making product selections. They can enhance customers' perceptions of the value of products by making buyers' shopping experiences easier or more convenient, such as by providing free delivery or offering a mobile shopping option. Retailers can facilitate comparison shopping, which allows customers to evaluate different options. For instance, car dealerships often cluster in the same general vicinity, as do furniture stores. The internet also allows consumers to comparison shop easily. Product value is also enhanced when retailers offer services, such as technical advice, delivery, credit, and repair. Finally, retail sales personnel are trained to be able to demonstrate to customers how products can satisfy their needs or solve problems.

Retailers can add significant value to the supply chain, representing a critical link between producers and ultimate consumers by providing the environment in which exchanges occur. Retailers play a major role in creating time, place, and possession and, in some cases, form utility. They perform marketing functions that benefit ultimate consumers by making available broad arrays of products that can satisfy their needs.

Historically, retail stores have offered consumers a place to browse and compare merchandise to find just what they need. However, such traditional retailing is evolving to meet changing consumer demographics and buying behavior and is adopting new technologies to improve the shopping experience. Many retailers now engage in **multichannel retailing** by employing multiple distribution channels that complement their brick-and-mortar stores with websites, catalogs, and apps where consumers can research products, read other buyers' reviews, and make actual purchases. The most effective multichannel retail strategies integrate the firm's goals, products, systems, and technologies seamlessly across all platforms. They make it possible for a customer to research a product through the firm's website at home, find specific information about the product and locate the nearest one through an app on their smartphone while in the car, and checkout in a store or online. Regardless of platform, the key to success in retailing is to have a strong customer focus with a retail strategy that provides the level of

retailing All transactions in which the buyer intends to consume the product through personal, family, or household use

retailer An organization that purchases products for the purpose of reselling them to ultimate consumers

multichannel retailing Employing multiple distribution channels that complement brick-and-mortar stores with websites, catalogs, and apps where consumers can research products, read other buyers' reviews, and make actual purchases

service, product quality, and innovation that consumers desire. New store formats, service innovations, and advances in information technology have helped retailers to serve customers better. For example, through Domino's AnyWare program, regular customers who have set up profiles with the firm can text or tweet a pizza slice emoji, ask Alexa or Google Home, send a message through some smart TVs and automobiles, use the company's app, or call their local Domino's store, and their favorite regular order will be promptly delivered.[3]

Retailing is also increasingly international. In particular, many retailers see significant growth potential in international markets. The market for a product category such as cell phones is mature in North America and Europe. However, demand remains strong in places like India, China, and Brazil. These countries all have large, relatively new middle classes with consumers hungry for goods and services. In India, for example, the fast-growing middle class with rising disposable income has led companies like Amazon, IKEA, Tesla, and McDonald's to enter the market or expand operations there.[4] Many major U.S. retailers have international outlets in order to capitalize on international growth. On the other hand, international retailers, such as Aldi, Uniqlo, and Zara, have also found receptive markets in the United States.

online retailing Retailing that makes products available to buyers through computer connections

Learning Objective 15-2

Describe online retailing and explain how it is changing the field of retailing.

15-2 ONLINE RETAILING

A significant factor in the rise of multichannel retailing is **online retailing**, which makes products available to buyers through internet connections. Online retailing is a rapidly growing segment that most retailers now view as vital to their businesses. Worldwide, online retailing has been growing at an average annual rate of 20 percent, and online sales are projected to grow from $2.3 trillion to $4.5 trillion by 2022.[5] Online retail sales in the United States are expected to pass $1 trillion by 2027, up from $445 billion in 2017, and they account for 12 percent of all U.S. sales as well as 50 percent of sales growth in the last year.[6] Amazon—shown in the advertisement—is arguably the best-known online retailer, with net sales in excess of $177 billion. The company has branched out from selling books and electronics to fashion and groceries, as well as streaming movies. As shown in the advertisement, Amazon is promoting its ability to deliver fashionable clothes, shoes, and accessories in the familiar Smile boxes.

Online retailing satisfies an increasing expectation among consumers to have multiple channels available to obtain the goods and services they desire at their convenience. Consumers can perform a wide variety of shopping-related tasks online, including purchasing virtually anything they wish. They can track down rare collectibles, refill their eyeglass prescriptions, and even purchase high-end jewelry or their weekly groceries. They can have their purchases delivered to their homes or offices or pick them up at the nearest store, often at curbside. Consider that online grocery shopping is the fastest growing form of retail, especially among millennials. Supermarket chains from Meijer and H-E-B to Target and Costco are now assembling customers' grocery list items for them to pick up

Amazon Fashion

Style, Delivered

Online Retailers
While Amazon sells primarily online, a number of other companies combine online marketing with other forms of retailing.

ENTREPRENEURSHIP IN MARKETING

Maiden Home Furniture Focuses on Quality, Customer Education, and Transparency

When Nidhi Kapur went shopping for living-room furniture that was stylish, crafted to last, and priced for mid-range budgets, she stumbled on a potential marketing opportunity. Kapur and her husband didn't want to spend thousands of dollars on a custom-upholstered chair or sofa. She also had questions about where each item was made, who made it, and how well it was made. Frustrated after visiting numerous showrooms and browsing popular furniture websites, she decided to found Maiden Home Furniture as an online retailer of furniture that is distinctively designed, reasonably priced, made in America, and ready in six weeks or less.

Kapur spent two years researching suppliers, studying competitors, designing products, and polishing her marketing plan before launching her business in 2017. By selling made-to-order furniture directly to consumers via a branded website, rather than stocking merchandise in a brick-and-mortar store, she kept costs down and allowed buyers to choose their own styles, colors, and fabrics. She added a 30-day money-back guarantee to reassure customers that complete satisfaction was her company's goal.

In addition, Kapur set aside space on the Maiden Home website to present detailed information about product quality and the craftspeople who produce each piece of furniture in the hills of North Carolina. Educating customers about hardwoods and fabric, and introducing the craftspeople who actually work on the furniture, is a key element of her retail strategy. "My generation demands transparency," Kapur explains. "We would love to buy products from a skilled artisan and know how our products are made."[a]

or have them delivered for a small fee.[7] Retailers frequently offer exclusive online sales, or may reward customers who visit their websites or use their apps with special in-store coupons and other promotions and discounts. Banks and brokerages offer consumers access to their accounts, where they can perform a wide variety of activities, such as money transfers and stock trading.

Some firms that were primarily catalog retailers are now primarily online retailers, such as Paul Frederick, which sells men's apparel and accessories online and does not sell in stores. Brick-and-mortar stores, like Lowe's, increasingly offer all their products through their websites for the convenience of their customers. Indeed, stores increasingly offer more merchandise on their websites than they stock in stores, allowing them to maintain availability of slower moving goods and out-of-season items that some customers still desire to purchase. And some online retailers, like Warby Parker, Casper, and Untuckit, have opened brick-and-mortar stores in strategic locations to gain exposure for their brands, obtain more insights into shoppers' behavior, and sell products wherever their customers want to buy them.[8] With ongoing advances in computer technology and consumers ever more pressed for time, online retailing will continue to escalate.

Learning Objective 15-3

Classify the major types of retailers.

15-3 BRICK-AND-MORTAR RETAILERS

The reality is that evolving consumer demographics and preferences are spurring retailers to adapt in a variety of ways that are blurring the line between the various types of retailers more than ever before. Consider that most shoppers now research products online and then head to the nearest store to make the actual purchase—a practice sometimes called *webrooming*. For most consumers, there is no clear line between the brick-and-mortar store, the store's website, and its app, and they move back and forth depending on their circumstances and desires. Online retailer Amazon has blurred the line even further by opening its own brick-and-mortar grocery store in Seattle, where a sophisticated system using cameras, microphones, and the Amazon

Go app lets shoppers enter, pick up their items, and leave without actually passing through a checkout stand.[9]

Many types of brick-and-mortar retail stores exist. One way to classify them is by the breadth of products they offer. Two general categories include general-merchandise retailers and specialty retailers.

15-3a General-Merchandise Retailers

A retail establishment that offers a variety of product lines that are stocked in considerable depth is referred to as a **general-merchandise retailer**. The types of product offerings, mixes of customer services, and operating styles of retailers in this category vary considerably. The primary types of general-merchandise retailers are department stores, discount stores, convenience stores, supermarkets, superstores, hypermarkets, warehouse clubs, and warehouse showrooms (see Table 15.1).

general-merchandise retailer
A retail establishment that offers a variety of product lines that are stocked in considerable depth

department stores Large retail organizations characterized by a wide product mix and organized into separate departments to facilitate marketing efforts and internal management

Department Stores

Department stores are large retail organizations with at least 25 employees that are characterized by wide product mixes. To facilitate marketing efforts and internal management in these stores, department stores like Macy's, Kohl's, and Nordstrom organize related product lines into separate departments such as cosmetics, housewares, apparel, home furnishings, and appliances. This arrangement facilitates marketing and internal management. Often, each department functions as a self-contained business, and buyers for individual departments are fairly autonomous in their decision making.

Department Stores
Department stores like Nordstrom offer a wide variety of product lines.

Table 15.1 General-Merchandise Retailers

Type of Retailer	Description	Examples
Department store	Large organization offering a wide product mix and organized into separate departments	Macy's, Kohl's, JCPenney
Discount store	Self-service, general-merchandise store offering brand-name and private-brand products at low prices	Walmart, Target, Dollar General
Convenience store	Small, self-service store offering narrow product assortment in convenient locations	7-Eleven
Supermarket	Self-service store offering complete line of food products and some non-food products	Kroger, Safeway, Publix
Superstore	Giant outlet offering all food and non-food products found in supermarkets, as well as most routinely purchased products	Walmart Supercenters, SuperTarget
Hypermarket	Combination supermarket and discount store; larger than a superstore	Carrefour
Warehouse club	Large-scale, members-only establishments combining cash-and-carry wholesaling with discount retailing	Sam's Club, Costco
Warehouse showroom	Facility in a large, low-cost building with large on-premises inventories and minimal service	IKEA

At typical department stores, a large proportion of sales comes from apparel, accessories, and cosmetics. These stores carry a broad assortment of other products as well, including luggage, electronics, home accessories, and sports equipment. Some department stores offer additional services such as automobile insurance, hair care, income tax preparation, and travel and optical services. In some cases, the department store leases space for these specialized services to other businesses, with proprietors managing their own operations and paying rent to the store. Most department stores also sell products through websites, which can service customers who live in smaller markets where no stores are located or who prefer to shop online or through apps.

Department stores are distinctly service-oriented. Their total product may include credit, delivery, personal assistance, merchandise returns, and a pleasant atmosphere. Although some so-called department stores are actually large, departmentalized specialty stores, most department stores are shopping stores. Consumers can compare price, quality, and service at one store with those at competing stores. Along with large discount stores, department stores are often considered retailing leaders in a community and are found in most places with populations of more than 50,000. However, in recent years, department stores have faced intense competition from discount stores and online retailing, and many chains have closed stores to reduce costs.

Discount Stores

Discount stores are self-service, general-merchandise outlets that regularly offer brand-name and private-brand products at low prices. Discounters accept lower profit margins than conventional retailers in exchange for high sales volume. To keep inventory turnover high, they carry a wide but carefully selected assortment of products, from appliances to housewares to clothing. Major discount establishments also offer food products, toys, automotive services, garden supplies, and sports equipment.

Walmart and Target have grown to become not only the largest discount stores in the country, but also some of the largest retailers in the world. Walmart is the world's largest retailer, with revenues almost seven times higher than Target, which is ranked thirteenth in retail sales.[10] Not all discounters are large and international, however. Some, such as Meijer Inc., which has stores in the Midwestern United States, are regional discounters. Most discount stores operate in large (50,000 to 80,000 square feet), no-frills facilities. They usually offer everyday low prices (discussed in Chapter 20), rather than relying on sales events.

Discount retailing developed on a large scale in the early 1950s, when postwar production caught up with strong consumer demand for goods. At first, they were often cash-only operations in warehouse districts, offering goods at savings of 20 to 30 percent over conventional retailers. Facing increased competition from department stores and other discount stores, some discounters improved store services, atmosphere, and location. Some also raised prices, blurring the distinction between discount store and department store. Consider Target, which has grown more upscale in appearance and offerings over the years. It regularly launches new brands like Magnolia Home's Hearth & Hand, and it has updated with more creative displays and eye-catching signage.[11] Target also offers fresh, organic groceries, a pharmacy, and trendy clothing, home goods, and electronics. These adjustments to the firm's strategy are designed to appeal to its customers, who are generally younger and have higher incomes than patrons of rival stores.

As conventional discount stores have grown larger and pricier in recent years, low-income and thrifty consumers have turned to extreme-value stores (also known as dollar stores and single-price stores). **Extreme-value stores** are a fraction of the size of conventional discount stores and typically offer very low prices—generally $1 to $10—on smaller size name-brand nonperishable household items. Dollar General, Dollar Tree, and 99¢ Only Stores offer lower per unit prices than discount stores but often charge considerably more when priced per ounce than stores whose customers can afford to stock up on supersized items.

discount stores Self-service, general-merchandise stores that offer brand-name and private-brand products at low prices

extreme-value stores Retailers that are a fraction of the size of conventional discount stores and typically offer very low prices on smaller size name-brand nonperishable household items

Convenience Stores

A **convenience store** is a small, self-service store that is open long hours and carries a narrow assortment of products, usually convenience items such as soft drinks and other beverages, snacks, newspapers, tobacco, and gasoline, as well as services such as ATMs. According to the National Association of Convenience Stores, there are more than 154,000 convenience stores in the United States alone, which together serve 160 million customers daily.[12] They are typically less than 5,000 square feet, open 24 hours a day and 7 days a week, and stock about 500 items. The convenience store concept was developed in 1927 when Southland Ice in Dallas began stocking basics like milk and eggs along with ice for iceboxes to serve customers who wanted to replenish their supplies. In addition to national chains, there are many family-owned independent convenience stores.

Supermarkets

Supermarkets are large, self-service stores that carry a complete line of food products and some non-food items such as cosmetics and nonprescription drugs. Supermarkets are arranged by department for maximum efficiency in stocking and handling products, but have central check-out facilities. They offer lower prices than smaller neighborhood grocery stores, usually provide free parking, and may also provide services such as check cashing, pharmacies, and curbside pickup of groceries.

Consumers make the majority of all their grocery purchases in supermarkets. However, increased availability of grocery items at discount stores, premium markets, other competitors, and online have eroded supermarkets' market share of the grocery segment. As mentioned earlier, online retailers have reduced the need to go to grocery stores and have put pressure on supermarkets to increase marketing efforts and make shopping more convenient. Meal kits like Blue Apron have also cut into supermarket sales. Retailers like H-E-B, Whole Foods, and Costco have responded by partnering with Instacart to provide personal shopping and pick-up or delivery services in many metropolitan areas. Increasingly, stores like Safeway and Publix are offering their own delivery or curbside pickup services. Whole Foods and Kroger are testing their own meal kits.[13]

Another type of supermarket that may take back market share from discount stores is the *hard discounter*. Hard discounters maintain a no-frills environment and have a minimal assortment of goods they can sell at very low prices. These supermarkets first emerged in Europe. Now German grocery chains Aldi and Lidl have expanded outside of Europe and into the United States.

Superstores

Superstores, which originated in Europe, are giant retail outlets that carry not only the food and non-food products ordinarily found in supermarkets, but routinely purchased consumer products such as housewares, hardware, small appliances, clothing, and personal-care products as well. Superstores combine features of discount stores and supermarkets and generally carry about four times as many items as supermarkets. Superstores also offer additional services, including dry cleaning, automotive repair, check cashing, and bill paying. Examples include Walmart Supercenters, some Kroger stores, SuperTarget stores, and Meijer.

To cut handling and inventory costs, superstores use sophisticated operating techniques and often have tall shelving that displays entire assortments of products. Superstores can have an area of as much as 200,000 square feet (compared with 20,000 square feet in traditional supermarkets). Sales volume is typically two to three times that of supermarkets, partly because locations near good transportation networks help generate the in-store traffic needed for profitability.

convenience store A small self-service store that is open long hours and carries a narrow assortment of products, usually convenience items

supermarkets Large, self-service stores that carry a complete line of food products, along with some non-food items

superstores Giant retail outlets that carry food and non-food products found in supermarkets, as well as most routinely purchased consumer products

Hypermarkets

Hypermarkets combine supermarket and discount store shopping in one location. Larger than superstores, they range from 225,000 to 325,000 square feet and offer 45,000 to 60,000 different types of low-priced products. They commonly allocate 40 to 50 percent of their space to grocery products and the remainder to general merchandise, including apparel, appliances, housewares, jewelry, hardware, and automotive supplies. Many also lease space to noncompeting businesses, such as banks, optical shops, and fast-food restaurants. All hypermarkets focus on low prices and vast selections.

Retailers have struggled with making the hypermarket concept successful in the United States. Although Kmart, Walmart, and Carrefour have operated hypermarkets in the United States, most of these stores ultimately closed. Such stores may be too large for time-constrained U.S. shoppers. Hypermarkets have been somewhat more popular in Europe, South America, Mexico, the Middle East, and parts of Asia.

Warehouse Clubs

Warehouse clubs, a rapidly growing form of mass merchandising, are large-scale, members-only operations that combine cash-and-carry wholesaling with discount retailing. Sometimes called *buying clubs*, warehouse clubs offer the same types of products as discount stores but in a limited range of sizes and styles. Whereas most discount stores carry around 40,000 items, a warehouse club handles only 3,500 to 5,000 products, usually brand leaders. Sam's Club stores, for example, stock about 4,000 items. Costco currently leads the warehouse club industry with sales of more than $126 billion. Sam's Club is second with around $57 billion in store sales.[14] These establishments offer a broad product mix, including food, beverages, books, appliances, housewares, automotive parts, hardware, and furniture.

To keep prices lower than those of supermarkets and discount stores, warehouse clubs offer few services. They also keep advertising to a minimum. Their facilities, frequently located in industrial areas, have concrete floors and aisles wide enough for forklifts. Merchandise is stacked on pallets or displayed on pipe racks. Customers must perform some marketing functions, like transportation of purchases, themselves. Warehouse clubs appeal to price-conscious consumers and small retailers unable to obtain wholesaling services from large distributors.

hypermarkets Stores that combine supermarket and discount store shopping in one location

warehouse clubs Large-scale, members-only establishments that combine features of cash-and-carry wholesaling with discount retailing

warehouse showrooms Retail facilities in large, low-cost buildings with large on-premises inventories and minimal services

Warehouse Showrooms

Warehouse showrooms are retail facilities with five basic characteristics: large, low-cost buildings, warehouse materials-handling technology, vertical merchandise displays, large on-premises inventories, and minimal services. IKEA, a Swedish company that is the world's largest furniture retailer, sells furniture, household goods, and kitchen accessories in warehouse showrooms and through catalogs around the world. These high-volume, low-overhead operations offer few services and retain few personnel. Lower costs are possible at warehouse showrooms because some marketing functions have been shifted to consumers, who must transport, finance, and perhaps assemble products. Most consumers carry away purchases in the manufacturer's carton, although stores will deliver for a fee.

15-3b **Specialty Retailers**

In contrast to general-merchandise retailers with their broad product mixes, specialty retailers emphasize narrow and deep assortments. Despite

Warehouse Clubs
Sam's Club is a warehouse club that has a wide product mix with limited depth.

their name, specialty retailers do not sell specialty items (except when specialty goods complement the overall product mix). Instead, they offer substantial assortments in a few product lines. We examine three types of specialty retailers: traditional specialty retailers, category killers, and off-price retailers.

Traditional Specialty Retailers

Traditional specialty retailers are stores that carry a narrow product mix with deep product lines. Sometimes called *limited-line retailers*, they may be referred to as *single-line retailers* if they carry unusual depth in one product category. Specialty retailers commonly sell such shopping products as apparel, jewelry, sporting goods, fabrics, computers, and pet supplies. The Limited, Gap, Sunglass Hut, and Foot Locker are examples of retailers offering limited product lines but great depth within those lines.

Because they are usually small, specialty stores may have high costs in proportion to sales, and satisfying customers may require carrying some products with low turnover rates. Successful specialty stores understand their customers and know what products to carry, which reduces the risk of unsold merchandise. Specialty stores usually offer better selections and more sales expertise than department stores, their main competitors. By capitalizing on fashion trends, service, personnel, atmosphere, and location, specialty retailers position themselves strategically to attract customers in specific market segments.

Category Killers

A more recent kind of specialty retailer is called the **category killer**, which is a very large specialty store that concentrates on a major product category and competes on the basis of low prices and broad product availability. These stores are referred to as category killers because they expand rapidly and gain sizable market shares, taking business away from smaller, higher-cost retail outlets. Examples of category killers include Home Depot and Lowe's (home improvement), Staples (office supply), Barnes & Noble (bookseller), Petco and PetSmart (pet supply), and Best Buy (consumer electronics). The advertisement for Home Depot emphasizes the firm's deep paint product lines, promoting that its paint experts can match any color with the very best paint. The ad also reminds customers that its prices are "unbeatable." However, just as category killers took business away from traditional specialty retailers by competing largely on price, online retailing has taken market share away from category killers in recent years.

Off-Price Retailers

Off-price retailers are stores that buy manufacturers' seconds, overruns, returns, and off-season production runs at below-wholesale prices for resale to consumers at deep discounts. Unlike true discount stores, which pay regular wholesale prices for goods and usually carry second-line brand names, off-price retailers offer limited lines of national-brand and designer merchandise, usually clothing, shoes, or housewares. Consumers appreciate the ability to purchase name-brand goods at discounted prices, and sales at off-price retailers, such as T.J. Maxx, Marshalls, Stein Mart, and Burlington Coat Factory,

traditional specialty retailers Stores that carry a narrow product mix with deep product lines

category killer A very large specialty store that concentrates on a major product category and competes on the basis of low prices and product availability

off-price retailers Stores that buy manufacturers' seconds, overruns, returns, and off-season merchandise for resale to consumers at deep discounts

Category Killer
Home Depot is an example of a category killer.

SOURCE: HOME DEPOT

have grown. Off-price retailers typically perform well in recessionary times, as consumers who want to own name-brand items search for good value.

Off-price stores charge 20 to 50 percent less than department stores for comparable merchandise but offer few customer services. They often feature community dressing rooms and central checkout counters. Some of these stores do not take returns or allow exchanges. Off-price stores may or may not sell goods with the original labels intact. They turn over their inventory up to a dozen times per year, three times as often as traditional specialty stores. They compete with department stores for many of the same price-conscious customers who are knowledgeable about brand names.

To ensure a regular flow of merchandise into their stores, off-price retailers establish long-term relationships with suppliers that can provide large quantities of goods at reduced prices. Manufacturers may approach retailers with samples, discontinued products, or items that have not sold well. Also, off-price retailers may seek out manufacturers, offering to pay cash for goods produced during the manufacturers' off-season. Although manufacturers benefit from such arrangements, they also risk alienating their specialty and department store customers. Department stores tolerate off-price stores as long as they do not advertise brand names, limit merchandise to last season's or lower-quality items, and are located away from the department stores. When off-price retailers obtain large stocks of in-season, top-quality merchandise, tension builds between department stores and manufacturers. The success of off-price retailers has led some department stores like Macy's to open their own off-price retail stores. Macy's is adding Macy's Backstage outlets inside select Macy's department stores. These stores-within-the store will sell merchandise at sharp discounts.[15]

Learning Objective 15-4

Explore strategic issues in retailing.

15-4 STRATEGIC ISSUES IN RETAILING

Whereas most business purchases are based on economic planning and necessity, consumer purchases are likely to be influenced by social and psychological factors. Because consumers shop for various reasons—to search for specific items, alleviate boredom, or learn about something new—retailers must do more than simply fill space with merchandise. They must make desired products available, create stimulating shopping environments, and develop marketing strategies that increase store patronage. In this section, we discuss how store location, franchising, retail technologies, retail positioning, store image, and category management are used strategically by retailers.

15-4a Location of Retail Stores

You have likely heard the phrase "Location, location, location," commonly used in the real estate business. Location is also critical to business success. Making a good location decision is even more important because, once decided, it is the least flexible variable of the marketing mix. Location is an important strategic decision that dictates the limited geographic trading area from which a store draws its customers. Retailers consider various factors when evaluating potential locations, including position of the firm's target market within the trading area, kinds of products being sold, availability of

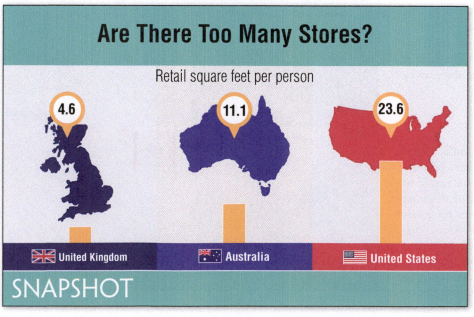

Are There Too Many Stores?

Retail square feet per person

4.6 — United Kingdom
11.1 — Australia
23.6 — United States

SNAPSHOT

Source: PwC, Quartz, and Financial Times.

public transportation, customer characteristics, and placement of competitors' stores. Increasingly, companies use marketing analytics of big data collected from their marketing information systems to identify optimal locations for new stores.

In choosing a location, a retailer must obviously consider the rental, leasing, or ownership terms of a potential property as well as the characteristics of the site itself. They research the types of stores in the area and the size, shape, and visibility of the lot or building under consideration. They usually evaluate the relative ease of movement to and from the site, including factors such as pedestrian and vehicular traffic, parking, and transportation. Retailers should look for compatibility with nearby retailers because stores that complement one another draw more customers with similar product needs for everyone.

Some retailers choose to locate in central business districts, whereas others prefer sites within shopping centers. Some retailers, including Walmart, Home Depot, and many fast-food restaurants, opt for freestanding structures that are not connected to other buildings, but may be located within planned shopping centers. Sometimes, retailers choose to locate in less orthodox settings where competition will be lower and where consumers have fewer other options. Pop-ups—which are located inside another retailer, stand alone, or at special events for just a few days or weeks—can generate consumer buzz and help restaurateurs and specialty retailers determine if there is sufficient interest in their concept before investing significant resources in a conventional space. Another cost-saving strategy is sharing a single store with a compatible retailer, which may enable multiple small retailers to afford a storefront in a more desirable location. In some parts of the United States, food trucks, sometimes organized into outdoor food courts, have become popular and may provide a less expensive opportunity to grow a small business.

There are several different types of shopping centers, including neighborhood, community, regional, superregional, lifestyle, power, and outlet centers. **Neighborhood shopping centers**, also called *strip malls,* usually consist of several small convenience and specialty stores, such as small grocery stores, gas stations, and fast-food restaurants. These retailers consider their target markets to be consumers who live within two to three miles of their stores, or 10 minutes' driving time. Because most purchases are based on convenience or personal contact, stores within a neighborhood shopping center generally do not coordinate selling efforts. Generally, product mixes consist of essential products, and depth of the product lines is limited. **Community shopping centers** include one or two department stores and some specialty stores, as well as convenience stores. They draw consumers looking for shopping and specialty

neighborhood shopping center
A type of shopping center usually consisting of several small convenience and specialty stores

community shopping center
A type of shopping center with one or two department stores, some specialty stores, and convenience stores

CREATIVE MARKETING

Pop-Up Stores: Now You See Them, Now You Don't

Pop-up retailing is big business, accounting for an estimated $50 billion in annual sales. Yet until recently, shopping centers rarely welcomed these temporary shops, preferring to sign long-term deals with established retail brands. Now, with online retailing gaining momentum, malls are inviting pop-ups to join the mix for a limited time, in a bid to fill empty spaces, build traffic, and add variety to the shopping experience.

Simon Property Group, the largest U.S. mall company, is welcoming an ever-revolving set of short-term pop-ups through a program known as "The Edit." Every three months, a different group of pop-ups opens in a Simon shopping center, adding an eclectic mix of brands and products to complement the existing roster of permanent stores. In Simon's Roosevelt

Field Shopping Center, for example, The Edit occupies a separate area where consumers are encouraged to browse and discover new products and new retail concepts, only steps from traditional anchor stores like Neiman Marcus, Nordstrom, and Bloomingdale's.

The Washington Prime Group, which operates malls from coast to coast, is also introducing a special marketplace for pop-up shops. Called "Tangible," the marketplace provides temporary retail space for e-commerce companies and for big brands that want to test new products or new markets. The idea is to add a fresh dimension to the shopping experience and bring consumers back to malls more frequently as they check out the latest pop-ups. For their part, the pop-ups enjoy the benefits of mall traffic and the ability to try something new for a short period.[b]

regional shopping center
A type of shopping center with the largest department stores, widest product mixes, and deepest product lines

superregional shopping center A type of shopping center with the widest and deepest product mixes that attracts customers from many miles away and often have special attractions

lifestyle shopping center
A type of shopping center that is typically open air and features upscale specialty stores, dining, and entertainment

power shopping center
A type of shopping center that combines off-price stores with category killers

products not available in neighborhood shopping centers. Because these offer a wider variety of stores, they serve larger geographic areas and consumers are willing to drive longer distances to community shopping centers to shop. Community shopping centers are planned, and retailer efforts are coordinated to attract shoppers. Special events, such as art exhibits, automobile shows, and sidewalk sales, stimulate traffic. Managers of community shopping centers look for tenants that complement the centers' total assortment of products. Such centers have wide product mixes and deep product lines.

Regional shopping centers usually have the largest department stores, widest product mixes, and deepest product lines of all shopping centers. Many shopping malls are regional shopping centers, although some are community shopping centers. With 150,000 or more consumers in their target market, regional shopping centers must have well-coordinated management and marketing activities. Target markets may include consumers traveling from a distance to find products and prices not available in their hometowns. Because of the expense of leasing space in regional shopping centers, tenants are likely to be national chains. Large centers usually advertise, have special events, furnish transportation to some consumer groups (such as seniors), maintain their own security forces, and carefully select the mix of stores. The largest of these centers, sometimes called **superregional shopping centers**, have the widest and deepest product mixes and attract customers from many miles away. Superregional centers often have special attractions beyond stores, such as skating rinks, amusement centers, or upscale restaurants. Mall of America, in the Minneapolis area, is the largest shopping mall in the United States with 520 stores, including Nordstrom and Bloomingdale's, and 50 restaurants. The shopping center also includes a walk-through aquarium, a miniature golf course, a seven-acre Nickelodeon theme park, a sports and virtual reality entertainment center, and a hotel, and the complex holds many special events each year.[16]

With traditional mall sales declining, some shopping center developers are looking to new formats that differ significantly from traditional shopping centers. A **lifestyle shopping center** is typically an open-air shopping center that features upscale specialty stores, dining, and entertainment, most usually owned by national chains. Like San Jose's Santana Row, they are often located near affluent neighborhoods and may have fountains, benches, and other amenities that encourage "casual browsing." Often resembling traditional "Main Street" shopping districts, lifestyle centers feature appealing architectural design and are designed to foster consumer loyalty by creating a sense of place. Some lifestyle shopping centers, like the Domain in Austin, Texas, include residences above the stores. To attract a wide variety of people, this type of center is designed to facilitate numerous types of activities and cultural events.

Some shopping center developers are bypassing the traditional department store anchor and combining off-price stores and small stores with category killers in **power shopping center** formats. These centers may be anchored by popular stores, such as the Gap, T.J. Maxx, PetSmart, and Home Depot. Power shopping centers can take a variety of formats, all vying for the same retail dollar.

Factory outlet malls feature discount and factory outlet stores carrying traditional manufacturer brands, such as Polo Ralph Lauren, Nike, and Guess. The advertisement promotes Tanger Outlets, which operates more than 40 factory outlet malls. This advertisement displays the

Factory Outlet Mall
Stores in factory outlet malls feature well-known brands, such as Banana Republic, and offer discounted prices.

many brands and factory outlet stores shoppers can find at a typical Tanger Outlet mall, such as Banana Republic, American Eagle Outfitters, and Under Armour. Many outlet centers feature upscale products from last season, discounted for quick sale. Manufacturers own these stores and make a special effort to avoid conflict with traditional retailers of their products. Manufacturers place these stores in noncompetitive locations, often outside of metropolitan areas. Factory outlet centers attract value-conscious customers seeking quality and major brand names. They operate in much the same way as regional shopping centers, but usually draw customers, some of whom may be tourists, from a larger shopping radius. Promotional activity is at the heart of these shopping centers. Craft and antique shows, contests, and special events attract a great deal of traffic.

15-4b **Franchising**

In addition to location, retailers need to decide on their form of ownership. You are probably familiar with chains such as Macy's, Red Lobster, and Staples, which own and operate multiple stores in many states. Other retailers are owned and operated as just one or a few stores in a single area, like your favorite locally owned coffee shop. A third form of ownership is **franchising**, an arrangement in which a supplier, or franchisor, grants a dealer, or franchisee, the right to sell products in exchange for some type of consideration. A franchisor such as KFC or Pizza Hut may receive a percentage of total sales in exchange for furnishing equipment, buildings, management know-how, and marketing assistance to the franchisee. The franchisee supplies labor and capital, operates the franchised business, and agrees to abide by the provisions of the franchise agreement. Table 15.2 lists the leading U.S. franchises as well as the types of products they sell and their start-up costs. Steak 'n Shake, shown in the

franchising An arrangement in which a supplier (franchisor) grants a dealer (franchisee) the right to sell products in exchange for some type of consideration

Table 15.2 Top U.S. Franchisors and Their Start-Up Costs

Rank	Franchise and Description	Start-Up Costs
1	**McDonald's** Burgers, chicken, salads, beverages	$1M–2.2M
2	**7-Eleven Inc.** Convenience stores	$38K–1.1M
3	**Dunkin' Donuts** Coffee, donuts	$229K–1.7M
4	**The UPS Store** Shipping and business services	$178K–403K
5	**RE/MAX LLC** Real estate	$38K–225K
6	**Sonic Drive-In Restaurants** Burgers, hot dogs, ice cream, beverages	$1.1M–2.4M
7	**Great Clips** Hair Salons	$137K–258K
8	**Taco Bell** Mexican food	$525K–2.6M
9	**Hardee's** Burgers, chicken, biscuits	$1.4M–1.9M
10	**Sport Clips** Men's hair salons	$189K–355K

Source: "2018 Franchise 500," *Entrepreneur*, https://www.entrepreneur.com/franchise500/2018 (accessed March 26, 2018).

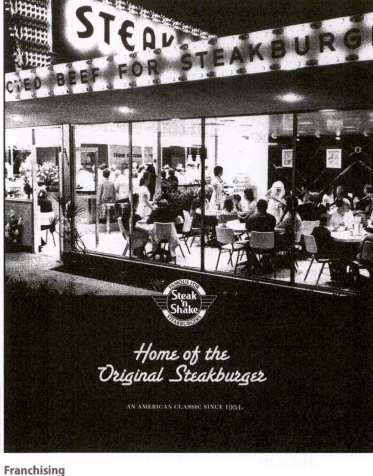

SOURCE: MAXIM MAGAZINE

Franchising
Steak 'n Shake is a fast-food franchise with more than 550 stores.

advertisement, is a hamburger chain that operates some company-owned stores and franchises others. The ad pictures a Steak 'n Shake location and highlights the fact that it has been the "home of the original steakburger" since 1934.

Because of changes in the international marketplace, shifting employment options in the United States, the large U.S. service economy, and corporate interest in more joint-venture activity, franchising is a very popular retail option. There are more than 745,290 franchise establishments in the United States, which provide 7.8 million jobs across a variety of industries, and generate $713 billion in sales.[17]

Franchising offers several advantages to both the franchisee and the franchisor. It enables a franchisee to start a business with limited capital and benefit from the business experience of others. Generally speaking, franchises may be more successful than independent stores because they can build on the established reputation of a national brand. However, franchise failure rates vary greatly depending on the particular franchise. Nationally advertised franchises, such as Subway and Burger King, are often assured of sales as soon as they open because customers already know what to expect. If business problems arise, the franchisee can obtain guidance and advice from the franchisor at little or no cost. Also, the franchisee receives materials to use in local advertising and can benefit from national promotional campaigns sponsored by the franchisor.

Through franchise arrangements, the franchisor gains fast and selective product distribution without incurring the high cost of constructing and operating its own outlets. The franchisor, therefore, has more available capital for expanding production and advertising. It can also ensure, through the franchise agreement, that outlets are maintained and operated according to its own standards. Some franchisors do permit their franchisees to modify their menus, hours, or other operating elements to better match their target market's needs. The franchisor benefits from the fact that the franchisee, being a sole proprietor in most cases, is likely to be very highly motivated to succeed. Success of the franchise means more sales, which translates into higher income for the franchisor.

Franchise arrangements also have several drawbacks. The franchisor can dictate many aspects of the business: décor, menu, design of employees' uniforms, types of signs, hours of operation, and numerous details of business operations. In addition, franchisees must pay to use the franchisor's name, products, and assistance. Usually, there is a one-time franchise fee and continuing royalty and advertising fees, often collected as a percentage of sales. Franchisees often must work very hard, putting in 10 to 12 hours a day, six or seven days a week. In some cases, franchise agreements are not uniform, meaning one franchisee may pay more than another for the same services. Finally, the franchisor gives up a certain amount of control when entering into a franchise agreement with an entrepreneur. Consequently, individual establishments may not be operated exactly according to the franchisor's standards.

15-4c **Retail Technologies**

Today's consumers expect to be able to research and shop for a product wherever and whenever they want—in a mall, subway train, classroom, living room, or anywhere else. Younger shoppers in particular expect retailers to offer convenience, information, and a seamless experience across multiple platforms. Consider Nordstrom, which is famously guided by its mission to "provide a fabulous customer experience by empowering customers and the employees who serve them." The retailer has made strategic investments into technologies such as point-of-sale systems that allow salespeople to view a customer's requests and needs online, an innovation lab, apps, mobile checkout, support for salespeople texting, a cloud-based men's personalized clothing service, and it began to use social media to build relationships with consumers and generate buzz. The firm's websites and apps are integrated with its inventory management control system so that customers can find an item in a store or online and have it delivered to a third place such as their home or office. Mobile checkout lets a salesperson who has been helping a customer in the store check them out on the spot rather than having to look for a register. All of these efforts contribute to Nordstrom's mission and ensure that customers have a great experience across all of the firm's platforms.[18]

There are a number of exciting new technologies designed to improve consumers' shopping experience, whether they are in the store or browsing on their smartphone. Amazon's Go store, as we saw earlier, uses cameras, microphones, and the Amazon Go app to enable shoppers to enter, pick up their items, and leave without passing through a checkout stand. Larger retailers are launching their own apps to draw customers into stores, guide them around, and give them tools for researching and making purchases wherever they may be. Starbucks' app, for example, allows customers to order and pay right from their phone, allowing them to bypass the line, and to accumulate loyalty reward points. Sephora's app offers beauty tips and reminds shoppers about their past purchases in case they need to restock. The app's Virtual Artist uses artificial intelligence and augmented reality to let shoppers "try on" various facial products so they can find the ideal products.[19] Augmented reality technology, now available in more recent smartphones, lets customers of Houzz, Lowe's, and Build.com view products in 3D, which is boosting orders for all three retailers.[20]

Retailers of all sizes can take advantage of technology to improve the store experience for a variety of customers. One way is through the use of *beacons* that can send real-time messages and offers to customers with Bluetooth-enabled smartphones. They are increasingly being used in airports, sports stadiums, hotels, fast-food restaurants, and bank branches. Citibank, for example, is using beacons in some branches to enable some customers after-hours entry using their iPhone or Apple Watch.[21] Beacon technology helps Target's app guide shoppers through Target stores right to the products on their list.[22]

Retailers are investing in a number of exciting new technologies to make shopping exciting or efficient. At some Ralph Lauren and Rebecca Minkoff stores, smart mirrors can improve the dressing room experience by letting customers view clothing in different light and request a clerk bring the item in different colors or sizes without having to leave the dressing room. Soon, they'll be able to purchase the item via their smartphone before leaving the dressing room as well.[23] Virtual fit lets shoppers see how a product, such as eyeglasses, might look on them, using the cameras built into today's computers and smart devices. Self-checkout lets shoppers scan the items in their own shopping cart with their smartphone and pay for the merchandise out of a digital wallet, such as Apple Pay, so they don't have to wait in line. The technology even allows shoppers who subscribe to loyalty programs to get their rewards as they scan their own items.[24]

15-4d **Retail Positioning**

The large variety of shopping centers and the expansion of product offerings by traditional stores, along with the increased use of retail technology, have all contributed to intense retailing competition. Retail positioning is, therefore, an important consideration. **Retail positioning**

retail positioning Identifying an unserved or underserved market segment and serving it through a strategy that distinguishes the retailer from others in the minds of consumers in that segment

involves identifying an unserved or underserved market segment and reaching it through a strategy that distinguishes the retailer from others in the minds of customers in the market segment. For instance, Japan-based Uniqlo is positioned as a retailer of stylish, well-designed, and technologically innovative clothing that is made for all people.[25] This is in contrast to a number of discount and specialty store chains that have positioned themselves to appeal to time- and cash-strapped consumers with convenient locations and layouts as well as low prices. This strategy has helped many retailers gain market share at the expense of large department stores.

15-4e **Store Image**

To attract customers, a retail store must project an image—a functional and psychological picture in the consumer's mind—that appeals to its target market. Store environment, merchandise quality, and service quality are key determinants of store image. **Atmospherics**, the physical elements in a store's design that appeal to consumers' emotions and encourage buying, help to create an image and position a retailer. Retailers can use different elements—music, color, and complexity of layout and merchandise presentation—to influence customer attention, mood, and shopping behavior.

Exterior atmospheric elements include the appearance of the storefront, display windows, store entrances, and degree of traffic congestion. Exterior atmospherics are particularly important to new customers, who tend to base their judgment of an unfamiliar store on its outside appearance and may not ever enter if they feel intimidated by the appearance of the façade or if the location is inconvenient or unhospitable.

Interior atmospheric elements include aesthetic considerations, such as lighting, wall and floor coverings, dressing facilities, and store fixtures. Interior sensory elements contribute significantly to atmosphere. Bars, for example, consider several factors when it comes to atmospherics, including music tempo and volume, lighting, cleanliness, and physical layout. Most bars tend to sell a similar range of products, so they use atmospherics extensively to differentiate themselves and create a unique environment. In order for a bar to be successful and retain customers, it must monitor atmospheric variables and focus on maintaining customer comfort levels, which may vary depending on target audience. Bar patrons tend to be recreationally and socially motivated, rather than task motivated, so the layout must create a sense of flow and spread the crowd to the right places so customers do not feel claustrophobic.[26]

Color can attract shoppers to a retail display. Many fast-food restaurants use bright colors because these have been shown to make customers feel hungrier and eat faster, which increases turnover.[27] For instance, red is associated with impulsivity and hunger, and yellow is associated with feeling good—both of these colors are common in fast-food restaurants. Green, on the other hand, is calming and associated with wellness, so it is more commonly seen in natural foods stores and restaurants.[28] Sound is another important sensory component of atmosphere. A low-end, family dining restaurant might play fast pop music to encourage customers to eat quickly and leave, increasing turnover and sales. A high-end restaurant, on the other hand, will opt to play soft classical music to enhance the

atmospherics The physical elements in a store's design that appeal to consumers' emotions and encourage buying

ISTOCK.COM/ADRIANHANCU

Atmospherics
Atmospherics can greatly influence customers' experiences. The colors, lighting, and spaciousness makes this restaurant attractive and inviting.

experience and encourage patrons to indulge in multiple courses. Retailers may even employ scent, especially food aromas, to attract customers. Most consumers expect the scent of a store to be congruent with the products that are sold there. Thus, Starbucks should smell like its coffee, Panera like its freshly baked bread, and Yankee Candle like its scented candles. Online retailers are not exempt from concern over atmospherics. Studies have demonstrated that such elements as the layout of a site and the content of digital ads that appear on that site can affect consumer mood and shopping behavior.[29]

15-4f Category Management

Category management is a retail strategy of managing groups of similar, often substitutable, products produced by different manufacturers. It first developed in the food industry because supermarkets were concerned about competitive behavior among manufacturers. Supermarkets use category management to allocate space for their many product categories, such as cosmetics, cereals, and soups. The strategy is effective for many different types of retailers. The assortment of merchandise a store chooses through category management is strategic and meant to improve sales and enhance customer satisfaction.

Category management is an important part of developing a collaborative supply chain, which enhances value for customers. Successful category management involves collecting and analyzing data on sales and consumers and sharing the information between the retailer and manufacturer. Walmart, for example, has developed strong supplier relationships with many of its manufacturers, like Procter & Gamble. Collaborative supply chains should designate a single source to develop a system for collecting information on demand, consumer behavior, and optimal product allocations. The key is cooperative interaction between the manufacturers of category products and the retailer to create maximum success for all parties in the supply chain.

15-5 DIRECT MARKETING, DIRECT SELLING, AND VENDING

Learning Objective 15-5
Identify the various forms of direct marketing, direct selling, and vending.

Although retailers are the most visible members of the supply chain, many products are sold outside the confines of a retail store. As we saw earlier, online selling now accounts for a rising percentage of retail sales, but direct selling and direct marketing also account for a huge proportion of the sale of goods globally. Products also may be sold in vending machines, but these account for a very small minority of total retail sales.

15-5a Direct Marketing

Direct marketing is the use of the telephone, internet, and nonpersonal media to communicate product and organizational information to customers, who can then purchase products via mail, telephone, or the internet. Direct marketing is one type of nonstore retailing. Sales through direct marketing activities are significant, accounting for about 8.5 percent of the entire U.S. GDP.[30] Direct marketing can occur through online retailing, catalog marketing, direct-response marketing, telemarketing, and television home shopping.

Catalog Marketing

In **catalog marketing**, an organization provides a catalog from which customers make selections and place orders by mail, telephone, or the internet. Catalog marketing began in 1872, when Montgomery Ward issued its first catalog to rural families. There are thousands of catalog marketing companies in the United States, many of which also publish online. Some catalog marketers sell products spread over multiple product lines, while others are more

category management A retail strategy of managing groups of similar, often substitutable products produced by different manufacturers

direct marketing The use of the telephone, internet, and nonpersonal media to introduce products to customers, who can then purchase them via mail, telephone, or the internet

catalog marketing A type of marketing in which an organization provides a catalog from which customers make selections and place orders by mail, telephone, or the internet

SLEEP 2017

SHARPER IMAGE®

SLEEP SMART & FEEL GREAT

Temperature Regulating Bedding
Page 18

SAVE UP TO 50%
5% 10% 20% 30% 50%
Apply Mystery Coupon code on back
cover for instant savings!

SOURCE: SHARPER IMAGE

Catalog Marketing
Sharper Image utilizes catalog marketing to sell its electronic toys and home goods.

specialized. Take, for example, this catalog cover for the Sharper Image, which highlights the firm's temperature regulating bedding, a product available in the catalog. Sharper Image is a catalog marketer specializing in home electronics and high-tech home goods. The catalog cover shows off some of the products a shopper can find via the catalog or the firm's website.

Many companies, including Lands' End, Pottery Barn, and Crate & Barrel, employ a multichannel strategy and sell via catalogs, online, and through retail stores in major metropolitan areas. These retailers generally offer considerable product depth for just a few lines of products. Still other catalog companies specialize in products from a single product line, such as seeds or automotive parts.

The advantages of catalog retailing include efficiency and convenience for customers because they do not have to visit a store. The retailer benefits by being able to locate in remote, low-cost areas, save on expensive store fixtures, and reduce both personal selling and store operating expenses. On the other hand, catalog retailing is inflexible, provides limited service, and is most effective for a select set of products.

Direct-Response Marketing

Direct-response marketing occurs when a retailer advertises a product and makes it available through mail or telephone orders. Generally, customers use a credit card, but other forms of payment may be permitted. Examples of direct-response marketing include a television commercial offering exercise machines, cosmetics, or household cleaning products available through a toll-free number, and a newspaper or magazine advertisement for a series of children's books available by filling out the form in the ad or calling a toll-free number. Direct-response marketing through television remains a multi-billion-dollar industry, although it now competes with the internet for customers' attention. This marketing method has resulted in many products gaining widespread popularity. Some firms, like Russ Reid, specialize in direct-response marketing and assist firms in developing successful promotions. Direct-response marketing is also conducted by sending letters, samples, brochures, or booklets to prospects on a mailing list and asking that they order the advertised products by mail or telephone. In general, products must be priced above $20 to justify the advertising and distribution costs associated with direct-response marketing.

Telemarketing

direct-response marketing
A type of marketing in which a retailer advertises a product and makes it available through mail or telephone orders

telemarketing The performance of marketing-related activities by telephone

A number of organizations use the telephone to strengthen the effectiveness of traditional marketing methods. **Telemarketing** is the performance of marketing-related activities by telephone. Some organizations use a prescreened list of prospective clients. Telemarketing can help to generate sales leads, improve customer service, speed up payments on past-due accounts, raise funds for nonprofit organizations, and gather marketing data.

However, increasingly restrictive telemarketing laws have made it a less appealing and less popular marketing method. In 2003, the U.S. Congress implemented a national do-not-call registry, which has more than 229 million numbers on it. The Federal Trade Commission (FTC) enforces violations, and companies are subject to fines of up to $16,000 for each call made to numbers on the list.[31] The Federal Communications Commission (FCC) has ruled that companies are no longer allowed to call customers using prerecorded marketing calls simply because they had done business in the past. The law also requires that an "opt-out" mechanism be embedded in the call for consumers who do not wish to receive the calls. Companies that are still allowed to make telemarketing phone calls must pay for access to the do-not-call registry and must obtain updated numbers from the registry at least every three days. Certain exceptions do apply to no-call lists. For example, charitable, political, and telephone survey organizations are not restricted by the national registry.[32] In spite of regulations, many consumers still find robocalls to be a nuisance, and Congress is seeking further measures to curb them.

Television Home Shopping

Television home shopping presents products to television viewers, encouraging them to order through toll-free numbers and pay with credit cards. The Home Shopping Network originated and popularized this format. The most popular products sold through television home shopping are jewelry, clothing, housewares, and electronics. Most homes in the United States have access to at least one home shopping channel, with the Home Shopping Network and QVC being the largest.

The television home shopping format offers several benefits. Products can be demonstrated easily, and an adequate amount of time can be spent showing the product so viewers are well-informed. The length of time a product is shown depends not only on the time required for performing demonstrations but also on whether the product is selling. Once the calls peak and begin to decline, hosts switch to a new product. Other benefits are that customers can shop at their convenience and from the comfort of their homes. This method is particularly popular among older consumers, who tend to be less comfortable with online shopping and are less mobile to physically go to a store.

15-5b **Direct Selling**

Direct selling is the marketing of products to ultimate consumers through face-to-face sales presentations at home or in the workplace. For example Cutco, as shown here, is a direct seller of high-quality cutlery. The ad shows a top-selling pair of shears to promote the company's holiday gift guide. This product is sold through face-to-face selling. The top five global direct selling companies are Amway, Avon, Herbalife, Vorwerk, and Mary Kay. Four of these companies are based in the United States.[33] Direct selling is a highly valuable industry. Amway alone has $8.6 billion in annual sales.[34] Direct selling was once associated with door-to-door sales, but it has evolved into a highly professional industry where most contacts with buyers are prearranged through electronic

television home shopping A form of selling in which products are presented to television viewers, who can buy them by calling a toll-free number and paying with a credit card

direct selling Marketing products to ultimate consumers through face-to-face sales presentations at home or in the workplace

SOURCE: CUTCO CORPORATION

Direct Selling
Cutco is a popular brand of cutlery sold on a person-to-person basis.

communication or another means of prior communication. Today, companies identify customers through the mail, telephone, internet, social networks, or shopping-mall intercepts and then set up appointments with salespeople. Direct selling is most successful in other countries, particularly collective societies like China, where Amway has achieved higher sales than in its domestic market, the United States. Collective societies prize the one-on-one attention and feeling like they are connecting with the salesperson.

Although the majority of direct selling takes place on an individual, or person-to-person, basis, it sometimes may be carried out in a group, or "party" plan, format. With a party plan, a consumer acts as a host and invites friends and associates to view merchandise, often at someone's home. The informal atmosphere helps to overcome customers' reluctance and encourages them to try out and buy products. Tupperware and Mary Kay were the pioneers of this selling technique and remain global leaders.

Direct selling has benefits and limitations. It gives the marketer an opportunity to demonstrate the product in a comfortable environment where it most likely would be used. The seller can give the customer personal attention, and the product can be presented to the customer at a convenient time and location. Product categories that have been highly successful for direct selling include cosmetics and personal-care products, health products, jewelry, accessories, and household products. Personal attention to the customer is the foundation on which many direct sellers have built their businesses. However, because commissions for salespeople are high, around 30 to 50 percent of the sales price, and great effort is required to identify promising prospects, overall costs of direct selling make it the most expensive form of retailing. Furthermore, some customers view direct selling negatively, owing to unscrupulous and fraudulent practices used by some direct sellers. Some communities even have local ordinances that control or, in some cases, prohibit direct selling. Despite these negative views held by some individuals, direct selling is still alive and well, bringing in annual revenues of more than $35 billion in the United States.[35]

15-5c **Vending**

Vending is the use of machines to dispense products. It is one of the most impersonal forms of retailing, and it accounts for a very small minority of all retail sales. Small, standardized, routinely purchased products (e.g., snacks and drinks) are best suited for sale in vending machines because consumers buy them out of convenience. Machines in areas of heavy foot traffic provide efficient and continuous service to consumers. High-volume areas, such as in commercial centers of large cities or in airports, may offer a wide range of vending product options. In some markets, vending machines have taken on cult popularity, particularly among urban-dwelling consumers. In larger cities around the world, customers can find a wide variety of products dispensed via vending machine, even high-end items such as gold bars, cars, and cell phones as well as cosmetics and food. Snap, the social media site, developed a unique smiling yellow vending machine to distribute its $130 Spectacles video sunglasses.[36]

Because vending machines need only a small amount of space and no sales personnel, this retailing method has some advantages over stores. The advantages are partly offset, however, by the high costs of equipment and frequent servicing and repairs. Many machines can now convey status reports via the internet, helping marketers identify which items are selling and need to be restocked and which may have spoiled and need to be replaced with items with a greater likelihood of selling.

vending The use of machines to dispense products

wholesaling Transactions in which products are bought for resale, for making other products, or for general business operations

wholesaler An individual or organization that sells products that are bought for resale, for making other products, or for general business operations

Learning Objective 15-6

Explain the nature and functions of wholesalers.

15-6　**WHOLESALING**

Wholesaling refers to all transactions in which products are bought for resale, making other products, or general business operations. It does not include exchanges with ultimate consumers. A **wholesaler** is an individual or organization that sells products that are bought for resale, making other products, or general business operations. In other words, wholesalers buy products and resell them to resellers, government, and institutional users. For instance, Sysco, the nation's number-one food-service distributor, supplies restaurants, hotels, schools, industrial caterers, and hospitals with everything from frozen and fresh food and paper products to medical and cleaning supplies. Wholesaling activities are not limited to goods. Service companies, such as financial institutions, also use active wholesale networks. There are 413,437 wholesaling establishments in the United States, and more than half of all products sold in this country pass through these firms.[37]

Wholesalers may engage in many supply chain management activities, which we will discuss. In addition to bearing the primary responsibility for the physical distribution of products from manufacturers to retailers, wholesalers may establish information systems that help producers and retailers manage the supply chain from producer to customer. Many wholesalers use information technology and the internet to share information among intermediaries, employees, customers, and suppliers and facilitating agencies, such as trucking companies and warehouse firms. Some firms make their databases and marketing information systems available to their supply chain partners to facilitate order processing, shipping, and product development and to share information about changing market conditions and customer desires. As a result, some wholesalers play a key role in supply chain management decisions.

15-6a Services Provided by Wholesalers

Wholesalers provide essential services to both producers and retailers. By initiating sales contacts with a producer and selling diverse products to retailers, wholesalers serve as an extension of the producer's sales force. Wholesalers also provide financial assistance. They often pay for transporting goods, reduce a producer's warehousing expenses and inventory investment by holding goods in inventory, extend credit and assume losses from buyers who turn out to be poor credit risks, and can be a source of working capital when they buy a producer's output. Wholesalers also serve as conduits for information within the marketing channel, keeping producers up to date on market developments and passing along the manufacturers' promotional plans to other intermediaries. Using wholesalers, therefore, gives producers a distinct advantage because the specialized services wholesalers perform allow producers to concentrate on developing and manufacturing products that match customers' needs and wants.

Wholesalers support retailers by assisting with marketing strategy, especially the distribution component. Wholesalers also help retailers select inventory. They are often specialists on market conditions and experts at negotiating final purchases. In industries in which obtaining supplies is important, skilled buying is indispensable. Effective wholesalers make an effort to understand the businesses of their customers. They also must now understand digital marketing and digital communications. Firms such as Williams Commerce specialize in helping wholesalers to adapt to an increasingly digital environment while maintaining the high level of customer contact that is sometimes required.[38]

Wholesalers can also reduce a retailer's burden of looking for and coordinating supply sources. If the wholesaler purchases for several different buyers, expenses can be shared by all customers. Furthermore, whereas a manufacturer's salesperson offers retailers only a few products at a time, independent wholesalers always have a wide range of products available. Thus, through partnerships, wholesalers and retailers can forge successful relationships for the benefit of customers.

The distinction between services performed by wholesalers and those provided by other businesses has blurred in recent years. Changes in the competitive nature of business, especially the growth of strong retail chains like Walmart, Home Depot, and Best Buy, are changing supply chain relationships. In many product categories, such as electronics, furniture, and even food products, retailers have discovered that they can deal directly with producers, performing wholesaling activities themselves at a lower cost. However, when a wholesaler is eliminated from a marketing channel, wholesaling activities still have to be performed by a member of the supply chain, whether a producer, retailer, or facilitating agency. Most retailers rely on computer technology to expedite ordering, track deliveries, and monitor handling of goods. Thus, technology has allowed retailers to take over some wholesaling functions.

15-6b Types of Wholesalers

Wholesalers are classified according to several criteria: whether a wholesaler is independently owned or owned by a producer, whether it takes title to (owns) the products it handles, the range of services provided, and the breadth and depth of its product lines. Using these criteria, we discuss three general types of wholesaling establishments including merchant wholesalers, agents and brokers, and manufacturers' sales branches and offices.

Merchant Wholesalers

Merchant wholesalers are independently owned businesses that take title to goods, assume risks associated with ownership, and generally buy and resell products to other wholesalers, business customers, or retailers. A producer is likely to rely on merchant wholesalers when selling directly to customers would not be economically feasible. Merchant wholesalers are also useful for providing market coverage, making sales contacts, storing inventory, handling orders, collecting market information, and furnishing customer support. Some merchant wholesalers are even involved in packaging and developing private brands. Merchant wholesalers go by various names, including *wholesaler, jobber, distributor, assembler, exporter,* and *importer*. They fall into two broad categories: full service and limited service (see Figure 15.1).

Full-Service Wholesalers **Full-service wholesalers** perform the widest possible range of wholesaling functions. Customers rely on them for product availability, suitable product assortments, breaking large quantities into smaller ones, financial assistance, and technical advice and service. Full-service wholesalers handle either consumer or business products and provide numerous marketing services to their customers. Many large grocery wholesalers, for instance, help retailers with store design, site selection, personnel training, financing, merchandising, advertising, coupon redemption, and scanning. Macdonalds Consolidated is a full-service wholesaler of meat, dairy, and produce goods for grocery retailers in North America. Macdonalds offers many services, including communication management, document management, retailer flyers and merchandising, and rebates for valued customers.[39] Although full-service wholesalers often earn higher gross margins than other wholesalers, their operating expenses are also higher because they perform a wider range of functions.

Full-service wholesalers are categorized as general-merchandise, limited-line, and specialty-line wholesalers. **General-merchandise wholesalers** carry a wide product mix but offer limited depth within product lines. They deal in products such as drugs, nonperishable foods, cosmetics, detergents, and tobacco. **Limited-line wholesalers** carry only a few product

merchant wholesalers
Independently owned businesses that take title to goods, assume ownership risks, and buy and resell products to other wholesalers, business customers, or retailers

full-service wholesalers
Merchant wholesalers that perform the widest range of wholesaling functions

general-merchandise wholesalers Full-service wholesalers with a wide product mix but limited depth within product lines

limited-line wholesalers Full-service wholesalers that carry only a few product lines but many products within those lines

Figure 15.1   **Types of Merchant Wholesalers**

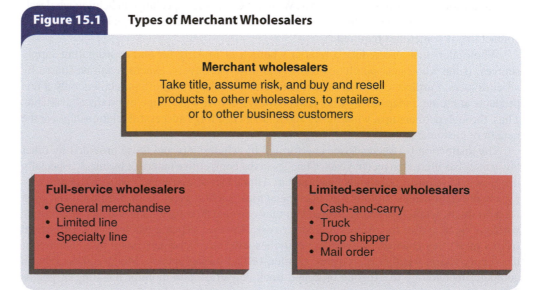

Merchant wholesalers
Take title, assume risk, and buy and resell products to other wholesalers, to retailers, or to other business customers

Full-service wholesalers
- General merchandise
- Limited line
- Specialty line

Limited-service wholesalers
- Cash-and-carry
- Truck
- Drop shipper
- Mail order

lines, such as groceries, lighting fixtures, or oil-well drilling equipment, but offer an extensive assortment of products within those lines. AmerisourceBergen Corporation, for example, is a limited-line wholesaler of pharmaceuticals and health products.[40]

General-line wholesalers provide a range of services similar to those of general-merchandise wholesalers. **Specialty-line wholesalers** offer the narrowest range of products, usually a single product line or a few items within a product line. **Rack jobbers** are full-service, specialty-line wholesalers that own and maintain display racks in supermarkets, drugstores, and discount and variety stores. Retailers provide the space, and they set up displays, mark merchandise, stock shelves, and keep billing and inventory records. Rack jobbers specialize in non-food items with high profit margins, such as health and beauty aids, books, magazines, hosiery, and greeting cards.

Merchant Wholesaler
Grainger is a full-service, limited-line wholesaler of electrical equipment and supplies.

Limited-Service Wholesalers **Limited-service wholesalers** provide fewer marketing services than do full-service wholesalers and specialize in just a few functions. Producers perform the remaining functions or pass them on to customers or other intermediaries. Limited-service wholesalers take title to merchandise but often do not deliver merchandise, grant credit, provide marketing information, store inventory, or plan ahead for customers' future needs. Because they offer restricted services, limited-service wholesalers charge lower rates and have smaller profit margins than full-service wholesalers. The decision about whether to use a limited-service or a full-service wholesaler depends on the structure of the marketing channel and the need to manage the supply chain to create a competitive advantage. Although limited-service wholesalers are less common than other types, they are important in the distribution of products like specialty foods, perishable items, construction materials, and coal.

Table 15.3 summarizes the services provided by four typical limited-service wholesalers: cash-and-carry wholesalers, truck wholesalers, drop shippers, and mail-order wholesalers. **Cash-and-carry wholesalers** are intermediaries whose customers—often small businesses—pay cash and furnish transportation. Cash-and-carry wholesalers usually handle a limited line of products with a high turnover rate, such as groceries, building materials, and electrical or office supplies. Many small retailers that other types of wholesalers will not take on because of their small size

specialty-line wholesalers Full-service wholesalers that carry only a single product line or a few items within a product line

rack jobbers Full-service, specialty-line wholesalers that own and maintain display racks in stores

limited-service wholesalers Merchant wholesalers that provide some services and specialize in a few functions

cash-and-carry wholesalers Limited-service wholesalers whose customers pay cash and furnish transportation

Table 15.3   **Services That Limited-Service Wholesalers Provide**

	Cash-and-Carry	Truck	Drop Shipper	Mail Order
Physical possession of merchandise	Yes	Yes	No	Yes
Personal sales calls on customers	No	Yes	No	No
Information about market conditions	No	Some	Yes	Yes
Advice to customers	No	Some	Yes	No
Stocking and maintenance of merchandise in customers' stores	No	No	No	No
Credit to customers	No	No	Yes	Some
Delivery of merchandise to customers	No	Yes	No	No

survive because of cash-and-carry wholesalers. **Truck wholesalers**, sometimes called *truck jobbers,* transport a limited line of products directly to customers for on-the-spot inspection and selection. They are often small operators who own and drive their own trucks. They usually have regular routes, calling on retailers and other institutions to determine their needs. **Drop shippers**, also known as *desk jobbers,* take title to products and negotiate sales but never take actual possession of products. They forward orders from retailers, business buyers, or other wholesalers to manufacturers and arrange for carload shipments of items to be delivered directly from producers to these customers. They assume responsibility for products during the entire transaction, including the costs of any unsold goods. **Mail-order wholesalers** use catalogs instead of a sales force to sell products to retail and business buyers. Wholesale mail-order houses generally feature cosmetics, specialty foods, sporting goods, office supplies, and automotive parts. Mail-order wholesaling enables buyers to choose and order particular catalog items for delivery through various mail carriers. This is a convenient and effective method of selling items to customers in remote areas that other wholesalers might find unprofitable to serve. The internet has provided an opportunity for mail-order wholesalers to serve a larger number of buyers, selling products over their websites and having the products shipped by the manufacturers.

Agents and Brokers

Agents and brokers negotiate purchases and expedite sales but do not take title to products (see Figure 15.2 for types of agents and brokers). Sometimes called *functional middlemen,* they perform a limited number of services in exchange for a commission, which generally is based on the product's selling price. **Agents** represent either buyers or sellers on a permanent basis, whereas **brokers** are intermediaries that buyers or sellers employ temporarily.

Although agents and brokers perform even fewer functions than limited-service wholesalers, they are usually specialists in particular products or types of customers and can provide valuable sales expertise. They know their markets well and often form long-lasting associations with customers. Agents and brokers enable manufacturers to expand sales when resources are limited, benefit from the services of a trained sales force, and hold down personal selling costs. Table 15.4 summarizes the services provided by agents and brokers.

Manufacturers' agents, which account for more than half of all agent wholesalers, are independent intermediaries that represent two or more sellers and usually offer complete product lines to customers. They sell and take orders year-round, much as a manufacturer's sales force does. Restricted to a particular territory, a manufacturer's agent handles noncompeting

truck wholesalers Limited-service wholesalers that transport products directly to customers for inspection and selection

drop shippers Limited-service wholesalers that take title to goods and negotiate sales but never actually take possession of products

mail-order wholesalers Limited-service wholesalers that sell products through catalogs

agents Intermediaries that represent either buyers or sellers on a permanent basis

brokers Intermediaries that bring buyers and sellers together temporarily

manufacturers' agents Independent intermediaries that represent two or more sellers and usually offer customers complete product lines

Figure 15.2	Types of Agents and Brokers

Agents and brokers
Do not take title to products and are compensated with commissions for negotiating exchanges between sellers and buyers

Agents
Represent either buyer or seller, usually on a permanent basis
- Manufacturers' agents
- Selling agents
- Commission merchants

Brokers
Bring buyers and sellers together on a temporary basis
- Food brokers
- Real estate brokers
- Other brokers, e.g., securities, insurance

Table 15.4 Services That Agents and Brokers Provide

	Manufacturers' Agents	Selling Agents	Commission Merchants	Brokers
Physical possession of merchandise	Some	Some	Yes	No
Long-term relationship with buyers or sellers	Yes	Yes	Yes	No
Representation of competing product lines	No	No	Yes	Yes
Limited geographic territory	Yes	No	No	No
Credit to customers	No	Yes	Some	No
Delivery of merchandise to customers	Some	Yes	Yes	No

and complementary products. The relationship between the agent and the manufacturer is governed by written contracts that outline territories, selling price, order handling, and terms of sale relating to delivery, service, and warranties. Manufacturers' agents have little or no control over producers' pricing and marketing policies. They do not extend credit and may be unable to provide technical advice. Manufacturers' agents are commonly used in sales of apparel, machinery and equipment, steel, furniture, automotive products, electrical goods, and some food items.

Selling agents market either all of a specified product line or a manufacturer's entire output. They perform every wholesaling activity except taking title to products. Selling agents usually assume the sales function for several producers simultaneously, and some firms may use them in place of a marketing department. In fact, selling agents are used most often by small producers or by manufacturers that have difficulty maintaining a marketing department because of such factors as seasonal production. In contrast to manufacturers' agents, selling agents generally have no territorial limits and have complete authority over prices, promotion, and distribution. To avoid conflicts of interest, selling agents represent noncompeting product lines. They play a key role in advertising, marketing research, and credit policies of the sellers they represent, at times even advising on product development and packaging.

Commission merchants receive goods on consignment from local sellers and negotiate sales in large, central markets. Sometimes called *factor merchants,* these agents have broad powers regarding prices and terms of sale. They specialize in obtaining the best price possible under market conditions. Most often found in agricultural marketing, commission merchants take possession of truckloads of commodities, arrange for necessary grading or storage, and transport the commodities to auction or markets where they are sold. When sales are completed, the agents deduct commissions and the expense of making the sale and turn over profits to the producer. Commission merchants also offer planning assistance and sometimes extend credit but usually do not provide promotional support.

A broker's primary purpose is to bring buyers and sellers together. Thus, brokers perform fewer functions than other intermediaries. They are not involved in financing or physical possession, have no authority to set prices, and assume almost no risks. Instead, they offer customers specialized knowledge of a particular commodity and a network of established contacts. Brokers are especially useful to sellers of products such as supermarket goods and real estate. Food brokers, for example, connect food and general merchandise to retailer-owned and merchant wholesalers, grocery chains, food processors, and business buyers.

Manufacturers' Sales Branches and Offices

Sometimes called *manufacturers' wholesalers,* manufacturers' sales branches and offices resemble merchant wholesalers' operations. **Sales branches** are manufacturer-owned intermediaries that sell products and provide support services to the manufacturers' sales forces. Situated away from the manufacturing plant, they are usually located where large customers are concentrated and demand is high. They offer credit, deliver goods, give promotional assistance,

selling agents Intermediaries that market a whole product line or a manufacturer's entire output

commission merchants Agents that receive goods on consignment from local sellers and negotiate sales in large, central markets

sales branches Manufacturer-owned intermediaries that sell products and provide support services to the manufacturers' sales forces and furnish other services. Customers include retailers, business buyers, and other wholesalers. Manufacturers of electrical supplies, plumbing supplies, lumber, and automotive parts often have branch operations.

Sales offices are manufacturer-owned operations that provide services normally associated with agents. Like sales branches, they are located away from manufacturing plants, but unlike sales branches, they carry no inventory. A manufacturer's sales office (or branch) may sell products that enhance the manufacturer's own product line.

Manufacturers may set up these branches or offices to reach their customers more effectively by performing wholesaling functions themselves. A manufacturer also might set up such a facility when specialized wholesaling services are not available through existing intermediaries. Performing wholesaling and physical distribution activities through a manufacturer's sales branch or office can strengthen supply chain efficiency. In some situations, though, a manufacturer may bypass its sales office or branches entirely—for example, if the producer decides to serve large retailer customers directly.

sales offices Manufacturer-owned operations that provide services normally associated with agents

Summary

15-1 Explain the purpose and function of retailers in the marketing channel.

Retailing includes all transactions in which buyers intend to consume products through personal, family, or household use. Retailers, organizations that sell products primarily to ultimate consumers, are important links in the marketing channel, because they are both marketers for and customers of wholesalers and producers. Retailers add value, provide services, and assist in making product selections. Many retailers now engage in multichannel retailing by employing multiple distribution channels that complement their brick-and-mortar stores with websites, catalogs, and apps.

15-2 Describe online retailing and explain how it is changing the field of retailing.

A significant factor in the rise of multichannel retailing is online retailing, which makes products available to buyers through computer connections. Online purchases are growing rapidly. Online retailing satisfies a growing expectation among consumers to have multiple channels available to obtain the goods and services they desire at their convenience. Consumers can perform a wide variety of shopping-related tasks online.

15-3 Classify the major types of retailers.

Retail stores can be classified according to the breadth of products offered. Two broad categories are general-merchandise retailers and specialty retailers. There are several primary types of general-merchandise retailers. Department stores are large retail organizations arranged by departments and characterized by wide product mixes in considerable depth. Discount

stores are self-service, low-price, general-merchandise outlets. Extreme-value stores are much smaller than conventional discount stores and offer even lower prices on smaller size name-brand nonperishable household items. Convenience stores are small self-service stores that are open long hours and carry a narrow assortment of products, usually convenience items. Supermarkets are large self-service food stores that carry some non-food products. Superstores are giant retail outlets that carry all the products found in supermarkets and most consumer products purchased on a routine basis. Hypermarkets offer supermarket and discount store shopping at one location. Warehouse clubs are large-scale, members-only discount operations. Warehouse and catalog showrooms are low-cost operations characterized by warehouse methods of materials handling and display, large inventories, and minimal services.

Specialty retailers offer substantial assortments in a few product lines. They include traditional specialty retailers, which carry narrow product mixes with deep product lines. Category killers are large specialty stores that concentrate on a major product category and compete on the basis of low prices and enormous product availability. Off-price retailers sell brand-name manufacturers' seconds and product overruns at deep discounts.

15-4 Explore strategic issues in retailing.

To increase sales and store patronage, retailers must consider strategic issues. Location determines the trading area from which a store draws its customers and should be evaluated carefully. When evaluating potential sites, retailers take into account a variety of factors, including the location of the firm's target market within the trading area, kinds of products sold, availability of public transportation, customer characteristics, and competitors' locations. Retailers can choose among several types of locations, including freestanding structures, traditional business districts, traditional planned shopping centers (neighborhood, community, regional, and superregional), or nontraditional shopping centers (lifestyle, power, and outlet).

Franchising is an arrangement in which a supplier grants a dealer the right to sell products in exchange for some type of consideration. Franchising enables a franchisee to start a business with limited capital and benefit from the business experience of others. The franchisee can obtain guidance and advice from the franchisor at little or no cost. Also, the franchisee receives materials to use in local advertising and can benefit from national promotional campaigns. However, the franchisor can dictate many aspects of the business. Franchisees must pay to use the franchisor's name, products, and assistance. Franchisees often must work very hard, putting in long days without breaks. In some cases, franchise agreements are not uniform, meaning one franchisee may pay more than another for the same services. Finally, the franchisor gives up control when entering into a franchise agreement.

As consumer demographics and shopping trends change, retailers are adjusting by exploiting new technologies—including integrated apps, beacons, virtual fit, and more—to improve the store experience and give consumers more shopping platforms. Retail positioning involves identifying an unserved or underserved market segment and serving it through a strategy that distinguishes the retailer from others in those customers' minds. Store image, which various customers perceive differently, derives not only from atmospherics but also from location, products offered, customer services, prices, promotion, and the store's overall reputation. Atmospherics refers to the physical elements of a store's design that can be adjusted to appeal to consumers' emotions and thus induce them to buy. Category management is a retail strategy of managing groups of similar, often substitutable, products produced by different manufacturers.

15-5 Identify the various forms of direct marketing, direct selling, and vending.

Direct marketing is the use of the telephone, internet, and nonpersonal media to communicate product and organizational information to customers, who can then purchase products via mail, telephone, or the internet. Direct marketing is a type of nonstore retailing, the selling of goods or services outside the confines of a retail facility. Direct marketing may occur online (online retailing), through a catalog (catalog marketing), and via advertising (direct-response marketing), telephone (telemarketing), and television (television home shopping). Two other types of nonstore retailing are direct selling and vending. Direct selling is the marketing of products to ultimate consumers through face-to-face sales

presentations at home or in the workplace. Vending is the use of machines to dispense products.

15-6 Explain the nature and functions of wholesalers.

Wholesaling consists of all transactions in which products are bought for resale, making other products, or general business operations. Wholesalers are individuals or organizations that facilitate and expedite exchanges that are primarily wholesale transactions. For producers, wholesalers are a source of financial assistance and information. By performing specialized accumulation and allocation functions, they allow producers to concentrate on manufacturing products. Wholesalers provide retailers with buying expertise, wide product lines, efficient distribution, and warehousing and storage.

Merchant wholesalers are independently owned businesses that take title to goods and assume ownership risks. They are either full-service wholesalers, offering the widest possible range of wholesaling functions, or limited-service wholesalers, providing only some marketing services and specializing in a few functions. There are several full-service merchant wholesaler types. General-merchandise wholesalers offer a wide but relatively shallow product mix. Limited-line wholesalers offer extensive assortments within a few product lines. Specialty-line wholesalers carry only a single product line or a few items within a line. Rack jobbers own and service display racks in supermarkets and other stores. Limited-service merchant wholesalers include cash-and-carry wholesalers, which sell to small businesses, require payment in cash, and do not deliver. Truck wholesalers sell a limited line of products from their own trucks directly to customers. Drop shippers own goods and negotiate sales, but never take possession of products. Finally, mail-order wholesalers sell to retail and business buyers through direct-mail catalogs.

Agents and brokers negotiate purchases and expedite sales in exchange for a commission, but they do not take title to products. Usually specializing in certain products, they can provide valuable sales expertise. Whereas agents represent buyers or sellers on a permanent basis, brokers are intermediaries that buyers and sellers employ on a temporary basis to negotiate exchanges. Manufacturers' agents offer customers the complete product lines of two or more sellers. Selling agents market a complete product line or a producer's entire output and perform every wholesaling function except taking title to products. Commission merchants are agents that receive goods on consignment from local sellers and negotiate sales in large, central markets.

Manufacturers' sales branches and offices are owned by manufacturers. Sales branches sell products and provide support services for the manufacturer's sales force in a given location. Sales offices carry no inventory and function much as agents do.

Important Terms

retailing 434
retailer 434
multichannel retailing 434
online retailing 435
general-merchandise
    retailer 437
department stores 437
discount stores 438
extreme-value stores 438
convenience store 439
supermarkets 439
superstores 439
hypermarkets 440
warehouse clubs 440
warehouse showrooms 440
traditional specialty
    retailers 441
category killer 441

off-price retailers 441
neighborhood shopping
    center 443
community shopping
    center 443
regional shopping center
    444
superregional shopping
    center 444
lifestyle shopping center
    444
power shopping center
    444
franchising 445
retail positioning 447
atmospherics 448
category management 449
direct marketing 449

catalog marketing 449
direct-response
    marketing 450
telemarketing 450
television home shopping
    451
direct selling 451
vending 452
wholesaling 452
wholesaler 452
merchant wholesalers 454
full-service wholesalers 454
general-merchandise
    wholesalers 454
limited-line wholesalers
    454
specialty-line wholesalers
    455

rack jobbers 455
limited-service
    wholesalers 455
cash-and-carry
    wholesalers 455
truck wholesalers 456
drop shippers 456
mail-order wholesalers
    456
agents 456
brokers 456
manufacturers'
    agents 456
selling agents 457
commission merchants
    457
sales branches 457
sales offices 458

Discussion and Review Questions

1. What value is added to a product by retailers? What value is added by retailers for producers and ultimate consumers?
2. How is online retailing integrated with other forms of retailing?
3. What are the major differences between discount stores and department stores?
4. In what ways are traditional specialty stores and off-price retailers similar? How do they differ?
5. What major issues should be considered when determining a retail site location?
6. Describe the three major types of traditional shopping centers. Give an example of each type in your area.
7. If you were opening a retail business, would you prefer to open an independent store or own a store under a franchise arrangement? Explain your preference.
8. Discuss the major factors that help to determine a retail store's image. How does atmosphere add value to products sold in a store?

9. How is door-to-door selling a form of retailing? Some consumers believe that direct-response orders bypass the retailer. Is this true?
10. What services do wholesalers provide to producers and retailers?
11. What is the difference between a full-service merchant wholesaler and a limited-service merchant wholesaler?
12. Drop shippers take title to products but do not accept physical possession of them, whereas commission merchants take physical possession of products but do not accept title. Defend the logic of classifying drop shippers as merchant wholesalers and commission merchants as agents.
13. Why are manufacturers' sales offices and branches classified as wholesalers? Which independent wholesalers are replaced by manufacturers' sales branches? By sales offices?

Developing Your Marketing Plan

Distribution decisions in the marketing plan entail the movement of your product from the producer to the final consumer. An understanding of how and where your customer prefers to purchase products is critical to the development of the marketing plan. As you apply the information in this chapter to your plan, focus on the following issues:

1. Considering your product's attributes and your target market's (or markets') buying behavior, will your product likely be sold to the ultimate customer or to another member of the marketing channel?
2. If your product will be sold to the ultimate customer, what type of retailing establishment is most suitable to

your product? Consider the product's characteristics and your target market's buying behavior. Refer to Table 15.1 for retailer types.

3. Discuss how the characteristics of the retail establishment, such as location and store image, have an impact on the consumer's perception of your product.

4. Are direct marketing or direct selling methods appropriate for your product and target market?

5. If your product will be sold to another member in the marketing channel, discuss whether a merchant wholesaler, agent, or broker is most suitable as your channel customer.

Video Case 15.1

Rebecca Minkoff's Cutting-Edge Retail Technology

At a time when many retail organizations are favoring e-commerce and cutting back on store locations, the upscale fashion retailer Rebecca Minkoff is on the cutting edge of brick-and-mortar retailing. The New York–based firm was cofounded by designer Rebecca Minkoff and her brother, Uri Minkoff, who has a background in software. She kicked off her design career in 2001 with a line of women's apparel, followed by a line of stylish handbags that made her name in the fashion world.

Today, Rebecca Minkoff is the creative force behind the branded clothing, watches, and other accessories sold in her stores, while her brother concentrates on the retail side of the business, overseeing both the stores and the e-commerce operation. The company has opened Rebecca Minkoff stores in New York City, Chicago, Los Angeles, and San Francisco, plus nine stores overseas. To reach a wider audience, the designer also wholesales her products to dozens of department stores for resale worldwide.

LENTAMART/SHUTTERSTOCK.COM

CEO Uri Minkoff is always looking for ways to attract and retain customers by making the in-store experience more engaging and more convenient. For example, in partnership with eBay, Rebecca Minkoff stores feature an interactive wall where customers can touch to view the latest products, request refreshments, and order clothing to try on in the fitting room. Customers receive a text when their requested items are set up in the fitting room, ready to be tried on.

Each fitting room is outfitted with sophisticated technology that helps customers make more informed buying decisions, while generating data that helps the retailer learn more about its customers. Customers can tap the "smart" mirror to see various styles in stock, view styling suggestions, request a different size, ask for assistance, or add selected items and personal preferences to a "saved" menu for future visits. Customers can also touch the mirror to change the lighting, enabling them to see how the new outfit they're considering

would look on a "Brooklyn morning" or a "Hudson River sunset."

These tech tools allow Rebecca Minkoff to collect data about the products that customers try on and the mix-and-match combinations they try, which items they buy, and what they don't buy. If customers tend to pair certain tops and bottoms, for instance, this may give the company insights into how to merchandise differently or spark design ideas for future fashion collections. Uri Minkoff emphasizes that information collected through such customer interactions serves as a starting point in understanding and anticipating what the retailer's customers will need and want in the future.

Rebecca Minkoff is in the vanguard of a trend known as "see now, buy now." In the past, designers would introduce a new seasonal collection with a splashy fashion show, but ship the new styles to stores months later. Since 2016, Rebecca Minkoff's latest fashions have been stocked in her stores, ready for immediate purchase, as soon as the styles are shown on the runway.

The retailer has built a huge social-media audience of more than 800,000 Instagram followers, 435,000 Facebook likes, and 900,000 Twitter followers. This enthusiastic audience spreads the word about the designer's products and special in-store events, such as art shows and talks by female entrepreneurs. "We want to make our stores a hub of community," explains Rebecca Minkoff. Despite the dramatic rise of e-commerce, she knows many customers still want to walk into her stores, see the products in person, consult with an employee, and try on clothing before they buy.[41]

Questions for Discussion

1. What role does technology such as customer-controlled lighting in fitting rooms play in the store image of Rebecca Minkoff?
2. What are the advantages and disadvantages of Rebecca Minkoff operating its own stores and e-commerce business as well as selling products wholesale to hundreds of other retailers?
3. Would you recommend that Rebecca Minkoff test direct selling through at-home consultants? Explain your answer.

Case 15.2

Lowe's Taps Technology for Retailing Edge

From ladders to lumber to light bulbs, Lowe's sells just about everything a consumer or contractor would need to build, repair, and maintain a home. The North Carolina–based home-improvement retailer operates more than 1,800 cavernous stores across North America. With hundreds of thousands of products in inventory and acres of free parking for its stores, Lowe's serves 17 million customers weekly and rings up $65 billion in yearly revenue.

Consumers can walk into any Lowe's location and receive expert help buying tools, materials, and accessories for do-it-yourself projects like installing a floor and replacing a kitchen sink. For those who don't want to tackle projects on their own, Lowe's offers the option of hiring a local professional through the store. The retailer also caters to contractors and others in the building trade, with a separate store checkout area and an information desk for business orders, credit accounts, pickup, and delivery.

Both consumers and professionals can browse and buy through separate websites designed specifically for their needs. Lowes.com, the company's website for consumers, offers thousands of how-to guides and videos demonstrating do-it-yourself techniques, plus photos of sample rooms and other finished projects for inspiration and ideas. Consumers can use online calculators to estimate how many gallons of paint are needed for a room or how many pounds of grass seed are needed for a lawn. LowesForPros.com, the website for building professionals, includes handy features such as customizable lists of frequently ordered products and interactive calculators for estimating project time and materials.

Facing competition from other category killers like Home Depot and from smaller hardware stores, Lowe's

DAVID NELSON/ALAMY STOCK PHOTO

is harnessing technology to enhance the customer experience before, during, and after a store or website visit. The Measured by Lowe's app enables consumers (and professionals such as interior designers) to use their smartphones and tablet computers as a tape measure for calculating length, width, and height. Another Lowe's app allows users to "visualize" how a piece of furniture would look in their own home or office, via augmented reality. A third app helps consumers navigate the aisles inside a Lowe's location to find the exact shelf where a product is stored or the aisle housing a certain product category. Apps are only some of the technologies being explored by Lowe's Innovation Lab, staffed by scientists and digital experts who study consumer behavior and experiment with cutting-edge software and equipment.

Lowe's chief customer officer sees apps and other digital tools as part of "the fabric of a fully integrated customer experience, from project inspiration to customer relationship management to how we present products and services and create engaging content." Looking ahead, he says the retailer plans to "become even faster at anticipating customer needs and providing relevant solutions leveraging technology."

As more products for the home incorporate digital elements, Lowe's is helping its customers understand how to choose and use these devices. It has partnered with the software retailer b8ta to set up "store within a store" SmartSpot departments in dozens of Lowe's stores, staffed by representatives trained to demonstrate and explain smart-home items like digital thermostats and digital security systems. In the store, consumers can try operating some of these products with experts standing by to assist. This gives consumers more confidence that they are making an informed decision and that they will be able to make full use of their purchases

once they get home. Lowe's also gains new insights from the questions and comments of customers who visit the SmartSpot department, adding to its in-depth knowledge of needs and buying behavior.[42]

Questions for Discussion

1. As a major retailer specializing in home-improvement products, Lowe's is considered a category killer. Does that label apply to Lowe's websites? Explain your answer.
2. How important are exterior and interior atmospherics to the image of a home-improvement store like Lowe's?
3. Lowe's partnered with a software retailer to set up smart-home departments inside some of its stores. What are the implications for Lowe's retail positioning?

Strategic Case 6

Gelson's Markets—Where Superior Quality Meets Convenience

Bernard and Eugene Gelson, the founders of Gelson's Markets, grew up helping their parents operate a grocery store in Iowa. As the Depression wound down in the late 1930s, the family moved to Los Angeles and opened a new grocery. The entrepreneurial brothers were eager to launch their own business and soon began running their own small grocery store. But at a time when ever-larger, self-service supermarkets were popping up from coast to coast, the Gelson brothers dreamed of cutting the ribbon on a stylishly modern supermarket differentiated by superior quality and service.

They hired a well-known architect to design the first Gelson's supermarket, a 25,000-square-foot retail store with many innovations. Opened in 1951, that first store featured wide aisles for easy browsing, air conditioning throughout, and a meat-cutting department in full view of customers, visually reinforcing the emphasis on freshness and quality. In less than a decade, the company was successful enough to open a second supermarket. Today, through store openings, acquisitions, and mergers, Gelson's Markets owns 28 stores in Southern California. Each store reflects the tastes and preferences of the neighborhood and offers full-service supermarket amenities.

Marketing Driven by Mission

The Gelson brothers knew from long experience that good service builds customer loyalty, which is why service has always been an integral part of the company's mission. The formal mission statement of Gelson's Markets is: "To make shopping anywhere else unacceptable for consumers who value quality products, cleanliness, convenience, and

personal service." As this statement indicates, top-quality food products—particularly fresh meats and seafood, fresh vegetables, and fresh fruit—are also key ingredients. The mission statement touches on two additional elements that customers expect in a world-class supermarket: cleanliness, which is a must in any food store, and convenience.

Gelson's Markets focuses on convenience in several ways. Consumers with busy lifestyles are increasingly interested in prepared foods, specialty takeout, and meal kits. Gelson's caters to these customers with distinctive and convenient offerings. For example, shoppers can customize takeout pizzas baked on the premises and order other signature favorites at the Wolfgang Puck Express takeout counter. In some stores, customers can create their own omelet and other breakfast or lunch items to eat there or pack for home or office. At the charcuterie station, customers can watch as carvers slice specialty cold cuts to order. They can also order healthy, flavorful cold-pressed juices made from fresh fruits and vegetables at a Liquiteria counter in select Gelson's stores.

In addition, Gelson's has begun selling a rotating, seasonal selection of fresh meal kits from Chef'd. The kits package recipes from famous chefs with fresh meat or seafood, fresh produce, and tasty herbs, making it simple and easy to cook a great meal at home. Although meal kits are usually ordered in advance and shipped to the customer's door, selling them in local Gelson's Markets adds convenience for consumers who decide to buy and cook on the same day. Other supermarkets have also noticed the popularity of meal kits and begun offering their own. For example,

Kroger recently introduced its own branded 20-minute meal kits for two, and Publix markets its private-brand meal kits to feed two or four people.

Serving a wide range of customer needs, Gelson's offers catering for every occasion, from birthdays and weddings to picnics and holiday banquets, with recipes developed by the in-house executive chef. The company has a dietician on staff to provide guidance about foods for gluten-free diets, vegan and vegetarian diets, dairy-free diets, low-sodium diets, and cooking with locally sourced ingredients, among other customer concerns. Customers are encouraged to visit the company's website for healthy-eating tips and recipes, advice about pairing wines with meals, selecting and storing fresh produce, and child-friendly menus. Thanks to a partnership with Instacart, customers can also order groceries online and receive delivery within one or two hours. Alternatively, they can click to buy fresh meats, floral arrangements, gift baskets, and other items on the Gelson's website, and specify pickup at a convenient Gelson's store.

Engaging with Customers, the Community, and Suppliers

Gelson's Markets engages with consumers and groups in each local community. It invites nonprofit organizations to apply for charitable donations, and contributes more than $2 million annually to good causes. Many of its stores host cat and dog adoption events throughout the year. The company also distributes a *Pet Gazette* quarterly newsletter for pet owners and sponsors periodic pet photo contests. With families in mind, the Gelson's Markets website has a "Kids Corner" section with downloadable coloring pages and a downloadable guide to healthy children's products. The stores also offer behind-the-scenes tours for school groups. Students have the opportunity to see how shipments are received from local farms, watch bakers at work, and learn how recyclables are handled, as well as sample some foods during the tour.

In addition to two email newsletters for customers—one filled with coupons, the other filled with recipes and new product news—Gelson's Markets has an active presence on Facebook, Pinterest, Instagram, and Twitter. Tens of thousands of followers watch for the company's latest nutrition and cooking tips, entertaining ideas, photos of special meals, and holiday food suggestions. Communication flows both ways: Gelson's Markets asks customers for feedback on its website, on its social media accounts, and in its stores, as well as inviting customers to rate its stores on Yelp.

Always on the lookout for new products and new suppliers, the supermarket invites companies to "pitch" themselves and their offerings through Gelson's link to the RangeMe online portal. First, a prospective supplier submits contact information and a product profile describing what it is offering, along with photos and a target-market description. Next, the system analyzes the product(s) and automatically transmits the information to the store buyer in charge of that category or department. Once the buyer has reviewed the supplier and the product details, he or she can get in touch for further discussion, to request product samples, or to set up a meeting. Although buyers also hunt for new products at specialty food shows and other industry events, the portal provides a convenient digital framework for suppliers to introduce themselves to the supermarket's decision makers.

Many supermarkets and specialty food stores operate in the highly competitive Southern California market. For differentiation and advantage in this marketing environment, Gelson's Markets is building on its decades of retailing experience, its dedication to service and quality, and its brand reputation to keep customers loyal.[43]

Questions for Discussion

1. How is the mission statement of Gelson's Markets reflected in its decisions about products and in-store features?

2. Why would Gelson's Markets create in-store departments for customers to create their own pizzas, cook their own omelets, and obtain fresh-squeezed juices?

3. What are the marketing challenges and opportunities of a retailer like Gelson's Markets partnering with a company like Instacart to offer home delivery of food products within about two hours?

4. How is Gelson's Markets keeping its supply chain efficient and effective as it seeks to serve customers and counter competition?

STARTS NOW

50% OFF

HOLIDAY SALE

ONLINE ONLY.
ALL SALES FINAL.

SHOP NOW

PART 7 focuses on communication with target market members and other relevant groups. A specific marketing mix cannot satisfy people in a particular target market unless they are aware of the product and know where to find it. Some promotion decisions relate to a specific marketing mix; others are geared toward promoting the entire organization.

CHAPTER 16 discusses integrated marketing communications. It describes the communication process and the major promotional methods that can be included in promotion mixes.

CHAPTER 17 analyzes the major steps in developing an advertising campaign. It also explains what public relations is and how it can be used.

CHAPTER 18 deals with personal selling and sales promotion efforts, exploring the general characteristics of sales promotion and sales promotion techniques.

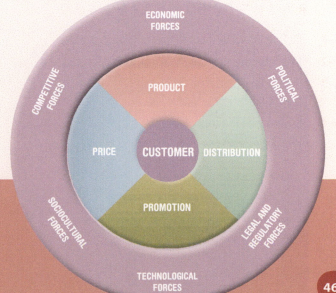

JR.BORDIO/SHUTTERSTOCK.COM

CHAPTER

16 Integrated Marketing Communications

LEARNING OBJECTIVES

16-1 Define integrated marketing communications.

16-2 Describe the steps of the communication process.

16-3 Recognize the definition and objectives of promotion.

16-4 Summarize the four elements of the promotion mix.

16-5 Explain the factors that are used to determine a product's promotion mix.

16-6 Describe how word-of-mouth communication affects promotion.

16-7 Discuss how product placement impacts promotion.

16-8 List major criticisms and defenses of promotion.

DARREN BRODE/SHUTTERSTOCK.COM

Toyota Camry Finds the Key to Integrated Marketing

When Toyota was about to introduce a new Camry model, it knew it needed to invest heavily in promotion. The company partnered with advertising agency Saatchi & Saatchi to develop an effective integrated marketing communications campaign. The team centered its campaign on the theme of love. It desired to portray its newer model as being sexy and edgy—a theme that would resonate with younger buyers.

The first step was to sell off the previous year's inventory. Using data collected from interested consumers, the team sent emails encouraging consumers to purchase the previous Camry model before it was gone. Interested consumers were directed to a sell-down landing page where they were encouraged to schedule test drives of the Camry.

The second step was to build buzz around its newest Camry model. In addition to traditional media, the team used internet and mobile channels to portray the special bond between owners and the Toyota Camry. For instance, it released "teasers" on social media sites prompting consumers to consider their relationships with their vehicles. A microsite was created that used the idea of courtship to interact with users and take them through the improved features of the new Camry model.

Customer engagement soared. About 150,000 consumers interacted with the campaign, more than 11,000 consumers scheduled test drives, and the amount of sales generated as a result of the campaign was estimated at more than $27 million for dealers involved in the project. The campaign was so effective that it earned nine international marketing awards, including an Internet Advertising Competition (IAC) Award for Outstanding Achievement in Internet Advertising from the Web Marketing Association.[1]

Organizations such as Toyota employ a variety of promotional methods to communicate with target markets. Sometimes the messages are planned in advance. Other times, they may be a response to a dramatic change in the marketing environment. Providing information to customers and other stakeholders is vital to initiating and developing long-term relationships with them.

This chapter looks at the general dimensions of promotion. First, we discuss the nature of integrated marketing communications. Next, we analyze the meaning and process of communication. We then define and examine the role of promotion and explore some of the reasons promotion is used. We consider major promotional methods and the factors that influence marketers' decisions to use particular methods. Next, we explain the positive and negative effects of personal and electronic word-of-mouth communication. Finally, we examine criticisms and benefits of promotion.

16-1 THE NATURE OF INTEGRATED MARKETING COMMUNICATIONS

Integrated marketing communications refer to the coordination of promotion and other marketing efforts to ensure maximum informational and persuasive impact on customers. Coordinating multiple marketing tools to produce this synergistic effect requires a marketer to employ a broad perspective. A major goal of integrated marketing communications is to send a consistent message to customers. Tide developed an integrated marketing campaign for the Super Bowl to highlight Tide's dominance in the detergent market as well as demonstrate its high performance. Tide's series of ads that ran during each quarter featured David Harbour (*Stranger Things*) and implied that any commercial with clean clothes is a Tide ad. The company coordinated social media posts with Old Spice spokesman Isaiah Mustafa as well as Betty White, Danica Patrick, Antonio Brown, and Drew Brees as part of the campaign. The result was more than 52,000 tweets during the game.[2]

Because various units both inside and outside most companies have traditionally planned and implemented promotional efforts, customers have not always received consistent messages. Integrated marketing communications allow an organization to coordinate and manage its promotional efforts to transmit consistent messages. Integrated marketing communications also enable synchronization of promotion elements and can improve the efficiency and effectiveness of promotion budgets. Thus, this approach not only creates long-term customer relationships but also enables the efficient use of promotional resources.

The concept of integrated marketing communications is increasingly effective for several reasons. Mass media advertising, a very popular promotional method in the past, is used less frequently today because of its high cost and lower effectiveness in reaching some target markets. Marketers can now take advantage of more precisely targeted promotional tools, such as television, direct mail, the internet, special-interest magazines, smartphones, mobile applications, social media, sales calls, and outdoor advertising. Database marketing and marketing analytics are also allowing marketers to target individual customers more precisely. Until recently, suppliers of marketing communications were specialists. Advertising agencies provided advertising campaigns, sales promotion companies provided sales promotion activities and materials, and public relations organizations engaged in publicity efforts. Today, a number of promotion-related companies provide one-stop shopping for the client seeking advertising, sales promotion, and public relations, thus reducing coordination problems for the sponsoring company. Because the overall cost of marketing communications has risen significantly, marketers demand systematic evaluations of communication efforts and a reasonable return on investment.

The types of communication used and the ways in which they are used are changing as both information technology and customer interests become increasingly dynamic. For instance, companies and politicians can hold press conferences where viewers can tweet their questions

integrated marketing communications Coordination of promotion and other marketing efforts for maximum informational and persuasive impact on customers

and have them answered on-screen. Some companies are creating their own branded content to exploit the many vehicles through which consumers obtain information. Under Armour teamed with famed Olympic athlete Michael Phelps to create a day in his life called "The Water Diviner." The writing, visuals, and lighting make this a compelling piece and won it recognition by *Advertising Age* as one of the top ten best branded content partnerships. As the most decorated Olympian in history (currently has won 28 medals), there remains significant fascination with Michael Phelps, and Under Armour has found an innovative way to create a partnership that enhances its branding.[3] Companies are turning toward branded content and other innovative communication media to engage users in ways that they can feel entertained without feeling the pressure of being inundated with traditional marketing messages.

Marketers and customers have almost unlimited access to data about each other. Integrating and customizing marketing communications while protecting customer privacy has become a major challenge. Through digital media, companies can provide product information and services that are coordinated with traditional promotional activities. In fact, gathering information about products is one of the main reasons people go online. This has made digital marketing a growing business. Marketers spend nearly 30 percent of their marketing budget on digital marketing.[4] The biggest concern of marketers is from fake news, questionable metrics, ethics issues which social media platforms have created, creator-perceived risk, and scrutiny. Almost 50 percent of advertisers will not spend money on risky platforms.[5] College students in particular say they are influenced by internet ads when buying online or just researching product purchases. The sharing of information and use of technology to facilitate communication between buyers and sellers are essential for successful customer relationship management.

16-2 PROMOTION AND THE COMMUNICATION PROCESS

Learning Objective 16-2

Describe the steps of the communication process.

Communication is essentially the transmission of information. For communication to take place, both the sender and receiver of information must share some common ground. They must have a common understanding of the symbols, words, and pictures used to transmit information. An individual transmitting the following message may believe he or she is communicating with you:

在工廠吾人製造化粧品,在商店吾人銷售希望。

However, communication has not taken place if you do not understand the language in which the message is written. Thus, we define **communication** as a sharing of meaning. Implicit in this definition is the notion of transmission of information because sharing necessitates transmission.

As Figure 16.1 shows, communication begins with a source. A **source** is a person, group, or organization with a meaning it attempts to share with an audience. A source could be an electronics salesperson wishing to communicate the attributes of OLED and 4K television to a buyer in the store or a television manufacturer using television ads to inform thousands of consumers about its products. Developing a strategy can enhance the effectiveness of the source's communication. For example, a strategy in which a salesperson attempts to influence a customer's decision by eliminating competitive products from consideration has been found to be effective. A **receiver** is the individual, group, or organization that decodes a coded message, and an *audience* is two or more receivers.

To transmit meaning, a source must convert the meaning into a series of signs or symbols representing ideas or concepts. This is called the **coding process**, or *encoding*. When coding meaning into a message, the source must consider certain characteristics of the receiver or audience. This is especially true for advertising. It is important to encode messages to prevent consumers from avoiding a conscious reception. Costs to the consumer in attention, time, and emotional response can diminish the impact of the message.[6] Therefore, signs or symbols must resonate with the receiver.

communication A sharing of meaning through the transmission of information

source A person, group, or organization with a meaning it tries to share with a receiver or an audience

receiver The individual, group, or organization that decodes a coded message

coding process Converting meaning into a series of signs or symbols

Figure 16.1 **The Communication Process**

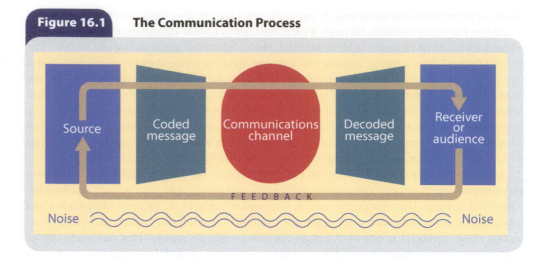

To share meaning, the source should use signs or symbols familiar to the receiver or audience. As marketers attempt to persuade consumers, they need to understand the specific lifestyles and attitudes that are acceptable to each target market to improve the effectiveness of their messaging. Marketers that understand this realize the importance of knowing their target market and ensuring that an advertisement or promotion uses language the target market understands and that shows behaviors acceptable within the culture. With the growth of the Hispanic market, marketers are increasingly using Spanish language media in their advertisements and messaging.

When coding a meaning, a source needs to use signs or symbols that the receiver or audience uses to refer to the concepts the source intends to convey. Instead of technical jargon, thoughtful language that helps consumers understand the message is more likely to result in positive attitudes and purchase intentions. Marketers try to avoid signs or symbols that may have several meanings for an audience. For instance, *soda* as a general term for soft drinks may not work well in national advertisements. Although in some parts of the United States the word means "soft drink," in other regions it may connote bicarbonate of soda, an ice cream drink, or something one mixes with alcoholic beverages.

communications channel The medium of transmission that carries the coded message from the source to the receiver

decoding process Converting signs or symbols into concepts and ideas

To share a coded meaning with the receiver or audience, a source selects and uses a **communications channel**, the medium of transmission that carries the coded message from the source to the receiver or audience. Transmission media include printed words (newspapers and magazines), broadcast media (television and radio), and digital communication (social media platforms such as Facebook and YouTube). Figure 16.2 shows how consumers are increasingly getting their news from social media sites.

When a source chooses an inappropriate communication channel, several problems may arise. The coded message may reach some receivers, but possibly the wrong receivers. Dieters who adopt the Weight Watchers diet may hear endorser Oprah Winfrey say that she ate bread every day and lost 26 pounds.[7] This may attract some consumers who are not serious about dieting and who think that it is easy. An advertiser that wants to reach a specific target market would need to take this information into account when choosing an appropriate communications message and channel. While the Weight Watchers diet may be effective in helping people to lose weight, the purpose is not to attract people that want an excuse to eat whatever they want. Thus, finding the right messages that target the right receivers can be a challenging process.

In the **decoding process**, signs or symbols are converted into concepts and ideas. Seldom does a receiver decode exactly the same meaning the source intended. When the result of decoding differs from what was coded, noise exists.

Figure 16.2 **Percentage of U.S. Adults Who Get Their News from Social Media Sites**

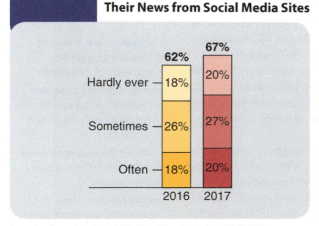

Source: Pew Research Center, Social Media and News Survey, August 8–21, 2017.

Noise is anything that reduces the clarity and accuracy of the communication; it has many sources and may affect any or all parts of the communication process. Noise sometimes arises within the communications channel itself. Radio or television transmission difficulties (satellite or cable) and poor or slow internet connections are sources of noise. Noise also occurs when a source uses signs or symbols that are unfamiliar to the receiver or have a meaning different from the one intended. Noise may also originate in the receiver; a receiver may be unaware of a coded message when perceptual processes block it out through a lack of understanding. Those who do not recycle, for instance, can block messages encouraging "green behaviors" such as recycling.

The receiver's response to a decoded message is **feedback** to the source. The source usually expects and normally receives feedback, although perhaps not immediately. During feedback, the receiver or audience provides the original source with a response to the message. Feedback is coded, sent through a communications channel, and decoded by the receiver, the source of the original communication. Thus, communication is a circular process, as indicated in Figure 16.1.

When marketers interact directly with consumers through personal selling sales promotions, feedback is provided immediately. Instant feedback lets marketers adjust messages quickly to improve the effectiveness of their communications. For example, when a salesperson realizes through feedback that a customer does not understand a sales presentation, the salesperson adapts the presentation to make it more meaningful to the customer. This is why face-to-face communication is the most adaptive and flexible, especially compared to digital, web-based, or other non-personal communications. In interpersonal communication, feedback occurs through talking, touching, smiling, nodding, eye movements, and other body movements and postures.

When mass communication like advertising is used, feedback is often slow and difficult to recognize. Also, it may be several months or even years before the effects of this promotion will be known. Some relevant and timely feedback can occur in the form of sales increases, inquiries about products, or online registrations for promotions or reward programs.

Each communication channel has a limit on the volume of information it can handle effectively. This limit, called **channel capacity**, is determined by the least efficient component of the communication process. Consider communications that depend on speech. An individual source can speak only so fast, and there is a limit to how much an individual receiver can take in through listening. Beyond that point, additional messages cannot be decoded; thus, meaning cannot be shared. To be effective, a 30-second advertising message should not exceed 75 words because most announcers cannot articulate words into understandable messages at a rate beyond 150 words per minute.

16-3 THE ROLE AND OBJECTIVES OF PROMOTION

Learning Objective 16-3

Recognize the definition and objectives of promotion.

Promotion is communication that builds and maintains favorable relationships by informing and persuading one or more audiences to view an organization positively and accept its products. Many organizations spend considerable resources on promotion to build and enhance relationships with current and potential customers as well as other stakeholders. Thoughtful promotion reinforces market positioning versus the competition and creates a reason for purchase. Chipotle Mexican Grill introduced a promotion designed to reinforce consumers' understanding of the quality and freshness of its guacamole and to create a reason for customers to visit or return to Chipotle. "'Cado Crusher" is a game that can be played online that allows you to make your own guacamole and appreciate Chipotle's fresh ingredients, and after playing you receive a coupon for free chips and guacamole with a purchase. Its promotional partner is Avocados from Mexico. Joint promotions support the goals of each partner, and Chipotle is a good customer, with each store using five cases of avocados a day.[8] Marketers also indirectly facilitate favorable relationships by focusing information about company activities and products on interest groups (such as environmental and consumer groups), current and potential investors, regulatory agencies, and society in general. For instance, some organizations

noise Anything that reduces a communication's clarity and accuracy

feedback The receiver's response to a decoded message

channel capacity The limit on the volume of information a communication channel can handle effectively

promotion Communication to build and maintain relationships by informing and persuading one or more audiences

Figure 16.3   **Information Flows Are Important in Integrated Marketing Communications**

promote responsible use of products criticized by society, such as tobacco, alcohol, and violent movies or video games. Companies sometimes promote programs that help selected groups. For example, Coca-Cola was a founding member of the Special Olympics, a sports organization for people with intellectual disabilities. It provides in-kind donations, volunteer hours, financial contributions, and publicity for the organization.[9] Such cause-related marketing links the purchase of products to philanthropic efforts for one or more causes. By contributing to causes that its target markets support, cause-related marketing can help marketers boost sales, increase loyalty, and generate goodwill.

To maximize promotional effectiveness, marketers strive for proper planning, implementation, coordination, and control of communications. Effective management of integrated marketing communications is based on information about, and feedback from, customers and the marketing environment, often obtained from an organization's marketing information system (see Figure 16.3). How successfully marketers use promotion to maintain positive relationships depends to some extent on the quantity and quality of information the organization receives and listens to from customers. Social media, blogging, and customer feedback through websites has been a very effective way to listen to customers. Because customers share information and opinions through many different sources, integrated marketing communications planning also takes into account these informal methods of communication. Because promotion is communication that can be managed, we now analyze what this communication is and how it works.

Promotional objectives vary considerably from one organization to another and within organizations over time. Large firms with multiple promotional programs operating simultaneously may have quite varied promotional objectives. For the purpose of analysis, we focus on the ten promotional objectives shown in Table 16.1. Although the list is not exhaustive, one or more of these objectives underlie many promotional programs.

16-3a Create Awareness

A considerable amount of promotion efforts focus on creating awareness. For an organization that is introducing a new product or a line extension, making customers aware of the product is crucial to initiating the product adoption process. A marketer that has invested

Table 16.1   **Possible Objectives of Promotion**

Create awareness	Retain loyal customers
Stimulate demand	Facilitate reseller support
Encourage product trial	Combat competitive promotional efforts
Identify prospects	Reduce sales fluctuations
Stimulate word of mouth	Generate positive social media posts

heavily in product development strives to create product awareness quickly to generate revenues to offset the high costs of product development and introduction. Apple often begins to build awareness about new products months before it releases them. It holds an annual developer conference, at which CEO Tim Cook creates interest and excitement about new products.[10] The Country Crock advertisement creates awareness around its new butter made with sunflower oil which does not require softening for baking. The advertisement shows a mother and her children mixing cookie dough with the headline, "Baking Made Easier."

Creating awareness is important for existing products, too. Promotional efforts may aim to increase awareness of brands, product features, image-related issues (such as ethical or socially responsive behavior), or operational characteristics (such as store hours, locations, and credit availability). Some promotional programs are unsuccessful because marketers fail to generate awareness of critical issues among a significant portion of target market members. Other times, the campaign itself is at fault. For example, when the state of Rhode Island launched a $5 million campaign to promote tourism they were not aware the footage in the 110-second video was of not only Rhode Island, but also Iceland. The company that cut the video was instructed to only use Rhode Island videos. Needless to say, those familiar with Rhode Island were confused when viewing the promotional materials, and the campaign's effectiveness was impacted.[11]

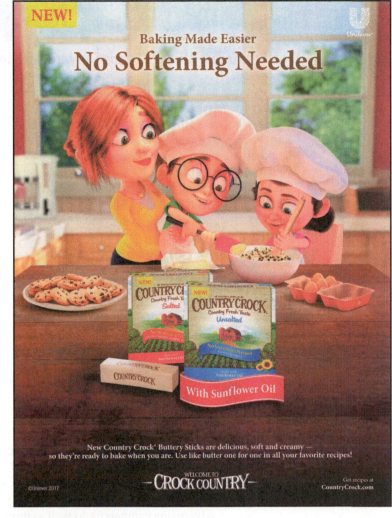

Creating Awareness
Country Crock uses a depiction of a mom and her children baking to show how easy it is to use its new butter. Country Crock is attempting to create awareness for its new butter product which does not require softening for baking.

16-3b Stimulate Demand

When an organization is the first to introduce an innovative product, it tries to stimulate **primary demand**—demand for a product category rather than for a specific brand of product—through **new introductory promotion**. New introductory promotion informs potential customers about the product: what it is, what it does, how it can be used, and where it can be purchased. Because this promotion is used in the introductory stage of the product life cycle, meaning there are no competing brands, it neither emphasizes brand names nor compares brands. This tactic was taken when introducing chia seeds to the food market. Less than a decade ago, the nutritional benefits of chia seeds were relatively unknown. Advertisers, therefore, had to engage in pioneer advertising to spread awareness of the product category before focusing on specific brands. Today, 37 percent of the U.S. population has heard of chia seeds as a food item.[12]

To build **selective demand**, demand for a specific brand, a marketer employs promotional efforts that point out the strengths and benefits of a specific brand. Building selective demand also requires singling out attributes important to potential buyers. Selective demand can be stimulated by differentiating the product from competing brands in the

primary demand Demand for a product category rather than for a specific brand

new introductory promotion Promotion that informs consumers about a new product

selective demand Demand for a specific brand

INTEGRITY IN MARKETING

The Rainforest Alliance Leaps Forward with Integrated Marketing

The Rainforest Alliance, a highly recognized nonprofit aiming to conserve biodiversity and promote sustainability, defies the traditional nonprofit mold. With thousands of members and supporters, the Rainforest Alliance has been fighting globally for wildlife and wild lands since 1987. As more consumers and businesses become interested in preserving the world's resources, the Rainforest Alliance has gained widespread support through its integrated marketing initiatives.

The Rainforest Alliance has many resources for businesses that partner with the organization. For example, the Rainforest Alliance provides the Rainforest Alliance Certified seal for use on product packaging which raises awareness for the program among consumers and other businesses. The Rainforest Alliance blog describes

how sustainability can positively impact a business, and its seal is one way businesses can inform consumers that they have incorporated sustainability principles into their operations. The non-profit also develops themed social media campaigns like #FollowTheFrog for partners to join in to amplify their reach. Additionally, the Rainforest Alliance offers resources to businesses who want to educate their own employees about sustainability.

The Rainforest Alliance uses many integrated marketing communications tactics to spread the word about its mission, send a consistent message to customers, and maximize the reach of the organization. For individuals looking to aid the environment and support small growers, the Rainforest Alliance is making a positive difference.[a]

minds of potential buyers. Consider the advertisement for GEICO. The advertisement lists strengths of the brand, such as its 24/7 licensed agents, while comparing it to "the other guy." It implies its competitors do not stack up against GEICO's attributes. Selective demand can also be stimulated by increasing the number of product uses and promoting them through advertising campaigns, as well as through price discounts, free samples, coupons, consumer contests and games, and sweepstakes. For example, Macy's Department Store uses One Day Sales to create demand for Macy's products, increase exposure to the brand, and build selective demand. In a time when traditional retailers are struggling to compete against online competitors, discounting can be a tactic that generates selective demand. In addition, selective demand can be stimulated by encouraging existing customers to use more of the product.

16-3c **Encourage Product Trial**

When attempting to move customers through the product adoption cycle, a marketer may successfully create awareness and interest, but customers may stall during the evaluation stage. In this case, certain types of promotion—such as free samples, coupons, test drives, or limited free-use offers, contests, and games—are employed to encourage product trial. Costco uses free sampling kiosks and demo kitchens to offer free samples throughout its stores.[13] Whether a marketer's product is the first in a new product category, a new brand in an existing category, or simply an existing brand seeking customers, trial-inducing promotional efforts aim to make product trial convenient and low risk for potential customers.

16-3d **Identify Prospects**

Certain types of promotional efforts aim to identify customers who are interested in the firm's product and are likely potential buyers. Television advertisements may encourage the viewer to visit the company's website and share personal information in order to receive something of value from the company. Customers who respond to such a message usually have higher interest in the product, making them potential customers. The organization can respond with phone calls, email, or personal contact by salespeople.

16-3e Retain Loyal Customers

Clearly, maintaining long-term customer relationships is a major goal of most marketers. Many companies, from fast-food companies such as Taco Bell to auto manufacturers such as BMW, know the long-term customer value for their products. Promotional efforts directed at customer retention can help an organization control its costs, because the costs of retaining customers are usually considerably lower than those of acquiring new ones. Frequent-user programs, such as those sponsored by airlines, car rental agencies, and hotels, aim to reward loyal customers and encourage them to remain loyal. Many supermarkets, such as Kroger and its affiliated brands, offer a loyalty program that gives one fuel point for every $1.00 spent in the store. Accumulated discounts range from $0.10 to $1.00 off per gallon of fuel. Some organizations employ special offers that only their existing customers can use. To retain loyal customers, marketers not only advertise loyalty programs but also use reinforcement advertising, which assures current users that they have made the right brand choice and tells them how to get the most satisfaction from the product.

16-3f Facilitate Reseller Support

Reseller support is a two-way street: producers generally want to provide support to resellers to assist in selling their products, and in turn they expect resellers to support their products. When a manufacturer, such as Procter & Gamble, advertises its home and health products to consumers, retailers and wholesalers should view this promotion as a form of strong manufacturer support. In some instances, a producer agrees to pay a certain proportion of retailers' advertising expenses for promoting its products. When a manufacturer is introducing a new consumer brand in a highly competitive product category, it may be difficult to persuade supermarket managers to carry this brand. However, if the manufacturer promotes the new brand with free samples and coupon distribution in the retailer's area, a supermarket manager views these actions as strong support and is much more likely to carry the product. To encourage wholesalers and retailers to increase their inventories of its products, a manufacturer may provide them with special offers and buying allowances. In certain industries, a producer's salesperson may provide support to a wholesaler by working with the wholesaler's customers (retailers) in the presentation and promotion of the products. Strong relationships with resellers are important to a firm's ability to maintain a sustainable competitive advantage. The use of various promotional methods can help support sales growth.

16-3g Combat Competitive Promotional Efforts

At times, a marketer's objective in using promotion is to challenge a competitor's promotional or marketing programs. This reactive approach is to prevent a sales or market share loss. A combative promotional objective is used most often by firms in extremely

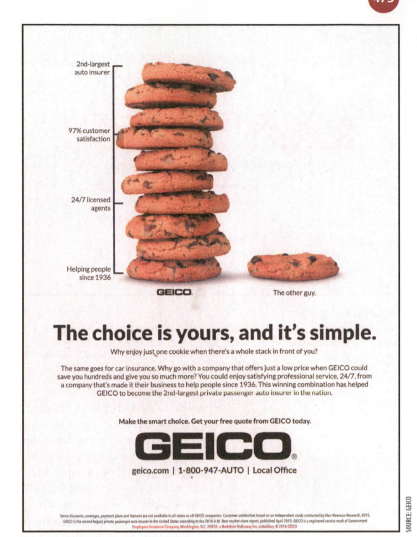

Building Selective Demand
This advertisement builds selective demand by pointing out the strengths and benefits of the brand—GEICO.

Seasonal Demand
Swimsuit apparel is subject to seasonal demand, with demand peaking in the summer and bottoming out in the fall and winter. To balance demand, marketers might use promotions such as coupons or advertisements that encourage consumers to purchase these products during off-peak periods.

competitive consumer markets, such as the fast-food, convenience store, and cable/internet/cell phone markets. Stores that offer price-matching programs include Best Buy, Fry's Electronics, The Home Depot, Lowes, Target, Walmart, Staples, Office Depot, and Office Max. It is not unusual for competitors to respond with a counter-pricing strategy or even match a competitor's pricing.

16-3h Reduce Sales Fluctuations

Product demand for many products varies from one month to another because of such factors as climate, holidays, seasons, and the economy. A business, however, cannot operate at peak efficiency when sales fluctuate rapidly. Changes in sales volume translate into changes in production, inventory levels, personnel needs, and financial resources. When promotional techniques reduce fluctuations by generating sales during slow periods, a firm can use its resources more efficiently.

Promotional techniques are often designed to stimulate sales during sales slumps. Hence, Snapper may offer sales prices on lawn mowers into the fall season to extend the selling season. During peak periods, a marketer may refrain from advertising to prevent stimulating sales to the point at which the firm cannot handle all of the demand. On occasion, a company advertises that customers can be better served by coming in on certain days. For example, in most states Logan's Road House allows kids 12 and under to receive one free kids meal for each adult meal purchased on Wednesdays.

To achieve the major objectives of promotion discussed here, companies must develop appropriate promotional programs. In the next section, we consider the basic components of such programs: the promotion mix elements.

INDIGO PHOTO CLUB/SHUTTERSTOCK.COM

16-4 THE PROMOTION MIX

Several promotional methods can be used to communicate with individuals, groups, and organizations. When an organization combines specific methods to manage the integrated marketing communications for a particular product, that combination is the product promotion mix for that product. The four possible elements of a **promotion mix** are advertising, personal selling, public relations, and sales promotion (see Figure 16.4). For some products, firms use all four elements; for others, they use only two or three. In this section, we provide an overview of each promotion mix element; they are covered in greater detail in the next two chapters.

16-4a Advertising

Advertising is a paid nonpersonal communication about an organization and its products transmitted to a target audience through mass media, including television, radio, the internet, newspapers, magazines, video games, direct mail, outdoor displays, and signs on mass transit vehicles. Advertising is changing as consumers' mass media consumption habits are changing. Companies are striving to maximize their presence and impact through digital media; ads are being designed that cater to smaller, more personalized audiences; and traditional media like newspapers are in a decline due to a drop in readership. Individuals and organizations use advertising to promote goods, services, ideas, issues, and people. Being highly flexible,

promotion mix A combination of promotional methods used to promote a specific product

Figure 16.4	The Four Possible Elements of a Promotion Mix

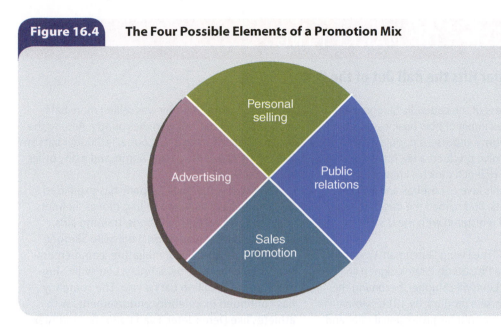

advertising can reach an extremely large target audience or focus on a small, precisely defined segment. For instance, Sonic's advertising focuses on a large audience of potential fast-food customers, ranging from children to adults, whereas advertising for Gulfstream jets aims at a much smaller and more specialized target market.

Advertising offers several benefits. It is extremely cost-efficient when it reaches a vast number of people at a low cost per person. For example, the cost of a 4-color, full-page advertisement in the national edition of *TIME* magazine costs $366,600. With a circulation of 3 million, this makes the cost of reaching roughly a thousand subscribers $122.[14] Advertising also lets the source repeat the message several times. For example, Subway promotes a different 6-inch sub of the day for $3.50 in its "Life's Important Days" campaign which relates significant life changes to the Subway Sub of the Day. Furthermore, advertising a product a certain way can add to the product's value, and the visibility an organization gains from advertising can enhance its image. For instance, incorporating touchable elements that generate positive sensory feedback in print advertising can be a positive persuasive tool.[15] At times, a firm tries to enhance its own or its product's image by including celebrity endorsers in advertisements. Peyton Manning, former quarterback for the Denver Broncos, does celebrity endorsements for Oreos, Gatorade, Direct TV, Nationwide Insurance, and Buick. Garnier partnered with actress Mandy Moore to endorse its Nutrisse Nourishing Color Creme hair dye. The advertisement shows Moore happily showing off her hair and notes that the actress uses shade #53 Medium Golden Brown. By using Moore as an endorser, Garnier is able to capitalize on her status as a celebrity. On the other hand, there are downsides to using celebrity endorsers when they act inappropriately. Nike has terminated or suspended contracts with celebrity endorsers for domestic violence allegations.

Celebrity Endorsers
Mandy Moore endorses Garnier Nutrisse. Garnier is able to capitalize on Moore's popularity as an actress to convince others to give it a try.

ENTREPRENEURISHIP IN MARKETING

Louisville Slugger Hits the Ball Out of the Park

The story and success of the Louisville Slugger baseball bat is a prime example of how businesses can capitalize on a celebrity endorser's popularity to convince others to give products a try. More than a century ago, Bud Hillerich took his knowledge of woodworking and his love of baseball and applied it to developing bats. Bud named the business "Louisville Slugger" and registered with the U.S. Patent Office.

In 1905, Honus "The Flying Dutchman" Wagner, a superstar with the Pittsburgh Pirates, signed an endorsement with Louisville Slugger, becoming the first athlete to endorse a product. By 1911, salesman Frank Bradsby had brought his professional sales and marketing expertise to the company. With his help,

by 1923, Louisville Slugger was selling more bats than any other bat maker in the country. Among the baseball legends who used Louisville Slugger bats are Babe Ruth, Lou Gehrig, Hank Aaron, and many other sports icons.

In recent years, the company has expanded beyond making bats into selling gloves, helmets, catcher's gear, equipment bags, training aids, and accessories. In addition, Louisville Slugger also offers personalized, miniature, commemorative, and collectable bats. Today, Louisville Slugger makes 1.8 million bats a year. The company has continued its celebrity endorsements with athletes like Derek Jeter, Evan Longoria, and Alex Rodriguez.[b]

Advertising has disadvantages as well. Even though the cost per person reached may be relatively low, the absolute dollar outlay can be extremely high, especially for commercials during popular television shows and those associated with popular websites. High costs can limit, and sometimes preclude, the use of advertising in a promotion mix. Moreover, advertising rarely provides rapid feedback. Measuring its effect on sales is often difficult, and it is generally less persuasive than personal selling. There are online sources, like RetailMeNot, that house coupon codes for many retailers. The use of a coupon code allows retailers to track the use and appeal of varying promotional offers.

16-4b Personal Selling

Personal selling is a paid personal communication that seeks to inform customers and persuade them to purchase products in an exchange situation. The phrase *purchase products* is interpreted broadly to encompass acceptance of ideas and issues. Personal selling is most extensively used in the business-to-business market and also in the business-to-consumer market for high-end products such as homes, cars, electronics, and furniture.

Personal selling has both advantages and limitations when compared with advertising. Advertising is general communication aimed at a relatively large target audience, whereas personal selling involves more specific communication directed at one or several individuals. Reaching one person through personal selling costs considerably more than through advertising, but personal selling efforts often have greater impact on customers. Personal selling also provides immediate feedback, allowing marketers to adjust their messages to improve communication. Such interaction helps them determine and respond to customers' information needs.

When a salesperson and a customer meet face-to-face, they use several types of interpersonal communication. The predominant communication form is language, both spoken and written. A salesperson and customer frequently use **kinesic communication**, or communication through the movement of head, eyes, arms, hands, legs, or torso. Winking, head nodding, hand gestures, and arm motions are some forms of kinesic communication. A good salesperson can often evaluate a prospect's interest in a product or presentation by noting eye contact and head

kinesic communication
Communicating through the movement of head, eyes, arms, hands, legs, or torso

nodding. **Proxemic communication**, a less obvious form of communication used in personal selling situations, occurs when either person varies the physical distance separating them. When a customer backs away from a salesperson, for example, he or she may be displaying a lack of interest in the product or expressing dislike for the salesperson. Touching, or **tactile communication**, is also a form of communication, although less popular in the United States than in many other countries. Handshaking is a common form of tactile communication both in the United States and elsewhere.

Sales managers need a variety of skills to oversee the sales force. These skills include interpersonal, technical, and strategic skills. The importance of these different types of skills depends largely on the level of management.[16] For instance, sales managers need strong leadership skills and must be able to use sales management technology to track and control sales strategies. A salesperson, however, needs extremely strong interpersonal skills, product knowledge, and needs to be likeable and responsive to customer needs.

Personal Selling
Expensive, personal selling is especially useful in high-risk transactions such as purchasing a new car.

16-4c **Public Relations**

Although many promotional activities focus on a firm's customers, other stakeholders—suppliers, employees, stockholders, the media, educators, potential investors, government officials, and society in general—are important to an organization as well. To communicate with customers and stakeholders, a company employs public relations. Public relations is a broad set of communication efforts used to create and maintain favorable relationships between an organization and its stakeholders. Maintaining a positive relationship with one or more stakeholders can affect a firm's current sales and profits, as well as its long-term survival. When United Record Pressing LLC announced its expansion in Nashville, it sent many signals for the company which produces 30 to 40 percent of all vinyl records available in stores. It signaled a resurgence in the sales of vinyl record albums to consumers; a strengthening business model and growth mode for this privately held company; and a commitment to the rich history, dating back to 1949, to retain the original building on Chestnut Street as "an important place in musical history."[17]

Public relations uses a variety of tools, including annual reports, brochures, event sponsorships, and sponsorship of socially responsible programs aimed at protecting the environment or helping disadvantaged individuals. The goal of public relations is to create and enhance a positive image of the organization. Increasingly, marketers are going directly to consumers with their public relations efforts through social media. Pampered Chef placed content on YouTube that shows consumers how to make certain recipes. This content familiarizes consumers with Pampered Chef and positions the organization as a helper in the kitchen.[18]

Other tools arise from the use of publicity, which is a component of public relations. Publicity is nonpersonal communication in news story form about an organization or its products, or both, transmitted through a mass medium at no charge. A few examples of publicity-based public relations tools are news releases, press conferences, feature articles, and social media sites such as YouTube and Twitter. For example, General Motors made headlines as the first automaker to broadcast on Facebook Live when they gave its Facebook fans an up-close look at a new car model.[19] To generate publicity, companies sometimes give away products to celebrities in the hope that the celebrities will be seen and photographed with the product, and those photos will stimulate awareness and product trial among their fans. Grammy nominees

proxemic communication
Communicating by varying the physical distance in face-to-face interactions

tactile communication
Communicating through touching

receive a gift bag known as the "Swag Bag." These bags can be worth around $30,000 and can consist of luxury products such as a 10-year supply of Oxygenetix Breathable Foundation and Oxygenated Moisturizer worth up to $13,400, a week-long trip to the Golden Door spa, worth $8,850, as well as other high-end products and services. Donors of the gifts count on the publicity to create awareness of their products and also hope high visibility entertainers will use their products.[20] Public relations efforts may be the responsibility of an individual or of a department within the organization, or the organization may hire an independent public relations agency.

Unpleasant situations and negative events, such as product tampering or an environmental disaster, may generate unfavorable public relations for an organization. Subway gained significant negative press for employing spokesperson Jared Fogle who lost around 200 pounds eating Subway sandwiches. Although the company made millions from the partnership, Subway had to sever ties with Fogle when he was charged with the possession and distribution of child pornography among other charges and was sentenced to 16 years in prison for his misconduct.[21] To minimize the damaging effects of unfavorable coverage, effective marketers have policies and procedures in place to help manage any public relations problems. Often these plans are called crisis management plans and attempt to anticipate what can go wrong and how to respond.

Public relations should not be viewed as a set of tools to be used only during crises. To get the most from public relations, an organization should have someone responsible for public relations either internally or externally and should have an ongoing public relations program.

16-4d Sales Promotion

Sales promotion is an activity or material that acts as a direct inducement, offering added value or incentive for the product to resellers, salespeople, or consumers. Examples include free samples, games, rebates, sweepstakes, contests, premiums, and coupons. *Sales promotion* should not be confused with *promotion*; sales promotion is just one part of the comprehensive area of promotion. Marketers spend more on sales promotion than on advertising, and sales promotion appears to be a faster-growing area than advertising. Coupons and coupon codes are important to retailers and manufacturers. Brands such as Werther's Original use coupons to promote their products as shown in the Werther's Original Sugar Free ad. The advertisement encourages consumers to try the product with a 50 cents off coupon.

Generally, when companies employ advertising or personal selling, they depend on these activities continuously or cyclically. However, a marketer's use of sales promotion tends to be less consistent. Many products are seasonal. Toys may be discounted in January after the holiday selling season to move excess inventory. Marketers frequently rely on sales promotion to improve the effectiveness of other promotion mix elements, especially advertising and personal selling. Coupons appear to be more effective for food and packaged goods marketers. Nine out of ten Millennials use coupons, using

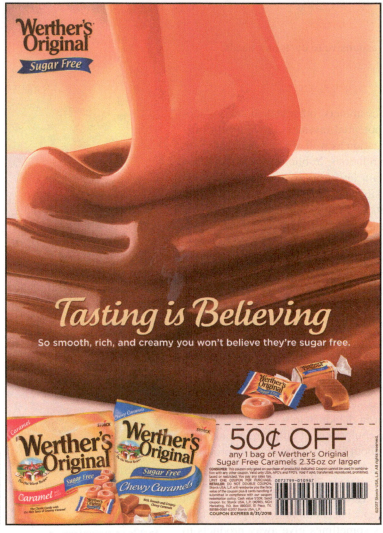

Sales Promotions

In addition to attracting customers with its depiction of smooth, creamy caramel, Werther's Original also offers a coupon for customers to redeem in-store.

coupon code websites such as coupons.com, Ebates, and traditional paper coupons.[22] Mobile devices are a personal technology, so they pose an unusual opportunity to reach consumers wherever they go. Mobile internet usage recently surpassed desktop usage.[23] Mobile apps are used as tools to engage the consumer through sales promotion items such as coupons in close proximity to the consumer and retailer.

An effective promotion mix requires the right combination of components. To see how such a mix is created, we now examine the factors and conditions affecting the selection of promotional methods that an organization uses for a particular product.

16-5 SELECTING PROMOTION MIX FACTORS

Learning Objective 16-5
Explain the factors that are used to determine a product's promotion mix.

Marketers vary the composition of promotion mixes for many reasons. Although a promotion mix can include all four elements, frequently, a marketer selects fewer than four. Many firms that market multiple product lines use several promotion mixes simultaneously.

16-5a Promotional Resources, Objectives, and Policies

The size of an organization's promotional budget affects the number and relative intensity of promotional methods included in a promotion mix. If a company's promotional budget is extremely limited, the firm is likely to rely on personal selling because it is easier to measure a salesperson's contribution to sales than to measure the sales effectiveness of advertising. Businesses must have significant promotional budgets to use regional or national advertising. Companies such as Procter & Gamble, Unilever, General Motors, and Coca-Cola are among the leaders in worldwide media spending. Organizations with extensive promotional resources generally include more elements in their promotion mixes, but having more promotional dollars to spend does not necessarily mean using more promotional methods. Researchers have found that resources spent on promotional activities have a positive influence on shareholder value.

An organization's promotional objectives and policies also influence the types of promotion selected. If a company's objective is to create mass awareness of a new convenience good, such as a breakfast cereal, its promotion mix probably leans heavily toward advertising, sales promotion, and possibly public relations. If a company hopes to educate consumers about the features of a

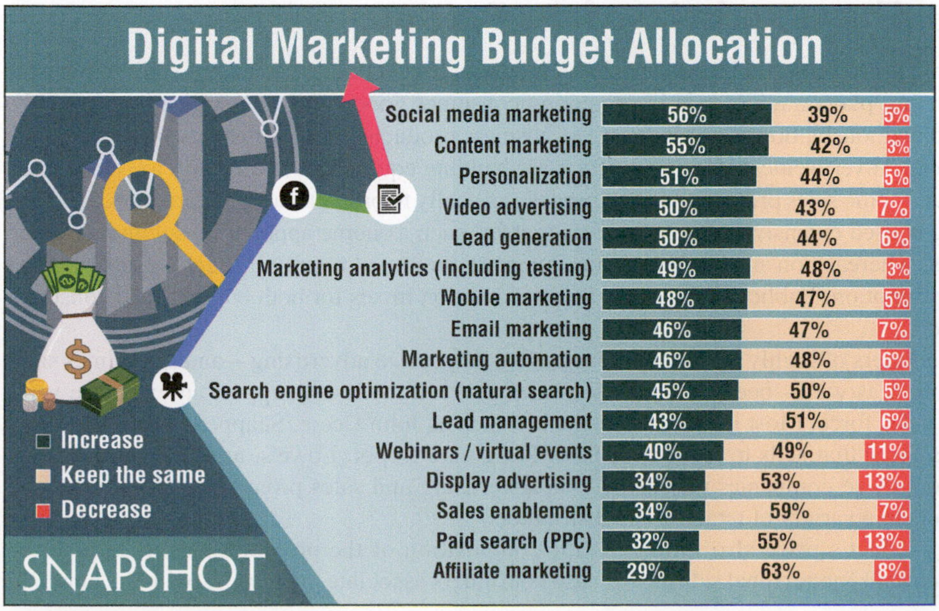

Digital Marketing Budget Allocation

	Increase	Keep the same	Decrease
Social media marketing	56%	39%	5%
Content marketing	55%	42%	3%
Personalization	51%	44%	5%
Video advertising	50%	43%	7%
Lead generation	50%	44%	6%
Marketing analytics (including testing)	49%	48%	3%
Mobile marketing	48%	47%	5%
Email marketing	46%	47%	7%
Marketing automation	46%	48%	6%
Search engine optimization (natural search)	45%	50%	5%
Lead management	43%	51%	6%
Webinars / virtual events	40%	49%	11%
Display advertising	34%	53%	13%
Sales enablement	34%	59%	7%
Paid search (PPC)	32%	55%	13%
Affiliate marketing	29%	63%	8%

□ Increase
■ Keep the same
■ Decrease

SNAPSHOT

Source: Econsultancy / Adobe

durable good, such as a home appliance, its promotion mix may combine a moderate amount of advertising, possibly some sales promotion designed to attract customers to retail stores, and a great deal of personal selling, because this method is an efficient way to inform customers about such products. If a firm's objective is to produce immediate sales of nondurable services, the promotion mix will probably stress advertising and sales promotion. For instance, dry cleaners and carpet-cleaning firms are more likely to use advertising with a coupon or discount rather than personal selling.

16-5b Characteristics of the Target Market

Size, geographic distribution, and sociocultural and demographic characteristics of an organization's target market help dictate the methods to include in a product's promotion mix. To some degree, market size and diversity determine composition of the mix. If the size is limited, the promotion mix will probably use a more targeted form of marketing such as personal selling, which can be very effective for reaching small numbers of people. With the low cost of social media, it is increasingly effective for small, niche markets. Organizations selling to industrial markets and firms marketing products through only a few wholesalers frequently make personal selling the major component of their promotion mixes. When a product's market consists of millions of customers, organizations rely on mass marketing through advertising and sales promotion, because these methods reach large groups of people at a low cost per person. When the population density is uneven around the country, marketers may use regional advertising to target smaller markets.

Geographic distribution of a firm's customers also affects the choice of promotional methods. Personal selling is more feasible if a company's customers are concentrated in a small area than if they are dispersed across a vast region. When the company's customers are numerous and dispersed, regional or national advertising may be more practical.

Distribution of a target market's demographic characteristics, such as age, income, or education, may affect the types of promotional techniques a marketer selects, as well as the messages and images employed. According to the U.S. Census Bureau, the percentage of children living in families with two parents is 69, down from 88 in 1960.[24] To reach the more than three-quarters of households consisting of single parents, unmarried couples, singles, and "empty nesters" (whose children have left home), more companies are modifying the images used in their promotions and marketing channels.

16-5c Characteristics of the Product

Generally, promotion mixes for business products concentrate on personal selling, whereas advertising plays a major role in promoting consumer goods. This generalization should be treated cautiously, however. Marketers of business products use some advertising to promote products. Advertisements for computers, road-building equipment, and aircraft are fairly common, and some sales promotion is also used occasionally to promote business products. Personal selling is used extensively for consumer durables, such as home appliances, automobiles, and houses, whereas consumer convenience items are promoted mainly through advertising and sales promotion. Public relations appears in promotion mixes for both business and consumer products.

Marketers of highly seasonal products often emphasize advertising—and sometimes sales promotion as well—because off-season sales generally will not support an extensive year-round sales force. Most lawn care companies, such as John Deere, Snapper, and Honda, have a sales force that sells to retailers such as The Home Depot, Lowe's, and Ace Hardware. In addition, these companies rely heavily on advertising and sales promotion to promote their products to a variety of retailers and distributors.

A product's price also influences the composition of the promotion mix. High-priced products call for personal selling, because consumers associate greater risk with the purchase of such products and usually want specific and comparative information from a salesperson. For low-priced convenience items, such as paper towels and deli meats, marketers use advertising rather than personal selling. Research suggests that consumers visiting a store specifically to purchase a product on sale are more likely to have read flyers and purchased other sale-priced products than consumers visiting the same store for other reasons.[25]

Another consideration in creating an effective promotion mix is the stage of the product's life cycle. During the introduction stage, advertising is used to create awareness for both business and consumer products. Apple released commercials promoting the ease and convenience of its Apple Watch. It released six different ads showing situations in which people from all walks of life can use the smart watch to manage and transform the messiness of life to achieve their objectives happily and efficiently.[26] For many products, personal selling and sales promotion are also helpful in this stage. In the growth and maturity stages, consumer products require heavy emphasis on advertising, whereas business products often call for a concentration of personal selling and some sales promotion. In the decline stage, marketers usually decrease all promotional activities, especially advertising.

Intensity of market coverage is still another factor affecting the composition of the promotion mix. When products are marketed through intensive distribution, firms depend strongly on advertising and sales promotion. Many convenience products like lotions, cereals, and coffee are promoted through samples, coupons, and refunds. When marketers choose selective distribution, promotion mixes vary considerably. Items handled through exclusive distribution—such as expensive watches, furs, and high-quality furniture—typically require a significant amount of personal selling.

A product's use also affects the combination of promotional methods. Manufacturers of highly personal products, such as laxatives, nonprescription contraceptives, and feminine hygiene products, depend on advertising because many customers do not want to talk with salespeople about these products. Service businesses often use tangible products to promote their intangible services. Unigo released an advertisement for Money College Planner depicting a bitten pencil to communicate that its tool will relieve the stress parents feel while planning for their children's future. The Money College Planner provides a customizable search for schools, one-on-one advice, and financial tools. The tangible element in the advertisement reassures parents about the value the tool provides.

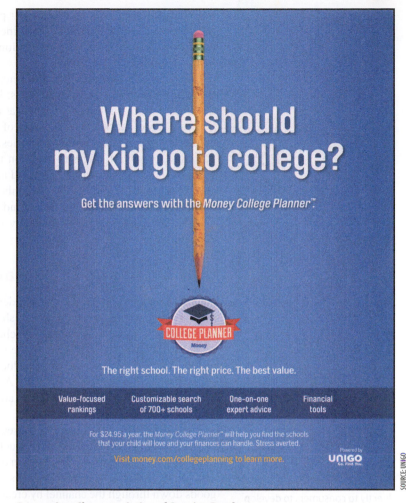

SOURCE: UNIGO

Portraying Characteristics of Service Products
Service products, such as Unigo's Money College Planner, are often portrayed using tangible goods that tell a story about the service. In this advertisement, Unigo uses a bitten pencil to show how its Money College Planner will relieve stress parents feel about college planning for their kids.

16-5d Costs and Availability of Promotional Methods

Costs of promotional methods are major factors to analyze when developing a promotion mix. National advertising and sales promotion require large expenditures. However, if these efforts succeed in reaching extremely large audiences, the cost per individual reached may be quite small, possibly a few pennies. Some forms of advertising are relatively inexpensive. Many small, local businesses advertise products through local newspapers, magazines, radio and television stations, outdoor boards, internet ads, and signs on mass transit vehicles.

Another consideration that marketers explore when formulating a promotion mix is the availability of promotional techniques. Despite the tremendous number of media vehicles in the United States, a firm may find that no available advertising medium effectively reaches a certain target market. The problem of media availability becomes more pronounced when marketers advertise in foreign countries. Some media, such as television, simply may not be available, or advertising on television may be highly regulated. For example, Sweden has some of the strictest controls for food advertising to children. Marketers have agreed to not target children 16 and under with unhealthy food or drink messages.[27] In some countries, advertisers are forbidden to make brand comparisons on television. Other promotional methods also have limitations. A firm may wish to increase its sales force but be unable to find qualified personnel.

16-5e Push and Pull Channel Policies

Another element that marketers consider when planning a promotion mix is whether to use a push policy or a pull policy. With a **push policy**, the producer promotes the product only to the next institution down the marketing channel. In a marketing channel with wholesalers and retailers, the producer promotes to the wholesaler because, in this case, the wholesaler is the channel member just below the producer (see Figure 16.5). Each channel member in turn promotes to the next channel member. A push policy normally stresses personal selling. Sometimes sales promotion and advertising are used in conjunction with personal selling to push the products down through the channel.

As Figure 16.5 shows, a firm that uses a **pull policy** promotes directly to consumers to develop strong consumer demand for its products. It does so primarily through advertising and sales promotion. Because consumers are persuaded to seek the products in retail stores, retailers in turn go to wholesalers or the producers to buy the products. This policy is intended to pull the goods down through the channel by creating demand at the consumer level. Consumers are told that if the stores do not have it, then they should request that the stores begin carrying the product. Push and pull policies are not mutually exclusive. At times, an organization uses both simultaneously.

push policy Promoting a product only to the next institution down the marketing channel

pull policy Promoting a product directly to consumers to develop strong consumer demand that pulls products through the marketing channel

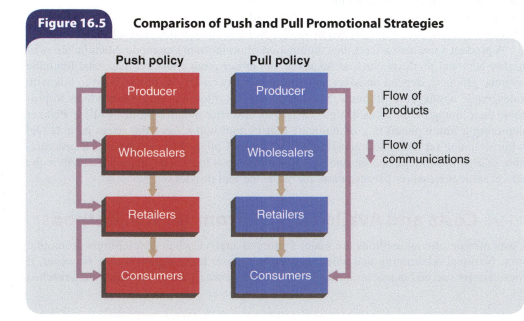

| Figure 16.5 | Comparison of Push and Pull Promotional Strategies |

Push policy / Pull policy

Producer → Wholesalers → Retailers → Consumers

Flow of products
Flow of communications

16-6 THE IMPACT OF WORD-OF-MOUTH COMMUNICATIONS ON PROMOTION

Learning Objective 16-6
Describe how word-of-mouth communication affects promotion.

When making decisions about the composition of promotion mixes, marketers should recognize that commercial messages, whether from advertising, personal selling, sales promotion, or public relations, are limited in the extent to which they can inform and persuade customers and move them closer to making purchases. Depending on the type of customers and the products involved, buyers to some extent rely on word-of-mouth communication from personal sources, such as family members and friends. **Word-of-mouth communication** is personal informal exchanges of communication that customers share with one another, either verbally or through social media, about products, brands, and companies. Most customers are likely to be influenced by friends and family members when they make purchases. In addition, customers are increasingly going online for information and opinions about products as well as about the companies. Electronic word of mouth is communicating about products through websites, blogs, email, social networks, or online forums. Buyers can peruse internet-based newsgroups, forums, and blogs to find word-of-mouth information. Users can go to a number of consumer-oriented websites, such as epinions.com and consumerreview.com, to learn about other consumers' feelings toward, and experiences with, specific products; some sites even encourage consumers to rate products they have tried. Users can also search within product categories and compare consumers' viewpoints on various brands and models. Not surprisingly, credibility has been identified as the most important attribute of a ratings website, and reducing risk and saving search effort were found to be the primary motives for using such sites.[28] For this reason, organizations should proactively manage their word-of-mouth communications.[29]

Hundreds of blogs and online news sites (such as BuzzFeed, TMZ, TechCrunch, Perez Hilton, and Engadget) play an essential role in propagating electronic word-of-mouth communications about everything from gossip to politics to consumer goods. They provide information on trends, reviews of products, and other information and have become so influential in introducing consumers to new products and shaping their views about them that marketers are increasingly monitoring them to identify new trends. Marketers must increasingly court bloggers, who wield growing influence over consumer perception of companies and products. Effective marketers who understand the importance of word-of-mouth communication attempt to identify opinion leaders and encourage them to try their products in the hope that they will spread favorable publicity about them. Apple, for example, has long relied on its nearly cult consumer following to spread by word of mouth their satisfaction with Apple products such as MacBooks, Apple Watches, iPhones, and iPads. The impact of consumer-generated communication—communication not made by companies—is powerful and is very effective compared to commercial messages. Celebrities that tweet about brands have source credibility if they have a large number of followers. Katy Perry and Justin Bieber have more than 100 million followers each. If followers have a social identification with the celebrity, they are more likely to engage in product involvement.[30] Interestingly, women—unlike men—are more likely to share negative word of mouth with those they have strong social ties with rather than those with which they have weak social ties. In general, consumers are much more likely to complain of a bad experience versus sharing praise for a good experience. Cadbury's Alien ad was voted one of the best viral ads. This Canadian ad focused upon the experience aliens had consuming Cadbury chocolate left behind by American astronauts. The aliens engage in wild dancing and excitement upon eating the chocolate.[31]

Buzz marketing is an attempt to incite publicity and public excitement surrounding a product through a creative event. Event attendance has a positive effect on brand equity.[32] Some marketers are piggybacking off the events of other companies, using long lines for an event or product launch as marketing opportunities. As long lines waited for the newest iPhones outside Apple's London store, a British apple juice brand carried a placard advertising "the latest in

word-of-mouth communication
Personal, informal exchanges of communication that customers share with one another about products, brands, and companies

buzz marketing An attempt to incite publicity and public excitement surrounding a product through a creative event

apple technology."[33] Buzz marketing can be an effective way of allowing a company to stand out from competing brands. Red Bull is another brand that excels at buzz marketing.

Buzz marketing works best as a part of an integrated marketing communication program that also uses advertising, personal selling, sales promotion, and publicity. However, marketers should also take care that buzz campaigns do not violate any laws or have the potential to be misconstrued and cause undue alarm. For instance, stenciling a brand's name or logo on the sidewalk might be an effective buzz marketing technique but can also be viewed as illegal graffiti by city authorities.

Viral marketing is a strategy to get consumers to share a marketer's message, often through email or online video, in a way that spreads dramatically and quickly. Blendtec, the powerful kitchen blender, developed videos showing its blender pulverizing everything from rakes to marbles and even Apple iPads. The "Will It Blend" videos have been viewed more than 100 million times and have attracted nearly 1 million subscribers. Humor and the unexpected are key contributors to viral marketing success.[34] Interestingly, viral marketing appears to be more effective for products that are less utilitarian (practical and functional) in nature. Promoting utilitarian products through social sharing mechanisms such as Facebook may actually be disadvantageous for practical no-frills products.[35]

Word of mouth, no matter how it is transmitted, is not effective in all product categories. It seems to be most effective for new-to-market and more expensive products. Despite the obvious benefits of positive word of mouth, marketers must also recognize the potential dangers of negative word of mouth. This is particularly important in dealing with online platforms that can reach more people and encourage consumers to "gang up" on a company or a product.

Learning Objective 16-7

Discuss how product placement impacts promotion.

16-7 PRODUCT PLACEMENT AS PROMOTION

A growing technique for reaching consumers is the selective placement of products within the context of television programs viewed by the target market. **Product placement** is a form of advertising that strategically locates products or product promotions within entertainment media to reach the product's target markets. For instance, the James Bond film *Spectre* featured the vehicles Aston Martin and Land Rover.[36] Apple is considered to be an expert at product placement, and its products are often seen in popular television shows and movies. Such product placement on television has become more important due to the increasing fragmentation of television viewers who have ever-expanding viewing options and technology that can screen advertisements (e.g., digital video recorders). A study found that 60 percent of respondents download or use digital video recorders so they can skip over the commercials.[37]

In-program product placements have been successful in reaching consumers as they are being entertained. Research demonstrates that a television series can impact consumers' intentions to purchase brands placed in those television shows. Of course, individual traits, such as consumer sensitivity to social influences, may increase or decrease intentions to purchase a specific brand.[38] As a result, product placement can be found in many of today's most popular shows. For instance, the show *Modern Family* featured a Toyota vehicle, while the Target brand has been featured prominently in episodes of *Jane the Virgin*.[39] Reality programming in particular has been a natural fit for product placements because of the close interchange between the participants and the product (*Tiny House* has partnered with many advertisers including 3M's Command brand of reusable wall hooks). Global spending for product placements is now more than $10.5 billion and growing.[40]

Product placement is not limited to U.S. movies and television shows. The European Parliament approved limited use of product placement, albeit only during certain types of programs and only if consumers were informed at the beginning of the segment that companies had paid to have their products displayed. In general, the notion of product placement has not been favorably viewed in Europe and has been particularly controversial in the United Kingdom. However, legislation has legalized product placement in U.K. television programs.[41] Supporting the use of product placement are findings that product placement can promote prosocial behavior such as healthy eating habits. For example, product placements are effective in promoting the consumption of fruits and vegetables among children.[42]

viral marketing A strategy to get consumers to share a marketer's message, often through email or online videos, in a way that spreads dramatically and quickly

product placement The strategic location of products or product promotions within entertainment media content to reach the product's target market

Learning Objective 16-8
List major criticisms and
defenses of promotion.

16-8 CRITICISMS AND DEFENSES OF PROMOTION

Even though promotional activities can help customers make informed purchasing decisions, social scientists, consumer groups, government agencies, and members of society in general have long criticized promotion. There are two main reasons for such criticism: Promotion does have flaws, and it is a highly visible business activity that pervades our daily lives. Although complaints about too much promotional activity are almost universal, a number of more specific criticisms have been lodged. In this section, we discuss some of the criticisms and defenses of promotion.

16-8a Is Promotion Deceptive?

One common criticism of promotion is that it is deceptive and unethical. During the 19th and early 20th centuries, much promotion was blatantly deceptive. Although no longer widespread, some deceptive promotion still occurs. For instance, the Federal Trade Commission (FTC) filed a lawsuit against dietary supplement maker Sunrise Nutraceuticals, LLC to stop it from advertising that its products could be used to alleviate opiate withdrawal symptoms and cure addiction. According to the FTC, these claims were unsubstantiated at best and downright false at worst.[43] Many industries suffer from claims of deception from time to time. One industry that is seemingly constantly bombarded with truthfulness-related claims is the diet products and exercise equipment industry. Some promotions are unintentionally deceiving; for instance, when advertising to children, it is easy to mislead them because they are more naïve than adults and less able to separate fantasy from reality. A promotion may also mislead some receivers because words can have diverse meanings for different people. However, not all promotion should be condemned because a small portion is flawed. Laws, government regulation, and industry self-regulation have helped decrease deceptive promotion.

16-8b Does Promotion Increase Prices?

Promotion is also criticized for raising prices, but in fact it can lower them. The ultimate purpose of promotion is to stimulate demand. If it does, the business should be able to produce and market products in larger quantities and thus reduce per-unit production research and development, overhead, and marketing costs, which can result in lower prices. As demand for flat-screen televisions and MP3 players increased, their prices dropped. When promotion fails to stimulate demand, the price of the promoted product increases because promotion costs must be added to other costs. Promotion also helps keep prices lower by facilitating price competition. When firms advertise prices, their prices tend to remain lower than when they are not promoting prices. Gasoline pricing illustrates how promotion fosters price competition. Service stations with the highest prices seldom have highly visible price signs. In addition, results of an analysis for the long-term economic growth for 64 countries indicated that there is a direct relationship between advertising and economic growth. The research findings indicate that advertising not only is related to economic growth but can also bring about economic growth.[44] A Deloitte study found that for every £1 billion ($1.64 billion) spent on advertising in the U.K., a £6 billion ($9.86 billion) increase in annual GDP occurs.[45] This should help clarify debates over the role of promotion in society.

16-8c Does Promotion Create Needs?

Some critics of promotion claim that it manipulates consumers by persuading them to buy products they do not need, hence creating "artificial" needs. In his theory of motivation, Abraham Maslow (discussed in Chapter 7) indicates that an individual tries to satisfy five levels of needs: physiological needs, such as hunger, thirst, and sex; safety needs; needs for love and affection; needs for self-esteem and respect from others; and self-actualization needs, or the need to realize one's potential. When needs are viewed in this context, it is difficult to demonstrate that promotion creates them. If there were no promotional activities, people would still have needs for food, water, sex, safety, love, affection, self-esteem, respect from others, and self-actualization.

Although promotion may not create needs, it does capitalize on them (which may be why some critics believe promotion creates needs). Many marketers base their appeals on these needs. For instance, several mouthwash, toothpaste, and perfume advertisements associate these products with needs for love, affection, and respect. These advertisers rely on human needs in their messages, but they do not create the needs.

16-8d Does Promotion Encourage Materialism?

Another frequent criticism of promotion is that it leads to materialism. The purpose of promoting goods is to persuade people to buy them; thus, if promotion works, consumers will want to buy more and more things. Marketers assert that values are instilled in the home and that promotion does not change people into materialistic consumers. However, the behavior of today's children and teenagers contradicts this view; many insist on high-priced, brand-name apparel, such as Gucci, Coach, Abercrombie & Fitch, 7 For All Mankind, and Ralph Lauren.

Marketing Harmful Products
Natural American Spirit markets its organic tobacco and lack of additives. Although it has a disclaimer stating that this does not mean it is a healthier cigarette, critics believe it is wrong to market the benefits of products that can cause harm.

16-8e Does Promotion Help Customers without Costing Too Much?

Every year, firms spend billions of dollars for promotion. The question is whether promotion helps customers enough to be worth the cost. Consumers do benefit because promotion informs them about product uses, features, advantages, prices, and locations where they can buy the products. Thus, consumers gain more knowledge about available products and can make more intelligent buying decisions. Promotion also informs consumers about services—for instance, health care, educational programs, and day care—as well as about important social, political, and health-related issues. For example, several organizations, such as the California Department of Health Services, inform people about the health hazards associated with tobacco use.

16-8f Should Potentially Harmful Products Be Promoted?

Finally, some critics of promotion, including consumer groups and government officials, suggest that certain products should not be promoted at all. Primary targets are products associated with violence and other possibly unhealthy activities, such as handguns, alcohol, and tobacco. Cigarette advertisements, for example, promote smoking, a behavior proven to be harmful and even deadly.

Tobacco companies, which spend billions on promotion, have countered criticism of their advertising by pointing out that advertisements for red meat and coffee are not censured, even though these products may also cause health problems. Consider the advertisement for Natural American Spirit. The company uses big letters to emphasize its American origins, organic tobacco, and lack of additives. The image of hands depicted as holding dirt reinforces this sustainability image. It also states in large letters that these benefits do not mean that its products are safer than other cigarettes. Despite these disclaimers, critics believe the marketing of these positive claims could deceive people into believing the cigarettes are safer because they are more eco-friendly. On the other hand, those who defend such promotion assert that, as long as it is legal to sell a product, promoting that product should be allowed.

Summary

16-1 Define integrated marketing communications.

Integrated marketing communications is the coordination of promotion and other marketing efforts to ensure maximum informational and persuasive impact on customers.

16-2 Describe the steps of the communication process.

Communication is a sharing of meaning. The communication process involves several steps. First, the source translates meaning into code, a process known as coding or encoding. The source should employ signs or symbols familiar to the receiver or audience. The coded message is sent through a communications channel to the receiver or audience. The receiver or audience then decodes the message and usually supplies feedback to the source. When the decoded message differs from the encoded one, a condition called noise exists.

16-3 Recognize the definition and objectives of promotion.

Promotion is communication to build and maintain relationships by informing and persuading one or more audiences. Although promotional objectives vary from one organization to another and within organizations over time, ten primary objectives underlie many promotional programs. Promotion aims to create awareness of a new product, a new brand, or an existing product; to stimulate primary and selective demand; to encourage product trial through the use of free samples, coupons, limited free-use offers, contests, and games; to identify prospects; to retain loyal customers; to facilitate reseller support; to combat competitive promotional efforts; to reduce sales fluctuations; and to generate positive social media posts.

16-4 Summarize the four elements of the promotion mix.

The promotion mix for a product may include four major promotional methods: advertising, personal selling, public relations, and sales promotion. Advertising is paid non-personal communication about an organization and its products transmitted to a target audience through a mass medium. Personal selling is paid personal communication that attempts to inform customers and persuade them to purchase products in an exchange situation. Public relations is a broad set of communication efforts used to create and maintain favorable relationships between an organization and its stakeholders. Sales promotion is an activity or material that acts as a direct inducement, offering added value or incentive for the product, to resellers, salespeople, or consumers.

16-5 Explain the factors that are used to determine a product's promotion mix.

The promotional methods used in a product's promotion mix are determined by the organization's promotional resources, objectives, and policies; characteristics of the target market; characteristics of the product; and cost and availability of promotional methods. Marketers also consider whether to use a push policy or a pull policy. With a push policy, the producer only promotes the product to the next institution down the marketing channel. Normally, a push policy stresses personal selling. Firms that use a pull policy promote directly to consumers, with the intention of developing strong consumer demand for the products. Once consumers are persuaded to seek the products in retail stores, retailers go to wholesalers or the producer to buy the products.

16-6 Describe how word-of-mouth communication affects promotion.

Most customers are likely to be influenced by friends and family members when making purchases. Word-of-mouth communication is personal informal exchanges of communication that customers share with one another about products, brands, and companies. Customers may also choose to go online to find electronic word of mouth about products or companies. Buzz marketing is an attempt to incite publicity and public excitement surrounding a product through a creative event. Viral marketing is a strategy to get consumers to share a marketer's message, often through email or online videos, in a way that spreads dramatically and quickly.

16-7 Discuss how product placement impacts promotion.

Product placement is the strategic location of products or product promotions within entertainment media content to reach the product's target market. In-program product placements have been successful in reaching consumers as they are being entertained rather than in the competitive commercial break time periods.

16-8 List major criticisms and defenses of promotion.

Promotional activities can help consumers make informed purchasing decisions, but they have also evoked many criticisms. Promotion has been accused of deception. Although some deceiving or misleading promotions do exist, laws, government regulation, and industry self-regulation minimize deceptive promotion. Promotion has been blamed for increasing prices, but it usually tends to lower them. When demand is high, production and marketing costs decrease, which can result in lower prices. Moreover, promotion helps keep prices lower by facilitating price competition. Other criticisms of promotional activity are that it manipulates consumers into buying products they do not need, that it leads to a more materialistic society, and that consumers do not benefit sufficiently from promotional activity to justify its high cost. Finally, some critics of promotion suggest that potentially harmful products, especially those associated with violence, sex, and unhealthy activities, should not be promoted at all.

Important Terms

integrated marketing
   communications 468
communication 469
source 469
receiver 469
coding process 469
communications channel
   470

decoding process 470
noise 471
feedback 471
channel capacity 471
promotion 471
primary demand 473
new introductory
   promotion 473

selective demand 473
promotion mix 476
kinesic communication
   478
proxemic communication
   479
tactile communication 479
push policy 484

pull policy 484
word-of-mouth
   communication 485
buzz marketing 485
viral marketing 486
product placement 486

Discussion and Review Questions

1. What does the term *integrated marketing communications* mean?
2. Define *communication* and describe the communication process. Is it possible to communicate without using all the elements in the communication process? If so, which elements can be omitted?
3. Identify several causes of noise. How can a source reduce noise?
4. What is the major task of promotion? Do firms ever use promotion to accomplish this task and fail? If so, give several examples.
5. Describe the possible objectives of promotion and discuss the circumstances under which each objective might be used.
6. Identify and briefly describe the four promotional methods an organization can use in its promotion mix.
7. What forms of interpersonal communication besides language can be used in personal selling?
8. How do target-market characteristics determine which promotional methods to include in a promotion mix? Assume a company is planning to promote a cereal to both adults and children. Along what major dimensions would these two promotional efforts have to differ from each other?
9. How can a product's characteristics affect the composition of its promotion mix?
10. Evaluate the following statement: "Appropriate advertising media are always available if a company can afford them."

11. Explain the difference between a pull policy and a push policy. Under what conditions should each policy be used?

12. In which ways can word-of-mouth communication influence the effectiveness of a promotion mix for a product?

13. Which criticisms of promotion do you believe are the most valid? Why?

14. Should organizations be allowed to promote offensive, violent, sexual, or unhealthy products that can be legally sold and purchased? Support your answer.

Developing Your Marketing Plan

A vital component of a successful marketing strategy is the company's plan for communicating with its stakeholders. One segment of the communication plan is included in the marketing mix as the promotional element. A clear understanding of the role that promotion plays, as well as the various methods of promotion, is important in developing the promotional plan. The following questions should assist you in relating the information in this chapter to several decisions in your marketing plan.

1. Review the communication process in Figure 16.1. Identify the various players in the communication process for promotion of your product.

2. What are your objectives for promotion? Use Table 16.1 as a guide in answering this question.

3. Which of the four elements of the promotional mix are most appropriate for accomplishing your objectives? Discuss the advantages and disadvantages of each.

4. What role should word-of-mouth communications, buzz marketing, or product placement play in your promotional plan?

Video Case 16.1

Napoletana: Taking a Bite at WOM Promotion

Frank Pepe's Pizzeria Napoletana has opened one of the most recognizable pizzerias in the United States using word of mouth (WOM). After returning from World War I, Pepe began making bread during the week and pizzas on the weekend. After seeing a demand for his product, he utilized his entrepreneurial spirit and focused solely on pizza. Pepe founded Pepe's Pizzeria in 1925, with a heavy influence from his Italian culture, in New Haven, CT.

Pepe developed the New Haven-style thin crust pizza that earned him a reputation as owner of one of the country's premiere pizzerias. Many people began referring to Pepe as "Old Reliable," which continued to generate positive feedback throughout different communities. Pepe's signature pizza, the White Clam Pizza, has been the most notable recipe since its development in the mid-1960s.

Since the beginning, Pepe's has been a family-run business. Frank's wife and children all worked in the original store and after retiring, they passed the business to their children, who still have a stake in the business today. Through the transition between generations, Pepe's has always aimed to deliver a premium product that is consistent and meets customer standards. As people come into the store, Pepe's employees engage in personal selling by communicating various menu items.

CEO Ken Berry places a high emphasis upon delivering the promise and guarantee of quality within their product every day. As chief executive operator, he sees the challenge of delivering this promise as a duty that helps protect and build the brand, which the Pepe family initially built. He strives to retain brand equity and rely upon feedback from loyal customers as the company continues to grow.

Including the first and flagship store, there are currently ten pizzerias within Connecticut and New York, Boston, and Rhode Island. With each new store came the difficult task of maintaining the original experience for new, prospective, and loyal customers. When Pepe's began to consistently pursue expansion tactics, some customers appeared dismayed. There were protests and boycotts occurring on opening days, as other happy customers waited in long lines to test the reputation of the premiere pizza.

To ensure customer satisfaction at the new locations, Ken Berry discussed the critical nature of replicating every aspect of the original idea. Everything from the recipes being virtually unchanged, to the layout and colors of the stores, needed to be congruent to ensure success. He describes Pepe's as an experience that allows customers to step back in time with a handcrafted product.

Another aspect of developing demand for the company in new locations was the advertising tactics used. As Pepe's has always done, it relied upon word of mouth to retain and gain new customers. It places emphasis upon the experience and listens to customer feedback on whether it is delivering a quality product. At times it uses direct mail, which can be an effective form of advertising, and tries to engage with consumers on Twitter and Facebook to remain connected with them. A major form of promotion comes in the form of free pizza, which is sales promotion. Generally, the week before a grand opening, Pepe's offers free pizza for a week at that location to allow new ovens to be broken in, workers to understand Pepe's culture, and to showcase the confidence that Pepe's has in its product to the local community. The business encourages repeat visits from its customers with the Frank Pepe Pizzeria Napoletana point-based rewards program that allows regulars to earn dollar discounts and a birthday reward. To allow customers to take the Frank Pepe brand home, the business started selling its own canned Genuine Italian Tomatoes.

For the public relations side of the company, Pepe's has a donation-request option on its website, where customers are welcome to fill out an application to receive, primarily, gift cards from the company. It also holds a good neighbor night, which allows an organization to hold a fundraiser at any location. Fifteen percent of proceeds made that night is given to the organization. While Pepe's loses out on some proceeds, these events create quality relationships in the community as well as potentially generating a new customer base. It also donates gift cards to nonprofit organizations for fundraising purposes.

Throughout the years Pepe's has strived to deliver a promise to customers by staying true to the original product. It has maintained its brand equity through its dedication and standards set by customers, family members, and all stakeholders associated with the product. For Pepe's, it is clear that, through positive word of mouth, advertising does not always need to be a costly expense.[46]

Questions for Discussion

1. What are the various promotion elements that Pepe's uses to communicate with customers?
2. What role does word of mouth play in Pepe's integrated marketing communications?
3. Evaluate free pizza as a form of sales promotion in Pepe's success.

Case 16.2

Picture Perfect: The Success of Product Placement

Watch a movie or television show carefully and you will likely identify several familiar product brands. These products are not there by accident. In fact, companies pay millions of dollars for screen time. The Subaru WRX in *Baby Driver*, Krispy Kreme in *Power Rangers*, and IHOP in the *Man of Steel* are just the tip of the iceberg for product placement, an advertising practice that strategically uses branded products within entertainment to reach a particular target market.

With the inundation of advertising consumers encounter on everything from television to social networking sites, it is becoming easier for them to ignore display ads or skip over video ads. Product placement provides marketers with the opportunity to present products to viewers as part of the show or movie without appearing too intrusive. Additionally, with more and more viewing options like Netflix, Hulu, and YouTube in addition to cable, television viewers have become fragmented.

Product placement is a growing business estimated to have surpassed $11 billion. In *Casino Royale*, James Bond drives a Ford Mondeo, a placement that cost Ford $14 million. *Man of Steel*, with more than 100 global marketing partners, attracted $160 million in promotional support including product placement. While strategic placements often include a hefty price tag, that is not always the case. For example, the infamous placement of Reese's Pieces in *E.T.*, which resulted in a 65 percent increase in sales, was given to the brand by the studio free of charge.

Product placement is not limited to television and videos. The Kluger Agency focuses on promoting brands in music. The agency is responsible for Hilary Duff's music video for "Sparks" which prominently features the Tinder dating app. The video has more than 14 million views. Familiar brands from Subway, Coca-Cola, and Pizza Hut have appeared in virtual worlds and video games. Coca-Cola was a longtime sponsor of *American Idol*. In the music video for the Bruno Mars song "Versace on the Floor" fashion brand Versace designed custom clothes for Bruno Mars and Zendaya. Product placement is also gaining popularity internationally. For instance, East Asian brands have been featured more in box-office movies. A Chinese firm acquired Propaganda GEM, showing the growing interest of marketers in China toward product placement as a marketing channel.

Product placement can also be found in video games. In "Mario Kart 8," gamers can unlock a Mercedes-Benz DLC. It marked the first time the franchise used a name brand vehicle. With advanced graphics and in-game physics, video game developers are able to create realistic digital replicas of real vehicles. For example, the Porsche 911 GT2 RS was revealed at the same time as the Forza Motorsport 7 game. Using video games to reveal new cars over traditional car

shows has allowed brands to stand apart from the competition. The BMW M5 made its world debut at Gamescom, an annual video game convention held in Germany. Ahead of the car's official launch, BMW also worked with EA Games on a smartphone app version of its vehicle in "Need for Speed No Limits" for a limited time only. According to BMW, gamers clocked more than 480,000 hours in the car.

Advertisers can even purchase storylines in television shows. For example, in the sitcom *Black-ish* Procter & Gamble payed for a plotline in which the characters discussed "The Talk," an award-winning P&G ad campaign. Sponsored storylines allow advertisers to move beyond fleeting product placements as well as 30-second ad slots for more prominent features.

Product placement does not come without challenges. Brands and agencies often battle for control. Understandably, brands want to send on-brand messages while artists and producers want creative control. Though product placement often feels authentic, advertising rules have attempted to regulate the practice. For example, in the U.K., shows with product placement must carry a "P" logo to signal its paid partnerships. U.K. broadcasters are also not permitted to use product placement in children's shows, news programs, or consumer advice shows. *The Great British Bake Off* decided to ban product placement deals to maintain the integrity of its show.[47]

Questions for Discussion

1. What are the strengths of product placement? The weaknesses?
2. What challenges do advertisers face with product placement?
3. How do you think product placement will evolve with new television viewing habits?

CHAPTER

17

Advertising and Public Relations

LEARNING OBJECTIVES

17-1 Describe advertising and its different types.

17-2 Summarize the eight major steps in developing an advertising campaign.

17-3 Identify who is responsible for developing advertising campaigns.

17-4 Define public relations.

17-5 Describe the different tools of public relations.

17-6 Analyze how public relations is used and evaluated.

CASIMIRO PT/SHUTTERSTOCK.COM

Spokescharacters Give Brands Big Personality

Flo from Progressive, Allstate Mayhem, the GEICO gecko—these spokescharacters have become indelibly linked to their brands. Companies develop spokescharacters because they help consumers remember their brands. This can significantly impact brand awareness, especially for new customers. Studies have shown that spokescharacters lead to more favorable attitudes among consumers who have little familiarity with the brand than those who are highly familiar with it.

Spokescharacters also assist brands by providing them with a personality to which consumers can relate and making brands more likable and fun. Consider Mayhem (played by actor Dean Winters), the spokescharacter for Allstate insurance, who personifies everyday insurable moments. He demonstrates accidents viewers can relate to and plays as the counterpart to the "In Good Hands" campaigns staring Dennis Haysbert. With a positive response from consumers, Mayhem enabled AdAge to improve its social media presence with a dedicated Mayhem profile on Twitter.

Another successful spokesperson is the Trivago Guy. German internet travel and hospitality firm Trivago hired Houston-born Tim Williams to be its spokesman. Americans seemed to find this scruffy-looking character highly relatable, so much so that Trivago's advertising awareness shot past competitors Orbitz and Expedia. Trivago also introduced a female spokesperson to the mix, Australian-born Gabrielle Miller. Miller's campaign marks another success for Trivago, generating more digital actions, from searches to social media posts, than previous campaigns.

While it is clear that spokescharacters increase brand awareness, does this actually result in increased sales? Just because consumers know about a brand does not mean they will necessarily purchase it. However, brand awareness does have a major impact in placing the brand into the consumer's consideration set. Brands in the initial consideration set are three times more likely to be purchased than those that are not. Perhaps this is why competitors such as Priceline announced they would increase their advertising expenditures after the Trivago Guy became such a success.[1]

Both large organizations and small companies use conventional and online promotional efforts like advertising to change their corporate images, build brand equity, launch new products, or promote current brands. In this chapter, we explore many dimensions of advertising and public relations. First, we focus on the nature and types of advertising. Next, we examine the major steps in developing an advertising campaign and describe who is responsible for developing the campaigns. Finally, we examine various public relations tools and ways to evaluate the effectiveness of public relations.

17-1 THE NATURE AND TYPES OF ADVERTISING

Advertising permeates our daily lives. At times, we view it positively; at other times, we feel bombarded and try to avoid it. Some advertising informs, persuades, or entertains us; some bores, annoys, or even offends us. Many companies are taking a different approach to their marketing, even using satire or criticism of their companies as a way to create awareness. Arby's bought two commercials in former television host Jon Stewart's final episode of *The Daily Show* despite the fact that Stewart poked fun at the company's products several times during his show. Rather than acting defensively to Stewart's ridicule, Arby's chose to use his popularity among younger people to reach this demographic.[2]

As mentioned in Chapter 16, **advertising** is a paid form of nonpersonal communication that is transmitted to a target audience through mass media, such as television, radio, the internet, newspapers, magazines, direct mail, outdoor displays, and signs or wraps on vehicles. Advertising can have a profound impact on how consumers view certain products. One example is locally grown and organic produce. Consumers are likely to view locally grown and organic produce as healthier. Whole Foods and other supermarkets promote locally grown food as being more sustainable because it eliminates emissions from transporting food long distances and supports local farmers. Advertisements even influence how a brand's own sales force views company products. Salesperson perception of brand advertising is positively related to effort and performance because it influences how the salesperson identifies with the brand.[3] Organizations use advertising to reach a variety of audiences ranging from small, specific groups, such as coin collectors in Wyoming, to extremely large groups, such as all athletic-shoe buyers in the United States.

When asked to name major advertisers, most people immediately mention business organizations. However, many nonbusiness organizations—including governments, churches, universities, and charitable organizations—employ advertising to communicate with stakeholders. Each year, the U.S. government spends hundreds of millions of dollars in advertising to advise and influence the behavior of its citizens. Although this chapter analyzes advertising in the context of business organizations, many of the following concepts apply to all types of organizations, including nonprofits.

Advertising is used to promote goods, services, ideas, images, issues, people, and anything else advertisers want to publicize or encourage. Depending on what is being promoted, advertising can be classified as institutional or product advertising. **Institutional advertising** promotes organizational images, ideas, and political issues. Institutional advertisements may deal with broad image issues, such as organizational strengths or the friendliness of employees. Monsanto, for instance, took out an advertisement to describe its supplier diversity. It shows photos of people from different backgrounds to demonstrate its commitment toward inclusion and diversity. Marketers may also aim to create a more favorable view of the organization in the eyes of noncustomer groups, such as shareholders, consumer advocacy groups, potential shareholders, or the general public. Institutional advertising can be proactive to create a favorable view of the organization or its industry or, in contrast, reactive, in response to something that may negatively impact an organization's reputation. For example,

advertising Paid nonpersonal communication about an organization and its products transmitted to a target audience through mass media

institutional advertising Advertising that promotes organizational images, ideas, and political issues

advocacy advertising Advertising that promotes a company's position on a public issue

product advertising Advertising that promotes the uses, features, and benefits of products

Wells Fargo created an incentive system for its sales force that resulted in many new, unauthorized accounts being opened for customers. In response to the negative news stories on the company's behavior, Wells Fargo ran an ad promoting their focus on customer relationships. The goal was to improve overall brand image in a time of extremely negative news.

When a company promotes its position on a public issue—for instance, a tax increase, sustainability, regulations, or international trade coalitions—institutional advertising is referred to as **advocacy advertising**. Such advertising may be used to promote socially approved behavior, such as recycling or moderation in consuming alcoholic beverages. AT&T, for instance, ran an advertising campaign called "It Can Wait" that showed a terrible car crash in reverse. Its intent was to discourage people from texting and driving.[4] This type of advertising not only has social benefits but also helps build an organization's image.

Product advertising promotes the uses, features, and benefits of products. There are two types of product advertising: pioneer and competitive. **Pioneer advertising** focuses on stimulating demand for a product category (rather than a specific brand) by informing potential customers about the product's features, uses, and benefits. Product advertising that focuses on products before they are available tends to cause people to think about the product more and evaluate it more positively.[5] Pioneer advertising is also employed when the product is in the introductory stage of the product life cycle, exemplified in the launch of the Samsung Galaxy Gear in the smartwatch category. When Tesla introduced a software update, version 7.0 and referred to as "autopilot," to its cars with a sophisticated technology and camera package, the cars could perform

Competitive Advertising
This Sally Hansen advertisement is an example of competitive advertising. Its purpose is to stimulate demand for Sally Hansen Miracle Gel nail polish by promoting its features, uses, and advantages.

tasks that normal automobiles could not. These Tesla vehicles could prevent drivers from being in accidents, steer, change lanes, adjust speed, and park. The early pioneers in this category had to educate consumers about the products and their benefits. **Competitive advertising** attempts to stimulate demand for a specific brand by promoting the brand's features, uses, and advantages through indirect or direct comparisons with competing brands. In the advertisement for Sally Hansen, features and advantages for its Miracle Gel are used. The ad states that Miracle Gel nail polish is more chip-resistant than regular nail polish, and it will last up to 14 days. Cable, satellite, and streaming internet television service providers use competitive advertising to position their brands such as Comcast, AT&T, Direct TV, and Sling TV. Advertising effects on sales must reflect competitors' advertising activities. The type and intensity of the competitive environment will determine the most effective approach.

To make direct product comparisons, marketers use a form of competitive advertising called **comparative advertising**, which compares the sponsored brand with one or more identified competing brands on the basis of one or more product characteristics. Surveys show that top creative advertising practitioners view comparative advertising favorably

pioneer advertising
Advertising that tries to stimulate demand for a product category rather than a specific brand by informing potential buyers about the product

competitive advertising Tries to stimulate demand for a specific brand by promoting its features, uses, and advantages relative to competing brands

comparative advertising
Compares the sponsored brand with one or more identified brands on the basis of one or more product characteristics

SOURCE: POND'S

Reminder Advertising

This Pond's advertisement is an example of reminder advertising. It promotes an established product to tell customers the advantages of its Cold Cream Cleanser.

reminder advertising
Advertising used to remind consumers about an established brand's uses, characteristics, and benefits

reinforcement advertising
Advertising that assures users they chose the right brand and tells them how to get the most satisfaction from it

native advertising Digital advertising that matches the appearance and purpose of the content in which it is embedded

when it clearly identifies the competition.[6] Samsung has used comparative advertising that compares its products' superior features to those of its rival, Apple. Often, the brands that are promoted through comparative advertisements have low market shares and are compared with competitors that have the highest market shares in the product category. Product categories that commonly use comparative advertising include soft drinks, toothpaste, pain relievers, foods, tires, automobiles, and detergents. Under the provisions of the 1988 Trademark Law Revision Act, marketers using comparative advertisements in the United States must not misrepresent the qualities or characteristics of competing products. Other countries may have laws that are stricter or less strict with regard to comparative advertising. For instance, Brazil has ruled that comparative advertising is acceptable as long as the comparison is fair and truthful. However, determining the fairness of an advertisement can be subjective and can vary in different situations.[7]

Other forms of competitive advertising include reminder and reinforcement advertising. **Reminder advertising** tells customers that an established brand is still around and still offers certain characteristics, uses, and advantages. In the advertisement, Pond's reminds customers about the many advantages of its Cold Cream Cleanser, such as its ability to easily lift away makeup and keep skin soft. Pond's communicates that this product has been around since 1907. **Reinforcement advertising** assures current users that they have made the right brand choice and tells them how to get the most satisfaction from that brand. Arm & Hammer baking soda does advertisements to remind purchasers to keep using the product for many different purposes. For example, if a box of baking soda is put into the refrigerator to reduce odors, then advertising reminds consumers to change out the baking soda on a periodic basis.

One growing trend among marketers has been the use of **native advertising**, or digital advertising that matches the appearance and purpose of the content in which it is embedded. The word "native" refers to the fact that this form of advertising is meant to resemble the content itself. Native advertising has been associated more with improved brand perception, awareness, and engagement than standard banner ads. Native advertising is expected to account for 74 percent of ad revenue within the next few years.[8] In a world inundated with advertisements, native advertising offers marketers the opportunity to reach consumers in new and innovative ways. It also increases advertising revenue for the sites that host them. On the other hand, native advertising is potentially misleading when consumers do not realize that a video or post is sponsored by an organization. One survey revealed that over 50 percent of consumers felt deceived upon realizing that an article or video was sponsored content.[9] To avoid deception and possible legal repercussions, brands should clearly identify sponsored content on digital media sites.

Learning Objective 17-2

Summarize the eight major steps in developing an advertising campaign.

17-2 DEVELOPING AN ADVERTISING CAMPAIGN

An **advertising campaign** involves designing a series of advertisements and placing them in various advertising media to reach a particular target audience. As Figure 17.1 shows, the major steps in creating an advertising campaign are (1) identifying and analyzing the target audience, (2) defining the advertising objectives, (3) creating the advertising platform, (4) determining the advertising appropriation, (5) developing the media plan, (6) creating the advertising message, (7) executing the campaign, and (8) evaluating advertising effectiveness. The number of steps and the exact order in which they are carried out may vary according to the organization's resources, the nature of its product, and the type of target audience to be reached. Nevertheless, these general guidelines for developing an advertising campaign are appropriate for all types of organizations.

17-2a Identifying and Analyzing the Target Audience

The **target audience** is the group of people at whom advertisements are aimed. Advertisements for the Dyson vacuum cleaner target more affluent home owners, whereas the Dirt Devil targets lower- to middle-income households. Identifying and analyzing the target audience are critical processes; the information yielded helps determine other steps in developing the campaign. The target audience may include everyone in the firm's target market. Marketers may, however, direct a campaign at only a portion of the target market. For instance, until recently, the upscale yoga apparel organization Lululemon Athletica focused mainly on women. However, the firm is extending its focus to men interested in fitness with new lines of menswear. It is estimated that nearly 30 percent of Americans practicing yoga are men. That number has doubled in the last four years, representing a rapidly growing market. Proactive companies like Lululemon Athletica are taking advantage of shifting demographics in this market.[10] Starbucks is well known for its retail coffee experience and ambiance.

advertising campaign The creation and execution of a series of advertisements to communicate with a particular target audience

target audience The group of people at whom advertisements are aimed

| Figure 17.1 | General Steps in Developing and Implementing an Advertising Campaign |

8 Evaluate advertising effectiveness
7 Execute campaign
6 Create advertising message
5 Develop media plan
4 Determine advertising appropriation
3 Create advertising platform
2 Define advertising objectives
1 Identify and analyze target audience

Target Audience
Blue Diamond associates itself with jumping rope to develop an image of fitness and healthy living that targets the health-conscious consumer.

Grocery stores now carry chilled, ready-to-drink Starbucks iced coffees and espressos. The market for Starbucks products is a more affluent target market than the market for Nescafe Taster's Choice, instant coffee. Starbucks' coffee is now sold, prepared, and sitting on a traditional grocery store shelf.

Advertisers research and analyze advertising targets to establish an information base for a campaign. Information commonly needed includes location and geographic distribution of the target group; the distribution of demographic factors, such as age, income, race, gender, and education; lifestyle information; and consumer attitudes regarding purchase and use of both the advertiser's products and competing products. The exact kinds of information an organization finds useful depend on the type of product being advertised, the characteristics of the target audience, and the type and amount of competition. Advertisers must be sure to create a campaign that will resonate with the target market. For instance, privacy concerns and irritating ads lead to avoidance, but when digital media and direct-mail advertising personalizes the information, acceptance of the ad tends to increase.[11] Generally, the more an advertiser knows about the target audience, the more likely the firm is to develop an effective advertising campaign. The advertisement for Blue Diamond almonds clearly demonstrates that its target audience is those who seek a healthy breakfast. Knowing the target market for a company helps in developing an effective marketing mix, including relevant promotions that specifically target this group. The advertisement shows a container of its almonds jumping rope to reinforce its association with healthy living. When the advertising target is not well understood and differentiated, the campaign is more likely to fail.

17-2b Defining the Advertising Objectives

The advertiser's next step is to determine what the firm hopes to accomplish with the campaign. Because advertising objectives guide campaign development, advertisers should define objectives carefully. Advertising objectives should be stated clearly, precisely, and in measurable terms. Quantifiable metrics allow advertisers to evaluate advertising success at the end of the campaign in terms of whether objectives have been met. To provide precision and measurability, advertising objectives should contain benchmarks and indicate what the advertiser hopes to accomplish. If the goal is to increase sales, the advertiser should state the current sales level (the benchmark) and the amount of sales increase sought through advertising. An advertising objective should also specify a time frame so that advertisers know exactly how long they have to accomplish the objective. An advertiser with average monthly sales of $450,000 (the benchmark) might set the following objective: "Our primary advertising objective is to increase average monthly sales from $450,000 to $540,000 (20 percent) within 12 months."

If an advertiser defines objectives on the basis of sales, the objectives focus on increasing absolute dollar sales or unit sales, increasing sales by a certain percentage, or increasing the firm's market share. Even though an advertiser's long-run goal is to increase sales, not all campaigns are designed to produce immediate sales. Some campaigns aim to increase product or brand awareness, make consumers' attitudes more favorable, heighten consumers' knowledge of product features, or create awareness of positive, healthy consumer behavior, such as a healthy lifestyle and diet. If the goal is to increase product awareness, the objectives are stated in terms of communication. A specific communication objective might be

DISRUPTIVE MARKETING

The Search Is On: Google AdWords Dominates Search Advertising

Google's ease of use and superior search results have propelled the search engine to its number one status, ousting the early dominance of competitors such as WebCrawler and Infoseek. As Google gained popularity, it began expanding into a number of different ventures, including multiple advertising platforms, a digital book publishing space, and social networking. Google's main source of revenue is advertising. In recent years the parent company of Google, Alphabet Inc., has earned more than $95 billion annually in advertising revenue.

Google's signature advertising platform is Google AdWords, first introduced in 2000. Google AdWords disrupted online advertising by changing the payment model and reducing barriers for businesses with small advertising budgets. Advertisers only pay when customers take action—either by viewing the ad (pay-per-impression), clicking on the ad (pay-per-click), or performing a certain predefined action such

as making an online purchase (pay-per-conversion). This model is attractive to advertisers because they only pay when their ad is effective, as determined by the metric of their choice. Advertisers also set their own budgets in the self-service platform.

Google continues to develop new and innovative ways to build upon the AdWords platform. For example, the company released AdWords Express to meet the needs of small businesses. To improve phone calls local businesses receive from search ads, Google introduced a feedback survey for the advertiser to leave feedback after each call to indicate the relevancy of the call. This feedback helps improve targeting and call quality. Improving the effectiveness of its AdWords service is a key driver of Google's collection of user information—the more it knows about its users, the more targeting options it can provide to advertisers and the more precisely it can serve targeted ads to the desired consumer segments.[a]

to increase new-product feature awareness, such as knowing that Southwest Rapid Rewards Premier Visa card offers 2 points for every dollar spent on Southwest flights and with travel partners.

17-2c Creating the Advertising Platform

Before launching a political campaign, party leaders develop a political platform stating major issues that are the basis of the campaign. Like a political platform, an **advertising platform** consists of the basic issues or selling points that an advertiser wishes to include in the advertising campaign. For example, McDonald's advertises all-day breakfasts as part of its advertising platform for its restaurants. A single advertisement in an advertising campaign may contain one or several issues from the platform. Although the platform sets forth the basic issues, it does not indicate how to present them.

An advertising platform should consist of issues important to customers. One of the best ways to determine those issues is to survey customers about what they consider most important in the selection and use of the product involved. Hulu surveyed its consumer panel, called the "Hulu Brain Trust" consisting of 500 members and asked for some 'true confessions' about the craziest places they have watched Hulu. The top 5 places include the bathroom, in a meeting, at a red light, wedding, and funeral. Hulu can use these interesting locations in digital media and other forms of advertising to better relate to its users.[12] Selling features must not only be important to customers, but also be strongly competitive features of the advertised brand. For example, Southwest Airlines has a great sales proposition versus many of its competitors in promoting that "bags fly free," whereas many other airlines charge for checked luggage. Although research is the most effective method for determining what issues to include in an advertising platform, customer research can be expensive. Often a competitor and market analysis can expose attractive selling features.

Because the advertising platform is a base on which to build the advertising message, marketers should analyze this stage carefully. It has been found that, if the message is viewed as useful, it will create greater brand trust.[13] A campaign can be perfect in terms of selection

advertising platform Basic issues or selling points to be included in an advertising campaign

and analysis of its target audience, statement of its objectives, media strategy, and the form of its message, but it will ultimately fail if the advertisements communicate information that consumers do not deem important when selecting and using the product. A Netflix ad was pulled from an outdoor board in Germany as it was deemed to have gone "a little too far." Netflix was using humor to promote its zombie comedy series *Santa Clarita Diet* and showed a billboard with a human finger sliced and seasoned as a special dish with a fork inside. Adolescents and children were particularly offended by the ads, disgusted and nauseated by the graphic. The ad may have backfired, but, significant publicity was achieved through the controversy.[14]

17-2d Determining the Advertising Appropriation

The **advertising appropriation** is the total amount of money a marketer allocates for advertising for a specific time period. GEICO is a leading television advertiser in the United States, outspending Verizon, Progressive, Ford, Lionsgate, T-Mobile, and AT&T in the same period.[15] Many factors affect a firm's decision about how much to appropriate for advertising. Geographic size of the market and the distribution of buyers within the market have a great bearing on this decision. Both the type of product advertised and the firm's sales volume relative to competitors' sales volumes also play roles in determining what proportion of revenue to spend on advertising. Advertising appropriations for business products are usually quite small relative to product sales, whereas consumer convenience items, such as the cosmetics sold by L'Oréal, generally have large advertising expenditures relative to sales. For instance, Procter & Gamble spends a relatively high percentage of sales to market its product mix of cosmetics, personal care products, appliances, detergents, and pet food. Retailers like Walmart usually have a much lower percent of sales spent on advertising.

Of the many techniques used to determine the advertising appropriation, one of the most logical is the **objective-and-task approach**. Using this approach, marketers determine the objectives a campaign is to achieve and then attempt to list the tasks required to accomplish them. The costs of the tasks are calculated and added to arrive at the total appropriation. This approach has one main problem: Marketers sometimes have trouble accurately estimating the level of effort needed to attain certain objectives. A chain of retail donut stores, for example, may find it extremely difficult to determine how much of an increase in national television advertising is needed to raise a brand's market share from 8 to 10 percent.

In the more widely used **percent-of-sales approach**, marketers simply multiply the firm's past sales, plus a factor for planned sales growth or decline, by a standard percentage based on both what the firm traditionally spends on advertising and the industry average. This approach, too, has a major flaw: It is based on the incorrect assumption that sales create advertising rather than the reverse. A marketer using this approach during declining sales will reduce the amount spent on advertising, but such a reduction may further diminish sales. Though illogical, this technique has been favored because it is easy to implement.

Another way to determine advertising appropriation is the **competition-matching approach**. Marketers following this approach try to match their major competitors' appropriations in absolute dollars or to allocate the same percentage of sales for advertising that their competitors do. Although a marketer should be aware of what competitors spend on advertising, this technique should not be used alone because the firm's competitors probably have different advertising objectives and different resources available for advertising. Many companies and advertising agencies review competitive spending on a quarterly basis, comparing competitors' dollar expenditures on print, radio, and television with their own spending levels. Competitive tracking of this nature occurs at both the national and regional levels.

At times, marketers use the **arbitrary approach**, which usually means a high-level executive in the firm states how much to spend on advertising for a certain period. The arbitrary approach often leads to underspending or overspending. Although hardly a scientific budgeting technique, it is expedient. In general, the corporate culture will drive advertising budget decisions but it is often not based on knowledge that will increase profits. However, budgeting is more complicated than relying on "rules of thumb."[16] A recent study showed that there is a need for unified measurement of consumers' consumption of traditional media and digital

---

advertising appropriation The advertising budget for a specific time period

objective-and-task approach Budgeting for an advertising campaign by first determining its objectives and then calculating the cost of all the tasks needed to attain them

percent-of-sales approach Budgeting for an advertising campaign by multiplying the firm's past and expected sales by a standard percentage

competition-matching approach Determining an advertising budget by trying to match competitors' advertising outlays

arbitrary approach Budgeting for an advertising campaign as specified by a high-level executive in the firm

media to allow marketers to properly allocate and optimize the effectiveness of their advertising spending.[17] It is challenging to know how much to spend and to measure advertising effectiveness.

Deciding how large the advertising appropriation should be is critical. If the appropriation is set too low, the campaign cannot achieve its full potential. When too much money is appropriated, overspending results, and financial resources are wasted.

17-2e Developing the Media Plan

Advertisers spend tremendous amounts on advertising media. These amounts have grown rapidly during the past two decades. Although television and print still comprise a greater share of advertising revenue than digital advertising, this last category is expected to grow rapidly during the next few years. Figure 17.2 shows how U.S. adults divide their time across different media. To derive maximum results from media expenditures, marketers must develop effective media plans. A **media plan** sets forth the exact media vehicles to be used (specific magazines, television stations, social media, newspapers, and so forth) and the dates and times the advertisements will appear. Reebok released an advertising campaign featuring J.J. Watt of the NFL's Houston Texans with magazine ads and content across digital and social media platforms as well as in-store activations.[18] The advertisement highlights that J.J. Watt is *Sports Illustrated*'s Sportsperson of the Year. The plan determines how many people in the target audience will be exposed to the message. The method also determines, to some degree, the effects of the message on those specific target markets. Media planning is a complex task requiring thorough analysis of the target audience. Sophisticated computer models have been developed to attempt to maximize the effectiveness of media plans.

To formulate a media plan, the planners select the media for the campaign and prepare a time schedule for each medium. The media planner's primary goal is to reach the largest number of people in the advertising target that the budget will allow. A secondary goal is to achieve

media plan A plan that specifies the media vehicles to be used and the schedule for running advertisements

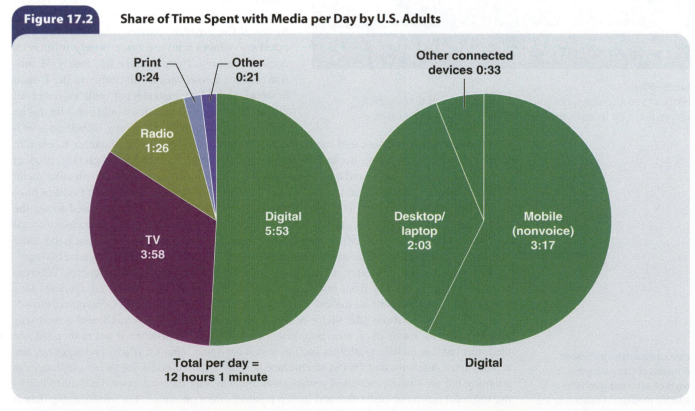

| **Figure 17.2** | **Share of Time Spent with Media per Day by U.S. Adults** |

Print 0:24 — Other 0:21

Other connected devices 0:33

Radio 1:26

Digital 5:53

Desktop/laptop 2:03

Mobile (nonvoice) 3:17

TV 3:58

Total per day = 12 hours 1 minute

Digital

Source: eMarketer, September 2017.

SOURCE: REEBOK

Media Plan
Reebok took out several print and digital advertisements to highlight its partnership with *Sports Illustrated*'s Sportsperson of the Year, J.J. Watt.

the appropriate message reach and frequency for the target audience while staying within budget. *Reach* refers to the percentage of consumers in the target audience actually exposed to a particular advertisement in a stated period. *Frequency* is the number of times these targeted consumers are exposed to the advertisement.

Media planners begin with broad decisions but eventually make very specific ones. They first decide which kinds of media to use: radio, television, newspapers, digital or online advertising, magazines, direct mail, outdoor displays, or signs on mass transit vehicles. Digital marketing in particular is growing, with spending on online and mobile advertising accounting for more than 38 percent of advertising dollars.[19] In fact, digital advertising sales have surpassed linear TV ad sales by more than $3 billion. The gap is expected to widen, with digital ad sales projected to increase to $80 billion as offline media sales decline.[20] Media planners assess different formats and approaches to determine which are most effective. Some media plans are highly focused and use just one medium. Others can be quite complex and dynamic.

Media planners take many factors into account when devising a media plan. They analyze location and demographic characteristics of consumers in the target audience, because people's tastes in media differ according to demographic groups and locations. Media planners also consider the sizes and types of audiences that specific media reach. For instance, *National Geographic* reaches relatively well-educated consumers who are often highly influential decision makers. The magazine has nearly 31 million readers across various platforms in the United States alone.[21] Many marketers of vehicles, nonprofit organizations, and electronics would consider this an attractive demographic. Declining broadcast television ratings and newspaper and magazine readership have led many companies to explore alternative media, including not only digital advertising but also ads on cell phones, product placements in video games, and advertisements in nontraditional venues. New media like social networking sites are also attracting advertisers due to their large reach. Research findings have found that, when advertising is a part of a social networking site, consumers need to see the advertising as beneficial, or it may lead them to abandon the site.[22] Advertisers are using social media as a tool for understanding customers and gaining insights.[23] On the other hand, even in this age of digital media, television remains the most successful medium for advertising.[24]

The rise in digital marketing is creating a dramatic shift for advertising agencies. Whereas competition came mostly from other agencies before, today, professional ad agencies face competition from amateur ad makers along with technology companies. For instance, crowdsourcing by organizations like Victor & Spoils is placing the roles of traditional advertising agencies into the hands of creative people worldwide. Digital marketing is not reduced to one medium, but can include platforms such as social networks, ebooks, iPads, geotargeting, and mobile apps. Agencies that choose to embrace new advertising media are facing challenges in adapting but are finding increased profits along the way. Big data can open the door to reaching the most desirable customers and have a positive effect on sales.[25] For instance, big data is allowing marketers to break up the Millennial generation into four categories marketers can use

cost comparison indicator
A means of comparing the costs of advertising vehicles in a specific medium in relation to the number of people reached

to target different products depending on their spending habits.[26] Digital marketing enables firms such as Coca-Cola to find more interactive ways to connect with specific target markets at a reasonable price.

The content of the message sometimes affects media choice. Print media can be used more effectively than broadcast media to present complex issues or numerous details in single advertisements. If an advertiser wants to promote beautiful colors, patterns, or textures, media offering high-quality color reproduction, such as magazines or television, should be used instead of newspapers. For instance, food can be effectively promoted in full-color magazine advertisements but far less effectively in black-and-white media. For example, the Keebler advertisement shows consumers several ways to use its Club Snack Crackers when preparing snacks for the family. The three options include The Veggie Club, The PB&J Club, and The Ham & Cheese Club. The food would look far less enticing in black-and-white media. By using magazine advertising, Keebler is able to create a colorful, visually compelling ad. Decisions are also made in selection for non-English-speaking audiences across multiple media platforms. Advertisers' evaluation of distinct cultural traits and preferences appears to be more important in the case of diverse ethnic cultures.[27]

The cost of media is an important but troublesome consideration. Planners try to obtain the best coverage possible for each dollar spent. However, there is no accurate way to compare the cost and impact of a television commercial with the cost and impact of a newspaper advertisement. Streaming advertisers are using big data from companies such as Nielsen to determine which shows interest their particular target market. Targeted, interactive ad technology has been available for years, but by finding out how campaigns perform on specific apps and devices, marketers are able to select the less costly medium while still reaching their target market.[28] Another common metric is the **cost comparison indicator**, which lets an advertiser compare the costs of several vehicles within a specific medium (such as two magazines) in relation to the number of people each vehicle reaches. The *cost per thousand impressions (CPM)* is the cost comparison indicator for magazines; it shows the cost of exposing 1,000 people to one advertisement.

SOURCE: KEEBLER CLUB SNACK CRACKERS

Turn your kitchen into the family snack bar with light, flaky, buttery **Club** Snack Crackers. For satisfied customers, every time.

Benefits of Magazine Advertising
Magazine advertisements allow marketers to show their advertisements using color. In this advertisement for Keebler Club Snack Crackers, various ways to prepare the crackers are displayed.

Top Ten Advertisers

$5.6 billion	$4.3 billion	$3.7 billion	$3.6 billion
1 Comcast	2 Procter & Gamble	3 General Motors Co.	4 AT&T

$2.7 billion $2.7 billion $2.7 billion

5 Nestlé

7 American Express Co. 6 Verizon Communications

8 Amazon 9 Ford Motor Co. 10 JPMorgan Chase & Co.

$2.6 billion $2.3 billion $2.2 billion

SNAPSHOT

Source: Compiled from *Ad Age's* annual "200 Leading Advertisers" report, June 26, 2017, http://adage.com/d/resources/system/files/resource/LNA%20Fact%20Pack%202017-online.pdf (accessed March 4, 2018).

Figure 17.3 shows the increase in digital ad spending worldwide. Emerging media are being used more extensively in light of media fragmentation and decline in traditional media (newspapers and radio). However, although the use of newer forms of media is increasing, many companies continue to spend significant amounts of their marketing dollars advertising in more traditional forums. It is estimated that seven out of ten consumers still use the Yellow Pages to call businesses, which continues to make it a viable option for some advertisers.[29] Media are selected by weighing the various advantages and disadvantages of each (see Table 17.1).

Like media selection decisions, media scheduling decisions are affected by numerous factors, such as target audience characteristics, product attributes, product seasonality, customer media behavior, and size of the advertising budget. There are three general types of media schedules: continuous, flighting, and pulsing. When a *continuous* schedule is used, advertising runs at a constant level with little variation throughout the campaign period. McDonald's is an example of a company that uses a continuous schedule. With a *flighting* schedule, advertisements run for set periods of time, alternating with periods in which no ads run. For instance, an advertising campaign might have an ad run for 2 weeks, then suspend it for 2 weeks, and then run it again for 2 weeks. Companies like Hallmark, John Deere, and Ray-Ban use a flighting schedule. A *pulsing* schedule combines continuous and flighting schedules: During the entire campaign, a certain portion of advertising runs continuously, and during specific time periods of the campaign, additional advertising is used to intensify the level of communication with the target audience.

17-2f Creating the Advertising Message

The basic content and form of an advertising message are a function of several factors. A product's features, uses, and benefits affect the content of the message. The intensity of the advertising can also have an impact. For instance, push advertising on digital devices refers to advertising that is not requested by the user. Although push advertising might alienate some

Figure 17.3 **Digital Ad Spending Worldwide (in Billions)**

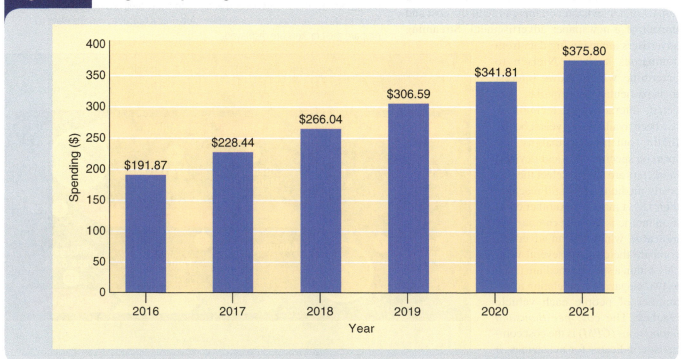

Source: eMarketer, September 2017

Table 17.1 **Advantages and Disadvantages of Major Media Classes**

Medium	Advantages	Disadvantages
Newspapers	Reach large audience; purchased to be read; geographic flexibility; short lead time; frequent publication; favorable for cooperative advertising; merchandising services	Not selective for socioeconomic groups or target market; short life; limited reproduction capabilities; large advertising volume limits exposure to any one advertisement
Magazines	Demographic selectivity; good reproduction; long life; prestige; geographic selectivity when regional issues are available; read in leisurely manner	High costs; 30- to 90-day average lead time; high level of competition; limited reach; communicates less frequently
Direct mail	Little wasted circulation; highly selective; circulation controlled by advertiser; few distractions; personal; stimulates actions; use of novelty; relatively easy to measure performance; hidden from competitors	Very expensive; lacks editorial content to attract readers; often thrown away unread as junk mail; criticized as invasion of privacy; consumers must choose to read the ad
Radio	Reaches 93 percent of U.S. adults; highly mobile and flexible; very low relative costs; ad can be changed quickly; high level of geographic and demographic selectivity; encourages use of imagination	Lacks visual imagery; short life of message; listeners' attention limited because of other activities; market fragmentation; difficult buying procedures; limited media and audience research
Television	Reaches large audiences; high frequency available; dual impact of audio and video; highly visible; high prestige; geographic and demographic selectivity; difficult to ignore; on-demand capabilities	Very expensive; highly perishable message; size of audience not guaranteed; amount of prime time limited; lack of selectivity in target market
Digital Media	Immediate response; potential to reach a precisely targeted audience; ability to track customers and build databases; highly interactive medium; real-time analytics	Costs of precise targeting are high; inappropriate ad placement; effects difficult to measure; concerns about security and privacy
Outdoor	Allows for frequent repetition; low cost; message can be placed close to point of sale; geographic selectivity; operable 24 hours a day; high creativity and effectiveness	Message must be short and simple; no demographic selectivity; seldom attracts readers' full attention; criticized as traffic hazard and blight on countryside; much wasted coverage; limited capabilities

Sources: Adapted from William F. Arens and Michael F. Weigold, *Contemporary Advertising* (Burr Ridge, IL: Irwin/McGraw-Hill, 2017); George E. Belch and Michael A. Belch, *Advertising and Promotion* (Burr Ridge, IL: Irwin/McGraw-Hill, 2015).

consumers, younger consumers are more accepting of push advertising if the source is trusted, permission has been given, and the messages are relevant or entertaining.[30] However, research has shown that advertising that pushes too hard to the point that consumers feel uncomfortable may cause consumers to consider the product negatively.[31] With the increase in digital technology, the cost of advertising for marketers is decreasing and advertising is becoming more frequent in venues such as mobile games and social media. As advertising becomes more embedded in our lives, advertisers must strive to not offend consumers by being too prevalent, obvious, or invasive.

Additionally, characteristics of the people in the target audience—gender, age, education, race, income, occupation, lifestyle, life stage, and other attributes—influence both content and form. For instance, gender affects how people respond to advertising claims that use hedging words like *may* and *probably* and pledging words, such as *definitely* and *absolutely*. Researchers have found that women respond negatively to both types of claims, but pledging claims have little effect on men.[32] When Procter & Gamble (P&G) promotes Crest toothpaste to children, the company emphasizes daily brushing and cavity control, focusing on fun and good flavors like bubblegum. When marketing Crest to adults, P&G focuses on functionality, stressing whitening, enamel protection, breath enhancement, and tartar and plaque control. To communicate effectively, advertisers use words, symbols, and illustrations that are meaningful, familiar, and appealing to people in the target audience.

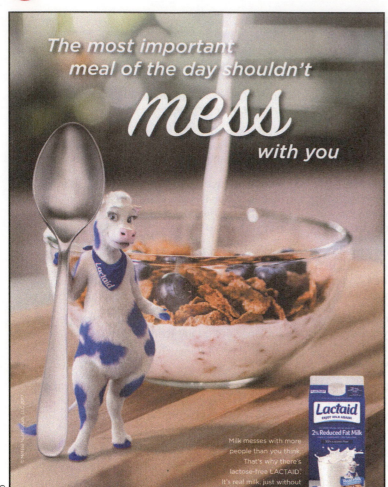

The most important
meal of the day shouldn't
mess
with you

Milk messes with more
people than you think.
That's why there's
lactose-free LACTAID.
It's real milk, just without
that annoying lactose.

Lactaid The milk that doesn't mess with you.

Lactaid
ENJOY MILK AGAIN!
2% Reduced Fat Milk
100% Lactose Free

SOURCE: LACTAID

Spokescharacter
Lactaid uses a cow in both its print and TV advertisements to feature its lactose-free milk.

Another controversy for advertisers is whether to advertise to children. Many countries have restrictions on advertising to this demographic. Sweden and Norway ban advertising directed at children, and Great Britain limits the advertising of foods high in fat, salt, or sugar on television and radio to children under the age of 16. Many firms in the European Union and the United States are attempting self-regulation, developing codes of conduct regarding this type of advertising. Coca-Cola, Unilever, Dannon, and General Mills are just a few examples of brands that have pledged under the Children's Food & Beverage Advertising Initiative to not target advertising toward children who are under 12 years old.[33]

An advertising campaign's objectives and platform also affect the content and form of its messages. If a firm's advertising objectives involve large sales increases, the message may include hard-hitting, high-impact language, symbols, and messages. Slogans such as Home Depot's basic message, "More saving. More doing," can aid in brand recall. When designing slogans, marketers should make them short, retain them for a long period of time, and provide large marketing budgets to make the slogan memorable.[34] The use of spokescharacters or design elements can also be highly effective. Spokescharacters are visual images that can convey a brand's features, benefits, or brand personality. Flo from Progressive Insurance and the GEICO gecko are examples of spokescharacters representing specific brands. The spokescharacter can provide a personality and improve brand equity by directly and indirectly enhancing excitement, sincerity, and trust.[35] Lactaid uses a cow as a spokescharacter for its lactose-free Lactaid. Viewers have come to associate the Lactaid Cow with the company. The advertisement emphasizes that Lactaid is real milk, but it's lactose-free. Thus, the advertising platform is the foundation on which campaign messages are built.

Choice of media obviously influences the content and form of the message. Effective outdoor displays and short broadcast spot announcements require concise, simple messages. Magazine and newspaper advertisements can include considerable detail and long explanations. Because several kinds of media offer geographic selectivity, a precise message can be tailored to a particular geographic section of the target audience. Some magazine publishers produce **regional issues**, in which advertisements and editorial content of copies appearing in one geographic area differ from those appearing in other areas. For instance, the AAA Publishing Network publishes 24 regional magazine titles, including *Home & Away* (Pennsylvania, Ohio, and New York), *GO Magazine* (North Carolina and South Carolina), and *Western Journey* (Idaho and Washington).[36] A company advertising with the AAA Publishing Network might decide to use one message in the New England region and another in the rest of the nation. A company may also choose to advertise in only one region. Such geographic selectivity lets a firm use the same message in different regions at different times.

regional issues Versions of a magazine that differ across geographic regions

17-2g **Copy**

Copy is the verbal portion of an advertisement and may include headlines, subheadlines, body copy, and a signature. Not all advertising contains all of these copy elements. Even handwritten notes on direct-mail advertising that say, "Try this. It works!" seem to increase requests for free samples.[37] The headline is critical because often it is the only part of the copy that people read. It should attract readers' attention and create enough interest to make them want to read the body copy or visit the website. The subheadline, if there is one, links the headline to the body copy and sometimes serves to explain the headline.

Body copy for most advertisements consists of an introductory statement or paragraph, several explanatory paragraphs, and a closing paragraph. Some copywriters have adopted guidelines for developing body copy systematically: (1) identify a specific desire or problem, (2) recommend the product as the best way to satisfy that desire or solve that problem, (3) state product benefits and indicate why the product is best for the buyer's particular situation, (4) substantiate advertising claims, and (5) ask the buyer to take action. When substantiating claims, it is important to present the substantiation in a credible manner. The proof of claims should help strengthen both the image of the product and company integrity. A shortcut explanation of what much advertising is designed to accomplish is the AIDA model. Advertising should create *awareness*, produce *interest*, create *desire*, and ultimately result in a purchase (*action*). Typeface selection can help advertisers create a desired impression using fonts that are engaging, reassuring, or very prominent.[38]

The signature identifies the advertisement's sponsor. It may contain several elements, including the firm's trademark, logo, name, and address. The signature should be attractive, legible, distinctive, and easy to identify in a variety of sizes.

Often, because radio listeners are not fully "tuned in" mentally to what they're hearing on the radio, radio copy should be informal and conversational to attract listeners' attention. Radio messages are highly perishable and should consist of short, familiar terms, which increase their impact. The length should not require a rate of speech exceeding approximately 2.5 words per second.

In television copy, the audio material must not overpower the visual material, and vice versa. However, a television message should make optimal use of its visual portion, which can be very effective for product use, applications, and demonstrations. Copy for a television commercial is sometimes initially written in parallel script form. Video is described in the left column and audio in the right. When the parallel script is approved, the copywriter and artist combine copy with visual material by using a **storyboard**, which depicts a series of miniature television screens showing the sequence of major scenes in the commercial. Beneath each screen is a description of the audio portion to be used with that video segment. Technical personnel use the storyboard as a blueprint when producing the commercial.

17-2h **Artwork**

Artwork consists of an advertisement's illustrations and layout. **Illustrations** are often photographs but can also be drawings, graphs, charts, and tables. Illustrations are used to draw attention, encourage audiences to read or listen to the copy, communicate an idea quickly, or convey ideas that are difficult to express. Illustrations can be more important in capturing attention than text or brand elements, independent of size.[39] They are especially important, because consumers tend to recall the visual portions of advertisements better than the verbal portions. Advertisers use a variety of illustration techniques. They may show the product alone, in a setting, or in use, or show the results of the product's use. For instance, the Home Depot advertisement shows a close-up of a customer shopping for blinds on a tablet. The advertisement reinforces that Home Depot customers can shop both online and in-store. Illustrations can also take the form of comparisons, contrasts, diagrams, and testimonials.

The **layout** of an advertisement is the physical arrangement of the illustration and the copy (headline, subheadline, body copy, and signature). These elements can be arranged in many

copy The verbal portion of advertisements

storyboard A blueprint that combines copy and visual material to show the sequence of major scenes in a commercial

artwork An advertisement's illustrations and layout

illustrations Photos, drawings, graphs, charts, and tables used to spark audience interest in an advertisement

layout The physical arrangement of an advertisement's illustration and copy

Components of a Print Ad
This Home Depot advertisement contains components of a print ad, including a headline, subheadline, body copy, signature, and illustration.

ways. The final layout is the result of several stages of layout preparation. As it moves through these stages, the layout promotes an exchange of ideas among people developing the advertising campaign and provides instructions for production personnel.

17-2i Executing the Campaign

Execution of an advertising campaign requires extensive planning and coordination, because many tasks must be completed on time and several people and firms are involved. Production companies, research organizations, media firms, printers, and commercial artists are just a few of the people and firms contributing to a campaign.

Implementation requires detailed schedules to ensure that various phases of the work are done on time. Advertising management personnel must evaluate the quality of the work and take corrective action when necessary. In some instances, changes are made during the campaign so it meets objectives more effectively. For example, an auto company focusing on fuel efficiency may need to add more information relative to the competition to achieve its objectives.

17-2j Evaluating Advertising Effectiveness

A variety of ways exist to test the effectiveness of advertising. They include measuring achievement of advertising objectives; assessing effectiveness of copy, illustrations, or layouts; and evaluating certain media.

Advertising can be evaluated before, during, and after the campaign. An evaluation performed before the campaign begins is called a **pretest**. A pretest usually attempts to evaluate the effectiveness of one or more elements of the message. To pretest advertisements, marketers sometimes use a **consumer jury**, a panel of existing or potential buyers of the advertised product. Jurors judge one or several dimensions of two or more advertisements. Such tests are based on the belief that consumers are more likely than advertising experts to know what influences them. Companies can also solicit the assistance of marketing research firms, such as Information Resources Inc. (IRI), to help assess ads.

To measure advertising effectiveness during a campaign, marketers usually rely on "inquiries" or responses. In a campaign's initial stages, an advertiser may use several advertisements simultaneously, each containing a coupon, form, toll-free phone number, QR code, social media, or website through which potential customers can request information. The advertiser records the number of inquiries or responses returned from each type of advertisement. If an advertiser receives 78,528 inquiries from advertisement A, 37,072 from advertisement B, and 47,932 from advertisement C, advertisement A is judged superior to advertisements B and C. Internet advertisers can also assess how many people "clicked" on an ad to obtain more product information. For the outdoor advertising industry, its independent auditor developed an out-of-home ratings system to determine the audiences likely to see an advertisement. Previous measurement systems used "Daily Effective Circulation," which essentially evolved around traffic counts, not on interested audiences. The industry has modified its rating system to account for new information, including vehicle speed and traffic congestion.[40]

pretest Evaluation of advertisements performed before a campaign begins

consumer jury A panel of a product's existing or potential buyers who pretest ads

Evaluation of advertising effectiveness after the campaign is called a **posttest**. Advertising objectives often determine what kind of posttest is appropriate. If the objectives' focus is on communication—to increase awareness of product features or brands or to create more favorable customer attitudes—the posttest should measure changes in these dimensions. Advertisers sometimes use consumer surveys or experiments to evaluate a campaign based on communication objectives. These methods are costly, however. In posttests, generalizations can be made about why advertising is failing or why media vehicles are not delivering the desired results.

For campaign objectives stated in terms of sales, advertisers should determine the change in sales or market share attributable to the campaign. Sales of Lincoln's MKZ sedan increased 5.1 percent in an eight-month period and is largely attributed to its advertising campaign featuring actor Matthew McConaughey.[41] However, changes in sales or market share brought about by advertising cannot be measured precisely; many factors independent of advertisements affect a firm's sales and market share. Competitors' actions, regulatory actions, and changes in consumer preferences, weather, and economic conditions are only a few factors that might enhance or diminish a company's sales or market share. For example, the statewide economic downturn in New Mexico has affected the state's ability to fund its very popular "New Mexico True" campaign. The campaign has successfully promoted the state's culture, people, and natural resources. However, the budget shortfall will not allow them to invest the $3.5 million needed to enter new markets like San Francisco.[42] By using data about past and current sales and advertising expenditures, advertisers can make gross estimates of the effects of a campaign on sales or market share.

Because it is difficult to determine the direct effects of advertising on sales, many advertisers evaluate print advertisements according to how well consumers can remember them. As more advertisers turn to mobile technology, total spending is estimated at $32 billion. Consumers are now dividing their attention between devices more than ever with 36 percent of Americans using more than one device simultaneously, from smartphones and tablets to computers and smart watches, so it's important to spend ad dollars wisely.[43] Researchers have found that ads that play on the theme of social desirability are more memorable when viewed in the presence of other people.

Posttest methods based on memory include recognition and recall tests. Such tests are usually performed by research organizations through surveys. In a **recognition test**, respondents are shown the actual advertisement and asked whether they recognize it. If they do, the interviewer asks additional questions to determine how much of the advertisement each respondent read. When recall is evaluated, respondents are not shown the actual advertisement but instead are asked about what they have seen or heard recently. For internet advertising, research suggests that the longer a person is exposed to a website containing a banner advertisement, the more likely he or she is to recall the ad.[44]

Recall can be measured through either unaided or aided recall methods. In an **unaided recall test**, respondents identify advertisements they have seen recently but are not shown any clues to help them remember. A similar procedure is used with an **aided recall test**, but respondents are shown a list of products, brands, company names, or trademarks to jog their memories. Many successful marketers have worked with advertising agencies to create catchy jingles to help consumers recall ads. Campbell's soup's "Mmm Mmm Good," McDonald's "You deserve a break today," and Coca-Cola's "I'd like to Teach the World to Sing" are all iconic jingles. Jingles are making a comeback. Working with Bacardi, iHeartMedia came up with a jingle "Drink Bacardi tonight." The campaign increased purchase intent by 54 percent.[45] However, targeted advertising can be viewed negatively by both consumers and regulators, and it is recommended that free websites that generate revenues through advertising remind consumers about the benefits their websites offer as they ask permission to display advertisements.[46]

The major justification for using recognition and recall methods is that people are more likely to buy a product if they can remember an advertisement about it than if they cannot. However, recalling an advertisement does not necessarily lead to buying the product or brand advertised. Researchers also use a sophisticated technique called *single-source data* to help evaluate advertisements. With this technique, individuals' behaviors are tracked from television sets to checkout counters. Monitors are placed in preselected homes, and microcomputers record when the television set is on and which station is being viewed. At the supermarket checkout, the individual in the sample household presents an identification card. Checkers then record the purchases by scanner, and data are sent to the research facility. Some single-source

posttest Evaluation of advertising effectiveness after the campaign

recognition test A posttest in which respondents are shown the actual ad and are asked if they recognize it

unaided recall test A posttest in which respondents are asked to identify advertisements they have seen recently but are not given any recall clues

aided recall test A posttest that asks respondents to identify recent ads and provides clues to jog their memories

data companies provide sample households with scanning equipment for use at home to record purchases after returning from shopping trips. Single-source data supplies information that links exposure to advertisements with purchase behavior.

17-3 WHO DEVELOPS THE ADVERTISING CAMPAIGN?

An advertising campaign may be handled by an individual, a few people within a firm, a firm's own advertising department, or an advertising agency. In very small firms, one or two individuals are responsible for advertising (and for many other activities as well). Usually, these individuals depend heavily on local media (TV, radio, and newspaper) for copywriting, artwork, and advice about scheduling media.

In certain large businesses, especially large retail organizations, advertising departments create and implement advertising campaigns. Depending on the size of the advertising program, an advertising department may consist of a few multiskilled individuals or a sizable number of specialists, including copywriters, artists, social media experts, media buyers, and technical production coordinators. Advertising departments sometimes obtain the services of independent research organizations and hire freelance specialists when a particular project requires it.

Many firms employ an advertising agency to develop advertising campaigns. When an organization uses an advertising agency, the firm and the agency usually develop the advertising campaign jointly. How much each participates in the campaign's total development

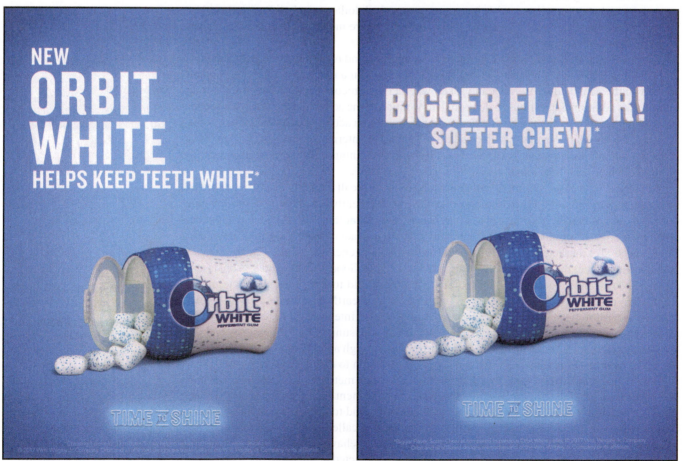

The Value of Advertising Agencies
Wrigley's advertising agency developed the tagline "Time to Shine" to support its Orbit White peppermint gum release. Wrigley printed a series of advertisements as part of the campaign.

depends on the working relationship between the firm and the agency. Ordinarily, a firm relies on the agency for copywriting, artwork, technical production, and formulation of the media plan. For example, for Orbit White advertisements, Wrigley worked with Energy BBDO and CLM BBDO to create its "Time to Shine" advertising campaign. The campaign consisted of both magazine advertisements and commercials. The new tagline was intended to be more aspirational than its older "just brushed clean feeling" tagline. The advertisements highlight Orbit White's big flavor, soft chew, and ability to keep teeth white.

Advertising agencies assist businesses in several ways. An agency, especially a large one, can supply the services of highly skilled specialists—not only copywriters, artists, and production coordinators, but also media experts, researchers, and legal advisers. Agency personnel often have broad advertising experience and are usually more objective than a firm's employees about the organization's products.

Because an agency traditionally receives most of its compensation from a 15 percent commission paid by the media from which it makes purchases, firms can obtain some agency services at low or moderate costs. If an agency contracts for $400,000 of television time for a firm, it receives a commission of $60,000 from the television station. Although the traditional compensation method for agencies is changing and now includes other factors, media commissions still offset some costs of using an agency. Like advertising, public relations can be a vital element in a promotion mix. We turn to this topic next.

17-4 PUBLIC RELATIONS

Learning Objective 17-4
Define public relations.

Public relations is a broad set of communication efforts used to create and maintain favorable relationships between an organization and its stakeholders. An organization communicates with various stakeholders, both internal and external, and public relations efforts can be directed toward any and all of them. A firm's stakeholders can include customers, suppliers, employees, shareholders, the media, educators, potential investors, government officials, and society in general. Public relations is also used to respond to negative events. How an organization uses public relations in a crisis often determines how quickly it will recover. Managers spend more resources understanding and responding to negative word of mouth than they do to the promotion of positive word of mouth.[47] Company scandals can often lead to the resignation of top officials such as the CEO or board members. Volkswagen's CEO stepped down after an emissions scandal revealed the company had duped regulators by placing defeat devices into its vehicles.[48] On the other hand, being honest with consumers and responsive to their needs develops a foundation for open communication and trust in the long run.

public relations
Communication efforts used to create and maintain favorable relations between an organization and its stakeholders

Public relations can be used to promote people, places, ideas, activities, and even countries. It is often used by nonprofit organizations to achieve their goals. Public relations focuses on enhancing the image of the total organization. Assessing public attitudes and creating a favorable image are no less important than direct promotion of the organization's products. Because the public's attitudes toward a firm are likely to affect the sales of its products, it is very important for firms to maintain positive public perceptions. In addition, employee morale is strengthened if the public perceives the firm positively.[49] Although public relations can make people aware of a company's products, brands, or activities, it can also create specific company images, such as innovativeness or dependability. Companies like Keurig, Green Mountain, Patagonia, Sustainable Harvest, and Honest Tea have reputations for being socially responsible not only because they engage in socially responsible behavior but also because their actions are reported through news stories and other public relations efforts. By getting the media to report on a firm's accomplishments, public relations helps the company maintain positive public visibility. Some firms use public relations for a single purpose; others use it for several purposes. Table 17.2 lists the top 10 public relations firms.

Table 17.2   Top 10 Public Relations Firms

Rank	PR Agency
1	Edelman
2	Weber Shandwick
3	FleishmanHillard
4	Ketchum
5	MSLGroup
6	Burson-Marsteller
7	Hill+Knowlton Strategies
8	Ogilvy PR
9	BlueFocus
10	Golin

Source: The Holmes Report, "Global Top 250 Firms," https://www.holmesreport.com/ranking-and-data/global-pr-agency-rankings/2017-pr-agency-rankings/top-250 (accessed March 4, 2018).

Learning Objective 17-5
Describe the different tools
of public relations.

17-5 PUBLIC RELATIONS TOOLS

Companies use a variety of public relations tools to convey messages and create images. Public relations professionals prepare written materials and use digital media to deliver brochures, newsletters, company magazines, news releases, blogs, managed social media sites, and annual reports that reach and influence their various stakeholders. Sometimes, organizations use less conventional tools in their public relations campaigns. AT&T's "It Can Wait" campaign spreads awareness about the dangers of texting and driving. Not only did it hold a pledge drive, but it also partnered with advertising agency BBDO to develop a documentary and held 400 local events to show individuals the impact their texting can have on their driving.[50] AT&T introduced the DriveMode app to silence incoming text messages while driving at 15 mph or faster. The campaign has resulted in more than 5 million app downloads and 14 million pledges.[51]

Public relations personnel also create corporate identity materials—such as logos, business cards, stationery, signs, and promotional materials—that make firms immediately recognizable. Speeches are another public relations tool. Because what a company executive says publicly at meetings or to the media can affect the organization's image, the speech must convey the desired message clearly. Event sponsorship, in which a company pays for part or all of a special event, like a benefit concert or a tennis tournament, is another public relations tool. One example is Pizza Hut's sponsorship of ESPN's College GameDay.[52] Sponsoring special events can be an effective means of increasing company or brand recognition with relatively minimal investment. Event sponsorship can gain companies considerable amounts of free media coverage. An organization tries to ensure that its product and the sponsored event target a similar audience and that the two are easily associated in customers' minds. Many companies as well as individuals assist in their charitable giving. Bill Daniels, the founder of Cablevision who passed away in 2000, set up a fund supported with more than a billion dollars to provide financial support for many causes, including business ethics.

INTEGRITY IN MARKETING

Patagonia Unzips Its Advertising Strategy: Don't Buy This Jacket

One of apparel store Patagonia's most popular advertisements features its popular R2 coat with the headline: "Don't Buy This Jacket." In the copy, the advertisement explains that although the R2 uses recycled materials, it is still harmful to the environment. Patagonia advocates for decreased consumption where consumers purchase less (also termed green demarketing).

Patagonia was founded upon environmental principles with a three-part mission: sell quality products, cause no unnecessary harm, and find business solutions to environmental issues. Because excessive consumption generates waste, encouraging consumers to purchase less demonstrates Patagonia's environmental commitment. Patagonia wants consumers to purchase apparel only as needed.

Patagonia has incorporated public relations activities into its campaign as well. For instance, it developed a film showing fans wearing old Patagonia clothing held together by duct tape, demonstrating the value of less consumption. Patagonia also announced it would donate 100 percent of proceeds from sales generated on the day after Thanksgiving to environmental causes.

Because Patagonia clothing lasts a long time, its marketing indirectly promotes its own products as a solution to the constant need to replace worn-out apparel. The company even urges consumers to return worn-out merchandise so Patagonia can recycle it into something else. This approach resonates with consumers as sustainable consumption becomes an important sociocultural value. Patagonia's revenue has increased by more than $250 million since it first launched its infamous campaign.[b]

Publicity is a part of public relations. **Publicity** is communication in news-story form about the organization, its products, or both, transmitted through a mass medium at no charge. For instance, each time Apple CEO Tim Cook announces that the company will introduce a new model of the iPhone and iPad, the story is covered in newspapers and television news shows throughout the world for months afterward. Although public relations has a larger, more comprehensive communication function than publicity, publicity is a very important aspect of public relations. Publicity can be used to provide information about goods or services; to announce expansions or contractions, acquisitions, research, or new-product launches; or to enhance a company's image.

The most common publicity-based public relations tool is the **news release**, sometimes called a *press release*, which is usually a single page of type-written copy containing fewer than 300 words and describing a company event or product. A news release gives the firm's or agency's name, address, phone number, and contact person. Companies sometimes use news releases when introducing new products or making significant announcements. Dozens of organizations, including Nike, Starbucks, and clean-energy companies, are partnering to create awareness of the economic benefits of national climate and energy legislation through press releases and other media. As Table 17.3 shows, news releases tackle a multitude of specific issues. A **feature article** is a manuscript of up to 3,000 words prepared for a specific publication. A **captioned photograph** is a photograph with a brief description explaining its contents. Captioned photographs are effective for illustrating new or improved products with highly visible features.

There are several other kinds of publicity-based public relations tools. For example, a **press conference** is a meeting called to announce major news events. Media personnel are invited to a press conference and are usually supplied with various written materials and photographs. Letters to the editor and editorials are sometimes prepared and sent to newspapers and magazines. Videos may be made available to broadcasters in the hope that they will be aired.

Publicity-based public relations tools offer several advantages, including credibility, news value, significant word-of-mouth communications, and a perception of media endorsement. The public may consider news coverage more truthful and credible than an advertisement

publicity A news-story type of communication about an organization and/or its products transmitted through a mass medium at no charge

news release A short piece of copy publicizing an event or a product

feature article A manuscript of up to 3,000 words prepared for a specific publication

captioned photograph A photograph with a brief description of its contents

press conference A meeting used to announce major news events

Table 17.3   Possible Issues for Publicity Releases

Support of a social cause	New products
Improved warranties	New slogan
Reports on industry conditions	Research developments
New uses for established products	Company's milestones and anniversaries
Product endorsements	Employment, production, and sales changes
Quality awards	Award of contracts
Company name changes	Opening of new markets
Interviews with company officials	Improvements in financial position
Improved distribution policies	Opening of an exhibit
International business efforts	History of a brand
Athletic event sponsorship	Winners of company contests
Visits by celebrities	Logo changes
Reports on new discoveries	Speeches of top management
Innovative business practices	Merit awards
Economic forecasts	Acquisitions and partnerships

because news media are not paid to provide the information. In addition, stories regarding a new-product introduction or a new environmentally responsible company policy, for example, are handled as news items and are likely to receive notice. Finally, the cost of publicity is low compared with the cost of advertising.[53]

Publicity-based public relations tools have some limitations. Media personnel must judge company messages to be newsworthy if the messages are to be published or broadcast at all. Consequently, messages must be timely, interesting, accurate, and in the public interest. It may take a great deal of time and effort to convince media personnel of the news value of publicity releases, and many communications fail to qualify. Although public relations personnel usually encourage the media to air publicity releases at certain times, they control neither the content nor the timing of the communication. Media personnel alter length and content of publicity releases to fit publishers' or broadcasters' requirements and may even delete the parts of messages that company personnel view as most important. Furthermore, media personnel use publicity releases in time slots or positions most convenient for them. Other outside public relations messages can be picked up during slow news times. Thus, messages sometimes appear in locations or at times that may not reach the firm's target audiences. Although these limitations can be frustrating, properly managed publicity-based public relations tools offer an organization substantial benefits.

Learning Objective 17-6

Analyze how public relations is used and evaluated.

17-6 EVALUATING PUBLIC RELATIONS EFFECTIVENESS

Because of the potential benefits of good public relations, it is essential that organizations evaluate the effectiveness of their public relations campaigns. Research can be conducted to determine how well a firm is communicating its messages or image to its target audiences. *Environmental monitoring* identifies changes in public opinion affecting an organization. A *public relations audit* is used to assess an organization's image among the public or to evaluate the effect of a specific public relations program. A *communications audit* may include a content analysis of messages, a readability study, or a readership survey. If an organization wants to measure the extent to which stakeholders view it as being socially responsible, it can conduct a *social audit*.

One approach to measuring the effectiveness of publicity-based public relations is to count the number of exposures in the media. To determine which releases are published in print media and how often, an organization can hire a clipping service, a firm that clips and sends news releases to client companies. To measure the effectiveness of television coverage, a firm can enclose a card with its publicity releases requesting that the television station record its name and the dates when the news item is broadcast (although station personnel do not always comply). Some multimedia tracking services exist, but they are quite costly.

Counting the number of media exposures does not reveal how many people have actually read or heard the company's message or what they thought about the message afterward. However, measuring changes in product awareness, knowledge, and attitudes resulting from the publicity campaign helps yield this information. To assess these changes, companies must measure these levels before and after public relations campaigns. Although precise measures are difficult to obtain, a firm's marketers should attempt to assess the impact of public relations efforts on the organization's sales. For example, critics' reviews of films can affect the films' box office performance. Interestingly, negative reviews (publicity) harm revenue more than positive reviews help revenue in the early weeks of a film's release.[54]

17-6a Dealing with Unfavorable Public Relations

Thus far, we have discussed public relations as a planned element of the promotion mix. However, companies may have to deal with unexpected and unfavorable publicity resulting from an unsafe product, an accident resulting from product use, controversial actions of employees, or some other negative event or situation. Product recalls or products that could harm consumers can create a crisis and damage a brand. The extent of negative publicity and whether the brand has to publicly take blame will affect the amount of damage.[55] Many companies have experienced unfavorable publicity connected with defective or contaminated products, such as faulty car parts, E. coli in fast food, and industrial compounds in pet foods. Unfavorable coverage can have quick and dramatic effects. Coca-Cola was forced to quickly pull an advertisement it featured in Germany to celebrate Fanta's 75th anniversary in the country. Its marketing referred to the 1940s as "the good old times." Coca-Cola experienced immediate backlash as the 1940s in Germany was marked by the Nazi era.[56]

Negative events that generate public relations can wipe out a company's favorable image and destroy positive customer attitudes established through years of expensive advertising campaigns and other promotional efforts. Target, for instance, suffered reputational damage after hackers hacked into its system and stole credit card information from millions of its customers. Reputation is often considered a valuable company asset. How an organization deals with unfavorable actions and outcomes can have a significant impact on firm valuation. Moreover, today's mass media, including online services and the internet, disseminate information faster than ever before, and bad news generally receives more media attention than corporate social responsibility.

To protect its image, an organization needs to prevent unfavorable public relations or at least lessen its effect if it occurs. First and foremost, the organization should try to prevent negative incidents and events through safety programs, inspections, training, and effective quality control procedures. Experts insist that sending consistent brand messages and images throughout all communications at all times can help a brand maintain its strength even during a crisis.[57] However, because negative events can strike even the most cautious firms, an organization should have plans in place to handle them when they occur. Firms need to establish policies and procedures for reducing the adverse impact of news coverage of a crisis or controversy. In most cases, organizations should expedite news coverage of negative events rather than try to discourage or block them. If news coverage is suppressed, rumors and other misinformation may replace facts and create public scrutiny.

An unfavorable event can easily balloon into serious problems or public issues and become very damaging. By being forthright with the press and public and taking prompt action, a firm may be able to convince the public of its honest attempts to deal with the situation, and news personnel may be more willing to help explain complex issues to the public. Dealing effectively with a negative event allows an organization to lessen, if not eliminate, the unfavorable impact on its image. Experts generally advise companies that are dealing with negative publicity to respond quickly and honestly to the situation and to keep the lines of communication with all stakeholders open. Digital media has enhanced the organizational ability to communicate with key stakeholders and develop dialogues on current issues.

Summary

17-1 Describe advertising and its different types.

Advertising is a paid form of nonpersonal communication transmitted to consumers through mass media, such as television, radio, the internet, newspapers, magazines, direct mail, outdoor displays, and signs on mass transit vehicles. Both business and nonbusiness organizations use advertising. Institutional advertising promotes organizational images, ideas, and political issues. When a company promotes its position

on a public issue such as taxation, institutional advertising is referred to as advocacy advertising. Product advertising promotes uses, features, and benefits of products. The two types of product advertising are pioneer advertising, which focuses on stimulating demand for a product category rather than a specific brand, and competitive advertising, which attempts to stimulate demand for a specific brand by indicating the brand's features, uses, and advantages. To make direct product comparisons, marketers use comparative advertising, which compares two or more brands. Two other forms of competitive advertising are reminder advertising, which reminds customers about an established brand's uses, characteristics, and benefits, and reinforcement advertising, which assures current users they have made the right brand choice. A newer form of advertising, native advertising, is digital advertising that matches the appearance and purpose of the content in which it is embedded.

17-2 Summarize the eight major steps in developing an advertising campaign.

Although marketers may vary in how they develop advertising campaigns, they should follow a general pattern. First, they must identify and analyze the target audience, the group of people at whom advertisements are aimed. Second, they should establish what they want the campaign to accomplish by defining advertising objectives. Objectives should be clear, precise, and presented in measurable terms. Third, marketers must create the advertising platform, which contains basic issues to be presented in the campaign. Advertising platforms should consist of issues important to consumers. Fourth, advertisers must decide how much money to spend on the campaign; they arrive at this decision through the objective-and-task approach, percent-of-sales approach, competition-matching approach, or arbitrary approach.

Advertisers must then develop a media plan, their fifth step, by selecting and scheduling media to use in the campaign. Some factors affecting the media plan are location and demographic characteristics of the target audience, content of the message, and cost of the various media. Sixth, the advertising message is created. The basic content and form of the advertising message are affected by product features, uses, and benefits; characteristics of the people in the target audience; the campaign's objectives and platform; and the choice of media. Advertisers use copy and artwork to create the message. Step seven, the execution of an advertising campaign requires extensive planning and coordination.

Finally, advertisers must devise one or more methods for evaluating advertisement effectiveness. Pretests are evaluations performed before the campaign begins; posttests are conducted after the campaign. Two types of posttests are a recognition test, in which respondents are shown the actual advertisement and asked whether they recognize it, and a recall test. In aided recall tests, respondents are shown a list of products, brands, company names, or trademarks to jog their memories. In unaided tests, no clues are given.

17-3 Identify who is responsible for developing advertising campaigns.

Advertising campaigns can be developed by personnel within the firm or in conjunction with advertising agencies. A campaign created by the firm's personnel may be developed by one or more individuals or by an advertising department within the firm. Use of an advertising agency may be advantageous because an agency provides highly skilled, objective specialists with broad experience in advertising at low to moderate costs to the firm.

17-4 Define public relations.

Public relations is a broad set of communication efforts used to create and maintain favorable relationships between an organization and its stakeholders. Public relations can be used to promote people, places, ideas, activities, and countries, and to create and maintain a positive company image. Some firms use public relations for a single purpose; others use it for several purposes.

17-5 Describe the different tools of public relations.

Public relations tools include written materials, such as brochures, newsletters, and annual reports; corporate identity materials, such as business cards and signs; speeches; event sponsorships; and special events. Publicity is communication in news-story form about an organization, its products, or both, transmitted through a mass medium at no charge. Publicity-based public relations tools include news releases, feature articles, captioned photographs, and press conferences. Problems that organizations confront in using publicity-based public relations include reluctance of media personnel to print or air releases and lack of control over timing and content of messages.

17-6 Analyze how public relations is used and evaluated.

To evaluate the effectiveness of their public relations programs, companies conduct research to determine how well their messages are reaching their audiences. Environmental monitoring, public relations audits, and counting the number of media exposures are all means of evaluating public relations effectiveness. Organizations should avoid negative public relations by taking steps to prevent negative events that result in unfavorable publicity.

Important Terms

advertising 496
institutional advertising
    496
advocacy advertising 497
product advertising 497
pioneer advertising 497
competitive advertising
    497
comparative advertising
    497
reminder advertising 498
reinforcement advertising
    498

native advertising 498
advertising
    campaign 499
target audience 499
advertising platform 501
advertising appropriation
    502
objective-and-task
    approach 502
percent-of-sales
    approach 502
competition-matching
    approach 502

arbitrary approach
    502
media plan 503
cost comparison
    indicator 505
regional issues 508
copy 509
storyboard 509
artwork 509
illustrations 509
layout 509
pretest 510
consumer jury 510

posttest 511
recognition
    test 511
unaided recall
    test 511
aided recall test 511
public relations 513
publicity 515
news release 515
feature article 515
captioned photograph
    515
press conference 515

Discussion and Review Questions

1. What is the difference between institutional and product advertising?
2. What is the difference between competitive advertising and comparative advertising?
3. What are the major steps in creating an advertising campaign?
4. What is a target audience? How does a marketer analyze the target audience after identifying it?
5. Why is it necessary to define advertising objectives?
6. What is an advertising platform, and how is it used?
7. What factors affect the size of an advertising budget? What techniques are used to determine an advertising budget?
8. Describe the steps in developing a media plan.
9. What is the function of copy in an advertising message?

10. Discuss several ways to posttest the effectiveness of advertising.
11. What role does an advertising agency play in developing an advertising campaign?
12. What is public relations? Whom can an organization reach through public relations?
13. How do organizations use public relations tools? Give several examples you have observed recently.
14. Explain the problems and limitations associated with publicity-based public relations.
15. In what ways is the effectiveness of public relations evaluated?
16. What are some sources of negative public relations?

Developing Your Marketing Plan

Determining the message that advertising is to communicate to the customer is an important part of developing a marketing strategy. A sound understanding of the various types of advertising and different forms of media is essential in selecting the appropriate methods for communicating the message. These decisions form a critical segment of the marketing plan. To assist you in relating the information in this chapter to the development of your marketing plan, consider the following issues:

1. What class and type of advertising would be most appropriate for your product?

2. Discuss the different methods for determining the advertising appropriation.
3. Using Table 17.1 as a guide, evaluate the different types of media and determine which would be most effective in meeting your promotional objectives (from Chapter 16).
4. What methods would you use to evaluate the effectiveness of your advertising campaign?
5. Review Table 17.3 and discuss possible uses for publicity in your promotional plan.

Video Case 17.1

Scripps Networks Interactive: An Expert at Connecting Advertisers with Programming

Television advertisers have faced challenges in the past decade. People tend to watch fewer television shows at the time of airing or choose to watch them on platforms such as Netflix or Hulu. The use of Digital Video Recorders (DVRs) has also contributed to this challenge as viewers can fast forward through commercials while watching their favorite shows. Scripps Networks Interactive, parent company to Food Network, HGTV, Travel Channel, DIY Network, Cooking Channel, and more, has found a way around this issue through product placement and integration, use of social media platforms, and promotion.

Scripps Networks Interactive is unique in that their programming appeals to similar target markets with similar interests. The director of Digital Media and Database Marketing for Scripps Networks Interactive states, "Our programming lends itself so well to speaking to lifestyle and what people are passionate and interested in, and I think our marketing communications strategy is a natural extension of that." This presents a strong opportunity for gaining real results through advertising. At the same time, these promotional initiatives do not always seem like advertising to viewers. One way this is accomplished is through cross-promotional activities across networks that appear to be natural extensions of the show rather than advertising that is deemed intrusive.

Product placement and integration works well with the lifestyle content of the company's programming because viewers are interested in the content being provided. In most cases, "our audiences . . . actually look to our advertisers' products for ideas and as resources," states the Senior Vice President of Interactive Ad Sales Marketing for Scripps. This creates an opportunity for the company to build strong relationships with advertisers. Advertisers seek out Scripps Networks not only for placement in their shows but also for integration into their social media space. The integration of television product placement and social media advertising has been a benefit for both parties. The Senior Vice President of Interactive Ad Sales Marketing explains, "If we tie a specific advertiser to *Iron Chef* or to *Chopped*, then there's opportunities for them to be driven from on-air to say 'check out the recipes from this specific episode online at foodnetwork.com.'" Despite the culinary nature of these shows, the advertising platform Scripps attracts other vendors, including automobile manufacturers.

Lexus, for example, was featured as the car driven by *Restaurant Impossible*'s host Robert Irvine. These clips were then shown on the show's webpage, packaged as a Lexus advertisement.

Scripps has also found a way to integrate product placement into brick-and-mortar locations as well as on digital space. After Food Network host Guy Fieri won recognition as "The Next Food Network Star," he partnered with TGI Fridays in an endorsement agreement. Fieri hosted a recipe showdown on the Food Network, and TGI Fridays promoted these recipes in their restaurants. Partnerships between chefs and brands have also been developed to create co-branded products. Alex Guarnaschelli, a judge on *Chopped*, was approached by Fisher Nuts to share recipes containing their products. These advertisements were shown on both the Food Network and the Cooking Channel.

Another benefit of this integration is that the company and the advertiser become cooperative marketing partners, where both are working from different directions to promote both the show and the product simultaneously. The General Manager of New Business for the Food Network explains an example of this kind of relationship with Kohl's and *Worst Cooks in America*: "Kohl's is advertising in it— they are sponsoring it. They are putting things on Pinterest or tweeting. We are doing the same thing in the context of the character, so you get both this top-down and bottom-up thing coming together."

Promotions also work well on this platform. A digital marketer for Scripps Networks describes the effectiveness of promotions. "What makes it more than just a giveaway for money is tying in hooks that engage people to not only sign up to a sweepstakes to win a trip . . . but making it part of the entertainment experience." For example, the Food Network ran a promotion for its show *The Great Food Truck Race*, where people were asked to go to the Facebook page and nominate or vote for their favorite local food truck. The winners would then be featured on the show's website. This event generated buzz and brought attention to the food trucks around the country that were being nominated. The nominees were featured on commercials aired during the show, where they asked viewers to vote for them online. The fans, businesses, and the show were all involved in generating buzz and promoting one another, creating an effect that is advantageous to all parties.

Scripps was recently acquired for $14.6 billion by Discovery Communications whose portfolio will be complemented by Scripps' lifestyle channels. The merger will give the companies greater market share with both domestic and international advertisers and further expand its cross-promotional opportunities. Combined, the companies reach 220 countries, represent 50 brands, and create 8,000 hours of original content annually.[58]

Questions for Discussion

1. Why is the Food Network such an important venue for many advertisers?
2. Why do you think even non-food advertisers are attracted to the Food Network?
3. Describe some of the ways that Discovery's acquisition of Scripps will create new advertising opportunities.

Case 17.2

The Rise of Native Advertising

Digital native advertising is online advertising that matches the appearance and purpose of the content in which it is embedded. For example, the wedding website The Knot may feature sponsored articles about wedding gowns that consumers can purchase through the website. Consumers find this advertising useful because the content is likely to follow the website's topics and style. Nearly 73 percent of internet users who are familiar with native advertising believe it is equally or more effective than non-sponsored ads.

The effectiveness of this type of digital advertising is causing marketers to take notice. For instance, the marketing agency of *The Wall Street Journal* partnered with Starz to develop an article—complete with video clips and an interactive timeline—that features the economics of romantic relationships throughout history. The sponsored content helped market Starz's show *The Girlfriend Experience*, while the focus on economics was meant to interest *The Wall Street Journal*'s business-savvy target market.

The increase in artificial intelligence (AI) technologies has the potential to improve the performance of native advertisements. AI tools can compile and analyze wide sets of data and create a variety of reports, freeing up marketers' time and improving the speed at which ad performance can be optimized. For example, *The Washington Post* uses a news-writing bot called Heliograf to generate welcome messages on native advertisements for readers to personalize the content.

However, because the advertisements are meant to resemble the surrounding content, consumers might not always recognize that an article or advertisement is sponsored. One report claims that 71 percent of native

advertising lacks sufficient transparency. The Federal Trade Commission (FTC) maintains that advertising must be distinguished from editorial content, but this line becomes blurred when the advertising resembles the content so closely. Industry self-regulatory guidelines are encouraging advertisers to label native ads as sponsored content to avoid confusion.

The FTC is still working toward establishing regulations that protect consumers. The FTC states: "Under the FTC Act, an act or practice is deceptive if there is a material misrepresentation or omission of information that is likely to mislead the consumer acting reasonably in the circumstances. A misrepresentation is material that is likely to affect consumers' choices or conduct regarding an advertised product or the advertising for the product." When advertisers and publishers fail to make appropriate disclosures, not only can the FTC take action, but so can the Federal Communications Commission (FCC) under its

GODFATHER/SHUTTERSTOCK.COM

Sponsorship ID Rule. This rule requires broadcast stations to make disclosures that identify any sponsors at the time of broadcasting. The FCC's reach includes radio, television, and video streaming. Recently, the FCC fined a U.S. television station operator $13.3 million for failing to disclose the sponsorship of a series of ads styled as news stories that aired more than 1,700 times.

Regulation on native advertising varies internationally. The Advertising Standards Authority (ASA) in the U.K. has developed regulations on digital advertising relatively recently, and has followed in the footsteps of the FTC, stating that native advertising cannot be camouflaged. Outbrain, a digital marketing platform that specialized in sponsored website links, came under fire from the ASA for a native advertising campaign that the organization said failed to clearly identify itself as an advertisement. The Internet Advertising Bureau (IAB UK) recently released new guidelines for native advertising and other sponsored content on social media and in influencer marketing. The guidelines require advertisers to "provide consumers with visual cues, or verbal brand mentions in audio formats, so consumers immediately know that they're engaging with marketing content."

It is estimated that these ads will account for 74 percent of all ad revenue by 2021. Though it seems native advertising is here to stay, advertisers will need to focus on developing genuine content and publishers will need to make clear disclosures to build and maintain consumer trust. Ad blockers may also prove themselves to be a challenge. Ad blockers, such as AdBlock, allow consumers to filter out banner ads, video ads, pop-ups, and more. When these services block native advertisements, the reach of the ads will drop significantly. With the growth of this form of advertising, publishers will need to carefully balance core content with sponsored content to avoid oversaturation which may deter site visitors. Despite these challenges, the future of native advertising is bright.[59]

Questions for Discussion

1. Why does native advertising need to be regulated?
2. What are some ways that advertisers can use native advertising to promote products?
3. What are the advantages of using native advertising over traditional digital advertising?

End of
SUMMER
SALE

60 % OFF

ALBOVK/SHUTTERSTOCK.COM

CHAPTER

18

Personal Selling and Sales Promotion

LEARNING OBJECTIVES

18-1 Describe the major goals of personal selling.

18-2 Summarize the seven basic steps in the personal selling process.

18-3 Identify the types of sales force personnel.

18-4 Describe team selling and relationship selling.

18-5 Discuss eight major decisions in sales force management.

18-6 Describe sales promotion.

18-7 Review consumer sales promotion methods.

18-8 Review trade sales promotion methods.

RAWPIXEL.COM/SHUTTERSTOCK.COM

Digital Discounting: The Demise of the Paper Coupon

Marketers are experiencing low redemption rates with print coupons in newspapers and magazines. The average redemption rate for these coupons during a six-month period was 0.34 percent. During times of prosperity, consumers are less likely to take the time to search for deals. However, there is potentially another explanation that marketers should consider: consumers' increased preference for convenience and their familiarity with the digital realm.

During this six-month period, only 0.6 percent of coupons distributed were digital. Yet the redemption rate for these coupons is projected to reach 10 percent in the next few years. For consumers, digital coupons are more convenient because they can pull up the coupons on their phones in-store. Grocery stores, department stores, and clothing stores are the top three locations for mobile coupon redemption. Websites such as RetailMeNot allow consumers to search for coupons they want at their leisure. More than half of consumers in a study remarked they would use more coupons if they were placed online.

Digital coupons also allow marketers to target markets more precisely. Through the use of apps, marketers can send mobile codes or coupons to consumers as they approach nearby stores. In fact, it is estimated that 10 percent of coupons sent through text messages are used. Marketers who use coupons as a form of sales promotion would do well to pay attention to this growing consumer interest in digital sales promotion.[1]

For many organizations, targeting customers with appropriate sales promotion and personal selling messages can play a major role in maintaining long-term, satisfying customer relationships, which in turn contribute to company success. Marketing strategy development should involve the sales organization during all stages of development and implementation. Top management needs extensive feedback from the sales force to better understand customers. Managers should strive to use sales data analytics to provide information for the sales force and sales promotion. Sales managers should communicate marketing strategy in a language with which salespeople feel comfortable.[2] As we saw in Chapter 16, personal selling and sales promotion are two important elements in a promotion mix. Personal selling is sometimes a company's sole promotional tool, and it is becoming increasingly professional and sophisticated, with sales personnel acting more as consultants, advisors, and sometimes as partners.

In this chapter, we focus on personal selling and sales promotion. We first consider the purposes of personal selling and then examine its basic steps. Next, we look at types of salespeople and how they are selected. After taking a look at several new types of personal selling, we discuss major sales force management decisions, including setting objectives for the sales force and determining its size; recruiting, selecting, training, compensating, and motivating salespeople; managing sales territories; and controlling and evaluating sales force performance. Then we examine several characteristics of sales promotion, reasons for using sales promotion, and sales promotion methods available for use in a promotion mix.

Learning Objective 18-1

Describe the major goals of personal selling.

18-1 THE NATURE AND GOALS OF PERSONAL SELLING

personal selling Paid personal communication that attempts to inform customers and persuade them to buy products in an exchange situation

Personal selling is paid personal communication that attempts to inform customers and persuade them to purchase products in an exchange situation. For instance, a Hewlett-Packard (HP) salesperson describing the benefits of the company's servers, PCs, and printers to a small-business customer is engaging in personal selling. Likewise, a member of the American Marketing Association (AMA) manning a table at an event engages in personal selling to inform interested parties about the benefits of joining the AMA. Personal selling gives marketers the greatest freedom to adjust a message to satisfy customers' information needs. It is the most precise of all promotion methods, enabling marketers to focus on the most promising sales prospects. Personal selling is also the most effective way to form relationships with customers. Personal selling is perhaps most important with business-to-business transactions involving the purchase of expensive products. Because of the high-risk factors involved, personal selling is often necessary to assure prospective customers about the quality of the product and answer any questions.[3] Despite these benefits, personal selling is generally the most expensive element in the promotion mix. The average cost of a sales call for industrial products and business-to-business sales is anywhere from $215 to $400.[4]

Millions of people earn their living through personal selling. Sales careers can offer high income, a great deal of freedom, a high level of training, and a high degree of job satisfaction. Salespeople who delight customers experience an improvement in customer orientation and job skills.[5] Although the public may harbor negative perceptions of personal selling, unfavorable

The Importance of Personal Selling
Financial advisors engage in personal selling as a way to provide financial advice and form relationships with customers.

MONKEY BUSINESS IMAGES/SHUTTERSTOCK.COM

stereotypes of salespeople are changing, thanks to the efforts of major corporations, professional sales associations, and academic institutions. Personal selling will continue to gain respect as professional sales associations develop and enforce ethical codes of conduct.[6] Developing ongoing customer relationships today requires sales personnel with high levels of professionalism as well as technical and interpersonal skills.[7]

Personal selling goals vary from one firm to another. However, they usually involve finding prospects, determining their needs, persuading prospects to buy, following up on the sale, and keeping customers satisfied. Identifying potential buyers interested in the organization's products is critical. Because most potential buyers seek information before making purchases, salespeople can ascertain prospects' informational needs and then provide relevant information. To do so, sales personnel must be well trained regarding both their products and the selling process in general.

Salespeople must be aware of their competitors. They must monitor the development of new products and keep abreast of competitors' sales efforts in their sales territories, how often and when the competition calls on their accounts, and what the competition is saying about their product in relation to its own. Salespeople must emphasize the benefits their products provide, especially when competitors' products do not offer those specific benefits. Salespeople often function as knowledge experts for the firm and provide key information for marketing decisions.[8]

Personal selling is changing today based on new technology, how customers gain information about products, and the way customers make purchase decisions. Customer information sharing through social media, mobile and web applications, and electronic sales presentations are impacting the nature of personal selling. Technology and social media provide an unprecedented level of transparency and communication between the salesperson and customers.[9] Many firms are using social media technology to reach business customers as well. "Social CRM" (customer relationship management) provides opportunities to manage data in discovering and engaging customers.[10] For instance, the cloud-computing models provided by Salesforce.com that enable firms to manage relationships with their customers can assist in sales management. Digital technology has become such an important part of our lives that it is not uncommon for salespersons to access their CRM systems through their smartphones. Consumer data can help salespeople understand and collaborate with customers in ways that did not exist in the past.

Using websites to manage orders and product information, track inventory, and train salespeople can save companies time and money. Twitter is a tool that can be used to post product information and updates, obtain prospects, recruit new salespeople, and communicate with salespeople. Facebook is another valuable tool that can supplement and support face-to-face contacts. On Facebook, salespeople can carry on conversations very similar to traditional face-to-face social networks. Mobile technology and applications provide salespeople with opportunities to offer service and connect with customers. CRM technology enables improved service, marketing and sales processes, and contact and data management and analysis. CRM can help facilitate the delivery of valuable customer experiences and provide the metrics to measure progress and sales successes.[11]

Few businesses survive solely on profits from one-time customers. For long-run survival, most marketers depend on repeat sales and thus need to keep their customers satisfied. In addition, satisfied customers provide favorable word-of-mouth and other communications, thereby attracting new customers. Although the whole organization is responsible for achieving customer satisfaction, much of the burden falls on salespeople, because they are almost always closer to customers than anyone else in the company and often provide buyers with information and service after the sale. Indeed, a firm's market orientation has a positive influence on salespeople's attitudes and commitment and on customer purchasing intentions.[12] Additionally, collaboration between sales and other marketing areas is positively related to market orientation that puts customers first, which positively impacts organizational performance.[13] Such contact gives salespeople an opportunity to generate additional sales and offers them a good vantage point for evaluating the strengths and weaknesses of the company's products and other marketing-mix components. Their observations help develop and maintain a marketing mix that better satisfies both the firm and its customers. Sales is no longer an isolated function in a global business world. The sales function is becoming part of a cross-functional strategic solution to customer management. This requires salespersons with both managerial and strategic skills.[14]

Learning Objective 18-2

Summarize the seven basic steps in the personal selling process.

18-2 STEPS OF THE PERSONAL SELLING PROCESS

The specific activities involved in the selling process vary among salespeople, selling situations, and cultures. No two salespeople use exactly the same selling methods. Nonetheless, many salespeople move through a general selling process. This process consists of seven steps, outlined in Figure 18.1: prospecting, preapproach, approach, making the presentation, overcoming objections, closing the sale, and following up.

18-2a Prospecting

Developing a database of potential customers is called **prospecting**. Salespeople seek names of prospects from company sales records, trade shows, commercial databases, newspaper announcements (of marriages, births, deaths, and so on), public records, telephone directories, trade association directories, and many other sources. Sales personnel also use responses to traditional and online advertisements that encourage interested persons to send in information request forms. Seminars and meetings targeted at particular types of clients, such as attorneys or accountants, may also produce leads.

prospecting Developing a database of potential customers

Most salespeople prefer to use referrals—recommendations from current customers—to find prospects. For instance, salespeople for Cutco Cutlery, which sells high-quality knives and kitchen cutlery, first make sales calls to their friends and families and then use referrals from them to seek out new prospects. Obtaining referrals requires that the salesperson have a good relationship with the current customer and, therefore, must have performed well before asking the customer for help. As might be expected, a customer's trust in and satisfaction with a salesperson influence his or her willingness to provide referrals. Research findings show that one referral is as valuable as 12 cold calls.[15] Also, 80 percent of clients are willing to give referrals, but only 20 percent are ever asked. Among the advantages of using referrals are more highly qualified sales leads, greater sales rates, and larger initial transactions. Some companies even award discounts off future purchases to customers who refer new prospects to their salespeople. Consistent activity is critical to successful prospecting. Salespeople must actively search the customer base for qualified prospects that fit the target market profile. After developing the prospect list, a salesperson evaluates whether each prospect is able, willing, and authorized to buy the product. Based on this evaluation, prospects are ranked according to desirability or potential.

Figure 18.1 **General Steps in the Personal Selling Process**

1. Prospecting
2. Preapproach
3. Approach
4. Making the presentation
5. Overcoming objections
6. Closing the sale
7. Following up

18-2b Preapproach

Before contacting acceptable prospects, a salesperson finds and analyzes information about each prospect's specific product needs, current use of brands, feelings about available brands, and personal characteristics. In short, salespeople need to know what potential buyers and decision makers consider most important and why they need a specific product. The most successful salespeople are thorough in their *preapproach*, which involves identifying key decision makers, reviewing account histories and problems, contacting other clients for information, assessing credit histories and problems, preparing sales presentations, identifying product needs, and obtaining relevant literature. Marketers are increasingly using marketing analytics and customer relationship management systems to comb through databases and thus identify their most profitable products and customers. CRM systems can also help sales departments manage leads, track customers, forecast sales, and assess performance. A salesperson with a lot of information about a prospect is better equipped to develop a presentation that precisely communicates with that prospect.

18-2c Approach

The **approach**—the manner in which a salesperson contacts a potential customer—is a critical step in the sales process. In more than 80 percent of initial sales calls, the purpose is to gather information about the buyer's needs and objectives. Creating a favorable impression and building rapport with prospective clients are important tasks in the approach because the prospect's first impressions of the salesperson are usually lasting ones. During the initial visit, the salesperson strives to develop a relationship rather than just push a product. Indeed, coming across as a "salesperson" may not be the best approach because some people are put off by strong selling tactics. The salesperson may have to call on a prospect several times before the product is considered. The approach must be designed to deliver value to targeted customers. If the sales approach is inappropriate, the salesperson's efforts are likely to have poor results.

One type of approach is based on referrals, as discussed in the section on prospecting. The salesperson who uses the "cold canvass" approach calls on potential customers without prior consent. This approach is decreasing. Social media is becoming more typical in gaining the initial contact with a prospect. Repeat contact is another common approach: When making the contact, the salesperson mentions a previous meeting. The exact type of approach depends on the salesperson's knowledge and preferences, the product being sold, the firm's resources, and the prospect's characteristics.

approach The manner in which a salesperson contacts a potential customer

18-2d Making the Presentation

During the sales presentation, the salesperson must attract and hold the prospect's attention, stimulate interest, and spark a desire for the product. Salespeople who carefully monitor the selling situation and adapt their presentations to meet the needs of prospects generally have more effective sales performance.[16] Salespeople should match their influencing tactics—such as information exchange, recommendations, deadlines, promises, ingratiation, and inspirational appeals—to their prospects. Different types of buyers respond to different tactics, but most respond well to information exchange and recommendations, and virtually no prospects respond to threats.[17] The salesperson should have the prospect view, examine, or see the benefits of the product. For some types of goods, it may be possible to touch or hold the product. If possible, the salesperson should demonstrate the product or invite the prospect to use it. If the customer is in a positive mood, suspicion will be eliminated and the presentation will gain strength.[18]

Prospecting
Companies often engage in prospecting at trade shows, which allow representatives to demonstrate the latest company products and collect information on consumers who might be interested in the firm's offerings. Company salespeople can later use this information in the preapproach and approach steps of the personal selling process.

During the presentation, the salesperson must not only talk, but also listen. Listening is half of the communication process and is often the most important part for a salesperson. Research indicates that salesperson listening and cognitive empathy developed through the sales interaction are linked, suggesting that listening positively affects the relationship between the buyer and seller during a sales presentation.[19] Nonverbal modes of communication are especially beneficial in building trust during the presentation.[20] Nonverbal signals provide a deeper understanding. The sales presentation gives the salesperson the greatest opportunity to determine the prospect's specific needs by listening to questions and comments and observing responses. Research findings show that complimenting the buyer on his or her questions adds to incremental sales.[21] Even though the salesperson plans the presentation in advance, she or he must be able to adjust the message to meet the prospect's informational needs. Adapting the message in response to the customer's needs generally enhances performance, particularly in new-task or modified-rebuy purchase situations.[22]

18-2e **Overcoming Objections**

An effective salesperson usually seeks out a prospect's objections in order to address them. If they are not apparent, the salesperson cannot deal with them, and the prospect may not buy. One of the best ways to overcome objections is to anticipate and counter them before the prospect raises them. However, this approach can be risky, because the salesperson may mention objections that the prospect would not have raised. If possible, the salesperson should handle objections as they arise. They can also be addressed at the end of the presentation.

18-2f **Closing the Sale**

Closing is the stage in the personal selling process when the salesperson asks the prospect to buy the product. During the presentation, the salesperson may use a *trial close* by asking questions that assume the prospect will buy. The salesperson might ask the potential customer about financial terms, desired colors or sizes, or delivery arrangements. Reactions to such questions usually indicate how close the prospect is to buying. Properly asked questions may allow prospects to uncover their own problems and identify solutions themselves. One questioning approach uses broad questions *(what, how, why)* to probe or gather information and focused questions *(who, when, where)* to clarify and close the sale. A trial close allows prospects to indicate indirectly that they will buy the product without having to say those sometimes difficult words: "I'll take it."

A salesperson should try to close at several points during the presentation because the prospect may be ready to buy. An attempt to close the sale may result in objections. Thus, closing can uncover hidden objections, which the salesperson can then address. One closing strategy involves asking the potential customer to place a low-risk, trial order.

18-2g **Following up**

After a successful closing, the salesperson must follow up the sale. In the follow-up stage, the salesperson determines whether the order was delivered on time and installed properly, if installation was required. If the product is a service, it is important to determine if there are any concerns or if improvements can be made in the experience. He or she should contact the customer to learn if any problems or questions regarding the product have arisen. The follow-up stage is also used to determine customers' future product needs.

Following up also aids the salesperson in creating a solid relationship with the customer. New salespeople might find it difficult to understand the reasons for following up on a sale if the customer seems satisfied with the product. However, a large number of customers who stop buying products do so not out of dissatisfaction but because the company neglected to contact them.[23] Thus, the follow-up stage is vital to establishing a strong relationship and creating loyalty on the part of the buyer.

closing The stage in the personal selling process when the salesperson asks the prospect to buy the product

18-3 TYPES OF SALESPEOPLE

Learning Objective 18-3
Identify the types of sales force personnel.

To develop a sales force, a marketing manager decides what kind of salesperson will sell the firm's products most effectively. Most business organizations use several different kinds of sales personnel. Based on the functions performed, salespeople can be classified into different groups. One salesperson can, and often does, perform multiple functions.

18-3a Sales Structure

Most companies have an inside sales force. Inside salespeople support personnel or take orders, follow up on deliveries, and provide technical information. An outside sales force is also important. Usually sales calls outside the firm are more consultative and are built on developing long-term relationships. Using both inside and outside salespersons to manage accounts is very typical. This task is sometimes called *creative selling*. It requires that salespeople recognize potential buyers' needs and give them necessary information. Increasingly, inside salespersons manage the digital approaches to sales and outside salespersons are more face-to-face and relationship-oriented.

Current-Customer Sales

Sales personnel who concentrate on current customers call on people and organizations that have purchased products from the firm before. These salespeople seek more sales from existing customers by following up on previous sales. Current customers can also be sources of leads for new prospects.

New-Business Sales

Business organizations depend to some degree on sales to new customers. New-business sales personnel locate prospects and convert them into buyers. Salespeople help generate new business in many organizations, but even more so in organizations that sell real estate, insurance, appliances, automobiles, and business-to-business supplies and services. These organizations depend in large part on new-customer sales.

support personnel Sales staff members who facilitate selling but usually are not involved solely with making sales

missionary salespeople Support salespeople, usually employed by a manufacturer, who assist the producer's customers in selling to their own customers

18-3b Support Personnel

Support personnel facilitate selling but usually are not involved solely with making sales. They engage primarily in marketing industrial products, locating prospects, educating customers, building goodwill, and providing service after the sale. There are many kinds of sales support personnel; the three most common are missionary, trade, and technical salespeople.

Missionary Salespeople

Missionary salespeople, usually employed by manufacturers, assist the producer's customers in selling to their own customers. Missionary salespeople may call on retailers to inform and persuade them to buy the manufacturer's products. When they succeed, retailers purchase products from wholesalers, which are the producer's

Inside Sales
Inside salespeople are highly important in personal selling. Their responsibilities include supporting personnel, taking orders, following up on deliveries, and providing technical information.

customers. Manufacturers of medical supplies and pharmaceuticals often use missionary sales-people, called *detail reps*, to promote their products to physicians, hospitals, and pharmacists.

Trade Salespeople

Trade salespeople are not strictly support personnel, because they usually take orders as well. However, they direct much effort toward helping customers—especially retail stores—promote the product. They are likely to restock shelves, obtain more shelf space, set up displays, provide in-store demonstrations, and distribute samples to store customers. Food producers and processors commonly employ trade salespeople.

Technical Salespeople

Technical salespeople give technical assistance to the organization's current customers, advising them on product characteristics and applications, system designs, and installation procedures. Because this job is often highly technical, the salesperson usually has formal training in one of the physical sciences, information technology, or in engineering. Technical sales personnel often sell technical industrial products, such as computers, heavy equipment, and steel.

When hiring sales personnel, marketers seldom restrict themselves to a single category, because most firms require different types of salespeople. Several factors dictate how many of each type a particular company should have. Product use, characteristics, complexity, and price influence the kind of sales personnel used, as do the number and characteristics of customers. The types of marketing channels and the intensity and type of advertising also affect the composition of a sales force.

trade salespeople Salespeople involved mainly in helping a producer's customers promote a product

technical salespeople Support salespeople who give technical assistance to a firm's current customers

team selling The use of a team of experts from all functional areas of a firm, led by a salesperson, to conduct the personal selling process

18-4 TEAM SELLING AND RELATIONSHIP SELLING

Personal selling has become an increasingly complex process due in large part to rapid technological innovation. Most importantly, the focus of personal selling is shifting from selling a specific product to building long-term relationships with customers by finding solutions to their needs, problems, and challenges. As a result, the roles of salespeople are changing. Among the newer philosophies for personal selling are team selling and relationship selling.

Team Selling
Team selling is becoming popular, especially in companies where the selling process is complex and requires a variety of specialized skills.

18-4a Team Selling

Many products, particularly expensive high-tech business products, have become so complex that a single salesperson can no longer be an expert in every aspect of the product and purchase process. **Team selling**, which involves the salesperson joining with people from the firm's financial, engineering, and other functional areas, is appropriate for such products. The salesperson takes the lead in the personal selling process, but other members of the team bring their unique skills, knowledge, and resources to the process to help customers find solutions to their own business challenges. Selling teams may be created to address a particular short-term situation, or they may be formal, ongoing teams. Team selling is advantageous in situations calling for detailed knowledge of new, complex, and dynamic technologies like jet aircraft and medical equipment. It is also used to engage clients in construction, consulting, and other professional services. It can be difficult, however, for highly competitive salespersons to adapt to a team selling environment.

18-4b Relationship Selling

Relationship selling, also known as consultative selling, involves building mutually beneficial long-term associations with a customer through regular communications over prolonged periods of time. Like team selling, it is especially used in business-to-business marketing. Relationship selling involves finding solutions to customers' needs by listening to them, gaining a detailed understanding of their organizations, understanding and caring about their needs and challenges, and providing support after the sale.

Sales representatives from organizations have begun to change their sales tactics to focus on building relationships. Pirch, a retailer that specializes in bathroom and kitchen appliances and fixtures, trains employees on the floor on how to encourage customers to enjoy themselves. Customers can take a cooking class on the store's stoves or don a bathing suit and try out its bath tubs. The philosophy behind this emphasis on experience is for Pirch to develop strong relationships and place customer needs first. Pirch claims this emphasis has led to average sales per square foot of $3,000, higher than Apple stores.[24] Relationships are also built on being able to recover when customers are concerned about services. Being proactive in identifying the need for recovery behavior is a major part of relationship selling.[25] Thus, contacting the customer if delivery time is longer than expected as well as explaining what happened and when the product will be delivered are important.

Relationship selling differs from traditional personal selling due to its adoption of a long-term perspective. Instead of simply focusing on short-term repeat sales, relationship selling

relationship selling The building of mutually beneficial long-term associations with a customer through regular communications over prolonged periods of time

INTEGRITY IN MARKETING

Eaton Sales Support Soars Like an Eagle

Eaton Corporation is a power management company with its U.S. headquarters in Cleveland, Ohio. The company produces more than 900,000 different industrial components and employs 95,000 people globally, selling products in 175 countries. Although the company sells mostly to industrial and government users, it also sells products to consumers for residences and recreation using social media sites to connect with users and spread awareness about its products.

Eaton uses many intermediaries such as distributors and retailers to sell products to businesses. Because Eaton's business products entail more risk of purchase, the company employs salespeople and has customer support available, including after-hours support, for its many different product lines. While the majority of Eaton's products are sold to business markets, some of its products, like its Golf Pride® golf club grip, also target end-use consumers. YouTube videos

help to demonstrate how Eaton products work, acting as a sales promotional tool.

Eaton is a truly multinational company with 55 percent of its revenues coming from outside the United States and 24 percent from developing countries. Eaton has faced environmental challenges in the Asia-Pacific region. By investing in energy-efficient operations and selling more sustainable products, Eaton has been meeting these environmental challenges head on. By creating more of a localized presence in places such as China, Eaton has the ability to increase managerial oversight and emphasize ethical expectations.

Eaton has a company-wide commitment to serving the needs of business, consumer, and global markets. It uses different marketing approaches to target its various markets, including advertising and digital media campaigns. Eaton's strong understanding of its customer markets is the key to its reputation and global success.[a]

Relationship Selling
Pharmaceutical companies have begun to change their sales tactics, spending more time listening to doctors and building relationships over simply promoting the benefits of the company's products.

involves forming long-term connections that will result in sales throughout the relationship.[26] Relationship selling is well poised to help sellers understand their customers' individual needs. It is particularly important in business-to-business transactions as businesses often require more "individualized solutions" to meet their unique needs than the individual consumer.[27]

Relationship selling has significant implications for the seller. Studies show that firms spend six times longer on finding new customers than in keeping current customers.[28] Thus, relationship selling that generates loyal long-term customers is likely to be extremely profitable for the firm both in repeat sales as well as the money saved in trying to find new customers. Finally, as the personal selling industry becomes increasingly competitive, relationship selling is one way that companies can differentiate themselves from rivals to create competitive advantages.[29]

Relationship selling efforts can be improved through sales automation technology tools that enhance interactive communication.[30] New applications for customer relationship management are also being provided through companies like Salesforce.com, whose cloud-computing model helps companies keep track of the customer life cycle without having to install any software (applications are downloaded). Social networks are being utilized in sales, adding new layers to the selling process. Salesforce CRM, for instance, now allows users to connect with their customers in real time through such networks as Twitter and Facebook. Sales force automation, which involves utilizing information technology to automatically track all stages of the sales process (a part of customer relationship management), has been found to increase salesperson professionalism and responsiveness, customer interaction frequency, and customer relationship quality.[31]

Learning Objective 18-5

Discuss eight major decisions in sales force management.

18-5　SALES FORCE MANAGEMENT

The sales force is directly responsible for generating one of an organization's primary inputs: sales revenue. Without adequate sales revenue, businesses cannot survive. In addition, a firm's reputation is often determined by the ethical conduct of its sales force. Indeed, a positive ethical climate, one component of corporate culture, has been linked with decreased role stress and turnover intention and improved job attitudes and job performance in sales.[32] Research has demonstrated that a negative ethical climate will trigger higher-performing salespeople to leave a company at a higher rate than those in a company perceived to be ethical.[33] The morale and ultimately the success of a firm's sales force depend in large part on adequate compensation, room for advancement, sufficient training, and management support—all key areas of sales management. Salespeople who are not satisfied with these elements may leave. Evaluating the input of salespeople is an important part of sales force management because of its strong bearing on a firm's success. Empowering leadership that makes salespeople feel like important contributors positively impacts how a sales team spreads knowledge among its customers.[34] Additionally, sales environments that stress creativity appear to place greater significance on the selection and placement of salespeople, sales force training, performance appraisals, and compensation systems.[35] Table 18.1 provides directions on how to attract and retain a top-quality sales force.

We explore eight general areas of sales management: establishing sales force objectives, determining sales force size, recruiting and selecting salespeople, training sales personnel, compensating salespeople, motivating salespeople, managing sales territories, and controlling and evaluating sales force performance.

Table 18.1   Directions for Attracting and Retaining a Top Sales Force

Training and development	• On-the-job training • Online individual instruction • Seminars • On-site classroom instruction
Compensation	• Make sure pay mix isn't too risky (high commission, low base) for sales role • Mix base salary with commission, bonus, or both • Base bonuses/commission on reaching sales goals rather than on individual sales dollars • Maintain competitive benefits and expense reimbursement practices
Work/life autonomy	• Offer flexible hours • Consider telecommuting/work-at-home options
Product quality and service	• Ensure goods and services meet customer needs • Provide the appropriate service after the sale

Source: "Attracting & Retaining a Top Sales Force," *Where Great Workplaces Start*, http://greatworkplace.wordpress.com/2010/02/10/attracting-retaining-a-top-sales-force (accessed March 11, 2018).

18-5a Establishing Sales Force Objectives

To manage a sales force effectively, sales managers must develop sales objectives. Sales objectives tell salespeople what they are expected to accomplish during a specified time period. They give the sales force direction and purpose and serve as standards for evaluating and controlling the performance of sales personnel. Sales objectives should be stated in precise, measurable terms; specify the time period and geographic areas involved; and be achievable.

Sales objectives are usually developed for both the total sales force and individual salespeople. Objectives for the entire force are normally stated in terms of sales volume, market share, or profit. Volume objectives refer to dollar or unit sales. The objective for an electric drill producer's sales force, for instance, might be to sell $18 million worth of drills, or 600,000 drills annually. When sales goals are stated in terms of market share, they usually call for an increase in the proportion of the firm's sales relative to the total number of products sold by all businesses in that industry. When sales objectives are based on profit, they are generally stated in terms of dollar amounts or return on investment. Sales objectives, or quotas, for individual salespeople are commonly stated in terms of dollar or unit sales volume. Other bases used for individual sales objectives include average order size, average number of calls per time period, and ratio of orders to calls.

18-5b Determining Sales Force Size

Sales force size is important because it influences the company's ability to generate sales and profits. Moreover, size of the sales force affects the compensation methods used, salespeople's morale, and overall sales force management. Sales force size must be adjusted periodically, because a firm's marketing plans change along with markets and forces in the marketing environment. One danger in cutting back the size of the sales force to increase profits is that the sales organization may lose strength and resiliency, preventing it from rebounding when growth occurs or better market conditions prevail.

Several analytical methods can help determine optimal sales force size. One method involves determining how many sales calls per year are necessary for the organization to serve customers effectively and then dividing this total by the average number of sales calls a salesperson makes annually. A second method is based on marginal analysis, in which additional salespeople are added to the sales force until the cost of an additional salesperson equals the additional sales generated by that person. Although marketing managers may use one or several analytical methods, they normally temper decisions with subjective judgments.

18-5c Recruiting and Selecting Salespeople

To create and maintain an effective sales force, sales managers must recruit the right type of salespeople. In **recruiting**, the sales manager develops a list of qualified applicants for sales

recruiting Developing a list of qualified applicants for sales positions

positions. Effective recruiting efforts are a vital part of implementing the strategic sales force plan and can help assure successful organizational performance. The costs of hiring and training a salesperson increase as product knowledge, service requirements, and technical skills are required. Thus, recruiting errors are expensive.

To ensure that the recruiting process results in a pool of qualified applicants, a sales manager establishes a set of qualifications before beginning to recruit. Although marketers have tried for years to identify a set of traits characterizing effective salespeople, no set of generally accepted characteristics exists yet. Experts agree that good salespeople exhibit optimism, flexibility, self-motivation, good time management skills, empathy, and the ability to network and maintain long-term customer relationships. There also seems to be a connection between high sales performance, motivational leadership, and employees who are coachable and highly competitive.[36] Today, companies are increasingly seeking applicants capable of employing relationship-building and consultative approaches as well as the ability to work effectively in team selling efforts. It is desirable to hire salespeople who are disciplined and adaptive with their time.[37]

Sales managers must determine what set of traits best fits their companies' particular sales tasks. Two activities help establish this set of required attributes. First, the sales manager should prepare a job description listing specific tasks salespeople are to perform. Second, the manager should analyze characteristics of the firm's successful salespeople, as well as those of ineffective sales personnel. From the job description and analysis of traits, the sales manager should be able to develop a set of specific requirements and be aware of potential weaknesses that could lead to failure.

A sales manager generally recruits applicants from several sources: departments within the firm, other firms, employment agencies, educational institutions, respondents to advertisements, websites (like Monster.com), and individuals recommended by current employees. The specific sources depend on the type of salesperson required and the manager's experiences and successes with particular recruiting tactics. In the advertisement, iCIMS promotes its applicant tracking system and recruiting software to help companies find the perfect candidates. The software helps companies build pools of talent, recruit and track new applicants, and onboard new hires.

The process of recruiting and selecting salespeople varies considerably from one company to another. Companies intent on reducing sales force turnover are likely to have strict recruiting and selection procedures. Sales management should design a selection procedure that satisfies the company's specific needs. Some organizations use the specialized services of other companies to hire sales personnel. The process should include steps that yield the information required to make accurate selection decisions. However, because each step incurs a certain amount of expense, there should be no more steps than necessary. Stages of the selection process should be sequenced so that the more expensive steps, such as a physical examination, occur near the end. Fewer people will then move through higher-cost stages.

Recruitment should not be sporadic; it should be a continuous activity aimed at reaching the best applicants. The selection process should systematically and effectively match applicants' characteristics and needs with the requirements of specific selling tasks. Finally, the selection process should ensure that new sales personnel are available where and when needed.

18-5d Training Sales Personnel

Many organizations have formal training programs; others depend on informal, on-the-job training. Some systematic training programs are quite extensive, whereas others are

A GOOD CATCH REQUIRES A SOPHISTICATED APPROACH

Attracting the perfect candidate requires a highly specialized set of talent acquisition tools. So iCIMS specifically designed software to proactively build pools of talent, recruit and track new applicants, and onboard the next great, new hire. To learn more, visit iCIMS.com.
©2016 iCIMS, Inc. All rights reserved.

iCIMS

Recruiting
iCIMS offers talent acquisition software for recruiting, tracking, and onboarding applicants.

rather short and rudimentary. Whether the training program is complex or simple, developers must consider what to teach, whom to train, and how to train them. Businesses that are considered to be the "best places to work" train their managers and professionals an average of 78 hours and their hourly and administrative staffers an average of 94 hours.[38]

A sales training program can concentrate on the company, its products, or its selling methods. Training programs often cover all three. Such programs can be aimed at newly hired salespeople, experienced salespeople, or both. The type of leadership is especially important for new salespeople who are just getting familiar with the selling process. Transformational leadership that involves coaching to foster trust and motivation has proven highly effective in training new hires when sales managers observe them making errors during customer interactions. This reduces feelings of helplessness among new salespeople when they encounter difficulties in the process.[39]

Training for experienced company salespeople usually emphasizes product information or the use of new technology, although salespeople must also be informed about new selling techniques and changes in company plans, policies, and procedures. Sales managers should use ethics training to institutionalize an ethical climate, improve employee satisfaction, and help prevent misconduct. Empowering the sales force through comprehensive training increases their effectiveness. The most successful sales forces tend to be those that clearly define the steps of the sales process, spend time each month on managing their sales representatives' networks, and train sales managers on how to manage efficiently.[40] Ordinarily, new sales personnel require comprehensive training, whereas experienced personnel need both refresher courses on established products and training regarding new-product information and technology changes. At The Container Store new full-time store employees are given 263 hours of training. Because retail store employees will be interacting with customers on a consistent basis, the organization believes extensive training will increase employees' personal selling skills and help them form relationships with customers. As the advertisement indicates, The Container Store places great emphasis on its employees' happiness.

Sales training may be done in the field, at educational institutions, in company facilities, and/or online using web-based technology. For many companies, online training saves time and money and helps salespeople learn about new products quickly. Sales managers might even choose to use online platforms with their sales force—GoToMeeting provides an online platform that enables sales training and meetings to be conducted face-to-face in HD video. Others put them into the field immediately, providing formal training only after they have gained some experience. Training programs for new personnel can be as short as several days or as long as three years; some are even longer. Sales training for experienced personnel is often scheduled when sales activities are not too demanding. Because experienced salespeople usually need periodic retraining, a firm's sales management must determine the frequency, sequencing, and duration of these efforts.

Sales managers, as well as other salespeople, often engage in sales training, whether daily on the job or periodically during sales meetings. In addition, a number of outside companies specialize in providing sales training programs. Materials for sales training programs range from videos, texts, online materials, manuals, and cases to programmed learning devices and digital media. Lectures, demonstrations, simulation exercises, role-plays, and on-the-job training can all be effective training

Sales Training
The Container Store provides 263 hours of training to each retail employee because the employees are the key to maintaining satisfied customers.

Top Challenges for Inside Sales Managers

Training & Development

Lead Quantity & Quality

Recruiting & Hiring

Tools & Technologies

Coaching

SNAPSHOT

Source: Aja Frost, "The Top 6 Challenges the Inside Sales Industry Is Facing," *HubSpot*, August 30, 2017, https://blog.hubspot.com/sales/top-challenges-inside-sales (accessed March 10, 2018).

methods. Self-directed learning to supplement traditional sales training has the potential to improve sales performance. The choice of methods and materials for a particular sales training program depends on the type and number of trainees, program content and complexity, length and location, size of the training budget, number of trainers, and a trainer's expertise.

18-5e Compensating Salespeople

To develop and maintain a highly productive sales force, an organization must formulate and administer a compensation plan that attracts, motivates, and retains the most effective individuals. The plan should give sales management the desired level of control and provide sales personnel with acceptable levels of income, freedom, and incentive. It should be flexible, equitable, easy to administer, and easy to understand. Good compensation programs facilitate and encourage proper treatment of customers. Obviously, it is quite difficult to incorporate all of these requirements into a single program. Figure 18.2 shows the average salaries for sales managers.

Figure 18.2 Average Salaries for Sales Managers

Annual mean wage

California	$130,450
Illinois	$127,650
Texas	$146,890
New York	$196,770
Georgia	$128,140

Note: States listed are those with the highest employment level in this occupation.
Source: Bureau of Labor Statistics, "Occupational Employment and Wages, May 2016," https://www.bls.gov/oes/current/oes112022.htm (accessed March 11, 2018).

Developers of compensation programs must determine the general level of compensation required and the most desirable method of calculating it. In analyzing the required compensation plan, sales management must ascertain a salesperson's value to the company on the basis of the tasks and responsibilities associated with the sales position. Sales managers may consider a number of factors, including salaries of other types of personnel in the firm, competitors' compensation plans, costs of sales force turnover, and non-salary selling expenses. The national average for sales representatives is $52,000 (including commissions and bonuses).[41] Salesperson compensation varies by industry and is often based on skills or knowledge needed to relate to customers. A high-level, high-performing salesperson or sales manager can make hundreds of thousands a year.

Sales compensation programs usually reimburse salespeople for selling expenses, provide some fringe benefits, and deliver the required compensation level. To achieve this, a firm may use one or more of three basic compensation methods: straight salary, straight commission, or a combination of the two. Table 18.2 lists the major characteristics, advantages, and disadvantages of each method. In a **straight salary compensation plan**, salespeople are paid a specified amount per time period, regardless of selling effort. This sum remains the same until they receive a pay increase or decrease. Although this method is easy to administer and affords salespeople financial security, it provides little incentive for them to boost selling efforts. In a **straight commission compensation plan**, salespeople's compensation is determined solely by sales for a given period. A commission may be based on a single percentage of sales or on a sliding scale involving several sales levels and percentage rates (e.g., sales under $500,000 a quarter would receive a smaller commission than sales over $500,000 each quarter). Although this method motivates sales personnel to escalate their selling efforts, it offers them little financial security, and it can be difficult for sales managers to maintain control over the sales force. Many new salespeople indicate a reluctance to accept the risks associated with straight commission. However, more experienced salespeople know this option can provide the greatest income potential. For these reasons, many firms offer a **combination compensation plan** in which salespeople receive a fixed salary plus a commission based on sales volume. Some combination programs require that a salesperson exceed a certain sales level before earning a commission; others offer commissions for any level of sales.

straight salary compensation plan Paying salespeople a specific amount per time period, regardless of selling effort

straight commission compensation plan Paying salespeople according to the amount of their sales in a given time period

combination compensation plan Paying salespeople a fixed salary plus a commission based on sales volume

Table 18.2 Characteristics of Sales Force Compensation Methods

Compensation Method	When Especially Useful	Advantages	Disadvantages
Straight salary	Compensating new salespeople; firm moves into new sales territories that require developmental work; sales requiring lengthy presale and post-sale services	Gives salespeople security; gives sales managers control over salespeople; easy to administer; yields more predictable selling expenses	Provides no incentive; necessitates closer supervision of salespeople; during sales declines, selling expenses remain constant
Straight commission	Highly aggressive selling is required; non-selling tasks are minimized; company uses contractors and part-timers	Provides maximum amount of incentive; by increasing commission rate, sales managers can encourage salespeople to sell certain items; selling expenses relate directly to sales resources	Salespeople have little financial security; sales managers have minimum control over sales force; may cause sales people to give inadequate service to smaller accounts; selling expenses less predictable
Combination	Sales territories have relatively similar sales potential; firm wishes to provide incentive but still control sales force activities	Provides certain level of financial security; provides some incentive; can move sales force efforts in profitable direction	Selling expenses less predictable; may be difficult to administer

Source: Charles Futrell, *Sales Management*, http://people.tamu.edu/~c-futrell/436/sm_home.html (accessed January 17, 2014).

When selecting a compensation method, sales management weighs the advantages and disadvantages listed in the table. Researchers have found that higher commissions are the most preferred reward, followed by pay increases. Yet preferences on pay tend to vary, depending upon the industry.[42] The Container Store prefers to pay its sales staff salaries that are 100 percent higher than those offered by rivals instead of basing pay on commission plans.[43]

18-5f **Motivating Salespeople**

Although financial compensation is an important incentive, additional programs are necessary for motivating sales personnel. The nature of the jobs, job security, and pay are considered to be the most important factors for the college student going into the sales area today.[44] A sales manager should develop a systematic approach for motivating salespeople to be productive. Sales managers act as models for their sales force. When salespeople perceive their managers as being more customer-oriented and adaptive, they are more likely to imitate these positive behaviors.[45] Salespeople who can identify with their sales managers tend to have higher sales performance and customer satisfaction.[46] Effective sales force motivation is achieved through an organized set of activities performed continuously by the company's sales management.

Sales personnel, like other people, join organizations to satisfy personal needs and achieve personal goals. Sales managers must identify those needs and goals and strive to create an organizational climate that allows each salesperson to fulfill them. Enjoyable working conditions, power and authority, job security, and opportunity to excel are effective motivators, as are company efforts to make sales jobs more productive and efficient. Sales managers who are emotionally intelligent tend to have a positive impact on the creativity of their workers.[47] A strong positive corporate culture leads to higher levels of job satisfaction and organizational commitment and lower levels of job stress.[48]

Sales contests and other incentive programs can also be effective motivators. These can motivate salespeople to increase sales or add new accounts, promote special items, achieve greater volume per sales call, and cover territories more thoroughly. However, companies need to understand salespersons' preferences when designing contests in order to make them effective in increasing sales. Some companies find such contests powerful tools for motivating sales personnel to achieve company goals. Managers should be careful to craft sales contests that support a strong customer orientation as well as motivate salespeople. In smaller firms lacking the resources for a formal incentive program, a simple but public "thank you" and the recognition from management at a sales meeting, along with a small-denomination gift card, can be very rewarding.

Motivating Salespeople
Trips or vacation packages are rewards that a high-performing salesperson might receive for surpassing his or her sales goals.

KASPARS GRINVALDS/SHUTTERSTOCK.COM

Salesperson turnover is one of the most critical concerns of organizations. Lower organizational commitment has been found to relate directly to job turnover. Identifying with the organization and performance are tied directly to organizational commitment that reduces turnover.[49] Properly designed incentive programs pay for themselves many times over, and sales managers are relying on incentives more than ever. Recognition programs that acknowledge outstanding performance with symbolic awards, such as plaques, can be very effective when carried out in a peer setting. The most common incentive offered by companies is cash, followed by gift cards and travel.[50] Travel reward programs can confer a high-profile honor, provide a unique experience that makes recipients feel special, and build camaraderie among award-winning salespeople. However, some recipients of travel awards may feel they already travel too much on the job. Limited travel packages might also be a turn-off. In one study, 70 percent of participants claimed they would be more motivated if they had more choices in travel destinations.[51] Cash rewards are easy to administer, are always appreciated by recipients, and appeal to all demographic groups. However, cash has no visible "trophy" value and provides few "bragging rights." The benefits of awarding merchandise are that the items have visible trophy value. In addition, recipients who are allowed to select the merchandise experience a sense of control, and merchandise awards can help build momentum for the sales force. The disadvantages of using merchandise are that employees may have a lower perceived value of the merchandise and the company may experience greater administrative problems. Some companies outsource their incentive programs to companies that specialize in the creation and management of such programs.

18-5g Managing Sales Territories

The effectiveness of a sales force that must travel to customers is somewhat influenced by management's decisions regarding sales territories. When deciding on territories, sales managers must consider size, geographic shape, routing, and scheduling.

Creating Sales Territories

Several factors enter into the design of a sales territory's size and geographic shape. First, sales managers must construct territories that allow sales potential to be measured. Sales territories often consist of several geographic units, such as census tracts, cities, counties, or states, for which market data are obtainable. Sales managers usually try to create territories with similar sales potential, or requiring about the same amount of work. If territories have equal sales potential, they will almost always be unequal in geographic size. Salespeople with larger territories have to work longer and harder to generate a certain sales volume. Conversely, if sales territories requiring equal amounts of work are created, sales potential for those territories will often vary. Think about the effort required to sell in New York and Connecticut versus the sales effort required in a larger, less populated area like Montana or Wyoming. If sales personnel are partially or fully compensated through commissions, they will have unequal income potential. Many sales managers try to balance territorial workloads and earning potential by using differential commission rates. At times, sales managers use commercial programs to help them balance sales territories. Although a sales manager seeks equity when developing and maintaining sales territories, some inequities always prevail. A territory's size and geographical shape should also help the sales force provide the best possible customer coverage and minimize selling costs. Customer density and distribution are important factors. It is important for territories to be designed so that salespeople contact customers with the frequency and consistency that feels ideal.[52]

Routing and Scheduling Salespeople

The geographic size and shape of a sales territory are the most important factors affecting the routing and scheduling of sales calls. Next in importance are the number and distribution of customers within the territory, followed by sales call frequency and duration. Those in charge of routing and scheduling must consider the sequence in which customers are called on, specific roads or transportation schedules to be used, number of calls to be made in a given period, and time of day the calls will occur. In some firms, salespeople plan their own routes and schedules with little or no assistance from the sales manager. In others, the sales manager maintains significant responsibility. No matter who plans the routing and scheduling, the major goals should be to minimize salespeople's non-selling time (time spent traveling and waiting) and maximize their selling time. Sales managers should try to achieve these goals so that a salesperson's travel and lodging costs are held to a minimum.

18-5h Controlling and Evaluating Sales Force Performance

To control and evaluate sales force performance properly, sales management needs information. A sales manager cannot observe the field sales force daily and, thus, relies on salespeople's call reports, customer feedback, contracts, and invoices. Call reports identify the customers called on and present detailed information about interactions with those clients. Sales personnel must often file work schedules indicating where they plan to be during specific time periods. Data about a salesperson's interactions with customers and prospects can be included in the company's customer relationship management system. This information provides insights about the salesperson's performance.

Dimensions used to measure a salesperson's performance are determined largely by sales objectives, normally set by the sales manager. If an individual's sales objective is stated in terms of sales volume, that person should be evaluated on the basis of sales volume generated. Even if a salesperson is assigned a major objective, he or she is ordinarily expected to achieve several related objectives as well. Thus, salespeople are often judged along several dimensions. Sales managers evaluate many performance indicators, including average number of calls per day, average sales per customer, actual sales relative to sales potential, number of new-customer orders, average cost per call, and average gross profit per customer. One survey found that 67 percent of sales managers use sales quotas as a form of measurement and 41 percent use winning new accounts.[53]

To evaluate a salesperson, a sales manager may compare one or more of these dimensions with predetermined performance standards. However, sales managers commonly compare a salesperson's performance with that of other employees operating under similar selling conditions or the salesperson's current performance with past performance. Sometimes, management judges factors that have less direct bearing on sales performance, such as personal appearance, product knowledge, and ethical standards. One concern is the tendency to reprimand top sellers less severely than poor performers for engaging in unethical selling practices.

After evaluating salespeople, sales managers take any needed corrective action to improve sales force performance. They may adjust performance standards, provide additional training, or try other motivational methods. Corrective action may demand comprehensive changes in the sales force.

Learning Objective 18-6

Describe sales promotion.

18-6 SALES PROMOTION

Sales promotion is an activity or material, or both, that acts as a direct inducement, offering added value or incentive for the product, to resellers, salespeople, or consumers. It encompasses all promotional activities and materials other than personal selling, advertising, and public relations. Retailers often offer buy-one-get-one-free sales, a sales promotion tactic known as a bonus or premium. In competitive markets, where products are very similar, sales promotion provides additional inducements that encourage product trial and purchase. Supermarkets such as Whole Foods provide food samples to encourage purchases.

Marketers often use sales promotion to facilitate personal selling, advertising, or both. Companies also employ advertising and personal selling to support sales promotion activities. Marketers frequently use advertising to promote contests, free samples, and premiums. The

sales promotion An activity and/or material intended to induce resellers or salespeople to sell a product or consumers to buy it

most effective sales promotion efforts are highly interrelated with other promotional activities. Decisions regarding sales promotion often affect advertising and personal selling decisions, and vice versa.

Sales promotion can increase sales by providing extra purchasing incentives. Many opportunities exist to motivate consumers, resellers, and salespeople to take desired actions. Some kinds of sales promotion are designed specifically to stimulate resellers' demand and effectiveness, some are directed at increasing consumer demand, and some focus on both consumers and resellers. Regardless of the purpose, marketers must ensure that sales promotion objectives are consistent with the organization's overall objectives, as well as with its marketing and promotion objectives.

When deciding which sales promotion methods to use, marketers must consider several factors, particularly product characteristics (price, size, weight, costs, durability, uses, features, and hazards) and target market characteristics (age, gender, income, location, density, usage rate, and shopping patterns). How products are distributed and the number and types of resellers may determine the type of method used. The competitive and legal environments may also influence the choice.

The use of sales promotion has increased dramatically over the past 30 years, primarily at the expense of advertising. This shift in how promotional dollars are used has occurred for several reasons. Heightened concerns about value have made customers more responsive to promotional offers, especially price discounts and point-of-purchase displays. Thanks to their size and access to checkout scanner data, retailers have gained considerable power in the supply chain and are demanding greater promotional efforts from manufacturers to boost retail profits. Declines in brand loyalty have produced an environment in which sales promotions aimed at persuading customers to switch brands are more effective. In addition, competition from online retailers, including Amazon, have pushed retailers to use more sales promotion incentives. Finally, a stronger emphasis placed on improving short-term performance calls for greater use of sales promotion methods that yield quick (although perhaps short-lived) sales increases.[54]

In the remainder of this chapter, we examine several consumer and trade sales promotion methods, including what they entail and what goals they can help marketers achieve.

18-7 CONSUMER SALES PROMOTION METHODS

Learning Objective 18-7
Review consumer sales promotion methods.

Consumer sales promotion methods encourage or stimulate consumers to patronize specific retail stores or try particular products. Online sales promotion can create a higher level of product and brand recall.[55] Consumer sales promotion methods initiated by retailers often aim to attract customers to specific locations, whereas those used by manufacturers generally introduce new products or promote established brands. In this section, we discuss coupons, cents-off offers, money refunds and rebates, frequent-user incentives, point-of-purchase displays, demonstrations, free samples, premiums, consumer contests and games, and consumer sweepstakes.

18-7a **Coupons**

Coupons reduce a product's price and aim to prompt customers to try new or established products, increase sales volume quickly, attract repeat purchasers, or introduce new package sizes or features. Savings are deducted from the purchase price. Coupons are the most widely used consumer sales promotion technique. Although coupons offer greater spending power, consumers have indicated that a primary reason for not using them is that they cannot find coupons for what they want to buy.[56] Digital coupons via websites and mobile apps are also becoming popular. Social deal sites like Groupon, while not exactly in the coupon area, are encouraging consumers to look for deals or better prices. Bed Bath & Beyond frequently

consumer sales promotion methods Sales promotion techniques that encourage consumers to patronize specific stores or try particular products

coupons Written price reductions used to encourage consumers to buy a specific product

sends 20-percent off coupons to consumers through the mail. However, these coupons are becoming so common that some analysts believe it could hurt Bed Bath & Beyond because consumers are so used to getting coupons that they will not shop without them.[57] Despite the growth in digital coupons, there are still plenty of people who are willing to clip coupons from printed sources. It is estimated that more than 90 percent of coupons come from free-standing inserts in booklets. Even Millennials use print coupons, although they are likely to use digital coupons more than any other age group. As a result, companies such as General Mills consider couponing to be a profitable sales promotion and will often increase its distribution of coupons close to major holidays.[58] To take advantage of renewed consumer interest in coupons, digital marketing—including mobile, social, and other platforms—is being used for couponing.[59] For example, Coupons.com appeals to bargain shoppers with both print and digital coupons. In the advertisement, Coupons.com promotes its website and app which connect users to a combination of printable grocery coupons, cash back offers, and digital coupon codes.

For best results, coupons should be easily recognized and state the offer clearly. The nature of the product (seasonal demand for it, life-cycle stage, and frequency of purchase) is the prime consideration in setting up a coupon promotion. Paper coupons are distributed on and inside packages, through freestanding inserts, in print advertising, on the back of cash register receipts, and through direct mail. Electronic coupons are distributed online, via in-store kiosks, through shelf dispensers in stores, and at checkout counters.[60] Figure 18.3 indicates that more than 130 million adults use digital coupons, and this number is projected to grow. When deciding on the distribution method for coupons, marketers should consider strategies and objectives, redemption rates, availability, circulation, and exclusivity. This advertisement for World Market provides a coupon that takes 10 percent off the purchase price. In addition to a barcode for in-store redemption, the coupon also lists an alphanumeric coupon code so it can be redeemed online. The company hopes this coupon will increase sales of its product. The coupon distribution and redemption arena has become very competitive. To avoid losing customers, many grocery stores will redeem any coupons offered by competitors. Also, to draw customers to their stores, grocers double and sometimes even triple the value of customers' coupons.

Coupons offer several advantages. Print advertisements with coupons are often more effective at generating brand awareness than print ads without coupons. Generally, the larger the coupon's cash offer, the better the recognition generated. Coupons reward current product users, win back former users, and encourage purchases in larger quantities. Because they are returned, coupons also help a manufacturer determine whether it reached the intended target market. The advantages of using electronic coupons over paper coupons include lower cost per redemption, greater targeting ability, improved data-gathering capabilities, and greater experimentation capabilities to determine optimal face values and expiration cycles.[61]

Hundreds of deals on the brands you love so you always get

more for today.™

Coupon codes for all your favorite stores, printable grocery coupons, mobile app and more at Coupons.com/morefortoday

COUPONS.COM

Online Couponing
This advertisement features Coupons.com, a hub for printable grocery coupons, cash back offers, and digital coupon codes.

Drawbacks of coupon use include fraud and misredemption, which can be expensive for manufacturers. Coupon fraud—including counterfeit internet coupons as well as coupons cashed in under false retailer names—costs manufacturers hundreds of millions in losses each year.[62] Another disadvantage, according to some experts, is that coupons are losing their value; because so many manufacturers offer them, consumers have learned not to buy without some incentive, whether that pertains to a coupon, a rebate, or a refund. Furthermore, brand loyalty among heavy coupon users has increased as many consumers redeem coupons only for products they normally buy. It is believed that about three-fourths of coupons are redeemed by people already using the brand on the coupon. Thus, coupons have questionable success as an incentive for consumers to try a new brand or product. An additional problem with coupons is that stores often do not have enough of the coupon item in stock. This situation generates ill will toward both the store and the product.

18-7b **Cents-Off Offers**

With **cents-off offers**, buyers pay a certain amount less than the regular price shown on the label or package. Like coupons, this method can serve as a strong incentive for trying new or unfamiliar products and is commonly used in product introductions. Hello Fresh and Blue Apron, two popular meal delivery services, often entice new customers by offering a price reduction on a subscriber's first box.

Print Coupons
This advertisement features a coupon from World Market.

SOURCE: WORLD MARKET

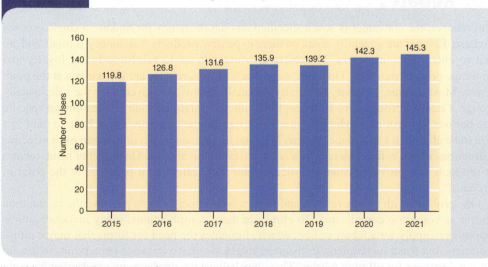

| **Figure 18.3** | **Number of U.S. Digital Coupon Users, 2015–2021 (in millions)** |

Number of Users

- 2015: 119.8
- 2016: 126.8
- 2017: 131.6
- 2018: 135.9
- 2019: 139.2
- 2020: 142.3
- 2021: 145.3

Note: Adults age 18 and up. This statistic gives information on the number of U.S. adults redeeming digital coupons from 2015 to 2021. In 2016, 126.8 million U.S. adults had redeemed online coupons. This figure is projected to grow to 145.3 million users in 2021.
Source: Statista, 2018.

cents-off offers Promotions that allow buyers to pay less than the regular price to encourage purchase

SOURCE: 1-800-FLOWERS.COM

Price Discounts
1-800-Flowers offers a 20 percent discount for customers who purchase flowers during a certain period of time.

Cents-off offers can stimulate product sales or multiple purchases, yield short-lived sales increases, and promote products during off-seasons. Grocery stores often promote food items with cents-off reductions at the point of purchase.

Cents-off offers are easy to control and are often used for specific purposes. If used on an ongoing basis, however, they reduce the price for customers who would buy at the regular price and may also cheapen a product's image. In addition, the method often requires special handling by retailers who are responsible for giving the discount at the point of sale. The advertisement for 1-800-Flowers offers a discount of 20 percent off its Graceful Lavender bouquet if customers place an order within a certain period of time. The advertisement is targeting people who need to purchase a gift for others. By encouraging consumers to purchase now, 1-800-Flowers is attempting to stimulate immediate sales.

18-7c **Money Refunds**

With **money refunds**, consumers submit proof of purchase and are mailed a specific amount of money. Usually, manufacturers demand multiple product purchases before consumers qualify for money refunds. Marketers employ money refunds as an alternative to coupons to stimulate sales. Money refunds, used primarily to promote trial use of a product, are relatively low in cost. However, they sometimes generate a low response rate and, thus, have limited impact on sales.

18-7d **Rebates**

With **rebates**, the consumer is sent a specified amount of money for making a single product purchase. Rebates are generally given on more expensive products than money refunds and are used to encourage customers. Marketers also use rebates to reinforce brand loyalty and encourage product purchase. On larger items, such as cars, rebates are often given at the point of sale. Most rebates, however, especially on smaller items, are given after the sale, usually through a mail-in process. For instance, Discount Tire might provide rebates during specific time periods for customers who purchase new tires, but the customer might have to mail in a form to be eligible for the rebate. Researchers find that these mail-in rebates are most effective in situations where consumers require a reason to purchase an item. On the other hand, rebates for products that provide instant gratification are more effective if provided at the point of purchase.[63]

One problem with money refunds and rebates is that many people perceive the redemption process as being too complicated. To eliminate these complications, many marketers allow customers to apply for a rebate online, which eliminates the need for forms that may confuse customers and frustrate retailers. Consumers might also have negative perceptions of manufacturers' reasons for offering rebates. They may believe the products are untested or have not sold well. If these perceptions are not changed, rebate offers may actually degrade product image and desirability.

money refunds Sales promotion techniques that offer consumers a specified amount of money when they mail in a proof of purchase, usually for multiple product purchases

rebates Sales promotion techniques in which a consumer receives a specified amount of money for making a single product purchase

18-7e Shopper, Loyalty, and Frequent-User Incentives

Various incentives exist for frequent product users and loyal customers. Organizations such as supermarkets often provide users with loyalty or shopper cards that allow them to track customer purchases while providing periodic discounts to shoppers for continued purchases. Shopper cards tend to have an impact on brand loyalty purchases for secondary brands, but not brands where there is strong brand performance.[64] A key purpose of shopper and frequent-user cards is to encourage continued loyalty. Whole Foods tested a rewards program for three years at select stores to see if it would make a difference on sales. The program allowed shoppers at these stores to earn points and discounts when they shopped.[65] Whole Foods ended up disbanding this program and moved to a digital coupons service instead.[66]

Many firms have similar incentives for rewarding customers who engage in repeat (frequent) purchases. For instance, major airlines offer frequent-flyer programs that reward customers who have flown a specified number of miles with free tickets for additional travel. Frequent-user incentives foster customer loyalty to a specific company or group of cooperating companies. They are favored by service businesses, such as airlines, auto rental agencies, hotels, and local coffee shops. Frequent-user programs not only reward loyal customers but also generate data that can contribute significant information about customers that helps marketers foster desirable customer relationships.

18-7f Point-of-Purchase Materials and Demonstrations

Point-of-purchase (POP) materials include outdoor signs, window displays, counter pieces, display racks, and self-service cartons. Innovations in POP displays include sniff-teasers, which give off a product's aroma in the store as consumers walk within a radius of 4 feet, and computerized interactive displays. These items, often supplied by producers, attract attention, inform customers, and encourage retailers to carry particular products. Retailers have also begun experimenting with new forms of POP technology, such as interactive kiosks allowing shoppers to browse through products. A retailer is likely to use point-of-purchase materials if they are attractive, informative, well-constructed, and in harmony with the store's image.

Demonstrations are excellent attention-getters. Manufacturers offer them temporarily to encourage trial use and purchase of a product or to show how a product works. Because labor costs can be extremely high, demonstrations are not used widely. They can be highly effective for promoting certain types of products, such as appliances, cosmetics, and cleaning supplies. Even automobiles can be demonstrated, not only by a salesperson but also by

point-of-purchase (POP) materials Signs, window displays, display racks, and similar devices used to attract customers

demonstrations Sales promotion methods a manufacturer uses temporarily to encourage trial use and purchase of a product or to show how a product works

ENTREPRENEURSHIP IN MARKETING

Tastefully Simple Takes a Bite Out of Family Meal Planning

Jill Blashack Strahan, founder and CEO of Tastefully Simple, is recognized for her entrepreneurial leadership that created a multimillion-dollar company. Before starting Tastefully Simple, Strahan had a small gift-basket business. However, when the gourmet foods she provided with her baskets proved more profitable than the baskets themselves, she shifted focus.

In 1995, Tastefully Simple was conceived with the idea of providing easy-to-prepare foods with a gourmet twist. The company's products are offered through independent sales consultants across the United States. Since its founding, the company's revenue has risen to between $50 and $100 million a year.

Consultants can earn up to 40 percent commissions for products, as well as other bonuses and incentives. Tastefully Simple received recognition for being ranked in the top five percent of companies nationwide in employee satisfaction for seven years running. Consultants are independent contractors. They develop sales promotions that introduce products, and they are compensated by sales commissions.[b]

the prospective buyer during a test drive. Cosmetics marketers, such as Estée Lauder and Clinique, sometimes offer potential customers "makeovers" to demonstrate product benefits and proper application.

18-7g Free Samples

Marketers use **free samples** to stimulate trial of a product, increase sales volume in the early stages of a product's life cycle, and obtain desirable distribution. Trader Joe's gives out free samples of its coffee, hoping to entice buyers to make a purchase. Sampling is the most expensive sales promotion method because production and distribution—at local events, by mail or door-to-door delivery, online, in stores, and on packages—entail high costs. However, it can also be one of the most effective sales promotion methods. In one survey, 92 percent of respondents said they would purchase a product if they liked it after getting a free sample. Samples eliminate the risk of trying a new product and allow consumers to feel as if they are getting something for free.[67]

Many consumers prefer to get their samples by mail. Other consumers like to sample new food products at supermarkets or try samples of new recipes featuring foods they already like. In designing a free sample, marketers should consider factors like seasonal demand for the product, market characteristics, and prior advertising. Free samples are usually inappropriate for slow-turnover products. Despite high costs, use of sampling is increasing. In a given year, almost three-fourths of consumer products companies may use sampling.

18-7h Premiums

Premiums are items offered free or at a minimal cost as a bonus for purchasing a product. Cracker Jack, introduced in 1896 as the first junk food, had a prize of trivial value inside. Now it has a QR code to download a baseball game to play on the customer's smartphone. Premiums are used to attract competitors' customers, introduce different sizes of established products, add variety to other promotional efforts, and stimulate consumer loyalty. Consumers appear to prefer premiums to discounts on products due to the perception that they are receiving something "free."[68] Creativity is essential when using premiums; to stand out and achieve a significant number of redemptions, the premium must match both the target audience and the brand's image. Premiums must also be easily recognizable and desirable. Consumers are more favorable toward a premium when the brand has high equity and there is a good fit between the product and the premium.[69] Premiums are placed on or inside packages and can also be distributed by retailers or through the mail. Examples include a service station giving a free car wash with a fill-up, a free shaving cream with the purchase of a razor, and a free plastic storage box with the purchase of Kraft Cheese Singles.

18-7i Consumer Contests

In **consumer contests**, individuals compete for prizes based on their analytical or creative skills. This method can be used to generate retail traffic and frequency of exposure to promotional messages. Contestants are usually more highly involved in consumer contests than in games or sweepstakes, even though total participation may be lower. Contests may also be used in conjunction with other sales promotional methods, such as coupons. Oreo is well known for its contests such as the Oreo Dunk Challenge, where consumers submitted photos or videos dunking Oreos in milk on social media in the hopes of meeting Christina Aguilera, Shaquille O'Neal, or Neymar da Silva Santos Júnior and winning $2,000.[70] More recently, Oreo welcomed fans to submit new flavor suggestions. The three finalists, Piña Colada, Kettle Corn, and Cherry Cola were released, and the person behind the winning flavor won $500,000.[71]

18-7j Consumer Games

In **consumer games**, individuals compete for prizes based primarily on chance—often by collecting game pieces like bottle caps or a sticker on a carton of french fries. Because collecting multiple pieces may be necessary to win or increase an individual's chances of winning, the

---

free samples Samples of a product given out to encourage trial and purchase

premiums Items offered free or at a minimal cost as a bonus for purchasing a product

consumer contests Sales promotion methods in which individuals compete for prizes based on their analytical or creative skills

consumer games Sales promotion methods in which individuals compete for prizes based primarily on chance

game stimulates repeated business. Development and management of consumer games is often outsourced to an independent public relations firm, which can help marketers navigate federal and state laws that regulate games. Although games may stimulate sales temporarily, there is no evidence to suggest that they affect a company's long-term sales.

Marketers considering games should exercise care. Problems or errors may anger customers and could result in a lawsuit. McDonald's wildly popular Monopoly game promotion, in which customers collect Monopoly real estate pieces on drink and french fry packages, has been tarnished by past fraud after a crime ring, including employees of the promotional firm running the game, was convicted of stealing millions of dollars in winning game pieces. McDonald's later reintroduced the Monopoly game with heightened security.

THE STATE/TRIBUNE NEWS SERVICE/GETTY IMAGES

Sweepstakes
HGTV's annual Dream Home sweepstakes gives viewers a chance to win a dream home.

18-7k Sweepstakes

Entrants in a **consumer sweepstakes** submit their names for inclusion in a drawing for prizes. HGTV offered consumers a chance to own a beachfront dream home by entering a sweepstakes through HGTV.com or DIYNetwork.com.[72] Sweepstakes are employed more often than consumer contests and tend to attract a greater number of participants. However, contestants are usually more involved in consumer contests and games than in sweepstakes, even though total participation may be lower. Contests, games, and sweepstakes may be used in conjunction with other sales promotion methods like coupons.

18-8 TRADE SALES PROMOTION METHODS

Learning Objective 18-8
Review trade sales promotion methods.

To encourage resellers, especially retailers, to carry their products and promote them effectively, producers use trade sales promotion methods. **Trade sales promotion methods** attempt to persuade wholesalers and retailers to carry a producer's products and market them more aggressively. Marketers use trade sales methods for many reasons, including countering the effect of lower-priced store brands, passing along a discount to a price-sensitive market segment, boosting brand exposure among target consumers, or providing additional incentives to move excess inventory or counteract competitors. These methods include buying allowances, buy-back allowances, scan-back allowances, merchandise allowances, cooperative advertising, dealer listings, free merchandise, dealer loaders, premium or push money, and sales contests.

18-8a Trade Allowances

Many manufacturers offer trade allowances to encourage resellers to carry a product or stock more of it. One such trade allowance is a **buying allowance**, a temporary price reduction offered to resellers for purchasing specified quantities of a product. A paper supplier could offer an office supply store $3 off of every case of paper purchased. Such offers provide an incentive for resellers to handle new products, achieve temporary price reductions, or stimulate purchase of items in larger-than-normal quantities. The buying allowance, which takes the form of money, yields profits to resellers and is simple and straightforward. There are no restrictions on how resellers use the money, which increases the method's effectiveness. One drawback of buying allowances is that customers may buy "forward"—that is, buy large amounts that keep

consumer sweepstakes A sales promotion in which entrants submit their names for inclusion in a drawing for prizes

trade sales promotion methods Methods intended to persuade wholesalers and retailers to carry a producer's products and market them aggressively

buying allowance A temporary price reduction to resellers for purchasing specified quantities of a product

them supplied for many months. Another problem is that competitors may match (or beat) the reduced price, which can lower profits for all sellers.

A **buy-back allowance** is a sum of money that a producer gives to a reseller for each unit the reseller buys after an initial promotional deal is over. This method is a secondary incentive in which the total amount of money resellers receive is proportional to their purchases during an initial consumer promotion, such as a coupon offer. Buy-back allowances foster cooperation during an initial sales promotion effort and stimulate repurchase afterward. If the retailer's inventory becomes low after the initial promotion, the buy-back allowance helps the retailer restock the inventory. This is often offered for bread and other perishable products. The main disadvantage of this method is expense.

A **scan-back allowance** is a manufacturer's reward to retailers based on the number of pieces moved through the retailers' scanners during a specific time period. To participate in scan-back programs, retailers are usually expected to pass along savings to consumers through special pricing. Scan-backs are becoming widely used by manufacturers because they link trade spending directly to product movement at the retail level.

A **merchandise allowance** is a manufacturer's agreement to pay resellers certain amounts of money for providing promotional efforts like advertising or point-of-purchase displays. This method is best suited to high-volume, high-profit, easily handled products. A drawback is that some retailers perform activities at a minimally acceptable level simply to obtain allowances. Before paying retailers, manufacturers usually verify their performance. Manufacturers hope that retailers' additional promotional efforts will yield substantial sales increases.

18-8b Cooperative Advertising and Dealer Listings

Cooperative advertising is an arrangement in which a manufacturer agrees to pay a certain amount of a retailer's media costs for advertising the manufacturer's products. The amount allowed is usually based on the quantities purchased. As with merchandise allowances, a retailer must show proof that advertisements did appear before the manufacturer pays the agreed-upon portion of the advertising costs. These payments give retailers additional funds for advertising. Some retailers exploit cooperative-advertising agreements by crowding too many products into one advertisement. Not all available cooperative-advertising dollars are used. Some retailers cannot afford to advertise, while others can afford it but do not want to advertise. A large proportion of all cooperative-advertising dollars is spent on newspaper advertisements.

Dealer listings are advertisements promoting a product and identifying participating retailers that sell the product. Dealer listings can influence retailers to carry the product, build traffic at the retail level, and encourage consumers to buy the product at participating dealers.

18-8c Free Merchandise and Gifts

Manufacturers sometimes offer **free merchandise** to resellers that purchase a stated quantity of products. Occasionally, free merchandise is used as payment for allowances provided through other sales promotion methods. To avoid handling and bookkeeping problems, the "free" merchandise usually takes the form of a reduced invoice.

A **dealer loader** is a gift to a retailer that purchases a specified quantity of merchandise. Dealer loaders are often used to obtain special display efforts from retailers by offering essential display parts as premiums. For example, New Belgium Brewing can provide a Fat Tire bicycle to hang in a pub. Marketers use dealer loaders to obtain new distributors and push larger quantities of goods.

18-8d Premium Money

Premium money (push money) is additional compensation offered by the manufacturer to salespeople as an incentive to push a line of goods. This method is appropriate when personal selling is an important part of the marketing effort; it is not effective for promoting products sold through self-service. Premium money often helps a manufacturer obtain a commitment from

---

buy-back allowance A sum of money given to a reseller for each unit bought after an initial promotional deal is over

scan-back allowance A manufacturer's reward to retailers based on the number of pieces scanned

merchandise allowance A manufacturer's agreement to pay resellers certain amounts of money for providing special promotional efforts, such as setting up and maintaining a display

cooperative advertising An arrangement in which a manufacturer agrees to pay a certain amount of a retailer's media costs for advertising the manufacturer's products

dealer listings Advertisements that promote a product and identify the names of participating retailers that sell the product

free merchandise A manufacturer's reward given to resellers that purchase a stated quantity of products

dealer loader A gift, often part of a display, given to a retailer that purchases a specified quantity of merchandise

premium money (push money) Extra compensation to salespeople for pushing a line of goods

the sales force, but it can be very expensive. The use of this incentive must be in compliance with retailers' policies as well as state and local laws.

18-8e **Sales Contests**

A **sales contest** is designed to motivate distributors, retailers, and sales personnel by recognizing outstanding achievements. To be effective, this method must be equitable for all individuals involved. One advantage is that it can achieve participation at all distribution levels. Positive effects may be temporary, however, and prizes are usually expensive.

sales contest A sales promotion method used to motivate distributors, retailers, and sales personnel through recognition of outstanding achievements

Summary

18-1 Describe the major goals of personal selling.

Personal selling is the process of informing customers and persuading them to purchase products through paid personal communication in an exchange situation. The five general goals of personal selling are finding prospects, determining their needs, persuading prospects to buy, following up on the sale, and keeping customers satisfied.

18-2 Summarize the seven basic steps in the personal selling process.

Many salespeople, either consciously or subconsciously, move through a general selling process as they sell products. In prospecting, the salesperson develops a database of potential customers. Before contacting prospects, the salesperson conducts a preapproach that involves finding and analyzing information about prospects and their needs. The approach is the manner in which the salesperson contacts potential customers. During the sales presentation, the salesperson must attract and hold the prospect's attention to stimulate interest and desire for the product. If possible, the salesperson should handle objections as they arise. During the closing, the salesperson asks the prospect to buy the product or products. After a successful closing, the salesperson must follow up on the sale.

18-3 Identify the types of sales force personnel.

The sales structure consists of the inside sales force and the outside sales force. The sales function focuses on both selling to current customers and generating new business sales. Sales support personnel facilitate selling, but their duties usually extend beyond making sales. The three types of support personnel are missionary, trade, and technical salespeople.

18-4 Describe team selling and relationship selling.

The roles of salespeople are changing, resulting in an increased focus on team selling and relationship selling. Team selling involves the salesperson joining with people from the firm's financial, engineering, and other functional areas. Relationship selling involves building mutually beneficial long-term associations with a customer through regular communications over prolonged periods of time.

18-5 Discuss eight major decisions in sales force management.

Sales force management is an important determinant of a firm's success because the sales force is directly responsible for generating the organization's sales revenue. Major decision areas and activities are establishing sales force objectives; determining sales force size; recruiting, selecting, training, compensating, and motivating salespeople; managing sales territories; and controlling and evaluating sales force performance.

Sales objectives should be stated in precise, measurable terms and specify the time period and geographic areas involved. The size of the sales force must be adjusted occasionally because a firm's marketing plans change along with markets and forces in the marketing environment.

Recruiting and selecting salespeople involve attracting and choosing the right type of salesperson to maintain an effective sales force. When developing a training program, managers must consider a variety of dimensions, such as who should be trained, what should be taught, and how training should occur. Compensation of salespeople involves formulating and administering a compensation plan that attracts, motivates, and retains the right types of salespeople. Motivated salespeople should translate into high productivity. Managing sales territories focuses on such factors as size, shape, routing, and scheduling. To control and evaluate sales force performance, sales managers use information obtained through salespeople's call reports, customer feedback, and invoices.

18-6 Describe sales promotion.

Sales promotion is an activity or a material (or both) that acts as a direct inducement, offering added value or incentive for the product to resellers, salespeople, or consumers. Marketers use sales promotion to identify and attract new customers, introduce new products, and increase reseller inventories. Sales promotion techniques fall into two general categories: consumer and trade.

18-7 Review consumer sales promotion methods.

Consumer sales promotion methods encourage consumers to patronize specific stores or try a particular product. These sales promotion methods include coupons; cents-off offers; money refunds and rebates; frequent-user incentives; point-of-purchase displays; demonstrations; free samples and premiums; and consumer contests, games, and sweepstakes.

18-8 Review trade sales promotion methods.

Trade sales promotion techniques can motivate resellers to handle a manufacturer's products and market them aggressively. These sales promotion techniques include buying allowances, buy-back allowances, scan-back allowances, merchandise allowances, cooperative advertising, dealer listings, free merchandise, dealer loaders, premium (or push) money, and sales contests.

Important Terms

personal selling 526
prospecting 528
approach 529
closing 530
support personnel 531
missionary salespeople 531
trade salespeople 532
technical salespeople 532
team selling 532
relationship selling 533
recruiting 535

straight salary
    compensation plan 539
straight commission
    compensation plan 539
combination
    compensation
    plan 539
sales promotion 542
consumer sales promotion
    methods 543
coupons 543
cents-off offers 545
money refunds 546

rebates 546
point-of-purchase (POP)
    materials 547
demonstrations 547
free samples 548
premiums 548
consumer contests 548
consumer games 548
consumer
    sweepstakes 549
trade sales promotion
    methods 549
buying allowance 549

buy-back allowance 550
scan-back allowance
    550
merchandise allowance
    550
cooperative advertising
    550
dealer listings 550
free merchandise 550
dealer loader 550
premium money
    (push money) 550
sales contest 551

Discussion and Review Questions

1. What is personal selling? How does personal selling differ from other types of promotional activities?
2. What are the primary purposes of personal selling?
3. Identify the steps of the personal selling process. Must a salesperson include all these steps when selling a product to a customer? Why or why not?
4. How does a salesperson find and evaluate prospects? Do you consider any of these methods to be ethically questionable? Explain.
5. Why are support personnel needed in the sales force?
6. Why are team selling and relationship selling becoming more prevalent?
7. Identify several characteristics of effective sales objectives.
8. How should a sales manager establish criteria for selecting sales personnel? What do you think are the general characteristics of a good salesperson?

9. What major issues or questions should management consider when developing a training program for the sales force?
10. Explain the major advantages and disadvantages of the three basic methods of compensating salespeople. In general, which method would you prefer? Why?
11. What major factors should be taken into account when designing the size and shape of a sales territory?
12. How does a sales manager, who cannot be with each salesperson in the field on a daily basis, control the performance of sales personnel?
13. What is sales promotion? Why is it used?
14. For each of the following, identify and describe three techniques and give several examples: (a) consumer sales promotion methods and (b) trade sales promotion methods.
15. What types of sales promotion methods have you observed recently? Comment on their effectiveness.

Developing Your Marketing Plan

When developing its marketing strategy, a company must consider the different forms of communication that are necessary to reach a variety of customers. Several types of promotion may be required. Knowledge of the advantages and disadvantages of each promotional element is necessary when developing the marketing plan. Consider the information in this chapter when evaluating your promotional mix:

1. Review the various types of salespeople described in this chapter. Given your promotional objectives (from Chapter 16), do any of these types of salespeople have a place in your promotional plan?

2. Identify the resellers in your distribution channel. Discuss the role that trade sales promotions to these resellers could play in the development of your promotional plan.

3. Evaluate each type of consumer sales promotion as it relates to accomplishing your promotional objectives.

Video Case 18.1

Nederlander Gives Audiences a Reason for a Standing Ovation

The Nederlander Organization has been managing Broadway-type theaters in several states and the U.K. for more than 100 years. It is a theatrical organization that owns concert venues and Broadway theaters. Nederlander describes itself as a lifestyle company, which puts it in a specific niche with a specific type of customer. Josh Lesnick, former President and CEO of Audience Rewards, explains, "I think with something like the arts, customers obviously want a good deal. They want a value-add, but it's really about the experience."

The organization engages in promotional activities for various concerts as well as production of Broadway shows. The success of such activities relies on building and maintaining strong relationships with the many theater owners and ticketing organizations. Nederlander Organization has leveraged these relationships with its Audience Rewards program, a type of sales promotion that has allowed it to build strong relationships with customers by enhancing their experience.

The unique nature of the industry and smaller size of its target market allows Nederlander to create a valuable experience for customers through personal selling and sales promotion activities. Josh Lesnick describes Audience Rewards as similar to a frequent-flyer program. Customers can become members for free and are entered into the ticketing system. When they buy tickets and go to shows, they collect points and are able to redeem them for free or discounted tickets and other rewards. The program was developed as an alternative to traditional discounting. "[It is] another way

to incentivize customers to go to the theater more, to spend more money, to try out new art."

Nederlander's sales promotion program strongly benefits smaller venues. The theater industry is composed of many small privately owned theaters, and each show is marketed individually. This can make it difficult and expensive for companies to advertise and promote their shows. Nederlander's Audience Rewards program helps ease this complexity because it works with many theater owners who support and take part in the program. Lesnick explains that it provides "a central platform to market across all the vendors and art."

The Audience Rewards program also depends on outside relationships with major companies who sponsor the rewards for the program. Acquiring such partnerships can be a challenge for most small companies; however, Nederlander's target market is an attractive opportunity for large companies. A market dominated by 30- to 59-year-old females with a high annual income of approximately $200,000 "appeals to our corporate partners because they want to get access to our customers," Lesnick explains. The program has also provided Nederlander with the opportunity to develop new products such as co-branded credit cards and Broadway-wide gift cards. With these new additions, customers and corporate partners are receiving valuable benefits. Customers are not only able to receive free and discounted tickets, but also able to redeem their points to participate in special red carpet events and backstage passes to meet performers. Corporate partners receive the benefit of access to a more specific and profitable target market.

Before the institution of the Audience Rewards program, Nederlander was bringing in hundreds of thousands of dollars in ticket sales without the use of technology or innovative customer relationship management techniques. Sean Free, Vice President of Sales and Ticketing, comments on the types of technologies used by businesses for marketing and business strategies. He states that "email blasts, and the retargeting efforts that people are now doing, and following people on the internet through IP addresses . . . is all very new . . . and Broadway is usually one of the last industries to follow through with the latest technology." Despite the tendency for the industry's slow reaction, Nederlander's implementation of the Audience Rewards program has served as a catalytic innovation for the company. For example, six months before the premier of the Broadway show *Evita*, Nederlander, in conjunction with some of its partners, sent out 5 million promotional emails to over 1 million members over a 10-day period. Lesnick explains that the emails "created a sense of urgency and an incentive to buy early." This "generated in the pre-sale [revenue] of over $1 million . . . which allowed the company to strategically realign their money to make other decisions."

In addition to the many benefits of this program, sales promotion has provided Nederlander Organization with a competitive advantage over other companies. Because this program relies on the relationships and support of the theater owners and outside companies with whom Nederlander has already solidified relationships, it has created a barrier to entry for other theater organizations due to its strong relationship marketing. This loyalty program has proven to be profitable and good for all partners and members involved with the company.[73]

Questions for Discussion

1. Why do you think more targeted promotional efforts, such as personal selling and sales promotion, are necessary for Nederlander's specific target market?

2. How does Nederlander's Audience Rewards program result in a competitive advantage?

3. Describe how Nederlander's strong customer relationship management results in increased loyalty to the organization.

Case 18.2

Salesforce.com Sold on Stakeholder Satisfaction

Salesforce.com strives to create mutually beneficial relationships with all of its stakeholders, including customers, employees, and communities. Salesforce.com is a customer relationship management (CRM) vendor that provides a cloud-computing model to enable businesses to manage relationships with their customers. Because it can be difficult to manage the sales process, Salesforce.com also offers additional services for companies, such as social media analytics.

Users obtain the company's software through a subscription and download it directly onto their computers. The massive growth of the company in recent years indicates that customers are happy with Salesforce.com's CRM solutions. It earns $10 billion in annual revenues and is one of the fastest growing software companies in the world. In fact, it is the largest company that exclusively sells cloud-based technology. The company sells many different tools including Sales Cloud, Service Cloud, Marketing Cloud, and Pardot. Its CRM users move sales data into the cloud, allowing them to easily access information and analytics. Salesforce.com then works to build deeper relationships with its users by cross-selling its other services. When customers use multiple Salesforce.com tools, it makes

them less likely to switch to a competitor like Oracle or Microsoft.

Digital transformation is a top priority for many CEOs. As a result of recent U.S. tax cuts, companies across all industries have been able to invest in new tools. Salesforce.com has been able to capitalize on this. One of the many ways Salesforce.com stays on top of demands for different types of software solutions is by partnering with other technology companies. For example, the company partnered with Dropbox, a cloud file hosting service, on an integration that allows users to upload assets to a Dropbox folder while automatically syncing the Salesforce.com CRM. Salesforce.com recognizes that companies often use many tools to accomplish tasks, especially when coordinated with other businesses such as outside marketing or advertising agencies, so it aims to simplify those processes. Both Dropbox and Salesforce.com announced the integration will extend to Quip, a collaborative word processing tool acquired for Salesforce.com to help users access content from anywhere.

Salesforce.com is also beloved by its employees and communities. The firm provides large bonuses and allows some of its employees to own stock in the company. Salesforce.com's 1/1/1 Model—which stands for 1 percent time (employees are given 1 percent time to volunteer), 1 percent equity (1 percent of its capital is given to the Salesforce Foundation), and 1 percent product (1 percent of its products are donated or discounted to organizations such as nonprofits)—has been recognized by top institutions for philanthropy, such as Fortune's "50 Best Workplaces for Giving Back." Salesforce.com has donated more than 1.3 million employee hours to community causes, has donated or discounted licenses for its software to over 29,000 nonprofit organizations, and has awarded over $100 million in grants.

Salesforce.com CEO Marc Benioff has a reputation for his social activism. Recently, the company added a new section to its annual report to highlight and stress its environmental, social, and governance activities for its stakeholders. For example, in recent years the company achieved net-zero greenhouse gas emissions and sourced 100 percent renewable energy for almost all of its campus in San Francisco. To offset greenhouse gas emissions at corporate events, such as employee travel, Salesforce.com purchases carbon credits. Benioff is also an outspoken supporter of gender equality in the workplace. These efforts, among others, continue to please stakeholders.

By selling quality CRM products and valuing its relationships with stakeholders, Salesforce.com has achieved both high growth and a positive reputation. Its ability to create a variety of cloud-based tools to support businesses, from sales tools to marketing analytics, and integrate with other services such as Dropbox, have contributed to the company's success.[74]

Questions for Discussion

1. How have Salesforce.com's CRM systems benefited its users?
2. Why is it a benefit for Salesforce.com to collaborate with other cloud-based services?
3. How can Salesforce.com prevent customers from switching to competing services?

Strategic Case 7

Patagonia Climbs into the World of IMC

When it comes to advertising, apparel manufacturer and retailer Patagonia takes a different approach. The headlines of its popular advertisements feature in big, bold letters "Don't Buy This Jacket." Underneath is a photo of a Patagonia jacket made from recycled materials. The copy of the ad describes how much water, carbon dioxide, and waste is expended in manufacturing and transporting the jacket. Patagonia acknowledges that even its eco-conscious products are environmentally damaging.

Patagonia is not trying to put itself out of business with these types of ads. Rather, it is reinforcing its mission of environmental protection and sustainability. Patagonia uses this type of promotion to cause consumers to think about whether they really need a brand-new product. If the answer is yes, then Patagonia encourages them to purchase products that will last them a long time. This is where its products come in.

Background

The idea behind Patagonia, headquartered in Ventura, California, started from one man's passion for rock climbing. Outdoor enthusiast Yvon Chouinard loved rock climbing but lacked reusable climbing gear. He began developing his own reusable rock climbing pitons and selling them out of his car. In 1965, he co-founded Chouinard Equipment.

Eventually, the company began selling more eco-friendly chocks to replace pitons. These chocks were designed to eliminate rock damage when climbing. This was the company's first major foray into environmental consciousness.

Chouinard and his wife had begun to sell durable climbing clothing as a way to supplement their hardware business, but by 1972 the clothing had become its own line. They called their clothing line Patagonia to reflect the mysticism of far off lands and adventurous places. Customers appreciated the bright colors and durability of Patagonia clothing. The company decided to align its brand with environmental responsibility and switched to more expensive organic cotton in 1996.

Today, Patagonia sells its gear through its own branded stores, online, and through retailers such as Dick's Sporting Goods and REI. Patagonia has 75 branded stores, profits exceeding $600 million, and 1,200 employees. Patagonia has become known for its environmental consciousness, employee-friendly workplace, and high-quality, long-lasting clothing.

As with all well-known firms, Patagonia's success would not be possible without a carefully integrated promotion mix that educates consumers about what the brand and its products represent. Word-of-mouth communication is highly encouraged, and Patagonia encourages

ISTOCK.COM/ELECTRA-K-VASILEIADOU

viral marketing through the use of social media including Facebook, YouTube, Twitter, mobile marketing, and its own corporate blog. A strong mix of advertising, public relations, personal selling, and sales promotions is used to keep its brand relevant, both for retailers that sell their products and for customers that buy from them directly.

Patagonia's "Do Not Buy" Advertising

Patagonia freely admits that advertising is not a high priority in its mission to change the world. The company does not employ an outside ad agency, instead choosing to develop promotions in-house. Much of the advertising that Patagonia does involves advocacy advertising rather than product advertising. For instance, its short film "DamNation" was geared toward demonstrating how removing dams in the United States is important to restoring our rivers. Although this type of promotion promotes a cause rather than a company brand, the advertising's affiliation with the company helps to promote the firm indirectly and give it a reputation for sustainability.

All of Patagonia's advertising reflects the company's mission statement: "Build the best product, cause no unnecessary harm, use business to inspire and implement solutions to the environmental crisis." Encouraging consumers to purchase their products if they do not need them conflicts with Patagonia's mission. As a result, it does the opposite and

releases advertisements advising consumers to avoid purchasing what they do not need, even if that means forgoing Patagonia products. Additionally, Patagonia's "Buy Less" campaign encourages consumers to sell their used Patagonia gear on eBay or through Patagonia's website. Patagonia is declaring a war against consumerism.

It might seem that Patagonia's advertising discourages sales. However, its advertising platform of a war against consumerism serves to demonstrate the appeal of its products. Patagonia offers products that last for a lifetime, and by encouraging consumers to purchase less, they are simultaneously encouraging them to make sure that what they do purchase lasts for a long time. Because customers can trust that Patagonia will sell them a high-quality product, they are more likely to become long-term customers of the firm.

Patagonia's Public Relations Image

Much of the publicity surrounding Patagonia involves the numerous sustainability initiatives in which it participates. For instance, in 1985 Patagonia started giving 1 percent of its total sales to environmental organizations. The organization 1% for the Planet is an alliance of businesses that donate part of their proceeds to environmental organizations to support sustainability and the preservation of the environment. Since it started, Patagonia has made $58 million in grants and in-kind donations.

Patagonia's Common Threads Initiative seeks to get employees and customers involved in the process of environmental responsibility. The company partnered with eBay to allow employees and consumers to sell their used products through eBay's "Common Threads" partner site. Those wishing to sell their products must take the pledge to reduce, reuse, and recycle. The Common Threads Initiative reinforces Patagonia's mission statement and is also an effective public relations tool to get employees and consumers involved in working with the organization.

Patagonia also reaches out to the public through its digital sites. Its blog thecleanestline.com serves as a weblog for customers, employees, and friends of Patagonia to share environmental activism activities and stories of the outdoors. Its Worn Wear program encourages customers to celebrate their stories of their experiences with treasured, well-worn apparel. Patagonia's initiatives and customer relationships have led it to be covered in numerous news and feature articles, from *Fast Company* magazine to *The Wall Street Journal.*

Personal Selling and Sales Promotions at Patagonia

Patagonia relies heavily on the sales function for its wholesale business. It employs a wholesale management team to build relationships and promote its brand among specialty retailers. As Patagonia expands globally, it is reorganizing and expanding its sales force to meet the needs of stores in different countries. In Europe, Patagonia added sales positions and reorganized its sales force into four regions. Sales members are given iPhones and iPads to enhance communication as they travel.

Patagonia also uses personal selling in its retail stores. Retail sales associates are trained to greet customers courteously, assist them in shopping for products, and provide them with accurate information in response to customer inquiries. They must also honor the company's "ironclad guarantee" for product returns. Sales training for Patagonia employees involves a combination of in-person training and online video.

Additionally, Patagonia offers a number of incentives or inducements to attract customers to its online and physical stores. Because Patagonia products can be expensive, the company mitigates the risk of purchase with liberal return and replacement policies. If the person decides she or he is not happy with the product, the customer may return it to the company to be repaired, replaced, or refunded. Products with wear and tear will be repaired at a reasonable charge. For online purchases Patagonia offers free deliveries for purchases over $75.

Above all, Patagonia wants to ensure that its sales promotions are completely transparent to customers. For this reason, it warns consumers about the authenticity of online coupons offering discounts for Patagonia products. Instead of offering online coupons, Patagonia has a link that will take the customer directly to its discounted product offerings. This eliminates the possibilities of coupon fraud and maintains a transparent, trusting relationship between the company and the customer.

Patagonia has developed an effective integrated marketing communications mix using advertising, public relations, personal selling, and sales promotion. Its promotion mix serves to establish and maintain long-term relationships with both customers and specialty stores. It also informs stakeholders about the company's avid support for environmental consciousness. Rather than promoting specific products, Patagonia prefers to promote environmental causes and combat the idea of consumerism. Although it might take some unconventional approaches to promotion, Patagonia has developed campaigns that resonate with customers and inspire long-term loyalty.[75]

Questions for Discussion

1. Describe how Patagonia uses different elements of the promotion mix.
2. Why do you think Patagonia tends to use advocacy advertising instead of product advertising?
3. How do Patagonia's marketing promotion activities serve to reinforce its primary mission?

Pricing Decisions

To provide a satisfying marketing mix, an organization must set a price that is acceptable to the target market.

PART 8 examines pricing decisions that can have numerous effects on other parts of the marketing mix. For instance, price can influence how customers perceive the product, what types of marketing institutions are used to distribute the product, and how the product is promoted.

CHAPTER 19 explores the importance of price and looks at some characteristics of price and nonprice competition. It examines fundamental concepts, such as demand, elasticity, marginal analysis, and breakeven analysis. The chapter then examines the major factors that affect marketers' pricing decisions.

CHAPTER 20 discusses six major stages that marketers use to establish prices.

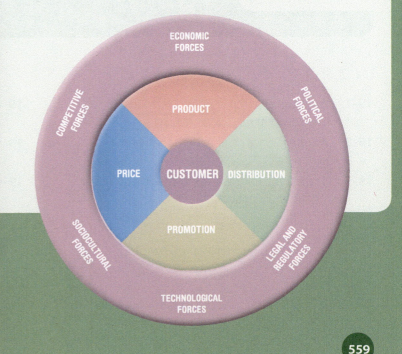

19

Pricing Concepts

LEARNING OBJECTIVES

19-1 Summarize why price is important to the marketing mix.

19-2 Compare price competition with nonprice competition.

19-3 Explore the role of demand curves and the price elasticity of demand.

19-4 Describe the relationships among demand, costs, and profits.

19-5 Describe eight key factors that may influence marketers' pricing decisions.

19-6 Identify seven methods companies can use to price products for business markets.

SLAVA296/SHUTTERSTOCK.COM

Can't Spend Enough on a Car?

Imagine a stylish and speedy sports car so personalized that each is made to fit the individual buyer's size, shape, and reach. Each of these 150 customized "hypercars" is outfitted with a V-12 engine rated at more than 1,000 horsepower. This unique sports car comes with an even more unique price tag of $2.6 million.

Welcome to the marketing world of Aston Martin's new Valkyrie. Based in Britain, Aston Martin is well known for its high-end sports cars. Although the firm produces only about 4,000 cars every year, its attention to design, engineering, and customer satisfaction enable it to set prices that result in profitability and fuel future investments in product development. The price of its entry-level Vantage model, for example, starts at more than $100,000.

The Valkyrie takes luxury customization and pricing to new levels, further burnishing the parent's image. Developed with the assistance of a Formula One racing expert, the Valkyrie is highly aerodynamic and capable of speeds far in excess of typical street or highway driving. Buyers have a lot of latitude in personalizing the interior and exterior. Each customer receives a scale model of the Valkyrie as ordered, allowing time to examine and adjust colors and other details before production begins.

Aston Martin introduced the Valkyrie at special international events attended by prospects who were prequalified on the basis of buying power and brand loyalty. The company knows its market. More than a year before the first car was built, the entire run of 150 cars was completely sold out.[1]

Many firms, including luxury auto makers, use pricing as a tool to make their products stand out from those of other firms. However, rival firms may likewise employ pricing as a major competitive tool, potentially leading to price wars. In other industries, firms can be very successful even if they don't have the lowest prices. The best price is not always the lowest price.

In this chapter, we focus first on the nature of price and its importance to marketers. We then consider some characteristics of price and nonprice competition. Next, we discuss several pricing-related concepts, such as demand, elasticity, and breakeven analysis. Then we examine in some detail the numerous factors that can influence pricing decisions. Finally, we discuss selected issues related to pricing products for business markets.

Learning Objective 19-1

Summarize why price is important to the marketing mix.

19-1 THE IMPORTANCE OF PRICE IN MARKETING

Price is the value paid for a product in a marketing exchange. Remember that we defined value in Chapter 1 as a customer's subjective assessment of benefits relative to costs in determining the worth of a product. Many factors influence the assessment of value, including time constraints, price levels, perceived quality, and motivations to use available information about prices.[2] In most marketing situations, the price is apparent to both buyer and seller. However, price does not always take the form of money paid. In fact, **barter**, the trading of products, is the oldest form of exchange. Money may or may not be involved. Barter among businesses, because of the relatively large values of the exchanges, usually involves trade credit.

Buyers' interest in price stems from their expectations about the usefulness of a product or the satisfaction they may derive from it. Because consumers have limited resources, they must allocate those resources to obtain the products they most desire. They must decide whether the utility gained in an exchange is worth the buying power sacrificed. Almost anything of value—ideas, services, rights, and goods—can be assessed by a price. In our society, financial price is the measurement of value commonly used in exchanges.

As pointed out in Chapter 11, developing a product may be a lengthy process. It takes time to plan promotion and to communicate benefits. Distribution usually requires a long-term commitment to dealers that will handle the product. Price is often the only thing a marketer can change quickly to respond to changes in demand, the actions of competitors, or the marketing environment. Under certain circumstances, however, the price variable may be relatively inflexible.

Price is a key element in the marketing mix because it relates directly to the generation of total revenue. The following equation is an important one for the entire organization:

$$\text{profit} = \text{total revenue} - \text{total costs}$$

$$\text{profit} = (\text{price} \times \text{quantity sold}) - \text{total costs}$$

Price affects an organization's profits in several ways because it is a key component of the profit equation and can be a major determinant of quantities sold. For instance, Target reduced the price of thousands of items in order to sell more of them and thereby boost revenue.[3] Furthermore, total costs are influenced by quantities sold. Consider Fossil watches that are priced under $300 versus Rolex watches that can cost tens of thousands of dollars. You would need to sell many more Fossil watches to reach your sales objectives than Rolex watches because of the dramatic difference in price.

Because price has a psychological influence on customers, marketers can use it symbolically. By pricing high, they can emphasize the quality of a product and try to increase the prestige associated with its ownership. By lowering a price, marketers can emphasize a bargain and attract customers who go out of their way to save a small amount of money. Thus, as this chapter details, price can have strong effects on a firm's sales and profitability.

price The value paid for a product in a marketing exchange

barter The trading of products

19-2 PRICE AND NONPRICE COMPETITION

The competitive environment strongly influences the marketing-mix decisions associated with a product. Pricing decisions are often made according to the price or nonprice competitive situation in a particular market.

19-2a Price Competition

When choosing to engage in **price competition**, a marketer emphasizes price as an issue and matches or beats competitors' prices. Planet Fitness, for example, has experienced dramatic growth by offering $10/month gym memberships when other sport club memberships average $50 a month. Although Planet Fitness offers fewer amenities, its lower price is appealing to consumers who won't use most gym amenities.[4] To compete effectively on a price basis, a firm should be the low-cost seller of the product. If all firms producing the same product charge the same price for it, the firm with the lowest costs is the most profitable. Consider the advertisement for The Dump furniture store, which boasts that it can sell products for 50–75 percent less than other firms by having very low overhead and buying below manufacturers' prices.

By focusing on overstocks, showroom models, design samples, and one-of-a-kinds, The Dump can pay significantly below famous brand manufacturer prices and pass the savings along to customers. Firms that stress low price as a key marketing-mix element tend to market standardized products. A seller competing on price may change prices frequently, or at least must be willing and able to do so. In a competitive pricing environment, whenever one firm changes its prices, its rivals usually respond quickly and aggressively.

Price competition gives marketers flexibility. They can alter prices in response to changes in their costs or demand for the product. If competitors try to gain market share by cutting prices, a company competing on a price basis can react quickly to such efforts. A major drawback of price competition is that competitors have the flexibility to adjust prices, too. If they quickly match or beat a company's price cuts, a price war may ensue. A **price war** involves two or more companies engaging in intense price competition, often in an effort to boost market share. For instance, the introduction of two German low-price grocers—Aldi and Lidl—has sparked a grocery price war in U.S. markets where the new chains have opened stores. Additionally, competition from extreme-value stores such as Dollar General along with lower prices from Amazon-owned Whole Foods have forced Walmart and traditional supermarkets to lower prices and cut into profit margins in order to remain competitive.[5] Chronic price wars often benefit consumers in the form of lower prices in the short run, but the constant price cutting is seldom sustainable, so they can substantially weaken organizations by slashing profit margins for everyone.

price competition Emphasizing price as an issue and matching or beating competitors' prices

price war involves two or more companies engaging in intense price competition, often in an effort to boost market share

Take away their LABELS. Take away their CATALOGS. Take away their OVERHEAD. Take away their MARKUP.

TAKE 50–75% OFF THEIR PRICES
the same furniture. the same makers.

$795
AT THE DISTRICT

SELLS FOR
$4000
IN THEIR CATALOG

Solid Reclaimed Wood Platform Bed
Handmade in Queen Size

FAMOUS BRAND NAMES. Up to 80% off only. The most respected designers and manufacturers. We can't always use their names, but you will know them when you see them.

NEVER PAY FULL PRICE. We buy closeouts, overstocks, design samples, one-of-a-kinds, and canceled orders. All just quality, brand new merchandise at a true 60–80% off price. The stuff regular stores don't want you to know about.

EVER CHANGING SELECTION. Every weekend, new items fill our showrooms. We are constantly searching the globe to bring you the best deals, but they come and go in a single weekend. Living, dining, bedroom, genuine leather and motion, fine rugs, and luxury mattresses.

OPEN 3 DAYS A WEEK. We dump all unnecessary costs. Regular stores open every day of the week and you pay for it. We are only open Friday, Saturday, and Sunday, which keeps our costs of doing business down. No fancy showroom or high pressure salespeople.

THE DUMP AMERICA'S FURNITURE OUTLET

ATLANTA • CHICAGO • DALLAS • HOUSTON • PHOENIX • PHILADELPHIA • VIRGINIA
www.thedump.com | FRIDAY 10-9 SATURDAY 10-9 SUNDAY 11-7

THE DISTRICT
High Design, Not High Markup
at The Dump

SOURCE: TEXAS MONTHLY

Price Competition
Furniture retailers frequently engage in price competition.

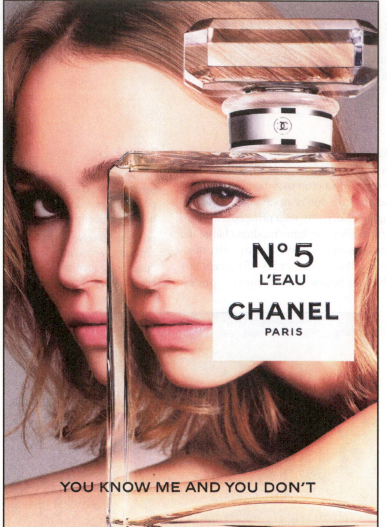

Nonprice Competition
Chanel does not mention price anywhere on this advertisement. Rather, it uses nonprice competition.

nonprice competition
Emphasizing factors other than price to distinguish a product from competing brands

19-2b Nonprice Competition

Nonprice competition occurs when a seller decides not to focus on price and instead emphasizes distinctive product features, service, product quality, promotion, packaging, or other factors to distinguish its product from competing brands. Thus, nonprice competition allows a company to increase its brand's unit sales through means other than changing the brand's price. Mars, for example, not only markets Snickers and M&M's but also has an upscale candy line called Ethel's Chocolate. With the tagline "eat chocolate, not preservatives," Ethel's Chocolate competes on the basis of taste, attractive appearance, and hip packaging, and, thus, has little need to engage in price competition.[6] A major advantage of nonprice competition is that a firm can build customer loyalty toward its brand.

Nonprice competition is effective only under certain conditions. A company must be able to distinguish its brand through unique product features, higher product quality, effective promotion, distinctive packaging, and/or excellent customer service. Chanel commands a premium price due to its status as a luxury brand. Notice the advertisement showing model Lily-Rose Depp peering through a large bottle of N° 5 L'Eau perfume with the tag line, "You know me and you don't." The price of the perfume is never mentioned in the advertisement. Buyers must not only be able to perceive these distinguishing characteristics but also deem them important. The distinguishing features that set a particular brand apart from competitors should be difficult, if not impossible, for competitors to imitate. Finally, the firm must extensively promote the brand's distinguishing characteristics to establish its superiority and set it apart from competitors in the minds of buyers.

Even a marketer that is competing on a nonprice basis cannot ignore competitors' prices. The organization must be aware of them and sometimes be prepared to price its brand near or slightly above competing brands. Therefore, price remains a crucial marketing-mix component even in environments that call for nonprice competition.

19-3 DEMAND CURVES AND PRICE ELASTICITY

Another significant factor in pricing decisions is demand. Marketers use marketing research and forecasting techniques to estimate sales potential and determine the relationship between a product's price and the quantity demanded.

19-3a **The Demand Curve**

For most products, the quantity buyers demand goes up as the price goes down, and the quantity demanded goes down as the price goes up. Case in point, prices have fallen precipitously for flat-screen television sets in recent years. This change in price is largely due to strong competition and newer technologies such as 4K and curved screens. In order to compensate, most makers of flat-screen televisions responded by continuing to lower prices. Thus, an inverse relationship exists between price and quantity demanded. As long as the marketing environment and buyers' needs, ability (purchasing power), willingness, and authority to buy remain stable, this fundamental inverse relationship holds.

Figure 19.1 illustrates the effect of price on the quantity demanded. The classic **demand curve** ($D1$) is a graph of the quantity of products a firm expects to sell at various prices if other factors remain constant. As you can see, as price falls, quantity demanded usually rises. Demand depends on other factors in the marketing mix, including product quality, promotion, and distribution. An improvement in any of these factors may cause a shift to demand curve $D2$. In such a case, an increased quantity ($Q2$) will be sold at the same price (P).

Many types of demand exist, and not all conform to the classic demand curve shown in Figure 19.1. Prestige products, such as selected perfumes and jewelry, tend to sell better at higher prices than at lower ones. This advertisement for Dooney & Bourke handbags provides a close-up of the high-priced Cowboys Zip Zip Satchel handbag to demonstrate its style and craftsmanship. These products are desirable partly because their expense makes buyers feel elite. If the price fell drastically and many people owned these products, they would lose some of their appeal. The demand curve in Figure 19.2 shows the relationship between price and quantity

Prestige Pricing
Luxury products such as Dooney & Bourke handbags sell better at higher prices than lower prices because they are considered to be exclusive products as they are unaffordable for many consumers.

Figure 19.1 **Demand Curve Illustrating the Price/ Quantity Relationship and Increase in Demand**

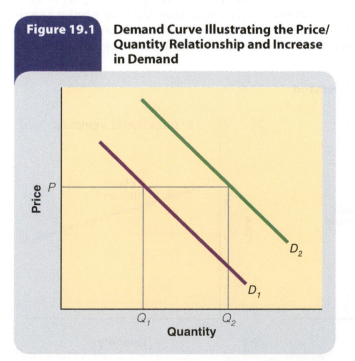

Figure 19.2 **Demand Curve Illustrating the Relationship between Price and Quantity for Prestige Products**

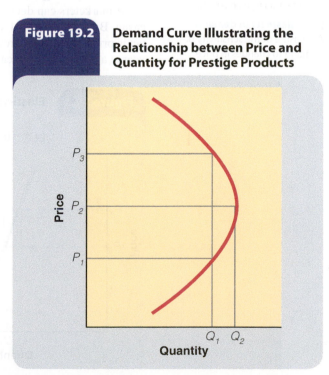

demanded for prestige products. Quantity demanded is greater, not less, at higher prices. For a certain price range—from $P1$ to $P2$—the quantity demanded ($Q1$) goes up to $Q2$. After a certain point, however, raising the price backfires. If the price goes too high, the quantity demanded goes down. The figure shows that if price is raised from $P2$ to $P3$, quantity demanded goes back down from $Q2$ to $Q1$.

19-3b Demand Fluctuations

Changes in buyers' needs, variations in the effectiveness of other marketing-mix variables, the presence of substitutes, and dynamic environmental factors can influence demand. Restaurants and utility companies experience large fluctuations in demand daily. Toy manufacturers, fireworks suppliers, and air-conditioning and heating contractors also face demand fluctuations because of the seasonal nature of their products. In some cases, demand fluctuations are predictable. It is no surprise to restaurants and utility company managers that demand fluctuates. However, changes in demand for other products may be less predictable, leading to problems for some companies. Other organizations anticipate demand fluctuations and develop new products and prices to meet consumers' changing needs.

19-3c Assessing Price Elasticity of Demand

We have seen how marketers identify the target market's evaluation of price and how they examine demand to learn whether price is related inversely or directly to quantity. The next step is to assess price elasticity of demand. **Price elasticity of demand** provides a measure of the sensitivity of demand to changes in price. It is formally defined as the percentage change in quantity demanded relative to a given percentage change in price (see Figure 19.3).[7] The percentage change in quantity demanded caused by a percentage change in price is much greater for products with elastic demand than for inelastic demand. For a product like electricity, demand is relatively inelastic. When its price increases from $P1$ to $P2$, quantity demanded goes down only a little, from $Q1$ to $Q2$. For products like recreational vehicles, demand is relatively elastic. When price rises sharply, from $P1$ to $P2$, quantity demanded goes down a great deal, from $Q'1$ to $Q'2$.

If marketers can determine a product's price elasticity of demand, setting a price is much easier. By analyzing total revenues as prices change, marketers can determine whether a product is price elastic. Total revenue is price times quantity. Thus, 10,000 cans of paint sold in one year at a price of $10 per can equals $100,000 of total revenue. If demand is *elastic*, a change in

demand curve A graph of the quantity of products a firm expects to sell at various prices if other factors remain constant

price elasticity of demand A measure of the sensitivity of demand to changes in price

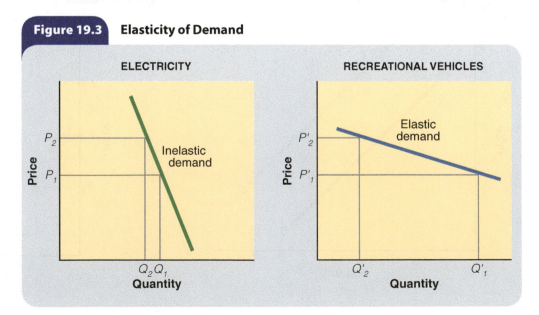

Figure 19.3   **Elasticity of Demand**

price causes an opposite change in total revenue. An increase in price will decrease total revenue, and a decrease in price will increase total revenue. *Inelastic* demand results in a change in the same direction as total revenue. An increase in price will increase total revenue, and a decrease in price will decrease total revenue. Demand for gasoline, for example, is relatively inelastic—even when prices are close to $4 per gallon—because people must still drive to work, run errands, and shop, all of which require fuel for their vehicles. Although higher gasoline prices force more consumers to change some behaviors in an effort to reduce the amount of gasoline they use, most cut spending in other areas instead because they require a certain level of fuel for weekly activities like commuting. The following formula determines the price elasticity of demand:

More Money, More Fun!

Year	Price of one-day, one-park admission to Disney's Magic Kingdom in Florida
1971	$3.50
1991	$33
2011	$85
2017	PEAK $124
	REGULAR $115
	VALUE $107

SNAPSHOT

Source: "WDW Ticket Increase Guide," http://allears.net/tix/tixincrease.htm.

$$\text{price elasticity of demand} = \frac{\% \text{ change in quantity demanded}}{\% \text{ change in price}}$$

For instance, if demand falls by 8 percent when a seller raises the price by 2 percent, the price elasticity of demand is –4 (the negative sign indicates the inverse relationship between price and demand). If demand falls by 2 percent when price is increased by 4 percent, elasticity is –1/2. The less elastic the demand, the more beneficial it is for the seller to raise the price. Products without readily available substitutes and for which consumers have strong needs (e.g., electricity or appendectomies) usually have inelastic demand. Marketers cannot base prices solely on elasticity considerations. They must also examine the costs associated with different sales volumes and evaluate what happens to profits.

19-4 DEMAND, COST, AND PROFIT RELATIONSHIPS

Learning Objective 19-4

Describe the relationships among demand, costs, and profits.

Understanding the relationship between demand, cost, and profit is imperative. To stay in business, a company must set prices that not only cover its costs but also meet customers' expectations. Consumers are becoming less tolerant of price increases, forcing manufacturers to find new ways to control costs. In the past, many customers who desired premium brands were willing to pay extra for those products. Today, customers pass up certain brand names if they can pay less without sacrificing quality. In this section, we explore two approaches to understanding demand, cost, and profit relationships: marginal analysis and breakeven analysis.

19-4a Marginal Analysis

Marginal analysis examines what happens to a firm's costs and revenues when production (or sales volume) changes by a single unit. Both production costs and revenues must be evaluated. To determine the costs of production, it is necessary to distinguish among several types of costs.

Fixed costs do not vary with changes in the number of units produced or sold. Consequently, a paint manufacturer's cost of renting a factory does not change because production increases from one to two shifts a day or because twice as much paint is sold. Rent may go up, but not because the factory has doubled production or revenue. **Average fixed cost** is the fixed cost per unit produced and is calculated by dividing fixed costs by the number of units produced.

Variable costs vary directly with changes in the number of units produced or sold. The wages for a second shift and the cost of twice as much paint are extra costs incurred when production is doubled. Variable costs are usually constant per unit; that is, twice as many workers and twice as much material produce twice as many cans of paint. **Average variable cost**, the variable cost per unit produced, is calculated by dividing the variable costs by the number of units produced.

Total cost is the sum of average fixed costs and average variable costs times the quantity produced. The **average total cost** is the sum of the average fixed cost and the average variable cost. **Marginal cost (MC)** is the extra cost a firm incurs when it produces one more unit of a product.

Table 19.1 illustrates various costs and their relationships. Notice that average fixed cost declines as output increases. Average variable cost follows a U shape, as does average total cost. As quantity increases, these costs initially decline and then rise. Because average total cost continues to fall after average variable cost begins to rise, its lowest point is at a higher level of output than that of average variable cost. Average total cost is lowest at five units at a cost of $22.00, whereas average variable cost is lowest at three units at a cost of $10.67. As Figure 19.4 shows, marginal cost equals average total cost at the latter's lowest level. In Table 19.1, this occurs between five and six units of production. Average total cost decreases as long as marginal cost is less than average total cost and increases when marginal cost rises above average total cost.

Marginal revenue (MR) is the change in total revenue that occurs when a firm sells an additional unit of a product. Figure 19.5 depicts marginal revenue and a demand curve. Most firms in the United States face downward-sloping demand curves for their products; in other words, they must lower their prices to sell additional units. This situation means that each additional

fixed costs Costs that do not vary with changes in the number of units produced or sold

average fixed cost The fixed cost per unit produced

variable costs Costs that vary directly with changes in the number of units produced or sold

average variable cost The variable cost per unit produced

total cost The sum of average fixed and average variable costs times the quantity produced

average total cost The sum of the average fixed cost and the average variable cost

marginal cost (MC) The extra cost incurred by producing one more unit of a product

marginal revenue (MR) The change in total revenue resulting from the sale of an additional unit of a product

Table 19.1   Costs and Their Relationships

1 Quantity	2 Fixed Cost	3 Average Fixed Cost (2) ÷ (1)	4 Average Variable Cost	5 Average Total Cost (3) + (4)	6 Total Cost (5) × (1)	7 Marginal Cost
1	$40	$40.00	$20.00	$60.00	$60	
						$10
2	40	20.00	15.00	35.00	70	
						2
3	40	13.33	10.67	24.00	72	
						18
4	40	10.00	12.50	22.50	90	
						20
5	40	8.00	14.00	22.00	110	
						30
6	40	6.67	16.67	23.33	140	
						40
7	40	5.71	20.00	25.71	180	

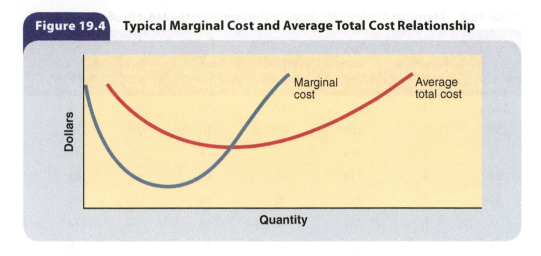

Figure 19.4 **Typical Marginal Cost and Average Total Cost Relationship**

unit of product sold provides the firm with less revenue than the previous unit sold. MR then becomes less-than-average revenue, as Figure 19.5 shows. Eventually, MR reaches zero, and the sale of additional units actually hurts the firm.

However, before the firm can determine whether a unit makes a profit, it must know its cost, as well as its revenue, because profit equals revenue minus cost. If MR is a unit's addition to revenue and MC is a unit's addition to cost, MR minus MC tells us whether the unit is profitable. Table 19.2 illustrates the relationships among price, quantity sold, total revenue, marginal revenue, marginal cost, and total cost. It indicates where maximum profits are possible at various combinations of price and cost. Notice that the total cost and the marginal cost figures in Table 19.2 are calculated and appear in Table 19.1.

Profit is the highest where MC = MR. In Table 19.2, note that at a quantity of four units, profit is the highest and MR − MC = 0. The best price is $33, and the profit is $42. Up to this point, the additional revenue generated from an extra unit sold exceeds the additional cost of producing it. Beyond this point, the additional cost of producing another unit exceeds the additional revenue generated, and profits decrease. If the price were based on minimum average total cost—$22 (Table 19.1)—it would result in a lower profit of $40 (Table 19.2) for five units priced at $30 versus a profit of $42 for four units priced at $33.

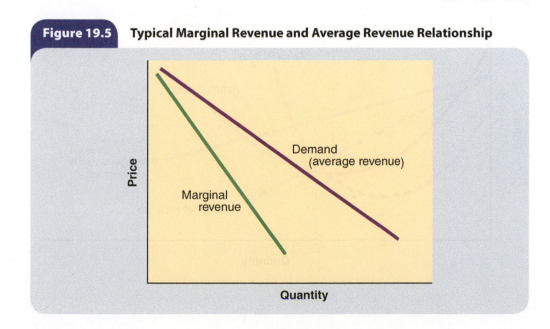

Figure 19.5 **Typical Marginal Revenue and Average Revenue Relationship**

Table 19.2   Marginal Analysis Method for Determining the Most Profitable Price*

1 Price	2 Quantity Sold	3 Total Revenue (1) × (2)	4 Marginal Revenue	5 Marginal Cost	6 Total Cost	7 Profit (3) − (6)
$57	1	$ 57	$57	$60	$60	$−3
50	2	100	43	10	70	30
38	3	114	14	2	72	42
33*	**4**	**132**	**18**	**18**	**90**	**42**
30	5	150	18	20	110	40
27	6	162	12	30	140	22
25	7	175	13	40	180	−5

*Boldface indicates the best price–profit combination.

Graphically combining Figures 19.4 and 19.5 into Figure 19.6 shows that any unit for which MR exceeds MC adds to a firm's profits, and any unit for which MC exceeds MR subtracts from profits. The firm should produce at the point where MR equals MC, because this is the most profitable level of production.

This discussion of marginal analysis may give the false impression that pricing can be highly precise. If revenue (demand) and cost (supply) remained constant, prices could be set for maximum profits. In practice, however, cost and revenue change frequently. The competitive tactics of other firms or government action can quickly undermine a company's expectations of revenue, as can changing economic conditions. Thus, marginal analysis is only a model from which to work. Moreover, it offers little help in pricing new products before costs and revenues are established. On the other hand, in setting prices of existing products, especially in competitive situations, most marketers can benefit by understanding the relationship between marginal cost and marginal revenue.

Figure 19.6   **Combining the Marginal Cost and Marginal Revenue Concepts for Optimal Profit**

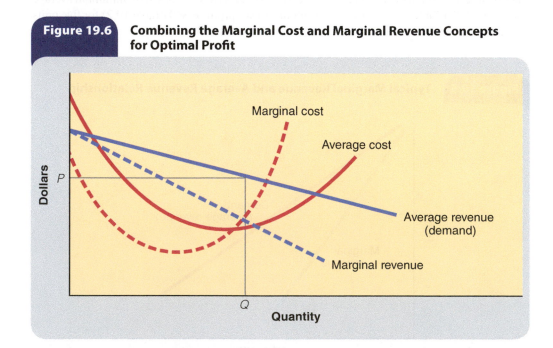

19-4b **Breakeven Analysis**

The point at which the costs of producing a product equal the revenue made from selling the product is the **breakeven point**. If a paint manufacturer has total annual costs of $100,000 and sells $100,000 worth of paint in the same year, the company has broken even.

Figure 19.7 illustrates the relationships among costs, revenue, profits, and losses involved in determining the breakeven point. Knowing the number of units necessary to break even is important in setting the price. If a product priced at $100 per unit has an average variable cost of $60 per unit, the contribution to fixed costs is $40. If total fixed costs are $120,000, the breakeven point in units is determined as follows:

$$\text{breakeven point} = \frac{\text{fixed costs}}{\text{per-unit contribution to fixed costs}}$$

$$= \frac{\text{fixed costs}}{\text{price-variable costs}}$$

$$= \frac{\$120,000}{\$40}$$

$$= 3,000 \text{ units}$$

To calculate the breakeven point in terms of dollar sales volume, the seller multiplies the breakeven point in units by the price per unit. In the preceding example, the breakeven point in terms of dollar sales volume is 3,000 (units) times $100, or $300,000.

To use breakeven analysis effectively, a marketer should determine the breakeven point for each of several alternative prices. This determination allows the marketer to compare the effects on total revenue, total costs, and the breakeven point for each price under consideration. Although this comparative analysis may not tell the marketer exactly what price to charge, it will identify highly undesirable price alternatives that should definitely be avoided.

Breakeven analysis is simple and straightforward. It does assume, however, that the quantity demanded is basically fixed (inelastic) and that the major task in setting prices is to recover

breakeven point The point at which the costs of producing a product equal the revenue made from selling the product

| Figure 19.7 | **Determining the Breakeven Point** |

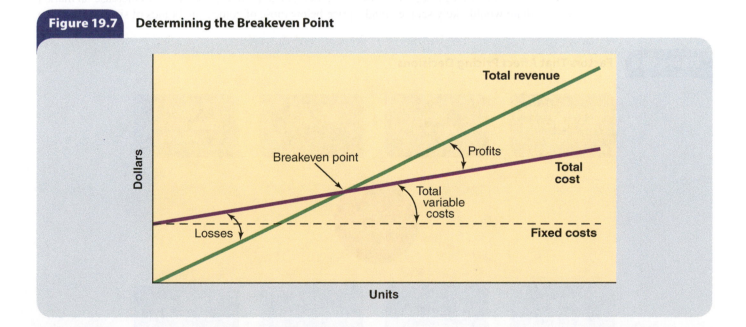

costs. It focuses more on how to break even than on how to achieve a pricing objective, such as percentage of market share or return on investment. Nonetheless, marketing managers can use this concept to determine whether a product will achieve at least a breakeven volume.

19-5 FACTORS THAT AFFECT PRICING DECISIONS

Pricing decisions can be complex due to the number of factors to consider. Frequently, there is considerable uncertainty about the reactions to price among buyers, channel members, and competitors. Price is also an important consideration in marketing planning, market analysis, and sales forecasting. It is a major issue when assessing a brand's position relative to competing brands. Most factors that affect pricing decisions can be grouped into one of the eight categories shown in Figure 19.8. In this section, we explore how each of these groups of factors enters into price decision making.

19-5a Organizational and Marketing Objectives

Marketers should set prices that are consistent with the organization's goals and mission. For example, a retailer trying to position itself as being value-oriented may wish to set prices that are quite reasonable relative to product quality. In this case, a marketer would not want to set premium prices on products but would strive to price products in line with this overall organizational goal.

Pricing decisions should also be compatible with the firm's marketing objectives. For instance, suppose one of a producer's marketing objectives is a 12 percent increase in unit sales by the end of the following year. Assuming buyers are price sensitive, increasing the price or setting a price above the average market price would not be in line with this objective.

19-5b Types of Pricing Objectives

The types of pricing objectives a marketer uses obviously have considerable bearing on the determination of prices. For instance, an organization that uses pricing to increase its market share would likely set the brand's price below those of competing brands of similar quality to

Figure 19.8 **Factors That Affect Pricing Decisions**

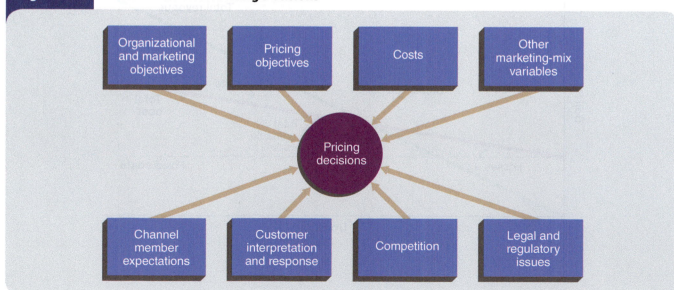

attract competitors' customers. Walmart's price objectives are illustrated by its slogan, "Save Money. Live Better." Walmart strives to help consumers save 25 percent or more on organic groceries. A marketer sometimes uses temporary price reductions in the hope of gaining market share. We examine pricing objectives in greater detail in Chapter 20.

19-5c Costs

Clearly, costs must be an issue when establishing price. A firm may temporarily sell products below cost to match competition, generate cash flow, or even increase market share, but in the long run, it cannot survive by selling its products below cost. Even a firm that has a high-volume business cannot survive if each item is sold slightly below its cost. A marketer should be careful to analyze all costs so they can be included in the total cost associated with a product.

To maintain market share and revenue in an increasingly price-sensitive market, many marketers have concentrated on reducing costs. For example, after losing market share to Airbus, Boeing embarked upon a number of cost-cutting measures. These measures included letting go more than a thousand employees.[8] Although many companies choose to cut costs by reducing their workforce, such a move should not be taken without careful consideration. Labor-saving technologies, a focus on quality, and efficient manufacturing processes have brought productivity gains that translate into reduced costs and lower prices for customers.

Besides considering the costs associated with a particular product, marketers must take into account the costs the product shares with others in the product line. Products often share some costs, particularly the costs of research and development, production, and distribution. Most marketers view a product's cost as a minimum, or floor, below which the product cannot be priced.

19-5d Marketing-Mix Variables

All marketing-mix variables are highly interrelated. Pricing decisions can influence evaluations and activities associated with product, distribution, and promotion variables. A product's price frequently affects the demand for that item, particularly for products with elastic demand. In such cases, a high price may result in lower unit sales, which in turn may lead to higher production costs per unit. Conversely, lower per-unit production costs may result in a lower price and higher unit sales. As noted, buyers may associate better product quality with a high price and poorer product quality with a low price. This perceived price–quality relationship influences customers' overall image of products or brands. Case in point, some individuals view Mercedes Benz vehicles as higher quality than other brands and are willing to pay a higher price to acquire them. Individuals who associate quality with a high price are likely to purchase products with well-established and recognizable brand names.

Selective Distribution
The maker of Solgar vitamins and supplements uses selective distribution to facilitate charging a higher price for its supplements.

The price of a product is linked to several dimensions of its distribution. Premium-priced products are often marketed through selective or exclusive distribution. Solgar, for instance, focuses on health food outlets to get its products to the consumer. The advertisement plays off the idiom "body and soul" by showing a large ampersand connecting "Body" and "Solgar." Solgar positions its vitamins and supplements as being pure, natural, and healthy and uses selective distribution. On the other hand, lower-priced products in the same product category may be sold through intensive distribution.

An increase in physical distribution costs, such as shipping, may have to be passed on to customers. When fuel prices increase significantly, shipping companies and airlines pass on these additional costs through surcharges or higher prices. When setting a price, the profit margins of marketing channel members, such as wholesalers and retailers, must also be considered. Channel members must be adequately compensated for the functions they perform.

Price may influence how a product is promoted. Bargain prices often appear in advertisements. Premium prices are less likely to be promoted, though they are sometimes included in advertisements for upscale items like luxury cars or fine jewelry. Higher-priced products are more likely than lower-priced ones to require personal selling. Furthermore, the price structure can affect a salesperson's relationship with customers. A complex pricing structure takes longer to explain to customers, is more likely to confuse potential buyers, and may cause misunderstandings that result in long-term customer dissatisfaction. Anyone who has tried to decipher his or her cell phone bill will empathize with the frustration that complex pricing structures can bring about. Trying to decipher charges for anytime, weekend, daytime, and roaming minutes, not to mention charges for smartphone data usage, can be confusing.

19-5e **Channel Member Expectations**

When making price decisions, a producer must consider what members of the distribution channel expect. A channel member certainly expects to receive a profit for the functions it performs. The amount of profit expected depends on what the intermediary could make if it were handling a competing product instead. Also, the amount of time and the resources required to carry the product influence intermediaries' expectations.

Channel members often expect producers to give discounts for large orders and prompt payment. For example, if POM Wonderful is selling directly to military bases, the government might expect the lowest possible price. At times, resellers expect producers to provide several support activities, such as sales training, service training, repair advisory service, cooperative advertising, sales promotions, and perhaps a program for returning unsold merchandise to the producer. These support activities clearly have associated costs that a producer must consider when determining prices.

19-5f **Customers' Interpretation and Response**

When making pricing decisions, marketers should address a vital question: How will our customers interpret our prices and respond to them? *Interpretation* in this context refers to what the price means or what it communicates to customers. Does the price signal "high quality" or "low quality;" or "great deal," "fair price," or "rip-off"? Customer *response* refers to whether the price will move customers closer to purchase of the product and the degree to which the price enhances their satisfaction with the purchase experience and with the product after purchase.

Customers' interpretation of, and response to, a price are to some degree determined by their assessment of value, or what they receive compared with what they give up to make the purchase. In evaluating what they receive, customers consider product attributes, benefits, advantages, disadvantages, the probability of using the product, and possibly the status

ENTREPRENEURSHIP IN MARKETING

Up, Up, and Away for Smart and Strong Luggage

Stephanie Korey and Jen Rubio began their luggage company, Away, after Rubio's suitcase broke during a trip and she couldn't find a replacement that was both well made and reasonably priced. The two friends, formerly coworkers at a successful e-business, conducted research to uncover consumers' problems with luggage. They heard complaints about lugging heavy bags to the airport, worries about being charged for overweight baggage, and frustration about wheels and zippers that break too soon. They also heard consumers wishing for a way to charge mobile gadgets while traveling.

Based on their research, Korey and Rubio developed a sturdy yet lightweight hard-shell suitcase that would stand up to the wear and tear of frequent travel. Then they added one more special feature: a built-in charging dock for phones and other digital

devices, powered by a removable battery. Customers can easily remove the charger from this "smart" luggage and use it to keep devices powered while in flight or on the road.

The entrepreneurs set up the Away website to sell directly to consumers rather than distributing through wholesalers and retailers, avoiding intermediary markups and keeping the final price reasonable. Their product line includes luggage priced from $225 to $295, depending on size, and all items are guaranteed for life. Customers can try the luggage for 100 days and return anything they don't like for a full refund if they're not completely satisfied. Thanks to high-quality materials, a "smart" design, and prices that don't break the bank, Away has already sold more than 100,000 pieces of luggage.[a]

associated with the product. In assessing the cost of the product, customers will likely consider its price, the amount of time and effort required to obtain it, and perhaps the resources required to maintain it after purchase.

When interpreting and responding to prices, how do customers determine if the price is too high, too low, or about right? In general, they compare prices with internal or external reference prices. An **internal reference price** is a price developed in the buyer's mind through experience with the product. It reflects a belief that a product should cost approximately a certain amount. To arrive at an internal reference price, consumers may consider one or more values, including what they think the product "ought" to cost, the price usually charged for it, the last price they paid, the highest and lowest amounts they would be willing to pay, the price of the brand they usually buy, the average price of similar products, the expected future price, and the typical discounted price.[9] Researchers have found that less-confident consumers tend to have higher internal reference prices than consumers with greater confidence, and frequent buyers—perhaps because of their experience and confidence—are more likely to judge high prices unfairly.[10] As consumers, our experiences have given each of us internal reference prices for a number of products. For instance, most of us have a reasonable idea of how much to pay for a 12-pack of soft drinks, a loaf of bread, or a cup of coffee.

For the product categories with which we have less experience, we rely more heavily on external reference prices. An **external reference price** is a comparison price provided by others, such as retailers or manufacturers. Some grocery and electronics stores, for example, will show other stores' prices next to their price of a particular good if their price is lower than the competitor's price. This provides a reference point for consumers unfamiliar with the product category. Customers' perceptions of prices are also influenced by their expectations about future price increases, what they paid for the product recently, and what they would like to pay for the product. Other factors affecting customers' perceptions of whether the price is right

internal reference price
A price developed in the buyer's mind through experience with the product

external reference price
A comparison price provided by others

For mom's birthday, they frosted ~~cupcakes.~~ *themselves.*

ARM & HAMMER™ PLUS OXICLEAN™
The **only** detergent to combine ARM & HAMMER™ Freshness with OxiClean™, America's #1 Stain Fighter Additive Brand.*

THE CLEAN YOU NEED AT A FRACTION OF THE COST.

armandhammer.com   *based on units sold. †per load vs. the leading detergent.

Value-Conscious Consumers
Arm & Hammer Plus Oxiclean is aimed at value-conscious consumers. The advertising message emphasizes high quality and low price.

include time or financial constraints, the costs associated with searching for lower-priced products, and expectations that products will go on sale.

Buyers' perceptions of a product relative to competing products may allow the firm to set a price that differs significantly from rivals' prices. If the product is deemed superior to most of the competition, a premium price may be feasible. However, even products with superior quality can be overpriced. Strong brand loyalty sometimes provides the opportunity to charge a premium price. On the other hand, if buyers view a product less than favorably (though not extremely negatively), a lower price may generate sales.

In the context of price, buyers can be characterized according to their degree of value consciousness, price consciousness, and prestige sensitivity. Marketers who understand these characteristics are better able to set pricing objectives and policies. **Value-conscious** consumers are concerned about both price and quality of a product.[11] The advertisement for Arm & Hammer uses humor in its Arm & Hammer Plus Oxiclean to convey that it cleans messes for a low price. The advertisement, which pictures children making a mess, emphasizes that the product is "the clean you need at a fraction of the cost." Value-conscious consumers may perceive value as quality per unit of price or as not only economic savings but also the additional gains expected from one product over a competitor's brand. The first view is appropriate for commodities like bottled water, bananas, and gasoline. If a value-conscious consumer perceives the quality of gasoline to be the same for Exxon and Shell, he or she will go to the station with the lower price. For consumers looking not just for economic value but additional gains they expect from one brand over another, a product differentiation value could be associated with benefits and features that are believed to be unique.[12] For instance, a BMW may be perceived to be better than a Cadillac.

Price-conscious individuals strive to pay low prices. They want the lowest prices, even if the products are not of the highest quality. Amazon.com has long been known for a willingness to sacrifice profit margins in favor of offering the lowest prices. Price-conscious consumers might also shop at extreme-value stores such as Dollar General and 99 Cents Only Stores. Commodity markets also tend to compete on price because consumers may not be able to tell the difference between competing products. Increasingly, department stores are opening discount outlets as a way to capture these price-conscious consumers. For instance, Macy's is opening off-price Backstage stores within a number of existing Macy's stores.[13] During uncertain economic periods, customers become more value and price conscious and tend to limit discretionary spending.

Prestige-sensitive buyers focus on purchasing products that signify prominence and status. For instance, Bentley, known for its luxury cars, introduced the Bentayga SUV with a W12 gasoline engine starting at $195,000.[14] The higher prices of prestige products convey a sense of exclusivity, creating demand among consumers who value the status associated with the product.

value-conscious Concerned about price and quality of a product

price-conscious Striving to pay low prices

prestige-sensitive Drawn to products that signify prominence and status

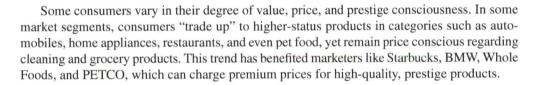

DISRUPTIVE MARKETING

Rent, Return, Repeat, or Try and Buy?

When Rent the Runway debuted in 2009, it pioneered the concept of renting designer fashions for special occasions. These days, CEO and co-founder Jennifer Hyman has an even more ambitious marketing plan that encourages consumers to rent stylish clothing for work or for everyday wear. If rentals become more widely popular, rental businesses could be on a collision course with the retail industry. Hyman understands the implications: "I want to put H&M and Zara out of business," she recently told a reporter.

Although the exact pricing differs from business to business, rental firms typically require consumers to set up an online account before they can select items to rent. Le Tote, for example, has three subscription plans, allowing either three, four, or five garment rentals per month for a flat fee. Subscribers can return any item at any time and receive a fresh item from their "virtual closet." If they want to own something they've rented, they pay a discounted price.

Now fashion manufacturers and retailers are trying rental plans. Ann Taylor offers a flat-fee subscription for renting its women's clothing, with unlimited exchanges and no deadlines for returns. Discount shoe retailer DSW is planning to offer shoe rentals. Amazon is taking a different approach. With Amazon Prime Wardrobe, customers can choose three or more apparel items to try on at home for seven days. Shipping and returns are free, and customers are charged only for what they keep. The more items they purchase, the bigger the discount. What's the future for "try and buy" and clothing rental plans?[b]

Some consumers vary in their degree of value, price, and prestige consciousness. In some market segments, consumers "trade up" to higher-status products in categories such as automobiles, home appliances, restaurants, and even pet food, yet remain price conscious regarding cleaning and grocery products. This trend has benefited marketers like Starbucks, BMW, Whole Foods, and PETCO, which can charge premium prices for high-quality, prestige products.

19-5g Competition

A marketer needs to know competitors' prices so the company's prices can be adjusted accordingly. This does not mean a company will necessarily match competitors' prices; it may set its price above or below theirs. However, for some organizations, matching competitors' prices is an important strategy for survival. United Airlines, for instance, planned to use larger aircraft and add more flights to allow it to lower fares to match those of low-cost airlines.[15] When adjusting prices, a marketer must assess how competitors will respond. Will competitors change their prices and, if so, will they raise or lower them? In Chapter 3, we described several types of competitive market structures. The structure that characterizes the industry to which a firm belongs affects the flexibility of price setting. Because of reduced pricing regulation, for instance, firms in the telecommunications industry have moved from a monopolistic market structure to an oligopolistic one, which has resulted in significant price competition for cell phone customers.

When an organization operates as a monopoly and is unregulated, it can set whatever prices the market will bear. However, the company may not price the product at the highest-possible level to avoid government regulation or penetrate a market by using a lower price. If the monopoly is regulated, it normally has less pricing flexibility; the regulatory body lets it set prices that generate a reasonable but not excessive return. A government-owned monopoly may price products below cost to make them accessible to people who otherwise could not afford them. Transit systems, for example, sometimes operate this way. However, government-owned monopolies sometimes charge higher prices to control demand. In some states with state-owned liquor stores, the price of liquor is higher than in states where liquor stores are not owned by a government body.

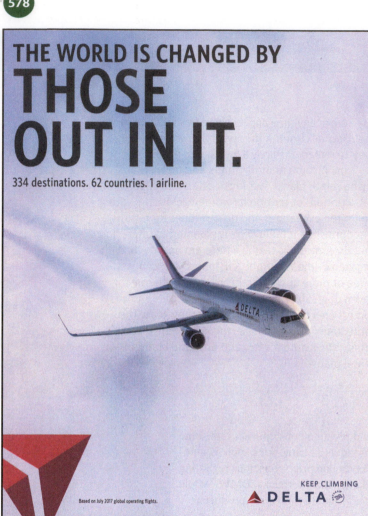

THE WORLD IS CHANGED BY
THOSE
OUT IN IT.

334 destinations. 62 countries. 1 airline.

Based on July 2017 global operating flights.

KEEP CLIMBING
DELTA

SOURCE: DELTA AIRLINES

Oligopolistic Competition

Airlines, such as Delta, engage in oligopolistic competition in the United States. The pricing of airline tickets can be affected by this type of competitive market structure. If an airline increases ticket prices by a small amount, one or more competitors may decide to increase ticket prices up to the same level. If competitors do not increase their ticket prices, the airline that initiated the price increase is likely to reduce its prices back to the original price level.

The automotive and airline industries exemplify oligopolies, in which only a few sellers operate and barriers to competitive entry are high. Companies in such industries can raise their prices in the hope that competitors will do the same. When an organization cuts its price to gain a competitive edge, other companies are likely to follow suit. This happens frequently in the airline industry. Consider the advertisement for Delta Airlines, which pictures a jetliner and describes the places to which passengers can fly on Delta. The advertisement promotes that "the world is changed by those out in it" to try to differentiate itself from other major competitors in the industry. However, generally there is very little advantage gained through price cuts in an oligopolistic market structure because competitors will often follow suit.

A market structure characterized by monopolistic competition has numerous sellers with product offerings that are differentiated by physical characteristics, features, quality, and brand images. The distinguishing characteristics of its products may allow a company to set a different price from its competitors. Firms in a monopolistic competitive market structure are likely to practice nonprice competition, discussed earlier in this chapter.

Under conditions of perfect competition, many sellers exist. Buyers view all sellers' products as the same. All firms sell their products at the going market price, and buyers will not pay more than that. This type of market structure, then, gives a marketer no flexibility in setting prices. Farming, as an industry, has some characteristics of perfect competition. Farmers sell their products at the going market price. At times, for example, corn, soybean, and wheat growers have had bumper crops and have been forced to sell them at depressed market prices. In countries in which farm subsidies are provided, the effects of perfect competition are reduced.

19-5h   Legal and Regulatory Issues

Legal and regulatory issues also influence pricing decisions. To curb inflation, the federal government can invoke price controls, freeze prices at certain levels, or determine the rates at which firms may increase prices. In some states and many other countries, regulatory agencies set prices on such products as insurance, dairy products, and liquor. Many regulations and laws affect pricing decisions and activities in the United States. Many other nations and trade agreements have similar prohibitions.

The Sherman Antitrust Act prohibits conspiracies to control prices, and in interpreting the act, courts have ruled that price fixing among firms in an industry is illegal. **Price fixing** is an agreement among competing firms to raise, lower, or maintain prices for mutual benefit. To avoid the appearance of price fixing, marketers must develop independent pricing policies and set prices in ways that do not even hint at collusion. Bumble Bee Foods pleaded guilty to

price fixing An agreement among competing firms to raise, lower, or maintain prices for mutual benefit conspiring to fix the price of packaged tuna products over a period of two years. The company paid a criminal fine of $25 million, changed its corporate policies, and hired a compliance officer to help it regain consumers' trust.[16]

Both the Federal Trade Commission Act and the Wheeler-Lea Act prohibit deceptive pricing. **Deceptive pricing** is the use of false or misleading statements or practices to persuade buyers that a product is a better deal than it really is. As an example, TJX Companies agreed to pay $8.5 million to settle a class-action lawsuit that claimed that its Marshalls, T.J. Maxx, and HomeGoods stores used misleading price tags to deceive shoppers into believing they were getting a better bargain. The three stores had been accused of using fabricated higher-than-actual prices on its "Compare At" price tags to make shoppers think the stores' sale prices were a better deal than they really were.[17] In establishing prices, marketers must guard against deceiving customers.

Another law with a strong impact on pricing decisions is the Robinson-Patman Act. For various reasons, marketers may wish to sell the same type of product at different prices. Provisions in the Robinson-Patman Act, as well as those in the Clayton Act, limit the use of such price differentials. **Price discrimination**, the practice of employing price differentials that tend to injure competition by giving one or more buyers a competitive advantage over other buyers, is prohibited by law. Many people are surprised to learn that they may be charged a different price for the same product than somebody else. Companies selling online have used user information on geographic location, platform (PC versus Mac, desktop versus mobile), frequency of purchase, browser history, and/or other characteristics to determine which price to present to an online shopper. Although this practice is not illegal, many internet shoppers have expressed dismay because they view the practice as unfair.[18] A marketer may use price differentials if they result from differences in the costs of selling or transportation to various customers, arise because the firm has had to cut its price to a particular buyer to meet competitors' prices, or do not hinder competition. Airlines, for example, may charge different customers different prices for the same flights based on the availability of seats at the time of purchase. As a result, flyers sitting in adjacent seats may have paid vastly different fares because one passenger booked weeks ahead, whereas the other booked on the spur of the moment a few days before when only a few seats were still available.

Another practice that can be illegal is predatory pricing. **Predatory pricing**, also called undercutting, involves the intent to set a product's price so low that rival firms cannot compete and, therefore, withdraw from the marketplace. Determining whether predatory pricing is occurring can be difficult in actual practice and thus actionable charges have been rare. It is not unusual for a company to set a price that is below cost temporarily in order to sell off unsalable products or excess capacity; without the intent to drive out competitors, there is no predatory pricing.

A global problem affecting business pricing strategies is the growing market for counterfeit goods. These products are typically bought because of their significantly lower prices. Such low prices should signal that the products are fake and of lower quality, but some bargain shoppers actually seek them out. Counterfeit prescription drugs sold through websites are especially problematic as they seldom contain the promoted drug and may even contain dangerous ingredients. Counterfeit goods are regulated on a country-by-country basis. More sales that are lost to the "gray market" means lower profits and potentially higher prices for the legitimate goods.

deceptive pricing The use of false or misleading statements or practices to persuade buyers that a product is a better deal than it really is

price discrimination Employing price differentials that injure competition by giving one or more buyers a competitive advantage

predatory pricing Also called undercutting, involves the intent to set a product's price so low that rival firms cannot compete and, therefore, withdraw from the marketplace

Counterfeit Products
Efforts to copy luxury goods result in declining profits for manufacturers and potentially higher prices for watch buyers who want authentic products.

LAUGHINGMANGO/ISTOCK UNRELEASED/GETTY IMAGES

Learning Objective 19-6

Identify seven methods companies can use to price products for business markets.

19-6 **PRICING FOR BUSINESS MARKETS**

As we saw in Chapter 8, establishing prices for business buyers that purchase products for resale, use those products in their own operations, or produce other products sometimes differs from setting prices for consumers. Differences in the size of purchases, geographic factors, and transportation considerations require sellers to adjust prices. In this section, we discuss several issues unique to the pricing of business products, including discounts, geographic pricing, and transfer pricing.

19-6a **Price Discounting**

Producers commonly provide intermediaries with discounts, or reductions, from list prices. Although many types of discounts exist, they usually fall into one of five categories: trade, quantity, cash, seasonal, and allowance. Table 19.3 summarizes some reasons to use each type of discount and provides examples. Such discounts can be a significant factor in a marketing strategy.

Trade Discounts

A reduction off the list price given by a producer to an intermediary for performing certain functions is called a **trade (functional) discount**. A trade discount is usually stated in terms of a percentage or series of percentages off the list price. Intermediaries are given trade discounts as compensation for performing various functions, such as selling, transporting, storing, final processing, and perhaps providing credit services. Although certain trade discounts are often standard practice within an industry, discounts vary considerably among industries. It is important that a manufacturer provide a trade discount large enough to offset the intermediary's costs, plus a reasonable profit, to entice the reseller to carry the product.

trade (functional) discount
A reduction off the list price a producer gives to an intermediary for performing certain functions

Table 19.3   **Discounts Used for Business Markets**

Type	Reasons for Use	Examples
Trade	To attract and keep effective resellers by compensating them for performing certain functions, such as transportation, warehousing, selling, and providing credit	A college bookstore pays about (functional) one-third less for a new textbook than the retail price a student pays.
Quantity	To encourage customers to buy large quantities when making purchases and, in the case of cumulative discounts, to encourage customer loyalty	Large department store chains purchase some women's apparel at lower prices than do individually owned specialty stores.
Cash	To reduce expenses associated with accounts receivable and collection by encouraging prompt payment of accounts	Numerous companies serving business markets allow a 2 percent discount if an account is paid within 10 days.
Seasonal	To allow a marketer to use resources more efficiently by stimulating sales during off-peak periods	Florida hotels provide companies holding national and regional sales meetings with deeply discounted accommodations during the summer months.
Allowance	In the case of a trade-in allowance, to assist the buyer in making the purchase and potentially earning a profit on the resale of used equipment; in the case of a promotional allowance, to ensure that dealers participate in advertising and sales support programs	A farm equipment dealer takes a farmer's used tractor as a trade-in on a new one. Nabisco pays a promotional allowance to a supermarket for setting up and maintaining a large, end-of-aisle display for a 2-week period.

Quantity Discounts

Deductions from list price that reflect the economies of purchasing in large quantities are called **quantity discounts**. Quantity discounts are used in many industries and pass on to the buyer cost savings gained through economies of scale. Quantity discounts can be either cumulative or noncumulative. **Cumulative discounts** are quantity discounts aggregated over a stated time period. Purchases totaling $10,000 in a 3-month period, for example, might entitle the buyer to a 5 percent, or $500, rebate. Such discounts are intended to reflect economies in selling and encourage the buyer to purchase from one seller. **Noncumulative discounts** are one-time reductions in prices based on the number of units purchased, the dollar value of the order, or the product mix purchased. Like cumulative discounts, these discounts should reflect some economies in selling or trade functions.

Cash Discounts

A **cash discount**, or price reduction, is given to a buyer for prompt payment or cash payment. Accounts receivable are an expense and a collection problem for many organizations. A policy to encourage prompt payment is a popular practice and sometimes a major concern in setting prices. Discounts are based on cash payments or cash paid within a stated time. For instance, "2/10 net 30" means that a 2 percent discount will be allowed if the account is paid within 10 days. If the buyer does not make payment within the 10-day period, the entire balance is due within 30 days without a discount. If the account is not paid within 30 days, interest may be charged.

Seasonal Discounts

A price reduction to buyers who purchase goods or services out of season is a **seasonal discount**. These discounts let the seller maintain steadier production during the year. Thus, it is usually much cheaper to purchase and install an air-conditioning unit in the winter than it is in the summer. This is because demand for air conditioners is very low during the winter in most parts of the country, and price, therefore, is also lower than in peak-demand season.

Allowances

Another type of reduction from the list price is an **allowance**, a concession in price to achieve a desired goal. Trade-in allowances, for example, are price reductions granted for turning in a used item when purchasing a new one. Allowances help make the buyer better able to make the new purchase. Another example is a promotional allowance, a price reduction granted to dealers for participating in advertising and sales support programs intended to increase sales of a particular item.

19-6b **Geographic Pricing**

Geographic pricing involves reductions for transportation costs or other costs associated with the physical distance between buyer and seller. Prices may be quoted as F.O.B. (free-on-board) factory or destination. An **F.O.B. factory** price indicates the price of the merchandise at the factory, before it is loaded onto the carrier, and thus excludes transportation costs. The buyer must pay for shipping. An **F.O.B. destination** price means the producer absorbs the costs of shipping the merchandise to the customer. This policy may be used to attract distant customers. Although F.O.B. pricing is an easy way to price products, it is sometimes difficult to administer, especially when a firm has a wide product mix or when customers are widely dispersed. Because customers will want to know about the most economical method of shipping, the seller must be informed about shipping rates.

---

quantity discounts Deductions from the list price for purchasing in large quantities

cumulative discounts Quantity discounts aggregated over a stated time period

noncumulative discounts One-time price reductions based on the number of units purchased, the dollar value of the order, or the product mix purchased

cash discount A price reduction given to buyers for prompt payment or cash payment

seasonal discount A price reduction given to buyers for purchasing goods or services out of season

allowance A concession in price to achieve a desired goal

geographic pricing Reductions for transportation and other costs related to the physical distance between buyer and seller

F.O.B. factory The price of merchandise at the factory before shipment

F.O.B. destination A price indicating the producer is absorbing shipping costs

To avoid the problems involved in charging different prices to each customer, **uniform geographic pricing**, sometimes called *postage-stamp pricing*, may be used. The same price is charged to all customers regardless of geographic location, and the price is based on average shipping costs for all customers. Paper products and office equipment are often priced on a uniform basis.

Zone pricing sets uniform prices for each of several major geographic zones; as the transportation costs across zones increase, so do the prices. For instance, a Florida manufacturer's prices may be higher for buyers on the Pacific coast and in Canada than for buyers in Georgia.

Base-point pricing is a geographic pricing policy that includes the price at the factory, plus freight charges from the base point nearest the buyer. This approach to pricing has virtually been abandoned because of its questionable legal status. The policy resulted in all buyers paying freight charges from one location, such as Detroit or Pittsburgh, regardless of where the product was manufactured.

When the seller absorbs all or part of the actual freight costs, it is using **freight absorption pricing**. The seller might choose this method because it wishes to do business with a particular customer or to get more business; more business will cause the average cost to fall and counterbalance the extra freight cost. This strategy is used to improve market penetration and retain a hold in an increasingly competitive market.

uniform geographic pricing
Charging all customers the same price, regardless of geographic location

zone pricing Pricing based on transportation costs within major geographic zones

base-point pricing Geographic pricing that combines factory price and freight charges from the base point nearest the buyer

freight absorption pricing Absorption of all or part of actual freight costs by the seller

transfer pricing Prices charged in sales between an organization's units

19-6c Transfer Pricing

Transfer pricing occurs when one unit in an organization sells a product to another unit. The price is determined by one of the following methods:

- *Actual full cost:* calculated by dividing all fixed and variable expenses for a period into the number of units produced.
- *Standard full cost:* calculated based on what it would cost to produce the goods at full plant capacity.
- *Cost plus investment:* calculated as full cost plus the cost of a portion of the selling unit's assets used for internal needs.
- *Market-based cost:* calculated at the market price less a small discount to reflect the lack of sales effort and other expenses.

The choice of transfer pricing method depends on the company's management strategy and the nature of the units' interaction. An organization must also ensure that transfer pricing is fair to all units involved in the transactions.

Summary

19-1 Summarize why price is important to the marketing mix.

Price is the value paid for a product in a marketing exchange. Barter, the trading of products, is the oldest form of exchange. Price is a key element in the marketing mix, because it relates directly to generation of total revenue. The profit factor can be determined mathematically by multiplying price by quantity sold to get total revenue and then subtracting total costs. Price is the only variable in the marketing mix that can be adjusted quickly and easily to respond to changes in the external environment.

19-2 Compare price competition with nonprice competition.

A product offering can compete on either a price or a nonprice basis. Price competition emphasizes price as the product differential. Prices fluctuate frequently, and price competition among sellers is aggressive. A price war involves two or more companies engaging in intense price competition. Nonprice competition emphasizes product differentiation through distinctive features, service, product quality, or other factors. Establishing brand loyalty by using nonprice competition works best when the product can be physically differentiated and the customer can recognize these differences.

19-3 Explore the role of demand curves and the price elasticity of demand.

An organization must determine the demand for its product. The classic demand curve is a graph of the quantity of products expected to be sold at various prices if other factors hold constant. It illustrates that, as price falls, the quantity demanded usually increases. However, for prestige products, there is a direct positive relationship between price and quantity demanded. Demand increases as price increases. Next, price elasticity of demand, the percentage change in quantity demanded relative to a given percentage change in price, must be determined. If demand is elastic, a change in price causes an opposite change in total revenue. Inelastic demand results in a parallel change in total revenue when a product's price is changed.

19-4 Describe the relationships among demand, costs, and profits.

Analysis of demand, cost, and profit relationships can be accomplished through marginal analysis or breakeven analysis. Marginal analysis examines what happens to a firm's costs and revenues when production (or sales volume) is changed by one unit. Marginal analysis combines the demand curve with the firm's costs to develop a price that yields maximum profit. Fixed costs do not vary with changes in the number of units produced or sold; average fixed cost is the fixed cost per unit produced. Variable costs vary directly with changes in the number of units produced or sold. Average variable cost is the variable cost per unit produced. Total cost is the sum of average fixed cost and average variable cost times the quantity produced. The optimal price is the point at which marginal cost (the cost associated with producing one more unit of the product) equals marginal revenue (the change in total revenue that occurs when one additional unit of the product is sold). Marginal analysis is only a model; it offers little help in pricing new products before costs and revenues are established.

Breakeven analysis, determining the number of units that must be sold to break even, is important in setting price. The point at which the costs of production equal the revenue from selling the product is the breakeven point. To use breakeven analysis effectively, a marketer should determine the breakeven point for each of several alternative prices. This makes it possible to compare the effects on total revenue, total costs, and the breakeven point for each price under consideration. However, this approach assumes the quantity demanded is basically fixed and the major task is to set prices to recover costs.

19-5 Describe eight key factors that may influence marketers' pricing decisions.

Eight factors enter into price decision making: organizational and marketing objectives, pricing objectives, costs, other marketing-mix variables, channel member expectations, customer interpretation and response, competition, and legal and regulatory issues. When setting prices, marketers should make decisions consistent with the organization's goals and mission. Pricing objectives heavily influence price-setting decisions. Most marketers view a product's cost as the floor below which a product cannot be priced. Because of the interrelationship among the marketing-mix variables, price can affect product, promotion, and distribution decisions. What the revenue channel members expect for their functions must also be considered when making price decisions.

Buyers' perceptions of price vary. Some consumer segments are sensitive to price, but others may not be. Thus, before determining price, a marketer needs to be aware of its importance to the target market. Knowledge of the prices charged for competing brands is essential to allow the firm to adjust its prices relative to competitors' prices. Government regulations and legislation also influence pricing decisions, especially with regard to practices such as price fixing, deceptive pricing, and predatory pricing.

19-6 Identify seven methods companies can use to price products for business markets.

The categories of discounts include trade, quantity, cash, seasonal, and allowance. A trade discount is a price reduction for performing such functions as storing, transporting, final processing, or providing credit services. If an intermediary purchases in large enough quantities, the producer gives a quantity discount, which can be either cumulative or noncumulative. A cash discount is a price reduction for prompt payment or payment in cash. Buyers who purchase goods or services out of season may be granted a seasonal discount. An allowance, such as a trade-in allowance, is a concession in price to achieve a desired goal.

Geographic pricing involves reductions for transportation costs or other costs associated with the physical distance between buyer and seller. With an F.O.B. factory price, the buyer pays for shipping from the factory. An F.O.B. destination price means the producer pays for shipping; this is the easiest way to price products, but it is difficult to administer. When the seller charges a fixed average cost for transportation, it is using uniform geographic pricing. Zone prices are uniform within major geographic zones; they increase by zone as transportation costs increase. With base-point pricing, prices are adjusted for shipping expenses incurred by the seller from the base point nearest the buyer. Freight absorption pricing occurs when a seller absorbs all or part of the freight costs.

Transfer pricing occurs when a unit in an organization sells products to another unit in the organization. Methods used for transfer pricing include actual full cost, standard full cost, cost plus investment, and market-based cost.

Important Terms

price 562
barter 562
price competition 563
price war 563
nonprice competition 564
demand curve 565
price elasticity of demand 566
fixed costs 568
average fixed cost 568
variable costs 568
average variable cost 568

total cost 568
average total cost 568
marginal cost (MC) 568
marginal revenue (MR) 568
breakeven point 571
internal reference price 575
external reference price 575
value-conscious 576
price-conscious 576

prestige-sensitive 576
price fixing 578
deceptive pricing 579
price discrimination 579
predatory pricing 579
trade (functional) discount 580
quantity discounts 581
cumulative discounts 581
noncumulative discounts 581
cash discount 581

seasonal discount 581
allowance 581
geographic pricing 581
F.O.B. factory 581
F.O.B. destination 581
uniform geographic pricing 582
zone pricing 582
base-point pricing 582
freight absorption pricing 582
transfer pricing 582

Discussion and Review Questions

1. Why are pricing decisions important to an organization?
2. Compare and contrast price and nonprice competition. Describe the conditions under which each form works best.
3. Why do most demand curves demonstrate an inverse relationship between price and quantity?
4. List the characteristics of products that have inelastic demand, and give several examples of such products.
5. Explain why optimal profits should occur when marginal cost equals marginal revenue.
6. Chambers Company has just gathered estimates for conducting a breakeven analysis for a new product. Variable costs are $7 a unit. The additional plant will cost $48,000. The new product will be charged $18,000 a year for its share of general overhead. Advertising expenditures will be $80,000, and $55,000 will be spent on distribution. If the product sells for $12, what is the breakeven point in units? What is the breakeven point in dollar sales volume?
7. In what ways do other marketing-mix variables affect pricing decisions?
8. What types of expectations may channel members have about producers' prices? How might these expectations affect pricing decisions?
9. How do legal and regulatory forces influence pricing decisions?
10. Compare and contrast a trade discount and a quantity discount.
11. What is the reason for using the term *F.O.B.*?
12. What are the major methods used for transfer pricing?

Developing Your Marketing Plan

The appropriate pricing of a product is an important factor in developing a successful marketing strategy. The price contributes to the profitability of the product and can deter competition from entering the market. A clear understanding of pricing concepts is essential in developing a strategy and marketing plan. Consider the information in this chapter when focusing on the following issues:

1. Does your company currently compete based on price or nonprice factors? Should your new product continue with this approach?

2. Discuss the level of elasticity of demand for your product. Is additional information needed for you to determine its elasticity?
3. At various price points, calculate the breakeven point for sales of your product.
4. Using Figure 19.8 as a guide, discuss the various factors that affect the pricing of your product.

Video Case 19.1

Louis Vuitton Bags the Value Shopper

For luxury-goods maker Louis Vuitton, price is a critical part of its marketing strategy. However, unlike most other companies, demand for Louis Vuitton products tends to rise with price increases. This is because its target market focuses on prestige-sensitive buyers—those who purchase products that signify prominence and status. These types of products carry an air of exclusivity because they demonstrate to others that the buyer has enough money to afford them. Louis Vuitton has targeted the elite since its founding in 1854 when it began selling luxury luggage to the rich. Today, the company sells leather goods, handbags, trunks, watches, and other accessories.

It would be a mistake, however, to assume that Louis Vuitton products are completely price inelastic. While demand for its products may increase as the price increases, this will occur only to a certain level. Afterward, demand will begin decreasing. Luxury brands like Louis Vuitton also face a constant balancing act. While they can price their products top dollar to attract the elite, this market is relatively small. On the other hand, there are many prestige-conscious customers willing to pay higher prices for Louis Vuitton products but who cannot afford a $50,000 price tag. In order to reach these consumers, it must develop products that are priced lower but still carry enough prestige that consumers will desire their brand. Darla Thomas, a researcher into luxury brands, describes this pricing strategy as "a delicate balance of selling to the masses while still remaining exclusive to the rich."

To retain this exclusive image, Louis Vuitton works hard to make its brand seem expensive and somewhat unattainable. Price is a critical factor, and Louis Vuitton often raises prices to try and jumpstart sales by emphasizing its exclusive, top-quality image. For instance, Louis Vuitton raised its prices 13 percent during a time when sales were flatlining to increase demand for its leather and canvas monogrammed bags. It also engages in nonprice competition through promotion, especially when it comes to celebrities endorsing the product. Famous endorsers have included actress Angelina Jolie, musician Bono, and athlete Michael Phelps.

Darla Thomas describes Louis Vuitton's product and pricing strategies as similar to a pyramid. "At the top you have the very beautifully made, exclusive, limited amount of product. They will make anything you want. From there you have the middle range that you can walk into a store and you can buy it. . . . And then you have the bottom range where the money comes in."

For many years, developing countries such as China were top markets for luxury brands. As the middle classes increased, so did the desire to demonstrate the ability to

afford nice products. Darla Thomas uses an example of a Chinese secretary "who wants to put the bag on her desk to show that she can afford a Louis Vuitton bag" as an example of this emerging middle class. These pricing strategies have worked well for Louis Vuitton. With a value of $28.8 billion, Louis Vuitton is one of the most profitable luxury brands with profit margins of 40 percent.

On the other hand, this means that luxury brand makers like Louis Vuitton are highly dependent upon a thriving economy. As economies slow in China, Russia, and Brazil, demand for luxury goods falls. In harder economic times, consumers become more value-conscious, desiring quality products at more affordable prices. In recent years, a weaker euro has encouraged consumers from China to come to France and purchase Louis Vuitton products, keeping sales stable. However, desire for Louis Vuitton could be diminishing, prompting the brand to reassess its marketing strategy.

Part of the problem could be that Louis Vuitton has over-expanded. While it only had two stores in 1977, today it has more than 460. This not only creates costs for Louis Vuitton, but could also cheapen its image as an exclusive brand. Competition is also intense, with major competitors including Kering, Gucci, and Hermes. Whatever the cause, pricing remains a key component in developing demand. Louis Vuitton is, therefore, constantly monitoring, reevaluating, and updating its pricing policies to compete with competitors and increase global demand.[19]

Questions for Discussion

1. Are Louis Vuitton products price elastic or inelastic? Why?
2. What type of factors do you think most affect Louis Vuitton's pricing decisions?
3. Generally, what should happen when Louis Vuitton raises its prices? Why is there a limit to how high it can increase its pricing?

Case 19.2

CVS: Continuous Value Strategy

In the United States, the retail pharmacy field is dominated by two large firms, Walgreens and CVS. CVS, the second largest pharmacy chain, is constantly competing against Walgreens for market share, especially in its quest to become more of a health-care management company.

One way in which CVS attracts customers is through its pricing strategies. CVS employs price discounts through several methods, including in-store discounts. Retail stores often display discounted prices through the use of shelf signs on individual products. In addition, CVS mails coupons and store-wide purchase discounts to customers and offers a number of online discounts through CVS.com. When customers link their CVS ExtraCare® cards to the company's myWeekly Ad website, they receive weekly sales updates. The ExtraCare® card also gives customers access to personalized coupons in-store and through mobile apps.

CVS provides other consumer sales promotions as well. For instance, customers can save money and get free shipping if they order their prescriptions through the mail with its CVS Caremark Mail Service Pharmacy. Its iSave program also helps consumers save on costs. In this program, CVS has partnered with more than 270,000 providers in different areas of health care. Customers who make appointments with these providers and identify themselves as iSave members can save money on these services. CVS's website also offers information on rebates for selected products. Additionally, CVS shows its commitment toward veterans

with its Veterans Advantage program. Under this program, veterans can receive 20 percent discounts on products and free shipping on online orders.

CVS's MinuteClinics are also important to consumers because they provide basic care at less cost than going to the doctor. Many people visit MinuteClinics when they are sick or wish to get basic services such as flu shots. The clinics are staffed with certified nurse practitioners and physician assistants qualified in medicine. One major criticism against CVS's MinuteClinics is that customers might choose to go to the clinics when they have extreme illnesses rather than the hospital or doctor's office. However, the CVS MinuteClinic website contains information that describes their limitations and when consumers should visit their doctors. CVS's MinuteClinics accept most types of insurance and have had more than 37 million patient visits.

CVS assists patients in another important—albeit behind-the-scenes—way. The company has been a tough negotiator when negotiating drug prices with pharmaceutical companies. CVS negotiates drug prices for more than 94 million people across the nation. Sometimes this has required CVS to take a tough stance and be willing to drop drugs from its insurance unless the drug makers lower the prices. For example, CVS dropped 26 drugs, including Viagra, from its prescription drug insurance in favor of comparable drugs with lower costs. An analysis has revealed that the attempts of drug makers to raise prices have been

JETCITYIMAGE/ISTOCK EDITORIAL/GETTY IMAGES

mitigated by the strong negotiation tactics of companies such as CVS and Express Scripts. During a time when some drug makers are raising the prices of medications 50-fold, the use of negotiation is crucial toward keeping prices affordable for consumers.

In 2015, CVS acquired Target's in-store pharmacy and clinic. This has raised some concerns that prices could increase for Target pharmacy customers. Whenever two large companies merge, there is less competition in the marketplace. Firms with more control could, therefore, raise prices. Some believe that the prices will increase for Target pharmacy customers because Target—as a discount store—has traditionally been more focused on keeping prices low than CVS has. However, others believe the merger might result in savings for the customer. One health industry economic analyst suggests that the merger of the two big firms will improve relationships with wholesalers and suppliers of drugs, which could result in cost savings that CVS could then pass on to the customer.

It is clear that pharmacies such as CVS are important in negotiating prices of prescription drugs. The discounts and programs they offer are also important in helping consumers to afford their medications. The cost savings CVS has to offer has made it a popular pharmacy destination for American consumers.[20]

Questions for Discussion

1. Why is price competition such an issue for CVS as it fights to gain market share?
2. Describe ways CVS uses sales promotion techniques to provide price discounts.
3. Why is it important for CVS to negotiate with pharmaceutical companies on the prices of drugs?

20

Setting Prices

LEARNING OBJECTIVES

20-1 Identify issues related to developing pricing objectives.

20-2 Discuss the importance of identifying the target market's evaluation of price.

20-3 Explain how marketers analyze competitors' prices.

20-4 Analyze the bases used for setting prices.

20-5 Compare the different types of pricing strategies.

20-6 Describe the selection of a specific price.

JETCITYIMAGE/ISTOCK EDITORIAL/GETTY IMAGES

Aldi Spotlights Low Grocery Prices

Aldi, based in Germany, wants to shake up the U.S. supermarket industry with hundreds of new stores featuring deeply discounted groceries and low-priced private brands. The company has had a U.S. presence for more than 40 years. Now Aldi is expanding from its current network of 1,600 stores in 35 states to at least 2,500 stores by 2022. The goal is to sharply boost market share by targeting price-sensitive consumers at all income levels. Every store will put the spotlight on low prices, turning up the competitive heat on such well-known retail rivals as Kroger, Walmart, and Albertsons.

Aldi originally featured a limited selection of private brands and fresh produce in a low-frills retail environment. In recent years, it has broadened its appeal to mainstream U.S. consumers by renovating some stores, adding more manufacturers' brands, and increasing its assortment of organic foods, fresh fish, and fresh meats. Aldi is also testing home delivery in Dallas, Atlanta, and Los Angeles, with an eye toward the possibility of adding an online grocery service in the future.

However, Aldi isn't the only deep-discount grocery retailer from Germany with big plans for the U.S. market. Lidl, another German supermarket company known for super-low prices and private brands, opened more than three dozen U.S. stores in 2017. As a result of increasingly intense retail competition across the country, Aldi could very well find itself in the middle of a supermarket price war. No matter what happens, a spokesperson says Aldi is ready "to ensure we're the low-cost leader."[1]

Because price has such a profound impact on a firm's bottom line, finding the right pricing strategy is crucial, especially for firms employing a strategy of price competition. Marketers must carefully select a pricing strategy that is both profitable for the company and reasonable to the customers. Selecting a pricing strategy is one of the fundamental components of the process of setting prices.

In this chapter, we examine six stages of a process that marketers can use when setting prices. Figure 20.1 illustrates these stages. Stage 1 is the development of a pricing objective that is compatible with the organization's overall marketing objectives. Stage 2 entails assessing the target market's evaluation of price. Stage 3 involves evaluating competitors' prices, which helps determine the role of price in the marketing strategy. Stage 4 requires choosing a basis for setting prices. Stage 5 is the selection of a pricing strategy, or the guidelines for using price in the marketing mix. Stage 6, determining the final price, depends on environmental forces and marketers' understanding and use of a systematic approach to establishing prices. These stages are guidelines that provide a logical sequence for establishing prices, not rigid steps that must be followed in a particular order.

Learning Objective 20-1

Identify issues related to developing pricing objectives.

20-1 DEVELOPMENT OF PRICING OBJECTIVES

The first step in setting prices is developing **pricing objectives**—goals that describe what a firm wants to achieve through pricing. Specifying pricing objectives is an important task because these form the basis for decisions for other stages of the pricing process. Thus, pricing objectives must be stated explicitly and in measurable terms. Objectives should also include a time frame for accomplishing them.

Marketers must ensure that pricing objectives are consistent with the firm's marketing and overall objectives because pricing objectives influence decisions in many functional areas, including finance, accounting, and production. A marketer can use both short- and long-term pricing objectives and can employ one or multiple pricing objectives. For instance, a firm may wish to increase market share by 18 percent over the next three years, achieve a 15 percent return on investment, and promote an image of quality in the marketplace. In this section, we identify some of the pricing objectives companies might set. Table 20.1 shows the major pricing objectives and typical actions associated with them.

pricing objectives Goals that describe what a firm wants to achieve through pricing

| **Figure 20.1** | **Stages for Establishing Prices** |

1. Development of pricing objectives
2. Assessment of target market's evaluation of price
3. Evaluation of competitors' prices
4. Selection of a basis for pricing
5. Selection of a pricing strategy
6. Determination of a specific price

Table 20.1 Pricing Objectives and Typical Actions Taken to Achieve Them

Objective	Possible Action
Survival	Adjust price levels so the firm can increase sales volume to match organizational expenses.
Profit	Identify price and cost levels that allow the firm to maximize profit.
Return on investment	Identify price levels that enable the firm to yield targeted ROI.
Market share	Adjust price levels so the firm can maintain or increase sales relative to competitors' sales.
Cash flow	Set price levels to encourage rapid sales.
Status quo	Identify price levels that help stabilize demand and sales.
Product quality	Set prices to recover research and development expenditures and establish a high-quality image.

20-1a Survival

Survival is one of the most fundamental pricing objectives. Achieving this objective generally involves temporarily setting prices low, at times below costs, in order to attract more sales. Because price is a flexible ingredient in the marketing mix, survival strategy can be useful in keeping a company afloat by increasing sales volume. Most organizations will tolerate setbacks, such as short-run losses and internal upheaval, if necessary for survival.

20-1b Profit

Although a business may claim that its objective is to maximize profits for its owners, the objective of profit maximization is rarely operational because its achievement is difficult to measure. Therefore, profit objectives tend to be set at levels that the owners and top-level decision makers view as satisfactory and attainable. Specific profit objectives may be stated in terms of either actual dollar amounts or a percentage of sales revenues.

20-1c Return on Investment

Pricing to attain a specified rate of return on the company's investment is a profit-related pricing objective. A return on investment (ROI) pricing objective generally requires some trial and error, as it is unusual for all data and inputs required to determine the necessary ROI to be available when first setting prices. Many pharmaceutical companies use ROI pricing objectives because of the high level of investment in research and development required.

20-1d Market Share

Many firms establish pricing objectives to maintain or increase market share, which is a product's sales in relation to total industry sales. For instance, Gillette reduced prices on its razors in a bid to regain some market share lost to start-up razor clubs like Harry's and Dollar Shave Club. Gillette's market share fell from 70 percent to 54 percent after Dollar Shave Club entered the market with its subscription razor refill service.[2] High relative market shares often translate into high profits for firms. The Profit Impact of Market Strategies (PIMS) studies, conducted annually since the 1960s, have shown that both market share and product quality influence profitability.[3] Thus, marketers often use an increase in market share as a primary pricing objective.

Maintaining or increasing market share need not depend on growth in industry sales. An organization can increase its market share even if sales for the total industry are flat or

At STIHL Incorporated, the real story is the team behind our world-class machines. It's a team made up of real people – our employees who build the product, the STIHL Dealers who sell and service the product, and of course our customers who depend on STIHL quality for use at their homes and businesses. It is those relationships that have made STIHL an industry leader for over 90 years, and that will continue to drive our success with current and future technology like Lithium-Ion powered products.

Bjoern Fischer
PRESIDENT | STIHL INC.

Product Quality Pricing Objective
The high level of quality built into STIHL equipment helps to support a product quality pricing objective.

decreasing. On the other hand, a firm's sales volume can increase while its market share decreases if the overall market grows.

20-1e Cash Flow

Some companies set prices so they can recover cash as quickly as possible. Financial managers understandably want to recover quickly the capital spent to develop products. Choosing this pricing objective may have the support of a marketing manager if he or she anticipates a short product life cycle. Although it may be acceptable in some situations, the use of cash flow and recovery as an objective oversimplifies the contribution of price to profits. If this pricing objective results in high prices, competitors with lower prices may gain a large share of the market.

20-1f Status Quo

In some cases, an organization is in a favorable position and desires nothing more than to maintain the status quo. Status quo objectives can focus on several dimensions, such as maintaining a certain market share, meeting (but not beating) competitors' prices, achieving price stability, and maintaining a favorable public image. A status quo pricing objective can reduce a firm's risks by helping to stabilize demand for its products. A firm that chooses status quo pricing objectives risks minimizing pricing as a competitive tool, which could lead to a climate of nonprice competition. Professionals such as accountants and attorneys often operate in such an environment.

20-1g Product Quality

A company may have the objective of leading its industry in product quality. A high price may signal to customers that the product is of a high quality. Attaining a high level of product quality is generally more expensive for the firm, as the costs of materials, research, and development may be greater. In the advertisement, STIHL Incorporated emphasizes the quality of its power equipment by highlighting the people who build, sell, service, and use its world class machines. The ad pictures the president of the German company describing how the firm's relationships have made the company an industry leader. This reputation for quality allows STIHL to command higher prices. The products and brands that customers perceive to be of high quality are more likely to survive in a competitive marketplace because they trust these products more, even if the prices are higher.

Learning Objective 20-2

Discuss the importance of identifying the target market's evaluation of price.

20-2 ASSESSMENT OF THE TARGET MARKET'S EVALUATION OF PRICE

After developing pricing objectives, marketers must next assess the target market's evaluation of price. Despite the general assumption that price is a major issue for buyers, the importance of price varies depending on the type of product, the target market, and the purchase situation. For instance, buyers are probably more sensitive to gasoline prices than luggage prices.

Table 20.2 **Examples of Perceptions of Product Value**

Basic, Cost-Effective Product	Expensive, Time-Saving Product
Whole loose bagels, $0.59 each	Sliced packaged bagels, $0.65 each
Whole broccoli, $1.49/lb	Florets broccoli, $3.99/lb
Whole carrots, $1.49/lb	Baby carrots, $3.99/lb
Whole chicken, $1.49/lb	Cut-up chicken, $1.99/lb
Whole feta cheese, $3.23/8 oz	Crumbled feta cheese, $8.65/8 oz
Whole Granny Smith apples, $1.99/lb	Sliced Granny Smith apples, $3.97/lb
Lean ground chuck (ground), $3.99/lb	Lean ground chuck (patties), $5.99/lb

Note: Prices are based on a report from 2013.

Source: "Supermarket Smarts," *Consumer Reports ShopSmart*, www.shopsmartmag.org/files/Supermarket_smarts.pdf (accessed December 28, 2013).

We purchase gasoline regularly and notice fluctuations in price, but because luggage is more likely to be perceived as a long-term investment, we expect to pay more for it. With respect to the type of target market, adults frequently must pay more than children for goods and services, including clothing, meals, and movie tickets, because they consume a larger quantity.

The purchase situation also affects the buyer's view of price. Most moviegoers would never pay, in other situations, the prices charged for soft drinks, popcorn, and candy at concession stands. The markup for popcorn in movie theaters can be up to 1,275 percent.[4] Nevertheless, consumers are willing to pay the markup to enhance their movie experience by enjoying buttery popcorn at the theater. By assessing the target market's evaluation of price, a marketer is in a better position to know how much emphasis to put on price in the overall marketing strategy. Information about the target market's price evaluation may also help a marketer determine how far above the competition the firm can set its prices.

Today, because some consumers seek less-expensive products and the internet allows consumers to shop more selectively than ever before, some manufacturers and retailers focus on the value of products in their communications with customers. Remember that value is more than just a product's price. It combines price with quality attributes, which customers use to differentiate among competing brands. Generally, consumers want to maximize the value they receive for their money. Consumers may even perceive relatively expensive products, such as organic produce, to have great value if the products have desirable features or characteristics. Consumers may also be willing to pay a higher price for products that offer convenience and save time. Table 20.2 illustrates this point by showing the unit price difference between basic food products and time-saving food products. Companies that offer both affordable prices and high quality, like Target, have altered consumers' expectations about how much quality they must sacrifice for low prices. Understanding the importance of a product to customers, as well as their expectations about quality and value, helps marketers assess correctly the target market's evaluation of price.

20-3 EVALUATION OF COMPETITORS' PRICES

Learning Objective 20-3

Explain how marketers analyze competitors' prices.

In most cases, marketers are in a better position to establish prices when they know the prices charged for competing brands, which is the next step in establishing prices. Identifying competitors' prices should be a regular part of marketing research. Some grocery and department stores even employ comparative shoppers who systematically collect data on prices at competitors' stores. Companies may also purchase price lists from syndicated marketing research services. Even if a marketer has access to competitors' price lists, they may not reflect the actual prices at which competitive products sell because negotiation is involved.

Knowing the prices of competing brands is essential for a marketer. Regardless of its actual costs, a firm does not want to sell its product at a price that is significantly above competitors' prices because the products may not sell as well, or at a price that is significantly below because customers may believe the product is of low quality. Particularly in an industry in which price competition prevails, a marketer needs competitive price information to ensure that a firm's prices are the same as, or slightly lower than, competitors' prices. In some instances, an organization's prices are designed to be slightly above competitors' prices, such as with Apple brand products, to lend an exclusive image and to signal product quality to consumers. Apple, therefore, set the price of its new iPhone X at $999, an astonishing price at the time, to establish an expectation of quality and creative design in consumers' minds.[5]

20-4 SELECTION OF A BASIS FOR PRICING

The fourth step in establishing prices involves selecting a basis for pricing: cost, demand, and/or competition. Marketers determine the appropriate pricing basis by analyzing the type of product, the market structure of the industry, the brand's market share position relative to competing brands, and customer characteristics. Although we discuss each basis separately in this section, an organization generally considers at least two, or perhaps all three, dimensions. Thus, if a company uses cost as a primary basis for setting prices, its marketers are still aware of, and concerned about, competitors' prices. If a company uses demand as a basis for pricing, marketers still must consider costs and competitors' prices. Indeed, cost is a factor in every pricing decision because it establishes a price minimum below which the firm will not be able to recoup its production and other costs. Demand, likewise, sets an effective price maximum above which customers are unlikely to buy the product. Setting appropriate prices can be a difficult balance for firms. A high price may reduce demand for the product, but a low price will hurt profit margins and may instill in customers a perception that the product is of low quality. Firms must weigh many different factors when setting prices, including costs, competition, customer buying behavior and price sensitivity, manufacturing capacity, and product life cycles.

20-4a Cost-Based Pricing

With **cost-based pricing**, a flat dollar amount or percentage is added to the cost of the product, which means marketers calculate and apply a desired level of profit to the cost of the product and apply it uniformly. Cost-based pricing does not necessarily take into account the economic aspects of supply and demand, nor must it relate to just one pricing strategy or pricing objective. It is a straightforward and easy-to-implement method. Two common forms of cost-based pricing are cost-plus and markup pricing.

Cost-Plus Pricing

With **cost-plus pricing**, the seller's costs are determined (usually during a project or after a project is completed), and then a specified dollar amount or percentage of the cost is added to the seller's cost to establish the price. When production costs are difficult to predict, cost-plus pricing is appropriate. Projects involving custom-made equipment and commercial construction are often priced using this technique. The government also frequently expects cost-plus pricing from defense contractors. One pitfall for the buyer is that the seller may increase stated costs to gain a larger profit base. Furthermore, some costs, such as overhead, may be difficult to determine. In periods of rapid inflation, cost-plus pricing is popular, especially when the producer must use raw materials that frequently fluctuate in price. In industries in which cost-plus pricing is common and sellers have similar costs, price competition will not be especially intense.

cost-based pricing Adding a dollar amount or percentage to the cost of the product

cost-plus pricing Adding a specified dollar amount or percentage to the seller's cost

Markup Pricing

With **markup pricing**, commonly used by retailers, a product's price is derived by adding a predetermined percentage of the cost, called *markup,* to the cost of the product. For instance, most liquor stores mark up prices by 25 to 45 percent, whereas warehouse club Costco has a lower average markup of 10 to 14 percent on beer, wine, and spirits.[6] Markups can vary a great deal depending on the product and the situation. Although the percentage markup in a retail store varies from one category of goods to another—35 percent of cost for hardware items and 100 percent of cost for greeting cards, for example—the same percentage is often used to determine the prices on items within a single product category, and the percentage markup may be largely standardized across an industry at the retail level. Using a rigid percentage markup for a specific product category reduces pricing to a routine task that can be performed quickly.

What Is the Markup on Your Pizza?

Average cost of items on a supreme pizza

Tomato sauce · Red onion · Kosher salt · Active dry yeast · Mozzarella · Parmesan · Pepperoni · Italian sausage · "00" Flour · Olive oil · Black olives · Mushrooms · Green bell pepper · AP Flour

$0.05 · $0.02 · $0.01 · $0.00* · $0.60 · $0.35 · $0.24 · $0.18 · $0.15 · $0.09 · $0.08 · $0.05 · $0.05 · $0.05

Total Cost $1.90

Price (average) $14.00
Markup 636%

*Cost is less than $0.01

SNAPSHOT

Source: Priceonomics, "How Much Do the Ingredients Cost in Your Favorite Foods?" *Forbes,* April 7, 2017, https://www.forbes.com/sites/priceonomics/2017/04/07/how-much-do-the-ingredients-cost-in-your-favorite-foods/#2079e09b11ed (accessed March 14, 2018).

The following example illustrates how percentage markups are determined and distinguishes between two methods of stating a markup. Assume a retailer purchases a can of tuna at 45 cents and adds 15 cents to the cost, making the price 60 cents. There are two ways to look at the markup, as a percentage of cost or as a percentage of selling price:

$$\text{markup as percentage of cost} = \frac{\text{markup}}{\text{cost}}$$

$$= \frac{15}{45}$$

$$= 33.3\%$$

$$\text{markup as percentage of selling price} = \frac{\text{markup}}{\text{selling price}}$$

$$= \frac{15}{60}$$

$$= 25.0\%$$

The markup as a percentage of cost is 33.3 percent, while the markup as a percentage of price is only 25 percent. Obviously, when discussing a percentage markup, it is important to know whether the markup is based on cost or selling price.

Markups normally reflect expectations about operating costs, risks, and stock turnovers. Wholesalers and manufacturers often suggest standard retail markups that are considered profitable. To the extent that retailers use similar markups for the same product category, price competition is reduced. In addition, using rigid markups is convenient and is the major reason retailers favor this method.

20-4b **Demand-Based Pricing**

Marketers sometimes base prices on the level of demand for the product. When **demand-based pricing** is used, customers pay a higher price at times when demand for the product is strong and a lower price when demand is weak. Many entertainment venues have implemented

markup pricing Adding to the cost of the product a predetermined percentage of that cost

demand-based pricing Pricing based on the level of demand for the product

Demand-Based Pricing
Hotels engage in demand-based pricing. When demand at a hotel for a specific night is high, the prices will be higher, and when demand at a hotel is lower on a specific night, the prices will be lower.

demand-based pricing for ticket sales. The Walt Disney Company, for example, implemented demand-based pricing for Disney theme parks and resorts, offering cheaper tickets or extra perks on traditionally slow days and more expensive tickets or greater restrictions on traditionally crowded days, such as summer weekends.[7] The belief behind this pricing basis is that it is better to take a lower profit margin on a sale than no revenue at all.

Many service industries, including the airline, hotel, bus, car rental, ride sharing, and entertainment venues, use *dynamic pricing* to balance supply and demand. For instance, all tickets for Los Angeles Dodgers' baseball games are sold using dynamic pricing. Ticket prices are adjusted based on real-time market conditions that include seat location, the popularity of time and day, as well as whether there are special promotions like bobblehead giveaways.[8] Likewise, in some industries, *yield management* is a strategy of maximizing revenues by making numerous price changes in response to demand, competitors' prices, or environmental conditions. For example, Uber, like many firms in the transportation and travel industries, continually adjusts fares based on factors such as estimated traffic, estimated time and distance of the expected route, and the number of drivers available in order to ensure that the supply of drivers matches rider demand in real time.[9]

To use demand-based pricing, a marketer must be able to estimate the quantity of a product consumers will demand at different times and how demand will be affected by changes in the price. The marketer then chooses the price that generates the highest total revenue.

CREATIVE MARKETING

The Ups and Downs of Dynamic Toll Pricing

A growing number of cash-strapped states are turning to dynamic toll pricing to support highway upgrades and speed drivers on their way—for a price that varies every few minutes. In Virginia, for example, the Department of Transportation partnered with an Australian firm to develop new express lanes for crowded roads surrounding Washington, D.C. The goal was to keep express-lane traffic moving at a minimum of 45 miles per hour on I-495 and 55 miles per hour on I-95 by adjusting the toll amount as actual traffic patterns change.

During non-peak periods, Virginia drivers pay as little as 20 cents per mile in the express lane. However, at the height of rush hour, the toll can rise to $1 per mile or even higher. Drivers willing to pay (the current toll rate is displayed at each express-lane entrance) generally encounter less traffic and travel more quickly than price-sensitive drivers who choose toll-free routes.

Dynamic toll pricing is also being adopted in other areas. Along Interstate 580 through Alameda County, California, new express lanes double as high-occupancy vehicle lanes where carpoolers get a free ride at any hour. During the first year of operation, the highest toll for a full westbound trip was less than $10. Compare that with Virginia tolls that can exceed $30, depending on traffic conditions. In the end, it's up to each driver to weigh the value of saving time by paying the express-lane toll for a faster ride or saving the money by using free roads.[a]

Demand-based pricing is appropriate for industries in which companies have a fixed amount of available resources that are perishable, such as airline seats, hotel rooms, concert seats, and so on. The effectiveness of demand-based pricing depends on the marketer's ability to estimate demand accurately. Compared with cost-based pricing, demand-based pricing places a firm in a better position to reach high profit levels, as long as demand is strong at times and buyers value the product at levels sufficiently above the product's cost.

20-4c Competition-Based Pricing

With **competition-based pricing**, an organization considers costs to be secondary to competitors' prices. This is a common method among producers of relatively homogeneous products, particularly when the target market considers price to be an important purchase consideration. A firm that uses competition-based pricing may choose to set their prices below competitors' or at the same level. Consider the advertisement for Walgreens, which has long engaged in a price war with CVS and others. As shown in the ad, Walgreens has taken some steps to differentiate itself from its rivals, such as highlighting its charitable giving, after years of competing for market share on the basis of price. Likewise, competitors believe that Amazon's competition-based pricing model in industry after industry has been an attempt to gain monopoly control of many retail markets. Amazon uses highly sophisticated analytics to gauge consumer demand and compare its prices to competitors. To stay ahead of the competition, Amazon adjusts its prices millions of times each day, to ensure that it undercuts competitors on the most popular items.[10]

Competition-Based Pricing

Walgreens engages in competition-based pricing to directly compete with CVS, grocery retailers such as Kroger, and supercenters such as Target and Walmart.

20-5 SELECTION OF A PRICING STRATEGY

Learning Objective 20-5

Compare the different types of pricing strategies.

A *pricing strategy* is a course of action designed to achieve pricing objectives, which are set to help marketers solve the practical problems of setting prices. The extent to which a business uses any of the following strategies depends on its pricing and marketing objectives, the markets for its products, the degree of product differentiation, the product's life-cycle stage, and other factors. Generally, pricing strategies help marketers solve the practical problems of establishing prices. Table 20.3 lists the most common pricing strategies, which we discuss in this section.

20-5a Differential Pricing

An important issue in pricing decisions is whether to use a single price or different prices for the same product. Using a single price has several benefits. A primary advantage is simplicity. A single price is easily understood by both employees and customers. Because many salespeople and customers dislike negotiating prices, having a single price reduces the risk of a marketer developing an adversarial relationship with customers. The use of a single price does create some challenges, however. If the single price is too high, some potential customers may be unable to afford the product. If it is too low, the organization loses revenue from those customers who would have paid more had the price been higher.

competition-based pricing
Pricing influenced primarily by competitors' prices

Table 20.3   Common Pricing Strategies

Differential Pricing	Psychological Pricing
Negotiated pricing	Reference pricing
Secondary-market pricing	Bundle pricing
Periodic discounting	Multiple-unit pricing
Random discounting	Everyday low pricing
	Odd-even pricing
New-Product Pricing	Customary pricing
Price skimming	Prestige pricing
Penetration pricing	
	Professional Pricing
Product-Line Pricing	
Captive pricing	**Promotional Pricing**
Premium pricing	Price leaders
Bait pricing	Special-event pricing
Price lining	Comparison discounting

Differential pricing means charging different prices to different buyers for the same quality and quantity of product. For example, many movie theaters offer discounted tickets for daytime matinee performances, and airlines have different pricing tiers for airline seats depending on whether customers paid extra to board early or to obtain other perks. For differential pricing to be effective, the market must consist of multiple segments with different price sensitivities. When this method is employed, caution should be used to avoid confusing or antagonizing customers. Differential pricing can occur in several ways, including negotiated pricing, secondary-market pricing, periodic discounting, and random discounting.

Negotiated Pricing

Negotiated pricing occurs when the final price is established through bargaining between the seller and the customer. Negotiated pricing occurs in a number of industries and at all levels of distribution. Even when there is a predetermined stated price or a price list, manufacturers, wholesalers, and retailers still may negotiate to establish the final sales price. Consumers commonly negotiate prices for houses, cars, and used equipment. Customers rarely pay the list price on a car, for instance, because they go to a car dealership expecting to negotiate with the seller until they arrive at a price that is satisfactory to both the customer and the seller. Managing personal chemistry between the negotiators is just as important as settling on prices. The negotiation process can help build relationships and increase understanding between different parties in a supply chain relationship.

Secondary-Market Pricing

Secondary-market pricing means setting one price for the primary target market and a different price for another market. Often the price charged in the secondary market is lower. However, when the costs of serving a secondary market are higher than normal, secondary-market customers may have to pay a higher price. Examples of secondary markets include a geographically isolated domestic market, a market in a foreign country, and a segment willing to purchase a product during off-peak times (such as "early-bird" diners at restaurants and off-season vacation rentals). Secondary markets give an organization an opportunity to use excess capacity and stabilize the allocation of resources.

differential pricing Charging different prices to different buyers for the same quality and quantity of product

negotiated pricing Establishing a final price through bargaining between the seller and the customer

secondary-market pricing Setting one price for the primary target market and a different price for another market

Periodic Discounting

Periodic discounting is the temporary reduction of prices on a patterned or systematic basis. As a result, many retailers have annual holiday sales, and some apparel stores have regular seasonal sales. From the marketer's point of view, a major problem with periodic discounting is customers can predict when the reductions will occur and may delay their purchases until they can take advantage of the lower prices. Periodic discounting is less effective in an environment where many consumers shop online because they can more easily comparison shop for a better deal even during non-sale times.

Random Discounting

To alleviate the problem of customers knowing when discounting will occur, some organizations employ **random discounting**—that is, they reduce their prices temporarily on a non-systematic basis. When price reductions of a product occur randomly, current users of that brand are not able to predict when the reductions will occur. Therefore, they are less likely to delay their purchases in anticipation of buying the product at a lower price. Marketers also use random discounting to attract new customers. Random discounting can also be useful to draw attention to a relatively new product. Many grocery store items, such as a new kind of yogurt or cereal, will use random discounting. Marketers must be careful not to use random discounting too often, however, because customers will learn to wait for the discounts.

Whether they use periodic discounting or random discounting, retailers often employ tensile pricing when putting products on sale. *Tensile pricing* involves making a broad statement about price reductions, as opposed to detailing specific price discounts. Examples of tensile pricing would be statements like "20 to 50 percent off," "up to 75 percent off," and "save 10 percent or more." Generally, the tensile price that mentions only the maximum reduction (such as "up to 50 percent off") generates the highest customer response.[11]

20-5b New-Product Pricing

Setting the base price for a new product is a necessary part of formulating a marketing strategy. Marketers can easily adjust the base price in industries that are not subject to government price controls, and its establishment is one of the most fundamental decisions in the marketing mix.

periodic discounting
Temporary reduction of prices on a patterned or systematic basis

random discounting
Temporary reduction of prices on an unsystematic basis

DISRUPTIVE MARKETING

Flash Sales: You've Got to Be Fast!

From footwear to flights, marketers of goods and services are grabbing attention through "flash sales" that slash prices with no advance warning and restore regular prices within hours. Market leader Nike has implemented occasional flash sales to build buzz and boost unit sales of a handful of carefully selected items. During one flash sale, for example, Nike offered an unusually steep discount of 40 percent on some Air Jordan athletic shoes, among other items, catching the eye of brand fans.

The startup shoe company True Gault uses flash sales differently. Founder and CEO Sandra Gault markets custom-made high heels, regularly priced from $250 per pair and up. To reassure customers of the quality and comfort of her products, Gault offers to remake any shoes that don't fit properly. Then she uses flash sales to resell shoes returned in "original condition" at a discount and recoup some of the cost.

Some airlines use flash sales to stimulate purchasing during slow periods or to fill seats on certain routes. When JetBlue Airways tweets about flash sales with fares as low as $20, travelers rush to buy, knowing that prices could change in less than an hour. Southwest Airlines has been known to use flash sales, as well. "Flash sales are a great way to generate demand for Southwest's world-class product," a spokesperson explains. On the other hand, American Airlines prefers to reduce fares "when needed, based on demand," according to a spokesperson. "For us, flash sales are just not a great way to do that."[b]

The base price can be set high to recover development costs quickly or provide a reference point for developing discount prices for different market segments. When a marketer sets base prices, he or she considers how quickly competitors are expected to enter the market, whether they will mount a strong campaign on entry, and what effect their entry will have on the development of primary demand. Two strategies used in new-product pricing are price skimming and penetration pricing. Research into the pricing of new digital cameras hints that marketers use a skimming strategy about 20 percent of the time, a penetration strategy about 20 percent of the time, and a straightforward competition- or market-based strategy most of the time, especially for later entrants to the market.[12]

Price Skimming

Some consumers are willing to pay a high price for an innovative product, either because of its novelty or because of the prestige or status that ownership confers. **Price skimming** is the strategy of charging the highest possible price for a product during the introduction stage of its life cycle. The seller essentially "skims the cream" off the market, which helps a firm to recover the high costs of R&D more quickly. This approach provides the most flexible introductory base price. Demand tends to be inelastic in the introductory stage of the product life cycle.

Price skimming can provide several benefits. A skimming policy can generate much-needed initial cash flows to help offset development costs. Price skimming protects the marketer from problems that arise when the price is set too low to cover costs. When a firm introduces a product, its production capacity may be limited. A skimming price can help keep demand consistent with the firm's production capabilities. However, price skimming strategies can be dangerous because they may make the product appear more lucrative than it actually is to potential competitors. A firm also risks misjudging demand and facing insufficient sales at the higher price. New-product prices should be based on both the value to the customer and competitive products.

Penetration Pricing

At the opposite extreme, **penetration pricing** is the strategy of setting a low price for a new product. The main purpose of setting a low price is to build market share quickly to encourage product trial by the target market and discourage competitors from entering the market. This approach is less flexible for a marketer than price skimming, because it is more difficult to raise the price of a product from a penetration price than to lower or discount a skimming price. It is not unusual for a firm to use a penetration price after having skimmed the market with a higher price.

Penetration pricing can be especially beneficial when a marketer suspects that competitors could enter the market easily. If the low price stimulates sales, the firm may be able to order longer production runs, increasing economies of scale and resulting in decreased production costs per unit. If penetration pricing allows the marketer to gain a large market share quickly, competitors may be discouraged from entering the market. In addition, because the lower per-unit penetration price results in lower per-unit profit, the market may not appear to be especially lucrative to potential new entrants. A disadvantage of penetration pricing is that it places a firm in a less-flexible pricing position. Again, it is more difficult to raise prices significantly than it is to lower them.

20-5c **Product-Line Pricing**

Rather than considering products on an item-by-item basis when determining pricing strategies, some marketers employ product-line pricing. **Product-line pricing** means establishing and adjusting the prices of multiple products within a product line. When marketers use product-line pricing, their goal is to maximize profits for an entire product line rather than to focus on the profitability of an individual product item. Product-line pricing can provide marketers with

price skimming Charging the highest possible price that buyers who most desire the product will pay

penetration pricing Setting prices below those of competing brands to penetrate a market and gain a significant market share quickly

product-line pricing Establishing and adjusting prices of multiple products within a product line

pricing flexibility. Thus, marketers can set prices so that one product is profitable, whereas another is less profitable but increases market share by virtue of having a low price and, therefore, selling more units.

Before setting prices for a product line, marketers evaluate the relationship among the products in the line. When products in a line are complementary, sales increases in one item raise demand for other items. For instance, desktop printers and toner cartridges are complementary products. However, when products in a line function as substitutes for one another, buyers of one product in the line are unlikely to purchase one of the other products in the same line. In this case, marketers must be sensitive to how a price change for one of the brands may affect the demand not only for that brand but also for the substitute brands. For instance, if decision makers at Procter & Gamble were considering a price change for Tide detergent, they would likely also be concerned about how the price change might influence sales of other detergents, such as Cheer, Bold, and Gain.

When marketers employ product-line pricing, they have several strategies from which to choose. These include captive pricing, premium pricing, bait pricing, and price lining.

captive pricing Pricing the basic product in a product line low, while pricing related items higher

premium pricing Pricing the highest-quality or most versatile products higher than other models in the product line

Captive Pricing

When marketers use **captive pricing**, the basic product in a product line is priced low, but the price on the items required to operate or enhance it are higher. A common example of captive pricing is printer ink. The printer is priced quite low to attract sales, but the printer ink replacement cartridges are very expensive. Look at the advertisement for the Gillette Fusion 5 razor cartridges for another example. The Fusion 5 itself is not very expensive, but the replacement blades are highly specialized and retail for about $5 per blade cartridge. Because the razor requires specific replacement cartridges, consumers cannot purchase generic or off-brand replacements to save money. To compete against low-price subscription services like Dollar Shave Club, Gillette is advertising its own subscription service with lower prices for razor cartridges for the Fusion 5 and other Gillette razors. The ad touts, "Keep saving with the blades you love" to draw back customers who have turned to shaving subscription services.

Premium Pricing

Premium pricing occurs when the highest-quality product, or the most versatile and most desirable version of a product in a product line, is assigned the highest price. Other products in the line are priced to appeal to price-sensitive shoppers or to those who seek product-specific features. Marketers that use premium pricing often realize a significant portion of their profits from the premium-priced products. Examples of product categories in which premium pricing is common are small kitchen appliances, beer, ice cream, and television cable service. For example, tax software, such as TurboTax and H&R Block, are marketed in

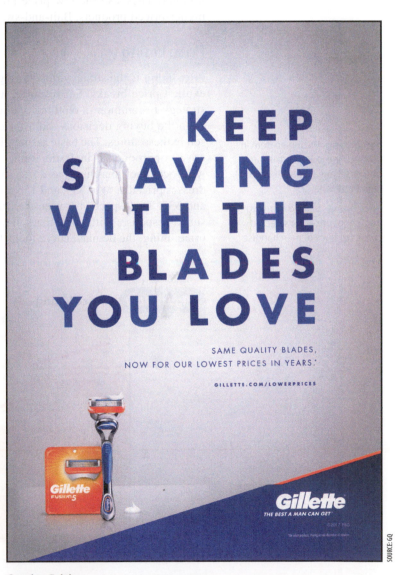

KEEP SHAVING WITH THE BLADES YOU LOVE

SAME QUALITY BLADES, NOW FOR OUR LOWEST PRICES IN YEARS.

GILLETTE.COM/LOWERPRICES

Gillette
THE BEST A MAN CAN GET

SOURCE: GQ

Captive Pricing
The Gillette Fusion 5 razor is an example of a captive pricing strategy because the original razor is sold at a relatively low price, but replacement blades are more expensive. Consumers cannot substitute another brand of blades.

multiple versions; the least expensive versions handle the most basic tax-preparation and forms, while more expensive versions include more tax forms, state tax forms, planning assistance, and more.

Bait Pricing

To attract customers, marketers may put a low price on one item in the product line with the intention of selling a higher-priced item in the line. This strategy is known as **bait pricing**. For example, a retailer may promote an inexpensive Chromebook in the expectation that consumers coming in to look at that product will wind up buying a more expensive one with more features than the advertised model. As long as a retailer has sufficient quantities of the advertised low-priced model available for sale, this strategy is acceptable. However, it may generate customer resentment if customers go to the store looking for the low-priced model and find only the high-priced model in stock. If this is done intentionally, it is called *bait-and-switch*. Bait-and-switch occurs when retailers have no intention of selling the bait product. They use the low price merely to entice customers into the store to sell them higher-priced products. Bait-and-switch is unethical, and in some states it is even illegal.

Price Lining

Price lining is the strategy of selling goods only at certain predetermined prices that reflect explicit price breaks. For instance, a shop may sell men's ties only at $22 and $37. This strategy is common in clothing and accessory stores. It eliminates minor price differences from the buying decision—both for customers and for managers who buy merchandise to sell in these stores. The basic assumption in price lining is that the demand for various groups or sets of products is inelastic. Rather than responding to slight changes in prices, customers will focus their purchases as a specific price level. Thus, a women's dress shop that carries dresses priced at $85, $55, and $35 may not attract many more sales with a drop to $83, $53, and $33. The "space" between the price of $85 and $55, however, can stir changes in consumer response, with consumers viewing the higher-priced item as of higher quality. With price lining, the demand curve looks like a series of steps, as shown in Figure 20.2.

bait pricing Pricing an item in a product line low with the intention of selling a higher-priced item in the line

price lining Setting a limited number of prices for selected groups or lines of merchandise

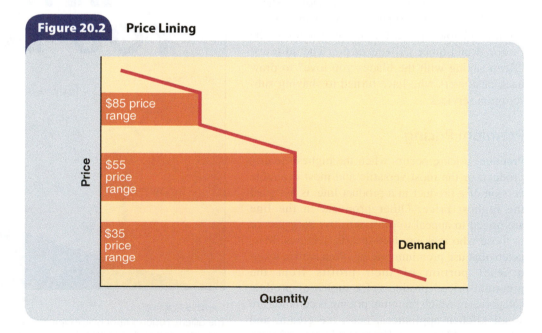

| Figure 20.2 | Price Lining |

20-5d **Psychological Pricing**

Psychological pricing attempts to influence a customer's perception of price to make a product's price more attractive. Psychological pricing strategies encourage purchases based on consumers' emotional responses, rather than on economically rational ones. These strategies are used primarily for consumer products, rather than business products, because most business purchases follow a systematic and rational approach. In this section, we consider several forms of psychological pricing: reference pricing, bundle pricing, multiple-unit pricing, everyday low pricing (EDLP), odd-even pricing, customary pricing, and prestige pricing.

Reference Pricing

Reference pricing means pricing a product at a moderate level and physically positioning it next to a more expensive model or brand in the hope that the customer will use the higher price as a reference price (i.e., a comparison price). Because of the comparison, the customer is expected to view the moderate price more favorably than he or she would if the product were considered alone. Reference pricing is based on the "isolation effect," meaning an alternative is less attractive when viewed by itself than when compared with other alternatives.

Bundle Pricing

Bundle pricing is the packaging together of two or more products, usually of a complementary nature, to be sold for a single price. To be attractive to customers, the single price generally is markedly less than the sum of the prices of the individual products. Being able to buy the bundled combination may be of value to the customer, increasing convenience and reducing the time required to shop. Bundle pricing is common for banking and travel services, computers, and automobiles with option packages. Bundle pricing is also common among products that are used in tandem. Comcast Xfinity, for instance, offers a special rate when consumers bundle television, internet, and phone service. Bundle pricing can help to increase customer satisfaction. It can also help firms sell slow-moving inventory and increase revenues by bundling it with products with a higher turnover.

Multiple-Unit Pricing

Many retailers (especially supermarkets) practice **multiple-unit pricing**, which is setting a single price for two or more units of a product, such as two cans for 99 cents, rather than 50 cents per can. Especially for frequently purchased products, this strategy can increase sales by encouraging consumers to purchase multiple units when they might otherwise have only purchased one at a time. Customers benefit from the cost savings and convenience this pricing strategy affords. A company may use multiple-unit pricing to attract new customers to its brands and, in some instances, to increase consumption. When customers buy in larger quantities, their consumption of the product may increase as it is more available. Customers who see the single price and who expect eventually to use more than one unit of the product will likely be inclined to purchase multiple units.

Discount stores and especially warehouse clubs, such as Sam's Club and Costco, are major users of multiple-unit pricing. For certain products in these stores, customers receive significant per-unit price reductions when they buy packages containing multiple units of the same product.

Everyday Low Pricing (EDLP)

To reduce or eliminate the use of frequent short-term price reductions, some organizations use an approach referred to as **everyday low pricing (EDLP)**. When EDLP is used, a marketer sets a low price for its products on a consistent basis, rather than setting higher prices and frequently

psychological pricing Pricing that attempts to influence a customer's perception of price to make a product's price more attractive

reference pricing Pricing a product at a moderate level and displaying it next to a more expensive model or brand

bundle pricing Packaging together two or more complementary products and selling them at a single price

multiple-unit pricing Packaging together two or more identical products and selling them at a single price

everyday low pricing (EDLP) Pricing products low on a consistent basis

Everyday Low Pricing

In this advertisement, Target encourages consumers to "get everyday low prices on everyday essentials."

discounting them. Everyday low pricing, though not deeply discounted, is set low enough to make customers feel confident they are receiving a good deal. EDLP is employed by retailers such as Walmart and by manufacturers such as Procter & Gamble. Look at the advertisement for Target, which promotes that customers can "get everyday low prices on everyday essentials." The advertisement, which shows products falling into a Target basket, reminds consumers that they can get everything on their list. A company that uses EDLP benefits from reduced promotional costs, reduced losses from frequent markdowns, and more stable sales.

A major issue with this approach is that customers can have mixed responses. In some instances, customers believe that everyday low pricing is a marketing gimmick and not truly the good deal that they proclaim. Some retailers have encountered a backlash against EDLP from consumers who enjoy the thrill of hunting down the best sales. For instance, when JCPenney opted to stop promotions and coupons in favor of an EDLP strategy, some customers stopped shopping there. JCPenney marketers discovered the hard way that many consumers want to see the 20 percent off markdown and use coupons because it helps to reinforce the feeling that they are getting a good deal. The company ultimately backtracked on the EDLP policy after seeing sharp declines in sales.[13]

Odd-Even Pricing

Odd-even pricing involves ending a price with certain numbers. Through this strategy, marketers try to influence buyers' perceptions of the product. It aligns with the belief among many retailers that consumers respond more positively to odd-number prices, such as $4.99, than to whole-dollar prices, such as $5, for items where customers are looking for value. Odd pricing is the strategy of setting prices using odd numbers that are slightly below whole-dollar amounts. Nine and five are the most popular ending figures for odd-number prices. This strategy assumes more of a product will be sold at $99.95 than at $100. Sellers who use this odd pricing believe that odd numbers increase sales because consumers register the dollar amount, not the cents. Odd-number pricing has been the subject of various psychological studies, but the results have been inconclusive.

Even prices, on the other hand, are often used to give a product an exclusive or upscale image. An even price is believed to influence a customer to view the product as being a high-quality, premium brand. A shirt maker, for example, may print on a premium shirt package a suggested retail price of $42.00 instead of $41.95.

Customary Pricing

With **customary pricing**, certain goods are priced on the basis of tradition. This is a less common pricing strategy now than it was in the past. An example would be the 25-cent gumballs sold in gumball machines—the price has remained at that level for probably as long as you can

odd-even pricing Ending the price with certain numbers to influence buyers' perceptions of the price or product

customary pricing Pricing on the basis of tradition

remember. Indeed, candy like the Skittles in the advertisement has long used customary pricing. The ad pictures a grumpy character that turns into a silly character when you "flip the rainbow." In cases of customary pricing, it is usual for the size of the product sold at the customary price to shrink over time to compensate for rising costs of raw materials.

Prestige Pricing

With **prestige pricing**, prices are set at an artificially high level to convey a quality image. Prestige pricing is used especially when buyers associate a higher price with higher quality. Maserati is a brand that has successfully used prestige pricing to set prices extremely high to convey an aura of ultra-luxury. Typical product categories that are subject to prestige pricing include perfumes, liquor, jewelry, cars, and some food items. Upscale appliances or furniture capitalize on the desire of some consumer segments to "trade up" for high-quality products. These consumers are willing to pay extra for a Sub-Zero refrigerator or a Viking commercial range because these products are high quality and project an image that the customers can afford the best.

20-5e Professional Pricing

Professional pricing is used by people who have great skill or experience in a particular field. Although costs are considered when setting prices, professionals often believe their fees should not relate directly to the time and/or effort spent in specific cases. Rather, professionals may charge a standard fee regardless of the problems involved in performing the job. Some doctors' and lawyers' fees are prime examples, such as $75 for an office visit, $2,000 for an appendectomy, and $995 for a divorce. Other professionals set prices using different methods. Like other marketers, professionals have costs associated with facilities, labor, insurance, equipment, and supplies. Professionals have an ethical responsibility not to overcharge customers.

SOURCE: SEVENTEEN MAGAZINE

Customary Pricing

Candy, such as Skittles, is often sold based on customary pricing. Generally, consumers expect to pay a certain price for a specified amount of candy, irrespective of the type of candy.

20-5f Promotional Pricing

Price—as an ingredient in the marketing mix—often is coordinated with promotion. The two variables are sometimes so interrelated that the pricing policy is promotion-oriented. Examples of promotional pricing include price leaders, special-event pricing, and comparison discounting.

Price Leaders

Sometimes a firm prices a few products below the usual markup, near cost, or below cost, which results in what are known as **price leaders**. This type of pricing is used most often in supermarkets and restaurants to attract customers by offering them especially low prices on a

prestige pricing Setting prices at an artificially high level to convey prestige or a quality image

professional pricing Fees set by people with great skill or experience in a particular field

price leaders Products priced near or even below cost

SimpliSafe

BLACK FRIDAY SALE

$200 OFF

OUR HOLIDAY PACKAGE

Whether you're home for the holidays or away.
Protect your home with SimpliSafe's special
holiday package. At $200 off, it's our biggest
holiday offer ever!

Designed for comprehensive home protection,
this 13-piece system keeps your home and
family safe around the clock. Alarm monitoring
is just $15 a month. And there's no long-term
contract, so you're never locked in.

Redeem this exclusive offer only at

SimpliSafe.com/EC

HURRY! OFFER ENDS SOON

Special-Event Pricing
Black Friday is a special event. The maker of SimpliSafe Home Security offers its
services for $200 off regular price on Black Friday.

few items, with the expectation that they will purchase other items as well. Management expects that
sales of regularly priced products will more than
offset the reduced revenues from the price leaders.

Special-Event Pricing

To increase sales volume, many organizations coordinate price with advertising or sales promotions for
seasonal or special situations. **Special-event pricing**
involves advertised sales or price cutting linked to a
holiday, a season, or an event. Consider the advertisement for the SimpliSafe home security system.
The ad offers $200 off select systems for Black Fri-
day, the major post-Thanksgiving sales holiday. If
the pricing objective is survival, then special sales
events may be designed to generate the necessary
operating capital. Special-event pricing entails coordination of production, scheduling, storage, and
physical distribution. Special-event pricing can be
an effective strategy to combat sales lags.

Comparison Discounting

Comparison discounting sets the price of a product
at a specific level and simultaneously compares it
with a higher price. The higher price may be the
product's previous price, the price of a competing
brand, the product's price at another retail outlet, or
a manufacturer's suggested retail price. Customers
may find comparative discounting informative, and
it can have a significant impact on their purchases.

However, because this pricing strategy on occasion has led to deceptive pricing practices, the Federal Trade Commission has established guidelines
for comparison discounting. If the higher price
against which the comparison is made is the price formerly charged for the product, the seller
must have made the previous price available to customers for a reasonable time period. If sellers present the higher price as the one charged by other retailers in the same trade area, they
must be able to demonstrate that this claim is true. When they present the higher price as the
manufacturer's suggested retail price, the higher price must be close to the price at which a
reasonable proportion of the product was sold. Some manufacturers' suggested retail prices
are so high that very few products are actually sold at those prices. In such cases, it is deceptive to use comparison discounting. The internet has allowed consumers to be more wary of
comparison discounting and less susceptible to being fooled, as they can easily compare the
listed price for a product with comparable products online.

special-event pricing
Advertised sales or price cutting
linked to a holiday, a season, or
an event

comparison discounting
Setting a price at a specific level
and comparing it with a higher
price

Describe the selection of a
specific price.

20-6 DETERMINATION OF A SPECIFIC PRICE

A pricing strategy will yield a certain price or range of prices, which is the final step in the
pricing process. However, marketers may need to refine this price in order to make it consistent
with circumstances (such as a sluggish economy) and with pricing practices in a particular
market or industry. As an example, Johnson & Johnson pledged to be transparent with its
pricing strategies for pharmaceutical products at a time when other firms came under fire

for rapidly escalating prices on life-saving drugs. The company even releases a transparency report demonstrating that it has held average list price increases below 10 percent for five years.[14] Pricing strategies should help in setting a final price. If they are to do so, marketers must establish pricing objectives, have considerable knowledge about target market customers, and determine demand, price elasticity, costs, and competitive factors. Additionally, the way marketers use pricing in the marketing mix will affect the final price.

In the absence of government price controls, pricing remains a flexible and convenient way to adjust the marketing mix. In many situations, marketers can adjust prices quickly—over a few days or even in minutes. Such flexibility is unique to this component of the marketing mix.

Summary

20-1 Identify issues related to developing pricing objectives.

Setting pricing objectives is critical because pricing objectives form a foundation on which the decisions of subsequent stages are based. Organizations may use numerous pricing objectives, including short-term and long-term ones, and different objectives for different products and market segments. Pricing objectives are overall goals that describe the role of price in a firm's long-range plans. There are several major types of pricing objectives. The most fundamental pricing objective is the organization's survival. Price can usually be easily adjusted to increase sales volume or combat competition to help the organization stay alive. Profit objectives, which are usually stated in terms of sales dollar volume or percentage change, are normally set at a satisfactory level rather than at a level designed to maximize profits. A sales growth objective focuses on increasing the profit base by raising sales volume. Pricing for return on investment (ROI) has a specified profit as its objective. A pricing objective to maintain or increase market share links market position to success. Other types of pricing objectives include cash flow, status quo, and product quality.

20-2 Discuss the importance of identifying the target market's evaluation of price.

Assessing the target market's evaluation of price tells the marketer how much emphasis to place on price and may help determine how far above the competition the firm can set its prices. Understanding how important a product is to customers relative to other products, as well as customers' expectations of quality, helps marketers correctly assess the target market's evaluation of price.

20-3 Explain how marketers analyze competitors' prices.

A marketer needs to be aware of the prices charged for competing brands. This allows the firm to keep its prices in line with competitors' prices when nonprice competition is used.

If a company uses price as a competitive tool, it can price its brand below competing brands.

20-4 Analyze the bases used for setting prices.

The three major dimensions on which prices can be based are cost, demand, and competition. When using cost-based pricing, the firm determines price by adding a dollar amount or percentage to the cost of the product. Two common cost-based pricing methods are cost-plus and markup pricing. Demand-based pricing is based on the level of demand for the product. To use this method, a marketer must be able to estimate the amounts of a product that buyers will demand at different prices. Demand-based pricing results in a high price when demand for a product is strong and a low price when demand is weak. In the case of competition-based pricing, costs and revenues are secondary to competitors' prices.

20-5 Compare the different types of pricing strategies.

A pricing strategy is an approach or a course of action designed to achieve pricing and marketing objectives. Pricing strategies help marketers solve the practical problems of establishing prices. The most common pricing strategies are differential pricing, new-product pricing, product-line pricing, psychological pricing, professional pricing, and promotional pricing.

When marketers employ differential pricing, they charge different buyers different prices for the same quality and quantity of products. For example, with negotiated pricing, the final price is established through bargaining between the seller and the customer. Secondary-market pricing involves setting one price for the primary target market and a different price for another market. Oftentimes the price charged in the secondary market is lower. Marketers employ periodic discounting when they temporarily lower their prices on a patterned or systematic basis because of such reasons as a seasonal change, a model-year change, or a holiday. Random discounting occurs on an unsystematic basis.

Two strategies used in new-product pricing are price skimming and penetration pricing. With price skimming, the organization charges the highest price that buyers who most desire the product will pay. A penetration price is a low price designed to penetrate a market and gain a significant market share quickly.

Product-line pricing establishes and adjusts the prices of multiple products within a product line. This strategy includes captive pricing, in which the marketer prices the basic product in a product line low and prices related items higher. Premium pricing is setting prices on higher-quality or more versatile products higher than those on other models in the product line. Bait pricing is when the marketer tries to attract customers by pricing an item in the product line low with the intention of selling a higher-priced item in the line. Price lining is when the organization sets a limited number of prices for selected groups or lines of merchandise.

Psychological pricing attempts to influence customers' perceptions of price to make a product's price more attractive. With reference pricing, marketers price a product at a moderate level and position it next to a more expensive model or brand. Bundle pricing is packaging together two or more complementary products and selling them at a single price. With multiple-unit pricing, two or more identical products are packaged together and sold at a single price. To reduce or eliminate use of frequent short-term price reductions, some organizations employ everyday low pricing (EDLP), setting a low price for products on a consistent basis. When employing odd-even pricing, marketers try to influence buyers'

perceptions of the price or the product by ending the price with certain numbers. Customary pricing is based on traditional prices. With prestige pricing, prices are set at an artificially high level to convey prestige or a quality image.

Professional pricing is used by people who have great skill or experience in a particular field, therefore allowing them to set the price. This concept carries the idea that professionals have an ethical responsibility not to overcharge customers.

As an ingredient in the marketing mix, price is often coordinated with promotion. The two variables are sometimes so closely interrelated that the pricing policy is promotion-oriented. Promotional pricing includes price leaders, special-event pricing, and comparison discounting. Price leaders are products priced below the usual markup, near cost, or below cost. Special-event pricing involves advertised sales or price cutting linked to a holiday, a season, or an event. Marketers that use a comparison discounting strategy price a product at a specific level and compare it with a higher price.

20-6 Describe the selection of a specific price.

A pricing strategy will yield a certain price or range of prices. Pricing strategies should help in setting a final price. If they are to do so, marketers must establish pricing objectives, have considerable knowledge about target market customers, and determine demand, price elasticity, costs, and competitive factors. Additionally, the way marketers use pricing in the marketing mix will affect the final price. Pricing remains a flexible and convenient way to adjust the marketing mix.

Important Terms

pricing objectives 590
cost-based pricing 594
cost-plus pricing 594
markup pricing 595
demand-based
    pricing 595
competition-based
    pricing 597
differential pricing 598
negotiated pricing 598

secondary-market
    pricing 598
periodic discounting 599
random discounting 599
price skimming 600
penetration
    pricing 600
product-line
    pricing 600
captive pricing 601

premium pricing 601
bait pricing 602
price lining 602
psychological
    pricing 603
reference pricing 603
bundle pricing 603
multiple-unit pricing 603
everyday low pricing
    (EDLP) 603

odd-even pricing 604
customary pricing 604
prestige pricing 605
professional
    pricing 605
price leaders 605
special-event
    pricing 606
comparison
    discounting 606

Discussion and Review Questions

1. Identify the six stages in the process of establishing prices.
2. How does a return on investment pricing objective differ from an objective of increasing market share?
3. Why must marketing objectives and pricing objectives be considered when making pricing decisions?
4. Why should a marketer be aware of competitors' prices?

5. What are the benefits of cost-based pricing?
6. Under what conditions is cost-plus pricing most appropriate?
7. A retailer purchases a can of soup for 24 cents and sells it for 36 cents. Calculate the markup as a percentage of cost and as a percentage of selling price.
8. What is differential pricing? In what ways can it be achieved?
9. For what types of products would price skimming be most appropriate? For what types of products would penetration pricing be more effective?
10. Describe bundle pricing, and give three examples using different industries.
11. What are the advantages and disadvantages of using everyday low pricing?
12. Why do customers associate price with quality? When should prestige pricing be used?
13. Are price leaders a realistic approach to pricing? Explain your answer.

Developing Your Marketing Plan

Setting the right price for a product is a crucial part of a marketing strategy. Price helps to establish a product's position in the mind of the consumer and can differentiate a product from its competition. Several decisions in the marketing plan will be affected by the pricing strategy that is selected. To assist you in relating the information in this chapter to the development of your marketing plan, focus on the following:

1. Using Table 20.1 as a guide, discuss each of the seven pricing objectives. Which pricing objectives will you use for your product? Consider the product life cycle, competition, and product positioning for your target market during your discussion.
2. Review the various types of pricing strategies in Table 20.3. Which of these is the most appropriate for your product?
3. Select a basis for pricing your product (cost, demand, and/or competition). How will you know when it is time to revise your pricing strategy?

Video Case 20.1

Warby Parker Puts Affordable Eyewear in Focus

Bringing down the high price of fashion eyeglasses was the goal that four friends set out to achieve when they founded Warby Parker in 2010. The business idea grew out of co-founder Dave Gilboa's personal experience. When he was a graduate student, he lost his glasses while hiking and was so outraged by the high price of replacing them that he squinted for months rather than buy new glasses. Eyeglasses are made from wire, plastic, screws, and glass, yet the retail price is often many times the actual cost of the materials, yielding a hefty profit margin. Adding a designer logo to a pair of frames pushes the final price even higher. Talking with friends, Gilboa learned he wasn't the only person unhappy about having to spend a lot for eyeglasses. So Gilboa teamed up with Neil Blumenthal, Andy Hunt, and Jeff Raider to create a business plan for a new kind of eyewear company, selling quality eyeglasses directly to customers with a price tag below $100 per pair.

Direct marketing keeps Warby Parker's distribution costs low and avoids the kind of intermediary markups that typically increase the final price. In-house designers develop all frame styles, which means no licensing fees for the right to use famous fashion logos. Customers benefit because Warby Parker passes the savings along in the form of affordable price tags for quality eyewear. The company also has a social conscience: It donates a pair of glasses to someone in need for every pair it sells.

Customers in Warby Parker's target market recognize the value of paying less for glasses by changing their buying behavior. The customer can select up to five eyeglass frames from online inventory and have these choices delivered for a five-day free at-home trial before purchasing a pair. Warby Parker pays the postage both ways, so the customer risks nothing. Frame prices begin at $95 per pair, although optional extras such as progressive lenses will increase the final price. After deciding on a frame, the customer submits a prescription, clicks to finalize the order, and receives new glasses by mail within one to two weeks.

Originally, Warby Parker marketed its eyeglasses only online. Initial sales were so brisk that the startup surpassed its first-year sales objectives by the end of the first three weeks. Six months after its online debut,

Warby Parker had already sold 85,000 pairs—and donated an equal amount to people in need. But not everything is online. Customers have always been able to visit the company's New York City headquarters, see frames in person, and try them on before ordering. This proved so popular that after a few years, the co-founders decided to open small showrooms in large cities so more customers could try on frames and consult with staff before ordering.

Now Warby Parker has embarked on an ambitious strategy of opening its own stores in cities where the company's database shows high concentrations of customers. The company has 64 stores so far and plans to have 100 locations by the end of 2018. The company has also used pop-up stores and stores on wheels. Some of Warby Parker's stores are equipped for optical examinations. Some include photo kiosks so customers can snap fun photos of themselves wearing different frames and post to social media for advice from friends. The photos don't just help customers make buying decisions—they keep the Warby Parker brand in the public eye and help the firm stay in touch with customers who opt to receive communications. What's next for Warby Parker as it shakes up the eyewear industry with direct marketing, retail stores, low prices, fun styles, and social responsibility?[15]

WARBY PARKER
eyewear

360B/SHUTTERSTOCK.COM

Questions for Discussion

1. Based on your knowledge of pricing concepts, why does Warby Parker stress that the price tag for frames starts at $95?
2. Given Warby Parker's original idea of selling online to minimize distribution costs and keep prices low, do you agree with its more recent decision to open dozens of stores? Explain your answer.
3. Should Warby Parker charge more for frames purchased in stores than for frames purchased online, to offset the higher cost of rent and store employees? Why or why not?

Case 20.2

Norwegian Air Shuttle Continues to Climb with Low Costs and Low Prices

In 1993, Norwegian Air Shuttle was a tiny airline with three small planes flying to local destinations. Within a decade, the company had changed marketing direction and was beginning its ascent into the top tier of discount carriers with an ambitious new strategy that led to lower costs, lower fares, and longer-distance operations. Today, the award-winning company, based just outside Oslo, Norway, has become Europe's third-largest budget airline, serving 30 million passengers every year.

Norwegian's dramatic growth was fueled by its decision to buy dozens of new jets. These longer-range, fuel-efficient aircraft could carry more passengers to more destinations at far lower costs than the company's old fleet. Whether fuel costs went up or down, Norwegian's new aircraft could keep operating costs under control. This enabled the airline to promote low airfares, attract price-conscious business

travelers and vacationers, and build its brand beyond Scandinavia. Now Norwegian has a fleet of 200 jets flying to New York, London, and hundreds of other international destinations, with more jets on order to support the airline's future expansion plans.

Investing in new aircraft also helped the company enter new markets and manage costs on the ground. Norwegian's young fleet has a longer range, giving the airline new opportunities to compete in the busy and lucrative trans-Atlantic market, among other popular international routes. What's more, the new planes are capable of landing on shorter runways in smaller airports. This is important because larger airports generally charge higher landing fees than smaller airports. So, although Norwegian flies to major hubs like New York, Chicago, and Los Angeles, it also flies to smaller, less-expensive airports such as Providence,

Rhode Island, and Orange County, New York. These airports are less centrally located than their big-city counterparts, but millions of passengers are willing to put up with a bit of inconvenience to save a lot of money.

Another way Norwegian keeps costs low is by steering customers to its website to buy tickets. In fact, the airline charges more for tickets purchased via phone or at the airport. Rather than bundling everything into the price of the ticket, it says it wants to give customers control over the decision of which options they will pay for. Therefore, Norwegian sets a separate price for every extra, from checked luggage and reserved seating to inflight snacks and meals. This means passengers who want to reserve a seat in advance or check a suitcase at the airport can choose those options, for a fee. On the other hand, Norwegian has a frequent-flyer program that rewards loyal customers with points for choosing to travel with the airline and book with its hotel and rental-car partners. And whenever the airline inaugurates a new route, it offers a limited number of seats at bargain prices to build awareness and boost demand.

With a large number of businesses and households trying to stretch their travel budgets, Norwegian has to navigate in global skies increasingly crowded with no-frills, low-fare airlines. In addition to European market leaders like Ryanair and easyJet, other budget airlines flying European routes include Wizz Air and Wow Air. Long-established full-service airlines are getting into the budget business, too. Germany's Lufthansa, for example, operates Eurowings as a low-price subsidiary, and the parent of British Airways operates Level as a low-price subsidiary.

U.S.-based airlines like American Airlines and Delta have unbundled pricing to give price-sensitive passengers the option of paying only for services they need. Then

REBIUS/ISTOCK EDITORIAL/GETTY IMAGES

there's Texas-based Southwest Airlines, well known for its low-cost, low-price positioning. Southwest doesn't yet fly to Europe, but it does serve Mexico and the Caribbean, and its bundle pricing includes two pieces of checked luggage per passenger. As the airline refreshes its fleet with newer jets, will it expand to destinations in Europe? Norwegian Air Shuttle is continuing to watch closely for signs of new competition as it expands its fuel-efficient fleet and adds new routes, year after year.[16]

Questions for Discussion

1. Why is bargain pricing appropriate when Norwegian begins service to a new destination?

2. Which of the major pricing objectives does Norwegian appear to be pursuing, and why?

3. Given Norwegian's positioning as a no-frills, low-fare airline, how much weight should its marketers give to competitors' pricing when they set prices? Explain your answer.

Strategic Case 8

To Rent or to Own? That Is the Question

Rent or own? That's the question as U.S. consumers in all income brackets consider whether to plunk down money (or borrow money) to make purchases that carry a high price tag. Ownership allows consumers the freedom to use a possession whenever they wish, and to make their own decisions

about personalizing it. Still, the purchase price isn't always the only outlay. Car owners, for example, are responsible for insurance, fuel, maintenance, and repairs.

What are the alternatives for consumers who don't want to empty their wallets or pay ongoing costs month after

ASTRID STAWIARZ/GETTY IMAGES

month? A growing number of consumers—Millennials in particular—are flocking to innovators like Rent the Runway for access to pricey goods by renting as needed, rather than paying to own vehicles, designer fashions, or other expensive items.

Rent to Wear

Rent the Runway, founded in 2009, is a pioneer in fashion rental, with more than 5 million customers. From their own experiences, co-founders Jennifer Hyman and Jennifer Fleiss know about the high cost of buying special occasion clothes, only to wear them a few times. They envisioned an e-business with a different approach to dressing up without going broke or going out of style. Customers rent daytime, evening, or bridal fashions from the firm's website or at a Rent the Runway showroom in New York, Chicago, Beverly Hills, Topanga, Ca., San Francisco, or Washington, D.C. The cost of renting is much lower than the actual purchase price. For example, a $5,000 Naeem Khan dress rents for $800, including prepaid shipping both ways. Rent the Runway also offers an unlimited subscription service for customers who elect to receive new rentals on a regular basis.

Gwynnie Bee, founded by Christine Hunsicker, caters to plus-size women who want more wardrobe choices with the convenience of home delivery. It offers different subscription plans that allow customers to rent one, two, or up to ten pieces of clothing at a time, for as long as they like. When they want to rent something new, customers return clothing in the firm's prepaid packaging and receive another shipment of rented clothing in short order. Gwynnie Bee's slogan, "Clothing without Commitment," sums up the founder's dedication to providing a wide variety of fashion choices so plus-size women can update their wardrobes without having to buy and own.

Rent for the Road

Car-sharing services like Zipcar and Turo, both facilitated by smartphone apps, are making it quick and easy for consumers to rent wheels for a short time, when and where they please. A pioneer of car sharing, Zipcar has nearly 1 million members who pay a fee for the right to rent a car, minivan, or earth-friendly hybrid by the hour. Instead of going to a rental office, members pick up a vehicle from a convenient local parking spot and return it locally.

Turo connects consumers who want to rent a car for a limited time with individual car owners willing to let renters use their cars at prices set by the hour, day, or week. This is a more personal experience, because the car owner meets with the rental customer to turn over the keys and, at the end of the rental period, receives the keys back from the customer. No visits to rental offices, no lengthy contracts to sign, just an app to connect with a car owner, followed by a meeting to transfer keys.

Compared with the rental pricing of traditional car-rental companies, or the price of car ownership, the pricing of vehicles rented through services such as Turo and Zipcar are generally lower. These services even offer exotic vehicles for rent, at higher prices, to consumers who want to treat themselves or who need a special set of wheels for a special occasion. Just as important, these car-sharing services generally include basic car-insurance coverage—another money-saving benefit that renters appreciate.

Despite the popular buzz about car-sharing, projections indicate that the majority of consumers will still want to own their own vehicles in the future. One study suggests that by 2021, when worldwide car sales are expected to reach 100 million vehicles, car-sharing will mean the loss of only 550,000 vehicle purchases. Already, an estimated 1.5 million consumers are using car-sharing services in North America. As a result, automakers like General Motors and Ford see new marketing opportunities. They are testing their own car-sharing services to introduce their branded vehicles to renters who may, at some point in the future, choose to buy and own.

Rent a Gadget

Entrepreneur Aarthi Ramamurthy launched Lumoid in 2014 as a "try before you buy" rental site for expensive fitness-tracking wristbands, headphones, cameras, and other high-tech gadgets, including drones. However, in mid-2017 after news of a partnership with Best Buy spread, Ramamurthy experienced funding difficulties scaling up for the launch and decided to end Lumoid's operation. The idea was to allow consumers to test the gadget at home or at work for two weeks, to be sure that actual performance meets expectations. Before buying headphones that sell for $399, for example, one renter might want to see whether the product feels comfortable when worn during a long workout. Another renter might want to test the same headphones' volume during an airplane flight. Many popular brands of headphones could be rented for two weeks as part of a three-for-$45 offer, so consumers could alternate various headphones during the trial period. At the end of the trial, consumers simply returned the rented gear, with no obligation to buy. However, if they did decide to buy through Lumoid, part or all of the rental fee was applied to the purchase price.[17]

Questions for Discussion

1. How would you expect seasonal fluctuations in demand to affect a rental company's decisions about pricing rented products such as wedding dresses or convertible cars?

2. In terms of pricing principles, why do rental companies often display the retail price alongside the rental price for products they feature?

3. From a marketing perspective, why do Rent the Runway and other rental companies offer a discount to first-time customers?

4. What elements are consumers likely to consider when evaluating the purchase price of a product they want to own compared with the price of renting that product for a limited time?

Glossary

accessory equipment Equipment that does not become part of the final physical product but is used in production or office activities

advertising Paid nonpersonal communication about an organization and its products transmitted to a target audience through mass media

advertising appropriation The advertising budget for a specific time period

advertising campaign The creation and execution of a series of advertisements to communicate with a particular target audience

advertising platform Basic issues or selling points to be included in an advertising campaign

advocacy advertising Advertising that promotes a company's position on a public issue

aesthetic modifications Changes relating to the sensory appeal of a product

agents Intermediaries that represent either buyers or sellers on a permanent basis

aided recall test A posttest that asks respondents to identify recent ads and provides clues to jog their memories

allowance A concession in price to achieve a desired goal

approach The manner in which a salesperson contacts a potential customer

arbitrary approach Budgeting for an advertising campaign as specified by a high-level executive in the firm

artwork An advertisement's illustrations and layout

Asia-Pacific Economic Cooperation (APEC) An alliance that promotes open trade and economic and technical cooperation among member nations throughout the world

Association of Southeast Asian Nations (ASEAN) An alliance that promotes trade and economic integration among member nations in Southeast Asia

atmospherics The physical elements in a store's design that appeal to consumers' emotions and encourage buying

attitude An individual's enduring evaluation of feelings about, and behavioral tendencies toward, an object or idea

attitude scale A means of measuring consumer attitudes by gauging the intensity of individuals' reactions to adjectives, phrases, or sentences about an object

average fixed cost The fixed cost per unit produced

average total cost The sum of the average fixed cost and the average variable cost

average variable cost The variable cost per unit produced

B2B e-commerce sites Online marketplaces where business buyers and sellers from around the world can exchange information, goods, services, ideas, and payments

bait pricing Pricing an item in a product line low with the intention of selling a higher-priced item in the line

balance of trade The difference in value between a nation's exports and its imports

barter The trading of products

base-point pricing Geographic pricing that combines factory price and freight charges from the base point nearest the buyer

benefit segmentation The division of a market according to benefits that consumers want from the product

Better Business Bureau (BBB) A system of nongovernmental, independent, local regulatory agencies supported by local businesses that helps settle problems between customers and specific business firms

big data Massive data files that can be obtained from both structured and unstructured databases

blogs Short for "weblogs," these are web-based journals in which writers editorialize and interact with other internet users

brand A name, term, design, symbol, or other feature that identifies one seller's product as distinct from those of other sellers

brand competitors Firms that market products with similar features and benefits to the same customers at similar prices

brand equity The marketing and financial value associated with a brand's strength in a market

brand extension An organization uses one of its existing brands to brand a new product in a different product category

brand insistence The degree of brand loyalty in which a customer strongly prefers a specific brand and will accept no substitute

brand licensing An agreement whereby a company permits another organization to use its brand on other products for a licensing fee

brand loyalty A customer's favorable attitude toward a specific brand

brand manager The person responsible for a single brand

brand mark The part of a brand that is not made up of words, such as a symbol or design

brand name The part of a brand that can be spoken, including letters, words, and numbers

brand preference The degree of brand loyalty in which a customer prefers one brand over competitive offerings

brand recognition The degree of brand loyalty in which a customer is aware that a brand exists and views the brand as an alternative purchase if their preferred brand is unavailable

breakdown approach Measuring company sales potential based on a general economic forecast for a specific period and the market potential derived from it

breakeven point The point at which the costs of producing a product equal the revenue made from selling the product

brokers Intermediaries that bring buyers and sellers together temporarily

buildup approach Measuring company sales potential by estimating how much of a product a potential buyer in a specific geographic area will purchase in a given period, multiplying the estimate by the number of potential buyers, and adding the totals of all the geographic areas considered

bundle pricing Packaging together two or more complementary products and selling them at a single price

business analysis Evaluating the potential impact of a product idea on the firm's sales, costs, and profits

business (organizational) buying behavior The purchase behavior of producers, government units, institutions, and resellers

business cycle A pattern of economic fluctuations that has four stages: prosperity, recession, depression, and recovery

business market Individuals, organizations, or groups that purchase a specific kind of product for resale, direct use in producing other products, or use in general daily operations

business products Products bought to use in a firm's operations, to resell, or to make other products

business services Intangible products that many organizations use in their operations

buy-back allowance A sum of money given to a reseller for each unit bought after an initial promotional deal is over

buying allowance A temporary price reduction to resellers for purchasing specified quantities of a product

buying behavior The decision processes and actions of people involved in buying and using products

buying center The people within an organization who make business purchase decisions

buying power The size of the resources, such as money, goods, and services that can be traded in an exchange, that enable the individual to make purchases

buzz marketing An attempt to incite publicity and public excitement surrounding a product through a creative event

captioned photograph A photograph with a brief description of its contents

captive pricing Pricing the basic product in a product line low, while pricing related items higher

cash discount A price reduction given to buyers for prompt payment or cash payment

cash-and-carry wholesalers Limited-service wholesalers whose customers pay cash and furnish transportation

catalog marketing A type of marketing in which an organization provides a catalog from which customers make selections and place orders by mail, telephone, or the internet

category killer A very large specialty store that concentrates on a major product category and competes on the basis of low prices and product availability

category management A retail strategy of managing groups of similar, often substitutable products produced by different manufacturers

cause-related marketing The practice of linking products to a particular social cause on an ongoing or short-term basis

centralized organization A structure in which top-level managers delegate little authority to lower levels

cents-off offers Promotions that allow buyers to pay less than the regular price to encourage purchase

channel capacity The limit on the volume of information a communication channel can handle effectively

channel captain The dominant leader of a marketing channel or a supply channel

channel power The ability of one channel member to influence another member's goal achievement

client publics Direct consumers of a product of a nonprofit organization

client-based relationships Interactions that result in satisfied customers who use a service repeatedly over time

closing The stage in the personal selling process when the salesperson asks the prospect to buy the product

co-branding Using two or more brands on one product

codes of conduct Formalized rules and standards that describe what the company expects of its employees

coding process Converting meaning into a series of signs or symbols

cognitive dissonance A buyer's doubts shortly after a purchase about whether the decision was the right one

combination compensation plan Paying salespeople a fixed salary plus a commission based on sales volume

commercialization Refining and finalizing plans and budgets for full-scale manufacturing and marketing of a product

commission merchants Agents that receive goods on consignment from local sellers and negotiate sales in large, central markets

communication A sharing of meaning through the transmission of information

communications channel The medium of transmission that carries the coded message from the source to the receiver

community shopping center A type of shopping center with one or two department stores, some specialty stores, and convenience stores

company sales potential The maximum percentage of a market that an individual firm within an industry can expect to obtain for a specific product

comparative advertising Compares the sponsored brand with one or more identified brands on the basis of one or more product characteristics

comparison discounting Setting a price at a specific level and comparing it with a higher price

competition Other organizations that market products that are similar to or can be substituted for a marketer's products in the same geographic area

competition-based pricing Pricing influenced primarily by competitors' prices

competition-matching approach Determining an advertising budget by trying to match competitors' advertising outlays

competitive advantage The result of a company matching a core competency to opportunities it has discovered in the marketplace

competitive advertising Tries to stimulate demand for a specific brand by promoting its features, uses, and advantages relative to competing brands

component parts Items that become part of the physical product and are either finished items ready for assembly or items that need little processing before assembly

concentrated targeting strategy A market segmentation strategy in which an organization targets a single market segment using one marketing mix

concept testing Seeking a sample of potential buyers' responses to a product idea

conclusive research Research designed to verify insights through objective procedures and to help marketers in making decisions

consideration set A group of brands within a product category that a buyer views as alternatives for possible purchase

consistency of quality The degree to which a product has the same level of quality over time

consumer buying behavior The decision processes and purchasing activities of people who purchase products for personal or household use and not for business purposes

consumer buying decision process A five-stage purchase decision process that includes problem recognition, information search, evaluation of alternatives, purchase, and postpurchase evaluation

consumer contests Sales promotion methods in which individuals compete for prizes based on their analytical or creative skills

consumer games Sales promotion methods in which individuals compete for prizes based primarily on chance

consumer jury A panel of a product's existing or potential buyers who pretest ads

consumer market Purchasers and household members who intend to consume or benefit from the purchased products and do not buy products to make a profit

consumer misbehavior Behavior that violates generally accepted norms of a particular society

consumer products Products purchased to satisfy personal and family needs

consumer sales promotion methods Sales promotion techniques that encourage consumers to patronize specific stores or try particular products

consumer socialization The process through which a person acquires the knowledge and skills to function as a consumer

consumer sweepstakes A sales promotion in which entrants submit their names for inclusion in a drawing for prizes

consumerism Organized efforts by individuals, groups, and organizations to protect consumers' rights

contract manufacturing The practice of hiring a foreign firm to produce a designated volume of the domestic firm's product, or a component of it, to specification; the final product carries the domestic firm's name

convenience products Relatively inexpensive, frequently purchased items for which buyers exert minimal purchasing effort

convenience store A small self-service store that is open long hours and carries a narrow assortment of products, usually convenience items

cooperative advertising An arrangement in which a manufacturer agrees to pay a certain amount of a retailer's media costs for advertising the manufacturer's products

copy The verbal portion of advertisements

core competencies Things a company does extremely well, which sometimes give it an advantage over its competition

corporate strategy A strategy that determines the means for utilizing resources in the various functional areas to reach the organization's goals

cost comparison indicator A means of comparing the costs of advertising vehicles in a specific medium in relation to the number of people reached

cost-based pricing Adding a dollar amount or percentage to the cost of the product

cost-plus pricing Adding a specified dollar amount or percentage to the seller's cost

coupons Written price reductions used to encourage consumers to buy a specific product

credence qualities Attributes that customers may be unable to evaluate even after purchasing and consuming a service

crowdsourcing Combines the words *crowd* and *outsourcing* and calls for taking tasks usually performed by a marketer or researcher and outsourcing them to a crowd, or potential market, through an open call

cultural relativism The concept that morality varies from one culture to another and that business practices are, therefore, differentially defined as right or wrong by particular cultures

culture The accumulation of values, knowledge, beliefs, customs, objects, and concepts that a society uses to cope with its environment and passes on to future generations

cumulative discounts Quantity discounts aggregated over a stated time period

customary pricing Pricing on the basis of tradition

customer advisory boards Small groups of actual customers who serve as sounding boards for new product ideas and offer insights into their feelings and attitudes toward a firm's products and other elements of its marketing strategy

customer contact The level of interaction between provider and customer needed to deliver the service

customer forecasting survey A survey of customers regarding the types and quantities of products they intend to buy during a specific period

customer lifetime value (CLV) A key measurement that forecasts a customer's lifetime economic contribution based on continued relationship marketing efforts

customer relationship management (CRM) Using information about customers to create marketing strategies that develop and sustain desirable customer relationships

customer services Human or mechanical efforts or activities that add value to a product

customers The purchasers of organizations' products; the focal point of all marketing activities

cycle analysis An analysis of sales figures for a three- to five-year period to ascertain whether sales fluctuate in a consistent, periodic manner

cycle time The time needed to complete a process

database A collection of information arranged for easy access and retrieval

dealer listings Advertisements that promote a product and identify the names of participating retailers that sell the product

dealer loader A gift, often part of a display, given to a retailer that purchases a specified quantity of merchandise

decentralized organization A structure in which decision-making authority is delegated as far down the chain of command as possible

deceptive pricing The use of false or misleading statements or practices to persuade buyers that a product is a better deal than it really is

decline stage The stage of a product's life cycle during which sales fall rapidly

decoding process Converting signs or symbols into concepts and ideas

Delphi technique A procedure in which experts create initial forecasts, submit them to the company for averaging, and then refine the forecasts

demand curve A graph of the quantity of products a firm expects to sell at various prices if other factors remain constant

demand-based pricing Pricing based on the level of demand for the product

demonstrations Sales promotion methods a manufacturer uses temporarily to encourage trial use and purchase of a product or to show how a product works

department stores Large retail organizations characterized by a wide product mix and organized into separate departments to facilitate marketing efforts and internal management

depression A stage of the business cycle during which unemployment is extremely high, wages are very low, total disposable income is at a minimum, and consumers lack confidence in the economy

depth of product mix The average number of different products offered in each product line

derived demand Demand for business products that stems from demand for consumer products

descriptive research Research conducted to clarify the characteristics of certain phenomena to solve a particular problem

differential pricing Charging different prices to different buyers for the same quality and quantity of product

differentiated targeting strategy A strategy in which an organization targets two or more segments by developing a marketing mix for each segment

digital distribution Delivering content through the internet to a computer or other device

digital marketing The use of all digital media, including the internet and mobile and interactive channels, to develop communication and exchanges with customers

digital media Electronic media that function using digital codes—media available via computers, cellular phones, smartphones, and other digital devices that have been released in recent years

direct marketing The use of the telephone, internet, and nonpersonal media to introduce products to customers, who can then purchase them via mail, telephone, or the internet

direct ownership A situation in which a company owns subsidiaries or other facilities overseas

direct selling Marketing products to ultimate consumers through face-to-face sales presentations at home or in the workplace

direct-response marketing A type of marketing in which a retailer advertises a product and makes it available through mail or telephone orders

discount stores Self-service, general-merchandise stores that offer brand-name and private-brand products at low prices

discretionary income Disposable income available for spending and saving after an individual has purchased the basic necessities of food, clothing, and shelter

disposable income After-tax income

disruptive innovation A new way of exploiting old technologies—or a new business model developed—to give customers more than they've come to expect from current products in a specific market

distribution The decisions and activities that make products available to customers when and where they want to purchase them

distribution centers Large, centralized warehouses that focus on moving rather than storing goods

drop shippers Limited-service wholesalers that take title to goods and negotiate sales but never actually take possession of products

dumping Selling products at unfairly low prices

early adopters People who adopt new products early, choose new products carefully, and are viewed as "the people to check with" by later adopters

early majority Individuals who adopt a new product just prior to the average person

electronic data interchange (EDI) A computerized means of integrating order processing with production, inventory, accounting, and transportation

electronic marketing or **e-marketing** The strategic process of distributing, promoting, and pricing products, and discovering the desires of customers using digital media and digital marketing

embargo A government's suspension of trade in a particular product or with a given country

environmental analysis The process of assessing and interpreting the information gathered through environmental scanning

environmental scanning The process of collecting information about forces in the marketing environment

ethical issue An identifiable problem, situation, or opportunity requiring a choice among several actions that must be evaluated as right or wrong, ethical or unethical

European Union (EU) An alliance that promotes trade among its member countries in Europe

evaluative criteria Objective and subjective product characteristics that are important to a buyer

everyday low pricing (EDLP) Pricing products low on a consistent basis

exchange controls Government restrictions on the amount of a particular currency that can be bought or sold

exchanges The provision or transfer of goods, services, or ideas in return for something of value

exclusive dealing A situation in which a manufacturer forbids an intermediary from carrying products of competing manufacturers

exclusive distribution Using a single outlet in a fairly large geographic area to distribute a product

executive judgment A sales forecasting method based on the intuition of one or more executives

experience qualities Attributes that can be assessed only during purchase and consumption of a service

experimental research Research that allows marketers to make causal inferences about relationships between variables

expert forecasting survey Sales forecasts prepared by experts outside the firm, such as economists, management consultants, advertising executives, or college professors

exploratory research Research conducted to gather more information about a problem or to make a tentative hypothesis more specific

exporting The sale of products to foreign markets

extended decision making A consumer decision-making process employed when purchasing unfamiliar, expensive, or infrequently bought products

external reference price A comparison price provided by others

external search An information search in which buyers seek information from sources other than their memories

extreme-value stores Retailers that are a fraction of the size of conventional discount stores and typically offer very low prices on smaller size name-brand nonperishable household items

family branding Branding all of a firm's products with the same name or part of the name

family packaging Using similar packaging for all of a firm's products or packaging that has one common design element

feature article A manuscript of up to 3,000 words prepared for a specific publication

Federal Trade Commission (FTC) An agency that regulates a variety of business practices and curbs false advertising, misleading pricing, and deceptive packaging and labeling

feedback The receiver's response to a decoded message

first-mover advantage The ability of an innovative company to achieve long-term competitive advantages by being the first to offer a certain product in the marketplace

fixed costs Costs that do not vary with changes in the number of units produced or sold

F.O.B. destination A price indicating the producer is absorbing shipping costs

F.O.B. factory The price of merchandise at the factory before shipment

focus group A small group of 8 to 12 people who are brought together to participate in an interview that is often conducted informally, without a structured questionnaire, to observe interaction when members are exposed to an idea or a concept

franchising An arrangement in which a supplier (franchisor) grants a dealer (franchisee) the right to sell products in exchange for some type of consideration

free merchandise A manufacturer's reward given to resellers that purchase a stated quantity of products

free samples Samples of a product given out to encourage trial and purchase

freight absorption pricing Absorption of all or part of actual freight costs by the seller

freight forwarders Organizations that consolidate shipments from several firms into efficient lot sizes

full-service wholesalers Merchant wholesalers that perform the widest range of wholesaling functions

functional modifications Changes affecting a product's versatility, effectiveness, convenience, or safety

General Agreement on Tariffs and Trade (GATT) An agreement among nations to reduce worldwide tariffs and increase international trade

general publics Indirect consumers of a product of a nonprofit organization

general-merchandise retailer A retail establishment that offers a variety of product lines that are stocked in considerable depth

general-merchandise wholesalers Full-service wholesalers with a wide product mix but limited depth within product lines

generic brands Brands indicating only the product category

generic competitors Firms that provide very different products that solve the same problem or satisfy the same basic customer need

geodemographic segmentation A way of segmenting the market that clusters people by zip codes or neighborhood units based on lifestyle and demographic information

geographic pricing Reductions for transportation and other costs related to the physical distance between the buyer and the seller

globalization The development of marketing strategies that treat the entire world (or its major regions) as a single entity

good A tangible physical entity

government markets Federal, state, county, or local governments that buy goods and services to support their internal operations and provide products to their constituencies

green marketing A strategic process involving stakeholder assessment to create meaningful long-term relationships with customers while maintaining, supporting, and enhancing the natural environment

gross domestic product (GDP) The market value of a nation's total output of goods and services for a given period; an overall measure of economic standing

growth stage The product life-cycle stage during which sales rise rapidly, profits reach a peak, and then profits start to decline

heterogeneity Variation in quality

heterogeneous market A market made up of individuals or organizations with diverse needs for products in a specific product class

homesourcing A practice whereby customer-contact jobs are outsourced into workers' homes

homogeneous market A market in which a large proportion of customers have similar needs for a product

horizontal channel integration Combining organizations at the same level of operation under one management

hypermarkets Stores that combine supermarket and discount store shopping in one location

hypothesis An informed guess or assumption about a certain problem or a set of circumstances

idea A concept, a philosophy, an image, or an issue

idea generation Seeking product ideas to achieve organizational objectives

illustrations Photos, drawings, graphs, charts, and tables used to spark audience interest in an advertisement

import tariff A duty levied by a nation on goods bought outside its borders and brought into the country

importing The purchase of products from a foreign source

impulse buying An unplanned buying behavior, involving no conscious planning, resulting from a powerful urge to buy something immediately

income For an individual, the amount of money received through wages, rents, investments, pensions, and subsidy payments for a given period

individual branding A branding strategy in which each product is given a different name

industrial distributor An independent business organization that takes title to industrial products and carries inventories

inelastic demand Demand that is not significantly altered by a price increase or decrease

information inputs Sensations received through sight, taste, hearing, smell, and touch

in-home (door-to-door) interview A personal interview that takes place in the respondent's home

innovators First adopters of new products

inseparability The quality of being produced and consumed at the same time

installations Facilities and nonportable major equipment

institutional advertising Advertising that promotes organizational images, ideas, and political issues

institutional markets Organizations with charitable, educational, community, or other nonbusiness goals

intangibility The characteristic that a service is not physical and cannot be perceived by the senses

integrated marketing communications Coordination of promotion and other marketing efforts for maximum informational and persuasive impact on customers

intensive distribution Using all available outlets to distribute a product

intermodal transportation Two or more transportation modes used in combination

internal reference price A price developed in the buyer's mind through experience with the product

internal search An information search in which buyers search their memories for information about products that might solve their problem

international marketing Developing and performing marketing activities across national boundaries

introduction stage The initial stage of a product's life cycle; its first appearance in the marketplace, when sales start at zero and profits are negative

inventory management Developing and maintaining adequate assortments of products to meet customers' needs

joint demand Demand involving the use of two or more items in combination to produce a product

joint venture A partnership between a domestic firm and a foreign firm or government

just-in-time (JIT) An inventory management approach in which supplies arrive just when needed for production or resale

kinesic communication Communicating through the movement of head, eyes, arms, hands, legs, or torso

labeling Providing identifying, promotional, or other information on package labels

laggards The last product adopters, who distrust new products

late majority Skeptics who adopt new products when they feel it is necessary

late-mover advantage The ability of later market entrants to achieve long-term competitive advantages by not being the first to offer a certain product in a marketplace

layout The physical arrangement of an advertisement's illustration and copy

learning Changes in an individual's thought processes and behavior caused by information and experience

level of involvement An individual's degree of interest in a product and the importance of the product for that person

level of quality The amount of quality a product possesses

licensing An alternative to direct investment that requires a licensee to pay commissions or royalties on sales or supplies used in manufacturing

lifestyle An individual's pattern of living expressed through activities, interests, and opinions

lifestyle shopping center A type of shopping center that is typically open air and features upscale specialty stores, dining, and entertainment

limited decision making A consumer decision-making process used when purchasing products occasionally or needing information about an unfamiliar brand in a familiar product category

limited-line wholesalers Full-service wholesalers that carry only a few product lines but many products within those lines

limited-service wholesalers Merchant wholesalers that provide some services and specialize in a few functions

line extension Development of a product that is closely related to existing products in the line but is designed specifically to meet different customer needs

logistics management Managing the efficient and effective flow of materials, products, and information from the point of origin to consumption

mail survey A research method in which respondents answer a questionnaire sent through the mail

mail-order wholesalers Limited-service wholesalers that sell products through catalogs

manufacturer brands A brand initiated by producers to ensure that producers are identified with their products at the point of purchase

manufacturers' agents Independent intermediaries that represent two or more sellers and usually offer customers complete product lines

marginal cost (MC) The extra cost incurred by producing one more unit of a product

marginal revenue (MR) The change in total revenue resulting from the sale of an additional unit of a product

market A group of individuals and/or organizations that have needs for products in a product class and have the ability, willingness, and authority to purchase those products

market density The number of potential customers within a unit of land area

market growth/market share matrix A helpful business tool, based on the philosophy that a product's market growth rate and its market share are important considerations in determining its marketing strategy

market manager The person responsible for managing the marketing activities that serve a particular group of customers

market opportunity A combination of circumstances and timing that permits an organization to take action to reach a particular target market

market orientation An organization-wide commitment to researching and responding to customer needs

market potential The total amount of a product that customers will purchase within a specified period at a specific level of industry-wide marketing activity

market segment Individuals, groups, or organizations sharing one or more similar characteristics that cause them to have similar product needs

market segmentation The process of dividing a total market into groups consisting of people or organizations with relatively similar product needs in order to design a marketing mix that matches those needs

market share The percentage of a market that actually buys a specific product from a particular company

market test Making a product available to buyers in one or more test areas and measuring purchases and consumer responses to marketing efforts

marketing The process of creating, distributing, promoting, and pricing goods, services, and ideas to facilitate satisfying exchange relationships with customers and to develop and maintain favorable relationships with stakeholders in a dynamic environment

marketing analytics The use of tools and methods to measure and interpret the effectiveness of a firm's marketing activities

marketing channel A group of individuals and organizations that direct the flow of products from producers to customers within the supply chain

marketing citizenship The adoption of a strategic focus for fulfilling the economic, legal, ethical, and philanthropic social responsibilities expected by stakeholders

marketing concept A managerial philosophy that an organization should try to satisfy customers' needs through a coordinated set of activities that also allows the organization to achieve its goals

marketing cost analysis Analysis of costs to determine which are associated with specific marketing efforts

marketing decision support system (MDSS) Customized computer software that aids marketing managers in decision making

marketing environment The competitive, economic, political, legal and regulatory, technological, and sociocultural forces that surround the customer and affect the marketing mix

marketing ethics Principles and standards that define acceptable marketing conduct as determined by various stakeholders

marketing implementation The process of putting marketing strategies into action

marketing information system (MIS) A framework for managing and structuring information gathered regularly from sources inside and outside the organization

marketing intermediaries Middlemen that link producers to other intermediaries or ultimate consumers through contractual arrangements or through the purchase and resale of products

marketing mix Four marketing activities—product, distribution, promotion, and pricing—that a firm can control to meet the needs of customers within its target market

marketing objective A statement of what is to be accomplished through marketing activities

marketing plan A written document that specifies the activities to be performed to implement and evaluate the organization's marketing strategies

marketing research The systematic design, collection, interpretation, and reporting of information to help marketers solve specific marketing problems or take advantage of marketing opportunities

marketing strategy A plan of action for identifying and analyzing a target market and developing a marketing mix to meet the needs of that market

markup pricing Adding to the cost of the product a predetermined percentage of that cost

Maslow's hierarchy of needs The five levels of needs that humans seek to satisfy, from most to least important

materials handling Physical handling of tangible goods, supplies, and resources

maturity stage The stage of a product's life cycle during which the sales curve peaks and starts to level off or decline, and profits continue to fall

media plan A plan that specifies the media vehicles to be used and the schedule for running advertisements

megacarriers Freight transportation firms that provide several modes of shipment

merchandise allowance A manufacturer's agreement to pay resellers certain amounts of money for providing special promotional efforts, such as setting up and maintaining a display

merchant wholesalers Independently owned businesses that take title to goods, assume ownership risks, and buy and resell products to other wholesalers, business customers, or retailers

micromarketing A way of segmenting a market that focuses precise marketing efforts on very small geographic markets, such as communities or neighborhoods

mission statement A long-term view, or vision, of what the organization wants to become

missionary salespeople Support salespeople, usually employed by a manufacturer, who assist the producer's customers in selling to their own customers

mobile applications Software programs that run on mobile devices and give users access to certain content

modified rebuy purchase A new-task purchase that is changed on subsequent orders or when the requirements of a straight rebuy purchase are modified

money refunds Sales promotion techniques that offer consumers a specified amount of money when they mail in a proof of purchase, usually for multiple product purchases

monopolistic competition A competitive structure in which a firm has many potential competitors and tries to develop a marketing strategy to differentiate its product

monopoly A competitive structure in which an organization offers a product that has no close substitutes, making that organization the sole source of supply

motivation The inner driving forces or reasons behind an individual's actions and behaviors

MRO supplies Maintenance, repair, and operating items that facilitate production and operations but do not become part of the finished product

multichannel distribution The use of a variety of marketing channels to ensure maximum distribution

multichannel retailing Employing multiple distribution channels that complement brick-and-mortar stores with websites, catalogs, and apps where consumers can research products, read other buyers' reviews, and make actual purchases

multinational enterprise A firm that has operations or subsidiaries in many countries

multiple sourcing An organization's decision to use several suppliers

multiple-unit pricing Packaging together two or more identical products and selling them at a single price

National Advertising Review Board (NARB) A self-regulatory unit that considers challenges to issues raised by the National Advertising Division (an arm of the Council of Better Business Bureaus) about an advertisement

native advertising Digital advertising that matches the appearance and purpose of the content in which it is embedded

negotiated pricing Establishing a final price through bargaining between the seller and the customer

neighborhood shopping center A type of shopping center usually consisting of several small convenience and specialty stores

new introductory promotion Promotion that informs consumers about a new product

new-product development process A seven-phase process for introducing products: idea generation, screening, concept testing, business analysis, product development, test marketing, and commercialization

new-task purchase An organization's initial purchase of an item to be used to perform a new job or solve a new problem

news release A short piece of copy publicizing an event or a product

noise Anything that reduces a communication's clarity and accuracy

noncumulative discounts One-time price reductions based on the number of units purchased, the dollar value of the order, or the product mix purchased

nonprice competition Emphasizing factors other than price to distinguish a product from competing brands

nonprobability sampling A sampling technique in which there is no way to calculate the likelihood that a specific element of the population being studied will be chosen

nonprofit marketing Marketing activities conducted to achieve some goal other than ordinary business goals such as profit, market share, or return on investment

North American Free Trade Agreement (NAFTA) An alliance that merges Canada, Mexico, and the United States into a single market

North American Industry Classification System (NAICS) An industry classification system that generates comparable statistics among the United States, Canada, and Mexico

objective-and-task approach Budgeting for an advertising campaign by first determining its objectives and then calculating the cost of all the tasks needed to attain them

odd-even pricing Ending the price with certain numbers to influence buyers' perceptions of the price or product

off-peak pricing The practice of reducing prices of services used during slow periods in order to boost demand

off-price retailers Stores that buy manufacturers' seconds, overruns, returns, and off-season merchandise for resale to consumers at deep discounts

offshore outsourcing The practice of contracting with an organization to perform some or all business functions in a country other than the country in which the product will be sold

offshoring The practice of moving a business process that was done domestically at the local factory to a foreign country, regardless of whether the production accomplished in the foreign country is performed by the local company (e.g., in a wholly owned subsidiary) or a third party (e.g., subcontractor)

oligopoly A competitive structure in which a few sellers control the supply of a large proportion of a product

omni-channel Various marketing channels, including mobile, desktop, or traditional retail spaces, providing seamless customer experiences

on-site computer interview A variation of the shopping mall intercept interview in which respondents complete a self-administered questionnaire displayed on a computer monitor

online fraud Any attempt to conduct dishonest activities online, including deceiving consumers into releasing personal information

online retailing Retailing that makes products available to buyers through computer connections

online survey A research method in which respondents answer a questionnaire via email or on a website

operations management Managing activities from production to final delivery through system-wide coordination

opinion leader A member of an informal group who provides information about a specific topic to other group members

opportunity cost The value of the benefit given up by choosing one alternative over another

order processing The receipt and transmission of sales order information

organizational (corporate) culture A set of values, beliefs, goals, norms, and rituals that members of an organization share

outsourcing The practice of contracting noncore operations with an organization that specializes in that operation

penetration pricing Setting prices below those of competing brands to penetrate a market and gain a significant market share quickly

percent-of-sales approach Budgeting for an advertising campaign by multiplying the firm's past and expected sales by a standard percentage

perception The process of selecting, organizing, and interpreting information inputs to produce meaning

performance standard An expected level of performance against which actual performance can be compared

periodic discounting Temporary reduction of prices on a patterned or systematic basis

perishability The inability of unused service capacity to be stored for future use

personal interview survey A research method in which participants respond to survey questions face-to-face

personal selling Paid personal communication that attempts to inform customers and persuade them to buy products in an exchange situation

personality A set of internal traits and distinct behavioral tendencies that result in consistent patterns of behavior in certain situations

pioneer advertising Advertising that tries to stimulate demand for a product category rather than a specific brand by informing potential buyers about the product

podcasts Audio or video files that can be downloaded from the internet with a subscription that automatically delivers new content to listening devices or personal computers

point-of-purchase (POP) materials Signs, window displays, display racks, and similar devices used to attract customers

population All the elements, units, or individuals of interest to researchers for a specific study

posttest Evaluation of advertising effectiveness after the campaign

power shopping center A type of shopping center that combines off-price stores with category killers

predatory pricing Also called undercutting, involves the intent to set a product's price so low that rival firms cannot compete and, therefore, withdraw from the marketplace

premium money (push money) Extra compensation to salespeople for pushing a line of goods

premium pricing Pricing the highest-quality or most versatile products higher than other models in the product line

premiums Items offered free or at a minimal cost as a bonus for purchasing a product

press conference A meeting used to announce major news events

prestige pricing Setting prices at an artificially high level to convey prestige or a quality image

prestige-sensitive Drawn to products that signify prominence and status

pretest Evaluation of advertisements performed before a campaign begins

price The value paid for a product in a marketing exchange

price competition Emphasizing price as an issue and matching or beating competitors' prices

price discrimination Employing price differentials that injure competition by giving one or more buyers a competitive advantage

price elasticity of demand A measure of the sensitivity of demand to changes in price

price fixing An agreement among competing firms to raise, lower, or maintain prices for mutual benefit

price leaders Products priced near or even below cost

price lining Setting a limited number of prices for selected groups or lines of merchandise

price skimming Charging the highest possible price that buyers who most desire the product will pay

price war Involves two or more companies engaging in intense price competition, often in an effort to boost market share

price-conscious Striving to pay low prices

pricing objectives Goals that describe what a firm wants to achieve through pricing

primary data Data observed and recorded or collected directly from respondents

primary demand Demand for a product category rather than for a specific brand

private distributor brands Brands initiated and owned by a reseller

private warehouses Company-operated facilities for storing and shipping their own products

probability sampling A type of sampling in which every element in the population being studied has a known chance of being selected for study

process materials Materials that are used directly in the production of other products but are not readily identifiable

procurement Processes to obtain resources to create value through sourcing, purchasing, and recycling, including materials and information

producer markets Individuals and business organizations that purchase products to make profits by using them to produce other products or using them in their operations

product A good, a service, or an idea

product adoption process The five-stage process of buyer acceptance of a product: awareness, interest, evaluation, trial, and adoption

product advertising Advertising that promotes the uses, features, and benefits of products

product competitors Firms that compete in the same product class but market products with different features, benefits, and prices

product deletion Eliminating a product from the product mix when it no longer satisfies a sufficient number of customers

product design How a product is conceived, planned, and produced

product development Determining if producing a product is technically feasible and cost-effective

product differentiation Creating and designing products so customers perceive them as different from competing products

product features Specific design characteristics that allow a product to perform certain tasks

product item A specific version of a product that can be designated as a distinct offering among a firm's products

product life cycle The progression of a product through four stages: introduction, growth, maturity, and decline

product line A group of closely related product items viewed as a unit because of marketing, technical, or end-use considerations

product manager The person within an organization who is responsible for a product, a product line, or several distinct products that make up a group

product mix The composite, or total, group of products that an organization makes available to customers

product modification Changes in one or more characteristics of a product

product placement The strategic location of products or product promotions within entertainment media content to reach the product's target market

product positioning The decisions and activities intended to create and maintain a certain concept of the firm's product, relative to competitive brands, in customers' minds

product specifications Written statements describing a product's necessary characteristics, standards of quality, and other information essential to identifying the best supplier for the needed product

product-line pricing Establishing and adjusting prices of multiple products within a product line

professional pricing Fees set by people with great skill or experience in a particular field

promotion Communication to build and maintain relationships by informing and persuading one or more audiences

promotion mix A combination of promotional methods used to promote a specific product

prospecting Developing a database of potential customers

prosperity A stage of the business cycle characterized by low unemployment and relatively high total income, which together ensure high buying power (provided the inflation rate stays low)

proxemic communication Communicating by varying the physical distance in face-to-face interactions

psychological influences Factors that in part determine people's general behavior, thus influencing their behavior as consumers

psychological pricing Pricing that attempts to influence a customer's perception of price to make a product's price more attractive

public relations Communication efforts used to create and maintain favorable relations between an organization and its stakeholders

public warehouses Storage space and related logistics facilities that can be leased by companies

publicity A news-story type of communication about an organization and/or its products transmitted through a mass medium at no charge

pull policy Promoting a product directly to consumers to develop strong consumer demand that pulls products through the marketing channel

purchasing The act of negotiating and executing transactions to buy and sell goods, materials, and services

pure competition A market structure characterized by an extremely large number of sellers, none strong enough to significantly influence price or supply

push policy Promoting a product only to the next institution down the marketing channel

quality The overall characteristics of a product that allow it to perform as expected in satisfying customer needs

quality modifications Changes relating to a product's dependability and durability

quantity discounts Deductions from the list price for purchasing in large quantities

quota A limit on the amount of goods an importing country will accept for certain product categories in a specific period of time

quota sampling A nonprobability sampling technique in which researchers divide the population into groups and then arbitrarily choose participants from each group

rack jobbers Full-service, specialty-line wholesalers that own and maintain display racks in stores

radio frequency identification (RFID) Using tags and readers that use radio waves to identify and track tagged materials

random discounting Temporary reduction of prices on an unsystematic basis

random factor analysis An analysis attempting to attribute erratic sales variations to random, nonrecurring events

random sampling A form of probability sampling in which all units in a population have an equal chance of appearing in the sample, and the various events that can occur have an equal or known chance of taking place

raw materials Basic natural materials that become part of a physical product

rebates Sales promotion techniques in which a consumer receives a specified amount of money for making a single product purchase

receiver The individual, group, or organization that decodes a coded message

recession A stage of the business cycle during which unemployment rises and total buying power declines, stifling both consumer and business spending

reciprocity An arrangement unique to business marketing in which two organizations agree to buy from each other

recognition test A posttest in which respondents are shown the actual ad and are asked if they recognize it

recovery A stage of the business cycle during which the economy moves from recession or depression toward prosperity

recruiting Developing a list of qualified applicants for sales positions

recycling Converting waste into reusable material, reprocessing, reclaiming, or reusing supplies and final products

reference group A group that a person identifies with so strongly that he or she adopts the values, attitudes, and behavior of group members

reference pricing Pricing a product at a moderate level and displaying it next to a more expensive model or brand

regional issues Versions of a magazine that differ across geographic regions

regional shopping center A type of shopping center with the largest department stores, widest product mixes, and deepest product lines

regression analysis A method of predicting sales based on finding a relationship between past sales and one or more independent variables, such as population or per capita income

reinforcement advertising Advertising that assures users they chose the right brand and tells them how to get the most satisfaction from it

relationship marketing Establishing long-term, mutually satisfying buyer–seller relationships

relationship selling The building of mutually beneficial long-term associations with a customer through regular communications over prolonged periods of time

reliability A condition that exists when a research technique produces almost identical results in repeated trials

reminder advertising Advertising used to remind consumers about an established brand's uses, characteristics, and benefits

research design An overall plan for obtaining the information needed to address a research problem or issue

reseller markets Intermediaries that buy finished goods and resell them for a profit

retail positioning Identifying an unserved or underserved market segment and serving it through a strategy that distinguishes the retailer from others in the minds of consumers in that segment

retailer An organization that purchases products for the purpose of reselling them to ultimate consumers

retailing All transactions in which the buyer intends to consume the product through personal, family, or household use

roles Actions and activities that a person in a particular position is supposed to perform based on expectations of the individual and surrounding people

routinized response behavior A consumer decision-making process used when buying frequently purchased, low-cost items that require very little search-and-decision effort

sales analysis Analysis of sales figures to evaluate a firm's performance

sales branches Manufacturer-owned intermediaries that sell products and provide support services to the manufacturers' sales forces

sales contest A sales promotion method used to motivate distributors, retailers, and sales personnel through recognition of outstanding achievements

sales force forecasting survey A survey of a firm's sales force regarding anticipated sales in their territories for a specified period

sales forecast The amount of a product a company expects to sell during a specific period at a specified level of marketing activity

sales offices Manufacturer-owned operations that provide services normally associated with agents

sales promotion An activity and/or material intended to induce resellers or salespeople to sell a product or consumers to buy it

sample A limited number of units chosen to represent the characteristics of a total population

sampling The process of selecting representative units from a total population

scan-back allowance A manufacturer's reward to retailers based on the number of pieces scanned

screening Selecting the ideas with the greatest potential for further review

search qualities Tangible attributes that can be judged before the purchase of a product

seasonal analysis An analysis of daily, weekly, or monthly sales figures to evaluate the degree to which seasonal factors influence sales

seasonal discount A price reduction given to buyers for purchasing goods or services out of season

secondary data Data compiled both inside and outside the organization for some purpose other than the current investigation

secondary-market pricing Setting one price for the primary target market and a different price for another market

segmentation variables Characteristics of individuals, groups, or organizations used to divide a market into segments

selective demand Demand for a specific brand

selective distortion An individual's changing or twisting of information that is inconsistent with personal feelings or beliefs

selective distribution Using only some available outlets in an area to distribute a product

selective exposure The process by which some inputs are selected to reach awareness and others are not

selective retention Remembering information inputs that support personal feelings and beliefs and forgetting inputs that do not

self-concept A perception or view of oneself

selling agents Intermediaries that market a whole product line or a manufacturer's entire output

service An intangible result of the application of human and mechanical efforts to people or objects

service quality Customers' perceptions of how well a service meets or exceeds their expectations

shopping mall intercept interview A research method that involves interviewing a percentage of individuals passing by "intercept" points in a mall

shopping products Items for which buyers are willing to expend considerable effort in planning and making purchases

single-source data Information provided by a single marketing research firm

situational influences Influences that result from circumstances, time, and location that affect the consumer buying decision process

social class An open group of individuals with similar social rank

social influences The forces other people exert on one's buying behavior

social network A website where users can create a profile and interact with other users, post information, and engage in other forms of web-based communication

social responsibility An organization's obligation to maximize its positive impact and minimize its negative impact on society

sociocultural forces The influences in a society and its culture(s) that change people's attitudes, beliefs, norms, customs, and lifestyles

sole sourcing An organization's decision to use only one supplier

source A person, a group, or an organization with a meaning it tries to share with a receiver or an audience

sourcing The process of determining what materials a firm needs, where those materials come from, and how they impact marketing integrity

Southern Common Market (MERCOSUR) An alliance that promotes the free circulation of goods, services, and production factors, and has a common external tariff and commercial policy among member nations in South America

special-event pricing Advertised sales or price cutting linked to a holiday, a season, or an event

specialty products Items, with unique characteristics, that buyers are willing to expend considerable effort to obtain

specialty-line wholesalers Full-service wholesalers that carry only a single product line or a few items within a product line

stakeholders Constituents who have a "stake," or claim, in some aspect of a company's products, operations, markets, industry, and outcomes

statistical interpretation Analysis of what is typical and what deviates from the average

storyboard A blueprint that combines copy and visual material to show the sequence of major scenes in a commercial

straight commission compensation plan Paying salespeople according to the amount of their sales in a given time period

straight rebuy purchase A routine purchase by a business buyer of the same products under approximately the same terms of sale

straight salary compensation plan Paying salespeople a specific amount per time period, regardless of selling effort

strategic alliances Partnerships that are formed to create a competitive advantage on a worldwide basis

strategic business unit (SBU) A division, product line, or other profit center within the parent company

strategic channel alliance An agreement whereby the products of one organization are distributed through the marketing channels of another

strategic marketing management The process of planning, implementing, and evaluating the performance of marketing activities and strategies, both effectively and efficiently

strategic performance evaluation Establishing performance standards, measuring actual performance, comparing actual performance with established standards, and modifying the marketing strategy, if needed

strategic philanthropy The synergistic use of organizational core competencies and resources to address key stakeholders' interests and achieve both organizational and social benefits

strategic planning The process of establishing an organizational mission and formulating goals, a corporate strategy, marketing objectives, and a marketing strategy

strategic windows Temporary periods of optimal fit between the key requirements of a market and the particular capabilities of a company competing in that market

stratified sampling A type of probability sampling in which the population is divided into groups with a common attribute, and a random sample is chosen within each group

styling The physical appearance of a product

subculture A group of individuals whose characteristics, values, and behavioral patterns are similar within the group and different from those of people in the surrounding culture

supermarkets Large, self-service stores that carry a complete line of food products, along with some non-food items

superregional shopping center A type of shopping center with the widest and deepest product mixes that attracts customers from many miles away and often has special attractions

superstores Giant retail outlets that carry food and non-food products found in supermarkets, as well as most routinely purchased consumer products

supply chain All the organizations and activities involved with the flow and transformation of products from raw materials through to the end customer

supply chain management (SCM) The coordination of all the activities involved with the flow and transformation of supplies, products, and information throughout the supply chain to the ultimate consumer

support personnel Sales staff members who facilitate selling but usually are not involved solely with making sales

sustainability The potential for the long-term well-being of the natural environment, including all biological entities, as well as the interaction among nature and individuals, organizations, and business strategies

sustainable competitive advantage An advantage that the competition cannot copy

SWOT analysis Assessment of an organization's strengths, weaknesses, opportunities, and threats

tactile communication Communicating through touching

target audience The group of people at whom advertisements are aimed

target market A specific group of customers on whom an organization focuses its marketing efforts

target public A collective of individuals who have an interest in or concern about an organization, a product, or a social cause

team selling The use of a team of experts from all functional areas of a firm, led by a salesperson, to conduct the personal selling process

technical salespeople Support salespeople who give technical assistance to a firm's current customers

technology The application of knowledge and tools to solve problems and perform tasks more efficiently

telemarketing The performance of marketing-related activities by telephone

telephone depth interview An interview that combines the traditional focus group's ability to probe with the confidentiality provided by telephone surveys

telephone survey A research method in which respondents' answers to a questionnaire are recorded by an interviewer on the phone

television home shopping A form of selling in which products are presented to television viewers, who can buy them by calling a toll-free number and paying with a credit card

test marketing A limited introduction of a product in geographic areas chosen to represent the intended market

third-party logistics (3PL) firms Firms that have special expertise in core logistics activities such as warehousing, transportation, inventory management, and information technology and can often perform these activities more efficiently

time series analysis A forecasting method that uses historical sales data to discover patterns in the firm's sales over time and generally involves trend, cycle, seasonal, and random factor analyses

total budget competitors Firms that compete for the limited financial resources of the same customers

total cost The sum of average fixed and average variable costs times the quantity produced

trade (functional) discount A reduction off the list price a producer gives to an intermediary for performing certain functions

trade name The full legal name of an organization

trade sales promotion methods Methods intended to persuade wholesalers and retailers to carry a producer's products and market them aggressively

trade salespeople Salespeople involved mainly in helping a producer's customers promote a product

trademark A legal designation of exclusive use of a brand

trading company A company that links buyers and sellers in different countries

traditional specialty retailers Stores that carry a narrow product mix with deep product lines

transfer pricing Prices charged in sales between an organization's units

transportation The movement of products from where they are made to intermediaries and end users

trend analysis An analysis that focuses on aggregate sales data over a period of many years to determine general trends in annual sales

truck wholesalers Limited-service wholesalers that transport products directly to customers for inspection and selection

tying agreement An agreement in which a supplier furnishes a product to a channel member with the stipulation that the channel member must purchase other products as well

unaided recall test A posttest in which respondents are asked to identify advertisements they have seen recently but are not given any recall clues

undifferentiated targeting strategy A strategy in which an organization designs a single marketing mix and directs it at the entire market for a particular product

uniform geographic pricing Charging all customers the same price, regardless of geographic location

unsought products Products purchased to solve a sudden problem, products of which customers are unaware, and products that people do not necessarily think of buying

validity A condition that exists when a research method measures what it is supposed to measure

value A customer's subjective assessment of benefits relative to costs in determining the worth of a product

value analysis An evaluation of each component of a potential purchase

value-conscious Concerned about price and quality of a product

variable costs Costs that vary directly with changes in the number of units produced or sold

vending The use of machines to dispense products

vendor analysis A formal, systematic evaluation of current and potential vendors

venture team A cross-functional group that creates entirely new products that may be aimed at new markets

vertical channel integration Combining two or more stages of the marketing channel under one management

vertical marketing system (VMS) A marketing channel managed by a single channel member to achieve efficient, low-cost distribution aimed at satisfying target market customers

viral marketing A strategy to get consumers to share a marketer's message, often through email or online videos, in a way that spreads dramatically and quickly

warehouse clubs Large-scale, members-only establishments that combine features of cash-and-carry wholesaling with discount retailing

warehouse showrooms Retail facilities in large, low-cost buildings with large on-premises inventories and minimal services

warehousing The design and operation of facilities for storing and moving goods

wealth The accumulation of past income, natural resources, and financial resources

wholesaler An individual or an organization that sells products that are bought for resale, for making other products, or for general business operations

wholesaling Transactions in which products are bought for resale, for making other products, or for general business operations

widgets Small bits of software on a website, desktop, or mobile device that perform a simple task, such as providing stock quotes or blog updates

width of product mix The number of product lines a company offers

wiki Type of software that creates an interface that enables users to add to or edit the content of some types of websites

willingness to spend An inclination to buy because of expected satisfaction from a product, influenced by the ability to buy and numerous psychological and social forces

word-of-mouth communication Personal, informal exchanges of communication that customers share with one another about products, brands, and companies

World Trade Organization (WTO) An entity that promotes free trade among member nations by eliminating trade barriers and educating individuals, companies, and governments about trade rules around the world

zone pricing Pricing based on transportation costs within major geographic zones

Endnotes

Chapter 1

1. Catherine Clifford, "How Amazon Founder Jeff Bezos Went from the Son of a Teen Mom to the World's Richest Person," *CNBC*, October 27, 2017, https://www.cnbc.com/2017/10/27/how-amazon-founder-jeff-bezos-went-from-the-son-of-a-teen-mom-to-the-worlds-richest-person.html (accessed December 18, 2017); Caroline Cakebread, "Amazon Launched 22 Years Ago This Week — Here's What Shopping on Amazon Was Like Back in 1995," *Business Insider*, July 20, 2017, www.businessinsider.com/amazon-opened-22-years-ago-see-the-business-evolve-2017-7 (accessed December 18, 2017); Charisse Jones, "Amazon Wants Your Teen to Spend Your Money But Parents Have the Final Say," *USA Today*, October 11, 2017, https://www.usatoday.com/story/money/2017/10/11/amazon-let-parents-hand-over-shopping-keys-kids/751594001/ (accessed December 18, 2017); Daniel Keyes, "Amazon Prime May Be Reaching Saturation in the U.S.," *Business Insider*, December 18, 2017, www.businessinsider.com/amazon-prime-may-be-reaching-saturation-in-the-us-2017-12 (accessed December 18, 2017); Amazon, "About A-to-z Guarantee," Amazon.com, https://www.amazon.com/gp/help/customer/display.html?nodeId=201889410 (accessed December 18, 2017); Alison Griswold, "Amazon Just Explained How Whole Foods Fits Into Its Plan for World Domination," *Quartz*, October 27, 2017, https://qz.com/1113795/amazon-amzn-just-explained-how-whole-foods-fits-into-its-plan-for-world-domination/ (accessed December 23, 2017); Ry Crist, "After a Busy 2017, Alexa Is Still on Top—and Still Evolving," *CNET*, December 20, 2017, https://www.cnet.com/news/after-a-busy-2017-alexa-is-still-on-top-and-still-evolving/ (accessed December 24, 2017).

2. "Definition of Marketing," American Marketing Association, https://www.ama.org/AboutAMA/Pages/Definition-of-Marketing.aspx (accessed December 10, 2017).

3. Isaac Mizrahi, "The Hispanic Market 'Long Tail': Five Hidden Growth Opportunities for U.S. CMOs to Win in 2017," *Forbes*, January 18, 2017, https://www.forbes.com/sites/onmarketing/2017/01/18/the-hispanic-market-long-tail-five-hidden-growth-opportunities-for-u-s-cmos-to-win-in-2017/#4e14aa5e22ca (accessed December 10, 2017).

4. Tessa Berenson, "Amazon Is Adding Spanish to Its U.S. Website," *Fortune*, March 10, 2017, http://fortune.com/2017/03/10/amazon-spanish-website/ (accessed December 10, 2017).

5. "Comcast Places a Bigger Bet on Selling to Businesses," *Fortune*, September 13, 2017, http://fortune.com/2017/09/13/comcast-selling-to-businesses/ (accessed December 10, 2017).

6. Rick Lingle, "Skyr Retells Its Story via Innovative Packaging," *Packaging Digest*, December 5, 2017, www.packagingdigest.com/food-packaging/skyr-retells-story-innovative-pkg1712 (accessed December 10, 2017).

7. Joyce Chepkemoi, "The World's Largest Fast Food Restaurant Chains," *World Atlas*, April 25, 2017, www.worldatlas.com/articles/the-world-s-largest-fast-food-restaurant-chains.html (accessed December 10, 2017).

8. Hugh McIntyre, "Pandora Has Lost Nearly 8 Million Listeners in 9 Months," *Forbes*, November 3, 2017, https://www.forbes.com/sites/hughmcintyre/2017/11/03/pandora-is-losing-850000-listeners-every-month/#25ef89955a93 (accessed December 10, 2017); Micah Singleton, "Spotify Now Has 140 Million Active Users," *The Verge*, June 15, 2017, https://www.theverge.com/2017/6/15/15807826/spotify-140-million-active-users (accessed December 10, 2017).

9. Molly Soat, "Turning Heads," *Marketing News*, July 2015, pp. 12–13.

10. "About Us," Makeup.com, https://www.makeup.com/about (accessed December 10, 2017).

11. Rajneesh Suri, Chiranjeev Kohli, and Kent B. Monroe, "The Effects of Perceived Scarcity on Consumers' Processing of Price Information," *Journal of the Academy of Marketing Science* 35, 1 (2007): pp. 89–100.

12. Natalie Mizik and Robert Jacobson, "Trading Off Between Value Creation and Value Appropriation: The Financial Implications and Shifts in Strategic Emphasis," *Journal of Marketing* 67, 1 (January 2003): pp. 63–76.

13. Peter Economy, "5 Remarkably Powerful Customer Service Secrets from the Hospitality Industry," *Inc.*, January 1, 2017, https://www.inc.com/peter-economy/5-remarkably-powerful-customer-service-secrets-from-the-hospitality-industry.html (accessed December 12, 2017).

14. O. C. Ferrell and Michael Hartline, *Marketing Strategy*, 5th ed. (Mason, OH: Cengage Learning, 2011), p. 370.

15. Sara Leroi-Werelds, Sandra Streukens, Michael K. Brady, and Gilbert Swinnen, "Assessing the Value of Commonly Used Methods for Measuring Customer Value: A Multi-setting Empirical Study," *Journal of the Academy of Marketing Science* 42, 4 (July 2014): pp. 430–451.

16. Isabelle Maignan, Tracy Gonzalez-Padron, G. Tomas Hult, and O. C. Ferrell, "Stakeholder Orientation: Development and Testing of a Framework for Socially Responsible Marketing," *Journal of Strategic Marketing* 19, 4 (2011): pp. 313–338.

17. Vijay K. Patel, Scott. C. Manley, O. C. Ferrell, Torsten M. Pieper, and Joseph F. Hair, Jr., "Stakeholder Orientation: Proactive and Responsive Components and Firm Performance," Working paper, 2016.

18. Mike Esterl, "New Diet Pepsi Leaves Some Loyalists with Bad Taste," *The Wall Street Journal*, October 8, 2015, www.wsj.com/articles/new-diet-pepsi-leaves-some-loyalists-with-bad-taste-1444327691 (accessed December 9, 2015); John Kell, "PepsiCo's CEO: Why I'm Bringing Back Diet Pepsi with Aspartame," *Fortune*, July 7, 2016, http://fortune.com/2016/07/07/pepsi-ceo-diet-pepsi-aspartame/ (accessed December 10, 2017).

19. Ajay K. Kohli and Bernard J. Jaworski, "Market Orientation: The Construct, Research Propositions, and Managerial Implications," *Journal of Marketing* 54, 2 (April 1990): pp. 1–18; O. C. Ferrell, "Business Ethics and Customer Stakeholders," *Academy of Management Executive* 18, 2 (May 2004): pp. 126–129.

20. "Starbucks CEO Howard Schultz Is All Abuzz," *CBS News*, June 5, 2012, https://www.cbsnews.com/news/

starbucks-ceo-howard-schultz-is-all-abuzz/ (accessed December 12, 2017).

21 Xeuming Luo and Christian Homburg, "Neglected Outcomes of Customer Satisfaction," *Journal of Marketing* 71, 2 (April 2007): pp. 133–149.

22 O. C. Ferrell, Joe F. Hair, Jr., Greg W. Marshall, and Robert D. Tamilia, "Understanding the History of Marketing Education to Improve Classroom Instruction," *Marketing Education Review* 25, 2 (2015): pp. 159–175; Eugene W. Anderson, Claes Fornell, and Sanal K. Mazvancheryl, "Customer Satisfaction and Shareholder Value," *Journal of Marketing* 68, 4 (October 2004): pp. 172–185.

23 Ajay K. Kohli and Bernard J. Jaworski, "Market Orientation: The Construct, Research Propositions, and Managerial Implications," *Journal of Marketing* 54, 2 (April 1990): pp. 1–18.

24 Kwaku Atuahene-Gima, "Resolving the Capability-Rigidity Paradox in New Product Innovation," *Journal of Marketing* 69, 4 (October 2005): pp. 61–83.

25 Maryalene LaPonsie, "15 Stores with the Best Return Policies," *CBS*, November 22, 2017, https://www.cbsnews.com/news/15-stores-with-the-best-return-policies/ (accessed January 6, 2018).

26 Gary F. Gebhardt, Gregory S. Carpenter, and John F. Sherry Jr., "Creating a Market Orientation," *Journal of Marketing* 70 (October 2006): pp. 37–55.

27 James D. Doyle and Anahit Armenakyan, "Value-creating Mechanisms Within the Market Orientation—Performance Relationship: A Meta-Analysis," *Journal of Strategic Marketing* 22, 3 (2014): pp. 193–205.

28 Erin Bunch, "Weight Watchers Adds Proteins to Its List of Zero Points Foods," *Well + Good*, December 4, 2017, https://www.wellandgood.com/good-food/weight-watchers-freestyle-zero-points/ (accessed January 6, 2018).

29 "A Winning Team for College Football," SAP, www.sap.com/customer-testimonials/sports-entertainment/dfb.html (accessed December 8, 2015).

30 Mark Matousek, "Elon Musk Reveals Tesla Is Making Its Own AI Chips for Self-Driving Cars—and He Claims the Technology Will Be the 'Best in the World,'" *Business Insider*, December 8, 2017, www.businessinsider.com/elon-musk-says-tesla-is-making-ai-chips-for-its-self-driving-cars-2017-12 (accessed January 6, 2018).

31 Jacquelyn S. Thomas, Robert C. Blattberg, and Edward J. Fox, "Recapturing Lost Customers," *Journal of Marketing Research* 41, 1 (February 2004): pp. 31–45.

32 Jagdish N. Sheth and Rajendras Sisodia, "More Than Ever Before, Marketing Is under Fire to Account for What It Spends," *Marketing Management* (Fall 1995): pp. 13–14.

33 Stephen L. Vargo and Robert F. Lusch, "Service-Dominant Logic: Continuing the Evolution," *Journal of the Academy of Marketing Science* 36 (2008): pp. 1–10.

34 Cherene Etemadi, "The Top 4 Relationship Marketing Examples You Need to Try," *Human Marketing*, November 27, 2017, http://inbound.human.marketing/the-top-4-relationship-marketing-examples (accessed January 6, 2018).

35 Chezy Ofir and Itamar Simonson, "The Effect of Stating Expectations on Customer Satisfaction and Shopping Experience," *Journal of Marketing Research* XLIV (February 2007): pp. 164–174.

36 Robert W. Palmatier, Lisa K. Scheer, and Jan-Benedict E. M. Steenkamp, "Customer Loyalty to Whom? Managing the Benefits and Risks of Salesperson-Owned Loyalty," *Journal of Marketing Research* XLIV (May 2007): pp. 185–199.

37 Ruth M. Stock and Marei Bednareck, "As They Sow, So Shall They Reap: Customers' Influence on Customer Satisfaction at the Customer Interface," *Journal of the Academy of Marketing Science* 42, 4 (July 2014): pp. 400–414.

38 Werner J. Reinartz and V. Kumar, "On the Profitability of Long-Life Customers in a Non-contractual Setting: An Empirical Investigation and Implications for Marketing," *Journal of Marketing* 64, 4 (October 2000): pp. 17–35.

39 Jeff Desjardins, "This Is the Lifetime Value of a Starbucks Customer," *Business Insider*, January 28, 2016, www.businessinsider.com/lifetime-value-of-a-starbucks-customer-2016-1 (accessed December 12, 2017).

40 V. Kumar and Morris George, "Measuring and Maximizing Customer Equity: A Critical Analysis," *Journal of the Academy of Marketing Science* 35 (2007): pp. 157–171.

41 Rajkumar Venkatesan and V. Kumar, "A Customer Lifetime Value Framework for Customer Selection and Resource Allocation Strategy," *Journal of Marketing* 68, 4 (October 2004): pp. 106–125.

42 Richard Waters and Hannah Kuchler, "Social Networks Now a Staple of Office Life," *Financial Times*, November 19, 2014, p. 15.

43 Arun Sundararajan, "The 'Gig Economy' Is Coming. What Will It Mean for Work?" *The Guardian*, July 25, 2015, www.theguardian.com/commentisfree/2015/jul/26/ will-we-get-by-gig-economy (accessed December 12, 2017).

44 David Weil, "Lots of Employees Get Misclassified as Contractors. Here's Why It Matters," *Harvard Business Review*, July 5, 2017, https://hbr.org/2017/07/lots-of-employees-get-misclassified-as-contractors-heres-why-it-matters (accessed December 12, 2017).

45 Richard Waters and Hannah Kuchler, "Social Networks Now a Staple of Office Life," *Financial Times*, November 19, 2014, p. 15.

46 Greenpeace, "Guide to Greener Electronics 2017," www.greenpeace.org/international/en/campaigns/detox/electronics/Guide-to-Greener-Electronics/ (accessed December 12, 2017).

47 Anis Ben Brik, Belaid Rettab, and Kemel Mallahi, "Market Orientation, Corporate Social Responsibility, and Business Performance," *Journal of Business Ethics* 99 (2011): pp. 307–324.

48 "Giving Statistics," *Charity Navigator*, https://www.charitynavigator.org/index.cfm?bay=content.view&cpid=42 (accessed December 12, 2017).

49 Kif Leswing, "Apple Just Broke Its Own Record as the Most Valuable Publicly Traded Company of All Time," *Business Insider*, May 8, 2017, www.businessinsider.com/apple-becomes-the-most-valuable-publicly-traded-company-of-all-time-2017-5 (accessed December 24, 2017); Aaron Pressman, "Why Wall Street Is Getting Worried about Apple's Stock Price," *Fortune*, November 27, 2017, http://fortune.com/2017/11/27/wall-street-apple-stock/ (accessed December 6, 2017); "The World's Most Valuable Brands," *Forbes*, https://www.forbes.com/powerful-brands/list/ (accessed December 6, 2017); Gina Hall, "These Silicon Valley Firms Make Top 10 List of the Best Managed Companies in the U.S.," *Silicon Valley Business Journal*, December 6, 2017, https://www.bizjournals.com/sanjose/news/2017/12/06/wsj-management-top-250-amzn-aapl-goog-jnj-ibm-msft.html (accessed December 6, 2017); Kaitlyn Wang, "Tim Cook Credits Apple's Success to Two Basic Principles," *Inc.*, June 15, 2017, https://www.inc.com/kaitlyn-wang/apple-tim-cook-people.html (accessed December 6, 2017); Adam Lashinsky, "Apple's Tim Cook Leads Different," *Fortune*, March 26, 2015, http://fortune.com/2015/03/26/tim-cook/ (accessed December 6, 2017); "Apple Chronology," *CNNMoney*, January 6, 1998, http://money.cnn.com/1998/01/06/technology/apple_chrono/ (accessed June 6, 2011); Apple History, www.apple-history.com/ (accessed June 6, 2011); "Apple Introduces iTunes—World's Best and Easiest to Use Jukebox

Software," Apple, January 9, 2001, www .apple.com/pr/library/2001/jan/09itunes.html (accessed June 6, 2011); John Brownlee, "What It's Like to Work at Apple," *Cult of Mac*, July 7, 2010, www.cultofmac.com/ what-its-like-to-work-at-apple (accessed June 6, 2011); "The Evangelist's Evangelist," Creating Customer Evangelists, www.creatingcus-tomerevangelists.com/resources/evangelists/ guy_kawasaki.asp (accessed June 6, 2011); "Former Apple Evangelist on Company's History," *CNET News*, March 29, 2006, http://news.cnet.com/1606-2_3-6055676. html (accessed June 6, 2011); "World's Most Admired Companies: Apple," *CNNMoney*, http://money.cnn.com/magazines/fortune/ mostadmired/2011/snapshots/670.html (accessed June 6, 2011); Pamela N. Danziger, "3 Things Retailers Need to Learn from Apple about the Experience Economy," *Forbes*, December 13, 2017, https://www .forbes.com/sites/pamdanziger/2017/12/13/ three-things-retailers-need-to-learn-from-apple-about-the-experience-economy/#48f0ecda1307 (accessed January 11, 2018).

50 Blake Mycoskie, "The Founder of TOMS on Reimagining the Company's Mission," *Harvard Business Review*, January/ February 2016, pp. 41–44; Ashley Fahey, "TOMS Founder Reflects on Conscious Capitalism, Entrepreneurship Ahead of Talk in Charlotte," *Charlotte Business Journal*, November 22, 2017, https://www.bizjournals .com/charlotte/news/2017/11/22/ toms-founder-reflects-on-conscious-capital-ism.html (accessed November 30, 2017); Patrick Cole, "TOMS Free Shoe Plan, Boosted by Clinton, Reaches Million Mark," *Bloomberg*, September 15, 2010, www .bloomberg.com/news/2010-09-16/toms-shoe-giveaway-for-kids-boosted-by-bill-clinton-reaches-million-mark.html (accessed November 30, 2017); TOMS, "One for One," www.toms.com/one-for-one-en/ (accessed November 30, 2017); Booth Moore, "Toms Shoes' Model Is Sell a Pair, Give a Pair Away," *The Los Angeles Times*, April 19, 2009, www.latimes.com/features/image/ la-ig-greentoms19-2009apr19,0,3694310. story (accessed December 10, 2017); Stacy Perman, "Making a Do-Gooder's Business Model Work," *Bloomberg Businessweek*, January 23, 2009, www .businessweek.com/smallbiz/content/ jan2009/sb20090123_264702.htm (accessed November 6, 2014); Michelle Prasad, "TOMS Shoes Always Feel Good," *KENTON Maga-zine*, March 19, 2011, http://kentonmagazine. com/toms-shoes-always-feel-good/ (accessed November 6, 2014); Craig Sharkton, "Toms Shoes—Philanthropy as a Business Model," sufac.com, August 23, 2008, http://sufac

.com/2008/08/toms-shoes-philanthropy-as-a-business-model/ (accessed June 3, 2011); Mike Zimmerman, "The Business of Giving: TOMS Shoes," *Success Magazine*, September 30, 2009, www.successmagazine.com/the-business-of-giving/PARAMS/article/852 (accessed June 3, 2011); "TOMS Founder Shares Sole-ful Tale," *North Texas Daily*, April 14, 2011, www.ntdaily.com/?p=53882 (accessed March 5, 2012); Scott Gerber, "Exit Inter-view: Blake Mycoskie," *Inc.*, December 2014/ January 2015, p. 144; PR Newswire, "TOMS Is on a Mission to Brew Something Greater: TOMS Roasting Co. Launches as the Next One for One® Product," *Cision*, March 12, 2014, https://www.prnewswire .com/news-releases/toms-is-on-a-mission-to-brew-something-greater-toms-roasting-co-launches-as-the-next-one-for-one-product-249740051.html (accessed December 10, 2017); Rick Tetzeli, "Behind Toms Founder Blake Mycoskie's Plan to Build an Army of Social Entrepreneurs," *Fast Company*, January 11, 2016, https://www.fastcompany .com/3054929/behind-toms-founder-blake-mycoskies-plans-to-build-an-army-of-social-entrepr (accessed December 10, 2017).

Chapter 2

1 Jeremy C. Owens, "Tesla Model 3 Runs into 'Production Bottleneck,'" *MarketWatch*, October 3, 2017, www.marketwatch.com/story/ tesla-model-3-hit-by-production-bottleneck-that-slowed-initial-deliveries-2017-10-02 (accessed January 5, 2018); Bill Vlasic, "In Pivotal Moment, Tesla Unveils Its First Mass-Market Sedan," *The New York Times*, July 29, 2017, www.nytimes.com/2017/07/29/business/ tesla-model-3-elon-musk.html (accessed January 5, 2018); Neal E. Boudette, "Tesla's First Mass-Market Car, the Model 3, Hits Pro-duction This Week," *The New York Times*, July 3, 2017, www.nytimes.com/2017/07/03/business/ tesla-model-3-elon-musk.html (accessed January 5, 2018); Eddie Yoon, "Tesla Shows How Traditional Business Metrics Are Out-dated," *Harvard Business Review*, August 8, 2017, https://hbr.org/2017/08/tesla-shows-how-traditional-business-metrics-are-outdated (accessed January 5, 2018).

2 O. C. Ferrell and Michael Hartline, *Marketing Strategy*, 6th ed. (Mason, OH: Cengage Learning, 2014), p. 9.

3 Christian Homburg, Karley Krohmer, and John P. Workman, Jr., "A Strategy Implemen-tation Perspective of Market Orientation," *Journal of Business Research* 57, 12 (2004): pp. 1331–1340.

4 "About," Facebook, https://www.facebook. com/pg/facebook/about/ (accessed April 13, 2018).

5 Peter High, "Slack's CEO on the Future of the Fastest Growing Workplace Software Ever," *Forbes*, November 7, 2016, http://www .forbes.com/sites/peterhigh/2016/11/07/ slacks-ceo-on-the-future-of-the-fastest-growing-workplace-software-ever/# 53ea2e812641 (accessed December 6, 2017); Carrie Melissa Jones, "What a Mission-Driven Company Looks Like," *CMS Wire*, February 16, 2016, http://www.cmswire. com/social-business/what-a-mission-driven-company-looks-like/ (accessed December 6, 2017).

6 Keshia Hannam, "These Are the Three Divisions GE's New CEO Will Focus On," *Fortune*, November 13, 2017, http://fortune .com/2017/11/13/ge-new-ceo-focus-three-key-units/ (accessed December 6, 2017).

7 Kirsten Korosec, "Ford CEO Jim Hackett's 6-Point Plan to Turnaround the Automaker," *Fortune*, October 3, 2017, http://fortune .com/2017/10/03/ford-jim-hackett-strategy/ (October 20, 2017).

8 "Global Divisions," PepsiCo, http://www .pepsico.com/Company/Global-Divisions (accessed October 20, 2017).

9 Stanley F. Slater, G. Tomas, M. Hult, and Eric M. Olson, "On the Importance of Matching Strategic Behavior and Target Market Selection to Business Strategy in High-Tech Markets," *Journal of the Academy of Marketing Science* 35, 1 (2007): pp. 5–17.

10 "Search Engine Market Share United States of America," *GlobalStats Statcounter*, March 2018, http://gs.statcounter.com/search-engine-market-share/all/united-states-of-america (accessed April 13, 2018).

11 Robert D. Buzzell, "The PIMS Program of Strategy Research: A Retrospective Appraisal," *Journal of Business Research* 57, 5 (2004): pp. 478–483.

12 Dee DePass, "Polaris Says It's the End of the Line for Victory Motorcycle Brand," *The Star Tribune*, January 9, 2017, http:// www.startribune.com/polaris-says-it-s-the-end-of-the-line-for-victory-motorcycle-brand/410139155/ (accessed October 23, 2017).

13 Mike Esterl, "'Share a Coke' Credited with a Pop in Sales," *The Wall Street Journal*, September 25, 2014, http://www.wsj.com/ articles/share-a-coke-credited-with-a-pop-in-sales-1411661519 (accessed October 23, 2017); Coca-Cola Company, "'Share a Coke' Returns with More Names, More Flavors and More Ways to Enjoy Ice-Cold Summer Refreshment," press release, April 18, 2017, http://www.coca-colacompany.com/press-center/press-releases/-share-a-coke—returns-with-more-names—more-flavors-and-more-wa (accessed October 23, 2017).

14. Lindsay September, "South Africa's First Baskin Robbins Store to Open This Month," *EatOut*, December 1, 2016, http://www.eatout.co.za/article/south-africas-first-baskin-robbins-store-open-december/ (accessed October 23, 2017).

15. Matthew DeBord, "Fender Created a Clever New Product to Tackle Its Biggest Business Challenge," *Business Insider*, July 26, 2017, http://www.businessinsider.com/how-fender-is-getting-into-digital-2017-7 (accessed October 23, 2017).

16. "Nokia, Onetime Cell-Phone Champ, Turns to Bathroom Scales," *Fox Business*, April 27, 2017, http://www.foxbusiness.com/markets/2017/04/27/nokia-onetime-cell-phone-champ-turns-to-bathroom-scales.html (accessed October 23, 2017).

17. Eliza Brooke, "Tommy Hilfiger Is Launching Clothing for Adults with Disabilities," *Racked*, October 17, 2017, https://www.racked.com/2017/10/17/16489394/tommy-hilfiger-adaptive-clothing (accessed October 23, 2017).

18. Derek F. Abell, "Strategic Windows," *Journal of Marketing* 42, 3 (1978): p. 21.

19. Nat Levy, "Look Out, Amazon? Walmart's $3.3B Jet.com Deal Starts to Pay Off with Big Growth in Online Sales," *Geekwire*, February 21, 2017, https://www.geekwire.com/2017/look-out-amazon-walmarts-3-3b-jet-com-deal-starts-to-pay-off-with-big-growth-in-online-sales/ (accessed October 23, 2017).

20. Robert F. Everett, "A Crack in the Foundation: Why SWOT Might Be Less Than Effective in Market Sensing Analysis," *Journal of Marketing and Management*, Special Issues 1, 1 (2014): pp. 58–78.

21. Swapnil Bhartiya, "Amazon's Echo vs. Google Home: The Choice Is Obvious," *CIO*, November 22, 2016, https://www.cio.com/article/3143137/open-source-tools/amazon-echo-vs-google-home-the-choice-is-obvious.html (accessed October 23, 2017).

22. Jared M. Hansen, Robert E. McDonald, and Ronald K. Mitchell, "Competence Resource Specialization, Causal Ambiguity, and the Creation and Decay of Competitiveness: The Role of Marketing Strategy in New Product Performance and Shareholder Value," *Journal of the Academy of Marketing Science*, 41, 3 (2013): pp. 300–319.

23. Tilottama G. Chowdhury, Sreedhar Madhavaram, S. Ratneshwar, and Rhetta Standifer, "The Appropriateness of Different Modes of Strategy from a Product-Market Perspective," *Journal of Strategic Marketing*, 22, 5 (2014): pp. 442–468.

24. Arif Durrani, "London Live to Move Closer to Evening Standard," *Campaign*, August 14, 2014, http://www.campaignlive.co.uk/news/1307558/london-live-move-closer-evening-standard/ (accessed February 5, 2018).

25. James Brightman, "Mobile Games Booming as Global Games Market Hits $108.9B in 2017 - NewZoo," *gamesindustry.biz*, April 20, 2017, http://www.gamesindustry.biz/articles/2017-04-20-mobile-games-booming-as-global-games-market-hits-usd108-9b-in-2017-newzoo (accessed February 5, 2018).

26. Myles Edwin Mangram, "The Globalization of Tesla Motors: A Strategic Marketing Plan Analysis," *Journal of Strategic Marketing*, 20, 4 (2012): pp. 289–312.

27. Kyle Stock, "Millennials Hit the Road in a Sleek New Generation of RVs," *Bloomberg*, December 5, 2016, https://www.bloomberg.com/news/articles/2016-12-05/millennials-hit-the-road-in-a-sleek-new-generation-of-rvs (accessed October 24, 2017).

28. Shikhar Sarin, Goutam Challagalla, and Ajay K. Kohli, "Implementing Changes in Marketing Strategy: The Role of Perceived Outcome- and Process-Oriented Supervisory Actions," *Journal of Marketing Research*, 49, 4 (2012): pp. 564–580.

29. Jessica Wohl, "McDonald's: 'There's a Big Mac for That' Boosted Results," *AdAge*, April 25, 2017, http://adage.com/article/cmo-strategy/mcdonald-s-h-a-big-mac-boosted-results/308795/ (accessed October 24, 2017).

30. Aparna Narayanan, "What Model 3 Problem? Tesla Designer Says Cars 'Age into the Future,'" *Investors Business Daily*, May 4, 2018, www.investors.com/news/tesla-design-chief-model-3-thinks-forward-to-autonomous-driving/; Dana Hull and Hannah Recht, "Tesla Doesn't Burn Fuel, It Burns Cash," *Bloomberg.com*, April 30, 2018, www.bloomberg.com/graphics/2018-tesla-burns-cash/; Chris Woodyard, "Tesla's Elon Musk Vows '24/7' Model 3 Production, Lots of New Jobs," *USA Today*, April 17, 2018, www.usatoday.com/story/money/cars/2018/04/17/teslas-elon-musk-vows-24-7-model-3-production-lots-new-jobs/526786002/; Russ Mitchell, "Tesla's Head Designer on the Model 3: 'It's Based on the Idea of Minimalism, That Less Is More,'" *Los Angeles Times*, Mary 3, 2018, www.latimes.com/business/autos/la-fi-hy-tesla-design-chief-20180502-story.html; Lora Kolodny, "Tesla Promises Profits in the Second Half of This Year—If It Can Meet Model 3 Production Goals," *CNBC*, May 2, 2018, www.cnbc.com/2018/05/02/tesla-profits-depend-on-meeting-model-3-goals.html; www.tesla.com; Video: "The Tesla Model 3: The Culmination of Elon Musk's Master Plan," *Wired*, July 27, 2017, www.youtube.com/watch?v=z G7uLvtzGJc&index=28&t=2s&list=PLibNZ v5Zd0dxcjS2fN-z6Pes82V0jeRHr.

31. Robert Klara, "How Crayola Crayons Gave Its Century-Old Product Renewed Relevance in the Age of iPads," *Adweek*, September 5, 2017, www.adweek.com/brand-marketing/crayola-has-given-its-century-old-product-a-contemporary-relevance-even-in-the-age-of-ipads (accessed January 5, 2018); Adrianne Pasquarelli, "Crayola Colors Outside the Lines," *Advertising Age*, July 31, 2017, http://adage.com/article/cmo-strategy/crayola-aims-maintain-relevance-tech-savvy-kids/309960/ (accessed January 5, 2018); John Kell, "Crayola Is Retiring This Classic Crayon," *Fortune*, March 30, 2017, http://fortune.com/2017/03/30/crayolas-retires-dandelion-crayon/ (accessed January 5, 2018); Jon Harris, "Crayola Partners with Clinique to Create Colorful Crayons for Your Lips," *The Morning Call (Allentown, PA)*, January 5, 2017, www.mcall.com/business/mc-crayola-clinique-partnership-20170105-story.html (accessed January 5, 2018).

32. "Why We're a Great Place to Work," http://www.wholefoodsmarket.com/careers/why-were-great-place-work (accessed December 30, 2017); "Whole Foods Market's Core Values," www.wholefoodsmarket.com/values/corevalues.php#supporting (accessed December 30, 2017); "100 Best Companies to Work For: Whole Foods Market," *CNN Money*, 2011, http://money.cnn.com/magazines/fortune/bestcompanies/2011/snapshots/24.html (accessed December 30, 2017); "100 Best Companies to Work For: Whole Foods Market," *CNN Money*, 2013, http://money.cnn.com/magazines/fortune/best-companies/2013/snap-shots/71.html?iid=bc_fl_list (accessed September 9, 2013); Kerry A. Dolan, "America's Greenest Companies 2011," *Forbes*, April 18, 2011, www.forbes.com/2011/04/18/americas-greenest-companies.html (accessed December 30, 2017); Joseph Brownstein, "Is Whole Foods' Get Healthy Plan Fair?" *ABC News*, January 29, 2010, http://abcnews.go.com/Health/w_DietAndFitnessNews/foods-incentives-make-employees-healthier/story?id=9680047 (accessed December 30, 2017); Deborah Dunham, "At Whole Foods Thinner Employees Get Fatter Discounts," *That's Fit*, January 27, 2010, www.thatsfit.com/2010/01/27/whole-foods-thin-employees-get-discounts/ (accessed September 9, 2013); David Burkus, "Why Whole Foods Builds Its Entire Business On Teams," *Forbes*, June 8, 2016, https://www.forbes.com/sites/david-burkus/2016/06/08/why-whole-foods-build-their-entire-business-on-teams/#47872abc3fa1 (accessed December 30, 2017); Kate Taylor, "Here Are All the Changes Amazon Is Making to Whole Foods," *Business Insider*, November

15, 2017, http://www.businessinsider.com/amazon-changes-whole-foods-2017-9/#whole-foods-immediately-slashed-prices-and-announced-another-round-of-price-cuts-in-november-1 (accessed December 30, 2017); "Whole Foods' Target Market," https://storify.com/abastian/whole-foods-target-market (accessed March 20, 2018); Deborah Abrams Kaplan, "Is Amazon Changing Whole Foods' Identity?" *Supply Chain Dive*, January 23, 2018, https://www.supplychaindive.com/news/amazon-whole-foods-identity-culture-change-inventory-management/515293/ (accessed on March 20, 2018); Nick Wingfield, "Here's How the Amazon Takeover Has Changed Whole Foods – So Far," *Boston*, March 1, 2018, https://www.boston.com/news/food/2018/03/01/amazon-whole-foods-changes (accessed March 24, 2018).

Chapter 3

1. FDA, "FDA Investigates Multistate Outbreak of E. Coli O26 Infections Linked to Chipotle Mexican Grill Restaurant," U.S. Food and Drug Administration, https://www.fda.gov/food/recallsoutbreaksemergencies/outbreaks/ucm470410.htm (accessed October 17, 2017); Diana Bradley, "Chris Arnold Guides Chipotle's Crisis Comeback," *PR Week*, July 5, 2017, https://www.prweek.com/article/1438230/chris-arnold-guides-chipotles-crisis-comeback# AB5RGAbJL-BziCe3l.99 (accessed October 17, 2017); Erin Douglas, "Chipotle Shows Signs of Recovery with New Menu Items in Testing, but Is It Enough?" *The Denver Post*, www.denverpost.com/2017/07/14/chipotle-new-menu-items-revenue-ecoli/ (accessed October 17, 2017); Jim Edwards, "How Chipotle's Business Model Depends on NEVER Running TV Ads," *Business Insider*, March 16, 2012, www.businessinsider.com/how-chipotles-business-model-relies-on-never-doing-tv-advertising-2012-3 (accessed November 22, 2017); Joel Stein, "The Fast Food Ethicist," *Time*, July 23, 2012, pp. 39–44; "Investor Relations Press Release," Chipotle Grill, February 5, 2013, http://ir.chipotle.com/phoenix.zhtml?c=194775&p=irol-newsArticle&id=1781728 (accessed November 22, 2017); Duff McDonald, "Esquire's Most Inspiring CEO in America: Steve Ells, Founder and Co-CEO, Chipotle," *Esquire*, 2012, www.esquire.com/features/most-inspiring-ceo-1012-steve-ells#slide-12 (accessed June 24, 2013); Seeking Alpha, "Chipotle's CEO Discusses Q1 2013 Results—Earnings Call Transcript," *Seeking Alpha*, April 18, 2013, http://seekingalpha.com/article/1353311-chipotle-s-ceo-discusses-q1-2013-results-earnings-call-transcript?part=single (accessed November 22, 2017);

Hollis Johnson, "I Compared Chipotle's Food to Another Major Mexican-Food Competitor—and the Winner Shocked Me," *Business Insider*, October 14, 2015, www.businessinsider.com/chipotle-vs-qdoba-review-2015-10 (accessed November 22, 2017); Sarah Begley, "Chipotle Customer Who Got E. Coli Asks for Free Burritos in Settlement," *Time*, September 14, 2016, http://time.com/4490672/chipotle-ecoli-free-burritos-settlement/ (accessed November 22, 2017); Jen Wieczner, "Chipotle's 'Free Burrito' Coupons Are Making People Less Scared to Eat There," *Fortune*, May 4, 2016, http://fortune.com/2016/03/04/chipotle-coupons-ecoli/ (accessed November 22, 2017); Ziati Meyer, "After Chipotle's Queso-Gate and Food Safety Issues, Can a New CEO Help?" *USA Today*, December 29, 2017, https://www.usatoday.com/story/money/2017/12/29/after-chipotles-queso-gate-and-food-safety-issues-can-new-ceo-help/982684001/ (accessed December 31, 2017).

2. Ryan Faughnder, "Disney Sues Redbox to Stop Digital Movie Sales, in the Latest Feud between the Companies," *Los Angeles Times*, December 1, 2017, http://beta.latimes.com/business/hollywood/la-fi-ct-disney-redbox-feud-20171201-story.html (accessed December 26, 2017).

3. Lisa Eadicicco, Matt Peckham, John Patrick Pullen, and Alex Fitzpatrick, "TIME's 20 Most Successful Technology Failures of All Time," *TIME*, April 3, 2017, http://time.com/4704250/most-successful-technology-tech-failures-gadgets-flops-bombs-fails/ (accessed December 26, 2017).

4. P. Varadarajan, Terry Clark, and William M. Pride, "Controlling the Uncontrollable: Managing Your Market Environment," *Sloan Management Review* 33, 2 (Winter 1992): pp. 39–47.

5. MuiChing Carina Chan, John Watson, and David Woodliff, "Corporate Governance Quality and CSR Disclosures," *Journal of Business Ethics* 125, 1 (2014): pp. 59–73.

6. Lynn Beavis, "Kingfisher Pioneers Environmental Philosophy," *The Guardian*, May 15, 2014, https://www.theguardian.com/sustainable-business/sustainability-case-studies-kingfisher-environmental-philosophy (accessed December 28, 2017).

7. O. C. Ferrell and Michael D. Hartline, *Marketing Strategy* (Mason, OH: Cengage Learning, 2008), p. 58.

8. Ibid.

9. Ibid.

10. Economist staff, "The World's Biggest Economic Problem," *The Economist*, October 25, 2014, p. 15.

11. Lara Ewen, "Nordstrom Rack Opens Second Manhattan Store," *Retail Dive*, October 26, 2017, https://www.retaildive.com/news/

nordstrom-rack-opens-second-manhattan-store/508192/ (accessed December 26, 2017).

12. Tanza Loudenback, "Middle-Class Americans Made More Money Last Year Than Ever Before," *Business Insider*, September 12, 2017, www.businessinsider.com/us-census-median-income-2017-9 (accessed December 26, 2017).

13. "The Number of Millionaires Worldwide Is at an All-Time High," *New York Post*, September 28, 2017, https://nypost.com/2017/09/28/the-number-millionaires-worldwide-is-at-an-all-time-high/ (accessed December 26, 2017).

14. Joshua Gallu, "Dodd-Frank May Cost $6.5 Billion and 5,000 Workers," *Bloomberg*, February 14, 2011, https://www.bloomberg.com/news/articles/2011-02-14/dodd-frank-s-implementation-calls-for-6-5-billion-5-000-staff-in-budget (accessed December 28, 2017); Binyamin Appelbaum and Brady Dennis, "Dodd's Overhaul Goes Well Beyond Other Plans," *The Washington Post*, November 11, 2009, www.washingtonpost.com/wp-dyn/content/article/2009/11/09/AR2009110901935.html?hpid=topnews&sid=ST2009111003729 (accessed December 28, 2017).

15. "Wall Street Reform: Bureau of Consumer Financial Protection (CFPB)," U.S. Treasury, www.treasury.gov/initiatives/Pages/cfpb.aspx (accessed January 19, 2016).

16. "Trade Mission," BusinessDictionary.com, www.businessdictionary.com/definition/trade-mission.html (accessed January 19, 2016).

17. OpenSecrets.org, "Top Organization Contributors," www.opensecrets.org/orgs/list.php (accessed December 11, 2015).

18. "Campaign Finance," *The New York Times*, http://topics.nytimes.com/top/reference/timestopics/subjects/c/campaign_finance/index.html (accessed January 19, 2016).

19. Federal Trade Commission, "Mallinckrodt Will Pay $100 Million to Settle FTC, State Charges It Illegally Maintained Its Monopoly of Specialty Drug to Treat Infants," January 18, 2017, https://www.ftc.gov/news-events/press-releases/2017/01/mallinckrodt-will-pay-100-million-settle-ftc-state-charges-it (accessed December 28, 2017).

20. The United States Department of Justice, "Telia Company AB and Its Uzbek Subsidiary Enter into a Global Foreign Bribery Resolution of More than $965 Million for Corrupt Payments in Uzbekistan," September 21, 2017, https://www.justice.gov/opa/pr/telia-company-ab-and-its-uzbek-subsidiary-enter-global-foreign-bribery-resolution-more-965 (accessed December 28, 2017).

21. Dionne Searcey, "U.K. Law on Bribes Has Firms in a Sweat," *The Wall Street Journal*,

December 28, 2010, p. B1; Julius Melnitzer, "U.K. Enacts 'Far-Reaching' Anti-Bribery Act," *Law Times*, February 13, 2011, www .lawtimesnews.com/201102141679/headline-news/uk-enacts-far-reaching-anti-bribery-act (accessed December 28, 2017).

22 Julius Melnitzer, "U.K. Enacts 'Far-Reaching' Anti-Bribery Act," *Law Times*, February 13, 2011, www.lawtimesnews.com/ 201102141679/headline-news/uk-enacts-far-reaching-anti-bribery-act (accessed December 28, 2017).

23 Levon Sevunts, "Canada Bans 'Grease Payments' to Foreign Officials," *Radio International Canada*, October 30, 2017, www.rcinet.ca/en/2017/10/30/canada-bans-grease-payments-to-foreign-officials/ (accessed December 28, 2017).

24 Samuel Rubenfeld, "Lockheed Martin Gets into Step with UK Bribery Act with New Policy," *The Wall Street Journal*, June 8, 2011, http://blogs.wsj.com/corruption-currents/2011/06/08/lockheed-martin-gets-into-step-with-uk-bribery-act-with-new-policy/ (accessed December 28, 2017).

25 "TRUSTe Will Pay $100,000 in Deal Over COPPA Violations," *Lexology*, April 27, 2017, https://www.lexology.com/library/ detail.aspx?g=7dc03832-3f5d-4f8a-9cb0-168b08d201fa (accessed December 28, 2017).

26 Diane Bartz, "Google Faces Renewed U.S. Antitrust Scrutiny, This Time over Android," *Reuters*, September 25, 2015, www.reuters .com/article/google-antitrust-idUSL1N11V0PJ20150925 (accessed December 28, 2017).

27 Jesse Newman, "FDA Tightens Its Food-Safety Rules," *The Wall Street Journal*, September 11, 2015, p. B3.

28 Anica Zeyen, Markus Beckmann, and Stella Wolters, "Actor and Institutional Dynamics in the Development of Multi-stakeholder Initiatives," *Journal of Business Ethics*, accepted November 11, 2014, DOI 10.1007/ s10551-014-2468-1.

29 Home Builders Association of Central Missouri, "Code of Ethics," www .hbacentralmo.com/about-us/code-of-ethics/ (accessed December 28, 2017).

30 Aric Jenkins, "Comcast Is No Longer Allowed to Say It Has the 'Fastest Internet in America,'" *Money*, February 9, 2017, http:// time.com/money/4665464/comcast-verizon-marketing-advertising-xfinity-fios-fastest-internet/ (accessed December 28, 2017).

31 Council of Better Business Bureaus, "National Advertising Review Board Recommends Philosophy Modify or Discontinue Certain Claims for 'Time in a Bottle,'" *ASRC*, May 14, 2015, www.asrcreviews.org/2015/05/ national-advertising-review-board-recommends-philosophy-modify-or-discontinue-certain-claims-for-time-in-a-bottle/ (accessed December 15, 2015).

32 "NARB Recommends Rust-Oleum Discontinue Use of 2X Ultra Cover Product Names," *Coatings World*, September 21, 2016, www .coatingsworld.com/contents/view_breaking-news/2016-09-21/narb-recommends-rust-oleum-discontinue-use-of-2x-ultra-cover-product-name (accessed December 28, 2016); "National Advertising Review Board Refers Rust-Oleum to the FTC," *Lexology*, June 20, 2017, https://www.lexology.com/library/ detail.aspx?g=f3d6ae31-4e2a-4298-80ab-cbef064fa992 (accessed December 28, 2017).

33 Associated Press, "Why Nearly 46 Percent of Households Still Have Landlines," *New York Post*, May 4, 2017, https://nypost .com/2017/05/04/why-nearly-46-percent-of-household-still-have-landlines/ (accessed December 28, 2017).

34 "Salesforce.com," *Forbes*, May 2015, www.forbes.com/companies/salesforce/ (accessed January 19, 2016).

35 William M. Pride and O. C. Ferrell, *Marketing: Concepts and Strategies*, 12th ed. (Boston: Houghton Mifflin, 2003), p. 493.

36 Economist staff, "Home, Hacked Home," *The Economist: Special Report on Cyber-Security*, July 12, 2014, pp. 14–15; Economist staff, "Prevention Is Better than Cure," *The Economist: Special Report on Cyber-Security*, July 12, 2014, p. 16.

37 Sarah Perez, "U.S. Consumers Now Spend 5 Hours Per Day on Mobile Devices," *Tech Crunch*, March 3, 2017, https://techcrunch .com/2017/03/03/u-s-consumers-now-spend-5-hours-per-day-on-mobile-devices/ (accessed December 28, 2017).

38 Sean Casey, "2016 Nielsen Social Media Report," Nielsen, January 17, 2017, www.nielsen.com/us/en/insights/ reports/2017/2016-nielsen-social-media-report.html?afflt=ntrt15340001&afflt_uid=eTMrtc4ZTtk.X3uAH4dVl-iyV8he9-07dCML7rsy7qxa&afflt_uid_2=AFFLT_ID_2 (accessed December 28, 2017).

39 Derek Thompson, "What in the World Is Causing the Retail Meltdown of 2017?" *The Atlantic*, April 10, 2017, https://www .theatlantic.com/business/archive/2017/04/ retail-meltdown-of-2017/522384/ (accessed January 14, 2018).

40 Debbie McAlister, Linda Ferrell, and O. C. Ferrell, *Business and Society* (Mason, OH: Cengage Learning, 2011), pp. 352–353.

41 Ibid.

42 Vladmir Zwass, "Electronic Commerce: Structures and Issues," *International Journal of Electronic Commerce* (Fall 2000): pp. 3–23.

43 Lauren Gensler, "The World's Largest Retailers 2017: Amazon & Alibaba Are Closing in on Wal-Mart," *Forbes*, May 24, 2017, https://www.forbes.com/sites/ laurengensler/2017/05/24/the-worlds-largest-retailers-2017-walmart-cvs-amazon/#11146e2920b5 (accessed January 14, 2018).

44 United States Census Bureau, "Facts for Features: Older Americans Month: May 2017," Newsroom, April 10, 2017, https:// www.census.gov/newsroom/facts-for-features/2017/cb17-ff08.html (accessed December 28, 2017).

45 SeniorPeopleMeet, www.seniorpeoplemeet .com (accessed December 15, 2015); BabyBoomerPeopleMeet, www .babyboomerpeoplemeet.com (accessed December 15, 2015).

46 Allison Schrager, "Most Americans Are Single, and They're Changing the Economy," *Bloomberg Business*, September 12, 2014, www.bloomberg.com/bw/articles/2014-09-12/ most-americans-are-single-dot-what-does-it-mean-for-the-economy (accessed December 28, 2017).

47 Neil Shah, "Baby Bust Threatens Growth," *The Wall Street Journal*, December 4, 2014, p. A3.

48 Haya El Nasser, Gregory Korte, and Paul Overberg, "308.7 Million," *USA Today*, December 22, 2010, p. 1A; "U.S. and World Population Clocks," U.S. Census Bureau, www.census.gov/popclock/ (accessed February 6, 2018).

49 CAP Immigration Team and Michael D. Nicholson, "The Facts on Immigration Today: 2017 Edition," *American Progress*, April 20, 2017, https://www .americanprogress.org/issues/ immigration/reports/2017/04/20/430736/ facts-immigration-today-2017-edition/ (accessed February 6, 2018).

50 U.S. Census Bureau, Statistical Abstract of the United States, 2010, p. 58.

51 Pew Research Center, "Projected U.S. Population by Race and Hispanic Origin, 2015-2065, with and without Immigrants Entering 2015-2065," September 24, 2015, www.pewhispanic.org/2015/09/28/ modern-immigration-wave-brings-59-million-to-u-s-driving-population-growth-and-change-through-2065/ph_2015-09-28_ immigration-through-2065-a2-06/ (accessed December 28, 2017).

52 Anne Marie Chaker, "Even Barbie Wants a Makeover," *The Wall Street Journal*, November 19, 2015, p. D1.

53 Tim Henderson, "Why Many Teens Don't Want to Get a Driver's License," *PBS*, March 6, 2017, https://www.pbs.org/newshour/nation/many-teens-dont-want-get-drivers-license (accessed December 28, 2017).

54 "Parents Grossly Underestimate the Influence Their Children Wield Over In-Store Purchases," *Science News*, March 17, 2009, www.sciencedaily.com/releases/2009/03/090316075853.htm (accessed December 28, 2017).

55 "About Seventh Generation," www.seventhgeneration.com/about (accessed January 19, 2016).

56 Kurt Eichenwald, "The Great Smartphone War," *Vanity Fair*, June 2014, www.vanityfair.com/business/2014/06/apple-samsung-smartphone-patent-war (accessed January 11, 2016); "Samsung Ordered to Pay Apple $120m for Patent Violation," *The Guardian*, May 2, 2014, www.theguardian.com/technology/2014/may/03/samsung-ordered-to-pay-apple-120m-for-patent-violation?CMP=EMCNEWEML6619I2 (accessed January 11, 2016); Dan Levine, "Apple, Google Agree to Settle Lawsuit Alleging Hiring Conspiracy," *Reuters*, April 24, 2014, www.reuters.com/article/2014/04/24/us-apple-google-settlement-idUSBREA3N1Y120140424 (accessed January 11, 2016); Ian Scerr, "Apple, Samsung Square off over Patent Damages," *The Wall Street Journal*, December 6, 2012, http://online.wsj.com/article/SB10001424127887323501404578164021886466686.html?mod=WSJ_article_comments#articleTabs%3Darticle (accessed January 11, 2016); Evan Ramstad, "Award to Apple Isn't Raised," *The Wall Street Journal*, June 30, 2012, http://online.wsj.com/article/SB10001424127887324329204578272870432069736.html?KEYWORDS=apple=samsungKEYWORDS%3Dapple=samsung (accessed January 11, 2016); Dino Grandoni, "How the Apple Samsung Lawsuit Hurt Consumers," *The Huffington Post*, July 31, 2012, www.huffingtonpost.com/2012/07/31/apple-samsung-lawsuit-consumers_n_1721623.html (accessed January 11, 2016); Paul Elias, "Apple's Samsung Verdict Nearly Cut in Half by Federal Judge," *The Huffington Post*, March 1, 2013, www.huffingtonpost.com/2013/03/01/half-of-billion-apple-samsung-settlement-invalidated_n_2792624.html (accessed January 11, 2016); Scott Bicheno, "Global smartphone market Q3 2015—Samsung strikes back," *Telecoms*, October 29, 2015, http://telecoms.com/450101/global-smartphone-market-q3-2015-samsung-strikes-back/ (accessed January 11, 2016); Based off a news clip from the BBC, May 2014, https://vimeo.com

57 Hayley Peterson, "Dollar General Is Defying the Retail Apocalypse and Opening 1,000 Stores," *AOL*, April 8, 2017, https://www.aol.com/article/finance/2017/04/08/dollar-general-is-defying-the-retail-apocalypse-and-opening-1-00/22031477/ (accessed November 22, 2017); Krystina Gustafson, "Dollar General Is Starting to Look a Lot Like Walmart," *CNBC*, March 16, 2017, https://www.cnbc.com/2017/03/16/dollar-general-is-starting-to-look-a-lot-like-walmart.html (accessed November 22, 2017); *Yahoo! Finance*, "Dollar General (DG)," https://finance.yahoo.com/quote/DG/financials?p=DG (accessed November 22, 2017); Mya Frazier, "Dollar General Hits a Goldmine in America," *Bloomberg Businessweek*, October 11, 2017, https://www.bloomberg.com/news/features/2017-10-11/dollar-general-hits-a-gold-mine-in-rural-america (accessed November 22, 2017).

Chapter 4

1 Sam Abuelsamid, "Does VW Diesel Cheating Threaten Consumer Trust of Automotive Software?" *Forbes*, October 21, 2015, www.forbes.com/sites/pikeresearch/2015/10/21/vw-diesel/ (accessed April 15, 2017); Paul Argenti, "The Biggest Culprit in VW's Emissions Scandals," *Fortune*, October 13, 2015, http://fortune.com/2015/10/13/biggest-culprit-in-volkswagen-emissions-scandal/ (accessed April 15, 2017); Associated Press, "VW Scandal Widens: Vehicles Don't Meet Standard for Second Pollutant," *NBC News*, November 3, 2015, www.nbcnews.com/business/autos/vw-scandal-widens-vehicles-dont-meet-standard-second-pollutant-n456726 (accessed April 15, 2017); Bloomberg News with E.J. Schultz, "VW's $14.7 Billion Settlement Resolves False Ad Claims," *Advertising Age*, June 28, 2016, http://adage.com/article/news/volkswagen-15-billion-emissions-settlement-includes-ftc-fals-advertising-claims/304733/ (accessed April 15, 2017); Department of Justice, Office of Public Affairs, "Volkswagen AG Agrees to Plead Guilty and Pay $4.3 Billion in Criminal and Civil Penalties; Six Volkswagen Executives and Employees Are Indicted in Connection with Conspiracy to Cheat U.S. Emissions Tests," *Justice News*, January 11, 2017, https://www.justice.gov/opa/pr/volkswagen-ag-agrees-plead-guilty-and-pay-43-billion-criminal-and-civil-penalties-six (accessed April 15, 2017); Sonari Glinton, "How a Little Lab in West Virginia Caught Volkswagen's Big Cheat," *NPR*, September 25, 2015, www.npr.org/2015/09/24/443053672/how-a-little-lab-in-west-virginia-caught-volkswagens-big-cheat (accessed April 15, 2017); Sarah Griffiths, "The Most Fuel-Efficient Car in the World: Volkswagen XL1 Does 300 MILES to the Gallon (And It Looks Cool Too)," *Daily Mail*, January 16, 2014, www.dailymail.co.uk/sciencetech/article-2540618/The-fuel-efficient-car-world-Volkswagen-XL1-does-300-MILES-gallon-looks-cool-too.html (accessed April 15, 2017); Russell Hotten, "Volkswagen: The Scandal Explained," *BBC News*, November 4, 2015, www.bbc.com/news/business-34324772 (accessed April 15, 2017); Steve Innskeep, "The Volkswagen Scandal and Germany's Reputation," *NPR*, October 1, 2015, www.npr.org/2015/10/01/444912600/the-volkswagen-scandal-and-germanys-reputation (accessed April 15, 2017); Bourree Lam, "The Academic Paper that Broke the Volkswagen Scandal," *The Atlantic*, September 25, 2015, www.theatlantic.com/business/archive/2015/09/volkswagen-scandal-cheating-emission-virginia-epa/407425/ (accessed April 15, 2017); Joanne Muller, "A Guilty Plea in Emissions Case Won't Fix VW's Reputation, But These New Models Will Help," *Forbes*, January 10, 2017, https://www.forbes.com/sites/joannmuller/2017/01/10/a-guilty-plea-in-emissions-case-wont-fix-vws-reputation-but-these-new-models-will-help/#58056ae42c4f (accessed April 15, 2017); Jeff Plungis and Dana Hull, "VW's Emissions Cheating Found by Curious Clean-Air Group," *Bloomberg Businessweek*, September 19, 2015, www.bloomberg.com/news/articles/2015-09-19/volkswagen-emissions-cheating-found-by-curious-clean-air-group (accessed April 15, 2017); Bertel Schmitt, "It's Official: Volkswagen Is World's Largest Automaker in 2016. Or Maybe Toyota." *Forbes*, January 30, 2017, https://www.forbes.com/sites/bertelschmitt/2017/01/30/its-official-volkswagen-worlds-largest-automaker-2016-or-maybe-toyota/#409806c976b0 (accessed April 15, 2017); Sarah Sloat, "Volkswagen to Offer $1,000 Package to U.S. Customers Hit by Emissions Scandal," *The Wall Street Journal*, November 9, 2015, www.wsj.com/articles/volkswagen-to-offer-1-000-package-to-u-s-customers-hit-by-emissions-scandal-1447088254?alg=y (accessed April 15, 2017); Mike Spector and Mike Colias, "Volkswagen Faces Up to Penalties," *The Wall Street Journal*, March 1–12, 2017, pp. B1-B2; Jackie Wattles, "Volkswagen

Stripped of Two 'Green Car of the Year' Titles," *CNNMoney*, October 1, 2015, http://money.cnn.com/2015/10/01/news/companies/volkswagen-green-car-of-year-awards-rescinded/ (accessed April 15, 2017); William Wilkes, "Volkswagen Adds to Scandal Cost," *The Wall Street Journal*, February 2, 2017, p. B3; Chris Woodyard, "Volkswagen Faces Lawsuits over Emissions Deception," *USA Today*, September 22, 2015, www.usatoday.com/story/money/cars/2015/09/22/volkswagen-vw-emissions-lawsuits/72604396/ (accessed April 15, 2017).

2 Peter R. Darke and Robin J. B. Ritchie, "The Defensive Consumer: Advertising Deception, Defensive Processing, and Distrust," *Journal of Marketing Research* 4, 1 (February 2007): pp. 114–127.

3 Isabelle Maignan and O. C. Ferrell, "Corporate Social Responsibility and Marketing: An Integrative Framework," *Journal of the Academy of Marketing Science* 32 (January 2004): pp. 3–19.

4 Robert Reiss, "Top CEOs Place High Value on Corporate Ethics and Social Responsibility to Drive Business," *Forbes*, September 11, 2017, https://www.forbes.com/sites/robertreiss/2017/09/11/top-ceos-place-high-value-on-corporate-ethics-and-social-responsibility-to-drive-business/#6eb97cbb4473 (accessed January 21, 2018).

5 Daniel Korschun, C. B. Bhattacharya, and Scott D. Swain, "Corporate Social Responsibility, Customer Orientation, and the Job Performance of Frontline Employees," *Journal of Marketing* 78 (May 2014): pp. 20–37.

6 3M, "3Mgives," https://www.3m.com/3M/en_US/gives-us/ (accessed January 21, 2018).

7 Isabelle Maignan and O. C. Ferrell, "Antecedents and Benefits of Corporate Citizenship: An Investigation of French Businesses," *Journal of Business Research* 51 (2001): pp. 37–51.

8 Debbie Thorne, Linda Ferrell, and O. C. Ferrell, *Business and Society: A Strategic Approach to Social Responsibility*, 4th ed. (Boston: Houghton Mifflin, 2011), pp. 38–40.

9 O. C. Ferrell, "Business Ethics and Customer Stakeholders," *Academy of Management Executive* 18 (May 2004): pp. 126–129.

10 "In the Community," *Panera Bread*, https://www.panerabread.com/en-us/en_us/community/community-giving.html (accessed January 23, 2018).

11 Archie Carroll, "The Pyramid of Corporate Social Responsibility: Toward the Moral Management of Organizational Stakeholders," *Business Horizons* (July/August 1991): p. 42.

12 Jiyun Kang and Gwendolyn Hustvedt, "Building Trust Between Consumers and Corporations: The Role of Consumer Perceptions of Transparency and Social Responsibility," *Journal of Business Ethics* 125, 2 (2014): pp. 253–265.

13 Giving USA, "Giving USA 2017: Total Charitable Donations Rise to New High of $390.05 Billion," June 12, 2017, https://givingusa.org/giving-usa-2017-total-charitable-donations-rise-to-new-high-of-390-05-billion/ (accessed January 23, 2018).

14 New Belgium, "Grants Program," http://www.newbelgium.com/Sustainability/Community/Grants (accessed January 31, 2018).

15 "BMW Ultimate Drive for the Cure," National Capital Chapter BMW Car Club of America, http://old.nccbmwcca.org/index.php?cure (accessed January 23, 2018).

16 Cone Communications, "Research & Insights," www.conecomm.com/research (accessed December 17, 2015).

17 Thorne, Ferrell, and Ferrell, *Business and Society*, p. 335.

18 Douglas MacMillan, "Warby Parker Adds Storefronts to Its Sales Strategy," *The Wall Street Journal*, November 17, 2014, http://online.wsj.com/articles/warby-parker-adds-storefronts-to-its-sales-strategy-1416251866 (accessed January 23, 2018); Warby Parker, "Buy a Pair, Give a Pair," www.warbyparker.com/buy-a-pair-give-a-pair (accessed February 8, 2018).

19 Dinah Eng [interviewer], "Mopping Up with Green Cleaners," *Fortune*, October 28, 2013, pp. 47–48; SC Johnson, *The SC Johnson Greenlist™ Process*, 2014, http://fortune.com/2013/10/10/mopping-up-with-method/ (accessed January 23, 2018).

20 Simona Romani, Silvia Grappi, and Richard P. Bagozzi, "Corporate Socially Responsible Initiatives and Their Effects on Consumption of Green Products," *Journal of Business Ethics*, accepted November 19, 2014, DOI: 10.1007/s10551-014-2485-0.

21 Forest Stewardship Council, "Kimberly-Clark Grows Its Commitment to FSC," *Newsletter Stories*, January 23, 2014, https://us.fsc.org/newsletter.239.809.htm (accessed January 23, 2018).

22 Gergely Nyilasy, Harsha Gangadharbatla, and Angela Paladino, "Perceived Greenwashing: The Interactive Effects of Green Advertising and Corporate Environmental Performance on Consumer Reactions," *Journal of Business Ethics*, 125, 4 (2014): pp. 693–707.

23 Paul Hawken and William McDonough, "Seven Steps to Doing Good Business," *Inc.* (November 1993): pp. 79–90.

24 Jill Gabrielle Klein, N. Craig Smith, and Andrew John, "Why We Boycott: Consumer Motivations for Boycott Participation," *Journal of Marketing* 68 (July 2004): pp. 92–109.

25 Christian Homburg and Andreas Fürst, "How Organizational Complaint Handling Drives Customer Loyalty: An Analysis of the Mechanistic and the Organic Approach," *Journal of Marketing* 69 (July 2005): pp. 95–114.

26 Jon Kamp and Jennifer Levitz, "Johnson & Johnson Pulls Hysterectomy Device from Hospitals," *The Wall Street Journal*, July 30, 2014, www.wsj.com/articles/johnson-johnson-to-call-for-voluntary-return-of-morcellators-1406754350 (accessed December 17, 2015); Jennifer Levitz, "FBI Is Investigating Hysterectomy Device Found to Spread Uterine Cancer," *The Wall Street Journal*, May 27, 2015, www.wsj.com/articles/fbi-is-investigating-surgical-device-1432746641 (accessed January 23, 2018).

27 "Burlington's Corporate Social Responsibility," Burlington, https://www.burlingtoncoatfactory.com/aboutus/communityrelations.aspx (accessed January 26, 2018).

28 CenturyLink, "CenturyLink Community," www.centurylink.com/aboutus/community.html (accessed January 26, 2018).

29 Sara Spruch-Feiner, "10 Feel-Good Beauty Brands That Give Back," *Observer*, December 19, 2017, http://observer.com/2017/12/10-feel-good-beauty-brands-that-give-back/ (accessed January 27, 2018).

30 Edelman, 2018 Edelman Trust Barometer Global Report, http://cms.edelman.com/sites/default/files/2018-01/2018_Edelman_Trust_Barometer_Global_Report_Jan.PDF (accessed January 27, 2018).

31 Martín Caballero, "Judge Approves $8.25 Million Settlement in GT's Kombucha and Whole Foods Suit," Bevnet, February 3, 2017, https://www.bevnet.com/news/2017/judge-approves-8-25-million-settlement-gts-kombucha-whole-foods-suit (accessed January 27, 2018).

32 Tim Barnett and Sean Valentine, "Issue Contingencies and Marketers' Recognition of Ethical Issues, Ethical Judgments and Behavioral Intentions," *Journal of Business Research* 57 (2004): pp. 338–346.

33 Trefis Team, "Can Chipotle Mexican Grill Recover from the E.Coli Outbreak Impact?" *Forbes*, December 14, 2015, www.forbes.com/sites/greatspeculations/2015/12/14/can-chipotle-mexican-grill-recover-from-the-e-coli-outbreak-impact/ (accessed December 16, 2015).

34 David E. Sprott, Kenneth C. Manning, and Anthony D. Miyazaki, "Grocery Price

Setting and Quantity Surcharges," *Journal of Marketing* (July 2003): pp. 34–46.

35 Stephen Taub, "SEC Probing Harley Statements," *CFO.com*, July 14, 2005, http://ww2.cfo.com/accounting-tax/2005/07/sec-probing-harley-statements (accessed January 27, 2018).

36 Kathy Chu and Trefor Moss, "Call Centers: New Battle Front for Fake Drugs," *The Wall Street Journal*, June 7, 2015, www.wsj.com/articles/call-centers-new-battle-front-for-fake-drugs-1433712783 (accessed January 27, 2018).

37 Lynnley Browning, "Companies Struggle to Comply with Rules on Conflict Minerals," *The New York Times*, September 7, 2015, www.nytimes.com/2015/09/08/business/dealbook/companies-struggle-to-comply-with-conflict-minerals-rule.html?_r=0 (accessed January 27, 2018).

38 Ben Dipietro, "Slave Labor Concerns Give Companies More Supply Chain Worries," *The Wall Street Journal*, September 3, 2015, http://blogs.wsj.com/riskandcompliance/2015/09/03/slave-labor-concerns-give-companies-more-supply-chain-worries/ (accessed January 27, 2018); Emma Richards, "Forced Labour Persists in the Thai Fishing Industry," *Asian Correspondent*, January 24, 2018, https://asiancorrespondent.com/2018/01/forced-labour-trafficking-persists-thai-fishing-industry-report/#53lyTPPV1h5BoM68.97 (accessed January 26, 2018); Sebastian Malo, "Retail Giant Costco Wins Dismissal of Prawn Lawsuit Over Thai Forced Labor," *Reuters*, January 25, 2017, https://www.reuters.com/article/us-usa-lawsuit-costco/retail-giant-costco-wins-dismissal-of-prawn-lawsuit-over-thai-forced-labor-idUSKBN1592JC (accessed January 26, 2018).

39 Telegraph Reporters, "M&S and ASOS Among British Retailers Found Employing Child Refugees in Factories," *Telegraph*, October 24, 2016, www.telegraph.co.uk/news/2016/10/24/ms-and-asos-among-british-retailers-found-employing-child-refuge/ (accessed January 26, 2018).

40 "Health Care Supply Company Novation Earns Ethics Inside Certification," *Ethisphere*, November 8, 2011, https://ethisphere.com/novation-llc-again-earns-ethics-inside-certification/ (accessed January 26, 2018).

41 Maxwell Murphy, "Reinforcing the Supply Chain," *The Wall Street Journal*, January 11, 2012, p. B6; "Monitoring and Auditing Global Supply Chains Is a Must," pp. 38–45.

42 "Monitoring and Auditing Global Supply Chains Is a Must," *Ethisphere*, Q3, (2011): pp. 38–45.

43 Peggy H. Cunningham and O. C. Ferrell, "The Influence of Role Stress on Unethical Behavior by Personnel Involved in the Marketing Research Process" (working paper, Queens University, Ontario, 2004), p. 35.

44 Joseph W. Weiss, *Business Ethics: A Managerial, Stakeholder Approach* (Belmont, CA: Wadsworth, 1994), p. 13.

45 O. C. Ferrell, Larry G. Gresham, and John Fraedrich, "A Synthesis of Ethical Decision Models for Marketing," *Journal of Macromarketing* (Fall 1989): pp. 58–59.

46 Ethics and Compliance Initiative, *2016 Global Business Ethics Survey™: Measuring Risk and Promoting Workplace Integrity* (Arlington, VA: Ethics and Compliance Initiative, 2016), p. 43.

47 Barry J. Babin, James S. Boles, and Donald P. Robin, "Representing the Perceived Ethical Work Climate Among Marketing Employees," *Journal of the Academy of Marketing Science* 28 (2000): pp. 345–358.

48 Ferrell, Gresham, and Fraedrich, "A Synthesis of Ethical Decision Models for Marketing."

49 Lawrence B. Chonko and Shelby D. Hunt, "Ethics and Marketing Management: A Retrospective and Prospective Commentary," *Journal of Business Research* 50 (2000): pp. 235–244.

50 Linda K. Trevino and Stuart Youngblood, "Bad Apples in Bad Barrels: A Causal Analysis of Ethical Decision Making Behavior," *Journal of Applied Psychology* 75 (1990): pp. 378–385.

51 Pfizer, "Pfizer's International Anti-Bribery and Anti-Corruption Business Principles," https://www.pfizer.com/sites/default/files/corporate_citizenship/pfizer_antibribery_anticorruption91112.pdf (accessed December 17, 2015); Pfizer, *The Blue Book: Summary of Pfizer Policies on Business Conduct*, www.pfizer.com/files/investors/corporate/bluebook_english.pdf (accessed December 17, 2015).

52 Ethics Resource Center, "The Ethics Resource Center's 2009 National Business Ethics Survey," p. 41.

53 Ethics Resource Center, "The Ethics Resource Center's 2007 National Business Ethics Survey," p. ix.

54 Ethics and Compliance Initiative, *2016 Global Business Ethics Survey™: Measuring Risk and Promoting Workplace Integrity* (Arlington, VA: Ethics and Compliance Initiative, 2016), p. 18.

55 Sir Adrian Cadbury, "Ethical Managers Make Their Own Rules," *Harvard Business Review* (September/October 1987): p. 33.

56 Isabelle Maignan, Tracy L. Gonzalez-Padron, G. Tomas M. Hult, and O. C. Ferrell, "Stakeholder Orientation: Development and Testing of a Framework for Socially Responsible Marketing," *Journal of Strategic Marketing*, vol. 19, 4 (July 2011): pp. 313–338.

57 Ferrell, Fraedrich, and Ferrell, *Business Ethics*, pp. 27–30.

58 CH2M, "CH2M Named a 2017 World's Most Ethical Company for 9 Years Running," March 13, 2017, https://www.ch2m.com/newsroom/news/ch2m-named-2017-worlds-most-ethical-company-9-years-running (accessed January 27, 2018).

59 G. Thomas Hult, Jeannette Mena, O. C. Ferrell, and Linda Ferrell, "Stakeholder Marketing: A Definition and Conceptual Framework," *AMS Review* 1, 1 (2011): pp. 44–65.

60 Marjorie Kelly, "Holy Grail Found: Absolute, Definitive Proof That Responsible Companies Perform Better Financially," *Business Ethics*, Winter 2004: pp. 4–5; Xueming Luo and C. B. Bhattacharya, "Corporate Social Responsibility, Customer Satisfaction, and Market Value," *Journal of Marketing* 70 (October 2006): pp. 1–18; Isabelle Maignan, O. C. Ferrell, and Linda Ferrell, "A Stakeholder Model for Implementing Social Responsibility in Marketing," *European Journal of Marketing* 39 (September/October 2005): pp. 956–977.

61 Cone Communications, "2017 Cone Communications CSR Study," www.conecomm.com/2017-cone-communications-csr-study-pdf (accessed January 27, 2018).

62 Maignan, Ferrell, and Ferrell, "A Stakeholder Model for Implementing Social Responsibility in Marketing."

63 Jacob Laxen, "New Belgium Adds Specialized Brewery Tours in Fort Collins," *Coloradan*, January 12, 2018, https://www.coloradoan.com/story/life/food-drink/2018/01/12/new-belgium-adds-specialized-brewery-tours-fort-collins/ 1028114001 (accessed January 26, 2018); New Belgium, www.newbelgium.com/brewery/company/craft-beer-rankings-and-financials (accessed January 26, 2018); "New Belgium Brewing: Ethical and Environmental Responsibility," O. C. Ferrell, John Fraedrich, and Linda Ferrell, *Business Ethics: Ethical Decision Making and Cases*, 9th ed. (Mason, OH: South-Western Cengage Learning, 2013), pp. 355–363; New Belgium, "The Tinkerer," *YouTube*, https://www.youtube.com/watch?v=8UfTzXhdz5Y (accessed January 26, 2018); Susan Adams, "New Belgium Brewing Hires a New CEO from the Liquor Industry," *Forbes*, July 17, 2017, https://www.forbes.com/sites/susanadams/2017/07/17/new-belgium-brewing-hires-a-new-ceo-from-the-liquor-industry/#65b7f66d5e7a (accessed

January 31, 2018); Devin Leonard, "New Belgium and the Battle of the Microbrews," *Bloomberg Businessweek*, December 1, 2011, www.businessweek.com/magazine/new-belgium-and-the-battle-of-the-micro-brews-12012011.html (accessed January 26, 2018); New Belgium, "Kim's Joy Ride: Fat Tire Ale," *YouTube*, https://www.youtube.com/watch?v=L94PE12VaFY (accessed January 26, 2018); "Case 15: New Belgium Brewing: Engaging in Sustainable Social Responsibility," in O. C. Ferrell, Debbie Thorne, and Linda Ferrell, *Business & Society A Strategic Approach to Social Responsibility and Ethics*, 5th ed. (Chicago: Chicago Business Press, 2016), pp. 556–563; Eric Gorski, "U.S. Craft Brewers Exporting Beer – and Ideas – Around the World," *Denver Post*, April 8, 2014, www.denverpost.com/news/ci_25517990/u-s-craft-brewers-exporting-beer-and-ideas (accessed January 26, 2018); New Belgium, "New Belgium President and Christine Perich to Assume CEO Position," August 10, 2015, www.newbelgium.com/community/Blog/new-belgium-brewing/2015/08/10/New-Belgium-President-and-COO-Christine-Perich-to-assume-CEO-position (accessed January 26, 2018); Charles Sizemore, "Why Big Beer Is Struggling in the Age of Craft Beer," *Forbes*, June 9, 2015, www.forbes.com/sites/moneybuilder/2015/06/09/why-big-beer-is-struggling-in-the-age-of-craft-beer/ (accessed January 26, 2018).

64 Dianne Kroncke, interview by Kayla Joy Asbury, October 2017; Radio Interview, "Sseko Designs – Brianna Leever," Net .Work. Master!, www.hombabiz.com/sseko-designs-brianna-leever/ (accessed October 12, 2017); Malia Spencer, "Life After 'Shark Tank' Is Pretty Good for One Portland Startup," *Portland Business Journal*, February 17, 2015, https://www.bizjournals.com/portland/blog/techflash/2015/02/life-after-shark-tank-is-pretty-good-for-one.html (accessed October 12, 2017); Sseko Designs, https://ssekodesigns.com/ (accessed January 26, 2018); "Like Sseko Designs, You Too Can Take Advantage of the African Growth and Opportunity Act," *U.S. Embassy in Uganda*, https://ug.usembassy.gov/learn-ugandans-taking-advantage-african-growth-opportunity-act/ (accessed January 26, 2018); "Sseko Designs, Uganda: An AGOA Success Story," United States AID, https://www.usaid.gov/news-information/videos/node/218021 (accessed October 12, 2017); Pete Williams, "Liz Forkin Bohannon from Sseko and the Future of Retail," *YouTube*, https://www.youtube.com/watch?v=X11t0vy6wiY (accessed October 12, 2017).

65 Matt Egan, "Wells Fargo Plans to Close 800 More Branches by 2020," *CNN*, January 12, 2018, http://money.cnn.com/2018/01/12/investing/wells-fargo-shutting-branches/index.html (accessed January 26, 2018); Stacy Cowley, "Wells Fargo Review Finds 1.4 Million More Suspect Accounts," *The New York Times*, August 31, 2017, https://www.nytimes.com/2017/08/31/business/dealbook/wells-fargo-accounts.html (accessed January 26, 2018); Matt Egan, "Wells Fargo Admits to Signs of Worker Retaliation," *CNN*, January 24, 2017, http://money.cnn.com/2017/01/23/investing/wells-fargo-retaliation-ethics-line/ (accessed April 19, 2017); Matt Egan, "Letter Warned Wells Fargo of 'Widespread' Fraud in 2007 – Exclusive," *CNN Money*, October 18, 2016, http://money.cnn.com/2016/10/18/investing/wells-fargo-warned-fake-accounts-2007/ (accessed January 6, 2017); Stacy Cowley, "At Wells Fargo, Complaints about Fraudulent Accounts Since 2005," *The New York Times*, October 11, 2016, www.nytimes.com/2016/10/12/business/dealbook/at-wells-fargo-complaints-about-fraudulent-accounts-since-2005.html (accessed January 6, 2017); Mark Snider, "Ex-Wells Fargo Bankers Sue Over Firing Amid Fraud," *USA Today*, September 25, 2016, www.usatoday.com/story/money/2016/09/25/ex-wells-fargo-employees-sue-over-scam/91079158/ (accessed January 6, 2017); Winston Craver, "Wells Fargo Draws Senators' Ire on Fraud Accounts Response," *Winston-Salem Journal*, December 23, 2016, www.journalnow.com/news/local/wells-fargo-draws-senators-ire-on-fraud-accounts-response/article_b2c44587-e2cf-5cb1-966e-6e20c89fa9d8.html (accessed January 6, 2017); Maria Armental, "Wells Fargo Reaches $110 Million Class-Action Settlement," *The Wall Street Journal*, March 28, 2017, p. A1; Shah Gilani, "The Situation at Wells Fargo Is Worse Than We Thought," *Wall Street Insights & Indictments*, September 16, 2016, http://wallstreetinsightsandindictments.com/2016/09/the-situation-at-wells-fargo-is-worse-than-we-thought/ (accessed April 16, 2017); Matt Egan, "5,300 Wells Fargo Employees Fired Over 2 Million Phony Accounts," *CNN*, September 8, 2016, http://money.cnn.com/2016/09/08/investing/wells-fargo-created-phony-accounts-bank-fees/ (accessed April 16, 2017); George Khoury, "Will Wells Fargo's CEO Face Criminal Charges?" FindLaw, October 17, 2016, http://blogs.findlaw.com/blotter/2016/10/will-wells-fargos-ceo-face-criminal-charges.html (accessed April 16, 2017); *United States v. Park*, 421 U.S. 658 (1975); Matt Egan, "Wells Fargo Admits to Signs of Worker Retaliation," *CNN*, January 24, 2017, http://money.cnn.com/2017/01/23/investing/wells-fargo-retaliation-ethics-line/?iid=EL (accessed April 16,

2017); Emily Glazer, "Wells Fargo Digs Deeper into its Culture Issues," *The Wall Street Journal*, March 21, 2017, p. A1; Lucinda Shen, "Here's How Much Wells Fargo CEO John Stumpf Is Getting to Leave the Bank," *Fortune*, October 13, 2016, http://fortune.com/2016/10/13/wells-fargo-ceo-john-stumpfs-career-ends-with-133-million-payday/ (accessed January 26, 2018); Wilfred Frost, "Wells Fargo Board Slams Former CEO Stumpf and Tolstedt, Claws Back $75 Million," *CNBC*, April 10, 2017, https://www.cnbc.com/2017/04/10/wells-fargo-board-slams-stumpf-and-tolstedt-claws-back-millions.html (accessed January 26, 2018); Andrea Riquier, "SEC Fines Wells Fargo Advisors for Failing to Report on Money Laundering," *MarketWatch*, November 14, 2017, https://www.marketwatch.com/story/sec-fines-wells-fargo-advisors-for-failing-to-report-on-money-laundering-2017-11-14 (accessed January 26, 2018); Wilfred Frost, "Wells Fargo Report Gives Inside Look at the Culture that Crushes the Bank's Reputation," *CNBC*, April 10, 2017, https://www.cnbc.com/2017/04/10/wells-fargo-report-shows-culture-that-crushed-banks-reputation.html (accessed January 26, 2018); Matt Egan, "Wells Fargo's Notorious Sales Goals to Get Makeover," *CNN*, January 6, 2017, http://money.cnn.com/2017/01/06/investing/wells-fargo-replace-sales-goals-fake-accounts/index.html (accessed January 26, 2018); Stacy Cowley, "Wells Fargo Whistle-Blower Wins $5.4 Million and His Job Back," *The New York Times*, April 3, 2017, https://www.nytimes.com/2017/04/03/business/04-wells-fargo-whistleblower-fired-osha.html (accessed January 26, 2018).

Chapter 5

1 Sarah Elbert, "Food for Thought," *Delta Sky*, December 2016, pp. 66–70; Annie Gasparro, "General Mills Starts Making Some Cheerios Without GMOs," *The Wall Street Journal*, January 2, 2014, www.wsj.com/articles/SB10001424052702303370904579297211874270146 (accessed January 6, 2017); Hadley Malcolm, "General Mills to Label GMOs on Products Across Country," *USA Today*, March 18, 2016, www.usatoday.com/story/money/2016/03/18/general-mills-to-label-gmos-on-products/81981314/ (accessed January 6, 2017); Stephanie Strom, "Paying Farmers to Go Organic, Even Before the Crops Come In," *The New York Times*, July 14, 2016, www.nytimes.com/2016/07/15/business/paying-farmers-to-go-organic-even-before-the-crops-come-in.html (accessed January 6, 2017); Mark Thomas, "How 'GMO-Free' Gave Cheerios a Competitive Advantage," *Michigan State University*, February 5, 2014, http://msue.anr.msu.edu/news/how_gmo_free_gave_cheerios_a_competitive_advantage

(accessed February 5, 2018); Eli Fish, "Insight into Marketing Research at General Mills," *Wisconsin School of Business*, November 13, 2014, https://bus.wisc.edu/mba/current-students/mba-specializations/marketing-research/blog/2014/11/13/insight-into-marketing-research-at-general-mills (accessed February 10, 2018).

2. Ellen Byron, "The Slower You Shop, the More You Spend," *The Wall Street Journal*, October 20, 2015, www.wsj.com/articles/the-slower-you-shop-the-more-you-spend-1445359614 (accessed December 21, 2015).

3. Tripp Mickle and Valerie Bauerlein, "Nascar, Once a Cultural Icon, Hits the Skids," *The Wall Street Journal*, February 21, 2017, www.wsj.com/articles/long-in-victory-lane-nascar-hits-the-skids-1487686349?tesla=y (accessed March 12, 2017); Andrew Lawrence, "More Than a Kneeling: Nascar's TV Ratings Decline Is as Worrying as the NFL's. Why?" *The Guardian*, November 17, 2017, www.theguardian.com/sport/2017/nov/17/more-than-a-kneeling-nascars-tv-ratings-decline-is-as-worrying-as-the-nfls-why (accessed February 4, 2018).

4. Allison Enright, "Surviving 2010," *Marketing News*, February 28, 2010, pp. 30–33.

5. Jens Hansegard, "IKEA Slides Into Cramped Quarters," *The Wall Street Journal*, October 1, 2015, pp. B1, B6.

6. Dhruv Grewal Parasuraman and R. Krishnan, *Marketing Research* (Boston: Houghton Mifflin, 2007).

7. Barry Babin and William Zikmund, *Exploring Marketing Research* (Mason, OH: Cengage Learning, 2016), p. 113.

8. Oracle, "About the Customer Advisory Board," Oracle Communications, www.oracle.com/communications-customer-advisory-board/about.html (accessed December 22, 2015).

9. Phil Wahba, "The Change Agent Inside CVS," *Fortune*, September 11, 2015, http://fortune.com/2015/09/11/cvs-health-helena-foulkes/ (accessed December 21, 2015).

10. Daniel Gross, "Lies, Damn Lies, and Focus Groups," *Slate*, October 10, 2003, www.slate.com/articles/business/moneybox/2003/10/lies_damn_lies_and_focus_groups.html (accessed July 9, 2012).

11. Babin and Zikmund, p. 113.

12. Peter Frost, "Here's the Next Step in McDonald's Turnaround Plan," *Chicago Business*, October 21, 2015, www.chicagobusiness.com/article/20151021/NEWS07/151029955/heres-the-next-step-in-mcdonalds-turnaround-plan (accessed December 21, 2015); Lori Weisberg, "McDonald's Tests New Menu in SD," *The San Diego Union-Tribune*, September 25, 2015, http://www.sandiegouniontribune.com/news/2015/sep/25/mcdonalds-launches-customized-sandwich-test/ (accessed December 21, 2015).

13. Andreas Persson and Lynette Ryals, "Making Customer Relationship Decisions: Analytics v Rules of Thumb," *Journal of Business Research*, 67(8) (August 2014), pp. 1725–1732.

14. Donna F. Davis, Susan L. Golicic, Courtney N. Boerstler, Sunny Choi, and Hanmo Oh, "Does Marketing Research Suffer from Methods Myopia?" *Journal of Business Research*, 66(9), pp. 1245–1250.

15. Vikas Mittal and Wagner A. Kamakura, "Satisfaction, Repurchase Intent, and Repurchase Behavior: Investigating the Moderating Effects of Customer Characteristics," *Journal of Marketing Research* (February 2001): pp. 131–142.

16. U.S. Census Bureau, *American Community Survey*, www.census.gov/acs/www (accessed January 20, 2011).

17. Aaron Gilchrist, "Census Forms Confusion: 'American Community Survey' Is Legit," *nbc12.com*, January 27, 2010, www.nbc12.com/Global/story.asp?S=11890921 (accessed January 21, 2011).

18. Symphony IRI Group, "About Us," http://symphonyiri.com/About/History/tabid/60/Default.aspy (accessed January 21, 2011).

19. David Lieberman, "TiVo to Sell Data on What People Watch, Fast-Forward," *USA Today*, April 20, 2010, www.usatoday.com/tech/news/2009-04-20-tivo-data-new-plan_N.htm (accessed March 19, 2010).

20. Procter & Gamble 2009 Annual Report, February 24, 2010, p. 3, http://annualreport.pg.com/annualreport2009/index.shtml (accessed March 20, 2010); Kelly Tay, "Marketing in a Digital Age," *Business Intelligence*, September 25, 2013, www.businesstimes.com.sg/specials/forward-thinkers/marketing-digital-age-20130925 (accessed November 26, 2013); Brian Terran, "Insights Key to Sustainability Cause, Says P&G Chief Executive," *Research*, September 27, 2012, www.research-live.com/news/news-headlines/insights-key-to-sustainability-cause-says-pg-chief-executive/4008338.article (accessed November 25, 2013).

21. Warren Davies, "How to Increase Survey Response Rates Using Post-It Notes," *GenerallyThinking.com*, August 3, 2009, http://generallythinking.com/blog/how-to-increase-survey-response-rates-using-post-it-notes (accessed March 9, 2010); Randy Garner, "Post-It Note Persuasion: A Sticky Influence," *Journal of Consumer Psychology* 15 (2005): pp. 230–237.

22. Kurt Schlosser, "GeekWire Poll: Do You Still Have a Landline Phone? Survey Finds 52 Percent of U.S. Adults Are Cell Only," *GeekWire*, January 17, 2017, www.geekwire.com/2017/geekwire-poll-still-landline-phone-survey-finds-52-percent-u-s-adults-cell/ (accessed February 4, 2018).

23. "About Qualtrics," Qualtrics, www.qualtrics.com/about/ (accessed February 4, 2018); Joshua Brustein, "How an Online Survey Company Joined the $1 Billion Club," *Bloomberg Businessweek*, September 24, 2014, www.businessweek.com/articles/2014-09-24/how-qualtrics-turned-online-surveys-into-a-1-billion-business (accessed December 16, 2014); "After Snap, Will One of These 12 Tech Companies be the Next to IPO?" *Silicon Republic*, February 10, 2017, www.siliconrepublic.com/companies/snapchat-ipo-who-is-next (accessed March 17, 2017).

24. Joshua Brustein, "How an Online Survey Company Joined the $1 Billion Club," *Bloomberg Businessweek*, September 24, 2014, www.businessweek.com/articles/2014-09-24/how-qualtrics-turned-online-surveys-into-a-1-billion-business (accessed December 16, 2014).

25. Ray Poynter, "Mobile Market Research, 2014," *International Journal of Market Research*, 56(6), pp. 705–707.

26. David Robertson, "Building Success: How Thinking 'Inside the Brick' Saved Lego," *Wired*, October 9, 2013, www.wired.co.uk/magazine/archive/2013/10/features/building-success (accessed November 19, 2014); Lego Ideas, https://ideas.lego.com/ (accessed November 19, 2014).

27. Charlene Li, "Why No One Uses the Corporate Social Network," *Harvard Business Review*, April 7, 2015, https://hbr.org/2015/04/why-no-one-uses-the-corporate-social-network (accessed December 21, 2015).

28. Amazon Mechanical Turk, http://aws.amazon.com/mturk/ (accessed December 16, 2014).

29. Michael Buhrmester, Tracy Kwang, and Samuel B. Gosling, "Amazon's Mechanical Turk: A New Source of Inexpensive, Yet High-Quality Data?" *Perspectives on Psychological Science*, doi: 10.1177/1745691610393980.

30. James Vincent, "Amazon's Mechanical Turkers want to be recognized as 'actual human beings,'" *The Verge*, December 4, 2014, www.theverge.com/2014/12/4/7331777/amazon-mechanical-turk-workforce-digital-labor (accessed January 11, 2016); Utpal Dholakia, "My Experience as an Amazon Mechanical Turk (MTurk) Worker," July 20, 2015, www.linkedin.com/pulse/my-experience-amazon-mechanical-turk-mturk-worker-utpal-dholakia (accessed January 11, 2016).

31 Sue Shellenbarger, "A Few Bucks for Your Thoughts?" *The Wall Street Journal*, May 18, 2011, http://online.wsj.com/news/articles/SB10001424052748703509104576329110724411724 (accessed March 28, 2014).

32 Bas Donkers, Philip Hans Franses, and Peter C. Verhoef, "Selective Sampling for Binary Choice Models," *Journal of Marketing Research* (November 2003): pp. 492–497.

33 Elizabeth Weise, "Online Retailers Getting Physical," *USA Today*, November 6, 2015, www.usatoday.com/story/tech/2015/11/06/amazon-brick-and-mortar-bonobos-modcloth/75235308/ (accessed December 21, 2015).

34 Hsin-Hui Lin and Shu-Fei Yang, "An Eye Movement Study of Attribute Framing in Online Shopping," *Journal of Marketing Analytics*, 2(2) (June 2014): pp. 72–80.

35 Piet Levy, "10 Minutes with . . . Gregory A. Reid," *Marketing News*, February 28, 2010, p. 34.

36 *Reputation.com*, "How to Make a Negative Review Work in Your Favor," www.reputation.com/reputationwatch/articles/how-make-negative-review-work-your-favor (accessed November 25, 2013).

37 Lauren Coleman-Lochner, "Why Procter & Gamble Needs to Shave More Indians," *Bloomberg Buinessweek*, June 9, 2011, www.businessweek.com/magazine/content/11_25/b4233021703857.htm (accessed April 15, 2016).

38 David Aaker, V. Kumar, George Day, and Robert Lane, *Marketing Research*, 10th ed. (New York: Wiley & Sons, 2010).

39 "BehaviorScan Rx," IRI, www.iriworldwide.com/default.aspx?TabId=159&0026;productid=75 (accessed November 19, 2014).

40 Douglas Laney, "The Importance of 'Big Data': A Definition," Gartner, June 2012.

41 Peter Daboll, "5 Reasons Why Big Data Will Crush Big Research," *Forbes*, December 3, 2013, www.forbes.com/sites/onmarketing/2013/12/03/5-reasons-why-big-data-will-crush-big-research (accessed December 5, 2013).

42 Danny Bradbury and Tim Anderson, "Big Data and Marketing: An Inevitable Partnership," *The Guardian*, October 16, 2013, www.theguardian.com/technology/2013/oct/16/big-data-and-marketing-an-inevitable-partnership (accessed December 5, 2013).

43 Steven Norton, "Big Companies Rein In Data Sprawl," *The Wall Street Journal*, October 22, 2015, p. B4.

44 Paula B. Goes, "Editor's Comments: Big Data and IS Research," *MIS Quarterly*, 38(3) (September 2014): pp. iii–viii.

45 Randy Bean, "How Companies Say They're Using Big Data," *Harvard Business Review*, April 28, 2017, https://hbr.org/2017/04/how-companies-say-theyre-using-big-data (accessed February 5, 2018).

46 Bradbury and Anderson, "Big Data and Marketing: An Inevitable Partnership."

47 Camille Chatterjee, "5 Ways Johnson & Johnson Is Blazing Technological Trails," Johnson & Johnson, March 15, 2016, www.jnj.com/innovation/5-ways-johnson-johnson-is-blazing-technological-trails (accessed February 5, 2018); Mehboob Feelani, "Watson, Come Here. I Want You," *Fortune*, October 27, 2014, p. 36.

48 Kashmir Hill, "How Target Figured Out a Teen Girl Was Pregnant Before Dad Did," *Forbes*, February 16, 2012, www.forbes.com/sites/kashmirhill/2012/02/16/how-target-figured-out-a-teen-girl-was-pregnant-before-her-father-did (accessed December 5, 2013).

49 SAS, "Big Data, Bigger Marketing," www.sas.com/software/customer-intelligence/big-data-marketing.html (accessed December 5, 2013).

50 James Rubin, "Survey Demonstrates the Benefits of Big Data," *Forbes*, November 15, 2013, www.forbes.com/sites/forbesinsights/2013/11/15/survey-demonstrates-the-benefits-of-big-data (accessed December 5, 2013).

51 Peter Daboll, "5 Reasons Why Big Data Will Crush Big Research."

52 Melissa S. Barker, Donald I. Barker, Nicolas F. Bormann, Mary Lou Roberts, and Debra Zahay, *Social Media Marketing* (Mason, OH: Cengage Learning, 2016), pp. 25–26.

53 Jayson DeMers, "2014 Is the Year of Digital Marketing Analytics: What It Means for Your Company," *Forbes*, February 10, 2014, www.forbes.com/sites/jaysondemers/2014/02/10/2014-is-the-year-of-digital-marketing-analytics-what-it-means-for-your-company/ (accessed December 15, 2014).

54 Marketing Science Institute, "MSI Closes Knowledge Gap on Marketers' Top Concerns," *Marketing Science Institute Review* (Fall 2014): pp. 1–2.

55 Elisabeth A. Sullivan, "Marketing Analytics," *Marketing News*, December 2014, pp. 24–33.

56 Regina Pefanis Schlee and Katrin R. Harich, "Teaching Students How to Integrate and Assess Social Networking Tools in Marketing Communications," *Marketing Education Review* 23, 3 (2013): pp. 209–223.

57 Sullivan, pp. 24–33.

58 Doug Henschen, "Big Data Success: 3 Companies Share Secrets," *Information Week*, October 4, 2013, www.informationweek.com/big-data/big-data-analytics/big-data-success-3-companies-share-secrets/d/d-id/1111815? (accessed December 15, 2014).

59 Frank Germann, Gary L. Lilien, and Arvind Rangaswamy, "Performance Implications of Deploying Marketing Analytics," *International Journal of Research in Marketing*, 30 (2), (June 2013), pp. 114–128.

60 Chares Duhigg, "How Companies Learn Your Secrets," *The New York Times*, February 15, 2012, www.nytimes.com/2012/02/19/magazine/shopping-habits.html?_r=1& pagewanted=all (accessed February 28, 2012).

61 "We Snoop to Conquer," *The Economist*, February 9, 2013, p. 64.

62 Emily Steel and Julia Angwin, "The Web's Cutting Edge, Anonymity in Name Only," *The Wall Street Journal*, August 4, 2010, http://online.wsj.com/article/SB10001424052748703294904575385532109190198.html (accessed February 7, 2012).

63 Diane Bowers, "The 2015 AMA Gold Top 50 Report," *Marketing News*, June 2015, pp. 36–93.

64 Reprinted with permission of The Marketing Research Association, P.O. Box 230, Rocky Hill, CT 06067-0230, 860-257-4008.

65 Yoni Heisler, "Once Mocked, Facebook's $1 Billion Acquisition of Instagram was a Stroke of Genius," *BGR*, December 29, 2016, http://bgr.com/2016/12/29/facebook-instagram-acquisition-1-billion-genius/ (accessed March 5, 2017); Bryan Clark, "Snapchat Growth Slowed Significantly after Launch of Instagram Stories," The Next Web, February 3, 2017, https://thenextweb.com/socialmedia/2017/02/03/snapchat-growth-slowed-significantly-after-the-launch-of-instagram-stories/#.tnw_0IAEa2YL (accessed March 5, 2017); Tribune wire reports, "Instagram Expands Marketing Reach for Businesses," *Chicago Tribune*, September 9, 2015, www.chicagotribune.com/bluesky/technology/ct-instagram-marketing-business-20150909-story.html (accessed January 8, 2016); "How Instagram Uses Machine Learning to Help You Explore," *Fast Company*, November 17, 2017, https://www.fastcompany.com/video/how-instagram-uses-machine-learning-to-help-you-explore/5EIAMya0 (accessed May 20, 2018); Bernard Marr, "The Amazing Ways Instagram Uses Big Data and Artificial Intelligence," *Forbes*, March 16, 2018, https://www.forbes.com/sites/bernardmarr/2018/03/16/the-amazing-ways-instagram-uses-big-data-and-artificial-intelligence/#6f46f76a5ca6 (accessed May 20, 2018); Nicholas Thompson, "Instagram Unleashes an AI System to Blast away Nasty Comments," *Wired*, June 29, 2017, https://

www.wired.com/story/instagram-launches-ai-system-to-blast-nasty-comments/ (accessed May 20, 2018).

66 "Church's Chicken Taps Market Force as Partner," *QSR*, February 7, 2018, www .qsrmagazine.com/news/church-s-chicken-taps-market-force-partner (accessed February 10, 2018); "Rent-A-Center Taps Market Force Information for Customer Experience Management," *Market Force Information*, December 20, 2017, www .marketforce.com/RAC-taps-market-force-for-customer-experience-management (accessed February 10, 2018); Marcia Layton Turner, "Publix and Wegmans Named America's Favorite Grocery Stores," *Forbes*, January 18, 2018, www.forbes.com/ sites/marciaturner/2018/01/18/publix-and-wegmans-named-americas-favorite-grocery-stores/#5246aa36d696 (accessed February 10, 2018); "Market Force Infor-mation," *Crunchbase*, www.crunchbase. com/organization/market-force-information (accessed February 10, 2018); "Church's Chicken: Catching Staff Doing Something Right," *Market Force Information*, www .marketforce.com/case-study-churchs-chicken-cups-cash (accessed February 10, 2018); "Who We Are," *Market Force Information*, www.marketforce.com/ about-us (accessed February 10, 2018); Scott Griffith, "Food Delivery Services Are Exploding," *Market Force Information*, October 10, 2017, www.marketforce.com/ blog/food-delivery-services-are-exploding (accessed February 10, 2018).

Chapter 6

1 Katie Morley, "Male Cosmetics Counters Could Hit Department Stores in Five Years, L'Oréal Boss Says," *The Telegraph (UK)*, August 6, 2017, www.telegraph.co.uk/ news/2017/08/06/male-cosmetics-counters-could-hit-department-stores-five-yearsloreal (accessed February 7, 2018); Leonie Roderick, "L'Oréal on How the 'Power' of Diversity Transformed the Brand," *Marketing Week*, March 1, 2017, www.marketingweek .com/2017/03/01/loreal-power-diversity (accessed February 7, 2018); Allison Collins, "WWD's 10 of Tomorrow: Beauty Innovator Sam Cheow," *Women's Wear Daily*, January 30 2017, http://wwd.com/beauty-industry-news/beauty-features/wwd-10-tomorrow-sam-cheow-beauty-loreal-10767789/ (accessed February 7, 2018).

2 Aaron Ricadela and Michael Ross, "Adidas Is a Late Starter in the Race for the Women's Market," *Bloomberg*, March 1, 2016, https://www.bloom-berg.com/news/articles/2016-03-01/

adidas-makes-late-sprint-in-crowded-race-to-sell-women-sneakers (accessed November 2, 2017).

3 Cheerwine, www.cheerwine.com (accessed February 7, 2018).

4 Art Weinstein, "Target Market Selection in B2B Technology Markets," *Journal of Marketing Analytics*, 2, 1 (2014): pp. 59–69.

5 Richard Fry, "5 Facts about Millennial Households," Pew Research Center, September 6, 2017, http://www.pewresearch. org/fact-tank/2017/09/06/5-facts-about-millennial-households/ (accessed April 19, 2018).

6 "Median Age of the Resident Population of the United States from 1960 to 2016," *Statista*, https://www.statista.com/ statistics/241494/median-age-of-the-us-population/ (accessed February 7, 2018).

7 Lucinda Shen, "Hilton's New 'Hostel on Steroids' Could Help It Steal Millennials from Airbnb," *Fortune*, September 26, 2017, http://fortune.com/2017/09/26/hilton-hostel-hotel-cheap/ (accessed April 19, 2018).

8 "QuickFacts," United States Census Bureau, July 1, 2016, http://www.census.gov/ quickfacts/table/PST045215/00 (accessed February 7, 2018).

9 "Marketing to Women—Quick Facts," She-Conomy, http://she-conomy.com/report/ marketing-to-women-quick-facts (accessed November 7, 2017).

10 "FAQ," Iman Cosmetics, www.imancosmet-ics.com/faq (accessed November 7, 2017).

11 Molly Soat, "Inside the Mind of a Wedding Consumer," *Marketing News*, November 2015, https://www.ama.org/publications/ MarketingNews/Pages/inside-mind-wedding-consumer.aspx (accessed November 7, 2017); Kathryn Vasel, "Couples Are Spending a Record Amount to Get Married," *CNN*, February 2, 2017, http://money.cnn .com/2017/02/02/pf/cost-of-wedding-budget-2016-the-knot/index.html (accessed November 7, 2017).

12 "The American Family Today," Pew Research Center, December 17, 2015, http://www .pewsocialtrends.org/2015/12/17/1-the-american-family-today/ (accessed November 2, 2017); U.S. Census Bureau, "The Majority of Children Live with Two Parents, Census Bureau Reports," press release, November 17, 2016, https://www .census.gov/newsroom/press-releases/2016/ cb16-192.html (accessed November 7, 2017).

13 Aaron Terrazos, "All Ages Welcome: Why Living Alone Isn't Just for America's Young and Old Anymore," Zillow, June 28, 2016, http://www.zillow.com/research/

americans-living-alone-12639/ (accessed November 7, 2017).

14 "For Couples Skipping the Ring, It Pays to Plot Out Finances, *NPR*, April 17, 2016, http://www.npr.org/2016/04/17/473498335/ for-couples-skipping-the-ring-it-pays-to-plot-out-finances (accessed December 19, 2016).

15 "American Community Survey Data on Same Sex Couples," U.S. Census Bureau, https:// www.census.gov/hhes/samesex/data/acs.html (accessed November 7, 2017).

16 "Claritas PRIZM," Claritas, https:// segmentationsolutions.nielsen.com/my bestsegments/Default.jsp?ID=70 (accessed November 7, 2017).

17 Alexandra Samuel, "Psychographics Are Just as Important for Marketers as Demographics," *Harvard Business Review*, March 11, 2016, https://hbr.org/2016/03/psychographics-are-just-as-important-for-marketers-as-demographics (accessed November 2, 2017).

18 Joseph T. Plummer, "The Concept and Appli-cation of Life Style Segmentation," *Journal of Marketing*, 38, 1 (1974): p. 33.

19 Claritas PRIZM, https:// segmentationsolutions.nielsen.com/my bestsegments/Default.jsp?ID=70 (accessed November 7, 2017).

20 Philip Kotler and Kevin Keller, *Marketing Management*, 14th ed. (Englewood Cliffs, NJ: Prentice Hall, 2012).

21 Charles W. Chase, Jr., "Selecting the Appropri-ate Forecasting Method," *Journal of Business Forecasting*, 16, 3 (1997): pp. 2, 23, 28–29.

22 "Chick-Fil-A Testing 'Spicy' Entrees in Cen-tral, South Texas," *KVUE*, October 18, 2017, http://www.kvue.com/life/food/chickfila-testing-spicy-chicken-entrees-central-south-texas/484228180 (accessed November 8, 2017).

23 Nicholas Thompson, "Do Nike's New Marathon Shoes Actually Make You Run Faster?" *Wired*, November 7, 2017, www .wired.com/story/do-nike-zoom-vaporfly-make-you-run-faster; Carola Long, "Sole Woman: Nike Embraces Female Footwear," *Financial Times*, February 28, 2018, www .ft.com/content/564eb2ec-1bcf-11e8-956a-43db76e69936; Jonathan Ringen, "Nike Has a New Digital Playbook—and It Starts with Sneakerheads," *Fast Company*, April 17, 2018, www.fastcompany.com/40547805/ nike-has-a-new-digital-playbook-and-it-starts-with-sneakerheads; Andy Giegerich, "Nike Revenue Rises by 5%, Net Income Falls as North American Sales Continue to Lag," *Portland Business Journal*, December 21, 2017, www.bizjournals.com/portland/ news/2017/12/21/nike-revenue-rises-by-5-percent-net-income-falls.html; Jake Woolf,

"These 4 Nike Sneakers Are Why the Swoosh Won 2017," GQ, December 21, 2017, www.gq.com/story/nike-sneakers-2017-vapormax-vaporfly-lebron-off-white; www.nike.com; Video: "The Shoe That Could Make a Sub-Two-Hour Marathon Possible," Wired, March 7, 2017, www.youtube.com/watch?v=8q1XCW_9F50&t=0s&list=PLibNZv5Zd0dxcjS2fN-z6Pes82V0jeRHr&index=37.

24 Julia Anderson, "Umpqua Bank to Close Three Clark County Branches," *Vancouver-Southwest Washington Business Journal*, November 10, 2017, www.vbjusa.com/news/top-stories/umpqua-bank-close-three-clark-county-branches/ (accessed February 5, 2018); Penny Crosman, "What's 'Human Digital Banking'? Umpqua's O'Haver Explains," *American Banker*, October 25, 2017, www.americanbanker.com/news/whats-human-digital-banking-umpquas-ohaver-explains (accessed February 5, 2018); Penny Crosman, "Where Your Teller Is Also Your Digital Banker," *American Banker*, September 21, 2017, www.americanbanker.com/news/where-your-teller-is-also-your-digital-banker (accessed February 5, 2018); www.umpquabank.com.

25 Eric Auchard and Christoph Steitz, "German Court Bans Uber's Unlicensed Taxi Services," *Reuters*, March 18, 2015, http://www.reuters.com/article/2015/03/18/us-uber-germany-ban-idUSKBN0ME1L820150318 (accessed April 15, 2017); Nick Bilton, "Disruptions: Taxi Supply and Demand, Priced by the Mile," *The New York Times*, January 8, 2012, http://bits.blogs.nytimes.com/2012/01/08/disruptions-taxi-supply-and-demand-priced-by-the-mile/ (accessed April 15, 2017); Michael Carney, "Playing Favorites: Uber Adds New Security Features, but Only in Select Crisis-Riddled Markets," *Pando Daily*, January 2, 2015, http://pando.com/2015/01/02/playing-favorites-uber-adds-new-security-features-but-only-in-select-crisis-riddled-markets/ (accessed April 15, 2017); Rob Davies, "Uber Suffers Legal Setbacks in France and Germany," *The Guardian*, June 9, 2016, https://www.theguardian.com/technology/2016/jun/09/uber-suffers-legal-setbacks-in-france-and-germany (accessed April 15, 2017); Economist staff, "Uberworld," *The Economist*, September 3, 2016, p. 9; Matt Flegenheimer, "For Now, Taxi Office Says, Cab-Hailing Apps Aren't Allowed," *The New York Times*, September 6, 2012, http://www.nytimes.com/2012/09/07/nyregion/cab-hailing-apps-not-allowed-by-new-york-taxi-commission.html?_r=0 (accessed April 15, 2017); Anja Floetenmeyer, "Taxi Deutschland - Taxi Deutschland App Got Uber Banned throughout Germany," *Taxi Deutschland*, http://www.taxi-deutschland.net/index.php/pressemitteilung/121-taxi-deutschland-app-got-uber-banned-throughout-germany (accessed May 21, 2015); Anna Gallegos, "The Four Biggest Legal Problems Facing Uber, Lyft and Other Ridesharing Services," *LXBN*, June 4, 2014, http://www.lxbn.com/2014/06/04/top-legal-problems-facing-uber-lyft-ridesharing-services/ (accessed April 15, 2017); Jefferson Graham, "App Greases the Wheels," *USA Today*, May 27, 2015, p. 5B; Felicitas Hackmann, "uberPOP, Uber's ride-sharing service, pops up in more EU cites" *VentureBeat*, April 15, 2014, http://venturebeat.com/2014/04/15/uberpop-ubers-peer-to-peer-service-pops-up-in-more-eu-cities/ (accessed April 15, 2017); Karun, "Times Internet and Uber Enter Into a Strategic Partnership, *Uber Blog*, March 22, 2015, http://blog.uber.com/times-internet (accessed April 15, 2017); R. Jai Krishna and Joanna Sugden, "India Asks Internet Service Providers to Block Uber Website in Delhi," *The Wall Street Journal*, May 14, 2015, http://www.wsj.com/articles/india-asks-internet-service-providers-to-block-uber-website-in-delhi-1431606032 (accessed April 15, 2017); Christopher Mims, "At Startups, People Are 'New Infrastructure,'" *The Wall Street Journal*, March 8, 2015, http://www.wsj.com/articles/at-startups-people-are-new-infrastructure-1425858978 (accessed April 15, 2017); Saritha Rai, "Uber Gets Serious About Passenger Safety in India, Introduces Panic Button," *Forbes*, February 12, 2015, http://www.forbes.com/sites/saritharai/2015/02/12/uber-gets-serious-about-passenger-safety-in-india-introduces-panic-button/ (accessed April 15, 2017); Sam Schechner and Tom Fairless, "Europe Steps Up Pressure on Tech Giants," *The Wall Street Journal*, April 2, 2015, http://www.wsj.com/articles/europe-steps-up-pressure-on-technology-giants-1428020273 (accessed April 15, 2017); Joana Sugden and Aditi Malhotra, "Indian Officials Drafting National Rules for Uber, Other Taxi Apps," *The Wall Street Journal*, April 7, 2015, http://www.wsj.com/articles/indian-officials-drafting-national-rules-for-uber-other-taxi-apps-1428427528 (accessed April 15, 2017); Sam Schechner, "Uber Wins French Court Reprieve Over Legality of Low-Cost Service," *The Wall Street Journal*, March 31, 2015, http://www.wsj.com/articles/uber-wins-french-court-reprieve-over-legality-of-low-cost-service-1427794312 (accessed April 15, 2017); Samantha Shankman, "Uber Gets into Ride-Sharing Game in Paris," *Skift*, February 4, 2014, http://skift.com/2014/02/04/uber-gets-into-the-ride-sharing-game-in-paris/ (accessed May 21, 2015); Aditi Shrivastava, "Uber Resumes Operations in Delhi Post 1.5 Months Ban," *The Economic Times*, January 23, 2015, http://articles.economictimes.indiatimes.com/2015-01-23/news/58382689_1_indian-taxi-market-radio-taxi-scheme-uber-spokesman (accessed April 15, 2017); "Vermittlung Privater Fahrer: Gericht Verbietet Uber Deutschlandweit," *der Spiegel*, http://www.spiegel.de/wirtschaft/unternehmen/uber-urteil-gericht-verbietet-uber-deutschlandweit-a-1024214.html (accessed April 15, 2017); Taxi Deutschland, "Uber Legal Problems Worldwide," http://www.taxi-deutschland.net/images/presse/Infografik_Uber-legal-issues_EN_v12_2015-02-06_final.pdf (accessed May 21, 2015); Uber, https://www.uber.com/ (accessed April 15, 2017); UNM Daniels Fund Ethics Initiative, "Truth, Transparency, and Trust: Uber Important in the Sharing Economy," PPT presentation, https://danielsethics.mgt.unm.edu/teaching-resources/presentations.asp (accessed April 15, 2017); Maria Vega Paul, "Uber Returns to Spanish Streets in Search of Regulatory U-Turn," *Reuters*, March 30, 2016, http://www.reuters.com/article/us-spain-uber-tech-idUSKCN0WW0AO (accessed April 15, 2017); Artyom Dogtiev, "Uber Revenue and Usage Statistics 2017," *Business of Apps*, November 21, 2017, http://www.businessofapps.com/data/uber-statistics/ (accessed December 29, 2017); Felim McGrath, "The Demographics of Uber's US Users," Global Web Index, August 16, 2017, https://blog.globalwebindex.net/chart-of-the-day/uber-demographics/ (accessed March 18, 2018); Chris O'Brien, "Uber CEO Slams Founders' 'Pirate' Culture, Pledges to Grow 'Responsibly,'" *Venture Beat*, January 22, 2018, https://venturebeat.com/2018/01/22/uber-ceo-slams-founders-pirate-culture-pledges-to-grow-responsibly/ (accessed March 24, 2018); "Tempe, Arizona, Police Release Footage from Deadly Crash involving Self-Driving Uber," *CBS News*, March 21, 2018, https://www.cbsnews.com/news/tempe-arizona-police-release-footage-deadly-crash-self-driving-uber/ (accessed March 24, 2018).

Chapter 7

1 "Dunkin' Donuts Scales Back Menu, Cuts Artificial Dyes from Donuts," *The Chicago Tribune*, January 9, 2018, http://www.chicagotribune.com/business/ct-biz-dunkin-donuts-menu-20180109-story.html (accessed January 9, 2018); Joseph Pisani, "Dunkin' CEO: We Will Always Make the Doughnuts," *USA Today*, October 26, 2017, www.usatoday.com/story/money/business/2017/10/26/

dunkin-ceo-we-always-make-dough-nuts/803699001/ (accessed January 9, 2018); Kristina Monllos, "Dunkin' Donuts Is Considering Losing 'Donuts' from Its Name," *Adweek*, August 4, 2017, www.adweek.com/brand-marketing/dunkin-donuts-is-considering-losing-donuts-from-its-name/ (accessed January 9, 2018); Kristi Palma, "Dunkin' Donuts Is Reducing Its Doughnut Menu at 100 Mass. Locations," *Boston Globe*, October 9, 2017, www.boston.com/culture/restaurants/2017/10/09/dunkin-donuts-is-reducing-its-doughnut-menu-at-100-mass-locations (accessed January 9, 2018); Steve Olenski, "Time to Make the Donuts: How the Dunkin' Donuts Brand Stays Relevant," *Forbes*, March 6, 2017, https://www.forbes.com/sites/steveolenski/2017/03/06/time-to-make-the-donuts-how-the-dunkin-donuts-brand-stays-relevant/#322909305556 (accessed January 9, 2018); www.dunkindonuts.com (accessed January 9, 2018).

2. Kathleen Mortimer and Andrew Pressey, "Customer Information Search and Credence Services: Implications for Service Providers," *Journal of Services Marketing* 27, 1 (2013): pp. 49–58.

3. Björn Frank, Takao Enkawa, and Shane J. Schvaneveldt, "How Do the Success Factors Driving Repurchase Intent Differ between Male and Female Customers?" *Journal of the Academy of Marketing Science* 42, 2 (2014): pp. 171–185.

4. Michelle Crouch, "Poll: 9 out of 10 Millennials Admit to Impulse Buys," *CreditCards.com*, January 25, 2017, https://www.creditcards.com/credit-card-news/impulse-buying-poll.php (accessed January 11, 2018).

5. Athina Nella and Christou Evangelos, "Segmenting Wine Tourists on the Basis of Involvement with Wine," *Journal of Travel & Tourism Marketing* 31, 7 (2014): pp. 783–798.

6. Russell W. Belk, "Situational Variables and Consumer Behavior," *Journal of Consumer Research* 2, 3 (1975): pp. 157–164.

7. Nathan Bomey, "Here's the Fitting Room Where You Can Bring a Friend," *USA Today*, February 6, 2017, https://www.usatoday.com/story/money/2017/02/06/abercrombie-fitch-concept-store/97542300/ (accessed January 11, 2018).

8. Tracey S. Dagger and Peter J. Danaher, "Comparing the Effect of Store Remodeling on New and Existing Customers," *Journal of Marketing* 78, 3 (2014): pp. 62–80.

9. Lauren Johnson, "These Digital Billboards from McDonald's Change Depending on How Bad the Traffic Is," *Adweek*, November 6, 2017, http://www.adweek.com/digital/these-digital-out-of-home-ads-from-mcdonalds-change-depending-on-how-bad-the-traffic-is/ (accessed January 11, 2018).

10. Ryan S. Elder and Ariadna Krishna, "The Effects of Advertising Copy on Sensory Thoughts and Perceived Taste," *Journal of Conumer Research* 36, 5 (2010): pp. 748–756.

11. George E. Newman, Margarita Gorlin, and Ravi Dhar, "When Going Green Backfires: How Firm Intentions Shape the Evaluation of Socially Beneficial Product Enhancements," *Journal of Consumer Research* 41, 3 (2014): pp. 823–839.

12. "What to Learn from Tropicana's Packaging Redesign Failure," *The Branding Journal*, May 2015, http://www.thebrandingjournal.com/2015/05/what-to-learn-from-tropicanas-packaging-redesign-failure/ (accessed January 11, 2018).

13. Some of this information was adapted from Barry J. Babin and Eric G. Harris, *CB8* (Boston: Cengage Learning, 2018), pp. 92–95; Wayne D. Hwer, Deborah J. MacInnis, and Rik Pieters, *Consumer Behavior*, 7th ed. (Boston: Cengage, 2018), pp. 44–48.

14. Sojung Kim and Matthew S. Eastin, "Hedonic Tendencies and the Online Consumer: An Investigation of the Online Shopping Process," *Journal of Internet Commerce* 10, 1 (2011): pp. 68–90.

15. Brendan Murphy and Emma DeFelice, "Permission to Connect: How 'Human Era' Brands Become More Likeable," *CampaignUS*, December 15, 2016, http://www.campaignlive.com/article/permission-connect-human-era-brands-become-likable/1418763 (accessed January 11, 2018).

16. Babin and Harris, *CB8*, p. 135.

17. Aric Rindfleisch, James E. Burroughs, and Nancy Wong, "The Safety of Objects: Materialism, Existential Insecurity, and Brand Connection," *Journal of Consumer Research* 36, 1 (2009): pp. 1–16.

18. Claritas PRIZM, https://segmentationsolutions.nielsen.com/mybestsegments/Default.jsp?ID=70&pageName=Learn%2BMore&menuOption=learnmore (accessed January 12, 2018).

19. Claritas ConneXions, https://segmentationsolutions.nielsen.com/mybestsegments/Default.jsp?ID=90&menuOption=learnmore (accessed January 12, 2018).

20. Harry L. Davis and Benny P. Rigaux, "Perception of Marital Roles in Decision Processes," *Journal of Consumer Research* 1, (June 1974): 5–14; Mandy Putnam and William R. Davidson, *Family Purchasing Behavior: 11 Family Roles by Product Category* (Columbus, Ohio: Management Horizons, Inc., A Division of Price Waterhouse, 1987).

21. "Marketing to Women Quick Facts," She-Conomy, http://she-conomy.com/facts-on-women (accessed January 12, 2018).

22. Paul A. Eisenstein, "A Minivan for Millennials? Is That, Like, Even Possible?" *NBC News*, January 5, 2017, http://www.nbcnews.com/business/autos/minivan-millennials-even-possible-n702641 (accessed January 12, 2018).

23. Nicolas Cole, "Sprint Is Betting Big on Influencer Marketing with Its #LiveUnlimited Campaign," *Inc.*, https://www.inc.com/nicolas-cole/sprint-is-betting-big-on-influencer-marketing-with.html, August 24, 2017 (accessed January 15, 2018).

24. Jimmy Rohampton, "How Does Social Media Influence Millennials' Shopping Behavior?" *Forbes*, May 3, 2017, https://www.forbes.com/sites/jimmyrohampton/2017/05/03/does-social-media-influence-millennials-shopping-decisions/#48090d974cf3 (accessed January 15, 2018).

25. Gavin O'Malley, "Women's Purchasing Influenced by Social Media," *Social Media Daily*, July 18, 2016, http://www.mediapost.com/publications/article/280569/womens-purchasing-influenced-by-social-media.html (accessed January 15, 2018).

26. Kasey Lobaugh, "Digital Influence Report: Global Findings from Nine Countries," *Deloitte Digital*, February 24, 2016, http://www.deloittedigital.com/us/blog/digital-influence-report-global-findings-from-nine-countries (accessed January 15, 2018).

27. "Hilton Will Target Africa's Middle Class in New Expansion Strategy," *Business Day The Weekender*, November 3, 2017, https://businessdayonline.com/theweekender/2017/11/03/hilton-will-target-africas-middle-class-in-new-expansion-strategy/ (accessed January 16, 2018).

28. Hayley FitzPatrick, "Target Announces Its Next Designer Collaboration: Victoria Beckham," *Yahoo Style*, October 20, 2016, https://www.yahoo.com/style/target-announces-its-next-designer-collaboration-135106778.html (accessed January 16, 2018).

29. Sandra L. Colby and Jennifer M. Ortman, "Projections of the Size and Composition of U.S. Population: 2014 to 2060," United States Census Bureau, March 2015, https://www.census.gov/content/dam/Census/library/publications/2015/demo/p25-1143.pdf (accessed January 16, 2018).

30 Lucy Handley, "'I Suppressed My Mexican Heritage for Fear of Being Labeled,' Says P&G Chief Marketer," *CNBC*, November 13, 2017, https://www.cnbc.com/2017/11/13/pgs-chief-marketer-marc-pritchard-has-feared-racial-bias-at-work.html (accessed January 16, 2018); "Tide's Multicultural Marketing Formula," WARC, November 14, 2017, https://www.warc.com/newsandopinion/news/tides_multicultural_marketing_formula/39594 (accessed January 16, 2018).

31 United States Census Bureau, "QuickFacts," https://www.census.gov/quickfacts/table/PST045216/00 (accessed January 16, 2018).

32 Colby and Ortman, "Projections of the Size and Composition of U.S. Population: 2014 to 2060."

33 Matt Weeks, "UGA Report: Minority Groups Driving US Economy," *UGA Today*, March 2, 2017, https://news.uga.edu/Multicultural-economy-report-17/ (accessed January 16, 2018); Janie Boschma, "Black Consumers Have 'Unprecedented Impact' in 2015," *The Atlantic*, February 2, 2016, http://www.theatlantic.com/politics/archive/2016/02/black-consumers-have-unprecedented-impact-in-2015/433725/ (accessed January 16, 2018).

34 "Allstate Black History Month Campaign Highlights Modern-Day African Americans Whose Stories Are 'Worth Telling,'" Allstate, press release, January 30, 2017, https://www.prnewswire.com/news-releases/allstate-black-history-month-campaign-highlights-modern-day-african-americans-whose-stories-are-worth-telling-300397259.html (accessed January 16, 2018).

35 United States Census Bureau, "QuickFacts;" Sandra L. Colby and Jennifer M. Ortman; "Hispanic Dollars Continue to Drive U.S. FMCG Dollars," Nielsen, July 31, 2017, http://www.nielsen.com/us/en/insights/news/2017/hispanic-consumers-continue-to-drive-us-fmcg-dollars.html (accessed January 17, 2018).

36 Cecilia M. O. Alvarez, Peter R. Dickson, and Gary K. Hunter, "The Four Faces of the Hispanic Consumer: An Acculturation-Based Segmentation," *Journal of Business Research*, 67, 2 (2014): pp. 108–115.

37 Parker Morse, "What Brands Can Learn from Target's Approach to Hispanic Marketing," *Mobile Marketing Watch*, December 21, 2017, https://mobilemarketingwatch.com/brands-can-learn-targets-approach-hispanic-marketing-74245/ (accessed January 17, 2018); Ashley Rodriguez, "Retailers Duke It Out for Hispanic Shoppers' Dollars," *Advertising Age*, April 6, 2015, http://adage.com/article/cmo-strategy/retailers-duke-hispanic-shoppers-dollars/297902/ (accessed January 21, 2018).

38 Jessica Binns, "Macy's Latin Explosion," *The Robin Report*, July 18, 2016, http://www.therobinreport.com/macys-latin-explosion/ (accessed January 17, 2018); Rick Wartzman, How Macy's Found Its Fit in the Hispanic Market," *Fortune*, April 17, 2015, http://fortune.com/2015/04/17/macys-diversity-hispanic-consumers/ (accessed January 17, 2018).

39 Eli Bishop, "6 Brands That Succeed at Understanding Hispanic Marketing," *Business 2 Community*, October 7, 2014, http://www.business2community.com/marketing/6-brands-succeed-understanding-hispanic-marketing-01030311 (accessed January 17, 2018).

40 "Asian-Americans Are Expanding Their Footprint in the U.S. and Making an Impact," Nielsen, May 19, 2016, http://www.nielsen.com/us/en/insights/news/2016/asian-americans-are-expanding-their-footprint-and-making-an-impact.html (accessed January 17, 2018); United States Census Bureau, "State & Country QuickFacts."

41 "Asian-Americans Are Not One Big Group," *Washington Examiner*, March 16, 2015, http://www.washingtonexaminer.com/asian-americans-are-not-one-big-group/article/2561445 (accessed January 24, 2017).

42 Alexia Fernandez Campbell, "The Overlooked Consumer with Billions to Spend," *The Atlantic*, August 24, 2016, http://www.theatlantic.com/business/archive/2016/08/the-overlooked-consumer-group-with-billions-to-spend/497105/ (accessed January 17, 2018).

43 Amy Jo Coffey, "Understanding the Invisibility of the Asian-American Television Audience: Why Marketers Often Overlook an Audience of 'Model' Consumers," *Journal of Advertising Research*, 53, 1 (2013): pp. 101–118.

44 Paul Lucas, "AIG Opens Office to Target Asian Americans," *Insurance Business*, November 7, 2016, http://www.ibamag.com/us/news/breaking-news/aig-opens-office-to-target-asian-americans-40118.aspx (accessed January 17, 2018).

45 Katie Reilly, "Shoplifting and Other Fraud Cost Retailers Nearly $50 Billion Last Year," *Time*, June 22, 2017, http://time.com/money/4829684/shoplifting-fraud-retail-survey/ (accessed January 17, 2018).

46 Kelly Kasulis, "Sophisticated Shoplifting Gangs Are Costing US Retailers $30 Billion a Year," *Quartz*, February 8, 2017, https://qz.com/905169/sophisticated-shoplifting-gangs-are-costing-us-retailers-30-billion-a-year/ (accessed January 17, 2018).

47 Lauren Thomas, "Retail Fraud Is on the Rise as Companies Grapple for Solutions," *CNBC*, December 7, 2017, https://www.cnbc.com/2017/12/07/retail-fraud-is-on-the-rise-as-companies-grapple-for-solutions.html (accessed January 17, 2018).

48 Don Reisinger, "Microsoft Touts Study Showing the Cost of Pirated Software," *CNET*, March 19, 2014, http://www.cnet.com/news/microsoft-touts-study-showing-the-cost-of-pirated-software/ (accessed January 17, 2018).

49 "Ford's 'Futurist' Predicts Upcoming Trends," *CBS This Morning*, December 12, 2014, www.cbsnews.com/videos/fords-futurist-predicts-upcoming-trends (accessed February 2, 2016); Melissa Wylie, "What It Means to Be Ford's 'Futurist'—No Crystal Ball," *Business Journals*, December 14, 2015, www.bizjournals.com/bizwomen/news/profiles-strategies/2015/12/what-it-means-to-be-fords-futurist-no-crystal-ball.html?page=all (accessed February 2, 2016); Dale Buss, "Ford Futurist Sheryl Connelly Issues 2016 Trends Report," *Brand Channel*, December 9, 2015, http://brandchannel.com/2015/12/09/ford-future-trends-sheryl-connelly-120915/ (accessed February 2, 2016); Michael Martinez, "Ford at CES: Dramatic Change on Way," *Detroit News*, January 5, 2016, www.detroitnews.com/story/business/autos/ford/2016/01/04/ford-tout-drones-driverless-cars-ces/78289104 (accessed February 2, 2016); Bradley Berman, "Big Auto Searches for Meaning Beyond Selling Cars," *MIT Technology Review*, January 21, 2016, www.technologyreview.com/s/545646/big-auto-searches-for-meaning-beyond-selling-cars/ (accessed February 2, 2016); Jonathan Camhi, "Ford Has Shed Some Light on Its Self-Driving Car Strategy," *Business Insider*, December 11, 2017. http://www.businessinsider.com/ford-self-driving-car-strategy-2017-12 (accessed January 17, 2018).

50 Beth Howitt, "Consumers' Obsession with Snacking Is Reshaping the Food Industry," *Fortune*, December 18, 2017, http://fortune.com/2017/12/18/cambell-hershey-snacking-acquisitions/ (accessed January 17, 2018); Monica Watrous, "Campbell Soup Completes Pacific Foods Acquisition," *Food Business News*, December 14, 2017, www.foodbusinessnews.net/articles/news_home/Business_News/2017/12/Campbell_Soup_completes_Pacifi.aspx?ID=%7B441BBC89-62E4-40D5-A718-FCC9988419AE%7D (accessed January 17, 2018); Mark Gurman and Craig Giammona, "Campbell Is Testing Online Soup Delivery," *Bloomberg News*, December 1, 2017, www.bloomberg.com/news/articles/2017-12-01/campbell-is-testing-online-soup-ordering-as-part-of-comeback-bid (accessed January 17, 2018);

Monica Watrous, "Campbell Soup Is Watching These Six Trends in 2018," *Food Business News,* December 15, 2017, www .foodbusinessnews.net/articles/news_home/ Consumer_Trends/2017/12/Campbell_Soup_ is_watching_thes.aspx?ID=%7B81F95CEA-51A9-464E-9374-D7867985C55D%7D (accessed January 17, 2018); www.campbells .com (accessed January 17, 2018).

Chapter 8

1 Matt Weinberger, "Google and Cisco Have Teamed up in the Cloud Wars against Amazon and Microsoft," *Business Insider,* October 25, 2017, www.businessinsider. com/google-cloud-and-cisco-sign-partner-ship-2017-10 (accessed January 19, 2018); Stig Øyvann, "First Self-Driving Cars, Now Google AI Is Helping Rolls-Royce with Autonomous Ships," *ZDNet,* October 9, 2017, www.zdnet.com/article/first-self-driving-cars-now-google-ai-is-helping-rolls-royce-with-autonomous-ships/ (accessed January 19, 2018); "How Amazon, Google, Microsoft, and IBM Sell AI as a Service," *Fast Company,* October 11, 2017, www.fastcompany.com/ 40474593/how-amazon-google-microsoft-and-ibm-sell-ai-as-a-service (accessed January 19, 2018); Mark Bergen, "Google Wants to Train Other Companies to Use Its AI Tools," *Bloomberg News,* October 19, 2017, www. bloomberg.com/news/articles/2017-10-19/ google-wants-to-train-other-companies-to-use-its-ai-tools (accessed January 19, 2018).

2 "SUSB Annual Data Tables by Establishment Industry," U.S. Census Bureau, https://www .census.gov/data/tables/2015/econ/susb/2015-susb-annual.html (accessed January 18, 2018).

3 "SUSB Annual Data Tables," U.S. Census Bureau; Kimberly Amadeo, "U.S. Retail Sales Report: Current Statistics and Recent Trends," *The Balance,* January 15, 2018, https://www.thebalance.com/u-s-retail-sales-statistics-and-trends-3305717 (accessed January 19, 2018).

4 Deloitte, "Global Powers of Retailing 2018: Transformative Change, Reinvigorated Commerce," January 2018, https://www2 .deloitte.com/content/dam/Deloitte/global/ Documents/consumer-industrial-products/ cip-2018-global-powers-retailing.pdf, p. 16.

5 "What Is the Total Government Spending?" US Government Spending, http://www .usgovernmentspending.com/percent_gdp (accessed January 18, 2018).

6 Aramark, "Aramark Named to Fortune's 'World's Most Admired Companies' List in 2017," press release, March 2, 2017, https:// www.aramark.com/about-us/news/ aramark-general/fortune-worlds-most-admired-companies-2017 (accessed January 19, 2018).

7 "North American Industry Classification System," U.S. Census Bureau, http://www .census.gov/eos/www/naics/ (accessed January 19, 2018).

8 "Notable Contract Awards," Booz Allen Hamilton, https://www.boozallen.com/ e/contracts/notable-contract-awards.html (accessed January 18, 2018).

9 Jethro Mullen, "Boeing vs Airbus: $77 Billion in Deals in Under 2 Hours," *CNN,* November 15, 2017, http://money.cnn.com/2017/11/15/ investing/boeing-flydubai-order/index .html?iid=EL (accessed January 19, 2018).

10 Kate Maddox, "Staples Reworks Its Market-ing to Target Business Customers," *Digital Commerce 360,* May 3, 2017, https://www .digitalcommerce360.com/2017/05/03/ staples-reworks-marketing-target-business-customers-2/ (accessed January 18, 2018).

11 Anne Maarit Jalkala and Joona Keränen, "Brand Positioning Strategies for Industrial Firms Providing Customer Solutions," *Journal of Business & Industrial Marketing* 29, 3 (2014): pp. 253–264.

12 Hannu Sakari Makkonen and Wesley J. Johnston, "Innovation Adoption and Diffusion in Business-to-Business Marketing," *Journal of Business & Industrial Marketing* 29, 4 (2014): pp. 324–331.

13 Das Narayandas and V. Kasturi Rangan, "Building and Sustaining Buyer–Seller Relationships in Mature Industrial Markets," *Journal of Marketing* (July 2004): p. 63.

14 "Food for Thought," Jet Blue, https://www .jetblue.com/green/food/ (accessed January 18, 2018).

15 Bain & Company, "Service Design & Operations," http://www.bain.com/ consulting-services/performance-improve-ment/service-operations.aspx (accessed January 22, 2018); Oliver Straehle, Michael Fuellemann, and Oliver Bendig, "Service Now! Time to Wake Up the Sleeping Giant," November 27, 2012, http://www.bain .com/Images/Bain%20study_Service_Now .pdf (accessed January 22, 2018).

16 Elena Fraj, Eva Martinez, and Jorge Matute, "Green Marketing in B2B Organisations: An Empirical Analysis from the Natural-Resource-Based View of the Firm," *Journal of Business & Marketing* 28, 5 (2013): pp. 396–410.

17 United States Environmental Protection Agency, "About the Environmentally Prefer-able Purchasing Program," https://www.epa .gov/greenerproducts/ about-environmentally-preferable-purchasing-program (accessed January 22, 2018).

18 Ali Jahromi Tamaddoni, Stanislav Stakhovych, and Michael Ewing, "Managing B2B Customer Churn, Retention and Profitability," *Industrial Marketing Management* 43, 7 (2014): pp. 1258–1268.

19 Agnieszka De Souza and Isis Almeida, "War on Sugar Turns Years of Growth into Market Tipping Point," *Bloomberg,* May 22, 2017, https://www.bloomberg.com/news/articles/ 2017-05-22/war-on-sugar-turns-decades-of-growth-into-industry-tipping-point (accessed January 22, 2018).

20 Frederick E. Webster, Jr., and Yoram Wind, "A General Model for Understanding Orga-nizational Buyer Behavior," *Marketing Management* (Winter/Spring 1996): pp. 52–57.

21 Kate Maddox, "Cintas Launches First National Brand Campaign in Its 87-Year History," *Advertising Age,* January 26, 2016, http://adage.com/article/btob/cintas-launches-national-brand-campaign-history/302356/ (accessed January 23, 2018).

22 Kunal Swani, Brian P. Brown, and George R. Milne, "Should Tweets Differ for B2B and B2C? An Analysis of Fortune 500 Companies' Twitter Communications," *Industrial Marketing Management* 43, 4 (2014): pp. 873–881.

23 "US B2B eCommerce Will Hit $1.2 Trillion by 2021," *Forrester,* June 5, 2017, https:// www.forrester.com/report/US+B2B+eComme rce+Will+Hit+12+Trillion+By+2021/-/ E-RES136173 (accessed January 24, 2018).

24 "B2B Online Buying: 68% of Buyers Make Purchases Online," V12Data, March 23, 2017, http://www.v12data.com/blog/b2b-online-buying-68-buyers-make-purchases-online/ (accessed January 24, 2018).

25 Bill Briggs, "How a Paper Distributor Grows e-commerce," *Digital Commerce 360,* January 22, 2018, https://www.digitalcommerce360 .com/2018/01/22/paper-distributor-grows-ecommerce/ (accessed January 24, 2018).

26 Bill Briggs, "How a Coffee Roaster's E-commerce Site Serves B2B and B2C Clients," *Digital Commerce 360,* January 8, 2018, https://www.digitalcommerce360 .com/2018/01/08/coffee-roasters-e-commerce-site-serves-b2b-b2c-clients/ (accessed January 24, 2018).

27 "About Us," Amazon Business, http://www .amazon.com/b?ie=UTF8&node= 11261610011 (accessed January 24, 2018); Sarah Perez, "Amazon Takes on Office Supply Retailers with Launch of Business Prime Shipping," *Tech Crunch,* October 24, 2017, https://www .digitalcommerce360.com/2018/01/08/

coffee-roasters-e-commerce-site-serves-b2b-b2c-clients/ (accessed January 24, 2018).

28 AutoWurld.com, https://www.autowurld.com/page/show/pagename/about-us (accessed January 25, 2018).

29 Alibaba, http://activities.alibaba.com/alibaba/following-about-alibaba.php?spm=a2700.784 8340.0.0.zec1aK (accessed January 25, 2018).

30 Ingrid Lunden, "Apple Pay Now in 20 Markets, Nabs 90% of All Mobile Contactless Trans-actions Where Active," *Tech Crunch*, October 23, 2017, https://techcrunch.com/2017/10/23/apple-pay-now-in-20-markets-nabs-90-of-all-contactless-transactions-where-active/ (accessed January 25, 2018); Menchie Mendoza, "Apple Pay Availability Tops 2 Million Locations, Soon Adding Chains Like Chick-Fil-A," *Tech Times*, February 4, 2016, www.techtimes.com/articles/130671/20160204/apple-pay-availability-tops-2-million-locations-soon-adding-chains-like-chick-fil-a.htm (accessed February 4, 2016); Caitlin McGarry, "Why Your Favorite Stores Still Don't Support Apple Pay," *MacWorld*, June 5, 2015, www.macworld.com/article/2932356/ios/why-your-favorite-stores-still-dont-support-apple-pay.html (accessed February 4, 2016); James F. Peltz, "Mobile-Payment Systems Draw More Shoppers and Merchants," *Los Angeles Times*, January 18, 2016, www.latimes.com/business/la-fi-agenda-mobile-payments-20160118-story.html (accessed February 4, 2016); Bill Snyder, "McDonald's CIO on Why It's Supporting Apple Pay on Launch Day," *CIO*, October 16, 2014, www.cio.com/article/2834502/consumer-technology/mcdonalds-cio-on-why-its-supporting-apple-pay-on-launch-day.html (accessed February 4, 2016); Sarah Perez, "Walgreens Becomes First Retailer to Inte-grate Its Loyalty Program with Apple Pay," *Tech Crunch*, November 5, 2015, http://techcrunch.com/2015/11/05/walgreens-becomes-first-retailer-to-integrate-its-loyalty-program-with-apple-pay (accessed February 4, 2016).

31 "Masterful Salesmanship Has Pushed Salesforce to Ever-Greater Heights," *The Economist*, January 4, 2018, www.economist.com/news/business/21734037-will-worlds-fourth-largest-software-firm-live-up-its-founders-soaring; Ron Miller, "Salesforce Wants to Reach $60 Billion Revenue Goal by 2034," *TechCrunch*, January 4, 2018, https://techcrunch.com/2018/01/04/salesforce-wants-to-be-a-60-billion-company-by-2034/; Matt Rosoff, "Salesforce COO Keith Block Explains How to Win Even If You're Not One of the 'Big Five,'" *CNBC*, November 11,

2017, www.cnbc.com/2017/11/11/salesforce-coo-keith-block-interview-at-dreamforce-2017.html; Brent Leary, "Small Business Takeaways from Dreamforce 2017," *Small Business Trends*, November 29, 2017, https://smallbiztrends.com/2017/11/small-business-takeaways-from-dreamforce-2017.html; www.salesforce.com

Chapter 9

1 Jon Ostrower, "Emirates Looks Past Turmoil with Boeing Deal," *CNN*, November 13, 2017, http://money.cnn.com/2017/11/13/news/companies/emirates-dubai-boeing-787-deal/index.html (accessed July 8, 2018); Emirates, "About Us," https://www.emirates.com/us/english/about-us/history.aspx#2296562 (accessed March 24, 2018); Emirates, "Our Business Model," https://www.emirates.com/us/english/about/int-and-gov-affairs/our-business-model/our-business-model.aspx (accessed March 24, 2018); Issac John, "Emirates Posts 29th Straight Year of Profitability," *Khaleej Times*, May 11, 2017, https://www.khaleejtimes.com/business/aviation/emirates-posts-29th-straight-year-of-profitability (accessed March 24, 2018); Sananda Sahoo, "Emirates and Etihad Sus-pend Flights to and from Qatar Amid Diplo-matic Dispute," *The National*, June 5, 2017, https://www.thenational.ae/business/emirates-and-etihad-suspend-flights-to-and-from-qatar-amid-diplomatic-dispute-1.57775 (accessed March 25, 2018); Sarah Diaa, "Emirates Says Demand for First Class Still 'Very Strong,'" *Gulf News*, November 12, 2017, http://gulfnews.com/business/aviation/dubai-airshow/emirates-says-demand-for-first-class-still-very-strong-1.2123187 (accessed March 25, 2018).

2 "Percentage of Procter & Gamble's Net Sales Worldwide in 2017, by Region," *Statista*, https://www.statista.com/statistics/244122/percentage-of-procter-und-gambles-net-sales-worldwide-by-region/ (accessed February 11, 2018).

3 "Our Story," Walmart, http://corporate.walmart.com/our-story/ (accessed February 11, 2018); "Starbucks Coffee Inter-national," Starbucks, www.starbucks.com/business/international-stores (accessed February 11, 2018).

4 "Export Assistance," Office of the United States Trade Representative, www.ustr.gov/trade-topics/trade-toolbox/export-assistance (accessed September 1, 2015).

5 Gary A. Knight and S. Tamer Cavusgil, "Inno-vation, Organizational Capabilities, and the Born-Global Firm," *Journal of International Business Studies* 35, 2 (2004): pp. 124–141.

6 Kate Taylor, "Taco Bell Has Created a Wildly Popular Hit Overseas – But It Won't be Coming to America Anytime Soon," *Business Insider*, October 11, 2016, www.businessinsider.com/taco-bell-kimchi-quesadilla-thrives-in-korea-2016-10 (accessed January 31, 2017).

7 Wayne Ma and Julie Jargon, "McDonald's Pulls Back in China with Deal," *The Wall Street Journal*, January 10, 2017, p. B1.

8 Olga Kravets and Ozlem Sandikci, "Compe-tently Ordinary: New Middle Class Consum-ers in the Emerging Markets," *Journal of Marketing* 78 (July 2014): pp. 125–140.

9 Geoffrey James, "20 Epic Fails in Global Branding," *Inc.*, October 29, 2014, www.inc.com/geoffrey-james/the-20-worst-brand-translations-of-all-time.html (accessed January 5, 2016).

10 John Revill and Annie Gasparro, "Cereal Makers Tweak Recipes for Emerging Markets," *The Wall Street Journal*, September 28, 2015, p. B6.

11 Xiaoling Guo, "Living in a Global World: Influence of Consumer Global Orientation on Attitudes Toward Global Brands from Developed Versus Emerging Countries," *Journal of International Marketing* 21, 1 (March 2013): pp. 1–22.

12 Sadrudin A. Ahmed and Alain D'Astous, "Moderating Effects of Nationality on Country-of-Origin Perceptions: English-Speaking Thailand Versus French-Speaking Canada," *Journal of Business Research* 60, 3 (2007): pp. 240–248; George Balabanis and Adamantios Diaman-topoulos, "Domestic Country Bias, Country-of-Origin Effects, and Consumer Ethnocentrism: A Multidimen-sional Unfolding Approach," *Journal of the Academy of Marketing Science* 32, 1 (2004): pp. 80–95; Harri T. Luomala, "Exploring the Role of Food Origin as a Source of Mean-ings for Consumers and as a Determinant of Consumers' Actual Food Choices," *Journal of Business Research* 60, 2 (2007): pp. 122–129; Durdana Ozretic-Dosen, Vatroslav Skare, and Zoran Krupka, "Assessments of Country of Origin and Brand Cues in Evaluating a Croatian, Western and Eastern European Food Product," *Journal of Business Research* 60, 2 (2007): pp. 130–136.

13 Chris Isidore, "Despite Trump's Latest Threat, BMW Won't Budge on Mexican Plant," *CNN Money*, January 16, 2017, http://money.cnn.com/2017/01/16/news/companies/trump-bmw-mexico/ (accessed January 25, 2016).

14 David A. Griffith, Goksel Yalcinkaya, and Gaia Rubera, "Country-Level Perfor-mance of New Experience Products in a Global Rollout: The Moderating Effects of Economic Wealth and National Culture,"

Journal of International Marketing 22, 4 (2014): pp. 1–20.

15 Philip Coggan, "Markets in a Muddle," *The Economist: The World in 2011 Special Edition*, p. 145.

16 John Hilsenrath and Brian Blackstone, "Cheaper Chinese Currency Has Global Impact," *The Wall Street Journal*, April 11, 2015, www.wsj.com/articles/cheaper-chinese-currency-has-global-impact-1439336422 (accessed January 6, 2016); Adam Shell, "Currency War: What You Need to Know," *USA Today*, August 13, 2015, p. 3B.

17 Inti Landauro, "Colombia, Mexico Criticize Rich Countries on Monetary, Fiscal Policies," *The Wall Street Journal*, January 24, 2011, http://online.wsj.com/article/BT-CO-20110124-710562.html (accessed January 20, 2012).

18 Peter Coy, "Dollar So Ripped, It Might Actually Rip," *Bloomberg Businessweek*, January 9–15, 2017, p. 12.

19 "Gross Domestic Product (GDP) Ranking by Country 2017 (in Billion U.S. Dollars)," *Statista*, https://www.statista.com/statistics/268173/countries-with-the-largest-gross-domestic-product-gdp/ (accessed February 11, 2018).

20 "The World Factbook," *Central Intelligence Agency*, https://www.cia.gov/library/publications/the-world-factbook/rankorder/2004rank.html (accessed February 11, 2018).

21 Ibid.

22 Stephen A. Samaha, Joshua T. Beck, and Robert W. Palmatier, "The Role of Culture in International Relationship Marketing," *Journal of Marketing* 78 (September 2014): pp. 78–98.

23 James Hookway and Samuel Rubenfeld, "U.S. Temporarily Lifts Trade Restrictions on Myanmar," *The Wall Street Journal*, December 7, 2015, www.wsj.com/articles/u-s-temporarily-lifts-trade-restrictions-on-myanmar-1449539262 (accessed January 6, 2016).

24 "The Rise of Capitalism," *The Economist*, January 21, 2012, p. 11.

25 "Emirates," The Emirates Group, www.theemiratesgroup.com/english/our-brands/air-transportation/emirates-airline.aspx (accessed January 6, 2016).

26 American Marketing Association, "Statement of Ethics," www.marketingpower.com/AboutAMA/Pages/Statement%20of%20Ethics.aspx (accessed January 5, 2016).

27 Felicia Schwartz, "U.S. and Cuba Renew Diplomatic Relations," *The Wall Street Journal*, July 2, 2015, p. A8.

28 Kimberly Amadeo, "How the U.S. Trade Deficit Hurts the Economy," *The Balance*, December 26, 2017, https://www.thebalance.com/u-s-trade-deficit-causes-effects-trade-partners-3306276 (accessed February 11, 2018).

29 Charles R. Taylor, George R. Franke, and Michael L. Maynard, "Attitudes toward Direct Marketing and Its Regulation: A Comparison of the United States and Japan," *Journal of Public Policy & Marketing* 19, 2 (2000): pp. 228–237.

30 Tom Schoenberg and Matt Robinson, "Walmart Balks at Paying $600-Million-Plus in Bribery Case," *Bloomberg Markets*, October 6, 2016, https://www.bloomberg.com/news/articles/2016-10-06/wal-mart-said-to-balk-at-paying-600-million-plus-in-bribe-case (accessed January 17, 2017).

31 "Measuring the Magnitude of Global Counterfeiting," *U.S. Chamber of Commerce's Global Intellectual Property Center*, www.theglobalipcenter.com/wp-content/themes/gipc/map-index/assets/pdf/2016/Global Counterfeiting_Report.pdf (accessed January 28, 2017).

32 Gillian Wong, "Counterfeits Test Alibaba's Goals," *The Wall Street Journal*, November 11, 2015, p. B8.

33 Business for Social Responsibility, www.bsr.org (accessed February 5, 2016).

34 Natalia Drozdiak and Sam Schechner, "EU Files Additional Formal Charges Against Google," *The Wall Street Journal*, July 16, 2016, www.wsj.com/articles/google-set-to-face-more-eu-antitrust-charges-1468479516 (accessed January 17, 2017).

35 "This Is Systembolaget," https://www.systembolaget.se/English/ (accessed January 5, 2016).

36 The CIA, *The World Fact Book*, https://www.cia.gov/library/publications/the-world-factbook/rankorder/rankorderguide.html (accessed January 31, 2017); Internet World Stats, https://www.internetworldstats.com/top20.htm (accessed February 22, 2018).

37 Alexandra Wexler, "Mobile Money Gets Easier in Africa," *The Wall Street Journal*, July 17, 2015, p. B5.

38 Economist staff, "Special Report: The World Economy," *The Economist*, October 4, 2014, pp. 1–18.

39 "The North American Free Trade Agreement (NAFTA)," export.gov, http://export.gov/FTA/nafta/index.asp (accessed January 5, 2016).

40 Central Intelligence Agency; "Population, Total," *The World Bank*, https://data .worldbank.org/indicator/SP.POP.TOTL (accessed February 11, 2018).

41 "Population by Year, Province and Territory," *Statistics Canada*, September 28, 2016, www.statcan.gc.ca/tables-tableaux/sum-som/l01/cst01/demo02a-eng.htm (accessed January 28, 2017); "Canada GDP Per Capita," *Trading Economics*, www.tradingeconomics.com/canada/gdp-per-capita (accessed January 28, 2017); "Canada," *Office of the United States Trade Representative*, https://ustr.gov/countries-regions/americas/canada (accessed January 28, 2017).

42 Statistics Canada, "Table 1 Merchandise trade: Canada's top 10 principal trading partners – Seasonally adjusted, current dollars," December 5, 2014, www.statcan.gc.ca/daily-quotidien/141205/t141205b001-eng.htm (accessed January 5, 2016).

43 The CIA, *The World Fact Book*, https://www.cia.gov/library/publications/the-world-factbook/rankorder/rankorderguide.html (accessed January 28, 2017).

44 Office of the United States Trade Representative, "Mexico," May 1, 2014, www.ustr.gov/countries-regions/americas/mexico (accessed January 28, 2017).

45 Office of the United States Trade Representative, "CAFTA-DR (Dominican Republic-Central America FTA)," www.ustr.gov/trade-agreements/free-trade-agreements/cafta-dr-dominican-republic-central-america-fta (accessed February 11, 2018).

46 Economist staff, "Crisis Revisited," *The Economist*, December 13, 2014, p. 17; "Euro Area," European Commission, https://ec.europa.eu/info/business-economy-euro/euro-area_en (accessed January 28, 2017).

47 "Euro Area 1999-2015," *European Central Bank*, https://www.ecb.europa.eu/euro/intro/html/map.en.html (accessed January 28, 2017); "Europe in 12 Lessons," *Europa*, http://europa.eu/abc/12lessons/lesson_2/index_en.htm (accessed January 28, 2017).

48 "IMF World Economic Outlook Database," *International Monetary Fund*, October 2017, www.imf.org/external/pubs/ft/weo/2017/02/weodata/weorept.aspx?pr.x=89&pr.y=6&sy=2017&ey=2017&scsm=1&ssd=1&sort=country&ds=.&br=1&c=998&s=NGDPD%2CPPPGDP%2CPPPPPC&grp=1&a=1 (accessed February 11, 2018).

49 "About the EU," *Europa*, http://europa.eu/about-eu/index_en.htm (accessed January 5, 2016).

50 "Special Advertising Section: The European Union and the United States," *Foreign Policy*, January 2013, p. 1.

51 Ibid.

52 "In a Nutshell," MERCOSUR, www.mercosur
.int/innovaportal/v/3862/2/innova.front/
en-pocas-palabras (accessed and translated
from Spanish via Chrome on September 2,
2015); Thomas Favaro, "Don't Hold Your
Breath for Mercosur's Changes," *Forbes*,
July 27, 2015, www.forbes.com/sites/
riskmap/2015/07/27/dont-hold-your-breath-
for-mercosurs-changes/ (accessed
February 5, 2016).

53 Joanna Klonsky, Stephanie Hanson, and
Brianna Lee, "Mercosur: South America's
Fractious Trade Bloc," Council on Foreign
Relations, July 31, 2012, www.cfr.org/
trade/mercosur-south-americas-fractious-
trade-bloc/p12762 (accessed January 5,
2016); "Agri-Food Regional of the South
(Mercosur): Brazil, Argentina, Paraguay,"
Agriculture and Agrifood Canada, January
2011, www.ats.agr.gc.ca/lat/3947-eng.htm
(accessed January 5, 2016); TeleSur,
"MERCOSUR: Paving the Way for Latin
American Integration," December 15, 2014,
www.telesurtv.net/english/analysis/
MERCOSUR-Paving-the-Way-for-Latin-
American-Integration-20141213-0025.html
(accessed January 5, 2016); "MERCOSUR,"
Ministry of Foreign Affairs, www.itamaraty.
gov.br/en/politica-externa/integracao-
regional/6347-mercosur-en (accessed
January 31, 2017).

54 Juan Forero, "Cuba's Private Sector Braces
for Change," *The Wall Street Journal*, January
11, 2017, p. A18.

55 Tim Padgett, "How Business Can Change
Cuba," *Bloomberg Businessweek*, October 16,
2014, pp. 8–9.

56 "About APEC," www.apec.org/About-Us/
About-APEC.aspx (accessed November 21,
2014); "U.S.-APEC Trade Facts," *Office
of the United States Trade Representative*,
https://ustr.gov/trade-agreements/other-
initiatives/asia-pacific-economic-cooperation-
apec/us-apec-trade-facts (accessed January
31, 2017).

57 "About APEC," Asia-Pacific Economic
Cooperation, www.apec.org/home.aspx
(accessed January 5, 2016).

58 Juro Osawa, "China Steps Up Fight Against
Online Music Piracy," *The Wall Street
Journal*, August 10, 2015, http://blogs.wsj
.com/digits/2015/08/10/china-steps-up-
fight-against-online-music-piracy/ (accessed
January 6, 2016).

59 Kathy Chu, "China Loses Edge on Labor
Costs," *The Wall Street Journal*, December 3,
2015, pp. B1, B4.

60 Kevin Granville, "The Trans-Pacific Partnership Trade Deal Explained," *The New York
Times*, May 11, 2015, www.nytimes
.com/2015/05/12/business/

unpacking-the-trans-pacific-partnership-trade-
deal.html?_r=0 (accessed February 5, 2016).

61 Paul Davidson, "Trade Deal May Lift Consumers," *The Wall Street Journal*, October 6, 2015,
pp. 1B–2B; Office of the United States Trade
Representative, "Overview of the Trans-Pacific
Partnership," https://ustr.gov/tpp/overview-of-
the-TPP (accessed January 6, 2016).

62 Colin Dwyer, "The TPP Is Dead. Long
Live The Trans-Pacific Trade Deal," NPR,
March 8, 2018, https://www.npr.org/sections/
thetwo-way/2018/03/08/591549744/the-tpp-
is-dead-long-live-the-trans-pacific-trade-deal
(accessed March 18, 2018).

63 Association of Southeast Asian Nations,
www.asean.org/ (accessed February 5, 2016).

64 "ASEAN Economic Community: 12 Things
to Know," *Asian Development Bank*,
December 29, 2015, www.adb.org/features/
asean-economic-community-12-things-know
(accessed January 6, 2016); "4 ASEAN
Infographics: Population, Market, Economy,"
ASEAN UP, https://aseanup.com/asean-
infographics-population-market-economy/
(accessed February 22, 2018).

65 Association of Southeast Asian Nations,
www.asean.org/asean/about-asean/ (accessed
January 5, 2016).

66 Simon Long, "Safety in Numbers," *The
Economist*, The World in 2015 Edition, p. 68.

67 Nick Mead, "OECD: South-East Asian
Economic Outlook to Return to Pre-crisis
Levels," *The Guardian*, November 18,
2012, www.theguardian.com/global-
development/datablog/2012/nov/18/oecd-
south-east-asia-economic-outlook (accessed
February 5, 2016); Kathy Quiano, "ASEAN
Summit Starts amid Cloud of Thai-Cambodia
Border Row," *CNN*, May 7, 2011, www.cnn
.com/2011/WORLD/asiapcf/05/07/asia.asean
.summit/index.html (accessed February 5,
2016).

68 Shelley Goldberg, "PTT Chemical Public
Company to Benefit from ASEAN Growth,"
Seeking Alpha, August 17, 2015, http://
seekingalpha.com/article/3445536-ptt-
chemical-public-company-to-benefit-from-
asean-growth (accessed January 19,
2016).

69 Eric Bellman, "Asia Seeks Integration despite
EU's Woes," *The Wall Street Journal*, July 22,
2011, p. A9.

70 World Trade Organization, "What Is the
WTO?" https://www.wto.org/english/
thewto_e/whatis_e/whatis_e.htm (accessed
September 3, 2015).

71 Ibid.

72 Tennille Tracy, "WTO Rules Against U.S.
Meat Labels," *The Wall Street Journal*,
May 19, 2015, p. A5.

73 Jan Johanson and Finn Wiedersheim-Paul,
"The Internationalization of the Firm," *Journal of Management Studies* 12, 3 (1975):
pp. 305–322; Jan Johanson and Jan-Erik
Vahlne, "The Internationalization Process of
the Firm—A Model of Knowledge Development and Increasing Foreign Commitments,"
Journal of International Business Studies 8,
1 (1977): pp. 23–32; S. Tamer Cavusgil and
John R. Nevin, "Internal Determinants of
Export Marketing Behavior: An Empirical
Investigation," *Journal of Marketing Research*
18, 1 (1981): pp. 114–119.

74 Pradeep Tyagi, "Export Behavior of Small
Business Firms in Developing Economies:
Evidence from the Indian Market," *Marketing
Management Journal* 10, 2 (2000): pp. 12–20.

75 Berrin Dosoglu-Guner, "How Do Exporters and Non-Exporters View Their 'Country of Origin' Image Abroad?" *Marketing
Management Journal* 10, 2 (2000): pp. 21–27.

76 WTSC Industrial Group, www.wtsc
.eu/ (accessed January 6, 2016).

77 Farok J. Contractor and Sumit K. Kundu,
"Franchising Versus Company-Run Operations: Model Choice in the Global Hotel
Sector," *Journal of International Marketing* 6,
2 (1998): pp. 28–53.

78 Greg Ip, "We Are Not the World," *The
Wall Street Journal*, January 7–8, 2017,
C1; Jennifer Alsever, "Smaller Businesses
Struggle to Make It in the U.S.A.," *Fortune*,
November 17, 2014, pp. 29–32.

79 James R. Hagerty, "Offshoring Outpaces
'Reshoring,'" *The Wall Street Journal*,
December 15, 2014, p. B3.

80 Paul Mozer, "Qualcomm in Venture with
Chinese Chip Maker," *The New York
Times*, June 23, 2015, www.nytimes
.com/2015/06/24/business/international/
qualcomm-in-venture-with-chinese-chip-
maker.html?_r=0 (accessed January 6, 2016).

81 Calum Fuller, "EY and LinkedIn Announce
Strategic Alliance," *Accountancy Age*,
October 30, 2015, www.accountancyage.
com/aa/news/2432737/ey-and-linkedin-
announce-strategic-alliance (accessed
January 6, 2016).

82 Matt Krantz, "As Europe Reels, 9 U.S.
Companies Under Pressure," *The Wall Street
Journal*, November 17, 2015, p. 1B.

83 "Export," Lone Star Distribution, http://
lonestardistribution.com/export/ (accessed
February 5, 2016).

84 Abbott, "Abbott Global," www.abbott.com/
global/url/content/en_US/10.17:17/
general_ content/General_Content_00054
.htm (accessed February 5, 2016).

85 Dana L. Alden, James B. Kelley, Petra
Riefler, Julie A. Lee, and Geoffrey N. Soutar,
"The Effect of Global Company Animosity

on Global Brand Attitudes in Emerging and Developed Markets: Does Perceived Value Matter?" *Journal of International Marketing* 21, 2 (2013): pp. 17–38.

86 Deborah Owens, Timothy Wilkinson, and Bruce Keillor, "A Comparison of Product Attributes in a Cross-Cultural/Cross-National Context," *Marketing Management Journal* 10, 2 (2000): pp. 1–11.

87 PR Newswire, "First 7-Eleven Store Opens in Middle East," *PR Newswire*, October 13, 2015, www.prnewswire.com/news-releases/first-7-eleven-store-opens-in-middle-east-300158789.html (accessed January 6, 2016).

88 Larry Light, "How Organisations Manage Global Brands in an Increasingly Global World," *Journal of Brand Strategy* 2, 3 (Fall 2013): pp. 228–235.

89 Anil K. Gupta, Vijay Govindarajan, and Peter Roche, "Converting Global Presence into Global Competitive Advantage," *Academy of Management Executive* 15, 2 (2001): pp. 45–58.

90 Lulu Yilun Chen, "Online Giant Alibaba Aims Beyond China and E-Commerce: QuickTake," The *Washington Post*, November 13, 2017, https://www.washingtonpost.com/business/online-giant-alibaba-aims-beyond-china-and-e-commerce-quicktake/2017/11/13/9147da86-c846-11e7-b506-8a10ed11ecf5_story.html (accessed November 19, 2017); Aaron Pressman and Adam Lashinsky, "Data Sheet–Alibaba's Vast and Growing Reach," *Fortune*, November 13, 2017, http://fortune.com/2017/11/13/data-sheet-alibaba-payments-shopping/ (accessed November 19, 2017); Daniel Keyes, "Amazon is Struggling to Find its Place China," *Business Insider*, August 30, 2017, www.businessinsider.com/amazon-is-struggling-to-find-its-place-china-2017-8 (accessed November 19, 2017); Susanna Kim, "Alibaba: How Did the Chinese Company Gets Its Name?" *ABC News*, September 18, 2014, http://abcnews.go.com/Business/alibaba-chinese-company/story?id=25591454 (accessed January 13, 2016); Bloomberg News, "Alibaba to Open Offices in Europe as U.S. Expansion Continues," *Bloomberg*, October 13, 2015, www.bloomberg.com/news/articles/2015-10-13/alibaba-to-open-offices-in-europe-as-u-s-expansion-continues (accessed January 13, 2016); Helen H. Wang, "Why Amazon Should Fear Alibaba," *Forbes*, July 8, 2015, www.forbes.com/sites/helenwang/2015/07/08/why-amazon-should-fear-alibaba/ (accessed January 13, 2016); John Watling, "China's Internet Giants Lead in Online Finance," *The Financialist*, February 14, 2014, https://www.thefinancialist.com/not-just-a-paypal-clone-chinas-internet-giants-chart-their-own-

course/ (accessed January 13, 2016); Juro Osawa, Paul Mozur, and Rolfe Winkler, "Alibaba Flexes Muscles Before IPO," *The Wall Street Journal*, April 15, 2015, www.wsj.com/news/articles/SB100014240527023038878045795014119325587 76 (accessed January 13, 2016); Bloomberg News, "Alibaba's IPO Filing: Everything You Need to Know," *The Wall Street Journal*, May 6, 2014, http://blogs.wsj.com/digits/2014/05/06/alibabas-ipo-filing-everything-you-need-to-know/ (accessed January 13, 2016); Gillian Wong, "Alibaba's Global Ambitions Face Counterfeit Challenge," *The Wall Street Journal*, November 10, 2015, www.wsj.com/articles/alibabas-global-ambitions-face-genuine-counterfeit-challenge-1447147654 (accessed January 13, 2016); Steven Davidoff Solomon, "Alibaba Investors Will Buy a Risky Corporate Structure," *The New York Times*, May 6, 2014, http://dealbook.nytimes.com/2014/05/06/i-p-o-revives-debate-over-a-chinese-structure/?_php=true&_type=blogs&_r=1 (accessed January 13, 2016).

91 "Netflix (NFLX) Expands Global Original Content Portfolio," *Nasdaq*, September 14, 2017, https://www.nasdaq.com/article/netflix-nflx-expands-global-original-content-portfolio-cm845858 (accessed February 11, 2018); Dana Feldman, "According to Netflix, These Are The Top 10 Shows New Members Binge First," *Forbes*, February 7, 2018, https://www.forbes.com/sites/danafeldman/2018/02/07/according-to-netflix-these-are-the-top-10-shows-new-members-binge-first/#213e7e3515bb (accessed February 11, 2018).

Chapter 10

1 O. C. Ferrell, John Fraedrich, and Linda Ferrell, *Business Ethics: Ethical Decision Making and Cases*, 9th ed, (Mason, Ohio: South-Western Cengage Learning, 2013), pp. 506–507; Jen Wieczner, "Best Buy CEO on How to Lead a Corporate Culture Turnaround (Without Making Employees Hate You)," *Fortune*, October 29, 2015, http://fortune.com/2015/10/29/best-buy-ceo-turn-around-tips/ (accessed November 24, 2017); Jennifer Calfas, "Best Buy Wants You to Try Gadgets Before You Buy Them," *Fortune*, June 13, 2017, http://fortune.com/2017/06/13/best-buy-amazon-apple-rent-try-buy/ (accessed November 24, 2017); Business Wire, "Best Buy Investor Day Details 'Best Buy 2020: Building the New Blue' Strategy," *Nasdaq*, September 19, 2017, www.nasdaq.com/press-release/best-buy-investor-day-details-best-buy-2020-building-the-new-blue-growth-strategy-20170919-00568 (accessed November 24, 2017); Kavita Kumar, "Best Buy Moves from Renew Blue Turnaround

to Growth Phase," *Star Tribune*, March 4, 2017, www.startribune.com/best-buy-moves-from-renew-blue-turnaround-to-growth-phase/415357004/ (accessed November 24, 2017); Courtney Reagan, "Best Buy CEO Sees 'Growth Opportunities' Ahead, Wall Street Isn't Buying It," *CNBC*, September 19, 2017, https://www.cnbc.com/2017/09/19/best-buy-ceo-weve-fixed-what-was-broken-now-focus-is-on-growth.html (accessed November 24, 2017); Judy Mottl, "Best Buy Embraces Innovative Tech to Deliver a Richer Customer Experience," *Retail Customer Experience*, December 15, 2017, https://www.retailcustomerexperience.com/articles/best-buy-embraces-innovative-tech-to-deliver-a-richer-customer-experience/ (accessed February 17, 2018); Yuyu Chen, "How Best Buy Is Holding Its Own in an Amazon World," *Digiday*, July 31, 2017, https://digiday.com/marketing/best-buy-holding-amazon-world/ (accessed February 17, 2018); Giselle Tsirulnik, "Best Buy Utilizes Mobile Marketing," *Strategic Growth Concepts*, www.strategicgrowthconcepts.com/marketing/marketing-resources/marketing-information-articles/Best-Buy-Utilizes-Mobile-Marketing_AE102.html (accessed February 17, 2018).

2 Lauren I. Labrecque, Jonas vor dem Esche, Charla Mathwick, Thomas P. Novak, and Charles F. Hofacker, "Consumer Power: Evolution in the Digital Age," *Journal of Interactive Marketing* 27, 4 (November 2013): pp. 257–269.

3 "Internet Users," Internet Live Stats, 2018, www.internetlivestats.com/internet-users/ (accessed February 17, 2018).

4 Piet Levy, "The State of Digital Marketing," *Marketing News*, March 15, 2010, pp. 20–21.

5 Maria Teresa Pinheiro Melo Borges Tiago and José Manuel Cristóvão Veríssimo, "Digital Marketing and Social Media: Why Bother?" *Business Horizons* 57, 6 (November 2014): pp. 703–708.

6 Charisse Jones, "Department Stores Become Endangered," *USA Today*, January 6–8, 2017: p. 1A.

7 Sanjit Kumar Roy and Gul T. Butaney, "Customer's Relative Loyalty: An Empirical Examination," *Journal of Strategic Marketing* 22, 3 (2014): pp. 206–221.

8 Melissa S. Barker, Donald I. Barker, Nicholas F. Bormann, Mary Lou Roberts, and Debra Zahay, *Social Media Marketing*, 2nd ed. (Mason, OH: Cengage Learning, 2017).

9 Ken Yeung, "Now with 2.5M Advertisers, Facebook Targets TV Budgets with New Ad-Buy Offering," *Venture Beat*, September 27, 2015, http://venturebeat.com/2015/09/27/now-with-2-5m-advertisers-facebook-targets-tv-budgets-with-new-ad-buying-offering/

(accessed March 2, 2017); *Business Insider*, April 12, 2017, http://www.businessinsider.com/facebook-adds-a-million-advertisers-in-7-months-2017-4 (accessed March 1, 2018).

10 Melissa S. Barker, Donald I. Barker, Nicholas F. Bormann, Mary Lou Roberts, and Debra Zahay, *Social Media Marketing*, 2nd ed. (Mason, OH: Cengage Learning, 2017).

11 Darius Fisher, "How to Handle Negative Yelp Reviews," *The Huffington Post*, June 7, 2016, www.huffingtonpost.com/darius-fisher/how-to-handle-negative-ye_b_10324196.html (accessed March 2, 2017).

12 "Dodge Brand Connecting with Its Fans by Inviting a Limited Number to the Hotly Anticipated Reveal of the All-New 2018 Dodge Challenger SRT Demon in NYC," *Yahoo! Finance*, February 22, 2017, http://finance.yahoo.com/news/dodge-brand-connecting-fans-inviting-130000410.html (accessed March 2, 2017).

13 V. Kumar, Xi Zhang, and Anita Luo, "Modeling Customer Opt-In and Opt-Out in a Permission-Based Marketing Context," *Journal of Marketing Research* 51, 4 (2014): pp. 403–419.

14 Michael Durkheimer, "For Young Investors with at Least $50,000, Snapchat Usage Almost Ties Facebook," *Forbes*, March 5, 2017, https://www.forbes.com/sites/michaeldurkheimer/2017/03/05/for-young-investors-with-at-least-50000-snapchat-usage-almost-ties-facebook/#ea016564886d (accessed March 5, 2017).

15 Christie Baraket, "QZone Tops WeChat as China's Biggest Open-Platform Social Network," *Adweek*, March 12, 2014, www.adweek.com/digital/qzone-tops-wechat-chinas-biggest-open-platform-social-network/ (accessed March 5, 2017); Jessica Davies, "How People Spend Time on Social Platforms Globally, in 5 Charts," *Digiday*, August 11, 2017, https://digiday.com/marketing/people-spend-time-social-platforms-globally-5-charts/ (accessed March 1, 2018).

16 Shannon Greenwood, Andrew Perrin, and Maeve Duggan, "Social Media Update 2016," Pew Research Center, November 11, 2016, www.pewinternet.org/2016/11/11/social-media-update-2016/ (accessed March 5, 2017).

17 Maria Vernuccio, "Communicating Corporate Brands Through Social Media: An Exploratory Study," *Journal of Business Communication* 51, 3 (2014): pp. 211–233.

18 Harry McCracken, "Inside Mark Zuckerberg's Bold Plan for the Future of Facebook," *Fast Company*, December 2015/January 2016, pp. 86–100, 136; Kaya Yurieff, "Facebook Hits 2 Billion Monthly Users," *CNN*, June 27, 2017, http://money.cnn.com/2017/06/27/technology/facebook-2-billion-users/index.html (accessed February 17, 2018).

19 Ivy Guerrero, "5 Most Popular Facebook Ads," *Insider Monkey*, November 1, 2016, www.insidermonkey.com/blog/5-most-popular-facebook-ads-484062/4/ (accessed March 5, 2017).

20 Anita Balakrishnan, "Facebook Ad Revenue Shoots Up 53%, Sending Shares Climbing Up," *CNBC*, February 1, 2017, www.cnbc.com/2017/02/01/facebook-earnings-q4-2016.html (accessed March 5, 2017); Tim Peterson, "Facebook's Q4 Ad Revenue Swells Despite Decreases in Time Spent and North American Daily Audience," MarTech, February 1, 2018, https://martechtoday.com/facebooks-q4-ad-revenue-swells-despite-time-spent-north-american-daily-audience-declines-210331 (accessed March 1, 2018).

21 Jeff Elder, "Facing Reality, Companies Alter Social-Media Strategies," *The Wall Street Journal*, June 23, 2014, pp. B1–B2.

22 Harriet Baskas, "Which Airlines Do Best on Facebook and Twitter?" *USA Today*, March 20, 2015, www.usatoday.com/story/todayinthesky/2015/03/20/airlines-facebook-twitter/25087101/ (accessed January 6, 2016).

23 Michael Liedtke, "Twitter Huddles with NFL to Tackle Audience Challenge," *Yahoo Finance!*, August 10, 2015, http://finance.yahoo.com/news/twitter-huddles-nfl-tackle-audience-130113486.html (accessed January 8, 2016).

24 Nathan McAlone, "Investors Are Going Nuts for Snapchat—Here's How Snap Thinks It Can Turn a $500 Million Loss into Profit," *Business Insider*, March 5, 2017, www.businessinsider.com/how-will-snapchat-make-money-2017-3 (accessed March 5, 2017); Kerry Flynn, "Snapchat's 2017 Earnings Impressed Everyone, App Is Growing with Android," *Mashable*, February 6, 2018, https://mashable.com/2018/02/06/snapchat-2017-earnings-evan-spiegel-187-million-daily-active-users/#z_dLRFRl3qqI (accessed March 1, 2018).

25 Haley Tsukayama, "Snapchat Files for Its Initial Public Offering: Here Are the 10 Most Interesting Things We've Learned So Far," *The Washington Post*, February 3, 2017, https://www.washingtonpost.com/news/the-switch/wp/2017/02/03/snapchat-files-for-its-initial-public-offering-here-are-the-10-most-interesting-things-weve-learned-so-far/?utm_term=.591d0ee20f98 (accessed March 5, 2017).

26 Kathleen Chaykowski, "Snapchat's Big Weakness: The Olds," *Forbes*, March 1, 2017, https://www.forbes.com/sites/kathleenchaykowski/2017/03/01/snapchats-big-weakness-the-olds/#15eb5908230b (accessed March 5, 2017).

27 Ryan Faughnder, "Is Snapchat a Media Company? Even Hollywood Can't Decide," *Los Angeles Times*, March 1, 2017, www.latimes.com/business/hollywood/la-fi-ct-snap-chat-studios-20170224-story.html (accessed March 5, 2017).

28 Douglas A. McIntyre, "YouTube Viewership Hits a Billion Hours of Content a Day," *24/7 Wall St.*, February 27, 2017, http://247wallst.com/apps-software/2017/02/27/youtube-viewership-hits-100-billion-hours-of-content-a-day/ (accessed March 5, 2017).

29 Rachel Strugatz, "Beauty's Battle for Views: Brands vs. Vloggers," *WWD*, February 23, 2017, http://wwd.com/beauty-industry-news/beauty-features/youtube-l2-beautys-battle-for-views-brands-vs-bloggers-10814639/ (accessed March 5, 2017).

30 Mike Snider, "How YouTube TV Compares to Rivals Sling, PlayStation, DirecTV," *USA Today*, March 5, 2017, www.usatoday.com/story/tech/talkingtech/2017/03/05/how-youtube-tv-compares-rivals-sling-playstation-directv/98551276/ (accessed March 5, 2017).

31 Sujan Patel, "How LinkedIn Uses LinkedIn for Marketing," *Forbes*, March 4, 2017, https://www.forbes.com/sites/sujanpatel/2017/03/04/how-linkedin-uses-linkedin-for-marketing/2/#3b96f9d3657f (accessed March 5, 2017).

32 Amanda Walgrove, "5 B2B Brands That Rock LinkedIn Marketing," *Contently*, February 24, 2017, https://contently.com/strategist/2015/02/24/5-b2b-brands-that-rock-linkedin/ (accessed March 5, 2017).

33 Dan Schwbel, "10 New Findings about the Millennial Consumer," *Forbes*, January 20, 2015, www.forbes.com/sites/danschawbel/2015/01/20/10-new-findings-about-the-millennial-consumer/#2715e4857a0b9cbb89c28a87 (accessed January 20, 2016).

34 Tumblr, "About Tumblr," www.tumblr.com/about (accessed January 15, 2016); Mike Shields, "Tumblr Rolls Out Network to Match Top Creators with Brands," *The Wall Street Journal*, January 22, 2015, http://blogs.wsj.com/cmo/2015/01/22/tumblr-rolls-out-network-to-match-top-creators-with-brands/ (accessed January 15, 2016).

35 Niall Harbison and Lauren Fisher, "40 of the Best Corporate Blogs to Inspire You," *Ragan's PR Daily*, September 13, 2012, www.prdaily.com/Main/

Articles/40_of_the_best_corporate_blogs_to_inspire_you_12645.aspx (accessed January 20, 2016).

36 Wikipedia, "Wikipedia: About," https://en.wikipedia.org/wiki/Wikipedia:About (accessed March 5, 2017).

37 Charlene Li and Josh Bernoff, *Groundswell* (Boston: Harvard Business Press, 2008), p. 24.

38 Ayaz Nanji, "Blog and Social Media Usage by Fortune 500 Companies," *Marketing Profs*, September 12, 2014, www.marketingprofs.com/charts/2014/25998/blog-and-social-media-usage-by-fortune-500-companies (accessed January 15, 2016).

39 Yoni Heisler, "Once Mocked, Facebook's $1 Billion Acquisition of Instagram Was a Stroke of Genius," *BGR*, December 29, 2016, http://bgr.com/2016/12/29/facebook-instagram-acquisition-1-billion-genius/ (accessed March 5, 2017).

40 Bryan Clark, "Snapchat Growth Slowed Significantly after Launch of Instagram Stories," The Next Web, February 3, 2017, https://thenextweb.com/socialmedia/2017/02/03/snapchat-growth-slowed-significantly-after-the-launch-of-instagram-stories/#.tnw_0IAEa2YL (accessed March 5, 2017).

41 Tribune wire reports, "Instagram Expands Marketing Reach for Businesses," *Chicago Tribune*, September 9, 2015, www.chicagotribune.com/bluesky/technology/ct-instagram-marketing-business-20150909-story.html (accessed January 8, 2016).

42 Laura Schlereth, "Marketers' Interest in Pinterest," *Marketing News*, April 30, 2012, pp. 8–9; Pinterest, http://pinterest.com (accessed January 20, 2016); http://pinterest.com/wholefoods/whole-planet-foundation (accessed January 20, 2016).

43 Jeff Bercovici, "Social Media's New Mad Men," *Forbes*, November 2014, pp. 71–82.

44 Nicole Lee, "Pinterest Uses AI and Your Camera to Recommend Pins," *Engadget*, February 8, 2017, https://www.engadget.com/2017/02/08/pinterest-uses-ai-and-your-camera-to-recommend-pins/ (accessed March 5, 2017).

45 Mike Shields, "Pinterest Narrows Its Advertising Focus," *The Wall Street Journal*, December 15, 2015, pp. B1–B2.

46 Douglas MacMillan and Elizabeth Dwoskin, "Smile! Marketers Are Mining Selfies," *The Wall Street Journal*, October 10, 2014, pp. B1–B2.

47 Cari Sommer, "YouTube Sensation Bethany Mota on How to Use Your Platform for Good," *Forbes*, December 12, 2016, https://www.forbes.com/sites/carisommer/2016/12/12/how-youtube-sensation-bethany-mota-is-using-her-platform-for-good/#2a6d839c322c (accessed March 5, 2016); Emma Oulton, "Bethany Mota's Book 'Make Your Mind Up' Promises to Be an Empowering Read," *Bustle*, October 17, 2016, https://www.bustle.com/articles/189997-bethany-motas-book-make-your-mind-up-promises-to-be-an-empowering-read (accessed March 5, 2017).

48 Kate Rockwood, "Why Spending $1,000 on an Instagram Post Might Actually Be Worth It," *Inc.*, February 2017, www.inc.com/magazine/201702/kate-rockwood/tip-sheet-social-media-influencers.html (accessed March 5, 2017).

49 "About Influenster," *Influenster*, https://www.influenster.com/about (accessed March 5, 2017).

50 "Mobile Fact Sheet," Pew Research Center, January 12, 2017, www.pewinternet.org/fact-sheet/mobile/ (accessed March 5, 2017).

51 Harry McCracken, "Inside Mark Zuckerberg's Bold Plan for the Future of Facebook," *Fast Company*, December 2015/January 2016, pp. 86–100, 136.

52 eMarketer, "US Ad Spending: The eMarketer Forecast for 2017," March 15, 2017, https://www.emarketer.com/Report/US-Ad-Spending-eMarketer-Forecast-2017/2001998 (accessed February 17, 2018).

53 Lauren Johnson, "Study with Major Brands Compares Ad Recall for Mobile and Desktop Promos," *Adweek*, July 16, 2015, http://www.adweek.com/news/technology/study-major-brands-compares-ad-recall-mobile-and-desktop-promos-165905 (accessed January 15, 2016).

54 Lauren Johnson, "How Capital One Used Instagram to Boost Ad Recall by 16 Percent," *Adweek*, August 11, 2015, www.adweek.com/news/technology/how-capital-one-used-instagram-boost-ad-recall-16-percent-166317 (accessed January 15, 2016).

55 Don E. Schultz, Varsha Jain, and Vijay Viswanathan, "Differential Gen Y's World of Apps," *Marketing News*, August 2015, pp. 14–15.

56 James Citron, "2014: The Year the MMS Upswing Arrives and How to Take Advantage of It," *Wired*, January 21, 2014, http://insights.wired.com/profiles/blogs/2014-the-year-the-mms-upswing-arrives-and-how-to-take-advantage#axzz3xLvg3dvO (accessed January 15, 2016).

57 "Mobile to Account for More than Half of Digital Ad Spending in 2015," *eMarketer*, September 1, 2015, www.emarketer.com/Article/Mobile-Account-More-than-Half-of-Digital-Ad-Spending-2015/1012930 (accessed January 15, 2016).

58 Jake Jeffries, "10 Incredible Mobile Marketing Stats 2015 [INFOGRAPHIC]," *Social Media Today*, January 13, 2015, www.socialmediatoday.com/content/10-incredible-mobile-marketing-stats-2015-infographic (accessed January 15, 2016).

59 Christopher Heine, "Foursquare Unleashes Location Data for Cross-Mobile Ad Targeting," *Adweek*, April 14, 2015, www.adweek.com/news/technology/foursquare-finally-unleashes-location-data-cross-mobile-ad-targeting-164069 (accessed January 19, 2016).

60 Kenneth Olmstead and Michelle Atkinson, "Chapter 1: The Majority of Smartphone Owners Download Apps," Pew Research Center, November 10, 2015, www.pewinternet.org/2015/11/10/the-majority-of-smartphone-owners-download-apps/ (accessed March 5, 2017).

61 Olga Khariff and Leslie Patton, "Starbucks Takes Its Pioneering Mobile-Phone App to Grande Level," *Bloomberg*, March 30, 2016, https://www.bloomberg.com/news/articles/2016-03-30/starbucks-takes-its-pioneering-mobile-phone-app-to-grande-level (accessed March 5, 2017).

62 Umika Pidaparthy, "Marketers Embracing QR Codes, for Better or Worse," *CNN Tech*, March 28, 2011, www.cnn.com/2011/TECH/mobile/03/28/qr.codes.marketing/ (accessed January 20, 2016).

63 Brad Tuttle, "The Creepy New Way Macy's Tempts You to Make Impulse Purchases," *Time*, September 16, 2014, http://time.com/money/3432693/macys-shopkick-ibeacon/ (accessed April 1, 2017).

64 Deanna Ting, "What Marriott Learned from Starwood's Loyalty and Digital Expertise," *Skift*, February 13, 2017, https://skift.com/2017/02/13/what-marriott-learned-from-starwoods-loyalty-and-digital-expertise/ (accessed April 1, 2017).

65 Greg Sterling, "Beacon Marketers Have New Ways Around App Download Requirement," *Marketing Land*, April 19, 2016, http://marketingland.com/beacon-market-matures-marketers-drop-173651 (accessed April 1, 2017).

66 Ann Zimmerman, "Check Out the Future of Shopping," *The Wall Street Journal*, May 18, 2011, p. D1.

67 "Google Wallet," www.google.com/wallet/what-is-google-wallet.html (accessed January 20, 2016).

68 Vangie Beal, "All about Widgets," Webopedia™, August 31, 2010, www.webopedia.com/DidYouKnow/Internet/2007/widgets.asp (accessed January 20, 2016).

69 Dylan Tweney, "Plyfe's Interactive Widgets for Your Site Have 46% Engagement—and They're Free," *Venture Beat*, June 25, 2015, http://venturebeat.com/2015/06/25/

plyfes-interactive-widgets-for-your-site-have-46-engagement-and-theyre-free/ (accessed January 19, 2016).

70 Melissa S. Barker, Donald I. Barker, Nicholas F. Bormann, Mary Lou Roberts, and Debra Zahay, *Social Media Marketing*, 2nd ed. (Mason, OH: Cengage Learning, 2017).

71 Matt McGee, "As Google Analytics Turns 10, We Ask: How Many Websites Use It?" *Marketing Land*, November 12, 2015, http://marketingland.com/as-google-analytics-turns-10-we-ask-how-many-websites-use-it-151892 (accessed March 5, 2017).

72 "By Tailoring the Features of Google Analytics, LunaMetrics Helps PBS Increase Both Conversions and Visits by 30%," *Google Analytics*, https://static.googleusercontent.com/media/www.google.com/en//intl/pt_ALL/analytics/customers/pdfs/pbs.pdf (accessed March 24, 2017).

73 Sonja Gensler, Franziska Völckner, Yuping Liu-Thompkins, and Caroline Wiertz, "Managing Brands in the Social Environment," *Journal of Interactive Marketing* 27, 4 (2013): pp. 242–256.

74 Emily Orofino, "Can This Genius Beauty Brand Crowdsource the Next Big Thing?" *POPSUGAR*, July 10, 2016, https://www.popsugar.com/beauty/Volition-Beauty-Custom-Made-Beauty-Products-41873521 (accessed March 25, 2017).

75 1-800-Flowers.com, www.1800flowers.com/flowers-same-day-delivery?gnavFlag+gnav_close&stateCode+&ddkey+http:FDFlowersControllerCmd (accessed January 19, 2016).

76 Emma Sopadjieva, Utpal M. Dholakia, and Beth Benjamin, "A Study of 46,000 Shoppers Shows that Omnichannel Retailing Works," *Harvard Business Review*, January 3, 2017, https://hbr.org/2017/01/a-study-of-46000-shoppers-shows-that-omnichannel-retailing-works (accessed March 5, 2017).

77 Cheryl Wischhover, "How ColourPop Became the Most Popular (and Most Mysterious) Beauty Brand on the Internet," *Fashionista*, January 22, 2016, http://fashionista.com/2016/01/colourpop-instagram-beauty (accessed March 5, 2017).

78 Athleta, "Our Mission," http://athleta.gap.com/browse/info.do?cid=1074426 (accessed February 17, 2018).

79 Lindsay Kolowich, "14 of the Best Brands on Instagram Right Now," *HubSpot*, February 21, 2017, https://blog.hubspot.com/marketing/instagram-best-brands#sm.000009ty2hnlotct2w4p7tr8o6gpc (accessed April 1, 2017).

80 Robert Hof, "Online Ad Revenues Blow Past Broadcast TV, Thanks to Mobile and Video," *Forbes*, April 10, 2014, www.forbes.com/sites/roberthof/2014/04/10/

online-ad-revenues-blow-past-broadcast-tv-thanks-to-mobile-and-video/ (accessed January 7, 2015); George Slefo, "Desktop and Mobile Ad Revenue Surpasses TV for the First Time," *AdAge*, April 26, 2017, http://adage.com/article/digital/digital-ad-revenue-surpasses-tv-desktop-iab/308808/ (accessed March 1, 2018).

81 Shawn D. Baron, Caryn Brouwer, and Amaya Garbayo, "A Model for Delivering Branding Value through High-Impact Digital Advertising," *Journal of Advertising Research* 54 (3), September 2014, pp. 286–291.

82 Alistair Barr, "Google Earnings: What to Watch," *The Wall Street Journal*, April 16, 2014, http://blogs.wsj.com/digits/2014/04/16/google-earnings-what-to-watch-4/ (accessed January 7, 2015); Conor Dougherty, "Analysts Ask What's Next for Google?" *The New York Times*, October 16, 2014, www.nytimes.com/2014/10/17/technology/google-search-ad-growth-slows.html (accessed January 7, 2015).

83 Corbin Davenport, "Instagram Is Expanding Its Shopping Feature to More Merchants," *Android Police*, October 2, 2017, https://www.androidpolice.com/2017/10/02/instagram-expanding-shopping-feature-merchants/ (accessed October 2, 2017).

84 "FTC Cracking Down on Social Influencers' Labeling of Paid Promotions," *AdAge*, August 5, 2016, http://adage.com/article/digital/ftc-cracking-social-influencers-labeling-promotions/305345/ (accessed March 5, 2017).

85 Aruna Viswanatha and Robert McMillan, "Yahoo Faces SEC Probe Over Data Breaches," *The Wall Street Journal*, January 23, 2017, p. A1.

86 O. C. Ferrell, "Broadening Marketing's Contribution to Data Privacy," *Journal of the Academy of Marketing Science*, p. 43, (March 2017).

87 Cecilia Kang, "Bills Would Curb Tracking of and Advertising to Children on Internet," *The Washington Post*, November 14, 2013, www.washingtonpost.com/business/technology/bills-would-curb-tracking-of-and-advertisingto-children-on-internet/2013/11/14/dee03382-4d58-11e3-ac54-aa84301ced81_story.html (accessed January 20, 2016); Anne Flaherty, "Senate Chairman Calls for 'Do Not Track' Bill," *Yahoo! News*, April 24, 2013, phys.org/news/2013-04-senate-chairman-track-bill.html (accessed January 20, 2016).

88 Jesse Brody, "Terms and Conditions," *Marketing News*, November 2014, pp. 34–41.

89 Will Bourne, "Birth of the Resistance," *Inc.*, July/August 2014, pp. 24–32, 110.

90 Brody, 34–41.

91 Nicole Hong, "Massive Cybertheft Scheme Is Alleged," *The Wall Street Journal*, November 11, 2015, p. A1.

92 Ben Rossen, "Ransomware—A Closer Look," *Federal Trade Commission*, November 10, 2016, https://www.ftc.gov/news-events/blogs/business-blog/2016/11/ransomware-closer-look (accessed March 25, 2017).

93 Sarah Needleman, "Social-Media Con Game," *The Wall Street Journal*, October 12, 2009, http://online.wsj.com/article/SB10001424052748704471504574445502831219412.html (accessed January 20, 2016).

94 BSA Software Alliance, "The Compliance Gap: BSA Global Software Survey," http://globalstudy.bsa.org/2016/index.html (accessed March 1, 2018).

95 Aubry R. Fowler III, Barry J. Babin, and May K. Este, "Burning for Fun or Money: Illicit Consumer Behavior in a Contemporary Context," presented at the Academy of Marketing Science Annual Conference, May 27, 2005, Tampa, FL.

96 Kevin Shanahan and Mike Hyman, "Motivators and Enablers of SCOURing: A Study of Online Piracy in the US and UK," *Journal of Business Research* 63, 9–10 (2010): pp. 1095–1102.

97 Paul Talbot, "Keeping Up With Change: How Marketers Give Customers What They Want," *Forbes*, June 20, 2018, https://www.forbes.com/sites/paultalbot/2018/06/20/keeping-up-with-change-how-marketers-give-customers-what-they-want/#12e0c8fc66bf (accessed July 15, 2018); Gabriel Beltrone, "Zappos Turned True Customer Stories Into Charming Low-Budget Ads," *Adweek*, November 7, 2017, www.adweek.com/creativity/zappos-turned-true-customer-stories-into-charming-low-budget-ads/ (accessed July 15, 2018); Todd Wasserman, "Zappos Facebook Activity over 2 Months Drives 85,000 Website Visits," *Mashable*, February 6, 2013, www.mashable.com/2013/02/06/zappos-facebook-results (accessed July 15, 2018); Laura Stampler, "Why Zappos Sees Sponsored Posts on Facebook as 'A Necessary Evil,'" *Business Insider*, February 6, 2013, www.businessinsider.com/zappos-on-facebook-and-social-media-2013-2 (accessed July 15, 2018); Mike Schoultz, "Zappos Marketing Strategy . . . What Is Their Difference Maker?" *Digital Spark Marketing*, November 12, 2013, www.digitalsparkmarketing.com/creative-marketing/brand/zappos-marketing-strategy (accessed December 6, 2013); Amy Porterfield, "9 Companies Doing Social Media Right and Why," *Social Media Examiner*, April 12, 2011, www.socialmediaexaminer.com/9-companies-doing-social-media-right-and-why (accessed July 15, 2018).

98 Oscar Williams-Grut, "Dollar Shave Club Is Entering the Cutthroat World of UK Razors: 'We Like Competition,'" *Business Insider*, January 30, 2018, www.businessinsider.com/

dollar-shave-club-is-entering-the-cutthroat-world-of-uk-razors-we-like-competition-2018-1?r=UK&IR=T (accessed February 17, 2018); Alan Livsey, "Dollar Shave Club Wins Market Share and Customers with Back-to-Basics Approach," *Financial Times*, March 16, 2017, https://www.ft.com/content/9bb5cc54-d368-11e6-b06b-680c49b4b4c0 (accessed February 18, 2018); Paresh Dave, "Dollar Shave Club Succeeded with Razors, but the Rest of the Bathroom Is a Challenge," *Los Angeles Times*, September 1, 2017, www.latimes.com/business/technology/la-fi-tn-dollar-shave-club-unilever-anniversary-20170828-htmlstory.html (accessed February 17, 2018); Jaclyn Trop, "How Dollar Shave Club's Founder Built a $1 Billion Company that Changed the Industry," *Entrepreneur*, March 28, 2017, https://www.entrepreneur.com/article/290539 (accessed February 17, 2018); "Dollar Shave Club Case Study," *Facebook*, 2017 https://www.facebook.com/business/success/dollar-shave-club (accessed February 17, 2018); Jeff Taylor, "Advertising Giant to Facebook & Google: Lose Fake News or Lose Us," *LGBTQ Nation*, February 12, 2018, https://www.lgbtqnation.com/2018/02/advertising-giant-facebook-google-lose-fake-news-lose-us/ (accessed February 17, 2018); Suzanne Vranica, "Unilever Threatens to Reduce Ad Spending on Tech Platforms That Don't Combat Divisive Content," *The Wall Street Journal*, February 11, 2018, https://www.wsj.com/articles/unilever-threatens-to-reduce-ad-spending-on-tech-platforms-that-dont-combat-divisive-content-1518398578 (accessed February 28, 2018).

99 Nancy Trejos, "Major Hotel Brand to Let Guests Earn Points for Ordering Food, Dining Out," *USA Today*, November 15, 2017, www.usatoday.com/story/travel/roadwarriorvoices/2017/11/15/major-hotel-brand-let-guests-earn-points-ordering-food-dining-out/865281001/; Elliott Mest, "Roundtable: Dissecting the Evolution of the Modern Business Traveler," December 12, 2017, www.hotelmanagement.net/operate/business-travel-roundtable-2017; Nancy Trejos, "IHG to Start New Midscale Hotel Brand," *USA Today*, September 22, 2017, www.usatoday.com/story/travel/roadwarriorvoices/2017/09/22/ihg-start-new-midscale-brand/692090001/; Ravneet Ahluwalia, "Intercontinental Hotels Launches New Budget Chain," *The Independent (UK)*, June 22, 2017, www.independent.co.uk/travel/news-and-advice/intercontinental-hotels-budget-resorts-holiday-inn-hilton-marriot-project-horizon-a7802316.html; Bernie Low, "CNBC Transcript: Interview with Richard Solomons, CEO, InterContinental Hotels Group," *CNBC*, April 26, 2017, www.cnbc.com/2017/04/26/cnbc-transcript-richard-solomons-ceo-intercontinental-hotels-group.html; Sheila Shayon, "ASOS Releases Fashion Collection for Hotel Indigo Properties," *BrandChannel*, September 22, 2017; http://brandchannel.com/2017/09/22/asos-hotel-indigo-092217/; Janice Tan, "IHG Says 2017 Was Its Strongest Performing Year Since 2010," *Marketing Magazine (Asia)*, November 7, 2017, www.marketing-interactive.com/ihg-forges-ahead-in-apac-new-hotel-launches-and-target-campaigns; www.ihgplc.com; https://littlebigtravellers.holidayinn.com/en.

Chapter 11

1 Ben Fox Rubin, "Amazon's Private-Label Diapers Are Back," *CNET*, November 7, 2017, www.cnet.com/news/amazons-private-label-diapers-are-back-mama-bear/ (accessed January 26, 2018); Matt Day, "Amazon Launches Two Furniture Lines as Private-Label Ambitions Grow," *Seattle Times*, November 7, 2017, www.seattletimes.com/business/amazon/amazon-launches-two-furniture-lines-as-private-label-ambitions-grow/ (accessed January 26, 2018); Sarah Perez, "Amazon Expands into Private Label Sportswear and Its First Home Furnishing Lines," *Tech Crunch*, November 7, 2017, https://techcrunch.com/2017/11/07/amazon-expands-into-private-label-sportswear-and-its-first-home-furnishing-lines/ (accessed January 26, 2018); Joseph Hansen and James Thomson, "The Impact Amazon Has (or Soon Will Have) on Your Brand: Do You Have a Plan?" *Entrepreneur*, October 10, 2017, www.entrepreneur.com/article/302410 (accessed January 26, 2018).

2 "Team Charity: Water," http://www.charitywater.org/about/ (accessed January 29, 2018).

3 "Drury Hotels Receives Record-Breaking 12th-Consecutive J.D. Power Award," Drury Hotels, press release, July 12, 2017, https://druryhotels.com/about/pressreleases/JDPower2017 (accessed January 29, 2018).

4 Sue Gleiter, "McDonald's Launches Line of 'Signature Crafted' Sandwiches with Higher-End Ingredients," *PennLive*, May 1, 2017, http://www.pennlive.com/food/index.ssf/2017/05/mcdonalds_signature_crafted.html (accessed January 30, 2018); "Here's How McDonald's Is Now Seeking to Attract Millennials," *Forbes*, November 17, 2016, http://www.forbes.com/sites/greatspeculations/2016/11/17/heres-how-mcdonalds-is-now-seeking-to-attract-millennials/#1d1312862d09 (accessed January 30, 2018).

5 He Huifeng, "The Asian Suppliers behind Some of the iPhone 7's Key Components," *South China Morning Post*, September 8, 2016, http://www.scmp.com/business/article/2017678/asian-suppliers-behind-some-iphone-7s-key-components (accessed January 31, 2018).

6 William P. Putsis Jr and Barry L. Bayus, "An Empirical Analysis of Firms' Product Line Decisions," *Journal of Marketing Research* 38, 1 (2001): pp. 110–118.

7 John Deere & Co., "Agriculture," https://www.deere.com/en_US/industry/agriculture/agriculture.page (accessed January 31, 2018).

8 Michael D. Johnson, Andreas Herrmann, and Frank Huber, "Evolution of Loyalty Intentions," *Journal of Marketing* 70, 2 (2006): pp. 122–132.

9 Jennifer Kaplan, "PepsiCo Takes on LaCroix in Sparkling-Water Battle," *Bloomberg*, February 8, 2018, https://www.bloomberg.com/news/articles/2018-02-08/pepsico-takes-on-lacroix-as-sparkling-water-battle-gathers-fizz (accessed February 8, 2018).

10 Richard L. Gruner, Christian Homburg, and Bryan A. Lukas, "Firm-Hosted Online Brand Communities and New Product Success," *Journal of the Academy of Marketing Science* 42, 1 (2014): pp. 29–48.

11 Joan Schneider and Julie Hall, "Why Most Product Launches Fail," *Harvard Business Review*, April 2011, https://hbr.org/2011/04/why-most-product-launches-fail (accessed January 31, 2018).

12 Michal Lev-Ram, "Can a Tech Makeover Save the Toy Industry?" *Fortune*, September 22, 2017, http://fortune.com/2017/09/22/mattel-ceo-most-powerful-women/ (accessed February 9, 2018); Matt Timms, "Life in Plastic, Not so Fantastic; the Tale of Barbie's Decline" *The New Economy*, January 7, 2015, http://www.theneweconomy.com/home/life-in-plastic-not-so-fantastic-barbies-great-decline (accessed February 24, 2016).

13 Beth Kowitt, "Stonyfield Gives Its Yogurt a Makeover," *Fortune*, February 13, 2017, http://fortune.com/2017/02/13/stonyfield-yogurt-sugar/ (accessed February 9, 2018).

14 Everett M. Rogers, *Diffusion of Innovations* (New York: Macmillan, 1962), pp. 81–86.

15 Arch G. Woodside and Wim Biemans, "Managing Relationships, Networks, and Complexity in Innovation, Diffusion, and Adoption Processes," *Business & Industrial Marketing* 20, 7 (2005): pp. 247–250.

16 Ibid, pp. 247–250.

17 "Common Language Marketing Dictionary," American Marketing Association, http://www.marketing-dictionary.org/ama (accessed February 24, 2016).

18 Warren Church, "Investment in Brand Pays Large Dividends," *Marketing News*, November 15, 2006, p. 21.

19 Ana Lucia Murillo, "Applebee's Gives Up on Millennials after Failed Rebranding Efforts," NPR's the Salt, August 15, 2017, https://www.npr.org/sections/thesalt/2017/08/15/543707953/applebees-ditches-millennials (accessed February 9, 2018).

20 Rosellina Ferraro, Amna Kirmani, and Ted Matherly, "Look At Me! Look At Me! Conspicuous Brand Usage, Self-Brand Connection, and Dilution," *Journal of Marketing Research* 50, 4 (2013): pp. 477–488.

21 C. D. Simms and P. Trott, "The Perceptions of the BMW Mini Brand: The Importance of Historical Associations and the Development of a Model," *Journal of Product & Brand Management* 15, 4 (2006): pp. 228–238.

22 Douglas Holt, "Branding as Cultural Activism," *How Brands Become Icons: The Principle of Cultural Branding* (Boston: Harvard Business School Press, 2004), p. 209.

23 Nigel Hollis, "Branding Unmasked," *Marketing Research* (Fall 2005): pp. 24–29.

24 David A. Aaker, "*Managing Brand Equity: Capitalizing on the Value of a Brand Name* (New York: Free Press, 1991), pp. 16–17.

25 Don E. Schulz, "The Loyalty Paradox," *Marketing Management* 14, 5 (2005): pp. 10–11.

26 "2018 Brand Keys Customer Loyalty Engagement Index," Brand Keys, http://brandkeys.com/wp-content/uploads/2018/01/2018-Category-Winners-tableFINAL.pdf (accessed February 9, 2018).

27 Mitchell C. Olsen, Rebecca J. Slotegraaf, and Sandeep R. Chandukala, "Green Claims and Message Frames: How Green New Products Change Brand Attitude," *Journal of Marketing* 78, 5 (2014): pp. 119–137.

28 Millward Brown, "2017 BrandZ Top 100 Global Brands," http://www.millwardbrown.com/brandz/top-global-brands/2017 (accessed February 9, 2018).

29 "Consumer Reports' Best and Worst Car Brands for Reliability in 2017," *Newsday,* January 18, 2018, https://www.newsday.com/classifieds/cars/consumer-reports-2018-best-and-worst-car-brands-for-reliability-include-toyota-lexus-and-kia-1.14536765 (accessed February 12, 2018).

30 Simone M. de Droog, Patti M. Valkenburg, and Moniek Buijzen, "Using Brand Characters to Promote Young Children's Liking of and Purchase Requests for Fruit," *Journal of Health Communication: International Perspectives* 26, 1 (2010): pp. 79–89.

31 "Consumers Continue to Reach for Store Brands, Producing Record Sales across Major U.S. Retail Channels," *PLMA,* http://plma.com/storeBrands/marketprofile2015.html (accessed February 12, 2018).

32 Pamela N. Danziger, "Growth in Store Brands and Private Label: It's Not about Price but Experience," *Forbes,* July 28, 2017, https://www.forbes.com/sites/pamdanziger/2017/07/28/growth-in-store-brands-and-private-label-its-not-about-price-but-experience/#84d8af4505fd (accessed February 12, 2018).

33 Chiranjeev S. Kohli, Katrin R. Harich, and Lance Lethesser, "Creating Brand Identity: A Study of Evaluation of New Brand Names," *Journal of Business Research* 58, 11 (2005): pp. 1506–1515.

34 Richard R. Klink and Gerard A. Athaide, "Creating Brand Personality with Brand Names," *Marketing Letters* 23, 1 (2012): pp. 109–117.

35 Sophia Yan, "What's in a Brand Name? In China, Everything," *CNN Money,* September 7, 2015, http://money.cnn.com/2015/09/07/news/foreign-firms-china-branding/ (accessed February 12, 2018).

36 Dorothy Cohen, "Trademark Strategy," *Journal of Marketing* 50, 1 (1986): p. 63.

37 Chiranjeev Kohli and Rajneesh Suri, "Brand Names That Work: A Study of the Effectiveness of Different Types of Brand Names," *Marketing Management Journal* 10, 2 (2000): pp. 112–120.

38 International Trademark Association, "Fact Sheets: Introduction to Trademarks," http://www.inta.org/TrademarkBasics/FactSheets/Pages/TrademarkUseFactSheet.aspx (accessed February 12, 2018).

39 Sophie Brown, "Brand Wars: Battling China's Trademark 'Squatters,'" *CNN,* July 17, 2014, http://www.cnn.com/2014/07/17/world/asia/china-trademark-squatters-penfolds/ (accessed February 12, 2018).

40 Rob Corben, "Economic Report Predicts Rise in Global Counterfeiting, Piracy," Voice of America, March 27, 2017, https://www.voanews.com/a/global-trend-in-counterfeiting-and-piracy/3783360.html (accessed February 12, 2018); "Counterfeit Goods: How to Tell the Real from the Ripoff," *Consumer Reports,* May 28, 2015, http://www.consumerreports.org/cro/magazine/2015/05/counterfeit-goods-how-to-tell-real-from-ripoff/index.htm (accessed February 12, 2018).

41 "Will Baileys' New Brand Extension, Baileys Iced Coffee, Grow the Brand?" *The Branding Journal,* September 4, 2017, http://www.thebrandingjournal.com/2017/09/will-baileys-new-brand-extension-baileys-iced-coffee-grow-brand/ (accessed February 12, 2018).

42 "The Worst Brand Extensions from Famous Companies," *To-market,* June 28, 2017, http://www.to-market.co.uk/worst-brand-extensions-famous-companies/ (accessed February 12, 2018).

43 Shantini Munthree, Geoff Bick, and Russell Abratt, "A Framework for Brand Revitalization through an Upscale Line Extension," *Journal of Product & Brand Management* 15, 3 (2006): pp. 157–167.

44 Kaleel Rahman and Charles S. Areni, "Generic, Genuine, or Completely New? Branding Strategies to Leverage New Products," *Journal of Strategic Marketing* 22, 1 (2014): pp. 3–15.

45 "Kids' Room Color Coordinator," Target, http://www.target.com/spot/kids-room-color-coordinator/landing (accessed February 12, 2018).

46 PR Newswire, "Best Western and Harley-Davidson Partnership Goes Global," press release, February 20, 2013, http://www.prnewswire.com/news-releases/best-western-and-harley-davidson-partnership-goes-global-192015471.html (accessed February 12, 2018).

47 "The Top 150 Global Licensors," *License Global,* April 1, 2017, http://www.licensemag.com/license-global/top-150-global-licensors-3 (accessed February 12, 2018).

48 SC Johnson, "Minimizing Packaging," http://www.scjohnson.com/en/commitment/focus-on/lesswaste/minimizingpackaging.aspx (accessed February 12, 2018).

49 "Rebrand Reflects Company's Farm-to-Jar Transparency," *Packaging World,* February 4, 2018, https://www.packworld.com/article/package-design/redesign/rebrand-reflects-companys-farm-jar-transparency (accessed February 12, 2018).

50 Anne Marie Mohan, "McCormick: Not Just Doing Well But Doing Good," *Packaging World,* January 28, 2018, https://www.packworld.com/article/sustainability/corporate-social-responsibility/mccormick-not-just-doing-well-doing-good (accessed February 13, 2018).

51 Lauren I. Labrecque and George R. Milne, "Exciting Red and Competent Blue: The Importance of Color in Marketing," *Journal of the Academy of Marketing Science* 40, 5 (2012): pp. 711–727.

52 Karlene Lukovitz, "Lean Cuisine Wins Top Prize in Nielsen's First Packaging Awards," *Media Post,* May 2, 2017, https://www.mediapost.com/publications/article/300225/lean-cuisine-wins-top-prize-in-nielsens-first-pac.html (accessed February 13, 2018).

53 "Laundry Detergent," Seventh Generation, www.seventhgeneration.com/laundry-detergent (accessed February 13, 2018).

54 Kimberly Janeway, "Laundry Pod Makers Are Facing More Pressure to Make Packaging Safer," *Consumer Reports,* February 7, 2018, https://www.consumerreports.org/

laundry-detergents/new-york-proposes-law-for-pod-packaging/ (accessed February 13, 2018); Barrett J. Brunsman, "P&G Redesigns Packaging, Launches New Ad Campaign as Poison Concerns Mount," *Cincinnati Business Courier*, April 21, 2016, http://www.bizjournals.com/cincinnati/news/2016/04/21/p-g-redesigns-packaging-launches-new-ad-campaign.html (accessed February 13, 2018); Serena Ng, "P&G, Other Laundry Pod Makers Agree to New Safety Standards," *The Wall Street Journal*, September 4, 2015, http://www.wsj.com/articles/p-g-other-laundry-pod-makers-agree-to-new-safety-standard-1441397456 (accessed February 13, 2018).

55. Kate Bertrand Connelly, "Valvoline's New Motor Oil Package Addresses Users' Pain Points," *Packaging Digest*, November 17, 2017, http://www.packagingdigest.com/packaging-design/valvolines-new-motor-oil-package-addresses-users-pain-points-2017-11-17 (accessed February 13, 2018).

56. Stack Wine, http://drinkstack.com (accessed February 13, 2018); Steve Ferree, "Take Stack Wine with You for International Picnic Day," *Examiner.com*, June 7, 2015, http://www.examiner.com/article/take-stack-wine-with-you-for-international-picnic-day (accessed February 26, 2016).

57. Valerie Folkes and Shashi Matta, "The Effect of Package Shape on Consumers' Judgments of Product Volume: Attention as a Mental Contaminant," *Journal of Consumer Research* 31, 2 (2004): pp. 390–401.

58. Caitlin Dewey, "The Raging Legal Battle over What Makes a Food 'Natural,'" *The Washington Post*, August 30, 2017, https://www.washingtonpost.com/news/wonk/wp/2017/08/30/the-raging-legal-battle-over-what-makes-a-food-natural/?utm_term=.6fd72ebe6f28 (accessed February 13, 2018).

59. Larry Loffer, "More Consumers Seeking Products Made in the USA," Wagner Meters, May 22, 2014, http://www.wagnermeters.com/wood-moisture-meter/more-consumers-seeking-products-made-in-the-usa/ (accessed February 13, 2018); Felix Gillette, "'Made in USA' Still Sells," *Bloomberg Businessweek*, October 11, 2012, www.businessweek.com/articles/2012-10-11-made-in-usa-still-sells (accessed February 13, 2018).

60. "Made in USA," Federal Trade Commission, https://www.ftc.gov/tips-advice/business-center/advertising-and-marketing/made-in-usa (accessed February 13, 2018).

61. Joseph Hincks, "Meet the Founder of Impossible Foods, Whose Meat-Free Burgers Could Transform the Way We Eat," *Time*, April 23, 2018, http://time.com/5247858/impossible-foods-meat-plant-based-agriculture/; Eustance Huang, "The Meatless 'Impossible Burger' Makes Its First Foray Outside the US," *CNBC*, April 19, 2018, https://www.cnbc.com/2018/04/19/the-meatless-impossible-burger-makes-its-first-foray-outside-the-us.html; Christina Troitino, "Impossible Foods Brings Its 'Bleeding' Veggie Burgers to White Castle," *Forbes*, April 12, 2018, https://www.forbes.com/sites/christinatroitino/2018/04/12/impossible-foods-brings-its-bleeding-veggie-burgers-to-white-castle/#ea79eb850927; www.impossiblefoods.com/; video: "The Strange Science of the Impossible Burger," *Wired*, September 20, 2017, www.youtube.com/watch?v=nIiLqNQOgPA&t=1s&list=PLibNZv5Zd0dxcjS2fN-z6Pes82V0jeRHr&index=11.

62. Nancy Trejos, "Hilton Announces New Affordable Hotel Brand, Tru," *USA Today*, January 25, 2016, www.usatoday.com/story/travel/hotels/2016/01/25/hilton-tru-new-hotel-brand/79185810 (accessed February 9, 2016); Nancy Trejos, "Hilton Marks a Milestone: Enters 100th Country," *USA Today*, January 21, 2016, www.usatoday.com/story/travel/2016/01/21/hilton-marks-milestone-enters-100th-country/79105564 (accessed February 9, 2016); Abha Bhattarai, "Hilton Tests Guest-Greeting Robots and Noise-Canceling Rooms," *The Washington Post*, January 15, 2016, www.washingtonpost.com/business/capitalbusiness/hilton-tests-guest-greeting-robots-and-noise-canceling-rooms/2016/01/15/1eb42e96-b48b-11e5-a76a-0b5145e8679a_story.html (accessed February 9, 2016); "Experience Canopy," Canopy by Hilton, http://canopy3.hilton.com/en/relax-to-revive/index.html (accessed February 13, 2018); "Our Story," Tru by Hilton, http://tru3.hilton.com/en/our-story/index.html (accessed February 13, 2018), www.hiltonworldwide.com.

Chapter 12

1. Jennifer Kaplan, "Coca-Cola's Next Big Bet May Be Spiffing Up Your Cocktail Mixers," *Bloomberg News*, November 6, 2017, www.bloomberg.com/news/articles/2017-11-06/coca-cola-s-next-big-bet-may-be-spiffing-up-your-cocktail-mixers (accessed February 15, 2018); Keith Nunes, "Change Is a Key Component of Coca-Cola's Growth Strategy," *Food Business News*, October 26, 2017, www.foodbusinessnews.net/articles/news_home/Financial-Performance/2017/10/Change_is_a_key_component_of_C.aspx?ID=%7BF06830F0-CC43-49E3-8EC0-FBAB06D2E7CC%7D&cck=1 (accessed February 15, 2018); Abha Bhattarai, "How Coca-Cola Got Americans to Drink Diet Soda Again," *The Washington Post*, October 25, 2017, www.washingtonpost.com/news/business/wp/2017/10/25/how-coca-cola-got-americans-to-drink-diet-soda-again/?utm_term=.4e96f0ec9b33 (accessed February 15, 2018).

2. Jeff Wells, "Wake-Up Call: Can Cereal Makers Revive a Flagging Category?" *Food Dive*, June 9, 2017, https://www.fooddive.com/news/wake-up-call-can-cereal-makers-revive-a-flagging-category/442743/ (accessed February 15, 2018).

3. "Pirate's Booty Line Extensions," *Progressive Grocer*, March 14, 2017, https://progressivegrocer.com/pirates-booty-line-extensions (accessed February 19, 2018).

4. Robert E. Carter and David J. Curry, "Perceptions versus Performance When Managing Extensions: New Evidence about the Role of Fit between a Parent Brand and an Extension," *Journal of the Academy of Marketing Science*, www.springerlink.com/content/8030v6q35851821t (accessed March 1, 2016).

5. Jeff Wells, "How Companies Find the Best Way to Innovate: Reformulation or a New Product Launch?" *Food Dive*, June 19, 2017, https://www.fooddive.com/news/how-companies-find-the-best-way-to-innovate-reformulation-or-a-new-product/445132/ (accessed February 19, 2018).

6. Todd Haselton, "These Are the Coolest New Features of the New iPhone X," *CNBC*, September 13, 2017, https://www.cnbc.com/2017/09/13/iphone-x-top-five-features.html (accessed February 19, 2018).

7. Scott Anthony, "Kodak's Downfall Wasn't about Technology," *Harvard Business Review*, July 15, 2016, https://hbr.org/2016/07/kodaks-downfall-wasnt-about-technology (accessed February 15, 2018).

8. "Buddy: The First Companion Robot," Blue Frog Robotics, http://www.bluefrogrobotics.com/en/buddy/ (accessed February 19, 2018).

9. Isis Almeida and Corinne Gretler, "Don't Call It Pink Chocolate," *Bloomberg*, https://www.bloomberg.com/news/articles/2017-09-05/chocolate-gets-first-addition-to-color-palette-in-80-years-ruby (accessed February 19, 2018).

10. Lanre Bakare, "The Best a Man Can Get? Dollar Shave Club, Harry's Lead Shaving's Young Turks," *The Guardian*, October 20, 2015, http://www.theguardian.com/fashion/2015/oct/20/dollar-shave-club-harrys-shaving-gillette-young-turks-razors (accessed February 19, 2018); Dollar Shave Club, https://www.dollarshaveclub.com/ (accessed February 19, 2018).

11 Christoph Fuchs and Martin Schreier, "Customer Empowerment in New Product Development," *Journal of Product Innovation Management* 28, 1 (2011): pp. 17–31.

12 Arina Soukhoroukova, Martin Spann, and Bernd Skiera, "Sourcing, Filtering, and Evaluating New Product Ideas: An Empirical Exploration of the Performance of Idea Markets," *Journal of Product Innovation Management* 29, 1 (2012): pp. 100–112.

13 Christoph Fuchs and Martin Schreier, "Customer Empowerment in New Product Development," *Journal of Product Innovation Management* 28, 1 (2011): pp. 17–31.

14 Madison Flager, "Exclusive: Lay's Debuts Its Next Potato Chip Flavor," *Delish,* October 10, 2017, http://www.delish.com/food-news/news/a56027/2017-lays-next-new-potato-chip-flavor/ (accessed February 19, 2017).

15 Kaleidoscope, http://kascope.com/ (accessed February 19, 2018).

16 Melissa McCart, "Chipotle Rolls Out Queso at NYC Test Kitchen," *Eater NY,* July 10, 2017, https://ny.eater.com/2017/7/10/15945712/chipotle-queso-margaritas-chelsea (accessed February 19, 2018).

17 Chloe Sorvino, "Inside Billionaire James Dyson's Reinvention Factory: From Vacuums to Hair Dryers and Now Batteries," *Forbes,* August 24, 2016, http://www.forbes.com/sites/chloesorvino/2016/08/24/james-dyson-exclusive-top-secret-reinvention-factory/#1172b604372c (accessed February 15, 2018).

18 JoAndrea Hoegg and Joseph W. Alba, "Seeing Is Believing (Too Much): The Influence of Product Form on Perceptions of Functional Performance," *Journal of Product Innovation Management* 28, 3 (2011): pp. 346–359.

19 Bob Guiliano, "KFC Test Markets Its New Hot-Honey Chicken Locally," *Bronx Times,* November 17, 2017, https://www.bxtimes.com/stories/2017/46/46-kfchothoney-2017-11-17-bx.html (accessed February 19, 2018).

20 Charles Passy, "How Fast-Food Chains Cook up New Menu Items," *The Wall Street Journal,* August 24, 2015, http://www.wsj.com/articles/how-fast-food-chains-cook-up-new-menu-items-1440381706 (accessed February 19, 2018).

21 Roger J. Calantone and C. Anthony Di Benedetto, "The Role of Lean Launch Execution and Launch Timing on New Product Performance," *Journal of the Academy of Marketing Science,* June 2011, http://rd.springer.com/article/10.1007/s11747-011-0258-1 (accessed January 20, 2014).

22 Denise DiMeglio, "Publix vs. Trader Joe's, Costco vs. BJ's, Target vs. Walmart: ACSI Scores Show Which Retailers Customers Prefer," American Customer Satisfaction Index, press release, February 27, 2018, http://www.theacsi.org/news-and-resources/press-releases/press-2018/press-release-retail-2017 (accessed March 8, 2018).

23 "Consumer Shipping Benchmarks by Industry," ACSI, www.theacsi.org/index.php?option=com_content&view=article&id=147&catid=&Itemid=212&i=Consumer+Shipping (accessed February 21, 2018).

24 Jeanne Bliss, "Trader Joe's Customer Experience Obsession," *1 to 1,* May 24, 2012, www.1to1media.com/weblog/2012/05/trader_joes_customer_experienc.html (accessed February 21, 2018); David DiSalvo, "What Trader Joe's Knows about Making Your Brain Happy," *Forbes,* February 19, 2015, http://www.forbes.com/sites/daviddisalvo/2015/02/19/what-trader-joes-knows-about-making-your-brain-happy/ (accessed February 21, 2018).

25 Marco Bertini, Elie Ofek, and Dan Ariely, "The Impact of Add-On Features on Consumer Product Evaluations," *Journal of Consumer Research* 36, 1 (2009): pp. 17–28.

26 Neeru Paharia, Jill Avery, and Anat Keinen, "Positioning Brands against Large Competitors to Increase Sales," *Journal of Marketing Research* 51, 6 (2014): pp. 647–656.

27 Deanna Ting, "Wyndham Is Repositioning All 16 of Its Brands to Appeal to Anyone and Everyone," *Skift,* June 8, 2016, https://skift.com/2016/06/08/wyndham-is-repositioning-all-16-of-its-brands-to-appeal-to-anyone-and-everyone/ (accessed February 16, 2017).

28 Scott Mervis, "As Sales Decline and Stores Discontinue Them, Should You Hang on to Your CDs?" *Pittsburg Post-Gazette,* February 22, 2018, http://www.post-gazette.com/ae/music/2018/02/21/CD-compact-disc-sales-decline-Juke-Records-Billboard-Best-Buy-Target/stories/201802210158 (accessed February 22, 2018).

29 Cutco, "The Cutco Story," https://www.cutco.com/ (accessed August 1, 2018); Dan Miner, "Long an Olean Anchor, Cutco Corp. Keeps Growing," *Buffalo Business First,* May 4, 2018, https://www.bizjournals.com/buffalo/news/2018/05/04/long-an-olean-anchor-cutco-corp-keeps-growing.html (accessed August 1, 2018); Bob Clark, "New, Former Cutco Heads Look to the Future," *Olean Times Herald,* December 3, 2017, http://www.oleantimesherald.com/news/new-former-cutco-heads-look-to-the-future/article_a7675356-d7d6-11e7-82da-3b9402086723.html (accessed August 1, 2018); John S. McClenahen, "The Cutting Edge: Cutco Cutlery Corp. Manufactures Knives in the United States to Maintain Quality and Flexibility," *Industry Week* 255.4, p. 11, April 2006, http://link.galegroup.com/apps/doc/A145161140/ITOF?u=naal_aub&sid=ITOF&xid=6eb7ea52 (accessed August 1, 2018); Barbara E. Stefano, "Spotlight: Cutco Cutlery," *Feast,* December 4, 2013, http://www.feastmagazine.com/dine-out/spot-light/article_7814337e-5d39-11e3-909b-0019bb30f31a.html (accessed August 1, 2018); Kavita Kumar, "Cutco Sharpens Its Business by Adding Retail Stores," *St. Louis Post-Dispatch*, April 27, 2012, https://www.stltoday.com/business/local/cutco-sharpens-its-business-by-adding-retail-stores/article_707e846c-8fbc-11e1-a44a-0019bb30f31a.html (accessed August 1, 2018); Karen Dybis, "Knife Seller Aims to Keep an Edge," *The Detroit News,* April 12, 2013, https://advance.lexis.com/document/index?crid=fd685b54-4284-47df-bb22-421d70cc90a1&pdpermalink=45f47ae0-2d07-4192-8256-e49ea25f4f1b&pdmfid=1516831&pdisurlapi=true (accessed August 1, 2018).

30 Lisa Gutierrez, "Hold the Cheese: Taco Bell Is Testing Quesadillas Stuffed with Twix and Kit Kats," *Kansas City Star,* October 24, 2017, http://www.kansascity.com/living/liv-columns-blogs/chow-town/article180629541.html (accessed February 22, 2018); Jonathan Ringen, "Epic Cheese Pull: How Taco Bell Nailed Its Innovative New Quesalupa," *Fast Company Create,* February 7, 2016, www.fastcocreate.com/3056059/most-innovative-companies/taco-bell-for-combining-corn-beans-meat-and-cheese-into-genius (accessed February 10, 2016); Michelle Castillo, "The Mystery Behind Taco Bell's Super Bowl 50 Ad," *CNBC,* February 5, 2016, www.cnbc.com/2016/02/05/the-mystery-behind-taco-bells-super-bowl-50-ad.html (accessed February 10, 2016); Beth Kowitt, "Fortune's 8 Most Extreme Foods of 2015," *Fortune,* January 14, 2016, http://fortune.com/2016/01/14/olive-garden-burger-king-extreme-food (accessed February 10, 2016); Tim Nudd, "Taco Bell Cleverly Crashed These 5 Local Super Bowl Ads with Its Quesalupa," *Adweek,* February 9, 2016, www.adweek.com/adfreak/taco-bell-cleverly-crashed-these-5-local-super-bowl-ads-its-quesalupa-169541 (accessed February 10, 2016).

Chapter 13

1 Ingrid Lunden, "Spotify Expands Merch to Beauty Products, Sells Out Tickets for Who We Be," *TechCrunch,* November 13, 2017, https://techcrunch.com/2017/11/13/spotify-expands-merch-to-beauty-products-sells-out-tickets-for-who-we-be/ (accessed February 26, 2018); Janko Roettgers,

"Microsoft Discontinues Groove Music, Partners with Spotify Instead," *Variety,* October 2, 2017, http://variety.com/2017/digital/news/microsoft-groove-music-deal-1202578189/ (accessed February 26, 2018); Hannah Carp, "Apple Music's Long Game: Why Jimmy Iovine Thinks They're 'Not Even Close' to Success with Streaming," *Billboard,* September 28, 2017, http://www.billboard.com/biz/articles/7981590/apple-musics-long-game-why-jimmy-iovine-thinks-theyre-not-even-close-to-success (accessed February 26, 2018); Sarah Lacy, "How Daniel Became Goliath," Startups.co, March 12, 2017, www.startups.co/articles/how-daniel-became-goliath (accessed February 26, 2018); www.spotify.com (accessed February 26, 2018).

2   Leonard L. Berry and A. Parasuraman, *Marketing Services: Competing through Quality* (New York: Free Press, 1991), p. 5.

3   Rhema Business Services, www.facebook.com/Homesourcing (accessed February 26, 2018).

4   Raymond P. Fisk, Stephen J. Grove, and Joby John, *Interactive Services Marketing* (Boston: Houghton Mifflin, 2008), p. 25.

5   "Your Satisfaction Matters," La Quinta Inns & Suites, http://www.lq.com/en/landing-pages/satisfaction-guarantee.html (accessed February 26, 2018).

6   K. Douglas Hoffman and John E. G. Bateson, *Services Marketing: Concepts, Strategies, and Cases,* 5th ed., (Mason, OH: Cengage Learning, 2017); Valarie A. Zeithaml, A. Parasuraman, and Leonard L. Berry, *Delivering Quality Service: Balancing Customer Perceptions and Expectations* (New York: Free Press, 1990).

7   J. Paul Peter and James H. Donnelly, *A Preface to Marketing Management* (Burr Ridge, IL: Irwin/McGraw-Hill, 2018).

8   Tim Nudd, "10 Things We Learned about Wendy's Twitter from Its Reddit AMA," *Adweek,* December 15, 2017, http://www.adweek.com/creativity/10-things-we-learned-about-wendys-twitter-from-its-reddit-ama/ (accessed February 26, 2018).

9   Michael D. Hartline and O. C. Ferrell, "Service Quality Implementation: The Effects of Organizational Socialization and Managerial Actions of Customer Contact Employee Behavior," *Marketing Science Institute Report,* no. 93–122 (Cambridge, MA: Marketing Science Institute, 1993).

10   David Kerly, Whitney Lloyd, Nathan A. Luna, and Jeffrey Cook, "Behind the Scenes with Southwest Airlines' Social Media 'Listening Center,'" *ABCNews,* November 21, 2017, http://abcnews.go.com/US/scenes-southwest-airlines-social-media-listening-center/story?id=51297908 (accessed February 26, 2018); Kare Anderson, "The Priceless Power of Socially Empowered Employees," *Forbes,* August 11, 2013, www.forbes.com/sites/kareanderson/2013/08/11/3000 (accessed February 26, 2018).

11   Hoffman and Bateson, *Services Marketing: Concepts, Strategies, and Cases,* 5th ed.

12   Fisk, Grove, and John, *Interactive Services Marketing,* p. 91.

13   Tracey Lien, "How Food Delivery Apps Have Changed the Game for Restaurants," *Los Angeles Times,* March 17, 2017, http://www.latimes.com/business/technology/la-fi-tn-app-restaurants-20170313-story.html (accessed February 27, 2018).

14   Stitch Fix, https://www.stitchfix.com/ (accessed February 27, 2018).

15   David Henry, "What's Zelle? Banks Hope the Commercials Get Customers to Notice the App," *Los Angeles Times,* January 29, 2018, https://www.reuters.com/article/us-usa-banks-payments-zelle/whats-zelle-banks-hope-commercials-get-customers-to-notice-the-app-idUSKBN1FI0GB (accessed February 27, 2018); Zelle on YouTube, https://www.youtube.com/channel/UCB1MzN2pFtOWKbd0Cks-Uyg/videos (accessed February 27, 2018).

16   Ashley Rodriguez, "Chase Relaunches Website with Focus on Branded Content, Simplicity," *Advertising Age,* July 20, 2015, http://adage.com/article/cmo-strategy/chase-unveils-website-redesign-brings-branded-content-homepage/299542/ (accessed February 27, 2018).

17   Bailey Bennett, "Spirit Airlines Is Turning to Disney for Help Improving Its Customer Service," *Travel + Leisure,* November 21, 2017, http://www.travelandleisure.com/airlines-airports/spirit-airlines-disney-institute-training (accessed February 27, 2018).

18   Hoffman and Bateson, *Services Marketing.*

19   Josh Cohen, "San Francisco Is Taking Demand-Based Parking Prices Citywide," *NextCity,* December 7, 2017, https://nextcity.org/daily/entry/san-francisco-demand-based-pricing (accessed February 27, 2018).

20   Samantha Raphelson, "High-End London Restaurant Launches Uber-Style Pricing Model," *NPR: The Salt,* February 6, 2018, https://www.npr.org/sections/thesalt/2018/02/06/583692650/high-end-london-restaurant-launches-uber-style-pricing-model (accessed February 27, 2018).

21   Brad Adgate, "The Future of Television Is a la Carte," *Forbes,* July 17, 2017, https://www.forbes.com/sites/bradadgate/2017/07/17/the-future-of-television-is-a-la-carte/#1170e1f47a81 (accessed February 27, 2018).

22   Zeithaml, Parasuraman, and Berry, *Delivering Quality Service.*

23   "#WellActually, Americans Say Customer Service Is Better Than Ever," American Express, news release, December 15, 2017, http://about.americanexpress.com/news/pr/2017/wellactually-americans-say-customer-service-better-than-ever.aspx (accessed February 27, 2018).

24   Valarie A. Zeithaml, "How Consumer Evaluation Processes Differ between Goods and Services," in *Marketing of Services,* eds., James H. Donnelly and William R. George (Chicago: American Marketing Association, 1981), pp. 186–190.

25   A. Parasuraman, Leonard L. Berry, and Valarie A. Zeithaml, "An Empirical Examination of Relationships in an Extended Service Quality Model," *Marketing Science Institute Working Paper Services,* no. 90–112 (Cambridge, MA: Marketing Science Institute, 1990), p. 29.

26   Steve Evans, "Visible Ink: The Mark of the Future Accountant?" *Accounting, Auditing & Accountability Journal* 25, 7 (2012): pp. 1234–1235.

27   Valarie A. Zeithaml, Leonard L. Berry, and A. Parasuraman, "Communication and Control Processes in the Delivery of Service Quality," *Journal of Marketing* 52, 2 (1988): pp. 35–48.

28   Valarie A. Zeithaml, Leonard L. Berry, and A. Parasuraman, "The Nature and Determinants of Customer Expectations of Service," *Journal of the Academy of Marketing Science* 21, 1 (1993): pp. 1–12.

29   "I'm Happy, You're Happy: Yet More Evidence that Satisfied Employees Make Satisfied, and Loyal, Customers," *Customer Service Psychology Research,* June 3, 2011, http://customerservicepsychology.wordpress.com/2011/06/03/i%e2%80%99m-happy-you%e2%80%99re-happy-yet-more-evidence-that-satisfied-employees-make-satisfied-and-loyal-customers (accessed March 1, 2018).

30   ACCION International, http://www.accion.org/ (accessed March 1, 2018).

31   Philip Kotler, *Marketing for Nonprofit Organizations,* 2nd ed. (Englewood Cliffs, NJ: Prentice-Hall, 1982), p. 37.

32   "Pacer's National Bullying Prevention Center," Pacer, www.pacer.org/bullying/about (accessed March 1, 2018).

33 Nick Morpus, "5 Nonprofits with Successful Content Marketing Campaigns," Capterra Nonprofit Technology Blog, April 21, 2017, https://blog.capterra.com/nonprofits-successful-content-marketing-campaigns/ (accessed March 1, 2018).

34 Ben Paynter, "How Will the Rise of Crowd-funding Reshape How We Give to Charity?" *Fast Company*, March 13, 2017, https://www.fastcompany.com/3068534/how-will-the-rise-of-crowdfunding-reshape-how-we-give-to-charity-2 (accessed March 1, 2018).

35 Caroline Earle, "Setting the Trend for the Future of Gyms with Boston-Based Strength Coach, Mike Boyle," *BostInno,* February 17, 2014, http://bostinno.streetwise.co/2014/02/17/interview-with-boston-coach-mike-boyle/ (accessed February 12, 2016); Jenni Whalen, "Q&A: Boston Trainer Mike Boyle," *Boston Magazine,* June 13, 2013, www.bostonmagazine.com/health/blog/2013/06/13/mike-boyle/ (accessed February 12, 2016); MBSC, http://www.bodybyboyle.com/ (accessed March 1, 2018); Cengage Learning, *Mike Boyle Strength and Conditioning* video.

36 Megan Nichols, "FedEx Delivery Service to Reach 34 Million People," *Memphis Business Journal* (October 9, 2017), www.bizjournals.com/memphis/news/2017/10/09/fedex-delivery-service-to-reach-34-million-people.html; Ron Maxey, "FedEx Worker Delivers Generators Ahead of Hurricane Irma," *The Commercial Appeal (Memphis, TX),* September 16, 2017, www.usnews.com/news/best-states/florida/articles/2017-09-16/fedex-worker-delivers-generators-ahead-of-hurricane-irma; Mary Schlangenstein and Michael Sasso, "FedEx, UPS Want to Steer Santa's Packages to the Local Drugstore," *Bloomberg,* December 14, 2017, www.bloomberg.com/news/articles/2017-12-14/fedex-ups-want-to-steer-santa-s-packages-to-the-local-drugstore; www.theacsi.org; www.fedex.com.

37 John Kell, "This Is the New Way Nike Is Going After Women," *Fortune,* January 28, 2016, http://fortune.com/2016/01/28/nike-youtube-margot-lily/ (accessed February 16, 2016); Matthew Kish, "A Q&A with Nike CEO Mark Parker, the PBJ's 2015 Executive of the Year," *Portland Business Journal,* January 29, 2016, www.bizjournals.com/portland/blog/threads_and_laces/2016/01/a-q-a-with-nike-ceo-mark-parker-the-pbjs-2015.html (accessed February 16, 2016); Jacob Pramuk, "Nike CEO: How We'll Reach $50B in Sales," *CNBC,* October 14, 2015, www.cnbc.com/2015/10/14/nike-ceo-how-well-reach-50b-in-sales.html (accessed February 16, 2016); Matt Townsend, "Nike Exceeds Estimates on New Products, Market-Share Gains," *Bloomberg,* June 25, 2015, www.bloomberg.com/news/articles/2015-06-25/nike-exceeds-profit-estimates-on-new-products-domestic-growth (accessed February 16, 2016); Elaine Low, "Nike Is Ramping Up Its Digital Strategy: What Does That Mean?" *Investor's Business Daily,* February 10, 2016, www.investors.com/news/nike-is-ramping-up-its-digital-strategy-what-does-that-mean (accessed February 16, 2016); Josh Peter, "Phil Knight Sees Finish Line as Nike's Leader," *USA Today,* September 30, 2015, www.usatoday.com/story/sports/2015/09/30/phil-knight-nike-michael-jordan-stepping-down-2016/72885302/ (accessed February 16, 2016); "Bill Bowerman: Nike's Original Innovator," *Nike News,* September 2, 2015, http://news.nike.com/news/bill-bowerman-nike-s-original-innovator (accessed February 16, 2016); "Nike CEO Mark Parker and Serena Williams on Competition: Tennis Great, Serena Williams, and Nike's Leader, Mark Parker, Trade Tales of Collaboration and Competition," *Fast Company,* January 27, 2016, www.fastcompany.com/3055401/nike-ceo-mark-parker-and-serena-williams-on-competition (accessed February 16, 2016); Megan Garber, "How Nike Turned Running Shoes into Fashion," *The Atlantic,* July 6, 2015, www.theatlantic.com/entertainment/archive/2015/07/how-nike-turned-sneakers-into-fashion/397610/ (accessed February 16, 2016); https://about.nike.com/ (accessed March 1, 2018).

Chapter 14

1 Tom Higgins, "Snowboarding Helps Fanatics Sell Thousands of Team USA Jackets," *Promo Marketing Magazine,* February 15, 2018, http://magazine.promomarketing.com/article/snowboarding-fanatics-team-usa-jackets/ (accessed February 18, 2018); Aliko Carter, "Obsolete Jerseys a Fear No More as American Express Partners with Fanatics," *Forbes,* January 25, 2018, https://www.forbes.com/sites/alikocarter/2018/01/25/obsolete-jerseys-a-fear-no-more-as-american-express-partners-with-fanatics/#59af6b7c3663 (accessed February 18, 2018); Ebon Novy-Williams, "Sports Champion T-Shirts, Delivered Just After the Buzzer," *Bloomberg,* March 15, 2017, https://www.bloomberg.com/news/articles/2017-03-15/sports-champion-t-shirts-delivered-just-after-the-buzzer (accessed March 22, 2017); Danny Ecker, "Retailers Prepare for Late-Night Cubs Frenzy," *Chicago Business,* November 2, 2016, www.chicagobusiness.com/article/20161102/BLOGS04/161109958/retailers-prepare-for-late-night-cubs-frenzy (accessed March 22, 2017); Tamara Chuang, "Prepping for Super Bowl Victory Means Weighing Economics of Losing," *Denver Post,* February 4, 2016, www.denverpost.com/2016/02/04/prepping-for-super-bowl-victory-means-weighing-economics-of-losing (accessed March 22, 2017).

2 Merrill Douglas, "Creating The Internet of Everything," *Inbound Logistics,* February 20, 2018, www.inboundlogistics.com/cms/article/creating-the-internet-of-everything/ (accessed March 10, 2018).

3 Mark Cox, "Industrial Technology and the Supply Chain: Is 2018 the Year We Turn a Corner?" *Inbound Logistics,* February 12, 2018, www.inboundlogistics.com/cms/article/industrial-technology-and-the-supply-chain-is-2018-the-year-we-turn-a-corner/ (accessed March 10, 2018).

4 Paul Vachon, "Golf Ball Maker Hits Supply Chain Sweet Spot," *Inbound Logistics,* September 21, 2017, www.inboundlogistics.com/cms/article/golf-ball-maker-hits-supply-chain-sweet-spot%20/ (accessed March 10, 2018).

5 Merrill Douglas, "Digital Supply Chain: What's Your Reality?" *Inbound Logistics,* February 22, 2018, www.inboundlogistics.com/cms/article/digital-supply-chain-whats-your-reality/ (accessed March 10, 2018).

6 Erica E. Phillips, "Consumers Triggering Major Changes in Retail Supply Chains," *The Wall Street Journal,* May 22, 2015, www.wsj.com/articles/consumers-driving-changes-in-retail-supply-chains-1432314236 (accessed March 11, 2016).

7 Tibbr, "Overview," www.tibbr.com/what-is-tibbr/overview/microblogging.php (accessed March 11, 2016); Yammer, "Overview," https://about.yammer.com (accessed March 11, 2016).

8 Patrick Burnson, "Supply Chain Managers Told to Prepare for Demand Surge in 2014," *Supply Chain Management Review,* November 16, 2013, www.scmr.com/article/supply_chain_managers_told_to_prepare_for_demand_surge_in_2014 (accessed March 11, 2016).

9 Lisa R. Melsted, "Delivering with Data: How Logistics Companies Are Shipping on Time," *Forbes,* February 16, 2015, www.forbes.com/sites/samsungbusiness/2015/02/16/delivering-with-data-how-logistics-companies-are-shipping-on-time/ (accessed March 11, 2016); Christina Ng, "Soap Opera: Amazon Moves In with P&G," *The Wall Street Journal,* October 14, 2013, http://online.wsj.com/news/articles/SB10001424052702304330904579135840230674458? (accessed March 11, 2016).

10 "Solution Highlights," MercuryGate, www.mercurygate.com/solution_highlights (accessed March 11, 2016); April Joyner,

"Best Industries 2012: Supply Chain | 6 Logistics Startups on the Move," *Inc.*, www .inc.com/ss/best-industries-2012/april-joyner/ supply-chain-management-companies-6-that-fill-a-niche (accessed March 11, 2016).

11 Jonathan Littman, "Supply-Chain Miseries Doom Target in Canada," *Supply Chain 24/7*, January 17, 2015, www.supplychain247.com/ article/supply_chain_miseries_doom_target_ in_canada (accessed March 11, 2016).

12 David Zax, "How Xerox Evolved from Copier Company to Creative Powerhouse," *Fast Company*, December 11, 2013, www .fastcompany.com/3023240/most-creative-people/dreaming-together-how-xerox-keeps-big-ideas-flowing (accessed March 14, 2016).

13 Applied Industrial Technologies, Inc., www .applied.com (accessed March 14, 2016).

14 Leo Aspinwall, "The Marketing Characteristics of Goods," in *Four Marketing Theories* (Boulder: University of Colorado Press, 1961), pp. 27–32.

15 Deloitte, "2016 Global Manufacturing Competitiveness Ranking," http://www2.deloitte .com/global/en/pages/about-deloitte/articles/ global-manufacturing-competitiveness-index .html (accessed March 15, 2016).

16 "2016 Global Manufacturing Competitiveness Index," *Deloitte*, https://www2.deloitte .com/global/en/pages/manufacturing/articles/ global-manufacturing-competitiveness-index .html (accessed March 3, 2017).

17 Adam Vaccaro, "Tell Your Customers about Your Responsible Supply Chain," *Inc.*, November 13, 2013, www.inc.com/adam-vaccaro/supply-chain-corporate-social-responsibility.html (accessed March 15, 2016).

18 Suppliers Partnership for the Environment, www.supplierspartnership.org (accessed March 15, 2016).

19 IGA, www.iga.com/about.aspx (accessed March 15, 2016).

20 Wroe Alderson, *Dynamic Marketing Behavior* (Homewood, IL: Irwin, 1965), p. 239.

21 Adam Rapp, Lauren Skinner Beitelspacher, Dhruv Grewal, and Douglas E. Hughes, "Understanding Social Media Effects across Seller, Retailer, and Consumer Interactions," *Journal of the Academy of Marketing Science*, 41, 31 (2013): pp. 547–566.

22 M. Kelly Cunningham, "Reducing Channel Conflict," *Journal of Marketing Development & Competitiveness* 7, 1 (2013): pp. 78–83.

23 "Keeping It Under Your Hat," *The Economist*, April 16, 2016, www.economist.com/news/ business-and-finance/21696911-tech-fashion-old-management-idea-back-vogue-vertical-integration-gets-new (accessed March 3, 2017); "Tesla Will Start Charging Money to

Use Its Supercharging Stations," *Los Angeles Times*, November 7, 2016, www .latimes.com/business/autos/la-fi-hy-tesla-charging-20161107-story.html (accessed March 3, 2017).

24 "Inditex Press Dossier," www.inditex.com/ en/media/press_dossier (accessed March 21, 2016), p. 6.

25 Clare O'Connor, "How Ace Hardware Turned Corner Stores into a $4.7 Billion Co-op," *Forbes*, March 2, 2015, www.forbes.com/ sites/clareoconnor/2015/02/11/how-ace-hardware-turned-corner-stores-into-a-4-7-billion co-op/ (accessed March 21, 2016).

26 "Sherwin Williams to Buy Valspar for $11.3 Billion," *Fortune*, March 20, 2016, http://fortune.com/2016/03/20/sherwin-williams-valspar/ (accessed March 21, 2016).

27 Noel Datko, "Supply Chain Basics: Managing Third Party Logistics and Embracing Technology," *Direct Selling News*, January 1, 2015, http://directsellingnews.com/index .php/view/supply_chain_basics_ managing_third_party_logistics_and_ embracing_technology#.VVzQQfnnuUk (accessed March 21, 2016); Karen M. Kroll, "3PLs Up the Ante," *Inbound Logistics*, January 2017, www.inboundlogistics.com/ cms/article/3pls-up-the-ante/ (accessed March 6, 2017).

28 Sarwant Singh, "Future of Logistics: Five Technologies That Will Self-Orchestrate the Supply Chain" *Forbes*, September 22, 2016, https://www.forbes.com/sites/ sarwantsingh/2016/09/22/future-of-logistics-5-technologies-that-will-self-orchestrate-the-supply-chain/#965b60b1d2b1 (accessed March 6, 2017).

29 Adam Lashinsky, "The Cutting Edge of Care," *Fortune*, March 9, 2015, http://fortune. com/2015/03/09/dollar-shave-club/ (accessed March 21, 2016); Darren Dahl, "Riding the Momentum Created by a Cheeky Video" *The Wall Street Journal*, April 11, 2013, www .nytimes.com/2013/04/11/business/ smallbusiness/dollar-shave-club-from-viral-video-to-real-business.html (accessed May 22, 2015).

30 Mark B. Solomon, "Hospital Chain Trinity Health, XPO Partner to Take Supply Chain in House," *DC Velocity*, March 9, 2016, www .dcvelocity.com/articles/20160309-hospital-chain-trinity-health-xpo-partner-to-take-supply-chain-in-house/ (accessed February 18, 2018).

31 Christopher Bjork, "Zara Builds Its Business around RFID," *The Wall Street Journal*, September 16, 2014, www.wsj.com/articles/ at-zara-fast-fashion-meets-smarter-inventory-1410884519?autologin=y (accessed March 6, 2017); "RFID Talking Blog," *RFID*

24-7, March 17, 2016, http://rfid24-7. com/2016/03/17/inditex-continues-rfid-rollout-to-2000-zara-locations/ (accessed March 6, 2017).

32 Bill C. Hardgrave and Justin Patton, "2016 State of RFID Adoption among U.S. Apparel Retailers, RFID Lab," Auburn University, 2016.

33 Distribution Unlimited Inc., http:// distributionunlimited.com/operations.php (accessed March 21, 2016).

34 Marilyn Moritz, "Robots Work Alongside Humans at Amazon Distribution Center," KSAT News, April 17, 2015, www.ksat.com/ content/pns/ksat/news/2015/04/17/robots-work-alongside-humans-at-amazon-distribution-center.html (accessed March 21, 2016); Marcus Wohlsen, "A Rare Peek Inside Amazon's Massive Wish-Fulfilling Machine," *Wired*, June 16, 2014, www.wired .com/2014/06/inside-amazon-warehouse/ (accessed March 21, 2016).

35 Sarah Perez, "Walmart Invests in E-Commerce, Next-Day Delivery Expansions with Two New Fulfillment Centers," *Tech Crunch*, October 15, 2014, http://techcrunch .com/2014/10/15/walmart-invests-in-e-commerce-next-day-delivery-expansions-with-two-new-fulfillment-centers (accessed March 21, 2016).

36 Maxim Vanhencxthoven, Michael Zimmerman, Balika Sonthalia, Sean T. Monahan, and Jeffrey Ward, "2017 State of Logistics Report," https://www.atkearney .com/transportation-travel/article?/a/2017-state-of-logistics-report-article (accessed March 19, 2018).

37 David Hummels and Georg Schaur, "Time as a Trade Barrier," *National Bureau of Economic Research*, January 2012, No. 17758, papers.nber.org/papers/w17758#fromrss (accessed March 21, 2016).

38 Expeditors International, "Our Company," https://www.expeditors.com/about-us/ company (accessed March 6, 2017).

39 International Cocoa Organization, "How Exactly Is Cocoa Harvested?" May 26, 1998, https://www.icco.org/faq/58-cocoa-harvesting/130-how-exactly-is-cocoa-harvested.html (accessed June 19, 2018); The Cocoa Exchange, "Sustainable and Responsibly-Sourced Cocoa," http://www .mytcesite.com/pws/homeoffice/tabs/ sustainable-cocoa.aspx (accessed June 19, 2018); Ashley Beyer, "The Cocoa Exchange Visits Fresh Living," KUTV, May 31, 2018, http://kutv.com/features/fresh-living/the-cocoa-exchange-visits-fresh-living (accessed June 19, 2018); Oliver Nieburg, "'The Cocoa Exchange': Mars Sets Up E-Commerce Party Program for

Chocolate," *Confectionary News*, May 16, 2017, https://www.confectionerynews.com/Article/2017/05/15/Cocoa-Exchange-Mars-sets-up-e-commerce-party-program-for-chocolate (accessed June 19, 2018); Keith Loria, "Candy Maker Mars Gets into the Party Business," *Food Dive*, May 10, 2017, https://www.fooddive.com/news/candy-maker-mars-gets-into-the-party-business/442160/ (accessed June 19, 2018); Bernie Pacyniak, "One-on-One: Berta de Pablos-Barbier, President of Mars Wrigley Confectionary U.S.," *Candy Industry*, November 1, 2017, https://www.candyindustry.com/articles/87940-one-on-one-berta-de-pablos-barbier-president-of-mars-wrigley-confectionery-us (accessed June 19, 2018).

40 Archer Daniels Midland Company, "ADM Expands Portfolio with Range of Wheat Protein Concentrates," November 28, 2017, https://www.adm.com/news/news-releases/adm-expands-portfolio-with-range-of-wheat-protein-concentrates (accessed December 2, 2017); Tony Reid, "ADM Planning Layoffs," *Herald & Review* (July 20, 2017), http://herald-review.com/business/agriculture/adm-planning-layoffs/article_26e525e5-f10d-5a5f-a4ae-fab3958340d8.html (accessed December 2, 2017); Javier Blas, "Commodity Trading Arm in Sleepy Swiss Village Trips up ADM Again," *Chicago Tribune*, February 8, 2017, www.chicagotribune.com/business/ct-archer-daniels-midland-commodity-trading-20170208-story.html (accessed December 5, 2017); "Partnerships across the Supply Chain Drive Continuous Improvement, Helping Meet Corporate Commitments," *Field to Market*, December 19, 2016, https://fieldtomarket.org/case-studies-series/partnerships-across-supply-chain/ (accessed December 5, 2017); Leah Guffey, "ADM Helps Unilever Bring Out the Best," *AgWired*, September 18, 2014, http://agwired.com/2014/09/18/adm-helps-unilever-bring-out-the-best/ (accessed July 6, 2015); Paul Demery, "Archer Daniels Midland Cultivates Its Handling of Purchase Orders and Invoices," *Digital Commerce 360*, September 9, 2014, https://www.digitalcommerce360.com/2014/09/09/archer-daniels-midland-cleans-its-handling-purchase-orders/ (accessed May 10, 2018); Gregory Meyer, "Archer Daniels Midland Buys Wild Flavors for €2.3 bn," *Financial Times*, July 7, 2014, www.ft.com/intl/cms/s/0/636b8732-05b4-11e4-9baa-00144feab7de.html#axzz3LYqkltWg (accessed July 6, 2015); Archer Daniels Midland, www.adm.com (accessed December 23, 2017); "ADM Announces Layoffs across the Country: 175 in Decatur," IllinoisHomePage.net, www.illinoishomepage.net/news/local-news/adm-annouces-layoffs-across-the-country-175-in-decatur/93355620 (accessed December 23, 2017).

Chapter 15

1   Suzette Parmley, "TJMaxx/HomeGoods Combo Store Marks Sunday Opening in South Philly," *Philadelphia Inquirer*, October 31, 2017, www.philly.com/philly/business/retail/tj-maxxhomegoods-combo-store-marks-sunday-opening-in-south-philly-20171031.html (accessed March 23, 2018); Laura Klepacki, "Why Off-Price Retail Is Rising as Department Stores Are Sinking," *Retail Dive*, February 1, 2017, www.retaildive.com/news/why-off-price-retail-is-rising-as-department-stores-are-sinking/434454/ (accessed March 23, 2018); Lauren Thomas, "The Owner of HomeGoods Just Opened Its First Home-Sense Store. Here's How the Two Compare," *CNBC*, August 21, 2017, www.cnbc.com/2017/08/21/tjx-the-owner-of-homegoods-just-opened-its-first-homesense.html (accessed March 23, 2018).

2   "2015 SUSB Annual Data Tables by Establishment Industry," U.S. Census Bureau, January 2018, https://www2.census.gov/programs-surveys/susb/tables/2015/us_6digitnaics_2015.xlsx (accessed March 20, 2018); "Industry Data," Bureau of Economic Analysis, November 2, 2017, https://bea.gov/iTable/iTable.cfm?reqid=51&step=51&isuri=1&5114=a&5102=1#reqid=51&step=51&isuri=1&5114=a&5102=1 (accessed March 20, 2018).

3   "Domino's AnyWare," Domino's Pizza, https://anyware.dominos.com/ (accessed March 20, 2018).

4   Rebecca Bundhun, "IKEA's India Launch Takes Shape," *The National* (AE), May 27, 2017, https://www.thenational.ae/business/ikea-s-india-launch-takes-shape-1.15035 (accessed March 20, 2018); Vicky Huang, "Tesla to Become Latest American Company to Target India's Monstrous Growth," *The Street*, February 11, 2017, https://www.thestreet.com/story/13994605/1/tesla-to-become-the-latest-american-company-to-target-india-s-monstrous-growth.html (accessed March 20, 2018).

5   "E-commerce Takes Off," *The Economist*, October 26, 2017, https://www.economist.com/news/special-report/21730546-e-commerce-transforming-business-and-daily-life-mostly-better-says-charlotte (accessed March 23, 2018); "A Brief Overview of the Global Ecommerce Market," *eMarketer*, July 13, 2017, https://retail.emarketer.com/article/brief-overview-of-global-ecommerce-market/59690010ebd40005284d5cc5 (accessed March 21, 2018).

6   "U.S. Online Retail Sales Likely to Surpass $1 Trillion by 2027: FTI," *Reuters*, October 17, 2017, https://www.reuters.com/article/us-usa-retail-internet/u-s-online-retail-sales-likely-to-surpass-1-trillion-by-2027-fti-idUSKBN1CM1LW (accessed March 20, 2018).

7   Joe Taschler and Sarah Hauer, "Online Grocery Shopping Is Revolutionizing Supermarkets," *USA Today*, October 27, 2017, https://www.usatoday.com/story/money/business/2017/10/27/online-grocery-shopping-revolutionizing-supermarkets/806496001/ (accessed March 21, 2018).

8   Lauren Thomas, "Warby Parker Aims to Run Nearly 100 Stores This Year, as Other Web Shops Follow," *CNBC*, February 15, 2018, https://www.cnbc.com/2018/02/15/as-warby-parker-approaches-100-stores-other-internet-brands-follow.html (accessed March 21, 2018).

9   Phil Wahba, "Amazon Dishes About Its First Amazon Go Cashier-Less Store," *Fortune*, March 19, 2018, http://fortune.com/2018/03/19/amazon-go/ (accessed March 21, 2018).

10 "Global Powers of Retailing 2018," *Deloitte*, https://www2.deloitte.com/global/en/pages/consumer-business/articles/global-powers-of-retailing.html (accessed March 22, 2018).

11 Warren Shoulberg, "5 Reasons Why Target Stores Look Better Than a Year Ago," *Forbes*, March 15, 2018, https://www.forbes.com/sites/warrenshoulberg/2018/03/15/5-reasons-why-target-stores-look-better-than-a-year-ago/#766122bf7664 (accessed March 22, 2018).

12 "About NACS," National Association of Convenience Stores, http://www.convenience.org/About_NACS/Pages/default.aspx (accessed March 23, 2018).

13 Angelica LaVito, "Grocery Stores Are Fighting Back Against Meal Kit Companies," *CNBC*, August 8, 2017, https://www.cnbc.com/2017/08/08/grocery-stores-are-fighting-back-against-meal-kit-companies.html (accessed March 28, 2018).

14 "Sam's Club Company Facts," Sam's Club, https://corporate.samsclub.com/our-story/company-facts (accessed March 23, 2018); "Why Become a Member," Costco, http://www.costco.com/membership-information.html (accessed March 23, 2018).

15 Ben Unglesbee, "Inside Backstage, Macy's Off-Price Hail Mary," *Retail Dive*, August 22,

2017, https://www.retaildive.com/news/inside-backstage-macys-off-price-hail-mary/503125/ (accessed March 23, 2018).

16 Mall of America, https://www.mallofamerica.com/about (accessed March 26, 2018); "Mall of America," Bloomington, https://www.bloomingtonmn.org/mallofamerica.html (accessed March 26, 2018).

17 "Franchise Business Economic Outlook for 2018," International Franchise Association Franchise Education and Research Foundation, January 2018, https://franchiseeconomy.com/files/Franchise_Business_Outlook_Jan_2018.pdf (accessed March 26, 2018).

18 Jeanne W. Ross, Cynthia M. Beath, and Ina Sebastian, "Why Nordstrom's Digital Strategy Works (and Yours Probably Doesn't)," *Harvard Business Review*, January 14, 2015, https://hbr.org/2015/01/why-nordstroms-digital-strategy-works-and-yours-probably-doesnt (accessed March 26, 2018).

19 Ann-Marie Alcantara, "How These 4 Brands Are Using Their Apps to Personalize Customer Experience," *Adweek*, February 19, 2018, http://www.adweek.com/digital/4-brands-explain-how-their-apps-improve-customer-experience/ (accessed March 26, 2018).

20 April Berthene, "Retailers Debut Augmented Reality Apps for Android," *Internet Retailer*, March 20, 2018 (accessed March 26, 2018).

21 Olga Kharif, "After Retail Stumble, Beacons Shine from Banks to Sports Arenas," *Bloomberg*, December 5, 2016, https://www.bloomberg.com/news/articles/2016-12-05/after-retail-stumble-beacons-shine-from-banks-to-sports-arenas (accessed March 26, 2018).

22 Sarah Perez, "Target Rolls out Bluetooth Beacon Technology in Stores to Power New Indoor Maps in Its App," *TechCrunch*, September 20, 2017, https://techcrunch.com/2017/09/20/target-rolls-out-bluetooth-beacon-technology-in-stores-to-power-new-indoor-maps-in-its-app/ (accessed March 26, 2018).

23 Matthew Townsend, "'Smart Mirrors' Come to the Fitting Room," *Bloomberg Businessweek*, February 16, 2017, https://www.bloomberg.com/news/articles/2017-02-16/-smart-mirrors-come-to-the-fitting-room (accessed March 26, 2018).

24 Sara Halzack, "5 New Technologies that May Change How You Shop," *The Washington Post*, January 14, 2015, http://www.washingtonpost.com/news/business/wp/2015/01/14/5-new-technologies-that-may-change-how-you-shop/ (accessed March 8, 2017).

25 Kieron Johnson, "Uniqlo's Four Secrets for Building a Global Brand," *Fortune*, October 12, 2017, http://fortune.com/2017/10/12/uniqlo-clothing-global/ (accessed March 27, 2018).

26 Rollo A. S. Grayson and Lisa S. McNeill, "Using Atmospheric Elements in Service Retailing: Understanding the Bar Environment," *Journal of Services Marketing* 23, 7 (2009): pp. 517–527.

27 Tom Buswell, "Restaurant Colors: Triggering Appetite with the Use of Colors," *Send Me the Manager*, January 21, 2013, www.sendmethemanager.com/blog/bid/199532/Restaurant-Colors-Triggering-Appetite-with-the-Use-of-Colors (accessed March 25, 2016).

28 Ibid.

29 Charles Dennis, J. Brakus, and Eleftherios Alamanos, "The Wallpaper Matters: The Influence of the Content of Digital Ads on Customer In-Store Experience," *Journal of Marketing Management* 29, 3/4 (2013): pp. 338–355.

30 "The Benefits of Direct Marketing," Humboldt Merchant Services, May 13, 2016, https://www.hbms.com/posts/the-benefits-of-direct-marketing (accessed March 27, 2018).

31 "Do Not Call Registry," Federal Trade Commission, www.donotcall.gov (accessed March 27, 2018); "What's Up with the National Do Not Call Registry," Federal Trade Commission, December 18, 2017, https://www.consumer.ftc.gov/blog/2017/12/whats-national-do-not-call-registry (accessed March 27, 2018).

32 Ibid.

33 "Latest Top 10," *Direct Selling News*, April 19, 2017, https://www.directsellingnews.com/global-100/ (accessed March 27, 2018).

34 Ibid.

35 "Industry Fact Sheets," Direct Selling Association, https://www.dsa.org/statistics-insights/factsheets (accessed March 27, 2018).

36 "25 Vending Machines You Won't Believe Exist," *MSN*, July 28, 2016, http://www.msn.com/en-in/money/gadgets/25-vending-machines-you-wont-believe-exist/ss-AA7zV4r (accessed March 27, 2018); Amina Elahi, "Snap Drops Spectacles Vending Machine at Woodfield Mall for Summer," *Chicago Tribune*, June 29, 2017, http://www.chicagotribune.com/bluesky/originals/ct-bsi-snapbot-woodfield-mall-summer-20170629-story.html (accessed March 27, 2018).

37 "Number of Firms, Number of Establishments, Employment, Annual Payroll by Enterprise Employment Size for the United States, All Industries," Statistics of U.S. Businesses (SUSB) Main, Bureau of the Census, September 29, 2017 release, https://www.census.gov/programs-surveys/susb/data/tables.html (accessed March 27, 2018).

38 "Williams Commerce Report on the Emerging Marketing Tactics Wholesalers Are Pursuing," *PR Web*, www.prweb.com/releases/2013/12/prweb11379890.htm (accessed March 27, 2018).

39 MacDonalds Consolidated, http://macdonaldsconsolidated.ca/ (accessed March 27, 2018).

40 AmerisourceBergen, www.amerisourcebergen.com/abc (accessed March 27, 2018).

41 Veronika Sonsev, "How Rebecca Minkoff Built a Fashion Brand Fueled by Female Empowerment," *Forbes.com*, February 6, 2018, www.forbes.com/sites/veronikasonsev/2018/02/06/how-rebecca-minkoff-built-a-fashion-brand-fueled-by-female-empowerment/#28d9e735f2ad; Jennifer Schlesinger, "Fashion Forward: How Rebecca Minkoff Uses Technology to Drive Triple-Digit Sales Growth," *CNBC.com*, September 9, 2017, www.cnbc.com/2017/09/09/how-rebecca-minkoff-uses-tech-to-drive-triple-digit-sales-growth.html; Christina Austin, "How Rebecca Minkoff Embraced Tech for Retail Success," *Fortune*, November 14, 2017, http://fortune.com/2017/11/14/rebecca-minkoff-amazon-tech-work-life-balance/; Lauren Olsen, "Rebecca Minkoff Releases Line of 'Smart' Bags," *Los Angeles Times*, November 14, 2017, www.latimes.com/fashion/la-ig-wwd-rebecca-minkoff-smart-handbags-20171114-story.html; "Rebecca Minkoff's Store of the Future Will Blow Your Mind," *Fast Company*, February 25, 2015, https://youtu.be/ugf6aDwgaU0.

42 Lauren Thomas, "Lowe's Is Bringing 'Smart Home' Centers to Its Stores Just in Time for the Holidays," *CNBC*, November 7, 2017, https://www.cnbc.com/2017/11/07/lowes-is-bringing-smart-home-centers-to-its-stores.html (accessed March 28, 2018); Natalie Gagliordi, "Lowe's Taps Former Amazon Exec for First Chief Digital Officer Role," *ZDNet*, December 19, 2017, www.zdnet.com/article/lowes-taps-former-amazon-exec-for-first-chief-digital-officer-role/ (accessed March 28, 2018); Jeremy Kaplan, "Lowe's Prints Comic Books Imagining Sci-Fi Futures—Then Makes Them Real," *Digital Trends*, September 6, 2017, www.digitaltrends.com/virtual-reality/lowes-innovation-lab-comics/ (accessed March 28, 2018); Natalie Gagliordi, "Lowe's Taps Apple's ARKit for New Home Improvement Apps," *ZDNet*, September 25, 2017, www.zdnet.com/article/lowes-taps-apples-arkit-for-new-home-improvement-apps/ (accessed March 28, 2018); www.lowes.com (accessed March 28, 2018).

43 Nancy Luna, "Sendero Marketplace in Rancho Mission Viejo, with Gelson's, Celebrates Grand Opening," *Orange County Register,* November 29, 2017, www.ocregister .com/2017/11/29/sendero-marketplace-in-rancho-santa-margarita-with-gelsons-celebrates-grand-opening/ (accessed March 28, 2018); "New Orange County Gelson's Gets Several Innovations," *Progressive Grocer,* November 3, 2017, https://progressivegrocer.com/new-orange-county-gelsons-gets-several-innovations (accessed March 28, 2018); Randy Hofbauer, "Gelson's to Sell Chef'd Meal Kits in Stores," *Progressive Grocer,* August 28, 2017, https://progressivegrocer.com/gelsons-sell-chefd-meal-kits-stores (accessed March 28, 2018); http://gelsons.com (accessed March 28, 2018).

Chapter 16

1 "Outsell and Agency Partner Saatchi & Saatchi's Integrated Marketing Campaign for Toyota North America Receives Top Industry Accolades," *Yahoo! Finance,* April 13, 2016, http://finance.yahoo.com/news/outsell-agency-partner-saatchi-saatchis-130000225 .html (accessed December 24, 2016); "Campaign: 2015 Toyota Camry Launch," Outsell, www.outsellauto.com/files/saatchi/Camry-Award2015/ (accessed December 24, 2016); "IAC Award," Internet Advertising Competition, www.iacaward.org/iac/winner/16084/outsell-and-saatchi—saatchi-wins-2016-webaward-for-2015-toyota-camry-launch .html (accessed December 26, 2016).

2 Ilyse Liffreing, "Brand Winners and Losers of Super Bowl LII," *Digiday,* February 4, 2018, https://digiday.com/marketing/brand-winners-losers-super-bowl-lii/ (accessed February 21, 2018); Marty Swant, "Every Ad Is a Tide Ad: Inside Saatchi and P&G's Clever Super Bowl Takeover Starring David Harbour," *Adweek,* February 4, 2018, www.adweek.com/brand-marketing/every-ad-is-a-tide-ad-inside-saatchi-and-pgs-clever-super-bowl-takeover-starring-david-harbour/ (accessed February 21, 2018); Jack Neff, "Tide Is Everywhere with Campaign to Own All Super Bowl Ads," *AdAge,* Febuary 4, 2018, http://adage.com/article/special-report-super-bowl/t/312249/ (accessed February 21, 2018).

3 Jerrid Grimm, "The 10 Best Branded Content Partnerships of 2016," *Advertising Age,* http://adage.com/article/agency-viewpoint/10-branded-content-partnerships-2016/307284/ (accessed January 26, 2017).

4 Chris Leone, "How Much Should You Budget for Marketing in 2017?" *Web Strategies,* October 20, 2016, www.webstrategiesinc.com/blog/how-much-budget-for-online-marketing-in-2014 (accessed January 26, 2017).

5 George Slefo, "40% of Marketers Say They Plan Facebook Audits," *Advertising Age,* January 19, 2017, http://adage.com/article/digital/marketers-facebook-audits-digital-ad-trust/307539/ (accessed January 26, 2017).

6 Pierre Berthon, Karen Robson, and Leyland Pitt, "The Theory and Practice of Advertising: Counting the Cost to the Consumer," *Journal of Advertising Research* 53, 3 (2013): pp. 244–246.

7 ABC News, "Oprah Winfrey Says She's Lost 26 Pounds, Eats Bread Every Day," January 27, 2016, http://abcnews.go.com/Health/oprah-winfrey-shes-lost-26-pounds-eats-bread/story?id=36539822 (accessed February 16, 2016).

8 E. J. Schultz, Jack Neff, Jessica Wohl, and Adrianne Pasquarelli, "Lowdown: First Reviews Are in on Bud Light's New Campaign," *Advertising Age,* January 25, 2017, http://adage.com/article/cmo-strategy/lowdown-reviews-bud-light-s-campaign/307693/ (accessed January 26, 2017).

9 Special Olympics, "Coca-Cola Company," www.specialolympics.org/Sponsors/Coca-Cola.aspx (accessed January 22, 2016).

10 Adi Robertson, Lizzie Plaugic, and Ariha Setalvad, "The 10 Most Important Things from Apple's iPhone 6S Event," *The Verge,* www.theverge.com/2015/9/9/9289963/apple-iphone-6s-highlights-announcements-recap (accessed January 22, 2016).

11 Lindsay Friedman, "The 12 Worst Social-Media Fails of 2016," *Entrepreneur,* September 22, 2016, https://www.entrepreneur.com/slideshow/272286 (accessed January 31, 2017).

12 Molly Soat, "Chia: From Pets to Protein Powder, the Marketing of the Chia Seed Is a Case Study on How a Superfood Trend Develops," *Marketing News,* January 2015, pp. 42–51.

13 Roger Dooley, "The Smartest Supermarket You've Never Heard Of," *Forbes,* January 28, 2014, www.forbes.com/sites/rogerdooley/2014/01/28/h-e-b/ (accessed January 8, 2015).

14 Time Media Kit, Advertising Rates, www.timemediakit.com/2016-advertising-rates/ (accessed February 12, 2017).

15 Joann Peck and Jennifer Wiggins, "It Just Feels Good: Customers' Affective Response to Touch and Its Influence in Persuasion," *Journal of Marketing,* 70 October 2006, pp. 56–69.

16 Thomas L. Powers, J'Aime C. Jennings, and Thomas E. DeCarlo, "An Assessment of Needed Sales Management Skills," *Journal of Personal Selling & Sales Management* 34, 3 (Summer 2014): pp. 206–222.

17 Ryan Burleson, "Vinyl Record Manufacturer in Nashville Is Said to Be Expanding," *The New York Times,* December 25, 2016, https://www.nytimes.com/2016/12/25/arts/music/vinyl-record-manufacturer-in-nashville-is-said-to-be-expanding.html?_r=0 (accessed February 12, 2017).

18 Pampered Chef, *YouTube,* https://www.youtube.com/user/PamperedChefVideo (accessed February 8, 2016).

19 Joel Comm, "What GM's Live Video Says about Content Marketing Strategy in 2017," *Forbes,* February 14, 2017, www.forbes.com/sites/forbescoachescouncil/2017/02/14/what-gms-live-video-says-about-content-marketing-strategy-in-2017/#24e70273cdac (accessed February 15, 2017).

20 Meghan Friedman, "Here's What's Inside the $30,000 Swag Bags at This Year's Grammys," *Harper's Bazaar,* February 7, 2017, www.harpersbazaar.com/culture/art-books-music/news/a20473/grammys-gift-bag-2017-distinctive-assets/ (accessed February 12, 2017).

21 Mallory Schlossberg, "Brands Are Playing a 'Deadly Game of Russian Roulette' with Celebrities That's Costing Them Millions," *Business Insider,* August 27, 2016, www.businessinsider.com/celebrity-endorsements-can-be-dangerous-2016-8 (accessed January 12, 2017).

22 Polly Mosendz, "Penny-Pinching Millennials Are Keeping the Coupon Alive," *Bloomberg,* June 16, 2016, https://www.bloomberg.com/features/2016-millennials-coupons/ (accessed February 12, 2017).

23 "Mobile and Tablet Internet Usage Exceeds Desktop for First Time Worldwide," StatCounter, November 1, 2016, http://gs.statcounter.com/press/mobile-and-tablet-internet-usage-exceeds-desktop-for-first-time-worldwide (accessed March 22, 2018).

24 "The Majority of Children Live with Two Parents, Census Bureau Reports," United States Census Bureau, November 17, 2016, www.census.gov/newsroom/press-releases/2016/cb16-192.html (accessed February 19, 2017).

25 Rockney G. Walters and Maqbul Jamil, "Exploring the Relationships between Shopping Trip Type, Purchases of Products on Promotion, and Shopping Basket Profit," *Journal of Business Research* 56 (2003): pp. 17–29.

26 Gabriel Beltrone, "Your Life Should Be This Dreamy, Say 6 Beautiful New Ads for the Apple Watch," October 9, 2015, www.adweek.com/adfreak/your-life-should-be-dreamy-say-6-beautiful-new-ads-apple-watch-167479 (accessed February 8, 2016).

27 "Restrictions of Food Marketing and Advertisements Aimed at Children," *Food Directions LLC.*, February 6, 2017, http://fooddirectionsllc.com/2017/02/06/restrictions-of-food-marketing-and-advertisements-aimed-at-children/ (accessed February 17, 2017).

28 Tomás Bayón, "The Chain from Customer Satisfaction via Word-of-Mouth Referrals to New Customer Acquisition," *Journal of the Academy of Marketing Science* 35 (June 2007): pp. 233–249.

29 Rodolfo Vázquez-Casielles, Leticia Suárez-Álvarez, and Ana-Belén Del Río-Lanza, "The Word of Mouth Dynamic: How Positive (and Negative) WOM Drives Purchase Probability: An Analysis of Interpersonal and Non-Interpersonal Factors," *Journal of Advertising Research* 53, 1 (2013): pp. 43–60.

30 Seung-A Annie Jin and Joe Phua, "Following Celebrities' Tweets About Brands: The Impact of Twitter-Based Electronic Word-of-Mouth on Consumers' Source Credibility Perception, Buying Intention, and Social Identification with Celebrities," *Journal of Advertising* 43, 2 (2014): pp. 181–195.

31 Dominic Powell, "The Top 10 Most Viral Advertisements of 2016 Revealed, December 12, 2016, www.smartcompany.com.au/marketing/advertising/79989-top-10-viral-advertisements-2016-revealed/ (accessed February 17, 2017).

32 Lia Zarantonello and Bernd H. Schmitt, "The Impact of Event Marketing on Brand Equity: The Mediating Roles of Brand Experience and Brand Attitude," *International Journal of Advertising* 32, 2 (2013): pp. 255–280.

33 Simon Zekaria, "Apple's Crowds Draw a Crowd of Guerilla Marketers," *The Wall Street Journal*, September 19, 2014, http://blogs.wsj.com/digits/2014/09/19/apples-crowds-draw-a-crowd-of-guerrilla-marketers/ (accessed February 8, 2016).

34 "Blendtec Celebrates 10 Years of Viral Marketing Success," *Nasdaq GlobeNewswire*, November 7, 2016, https://globenewswire.com/news-release/2016/11/07/887174/10165944/en/Blendtec-Celebrates-10-Years-of-Viral-Marketing-Success.html (accessed February 17, 2017).

35 Christian Schulze, Lisa Schöler, and Bernd Skiera, "Not All Fun and Games: Viral Marketing for Utilitarian Products," *Journal of Marketing* 78 (January 2014): pp. 1–19.

36 Nicholas Barber, "Does Bond's Product Placement Go Too Far?" *BBC*, October 1, 2015, www.bbc.com/culture/story/20151001-does-bonds-product-placement-go-too-far (accessed February 8, 2016).

37 Lynna Goch, "The Place to Be," *Best's Review*, February 2005, pp. 64–65.

38 Valeria Noguti and Cristel Antonia Russell, "Normative Influences on Product Placement Effects: Alcohol Brands in Television Series and the Influence of Presumed Influence," *Journal of Advertising* 43, 1 (2014): pp. 46–62.

39 Brian Steinberg, "TV's Old Product-Placement Era Could Be Nearing Its End," http://variety.com/2015/tv/news/tvs-old-product-placement-era-could-be-nearing-its-end-1201423710/ (accessed February 8, 2016).

40 Karine M. Charry, "Product Placement and the Promotion of Healthy Food to Preadolescents—When Popular TV Series Make Carrots Look Cool," *International Journal of Advertising* 33, 3 (2014): pp. 599–616.

41 Lilly Vitorovich, "Product Placement to Be Allowed in U.K. TV Programs," *The Wall Street Journal*, December 21, 2010, p. B5; Peter Shears, "Product Placement: The UK and the New Rules," *Journal of Production Management* 20 (2014): pp. 59–81.

42 Karine M. Charry, "Product Placement and the Promotion of Healthy Food to Pre-adolescents—When Popular TV Series Make Carrots Look Cool," *International Journal of Advertising* 33, 3 (2014): pp. 599–616.

43 Federal Trade Commission, "FTC Brings Action to Stop Marketer from Making Deceptive Opiate Addiction and Withdrawal Treatment Claims," November 17, 2015, https://www.ftc.gov/news-events/press-releases/2015/11/ftc-brings-action-stop-marketer-making-deceptive-opiate-addiction (accessed February 8, 2016).

44 Dennis A. Kopf, Ivonne M. Torres, and Carl Enomoto, "Advertising's Unintended Consequence," *Journal of Advertising* 40, 4 (Winter 2011): pp. 5–18.

45 Charles R. Taylor, "Editorial: On the Economic Effects of Advertising—Evidence That Advertising = Information," *International Journal of Advertising* 32, 3 (2013): pp. 339–342.

46 Florence Fabricant, "Tomatoes, Without the Pie," *The New York Times*, June 25, 2018, https://www.nytimes.com/2018/06/25/dining/canned-tomatoes-frank-pepe-pizza.html (accessed July 12, 2018); "Pepe's Pizza Launches New Rewards Program," *Pepe Pizzeria*, May 8, 2018, https://pepespizzeria.com/pepes-pizza-launches-new-rewards-program/ (accessed July 12, 2018); Pepe's Pizzeria, www.pepespizzeria.com/ (accessed July 12, 2018); Kara Baskin, "The Fireplace to Stay in Brookline Home; Pepe's Pizzeria Won't Move In," *Boston Globe*, September 18, 2014, www.bostonglobe.com/lifestyle/food-dining/2014/09/18/the-fireplace-stay-brookline-home-pepe-pizzeria-won-move/Bz2r5AdCR9jI1dNMH3eVkM/story.html (accessed February 8, 2016); "Good Neighbor Night: Avon Walk for Breast Cancer," http://pepespizzeria.com/pizza/category/pepes-pizza-good-neighbor-nights/ (accessed February 8, 2016).

47 Ronald Grover, "I Can Make Your Product a Star," *Businessweek*, July 13–20, 2009, pp. 68–69; Propaganda GEM, www.propagandagem.com/ (accessed December 23, 2016); Fast Company, "Why You Bought Those Reese's Pieces: A History of Product Placement in Movies," *YouTube*, March 19, 2015, https://www.youtube.com/watch?v=tGOeM4nB1Ys (accessed December 23, 2016); Abe Sauer, "China Product Placement: Q&A with Ruben Igielko-Herrlich, Propaganda GEM," *Brand Channel*, May 19, 2016, https://www.youtube.com/watch?v=tGOeM4nB1Ys (accessed December 23, 2016); Laurent Muzellec, "James Bond, Dunder Mifflin, and the Future of Product Placement," *Harvard Business Review*, June 23, 2016, https://hbr.org/2016/06/james-bond-dunder-mifflin-and-the-future-of-product-placement (accessed December 23, 2016); The Kluger Agency, www.klugeragency.com/ (accessed December 23, 2016); Will Freeman, "Six of the Best Product Placements in Video Games," *The Guardian*, July 13, 2014, https://www.theguardian.com/technology/2014/jul/03/six-of-the-best-product-placement-video-games (accessed December 23, 2016); Josh Halliday, "Product Placement: P Logo Stands for Puzzled Public," *The Guardian*, June 20, 2011, https://www.theguardian.com/media/2011/jun/20/product-placement-logo (accessed February 22, 2018); Mark Sweney, "Forget Product Placement: Now Advertisers Can Buy Storylines," *The Guardian*, January 20, 2018, https://www.theguardian.com/media/2018/jan/20/forget-product-placement-advertisers-buy-storylines-tv-blackish (accessed February 20, 2018); Hadeel Saab, "The Rise of Advertainment in the Music Industry," *Hollywood Branded*, August 17, 2017, https://blog.hollywoodbranded.com/the-rise-of-advertainment-in-the-music-industry (accessed February 22, 2018); Edward Wallace, "15 Unforgettable Examples of Product Placement in Movies," *Fortress*, June 21, 2017, www.fortressofsolitude.co.za/product-placement-movies/ (accessed February 22, 2018); Sophie Christie, "$45m for a Heineken Shot: The Big Business of Product Placement on Screen," *The Telegraph*, February 15, 2018, www.telegraph.co.uk/business/2018/02/15/45m-aheineken-shot-big-business-product-placement-screen/ (accessed February 22, 2018); Lindsay

Friedman, "5 Takeaways from the Million-aire Matchmaker Who Connects Brands to Artists," *Entrepreneur*, June 1, 2016, https://www.entrepreneur.com/article/276759 (accessed February 22, 2018); Martin Bigg, "Drive the New BMW M5 on Your Phone in Need For Speed No Limits," *Carbuzz*, February 6, 2018, https://carbuzz.com/news/drive-the-new-bmw-m5-on-your-phone-in-need-for-speed-no-limits (accessed February 22, 2018).

Chapter 17

1. David Court, Dave Elzinga, Susan Mulder, and Ole Jørgen Vetvik, "The Consumer Decision Journey," *McKinsey Quarterly*, June 2009, http://www.mckinsey.com/business-functions/marketing-and-sales/our-insights/the-consumer-decision-journey (accessed December 29, 2016); *CBS Sunday Morning*, "TV Commercial Spokespeople Tell All," *YouTube*, April 10, 2016, https://www.youtube.com/watch?v=Zx_2vm7NV8A (accessed December 29, 2016); Judith A. Garretson and Ronald W. Niedrich, "Spokes-Characters: Creating Character Trust and Positive Brand Attitudes," *Journal of Advertising* 33(2) (2004): pp. 25–36; Steven Perlberg, "People Are Oddly Mesmerized by the 'Trivago Guy'—and Now It's Helping Their Brand," *The Wall Street Journal*, August 11, 2014, http://blogs.wsj.com/cmo/2014/08/11/trivago-guy-ads/ (accessed December 29, 2016); Felix Gillette, "Branded for Life," *Bloomberg*, September 27, 2012, https://www.bloomberg.com/news/articles/2012-09-27/branded-for-life (accessed December 29, 2016); Sam Wolfson, "The Trivago Woman: 'People Have an Opinion, but Don't Know Me from a Bar of Soap,'" *The Guardian*, December 19, 2017, https://www.theguardian.com/lifeandstyle/2017/dec/19/trivago-girl-tv-adverts-gabrielle-miller-phenomenon (accessed March 3, 2018); Ashley Rodriguez, "How Allstate's Mayhem Disrupted the Chatter Around Insurance," *AdAge*, June 10, 2015, http://adage.com/article/cmo-strategy/mayhem-helped-allstate-disrupt-conversation-insurance/298779/ (accessed March 3, 2018).

2. Suzanne Vranica, "Arby's Swallows Pride for Jon Stewart," *The Wall Street Journal*, August 6, 2015, pp. B1, B8.

3. Douglas E. Hughes, "This Ad's for You: The Indirect Effect of Advertising Perceptions on Salesperson Effort and Performance," *Journal of the Academy of Marketing Science* 41, 1 (2013): pp. 1–18.

4. Tim Nudd, "AT&T's Latest 'It Can Wait' Ad Shows a Brutal Crash in Reverse, but There's No Going Back," *Adweek*, July 20, 2015, http://www.adweek.com/adfreak/atts-latest-it-can-wait-ad-shows-brutal-crash-reverse-theres-no-going-back-166004 (accessed February 10, 2016).

5. Micael Dahlén, Helge Thorbjørnsen, and Henrik Sjödin, "A Taste of 'Nextopia,'" *Journal of Advertising* 40, 1 (Winter 2011): pp. 33–44.

6. Fred K. Beard, "Practitioner Views of Comparative Advertising: How Practices Have Changed in Two Decades," *Journal of Advertising Research* 53, 3 (2013): pp. 313–323.

7. Andrew John Bellingall, "Comparative Advertising in Brazil," *Intellectual Property Magazine*, October 2010, pp. 27–30.

8. Ben Plomion, "Three Predictions for Native Advertising in 2017," *Forbes*, January 10, 2017, https://www.forbes.com/sites/forbescommunicationscouncil/2017/01/10/three-predictions-for-native-advertising-in-2017/#7fb5c1e6677e (accessed February 25, 2017).

9. Joe Lazauskas, "3 Ways Brands Can Make Native Advertising More Effective in 2017," *Contently*, January 4, 2017, https://contently.com/strategist/2017/01/04/better-native-advertising-2017/ (accessed February 25, 2017).

10. Marlynn Wei, "New Survey Reveals the Rapid Rise of Yoga and Why Some People Still Haven't Tried It," *Harvard Health Publications*, June 15, 2016, http://www.health.harvard.edu/blog/new-survey-reveals-the-rapid-rise-of-yoga-and-why-some-people-still-havent-tried-it-201603079179 (accessed February 25, 2017).

11. Tae Hyun Baek and Mariko Morimoto, "Stay Away from Me," *Journal of Advertising* 41, 1 (Spring 2012): pp. 59–76.

12. Sami Main, "Hulu Users Reveal the Weirdest Places They've Watched TV," *Adweek*, February 24, 2017, http://www.adweek.com/tv-video/hulu-users-reveal-the-weirdest-places-theyve-watched-tv/ (accessed February 25, 2017).

13. Daniel A. Sheinin, Sajeev Varki, and Christy Ashley, "The Differential Effect of Ad Novelty and Message Usefulness on Brand Judgments," *Journal of Advertising* 40, 3 (Fall 2011): pp. 5–17.

14. Tim Nudd, "Netflix's Ads for Santa Clarita Diet Are Good Gross Fun, but One Went a Little Too Far," February 22, 2017, http://www.adweek.com/creativity/netflixs-ads-for-santa-clarita-diet-are-good-gross-fun-but-one-went-a-little-too-far/ (accessed February 25, 2017).

15. "Leading TV Advertisers in the United States from February 17 to 23, 2017, by Weekly Advertising Spending (in million U.S. dollars)," *Statista*, https://www.statista.com/statistics/384835/estimated-tv-ad-spend-us-companies/ (accessed February 26, 2017).

16. Douglas West, John B. Ford, and Paul W. Farris, "How Corporate Cultures Drive Advertising and Promotion Budgets: Best Practices Combine Heuristics and Algorithmic Tools," *Journal of Advertising Research* (June 2014): pp. 149–162.

17. Amy Mitchell, "How Bad Data Can Blindside Your Marketing Analytics," *Adweek*, http://www.adweek.com/sponsored/where-data-projects-fall-short/ (accessed February 26, 2017).

18. Aaron Wilson, "Texans' J.J. Watt, Reebok Roll Out 'Hunt Greatness' Ad Campaign," *Houston Chronicle*, May 23, 2016, https://www.chron.com/sports/texans/article/Texans-J-J-Watt-unveils-personal-logo-new-7940308.php (accessed March 4, 2018).

19. "Digital Ad Spending to Surpass TV Next Year," *eMarketer*, March 8, 2016, https://www.emarketer.com/Article/Digital-Ad-Spending-Surpass-TV-Next-Year/1013671 (accessed March 12, 2017).

20. Jeanine Poggi, "Digital Advertising Tops TV in the U.S. for the First Time," *AdvertisingAge*, March 29, 2017, http://adage.com/article/advertising/magna-u-s-digital-ad-sales-top-tv-time-2016/308468/ (accessed April 5, 2017).

21. National Geographic Press room, "National Geographic Shows 30.9 Million Worldwide Audience via Consolidated Media Report," September 24, 2012, http://press.nationalgeographic.com/2012/09/24/national-geographic-shows-30-9-million-worldwide-audience-via-consolidated-media-report/ (accessed March 26 2018).

22. David G. Taylor, Jeffrey E. Lewin, and David Strutton, "Friends, Fans, and Followers: Do Ads Work on Social Networks? How Gender and Age Shape Receptivity," *Journal of Advertising Research* 51, 1 (2011): pp. 258–275.

23. Sonia Dickinson-Delaporte and Gayle Kerr, "Agency-Generated Research of Consumer-Generated Content: The Risks, Best Practices, and Ethics," *Journal of Advertising Research* (December 2014): pp. 469–478.

24. Geoffrey Precourt, "What We Know about TV Today (and Tomorrow)," *Journal of Advertising Research* 53, 1 (2013): pp. 3–4.

25. Gina A. Tran and David Strutton, "What Factors Affect Consumer Acceptance of In-Game Advertisements? Click 'Like' to Manage Digital Content for Players," *Journal of Advertising Research* 53, 4 (2013): pp. 455–469.

26. Marty Swant, "Infographic: Marketers Are Spending 500% More on Millennials than All

Others Combined," *Adweek*, November 17, 2015, http://www.adweek.com/news/technology/infographic-marketers-are-spending-500-more-millennials-all-others-combined-168176 (accessed February 11, 2016).

27 Amy Jo Coffey, "The Power of Cultural Factors in Spanish-Language Advertising: Ethnic-Group Traits and Metrics May Predict Advertiser Investment across Media Platforms," *Journal of Advertising Research*, pp. 346–355.

28 Mike Shields, "Advertising on Streaming TV Devices Is About to Get More Targeted," *The Wall Street Journal*, February 27, 2017, https://www.wsj.com/articles/advertising-on-streaming-tv-devices-is-about-to-get-more-targeted-1488193202 (accessed March 12, 2017).

29 DAS Group, "Old Skool: Why Print Yellow Pages Are Still Worth Considering as Part of Your Lead Generation Programs," January 5, 2016, http://www.das-group.com/blog/old-skool-why-print-yellow-pages-are-still-worth-considering-as-part-of-your-lead-generation-programs/ (accessed February 11, 2016).

30 Shintaro Okazaki and Patrick Barwise, "Has the Time Finally Come for the Medium of the Future? Research on Mobile Advertising," 50th Anniversary Supplement, *Journal of Advertising Research* 51, 1 (2011): pp. 59–71.

31 Chingching Chang, "Feeling Ambivalent about Going Green," *Journal of Advertising* 40, 4 (Winter 2011): pp. 19–31.

32 Ilona A. Berney-Reddish and Charles S. Areni, "Sex Differences in Responses to Probability Markers in Advertising Claims," *Journal of Advertising* 35 (Summer 2006): pp. 7–17.

33 Better Business Bureau, "Children's Food & Beverage Advertising Initiative," http://www.bbb.org/council/the-national-partner-program/national-advertising-review-services/childrens-food-and-beverage-advertising-initiative/ (accessed April 5, 2017).

34 Chiranjeev Kohli, Sunil Thomas, and Rajneesh Suri, "Are You in Good Hands? Slogan Recall: What Really Matters," *Journal of Advertising Research* 53, 1 (2013): pp. 31–42.

35 Judith Anne Garretson Folse, Richard G. Netemeyer, and Scot Burton, "Spokescharacters," *Journal of Advertising* 41, 1 (Spring 2012): pp. 17–32.

36 AAA Publishing Network, "Publishing Network," http://www.aaapublishingnetwork.com/pages.cfm?p=publications_all.cfm (accessed February 11, 2016).

37 Daniel J. Howard and Roger A. Kerin, "The Effects of Personalized Product Recommendations on Advertisement Response Rates: The 'Try This. It Works!' Technique," *Journal of Consumer Psychology* 14, 3 (2004): pp. 271–279.

38 Pamela W. Henderson, Joan L. Giese, and Joseph A. Cote, "Impression Management Using Typeface Design," *Journal of Marketing* 68 (October 2004): pp. 60–72.

39 Rik Pieters and Michel Wedel, "Attention Capture and Transfer in Advertising: Brand, Pictorial, and Text-Size Effects," *Journal of Marketing* 68 (April 2004): pp. 36–50.

40 Nathalie Tadena, "What Traffic Congestion, Car Speeds Mean for Outdoor Ads," *The Wall Street Journal*, June 17, 2014, http://blogs.wsj.com/cmo/2014/06/17/measuring-the-other-type-of-on-the-go-ads/ (accessed February 11, 2016).

41 Zach Doell, "Lincoln's Turnaround: 2014 Sales Up—Is It the McConaughey Bump?" *Kelley Blue Book*, http://www.kbb.com/car-news/all-the-latest/lincolns-turnaround-2014-sales-up_is-it-the-mcconaughey-bump/2000011621/ (accessed February 11, 2016).

42 Bruce Krasnow, "New Mexico Tourism Chief: No Funds to Grow Ad Campaign," *Taos News*, January 29, 2017, http://www.taosnews.com/stories/new-mexico-tourism-chief-no-funds-to-grow-ad-campaign,38564 (accessed April 5, 2017).

43 Marissa Delisle, "Mobile Marketing Trends 2017," *Digital Turbine*, January 6, 2017, https://www.digitalturbine.com/blog/mobile-marketing-trends-2017/ (accessed April 5, 2017).

44 Peter J. Danaher and Guy W. Mullarkey, "Factors Affecting Online Advertising Recall: A Study of Students," *Journal of Advertising Research* 43 (2003): pp. 252–267.

45 "The Power of the Jingle," *Advertising Age*, February 8, 2017, http://adage.com/article/iheart-media/power-jingle/307801/ (accessed April 5, 2017).

46 Jan H. Schumann, Florian von Wangenheim, and Nicole Groene, "Targeted Online Advertising: Using Reciprocity Appeals to Increase Acceptance among Users of Free Web Services," *Journal of Marketing* 78 (January 2014): pp. 59–75.

47 Martin Williams and Francis Buttle, "Managing Negative Word-of-Mouth: An Exploratory Study," *Journal of Marketing Management* 30, 13/14 (2014): pp. 1423–1447.

48 Russell Hotten, "Volkswagen: The Scandal Explained," *BBC*, December 10, 2015, http://www.bbc.com/news/business-34324772 (accessed February 11, 2016).

49 George E. Belch and Michael A. Belch, *Advertising and Promotion* (Burr Ridge, IL: Irwin/McGraw-Hill, 2008), p. 570.

50 "AT&T: It Can Wait: The Power of Movement," *PR Week Awards*, http://awards.prweekus.com/it-can-wait%C2%AE-power-movement (accessed January 21, 2015).

51 Carmen Gonzalez Caldwell, "AT&T Campaign: When Driving, Texting and Other Smartphone Activities Can Wait," *Miami Herald*, April 5, 2017, http://www.miamiherald.com/news/local/crime/article142979794.html (accessed April 5, 2017).

52 Korri Kezar, "Pizza Hut Will Be the Official Pizza Sponsor of ESPN College GameDay," *Dallas Business Journal*, http://www.bizjournals.com/dallas/news/2015/09/02/pizza-hut-will-be-the-official-pizza-sponsor-of.html (accessed February 11, 2016).

53 Belch and Belch, *Advertising and Promotion*, pp. 580–581.

54 Suman Basuroy, Subimal Chatterjee, and S. Abraham Ravid, "How Critical Are Critical Reviews? The Box Office Effects of Film Critics, Star Power, and Budgets," *Journal of Marketing* (October 2003): pp. 103–117.

55 Kathleen Cleeren, Harald J. van Heerde, and Marnik G. Dekimpe, "Rising from the Ashes: How Brands and Categories Can Overcome Product-Harm Crises," *Journal of Marketing* 77 (March 2013): pp. 58–77.

56 Zoe Szathmary, "Coca-Cola pulls 'Nazi' Fanta advertisement which referred to the 1940s as 'the good old times,'" *Daily Mail*, March 4, 2015, http://www.dailymail.co.uk/news/article-2979582/Coca-Cola-pulls-Nazi-Fanta-advertisement-referred-1940s-good-old-times.html (accessed February 11, 2016).

57 Deborah L. Vence, "Stand Guard: In Bad Times, an Ongoing Strategy Keeps Image Intact," *Marketing News*, November 16, 2006, p. 15.

58 Brian Steinberg, "Food Net's Endorsements Are Woven Inconspicuously into Its Programming Mix," *Variety*, November 5, 2013, http://variety.com/2013/tv/features/food-net-brand-tie-ins-that-sizzle-but-dont-burn-1200796087/ (accessed February 11, 2016); Carey Polis, "'From Scratch' Goes Behind the Scenes at the Food Network," *The Huffington Post*, October 1, 2013, http://www.huffingtonpost.com/2013/10/01/from-scratch-food-network_n_3984233.html (accessed February 11, 2016); Stuart Elliot, "Two Media Mainstays Expand Their Video Presence," *The New York Times*, October 2, 2013, http://www.nytimes.com/2013/10/03/business/media/two-media-mainstays-expand-their-video-presence.html (accessed February 11, 2016); John

Moulding, "Scripps Network Hails the Impact of Dynamic Advertising Insertion," *Videonet*, October 31, 2013, http://www.v-net .tv/scripps-networks-hails-the-impact-of-dynamic-advertising-insertion/ (accessed February 11, 2016).

59 Jayson DeMers, "Is Native Advertising Sustainable for the Long Haul?" *Forbes*, March 1, 2018, https://www.forbes.com/sites/jaysondemers/2018/03/01/is-native-advertising-sustainable-for-the-long-haul/2/#5a6b144868bf (accessed March 3, 2018); Mike Shields, "Publishers Worry that Native Ads Are Vulnerable to Blocking," *The Wall Street Journal*, October 5, 2015, http://www.wsj.com/articles/publishers-worry-that-native-ads-are-vulnerable-to-ad-blocking-1444039200 (accessed October 12, 2015); Lin Grensing-Pophal, "Consumers Coming to Accept Native Advertising Done Right," *EContent Magazine*, July/August 2014, pp. 8–10; Molly Soat, "The Native Frontier," *Marketing News*, May 2015, pp. 34–43; Suzanne Vranica, "Majority of Native Ads Lack Transparency," *The Wall Street Journal*, August 3, 2016, http://www .wsj.com/articles/majority-of-native-ads-lack-transparency-1470218409 (accessed December 23, 2016); Christine Birkner, "Why WSJ's Sponsored Content Features the Economics of Sex and Drugs," *Adweek*, April 7, 2016, http://www.adweek.com/news/advertising-branding/why-wsjs-sponsored-content-features-economics-sex-and-drugs-170666 (accessed December 23, 2016); Peter Trueman, "Native Advertising Laws in the UK & the US," *Native Ad Buzz*, http://www.nativeadbuzz.com/blog/native-advertising-laws-in-the-uk-the-us/ (accessed March 3, 2018); Emily Giller, "Native Advertising: An International Perspective," Professional Projects from the College of Journalism and Mass Communications, 2016, http://digitalcommons.unl.edu/journalismprojects/7; Ian D. Volner and Kathleen Sheridan, "United States: FCC Revives Its Own Native Advertising Rule: Sponsorship Identification," *Mondaq*, February 9, 2018, http://www .mondaq.com/unitedstates/x/672032/advertising+marketing+branding/FCC+Revives+Its+Own+Native+Advertising+Rule+Sponsorship+Identification (accessed March 3, 2018); David Murphy, "IAB UK Updates Content and Native Ad Guidelines," *Mobile Marketing*, February 13, 2018, http://mobilemarketingmagazine.com/iab-uk-updates-content-and-native-ad-guidelines (accessed March 3, 2018); "The Washington Post Brings Artificial Intelligence to Its Native Ads," *Digiday*, August 23, 2017, https://digiday.com/media/washington-post-brings-artificial-intelligence-native-ads/ (accessed March 3, 2018).

Chapter 18

1 Brandon Carter, "Coupon Statistics: The Ultimate Collection," *Access Development*, November 15, 2017, https://blog .accessdevelopment.com/ultimate-collection-coupon-statistics (accessed March 11, 2018); Joe Pinsker, "The Psychology Behind Costco's Free Samples," *The Atlantic*, October 1, 2014, www.theatlantic.com/business/archive/2014/10/the-psychology-behind-costcos-free-samples/380969/ (accessed September 15, 2015); Kelly Spors, "Why Giving Things Away for Free Can Boost Sales," *American Express*, October 3, 2014, https://www.americanexpress.com/us/small-business/openforum/articles/free-samples-can-boost-sales/ (accessed September 15, 2015); "Product Sampling," Interactions, www.interactionsmarketing .com/our-difference/product-sampling.html (accessed September 15, 2015); Brad Tuttle, "The Power of Freebies: Why Companies Pay to Give Free Samples to Supermarket Customers," *Time*, February 17, 2011, http://business.time.com/2011/02/17/the-power-of-freebies-why-companies-pay-to-give-free-samples-to-supermarket-customers/ (accessed September 15, 2015); Ilan Mochari, "Give It Away Now: Why Free Product Samples Always Pay Off," *Inc.*, www.inc.com/ilan-mochari/costco-sampling-free-food-giveaway.html (accessed September 15, 2015); Jeana Delano, "The Power of Product Sampling," *GCI Magazine*, www .gcimagazine.com/business/marketing/The-Power-of-Product-Sampling-280537262.html (accessed September 15, 2015); Annabelle Gurwitch, "The Treasure in a Small Package," *The New York Times*, October 17, 2014, www .nytimes.com/2014/10/19/fashion/want-a-free-sample-cosmetic-companies-are-onto-you.html (accessed September 15, 2015).

2 Avinash Malshe and Avipreet Sohi, "What Makes Strategy Making across the Sales-Marketing Interface More Successful?" *Journal of the Academy of Marketing Science* 37, 4 (Winter 2009): pp. 400–421.

3 "Advantages of Personal Selling," *KnowThis. com*, www.knowthis.com/principles-of-marketing-tutorials/personal-selling/advantages-of-personal-selling (accessed February 11, 2016).

4 Kim Zimmerman, "B2B Inside Sales Teams Leverage Social, Video and Data to Reach Top Prospects," *Demand Gen Report*, January 20, 2016, www.demandgenreport .com/features/industry-insights/b2b-inside-sales-teams-leverage-social-video-and-data-to-reach-top-prospects (accessed March 29, 2017).

5 Donald C. Barnes, Joel E. Collier, Nicole Ponder, and Zachary Williams, "Investigating the Employee's Perspective of Customer Delight," *Journal of Personal Selling & Sales Management* 33, 1 (Winter 2013): pp. 91–104.

6 Jon M. Hawes, Anne K. Rich, and Scott M. Widmier, "Assessing the Development of the Sales Profession," *Journal of Personal Selling & Sales Management* 24 (Winter 2004): pp. 27–37.

7 Dawn R. Deeter-Schmelz and Karen Norman Kennedy, "A Global Perspective on the Current State of Sales Education in the College Curriculum," *Journal of Personal Selling & Sales Management* 31, n1 (Winter 2011): pp. 55–76.

8 Willem Verbeke, Bart Dietz, and Ernst Verwaal, "Drivers of Sales Performance: A Contemporary Meta-Analysis. Have Salespeople Become Knowledge Brokers?" *Journal of the Academy of Marketing Science* 39 (2011): pp. 407–428.

9 Lisa Terry, "Customer Service," *Inbound Logistics*, December 2014, pp. 33–36.

10 Michael Rodriguez and Robert M. Peterson, "Generating Leads via Social CRM: Early Best Practices for B2B Sales," abstract in Concha Allen (ed.), "Special Abstract Section: 2011 National Conference in Sales Management," *Journal of Personal Selling* 31, 4 (Fall 2011): pp. 457–458.

11 Ed Peelena, Kees van Montfort, Rob Beltman, and Arnoud Klerkx, "An Empirical Study into the Foundation of CRM Success," *Journal of Strategic Marketing* 17, 6 (December 2009): pp. 453–471.

12 Eli Jones, Paul Busch, and Peter Dacin, "Firm Market Orientation and Salesperson Customer Orientation: Interpersonal and Intrapersonal Influence on Customer Service and Retention in Business-to-Business Buyer–Seller Relationships," *Journal of Business Research* 56 (2003): pp. 323–340.

13 Kenneth Le Meunier-FitzHugh and Nigel F. Piercy, "Exploring the Relationship between Market Orientation and Sales and Marketing Collaboration," *Journal of Personal Selling & Sales Management* 31, 3 (Summer 2011): pp. 287–296.

14 Kaj Storbacka, Pia Polsa, and Maria Sääksjärvi, "Management Practices in Solution Sales—Multilevel and Cross-Functional Framework," *Journal of Personal Selling & Sales Management* 31, 1 (Winter 2011): pp. 35–54.

15 Julie T. Johnson, Hiram C. Barksdale, Jr., and James S. Boles, "Factors Associated with Customer Willingness to Refer Leads to

Salespeople," *Journal of Business Research* 56 (2003): pp. 257–263.

16. Ralph W. Giacobbe, Donald W. Jackson, Jr., Lawrence A. Crosby, and Claudia M. Bridges, "A Contingency Approach to Adaptive Selling Behavior and Sales Performance: Selling Situations and Salesperson Characteristics," *Journal of Personal Selling & Sales Management* 26 (Spring 2006): pp. 115–142.

17. Richard G. McFarland, Goutam N. Challagalla, and Tasadduq A. Shervani, "Influence Tactics for Effective Adaptive Selling," *Journal of Marketing* 70 (October 2006): pp. 103–117.

18. Thomas E. DeCarlo and Michael J. Barone, "The Interactive Effects of Sales Presentation, Suspicion, and Positive Mood on Salesperson Evaluations and Purchase Intentions," *Journal of Personal Selling & Sales Management* 33, 1 (Winter 2013): pp. 53–66.

19. Susie Pryor, Avinash Malshe, and Kyle Paradise, "Salesperson Listening in the Extended Sales Relationship: An Exploration of Cognitive, Affective, and Temporal Dimensions," *Journal of Personal Selling & Sales Management* 33, 2 (Spring 2013): pp. 185–196.

20. John Andy Wood, "NLP Revisited: Nonverbal Communications and Signals of Trustworthiness," *Journal of Personal Selling & Sales Management* 26 (Spring 2006): pp. 198–204.

21. John Dunyon, Valerie Gossling, Sarah Willden, and John S. Seiter, "Compliments and Purchasing Behavior in Telephone Sales Interactions," abstract in Dawn R. Deeter-Schmelz (ed.), "Personal Selling & Sales Management Abstracts," *Journal of Personal Selling & Sales Management* 31, 2 (Spring 2011): p. 186.

22. Stephen S. Porter, Joshua L. Wiener, and Gary L. Frankwick, "The Moderating Effect of Selling Situation on the Adaptive Selling Strategy—Selling Effectiveness Relationship," *Journal of Business Research* 56 (2003): pp. 275–281.

23. Tammy Stanley, "Follow-Up: The Success Recipe Salespeople Don't See," *Direct Selling News*, May 2010, http://directsellingnews.com/index.php/view/follow_up_the_success_recipe_salespeople_dont_see#.Vr0hGlLd0cM (accessed February 11, 2016).

24. Dinah Eng, "Does Joy Help You Sell?" *Fortune*, January 1, 2016, p. 30.

25. Gabriel R. Gonzalez, K. Douglas Hoffman, Thomas N. Ingram, and Raymond W. LaForge, "Sales Organization Recovery Management and Relationship Selling: A Conceptual Model and Empirical Test," *Journal of Personal Selling & Sales Management* 30, 3 (Summer 2010): pp. 223–238.

26. Barton A. Weitz and Kevin D. Bradford, "Personal Selling and Sales Management: A Relationship Marketing Perspective," *Journal of the Academy of Marketing Science* 27, 2 (1999): pp. 241–254.

27. Eli Jones, Steven P. Brown, Andris A. Zoltners, and Barton A. Weitz, "The Changing Environment of Selling and Sales Management," *Journal of Personal Selling & Sales Management* 25, 2 (Spring 2005): pp. 105–111.

28. "The Right Questions and Attitudes Can Beef Up Your Sales, Improve Customer Retention," *Selling* (June 2001): p. 3.

29. Jones et al., 105–111.

30. Gary K. Hunter and William D. Perreault Jr., "Making Sales Technology Effective," *Journal of Marketing* 71 (January 2007): pp. 16–34.

31. Othman Boujena, Johnston J. Wesley, and Dwight R. Merunka, "The Benefits of Sales Force Automation: A Customer's Perspective," *Journal of Personal Selling & Sales Management* 29, 2 (2009): pp. 137–150.

32. Fernando Jaramillo, Jay Prakash Mulki, and Paul Solomon, "The Role of Ethical Climate on Salesperson's Role Stress, Job Attitudes, Turnover Intention, and Job Performance," *Journal of Personal Selling & Sales Management* 26 (Summer 2006): pp. 272–282.

33. Christophe Fournier, John F. Tanner, Jr., Lawrence B. Chonko, and Chris Manolis, "The Moderating Role of Ethical Climate on Salesperson Propensity to Leave," *Journal of Personal Selling & Sales Management* 3, 1 (Winter 2009–2010): pp. 7–22.

34. Bulent Menguc, Seigyoung Auh, and Aypar Uslu, "Customer Knowledge Creation Capability and Performance in Sales Teams," *Journal of the Academy of Marketing Science*, 41(2013): pp. 19–39.

35. Leonidas A. Zampetakis, "Sales Force Management Practices in Organizations with a Supportive Climate towards Creativity," *Journal of Strategic Marketing* 22 (1), 2014: pp. 59–72.

36. Kirby L. J. Shannahan, Alan J. Bush, and Rachelle J. Shannahan, "Are Your Salespeople Coachable? How Salesperson Coachability, Trait Competitiveness, and Transformational Leadership Enhance Sales Performance," *Journal of the Academy of Marketing Science* 41 (2013): pp. 40–54.

37. Christophe Fournier, William A. Weeks, Christopher P. Blocker, and Lawrence B. Chonko, "Polychronicity and Scheduling's Role in Reducing Role Stress and Enhancing Sales Performance," *Journal of Personal Selling & Sales Management* 33, 2 (Spring 2013): pp. 197–210.

38. Milton Moskowitz, "The Best Employers in the U.S. Say Their Greatest Tool Is Culture," *Fortune*, March 5, 2015, http://fortune.com/2015/03/05/best-companies-greatest-tool-is-culture/ (accessed February 12, 2016).

39. Jeffrey P. Boichuk, Willy Bolander, Zachary R. Hall, Michael Ahearne, William J. Zahn, and Melissa Nieves, "Learned Helplessness Among Newly Hired Salespeople and the Influence of Leadership," *Journal of Marketing* 78 (January 2014): pp. 95–111.

40. Jason Jordan and Robert Kelly, "Companies with a Formal Sales Process Generate More Revenue," *Harvard Business Review*, January 21, 2015, https://hbr.org/2015/01/companies-with-a-formal-sales-process-generate-more-revenue (accessed January 22, 2015).

41. Glassdoor, "Sales Salaries," March 24, 2017, https://www.glassdoor.com/Salaries/sales-salary-SRCH_KO0,5.htm (accessed March 29, 2017).

42. Tara Burnthorne Lopez, Christopher D. Hopkins, and Mary Anne Raymond, "Reward Preferences of Salespeople: How Do Commissions Rate?" *Journal of Personal Selling & Sales Management* 26 (Fall 2006): pp. 381–390.

43. Jolie Lee, "Container Store Pays Workers on Average $50,000," *USA Today*, October 17, 2014, www.usatoday.com/story/money/business/2014/10/17/container-store-salaries-retail/17426865/# (accessed February 12, 2016).

44. Denny Bristow, Douglas Amyx, Stephen B. Castleberry, and James J. Cochran, "A Cross-Generational Comparison of Motivational Factors in a Sales Career among Gen-X and Gen-Y College Students," *Journal of Personal Selling & Sales Management* 31, 1 (Winter 2011): pp. 35–54.

45. Subhra Chakrabarty, Gene Brown, and Robert E. Widing, "Distinguishing between the Roles of Customer-Oriented Selling and Adaptive Selling in Managing Dysfunctional Conflict in Buyer–Seller Relationships," *Journal of Personal Selling & Sales Management* 33, 3 (Summer 2013): pp. 245–260.

46. Michael Ahearne, Till Haumann, Forian Kraus, and Jan Wieseke, "It's a Matter of Congruence: How Interpersonal Identification between Sales Managers and Salespersons Shapes Sales Success," *Journal of the Academy of Marketing Science* 41 (2013): pp. 625–648.

47. Felicia G. Lassk and C. David Shephard, "Exploring the Relationship between Emotional Intelligence and Salesperson Creativity," *Journal of Personal Selling & Sales Management* 33, 1 (Winter 2013): pp. 25–38.

48. John W. Barnes, Donald W. Jackson, Jr., Michael D. Hutt, and Ajith Kumar, "The Role of Culture Strength in Shaping Salesforce Outcomes," *Journal of Personal Selling & Sales Management* 26 (Summer 2006): pp. 255–270.

49. James B. DeConinck, "The Effects of Leader–Member Exchange and Organizational Identification on Performance and Turnover among Salespeople," *Journal of Personal Selling & Sales Management* 31, 1 (Winter 2011): pp. 21–34.

50. Patricia Odell, "Motivating the Masses," *Promo*, September 1, 2005, http://promomagazine.com/research/pitrends/marketing_ motivating_ masses (accessed April 20, 2011).

51. Anne Hamilton, "Incentive Travel That Pays," *Direct Selling News*, 10(8), August 2014, pp. 60–61.

52. G. Alexander Hamwi, Brian N. Rutherford, Hiram C. Barksdale, Jr., and Julie T. Johnson, "Ideal Versus Actual Number of Sales Calls: An Application of Disconfirmation Theory," *Journal of Personal Selling & Sales Management* 33(3), (Summer 2013): pp. 307–318.

53. Alix Stuart, "Is Your Sales Team on Track?" *Inc.*, December 2014/January 2015, pp. 76–77.

54. George E. Belch and Michael A. Belch, *Advertising and Promotion* (Burr Ridge, IL: Irwin/McGraw-Hill, 2004), pp. 514–522.

55. Esmeralda Crespo-Almendros and Salvador Del Barrio-Garcia, "The Quality of Internet-User Recall: A Comparative Analysis by Online Sales-Promotion Types," *Journal of Advertising Research* 54 (1) (March 2014): pp. 46–60.

56. Brad Tuttle, "Why Americans Are Cutting Coupons out of Their Lives," *Time*, February 28, 2013, http://business.time.com/2013/02/28/why-americans-are-cutting-coupons-out-of-their-lives (accessed February 11, 2016).

57. Sarah Halzack, "The Trouble with Those 20 Percent Off Coupons from Bed, Bath & Beyond," *The Washington Post*, https://www.washingtonpost.com/news/business/wp/2015/09/30/the-trouble-with-those-20-percent-off-coupons-from-bed-bath-beyond/ (accessed February 12, 2016).

58. Venessa Wong, "Clipping Forever: Why the Humble Coupon Isn't Going Away," *Bloomberg Businessweek*, November 7, 2014, www.businessweek.com/articles/2014-11-07/clipping-forever-why-the-humble-coupon-isnt-going-away (accessed January 23, 2015).

59. Jiayue Huang, "Americans Still Prefer Their Paper Coupons," *USA Today*, November 2, 2015, p. 5B.

60. Arthur L. Porter, "Direct Mail's Lessons for Electronic Couponers," *Marketing Management Journal* (Spring/Summer 2000): pp. 107–115.

61. Ibid.

62. Coupon Information Corporation, www.couponinformationcenter.com/ (accessed February 11, 2016).

63. John T. Gourville and Dilip Soman, "The Consumer Psychology of Mail-in Rebates," *Journal of Product & Brand Management* 20, 2 (2011): pp. 147–157.

64. Don E. Schultz and Martin P. Block, "Sales Promotion Influencing Consumer Brand Preferences/Purchases," *Journal of Consumer Marketing* 31 (3): pp. 212–217.

65. Bruce Horovitz, "Whole Foods to Test First Rewards Program," *USA Today*, September 19, 2014, p. 4B; Whole Foods, "Introducing Whole Foods Market Rewards," www.wholefoodsmarket.com/wfm-rewards (accessed February 12, 2016).

66. Whole Foods Market, http://www.wholefoodsmarket.com/wfm-rewards (accessed March 28, 2018).

67. Jeana Delano, "The Power of Product Samples," *Global Cosmetic Industry*, November 2014, pp. 46–48.

68. Katherine Hobson, "A Sales Promotion That Works for Shoes May Not for Chocolate," *The Wall Street Journal*, February 8, 2011, http://blogs.wsj.com/health/2011/02/08/a-sales-promotion-that-works-for-shoes-may-not-for-chocolate (accessed February 11, 2016).

69. Teresa Montaner, Leslie de Chernatony, and Isabel Buil, "Consumer Response to Gift Promotions," *Journal of Product & Brand Management* 20, 2 (2011): pp. 101–110.

70. Jessica Wohl, "Oreo Enlists Celebs to Demonstrate the Perfect Dunk in Latest Global Push," *AdvertisingAge*, February 8, 2017, http://adage.com/article/cmo-strategy/oreo/307896/ (accessed April 1, 2017).

71. Joe McGauley, "Oreo Is Unleashing These 3 New Flavors Created by Fans," *Thrillist*, December 11, 2017, https://www.thrillist.com/news/nation/oreo-new-flavor-creation-contest-winners (accessed March 10, 2018).

72. HGTV, "HGTV Dream Home Giveaway 2016," www.hgtv.com/design/hgtv-dream-home/sweepstakes (accessed February 12, 2016).

73. Kenneth Jones, "Broadway's Major Producers Join with Regional Presenters for Audience Rewards Program," *Playbill*, June 28, 2007, www.playbill.com/news/article/109186-Broadways-Major-Producers-Join-with-Regional-Presenters-for-Audience-Rewards-Program (accessed December 11, 2013); Nederlander Organization–Announcements, "Audience Rewards Hits 1 Million Members," August 25, 2012, www.nederlander.com/press_03.html (accessed December 11, 2013); Audience Rewards, "Our History," https://www.audiencerewards.com/redeemcenter/infopage.cfm?id525 (accessed December 11, 2013).

74. Bob Evans, "Why Salesforce Is Soaring in the Cloud: 20 Eye-Popping Numbers," *Forbes*, March 5, 2018, https://www.forbes.com/sites/bobevans1/2018/03/05/20-eye-popping-stats-from-salesforce-com-as-it-soars-on-digital-transformation-boom/2/#1a69a66129a1 (accessed March 11, 2018); Teresa Kersten, "How Salesforce Captures and Keeps Its Massive Customer Base," *Madison*, March 10, 2018, http://host.madison.com/business/investment/markets-and-stocks/how-salesforce-captures-and-keeps-its-massive-customer-base/article_9156e73e-7d2b-5a29-8c20-06ca39227af6.html (accessed March 11, 2018); Ron Miller, "Dropbox Announces Deeper Integration with Salesforce Ahead of IPO," *TechCrunch*, March 9, 2018, https://techcrunch.com/2018/03/09/dropbox-announces-deeper-integration-with-salesforce-ahead-of-ipo/ (accessed March 11, 2018); Eugene Kim, "Salesforce Added a New Section to Its Annual Report Highlighting Its Social Activism," *CNBC*, March 9, 2018, https://www.cnbc.com/2018/03/09/salesforce-annual-report-emphasizes-social-activism.html (accessed March 11, 2018); Salesforce, "Join the Power of Us Program," www.salesforce.org/nonprofit/power-of-us/ (accessed December 26, 2016); *Fortune*, "100 Best Companies to Work For: Salesforce.com," 2016, http://fortune.com/best-companies/salesforce-23/ (accessed December 26, 2016); Salesforce, "Recognition," 2016, www.salesforce.com/company/awards/company.jsp (accessed December 26, 2016); Milton Moskowitz and Charles Kapelke, "25 Top-Paying Companies," *CNNMoney*, January 26, 2011, http://money.cnn.com/galleries/2011/pf/jobs/1101/gallery.best_companies_top_paying.fortune/index.html (accessed December 26, 2016); Salesforce, "Salesforce.org's 1-1-1 Integrated Philosophy," www.salesforce.org/ (accessed December 26, 2016); Chris Kanaracus, "Salesforce.com's Marc Benioff Talks Growth, Microsoft," *InfoWorld*, June 6, 2011, www.infoworld.com/article2621807/applications/salesforce-com-ceo-benioff-talks-growth—analytics—and-microsoft.html (accessed December 26, 2016);

Steve D. Jones, "Salesforce.com Shares Weaken on Concern about Billings Growth," *The Wall Street Journal*, November 18, 2011; Salesforce, "Salesforce.com Named to Ethisphere's 'World's Most Ethical Companies' List for Fifth Consecutive Year," April 27, 2011, www.salesforce.com/company/news-press/press-releases/2011/04/110427.jsp (accessed December 26, 2016).

75 Drake Baer, "How Patagonia's New CEO Is Increasing Profits While Trying to Save the World," *Fast Company*, February 28, 2014, www.fastcompany.com/3026713/lessons-learned/how-patagonias-new-ceo-is-increasing-profits-while-trying-to-save-the-world (accessed July 22, 2015); Meredith Debry Berg, "Why Advertising Is 'Dead Last' Priority at Outerwear Marketer Patagonia," *Advertising Age*, December 17, 2013, http://adage.com/article/cmo- strategy/advertising-dead-priority-patagonia/ 245712/ (accessed July 22, 2015); eBay, "Join Us in the Common Threads Partnership," http://campaigns.ebay.com/patagonia/join/ (accessed July 22, 2015).

Chapter 19

1 Alan Tovey, "Aston Martin Upgrades Forecasts as Demand for Luxury Sports Cars Moves into Fast Lane," *The Telegraph (U.K.)*, November 22, 2017, www.telegraph.co.uk/business/2017/11/22/aston-martin-upgrades-forecasts-demand-luxury-sports-cars-moves/ (accessed March 5, 2018); Peter Campbell, "Aston Martin Profits Rev Up under Plain-Speaking Chief Andy Palmer," *Financial Times*, November 24, 2017, www.ft.com/content/823477ea-d113-11e7-b781-794ce08b24dc (accessed March 5, 2018); Brett Berk, "A Hypercar Made to Measure," *Bloomberg Businessweek*, September 25, 2017, pp. 70–71.

2 Rajneesh Suri and Kent B. Monroe, "The Effects of Time Constraints on Consumers' Judgments of Prices and Products," *Journal of Consumer Research* 30, 1 (2003): pp. 92–104.

3 Tom Ryan, "Will Lower Everyday Prices Boost Target's Traffic and Sales?" *RetailWire*, September 11, 2017, http://www.retailwire.com/discussion/will-lower-everyday-prices-boost-targets-traffic-and-sales/ (accessed March 5, 2018).

4 Nathaniel Meyersohn, "Planet Fitness Is Winning by Charging $10 a Month," *CNN*, January 12, 2018, http://money.cnn.com/2018/01/12/news/companies/planet-fitness/index.html?iid=hp-stack-dom (accessed March 5, 2018).

5 Craig Giammona, "The Germans Are Escalating America's Grocery Price War," *Bloomberg*, January 3, 2018, https://www.bloomberg.com/news/articles/2018-01-03/amazon-gets-the-headlines-but-lidl-is-still-the-grocer-to-watch (accessed March 5, 2018).

6 "About Ethel M.® Chocolates," https://www.ethelm.com/category/customer+service/about+us.do (accessed March 5, 2018).

7 *Dictionary of Marketing Terms*, American Marketing Association, https://www.ama.org/resources/Pages/Dictionary.aspx (accessed March 6, 2018).

8 Bart Jansen, "Boeing Laying Off Hundreds More Engineers," *USA Today*, February 17, 2017, https://www.usatoday.com/story/money/2017/04/17/boeing-laying-off-hundreds/100573444/ (accessed March 6, 2018).

9 Russell S. Winer, *Pricing* (Cambridge, MA: Marketing Science Institute, 2005), p. 20.

10 Manoj Thomas and Geeta Menon, "When Internal Reference Prices and Price Expectations Diverge: The Role of Confidence," *Journal of Marketing Research* 44, 3 (August 2007): pp. 401–409.

11 Donald R. Lichtenstein, Nancy M. Ridgway, and Richard G. Netemeyer, "Price Perceptions and Consumer Shopping Behavior: A Field Study," *Journal of Marketing Research*, 30, 2 (1993): pp. 234–245.

12 Gerald E. Smith and Thomas T. Nagle, "A Question of Value," *Marketing Management* 14, 4 (2005): pp. 39–40.

13 Lisa Eckelbecker, "Macy's to Open In-Store Outlet at Solomon Pond Mall," *Telegram & Gazette*, March 5, 2018, http://www.telegram.com/news/20180305/macys-to-open-in-store-outlet-at-solomon-pond-mall (accessed March 6, 2018).

14 Hannah Elliott, "Why the 2018 Bentley Bentayga Justifies the Price Tag," *Bloomberg*, October 3, 2017, https://www.bloomberg.com/news/articles/2017-10-03/2018-bentley-bentayga-review-worth-the-230-000-price-tag (accessed March 7, 2018).

15 Chris Isadore, "Is a Fare War Coming? United Sparks Worries among Investors," *CNN*, January 24, 2018, http://money.cnn.com/2018/01/24/news/companies/united-airlines-fare-war/index.html (accessed March 7, 2018).

16 Julia Horowitz, "Bumble Bee Agrees to Plead Guilty in Tuna Price Fixing Scheme," *CNN*, May 8, 2017, http://money.cnn.com/2017/05/08/news/companies/bumble-bee-tuna-price-fixing/index.html (accessed March 7, 2018).

17 "TJX Cos. to Pay $8.5 Million to End Class Claims over Sale Prices," *Lexis Legal News*, December 13, 2017, https://www.lexislegalnews.com/articles/22749/tjx-cos-to-pay-8-5-million-to-end-class-claims-over-sale-prices (accessed March 7, 2018).

18 Christo Wilson, "If You Use a Mac or an Android, E-commerce Sites May Be Charging You More," *The Washington Post*, November 3, 2014, https://www.washingtonpost.com/posteverything/wp/2014/11/03/if-you-use-a-mac-or-an-android-e-commerce-sites-may-be-charging-you-more/ (accessed March 7, 2018).

19 "#20 Louis Vuitton," *Forbes*, May 2017, https://www.forbes.com/companies/louis-vuitton/ (accessed March 8, 2018); Jason Chow, "Weak Euro Masks Lingering Woes at LVMH, Kering," *The Wall Street Journal*, July 26, 2015, http://www.wsj.com/articles/low-euro-masks-lingering-woes-at-lvmh-kering-1437942805 (accessed February 15, 2016); "#14 Louis Vuitton," *Forbes*, May 2015, http://www.forbes.com/companies/louis-vuitton/ (accessed February 15, 2016); Christina Passariello, "Louis Vuitton Sports a Richer Price Tag," *The Wall Street Journal*, April 16, 2013, https://www.wsj.com/articles/SB10001424127887324345804578426902194074008 (accessed March 8, 2018); Lauren Milligan, "Would You Pay 70 Per Cent More for Chanel?" *Vogue*, March 5, 2014, http://www.vogue.co.uk/news/2014/03/05/price-increases-for-luxury-items—chanel-louis-vuitton-bags (accessed February 15, 2016); https://us.louisvuitton.com/ (accessed March 8, 2018).

20 Martin Moylan, "As Target Pharmacies Shift to CVS, Will Consumers Stick Around?" *MPR News*, July 29, 2015, http://www.mprnews.org/story/2015/07/29/target-cvs-pharmacy-switch (accessed February 4, 2016); Andrew Pollack, "Drug Goes from $13.50 a Tablet to $750, Overnight," *The New York Times*, September 20, 2015, http://www.nytimes.com/2015/09/21/business/a-huge-overnight-increase-in-a-drugs-price-raises-protests.html?_r=0 (accessed December 4, 2015); CVS Caremark, "Mail Order Direct," https://www2.caremark.com/nlc/mod.htm (accessed February 4, 2016); CVS, "CVS iSave," https://www.cvsisave.com/ (accessed February 4, 2016); Robert Langreth, "Big Pharma's Foe Takes Victory Lap as Drug Price Increases Slow," *Bloomberg*, September 10, 2015, http://www.bloomberg.com/news/articles/2015-09-10/big-pharma-s-foe-takes-victory-lap-as-drug-price-increases-slow (accessed February 4, 2016); Ransdell Pierson, "CVS Urges Cost Controls for New Cholesterol Drugs," *Reuters*, February 17, 2015, http://www.reuters.com/article/us-cvs-health-cholesterol-idUSKBN0LL1CQ20150217

(accessed February 4, 2016); CVS Pharmacy, "Deals," http://www.cvs.com/deals/deals .jsp (accessed February 9, 2016); Robert Langreth, "Good Drug Deals: CVS, Express Scripts Drive Hard Bargains with Manufacturers," *Providence Journal*, September 11, 2015, http://www.providencejournal. com/article/20150911/NEWS/150919716 (accessed February 4, 2016); Trisha Thadani, "CVS Drops Viagra, Other Drugs, from Insurance Coverage," *USA Today*, August 6, 2015, http://www.usatoday.com/story/news/ health/2015/08/06/cvs-drops-viagra/31227269/ (accessed February 4, 2016); CVS, "About Us," MinuteClinic, https://www.cvs.com/ minuteclinic/visit/about-us (accessed March 8, 2018); CVS, "Services," MinuteClinic, https:// www.cvs.com/minuteclinic/services (accessed March 8, 2018).

Chapter 20

1. Andrea Felsted and Sarah Halzack, "European Discounters Are Coming for Your Retail Sales, America," *Bloomberg*, October 16, 2017, www.bloomberg.com/ gadfly/articles/2017-10-16/aldi-lidl-and-primark-invade-u-s-retail (accessed March 12, 2018); Craig Giammona, "Aldi and Lidl Take Supermarket Battle to the U.S.," *Bloomberg*, June 11, 2017, https://www.bloomberg.com/ news/articles/2017-06-12/european-grocery-rivalry-expands-to-u-s-as-aldi-lidl-bulk-up (accessed March 12, 2018); Beth Kowitt, "Why Discount Grocer Aldi Is Getting into the Delivery Game," *Fortune*, August 14, 2017, http:// fortune.com/2017/08/13/aldi-instacart-amazon-whole-foods/ (accessed March 12, 2018).

2. Brad Tuttle, "Gillette Is Finally Slashing Its Crazy Razor Prices," *Time*, April 4, 2017, http://time.com/money/4724823/gillette-razor-prices-cut/ (accessed March 12, 2018).

3. "The Profit Impact of Market Strategies (PIMS) Overview," The Strategic Planning Institute, http://pimsonline.com/about_pims _db.htm (accessed February 20, 2017).

4. Ari Cetron, "19 of the Most Outrageously Overpriced Products," *MoneyTalks News*, August 29, 2017, https://www.moneytalksnews .com/19-of-the-most-outrageously-overpriced-products/ (accessed March 13, 2018).

5. Rafi Mohammed, "The Psychology Behind the New iPhone's Four-Digit Price," *Harvard Business Review*, September 21, 2017, https:// hbr.org/2017/09/the-psychology-behind-the-new-iphones-four-digit-price (accessed March 13, 2018).

6. "Costco's Kirkland Signature Alcohol Boosting Stores' Bottom Line in a Big Way," *Fox News*, March 17, 2017, http://www.foxnews .com/food-drink/2017/03/17/

costcos-kirkland-signature-alcohol-boosting-stores-bottom-line-in-big-way.html (accessed March 13, 2018).

7. Lizette Chapman, "Disney Raises Park Prices, Plans Fixed-Date Ticketing," *Bloomberg*, February 11, 2018, https://www.bloomberg .com/news/articles/2018-02-11/disney-raises-park-prices-weighs-plan-for-fixed-date-ticketing (accessed March 13, 2018).

8. Bill Shaikin, "What Does the Dodgers' Dynamic Pricing Schedule Mean for Fans? A Seat That Costs $33 One Day Will Cost $80 Another Day," *Los Angeles Times*, January 26, 2018, http://www.latimes. com/sports/dodgers/la-sp-dodgers-tickets-20180126-story.html (accessed March 13, 2018).

9. "What Is Dynamic Pricing?" Uber, https:// help.uber.com/h/34212e8b-d69a-4d8a-a923-095d3075b487 (accessed March 13, 2018).

10. Bill Snyder, "Report Analyzes Amazon's Dynamic Pricing Strategy," *CIO*, January 16, 2015, http://www.cio.com/article/2870961/ consumer-technology/report-analyzes-amazons-dynamic-pricing-strategy.html (accessed March 13, 2018).

11. Joan Lindsay Mullken and Ross D. Petty, "Marketing Tactics Discouraging Price Search: Deception and Competition," *Journal of Business Research* 64, 1 (2011): pp. 67–73.

12. Martin Spann, Marc Fischer, and Gerard J. Tillis, "Skimming or Penetration? Strategic Dynamic Pricing for New Products," *Marketing Science*, 34, 2 (2015): pp. 235–249; "New USC Marshall Study Challenges Marketing Strategy Assumptions," USC Marshall School of Business news release, March 15, 2015, https:// www.marshall.usc.edu/news/new-usc-marshall-study-challenges-marketing-strategy-assumptions (accessed March 14, 2018).

13. Stephanie Clifford and Catherine Rampell, "Sometimes, We Want Prices to Fool Us," *The New York Times*, April 14, 2013, www .nytimes.com/2013/04/14/business/for-penney-a-tough-lesson-in-shopper-psychology .html (accessed March 14, 2018).

14. Sy Mukherjee, "Johnson & Johnson Is Dialing Down Crazy Drug Price Hikes," *Fortune*, February 27, 2017, http://fortune .com/2017/02/27/pharma-drug-price-hikes/ (accessed March 14, 2018).

15. Lauren Thomas, "Warby Parker Aims to Run Nearly 100 Stores This Year, as Other Web Shops Follow," *CNBC*, February 15, 2018, https://www.cnbc.com/2018/02/15/ as-warby-parker-approaches-100-stores-other-internet-brands-follow.html (accessed March 14, 2018); Richard Benson, "Warby Parker Is Bringing Affordable Eyewear to the Developing World," *Wired UK*, June 1, 2016,

www.wired.co.uk/article/warby-parker-glasses-profit-purpose; Farnoosh Torabi, "Warby Parker: How to Limit Risk When You Try to Double Your Size," *CNBC*, May 3, 2016, www.cnbc.com/2016/05/03/warby-parker-how-to-limit-risk-when-you-try-to-double-your-size.html; Ginia Bellafante, "At Warby Parker, a Sense of Exclusion in a Low Price," *The New York Times*, May 20, 2016, www.nytimes.com/2016/05/22/nyregion/at-warby-parker-a-sense-of-exclusion-in-a-low-price.html; Courtney Rubin, "Smile! Photo Booths Prove You're a Happy Customer," *The New York Times*, October 6, 2015, www.nytimes.com/2015/ 10/08/fashion/photo-boots-warby-parker-topshop.html; *Innovation Agents: Dave Gilboa, co-founder, Warby Parker*, www .youtube.com/watch?v=jJSKGUPou8w; www.warbyparker.com.

16. Michael Thomas, "Low Fares and Snack Fees—How No-Frills Favorite Norwegian Air Went Global," *Fast Company*, August 14, 2017, www.fastcompany.com/40401500/ how-travel-favorite-norwegian-air-went-global-with-low-fares-and-snack-fees (accessed March 14, 2018); Tanya Powley and Richard Milne, "Investors Fret over Norwegian Air's Rapid Growth," December 8, 2017, www.ft.com/content/a013d226-daa8-11e7-a039-c64b1c09b482 (accessed March 14, 2018); Dan Reed, "Norwegian What? Little-Known Oslo-Based Discounter Is Disrupting Big Airlines' Profit Model," *Forbes*, November 7, 2017, https://www .forbes.com/sites/danielreed/2017/11/07/ norwegian-what-little-known-oslo-based-discounter-is-disrupting-big-airlines-profit-model/#6e2f402c1c30 (accessed March 14, 2018); www.norwegian.com, (accessed March 14, 2018).

17. Kerry Hannon, "Rent the Jet, or Island," *The New York Times*, February 14, 2016, p. F2; Lauren A. White, "The Sharing Economy's New Frontier: Everyday Clothing Rental," *CBS News*, January 20, 2016, www.cbsnews.com/ news/sharing-economy-gwynnie-bee-everyday-plus-size-clothing-rental/ (accessed February 29, 2016); Phil LeBeau, "Car-Sharing Impact Will Be Limited, Despite a Jump in Shared Mobility Start-ups, BCG Says," *CNBC*, February 23, 2016, www .cnbc.com/2016/02/23/car-sharing-impact-will-be-limited-despite-a-jump-in-shared-mobility-start-ups-bcg-says.html (accessed February 29, 2016); Rick Broida, "Rent Private Cars for Cheap with Turo," *CNET*, February 22, 2016, www.cnet.com/how-to/rent-private-cars-for-cheap-with-turo (accessed February 29, 2016); Zoe Henry, "How Rent the Runway Plans to Own Your

Closet," *Inc.,* November 13, 2015, www.inc
.com/zoe-henry/rent-the-runway-2015-
company-of-the-year-nominee.html (accessed
February 29, 2016); Drew Casey, "Lumoid
Pioneers a 'Try before You Buy' Model
of Buying Gadgets," *CNBC,* December
20, 2015, www.cnbc.com/2015/12/17/
lumoid-pioneers-a-try-before-you-buy-model-
of-buying-gadgets.html (accessed
February 29, 2016); Benny Evangelista, "As
Drones Take off, S.F. Startup Lumoid Teaches
Flight School," *San Francisco Chronicle,*
October 30, 2015, www.sfchronicle.com/
business/article/As-drones-take-off-S-F-
startup-Lumoid-teaches-6601990.php
(accessed February 29, 2016); Sarah Buhr,
"Why Gear Rental Marketplace Lumoid Shut
Down," *TechCrunch,* December 10, 2017,
https://techcrunch.com/2017/12/10/why-
gear-rental-marketplace-lumoid-shut-down
(accessed April 9, 2018).

Feature Notes

Chapter 1

[a] Adapted from "Zappos: Delivering Happiness to Stakeholders," Daniels Fund Ethics Initiative, http://danielsethics.mgt.unm .edu/pdf/Zappos%20Case.pdf (accessed December 24, 2017); Zappos.com, "Company Statement from Zappos.com," YouTube, April 1, 2016, https://www.youtube.com/ watch?v=3zieP6NUWL8 (accessed December 24, 2017); Steve Olenski, "Customer Relationships: Creating a Foundation for Successful Marketing Partnerships," *Forbes*, November 18, 2015, https://www.forbes. com/sites/steveolenski/2015/11/18/customer-relationships-creating-a-foundation-for-successful-marketing-partnerships/ (accessed December 24, 2017); Gabriel Beltrone, "Zappos Turned True Customer Stories Into Charming Low-Budget Ads," *Adweek*, November 7, 2017, www.adweek.com/ creativity/zappos-turned-true-customer-stories-into-charming-low-budget-ads/ (accessed December 24, 2017); Micah Solomon, "Tony Hsieh Reveals the Secret to Zappos' Customer Service Success in One Word," *Forbes*, June 12, 2017, https://www .forbes.com/sites/micahsolomon/2017/06/12/ tony-hsieh-spills-the-beans-the-one-word-secret-of-zappos-customer-service-success/ #7fb208401acc (accessed December 24, 2017).

[b] Abigail Abrams, "Nestlé Just Announced a Huge Blue Bottle Coffee Deal. What's That?" *TIME*, September 14, 2017, http://time .com/4942170/blue-bottle-coffee-nestle-stock/ (accessed December 24, 2017); Jonathan Kauffmann, "Blue Bottle Coffee Faces Challenges as It Moves to New Ground," *San Francisco Chronicle*, October 8, 2016, www .sfchronicle.com/business/article/ Blue-Bottle-Coffee-faces-challenges-as-it-moves-9952708.php (accessed December 24, 2017); Madeline Stone, "Why People Are Crazy about Blue Bottle, the Coffee Chain that Just Raised Another $70 Million from Tech Investors," *Business Insiders*, June 5, 2015, www.businessinsider.com/ what-blue-bottle-coffee-is-like-2015-6/ (accessed December 24, 2017); "Blue Bottle Coffee: Palo Alto," https://bluebottlecoffee. com/cafes/palo-alto (accessed December 3, 2016); Danielle Sacks, "Brewing the Perfect Cup," *Fast Company*, September 2014, pp. 86–91; Richard Reynolds, "Coffee's Third Wave," *Imbibe*, January 22, 2009, http://imbibemagazine.com/coffee-s-third-wave/ (accessed December 24, 2017); Joel Stein, "Blue Bottle Coffee and the Next Wave of Artisanal Coffee Shops," *Bloomberg Businessweek*, May 1, 2014, https://www .bloomberg.com/news/articles/2014-05-01/ blue-bottle-coffee-and-the-next-wave-of-artisanal-coffee-shops (accessed December 24, 2017); Blue Bottle Coffee, "Cafés," https:// bluebottlecoffee.com/cafes (accessed December 24, 2017); Clarissa Buch, "Blue Bottle Coffee Opens in the Design District and Aventura Mall," *Miami New Times*, October 18, 2017, www.miaminewtimes. com/restaurants/blue-bottle-coffee-opens-in-miamis-design-district-and-aventura-mall-9755247 (accessed December 24, 2017).

Chapter 2

[a] Robert Klara, "What Tiffany & Co. Learned About Mobile from Watching Its Competitors," *Adweek*, September 27, 2017, www.adweek.com/brand-marketing/ what-tiffany-co-learned-about-mobile-from-watching-its-competitors/ (accessed January 5, 2018); "Tiffany, Signet Shine after Fashion Jewelry Drives Sales Beat," *Reuters*, August 24, 2017, www.reuters.com/ article/us-tiffany-results/tiffany-signet-shine-after-fashion-jewelry-drives-sales-beat-idUSKCN1B416B (accessed January 5, 2018); Stephanie Hoi-Nga Wong, "Tiffany Makes Inroads with Millennials as Hepburn Era Fades," *Bloomberg News*, August 24, 2017, https://www.bloomberg.com/news/ articles/2017-08-24/tiffany-drops-as-sluggish-demand-hurt-sales-in-most-regions (accessed January 5, 2018); www.tiffany.com (accessed November 9, 2017).

[b] "The Future Is Still Unclear for Voice Shopping," *PYMNTS*, October 13, 2017, www .pymnts.com/voice-activation/2017/voice-shopping-artificial-intelligence (accessed January 5, 2018); Brian Barrett, "An Alexa and Cortana Team-Up Won't Get Far Without a Phone," *Wired*, August 30, 2017, www .businessinsider.com/amazon-microsoft-make-ai-virtual-assistants-alexa-cortana-talk-2017-8 (accessed January 5, 2018); Sarah Perez, "Amazon Adds Alexa to Its Main Shopping App," *TechCrunch*, March 16, 2017, https://techcrunch.com/2017/03/16/amazon-adds-alexa-to-its-main-shopping-app (accessed January 5, 2018); Penelope Green, "'Alexa, Where Have You Been All My Life?'" *The New York Times*, July 11, 2017, www.nytimes .com/2017/07/11/style/alexa-amazon-echo .html (accessed January 5, 2018); www .amazon.com (accessed November 9, 2017).

Chapter 3

[a] Kate Taylor, "The incredible story of how Chick-fil-A took over fast food," *Business Insider*, January 25, 2016, www .businessinsider.com/chick-fil-a-history-and-facts-2016-1/#chick-fil-a-has-its-roots-in-a-restaurant-called-the-dwarf-grill-opened-by-founder-truett-cathy-in-1946-1 (accessed November 2, 2017); Chick-fil-A, "Who We Are," https://www.chick-fil-a.com/About/ Who-We-Are (accessed November 2, 2017); Hayley Peterson, "Why Chick-fil-A's restaurants sell 4 times as much as KFC's," *Business Insider*, August 1, 2017, www .businessinsider.com/why-chick-fil-a-is-so-successful-2017-8 (accessed November 2, 2017).

[b] Caryn Ginsberg, "The Market for Vegetarian Foods," *The Vegetarian Resource Group*, www.vrg.org/nutshell/market.htm (accessed December 19, 2017); Jaag Korteweg, Founder of De Vegetarische Slager, November 2017 (J. Wienen, Interviewer); Nielsen, "Green Generation: Millennials Say Sustainability Is a Shopping Priority," November 5, 2015, www.nielsen.com/us/en/insights/news/2015/

green-generation-millennials-say-sustainability-is-a-shopping-priority.html (accessed December 19, 2017); The Vegetarian Butcher, "About Us," 2017, https://www .thevegetarianbutcher.com/about-us/since-1962 (accessed December 19, 2017); Niamh Michail, "Vegetarian Butcher Slams Dutch Food Authority for Double Standards Over 'Misleading' Meat Name Ban," *Food Navigator*, October 5, 2017, https://www.foodnavigator. com/Article/2017/10/05/Vegetarian-Butcher-slams-Dutch-food-authority-for-double-standards-over-misleading-meat-name-ban (accessed December 19, 2017); Bryan Walsh, "The Triple Whopper Environmental Impact of Global Meat Production," *TIME*, December 16, 2013, http://science.time. com/2013/12/16/the-triple-whopper-environmental-impact-of-global-meat-production/ (accessed February 6, 2018).

Chapter 4

a   Jennifer Kaplan, "Vita Coco to Near $1 Billion in Sales as Potential Buyers Circle," *Bloomberg*, February 14, 2017, https://www .bloomberg.com/news/articles/2017-02-14/vita-coco-to-near-1-billion-in-sales-as-potential-buyers-circle (accessed January 24, 2018); UNM Daniels Fund Ethics Initiative, "Harmless Harvest: First Fair Trade to Life Coconut Water," 2016, https://danielsethics. mgt.unm.edu/pdf/harmless-harvest.pdf (accessed December 17, 2016); Elaine Watson, "Harmless Harvest Raw Coconut Water: We're Not Competing with Vita Coco or Zico," *Food Navigator*, January 6, 2016, www.foodnavigator-usa.com/Manufacturers/Harmless-Harvest-raw-coconut-water-We-re-not-competing-with-Vita-Coco (accessed December 17, 2016); Liz Welch, "How These 2 Guys Are Winning the Hyper-Competitive Coconut Water Wars," *Inc.*, June 2016, www.inc.com/magazine/201606/liz-welch/harmless-harvest-coconut-water-sustainability. html (accessed December 17, 2016); Kat Odell, "Taste Test: The Best Coconut Water," *Eater*, March 18, 2016, www.eater .com/drinks/2016/3/18/11222874/taste-test-coconut-water-best (accessed December 17, 2016); Quality Assurance & Food Safety, "Harmless Harvest Takes 'Constructive Capitalism' Approach," August 16, 2016, www.qualityassurancemag.com/article/harmless-harvest-takes-constructive-capitalism-approach/ (accessed December 17, 2016).

b   Centers for Disease Control, "12 Month-Ending Provisional Counts of Drug Overdose Deaths," *Centers for Disease Control*, January 16,

2018, https://www.cdc.gov/nchs/nvss/vsrr/drug-overdose-data.htm (accessed January 16, 2018); Julie Hirschfeld Davis, "Trump Declares Opioid Crisis a 'Health Emergency' but Requests No Funds," *The New York Times*, October 26, 2017, https://www.nytimes .com/2017/10/26/us/politics/trump-opioid-crisis.html (accessed January 22, 2018); Eric Eyre, "Pill Rules Not Enforced," *The Pulitzer Prizes*, December 19, 2016, www .pulitzer.org/winners/eric-eyre (accessed January 22, 2018); Michael Kranz, "Deaths from Opioid Overdoses Are Especially Prevalent in 4 U.S. States," *Business Insider*, October 31, 2017, www.businessinsider.com/opioid-crisis-death-rates-four-states-us-average-trump-2017-10 (accessed January 11, 2018); Anders Melin and Jef Feeley, "McKesson Records Show Failed Opioid Oversight, Lawsuit Says," *Bloomberg*, December 8, 2017, https://www.bloomberg.com/news/articles/2017-12-08/mckesson-investor-claims-board-failed-oversight-duty-on-opioids (accessed January 21, 2018); Gretchen Morgenson, "Hard Questions for a Company at the Center of the Opioid Crisis," *The New York Times*, July 21 2017, https://www.nytimes.com/2017/07/21/business/mckesson-opioid-packaging.html (accessed January 22, 2018); Raymond Nate, "McKesson in Record $150 Million U.S. Settlement Over Suspicious Drug Orders," *Reuters*, January 17, 2017, https://www .reuters.com/article/us-mckesson-justice/mckesson-in-record-150-million-u-s-settlement-over-suspicious-drug-orders-idUSKBN15133J (accessed January 11, 2018); Charles Omstein, "Drug-Distributors Penalized for Turning Blind Eye in Opioid Epidemic," January 27, 2017, https://www .npr.org/sections/health-shots/2017/01/27/511858862/drug-distributors-penalized-for-turning-blind-eye-in-opioid-epidemic (accessed January 16, 2018); Open Secrets Organization, "Lobbying Spending Database - McKesson Corp, 2017," January 23, 2018, https://www.opensecrets.org/lobb/clientsum. php?id=D000022105 (accessed January 23, 2018); Sara Randazzo, "U.S. News: State Sues Drug Maker for Opioid Marketing," *The Wall Street Journal*, August 16, 2017, https://search.proquest.com/results/CA32B32728084 247PQ/1?accountid=8421 (accessed January 11, 2018); The United States Department of Justice, "McKesson Agrees to Pay Record $150 million settlement for Failure to Report Suspicious Orders for Pharmaceutical Drugs," The United States Department of Justice, January 17, 2017, https://www.justice.gov/

opa/pr/mckesson-agrees-pay-record-150-million-settlement-failure-report-suspicious-orders (accessed, January 12, 2018); Jeanne Whalen, "McKesson to Pay $150 Million for Failing to Report 'Suspicious' Drug Orders," *The Wall Street Journal*, January 17, 2017, https://www.wsj.com/articles/mckesson-to-pay-150-million-for-failing-to-report-suspicious-drug-orders-1484699478 (accessed January 18, 2018).

Chapter 5

a   Danny Bradbury, "Small Business, Big Data: How to Boost Your Marketing with Analytics," *Forbes*, June 5, 2015, www .forbes.com/sites/ramcommercial/2015/06/05/small-business-big-data-how-to-boost-your-marketing-with-analytics/#66e9645c79b3 (accessed December 17, 2016); Kimberly A. Whitler, "How the Best Marketers Are Using Analytics to Create Competitive Advantage," *Forbes*, July 18, 2015, www.forbes.com/sites/kimberlywhitler/2015/07/19/how-some-of-the-best-marketers-are-using-analytics-to-create-a-competitive-advantage/#3dd8d4ce4870 (accessed December 17, 2016); Louis Columbus, "Roundup of Analytics, Big Data & Business Intelligence Forecasts and Market Estimates, 2015," *Forbes*, May 25, 2015, www.forbes.com/sites/louiscolumbus/2015/05/25/roundup-of-analytics-big-data-business-intelligence-forecasts-and-market-estimates-2015/#74fa 33284869 (accessed December 17, 2016); Krystle Vermes, "84% of B2B Marketers Consider Analytics to Be Very Important to Success," *KoMarketing*, August 8, 2016, www.komarketingassociates.com/industry-news/report-84-b2b-marketers-consider-analytics-important-success-3172/ (accessed December 17, 2016).

b   Ellen Byron, "'From Diapers to 'Depends': Marketers Discreetly Retool for Aging Boomers," *The Wall Street Journal*, February 5, 2011, http://online.wsj.com/article/SB100014 24052748704013604576104394209062996.html (accessed November 19, 2014); Bruce Horovitz, "Big-Spending Baby Boomers Bend the Rules of Marketing," *USA Today*, November 16, 2010, www.usatoday.com/money/advertising/2010-11-16-1Aboomerbuyers16_CV_N.htm (accessed November 19, 2014); Matthew Boyle, "Aging Boomers Befuddle Marketers Aching for $15 Trillion Prize," *Bloomberg*, September 16, 2012, www.bloomberg.com/news/2013-09-17/aging-boomers-befuddle-marketers-eying-15-trillion-prize.html (accessed November 6, 2014).

Chapter 6

[a] Zoe Wood, "Introducing Halo Top: The 'Healthy' Ice-Cream Taking Over America," *The Guardian*, October 20, 2017, https://www.theguardian.com/lifeandstyle/2017/oct/20/introducing-halo-top-the-healthy-ice-cream-taking-over-america (accessed November 8, 2017); Ronald D. White, "How a Lawyer Turned His Homemade Treats into America's Best-Selling Ice Cream Pint," *Los Angeles Times*, October 18, 2017, http://www.duluthnewstribune.com/lifestyle/food/4345513-how-lawyer-turned-his-homemade-treats-americas-best-selling-ice-cream-pint (accessed November 8, 2017); www.halotop.com (accessed November 8, 2017).

[b] Amina Elahi, "Flowers for Dreams Brings Its Burlap-Wrapped Bouquets to Milwaukee," *Chicago Tribune*, January 24, 2017, www.chicagotribune.com/bluesky/originals/ct-flowers-for-dreams-expansion-milwaukee-bsi-20170124-story.html (accessed November 8, 2017); Micah Materre, "Friends Blooming Business Helps Charities Too," *WGN-TV*, March 31, 2017, http://wgntv.com/2017/03/31/friends-blooming-business-helps-charities-too/ (accessed November 8, 2017); Cassandra West, "Artisanal Bouquets Delivered by Bike Couriers: How Millennial, and Profitable," *Crain's Chicago Business*, June 23, 2016, www.chicagobusiness.com/article/20160623/ISSUE01/160629945/artisanal-bouquets-delivered-by-bike-couriers-how-millennial-and-profitable (accessed November 8, 2017); www.flowersfordreams.com (accessed November 8, 2017).

Chapter 7

[a] Becky Willan, "Why Unilever's Sustainable Living Brands Are Driving Growth," *Campaign Live*, May 25, 2017, https://www.campaignlive.co.uk/article/why-unilevers-sustainable-living-brands-driving-growth/1434506 (accessed November 13, 2017); Leonie Roderick, "Unilever's Sustainable Brands Grow 50% Faster than the Rest of the Business," *Marketing Week*, May 18, 2017, www.marketingweek.com/2017/05/18/unilever-sustainable-brands-growth/ (accessed November 13, 2017); Vivienne Walt, "Unilever CEO Paul Polman's Plan to Save the World," *Fortune*, February 17, 2017, http://fortune.com/2017/02/17/unilever-paul-polman-responsibility-growth (accessed November 13, 2017).

[b] Sarah Perez, "Target Is Adding Pinterest's Visual Search Tool to Its App and Website," *Techcrunch*, September 25, 2017, https://techcrunch.com/2017/09/25/target-is-adding-pinterests-visual-search-tool-to-its-app-and-website/ (accessed November 13, 2017); "Target Explores Visual Search with Pinterest," *WARC*, October 17, 2017, www.warc.com/newsandopinion/news/target_explores_visual_search_with_pinterest/39452 (accessed November 13, 2017); Adrianne Pasquarelli, "Target + Pinterest = a Quest for Holiday Dollars," *Advertising Age*, September 25, 2017, http://adage.com/article/cmo-strategy/target-pinterest-dollars/310606/# (accessed November 13, 2017).

Chapter 8

[a] Melissa Thompson, "6 Industries That Could Be Forever Changed by Blockchain," *Inc.*, October 10, 2017, www.inc.com/melissa-thompson/6-industries-that-could-be-forever-changed-by-blockchain.html (accessed January 19, 2018); Eva Grey, "Could Blockchain Technology Revolutionise Shipping?" *Ship Technology*, September 11, 2017, www.ship-technology.com/features/featurecould-blockchain-technology-revolutionise-shipping-5920391/ (accessed January 19, 2018); Robert Hackett, "Maersk and Microsoft Tested a Blockchain for Shipping Insurance," *Fortune*, September 5, 2017, http://fortune.com/2017/09/05/maersk-blockchain-insurance/; Gertrude Chavez-Dreyfuss, "IBM, Maersk in Blockchain Tie-up for Shipping Industry," *Reuters*, March 6, 2017, www.reuters.com/article/us-usa-blockchain-ibm/ibm-maersk-in-blockchain-tie-up-for-shipping-industry-idUSKBN16D26Q (accessed January 19, 2018).

[b] Yvelette Stines, "Brittni Brown Is Changing the Game of Public Relations," *Michipreneur*, March 29, 2017, www.michipreneur.com/brittni-brown-is-changing-the-game-of-public-relations/ (accessed January 19, 2018); Danielle D. Hughes, "'Bee-Coming Your Brand University' Is Educating Young Professionals and Entrepreneurs," *Black Enterprise*, March 24, 2017, www.blackenterprise.com/small-business-featured/bee-coming-your-brand-university-educate-professionals-entrepreneurs (accessed January 19, 2018); Janay Nicole, "Bee-Coming a BAUCE: Publicist Brittni Brown on Personal Branding and Entrepreneurship," *BAUCE*, March 27, 2017, http://baucemag.com/publicist-brittni-brown-personal-branding-entrepreneurship/ (accessed January 19, 2018); Teresa Duhl, "Making Their Mark: Brittni Brown (28), The Bee Agency," *Corp!*, November–December 2016, pp. 28–29; www.thebeeagency.com (accessed January 19, 2018).

Chapter 9

[a] Anmar Frangoul, "Here Are Six of China's Ambitious, Mind-Boggling, Renewable Energy Projects," *CNBC*, January 22, 2018, https://www.cnbc.com/2018/01/22/here-are-six-of-chinas-ambitious-mind-boggling-renewable-energy-projects.html (accessed February 11, 2018); Sherisse Pham and Matt Rivers, "China Is Crushing the U.S. in Renewable Energy," *CNN*, July 18, 2017, http://money.cnn.com/2017/07/18/technology/china-us-clean-energy-solar-farm/index.html (accessed February 11, 2018); Pete Engardio, "Cradle of a Green Revolution," *Businessweek*, November 2, 2009, pp. 40–41; Bryan Walsh, "Electric Cars: China's Power Play," *Time*, August 31, 2009, http://content.time.com/time/magazine/article/0,9171,1917647,00.html (accessed December 17, 2016); Daniel K. Gardner, "Meet China's Green Crusader," *The New York Times*, November 1, 2009, www.nytimes.com/2009/02/11/opinion/11iht-edgardner.1.20105872.html (accessed December 17, 2016); Adam Aston, "China's Surprising Clout in Cleantech," *Businessweek*, November 30, 2009, p. 56; Bloomberg News, "China to Slow Green Growth for First Time after Record Boom," *Bloomberg*, September 22, 2016, https://www.bloomberg.com/news/articles/2016-09-22/china-to-rein-in-green-growth-for-first-time-after-record-boom (accessed December 17, 2016); "Court in China Issues Record Pollution Fine," *BBC*, December 31, 2014, www.bbc.com/news/world-asia-china-30640385 (accessed December 17, 2016); Feng Hao, "China's EV Push Hurting Fuel Economy Standards," *China Dialogue*, November 21, 2016, https://www.chinadialogue.net/article/show/single/en/9414-China-s-EV-push-hurting-fuel-economy-standards (accessed December 17, 2016).

[b] Matt Levine, "Airbnb's Public Fight to Stay Private Is Complicated," *Bloomberg*, February 9, 2018, https://www.bloomberg.com/view/articles/2018-02-09/airbnb-ipo-woes-brian-chesky-fights-to-stay-private (accessed February 11, 2018); Marco della Cava, "Airbnb Pushes Itself Further and Farther," *USA Today*, August 20, 2015, p. 3B; Eric Newcomer, "Airbnb Overhauls Service for Business Travelers," *Bloomberg*, July 20, 2015, www.bloomberg.com/news/

articles/2015-07-20/airbnb-overhauls-service-for-business-travelers (accessed February 11, 2018); Airbnb, "About Us," https://press.atairbnb.com/about-us/ (accessed February 11, 2018); Tomio Geron, "Airbnb and the Unstoppable Rise of the Share Economy," *Forbes*, January 23, 2013, www.forbes .com/sites/tomiogeron/2013/01/23/airbnb-and-the-unstoppable-rise-of-the-share-economy/ (accessed February 11, 2018); Christine Lagorio-Chafkin, "Brian Chesky, Joe Gebbia, and Nathan Blecharczyk, Founders of Airbnb," *Inc.*, July 19, 2010, www.inc. com/30under30/2010/profile-brian-chesky-joe-gebbia-nathan-blecharczyk-airbnb.html (accessed February 11, 2018); Daniel Meesak, "Airbnb's Struggles Continue as China Head Leaves Company and Tujia Keeps Expanding," *Jing Travel*, October 24, 2017, https://jingtravel .com/airbnbs-struggles-continue-china-head-leaves-company-tujia-keeps-expanding/ (accessed February 11, 2018).

Chapter 10

[a] Mike Isaac, "Facebook Mounts Effort to Limit Tide of Fake News," *The New York Times*, December 15, 2016, www.nytimes. com/2016/12/15/technology/facebook-fake-news.html?_r=0 (accessed December 23, 2016); Andrew Higgins, Mike McIntire, and Gabriel J.X. Dance, "Inside a Fake News Sausage Factory: 'This Is All About Income'," *The New York Times*, November 25, 2016, www.nytimes.com/2016/11/25/world/europe/fake-news-donald-trump-hillary-clinton-georgia.html (accessed December 23, 2016); David Pierson, "Facebook Bans Fake News from Its Advertising Network—But Not Its News Feed," *Los Angeles Times*, November 15, 2016, www.latimes.com/business/la-fi-facebook-fake-news-20161115-story.html (accessed December 23, 2016); Suzanne Vranica, "Unilever Threatens to Reduce Ad Spending on Tech Platforms That Don't Combat Divisive Content," *The Wall Street Journal*, February 11, 2018, https://www.wsj.com/articles/unilever-threatens-to-reduce-ad-spending-on-tech-platforms-that-dont-combat-divisive-content-1518398578 (accessed February 28, 2018).

[b] Cheryl Wischhover, "Michelle Phan Is Leaving ipsy," *Racked*, September 22, 2017, https://www.racked.com/2017/9/22/16347820/michelle-phan-leaving-ipsy-shopper (accessed February 17, 2018); Elizabeth Segran, "Beauty Subscriptions Are a Tough Racket, but ipsy Is Sitting Pretty," *Fast Company*, March 8, 2017, https://

www.fastcompany.com/3068822/beauty-subscriptions-are-a-tough-racket-but-ipsy-is-sitting-pretty (accessed February 17, 2018); Erin Griffith, "YouTube Star Michelle Phan's Beauty Startup ipsy Raises $100 million," *Fortune*, September 14, 2015, http://fortune.com/2015/09/14/ipsy-glam-bag-michelle-phan-funding/ (accessed December 21, 2016); Geoff Weiss, "How ipsy, Michelle Phan's Million-Member Sampling Service, Is Giving Birchbox a Run for Its Money," *Entrepreneur*, March 31, 2015, https://www.entrepreneur.com/article/244536 (accessed December 21, 2016); Khadeeja Safdar, "Birchbox, a Pioneer in Subscription Beauty Sales, Scales Back," *The Wall Street Journal*, June 15, 2016, www.wsj.com/articles/birchbox-retrenches-amid-rapid-rise-in-competition-cash-squeeze-1465983002 (accessed December 21, 2016); ipsy, https://www .ipsy.com/subscribe (accessed December 21, 2016); Tamar Anitai, "Makeup Tutorial: Learn How to Get Lady Gaga's Scary 'Bad Romance' Eyes," *MTV News*, January 27, 2010, www.mtv.com/news/2295046/makeup-tutorial-learn-how-to-get-lady-gagas-scary-bad-romance-eyes/ (accessed December 21, 2016).

Chapter 11

[a] Vanessa Friedman, "Coach Inc. Is Dead. Long Live Tapestry," *The New York Times*, October 11, 2017, www.nytimes.com/2017/10/11/fashion/coach-inc-rebrands-tapestry-american-fashion-group.html (accessed January 29, 2017); Osman Ahmed, "The Art of Renaming à Business," *Business of Fashion*, November 3, 2017, www .businessoffashion.com/articles/intelligence/the-art-of-renaming-a-business (accessed January 29, 2018); Doreen McCallister, "Coach Changes Corporate Name to Tapestry; Brand Name Is Unchanged," *NPR*, October 12, 2017, www.npr.org/sections/thetwo-way/2017/10/12/557287019/coach-changes-corporate-name-to-tapestry-brand-name-is-unchanged (accessed January 29, 2018).

[b] "Eco-Friendly Toys Nab Environmental Award," *Plastics Technology*, October 11, 2017, www.ptonline.com/articles/eco-friendly-toys-nab-environmental-award (accessed January 29, 2018); Josh Egbert, "New Toys Made from Corn and Sugar to Hit Store Shelves," *Fox21 News*, June 27, 2017, http://fox21news.com/2017/06/27/new-toys-made-from-corn-and-sugar-to-hit-

store-shelves/ (accessed January 29, 2018; Pat Ferrier, "Fort Collins Toy Company Lands John Deere License," *USA Today*, March 8, 2016, www.usatoday.com/story/money/business/2016/03/08/fort-collins-toy-company-lands-john-deere-license/81478278/ (accessed January 29, 2018); Michael Lauzon, "Farm-to-Toy Molding," *Plastics News*, July 28, 2017, www.plasticsnews.com/article/20170728/NEWS/170729892/farm-to-toy-molding (accessed January 29, 2018).

Chapter 12

[a] Claire Coghlan, "How This Crowd-Sourced Startup Is Disrupting the Beauty Industry," *Forbes*, October 17, 2017, www.forbes.com/sites/clairecoghlan/2017/10/17/how-this-crowd-sourced-startup-is-disrupting-the-beauty-industry/#52cb58907ca1 (accessed February 15, 2018); Jean Bonchak, "Concord Township Innovator Appealing to Crowdsourcing with Product," *News-Herald (Willoughby, OH)*, July 12, 2017, www .news-herald.com/business/20170712/concord-township-innovator-appealing-to-crowdsourcing-with-product (accessed February 15, 2018); Danny Parisi, "Sephora to Launch 5 Products from Crowdsourced Beauty Brand Volition," *Luxury Daily*, June 26, 2017, www.luxurydaily.com/sephora-launches-volition-platform-to-crowdsource-new-product-ideas/ (accessed February 15, 2018); https://volitionbeauty.com/innovations (accessed February 15, 2018).

[b] Natasha Bach, "Starbucks Is Doing Something Different for National Coffee Day," *Fortune*, September 29, 2017, http://fortune.com/2017/09/29/starbucks-national-coffee-day/ (accessed February 15, 2018); Janet I. Tu, "New Starbucks CEO Aims to Build Company That Will Last a Century," *Seattle Times*, April 3, 2017, www.seattletimes.com/business/starbucks/new-starbucks-ceo-aims-to-build-company-that-will-last-a-century (accessed February 15, 2018); Sebastian Buck, "As Millennials Demand More Meaning, Older Brands Are Not Aging Well," *Fast Company*, October 5, 2017, www.fastcompany.com/40477211/as-millennials-demand-more-meaning-older-brands-are-not-aging-well (accessed February 15, 2018); www .starbucks.com (accessed September 29, 2017).

Chapter 13

[a] Tiffany Hsu, "IKEA Enters 'Gig Economy' by Acquiring TaskRabbit," *The New York*

Times, September 28, 2017, www.nytimes. com/2017/09/28/business/ikea-taskrabbit. html (accessed February 26, 2018); Oscar Williams-Grut, "IKEA U.K. CEO: Task Rabbit Deal Is Part of Plan to 'Become More Relevant,'" *Business Insider*, October 20, 2017, www.businessinsider.com/ikeas-uk-ceo-taskrabbit-acquisition-2017-10 (accessed February 26, 2018); Adam Rogers, "Struggling with IKEA Furniture? There's an App for That," *Wired*, September 29, 2017, www.wired.com/story/struggling-with-ikea-furniture-theres-an-app-for-that/ (accessed February 26, 2018); www.ikea.com (accessed February 26, 2018).

b Ernie Smith, "With New Initiative, Ad Council Moves into Pro Bono Marketing Help," *Associations Now*, October 18, 2017, https://associationsnow.com/2017/10/new-initiative-ad-council-moves-pro-bono-marketing-help/ (accessed March 1, 2018); Minda Smiley, "Ad Council Program Connects Advertisers with Nonprofits in Need of Marketing Chops," *The Drum*, November 10, 2017, www.thedrum.com/news/2017/11/10/ad-council-program-connects-advertisers-with-nonprofits-need-marketing-chops (accessed March 1, 2018); Megan Graham, "Ad Council Program Connects Creative and Media Pros with Nonprofits," *Advertising Age*, October 18, 2017, http://adage.com/article/agency-news/ad-council-program-connect-creative-media-types-nonprofits/310927/ (accessed March 1, 2018).

Chapter 14

a Haney's Appledale Farm, www.haneysappledalefarm.com/ (accessed December 8, 2017); Mark Haney, "Agriculture Takes Center Stage as Consumers Drive Local Food Movement," *Kentucky Farm Bureau Newsroom*, July 7, 2015, http://kyfbnewsroom.com/agriculture-takes-center-stage-as-consumers-drive-local-food-movement/ (accessed December 8, 2017); Mark Haney, "President's Column," *Kentucky Farm Bureau Magazine*, Volume 16, No. 8, October 2017, https://www.kyfb.com/federation/newsroom/kentucky-farm-bureau-news/kfbn-2017/october-2017/ (accessed December 8, 2017); Leticia Hendrikson, "Haney's Appledale Farm," *Kentucky Heir*, October 22, 2010, https://kentuckyheir.com/2010/10/22/haneys-appledale-farm-nancy-kentucky/ (accessed December 8, 2017); Kentucky Department of Agriculture, "Power of the Neighborhood Market," https://www.kyagr.com/marketing/documents/ EDU_Power-of-the-Neighborhood-Market. pdf (accessed December 8, 2017); Kentucky Farm Bureau, "Kentucky Farm Bureau, Voice of Kentucky Agriculture," July 31, 2017, https://www.kyfb.com/federation/newsroom/ kentucky-farm-bureau-the-voice-of-kentucky-agriculture/ (accessed December 8, 2017); Kentucky Farm Bureau, "Kentucky Farm Bureau, KFB President Mark Haney Announces Formation of Water Management Working Group," *Kentucky Farm Bureau Magazine*, December 9, 2014, https://www .kyfb.com/federation/newsroom/haney-announces-water-management-working-group/ (accessed December 8, 2017); Kentucky Farm Bureau, "KFB President Mark Haney Emphasizes KFB Loves KY During Annual Address," *Kentucky Farm Bureau Newsroom*, December, 2, 2016, https://www.kyfb .com/federation/newsroom/kfb-president-mark-haney-emphasizes-kfb-loves-ky-during-annual-address/ (accessed December 8, 2017); "Down on the Farm," *Kentucky Living*, April 1, 2003, https://www.kentuckyliving. com/archives/down-on-the-farm (accessed December 8, 2017); Kentucky Department of Travel, "Haney's Appledale Farm," 2017, https://www.kentuckytourism.com/haneys-appledale-farm/2267/ (accessed December 8, 2017); Dianne Kroncke, "Give More Than You're Taking—Appledale Farm Interview with Don Haney," Phone Interview, Auburn University, Alabama, November 13, 2017; Diane Kroncke, "Personal Interview, Be the Best, Appledale Farm Interview with Mark Haney," Phone Interview, Auburn University, Alabama, November 29, 2017; Dianne Kroncke, "Personal Interview with Kaycee Rader of Nancy, Kentucky," at Grand Floridian, Orlando, Florida, November 20, 2017; Lake Cumberland, Somerset Polaski County Tourism, "Agritourism," 2015, www .lakecumberlandtourism.com/explore/ agritourism (accessed December 8, 2017); Tricia Neal, "The Nancy Connection," *Commonwealth Journal*, December 9, 2010, www.somerset-kentucky.com/news/ local_news/the-nancy-connection/article_ fb7e5f3a-7366-5f36-bfe0-debdf1bb7960. html (accessed November 12, 2017); Mark Haney, "Mark Haney Association Plans Should Be Part of Health Care Reform; Would Provide Bargaining Power," *Northern Kentucky Tribune*, September 26, 2017, www.nkytribune. com/2017/09/mark-haney-association-plans-should-be-part-of-health-care-reform-would-provide-bargaining-power/ (accessed December 8, 2017); University of Kentucky, Agriculture, Integrated Pest Management Programs, College of Agriculture, Food and Environment, "Historical Data on Integrated Pest Management Programs," https://ipm. ca.uky.edu/trapdata (accessed November 27, 2017); Wikimedia Foundation, Inc., "Integrated Pest Management," Wikipedia, November 22, 2017, https://en.wikipedia.org/wiki/Integrated_ pest_management (accessed December 8, 2017); Words to Live By, "Haney's Appledale Farm," 2017, https://www.wordstoliveby.com/ blogs/words-we-live-by/haneys-appledale-farm (accessed December 8, 2017).

b REI, *2009 Stewardship Report*, https:// www.rei.com/content/dam/documents/pdf/ Stewardship-Report-2009.pdf (accessed November 26, 2016); REI, "REI Overview," https://www.rei.com/about-rei/business.html (accessed November 26, 2016); REI, "The REI Member Dividend," https://www.rei. com/membership/dividend (accessed November 26, 2016); "Outdoor Classes, Events & Outings," https://www.rei.com/learn. html (accessed November 26, 2016); Giselle Tsirulnik, "REI App Purpose Is Twofold: Sales and Service," *Mobile Commerce Daily*, March 25, 2011, www.mobilecommercedaily. com/rei-app-purpose-is-twofold-sales-and-service (accessed November 26, 2016); REI, "The REI Workplace," https://www.rei .com/stewardship/workplace.html (accessed November 26, 2016); "100 Best Companies to Work For: Recreational Equipment Inc. (REI)," 2016, http://fortune.com/best-companies/recreational-equipment-inc-rei-26/ (accessed November 26, 2016); REI, "REI Employees Earn Co-op a Spot on the 2016 Fortune 100 Best Companies to Work For," March 3, 2016, http://newsroom.rei.com/ news/corporate/rei-employees-earn-co-op-spot-on-2016-fortune-100-best-companies-to-work-for.htm (accessed November 26, 2016).

Chapter 15

a Elizabeth Segran, "This Furniture Startup Wants You to Meet the Craftsman Who Made Your Sofa," *Fast Company*, September 27, 2017, www.fastcompany.com/40461435/ this-furniture-startup-wants-you-to-meet-the-craftsman-who-made-your-sofa (accessed March 28, 2018); Angela Tafoya, "Design Disruptor: Nidhi Kapur, Maiden Home," *Lonny*, May 8, 2017, www.lonny.com/ See+It+Now/articles/HYJnXscuYps/Design+ Disruptor+Nidhi+Kapur+Maiden+Home (accessed March 28, 2018); James Gaddy, "The Startup for Sitting Down," *Bloomberg Businessweek*, October 30, 2017, p. 71.

b Lauren Thomas, "Pop-Up Shops Still Popular with Retailers for the Holidays," *CNBC*, November 10, 2017, www.cnbc .com/2017/11/10/pop-up-shops-still-popular-with-retailers-for-the-holidays.html (accessed March 26, 2018); Lauren Thomas, "Pop-Up Shops Find a Permanent Home at the Mall," *CNBC*, October 16, 2017, www.cnbc .com/2017/10/16/pop-up-shops-find-a-permanent-home-at-the-mall.html (accessed March 26, 2018); Sarah Steimer, "Capturing Momentary Retail Magic," *Marketing News*, October 2017, pp. 70–77.

Chapter 16

a Rainforest Alliance, "Annual Report 2012," 2012, www.rainforest-alliance.org/sites/ default/files/about/annual_reports/AR2012_ spreads-optimized.pdf (accessed June 24, 2013); Rainforest Alliance, "About Us," www.rainforest-alliance.org/about (accessed January 1, 2018); Kelly K. Spors, "Top Small Workplaces 2008," *The Wall Street Journal*, February 22, 2009, https://www .wsj.com/articles/SB122347733961315417 (accessed January 1, 2018); Richard Donovan, "Rainforest Alliance Launches TREES," Forest Stewardship Council, www.fscus.org/ news/index.php?article=169 (accessed May 29, 2009); Rainforest Alliance, "Marketing Your Commitment to Sustainability," https:// www.rainforest-alliance.org/business/ marketing (accessed January 1, 2018); Rainforest Alliance, "Raising Awareness . . . Among Employees," https://www .rainforest-alliance.org/business/marketing/ awareness/employees (accessed January 1, 2018); Rainforest Alliance, "What Does Rainforest Alliance Certified™ Mean?" October 25, 2016, https://www.rainforest-alliance.org/faqs/what-does-rainforest-alliance-certified-mean (accessed January 1, 2018).

b Louisville Slugger Museum and Factory, "About Us—FAQs," 2017, https://www .sluggermuseum.com/about-us/faqs (accessed December 26, 2017); Louisville Slugger, "Our History," 2017, www.slugger .com/en-us/our-history (accessed December 26, 2017); How Products Are Made, "Baseball Bat," www.madehow.com/Volume-2/ Baseball-Bat.html (accessed December 26, 2017); David Mielach, "Louisville Slugger's Unlikely Home Run," *Business News Daily*, July 8, 2012, https://www.business-newsdaily.com/2806-louisville-slugger-story.html (accessed December 26, 2017).

Chapter 17

a Susan Wenograd, "AdWords Express Launches Notifications for Calls from Search Ads," Search Engine Land, February 7, 2018, https:// searchengineland.com/adwords-express-launches-notifications-calls-search-ads-291485 (accessed March 3, 2018); Andy Rachleff, "What 'Disrupt' Really Means" *TechCrunch*, February 16, 2013, https:// techcrunch.com/2013/02/16/the-truth-about-disruption/ (accessed March 3, 2018); "Google's Ad Revenue from 2001 to 2017 (in Billion U.S. Dollars)," Statista, 2018, https:// www.statista.com/statistics/266249/advertising-revenue-of-google/ (accessed March 3, 2018); Doug Aamoth, "Google Turns 14, Was Initially Called 'BackRub,'" *Time*, September 27, 2012, http://techland.time.com/2012/o9/27/google-turns-14-today-was-initially-called-backrub/ (accessed March 3, 2018).

b Kevin Moss, "Don't Read This Article: How Ads Against Consumerism Help Sustainability," *Eco Business*, February 6, 2018, http://www.eco-business.com/opinion/ dont-read-this-article-how-ads-against-consumerism-help-sustainability/ (accessed March 3, 2018); Tim Nudd, "Ad of the Day: Patagonia," *Ad Week*, November 28, 2011, http://www.adweek.com/news/advertising-branding/ad-day-patagonia-136745 (accessed December 28, 2016); Kyle Stock, "Patagonia's Confusing and Effective Campaign to Grudgingly Sell Stuff," *Bloomberg*, November 25, 2013, https://www.bloomberg.com/news/ articles/2013-11-25/patagonias-confusing-and-effective-campaign-to-grudgingly-sell-stuff (accessed December 28, 2016); Andrew Cave, "'Don't Buy This Racket': Patagonia to Give Away All Retail Revenues on Black Friday," *Forbes*, November 21, 2016, http://www .forbes.com/sites/andrewcave/2016/11/21/ dont-buy-this-racket-patagonia-to-give-away-all-retail-revenues-on-black-friday/# 1ea56050230c (accessed December 28, 2016); Brandon J. Reich and Catherine A. Armstrong Soule (2016), "Green Demarketing in Advertisements: Comparing 'Buy Green' and 'Buy Less' Appeals in Product and Institutional Advertising Contexts," *Journal of Advertising* 45(4): pp. 441–458.

Chapter 18

a Eaton Corporation, "2014 Annual Report," www.eaton.com/ecm/groups/public/@ pub/@eaton/@corp/documents/content/ pct_1224149.pdf (accessed January 20, 2016); Eaton, "Fast Facts," www.eaton.com/Eaton/ OurCompany/AboutUs/CorporateInformation/ FastFacts/index.htm (accessed January 20, 2016); Eaton Corporation, "Global Ethics & Compliance," www.eaton.com/Eaton/ OurCompany/GlobalEthics (accessed January 20, 2016); Ethisphere Institute, "2013 World's Most Ethical Companies," *Ethisphere*, worldsmostethicalcompanies. ethisphere.com/honorees (accessed January 20, 2016); Eaton, www.eaton.com/ Eaton/index.htm (accessed January 20, 2016); Eaton, "Aerospace," www.eaton.com/ Eaton/ProductsServices/Aerospace/index. htm?wtredirect+www.eaton.com/aerospace (accessed January 20, 2016); Eaton, "Success Stories: Mushroom Farming Industry," www .eaton.com/Eaton/OurCompany/Success Stories/ManufacturingIndustrial/Mushroom-Farming-Industry/index.htm (accessed January 20, 2016); Fortune, "Most Admired: Industrial and Farm Equipment," *Fortune*, archive.fortune.com/magazines/fortune/most-admired/2012/industries/28.html (accessed January 20, 2016); Eaton, "Eaton Receives Eloqua Markie Award for Most Creative Marketing Campaign," November 21, 2012, www .eaton.com/Eaton/OurCompany/NewsEvents/ NewsReleases/PCT_403135 (accessed January 20, 2016); Eaton, "Eaton's LED Solutions Allow California Facility to Save More Than 50 Percent on Exterior," September 19, 2013, www.eaton.com/Eaton/OurCompany/ NewsEvents/NewsReleases/PCT_508987 (accessed January 20, 2016); Curt Hutchins, *A Transition in Global Markets: Asia-Pacific Is the Future*, 2012, www.amcham-shanghai. org/NR/rdonlyres/73F016E2-0E5F-4BC0-9B99-AC028BD9EA16/17086/CurtHutchins. pdf (accessed January 20, 2016); Anna Clark, "Mega-trends: The Power behind Eaton's Global Green Growth," *Green Biz*, June 19, 2013, www.greenbiz.com/blog/2013/06/19/ power-behind-eatons-global-green-growth (accessed January 20, 2016).

b "Tastefully Simple Founder and Founding Partner Recognized," *Echo Press*, October 19, 2012, http://dev1.echopress.com/event/article/ id/98803/ (accessed January 16, 2014); Beth Douglass Silcox and Barbara Seale, "The Most Influential Women in Direct Selling," *Direct Selling News*, October 2012, pp. 58–59; Tastefully Simple, https://www .tastefullysimple.com/ (accessed December 26, 2016); "DSN Global 100: The Top Direct Selling Companies in the World," *Direct Selling News*, June 1, 2012, http://directsellingnews.com/index.php/ view/dsn_global_100_the_top_direct_ selling_companies_in_the_world/P7#.

UIGzEPUmx8F (accessed December 26, 2016); "DSN Global 100," *Direct Selling News*, June 1, 2014, http://directsellingnews.com/index.php/view/the_2013_dsn_global_100_list?popup=yes#.UthLx_XLQ4k (accessed December 26, 2016); BestCompany.com, "Tastefully Simple," 2016, https://bestcompany.com/mlm/company/tastefully-simple/ (accessed December 26, 2016); Tastefully Simple, "Awards & Recognition," https://www.tastefullysimple.com/about-us/awards-recognition (accessed December 26, 2016); "Tastefully Simple Streamlines Operations," *Voice of Alexandria*, November 9, 2016, http://www.voiceofalexandria.com/news/local_business_news/tastefully-simple-streamlines-operations/article_933bbc28-a6bd-11e6-b33e-8fb44a689e7d.html (accessed December 26, 2016).

Chapter 19

a   Leslie Josephs, "Airlines Ban Some High-Tech Suitcases, Fearing Battery Fires," *CNBC*, Dec 1, 2017, www.cnbc.com/2017/12/01/american-airlines-bans-some-high-tech-suitcases.html (accessed March 6, 2018); Ahiza Garcia, "The Founders of Away Changed the Luggage Industry after a Travel Mishap," *Money*, October 24, 2017, http://money.cnn.com/2017/10/24/news/companies/away-jen-rubio-steph-korey-travel-fresh-money/index.html (accessed March 6, 2018); Burt Helm, "How This Company Launched with Zero Products—and Hit $12 Million in First-Year Sales," *Inc.*, June 28, 2017, www.inc.com/magazine/201707/burt-helm/how-i-did-it-steph-korey-jen-rubio-away.html (accessed March 6, 2018); "Network: From Bags to Riches," *Columbia Magazine*, Spring 2017, pp. 46–47; www.awaytravel.com (accessed March 6, 2018).

b   Kim Bhasin, "Soon You May Be Renting Your Work Clothes," *Bloomberg*, November 14, 2017, www.bloomberg.com/news/articles/2017-11-14/soon-you-may-be-renting-your-work-clothes (accessed March 7, 2018); Jennifer Jolly, "Stitch Fix? Rent the Runway? I Tried 5 Clothing Services in a Month. Here's What I Found," *USA Today*, November 9, 2017, www.usatoday.com/story/tech/columnist/2017/11/09/stitch-fix-rent-runway-clothing-services-booming-heres-how-choose/845394001/ (March 7, 2018); Jennifer Calfas, "This New Amazon Prime Benefit Will Let You Try on Clothes before Buying Them," *Time*, June 20, 2017, http://time.com/money/4824976/amazon-prime-wardrobe-clothes/ (accessed March 7, 2018).

Chapter 20

a   Dana Hedgpeth and Luz Lazo, "I-66 Toll Hits $40 on Day 2. Virginia Transportation Chief: 'No One Has to Pay a Toll,'" *Washington Post*, December 5, 2017, www.washingtonpost.com/news/dr-gridlock/wp/2017/12/05/i-66-toll-in-virginia-reaches-new-high-of-36-50-on-day-2/?utm_term=.f31de6d4a66d (accessed March 13, 2018); Frederick Kunkle, "Virginia's Price-Gouging Toll Collector Should Return $30 to Snow-bound Drivers," *Washington Post*, January 12, 2017, www.washingtonpost.com/news/tripping/wp/2017/01/12/virginias-price-gouging-toll-collector-should-return-30-to-snowbound-drivers/?utm_term=.5e7e86e3ef36 (accessed March 13, 2018); Jeremy Walsh, "Officials Praise I-580 Express Lanes for First-Year Results," *Pleasanton Weekly*, March 17, 2017, www.pleasantonweekly.com/news/2017/03/17/officials-praise-i-580-express-lanes-for-first-year-results (accessed March 13, 2018); Neil Irwin, "Why Surge Prices Make Us So Mad: What Springsteen, Home Depot, and a Nobel Winner Know," *The New York Times*, October 14, 2017, www.nytimes.com/2017/10/14/upshot/why-surge-prices-make-us-so-mad-what-springsteen-home-depot-and-a-nobel-winner-know.html (accessed March 13, 2018).

b   Hugo Martin, "Travelers Love Airline Flash Sales but the Ultra-Cheap Fares Are on the Decline," *Los Angeles Times*, November 12, 2017, www.latimes.com/business/la-fi-airline-sales-20171112-story.html (accessed March 14, 2018); Michael K. Conway, "Nike Launches Two-Day Flash Sale with 40 Percent Off," *Footwear News*, October 11, 2017, http://footwearnews.com/2017/focus/athletic-outdoor/nike-flash-sale-443366/ (accessed March 14, 2018); Jennie Bell, "This Startup Is Making High Heels More Comfortable with a Foot-Scanning Technology," *Footwear News*, July 12, 2017, http://footwearnews.com/2017/focus/womens/comfortable-high-heels-true-gault-custom-shoes-391516/ (accessed March 14, 2018).

Name Index

Organization Index

Subject Index